PAGE 46

ON THE ROAD

and insider tips

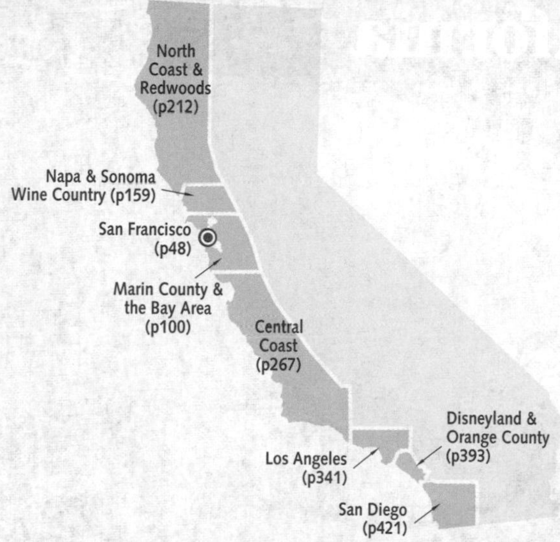

PAGE 503

SURVIVAL GUIDE

VITAL PRACTICAL INFORMATION TO HELP YOU HAVE A SMOOTH TRIP

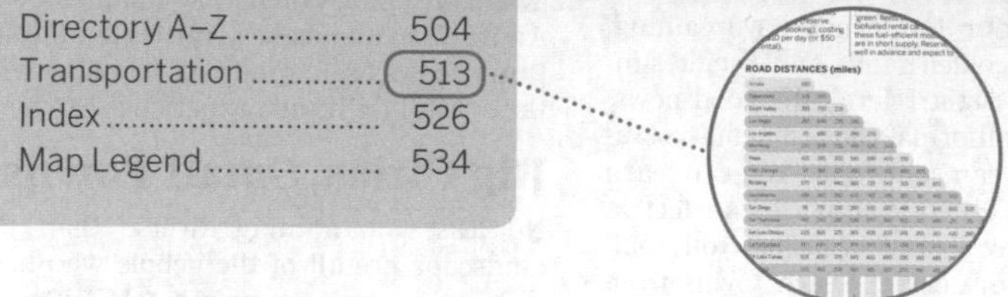

THIS EDITION WRITTEN AND RESEARCHED BY

Sara Benson

Andrew Bender, Alison Bing, Nate Cavalieri, Bridget Gleeson, Beth Kohn, John A Vlahides

welcome to Coastal California

Beaches & Outdoors

In all of your California daydreaming, palm trees, golden sands and Pacific sunsets beckon, right? Here's the good news: in coastal California, those cinematic fantasies really can come true. You can learn to surf, drink a cocktail with your feet in the sand, play a game of pickup volleyball or join a drum circle. Beach towns from Santa Cruz south to San Diego, each with its own idiosyncratic personality, give you perfect excuses to hit the road. Heading north of San Francisco, dramatically windswept beaches have inspired generations of poets and painters, offering miles of oceanfront for beachcombing and tramping in solitude. If you can tear yourself away from the ocean, myriad adventures await on land. When that infamous San Andreas Fault shakes, rattles and rolls, think of it as a reminder of just how wild the coastal California experience can be.

Big Cities, Small Towns

No less astoundingly diverse than the landscape are all of the people who have staked their fortunes on coastal California. Start out exploring San Francisco's eclectic neighborhoods, from beatnik North Beach and historic Chinatown to arty SoMa and the hipsterville Mission. Then join the star-crossed paparazzi as they chase TV and silver-screen celebrities with their glam entourages in LA. Hang with radical

From towering coast redwoods in foggy Northern California to the perfectly sun-kissed surf beaches of Southern California, these 1100 miles of Pacific Coast are a knockout beauty.

(left) Crescent Bay (p417), Orange County
(below) Outdoor dining, San Francisco (p48)

tree-sitting lefties in the Humboldt Nation, live the very good life in California's wine country towns, get groovy with modern-day hippies in Santa Cruz and new-age gurus in San Diego's North County, or talk fishing with salty dogs in old port towns like Eureka, Bodega Bay and Monterey.

Food & Drink

Maybe your coastal sojourn will be an epicurean quest. Finding the most-killer fish tacos in San Diego alone could take days or even weeks. San Francisco and Los Angeles are all-around global foodie capitals, where citizens passionately argue about the best sushi bar, gourmet food truck or pop-up kitchen. LA is also a melting pot of multicultural cooking, from Little Tokyo and Thai Town to the tamale shops of East LA. Follow your nose and let it lead you serendipitously up and down California's coastal highways, stopping at rollicking seafood shacks, brewpubs and farmers markets, or follow two-lane back roads that wind past pastoral vineyards. You'll never be able to eat or drink your fill here, but that just gives you an irresistable excuse to come back and do it all over again.

Coastal California

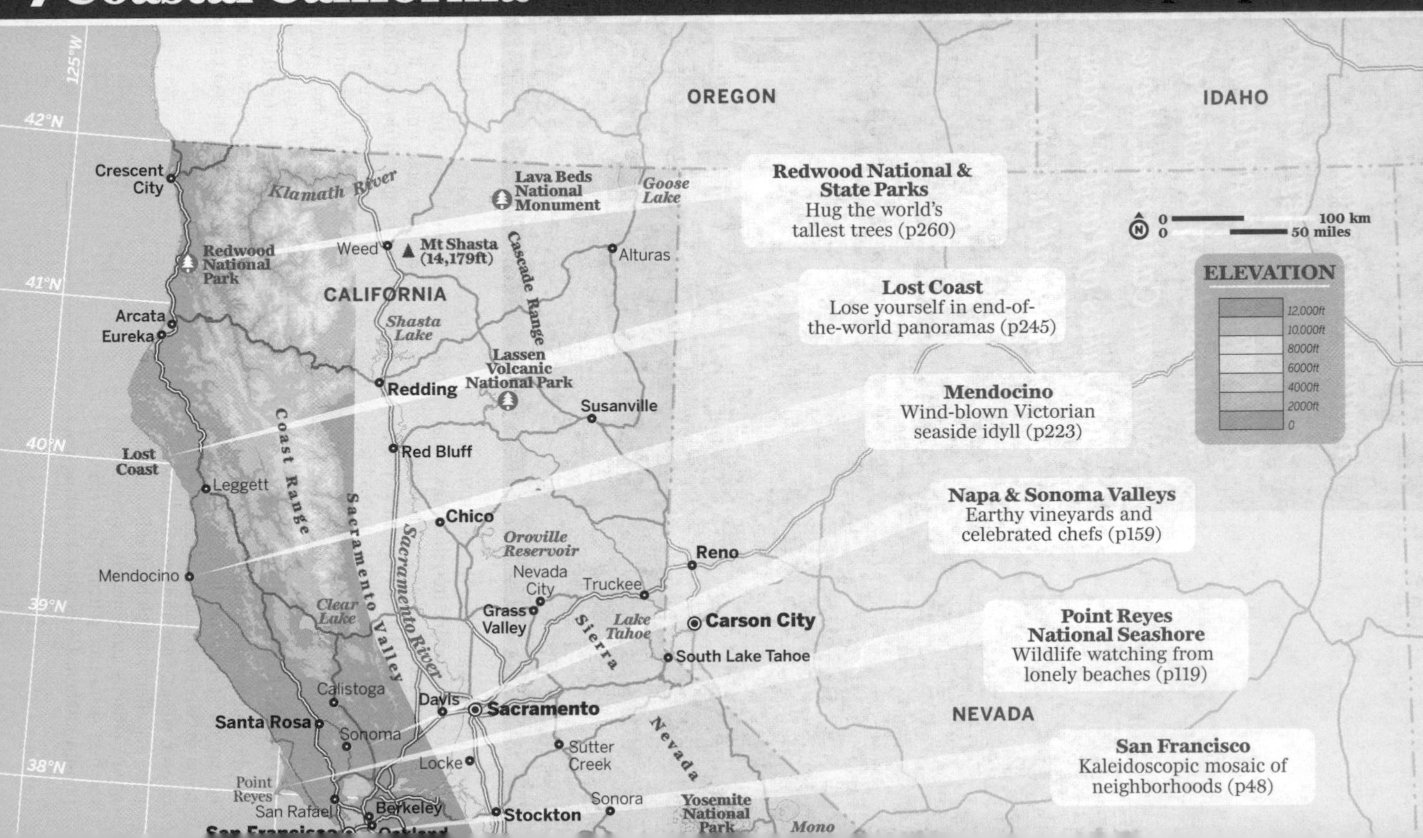
Redwood National & State Parks
Hug the world's tallest trees (p260)
Lost Coast
Lose yourself in end-of-the-world panoramas (p245)
Mendocino
Wind-blown Victorian seaside idyll (p223)
Napa & Sonoma Valleys
Earthy vineyards and celebrated chefs (p159)
Point Reyes National Seashore
Wildlife watching from lonely beaches (p119)
San Francisco
Kaleidoscopic mosaic of neighborhoods (p48)
OREGON
IDAHO
NEVADA
CALIFORNIA
ELEVATION
12,000ft
10,000ft
8000ft
6000ft
4000ft
2000ft
0
0
100 km
0
50 miles
125°W
42°N
41°N
40°N
39°N
38°N
Crescent City
Klamath River
Redwood National Park
Arcata
Eureka
Lost Coast
Leggett
Mendocino
Coast Range
Weed
Mt Shasta (14,179ft)
Lava Beds National Monument
Goose Lake
Alturas
Cascade Range
Shasta Lake
Redding
Lassen Volcanic National Park
Susanville
Red Bluff
Chico
Oroville Reservoir
Nevada City
Grass Valley
Truckee
Reno
Lake Tahoe
Carson City
South Lake Tahoe
Sierra
Nevada
Sacramento Valley
Sacramento River
Clear Lake
Calistoga
Santa Rosa
Sonoma
Davis
Sacramento
Sutter Creek
Locke
Point Reyes
San Rafael
Berkeley
Stockton
Sonora
Yosemite National Park
Mono

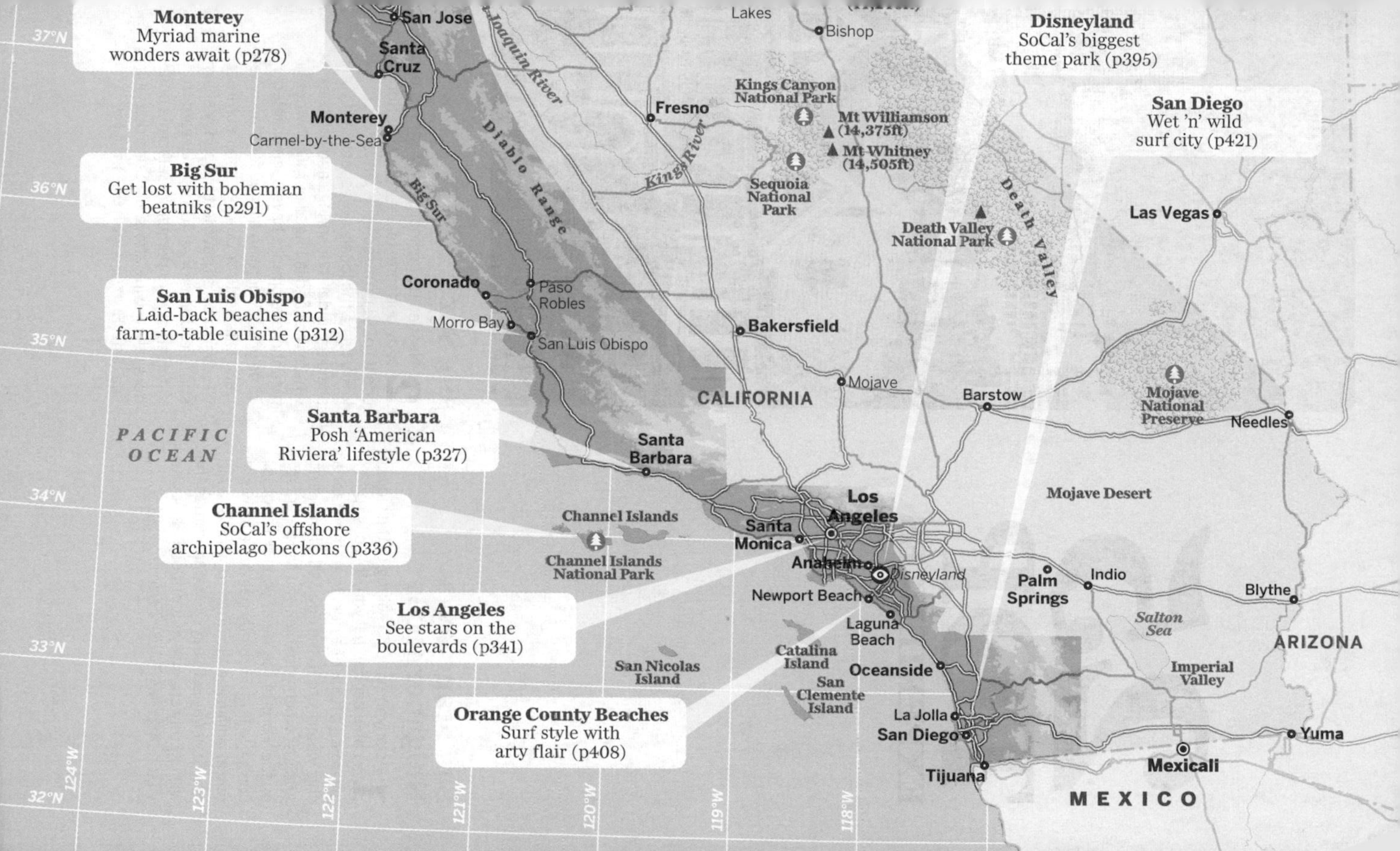

Monterey
Myriad marine wonders await (p278)
Big Sur
Get lost with bohemian beatniks (p291)
San Luis Obispo
Laid-back beaches and farm-to-table cuisine (p312)
Santa Barbara
Posh 'American Riviera' lifestyle (p327)
Channel Islands
SoCal's offshore archipelago beckons (p336)
Los Angeles
See stars on the boulevards (p341)
Orange County Beaches
Surf style with arty flair (p408)
Disneyland
SoCal's biggest theme park (p395)
San Diego
Wet 'n' wild surf city (p421)
PACIFIC OCEAN
CALIFORNIA
ARIZONA
MEXICO
San Jose
Santa Cruz
Monterey
Carmel-by-the-Sea
Big Sur
Diablo Range
San Joaquin River
Kings River
Fresno
Lakes
Bishop
Kings Canyon National Park
Mt Williamson (14,375ft)
Mt Whitney (14,505ft)
Sequoia National Park
Death Valley
Death Valley National Park
Las Vegas
Coronado
Paso Robles
Morro Bay
San Luis Obispo
Bakersfield
Mojave
Barstow
Mojave National Preserve
Needles
Santa Barbara
Mojave Desert
Los Angeles
Santa Monica
Anaheim
Disneyland
Channel Islands
Channel Islands National Park
Newport Beach
Laguna Beach
Palm Springs
Indio
Blythe
Salton Sea
Catalina Island
San Nicolas Island
Oceanside
San Clemente Island
Imperial Valley
La Jolla
San Diego
Tijuana
Mexicali
Yuma
37°N
36°N
35°N
34°N
33°N
32°N
124°W
123°W
122°W
121°W
120°W
119°W
118°W

25 TOP EXPERIENCES

San Francisco's Neighborhoods

1 As anyone who has clung to the side of a cable car can tell you, this city (p48) gives you a heck of a ride, from the Marina's chic waterfront to the edgy Mission district. And just when you think you have a grasp on the 'Paris of the West,' you turn another corner to find a brightly painted alleyway mural, a filigreed Victorian roofline or a hidden stairway with bay-view panoramas that will entirely change your outlook. Renovated Victorian terrace houses, San Francisco

Big Sur

2 Nestled up against mossy, mysterious redwood forests, the rocky Big Sur coast (p291) is a secretive place. Get to know it like the locals do, especially if you're seeking hidden hot springs and beaches where the sand is tinged purple or where gigantic jade chunks have been claimed. Time your bohemian escape for May, when waterfalls peak, or October, after summer-vacation crowds have left but sunny skies still rule. Don't forget to look skyward to catch sight of endangered California condors taking wing above Big Sur's dizzying sea cliffs. Bixby Bridge (p293), Big Sur

RICHARD I'ANSON/LONELY PLANET IMAGES ©

DOUG STEAKLEY/LONELY PLANET IMAGES ©

Los Angeles

3 LA (p341) runs deeper than her blond beaches, Botoxed celebutantes and reality-TV entourages would have you believe. True, she has spawned tons of pop culture, from skateboarding to gangsta rap, while popularizing silicone implants and spandex. But the City of Angels has also nurtured artists, architects, writers, performers and film directors alongside yogis, alternative-health gurus and meditative religions. Ultimately, it's LA's ethnic diversity and vibrant global-immigrant culture that make the biggest impression. Open your mind and you'll soon love La La Land as much as we do.

Disneyland

4 Walt Disney built his dream where orange groves and walnut trees once grew, throwing open the doors of his Magic Kingdom in 1955. Today, Disneyland (p395) is SoCal's most visited tourist attraction. Inside Anaheim's megapopular theme parks, beloved cartoon characters waltz arm-in-arm down Main Street USA and fireworks explode over Sleepy Beauty's castle on hot summer nights. If you're a kid, or just hopelessly young at heart, Disneyland could well be 'The Happiest Place on Earth.' Pirates of the Caribbean, Disneyland

LEE FOSTER/LONELY PLANET IMAGES ©

BRENT WINEBRENNER/LONELY PLANET IMAGES ©

PROEHL STUDIOS/CORBIS ©

₹edwood National & State Parks

5 Ditch the cell phone and hug a tree, starting ·ith the world's tallest, oast redwoods. California's owering giants grow all along ıe North Coast, up to the regon border. It's possible cruise past these trees – r even drive right through ıem at old-fashioned tourist aps – but nothing compares the awe you'll feel while eading underneath the ıost ancient ones protected y Redwood National and tate Parks (p260). When ıe mist floats over the forest oor, these serene groves rovide an almost mystical xperience. Horseback riding, edwood National Park

California Cuisine

6 The Golden State has seen more than its fair share of boom times and busts, and Hollywood starlets come and go, but for epicures, the prize remains the same: California's food and wine (p475). You'll have good reason to pat your belly blissfully as you travel up and down the coast, tasting everything from surfer-worthy fish tacos at seafood shacks to farm-to-table feasts on chefs' seasonal, organic and locavarian tasting menus. Agricultural abundance is the mother of invention in coastal kitchens here. Shrimp kebabs with tomato and zucchini

San Diego

7 New York has its cabbie and Chicago its bluesman. San Diego (p421) has the valet guy in a polo shirt and khaki shorts. With his perfectly tousled hair, bronzed skin and enthusiastic grin, he looks like he's on a perennial spring break. Likewise, San Diego's breezy confidence and sunny countenance are infectious. The only problem is that with 70 miles of coastline and a near-perfect climate, it's tough to decide where to start. When in doubt, do as locals do: grab a fish taco and a surfboard, then hit the beach. Scripps Institute of Oceanography, La Jolla, San Diego

Napa & Sonoma Wine Country

8 As winemaking in the neighboring Napa Valley (p163) grows ever richer, Sonoma's sun-dappled vineyards (p182) remain surrounded by pastoral ranchlands, but the uniqueness of terroir is what's valued most in both places. In California's best-known wine country, you can take a tour of biodynamic vineyards, shake hands with famous winemakers or sample new vintages from the barrel in naturally cooled underground cellars, then crack open a bottle in the fields outside. Who cares if it's not noon? This is California: conventions need not apply. Wine tasting, Sonoma Valley

Santa Barbara

9 Locals call it the 'American Riviera,' but honestly that's not such a stretch: Santa Barbara (p327) is so idyllic, you just have to sigh. Waving palm trees, sugar-sand beaches, boats bobbing by the harbor – it'd be a travel cliché if it wasn't the plain truth. California's 'Queen of the Missions' is a beauty, as are downtown's red-roofed, whitewashed adobe buildings, all rebuilt in harmonious Spanish colonial style after a devastating 1925 earthquake. Come aspire to the easy-breezy, rich-and-famous lifestyle here, even if just for a day. State St, Santa Barbara

Hearst Castle

10 More of a monumen to William Randolph Hearst's maniacal obsession with Old World treasures collected from Europe, Hearst Castle (p299) is the biggest showboat attraction on the Central Coast. Take a spin around Hearst's hilltop retreat with its sparkling outdoor Neptune Pool, interiors lavishly decorated in antiquities and jewels, and jaw-dropping coastal sunset viewed from the balcony. Evening living-history tours during the winter holidays wi take you back to the castle's 1930s heyday, when Hollywood celebrities hobnobbed here with heads of state. Outdoor pool, Hearst Castle

10

WITOLD SKRYPCZAK/LONELY PLANET IMAGES ©

:olden Gate Bridge

11 Sashay or pedal out onto San Francisco's :conic bridge (p51) to spy ·n cargo ships threading hrough pylons painted nternational Orange' and to nemorize the 360-degree iews of the rugged Marin leadlands, far-off downtown kyscrapers and the speck hat is Alcatraz Island. Back n solid ground, you can et another perspective on his 20th-century engineer- ıg feat by detouring out to vindy Fort Point, where Kim lovak and Jimmy Stewart ove into the chilly waters of ;an Francisco Bay in Hitch- ock's classic thriller *Vertigo*.

11

ORIEN HARVEY/LONELY PLANET IMAGES ©

AURORA PHOTOS/ALAMY ©

Lost Coast

12 Hellloooo? Anyone out there? This is the coast that time has just about forgotten. Buoyed by the wilderness peaks of the Kings Range and speckled by wild beaches of volcanic origin, the Lost Coast (p245) makes you earn its natural wonders. Time your multiday backpacking trek to match the flow of the tides and camp out by the crashing surf on a deserted beach along the Lost Coast Trail. Or just drive yourself to the coast's last outpost of civilization, tiny Shelter Cove.
Tidal pools, Lost Coast

Mendocino

13 Nothing restores the soul like a ramble out onto the craggy, salt-washed headlands of Mendocino (p223) on the North Coast. In summer, fragrant bursts of lavender and jasmine drift along fog-laden winds. Year-round churning surf is never out of earshot, and driftwood-littered beaches are potent reminders of the sea's power. Originally a 19th-century port built by New Englanders, Mendocino today belongs to bohemians who would scoff at the puritanical virtues of early settlers, instead favoring art and nature's outdoor temple for their modern-day religions.

Orange County Beaches

14 In Orange County (p408), there are beaches for all. Huntington draws the hang-loose, trust-fund surfer crowd, while bike rebels, bodacious babes and anti-establishment types hit Sunset Beach. Families with younger kids gravitate toward old-fashioned Seal Beach and its pier, but glamorous teens, trophy wives and yachties cavort in the fantasyland of Newport Beach. Furthest south, Laguna Beach beckons, with its sophisticated blend of money and culture. Oh, and natural beauty too: startlingly beautiful seascapes inspired an artists colony to bloom.
Seal Beach

oint Reyes National eashore

15 If just one park could encapsulate Northern California, Point Reyes (p119) ould get our vote. Step across the jagged ash of the San Andreas Fault, then stand out y the lighthouse at what truly feels like land's nd. Peer through binoculars at migratory hales, or witness the raucous birthing and ating antics of endangered elephant seals at himney Rock. Then hike among herds of tule k and drive out to more windswept beaches, here the horizon stretches toward eternity.

Santa Cruz

16 Nowhere else can you get in touch with NorCal's countercultural ethos faster than in flower-powered, surf-happy Santa Cruz (p269). White sandy beaches for wetsuit-wearing, board-riding dudes and chicks? Check. A carnivalesque downtown flush with boho cafes, one-of-a-kind shops and eccentric personalities? Yup. Tree-hugger hippie camps and outsider artists' cabins in the redwood forests? Uh-huh. Left-of-liberal politics, Rastafarian dreadlocks and New Age crystal readings? Of course, man. Beach boardwalk, Santa Cruz

15

LEE FOSTER/LONELY PLANET IMAGES ©

16

EDDIE BRADY/LONELY PLANET IMAGES ©

Monterey

17 Forget the Hollywood visions of SoCal beaches. In NorCal's fishing villages, think John Steinbeck and his novels of American realism instead of MTV's spring breakers. Hop aboard a whale-watching cruise into Monterey Bay's national marine sanctuary (p278), some of whose denizens of the deep also swim in Cannery Row's aquarium. Soak up the atmosphere at the West Coast's oldest lighthouse near the famous 17-Mile Drive to Pebble Beach, or head downtown among the gardens and adobe-walled buildings from California's Mexican past. Aquarium, Monterey Bay

San Luis Obispo

18 Almost exactly between San Francisc and Los Angeles, San Luis Obispo (p312) is often overlooked or merely dismissed by urban culture vultures. But this co lection of ranchlands, vineyards and organic farms is refreshingly down to earth. Detour here for laid-back beach towns, spectacular hiking and camping in state parks and elfin n ture preserves and, most of all, the locavariar bounty from more than a dozen farmers mar kets. You won't need a car – clamber aboard Amtrak's *Pacific Surfliner* or *Coast Starlight* trains for unforgettable coastal scenery.

19

ANN CECIL/LONELY PLANET IMAGES ©

20

STEPHEN SAKS/LONELY PLANET IMAGES ©

anta Barbara Wine ountry

19 Southern California features the Santa Ynez and Santa Maria Valleys, aka *deways* wine country (p322). Less than an our's drive from Santa Barbara, you can wan- er through fields of grapes, tipple pinot noir nd other prize-winning varietals, and sample e sun-drenched good life. Start in dandified os Olivos, overflowing with tasting rooms and fes. Then wind north along the Foxen Wine ail, a two-lane back road, where famous- ame wineries and boutique winemakers are enial neighbors. Santa Ynez Valley (p325)

Channel Islands

20 Tossed like so many lost pearls off the coast, the Channel Islands (p336) are SoCal's answer to the Galapagos. Centuries ago, seafaring Chumash tribes-people established villages on remote rocks. Today the islands support an abundance of marine life, from coral-reef creatures to giant colonies of pinnipeds. Get back to nature in Channel Islands National Park, a wildlife haven with sea kayaking and snorkeling opportunities, as well as challenging hiking trails and rustic campgrounds, or make a more civilized excursion to Catalina. Anacapa Island (p337)

EDDIE BRADY/LONELY PLANET IMAGES ©

La Jolla

21 On the most beautiful stretch of San Diego's coastline, La Jolla (p440) is definitely not just another SoCal beach town. Sitting pretty atop rocky bluffs just a whisper's breath from the sea, La Jolla's richly adorned downtown is crowded with fashion-forward boutiques, hideaway cafes and posh hotels. But what's right on the shoreline is even more of a treasure, especially the all-natural fish bowl of La Jolla Cove and windswept Torrey Pines State Reserve, further north along the ribbon of coastal highway. Wild seals, La Jolla

Whale-Watching

22 Thar she blows! All up and down the coast, and no matter what the season, you can spot migratory whales (p35) offshore from California. During summer and fall, blue, humpback and sperm whales cruise by. But the biggest parades happen every winter and spring when gray whales make their annual migrations between the arctic waters of Alaska and balmy breeding and birthing lagoons in the Gulf of Mexico. Jump aboard a whale-watching boat tour to observe these majestic marine mammals up close and personal. Humpback whale

Venice Beach

23 Muscled bodybuilders à la Arnold Schwarzenegger, goth punk and hippie tribal drummers all gravitate toward Venice Beach's Ocean Front Walk (p368). This is the place where SoCal's crazy side really lets it all hang out. Imagine an experimental human zoo and an outdoor year-round carnival in which audience participation is encouraged. So, strap on those rollerblades, hop on a pastel pink beach cruiser or just strut down the boardwalk and shake what yo' mama gave you. Cycling and skating, Venice Beach

olinas

24 Never mind that locals keep taking down the highway signs to prevent u from finding this paradisiacal hamlet by e sea in Marin County (p117). Once you ally find the spot, take time out to go beach-mbing along Agate Beach, drift around the acid waters of Bass Lake on an inner tube, gin up your courage enough to talk politics th the grizzled old fishers and Baby Boom-s at a saloon while slurping down oyster ooters and an icy beer. Murals on grocery ore wall, Bolinas

Sausalito

25 It's not just seabirds and seals – travelers also flock to this little fishing and houseboat community (p104) on San Francisco Bay, just north of the Golden Gate Bridge. Tool around Sausalito's little down-town on a bike and walk out onto the floating quays in the marina that bob up and down with the gentle waves. Feast on fresh sushi or sustainably grown and harvested comfort food before hopping on a ferry back across the bay, letting the salty maritime breezes lick your lips. Moored houseboats, Sausalito

24

25

need to know

Currency
» US dollars ($)

Language
» English

When to Go

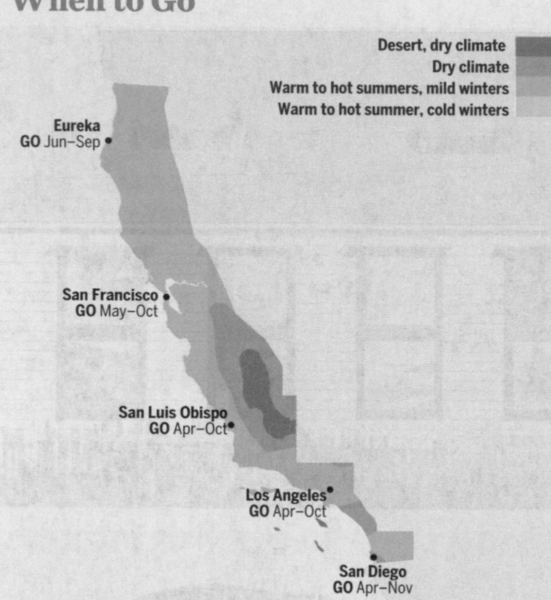

High Season (Jun–Aug)

» Accommodation prices up 50% to 100% on average

» Major holidays are even busier and more expensive

» Thick clouds may blanket the coast during 'May gray' and 'June gloom' (sometimes into July)

Shoulder Season (Apr–May & Sep–Oct)

» Crowds and prices drop off almost everywhere along the coast

» Mild temperatures, with many sunny, cloudless days

» Weather typically wetter in spring, drier in autumn

Low Season (Nov–Mar)

» Fewest crowds and lowest lodging rates, except around holidays and possibly in major coastal cities

» Chilly temperatures bring more frequent rainstorms throughout winter

Your Daily Budget

Budget less than
$75

» Hostel dorm beds $25-40

» Find farmers markets and *taquerías* for cheap eats

» Skip the theme parks, hit the beaches and plan around 'free admission' days at museums

Midrange
$75–200

» Two-star motel or hotel double room $100-200

» Rental car from $30 per day, excluding insurance and gas

Top end more than
$200

» Three-star lodging from $200 per night in summer high season

» Three-course meal in top restaurant $75 plus wine

Money

» ATMs are widely available. Credit cards normally required for hotel reservations, car rentals etc. Out-of-state checks rarely accepted. Tipping is customary, not optional.

Visas

» Generally not required for citizens of Visa Waiver Program (VWP) countries, but only with ESTA approval (apply online at least 72 hours in advance).

Cell Phones

» The only foreign phones that will work are GSM multiband models. Cell-phone coverage can be spotty in remote coastal areas, mountains and forests.

Driving

» Traffic in sprawling metro areas can be nightmarish. Avoid commuter rush hours (roughly 7am to 10am and 3pm and 7pm from Monday to Friday).

Websites

» **California Travel & Tourism Commission** (www.visitcalifornia.com) Multilingual trip-planning guides.

» **CalTrans** (www.dot.ca.gov) Highway conditions and construction updates.

» **Lonely Planet** (lonelyplanet.com/california) Destination info, hotel bookings, travelers forums and more.

» **SF Gate** (www.sfgate.com/travel) Travel features, weekend getaways and blogs.

» **LA Times** (www.latimes.com/travel) Daily news, travel deals and blogs.

Exchange Rates

Australia	A$1	$1.03
Canada	C$1	$0.98
Euro zone	€1	$1.38
China	Y10	$1.58
Japan	¥100	$1.30
Mexico	MXN10	$0.74
New Zealand	NZ$1	$0.79
UK	£1	$1.61

For current exchange rates see www.xe.com.

Important Numbers

Numbers have a three-digit area code then a seven-digit local number. For long-distance and toll-free calls, dial 1 plus all 10 digits.

Country code	1
International dialing code	011
Operator	0
Emergency (ambulance, fire & police)	911
Directory assistance (local)	411

Arriving in Coastal California

» **Los Angeles International Airport** (LAX; see p387)

Taxis $30-55, 30 minutes to one hour

Door-to-door shuttles $16-25; 24 hours

Bus Metro FlyAway bus ($7) to downtown LA or free Shuttle C to LAX Transit Center

» **San Francisco International Airport** (SFO; see p98)

Taxis $35-50, 25 to 50 minutes

Door-to-door shuttles $15-20; 24 hours

Train BART ($8.10, 30 minutes) to downtown every 20 minutes from 6am to 11:45pm

California State Parks

Most Californians rank outdoor recreation as vital to their quality of life. In fact, the amount of protected lands in California has steadily grown due to important pieces of legislation passed since the 1960s, notably the landmark 1976 California Coastal Act, which saved much of the coastline from further development. Today, state parks defend nearly a third of California's coastal beaches, as well as redwood forests, waterfalls, mountains, canyons, wildlife preserves and historic sites like lighthouses. In recent years, state budget shortfalls and chronic underfunding have led to temporary park closures, reduced opening hours and visitor services, as well as steadily increasing admission and recreation (eg camping) fees. As this book went to press, 70 state parks were slated to shut down in 2012. Visit www.parks.ca.gov for updates.

if you like...

Beaches

Northern California beaches are all about crashing waves, tidepools, rock collecting and (often) solitary strolls along the water's edge, but for the full-on *Baywatch* experience you need to head south. Bust out the surfboards and bikinis once you hit Santa Barbara.

Huntington Beach Orange County's 'Surf City USA' lives up to its moniker (p409)

Santa Monica Cycle LA's oceanfront bike path, ride a solar-powered Ferris wheel or dance under the stars (p361)

La Jolla Kayak sea caves, snorkel or scuba dive in an underwater park, or surf San Diego's legendary Windansea Beach (p440)

Santa Barbara Chic pocket beaches where you may even spot celebs (p327)

Santa Cruz Surf Steamer Lane, let the kids loose at Natural Bridges or spot the Pacific from a roller coaster (p269)

Sonoma Coast Rocky headlands, hidden coves and hiking trails atop 17 miles of wind-sculpted bluffs (p184)

Hot Springs & Spas

In California, you can get nekkid and soak in natural hot-springs pools, let your knotted-up muscles be teased into submission at a wine-country spa or rent your own private redwood hot tub under the stars.

Calistoga Volcanic mud baths are just what the doctor ordered before a day in the vineyards (p177)

Big Sur Take an oceanfront sea-cliff dip after midnight at Esalen, or trek into the wilderness to au-naturel Sykes Hot Springs (p291)

North Coast Find holistic health cures at Harbin Hot Springs, dip into naturally carbonated Vichy Hot Springs, bathe with tree-hugging hippies at Orr Hot Springs or go bohemian hot-tubbing in Arcata (p212)

Avila Beach Let the kids cavort in the hot-springs swimming pool and waterslide, or book a hillside hot tub for just the two of you (p317)

Parks & Preserves

Coastal California's natural glories don't stop with beaches. All along the coast, a chain of public parks protect an astonishing diversity of life zones, extending offshore to marine sanctuaries and wind-tossed islands. Just inland, misty redwood forests and mountain peaks beckon.

Redwood National & State Parks Get lost ambling among ancient groves of the world's tallest trees on the fog-laden North Coast (p260)

Channel Islands National Park Escape civilization on SoCal's far-flung islands, nicknamed 'California's Galapagos' for their unique and rare wildlife (p336)

Point Reyes National Seashore Step on the San Andreas Fault, hike to lonely end-of-the-world beaches and in winter, spy whales and elephant seals (p119)

Monterey Bay National Marine Sanctuary Cruise above an undersea canyon on a whale-watching boat, then paddle Elkhorn Slough nature preserve in a kayak (p278)

Big Sur State Parks Walk the sea cliffs where California condors fly, or tour a historic light station (p291)

STEPHEN SAKS/LONELY PLANET IMAGES ©

» Market, Ferry Building (p51), San Francisco

Fabulous Food

Infused by immigrant cultures for more than 200 years, California cuisine is all about creatively mixing it up, from kim-chi tacos to vegan soul food. Even rockstar chefs make sure their menus feature local farmers, fishers, ranchers and artisan producers.

Chez Panisse Chef Alice Waters revolutionized California cuisine back in the '70s with seasonal San Francisco Bay Area locavarian cooking (p135)

French Laundry High-wattage kitchen mastered by Thomas Keller is the Wine Country's gastronomic highlight (p173)

Ferry Building Marketplace Hit the thrice-weekly outdoor farmers market, or duck inside for a waterfront collection of Bay Area artisanal food vendors (p51)

LA's Food Trucks Food trucks may be everywhere now, but LA sparked the mobile gourmet revolution first with Kogi BBQ – and over 200 out-of-the-box chefs on wheels followed (p373)

San Diego's Fish Tacos Start your search for the perfect fish taco down south near the Mexico border (p448)

Wine

NorCal's Napa and Sonoma Valleys may be the most famous, but plenty of other California wine countries more than hold their own. Just crack open a bottle from these sun-kissed rural valleys and you'll soon become a believer.

Napa Valley Delve into the Wine Country's artisanal food scene while paying your respects to California's legendary big-name producers (p163)

Sonoma Valley Shake hands with independent-minded boutique winemakers in their sun-dappled biodynamic vineyards (p182)

Russian River Area Taste killer pinot noir and chardonnay at woodsy wineries after a lazy day of canoeing on the river (p193)

Santa Ynez & Santa Maria Valleys Pastoral country roads wind past some of Santa Barbara's most famous vintners (p325)

Paso Robles Dozens of down-to-earth vineyards heat up to produce rich, earthy zinfandels and many more diverse varietals (p310)

Hiking

Lace up those hiking boots! It's time to hit the trail, practically anywhere you go. Ever since Native Americans made the first footpaths through the wilderness, Californians have been walking. Oceanside rambles and verdant forest idylls still await today.

North Coast Hardy backpackers challenge the remote Lost Coast Trail, or take an easy ramble among old-growth redwood trees in fern-laden forests (p212)

Marin County Tawny headlands tempt hikers across San Francisco's Golden Gate Bridge, or explore the epic beaches at wild, windblown Point Reyes National Seashore (p119)

Central Coast Pound the beaches of Point Lobos, seek out the secret waterfalls of Big Sur and climb ocean-view volcanic peaks around San Luis Obispo (p267)

Los Angeles Run around LA's biggest urban greenspace, Griffith Park, or drive up into the wilder Santa Monica Mountains, where trails traipse past movie-worthy scenery (p367)

» Madonna Inn, San Luis Obispo (p306)

Offbeat & Kitsch

A capital of kookiness, coastal California lets you encounter eccentric characters, oddball places and bizarre experiences, especially on the North Coast. Even metro areas like loopy LA and bohemian SF are jam-packed with weird stuff you won't want to miss.

Venice Boardwalk Gawk at the human zoo of chainsaw-jugglers and Speedo-clad snake charmers by the sea in La La Land (p368)

Kinetic Grand Championship Outrageously whimsical, artistic and human-powered sculptures race along the North Coast (p255)

Madonna Inn Fantastically campy hotel in San Luis Obispo advertising 110 bizarrely themed rooms, from 'Caveman' to 'Hot Pink' (p306)

Mystery Spot Santa Cruz's shamelessly kitschy 1940s tourist trap will turn your whole world upside down (p270)

Solvang A Danish-flavored village in Santa Barbara's wine country spirited out of a Hans Christian Andersen fairytale (p325)

Small Towns

There's no denying that California, the biggest state in the nation, is a crowded place. If you tire of never-ending freeway traffic, make your escape to these in-between spots, whether by the beach or just down the road from bountiful vineyards.

Calistoga For the blue-jeans-and-boots crowd in Napa Valley, where quaint downtown streets are speckled with mud-bath spas (p177)

Bolinas Locals still tear down highway signs, but this end-of-the-road hamlet in Marin County is no longer a secret (p117)

Seal Beach Old-fashioned Orange County pit stop has a cute main street rolling out to a surf-worthy pier (p408)

Ferndale North Coast's charming Victorian farm town, filled with 'butterfat mansions,' puts on California's longest-running county fair (p249)

San Luis Obispo Oprah called it 'the happiest place in America,' with its bike-friendly downtown, exuberant weekly farmers market and sandy beaches nearby (p312)

Scenic Drives

Drop the convertible top, cue up the Red Hot Chili Peppers and step on it. Coastal highways deliver surreally beautiful ocean vistas and serpentine cliffside stretches. More unusual detours will tempt adventure and beauty-seeking road trippers too.

Pacific Coast Highway SoCal's official stretch of PCH famously hopscotches between beach towns in Orange County (p151)

Avenue of the Giants In the early morning mist, roll through groves of redwood trees in NorCal's Humboldt Redwoods State Park (p247)

17-Mile Drive Postcard Pacific vistas beckon all along this private Pebble Beach toll road on the rugged Monterey Peninsula (p289)

Mulholland Drive So famous David Lynch named a movie after it, LA's mountaintop way (p370) winds past movie-star mansions and vista points

San Diego North County Cruise lazily alongside the Pacific past surf beaches, alternative-minded small towns and sea cliffs where hot-air balloons take flight (p460)

If you like... traveling with your dog, Huntington Beach (p409), Carmel-by-the-Sea (p288) and Fort Bragg (p229) are happy havens for your four-legged friends.

Aquariums & Zoos

Coastal California is chockablock with old-fashioned boardwalks, futuristic theme parks and tons of other family-friendly attractions to keep little ones entertained for days, but for many kids, it's the local wildlife that are the real stars.

Monterey Bay Aquarium Watch otters and penguins cavort at feeding time, touch tidepool critters and get a big chill when sharks swim by (p278)

San Diego Zoo Safari Park Take a safari-style tram tour through an 'open-range' zoo where giraffes, lions and ostriches roam (p429)

Aquarium of the Pacific Meet more of coastal California's denizens of the deep in LA (p363)

Los Angeles Zoo Originally a refuge for retired circus animals, this conservation-minded zoo is active in species recovery efforts, including for California condors (p355)

Marine Mammal Center Marin County's wildlife hospital and marine education center has unbeatable eco-credentials; look in on the 'patients' out back (p103)

Historic Sites

Gold is usually the reason given for the madcap course of California's history, but Native American tribal villages, Spanish colonial *presidios* (forts), Catholic missions and Mexican *pueblos* (towns) have all left traces for you to dig into a little further.

Mission San Juan Capistrano A painstakingly restored jewel along 'El Camino Real,' California's mission trail (p)

Old Town San Diego Time travel back to the late 19th century on the site of California's first civilian Spanish colonial *pueblo* (p432)

El Pueblo de Los Angeles Get swept up by the atmosphere of LA's earliest days along lively Olvera St (p346)

Monterey State Historic Park Tour an unmatched collection of brick and adobe buildings from California's Spanish, Mexican and American periods (p279)

San Francisco Crawl along the back alleys of Chinatown, channel the Beats in North Beach or tour the flower-powered, hippie-psychedelic Haight (p48)

Nightlife

You've seen the red carpet rolled out for movie-star premieres. Now it's your turn to step out in style at urban nightclubs. Oh, you're not a fan of velvet ropes and attitudinous bouncers? No problem: thousands of bars up and down the coast have a California-casual style.

Los Angeles Hip-hop to world beats, techno to trance, DJs spin in Hollywood's glam club scene; nearby 'WeHo' is an LGBT nightlife hub (p380)

San Francisco Drink with artists and hipsters in the Mission, sip absinthe in Barbary Coast saloons or party with the rainbow-flag nation in the Castro (p88)

San Diego Go on a pub crawl in the Gaslamp Quarter, downtown's historic red-light district, or don your flip-flops and board shorts at surfer beach bars (p451)

North Coast Spend a week or just a weekend at only-in-California brewpubs, sampling award-winning ales, lagers, fruit beers and other inventive microbrews (p229)

month by month

Top Events

1 **Tournament of Roses**, January

2 **Miramar Air Show & Fleet Week**, September & October

3 **Pride Month**, June

4 **Festival of Arts & Pageant of the Masters**, July & August

5 **Kinetic Grand Championship**, May

January

Typically the wettest and coldest month in California, January is also the slowest season for coastal travel, except during the Martin Luther King Jr Day holiday weekend.

Tournament of Roses

Held before the Rose Bowl college football game, this famous New Year's parade of flower-festooned floats, marching bands and prancing equestrians draws over 100,000 spectators to Pasadena, a suburb of LA.

Chinese New Year

Firecrackers, parades, lion dances and street food celebrate the Chinese Lunar New Year, falling in late January or early February. Some of California's most colorful celebrations take place in San Francisco and Los Angeles.

March

Winter rains start to end. Coastal travel picks up again, especially over spring break (exact dates vary, depending on school schedules and the Easter holiday).

Mendocino Coast Whale Festivals

As the northbound winter migration of gray whales peaks, Mendocino and Fort Bragg celebrate over three weekends in March with food and wine tasting, art shows and naturalist-guided walks and talks.

Festival of the Swallows

After wintering in South America, the famous swallows return to Orange County's Mission San Juan Capistrano around March 19. The historic mission town celebrates its Spanish and Mexican heritage with events all month long.

May

California's weather starts to heat up, although some coastal areas are blanketed by fog ('May gray'). Travel peaks over the Memorial Day holiday weekend.

Bay to Breakers

On the third Sunday in May, costumed joggers make the annual pilgrimage from San Francisco's Embarcadero to Ocean Beach. Watch out for the participants dressed as salmon, who run 'upstream' from the finish line!

Kinetic Grand Championship

Over Memorial Day weekend, this 'triathlon of the art world' involves a three-day race from Arcata to Ferndale on the North Coast. Competitors outdo each other in inventing human-powered, self-propelled and sculptural contraptions.

June

Once school lets out for the summer, just about everywhere along the coast gets busy, even though fog ('June gloom') usually lingers in some areas.

Pride Month

Out and proud since 1970, many of California's Gay Pride events take place throughout June, with costumed parades, coming-out parties, live music, DJs and more. The biggest, bawdiest celebrations are in San Francisco and LA.

July

Beach season gets into full swing, especially in Southern California, where theme parks are mobbed by families. The July 4th holiday weekend is the busiest. Fog lingers in San Francisco.

Reggae on the River

Come party with the 'Humboldt Nation' of hippies, Rastafarians, tree huggers and other fun NorCal freaks for two days of live reggae bands, arts and crafts, barbecue, juggling, unicycling, camping and swimming in mid-July.

Festival of Arts & Pageant of the Masters

Exhibits by hundreds of working artists and a pageant of masterpiece paintings 're-created' by actors keep Orange County's Laguna Beach extremely busy during both July and August.

August

Sunny weather and warm water temperatures mean the beaches are packed. Kids go back to school, but everywhere along the coast stays busy through Labor Day.

Old Spanish Days Fiesta

Santa Barbara celebrates its early Spanish, Mexican and American rancho culture with flashy parades, cowboy rodeo events, arts-and-crafts shows and live music and dancing, all happening in early August.

September

Summer's last hurrah is the Labor Day holiday weekend, when everywhere is extremely crowded. Afterward, the beaches and coastal cities start seeing fewer visitors.

Miramar Air Show & Fleet Week

San Diego's military pride is on display for more than two weeks with parades, concerts, shipboard tours and the USA's largest air show in late September or early October.

October

Despite beautifully sunny and balmy weather, coastal travel slows down. Shoulder-season deals abound at beaches and in cities as temperatures begin to cool off.

Vineyard Festivals

All month long under sunny skies, California's wine counties celebrate bringing in the harvest from the vineyards with chefs' food-and-wine shindigs, grape-stomping 'crush' parties and barrel tastings. Some events start even earlier, in September.

November

Temperatures drop everywhere around California, with scattered winter rain and mountain snowstorms just beginning. Coastal travel slows even further, except around the Thanksgiving holiday.

Día de los Muertos

Mexican communities honor dead ancestors on November 2 with costumed parades, sugar skulls, graveyard picnics, candlelight processions and fabulous altars. The most memorable festivities are in San Francisco, LA and San Diego.

December

Winter rains start to drench coastal California. Christmas and New Year's Eve are extremely busy times, with a short-lived lull in travel between them.

Mavericks

Half Moon Bay's monster big-wave surfing competition only takes place if winter swells top 50ft, usually between December and March. When the surf's up, invited pro surfers have 24 hours to fly in from around the globe.

Parade of Lights

Ho, ho, ho! Spicing up the Christmas holiday season with nautical cheer, brightly bedecked and illuminated boats float through many coastal California harbors, most famously at Newport Beach and San Diego.

itineraries

Whether you've got six days or 60, these itineraries provide a starting point for the trip of a lifetime. Want more inspiration? Head online to lonelyplanet.com/thorntree to connect with other travelers.

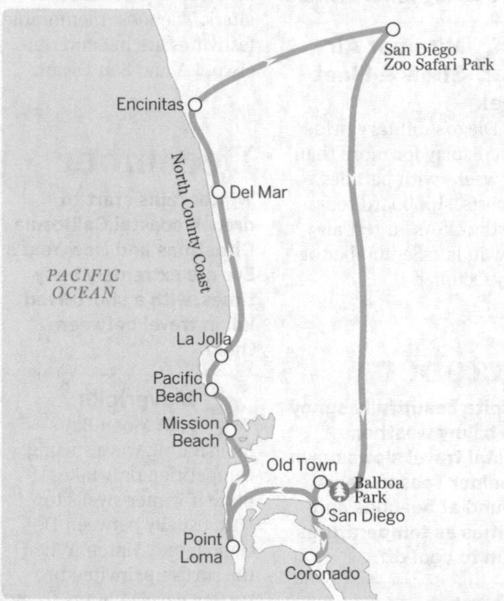

Three Days
San Diego & North County

The best part about San Diego? It's usually at least 68°F (20°C) and sunny. Add insanely good Mexican food, beaches of all stripes, historic sites and one of the best zoos in the world (plus a separate safari park). Are you sold yet?

Pearl-like beaches stretch all the way up San Diego's **North County Coast**. Before you head northward, drive out to **Point Loma** for sweeping views, or take a ferry over to old-fashioned **Coronado**, with its famous 'Hotel Del.' Ride the Giant Dipper roller coaster at family-friendly **Mission Beach**, join the funky surfers at **Pacific Beach**, dive or snorkel in **La Jolla**, bet on horse races or soar in a hot-air balloon at **Del Mar**, and get new-agey in **Encinitas**.

If you have kids, make a beeline to suburban **San Diego Zoo Safari Park**, where giraffes, lions and zebras roam. Otherwise, head back to the city to explore the zoo- and museum-loaded **Balboa Park** and atmospheric Spanish-Mexican **Old Town**. End your trip with a wild night out in **San Diego**'s Gaslamp Quarter or the trendy Hillcrest neighborhood.

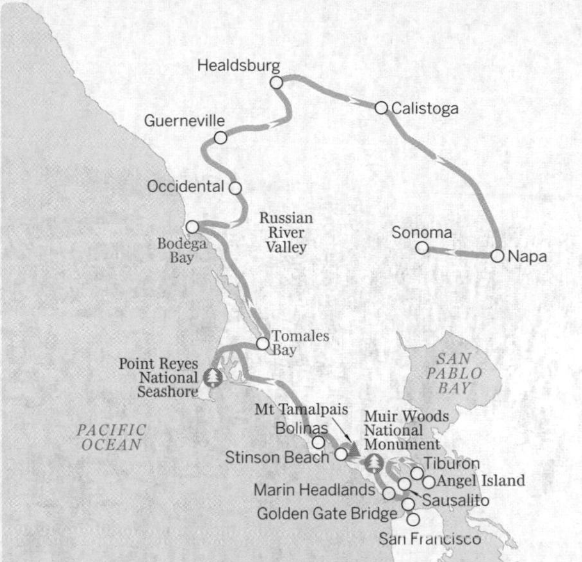

Five Days

San Francisco, Marin County & Wine Country

In the hilly 7-sq-mile peninsula that is dashing, innovative and ever-evolving **San Francisco**, you can spend a day uncovering the alleyways of **Chinatown**, wandering the mural-adorned **Mission District** and climbing **Coit Tower** above beatnik **North Beach**. Then brave the fog on a cruise over to **Alcatraz** from **Fisherman's Wharf**, or lose yourself on a sunny day in **Golden Gate Park**, stopping to smell the flowers where hippies danced during 1967's 'Summer of Love.' Wherever you roam, eat everything in sight – especially anything being hawked by organic farmers or artisanal cheese and olive-oil makers at the waterfront **Ferry Building Marketplace**.

Escape the city via the landmark **Golden Gate Bridge**, which you can trek, cycle or drive across. Safely on the far side of the bay, detour down to the waterfront to photograph the floating houseboats of picturesque **Sausalito**, or go hiking and mountain-biking across the **Marin Headlands**, stopping to check in on the 'patient' seals and sea lions at the Marine Mammal Center's wildlife hospital. To really get away from it all, hop aboard the ferry from **Tiburon** over to **Angel Island**, where you can pitch a tent within view of San Francisco's city lights.

Meander north along the Marin County coast, passing the tall redwood trees of **Muir Woods National Monument**, crescent-shaped **Stinson Beach** and the turnoff to quirky small-town **Bolinas**, or veer inland to conquer **Mt Tamalpais**. Make your way to wildly beautiful **Point Reyes National Seashore**, where end-of-the-world beaches lead to long rambles, and you can spy whales in winter from the historic lighthouse. Save time for sea kayaking and oyster shucking at nearby **Tomales Bay**.

From Bodega Bay, country roads wind inland to charming **Occidental** and the vineyards of the **Russian River Valley**. Paddle a canoe downriver to **Guerneville**, with its rustic redwood cottages and vibrant summertime festivals by the beach. Truck east across Hwy 101, then turn south to tipple in the heart of Northern California's wine country, orbiting stylish **Napa** and its countrified but still-chic cousin **Sonoma**, or head north to equally posh **Healdsburg**. Soak your road-weary bones in a volcanic mud bath at a hot-springs spa in **Calistoga** before looping back to San Francisco.

» (above) Huntington Beach (p40
Orange County

» (left) Hollywood Walk of Fame (p
Los Angeles

CHRISTINA LEASE/LONELY PLANET IMAGES ©

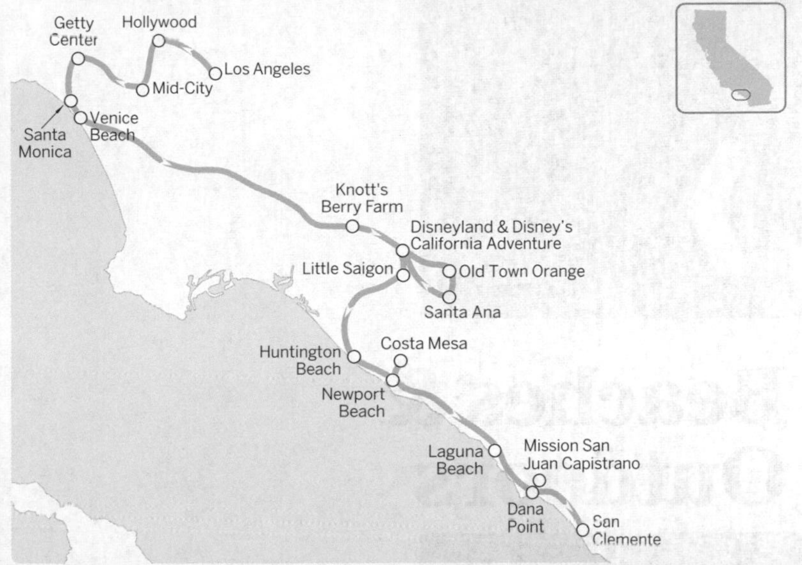

One Week

Los Angeles, Disneyland & Orange County

Kick things off in **Los Angeles**, where top-notch attractions, miles of beaches and tasty food form an irresistible trifecta. Traipse along the star-studded sidewalks of clubby **Hollywood**, dive into the arts and cultural scenes of **Downtown**, and browse the many museums of **Mid-City** and West LA's hilltop **Getty Center**. Out at the Pacific's edge, sophisticated **Santa Monica** beckons with a carnival seaside pier and creative restaurants, while artsy, alternative **Venice Beach** lives and breathes boho-chic style.

Forty miles inland, make a date with Mickey at perfectly 'imagineered' **Disneyland** and next-door **Disney's California Adventure**, celebrating the Golden State. Both parks are in Anaheim, not far from **Knott's Berry Farm**, America's oldest theme park, which pairs Old Western cowboy themes with futuristic roller coasters. If it's too darn hot, cool off at Knott's **Soak City USA**.

Just so you don't think Orange County is all about theme-park thrills, head to **Santa Ana** and drop by the interactive Discovery Science Center, where the whole family can virtually experience a 6.9-magnitude earthquake, or peruse the art galleries of the Bowers Museum. Catch your breath in time-warped **Old Town Orange**, clustered with vintage and antiques stores, before cruising west toward the Pacific. **Little Saigon** is not far away, where you can trade theme-park hot dogs and funnel cakes for a steaming bowl of pho.

In **Huntington Beach**, aka 'Surf City USA,' rent a board, play beach volleyball, build a bonfire after sunset – whatever, just kick back and chill, dude. Hit **Newport Beach** for soap opera–worthy people-watching by the piers and lazily pedaling a beach cruiser along the oceanfront bike path. Make a quick stop for power shopping and eclectic eats in **Costa Mesa**, then roll south to **Laguna Beach**, a former artists' colony with more than two dozen public beaches to spoil you, plus a fashionable downtown boutique shopping, gallery and cafe scene.

Slingshot back toward the I-5, stopping off at **Mission San Juan Capistrano** for a taste of Spanish colonial and Mexican rancho history. Or keep up the beach-bum attitude by slacking south to **Dana Point**, with its yacht-filled harbor and kid-friendly beach, and retro **San Clemente**, near Trestles, a year-round surf break.

Beaches & Outdoors

Best Times to Go...

Swimming Jul–Aug
Surfing Sep–Nov
Kayaking, snorkeling & diving Jul–Oct
Windsurfing Apr–Oct
Whale-watching Jan–Mar
Hiking Apr–Oct
Cycling & mountain-biking Apr–Oct

Top Outdoor Experiences

Surfing Santa Cruz, Malibu, Huntington Beach, Trestles or Rincon Point
Sea kayaking Channel Islands National Park
Snorkeling or **scuba diving** La Jolla in San Diego County
Whale-watching Monterey Bay National Marine Sanctuary
Beach volleyball Manhattan Beach in LA's South Bay
Hiking Redwood National & State Parks
Backpacking Lost Coast Trail in Northern California
Cycling Hwy 1 along the Big Sur coast
Mountain biking Marin County, especially around Mt Tamalpais

Coastal California is an all-seasons outdoor playground. Here you can go hiking among wildflowers in spring, swimming in the Pacific warmed by summer's sunshine, mountain-biking among fall foliage and whale-watching aboard a biodiesel-powered boat in winter. For bigger thrills, launch a glider off ocean bluffs, pull on a wet suit and scuba dive into underwater sanctuaries, or hook a kite onto a surfboard and launch yourself over foamy waves. Whatever your adrenaline fix, you'll find it here.

Beaches & Swimming

If lazing on the beach and taking quick dips in the Pacific is what you've got in mind, look to Southern California. Northern California beaches are cold year-round, with a dangerously high swell in places and rocky beaches with windy conditions that make swimming uninviting – if you try it, you'd best wear a wet suit!

With miles and miles of wide, sandy beaches, you won't find it hard to get wet and wild in Southern California, especially between Santa Barbara and Los Angeles and along both the Orange County and San Diego County coasts. Ocean temperatures become tolerably warm by May or June, peaking in July and August.

Another way to keep cool during the dog days of summer in SoCal is at a family-friendly water park like **Hurricane Harbor** north of LA, Knott's **Soak City USA** in Anaheim or **Legoland** north of San Diego.

Best Swimming Beaches

» **Los Angeles** Santa Monica, Venice, South Bay, Malibu, Zuma Beach

» **Orange County** Newport Beach, Laguna Beach, Seal Beach, Crystal Cove & Doheny State Beaches

» **San Diego** Coronado, Mission & Pacific Beaches, La Jolla, Cardiff

» **Central Coast** Ventura, Carpinteria, Santa Barbara, El Capitán & Refugio State Beaches

Top Family-Friendly Beaches

» Santa Monica, Los Angeles

» Newport Beach, Orange County

» Silver Strand State Beach, San Diego

» Leo Carrillo State Beach, Malibu

» Arroyo Burro (Hendry's) Beach, Santa Barbara

Best for Beach Volleyball

» Manhattan Beach, LA's South Bay

» Hermosa Beach, LA's South Bay

» Huntington Beach, Orange County

» Ocean Beach, San Diego

» East Beach, Santa Barbara

Safety Tips

» Popular beaches have lifeguards, but can still be dangerous places to swim. Obey all posted warning signs and ask about local conditions before venturing out.

» Many beaches also have flags to distinguish between swimming and surfer-only sections.

» Stay out of the ocean for at least three days after a major rainstorm because of dangerously high levels of pollutants flushed out through storm drains.

» Water quality varies from beach to beach, and day to day. Check the weekly **Beach Report Cards** (http://brc.healthebay.org) issued by the nonprofit organization Heal the Bay for current water conditions and beach closures statewide.

RIPTIDES

If you find yourself being carried offshore by an ocean current called a riptide, the important thing is to keep afloat. Don't panic or swim against the current, as this will quickly exhaust you and you could drown. Instead, swim parallel to the shoreline and once the current stops pulling you out, swim back to the beach.

Books & Maps

The outstanding *California Coastal Access Guide* (University of California Press, $30) has comprehensive maps and directions to every public beach, reef, harbor, cove, overlook and coastal campground. It's especially helpful for finding secret pockets of uncrowded sand.

Surfing

Surf's up! The most powerful swells arrive along California's coast during late fall and winter. May and June are generally the flattest months, although they do bring warmer water. Speaking of temperature, don't believe all those images of hot blondes surfing in skimpy bikinis; without a wet suit, you'll likely freeze your butt off except at the height of summer, especially in NorCal.

Crowds can be a problem at many surf spots, as can overly territorial gangs of surfers. Control your longboard or draw ire from aggro dudes in Malibu, San Diego's Windansea Beach and Orange County's Huntington Beach. Tip: befriend a local surfer for an introduction – and protection.

Sharks do inhabit California waters but attacks are rare. Most take place in the so-called 'Red Triangle' between Monterey on the Central Coast, Tomales Bay north of San Francisco and the offshore Farallon Islands.

Top Surf Spots for Pros

California comes fully loaded with easily accessible world-class surf spots, the lion's share of which are in SoCal, including:

» **Huntington Beach** in Orange County may have the West Coast's most consistent waves, with miles of breaks centered on the pier.

» The OC's **Trestles** is a premier summer spot with big but forgiving waves, a fast ride and both right and left breaks.

» San Diego's **Windansea Beach** is a powerful reef break, while nearby **Big Rock** churns out gnarly tubes.

» Malibu's **Surfrider Beach** is a clean right break that just gets better with bigger waves.

» Santa Barbara's **Rincon Point** is another legendary right point break that peels forever.

» Santa Cruz's **Steamer Lane** has glassy point breaks and rocky reef breaks.

» Half Moon Bay's **Mavericks** (www.maverickssurf.com) is world-famous for big-wave surfing, topping 50ft when the most powerful winter swells arrive.

Best Breaks for Beginners

The best spots to learn to surf are at beach breaks of long, shallow bays where waves are small and rolling, including:

» **San Diego** Mission Beach, Pacific Beach, Oceanside

» **Orange County** Seal Beach, Newport Beach, Dana Point

» **Los Angeles** Santa Monica, Manhattan Beach

» **Central Coast** Santa Cruz, Santa Barbara, Cayucos

Rentals & Lessons

You'll find board rentals on just about every patch of sand where surfing is possible. Expect to pay about $20 per half-day for a board, with wet-suit rental another $10.

Two-hour group lessons for beginners start around $75 per person, while private, two-hour instruction costs over $100. If you're ready to jump in the deep end, many surf schools offer pricier weekend surf clinics and week-long 'surfari' camps.

Stand-up paddle surfing (SUP) is easier than learning how to board surf, and it's skyrocketing in popularity. You'll find similarly priced board-and-paddle rentals and lessons all along the coast, from San Diego to north of San Francisco Bay.

Books, Maps & Online Resources

» Browse the comprehensive atlas, live webcams and surf reports at **Surfline** (www.surfline.com) for the low-down from San Diego to Santa Barbara.

» Orange County–based **Surfer** (www.surfermag.com) magazine's website has travel reports, gear reviews, newsy blogs and videos.

BODYSURFING & BODYBOARDING

If you don't have the time or inclination to master the art of surfing, there are other ways to catch your 'dream wave' at many SoCal beaches. Bodysurfing and bodyboarding (or boogie boarding) can extend your ride on the waves, sometimes as much as 100ft or more. Both sports benefit from the use of flippers to increase speed and control. If you're not sure how to do it, watch others or strike up a watery kinship and simply ask for pointers. It's really pretty easy, and you'll be howling with glee once you catch that first wave.

» Plan a coastal surfing adventure using **SurfMaps** (www.surfmaps.net), which even detail seasonal weather and water temperatures.

» Enlightened surfers can join up with **Surfrider** (www.surfrider.org), a nonprofit organization that aims to protect the coastal environment.

Windsurfing & Kiteboarding

Experienced windsurfers tear up the waves along the coast, while newbies (or those who want a mellower ride) skim along calm bays and protected beaches. There's almost always a breeze, but the best winds blow from April through October. Wet suits are a good idea year-round, especially in Northern California.

Best Places to Windsurf & Kiteboard

Usually any place that has good windsurfing also has good kiteboarding. Look for the people doing aerial acrobatics as their parachute-like kites yank them from the water. In wide-open spaces devoid of obstacles like piers and power lines, you won't have to worry about unexpected flights that could slam you into concrete.

» In San Diego, beginners should check out **Santa Clara Point** in Mission Bay.

» Santa Barbara's **Leadbetter Beach** is another good spot for beginners to learn.

» In LA County, you'll see lots of action off **Belmont Shores** near Long Beach and **Point Fermin** near San Pedro.

» San Francisco's **Crissy Field** is a favorite spot for experienced boarders, where the wind literally howls as it squeezes into the bay.

» Further north along the coast, **Bodega Bay** is another place to learn how to skim or to perfect your skills.

Rentals & Lessons

The learning curve in windsurfing is steeper than other board sports – imagine balancing on a fast-moving plank through choppy waters while trying to read the wind and angle the sail just so. At most windsurfing hot spots, you'll spend about $75 to $110 for a half-day beginner's lesson.

Although it's harder to get started kiteboarding, experts say it's easier to advance quickly once the basics are down. Beginner kiteboarding lessons ($175 to $400) usually last a few days. The first day is spent learning kite control on the beach and the second day gets you into the water.

Windsurfing gear rentals start at around $50 per day for a beginner's board, plus $15 to $25 for a wet suit and harness. Most windsurfing shops at least dabble in kiteboarding, but usually won't rent kite gear to people who aren't also taking lessons.

Online Resources

» Wind reports, weather forecasts, live windcams and active discussion forums are available at www.iwindsurf.com.

» Aspiring and experienced kiteboarders should check out www.ikitesurf.com and www.kitebeaches.com for primo locations, wind reports and more.

Scuba Diving & Snorkeling

All along the California coast, rock reefs, shipwrecks and kelp beds teem with sea creatures ready for their close-up. Underwater playgrounds are suited for all skill and experience levels. Ocean waters are warmest in Southern California and between July and September, but wet suits are recommended for divers year-round.

Local dive shops are your best resources for equipment, guides, instructors and boat trips. If you've already got your PADI certification, you can rent one-tank dive outfits or book a one-tank boat dive for $65 to $110 per person; reserve either at least a day in advance. If you just want to dabble in diving, ask about beginner scuba courses that include basic instruction, followed by a shallow beach or boat dive, for about $100 to $150. If you're serious about learning and have the time and money, sign up for a multiday open-water certificate course, which costs around $300 to $550.

Snorkel kits (including mask, snorkel, fins and maybe a wet suit) can be rented from beach concessionaires and many dive shops for around $20 to $40 per day. If you're going to be taking the plunge more than once or twice, it's probably worth buying your own mask and fins. Remember not to touch anything while you're out snorkeling, don't snorkel alone and always wear a T-shirt or sunblock on your back.

Best Scuba Diving & Snorkeling Spots

» San Diego's **La Jolla Underwater Park Ecological Reserve** is a great place for beginning divers, while **La Jolla Cove** attracts snorkelers.

» More experienced divers might want to steer towards **Crystal Cove State Park** just south of Newport Beach, **Divers Cove** in Laguna Beach and San Diego's **Mission Beach**, where you can explore a WWII military shipwreck.

» Some popular dive spots are also good for snorkeling, for example, offshore **Channel Islands National Park** and **Catalina Island**. Boats depart from Los Angeles, Orange County and Ventura on the Central Coast.

» With its national marine sanctuary, **Monterey Bay** offers world-renowned diving and snorkeling, although you'll need to wear a wet suit. It's chilly!

» Just south of Monterey on the Central Coast, **Point Lobos State Natural Reserve** is another gem for snorkelers and divers (permit reservations required).

Books & Online Resources

» **LA Diver** (http://ladiver.com) has encyclopedic listings of dive sites and shops, certification programs, safety resources and weather conditions for the LA area, with links to sister sites for Southern, Central and Northern California.

» Lonely Planet's *Diving & Snorkeling Southern California & the Channel Islands* by David Krival is a hands-on guide to happy encounters with marine critters.

» Published by PADI, the magazines **Scuba Diving** (www.scubadiving.com) and **Sport Diver** (www.sportdiver.com) have comprehensive websites dedicated to underwater adventures.

Kayaking

Few water-based sports are as accessible and fun for the whole gang as kayaking, and most people manage to get paddling along quickly and with minimal instruction. Whether you're looking for adventure exploring sea caves or just a serene paddle along coastal bluffs or inland rivers, opportunities abound in California.

Best Places to Kayak

» Sea kayaking is fabulous in the **Channel Islands National Park**, offshore from Ventura, and **Catalina Island**, closer to Los Angeles and Orange County.

» Further south, beginners can paddle the calm, protected waters of San Diego's **Mission Bay** or **Dana Point** in Orange County.

» Experienced paddlers can explore sea caves while floating above the kelp forests and reefs of **La Jolla Underwater Park Ecological Reserve** in San Diego.

» You'll find coastal kayaking in **Malibu**, among the coves of Orange County's **Laguna Beach** and around **Gaviota** near Santa Barbara.

» Beginners can take a spin around **Morro Bay**, whose waters are protected by a 4-mile sand spit, or float inland at **Elkhorn Slough** between Monterey and Santa Cruz.

» In Northern California, brave the choppy waters of **San Francisco Bay**, or head for more sheltered **Richardson Bay** in Sausalito, **Tomales Bay** near Point Reyes, **Bodega Bay** further north, or **Half Moon Bay** south along Hwy 1.

» Near the Napa and Sonoma wine country, the **Russian River** is a pretty place to paddle, with put-ins at Guerneville, Jenner and Healdsburg. Near Mendocino, the **Big River** tidal estuary is another peaceful float.

» All along the **North Coast**, various small towns offer challenging put-in points for experienced sea kayakers, as well as gentler lagoons, coves and bays for beginners.

BEWARE: POISON OAK

Watch out for western poison oak throughout California, especially in forests and foothills below 5000ft in elevation. This poisonous shrub is most easily identified by its shiny reddish-green tripartite leaves, which turn crimson in the fall, and its white berries. In winter, when the plant has no leaves, it looks brown and twiggy, but can still cause a serious allergic reaction if even one billionth of a gram of urushiol oil touches your skin. If you brush against poison oak, scrub the affected area immediately with soap and water or an over-the-counter remedy such as Tecnu, a soap specially formulated to remove the plant's itchy urushiol oils.

Rentals & Tours

Most outfitters offer a choice between sit-upon (open) kayaks and sit-in (closed-hull) ones; the latter are slightly more difficult to keep balanced and upright. Kayak rentals average $35 to $70 for the day, and you'll usually have a choice between single and tandem. Whatever kind of kayak you get, a reputable outfitter will make sure you're aware of the tide schedule and wind conditions for your proposed route.

Many kayaking outfitters give lessons and lead guided tours (from $50), including sunrise, sunset and full-moon paddles. There's nothing quite like seeing the reflection of the moon and stars glittering on the water and hearing the gentle splash of water on your kayak's hull. Small-group tours led by guides with natural-history knowledge are best.

Whether you're taking a guided tour or just renting kayaks, try to make reservations at least the day before.

Online Resources

» For dozens of links to local kayaking outfitters, schools and organizations, plus helpful advice, visit **Kayak Online** (www.kayakonline.com/california.html).

» **California Kayak Friends** (www.ckf.org) offers lots of information about everything from safety and popular paddling destinations to recent trip reports and upcoming events.

Whale-Watching

During their annual migration, gray whales can be spotted off the California coast from December to April, while blue, humpback and sperm whales pass by in summer and fall (see also p494). You can try your luck whale-watching while staying shore-bound (eg from lighthouses) – it's free, but you're less likely to see whales and you'll be removed from all the action.

Just about every port town worth its sea salt along the coast offers whale-watching boat excursions, especially during winter. Bring binoculars and dress in warm, waterproof layers.

Half-day whale-watching boat trips (from $30 to $45 per adult, $15 to $25 per child) last from 2½ to four hours; all-day trips average $65 to $100, sometimes including meals. Make reservations at least a day in advance.

Better tour boats limit the number of people and have a trained naturalist or marine biologist on board. Some tour companies will let you go again for free if you don't spot any whales during your first trip.

Choppy seas can be nauseating. To avoid seasickness, sit outside on the boat's second level – but not too close to the diesel fumes in back – and try staring ahead at the horizon. Over-the-counter motion-sickness pills (eg Dramamine) are effective against motion-sickness, but they can also make you drowsy; you'll usually need to take them a half hour in advance. Chewing ginger works for some people.

Hiking & Backpacking

No matter where you find yourself in coastal California, you're never far from a trail, even in busy metropolitan areas. The best trails are often in the jaw-dropping scenery of national and state parks, national forests, recreation areas and other public lands. Take your pick from a staggering variety of routes, easy strolls negotiable by wheelchairs and baby strollers to multiday backpacking treks through the wilderness. Don't miss a ramble among the world's tallest trees, coast redwoods, or spring wildflowers that bloom with all the colors of an Impressionist painter's palette.

Best Places to Hike

» **North Coast** Redwood National & State Parks and Humboldt Redwoods State Park offer misty walks through groves of old-growth coast redwoods, or you can trek to truly wild beaches along the challenging Lost Coast Trail.

» **San Francisco Bay Area** The Marin Headlands, Muir Woods, Mt Tamalpais and Point Reyes National Seashore, all within a 90-minute drive of San Francisco, are crisscrossed by dozens of superb trails.

» **Central Coast** Santa Cruz and Big Sur State Parks abound with redwood-forest trails, while Point Lobos State Natural Reserve and Channel Island National Park offer plenty of ocean-view trails with wildlife-watching. For peaks to climb, head to Montaña de Oro State Park or Pinnacles National Monument.

» **Los Angeles** Ditch your car in urban Griffith Park and the wilder Santa Monica Mountains National Recreation Area, or head out to the cooler climes of Big Bear Lake. Offshore, day hikers and backpackers trek across Catalina Island.

Fees & Wilderness Permits

» Coastal California's national parks, including Redwood National Park, Point Reyes National Seashore and Channel Islands National Park, are often free.

» Most California state parks charge a daily parking fee of $6 to $15, but there's often no charge if you walk or bike into these parks.

» You'll need a **National Forest Adventure Pass** (☎909-382-2622; www.fs.fed.us/r5/sanbernardino/ap/; per day/year $5/30) for parking in the San Bernardino, Cleveland, Angeles or Los Padres national forests. Buy these passes on the spot from USFS ranger stations and authorized local vendors (eg sporting-goods stores), or order in advance online or by phone.

» Often required for overnight hikes and backpacking trips, wilderness permits are issued at ranger stations and park visitor centers; fees range from free to $25.

» Daily trail quotas limiting the number of wilderness permits issued may be in effect during peak periods, usually from late spring through early fall.

» Some wilderness permits may be reserved in advance online or by phone, fax or mail. Permits for a few of the most popular trails sell out months beforehand.

Camping in Coastal California

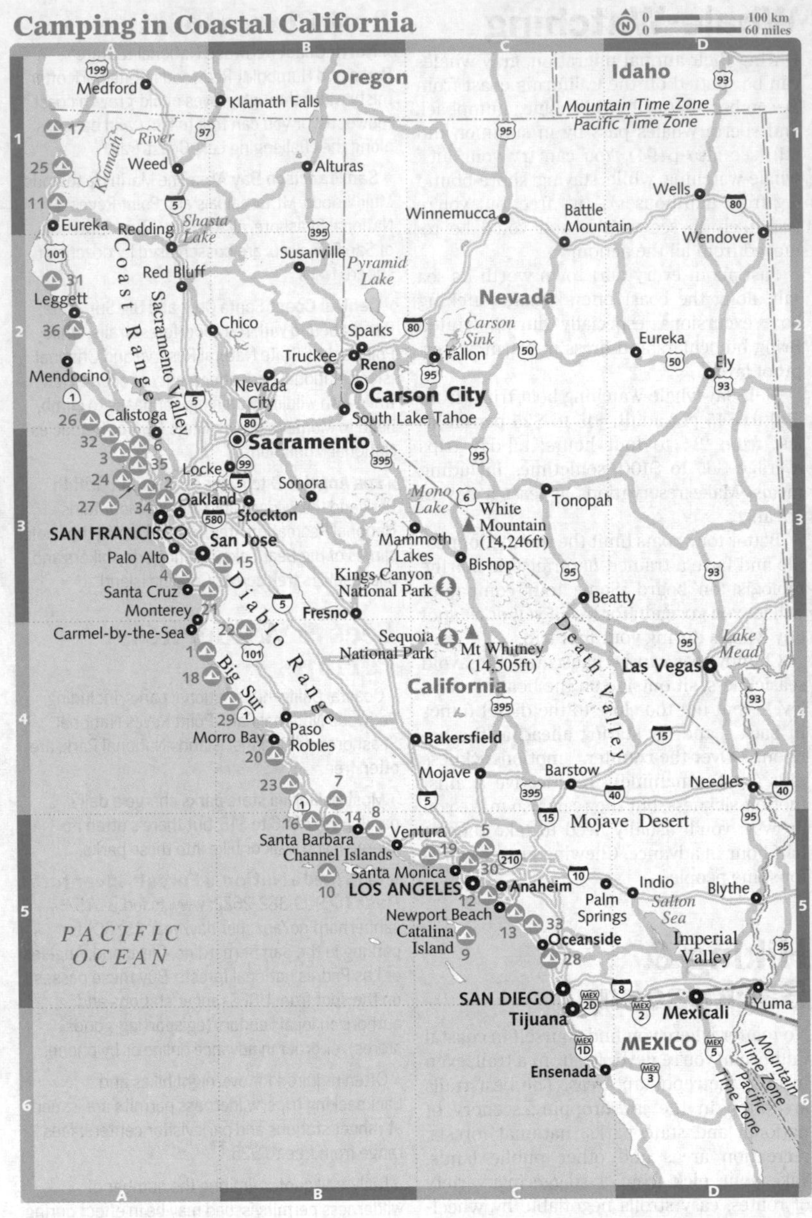

Maps & Online Resources

» At most major trailheads in national, state and regional parks, bulletin boards display basic trail maps and safety information.

» For short, well-established hikes, the free trail maps handed out at park visitor centers and ranger stations are usually sufficient.

» A more detailed topographical map may be necessary for longer backcountry hikes. Topo maps are sold at park bookstores, visitor centers,

Camping in Coastal California

Sleeping

1 Andrew Molera State Park A4
2 Angel Island State Park A3
3 Austin Creek State Recreation Area A3
4 Big Basin Redwoods State Park A3
5 Big Bear Lake C5
6 Bothe-Napa Valley State Park A3
7 Cachuma Lake Recreation Area B4
8 Carpinteria State Beach B5
Casini Ranch .... (see 3)
9 Catalina Island C5
10 Channel Islands National Park B5
11 Clam Beach County Park A1
12 Crystal Cove State Park C5
13 Doheny State Beach C5
14 El Capitán State Beach B5
Henry Cowell Redwoods State Park .... (see 4)
15 Henry W Coe State Park B3
16 Jalama Beach County Park B5
17 Jedediah Smith Redwoods State Park A1
Julia Pfeiffer Burns State Park .... (see 1)
18 Kirk Creek A4
19 Leo Carrillo State Beach C5
Limekiln State Park .... (see 1)
Los Padres National Forest .... (see 7)
Marin Headlands .... (see 34)
Montaña de Oro State Park .... (see 20)
20 Morro Bay State Park B4
21 New Brighton State Beach A3
Pfeiffer-Big Sur State Park .... (see 1)
22 Pinnacles National Monument B4
23 Pismo State Beach B4
Plaskett Creek .... (see 18)
24 Point Reyes National Seashore A4
25 Prairie Creek Redwoods State Park A1
Refugio State Beach .... (see 14)
26 Salt Point State Park A2
27 Samuel P Taylor State Park A3
28 San Elijo State Beach C5
29 San Simeon State Park B4
30 Santa Monica Mountains National Recreation Area C5
31 Sinkyone Wilderness State Park A2
32 Sonoma Coast State Beach A3
33 South Carlsbad State Beach C5
34 Steep Ravine A3
35 Sugarloaf Ridge State Park A3
36 Van Damme State Park A2

ranger stations and outdoor-gear shops including **REI** (www.rei.com).

» The **US Geological Survey** (USGS; www.store.usgs.gov) offers its topographic maps as free PDFs, or you can order print copies online.

» **Trails.com** (www.trails.com) lets you search for hundreds of multisport trails throughout California (trail summary overviews are free).

» **Coastwalk** (www.coastwalk.org) advocates for a long-distance trail all along California's shoreline. Join a group hike, or volunteer to do beach cleanup or trail maintenance.

» Learn how to minimize your impact on the environment while traipsing through the wilderness by visiting the **Leave No Trace Center for Outdoor Ethics** (www.lnt.org) online.

Cycling & Mountain-Biking

Strap on that helmet! Coastal California is outstanding cycling territory, no matter whether you're off for a leisurely spin along the beach, an adrenaline-fueled mountain ride or a multiday bike-touring coastal adventure. The cycling season runs year-round in Southern California, although coastal fog may rob you of views in winter and during 'May gray' and 'June gloom.' Winter in Northern California is colder, rainier and generally not ideal for cycling, with prime time from late spring until early fall.

Road Rules

» In national and state parks, bicycles are usually limited to paved and dirt roads and are not allowed on trails or in designated wilderness areas.

» Most national forests and Bureau of Land Management (BLM) areas are open to mountain-bikers. Stay on already established tracks and always yield to hikers and horseback riders.

» For road-cycling rules, emergency roadside assistance and transporting your bike, see p515; for rental information, see p519.

Best Places to Cycle

» Even the heavily trafficked urban areas of Southern California may sport some good cycling turf. Take, for example, the beachside South Bay

EVEN MORE ACTIVITIES!

ACTIVITY	LOCATION	REGION	PAGE
Bird-watching	Channel Islands National Park	Central Coast	p336
	Elkhorn Slough	Central Coast	p278
	Audubon Canyon Ranch	Marin County	p116
	Point Reyes National Seashore	Marin County	p119
	Point Lobos State Natural Reserve	Central Coast	p290
	Humboldt Bay National Wildlife Refuge	North Coast	p250
	Arcata Marsh & Wildlife Sanctuary	North Coast	p255
	Pinnacles National Monument	Central Coast	p309
Caving	Pinnacles National Monument	Central Coast	p309
Fishing*	San Diego	San Diego County	p444
	Bodega Bay	North Coast	p215
	Monterey Bay	Central Coast	p281
	Dana Point	Orange County	p420
Golf	Pebble Beach	Central Coast	p289
	Torrey Pines	San Diego	p442
	Pacific Grove	Central Coast	p288
Hang gliding & paragliding	Torrey Pines	San Diego	p441
	Santa Barbara	Central Coast	p331
Horseback Riding	Point Reyes National Seashore	Marin County	p119
	Santa Monica Mountains & Griffith Park	Los Angeles	p368
	Bodega Bay	North Coast	p215
	Big Sur	Central Coast	p294
Hot-air ballooning	Del Mar	San Diego	p459
	Napa Valley	Wine Country	p173
Rock climbing	Pinnacles National Monument	Central Coast	p309
Skiing	Big Bear Lake	Los Angeles	p391

*For fishing licenses, regulations and location information, consult the **California Department of Fish & Game** (www.dfg.ca.gov).

Trail in **Los Angeles** or oceanfront recreational paths at **Newport Beach** and **Huntington Beach** in Orange County.

» In Northern California's bike-friendly **San Francisco**, you can cruise through Golden Gate Park and over the Golden Gate Bridge, then hop the ferry back across the bay from **Sausalito**. Sitting right in the bay, **Angel Island** is another great bike-and-ferry combo.

» Along the Central Coast, the waterfront **Monterey Peninsula Recreational Trail** and scenic **17-Mile Drive** entice cyclists of all skill levels. Shorter seaside bike paths in **Santa Barbara** and **Santa Cruz** are an easy pedal for the whole family. For long-distance cyclists, nothing surpasses coastal **Highway 1**, especially the dizzying stretch through **Big Sur** on the Central Coast.

» Northern California's **Napa and Sonoma wine country** offers some beautiful bike tours past valley vineyards, farms and small towns.

» Further north, you can ride among the world's tallest trees along the winding **Avenue of Giants** in tranquil Humboldt Redwoods State Park.

Best Mountain-Biking Areas

» Just north of San Francisco, the **Marin Headlands** offers a bonanza of trails for fat-tire fans, while **Mt Tamalpais State Park** lays claim to being the sport's birthplace. Even **Point Reyes National Seashore** has some single-track.

» You'll find miles of backcountry roads and trails for mountain-biking in the **Santa Monica Mountains** north of LA. Also a day trip from LA, **Big Bear Lake** is another fat-tire playground, with national forest trails and a ski-resort chairlift that serves mountain-bikers in summer.

» State parks especially popular with mountain-bikers include Orange County's **Crystal Cove**; **McNee Ranch** south of San Francisco; NorCal's **Humboldt Redwoods** and **Prairie Creek Redwoods**; and **Wilder Ranch** near Santa Cruz, **Andrew Molera** in Big Sur and San Luis Obispo's **Montaña de Oro**, all on the Central Coast.

Maps & Online Resources

Local bike shops can supply you with more cycling route ideas, maps and advice.

» For online forums and reviews of mountain-biking trails throughout California, search **DirtWorld.com** (http://dirtworld.com) and **MTBR.com** (www.mtbr.com).

» **Adventure Cycling Association** (www.adventurecycling.org) sells long-distance cycling route guides and touring maps, including the Pacific Coast Highway (PCH).

» **California Bicycle Coalition** (www.calbike.org) links to free online cycling maps, bike-sharing programs and community bike shops.

» **California Association of Bicycling Organizations** (www.cabobike.org) offers free bicycle touring and freeway access information online.

» Find bicycle specialty shops, local cycling clubs, group rides and other special events with the **League of American Bicyclists** (www.bikeleague.org).

Travel with Children

Los Angeles

See stars in Hollywood and behind-the-scenes movie magic at Universal Studios, then hit the beaches for fun in the sun.

Orange County & San Diego

Theme parks: Disneyland, Knott's Berry Farm, San Diego Zoo Safari Park and more.

San Francisco Area

Explore the science museums, hear the barking sea lions at Pier 39, then amble through Golden Gate Park and over the city's iconic bridge.

Central Coast

Whale-watching boats and a giant aquarium in Monterey, Big Sur's forests and riverside campgrounds, and Santa Barbara's beaches and pint-sized museums all attract families.

North Coast & Redwoods

Go tide-pooling by NorCal's rocky beaches and coves, then let your kids stand next to the world's tallest trees, protected by state and national parks.

California is a tailor-made destination for traveling with kids. The kids will already be begging to go to Southern California's theme parks. Get those over with (you may well enjoy them too) and then introduce them to many other worlds, big and small. There's really not too much to worry about when traveling with your kids in coastal California, as long as you keep them covered in sunblock.

California's sunny skies lend themselves to outdoor activities of all kinds. Here's a start (big breath!): swimming, bodysurfing, snorkeling, kayaking, bicycling, horseback riding and hiking. In winter when it's cold and rainy, or when fog hugs the coast during 'May gray' and 'June gloom,' you'll find museums and indoor entertainment galore.

Coastal California with Kids

Children's discounts are widely available for everything from museum admission and movie tickets to bus fares and motel stays. The definition of a 'child' varies – in some places anyone under 18 is eligible, while at others the cut-off is age six. At amusement parks, some rides may have minimum-height requirements – let younger kids know about this in advance to avoid disappointment and tears.

It's perfectly fine to bring kids, even toddlers, along to casual restaurants, which often provide high chairs. Many diners and family restaurants break out paper placemats and crayons for drawing. Ask about cheaper children's menus too. At theme parks, pack a cooler in the car and have a picnic in the parking lot to save money. On the road, local supermarkets including Trader Joe's and Whole Foods have healthy, ready-to-eat takeout.

Baby food, infant formula, soy and cow's milk, disposable diapers (nappies) and other necessities are widely available in drugstores and supermarkets. Most women are discreet about breastfeeding in public. Many public toilets have a baby-changing table and some gender-neutral private 'family' bathrooms may be available at airports, museums, etc.

Children's Highlights

It's easy to keep kids entertained no matter where you travel in coastal California. Throughout this book, look for family attractions and other fun activities, all marked with the child-friendly icon (👪). At national and state parks, ask at visitor centers about ranger-led activities and self-guided 'Junior Ranger' programs, in which kids earn a badge after completing an activity. To make the most of coastal California's cities, see the special 'City for Children' sections in the San Francisco (p95) and Los Angeles (p368) destination chapters of this book.

Theme Parks

» **Disneyland & Disney's California Adventure** All ages of kids, even teens, and the eternally young at heart will adore the 'Magic Kingdom.'

» **Knott's Berry Farm** Near Disney, SoCal's original theme park offers thrills-a-minute, especially during spooky haunted Halloween nights.

» **Universal Studios Hollywood** Movie-themed rides, special-effects shows and a working studio backlot tram tour entertain tweens and teens.

» **Six Flags Magic Mountain & Hurricane Harbor** Drive outside LA for high-adrenaline roller coasters, thrill rides and twisting water slides that will terrify even teens.

» **Legoland** North of San Diego, this fantasyland of building blocks is designed for tots and youngsters.

Aquariums & Zoos

» **San Diego Zoo & Safari Park** Journey around the world with exotic wildlife and go on safari outdoors at California's best and biggest zoo.

» **Los Angeles Zoo** What was once the home of retired circus animals is today a center for endangered species conservation, most famously California condors.

» **Monterey Bay Aquarium** Get acquainted with coastal California's aquatic citizens next door to the Central Coast's biggest marine sanctuary.

» **Aquarium of the Pacific** Long Beach's high-tech aquarium houses critters from balmy Baja California to the chilly north Pacific.

» **Seymour Marine Discovery Center** Santa Cruz's university-run aquarium makes interactive science fun, with tidepools for exploring at the beach nearby.

» **Birch Aquarium** La Jolla's kids zone is as entertaining as it is educational, thanks to the stellar Scripps Institute of Oceanography.

Beaches

» **Los Angeles** Have carnival fun at Santa Monica Pier, drop by Manhattan Beach's pier aquarium and beach volleyball courts, or drive to Malibu's perfect beaches.

» **Orange County** Newport Beach offers kiddie-sized Balboa Pier rides, Laguna Beach miles of million-dollar sand, Huntington Beach (aka 'Surf City USA') wave-riding lessons, and old-fashioned Seal Beach calm waters for wading.

» **San Diego** Head over to Coronado's idyllic Silver Strand, play in Mission Bay by SeaWorld, lap up La Jolla's snorkeling pools and coves or unwind in surf-style North County beach towns.

» **Central Coast** Laze on Santa Barbara's golden sands, then roll north past San Luis Obispo's off-the-beaten track beach towns to Santa Cruz's famous boardwalk and pier.

» **San Francisco Bay Area** Travel north up to Marin County's crescent-shaped Stinson Beach and wilder Point Reyes National Seashore, or south along Hwy 1 past lighthouse hostels to Half Moon Bay.

Parks

» **Redwood National & State Parks** On the fog-laden North Coast, a string of nature preserves protects magnificent wildlife, beaches and the tallest trees on earth.

» **Griffith Park** Bigger than NYC's Central Park, this LA green space has tons of fun for younger kids, from miniature train rides and a merry-go-round to planetarium shows.

» **Balboa Park** Spend all day at the San Diego Zoo and museums, taking time out for the puppet theater or a model-railroad ride. Plazas, fountains and gardens offer plenty of space for younger kids to let off steam.

» **Golden Gate Park** With kids in tow, wander through the indoor rain forest at the California Academy of Sciences, tour the Japanese tea garden and spot the park's buffalo herd.

» **Channel Islands National Park** Sail across to California's Galapagos for wildlife watching, sea kayaking, hiking and camping adventures; best for teens.

Museums

» **San Francisco Bay Area** San Francisco is a mind-bending classroom for kids, with the hands-on Exploratorium, high-tech Children's Creative Museum and ecofriendly California Academy of Sciences. Then head over to the East Bay's star-powered Chabot Space & Science Center.

» **Los Angeles** See stars (the real ones) at the Griffith Observatory and dinosaur bones at the Natural History Museum of Los Angeles County and the Page Museum at the La Brea Tar Pits, then get hands-on at the energetic California Science Center.

» **San Diego** Balboa Park is jam-packed with museums such as the Reuben H Fleet Science Center and lunar-view San Diego Air & Space Museum, or take younger kids downtown to the engaging New Children's Museum.

» **Orange County** Bring budding lab geeks to the Discovery Science Center and get a pint-sized dose of arts and culture at the Bowers Kidseum, both near Disneyland.

» **Santa Barbara** Go virtually deep-sea fishing at the harborfront maritime museum, then meet stuffed wildlife and watch planetarium shows at uptown's natural history museum.

Just for Fun

» **Hollywood Walk of Fame** Let kiddos put their hands inside the prints of famous movie characters and stars outside Grauman's Chinese Theatre.

» **Musée Mechanique** Unload rolls of quarters inside this old-timey vintage game arcade at San Francisco's Fisherman's Wharf.

» **Santa Cruz Beach Boardwalk** Get your kicks aboard the Giant Dipper wooden roller coaster, old-fashioned carousel and other carnival rides by the sea.

» **Chandelier Drive-Thru Tree Park & Confusion Hill** Youngsters will squeal as you drive right through a redwood tree, then play inside a 1940s tourist trap in Northern California's redwood country.

» **Trees of Mystery** Another North Coast roadside attraction, with an aerial canopy ride through a redwood forest and a giant talking statue of Paul Bunyan and his blue ox, Babe.

Planning

When to Go

For the best times to visit coastal California and setting your family's vacation budget, see p18. For family-friendly festivals and events, see p24. A word of advice: don't pack your schedule too tightly. Traveling with kids always takes longer than expected, especially when navigating metro areas like LA and San Francisco, where you'll want to allow extra time for traffic jams and getting lost.

Accommodations

Motels and hotels typically have rooms with two beds or an extra sofa bed. They also may have roll-away beds or cots that can be brought into the room, usually for a surcharge. Some offer 'kids stay free' promotions, although this may apply only if no extra bedding is required. Many B&Bs don't allow children; ask when booking.

Resorts may have drop-off day camps for kids or on-call babysitting services. At other hotels, the front-desk staff or concierge might help you make arrangements. Be sure to ask whether babysitters are licensed and bonded, what they charge per hour per child, whether there's a minimum fee and if they charge extra for transportation and meals.

Transportation

Airlines usually allow infants (up to age two) to fly for free, while older children requiring a seat of their own qualify for reduced fares. Children receive substantial discounts on Amtrak trains and Greyhound buses. In California, any child under age six or weighing less than 60lb must be buckled up in the back seat of the car in a child or infant safety seat. Most car-rental agencies rent these seats for about $10 per day or $50 per trip, but you must specifically book them in advance.

What to Pack

Sunscreen. Lots of sunscreen.

If your family likes beach umbrellas and sand chairs, pails and shovels, you'll probably want to bring or buy your own at local supermarkets and drugstores. At many beaches, you can rent bicycles and all kinds of watersports gear (eg snorkel sets).

If you forget some critical piece of equipment, **Baby's Away** (www.babysaway.com) rents cribs, strollers, car seats, high chairs, backpacks, beach gear and more.

Before You Go

» Lonely Planet's *Travel with Children* is loaded with valuable tips and amusing anecdotes, especially for new parents and kids who haven't traveled before.

» **Lonelyplanet.com** (www.lonelyplanet.com) lets you ask questions and get advice from other travelers in the Thorn Tree's 'Kids to Go' and 'USA' forums.

» The state's official visitor website, **California Travel & Tourism** (www.visitcalifornia.com), lists family-friendly attractions, activities, special events and more.

» **Family Travel Files** (www.thefamilytravelfiles.com/locations/california) is an info-packed site with vacation-planning articles, tips and discounts for Northern and Southern California.

» **Parents Connect** (www.parentsconnect.com/family-travel) is a virtual encyclopedia of everything first-time family travelers need to know.

regions at a glance

Coastal California's cities have more flavors than a jar of jellybeans. Start in San Francisco, equal parts earth-mother and geek-chic, or Los Angeles, where nearly 90 independent cities are rolled into one multicultural mosaic. Later, kick back in surf-style San Diego.

But don't skip the features away from California's urban jungles: misty redwood forests along the North Coast, country lanes winding past vineyards in Napa and Sonoma wine country, the Central Coast's oceanfront vistas or Orange County's cinematic beaches.

On sunny days, when the coastal fog lifts, more than 1100 miles of Pacific beaches await.

San Francisco

Food ✓✓✓
Culture ✓✓✓
Museums ✓✓✓

California's 'Left Coast' reputation rests on SF, where DIY self-expression, sustainability and spontaneity rank among the highest virtues. Free thinkers, edgy neighborhoods, top-tier museums and ground-breaking arts scenes all thrive.

p48

Marin County & the Bay Area

Outdoor Sports ✓✓✓
Ecotourism ✓✓✓
Food ✓✓✓

Outdoors nuts adore Marin County and Hwy 1 south of San Francisco for their beaches, wildlife-watching, kayaking, and hiking and mountain-biking trails. Taste and tour organic farms that inspire chefs all around the Bay, too.

p100

Napa & Sonoma Wine Country

Wineries ✓✓✓
Food ✓✓✓
Cycling & Canoeing ✓✓✓

Amid fruit orchards and ranch lands, sunny valleys kissed by cool coastal fog have made the Napa, Sonoma and Russian River Valleys into California's premier wine-growing region and a showcase for rule-breaking cuisine.

p159

North Coast & the Redwoods

Wildlife ✓✓✓
Hiking ✓✓✓
Beaches ✓✓

Primeval redwood forests are the prize along NorCal's foggy, rocky and wild coastline. Let loose your inner hippie in Humboldt County, or explore bootstrap fishing villages and wind-tossed beaches from Bodega Bay to Eureka.

p212

Central Coast

Wildlife ✓✓✓
Beaches ✓✓✓
Scenic Drives ✓✓✓

Off serpentine Hwy 1, hike Big Sur's redwood forests, where waterfalls spring; hop aboard a whale-watching boat in Monterey Bay; surf anywhere from Santa Cruz to Santa Barbara; or escape to the prized Channel Islands.

p267

Los Angeles

Nightlife ✓✓✓
Food ✓✓✓
Beaches ✓✓✓

There's more to life in La La Land than just sunny beaches and air-kissing celebs. Get a dose of art and culture Downtown, then dive into diverse neighborhoods, from historic Little Tokyo to red-carpet Hollywood.

p341

Disneyland & Orange County

Theme Parks ✓✓✓
Beaches ✓✓✓
Surfing ✓✓✓

The OC's beaches are packed bronze-shoulder-to-shoulder with blond surfers, beach-volleyball nuts and soap opera-esque beauties. Inland, take the kids – heck, load up the whole minivan – to Disneyland Park and Disney's California Adventure.

p393

San Diego

Beaches ✓✓✓
Mexican Food ✓✓✓
Museums ✓✓✓

With a near perfect climate, lucky residents of California's southernmost city always seem to be slacking off – and who can blame them? Take a permanent vacation in laid-back beach towns while devouring fish tacos.

p421

❯ **Every listing is recommended by our authors, and their favourite places are listed first**

❯ **Look out for these icons:**

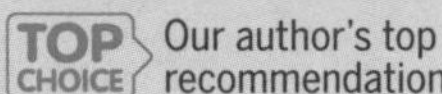

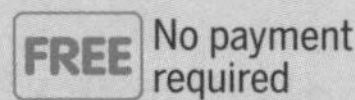

See the Index for a full list of destinations covered in this book.

On the Road

San Francisco

Best Places to Eat

» Coi (p79)
» Benu (p82)
» La Taquería (p82)
» Frances (p85)
» Aziza (p87)

Best Places to Stay

» Orchard Garden Hotel (p72)
» Hotel Vitale (p76)
» Hotel Bohème (p74)
» Inn San Fransisco (p76)
» Argonaut Hotel (p75)

Why Go?

Get to know the world capital of weird from the inside out, from mural-lined alleyways named after poets to clothing-optional beaches on a former military base. But don't be too quick to dismiss San Francisco's wild ideas. Biotech, gay rights, personal computers, cable cars and organic fine dining were once considered outlandish too, before San Francisco introduced these underground ideas into the mainstream decades ago. San Francisco's morning fog erases the boundaries between land and ocean, reality and infinite possibility.

Rules are never strictly followed here, but bliss is. Golden Gate Bridge and Alcatraz are entirely optional – San Franciscans mostly admire them from afar – leaving you free to pursue inspiration through Golden Gate Park, past flamboyantly painted Victorian homes and through Mission galleries. Just don't be late for your sensational, sustainable dinner: in San Francisco, you can find happiness and eat it too.

When to Go

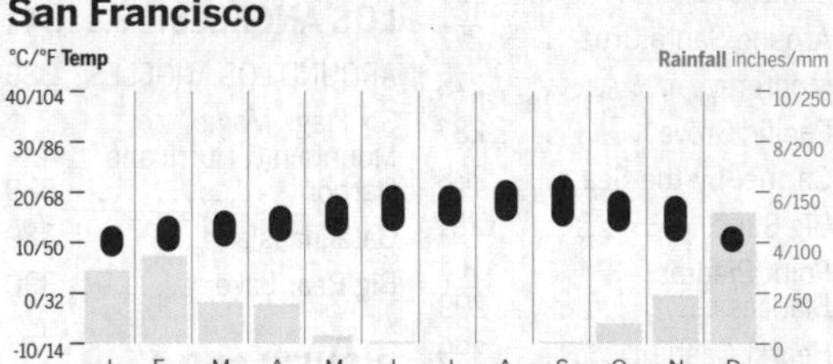

Jan–Mar Low-season rates, brisk but rarely cold days, and the colorful Lunar New Year parade.

May–Aug Farmers markets and festivals make up for high-season rates and chilly afternoon fog.

Sep–Nov Blue skies, free concerts, bargain hotel rates and flavor-bursting harvest cuisine.

Cable Cars

Groaning brakes and clanging brass bells only add to the thrills of San Francisco's cable cars, which have hardly changed since their introduction here in 1873. Cable cars still can't move in reverse, and require burly gripmen (and one buff gripwoman) to lean hard on hand-operated brakes to keep from careening downhill. The city receives many applicants for this job, but 80% fail the strenuous tests of upper-body strength and hand–eye coordination, and rarely try again. Today the cable car seems more like a steampunk carnival ride than modern transport, but it remains the killer app to conquer San Francisco's breakneck slopes. There are no seat belts, child seats or air bags on board – just jump onto the wooden sideboard, grab a strap, and enjoy the ride of your life.

DON'T MISS...

» **Saloons** The Barbary Coast is roaring back to life with historically researched whiskey cocktails and staggering absinthe concoctions in San Francisco's great Western saloon revival (p88).

» **Foraged fine dining** No SF tasting menu is complete without wild chanterelles, miner's lettuce from Berkeley hillsides or SF-backyard nasturtium flowers, from **Commonwealth** (p82) to **Coi** (p79).

» **Green everything** Recent reports rank San Francisco as the greenest city in North America, with its LEED-certified green hotels, pioneering citywide composting laws and America's biggest stretch of urban greenery: **Golden Gate Park** (p49).

» **Showtime** Bewigged satire, world premiere opera, year-round film festivals, Grammy-winning symphonies and legendary, jawdropping drag: no one puts on a show like San Francisco, and the cheering, back-talking local audiences demand encores in no uncertain terms.

SF's Best Free...

» **Music** Golden Gate Park (p49) hosts free concerts summer through fall, from opera to Hardly Strictly Bluegrass (p72).

» **Speech** City Lights Bookstore (p55) won a landmark free speech case over the publication of Allen Ginsberg's magnificent, incendiary *Howl;* take a seat in the designated Poet's Chair and celebrate your right to read freely.

» **Love** Pride (p71) fills San Francisco streets with free candy, free condoms, and over a million people freely smooching total strangers under rainbow flags.

» **Spirits** Anywhere within city limits, at any time – consider yourself warned.

DID YOU KNOW?

Despite slacker reputations cultivated at 30 medical marijuana clubs, San Franciscans hold more patents, read more books and earn more degrees per capita than residents of any other US city.

Fast Facts

» **Population** 805,235

» **Area** 7 square miles

» **Telephone area code** 415

Planning Your Trip

» **Three weeks before** Book Alcatraz trips and dinner at Coi or Frances.

» **Two weeks before** Build stamina for downtown hills, South of Market (SoMa) galleries and Mission bars.

» **One week before** Score tickets to San Francisco Symphony or Opera, and assemble your costume – SF throws parades whenever.

Resources

» **SF Bay Guardian** (www.sfbg.com) Hot tips on local entertainment, arts, politics.

» **SFGate** (www.sfgate.com) News and event listings.

San Francisco Highlights

1 Make yourself at home where the buffalo roam in **Golden Gate Park** (p49)

2 Reach new artistic heights at the **San Francisco Museum of Modern Art** (p60) rooftop sculpture garden

3 Watch fog dance atop the deco towers of the **Golden Gate Bridge** (p51)

4 Graze the **Ferry Building** (p51), SF's local, sustainable foodie destination

5 Plot your escape from **Alcatraz** (p71), SF's notorious island prison

6 Discover unlikely urban marine life along **Fisherman's Wharf** (p56): sea lions, sharks, and a WWII submarine

7 Unwind in Japanese baths and catch film screenings in **Japantown** (p57)

8 Get breathless from the climb, murals and panoramic views at **Coit Tower** (p57)

9 Wander through 150 years of California history in pagoda-topped **Chinatown** (p53)

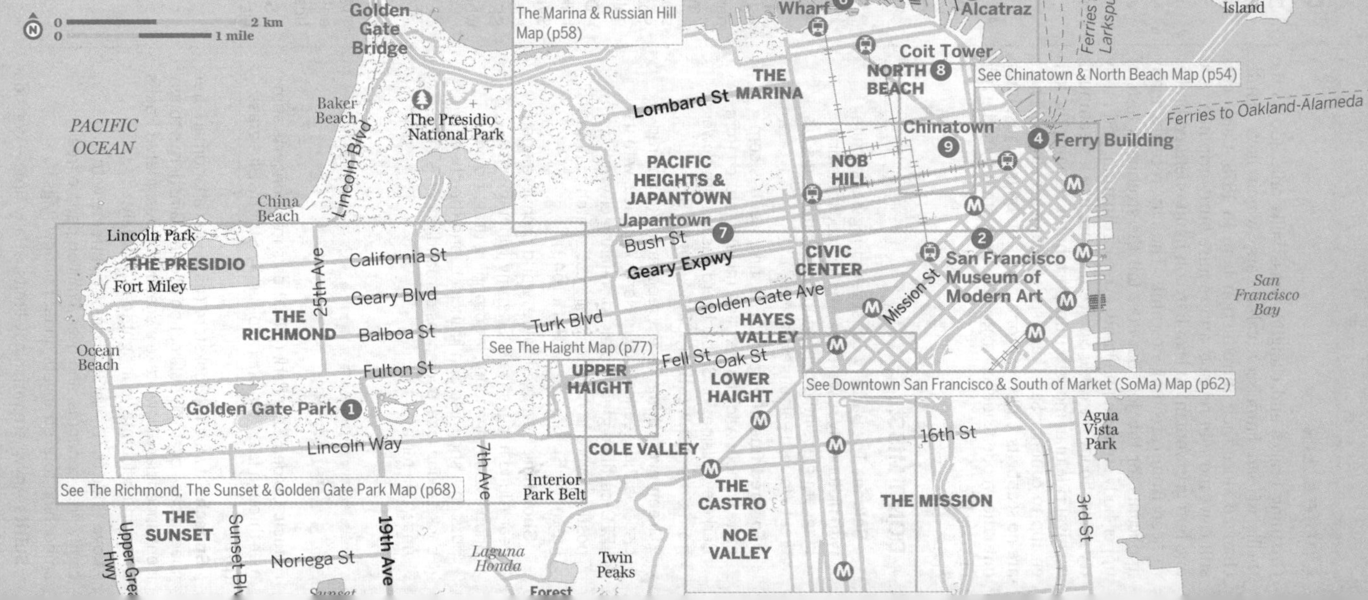

History

Oysters and acorn bread were prime dinner options in the Mexico-run Ohlone settlement of San Francisco circa 1848 – but a year and some gold nuggets later, Champagne and chow mein were served by the bucket. Gold found in the nearby Sierra Nevada foothills had turned a waterfront village of 800 into a port city of 100,000 prospectors, con artists, prostitutes and honest folk trying to make an honest living – good luck telling which was which. That friendly bartender might drug your drink, and you'd wake up a mile from shore, shanghaied into service on some ship bound for Argentina.

By 1850, California was nabbed from Mexico and fast-tracked for US statehood, and San Francisco attempted to introduce public order to 200 saloons and untold numbers of brothels and gambling dens. Panic struck when Australia glutted the market with gold in 1854, and ire turned irrationally on SF's Chinese community, who from 1877 to 1945 were restricted to living and working in Chinatown by anti-Chinese laws. The main way out of debt was dangerous work building railroads for the city's robber barons, who dynamited, mined and clear-cut their way across the Golden West, and built grand Nob Hill mansions above Chinatown.

The city's lofty ambitions and 20-plus theaters came crashing down in 1906, when earthquake and fire left 3000 dead, 100,000 homeless and much of the city reduced to rubble – including almost every mansion on Nob Hill. Theater troupes and opera divas performed for free amid smoldering ruins downtown, establishing SF's tradition of free public performances in parks.

Ambitious public works projects continued through the 1930s, when Diego Rivera, Frida Kahlo and federally funded muralists began the tradition of leftist politics in paint visible in some 400 Mission murals.

WWII brought seismic shifts to San Francisco's community as women and African Americans working in San Francisco shipyards created a new economic boom, and President Franklin Delano Roosevelt's Executive Order 9066 mandated the internment of the city's historic Japanese American community. A 40-year court battle ensued, ending in an unprecedented apology from the US government. San Francisco became a testing ground for civil rights and free speech, with Beat poet Lawrence Ferlinghetti and City Lights Bookstore winning a landmark 1957 ruling against book banning over the publication of Allen Ginsberg's splendid, incendiary *Howl and Other Poems*.

The Central Intelligence Agency (CIA) hoped an experimental drug called LSD might turn San Francisco test subject Ken Kesey into the ultimate fighting machine, but instead the author of *One Flew Over the Cuckoo's Nest* slipped some into Kool-Aid and kicked off the psychedelic '60s. The Summer of Love meant free food, love and music in The Haight until the '70s, when enterprising gay hippies founded an out-and-proud community in the Castro. San Francisco witnessed devastating losses from AIDS in the 1980s, but the city rallied to become a model for disease treatment and prevention.

Geeks and cyberpunks converged on SF in the mid-1990s, spawning the Web and dot-com boom – until the bubble popped in 2000. But risk-taking SF continues to float new ideas, and as recession hits elsewhere, social media, mobile apps and biotech are booming in San Francisco. Congratulations: you're just in time for San Francisco's next wild ride.

Sights

THE BAY & THE EMBARCADERO

TOP CHOICE Golden Gate Bridge BRIDGE
(Map p50; ☎415-921-5858; www.goldengate.org; Fort Point Lookout, Marine Dr; southbound car $6, carpools free) San Franciscans have passionate perspectives on every subject, but especially their signature landmark. Cinema buffs believe Hitchcock had it right: seen from below at **Fort Point**, the 1937 brige induces a thrilling case of *Vertigo*. Fog aficionados prefer the north-end lookout at Marin's **Vista Point**, to watch gusts billow through bridge cables like dry ice at a Kiss concert. Hard to believe the Navy almost nixed the soaring art deco design of architects Gertrude and Irving Murrow and engineer Joseph B Strauss in favor of a hulking concrete span painted with caution-yellow stripes.

To see both sides of the Golden Gate debate, hike or bike the 2-mile span. MUNI buses 28 and 29 run to the toll plaza, and pedestrians and cyclists can cross the bridge on the east side; Golden Gate Transit buses head back to SF from Marin.

Ferry Building HISTORIC BUILDING
(Map p62; www.ferrybuildingmarketplace.com; Embarcadero) Slackers have the right idea at the Ferry Building, the transport hub

NEIGHBORHOODS IN A NUTSHELL

North Beach & the Hills Poetry and parrots, top-of-the-world views, Italian gossip and opera on the jukebox.

Embarcadero & the Piers Gourmet treats, sea-lion antics, 19th-century video games, and getaways to and from Alcatraz.

Downtown & the Financial District The notorious Barbary Coast has gone legit with banks and boutiques, but reveals its wild side in provocative art galleries.

Chinatown Pagoda roofs, mahjong, and fortunes made and lost in historic alleyways.

Hayes Valley, Civic Center & the Tenderloin Grand buildings and great performances, dive bars and cable cars, foodie finds and local designs.

SoMa Where high technology meets higher art, and everyone gets down and dirty on the dance floor.

Mission A book in one hand, a burrito in the other, and murals all around.

Castro Out and proud with samba whistles, rainbow flags and policy platforms.

Haight Flashbacks and fashion-forwardness, free thinking, free music and pricey skateboards.

Japantown, the Fillmore & Pacific Heights Sushi in the fountains, John Coltrane over the altar, and rock at the Fillmore.

Marina & the Presidio Boutiques, organic dining, peace and public nudity at a former army base.

Golden Gate Park & the Avenues SF's mile-wide wild streak, surrounded by gourmet hangouts for hungry surfers.

turned gourmet emporium where no one's in a hurry to leave. Boat traffic tapered off after the grand hall and clock tower were built in 1898, and by the 1950s the building was literally overshadowed by a freeway overpass. But after the freeway collapsed in the 1989 Loma Prieta Earthquake, the city revived the Ferry Building as a tribute to San Francisco's monumental good taste. On weekends the **Ferry Building Farmers Market** (see the boxed text p80) fans out around the south end of the building like a fabulous garnish.

UNION SQUARE

Powell St Cable Car Turnaround CABLE CAR

(Map p62) Pause at Powell and Market to notice operators leap out of a century-old cable car, and slooowly turn it around on a revolving wooden platform by hand. As technology goes, this seems pretty iffy. Cable cars can't go in reverse, emit mechanical grunts on uphill climbs and require burly operators to lean hard on the handbrake to keep from careening down Nob Hill. For a city of risk-takers, this steampunk transport is the perfect joyride.

Folk Art International CULTURAL BUILDING

(Map p62; ☎415-392-9999; www.folkartintl.com; 140 Maiden Lane; ⊙10am-6pm Tue-Sat) Squeeze the Guggenheim into a brick box with a sunken Romanesque archway, and there you have Frank Lloyd Wright's 1949 Circle Gallery Building, which since 1979 has been the home of the **Xanadu Gallery**.

FINANCIAL DISTRICT

14, 49 and 77 Geary GALLERIES

(Map p62; www.sfada.com; ⊙most galleries 10:30am-5:30pm Tue-Fri, 11am-5pm Sat) Eccentric art collectors descend from hilltop mansions for First Thursday gallery openings of unpredictable art among outspoken crowds. Look for conceptual art at **Gallery Paule Anglim** at 14 Geary; four floors of contemporary art at 49 Geary, from installations by jailed Chinese artist Ai Weiwei at **Haines Gallery** to conceptual photography at **Fraenkel Gallery**; and at 77 Geary, Taravat Talepasand's Iranian-American superheroine portraits at **Marx & Zavattero Gallery** and Vik Muniz's collaged masterworks at **Rena Bransten Gallery**.

Transamerica Pyramid LANDMARK

(Map p62; 600 Montgomery St) Below the 1972 concrete rocketship that defines San Francisco's skyline, a half-acre redwood grove has taken root in the remains of old whaling ships. The building is off-limits to visitors, but the grove is open for daytime picnics on the site of a saloon frequented by Mark Twain and the newspaper office where Sun Yat-sen drafted his Proclamation of the Republic of China.

CIVIC CENTER & THE TENDERLOIN

TOP CHOICE **Asian Art Museum** MUSEUM

(Map p62; ☎415-581-3500; www.asianart.org; 200 Larkin St; adult/student $12/7; ⏰10am-5pm Tue, Wed, Fri-Sun, to 9pm Thu; 👪) Civic Center may be landlocked, but it has an unrivalled view of the Pacific thanks to this museum. Cover 6000 years and thousands of miles here in under an hour, from racy ancient Rajasthan miniatures to futuristic Japanese manga (graphic novels) via priceless Ming vases and even a Bhutan collection. The Asian has worked diplomatic wonders with a rotating collection of 17,000 treasures that bring Taiwan, China and Tibet together, unite Pakistan and India, and strike a harmonious balance among Japan, Korea and China. Stick around for outstanding educational events, from shadow-puppet shows and yoga for kids to First Thursday MATCHA nights from 5pm to 9pm, when soju cocktails flow, DJs spin Japanese hip-hop and guest acupuncturists assess visitors' tongues.

City Hall HISTORIC BUILDING

(Map p62; ☎415-554-4000, tour info 415-554-6023, art exhibit line 415-554-6080; www.ci.sf.ca.us/cityhall; 400 Van Ness Ave; ⏰8am-8pm Mon-Fri, tours 10am, noon & 2pm; 👪) From its Gilded Age dome to the avant-garde art in the basement, City Hall is quintessentially San Franciscan. Rising from the ashes of the 1906 earthquake, this Beaux Arts building has seen historic firsts under its splendid Tennessee pink marble and Colorado limestone rotunda: America's first sit-in on the grand staircase in 1960, protesting red-baiting McCarthy hearings; the 1977 election and 1978 assassination of openly gay Supervisor Harvey Milk; and 4037 same-sex marriages performed in 2004, until the state intervened. Intriguing art shows downstairs showcase local artists; weekly Board of Supervisors meetings are open to the public at 2pm on Tuesdays.

FREE **Luggage Store Gallery** GALLERY

(Map p62; ☎415-255-5971; www.luggagestoregallery.org; 1007 Market St; ⏰noon-5pm Wed-Sat) A dandelion pushing through cracks in the sidewalk, this plucky nonprofit gallery has brought signs of life to one of the toughest blocks in the Tenderloin for two decades. Streetwise art gets its due above an ex-luggage store in this second-floor gallery, which helped launch street satirists Barry McGee, Clare Rojas and Rigo. You'll recognize the place by its graffitied door and the rooftop mural by Brazilian duo Osgemeos of a defiant kid holding a lit firecracker. With such oddly touching works, poetry nights and monthly performing-arts events, this place puts the tender in the Tenderloin.

Glide Memorial United Methodist Church CHURCH

(Map p62; ☎415-674-6090; www.glide.org; 330 Ellis St; ⏰9am & 11am Sun) On Sundays, 1500 people add their voices to the electrifying gospel services at this GLBT-friendly (and just plain friendly) church. After the celebration ends in hearty handshakes and hugs, the radical Methodist congregation gets to work, providing one million free meals a year and homes for 52 formerly homeless families.

CHINATOWN

Chinese Historical Society of America Museum MUSEUM

(Map p54; ☎415-391-1188; www.chsa.org; 965 Clay St; adult/child $5/2, first Tue of month free; ⏰noon-5pm Tue-Fri, 11am-4pm Sat) Picture what it was like to be Chinese in America during the Gold Rush, the transcontinental railroad construction or in the Beat heyday at the nation's largest Chinese American historical institute. There are rotating exhibits across the courtyard in CHSA's graceful red-brick, green-tile-roofed landmark building, built as Chinatown's YWCA in 1932 by Julia Morgan, chief architect of Hearst Castle.

Chinese Culture Center CULTURAL CENTER

(Map p54; ☎415-986-1822; www.c-c-c.org; 3rd fl, Hilton Hotel, 750 Kearny St; gallery free, donation requested; ⏰10am-4pm Tue-Sat) You can see all the way to China on the 3rd floor of the Hilton inside this cultural center, which hosts exhibits of traditional Chinese arts; Xian Rui (Fresh & Sharp) cutting-edge art installations, such as Stella Zhang's discomfiting toothpick-studded pillows; and Art at Night, showcasing Chinese-inspired art, jazz, and food. Check the center's online

Chinatown & North Beach

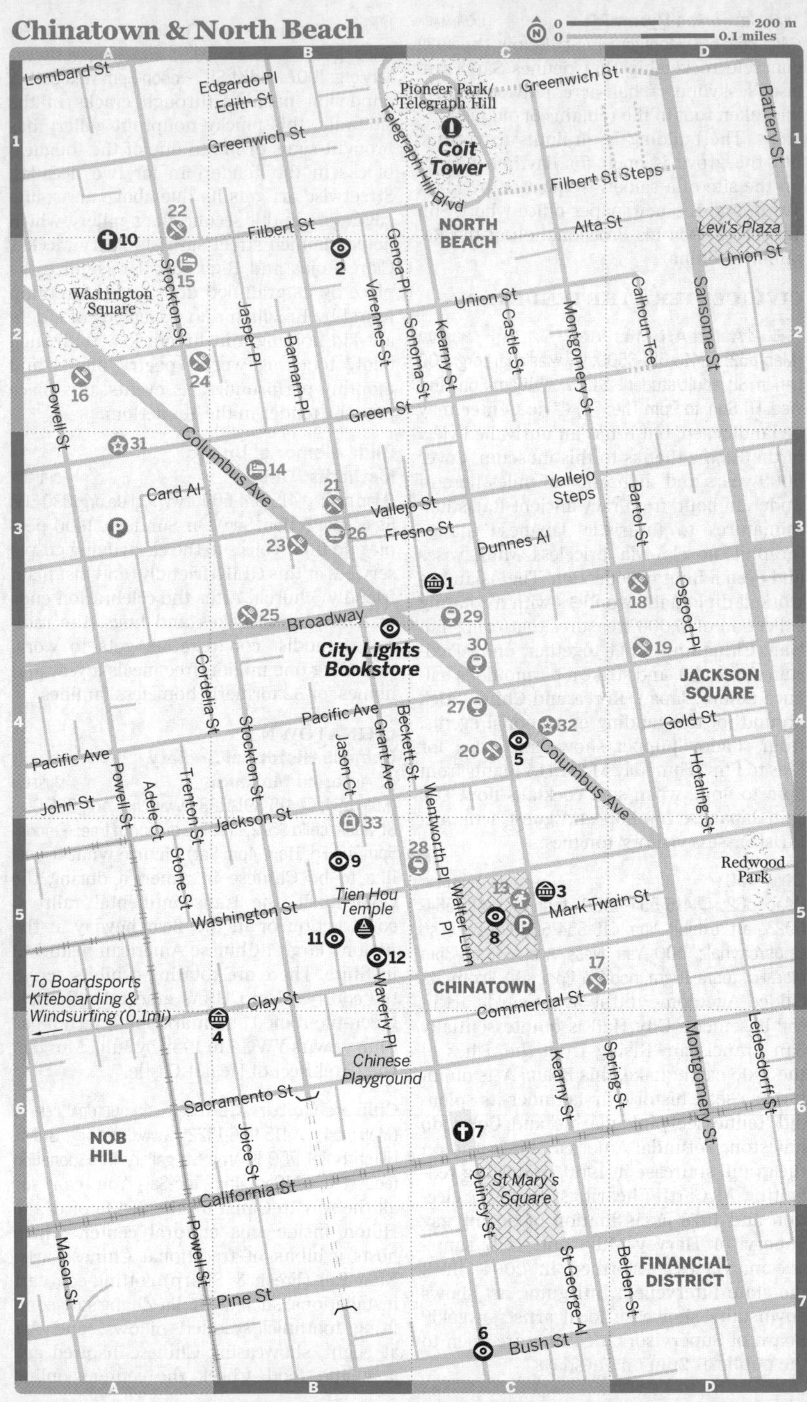

0 200 m
0 0.1 miles
Lombard St
Edgardo Pl
Edith St
Greenwich St
Pioneer Park/
Telegraph Hill
Coit Tower
Telegraph Hill Blvd
Battery St
Filbert St Steps
NORTH BEACH
Alta St
Levi's Plaza
Union St
Filbert St
Washington Square
Stockton St
Jasper Pl
Bannam Pl
Varennes St
Genoa Pl
Sonoma St
Kearny St
Castle St
Montgomery St
Calhoun Tce
Sansome St
Powell St
Green St
Columbus Ave
Card Al
Vallejo St
Fresno St
Vallejo Steps
Dunnes Al
Bartol St
Osgood Pl
Broadway
City Lights Bookstore
JACKSON SQUARE
Cordelia St
Pacific Ave
Jason Ct
Grant Ave
Beckett St
Gold St
Hotaling St
John St
Adele Ct
Trenton St
Jackson St
Wentworth Pl
Redwood Park
Stone St
Washington St
Tien Hou Temple
Walter Lum Pl
Mark Twain St
To Boardsports Kiteboarding & Windsurfing (0.1mi)
Clay St
Waverly Pl
CHINATOWN
Commercial St
Leidesdorff St
Chinese Playground
Sacramento St
Spring St
NOB HILL
Joice St
California St
St Mary's Square
Quincy St
Mason St
Pine St
St George Al
Belden St
FINANCIAL DISTRICT
Bush St

Chinatown & North Beach

Top Sights

City Lights Bookstore B4
Coit Tower C1

Sights

1 Beat Museum C3
2 Bob Kaufman Alley B2
3 Chinese Culture Center C5
4 Chinese Historical Society of America Museum B6
5 Columbus Tower C4
6 Dragon Gate C7
7 Old St Mary's Church C6
8 Portsmouth Square C5
9 Ross Alley B5
10 Saints Peter & Paul Church A2
11 Spofford Alley B5
12 Waverly Place B5

Activities, Courses & Tours

13 Chinatown Alleyways Tours C5

Sleeping

14 Hotel Bohème B3
15 Washington Square Inn A2

Eating

16 Cinecittà A2
17 City View C5
18 Coi D3
19 Cotogna D4
20 House of Nanking C4
21 Ideale B3
22 Liguria Bakery A1
23 Molinari B3
24 Tony's Coal-fired Pizza & Slice House A2
25 Yuet Lee B3

Drinking

26 Caffe Trieste B3
27 Comstock Saloon C4
28 Li Po C5
29 Specs' C3
30 Tosca Cafe C4

Entertainment

31 Beach Blanket Babylon A3
32 Purple Onion C4

Shopping

33 Golden Gate Fortune Cookie Company B5

schedule for concerts, hands-on arts workshops, Mandarin classes, genealogy services and Chinatown arts festivals.

Dragon Gate LANDMARK

(Map p54; at Bush St & Grant Ave) Enter the Dragon Gate donated by Taiwan in 1970, and you're on the once-notorious street known as Dupont in its red-light heyday. Forward-thinking Chinatown businessmen headed by Look Tin Ely pooled funds in the 1920s to reinvent the area as the tourist attraction you see today, hiring architects to create a signature 'Chinatown Deco' look with pagoda-style roofs and dragon lanterns lining Grant Ave.

Old St Mary's Church CHURCH

(Map p54; ☎415-288-3800; www.oldsaintmarys.org; 660 California St) For decades after its 1854 construction, the Catholic archdiocese valiantly tried to give this brothel district some religion. The 1906 fire destroyed one of the district's biggest bordellos directly across from the church, making room for St Mary's Sq, where skateboarders now ride handrails while Beniamino Bufano's 1929 **Sun Yat-sen statue** keeps a lookout.

Portsmouth Square SQUARE

(Map p54) Chinatown's outdoor living room is named after John B Montgomery's sloop that docked nearby in 1846, but the presiding deity at this people's park is the **Goddess of Democracy**, a bronze replica of the plaster statue made by Tiananmen Sq protesters in 1989. Historical markers dot the perimeter of the historic square, noting the site of San Francisco's first bookshop and newspaper, and the bawdy Jenny Lind Theater, which with a few modifications became San Francisco's first City Hall. A **night market** is held here from 6pm to 11pm each Saturday from July to October.

NORTH BEACH

TOP CHOICE **City Lights Bookstore** CULTURAL BUILDING

Map p54; www.citylights.com; 261 Columbus Ave; ⏲10am-midnight) Ever since manager Shigeyoshi Murao and founder and Beat poet Lawrence Ferlinghetti successfully defended their right to 'willfully and lewdly print' Allen Ginsberg's magnificent *Howl and Other Poems* in 1957, this bookstore has been a landmark. Celebrate your freedom to read freely in the designated Poet's Chair upstairs overlooking Jack Kerouac Alley, load up on 'zines on the mezzanine or entertain radical

THREE CHINATOWN ALLEYS THAT MADE HISTORY

» **Waverly Place** (Map p54) After the 1906 earthquake and fire devastated Chinatown, developers schemed to relocate Chinatown residents left homeless to less desirable real estate outside the city. But representatives from the Chinese consulate and several gun-toting merchants marched back to Waverly Place, holding temple services amid the rubble at still-smoldering altars. The alley is also the namesake for the main character in Amy Tan's bestselling *The Joy Luck Club*.

» **Spofford Alley** (Map p54) Sun Yat-sen plotted the overthrow of China's last emperor at No 36 and the 1920s brought bootleggers' gun battles to this alley, but Spofford has mellowed with age. In the evenings you'll hear the shuffling of mahjong tiles and an *erhu* (two-stringed Chinese fiddle) warming up at local senior centers.

» **Ross Alley** (Map p54) Alternately known as Manila, Spanish and Mexico St after the working girls who once worked this block, mural-lined Ross Alley is occasionally pimped out for Hollywood productions, including *Karate Kid II* and *Indiana Jones and the Temple of Doom*.

ideas downstairs in the Muckracking and Stolen Continents sections.

Beat Museum MUSEUM

(Map p54; ☎1-800-537-6822; www.thebeatmuseum.org; 540 Broadway; admission $5; ⏰10am-7pm Tue-Sun) For the complete Beat experience, stop by to check out City Lights' banned edition of Allen Ginsberg's *Howl,* Beat-era documentary footage in a makeshift theater, and tributes to authors who expanded the American outlook to include the margins – including a $10.18 check Jack Kerouac wrote for liquor.

Columbus Tower BUILDING

(Map p54; 916 Kearny St) Shady political boss Abe Ruef had only just finished this copper-clad building in 1905 when it was hit by the 1906 earthquake, and he restored it right before he was convicted of bribery and bankrupted in 1907. The Kingston Trio bought the building in the 1960s, and recorded reggae and the Grateful Dead in the basement. Since 1970 the building has belonged to filmmaker Francis Ford Coppola, who leases the top floors to fellow filmmakers Sean Penn and Wayne Wang and sells Italian fare and his own-label Napa wine at ground-level Café Niebaum-Coppola. Our advice: skip the pasta, take the cannoli.

Bob Kauffman Alley STREET

(Map p54; off Grant Ave near Filbert St) Enjoy a moment of profound silence courtesy of the Beat-bebop-jazz-poet-anarchist-voodoo-Jewish-biracial-African-all-American-streetcorner-prophet who refused to speak for 12 years after the assassination of John F Kennedy. The day the Vietnam War ended, he broke his silence by walking into a cafe and reciting his poem 'All Those Ships That Never Sailed'.

Saints Peter & Paul Church CHURCH

(Map p54; ☎415-421-0809; www.stspeterpaul.san-francisco.ca.us; 666 Filbert St; ⏰7:30am-4pm) Wedding-cake cravings are to be expected upon sight of this 1924 church, the frosting-white triple-decker cathedral where Joe Di Maggio and Marilyn Monroe famously posed for wedding photos (since they were both divorced, they were denied a church wedding here). The church overlooks Washington Sq, the North Beach park where nonagenarian *nonnas* (Italian grandmothers) feed wild parrots by the 1897 **Ben Franklin statue**.

FISHERMAN'S WHARF

Aquatic Park Bathhouse HISTORIC BUILDING

(Map p58; ☎415-447-5000; www.nps.gov/safr; 499 Jefferson at Hyde; adult/child $5/free; ⏰10am-4pm) A monumental hint to sailors in need of a scrub, this recently restored, ship-shape 1939 Streamline Moderne landmark is decked out with WPA art treasures: playful seal and frog sculptures by Beniamino Bufano, Hilaire Hiler's surreal underwater dreamscape murals and recently uncovered wood reliefs by Richard Ayer. Acclaimed African American artist Sargent Johnson created the stunning carved green slate marquee doorway and the veranda's mesmerizing aquatic mosaics, which he deliberately left unfinished on the east side to protest plans to include a private restaurant in this public facility. Johnson won: the east wing is now a maritime museum office.

FREE **Musée Mecanique** MUSEUM

(Map p58; ☎415-346-2000; www.museemecanique.org; Pier 45, Shed A; ⏰10am-7pm Mon-Fri, to 8pm Sat & Sun; 👪) A few quarters let you start bar brawls in coin-operated Wild West saloons, peep at belly-dancers through a vintage Mutoscope, save the world from Space Invaders and get your fortune told by an eerily lifelike wooden swami at this vintage arcade.

USS Pampanito HISTORIC SITE

(Map p58; ☎415-775-1943; www.maritime.org; Pier 45; adult/child $10/4; ⏰9am-5pm) Explore a restored WWII submarine that survived six tours of duty, while listening to submariners' tales of stealth mode and sudden attacks in a riveting audio tour ($2) that makes surfacing afterwards a relief (caution claustrophobes).

Pier 39 LANDMARK

(Map p58; ☎415-981-1280; www.pier39.com; Beach St & Embarcadero; 👪) Ever since they first hauled out here in 1990, 300 to 1300 sea lions have spent winter through summer bellyflopped on these yacht docks. While bulls jostle for prime sunning location on the piers, boardwalk B-boyers compete for street-dance supremacy and kids wage battles of the will with parents over souvenir teddy bears.

RUSSIAN HILL & NOB HILL

Grace Cathedral CHURCH

(Map p58; ☎415-749-6300; www.gracecathedral.org; 1100 California St; suggested donation adult/child $3/2; ⏰7am-6pm Mon-Fri, 8am-6pm Sat, 8am-7pm Sun, services with choir 8:30am & 11am Sun) Rebuilt three times since the Gold Rush, and still this progressive Episcopal church keeps pace with the times. Additions include the AIDS Interfaith Memorial Chapel, which features a bronze Keith Haring altarpiece; stained-glass 'Human Endeavor' windows that illuminate Albert Einstein in a swirl of nuclear particles; and pavement labyrinths offering guided meditation for restless souls.

San Francisco Art Institute GALLERY

(SFAI; Map p58; ☎415-771-7020; www.sfai.edu; 800 Chestnut St; ⏰9am-7:30pm) Founded during the 1870s, SFAI was the centre of the Bay Area's figurative art scene in the 1940s and '50s, turned to Bay Area Abstraction in the '60s and conceptual art in the '70s, and since the '90s has championed new media art in its **Walter and McBean Gallery** (⏰11am-6pm Mon-Sat). Also on campus, the **Diego Rivera Gallery** features Rivera's 1931 mural *The Making of a Fresco Showing a Building of a City*, a fresco within a fresco showing the back of the artist himself, as he pauses to admire the constant work in progress of San Francisco.

JAPANTOWN & PACIFIC HEIGHTS

Japan Center CULTURAL BUILDING

(off Map p58; www.sfjapantown.org; 1625 Post St; ⏰10am-midnight) Still looks much the way it did when it opened in 1968, with indoor wooden pedestrian bridges, *ikebana* (flower-arranging) displays and *maneki-neko* (waving cat) figurines beckoning from restaurant entryways.

Haas-Lilienthal House HISTORIC BUILDING

(Map p58; ☎415-441-3004; 2007 Franklin St; adult/child $8/5; ⏰noon-3pm Wed & Sat, 11am-4pm Sun) An 1882 Queen Anne with decor that looks

WORTH A TRIP

COIT TOWER

Adding an exclamation mark to San Francisco's landscape, **Coit Tower** (Map p54; ☎415-362-0808; Telegraph Hill; admission free, elevator rides $5; ⏰10am-6pm) offers views worth shouting about – especially after you climb the giddy, steep Filbert St or Greenwich St steps to the top of Telegraph Hill. This 210ft, peculiar projectile is a monument to San Francisco firefighters financed by eccentric heiress Lillie Hitchcock Coit. Lillie could drink, smoke and play cards as well as any off-duty firefighter, rarely missed a fire or a firefighter's funeral and even had the firehouse emblem embroidered on all her bedsheets.

When Lillie's totem was completed in 1934, the worker-glorifying, Diego Rivera–style WPA murals lining the lobby were denounced as Communist, as were the 25 artists who worked on them. Now protected as historic landmarks, the lobby murals broaden world-views just as surely as the 360-degree views of downtown from the tower-top viewing platform. To see more murals hidden inside Coit Tower's stairwell, take one of the free guided tours at 11am on Saturdays.

Fisherman's Wharf, The Marina & Russian Hill

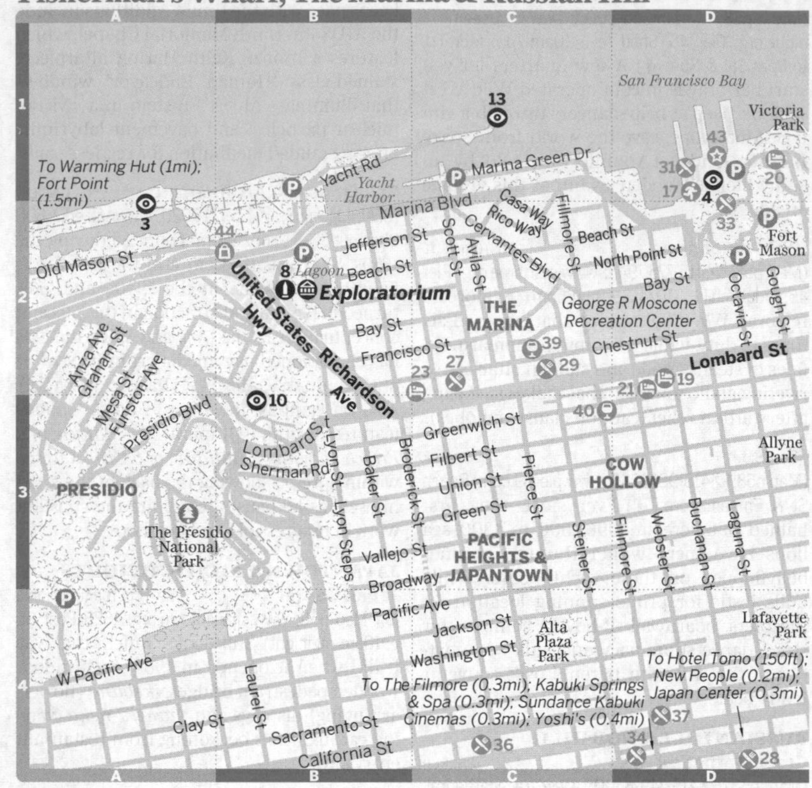

like a murder-mystery setting, including a dark-wood ballroom, red-velvet parlor and spooky stairways. One-hour tours are led by volunteers devoted to Victoriana.

Peace Pagoda MONUMENT

(off Map p62; Peace Plaza) San Francisco's sister city of Osaka in Japan gifted Yoshiro Taniguchi's striking minimalist concrete pagoda to the people of San Francisco in 1968.

THE MARINA

TOP CHOICE **Exploratorium** MUSEUM

(Map p58; 415-561-0360; www.exploratorium.edu; 3601 Lyon St; adult/child $15/10, incl. Tactile Dome $20; 10am-5pm Tue-Sun;) Budding Nobel Prize winners swarm this hands-on discovery museum that's been blowing minds since 1969, answering the questions you always wanted to ask in science class: does gravity apply to skateboarding, do robots have feelings and do toilets flush counterclockwise in Australia? One especially far-out exhibit is the **Tactile Dome**, a pitch-black space that you can crawl, climb and slide through (advance reservations required). It's moving to Piers 15 and 17 in 2013.

Palace of Fine Arts MONUMENT

(Map p58; www.lovethepalace.org; Palace Dr) When San Francisco's 1915 Panama-Pacific expo was over, SF couldn't bear to part with this Greco-Roman plaster palace. California Arts and Crafts architect Bernard Maybeck's artificial ruin was recast in concrete, so that future generations could gaze up at the rotunda relief to glimpse Art under attack by Materialists, with Idealists leaping to her rescue.

Wave Organ MONUMENT

(Map p58) Another intriguing Exploratorium project, this sound system of PVC tubes, concrete pipes and found marble from San Francisco's old cemetery was installed into the Marina Boat Harbor jetty by artist Peter

Richards in 1986. Depending on the waves, winds and tide, the tones emitted by the organ can sound like nervous humming, a gurgling baby or prank-call heavy breathing.

Fort Mason HISTORIC SITE

(Map p58; ☎415-345-7500; www.fortmason.org) Army sergeants would be scandalized by the frolicking at this former military outpost, including comedy improv workshops, vegetarian brunches at **Greens** (p81) and **Off the Grid** (p81), where gourmet trucks circle like pioneer wagons.

THE PRESIDIO

Presidio Visitors Center HISTORIC BUILDING

(Map p58; ☎415-561-4323; www.nps.gov/prsf; cnr Montgomery St & Lincoln Blvd; ⏰9am-5pm) San Francisco's official motto is still 'Oro in Paz, Fierro in Guerra' (Gold in Peace, Iron in War), but its main base hasn't seen much military action since it was built by conscripted Ohlone as a Spanish *presidio* (military post) in 1776. Jerry Garcia began and ended his ignominious military career here by going AWOL nine times in eight months and getting court-martialed twice before co-founding the Grateful Dead.

The Presidio's military role ended in 1994, when the 1480-acre plot became part of the Golden Gate National Recreation Area. The Visitors Center can direct you towards the **Pet Cemetery** off Crissy Field Ave, where handmade tombstones commemorate military hamsters who've completed their final tour of duty. Today the only wars waged around here are interstellar ones in George Lucas' screening room in the **Letterman Digital Arts Center**, right by the Yoda statue.

Crissy Field PARK

(Map p58; www.crissyfield.org; 603 Mason St; ⏰sunrise-sunset, Center 9am-5pm) War is now officially for the birds at this former military airstrip, restored as a tidal marsh and

Fisherman's Wharf, The Marina & Russian Hill

Top Sights

- Exploratorium ... B2
- Fisherman's Wharf ... F1

Sights

- 1 Aquarium of the Bay ... G1
- 2 Aquatic House Bathhouse ... E1
- 3 Crissy Field ... A2
- 4 Fort Mason ... D1
- 5 Grace Cathedral ... F4
- 6 Haas-Lilienthal House ... E3
- 7 Musée Mecanique ... F1
- 8 Palace of Fine Arts ... B2
- 9 Pier 39 ... F1
- 10 Presidio Visitors Center ... B3
- 11 San Francisco Art Institute ... F2
- 12 USS Pampanito ... F1
- 13 Wave Organ ... C1

Activities, Courses & Tours

- 14 Adventure Cat ... F1
- 15 Blazing Saddles ... F2
- 16 Fire Engine Tours ... E1
- 17 Oceanic Society ... D1

Sleeping

- 18 Argonaut Hotel ... E1
- 19 Coventry Motor Inn ... D2
- 20 HI San Francisco Fisherman's Wharf ... D1
- 21 Hotel Del Sol ... D2
- 22 Hotel Majestic ... E4
- 23 Marina Motel ... C2
- 24 Queen Anne Hotel ... E4
- 25 San Remo Hotel ... F2
- 26 Tuscan Inn ... F1

Eating

- 27 A16 ... C2
- 28 Benkyodo ... D4
- 29 Blue Barn Gourmet ... C2
- 30 Crown & Crumpet ... E1
- 31 Greens ... D1
- 32 In-N-Out Burger ... F1
- 33 Off the Grid ... D2
- 34 Out the Door ... D4
- 35 Swan Oyster Depot ... E4
- 36 Tataki ... C4
- 37 The Grove ... D4
- 38 Za ... E3

Drinking

- 39 California Wine Merchant ... C2
- 40 MatrixFillmore ... C3

Entertainment

- 41 Bimbo's 365 Club ... F2
- 42 Cobb's Comedy Club ... F2
- 43 Magic Theatre ... D1

Shopping

- 44 Sports Basement ... B2

reclaimed by knock-kneed coastal birds. On blustery days, bird-watch from the shelter of Crissy Field Center, which has a cafe counter facing the field with binoculars. Join joggers and puppies romping beachside trails that were once oil-stained asphalt, and on foggy days stop by the certified green **Warming Hut** (off Map p58; 983 Marine Dr; ⏲9am-5pm) to thaw out with Fair Trade coffee, browse field guides and sample honey made by Presidio honeybees.

Fort Point HISTORIC BUILDING

(off Map p58; ☎415-561-4395; www.nps.gov/fopo; Marine Dr; ⏲10am-5pm Thu-Mon) Despite its impressive guns, this Civil War fort saw no action – at least until Alfred Hitchcock shot scenes from *Vertigo* here, with stunning views of the Golden Gate Bridge from below.

Baker Beach BEACH

The city's best beach, with windswept pines uphill, craggy cliffs and a whole lot of exposed goosebumps on the breezy, clothing-optional north end.

SOUTH OF MARKET (SOMA)

TOP CHOICE **San Francisco Museum of Modern Art** MUSEUM

(SFMOMA; Map p62; ☎415-357-4000; www.sfmoma.org; 151 3rd St; adult/student/child $18/11/free, first Tue of month free; ⏲11am-6pm Fri-Tue, to 9pm Thu) Swiss architect Mario Botta's light-filled brick box leans full-tilt toward the horizon, with curators similarly inclined to take forward-thinking risks on Matthew Barney's poetic videos involving industrial quantities of Vaseline and Olafur Eliasson's outer-space light installations. SFMOMA has arguably the world's leading photography collection, with works by Ansel Adams, Daido Moriyama, Diane Arbus, Edward Weston, William Eggleston and Dorothea Lange, and since its 1995 grand reopening coincided with the tech boom, SFMOMA became an early champion of new media art. Sculpture sprouts from the new rooftop garden, and a $480 million expansion is underway to accommodate 1100 major modern works donated by the Fisher family (local founders of Gap). Go Thursday nights after 6pm for half-price admission and the most artful flirting in town.

Contemporary Jewish Museum MUSEUM
(Map p62; ☎415-655-7800; www.jmsf.org; 736 Mission St; adult/student/child $10/8/free; ⏰11am-5:30pm Fri-Tue, 1-8:30pm Thu) In 2008, architect Daniel Liebskind reshaped San Francisco's 1881 power plant with a blue steel extension to form the Hebrew word *l'chaim* ('to life'). Inside this architectural statement are lively shows, ranging from a retrospective of modern art instigator and Bay Area native Gertrude Stein to Linda Ellia's *Our Struggle: Artists Respond to Mein Kampf,* for which 600 artists from 17 countries were invited to alter one page of Hitler's book.

Cartoon Art Museum MUSEUM
(Map p62; ☎415-227-8666; www.cartoonart.org; 655 Mission St; adult/student $7/5, 'pay what you wish' first Tue of month; ⏰11am-5pm Tue-Sun; 👪) Comics fans need no introduction to the museum founded on a grant from Bay Area cartoon legend Charles M Schultz (of *Peanuts* fame). International and noteworthy local talent includes longtime Haight resident R Crumb and East Bay graphic novelists Daniel Clowes *(Ghostworld),* Gene Yang *(American Born Chinese)* and Adrian Tomine *(Optic Nerve).* Lectures and openings are rare opportunities to mingle with comics legends, Pixar studio heads and obsessive collectors.

Museum of the African Diaspora MUSEUM
(MoAD; Map p62; ☎415-358-7200; www.moadsf.org; 685 Mission; adult/student $10/5; ⏰11am-6pm Wed-Sat, noon-5pm Sun; 👪) An international cast of characters tell the epic story of the diaspora, from Ethiopian painter Qes Adamu Tesfaw's three-faced icons to quilts by India's Siddi community, descended from 16th-century African slaves. Themed interactive displays vary in interest and depth, but don't miss the moving video of slave narratives voiced by Maya Angelou.

Museum of Craft and Folk Art MUSEUM
(Map p62; ☎415-227-4888; www.mocfa.org; 51 Yerba Buena Lane; adult/child $5/free; ⏰11am-5pm Tue-Sun) Intricate handiwork with fascinating personal backstories, from sublime Shaker women's woodworking to contemporary Korean *bojagi* (wrapping textiles).

FREE **Catharine Clark Gallery** GALLERY
(Map p62; ☎415-399-1439; www.cclarkgallery.com; 150 Minna St; ⏰11am-6pm Tue-Sat) No material is too political or risqué at San Francisco's most cutting-edge gallery: Masami Teraoka paints geishas and goddesses as superheroines fending off wayward priests, and Packard Jennings offers instructional pamphlets for converting cities into wildlife refuges.

THE MISSION

Mission Dolores CHURCH
(Map p84; ☎415-621-8203; www.missiondolores.org; cnr Dolores & 16th Sts; adult/child $5/3; ⏰9am-4pm) The city's oldest building and its namesake, the whitewashed adobe Misión San Francisco de Asis was founded in 1776 and rebuilt in 1782 with conscripted Ohlone and Miwok labor in exchange – note the ceiling patterned after Native baskets. In the cemetery beside the adobe mission, a replica Ohlone hut is a memorial to the 5000 Ohlone and Miwok who died in 1814 and 1826 measles epidemics. The mission is overshadowed by the adjoining ornate 1913 **basilica,** where stained-glass windows commemorate the 21 original California missions, from Santa Cruz to San Diego.

826 Valencia CULTURAL BUILDING
(Map p84; ☎415-642-5905; www.826valencia.com; 826 Valencia St; ⏰noon-6pm; 👪) A mural by comic-artist Chris Ware graces the storefront housing this nonprofit youth writing program and purveyor of essential pirate supplies: eye patches, tubs of lard and tall tales for long nights at sea. Stop by the Fish Theater to see pufferfish immersed in Method acting. He's no Sean Penn, but as it says on the sign: 'Please don't judge the fish.' Check the website for workshops for kids and adults on scripting video games and starting up magazines, taught by industry experts.

Creativity Explored GALLERY
(Map p84; ☎415-863-2108; www.creativityexplored.org; 3245 16th St; donations welcome; ⏰10am-3pm Mon-Fri, until 7pm Thu, 1-6pm Sat) Fresh perspectives on themes ranging from superheroes to architecture by critically acclaimed, developmentally disabled artists – don't miss joyous openings with the artists, their families and fans.

Downtown San Francisco & South of Market (SoMa)

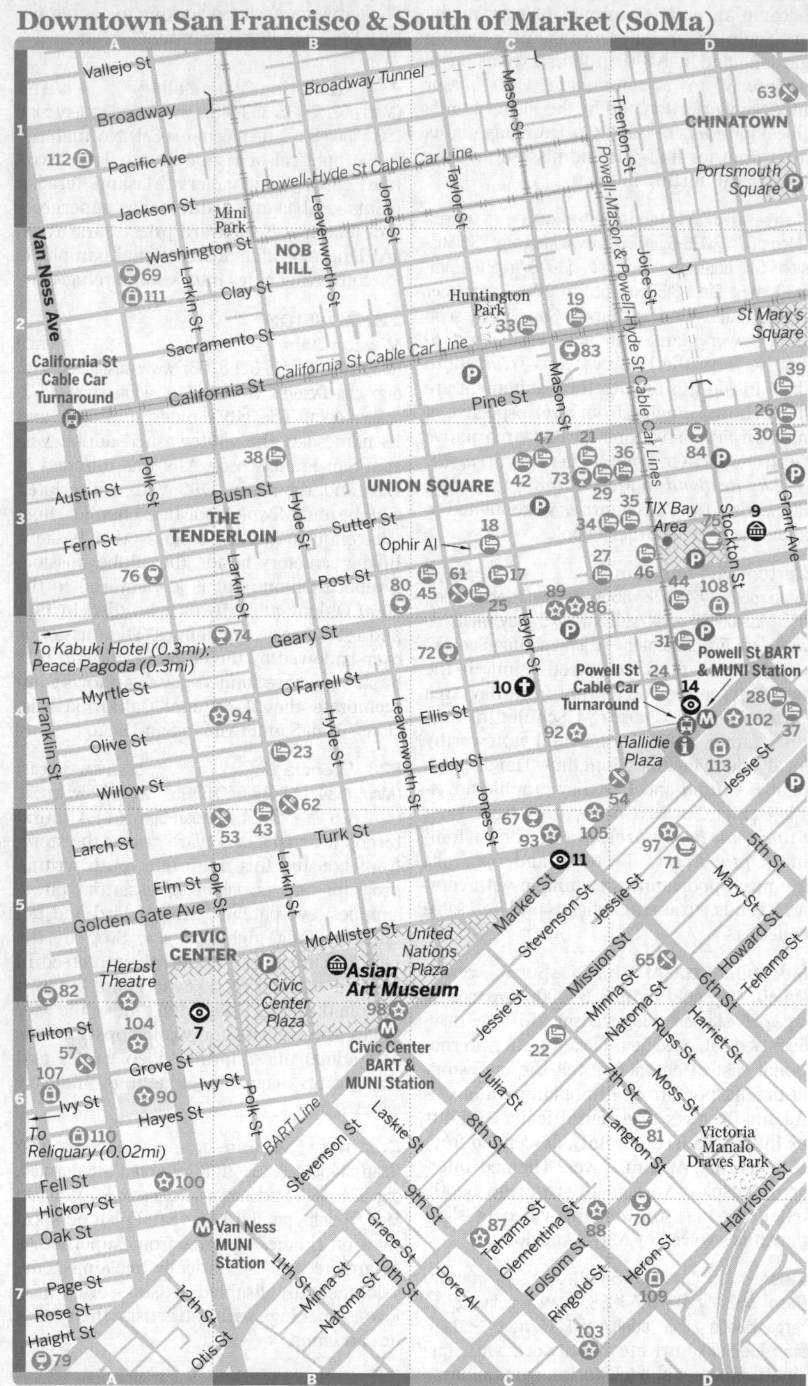

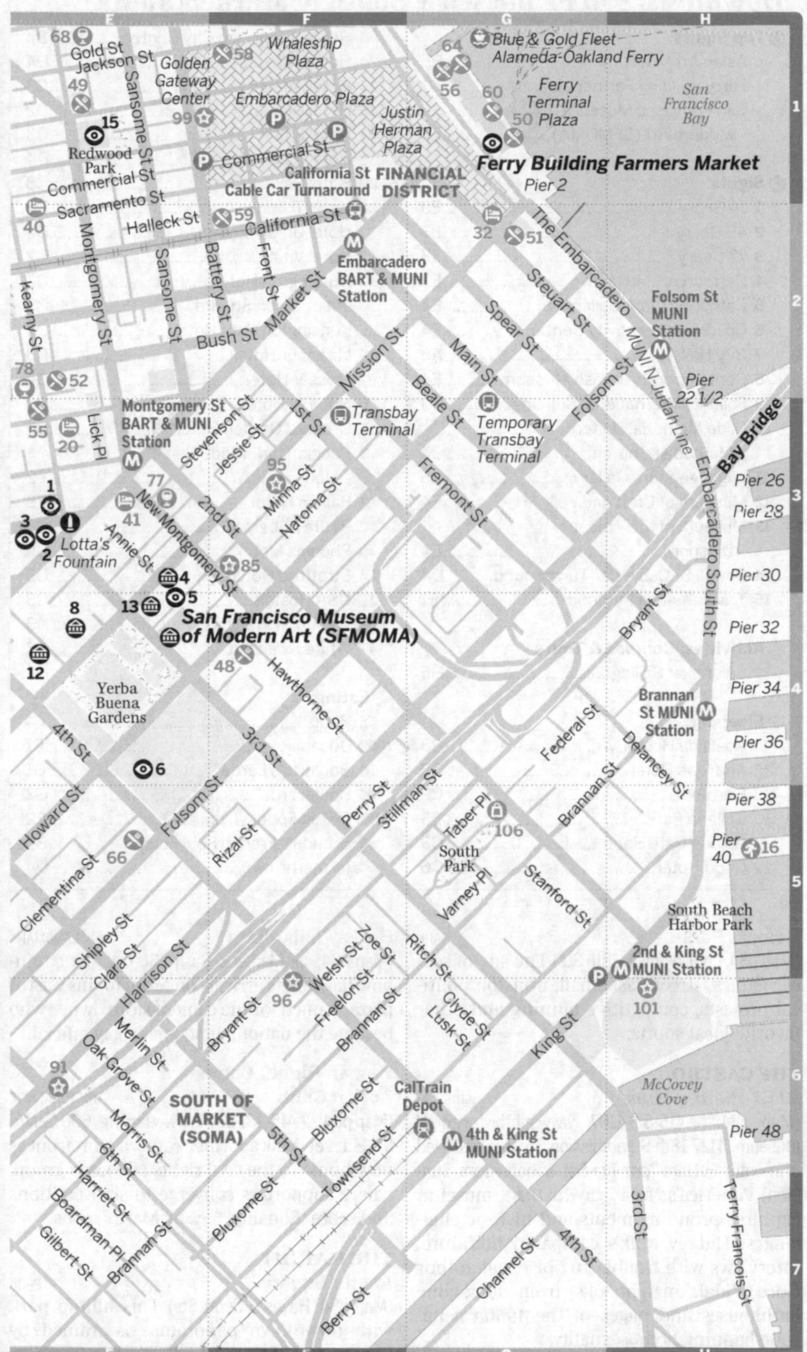

Gold St
Jackson St
Golden Gateway Center
Whaleship Plaza
Embarcadero Plaza
Justin Herman Plaza
Blue & Gold Fleet
Alameda-Oakland Ferry
Ferry Terminal Plaza
San Francisco Bay
Redwood Park
Commercial St
Sacramento St
California St
Cable Car Turnaround
FINANCIAL DISTRICT
Ferry Building Farmers Market
Pier 2
Halleck St
Embarcadero BART & MUNI Station
The Embarcadero
Steuart St
Spear St
Main St
Beale St
Folsom St MUNI Station
MUNI N-Judah Line
Pier 22 1/2
Bay Bridge
Kearny St
Montgomery St
Sansome St
Battery St
Front St
Market St
Bush St
Mission St
1st St
Transbay Terminal
Temporary Transbay Terminal
Folsom St
Montgomery St BART & MUNI Station
Lick Pl
Stevenson St
Jessie St
Minna St
Natoma St
Fremont St
Embarcadero South St
Pier 26
Pier 28
Pier 30
Pier 32
Pier 34
Pier 36
Pier 38
Pier 40
New Montgomery St
2nd St
Annie St
Lotta's Fountain
San Francisco Museum of Modern Art (SFMOMA)
Hawthorne St
Bryant St
Brannan St MUNI Station
Yerba Buena Gardens
4th St
3rd St
Federal St
Delancey St
Howard St
Folsom St
Rizal St
Perry St
Stillman St
Taber Pl
Brannan St
South Park
Varney Pl
Stanford St
Clementina St
South Beach Harbor Park
Shipley St
Clara St
Harrison St
Zoe St
Welsh St
Freelon St
Ritch St
Clyde St
Lusk St
2nd & King St MUNI Station
King St
Merlin St
Oak Grove St
Bryant St
Brannan St
McCovey Cove
SOUTH OF MARKET (SOMA)
Morris St
6th St
Harriet St
Boardman Pl
Gilbert St
Brannan St
Bluxome St
5th St
Townsend St
CalTrain Depot
4th & King St MUNI Station
Pier 48
3rd St
Terry Francois St
4th St
Channel St
Berry St
SAN FRANCISCO

Downtown San Francisco & South of Market (SoMa)

Top Sights
Asian Art Museum B5
Ferry Building Farmers Market G1
San Francisco Museum of Modern Art (SFMOMA) E4

Sights
1 14 Geary E3
2 49 Geary E3
3 77 Geary E3
4 Cartoon Art Museum E3
5 Catharine Clark Gallery E4
6 Children's Creativity Center E4
7 City Hall A6
8 Contemporary Jewish Museum E4
9 Folk Art International Building D3
10 Glide Memorial United Methodist Church C4
11 Luggage Store Gallery C5
12 Museum of Craft and Folk Art E4
13 Museum of the African Diaspora E4
14 Powell St Cable Car Turnaround D4
15 Transamerica Pyramid E1

Activities, Courses & Tours
16 Spinnaker Sailing H5

Sleeping
17 Adelaide Hostel C3
18 Andrews Hotel C3
19 Fairmont C2
20 Galleria Park E3
21 Golden Gate Hotel C3
22 Good Hotel C6
23 HI San Francisco City Center B4
24 Hotel Abri D4
25 Hotel Adagio C3
26 Hotel Des Arts D2
27 Hotel Frank C3
28 Hotel Palomar D4
29 Hotel Rex C3
30 Hotel Triton D3
31 Hotel Union Square D4
32 Hotel Vitale G2
33 Huntington Hotel C2
34 Inn at Union Square C3
35 Kensington Park Hotel D3
36 Larkspur Hotel D3
37 Mosser Hotel D4
38 Nob Hill Hotel B3
39 Orchard Garden Hotel D2
40 Pacific Tradewinds Guest House E2
41 Palace Hotel E3
42 Petite Auberge C3
43 Phoenix Motel B5
44 Stratford Hotel D3
45 USA Hostels C3
46 Westin St Francis Hotel D3
47 White Swan Inn C3

Eating
48 Benu F4
49 Bocadillos E1
50 Boulette's Larder G1
51 Boulevard G2
52 Boxed Foods E2
53 Brenda's French Soul Food B5
54 farmerbrown D4

Dolores Park PARK
(Map p84; cnr Dolores & 18th Sts) The site of soccer games, street basketball, nonstop political protests, competitive tanning and other favorite local sports.

THE CASTRO

GLBT History Museum MUSEUM
(Map p84; ☎415-621-1107; www.glbthistory.org/museum; 4127 18th St; admission $5, free first Wed of month; ⊙11am-7pm Tue-Sat & noon-5pm Sun-Mon) America's first gay-history museum captures proud moments and historic challenges: Harvey Milk's campaign literature, interviews with trailblazing bisexual author Gore Vidal, matchbooks from long-gone bathhouses and pages of the 1950s penal code banning homosexuality.

Harvey Milk Plaza LANDMARK
(Map p84; cnr Market & Castro Sts) A giant rainbow flag greets arrivals on Muni to this Castro plaza, named for the camera store owner who became the nation's first openly gay official.

Human Rights Campaign Action Center HISTORIC SITE
(Map p84; ☎415-431-2200; www.hrc.org; 600 Castro St) Harvey Milk's former camera storefront is now home to the civil rights advocacy group, where supporters converge to sign petitions and score 'Equality' tees by Marc Jacobs.

THE HAIGHT

Alamo Square PARK
(Map p84; Hayes & Scott Sts) This hilltop park with downtown panoramas is framed by picturesque 'Painted Ladies' – the flamboy-

55 Gitane.......E3
56 Hog Island Oyster Company.......G1
57 Jardinière.......A6
58 Kokkari.......F1
59 Michael Mina.......F2
60 Mijita.......G1
61 Millennium.......C3
62 Saigon Sandwich Shop.......B4
63 Sentinel.......D1
64 Slanted Door.......G1
65 Split Pea Seduction.......D5
66 Zero Zero.......E5

Drinking
67 Aunt Charlie's Lounge.......C5
68 Barrique.......E1
69 Bigfoot Lodge.......A2
70 Bloodhound.......D7
71 Blue Bottle Coffee Company.......D5
72 Bourbon & Branch.......C4
73 Cantina.......C3
74 Edinburgh Castle.......B4
75 Emporio Rulli Caffè.......D3
76 Hemlock Tavern.......A3
77 House of Shields.......E3
78 Irish Bank.......E2
79 Rebel.......A7
Rickhouse.......(see 52)
80 Rye.......B3
81 Sightglass Coffee.......D6
82 Smuggler's Cove.......A5
83 Top of the Mark.......C2
84 Tunnel Top Bar.......D3

Entertainment
85 111 Minna.......F3
86 American Conservatory Theater.......C3
87 AsiaSF.......C7
88 Cat Club.......C7
89 Curran Theatre.......C3
90 Davies Symphony Hall.......A6
91 EndUp.......E6
92 Exit Theatre.......C4
93 Golden Gate Theatre.......C5
94 Great American Music Hall.......B4
95 Harlot.......F3
96 Hotel Utah.......F6
97 Mezzanine.......D5
98 Orpheum Theatre.......B6
99 Punch Line.......E1
100 Rickshaw Stop.......A6
101 San Francisco Giants.......H6
102 Sisters of Perpetual Indulgence.......D4
103 The Stud.......C7
104 War Memorial Opera House.......A6
105 Warfield.......C5

Shopping
106 Jeremy's.......G5
107 MAC.......A6
108 Macy's.......D3
109 Madame S & Mr S Leather.......D7
110 Nancy Boy.......A6
111 Studio.......A2
112 Velvet da Vinci.......A1
113 Westfield Shopping Center.......D4

antly painted and outrageously ornamented Victorian homes that took San Franciscan liberties with the regal English style. The gingerbread-trimmed houses of Postcard Row facing the park along Steiner have been disappointingly repainted in innocuous neutrals, but stroll around the square between Steiner and Scott and you'll spot Painted Ladies with drag-diva color palettes.

Zen Center HISTORIC BUILDING
(Map p84; www.sfzc.org; 300 Page St) Find a moment of Zen at the largest Buddhist community outside Asia, headquartered in an elegant building designed by Julia Morgan.

THE RICHMOND

California Palace of the Legion of Honor MUSEUM
(Map p68; ☎415-750-3600; http://legionofhonor.famsf.org; 100 34th Ave; adult/child $10/6, $2 discount with Muni ticket, 1st Tue of month free; ⏲9:30am-5:15pm Tue-Sun) A nude sculptor's model who married well and collected art with a passion, 'Big Alma' de Bretteville Spreckels gifted this museum to San Francisco. Featured artworks range from Monet waterlilies to John Cage soundscapes, Iraqi ivories to R Crumb comics – part of the Legion's Achenbach Collection of 90,000 graphic artworks.

Cliff House HISTORIC BUILDING
(Map p68; www.cliffhouse.com; 1090 Point Lobos Ave) Built by populist millionaire Adolph Sutro in 1863 as a workingman's resort, Cliff House is now in its fourth incarnation as an upscale (overpriced) restaurant. Three of the resort's attractions remain: hiking trails around the splendid ruins of **Sutro Baths**, wintertime views of sea lions frolicking

MISSION MURALS

Inspired by visiting artist Diego Rivera and the WPA murals and outraged by US foreign policy in Central America, Mission *muralistas* set out in the 1970s to transform the political landscape, one alley at a time. Precita Eyes (p69) restores historic murals, commissions new ones, and offers muralist-led tours. Several of the most noteworthy Mission murals can be found in three locations:

» **Balmy Alley** (Map p84; www.balmyalley.com; off 24th St) Between Treat Ave and Harrison St, historic early works transform garage doors into artistic and political statements, from an early memorial for El Salvador activist Archbishop Òscar Romero to a homage to the golden age of Mexican cinema.

» **Clarion Alley** (Map p84; btwn 17th & 18th Sts, off Valencia St) Only the strongest street art survives in Clarion, where lesser works are peed on or painted over. Very few pieces have lasted years, such as Andrew Schoultz's mural of gentrifying elephants displacing scraggly birds, and topical murals like the new one honoring the Arab Spring usually go up on the west end.

» **Women's Building** (Map p84; ☎415-431-1180; www.womensbuilding.org; 3543 18th St) San Francisco's biggest mural is the 1994 *MaestraPeace*, a show of female strength painted by 90 *muralistas* that wraps around the Women's Building, with icons of female strength from Mayan and Chinese goddesses to modern trailblazers, including Nobel Peace Prize winner Rigoberta Menchu, poet Audre Lorde and former US Surgeon-General Dr Jocelyn Elders.

on **Seal Rock**, and the **Camera Obscura** (admission $2; ⏰11am-sunset), a Victorian invention projecting sea views inside a small building.

INSIDE GOLDEN GATE PARK

California Academy of Sciences AQUARIUM, WILDLIFE RESERVE
(Map p68; ☎415-321-8000; www.calacademy.org; 55 Concourse Dr; adult/child $30/25, $3 discount with Muni ticket, 6-10pm Thu over 21s $10; ⏰9:30am-5pm Mon-Sat, 11am-5pm Sun; 👪) Architect Renzo Piano's 2008 landmark LEED-certified green building houses 38,000 weird and wonderful animals in a four-story rainforest and split-level aquarium under a 'living roof' of California wildflowers. After the penguins nod off to sleep, the wild rumpus starts at kids'-only Academy Sleepovers and over-21 NightLife Thursdays, when rainforest-themed cocktails encourage strange mating rituals among shy Internet daters.

MH de Young Memorial Museum MUSEUM
(Map p68; ☎415-750-3600; www.famsf.org/deyoung; 50 Hagiwara Tea Garden Dr; adult/child $10/free, $2 discount with Muni ticket, 1st Tue of month free; ⏰9:30am-5:15pm Tue-Sun, until 8:45pm Fri) Follow sculptor Andy Goldsworthy's artificial fault-line in the sidewalk into Herzog & de Meuron's sleek, copper-clad building that's oxidizing to green, blending into the park. Don't be fooled by the de Young's camouflaged exterior: shows here boldly broaden artistic horizons from Oceanic ceremonial masks and Balenciaga gowns to sculptor Al Farrow's cathedrals built from bullets. Access to the tower viewing room is free, and worth the wait for the elevator.

Conservatory of Flowers GARDEN
(Map p68; ☎15-666-7001; www.conservatoryofflowers.org; Conservatory Dr West; adult/child $7/2; ⏰10am-4pm Tue-Sun) Flower power is alive inside the newly restored 1878 Victorian conservatory, where orchids sprawl out like Bohemian divas, lilies float contemplatively and carnivorous plants reek of insect belches.

Strybing Arboretum & Botanical Gardens GARDEN
(Map p68; ☎415-661-1316; www.strybing.org; 1199 9th Ave; admission $7; ⏰9am-6pm Apr-Oct, 10am-5pm Nov-Mar) There's always something blooming in these 70-acre gardens. The Garden of Fragrance is designed for the visually impaired, and the California native plant section explodes with color when the native wildflowers bloom in early spring, right off the redwood trail.

Japanese Tea Garden GARDEN
(Map p68; http://japaneseteagardensf.com; Hagiwara Tea Garden Dr; adult/child $7/5, Mon, Wed, Fri before 10am free; ⏰9am-6pm; 👪) Mellow out

in the Zen Garden, admire doll-sized trees that are pushing 100, and sip toasted-rice green tea under a pagoda in this picturesque 5-acre garden founded in 1894.

Stow Lake LAKE
(Map p68; http://sfrecpark.org/StowLake.aspx; paddleboats/canoes/rowboats/bikes per hr $24/20/19/8; ⌚rentals 10am-4pm) Huntington Falls tumble down 400ft Strawberry Hill into the lake, near a romantic Chinese pavilion and a 1946 boathouse offering boat and bike rentals.

Ocean Beach BEACH
(Map p68; ☎415-561-4323; www.parksconservancy.org; ⌚sunrise-sunset) The park ends at this blustery beach, too chilly for bikini-clad clambakes but ideal for wet-suited pro surfers braving rip tides (casual swimmers beware). Bonfires are permitted in designated fire-pits only; no alcohol allowed. One mile south of Ocean Beach, hang-gliders leap off 200ft cliffs and shorebirds nest in defunct Nike missile silos near the parking lot of **Fort Funston** (Skyline Blvd); follow the Great Hwy south, turn right onto Skyline Blvd and the entrance to the park is past Lake Merced on the right-hand side.

Activities

Cycling & Skating

Avenue Cyclery BICYCLE RENTAL
(Map p68; ☎415-387-3155; www.avenuecyclery.com; 756 Stanyan St; per hr/day $8/30; ⌚10am-6pm Mon-Sat, to 5pm Sun) Just outside Golden Gate Park in the Upper Haight; bike rental includes a helmet.

Blazing Saddles BICYCLE RENTAL
(Map p58; ☎415-202-8888; www.blazingsaddles.com; 2715 Hyde St; bikes per hr/day from $8/32; ⌚8am-7:30pm, weather permitting; 👪) From this bike rental shop's Fisherman's Wharf outposts, cyclists can cross the Golden Gate Bridge and take the Sausalito ferry back to SF.

Golden Gate Park Bike & Skate CYCLING, SKATING
(Map p68; ☎415-668-1117; www.goldengatepark bikeandskate.com; 3038 Fulton St; per hr/day skates from $5/20, bikes from $3/15; ⌚10am-6pm; 👪) To make the most of Golden Gate Park, rent wheels – especially Sundays and summer Saturdays, when JFK Dr is closed to vehicular traffic. Call ahead weekdays to make sure they're open if the weather's dismal.

Wheel Fun Rentals CYCLING, SKATING
(Map p68; ☎415-668-6699; www.wheelfunrentals.com; 50 Stow Lake Dr; per hr/day skates $6/20, bikes $8/25, tandems $12/40; ⌚9am-7pm) Glide around Golden Gate and dip into the Sunset on a reasonable rental. To cruise the waterfront, head to its second location in the Marina at Fort Mason.

Sailing, Kayaking, Windsurfing & Whale-Watching

Spinnaker Sailing SAILING
(Map p62; ☎415-543-7333; www.spinnaker-sailing.com; Pier 40; lessons $375; ⌚10am-5pm) Experienced sailors can captain a boat from Spinnaker and sail into the sunset, while landlubbers can charter a skippered vessel or take classes.

City Kayak KAYAKING
(☎415-357-1010; http://citykayak.com; South Beach Harbor; kayak rentals per hr $35-65, 3hr

DON'T MISS

GOLDEN GATE PARK

When San Franciscans refer to 'the park,' there's only one that gets the definite article. Everything that San Franciscans hold dear is in Golden Gate Park: free spirits, free music, redwoods, Frisbee, protests, fine art, bonsai and buffalo. An 1870 competition to design the park was won by 24-year-old William Hammond Hall, who spent the next two decades tenaciously fighting casino developers, theme-park boosters and slippery politicians to transform the 1017 acres of dunes into the world's largest developed park. Sporty and not-so-sporty types will appreciate the park's range of outdoor activities, with 7.5 miles of bicycle trails, 12 miles of equestrian trails, an archery range, baseball and softball diamonds, fly-casting pools, lawn bowling greens, four soccer fields and 21 tennis courts. There are places in and around the park to rent bicycles and skates.

Park information is available from **McLaren Lodge** (Map p68; ☎415-831-2700; cnr Fell & Stanyan Sts; ⌚8am-5pm Mon-Fri), and free park walking tours are organized by **Friends of Recreation & Parks** (☎415-263-0991).

The Richmond, The Sunset & Golden Gate Park

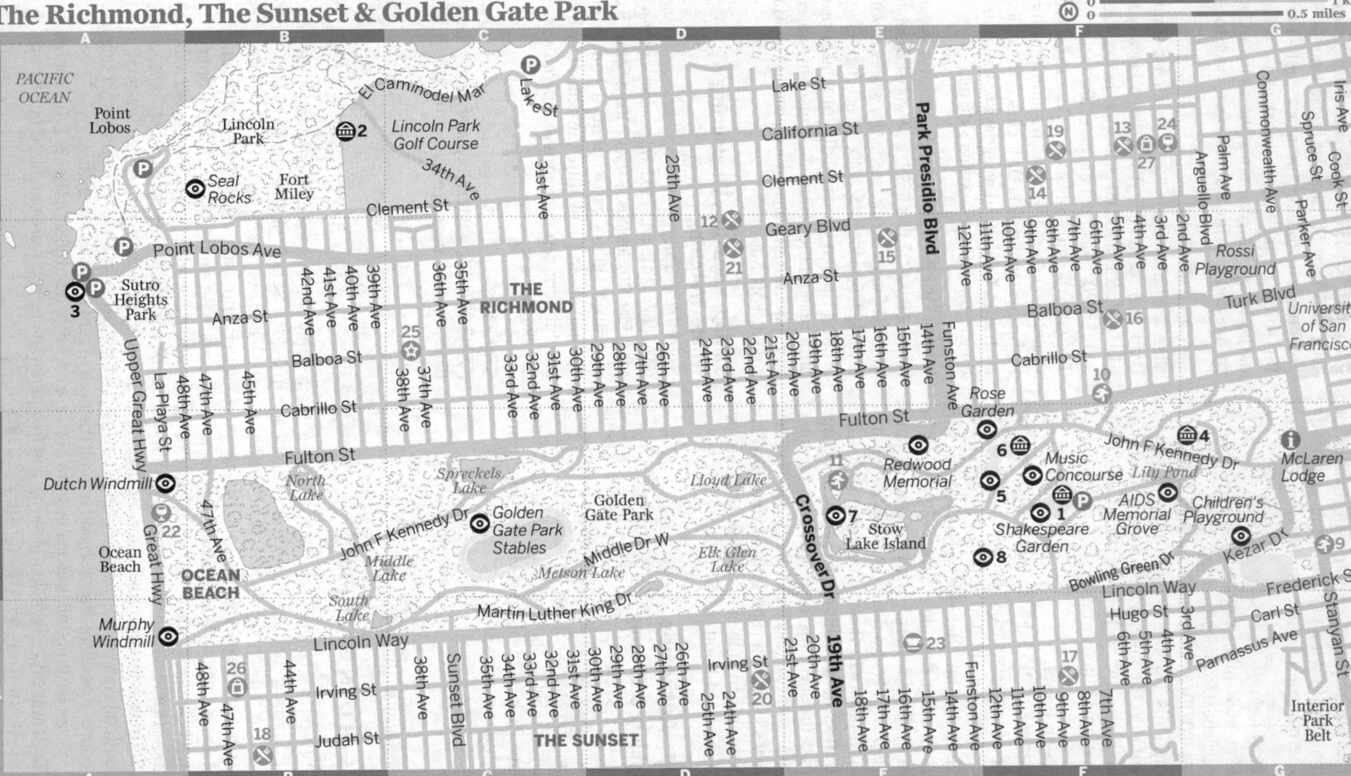

The Richmond, The Sunset & Golden Gate Park

Sights
1 California Academy of Sciences F3
2 California Palace of the Legion of Honor B1
3 Cliff House A2
4 Conservatory of Flowers G3
5 Japanese Tea Garden F3
6 MH de Young Memorial Museum F3
7 Stow Lake E3
8 Strybing Arboretum & Botanical Gardens F3

Activities, Courses & Tours
9 Avenue Cyclery G3
10 Golden Gate Park Bike & Skate F2
11 Wheel Fun Rentals E3

Eating
12 Aziza D2
13 Genki F1
14 Halu F1
15 Kabuto E2
16 Namu F2
17 Nanking Road Bistro F4
18 Outerlands B4
19 Spices F1
20 Sunrise Deli D4
21 Ton Kiang D2

Drinking
22 Beach Chalet Brewery A3
23 Hollow E4
24 Plough & Stars F1

Entertainment
25 Balboa Theater C2

Shopping
26 Mollusk B4
27 Park Life F1

lesson & rental package $59, tours $65-75) Experienced paddlers hit the choppy waters beneath the Golden Gate Bridge or take a moonlit group tour, while newbies venture calm waters near the Bay Bridge.

Adventure Cat SAILING
(Map p58; ☎415-777-1630; www.adventurecat.com; Pier 39; adult/child $35/15, sunset cruise $50) Three daily catamaran cruises depart March-October; weekends only November-February.

Boardsports Kiteboarding & Windsurfing WINDSURFING
(off Map p54; ☎415-385-1224; www.boardsportsschool.com; 1200 Clay St; 1.5-2hr lessons $50-220; ⏰by appointment) Offers kiteboarding and windsurfing rentals and lessons; experienced windsurfers take on the bay at the beach off Crissy Field. Most beginner classes are held east across the bay in Alameda.

Oceanic Society WHALE-WATCHING
(Map p58; ☎415-474-3385; www.oceanic-society.org; per person $100-120; ⏰office 8:30am-5pm Mon-Fri, trips Sat & Sun) Whale sightings aren't a fluke on naturalist-led, ocean-going weekend boat trips during mid-October through December migrations. In the off-season, trips run to the Farallon Islands, 27 miles west of San Francisco.

Spas

Kabuki Springs & Spa SPA
(off Map p58; ☎415-922-6000; www.kabukisprings.com; 1750 Geary Blvd; admission $22-25; ⏰10am-9:45pm) Soak muscles worked by SF's 43 hills in these Japanese baths for the ultimate cultural immersion experience. Men and women alternate days, and bathing suits are required on coed Tuesdays.

Tours

Precita Eyes Mural Tours WALKING
(Map p84; ☎415-285-2287; www.precitaeyes.org; 2981 24th St; adult/child $12-15/5; ⏰11am, noon, 1:30pm Sat & Sun) Muralists lead two-hour tours on foot or bike covering 60 to 70 murals in a 6 to 10 block radius of mural-bedecked Balmy Alley; proceeds fund mural upkeep.

Chinatown Alleyways Tours WALKING
(Map p54; ☎415-984-1478; www.chinatownalleywaytours.org; adult/child $18/5/; ⏰11am Sat & Sun) Neighborhood teens lead two-hour tours for up-close-and-personal peeks into Chinatown's past (weather permitting). Book five days ahead or pay double for Saturday walk-ins; cash only. Tour meeting points vary.

FREE **Public Library City Guides** WALKING
(www.sfcityguides.org) Volunteer local historians lead tours by neighborhood and theme: Art

Walking Tour
San Francisco Hilltops

Conquer San Francisco's three most famous hills – Telegraph, Russian and Nob – for views that are pure poetry.

Enter ❶ **Dragon Gate** and walk up dragon-lamp-lined Grant Ave to Sacramento St, where you'll turn left half a block up, then right onto ❷ **Waverly Place**, where prayer flags grace painted temple balconies. At Clay St, jog left and right again onto ❸ **Spofford Alley**, where Sun Yat-sen plotted revolution. At the end of the block on Washington, take a right and an immediate left onto ❹ **Ross Alley**, once San Francisco's bordello street.

Turn right down Jackson to Grant, then take the right-hand turnoff from Grant onto ❺ **Jack Kerouac Alley**, where the pavement echoes Kerouac's ode to San Francisco: 'The air was soft, the stars so fine, and the promise of every cobbled alley so great...' Ahead is literary landmark ❻ **City Lights**: head upstairs to Poetry, and read one poem.

Head left up Columbus to the corner of Vallejo and stop at ❼ **Molinari**, where you can get panini sandwiches for a picnic atop Telegraph Hill. Cross Columbus, veer right one block up Vallejo and fuel up with an espresso at ❽ **Caffe Trieste**, where Francis Ford Coppola drafted his script for *The Godfather*. Walk up Vallejo and scale the steps to Montgomery St. Go left three blocks, and turn left onto cottage-lined ❾ **Greenwich Street Steps** to summit Telegraph Hill. Inside ❿ **Coit Tower**, enjoy once-controversial murals downstairs and panoramic views of the bay up top.

Head downhill, past parrot-feeding *nonnas* (Italian grandmothers) at ⓫ **Washington Square**. Turn left on Columbus, right on Vallejo, up three blocks and another picturesque stairway path to ⓬ **Ina Coolbrith Park**. Any breath you have left will be taken away by sweeping views to Alcatraz. Summit your last hill of the day the easy way: catch the ⓭ **Mason-Powell Cable Car** up Nob Hill.

WORTH A TRIP

ALCATRAZ

Almost 150 years before Guantanamo, a rocky island in the middle of San Francisco Bay became the nation's first military prison: **Alcatraz** (Map p50; ☎415-981-7625; www.alcatrazcruises.com, www.nps.gov/alcatraz; adult/child day $26/16, night $33/19.50; ⏲call center 8am-7pm, ferries depart Pier 33 every 30min 9am-3:55pm, plus 6:10pm & 6:45pm). Civil War deserters were kept in wooden pens along with Native American 'unfriendlies,' including 19 Hopis who refused to send their children to government boarding schools where Hopi religion and language were banned.

In 1934 the Federal Bureau of Prisons took over Alcatraz to make a public example of bootleggers and other gangsters. 'The Rock' only averaged 264 inmates, but its A-list criminals included Chicago crime boss Al Capone, Harlem poet-mafioso 'Bumpy' Johnson, and Morton Sobell, found guilty of Soviet espionage along with Julius and Ethel Rosenberg. Though Alcatraz was considered escape-proof, in 1962 the Anglin brothers and Frank Morris floated away on a makeshift raft and were never seen again.

Since importing guards and supplies cost more than putting up prisoners at the Ritz, the prison was closed in 1963. Native American leaders occupied the island from 1969–71 to protest US occupation of Native lands; their standoff with the FBI is commemorated in a dockside museum and 'This is Indian Land' water-tower graffiti.

Ferries depart for Alcatraz behind the Pier 33 ticket booth, but book tickets online at least two weeks ahead in summer. Day visits include captivating audio tours with prisoners and guards recalling cellhouse life, while popular, creepy twilight tours are led by park rangers.

Deco Marina, Gold Rush Downtown, Pacific Heights Victorians, North Beach by Night and more. See website for upcoming tours.

Haight-Ashbury Flower Power Walking Tour WALKING
(Map p77; ☎415-863-1621; www.haightashburytour.com; adult/under 9yr $20/free; ⏲9:30am Tue & Sat, 2pm Thu, 11am Fri) Take a long, strange trip through 12 blocks of hippie history, following in the steps of Jimi, Jerry and Janis – if you have to ask for last names, you really need this tour, man. Tours meet at the corner of Stanyan and Waller Sts and last about two hours; reservations required. Meeting points vary.

Victorian Home Walk WALKING
(Map p62; ☎415-252-9485; www.victorianwalk.com; Westin St Francis Hotel, cnr Powell & Post Sts; per person $25; ⏲11am) Learn to tell your Queen Annes from your Sticks with prime examples in Pacific Heights. Tours last about 2½ hours; meeting points vary.

Festivals & Events

February

Lunar New Year CULTURAL
(www.chineseparade.com) Firecrackers, legions of tiny-tot martial artists and a 200ft dancing dragon make this parade at the end of February the highlight of San Francisco winters.

April & May

Cherry Blossom Festival CULTURAL
(www.nccbf.org) Celebrate spring mid-April with scrumptious food-stall yakitori, raucous taiko drums and origami flower kits from the street crafts fair.

San Francisco International Film Festival FILM
(www.sffs.org) Pace yourself: the nation's longest-running film fest is a marathon event, with 325 films, 200 directors and sundry actors and producers over two weeks from late April.

Bay to Breakers QUIRKY
(www.baytobreakers.com; race registration $44-48) Run costumed or naked from Embarcadero to Ocean Beach the third Sunday in May, while joggers dressed as salmon run upstream.

Carnaval CULTURAL
(www.carnavalsf.com) Shake your tail feathers through the Mission on Memorial Day weekend in late May.

June

Other towns have a gay day, but SF goes all out for **Pride Month**, better known elsewhere as the month of June.

DEALS AND HIDDEN COSTS

San Francisco is the birthplace of the boutique hotel, offering stylish rooms for a price: $100 to $200 rooms midrange, plus 15.5% hotel tax (hostels exempt) and $35-50 for overnight parking. For vacancies and deals, check San Francisco Visitor Information Center's **reservation line** (☎800-637-5196, 415-391-2000; www.onlyinSanFrancisco.com), **Bed & Breakfast SF** (☎415-899-0060; www.bbsf.com) and **Lonely Planet** (http://hotels.lonelyplanet.com).

Gay and Lesbian Film Festival FILM
(www.frameline.org) Here, queer and ready for a premiere: the world's oldest, biggest GLBT film fest launches new talents from 30 countries, with 200 film screenings over the last half of June.

Dyke March & Pink Saturday PARADE
(www.dykemarch.org & www.sfpride.org) Around 50,000 lesbian, bisexual and transgender women converge in Dolores Park at 7:30pm and head to Castro St to show some coed Pride at the Pink Saturday street party on the last Saturday in June.

Lesbian, Gay, Bisexual and Transgender Pride Parade PARADE
(www.sfpride.org) No one does Pride like San Francisco on the last Sunday in June: 1.2 million people, seven stages, tons of glitter, ounces of bikinis and more queens for the day than anyone can count.

September

SF Shakespeare Fest CULTURAL
(www.sfshakes.org; ⌚7:30pm Sat, 2:30pm Sun) The play's the thing in the Presidio, outdoors and free of charge on sunny September weekends.

Folsom Street Fair QUIRKY
(www.folsomstreetfair.com) Enjoy public spankings for local charities on the last Sunday in September. To answer the obvious question in advance: yes, people do actually get pierced there, but it's best not to stare unless you're prepared to strip down and compare.

October & November

Jazz Festival MUSIC
(www.sfjazz.org) Old schoolers and hot new talents jam around the city in late October.

Litquake CULTURAL
(www.litquake.org) Authors tell stories at the biggest lit fest in the West and spill trade secrets over drinks at the legendary Lit Crawl during the second week in October.

Hardly Strictly Bluegrass MUSIC
(www.strictlybluegrass.com) SF celebrates Western roots with three days of free Golden Gate Park concerts and headliners ranging from Elvis Costello to Gillian Welch in early October.

Diá de los Muertos CULTURAL
(Day of the Dead; www.dayofthedeadsf.org) Zombie brides, Aztec dancers and toddler Frida Kahlos with drawn-on unibrows lead the parade honoring the dead down 24th St on November 2.

Sleeping

UNION SQUARE

TOP CHOICE **Orchard Garden Hotel** BOUTIQUE HOTEL $$
(Map p62; ☎415-399-9807; www.theorchardgardenhotel.com; 466 Bush St; r $179-249; ❄@📶) SF's first all-green-practices hotel has soothingly quiet rooms with luxe touches, like Egyptian-cotton sheets, plus an organic rooftop garden.

Hotel Rex BOUTIQUE HOTEL $$
(Map p62; ☎415-433-4434; www.jdvhotels.com; 562 Sutter St; r $169-279; P❄@📶) Noir-novelist chic, with 1920s literary lounge and compact rooms with hand-painted lampshades, local art and sumptuous beds piled with down pillows.

Hotel Palomar BOUTIQUE HOTEL $$$
(Map p62; ☎415-348-1111, 866-373-4941; www.hotelpalomar-sf.com; 12 4th St; r $199-299; ❄@📶) The sexy Palomar is decked out with crocodile-print carpets, chocolate-brown wood and cheetah-print robes in the closet. Beds have feather-light down comforters and Frette linens, and there's floor space for in-room yoga (request mats and DVD at check-in). Smack downtown, but rooms have soundproof windows.

Hotel Triton BOUTIQUE HOTEL $$
(Map p62; ☎415-394-0500, 800-800-1299; www.hotel-tritonsf.com; 342 Grant Ave; r $169-239; ❄@📶) The lobby looks straight out of a comic book, and rooms are whimsically designed and ecofriendly; least-expensive rooms are tiny and celeb suites are named after Carlos Santana and Jerry Garcia. Don't miss tarot-card readings and chair massages during nightly happy hour.

Hotel Abri BOUTIQUE HOTEL $$
(Map p62; ☎415-392-8800, 866-823-4669; www.hotel-abri.com; 127 Ellis St; r $149-229; ❄@📶) Snazzy boutique hotel with bold black-and-tan motifs and ultra-mod cons: iPod docking stations, pillow-top beds, flat-screen TVs and rainfall showerheads.

Hotel des Arts QUIRKY $$
(Map p62; ☎415-956-3232; www.sfhoteldesarts.com; 447 Bush St; r $139-199, without bath $99-149; 📶) A budget hotel for art freaks, with specialty rooms painted by underground artists – it's like sleeping inside an art installation. Standard rooms are less exciting, but clean and good value; bring earplugs.

White Swan Inn BOUTIQUE HOTEL $$
(Map p62; ☎415-775-1755, 800-999-9570; www.jdvhotels.com; 845 Bush St; r $159-199; P@📶) An English country inn downtown, with cabbage-rose wallpaper, red-plaid flannel bedspreads and colonial-style furniture. Hipsters may find it stifling, but if you love Tudor style, you'll feel right at home. Every room has a gas fireplace.

Hotel Adagio BOUTIQUE HOTEL $$
(Map p62; ☎415-775-5000, 800-228-8830; www.thehoteladagio.com; 550 Geary St; r $159-249; ❄@📶) Huge rooms set the Adagio apart, along with the snappy style: chocolate-brown and off-white leather furnishings with bright-orange splashes. Sumptuous beds have Egyptian-cotton sheets and feather pillows; bathrooms are disappointing. Still, it's a hot address for a fair price – great bar, too.

Westin St Francis Hotel HISTORIC HOTEL $$$
(Map p62; ☎415-397-7000, 800-228-3000; www.westin.com; 335 Powell St; r $209-369; ❄@📶) One of the city's most famous hotels, the St Francis lords over Union Sq. Tower rooms have stellar views, but feel generic; we prefer the original building's old-fashioned charm, with its high ceilings and crown moldings. The Westin's beds set the industry standard for comfort.

Hotel Frank BOUTIQUE HOTEL $$
(Map p62; ☎415-986-2000, 800-553-1900; www.hotelfranksf.com; 386 Geary St; r $169-299; ❄📶) A block off Union Square, Frank has a snappy, swinging design aesthetic, with big black-and-white houndstooth rugs and faux-alligator headboards. The baths are tight, but extras like plasma-screen TVs compensate.

Larkspur Hotel BOUTIQUE HOTEL $$
(Map p62; ☎415-421-2865, 866-823-4669; www.larkspurhotelunionsquare.com; 524 Sutter St; r $169-199; @📶) Built in 1915 and overhauled in 2008, the understatedly fancy Larkspur has a monochromatic, earth-tone color scheme and simple, clean lines. Baths are tiny but have fab rainfall showerheads.

Golden Gate Hotel HOTEL $$
(Map p62; ☎415-392-3702, 800-835-1118; www.goldengatehotel.com; 775 Bush St; r $165, without bath $105; @📶) A homey Edwardian hotel with kindly owners, homemade cookies and a cuddly cat, safely uphill from the Tenderloin. Most rooms have private baths, some with clawfoot tubs.

Petite Auberge B&B $$
(Map p62; ☎415-928-6000, 800-365-3004; www.jdvhotels.com; 863 Bush St; r $169-219; 📶) French provincial charmer; some rooms have fireplaces.

Stratford Hotel HOTEL $
(Map p62; ☎415-397-7080; hotelstratford.com; 242 Powell St; r incl breakfast $89-149; @📶) Simple, smallish, clean rooms with rainfall showers; request rooms facing away from clanging Powell St cable cars.

Kensington Park Hotel BOUTIQUE HOTEL $$$
(Map p62; ☎415-788-6400; www.kensingtonparkhotel.com; 450 Post St; r $189-269; ❄@📶) Stellar location for shopping trips; great beds, stylish rooms.

Andrews Hotel HOTEL $$
(Map p62; ☎415-563-6877, 800-926-3739; www.andrewshotel.com; 624 Post St; r incl breakfast $109-199; 📶) Folksy character, great rates, good location.

Inn at Union Square HOTEL $$$
(Map p62; ☎415-397-3510, 800-288-4346; www.unionsquare.com; 440 Post St; r $229-289; ste

$309-359; ❄@🛜) Quiet, conservative elegance steps from Union Sq.

Hotel Union Square HOTEL $$
(Map p62; ☎415-397-3000, 800-553-1900; www.hotelunionsquare.com; 114 Powell St; r $150-220; ❄@🛜) Swank design touches such as concealed lighting, mirrored walls and plush fabrics complement the original brick walls, compensating for small, dark rooms. Convenient location near public transport; not all rooms have air-con.

Adelaide Hostel HOSTEL $
(Map p62; ☎415-359-1915, 877-359-1915; www.adelaidehostel.com; 5 Isadora Duncan Lane; dm $30-35, r $70-90, incl breakfast; @🛜) The 22-room Adelaide sets the standard for SF hostels, with up-to-date furnishings, marble-tiled bathrooms and optional $5 dinners and group activities. Private rooms may be in the nearby Dakota or Fitzgerald Hotels; request the Fitzgerald.

USA Hostels HOSTEL $
(Map p62; ☎415-440-5600, 877-483-2950; www.usahostels.com; 711 Post St; dm $30-34, r $73-83; 🛜) Built in 1909, this former hotel was recently converted into a spiffy hostel with great service. Private rooms sleep 3-4; on-site cafe serves inexpensive cafeteria-style dinners.

FINANCIAL DISTRICT

Palace Hotel HISTORIC HOTEL $$$
(Map p62; ☎415-512-1111, 800-325-3535; www.sfpalace.com; 2 New Montgomery St; r $199-329; ❄@🛜≋) The landmark Palace stands as a monument to turn-of-the-20th-century grandeur, aglow with century-old Austrian crystal chandeliers. Cushy (if staid) accommodations cater to expense-account travelers, but prices drop weekends. Even if you're not staying here, drop into the opulent Garden Court to sip tea.

Galleria Park BOUTIQUE HOTEL $$
(Map p62; ☎415-781-3060, 800-738-7477; www.jdvhotels.com; 191 Sutter St; r $189-229; ❄@🛜) A restyled 1911 hotel with contemporary art, Frette linens, high-end bath amenities, free evening wine hour, and – most importantly – good service. Rooms on Sutter St are noisier, but get more light; interior rooms are quietest.

Pacific Tradewinds Guest House HOSTEL $
(Map p62; ☎415-433-7970, 888-734-6783; www.Sanfranciscohostel.org; 680 Sacramento St; dm $29.50; @🛜) San Francisco's smartest-looking all-dorm hostel has a blue-and-white nautical theme, fully equipped kitchen and spotless glass-brick showers. The nearest BART station is Embarcadero, and you'll have to haul your bags up four flights – but service is terrific.

CIVIC CENTER & THE TENDERLOIN

Phoenix Motel MOTEL $$
(Map p62; ☎415-776-1380, 800-248-9466; www.jdvhospitality.com; 601 Eddy St; r $119-169 incl breakfast; P🛜≋) The city's rocker crash pad draws artists and hipsters to a vintage-1950s motor lodge with tropical décor in the gritty Tenderloin. Check out the shrine to actor Vincent Gallo, opposite Room 43, and happening lounge Chambers. Bring earplugs. Parking is free, as is weekday admission to Kabuki Springs & Spa (p69).

HI San Francisco City Center HOSTEL $
(Map p62; ☎415-474-5721; www.sfhostels.com; 685 Ellis St; dm incl breakfast $25-30, r $85-100; @🛜) A converted seven-story 1920s apartment building, this hostel sports 262 beds and 11 private rooms, all with private baths. The neighborhood is grim, but cheap eats and good bars are nearby.

NORTH BEACH

TOP CHOICE **Hotel Bohème** BOUTIQUE HOTEL $$
(Map p54; ☎415-433-9111; www.hotelboheme.com; 444 Columbus Ave; r $174-194; @🛜) Like a love letter to the jazz era, the Bohème has moody 1950s orange, black and sage-green color schemes. Inverted Chinese umbrellas hang from ceilings and photos from the Beat years decorate the walls. Rooms are smallish, and some front on noisy Columbus Ave, but the hotel is smack in the middle of North Beach's vibrant street scene.

San Remo Hotel HOTEL $
(Map p58; ☎415-776-8688, 800-352-7366; www.sanremohotel.com; 2237 Mason St; d $65-99; @🛜) One of the city's best values, the 1906 San Remo has old-fashioned charm. Rooms are simply done with mismatched turn-of-the-century furnishings, and all share bathrooms. Note: least-expensive rooms have windows onto the corridor, not the outdoors; no elevator.

Washington Square Inn B&B $$$
(Map p54; ☎415-981-4220, 800-388-0220; www.wsisf.com; 1660 Stockton St; r $179-329 incl breakfast; @🛜) On a leafy, sun-dappled park, this European-style inn has tasteful rooms and

a few choice antiques, including carved-wooden armoires; least-expensive rooms are tiny. Wine and cheese each evening, and breakfast in bed.

FISHERMAN'S WHARF

TOP CHOICE **Argonaut Hotel** HOTEL **$$$**
(Map p58; ☎415-563-0800, 866-415-0704; www.argonauthotel.com; 495 Jefferson St; r $205-325; P❄📶👪) Built as a cannery in 1908, the nautical-themed Argonaut has century-old wooden beams, exposed brick walls, and porthole-shaped mirrors. All rooms have ultra-comfy beds and CD players, but some are tiny and get limited sunlight; pay extra for mesmerizing bay views.

🍃 **Tuscan Inn** HOTEL **$$**
(Map p58; ☎415-561-1100, 800-648-4626; www.tuscaninn.com; 425 North Point St; r $169-229; P❄@📶👪) Way more character than the Wharf's other tourist hotels, with bold colors and mixed patterns – who says stripes and checks don't match? Managed by fashion-forward Kimpton Hotels, with character, spacious rooms, in-room Nintendo and wine hour for parents.

HI San Francisco Fisherman's Wharf HOSTEL **$**
(Map p58; ☎415-771-7277; www.sfhostels.com; Bldg 240, Fort Mason; dm $25-30, r $65-100; P@📶) Trade downtown convenience for a lush, green setting. Dorms range from four to 22 beds; some are coed. No curfew, and no heat on during the day in winter: bring warm clothes. Limited free parking.

NOB HILL

Huntington Hotel LUXURY HOTEL **$$$**
(Map p62; ☎415-474-5400, 800-227-4683; www.huntingtonhotel.com; 1075 California St; r from $325; ❄@📶🏊) The go-to address of society ladies who prefer the comfort of tradition over the garishness of style. Book a refurbished room and an appointment at on-site Nob Hill Spa, one of the city's best.

Fairmont HISTORIC HOTEL **$$$**
(Map p62; ☎415-772-5000, 800-441-1414; www.fairmont.com; 950 Mason St; r $219-339; ❄@📶) The historic lobby is decked out with crystal chandeliers and towering yellow-marble columns, and rooms are comfortably business-class; for maximum character, book a room in the original 1906 building. Tower rooms have stupendous views, but look generic.

HAVE YOUR SAY

Found a fantastic restaurant that you're longing to share with the world? Disagree with our recommendations? Or just want to talk about your most recent trip?

Whatever your reason, head to lonelyplanet.com, where you can post a review, ask or answer a question on the Thorntree forum, comment on a blog, or share your photos and tips on Groups. Or you can simply spend time chatting with like-minded travelers. So go on, have your say.

Nob Hill Hotel HOTEL **$$**
(Map p62; ☎415-673-6080; www.nobhillinn.com; 1000 Pine St; r $125-165, ste $195-275; 📶) A 1906 hotel dressed up in Victorian style, with brass beds and floral-print carpet. The look borders on grandma-lives-here, but it's definitely not cookie cutter. Rooms on Hyde St are loud; book in back. Friendly service. Wi-fi in lobby.

JAPANTOWN & PACIFIC HEIGHTS

Kabuki Hotel HOTEL **$$**
(off Map p62; ☎415-922-3200, 800-333-3333; www.radisson.com; 1625 Post St; r $189-249; ❄@📶) Shoji (rice-paper) screens, platform beds, deep Japanese soaking tubs and adjoining showers liven up boxy '60s architecture. Bonuses: bonsai garden and free weekday passes to Kabuki Springs & Spa (p69).

Hotel Tomo HOTEL **$$**
(of Map p58; ☎415-921-4000, 888-822-8666; www.jdvhotels.com/tomo; 1800 Sutter St; r $119-189; P❄@📶👪) Japanese pop culture makes a splash in minimalist, blond-wood rooms that look like cool college dorms, with *anime* murals and beanbags.

Hotel Majestic HOTEL **$$**
(Map p58; ☎415-441-1100, 800-869-8966; www.thehotelmajestic.com; 1500 Sutter St; r $100-175; @📶) Traditional elegance c 1902, with Chinese porcelain lamps beside triple-sheeted beds. Standard rooms are small and need updating, but good value; don't miss the clubby lobby bar.

Queen Anne Hotel B&B **$$**
(Map p58; ☎415-441-2828, 800-227-3970; www.queenanne.com; 1590 Sutter St; r incl breakfast

$123-169, ste $203-255; P@) The Queen Anne Hotel occupies a lovely former Victorian girls' school, built in 1890, with frills galore. Comfortable (if sometimes tiny) rooms are antique-filled; some have wood-burning fireplaces.

THE MARINA & COW HOLLOW

Hotel Del Sol MOTEL $$

(Map p58; 415-921-5520; www.thehoteldelsol.com; 3100 Webster St; d $149-199; P@) A colorful, revamped 1950s motor lodge, with heated outdoor pool, board games, and family suites with bunk-beds.

Marina Motel MOTEL $

(Map p58; 415-928-1000; www.marinainn.com; 3110 Octavia Blvd; r $79-109;) The Marina is a bougainvillea-bedecked 1939 motor court, offering some rooms with kitchens ($10 extra) and free parking. Request quiet rooms in back.

Coventry Motor Inn MOTEL $

(Map p58; 415-567-1200; www.coventrymotorinn.com; 1901 Lombard St; r $95-145; P) Of the motels lining Lombard St, the generic Coventry has the highest overall quality-to-value ratio, with spacious rooms and covered parking.

SOUTH OF MARKET (SOMA)

TOP CHOICE Hotel Vitale HOTEL $$$

(Map p62; 415-278-3700, 888-890-8688; www.hotelvitale.com; 8 Mission St; d $239-379; @) Behind that skyscraper exterior is a soothing spa-hotel, with silky-soft 450-thread-count sheets and rooftop hot tubs; upgrade to bay-view rooms.

Good Hotel MOTEL $$

(Map p62; 415-621-7001; www.thegoodhotel.com; 112 7th St; r $109-169; P@) A revamped motor lodge that places a premium on green, with reclaimed wood headboards, light fixtures of repurposed bottles, and fleece bedspreads made of recycled soda bottles. The vibe is upbeat and there's a pool across the street and bikes for rent, but the neighborhood is sketchy.

Mosser Hotel HOTEL $$

(Map p62; 415-986-4400, 800-227-3804; www.themosser.com; 54 4th St; r $129-159, with shared bath $69-99; @) Tiny rooms and tinier bathrooms, but with stylish details and central location.

THE MISSION

Inn San Francisco B&B $$

(Map p84; 415-641-0188; www.innsf.com; 943 S Van Ness Ave; r incl breakfast $175-285, with shared bath $120-145, cottage $335; P@) Impeccably maintained and packed with antiques, this 1872 Italianate-Victorian mansion has a redwood hot tub in the English garden, genteel guestrooms with fresh-cut flowers and featherbeds and limited parking.

THE CASTRO

Parker Guest House B&B $$

(Map p84; 415-621-3222; www.parkerguesthouse.com; 520 Church St; r incl breakfast $149-229; P@) SF's best gay B&B has cushy rooms with super-comfortable beds and down comforters in adjoining Edwardian mansions, plus a steam room and garden.

Belvedere House B&B $$

(off Map p84; 415-731-6654; www.belvederehouse.com; 598 Belvedere St; r incl breakfast $125-190; @) Castro's romantic getaway on a leafy side street, with vintage chandeliers and eclectic art in six cozy rooms. Though primarily for gay guests, all are welcome – kids get child-sized bathrobes. No elevator.

Inn on Castro B&B $$

(Map p84; 415-861-0321; www.innoncastro.com; 321 Castro St; r $165-195, without bath $125-155, breakfast incl; self-catering apt $165-220;) A portal to the Castro's disco heyday, this Edwardian townhouse is decked out with top-end '70s-mod furnishings, and the patio has a flower-festooned private deck. Breakfasts are exceptional – the owner is a chef. Also rents out nearby apartments.

Willows B&B $$

(Map p84; 415-431-4770; www.willowssf.com; 710 14th St; r $110-140;) Homey comforts of a B&B, without the frills or fuss. None of the 12 rooms has a private bathroom; all have sinks. Shared kitchenette. Rooms on 14th St are sunnier and have good street views, but they're noisier. No elevator.

THE HAIGHT & HAYES VALLEY

The Parsonnage B&B $$$

(Map p84; 415-863-3699, 888-763-7722; www.theparsonage.com; 198 Haight St; r incl breakfast $200-250; @) A 23-room Italiante-Victorian with original rose-brass chandeliers and Carrera-marble fireplaces, close to Market St. Spacious, airy rooms have oriental rugs and period antiques; some have wood-burning

The Haight

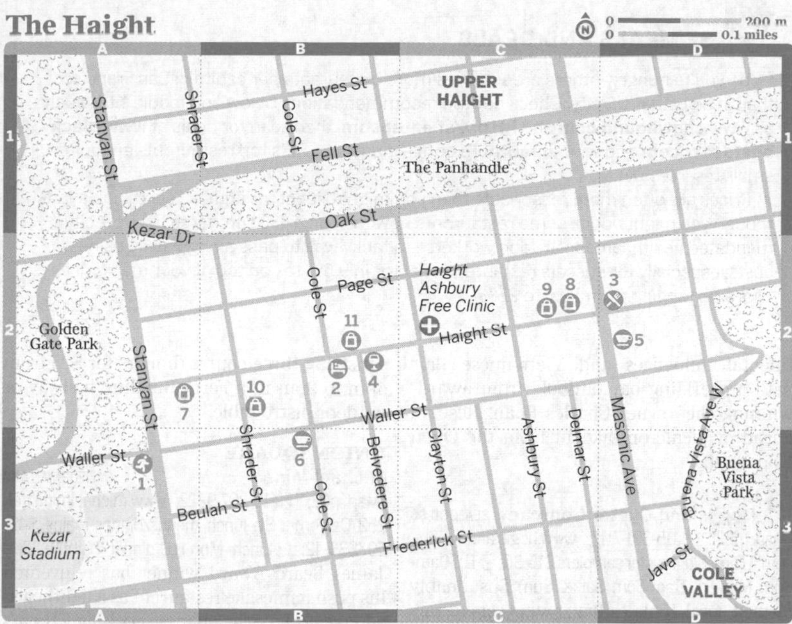

The Haight

Activities, Courses & Tours

1 Haight-Ashbury Flower Power Walking Tour A3

Sleeping

2 Red Victorian B2

Eating

3 Magnolia Brewpub........ D2

Drinking

4 Aub Zam Zam B2
5 Coffee to the People........ D2
6 Cole Valley Café........ B3

Shopping

7 Amoeba Records........ A2
8 Goorin Brothers Hats........ C2
9 Piedmont Boutique C2
10 SFO Snowboarding & FTC Skateboarding B2
11 Wasteland B2

fireplaces. Don't miss brandy and chocolates before bed.

Chateau Tivoli INN $$

(off Map p84; ☎415-776-5462, 800-228-1647; www.chateautivoli.com; 1057 Steiner St; r $140-200, r without bathroom $100-130, ste $250-290; 📶) The glorious turreted chateau has faded since the days when Mark Twain and Isadora Duncan visited, and rooms are modest, but the place is full of soul, character and – rumor has it – the ghost of a Victorian opera diva. Wi-fi in lobby.

Red Victorian QUIRKY $$

(Map p77; ☎415-864-1978; www.redvic.net; 1665 Haight St; r $149-229, without bath $89-129, incl breakfast; 📶) The '60s live on at the tripped-out Red Vic. The 18 rooms have themes such as Sunshine, Flower Children and the Summer of Love; only four have baths, but all come with breakfast in the organic cafe. Wi-fi in the lobby; no elevator.

Metro Hotel HOTEL $

(Map p84; ☎415-861-5364; www.metrohotelsf.com; 319 Divisadero St; r $76-120; 📶) No-frills rooms in the center of The Haight, with good pizza and a garden downstairs and bars and shopping just outside. Rooms in back are quietest.

Eating

THE EMBARCADERO

Slanted Door VIETNAMESE, CALIFORNIAN $$

(Map p62; ☎415-861-8032; www.slanteddoor.com; 1 Ferry Bldg; lunch/dinner mains $13-24/$18-36; ⏲lunch & dinner) California ingredients, Con-

SF MEALS AND DEALS

Hope you're hungry – there are 10 times more restaurants per capita in San Francisco than in any other US city. Check out the recommendations below and foodie sites such as **www.chowhound.com** and **http://sf.eater.com**, then scan for deals at **www.blackboardeats.com** and **www.opentable.com –** and since SF's top restaurants are quite small, reserve now.

Prices are often more reasonable than you might expect for organic, sustainable fare, though you might notice some restaurants now tack on a 4% surcharge to cover city-mandated healthcare for SF food workers – a tacky way to pass along basic business costs, especially for upscale restaurants. Factor in 9.5% tax on top of your meal price, plus a tip ranging from 15% to 25%.

tinental influences and Vietnamese flair with a sparkling bay outlook, from award-winning chef/owner Charles Phan. Reserve ahead or picnic on takeout from the Open Door stall.

Hog Island Oyster Company SEAFOOD **$$**
(Map p62; ☎415-391-7117; www.hogislandoysters.com; 1 Ferry Bldg; oyster samplers $15-30; ⊙11:30am-8pm Mon-Fri, 11am-6pm Sat & Sun) Sustainably farmed, local Tomales Bay oysters served raw or cooked to perfection, with superb condiments and a glass of Sonoma bubbly. From 5pm to 7pm on Mondays and Thursdays, oysters are half-price and pints are $4.

Mijita MEXICAN **$**
(Map p62; ☎415-399-0814; www.mijitasf.com; No 44, 1 Ferry Bldg; small plates $2-9; ⊙10am-7pm Mon-Wed, to 8pm Thu-Sat, 10am-4pm Sun;) Sustainable fish tacos reign supreme and *agua fresca* (fruit punch) is made with fresh juice at chef Traci des Jardins' thoughtful tribute to her Mexican grandmother's cooking, with bay views to be savored from your leather stool.

Boulette's Larder CALIFORNIAN **$$**
(Map p62; ☎415-399-1155; www.bouletteslarder.com; 1 Ferry Bldg; breakfast $7.50-16.50, lunch $9-20, brunch $7-22; ⊙breakfast Mon-Fri, lunch Mon-Sat, brunch Sun) Dinner theater doesn't get better than brunch at Boulette's communal table, amid the swirl of chefs preparing for dinner service. Inspired by the truffled eggs and beignets? Get spices and mixes at the counter.

Il Cane Rosso CALIFORNIAN **$$**
(Map p62; ☎415-391-7599; http://canerossosf.com; 1 Ferry Bldg; mains $13; ⊙breakfast, lunch & dinner) Farm-fresh breakfasts and lunches and soul-satisfying three-course dinners for $25 from 5pm to 9pm in a Ferry Building hallway or outdoor bistro table.

UNION SQUARE

Michael Mina CALIFORNIAN **$$$**
(Map p62; ☎415-397-9222; www.michaelmina.net; 252 California St; lunch menus/dinner mains $49-59/$35-42; ⊙lunch Mon-Fri, dinner nightly) The James Beard Award winner has reinvented his posh namesake restaurant as a lighthearted take on French-Japanese cooking – there's still caviar and lobster, but also foie gras PB&J and lobster pot pie. Reservations essential, or grab bar bites and cocktails at the bar.

farmerbrown MODERN AMERICAN, ORGANIC **$$**
(Map p62; ☎415-409-3276; www.farmerbrownsf.com; 25 Mason St; mains $12-23; ⊙6-10:30pm Tue-Sun, weekend brunch 11am-2pm) A rebel from the wrong side of the block, dishing up seasonal watermelon margaritas with a cayenne-salt rim, ribs that stick to yours and coleslaw with kick. Chef-owner Jay Foster works with local organic and African American farmers to provide food with actual soul, in a shotgun-shack setting with live funk bands.

Millennium VEGETARIAN, VEGAN **$$$**
(Map p62; ☎415-345-3900; www.millenniumrestaurant.com; 580 Geary St; menus $39-72; ⊙dinner;) Three words you're not likely to hear together outside these doors sum up the menu: opulent vegan dining. GMO-free and proud of it, with wild mushrooms and organic produce in succulent seasonal concoctions. Book ahead for aphrodisiac dinners and vegetarian Thanksgiving.

FINANCIAL DISTRICT

Kokkari GREEK **$$$**
(Map p62; ☎415-981-0983; www.kokkari.com; 200 Jackson St; mains $21-35; ⊙lunch Mon-Fri,

dinner nightly; ✎) This is one Greek restaurant where you'll want to lick your plate instead of break it, with starters such as grilled octopus with lemon-oregano zing, and a lamb and eggplant moussaka rich as the Pacific Stock Exchange. Reserve ahead, or make a meal of appetizers at the bar.

Bocadillos MEDITERRANEAN **$$**
(Map p62; ☎415-982-2622; www.bocasf.com; 710 Montgomery St; dishes $9-15; ⏲7am-10pm Mon-Fri, 5-10:30pm Sat) Lunchtime fine dining that won't break the bank or pop buttons, with just-right Basque bites of lamb burger, snapper ceviche with Asian pears, Catalan sausages and wines by the glass.

Gitane MEDITERRANEAN **$$**
(Map p62; ☎415-788-6686; www.gitanerestaurant.com; 6 Claude Lane; mains $15-25; ⏲5:30pm-midnight Tue-Sat, bar to 1am; ✎) Slip out of the Financial District and into something more comfortable at this boudoir-styled bistro, featuring Basque- and Moroccan-inspired stuffed squash blossoms, silky pan-seared scallops, herb-spiked lamb tartare and craft cocktails.

Boxed Foods SANDWICHES **$**
(Map p62; www.boxedfoodscompany.com; 245 Kearny St; dishes $8-10; ⏲8am-3pm Mon-Fri; ✎) The SF salad standard is set here daily, with organic greens topped by tart goat cheese, smoked bacon, wild strawberries and other local treats. Grab hidden seating in back, or get yours to go to the Transamerica Pyramid redwood grove.

CIVIC CENTER & THE TENDERLOIN

TOP CHOICE **Jardinière** CALIFORNIAN **$$$**
(Map p62; ☎415-861-5555; www.jardiniere.com; 300 Grove St; mains $18-38; ⏲dinner) Opera arias can't compare to the high notes hit by James Beard Award winner, Iron Chef and Top Chef Master Traci des Jardins, who lavishes braised oxtail ravioli with summer truffles and stuffs crispy pork belly with salami and Mission figs. Go Mondays, when $45 scores three market-inspired, decadent courses with wine pairings, or enjoy post-SF Opera meals in the bar downstairs.

Brenda's French Soul Food CREOLE **$**
(Map p62; ☎415-345-8100; www.frenchsoulfood.com; 652 Polk St; mains $8-12; ⏲8am-3pm Sun-Tue, 8am-10pm Wed-Sat) Chef-owner Brenda Buenviaje combines Creole cooking with French technique in hangover-curing Hangtown fry (omelette with cured pork and corn-breaded oysters), shrimp-stuffed po' boys, and fried chicken with collard greens and hot-pepper jelly – all worth inevitable waits on a sketchy stretch of sidewalk.

Saigon Sandwich Shop VIETNAMESE **$**
(Map p62; ☎415-475-5698; 560 Larkin St; sandwiches $3.50; ⏲6:30am-5:30pm) Might as well order two of those roast-pork *banh mi* (Vietnamese sandwiches) with housemade pickled vegetables now, so you don't have to wait in line on this sketchy sidewalk again.

Bar Jules CALIFORNIAN **$$**
(Map p84; ☎415-621-5482; www.barjules.com; 609 Hayes St; mains $10-26; ⏲6-10pm Tue, 11:30am-3pm & 6-10pm Wed-Sat, 11am-3pm Sun) Small and succulent is the credo at this dinky bistro, where the short daily menu packs a wallop of local flavor – think Sonoma duck breast with cherries, almonds and arugula, Napa wines and the dark, sinister 'chocolate nemesis.' Waits are a given, but so is unfussy, tasty food.

CHINATOWN

City View CHINESE **$**
(Map p54; ☎415-398-2838; 662 Commercial St; small plates $3-5; ⏲11am-2:30pm Mon-Fri, 10am-2:30pm Sat & Sun) Take your seat in a sunny dining room and your pick from carts loaded with delicate shrimp and leek dumplings, tender black-bean asparagus and crisp Peking duck and other tantalizing, ultrafresh dim sum.

Yuet Lee CHINESE, SEAFOOD **$$**
(Map p54; ☎415-982-6020; 1300 Stockton St; ⏲11am-3am Wed-Mon; 👪) That brash fluorescent lighting isn't especially kind on dates, but if you're willing to share Yuet Lee's legendary crispy salt-and-pepper crab or smoky-sweet roast duck with your booth mate, it must be love.

House of Nanking CHINESE **$$**
(Map p54; ☎415-421-1429; 919 Kearny St; starters $5-8, mains $9-15; ⏲11am-10pm Mon-Fri, noon-10pm Sat, noon-9pm Sun) Bossy service with bravura cooking. Supply the vaguest outlines for your dinner – maybe seafood, nothing deep-fried, perhaps some greens – and within minutes you'll be devouring pan-seared scallops, sautéed pea shoots and garlicky noodles.

NORTH BEACH

TOP CHOICE **Coi** CALIFORNIAN **$$$**
(Map p54; ☎415-393-9000; http://coirestaurant.com; 373 Broadway; set menu $145 per person;

TOP 5 SF FARMERS MARKETS

» **Fancy foods** **Ferry Building** (www.cuesa.org) showcases California-grown, organic produce, artisan meats and gourmet prepared foods at moderate-to-premium prices at markets held Tuesday, Thursday and Saturday mornings year-round.

» **Best value and selection** City-run **Alemany** (www.sfgov.org/site/alemany) has offered bargain prices on local and organic produce every Saturday year-round since 1943, plus stalls with ready-to-eat foods.

» **Most convenient** Sundays and Wednesdays from 7am to 5pm in UN Plaza, **Heart of the City** (www.hocfarmersmarket.org) offers local produce (some organics) at good prices and prepared-food stalls for downtown lunches at UN Plaza, which on other days is an obstacle course of skateboarders, Scientologists and raving self-talkers, plus a few crafts stalls.

» **Best for families** **Inner Sunset** (parking lot btwn 8th & 9th Ave, off Irving St; 9am-1pm) has local and some organic produce and artisan foods at moderate prices, plus kids' programs on Sundays April–September.

» **Best evening market** **Castro farmers market** (Market St at Noe St; 4-8pm Mar-Dec) has local and organic produce and artisan foods at moderate prices, cooking demos and live folk music.

6-10pm Tue-Fri, 5:30-10pm Fri & Sat;) Chef Daniel Patterson's wild tasting menu featuring foraged morels, wildflowers and Pacific seafood is like licking the California coastline. Black and green noodles are made from clams and Pacific seaweed, and purple ice-plant petals are strewn atop Sonoma duck's tongue, wild-caught abalone and just-picked arugula. Only-in-California flavors and intriguing wine pairings ($95; pours generous enough for two to share) will keep you California dreaming.

Cotogna ITALIAN $$
(Map p54; 415-775-8508; www.cotognasf.com; 470 Pacific Av; mains $14-24; noon-3pm & 7-10pm Mon-Sat;) No wonder chef-owner Michael Tusk won the 2011 James Beard Award: his rustic Italian pastas and toothsome pizzas magically balance a few pristine, local flavors. Book ahead; the $24 prix-fixe is among SF's best dining deals.

Ideale ITALIAN $$
(Map p54; 415-391-4129; 1315 Grant Ave; 5:30-10:30pm Mon-Sat, 5-10pm Sun) SF's most authentic Italian restaurant, with a Roman chef that grills a mean fish and whips up gorgeous truffled zucchini – but order anything with bacon or meat and Tuscan-staff-recommend wine, and everyone goes home happy.

Liguria Bakery ITALIAN, BAKERY $
(Map p54; 415-421-3786; 1700 Stockton St; focaccia $3; 8am-1pm Mon-Fri, 7am-1pm Sat, 7am-noon Sun) Bleary-eyed art students and Italian grandmothers are in line by 8am for the cinnamon-raisin focaccia, leaving 9am dawdlers a choice of tomato or classic rosemary, and noontime arrivals out of luck.

Cinecittà PIZZA $
(Map p54; 415-291-8830; 663 Union St; noon-10pm Sun-Thu, to 11pm Fri & Sat;) Squeeze in at the counter for your thin-crust pie and Anchor Steam on draft with a side order of sass from Roman owner Romina. Go with the two standouts: wild mushroom with sundried tomato for vegetarians, or the omnivore's delight with artichoke hearts, olives, prosciutto and egg.

Molinari ITALIAN, SANDWICHES $
(Map p54; 415-421-2337; 373 Columbus Ave; sandwiches $5-8; 9am-5:30pm Mon-Fri, 7:30am-5:30pm Sat) Grab a number and wait your turn ogling Italian wines and cheeses, and by the time you're called, the scent of house-cured salami dangling from the rafters and Parma prosciutto will have made your choice for you.

Tony's Coal-Fired Pizza Slice House PIZZA, SANDWICHES $
(Map p54; 415-835-9888; www.tonyspizzanapoletana.com; 1556 Stockton St; noon-11pm Wed-Sun) Get a meatball sub or cheesy, thin-crust slice to go from nine-time world champ pizza-slinger Tony Gemignani, and take that slice to sunny Washington Square Park to savor amid wild parrots.

FISHERMAN'S WHARF

Crown & Crumpet DESSERTS, SANDWICHES $$

(Map p58; ☎415-771-4252; www.crownandcrumpet.com; 207 Ghirardelli Square; dishes $8-12; ⏲10am-9pm Mon-Fri, 9am-9pm Sat, 9am-6pm Sun;) Designer style and rosy cheer usher teatime into the 21st century: dads and daughters clink teacups with crooked pinkies, Lolita Goth teens nibble cucumber sandwiches and girlfriends rehash dates over scones and champagne. Reservations recommended weekends.

In-N-Out Burger BURGERS $

(Map p58; ☎800-786-1000; www.in-n-out.com; 333 Jefferson St; burgers $3-6; ⏲10:30am-1am Sun-Thu, to 1:30am Fri & Sat;) Serving burgers for 60 years the way California likes them: with prime chuck ground onsite, fries and shakes made with pronounceable ingredients, served by employees paid a living wage.

RUSSIAN HILL & NOB HILL

Swan Oyster Depot SEAFOOD $$

(Map p58; ☎415-673-1101; 1517 Polk St; dishes $10-20; ⏲8am-5:30pm Mon-Sat) Superior freshness without the superior attitude of most seafood restaurants. Order yours to go, browse nearby boutiques and breeze past the line to pick up your crab salad and oysters with mignonette (wine and shallot) picnic.

Za PIZZA $

(Map p58; ☎415-771-3100; www.zapizzasf.com; 1919 Hyde St; ⏲noon-10pm Sun-Wed, to 11pm Thu-Sat) Pizza lovers brave the uphill climb for cornmeal-dusted, thin-crust pizza by the slice piled with fresh ingredients, a pint of Anchor Steam and a cozy bar setting with highly flirtatious pizza-slingers – all for under 10 bucks.

JAPANTOWN & PACIFIC HEIGHTS

Tataki SUSHI $$

(Map p58; ☎415-931-1182; www.tatakisushibar.com; 2815 California St; dishes $12-20; ⏲11:30am-2pm & 5:30-10:30pm Mon-Fri, 5-11:30pm Sat, 5-9:30pm Sun) Rescue dinner dates and the oceans with sensational, sustainable sushi: silky arctic char drizzled with yuzu-citrus and capers replaces dubious farmed salmon, and the Golden State Roll is a local hero with spicy line-caught scallop, Pacific tuna, organic apple slivers and edible gold.

Out the Door VIETNAMESE $$

(Map p58; ☎415-923 9575; www.outthedoors.com; 2232 Bush St; lunch/dinner mains $12-18/$18-28; ⏲8am-4:30pm & 5:30pm-10pm Mon Fri, 8am-3pm & 5:30pm-10pm Sat & Sun) Stellar French beignets and Vietnamese coffee, or salty-sweet dungeness-crab frittatas at this offshoot of famous Slanted Door (p77). Lunchtime's rice plates and noodles are replaced at dinner with savory clay-pot meats and fish.

Benkyodo JAPANESE, SANDWICHES $

(Map p58; ☎415-922-1244; www.benkyodocompany.com; 1747 Buchanan St; sandwiches $3-4; ⏲8am-5pm Mon-Sat) The perfect retro lunch counter cheerfully serves old-school egg salad and pastrami sandwiches, plus $1 chocolate-filled strawberry and green-tea mochi made in-house.

The Grove AMERICAN $

(Map p58; ☎415-474-1419; 2016 Fillmore St; dishes $8-12; ⏲7am-11pm;) Rough-hewn recycled wood and a stone fireplace give this Fillmore St cafe ski-lodge coziness for made-to-order breakfasts, working lunches with salads, sandwiches and wi-fi, and chat sessions with warm-from-the-oven cookies and hot cocoa.

THE MARINA & COW HOLLOW

Off the Grid FOOD TRUCKS $

(Map p58; http://offthegridsf.com; Fort Mason parking lot; dishes under $10; ⏲5-10pm Fri;) Some 30 food trucks circle their wagons at SF's largest mobile-gourmet hootenanny (other nights/locations attract less than a dozen trucks; see website). Arrive before 6:30pm or expect 20-minute waits for Chairman Bao's clamshell buns stuffed with duck and mango, Roli Roti's free-range herbed roast chicken, or dessert from The Crème Brûlée Man. Cash only; take dinner to nearby docks for Golden Gate Bridge sunsets.

Blue Barn Gourmet SANDWICHES $

(Map p58; ☎415-441-3232; www.bluebarngourmet.com; salads & sandwiches $8-10; 2105 Chestnut St; ⏲11am-8:30pm Sun-Thu, to 7pm Fri & Sat;) Toss aside thoughts of ordinary salads with organic produce, heaped with fixings: artisan cheeses, caramelized onions, heirloom tomatoes, candied pecans, pomegranate seeds, even Meyer grilled sirloin. For something hot, try the toasted panini oozing with Manchego cheese, fig jam and salami.

Greens VEGETARIAN $$

(Map p58; ☎415-771-6222; www.greensrestaurant.com; Fort Mason Center, bldg A; mains $7-20; ⏲noon-2:30pm Tue-Sat, 5:30-9pm Mon-Sat, 9am-4pm Sun;) In a converted army barracks, enjoy Golden Gate views, smoky-rich black bean chili with pickled jalapeños and roasted eggplant panini. All Greens' dishes are meat-free and organic, mostly raised on a Zen farm in Marin – sure beats army rations.

A16 ITALIAN **$$**
(Map p58; ☎415-771-2216; www.a16sf.com; 2355 Chestnut St; pizza $12-18, mains $18-26; ⊙lunch Wed-Fri, dinner nightly) SF's James Beard Award–winning Neapolitan pizzeria requires reservations, then haughtily makes you wait in the foyer like a high-maintenance date. The housemade mozzarella burata and chewy-but-not-too-thick-crust pizza topped with kicky calamari makes it worth your while.

Warming Hut CAFE
(off Map p58; Crissy Field; pastries $2-4; ⊙9am-5pm) When the fog rolls into Crissy Field, head here for Fair Trade coffee, organic pastries and organic hot dogs within walls insulated with recycled denim; all purchases support Crissy Field conservation.

SOUTH OF MARKET (SOMA)

TOP CHOICE **Benu** CALIFORNIAN, FUSION **$$$**
(Map p62; ☎415-685-4860; www.benusf.com; 22 Hawthorne St; mains $25-40; ⊙5:30-10pm Tue-Sat) SF has refined fusion cuisine over 150 years, but no one rocks it quite like chef Corey Lee, who remixes local fine-dining staples and Pacific Rim flavors with a SoMa DJ's finesse. Velvety Sonoma foie gras with tangy, woodsy yuzu-sake glaze makes tastebuds bust wild moves, while Dungeness crab and black truffle custard bring such outsize flavor to faux-shark's fin soup, you'll swear there's Jaws in there. The tasting menu is steep ($160) and beverage pairings add $110, but you won't want to miss star-sommelier Yoon Ha's flights of fancy – including a rare 1968 Madeira with your soup.

Boulevard CALIFORNIAN **$$$**
(Map p62; ☎415-543-6084; www.boulevardrestaurant.com; 1 Mission St; lunch $17-25, dinner $29-39; ⊙lunch Mon-Fri, dinner daily) Belle epoque decor adds grace notes to this 1889 building that once housed the Coast Seamen's Union, but chef Nancy Oakes has kept the menu honest with juicy pork chops, enough soft-shell crab to satisfy a sailor and crowd-pleasing desserts.

Zero Zero PIZZA **$$**
(Map p62; ☎415-348-8800; www.zerozerosf.com; 826 Folsom St; pizzas $12-17; ⊙noon-2:30pm & 5:30-10pm Sun-Thu, to 11pm Fri & Sat) The name is a throw-down of Neapolitan pizza credentials – '00' flour is used exclusively for Naples' puffy-edged crust – and these pies deliver, with inspired SF-themed toppings. The Geary is piled with Manila clams, bacon and chillis, but the real crowd-pleaser is the Castro, turbo-loaded with house-made sausage.

Juhu Beach Club INDIAN **$**
(Map p84; ☎415-298-0471; www.facebook.com/JuhuBeachClub; 320 11th St; dishes $4-8 ⊙11:30am-2:30pm Mon-Fri) SoMa's gritty streets are looking positively upbeat ever since reinvented *chaat* (Indian street snacks) popped up inside Garage Café, serving lunchtime pork vindaloo buns, aromatic grilled Nahu chicken salad, and the aptly named, slow-cooked shredded steak 'holy cow' sandwich.

Sentinel SANDWICHES **$**
(Map p62; ☎415-284-9960; www.thesentinelsf.com; 37 New Montgomery St; sandwiches $8.50-9; ⊙7:30am-2:30pm Mon-Fri) Rebel SF chef Dennis Leary takes on the classics: tuna salad gets radical with chipotle mayo, and corned beef crosses borders with Swiss cheese and housemade Russian dressing. Menus change daily; come prepared for about a 10-minute wait, since sandwiches are made to order.

Split Pea Seduction SANDWICHES **$**
(Map p62; ☎415-551-2223; www.splitpeaseduction.com; 138 6th St; lunches $6-9.75; ⊙8am-5pm Mon-Fri; ✎) Right off Skid Row are unexpectedly healthy, homey soup-and-sandwich combos, including seasonal soups such as potato with housemade pesto and a signature *crostata* (open-faced sandwich), such as cambozola cheese and nectarine drizzled with honey.

THE MISSION

TOP CHOICE **La Taquería** MEXICAN **$**
(Map p84; ☎415-285-7117; 2889 Mission St; burritos $6-8; ⊙11am-9pm Mon-Sat, 11am-8pm Sun) No debatable tofu, saffron rice, spinach tortilla or mango salsa here: just classic tomatillo or mesquite salsa, marinated, grilled meats and flavorful beans inside a flour tortilla – optional housemade spicy pickles and sour cream highly recommended.

Commonwealth CALIFORNIAN **$$**
(Map p84; ☎415-355-1500; www.commonwealthsf.com; 2224 Mission St; small plates $5-16; ⊙5:30-10pm Tue-Thu & Sun, to 11pm Fri & Sat; ✎) Califor-

VEGETARIANS: TURNING THE TABLES IN SF

San Francisco offers far more than grilled cheese and veggie burgers for vegetarians and vegans.

» **Vegan** Three organic vegan options could convert even committed carnivores: **Millennium** (p78), **Greens** (p81) and **Samovar Tea Lounge** (p91).

» **Vegetarian prix-fixe** Multicourse options featuring local, seasonal produce are offered at fancy restaurants like **Michael Mina** (p78) and **Benu** (p82).

» **Ethnic vegetarian** Omnivores veer to the vegetarian side of the menu at ethnic specialty joints like Ethiopian **Axum Café** (p86), Mexican **Pancho Villa** (p83), and Indian **Udupi Palace** (p83).

» **Vegetarian power lunches** Organic soup/salad/sandwich joints downtown offer fresh perspectives on lunch: **Boxed Foods** (p79), **Split Pea Seduction** (p82)

nia's most imaginative farm-to-table dining isn't in some quaint barn, but the converted cinderblock Mission dive where chef Jason Fox serves crispy hen with toybox carrots cooked in hay (yes, hay), and sea urchin floating on a bed of farm egg and organic asparagus that looks like a tidepool and tastes like a dream. Savor the $65 prix-fixe knowing $10 is donated to charity.

Locanda ITALIAN $$
(Map p84; ☎415-863-6800; www.locandasf.com; 557 Valencia St; share plates $10-24; ⌚5:30pm-midnight) The vintage Duran Duran Rome concert poster in the bathroom is your first clue that Locanda is all about cheeky, street-wise Roman fare. Scrumptious tripe melting into rich tomato-mint sauce is a must, piazza bianco with figs and prosciutto creates obsessions, and Roman fried artichokes and sweetbreads mean authenticity minus the airfare.

Pizzeria Delfina PIZZA $$
(Map p84; ☎415-437-6800; www.delfinasf.com; 3611 18th St; pizzas $11-17; ⌚11:30am-10pm Tue-Thu, to 11pm Fri, noon-11pm Sat & Sun, 5:30-10pm Mon; ✎) One bite explains why SF is obsessed with pizza lately: Delfina's thin crust supports the weight of fennel sausage and fresh mozzarella without drooping or cracking, while white pizzas let chefs freestyle with Cali-foodie ingredients like maitake mushrooms, broccoli rabe and artisan cheese. No reservations; sign up on the chalkboard and wait with wine at Delfina bar next door.

Range CALIFORNIAN $$
(Map p84; ☎415-282-8283; www.rangesf.com; 842 Valencia St; mains $20-28; ⌚5:30-10pm Sun-Thu, to 11pm Fri & Sat; ✎) Inspired American dining is alive and well within Range. The menu is seasonal Californian, prices are reasonable and the style is repurposed industrial chic – think coffee-rubbed pork shoulder served with microbrewed beer from the blood-bank refrigerator.

Bi-Rite Creamery ICE CREAM $$
(Map p84; ☎415-626-5600; http://biritecreamery.com; 3692 18th St; ice cream $3.25 7; ⌚11am-10pm Sun-Thu, to 11pm Fri & Sat) Velvet ropes at clubs seem pretentious in laid-back San Francisco, but at organic Bi-Rite Creamery they make perfect sense: lines wrap around the corner for legendary salted-caramel ice cream with housemade hot fudge. For a quick fix, get balsamic strawberry soft serve at the soft-serve window (⌚1-9pm).

Pancho Villa MEXICAN $
(Map p84; ☎415-864-8840; www.sfpanchovilla.com; 3071 16th St; burritos $7-8.50; ⌚10am-noon; ✎) The hero of the downtrodden and burrito-deprived, delivering tinfoil-wrapped meals the girth of your forearm and a worthy condiments bar. The line moves fast, and as you leave the door is held open for you and your Pancho's paunch.

Udupi Palace INDIAN $
(Map p84; ☎415-970-8000; www.udupipalaceca.com; 1007 Valencia St; mains $8-10; ⌚11am-10pm Mon-Thu, to 10:30pm Fri-Sun; ✎) Tandoori in the Tenderloin is for novices – SF foodies swoon over the bright, clean flavors of South Indian *dosa,* a light, crispy pancake made with lentil flour dipped in mildly spicy vegetable *sambar* (soup) and coconut chutney.

Mission Chinese CALIFORNIAN, CHINESE $$
(Map p84; Lung Shan; ☎415-863-2800; www.missionchinesefood.com; 2234 Mission St; dishes

The Castro & The Mission

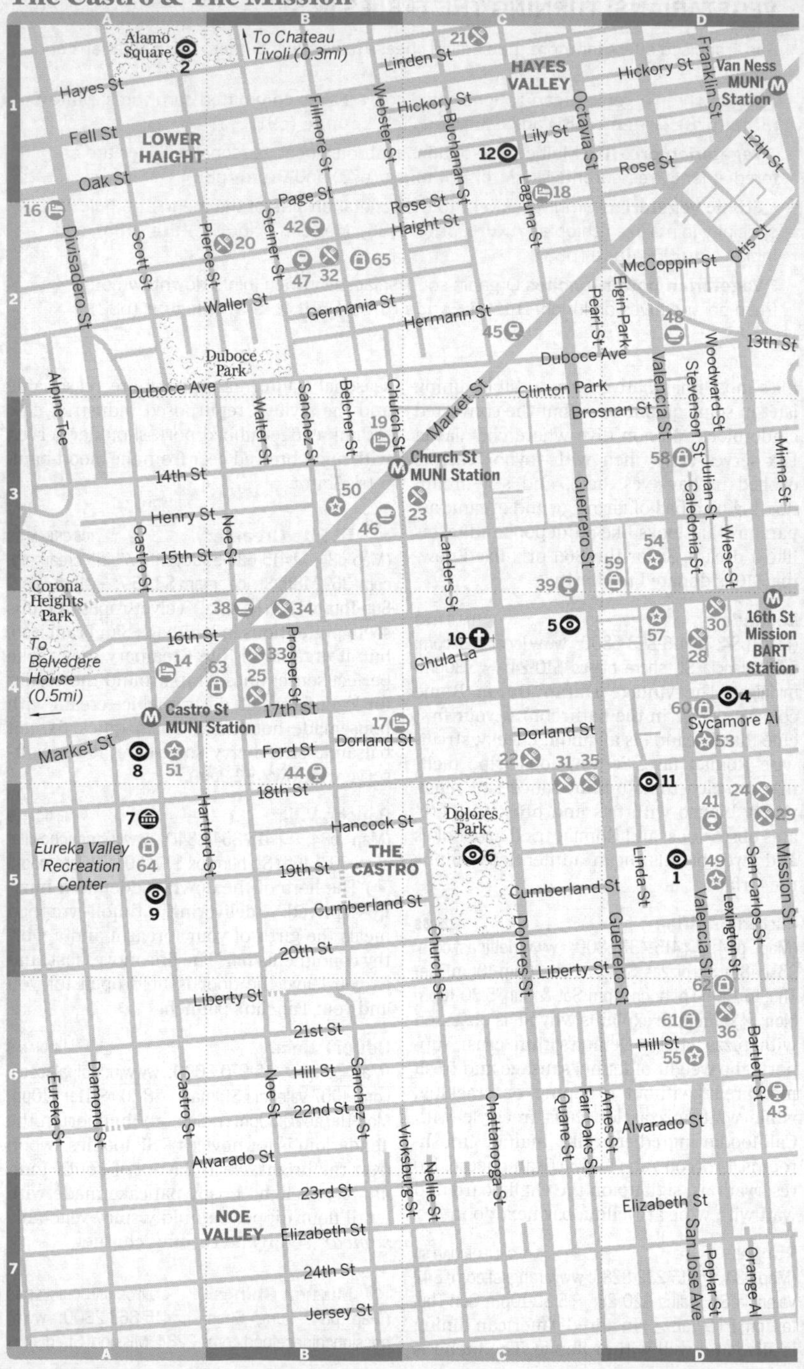

$9-16; ⏰11:30am-10:30pm Mon-Tue & Thu-Sun) Lovers of spicy food, Chinese takeout and sustainable meat converge on this gourmet dive. Creative, meaty mains such as tingly lamb noodles are big enough for two – if not for the salt-shy – and $0.75 from each main is donated to San Francisco Food Bank.

Tartine BAKERY **$**
(Map p84; ☎415-487-2600; www.tartinebakery.com; 600 Guerrero St; pastries $2-5; ⏰8am-7pm Mon-Wed, to 8pm Thu-Sat, 9am-8pm Sun) Lines out the door for pumpkin tea bread, Valrhona chocolate cookies and open-face *croques monsieurs* (toasted ham-and-cheese sandwiches) – all so loaded with butter that you feel fatter and happier just looking at them.

THE CASTRO

TOP CHOICE **Frances** CALIFORNIAN **$$**
(Map p84; ☎415-621-3870; www.frances-sf.com; 3870 17th St; mains $14-27; ⏰5-10.30pm Tue-Sun) Chef and owner Melissa Perello earned a Michelin star for fine dining, then ditched downtown to start this market-inspired neighborhood bistro. Daily menus showcase bright, seasonal flavors and luxurious textures: cloud-like sheep's milk ricotta gnocchi with crunchy breadcrumbs and broccolini, grilled calamari with preserved Meyer lemon, and artisan wine served by the ounce, directly from Wine Country.

Chilango MEXICAN **$$**
(Map p84; ☎415-552-5700; chilangorestaurantsf.com; 235 Church St; dishes $8-12; ⏰11am-10pm) Upgrade from to-go *taquerías* (Mexican fast-food restaurants) to organic *chilango* (Mexico City native) dishes worthy of a sit-down dinner, including grassfed filet mignon tacos, sustainable pork carnitas and sensational freerange chicken mole.

Starbelly CALIFORNIAN **$$**
(Map p84; ☎415-252-7500; www.starbellysf.com; 3583 16th St; dishes $6-19; ⏰11:30am-11pm, to midnight Fri & Sat) Reclaimed wood décor to match the food: market-fresh salads, scrumptious paté, roasted mussels with house-made sausage and juicy grassfed burgers. Reserve ahead to lounge amid flowering herbs on the heated patio, or join the communal table.

Sushi Time SUSHI **$**
(Map p84; ☎415-552-2280; www.sushitime-sf.com; 2275 Market St; rolls $4-10; ⏰dinner Mon-Sat) Devour sashimi and Barbie, GI Joe and Hello

The Castro & The Mission

Sights

1 826 Valencia ... D5
2 Alamo Square ... A1
3 Balmy Alley ... F7
Castro Theatre ... (see 51)
4 Clarion Alley ... D4
5 Creativity Explored ... C4
6 Dolores Park ... C5
7 GLBT History Museum ... A5
8 Harvey Milk Plaza ... A4
9 Human Rights Campaign Action Center ... A5
10 Mission Dolores Basilica ... C4
11 Women's Building ... D4
12 Zen Center ... C1

Activities, Courses & Tours

13 Precita Eyes ... F7

Sleeping

14 Inn on Castro ... A4
15 Inn San Francisco ... E5
16 Metro Hotel ... A2
17 Parker Guest House ... B4
18 The Parsonnage ... C1
19 Willows ... B3

Eating

20 Axum Café ... B2
21 Bar Jules ... C1
22 Bi-Rite Creamery ... C4
23 Chilango ... C3
24 Commonwealth ... D5
25 Frances ... B4
26 Juhu Beach Club ... F2
27 La Taquería ... E7
28 Locanda ... D4
29 Mission Chinese ... D5
30 Pancho Villa ... D4
31 Pizzeria Delfina ... C4
Range ... (see 1)
32 Rosamunde Sausage Grill ... B2
33 Starbelly ... B4
34 Sushi Time ... B4
35 Tartine ... C4
36 Udupi Palace ... D6

Drinking

37 Bar Agricole ... F2
38 Café Flore ... B4
39 Elixir ... C3
40 Homestead ... E5
41 Lexington Club ... D5
42 Mad Dog in the Fog ... B2
43 Make-Out Room ... D6
Ritual Coffee Roasters ... (see 55)
44 Samovar Tea Lounge ... B4
45 The Mint ... C2
46 Thorough Bread ... B3
47 Toronado ... B2
48 Zeitgeist ... D2

Entertainment

49 Amnesia ... D5
50 Cafe du Nord ... B3
51 Castro Theatre ... A4
52 DNA Lounge ... F2
53 Elbo Room ... D4
54 Intersection for the Arts ... D3
55 Marsh ... D6
56 ODC Theater ... E4
57 Roxie Cinema ... D4

Shopping

58 Accident & Artifact ... D3
59 Adobe Books & BackRoom Gallery ... D3
60 Community Thrift ... D4
61 Dema ... D6
62 Gravel & Gold ... D6
Human Rights Campaign Action Center ... (see 9)
63 Sui Generis ... B4
64 Under One Roof ... A5
65 Upper Playground ... B2

Kitty rolls in the tiny glassed-in patio like a shark in an aquarium. Happy-hour specials run from 5pm to 6:30pm.

THE HAIGHT & HAYES VALLEY

Rosamunde Sausage Grill SANDWICHES $
(Map p84; ☎415-437-6851; 545 Haight St; sausages $4-6; ⏲11:30am-10pm) Here's what they serve at baseball games in heaven: divine duck, spicy lamb or wild boar sausages, fully loaded with your choice of roasted peppers, grilled onions, mango chutney or wasabi mustard, washed down with microbrews at Toronado (p91).

Axum Café ETHIOPIAN $
(Map p84; ☎415-252-7912; www.axumcafe.com; 698 Haight St; $7-14; ⏲dinner; ✎) When you've got a hot date with a vegan, a marathoner's appetite and/or the salary of an activist, Axum's vegetarian platter for two is your saving grace: lip-tingling red lentils, fiery

mushrooms and mellow yellow chickpeas, scooped up with spongy *injera* bread.

Magnolia Brewpub CALIFORNIAN $$
(Map p77; ☎415-864-7468; www.magnoliapub.com; 1398 Haight St; mains $11-20; ⏰noon-midnight Mon-Thu, until 1am Fri, 10am-1am Sat, 10am-midnight Sun) Organic pub grub and homebrew samplers keep conversation flowing at communal tables, while grass-fed Prather Ranch burgers satisfy stoner appetites in side booths – it's like the Summer of Love is back, only with better food.

THE RICHMOND

TOP CHOICE **Aziza** CALIFORNIAN, NORTH AFRICAN $$
(Map p68; ☎415-752-2222; www.azizasf.com; 5800 Geary Blvd; mains $16-29; ⏰5:30-10:30pm Wed-Mon;) Mourad Lahlou's inspiration is Moroccan and his produce organic Californian, but his flavors are out of this world: Sonoma duck confit melts into caramelized onion in flaky pastry *basteeya* (savory phyllo pastry), while sour cherries rouse slow-cooked local lamb shank from its barley bed.

Namu KOREAN, CALIFORNIAN $$
(Map p68; ☎415-386-8332; www.namusf.com; 439 Balboa St; small plates $8-16; ⏰6-10:30pm Sun-Tue, 6pm-midnight Wed-Sat, 10:30am-3pm Sat & Sun) Organic ingredients, Silicon Valley inventiveness and Pacific Rim roots are showcased in Korean-inspired soul food, including housemade kimchee, umami-rich shitake mushroom dumplings and NorCal's definitive *bibimbap:* organic vegetables, grassfed steak and Sonoma farm egg served in a sizzling stone pot.

Ton Kiang DIM SUM $
(Map p68; ☎415-387-8273; www.tonkiang.net; 5821 Geary Blvd; dim sum $3-7; ⏰10am-9pm Mon-Thu, 10am-9:30pm Fri, 9:30am-9:30pm Sat, 9am-9pm Sun;) Don't bother asking what's in those bamboo steamers: choose some on aroma alone and ask for the legendary *gao choy gat* (shrimp and chive dumplings), *dao miu gao* (pea tendril and shrimp dumplings) and *jin doy* (sesame balls) by name.

Kabuto CALIFORNIAN, SUSHI $$
(Map p68; ☎415-752-5652; www.kabutosushi.com; 5121 Geary Blvd; sushi $2-7, mains $9-13; ⏰dinner Tue-Sun) Innovative sushi served in a converted vintage hot-dog drive-in: nori-wrapped sushi rice with foie gras and ollalieberry reduction, *hamachi* (yellowtail) with pear and wasabi mustard, and – eureka! – the 49er oyster with sea urchin, caviar, a quail's egg and gold leaf, chased with rare sake.

Spices CHINESE $
(Map p68; ☎415-752-8884; http://spicesrestaurantonline.com; 294 8th Ave; mains $7-13; ⏰lunch & dinner) The menu reads like an oddly dubbed Hong Kong action flick, with dishes labeled 'explosive!!' and 'stinky!', but the chefs can call zesty pickled Napa cabbage, silky ma-po tofu and brain-curdling spicy chicken whatever they want – it's all worthy of exclamation. Cash only.

Halu JAPANESE $
(Map p 68; ☎415-221-9165; 312 8th Ave; yakitori $2.50-4, ramen $10-11; ⏰5-10pm Tue-Sat) Dinner at this surreal, snug yakitori joint covered with Beatles memorabilia feels like stowing away on the Yellow Submarine. Small bites crammed onto sticks and barbecued, including bacon-wrapped scallops, quail eggs and mochi – and if you're up for offal, have a heart.

Genki DESSERT, SELF-CATERING $
(Map p68; ☎415-379-6414; www.genkicrepes.com; 330 Clement St; crepes $5; ⏰2-10:30pm Mon, 10:30am-10:30pm Tue-Thu & Sun, 10am-11:30pm Fri & Sat) A teen mob scene for French crepes by way of Tokyo with green-tea ice cream and Nutella, and tropical fruit tapioca bubble tea. Stock up in the beauty supply and Pocky aisle to satisfy sudden snack or hair-dye whims.

THE SUNSET

TOP CHOICE **Outerlands** CALIFORNIAN $
(Map p68; ☎415-661-6140; http://outerlandssf.com; 4001 Judah St; sandwiches & small plates $8-9; ⏰11am-3pm & 6-10pm Tue-Sat, 10am-2:30pm Sun) Drift into this beach-shack bistro for organic California comfort food: lunch means a $9 grilled artisan cheese combo with seasonal housemade soup, and dinner brings slow-cooked pork shoulder slouching into green-garlic risotto. Arrive early and sip wine outside until seats open up indoors.

Nanking Road Bistro CHINESE $
(Map p68; ☎415-753-2900; 1360 9th Ave; mains $7-12; ⏰11:30am-10pm Mon-Fri, noon-10pm Sat & Sun;) Northern regional Chinese food is underrepresented in historically Cantonese SF, but the breakaway stars of Nanking Road's menu are clamshell *bao* (bun) folded over crispy Beijing duck and a definitive *kung*

pao chicken lunch special ($7), with the right ratio of chili to roast peanuts.

Sunrise Deli MIDDLE EASTERN $
(Map p68; ☎415-664-8210; 2115 Irving St; dishes $4-7; ⊙9am-9pm Mon-Sat, 10am-8pm Sun; ✎) A hidden gem in the fog belt, Sunrise dishes up what is arguably the city's best smoky baba ghanoush, *mujeddrah* (lentil-rice with crispy onions), garlicky *foul* (fava bean spread) and crispy falafel, either to go or to enjoy in the old-school cafe atmosphere.

Drinking

DOWNTOWN & SOUTH OF MARKET (SOMA)

Emporio Rulli Caffè CAFE
(Map p62; www.rulli.com; 333 Post St; ⊙7:30am-7pm) Ideal people-watching atop Union Sq, with excellent espresso and pastries to fuel up for shopping, plus wine by the glass afterward.

Bar Agricole BAR
(Map p84; www.baragricole.com; 355 11th St; 6-10pm Sun-Wed, til late Thu-Sat) Drink your way to a history degree with well-researched cocktails: Bellamy Scotch Sour with egg whites passes the test, but Tequila Fix with lime, pineapple gum, and hellfire bitters earns honors.

Sightglass Coffee CAFE
(Map p62; http://sightglasscoffee.com; 270 7th St; ⊙7am-6pm Mon-Sat, 8am-6pm Sun) San Francisco's newest cult coffee is roasted in a SoMa warehouse – follow the wafting aromas of Owl's Howl Espresso, and sample their family-grown, high-end 100% Bourbon-shrub coffee.

Bloodhound BAR
(Map p62; www.bloodhoundsf.com; 1145 Folsom St; ⊙4pm-2am) The murder of crows painted on the ceiling is definitely an omen: nights at Bloodhound assume mythic proportions with top-shelf booze served in Mason jars and pool marathons. SF's best food trucks often park out front; ask the barkeep to suggest a pairing.

House of Shields BAR
(Map p62; 39 New Montgomery St; ⊙2pm-2am Mon-Fri, from 7pm Sat) Flash back a hundred years at this recently restored mahogany bar, with original c 1908 chandeliers hanging from high ceilings and old-fashioned cocktails without the frippery.

Blue Bottle Coffee Company CAFE
(Map p62; www.bluebottlecoffee.net; 66 Mint St; ⊙7am-7pm Mon-Fri, 8am-6pm Sat, 8am-4pm Sun) The microroaster with the crazy-looking $20,000 coffee siphon for superior Fair Trade organic drip coffee is rivaled only by the bittersweet mochas and cappuccinos with ferns drawn in the foam. Expect a wait and $4 for your fix.

UNION SQUARE

Rickhouse BAR
(Map p62; www.rickhousebar.com; 246 Kearny St; ⊙Mon-Sat) Like a shotgun shack plunked downtown, Rickhouse is lined with repurposed whisky casks imported from Kentucky, and backbar shelving from an Ozark Mountains nunnery that once secretly brewed hooch. The emphasis is on bourbon, but authentic Pisco Punch (Peruvian-liquor citrus cocktail) is served in garage-sale punchbowls.

Barrique BAR
(Map p62; www.barriquesf.com; 461 Pacific Ave; ⊙3pm-10pm Tue-Sat) Roll out the barrel: get your glass of high-end small-batch vino straight from the cask, directly from the vineyard. Settle into white-leather sofas in back, near the casks, with artisan cheese and charcuterie plates.

Irish Bank PUB
(Map p62; www.theirishbank.com; 10 Mark Lane; ⊙11:30am-2am) Perfectly pulled pints, thick-cut fries with malt vinegar and juicy sausages served in a hidden alleyway or church pews indoors. Irish owner Ronin bought the place from his boss, and is now every working stiff's close and personal friend.

Tunnel Top Bar BAR
(Map p62; www.tunneltop.com; 601 Bush St; ⊙Mon-Sat) Chill two-story bar with exposed beams, beer-bottle chandelier, and a balcony where you can spy on the crowd below, grooving to hip-hop. Cash only.

Cantina BAR
(Map p62; www.cantinasf.com; 580 Sutter St; ⊙Mon-Sat) Latin-inspired cocktails made with fresh juice – there's not even a soda gun behind the bar – make this a go-to bar for off-duty bartenders; DJs spin weekends.

CIVIC CENTER & THE TENDERLOIN

Hemlock Tavern BAR
(Map p62; www.hemlocktavern.com; 1131 Polk St; ⊙4pm-2am) Cheap drinks at the oval bar,

pogo-worthy punk rock in the back room, a heated smoking area and free peanuts in the shell to eat and throw at literary events.

Edinburgh Castle BAR

(Map p62; www.castlenews.com; 950 Geary St; ⏲7pm-1am) Photos of bagpipers, the *Trainspotting* soundtrack on the jukebox, dart boards and a service delivering vinegary fish and chips in newspaper are all the Scottish authenticity you could ask for, short of haggis.

Rye BAR

(Map p62; www.ryesf.com; 688 Geary St; ⏲5:30pm-2am Mon-Fri, 7pm-2am Sat & Sun) Polished cocktails with herb-infused spirits and fresh-squeezed juice in a sleek darkwood setting. Come early, drink something challenging involving dark rum or juniper gin, and leave before the smoking cage overflows.

Bourbon & Branch BAR

(Map p62; ☎415-346-1735; www.bourbonandbranch.com; 501 Jones St; ⏲Wed-Sat by reservation) 'Don't even think of asking for a cosmo' reads one of many House Rules at this revived speakeasy, complete with secret exits from its Prohibition-era heyday. For top-shelf gin and bourbon cocktails in the Library, use the buzzer and the password 'books.'

CHINATOWN

Li Po BAR

(Map p54; 916 Grant Ave; ⏲2pm-2am) Enter the grotto doorway and get the once-over by the dusty Buddha as you slide into red vinyl booths beloved of Beats for beer or Chinese Mai Tai, made with *baiju* (rice liquor).

NORTH BEACH

TOP CHOICE **Caffe Trieste** CAFE

(Map p54; www.caffetrieste.com; 601 Vallejo St; ⏲6:30am-11pm Sun-Thu, 6:30am-midnight Fri & Sat; 📶) Look no further for inspiration: Francis Ford Coppola drafted *The Godfather* here under the mural of Sicily, and Poet Laureate Lawrence Ferlinghetti still swings by en route to City Lights. With opera on the jukebox and weekend accordion jam sessions, this is North Beach at its best since 1956.

Specs' BAR

(Map p54; 12 William Saroyan Pl; ⏲5pm-2am) A saloon that doubles as a museum of nautical memorabilia gives neighborhood characters license to drink like sailors, tell tall tales to gullible newcomers and plot mutinies against last call.

Comstock Saloon BAR

(Map p54; 155 Columbus Ave; ⏲11:30am-2am Mon-Fri, 2pm-2am Sat) A Victorian saloon with period-perfect Pisco Punch with real pineapple gum and Hop Toads with Jamaican rum, bitters and apricot brandy – plus beef shank and bone marrow pot pie and maple bourbon cake in the adjacent restaurant.

Tosca Cafe COCKTAIL BAR

(Map p54; http://toscacafesf.com; 242 Columbus Ave; ⏲5pm-2am Tue-Sun) Come early for your pick of opera on the jukebox and red circular booths, and stay late for Irish coffee nightcap crowds and chance sightings of Sean Penn, Bono or Robert De Niro.

NOB HILL

Bigfoot Lodge BAR

(Map p62; ☎415-440-2355; www.bigfootlodge.com; 1750 Polk St; ⏲3pm-2am) Cure cabin fever at this log-cabin bar with happy hours in the shadow of an 8ft Sasquatch, getting nicely toasted on Toasted Marshmallows – vanilla vodka, Bailey's and a flaming marshmallow.

Top of the Mark BAR

(Map p62; www.topofthemark.com; 999 California St; cover $5-15; ⏲5pm-midnight Sun-Thu, 4pm-1am Fri & Sat) Sashay across the dance floor and feel on top of the world overlooking SF. Cocktails will set you back $15 plus cover, but watch the sunset and then try to complain.

THE MARINA

California Wine Merchant WINE BAR

(Map p58; www.californiawinemerchant.com; 2113 Chestnut St; ⏲10am-midnight Mon-Wed, to 1:30am Thu-Sat, 11am-11pm Sun) Pair local wines by the glass with mild flirting in this wine cave, and be surprised by the subtleties of Central Coast pinots and playboys improving their game.

MatrixFillmore LOUNGE

(Map p58; 3138 Fillmore St; ⏲6pm-2am) The one bar in town where the presumption is that you're straight and interested. Modern and sleek, if a little sharp around the edges – and the same can be said of the crowd.

GAY/LESBIAN/BI/TRANS SAN FRANCISCO

Singling out the best places to be queer in San Francisco is almost redundant. Though the Castro is a gay hub and the Mission is a magnet for lesbians, the entire city is gay-friendly – hence the number of out elected representatives in City Hall at any given time. New York Marys may label SF the retirement home of the young – indeed, the sidewalks roll up early – but for sexual outlaws and underground weirdness, SF trounces New York. Dancing queens and slutty boys head South of Market (SoMa), the location of most thump-thump clubs. In the 1950s, bars euphemistically designated Sunday afternoons as 'tea dances,' appealing to gay crowds to make money at an otherwise slow time. The tradition now makes Sundays one of the busiest times for SF's gay bars. Top GLBT venues include:

The Stud (Map p62; ☎415-252-7883; www.studsf.com; 399 9th St; admission $5-8; ⏲5pm-3am) Rocking the gay scene since 1966, and branching out beyond leather daddies with rocker-grrrl Mondays, Tuesday drag variety shows, raunchy comedy/karaoke Wednesdays, Friday art-drag dance parties, and performance-art cabaret whenever hostess/DJ Anna Conda gets it together.

Lexington Club (Map p84; ☎415-863-2052; 3464 19th St; ⏲3pm-2am) Odds are eerily high you'll develop a crush on your ex-girlfriend's hot new girlfriend here over strong drink, pinball and tattoo comparisons – go on, live dangerously at SF's most famous/notorious full-time lesbian bar.

Rebel Bar (Map p62; ☎415-431-4202; 1760 Market St; admission varies; ⏲5pm-3am Mon-Thu, to 4am Fri, 11am-4am Sat & Sun) Funhouse southern biker disco, complete with antique mirrored walls, Hell's Angel cocktails (Bulleit bourbon, Chartreuse, OJ) and exposed pipes. The crowd is mostly 30-something, gay and tribally tattooed; on a good night, poles get thoroughly worked.

Aunt Charlie's (Map p62; ☎415-441-2922; www.auntcharlieslounge.com; 133 Turk St; ⏲9am-2am) Total dive, with the city's best classic drag show Fridays and Saturdays at 10pm. Thursday nights, art-school boys freak for bathhouse disco at Tubesteak ($5).

Endup (Map p62; ☎415-646-0999; www.theendup.com; 401 6th St; admission $5-20; ⏲10pm-4am Mon-Thu, 11pm-11am Fri, 10pm Sat to 4am Mon) Home of Sunday 'tea dances' (gay dance parties) since 1973, though technically the party starts Saturday – bring a change of clothes and EndUp watching the sunrise Monday over the freeway on-ramp.

Sisters of Perpetual Indulgence (Map p62; ☎415-820-9697; www.thesisters.org) For guerrilla antics and wild fundraisers, check in with the self-described 'leading-edge order of queer nuns,' a charitable organization and San Francisco institution.

THE MISSION

TOP CHOICE Zeitgeist BAR

(Map p84; www.zeitgeistsf.com; 199 Valencia St; ⏲9am-2am) When temperatures tip over 70°F (21°C), bikers and hipsters converge on Zeitgeist's huge outdoor beer garden (minus the garden) for 40 brews on tap pulled by SF's toughest lady barkeeps and late-night munchies courtesy of the Tamale Lady.

Elixir BAR

(Map p84; www.elixirsf.com; 3200 16th St; ⏲3pm-2am Mon-Fri, noon-2am Sat & Sun) Drinking is good for the environment at SF's first certified green bar, with your choice of organic, green and even biodynamic cocktails – *ayiyi,* those peach margaritas with ancho-chili-infused tequila. Mingle over darts and a killer jukebox.

Homestead BAR

(Map p84; 2301 Folsom St; ⏲5pm-1am) Your friendly Victorian corner dive c 1893, complete with carved-wood bar, roast peanuts in the shell, cheap draft beer and Victorian tin-stamped ceiling.

Make-Out Room BAR
(Map p84; www.makeoutroom.com; 3225 22nd St) Between the generous pours and Pabst beer specials, the Make-Out has convinced otherwise sane people to leap onstage and read from their teen journals for Mortified nights, sing along to punk-rock fiddle and flail to '80s one-hit-wonder DJ mashups.

Ritual Coffee Roasters CAFE
(Map p84; www.ritualroasters.com; 1026 Valencia St; ⏲6am-10pm Mon-Fri, 7am-10pm Sat, 7am-9pm Sun; 📶) Cults wish they inspired the same devotion as Ritual, where lines head out the door for house-roasted cappuccino with ferns in the foam and deliberately limited electrical outlets to encourage conversation.

THE CASTRO

Café Flore CAFE
(Map p84; 2298 Market St; ⏲7am-1am; 📶) The see-and-be-seen, glassed-in corner cafe at the center of the gay universe. Eavesdrop on blind dates with bracing cappuccino or knee-weakening absinthe.

Thorough Bread CAFE, BAKERY
(Map p84; www.thoroughbreadandpastry.com; 248 Church St; ⏲7am-7pm Tue-Sat, to 3pm Sun) Pedigreed pastries and excellent breads from San Francisco Baking Institute chefs, plus powerful drip coffee.

Samovar Tea Lounge TEAHOUSE
(Map p84; 498 Sanchez St; ⏲10am-11pm; 📶) Iron pots of tea with scintillating side dishes, from savory pumpkin dumplings to chocolate brownies with green-tea mousse.

The Mint THEME BAR
(Map p84; www.themint.net; 1942 Market St; ⏲4pm-2am) Show tunes are serious stuff at karaoke sessions starting at 9pm nightly, where it takes courage and a vodka gimlet to attempt Barbra Streisand. Prepare to be upstaged by a banker with a boa and a mean falsetto.

THE HAIGHT & HAYES VALLEY

Cole Valley Café CAFE
(Map p77; www.colevalleycafe.com; 701 Cole St; ⏲6:30am-8:30pm Mon-Fri, 6:30am-8pm Sat & Sun; 📶) Powerful coffee and chai, free wifi, and hot gourmet sandwiches that are a bargain at any price, let alone $6 for lip-smacking thyme-marinated chicken with lemony avocado spread or the smoky roasted eggplant with goat cheese and sundried tomatoes.

Coffee to the People CAFE
(Map p77; www.coffeetothepeople.squarespace.com; 1206 Masonic Ave; ⏲6am-8pm Mon-Fri, to 9pm Sat & Sun; 📶✎👪) The people, united, will never be decaffeinated at this utopian coffee shop with free wireless, 3% pledged to coffee-growers' nonprofits, a radical reading library and enough Fair Trade coffee to revive the Sandinista movement.

TOP CHOICE **Smuggler's Cove** THEME BAR
(Map p62; http://smugglerscovesf.com; 650 Gough St; ⏲5pm-2am) Yo-ho-ho and a bottle of rum…or make that 200 at this Barbary Coast shipwreck of a tiki bar. With tasting flights and 70 historic cocktail recipes gleaned from rum-running around the world, you won't be dry-docked for long.

TOP CHOICE **Toronado** BAR
(Map p84; www.toronado.com; 547 Haight St; ⏲6pm-1am) Bow before the chalkboard altar listing 50 microbrews and hundreds more bottled, including spectacular seasonal microbrews. Bring cash, come early and stay late, with a sausage from Rosamunde next door to accompany seasonal ales.

Aub Zam Zam LOUNGE
(Map p77; 1633 Haight St; ⏲3pm-2am) Arabesque arches, jazz on the jukebox and enough paisley to make Prince feel right at home pay homage to the purist Persian charm of dearly departed cocktail fascist Bruno, who'd throw you out for ordering a vodka martini.

THE RICHMOND

Beach Chalet Brewery BREWERY
(Map p68; www.beachchalet.com; 1000 Great Hwy; ⏲9am-10pm Sun-Thu, to 11pm Fri & Sat) Brews with views: sunsets over the Pacific, a backyard bar, and recently restored 1930s WPA frescoes downstairs showing a condensed history of San Francisco.

Plough & Stars PUB
(Map p68; www.theploughandstars.com; 116 Clement St; ⏲3pm-2am Mon-Thu, 2pm-2am Fri-Sun, showtime 9pm) The Emerald Isle by the Golden Gate. Jigs are to be expected after the first couple of rounds and rousing Irish fiddle tunes are played most nights by top Celtic talent.

THE SUNSET

Hollow CAFE
(Map p68; http://hollowsf.com; 1493 Irving St; ⏲8am-5pm Mon-Fri, 9am-5pm Sat & Sun) Between

HOT TICKETS

Big events sell out fast in SF. Scan the free weeklies, the *San Francisco Bay Guardian* and the *SF Weekly*, and see what half-price and last-minute tickets you can find at **TIX Bay Area** (Map p62; ☎415-433-7827; Union Sq at 251 Stockton St; ⏲11am-6pm Tue-Thu, to 7pm Fri & Sat). Tickets are sold on the day of the performance for cash only. For tickets to theater shows and big-name concerts in advance, call **Ticketmaster** (☎415-421-8497) or **BASS** (☎415-478-2277).

simple explanations and Golden Gate Park, there's Hollow: cultish Ritual coffee and Guiness cupcakes served amid art-installation displays of magnifying glasses, tin pails, and monster etchings.

★ Entertainment

Nightclubs

El Rio CLUB
(off Map p84; ☎415-282-3325; www.elriosf.com; 3158 Mission St; admission $3-8) Free-form funky grooves worked by regulars of every conceivable ethnicity and orientation. 'Salsa Sundays' are legendary – arrive at 3pm for lessons – and other nights feature oyster happy hours, eclectic music, and shameless flirting on the garden patio.

Cat Club CLUB
(Map p62; www.catclubsf.com; 1190 Folsom St; admission $5 after 10pm; ⏲Tue-Sun) Thursday's '1984' is a euphoric straight/gay/bi/whatever party scene from a lost John Hughes movie; other nights vary from Saturday power pop to Bondage-a-Go-Go.

AsiaSF CLUB
(Map p62; ☎415-255-2742; www.asiasf.com; 201 9th St; $35 minimum per person; ⏲Wed-Sun) Cocktails and Asian-inspired dishes are served with a tall order of sass and one little secret: your servers are drag stars. Your hostesses rock the bar/runway hourly – but once inspiration and drinks kick in, everyone mixes it up on the downstairs dance floor. The three-course 'Menage á Trois Menu' runs $39, cocktails around $10, and honey, those tips are well-earned.

DNA Lounge CLUB
(Map p84; www.dnalounge.com; 375 11th St; admission $3-25) SF's mega-club hosts live bands and big-name DJs. Second and fourth Saturdays bring Bootie, the kick-ass original mashup party; Monday's Goth Death Guild means shuffle-dancing and free tea service.

Harlot CLUB
(Map p62; www.harlotsf.com; 46 Minna St; admission $10-20, free 5-9pm Wed-Fri; ⏲Wed-Sat) Aptly named after 10pm, when the bordello-themed lounge cuts loose to house Thursdays, indie-rock Wednesdays, and women-only Fem Bar parties.

111 Minna CLUB
(Map p62; www.111minnagallery.com; 111 Minna St) Street-wise art gallery by day, after-work lounge and club after 9pm, when '90s and '80s dance parties take the back room by storm.

Live Music

TOP CHOICE The Fillmore LIVE MUSIC
(off Map p58; www.thefillmore.com; 1805 Geary Blvd; tickets from $20) Hendrix, Zeppelin, Janis – they all played the Fillmore. The legendary venue that launched the psychedelic era has the posters to prove it upstairs, and hosts arena acts in a 1250-seat venue where you can squeeze in next to the stage.

Slim's LIVE MUSIC
(www.slims-sf.com; 333 11th St; tickets $11-28) Guaranteed good times by Gogol Bordello, Tenacious D, and AC/DShe (the hard-rocking female tribute band) fill the bill at this mid-sized club, where Prince and Elvis Costello have shown up to play sets unannounced.

Yoshi's JAZZ
(off Map p58; www.yoshis.com; 1300 Fillmore St; tickets $12-50) San Francisco's definitive jazz club draws the world's top talent to the historic African and Japanese American Fillmore jazz district, and serves pretty good sushi besides.

Mezzanine LIVE MUSIC
(Map p62; www.mezzaninesf.com; 444 Jessie St; admission $10-40) The best sound system in SF bounces off the brick walls at breakthrough hiphop shows by Quest Love, Method Man, Nas and Snoop Dogg, plus throwback alt-

classics like the Dandy Warhols and Psychedelic Furs.

Warfield LIVE MUSIC

(Map p62; www.thewarfieldtheatre.com; 982 Market St) Originally a vaudeville theater but now an obligatory stop for marquee acts from Beastie Boys and PJ Harvey to Furthur (formerly the Grateful Dead).

Great American Music Hall LIVE MUSIC

(Map p62; www.musichallsf.com; 859 O'Farrell St; admission $12-35) Previously a bordello and a dance hall, this ornate venue now hosts rock, country, jazz and world music artists. Arrive early to stake your claim to front-row balcony seats with a pint and a passable burger.

Bottom of the Hill LIVE MUSIC

(off Map p84; www.bottomofthehill.com; 1233 17th St; admission $5-12; ⏲Tue-Sat) Top of the list for breakthrough bands, from notable local alt-rockers like Deerhoof to newcomers worth checking out by name alone (Yesway, Stripmall Architecture, Excuses for Skipping) in *Rolling Stone*'s favorite SF venue; cash only.

Bimbo's 365 Club LIVE MUSIC

(Map p58; www.bimbos365club.com; 1025 Columbus Ave; tickets from $20) Anything goes behind these vintage-1931 speakeasy velvet curtains, lately including live shows by the likes of Cibo Matto, Ben Harper and Coldplay. Cash only, and bring something extra to tip the ladies' powder room attendant – this is a classy joint.

Hotel Utah LIVE MUSIC

(Map p62; www.thehotelutahsaloon.com; 500 4th St; bar admission free, shows $5-10) Whoopi Goldberg and Robin Williams broke in the stage of this historic Victorian hotel back in the '70s, and the thrill of finding SF's hidden talents draws crowds to singer-songwriter Open Mic Mondays, indie-label debuts and local favorites like Riot Earp, Saucy Monkey and The Dazzling Strangers.

Cafe du Nord LIVE MUSIC

(Map p84; www.cafedunord.com; 2170 Market St; admission $7-15) A 1930s downstairs speakeasy in the basement of the Swedish-American Hall serves 'em short and strong and glam-rocks, afrobeats, retro-rockabillies and indie-record-release parties almost nightly – plus pulled-on-stage performances by off-duty musicians and novelists.

Elbo Room LIVE MUSIC

(Map p84; www.elbo.com; 647 Valencia St; admission $5-8) Funny name, because there isn't much to speak of upstairs on show nights with crowd-favorite funk, dancehall dub, and offbeat indie bands like Uni and Her Ukelele.

Rickshaw Stop LIVE MUSIC

(Map p62; www.rickshawstop.com; 155 Fell St; admission $5-35) Noise-poppers, eccentric rockers and crafty DJs cross-pollinate hemispheres with something for everyone: badass banghra nights, Latin explosion bands, lesbian disco, and mainstay Thursday 18+ Popscene.

Amnesia LIVE MUSIC

(Map p84; www.amnesiathebar.com; 853 Valencia St) A teensy bar featuring nightly local music acts that may be playing in public for the first time, so show hardworking bands some love and buy that shy rapper a drink.

Theater

Musicals and Broadway spectaculars play at a number of downtown theaters. **SHN** (☎415-512-7770; www.shnsf.com) hosts touring Broadway shows at opulent **Orpheum Theatre** (Map p62; 1192 Market St), **Curran Theatre** (Map p62; 445 Geary St), and 1920s **Golden Gate Theatre** (Map p62; 1 Taylor St). But the pride of SF is its many indie theaters that host original, solo and experimental shows, including the following.

TOP CHOICE **American Conservatory Theater** THEATER

(Map p62; ACT; ☎415-749-2228; www.act-sf.org; 415 Geary St) San Francisco's most famous mainstream venue has put on original landmark productions of Tony Kushner's *Angels in America* and Robert Wilson's *Black Rider*, with a libretto by William S Burroughs and music by the Bay Area's own Tom Waits.

Beach Blanket Babylon COMEDY, CABARET

(Map p54; ☎415-421-4222; www.beachblanketbabylon.com; 678 Green St; seats $25-78) San Francisco's longest-running comedy cabaret keeps the belly laughs coming with giant hats, killer drag and social satire with bite. Spectators must be 21-plus, except at matinees.

Magic Theatre THEATER

(Map p58; ☎415-441-8822; www.magictheatre.org; Fort Mason, Bldg D) Risk-taking original productions from major playwrights, including Sam Shepard, Edna O'Brien and Terrence McNally, starring actors like Ed Harris and Sean Penn, plus staged works written by teenagers.

Cobb's Comedy Club COMEDY
(Map p58; ☎415-928-4320; www.cobbscomedy club.com; 915 Columbus Ave; admission $13-33 plus 2-drink minimum) Bumper-to-bumper shared tables make for an intimate (and vulnerable) audience for stand-up acts, from new talent to HBO's Dave Chapelle and NBC's Tracy Morgan.

Exit Theater THEATER
(Map p62; ☎415-673-3847; http://theexit.org; 156 Eddy St; admission $15-20) Hosts the SF Fringe Festival and avant-garde productions year-round.

Intersection for the Arts LIVE MUSIC, THEATER
(Map p84; ☎415-626-2787; www.theintersection.org; 446 Valencia; admission $5-20) Ambidextrous nonprofit art space with famous playwrights-in-residence, a major jazz showcase and a provocative upstairs gallery program since 1965.

Marsh THEATER
(Map p84; ☎415-826-5750; www.themarsh.org; 1062 Valencia St; tickets $15-35) Choose your seat wisely: you'll spend the evening on the edge of it, with one-acts, monologues and works-in-progress that involve the audience.

Punch Line COMEDY
(Map p62; ☎415-397-4337; www.punchlinecomedy club.com; 444 Battery St; admission $12-23, plus 2-drink minimum; ⏲Tue-Sun) Turns unknown comics into known names – Chris Rock, Ellen DeGeneres and David Cross, to name a few.

Purple Onion COMEDY
(Map p54; ☎415-956-1653; www.caffemacaroni.com; 140 Columbus Ave; admission $10-15) Woody Allen, Robin Williams and Phyllis Diller clawed their way up from underground at this grotto nightclub, and Zach Galifianakis shot an excruciatingly funny comedy special here.

Classical Music, Opera & Dance

TOP CHOICE **Davies Symphony Hall** CLASSICAL MUSIC
(Map p62; ☎415-864-6000; www.sfsymphony.org; 201 Van Ness Ave) Home of nine-time Grammy-winning SF Symphony, conducted with verve by Michael Tilson Thomas from September to May here – don't miss Beethoven.

War Memorial Opera House OPERA
(Map p62; ☎415-864-3330; www.sfopera.com; 301 Van Ness Ave) Rivaling City Hall's grandeur is the 1932 home to **San Francisco Opera** (www.sfopera.com) from June through December and the **San Francisco Ballet** (www.sfballet.org) from January through May. Student tickets and standing-room tickets go on sale two hours before performances.

TOP CHOICE **ODC Theater** DANCE
(Map p84; ☎415-863-9834; www.odctheater.org; 3153 17th St) For 40 years, redefining dance with risky, raw performances and the sheer joy of movement with performances September through December, and 200 dance classes a week.

Cinemas

TOP CHOICE **Castro Theatre** CINEMA
(Map p84; www.thecastrotheatre.com; 429 Castro St; adult/child $10/7.50) Showtunes on a Wurlitzer are the overture to independent cinema, silver-screen classics and unstoppable audience participation.

Sundance Kabuki Cinema CINEMA
(off Map p58; www.sundancecinemas.com/kabuki.html; 1881 Post St; adult/child $10-14) Trendsetting green multiplex with GMO-free popcorn, reserved seating in cushy recycled-fiber seats and the frankly brilliant Balcony Bar, where you can slurp seasonal cocktails during your movie.

Roxie Cinema CINEMA
(Map p84; www.roxie.com; 3117 16th St; adult/child $10/6.50) Independent gems, insightful documentaries and rare film noir you won't find elsewhere, in a landmark 1909 cinema recently upgraded with Dolby sound.

Balboa Theater CINEMA
(Map p68; www.balboamovies.com; 3630 Balboa St; double-features adult/child $10/7.50) Double-features perfect for foggy weather, including film fest contenders selected by the director of the Telluride Film Festival, in a renovated 1926 art deco cinema.

Sports

San Francisco Giants BASEBALL
(Map p62; http://Sanfrancisco.giants.mlb.com; AT&T Park; tickets $5-135; ⏲season Apr-Oct)

SAN FRANCISCO FOR CHILDREN

Imaginations come alive in this storybook city, with wild parrots squawking indignantly at passersby near **Coit Tower** (p57) on Telegraph Hill and sunning sea lions gleefully nudging one another off the docks at **Pier 39** (p57). For thrills, try rickety, seatbelt-free **cable cars** (p95), or pick up a dragon kite in Chinatown souvenir shops to fly at **Crissy Field** (p59) – just be sure to bundle up for the wind. Kids will find playmates in playgrounds at **Golden Gate Park** (p49) and **Portsmouth Square** (p55).

For organized activities, try these kid-friendly attractions:

» **Children's Creativity Museum** (Map p62; ☎415-820-3320; www.zeum.org; 221 4th St; admission $10; ⌚11am-5pm Tue-Sun; 👪) Technology that's too cool for school: robots, live-action video games, DIY music videos, and 3D animation workshops with Silicon Valley innovators. The vintage 1906 Loof Carousel out front operates until 6pm daily ($3 for two rides).

» **Aquarium of the Bay** (Map p58; www.aquariumofthebay.com; Pier 39; adult/child $17/8; ⌚9am-8pm summer, 10am-6pm winter; 👪) Glide through glass tubes underwater on conveyer belts as sharks circle and manta rays flutter overhead.

» **Fire Engine Tours** (Map p58; ☎415-333-7077; www.fireenginetours.com; Beach St at the Cannery; adult/child $50/30; ⌚tours depart 1pm; 👪) Hot stuff: a 75-minute, open-air vintage fire engine ride over Golden Gate Bridge.

See also: the **Exploratorium** (p58), **California Academy of Sciences** (p66), **Cartoon Art Museum** (p61), **Musée Mecanique** (p57) and **826 Valencia** (p61).

Watch and learn how the World Series is won – bushy beards, women's underwear and all. The city's National League baseball team draws crowds to AT&T Park and its solar-powered scoreboard; the Waterfront Promenade offers a free view of right field.

San Francisco 49ers FOOTBALL

(www.49ers.com; Candlestick Park; tickets from $59; ⌚season Aug-Dec) For NFL football, beer and garlic-fries, head to Candlestick Park. Lately they've been in a slump, but the '49ers are one of the most successful teams in National Football League history, with no fewer than five Super Bowl championships. Home games are played at cold and windy Candlestick Park, off Hwy 101 south of the city.

Shopping

San Francisco has big department stores and name-brand boutiques around Union Sq, including **Macy's** (Map p62; www.macys.com; 170 O'Farrell Street) and the sprawling new **Westfield Shopping Centre** (Map p62; www.westfield.com/SanFrancisco; 865 Market St; ⌚9:30am-9pm Mon-Sat, 10am-7pm Sun), but special, only-in-SF scores are found in the Haight, the Castro, the Mission and Hayes Valley (west of Civic Center).

TOP CHOICE **Adobe Books & BackRoom Gallery** BOOKS

(Map p84; http://adobebooksbackroomgallery.blogspot.com; 3166 16th St; ⌚11am-midnight) Come here for every book you never knew you needed used and cheap, plus 'zine launch parties, poetry readings, and BackRoom Gallery – but first you have to navigate the obstacle course of sofas, cats, art books and German philosophy.

TOP CHOICE **Under One Roof** GIFTS

(Map p84; www.underoneroof.org; 518a Castro St; ⌚10am-8pm Mon-Sat, 11am-7pm Sun) AIDS service organizations receive 100% of the proceeds from goods donated by local designers and retailers, so show volunteer salespeople some love for raising $11 million to date.

Reliquary CLOTHING, ACCESSORIES

(off Map p62; http://reliquarysf.com; 537 Octavia Blvd; ⌚11am-7pm Tue-Sat, noon-6pm Sun) Owner Leah Bershad was once a designer for Gap, but the folksy jet-set aesthetic here is the exact opposite of khaki-and-fleece global domination: Santa Fe woollen blankets, silver jewelry banged together by Humboldt hippies, Majestic tissue-tees and Clare Vivier pebble-leather clutches.

Piedmont Boutique ACCESSORIES
(Map p77; 1452 Haight St; ⊙11am-7pm) Glam up or get out at this supplier of drag fabulousness: pleather hot pants, airplane earrings and a wall of feather boas.

Amoeba Records MUSIC
(Map p77; www.amoeba.com; 1855 Haight St; ⊙10:30pm-10pm Mon-Sat, 11am-9pm Sun) Bowling-alley-turned-superstore of new and used records in all genres, plus free in-store concerts and Music We Like 'zine for great new finds.

MAC CLOTHING
(Map p62; http://modernappealingclothing.com; 387 Grove St; ⊙11am-7pm Mon-Sat, noon-6pm Sun) Impeccably structured looks for men from Belgian minimalist Dries Van Noten and Tsumori Chisato's Japanese luxe for the ladies; superb 40% to 75% off sales rack.

Velvet da Vinci JEWELRY
(Map p62; www.velvetdavinci.com; 2015 Polk St; ⊙11am-6pm Tue-Sat, to 4pm Sun) Ingenious jewelry by local and international artisans: Julia Turner's satellite-dish ring, Ben Neubauer's cage earrings, a drinking flask bracelet by William Clark.

Nancy Boy BEAUTY
(Map p62; www.nancyboy.com; 347 Hayes St; ⊙11am-7pm Mon-Fri, to 6pm Sat & Sun) Wear these highly effective moisturizers, pomades and sun balms with pride, all locally made with plant oils and tested on boyfriends, never animals.

New People CLOTHING, GIFTS
(off Map p58; www.newpeopleworld.com; 1746 Post St) An eye-popping three-story emporium devoted to Japanese art and pop culture, with contemporary art, Lolita fashions, traditional Japanese clothing with contemporary graphics, and *kawaii* (Japanese for all things cute).

Gravel & Gold HOUSEWARES, GIFTS
(Map p84; gravelandgold.com; 3266 21st St; ⊙noon-7pm Tue-Sat, noon-5pm Sun) A gallery/boutique celebrating the 1960s-1970s hippie homesteader movement, from stoneware teapots to hand-dyed smocked dresses – which you can try on among psychedelic murals behind a patched curtain.

Goorin Brothers Hats ACCESSORIES
(Map p77; www.goorin.com; 1446 Haight St; ⊙11am-7pm Sun-Fri, to 8pm Sat) Peacock feathers, high crowns and local-artist-designed embellishments make it easy to withstand the fog while standing out in a crowd in SF-designed fedoras, caps and cloches.

Accident & Artifact GIFTS, ACCESSORIES
(Map p84; www.accidentandartifact.com; 381 Valencia St; ⊙noon-6pm Thu-Sun) A most curious curiosity shop, even by Mission standards: decorative dried fungi, vintage Okinawan indigo textiles, artfully redrawn topographical maps and fur-covered televisions with antlers.

Dema CLOTHING
(Map p84; www.godemago.com; 1038 Valencia St; ⊙11am-7pm Mon-Fri, noon-6pm Sat & Sun) Wear-everywhere shifts in vintage-inspired prints by local designer Dema, plus clever cardigans and Orla Kiely tees.

Madame S & Mr S Leather CLOTHING
(Map p62; www.madame-s.com; 385 8th St; ⊙11am-7pm) S&M superstore, with such musts as leashes, dungeon furniture and for that special someone, a chrome-plated codpiece.

Wasteland VINTAGE, CLOTHING
(Map p77; www.thewasteland.com; 1660 Haight St; ⊙11am-8pm Mon-Sat, noon-7pm Sun) The catwalk of thrifting: psychedelic Pucci maxiskirts, barely worn Marc Jacobs smocks and a steady supply of go-go boots.

Jeremy's CLOTHING, ACCESSORIES
(Map p62; www.jeremys.com; 2 South Park St; ⊙11am-6pm Mon-Sat, to 5pm Sun) Window displays, photo shoot ensembles and department store customer returns translate to jaw-dropping bargains on major designers for men and women.

Park Life ARTWORK, BOOKS
(Map p68; www.parklifestore.com; 220 Clement St; ⊙11am-8pm) Design store, indie publisher and art gallery with gift options: tees with drawn-on pockets, Park Life's catalog of graffiti artist Andrew Schoultz, and Ian Johnson's portrait of Miles Davis radiating prismatic thought waves.

Sui Generis VINTAGE, CLOTHING
(Map p84; men's shop 2231 Market St, women's shop 2265 Market St; ⊙noon-7pm Tue-Thu, to 8pm Fri & Sat, to 4pm Sun) Straight-off-the-runway, lightly worn scores from Prada, Zegna, Armani & Co, some in the double-digit range.

Studio GIFTS
(Map p62; www.studiogallerysf.com; 1815 Polk St; ⏰11am-8pm Wed-Fri, to 6pm Sat & Sun) Winsome locally made arts and crafts at bargain prices, including Chiami Sekine's collages of boxing bears, SF architectural etchings by Alice Gibbons, and Monique Tse's fat-free glass cupcakes.

Golden Gate Fortune Cookie Company FOOD & DRINK
(Map p54; 56 Ross Alley; admission free; ⏰8am-7pm) Make a fortune in San Francisco at this bakery, where cookies are stamped out on old-fashioned presses and folded over your customized message (50c each). Cash only; 50c tip for photo requested.

Sports Basement OUTDOOR EQUIPMENT
(Map p58; www.sportsbasement.com; 610 Mason St; ⏰9am-8pm Mon-Fri, 8am-7pm Sat & Sun) There's 70,000 sq ft of sports and camping equipment housed in the Presidio's former US Army PX; free coffee and hot cider while you shop.

Community Thrift CLOTHING, HOUSEWARES
(Map p84; www.communitythriftsf.org; 623 Valencia St; ⏰10am-6:30pm) Vintage home furnishing scores and local retailer overstock, all sold to benefit local charities.

SFO Snowboarding & FTC Skateboarding OUTDOOR EQUIPMENT
(Map p77; 1630 Haight St; ⏰11am-7pm) State-of-the-art gear, snowboards and skateboards, some with designs by local artists.

Mollusk OUTDOOR EQUIPMENT
(Map p68; www.mollusksurfshop.com; 4500 Irving St; ⏰10am-6:30pm) For locally designed surf gear.

Information

Dangers & Annoyances

Keep your city smarts and wits about you, especially at night in SoMa, the Mission and the Haight. Unless you know where you're going, avoid the sketchy, depressing Tenderloin (bordered east–west by Powell and Polk Sts and north–south by O'Farrell and Market Sts), Skid Row (6th St between Market and Folsom Sts) and Bayview-Hunters Point. To cut through the Tenderloin, take Geary or Market Sts – still seedy, but tolerable. Panhandlers and homeless people are a fact of life in the city. People will probably ask you for spare change, but donations to local non-profits stretch further. For safety, don't engage with panhandlers at night or around ATMs. Otherwise, a simple 'I'm sorry,' is a polite response.

Emergency & Medical Services

San Francisco General Hospital (☎emergency room 415-206-8111, main 415-206-8000; www.sfdph.org; 1001 Potrero Ave) 24-hour care.

Walgreens (☎415-861-3136; www.walgreens.com 498 Castro St; ⏰24hr) Pharmacy and over-the-counter meds; dozens of locations citywide.

Internet Access

SF has free wi-fi hot spots citywide – locate one nearby with **www.openwifispots.com**. Connect for free in Union Sq and most cafes and hotel lobbies.

Apple Store (☎415-392-0202; www.apple.com/retail/SanFrancisco; 1 Stockton St; ⏰9am-9pm Mon-Sat, 10am-8pm Sun; 📶) Free wi-fi access and internet terminal usage.

Main Library (http://stpl.org; 100 Larkin St; ⏰10am-6pm Mon & Sat, 9am-8pm Tue-Thu, noon-5pm Fri & Sun; 📶) Free 15-minute internet terminal usage; spotty wi-fi access.

Brain Wash (www.brainwash.com; 1122 Folsom St; per wash from $2; ⏰7am-10pm Mon-Thu, to 11pm Fri & Sat, 8am-10pm Sun; 📶) Come with laundry, stay for lunch, beer, live entertainment, pinball, free wi-fi and internet terminals ($3 per 20 minutes).

Money

Bank of America (www.bankamerica.com; One Market Plaza; ⏰9am-6pm Mon-Fri)

Post

Rincon Center post office (Map p62; www.usps.com; 180 Steuart St; ⏰8am-6pm Mon-Fri, 9am-2pm Sat) Postal services plus historic murals.

Union Square post office (Map p62; www.usps.com; 170 O'Farrell St; ⏰10am-5:30pm Mon-Sat, 11am-5pm Sun) In the basement of Macy's department store.

Tourist Information

California Welcome Center (Map p58; ☎415-981-1280; www.visitcwc.com; Pier 39, Bldg P, ste 241b; ⏰10am-5pm) Handy for travel information, brochures, maps and help booking accommodations.

San Francisco Visitors Information Center (Map p62; ☎415-391-2000; www.onlyinSanFrancisco.com; lower level, Hallidie Plaza; ⏰9am-5pm Mon-Fri, 9am-3pm Sat & Sun) Maps, guidebooks, brochures, accommodations help.

Websites

http://sfbay.craigslist.org Events, activities, partners, freebies and dates.

http://sf.eater.com SF food, nightlife and bars.

www.flavorpill.com Live music, lectures, art openings and movie premieres.

www.urbandaddy.com Bars, shops, restaurants and events.

 Getting There & Away

Air

The Bay Area has three major airports: **San Francisco International Airport** (SFO; www.flysfo.com), 14 miles south of downtown SF, off Hwy 101; Oakland International Airport (see p128), a few miles across the bay; and San José International Airport (p128), at the southern end of the bay. The majority of international flights use SFO. Travelers from other US cities may find cheaper flights into Oakland on discount airlines such as JetBlue and Southwest.

Improvements over the last decade include a new international terminal, LEED-certified green Terminal 2 and a BART extension directly to the airport. All three SFO terminals have ATMs and information booths on the lower level, and **Travelers' Aid information booths** (9am-9pm) on the upper level. The airport paging and information line is staffed 24 hours; call from any white courtesy phone.

Bus

Until the new terminal is complete in 2017, SF's intercity hub remains the **Temporary Transbay Terminal** (Map p62; Howard & Main Sts), where you can catch buses on **AC Transit** (www.actransit.org) to the East Bay, **Golden Gate Transit** (http://goldengatetransit.org) north to Marin and Sonoma Counties, and **SamTrans** (www.samtrans.com) south to Palo Alto and the Pacific coast. **Greyhound** (800-231-2222; www.greyhound.com) buses leave daily for Los Angeles ($56.50, eight to 12 hours), Truckee near Lake Tahoe ($33, 5½ hours), and other destinations.

Car & Motorcycle

All major car-rental operators (Alamo, Avis, Budget, Dollar, Hertz, Thrifty) are represented at the airports, and many have downtown offices.

Ferry

For Alcatraz Cruises, see p71.

Blue & Gold Fleet Ferries (Map p62; www.blueandgoldfleet.com) The Alameda-Oakland Ferry runs from the Ferry Building to Jack London Sq in Oakland ($6.25, 30 minutes). Ferries to Tiburon, Sausalito and Angel Island run from Pier 41 at Fisherman's Wharf.

Golden Gate Ferries (Map p62; 415-923-2000; www.goldengateferry.org; 6am-10pm Mon-Fri, 10am-6pm Sat & Sun) Regular services run from the Ferry Building to Larkspur and Sausalito in Marin County. Transfers are available to MUNI bus services, and bicycles permitted.

Vallejo Ferries (Map p62; 415-773-1188; one way adult/child $15/7.50) Get to Napa car-free, with departures from Ferry Building docks about every hour from 6:30am through 7pm weekdays and every two hours from 11am through 7:30pm on weekends; bikes are permitted. From the Vallejo Ferry Terminal, take Napa Valley Vine bus 10 to downtown Napa, Yountville, St Helena or Calistoga. Also connects to Six Flags Marine World theme park in Vallejo.

Train

CalTrain (Map p62; www.caltrain.com; cnr 4th & King Sts) links San Francisco to the South Bay, including Palo Alto (Stanford University) and San Jose.

Amtrak (800-872-7245; www.amtrakcalifornia.com) offers low-emission, leisurely travel to and from San Francisco. *Coast Starlight*'s spectacular 35-hour run from Los Angeles to Seattle stops in Oakland, and the *California Zephyr* takes its sweet time (51 hours) traveling from Chicago through the Rockies to Oakland. Both have sleeping cars and dining/lounge cars with panoramic windows. Amtrak runs free shuttle buses to San Francisco's Ferry Building and CalTrain station.

 Getting Around

For Bay Area transit options, departures and arrivals, check 511 or www.511.org.

To/From the Airport

» **BART** (Bay Area Rapid Transit; www.bart.gov; one-way $8.10) offers a fast, direct ride to downtown San Francisco.

» **SamTrans** (www.samtrans.com; one-way $5) express bus KX gets you to Temporary Transbay Terminal in about 30 minutes.

» **SuperShuttle** (800-258-3826; www.supershuttle.com; one-way $17) door-to-door vans depart from baggage-claim areas, taking 45 minutes to most SF locations.

» **Taxis** to downtown San Francisco cost $35-50.

Bicycle

San Francisco is cyclable, but traffic downtown can be dangerous; bicycling is best east of Van Ness Ave and across the bay. For bike shops and rentals, see p67. Bicycles can be carried on BART, but not in the commute direction during weekday rush hours.

Car & Motorcycle

If you can, avoid driving in San Francisco: street parking is harder to find than true love, and meter readers are ruthless. Convenient downtown parking lots are at Embarcadero Center, 5th and Mission Sts, Union Sq, and Sutter and Stockton Sts. National car-rental agencies have airport and downtown offices.

Before you set out to any bridge or other traffic choke-point, call ☎511 toll-free for a traffic update. Members of the **American Automobile Association** (AAA; ☎415-773-1900, 800-222-4357; www.aaa.com; 160 Sutter St; ⊙8:30am-5:30pm Mon-Fri) can call the 800 number any time for emergency road service and towing. AAA also provides travel insurance and free road maps of the region.

Parking authorities are quick to tow cars. If this should happen to you, you'll have to retrieve your car at **Autoreturn** (☎415-865-8200; www.autoreturn.com; 450 7th St; ⊙24hr). Besides at least $73 in fines for parking violations, you'll also have to fork out a towing and storage fee ($392.75 for the first four hours, $61.75 for the rest of the first day, $61.75 for every additional day, plus a $25.50 transfer fee if your car is moved to a long-term lot). Cars are usually stored at 415 7th St, corner of Harrison St.

Some of the cheaper downtown parking garages are **Sutter-Stockton Garage** (Map p62; ☎415-982-7275; cnr Sutter & Stockton Sts), **Ellis-O'Farrell Garage** (Map p62; ☎415-986-4800; 123 O'Farrell St) and **Fifth & Mission Garage** (Map p62; ☎415-982-8522; 833 Mission St), near Yerba Buena Gardens. The parking garage under Portsmouth Sq in Chinatown is reasonably priced for shorter stops; ditto for the **St Mary's Square Garage** (☎415-956-8106; California St), under the square, at Grant and Kearny Sts. Daily rates range between $20 and $35.

BART

Bay Area Rapid Transit (BART; ☎415-989-2278; www.bart.gov; ⊙4am-midnight Mon-Fri, 6am-midnight Sat, 8am-midnight Sun) is a subway system linking SFO, the Mission District, downtown, San Francisco and the East Bay. The fastest link between Downtown and the Mission District also offers transit to SF airport, Oakland ($3.20) and Berkeley ($3.75). Within SF, one-way fares start at $1.75.

MUNI

MUNI (Municipal Transit Agency; www.sfmuni.com) operates bus, streetcar and cable-car lines. Two cable-car lines leave from Powell and Market Sts; a third leaves from California and Markets Sts. A detailed *MUNI Street & Transit Map* is available free online and at the Powell MUNI kiosk ($3). Standard fare for buses or streetcars is $2, and tickets are good on buses or streetcars (not BART or cable cars) for 90 minutes; cable-car fare is $6 for a single ride.

Tickets are available on board, but you'll need exact change. Hang onto your ticket – if you're caught without one, you're subject to a $75 fine.

A **MUNI Passport** (one-/three-/seven-days $14/21/27) allows unlimited travel on all MUNI transport, including cable cars; it's sold at San Francisco's Visitor Information Center (p72) and at the TIX Bay Area kiosk at Union Sq and from a number of hotels. A seven-day **City Pass** (adult/child $69/39) covers Muni and admission to five attractions.

Key MUNI routes include:

» F Fisherman's Wharf and Embarcadero to Castro

» J Downtown to Mission/Castro/Noe Valley

» K, L, M Downtown to Castro

» N Caltrain and SBC Ballpark to Haight, Golden Gate Park and Ocean Beach

» T Embarcadero to Caltrain and Bayview

Taxi

Fares run about $2.25 per mile, plus 10% tip (starting at $1); meters start at $3.50. Major cab companies include:

Green Cab (☎415-626-4733; www.626green.com) Fuel-efficient hybrids; worker-owned collective.

DeSoto Cab (☎415-970-1300)

Luxor (☎415-282-4141)

Yellow Cab (☎415-333-3333)

Marin County & the Bay Area

Includes »

Best Places to Eat

» Chez Panisse (p135)
» Fish (p108)
» Bakesale Betty (p125)
» Duarte's Tavern (p148)
» Gather (p134)

Best Places to Stay

» Cavallo Point (p105)
» Mountain Home Inn (p112)
» Hotel Shattuck Plaza (p134)
» Pigeon Point Lighthouse Hostel (p148)
» East Brother Light Station (p139)

Why Go?

The region surrounding San Francisco encompasses a bonanza of natural vistas and wildlife. Cross the Golden Gate Bridge to Marin and visit wizened ancient redwoods body-blocking the sun and herds of elegant tule elk prancing along the bluffs of Tomales Bay. Gray whales show some fluke off the cape of wind-scoured Point Reyes, and hawks surf the skies in the pristine hills of the Marin Headlands.

On the cutting edge of intellectual thought, Stanford University and the University of California at Berkeley draw academics and students from around the world. The city of Berkeley sparked the locavore food movement and continues to be on the forefront of environmental and left-leaning political causes. South of San Francisco, Hwy 1 traces miles of undeveloped coastline and sandy pocket beaches.

When to Go

Berkeley

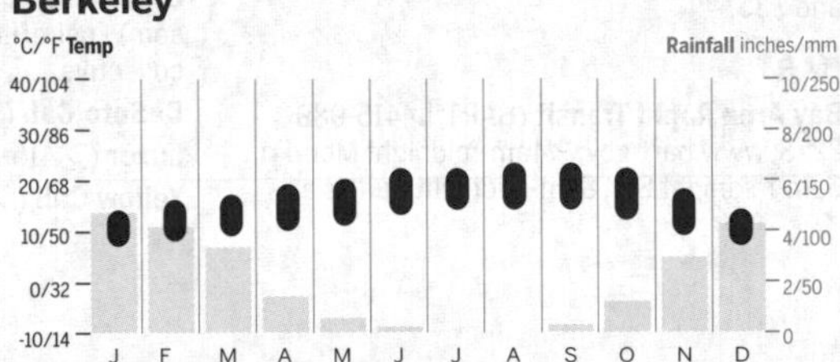

Dec–Mar Elephant seal pupping season and the peak of gray whale migrations.

Mar–Apr Wildflowers hit their peak on trails throughout the region.

Jun–Sep Farmers markets overflow with sweet seasonal fruit.

Getting Around

Visitors taking multiple forms of public transportation throughout the Bay Area should note that the regional **Clipper card** (www.clippercard.com) can be used on the Caltrain, BART, SamTrans, VTA, Golden Gate Transit and the Golden Gate Ferry systems. It can be a handy way to avoid buying multiple tickets, and offers some small discounts, plus almost 50% off on the Golden Gate Ferry system.

MARIN COUNTY

If there's a part of the Bay Area that consciously attempts to live up to the California dream, it's Marin County. Just across the Golden Gate Bridge from San Francisco, the region has a wealthy population that cultivates a seemingly laid-back lifestyle. Towns may look like idyllic rural hamlets, but the shops cater to cosmopolitan and expensive tastes. The 'common' folk here eat organic, vote Democrat and drive hybrids.

Geographically, Marin County is a near mirror image of San Francisco. It's a south-pointing peninsula that nearly touches the north-pointing tip of the city, and is surrounded by ocean and bay. But Marin is wilder, greener and more mountainous. Redwoods grow on the coast side of the hills, the surf crashes against cliffs, and hiking and cycling trails crisscross the blessed scenery of Point Reyes, Muir Woods and Mt Tamalpais. Nature is what makes Marin County such an excellent day trip or weekend escape from San Francisco.

Busy Hwy 101 heads north from the Golden Gate Bridge ($6 toll when heading back into San Francisco), spearing through Marin's middle; quiet Hwy 1 winds its way along the sparsely populated coast. In San Rafael, Sir Francis Drake Blvd cuts across west Marin from Hwy 101 to the ocean.

Hwy 580 comes in from the East Bay over the Richmond-San Rafael bridge ($5 toll for westbound traffic) to meet Hwy 101 at Larkspur.

Frequent **Marin Airporter** (☎415-461-4222; www.marinairporter.com; fare $20) buses connect from Marin stops to the San Francisco International Airport from 4am until about 10:30pm; SFO-Marin service departs every 30 minutes.

The **Marin Convention & Visitors Bureau** (☎415-925-2060, 866-925-2060; www.visitmarin.org; 1 Mitchell Blvd, San Rafael; ⊙9am-5pm Mon-Fri) provides tourist information for the entire county.

Marin Headlands

The headlands rise majestically out of the water at the north end of the Golden Gate Bridge, their rugged beauty all the more striking given the fact that they're only a few miles from San Francisco's urban core. A few forts and bunkers are left over from a century of US military occupation – which is, ironically, the reason they are protected parklands today and free of development. It's no mystery why this is one of the Bay Area's most popular hiking and cycling destinations. As the trails wind through the headlands, they afford stunning views of the sea, the Golden Gate Bridge and San Francisco, leading to isolated beaches and secluded spots for picnics.

Sights

After crossing the Golden Gate Bridge, exit immediately at Alexander Ave, then dip left under the highway and head out west for the expansive views and hiking trailheads. Conzelman Rd snakes up into the hills, where it eventually forks. Conzelman Rd continues west, becoming a steep, one-lane road as it descends to Point Bonita. From here it continues to Rodeo Beach and Fort Barry. McCullough Rd heads inland, joining Bunker Rd toward Rodeo Beach.

Hawk Hill HILL

About 2 miles along Conzelman Rd is Hawk Hill, where thousands of migrating birds of prey soar along the cliffs from late summer to early fall.

Point Bonita Lighthouse LIGHTHOUSE

(www.nps.gov/goga/pobo.htm; ⊙12:30-3:30pm Sat-Mon) At the end of Conzelman Rd, this light-

FAST FACTS

Population of Berkeley 112,500

Average temperature low/high in Berkeley Jan 43/56°F, Jul 54/70°F

Downtown Berkeley to Sacramento 80 miles, 1½ hours

San Jose to San Francisco 45 miles, one hour

San Francisco to Point Reyes Lighthouse 55 miles, 2½ hours

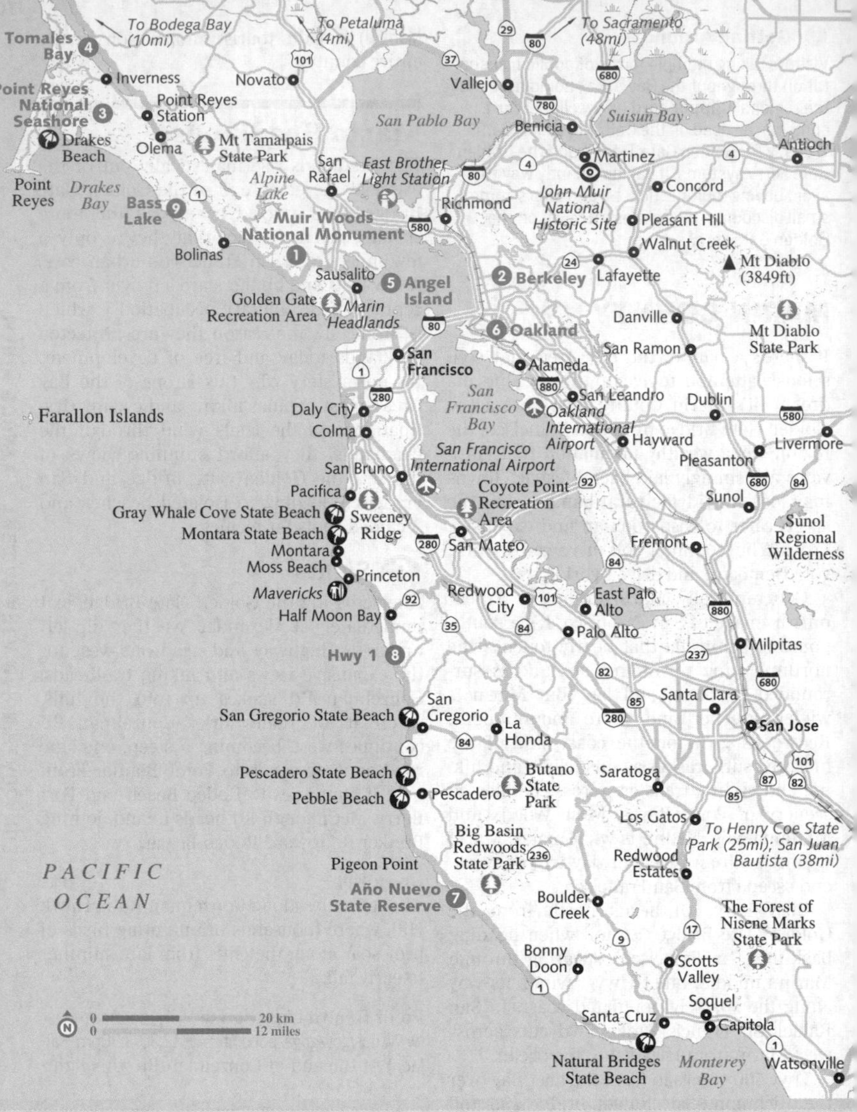

Marin County & the Bay Area Highlights

1. Gaze up at the majestic redwood canopy at **Muir Woods National Monument** (p115)

2. Feast your way through the delectable **Gourmet Ghetto** (p131) in Berkeley

3. Cavort with elk and gray whales at the **Point Reyes National Seashore** (p119)

4. Kayak **Tomales Bay** (p119) amid harbor seals and splendid shorelines

5. Hike or cycle the perimeter of panoramic **Angel Island** (p111)

6. Head to Oakland's **Chabot Space & Science Center** (p124) to marvel at the stars

7. Spy on the elephant seals at **Año Nuevo State Reserve** (p149)

8. Tour the beach cove coastline along **Hwy 1** (p146) from Pacifica to Santa Cruz

9. Cool off with a cannonball splash at blissful **Bass Lake** (p117)

house is a breathtaking half-mile walk from a small parking area. From the tip of Point Bonita, you can see the distant Golden Gate Bridge and beyond it the San Francisco skyline. It's an uncommon vantage point of the bay-centric city, and harbor seals haul out nearby in season. To reserve a spot on one of the free monthly full-moon tours of the promontory, call ☎415-331-1540.

FREE **Nike Missile Site SF-88** HISTORIC SITE
(☎415-331-1453; www.nps.gov/goga/nike-missile-site.htm; ⏰12:30-3:30pm Wed-Fri & 1st Sat of month) File past guard shacks with uniformed mannequins to witness the area's not-too-distant military history at this fascinating Cold War museum staffed by veterans. Watch them place a now-warhead-free missile into position, then ride a missile elevator to the cavernous underground silo to see the multikeyed launch controls that were thankfully never set in motion.

FREE **Marine Mammal Center** ANIMAL RESCUE CENTER
(☎415-289-7325; www.marinemammalcenter.org; ⏰10am-5pm; 👪) Set on the hill above Rodeo Lagoon, the newly expanded Marine Mammal Center rehabilitates injured, sick and orphaned sea mammals before returning them to the wild, and has educational exhibits about these animals and the dangers they face. During the spring pupping season the center can have up to several dozen orphaned seal pups on site and you can often see them before they're set free.

Headlands Center for the Arts ARTS CENTER
(☎415-331-2787; www.headlands.org) In Fort Barry, refurbished barracks converted into artist work spaces host open studios with its artists-in-residence, as well as talks, performances and other events.

Activities

Hiking

At the end of Bunker Rd sits Rodeo Beach, protected from wind by high cliffs. From here the **Coastal Trail** meanders 3.5 miles inland, past abandoned military bunkers, to the **Tennessee Valley Trail**. It then continues 6 miles along the blustery headlands all the way to Muir Beach.

All along the coastline you'll find cool old battery sites – abandoned concrete bunkers dug into the ground with fabulous views. Evocative **Battery Townsley**, a half-mile walk or bike ride up from the Fort Cronkite parking lot, opens for free subterranean tours from noon to 4pm on the first Sunday of the month.

Mountain-Biking

The Marin Headlands have some excellent mountain-biking routes, and it's an exhilarating ride across the Golden Gate Bridge to reach them (see the boxed text, p109).

For a good 12-mile dirt loop, choose the **Coastal Trail** west from the fork of Conzelman and McCullough Rds, bumping and winding down to Bunker Rd where it meets **Bobcat Trail**, which joins **Marincello Trail** and descends steeply into the Tennessee Valley parking area. The **Old Springs Trail** and the **Miwok Trail** take you back to Bunker Rd a bit more gently than the Bobcat Trail, though any attempt to avoid at least a couple of hefty climbs is futile.

Horseback Riding

For a ramble on all fours, **Miwok Livery Stables** (☎415-383-8048; www.miwokstables.com; 701 Tennessee Valley Rd; trail ride $75) offers hillside trail rides with stunning views of Mt Tam and the ocean.

Sleeping

There are four small campgrounds in the headlands, and two involve hiking (or cycling) in at least 1 mile from the nearest parking lot. **Hawk**, **Bicentennial** and **Haypress** campgrounds are inland, with free camping, but sites must be reserved through the Marin Headlands Visitors Center (p104).

Marin Headlands Hostel HOSTEL $
(☎415-331-2777; www.norcalhostels.org/marin; Bldg 941, Fort Barry, Marin Headlands; dm $22-26, r $72-92; @) Wake up to grazing deer and dew on the ground at this spartan 1907 military compound snuggled in the woods. It has comfortable beds and two well-stocked kitchens, and guests can gather round a fireplace in the common room, shoot pool or play ping-pong. Most importantly, the Hostelling International (HI) hostel is surrounded by hiking trails.

Kirby Cove Campground CAMPGROUND $
(☎877-444-6777; www.recreation.gov; tent sites $25; ⏰Apr-Oct) In a spectacular shady nook near the entrance to the bay, there's a small beach with the Golden Gate Bridge arching over the rocks nearby. At night you

WHY IS IT SO FOGGY?

When the summer sun's rays warm the air over the chilly Pacific, fog forms and hovers offshore; to grasp how it moves inland requires an understanding of California's geography. The vast agricultural region in the state's interior, the Central Valley, is ringed by mountains like a giant bathtub. The only substantial sea-level break in these mountains occurs at the Golden Gate, to the west, which happens to be the direction from which prevailing winds blow. As the inland valley heats up and the warm air rises, it creates a deficit of air at surface level, generating wind that gets sucked through the only opening it can find: the Golden Gate. It happens fast and it's unpredictable. Gusty wind is the only indication that the fog is about to roll in. But even this is inconsistent: there can be fog at the beaches south of the Golden Gate and sun a mile to the north. Hills block fog – especially at times of high atmospheric pressure, as often happens in summer. Because of this, weather forecasters speak of the Bay Area's 'microclimates.' In July it's not uncommon for inland areas to reach 100°F (38°C), while the mercury at the coast barely reaches 70°F (21°C).

can watch the phantom shadows of cargo ships passing by (and sometimes be lulled to sleep by the dirge of a fog horn). Reserve far ahead.

Information

Information is available from the **Golden Gate National Recreation Area** (GGNRA; ☎415-561-4700; www.nps.gov/goga) and the **Marin Headlands Visitors Center** (☎415-331-1540; www.nps.gov/goga/marin-headlands.htm; ⏲9:30am-4:30pm), in an old chapel off Bunker Rd near Fort Barry.

Getting There & Away

By car, take the Alexander Ave exit just after the Golden Gate Bridge and dip left under the freeway. Conzelman Rd, to the right, takes you up along the bluffs; you can also take Bunker Rd, which leads to the headlands through a one-way tunnel. It's also a snap to reach these roads from the bridge via bicycle.

Golden Gate Transit (☎415-455-2000, 511; www.goldengatetransit.org) bus 2 runs a limited weekday commuter service from the corner of Pine and Battery Sts in San Francisco's Financial District to Sausalito and the Headlands ($4.25). On Sunday and holidays **MUNI** (☎415-701-2311, 511; www.sfmta.com) bus 76 runs from the 4th St Caltrain depot in San Francisco to the Marin Headlands Visitors Center and Rodeo Beach.

Sausalito

Perfectly arranged on a secure little harbor on the bay, Sausalito is undeniably lovely. Named for the tiny willows that once populated the banks of its creeks, it's a small settlement of pretty houses that tumble neatly down a green hillside into a well-heeled downtown. Much of the town affords the visitor uninterrupted views of San Francisco and Angel Island, and due to the ridgeline at its back, fog generally skips past it.

Sausalito began as a 19,000-acre land grant to an army captain in 1838. When it became the terminus of the train line down the Pacific coast, it entered a new stage as a busy lumber port with a racy waterfront. Dramatic changes came in WWII when Sausalito became the site of Marinship, a huge shipbuilding yard. After the war a new bohemian period began, with a resident artists' colony living in 'arks' (houseboats moored along the bay). You'll still see dozens of these floating abodes.

Sausalito today is a major tourist haven, jam-packed with souvenir shops and costly boutiques. It's the first town you encounter after crossing the Golden Gate Bridge from San Francisco, so daytime crowds turn up in droves and make parking difficult. Ferrying over from San Francisco makes a more relaxing excursion.

Sights

Sausalito is actually on Richardson Bay, a smaller bay within San Francisco Bay. The commercial district is mainly one street, Bridgeway Blvd, on the waterfront.

FREE **Bay Model Visitor Center** MUSEUM
(☎415-332-3871; www.spn.usace.army.mil/bmvc; 2100 Bridgeway Blvd; ⏲9am-4pm Tue-Fri, plus 10am-5pm Sat & Sun in summer; 🚼) One of the coolest things in town, fascinating to both

kids and adults, is the Army Corps of Engineers' visitor center. Housed in one of the old Marinship warehouses, it's a 1.5-acre hydraulic model of San Francisco Bay and the delta region. Self-guided tours take you over and around it as the water flows.

Bay Area Discovery Museum MUSEUM
(415-339-3900; www.baykidsmuseum.org; adult/child $10/8; 9am-4pm Tue-Fri, 10am-5pm Sat & Sun;) Just under the north tower of the Golden Gate Bridge, at East Fort Baker, this excellent hands-on activity museum is specifically designed for children. Permanent (multilingual) exhibits include a wave workshop, a small underwater tunnel and a large outdoor play area with a shipwreck to romp around. A small cafe has healthy nibbles.

Plaza de Viña Del Mar PARK
Near the ferry terminal, the plaza has a fountain flanked by 14ft-tall elephant statues from the 1915 Panama–Pacific Exposition in San Francisco.

Activities

Sausalito is great for **bicycling**, whether for a leisurely ride around town, a trip across the Golden Gate Bridge or a longer-haul journey. From the ferry terminal, an easy option is to head south on Bridgeway Blvd, veering left onto East Rd toward the Bay Area Discovery Museum. Another nice route heads north along Bridgeway Blvd, then crosses under Hwy 101 to Mill Valley. At Blithedale Ave, you can veer east to Tiburon; a bike path parallels parts of Tiburon Blvd.

Sea Trek KAYAKING
(415-488-1000; www.seatrek.com; Schoonmaker Point Marina; single/double kayaks per hr $20/35) On a nice day, Richardson Bay is irresistible. Kayaks and stand-up paddleboards can be rented here, near the Bay Model Visitor Center. No experience is necessary, and lessons and group outings are also available.

Also on offer are guided kayaking excursions around Angel Island (see p111) from $75 per person, including overnight camping ($140). Tours include equipment and instructions. May through October is the best time to paddle.

Mike's Bikes BICYCLE RENTAL
(415-332-3200; 1 Gate 6 Rd; 24hr $40) At the north end of Bridgeway Blvd near Hwy 101, this shop rents out road and mountain bikes. Supplies are limited and reservations aren't accepted.

Sleeping

All of the lodgings below charge an additional $15 to $20 per night for parking.

Cavallo Point HOTEL $$$
(415-339-4700; www.cavallopoint.com; 601 Murray Circle, Fort Baker; r from $280;) Spread out over 45 acres of the Bay Area's most scenic parkland, Cavallo Point is a buzz-worthy lodge that flaunts a green focus, a full-service spa and easy access to outdoor activities. Choose from richly renovated rooms in the landmark Fort Baker officers' quarters or more contemporary solar-powered accommodations with exquisite bay views (including a turret of the Golden Gate Bridge).

Inn Above Tide INN $$$
(415-332-9535, 800-893-8433; www.innabovetide.com; 30 El Portal; r incl breakfast $320-595, ste $695-1100;) Next to the ferry terminal, ensconce yourself in one of the 29 modern and spacious rooms – most with private decks and wood-burning fireplaces – that practically levitate over the water. With envy-inducing bay views from your window, scan the horizon with the in-room binoculars. Free loaner bicycles available.

Gables Inn INN $$$
(415-289-1100; www.gablesinnsausalito.com; 62 Princess St; r incl breakfast $185-445;) Tranquil and inviting, this inn has nine guest rooms in a historic 1869 home, and six in a newer building. The more expensive rooms have Jacuzzi baths, fireplaces and balconies with spectacular views, but even the smaller, cheaper rooms are stylish and tranquil. Evening wine is included.

Hotel Sausalito HISTORIC HOTEL $$
(415-332-0700; www.hotelsausalito.com; 16 El Portal; r $155-195, ste $265-285;) Steps away from the ferry in the middle of downtown, this grand 1915 hotel has loads of period charm, paired with modern touches like MP3-player docking stations. Each guest room is decorated in Mediterranean hues, with sumptuous bathrooms and park or partial bay views.

Marin County

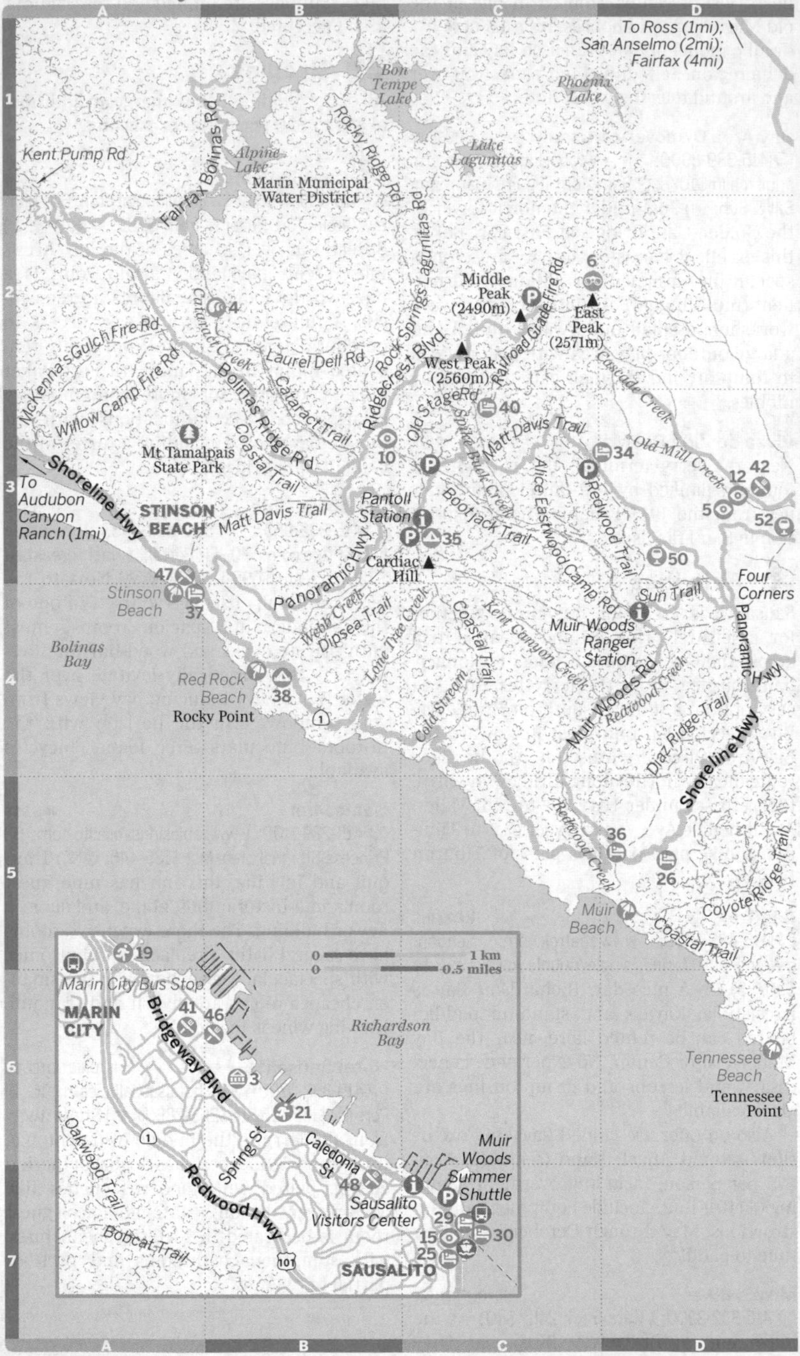

To Ross (1mi); San Anselmo (2mi); Fairfax (4mi)
Bon Tempe Lake
Phoenix Lake
Rocky Ridge Rd
Fairfax Bolinas Rd
Alpine Lake
Lake Lagunitas
Kent Pump Rd
Marin Municipal Water District
Lagunitas Rd
Middle Peak (2490m)
East Peak (2571m)
Railroad Grade Fire Rd
Rock Springs Lagunitas Rd
Ridgecrest Blvd
West Peak (2560m)
Cataract Creek
Laurel Dell Rd
McKenna's Gulch Fire Rd
Willow Camp Fire Rd
Bolinas Ridge Rd
Cataract Trail
Coastal Trail
Old Stage Rd
Spike Buck Creek
Matt Davis Trail
Cascade Creek
Old Mill Creek
Mt Tamalpais State Park
Shoreline Hwy
To Audubon Canyon Ranch (1mi)
STINSON BEACH
Matt Davis Trail
Pantoll Station
Bootjack Trail
Alice Eastwood Camp Rd
Redwood Trail
Panoramic Hwy
Cardiac Hill
Four Corners
Stinson Beach
Bolinas Bay
Webb Creek
Dipsea Trail
Lone Tree Creek
Coastal Trail
Kent Canyon Creek
Sun Trail
Muir Woods Ranger Station
Panoramic Hwy
Red Rock Beach
Rocky Point
Cold Stream
Muir Woods Rd
Redwood Creek
Diaz Ridge Trail
Shoreline Hwy
Redwood Creek
Muir Beach
Coastal Trail
Coyote Ridge Trail
Tennessee Beach
Tennessee Point
1 2 3 4 5 6 7 10 12 34 35 36 37 38 40 42 47 50 52 26

Marin City Bus Stop
MARIN CITY
Bridgeway Blvd
Richardson Bay
0 1 km
0 0.5 miles
Oakwood Trail
Spring St
Caledonia St
Redwood Hwy
Bobcat Trail
Sausalito Visitors Center
Muir Woods Summer Shuttle
SAUSALITO
101
3 15 19 21 25 29 30 41 46 48

A B C D

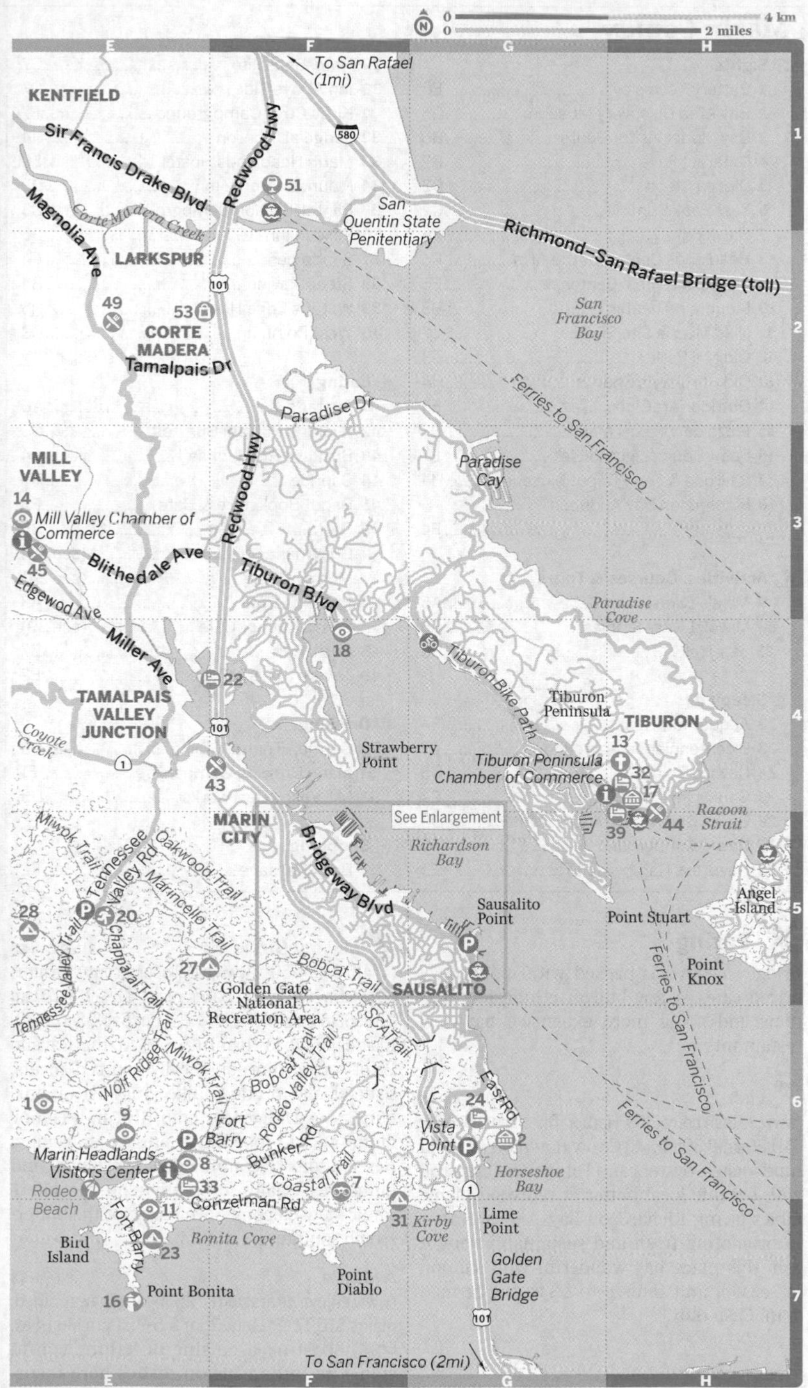

To San Rafael (1mi)
KENTFIELD
Sir Francis Drake Blvd
Redwood Hwy
Magnolia Ave
Corte Madera Creek
LARKSPUR
San Quentin State Penitentiary
Richmond–San Rafael Bridge (toll)
San Francisco Bay
CORTE MADERA
Tamalpais Dr
Paradise Dr
Ferries to San Francisco
Paradise Cay
MILL VALLEY
Mill Valley Chamber of Commerce
Blithedale Ave
Tiburon Blvd
Edgewod Ave
Miller Ave
Paradise Cove
Tiburon Bike Path
TAMALPAIS VALLEY JUNCTION
Coyote Creek
Strawberry Point
Tiburon Peninsula
TIBURON
Tiburon Peninsula Chamber of Commerce
Racoon Strait
MARIN CITY
See Enlargement
Richardson Bay
Bridgeway Blvd
Miwok Trail
Tennessee Valley Rd
Oakwood Trail
Marincello Trail
Sausalito Point
Point Stuart
Angel Island
Tennessee Valley Trail
Chapparal Trail
Bobcat Trail
Point Knox
Golden Gate National Recreation Area
SAUSALITO
SCA Trail
Wolf Ridge Trail
Bobcat Trail
Rodeo Valley Trail
East Rd
Fort Barry
Bunker Rd
Vista Point
Marin Headlands Visitors Center
Horseshoe Bay
Coastal Trail
Rodeo Beach
Conzelman Rd
Kirby Cove
Lime Point
Fort Barry
Bird Island
Bonita Cove
Golden Gate Bridge
Point Bonita
Point Diablo
To San Francisco (2mi)

Marin County

Sights

1	Battery Townsley	E6
2	Bay Area Discovery Museum	G6
3	Bay Model Visitor Center	B6
4	Cataract Falls	B2
5	Dipsea Steps	D3
6	East Peak Summit	C2
7	Hawk Hill	F6
8	Headlands Center for the Arts	E6
9	Marine Mammal Center	E6
10	Mountain Theater	B3
11	Nike Missile Site SF-88	E7
12	Old Mill Park	D3
13	Old St Hilary's Church	H4
14	Outdoor Art Club	E3
15	Plaza de Viña del Mar	C7
16	Point Bonita Lighthouse	E7
17	Railroad & Ferry Depot Museum	H4
18	Richardson Bay Audubon Center	F4

Activities, Courses & Tours

19	Mike's Bikes	A5
20	Miwok Livery Stables	E5
21	Sea Trek	B6

Sleeping

22	Acqua Hotel	F4
23	Bicentennial Campground	E7
24	Cavallo Point	G6
25	Gables Inn	C7
26	Green Gulch Farm & Zen Center	D5
27	Hawk Campground	E5
28	Haypress Campground	E5
29	Hotel Sausalito	C7
30	Inn Above Tide	C7
31	Kirby Cove Campground	F7
32	Lodge at Tiburon	H4
33	Marin Headlands Hostel	E6
34	Mountain Home Inn	D3
35	Pantoll Station Campground	C3
36	Pelican Inn	D5
37	Sandpiper	A4
38	Steep Ravine	B4
39	Water's Edge Hotel	H5
40	West Point Inn	C3

Eating

41	Avatar's	A6
42	Avatar's Punjabi Burritos	D3
43	Buckeye Roadhouse	F4
44	Caprice	H5
45	Depot Bookstore & Cafe	E3
46	Fish	B6
	Guaymas	(see 39)
	Murray Circle	(see 24)
47	Parkside Cafe	A3
	Sam's Anchor Cafe	(see 39)
48	Sushi Ran	B7
49	Tavern at Lark Creek	E2

Drinking

50	German Tourist Club	D3
51	Marin Brewing Company	F1
52	Mill Valley Beerworks	D3

Shopping

53	Book Passage	E2

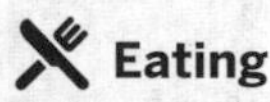

Eating

Bridgeway Blvd is packed with moderately priced cafes, a few budget ethnic food options and some more expensive bay-view restaurants.

Fish — SEAFOOD $$

(www.331fish.com; 350 Harbor Dr; mains $13-25; 11:30am-8:30pm;) Chow down on seafood sandwiches, oysters and Dungeness crab roll with organic local butter at redwood picnic tables facing Richardson Bay. A local leader in promoting fresh and sustainably caught fish, this place has wonderful wild salmon in season, and refuses to serve the farmed stuff. Cash only.

Murray Circle — AMERICAN $$

(415-339-4750; www.cavallopoint.com/dine.html; 601 Murray Circle, Fort Baker; mains $17-29; 7-11am & 11:30am-2pm Mon-Fri, to 2:30pm Sat & Sun, 5:30-10pm Sun-Thu, to 11pm Fri & Sat) At the Cavallo Point lodge, dine on locally sourced meats, seafood and produce, like grass-fed organic burgers or Dungeness crab BLT, in a clubby dining room topped by a pressed-tin ceiling. Reservations recommended for lunch and dinner, especially for seating on the panoramic-view balcony. Save room for the butterscotch soufflé.

Avatar's — INDIAN $$

(www.enjoyavatars.com; 2656 Bridgeway Blvd; mains $10-17; 11am-3pm & 5-9:30pm Mon-Sat;) Boasting a cuisine of 'ethnic confusion,' the Indian fusion dishes here incorporate Mexican, Italian and Caribbean ingredients and will bowl you over with their flavor and creativity. Think Punjabi enchilada with curried sweet potato or spinach and mushroom ravioli with mango and rose petal alfredo sauce. All diets (vegan, gluten-free, etc) are graciously accommodated.

Sushi Ran SUSHI **$$**
(☎415-332-3620; www.sushiran.com; 107 Caledonia St; sushi $4-19) Many Bay Area residents claim this place is the best sushi spot around. A wine and sake bar next door eases the pain of the long wait for a table.

Information

The **Sausalito Visitors Center** (☎415-332-0505; www.sausalito.org; 780 Bridgeway Blvd; ⌚11:30am-4pm Tue-Sun) has local information. There's also an information kiosk at the ferry terminal.

Getting There & Away

Driving to Sausalito from San Francisco, take the Alexander Ave exit (the first exit after the Golden Gate Bridge) and follow the signs into Sausalito. There are five municipal parking lots in town, and street parking is difficult to find.

Golden Gate Transit (☎415-455-2000; www.goldengatetransit.org) bus 10 runs daily to Sausalito from downtown San Francisco ($4.25).

The ferry is a fun and easy way to travel to Sausalito. **Golden Gate Ferry** (☎415-455-2000; www.goldengateferry.org; one-way $9.25) operates to and from the San Francisco Ferry Building six to nine times daily and takes 30 minutes. The **Blue & Gold Fleet** (☎415-705-8200; www.blueandgoldfleet.com; Pier 41, Fisherman's Wharf; one-way $10.50) sails to Sausalito four to five times daily from the Fisherman's Wharf area in San Francisco. Both ferries operate year-round and transport bicycles for free.

Tiburon

At the end of a small peninsula pointing out into the center of the bay, Tiburon is blessed with gorgeous views. The name comes from the Spanish *Punta de Tiburon* (Shark Point). Take the ferry from San Francisco, browse the shops on Main St, grab a bite to eat and you've seen Tiburon. The town is also a jumping-off point for nearby Angel Island (see p111).

Sights & Activities

The central part of town is comprised of Tiburon Blvd, with Juanita Lane and charming Main St arcing off. Main St, which is also known as Ark Row, is where the old houseboats have taken root on dry land and metamorphosed into classy shops and boutiques.

FREE **Railroad & Ferry Depot Museum** MUSEUM
(1920 Paradise Drive; www.landmarks-society.org; ⌚1-4pm Wed, Sat & Sun Mar-Oct) Formerly the terminus for a 3000-person ferry to San Francisco and a railroad that once reached north to Ukiah, this late 19th century building showcases a scale model of Tiburon's commercial hub, circa 1909. The restored

HIKING & CYCLING THE BRIDGE

Walking or cycling across the Golden Gate Bridge to Sausalito is a fun way to avoid traffic, get some great ocean views and bask in that refreshing Marin County air. It's a fairly easy journey, mostly flat or downhill when heading north from San Francisco (cycling back to the city involves one big climb out of Sausalito). You can also simply hop on a ferry back to SF (see p109).

The trip is about 4 miles from the south end of the bridge and takes less than an hour. Pedestrians have access to the bridge's east walkway between 5am and 9pm daily (until 6pm in winter). Cyclists generally use the west side, except on weekdays between 5am and 3:30pm, when they must share the east side with pedestrians (who have the right-of-way). After 9pm (6pm in winter), cyclists can still cross the bridge on the east side through a security gate. Check the bridge website (http://goldengatebridge.org/bikesbridge/bikes.php) for changes.

For more ambitious cyclists, the reopening of the Cal Park Hill Tunnel means a safe subterranean passage from Larkspur (another ferry terminus) to San Rafael.

More information and resources are available at the websites of the **San Francisco Bicycle Coalition** (www.sfbike.org) and the **Marin County Bicycle Coalition** (www.marinbike.org).

stationmaster's quarters can be visited upstairs.

Angel Island–Tiburon Ferry CRUISE
(☎415-435-2131; www.angelislandferry.com; adult/child $20/10) Runs sunset cruises on Friday and Saturday evenings from May through October. Reservations recommended.

Old St Hilary's Church CHURCH
(201 Esperanza; ⊙1-4pm Sun Apr-Oct) There are great views from the lovely hillside surrounding this fine 19th-century example of Carpenter Gothic.

Richardson Bay Audubon Center NATURE RESERVE
(☎415-388-2524; www.tiburonaudubon.org; 376 Greenwood Beach Rd; ⊙9am-5pm Mon-Sat) Off Tiburon Blvd, this center is home to a huge variety of water birds.

Sleeping

Water's Edge Hotel HOTEL $$
(☎415-789-5999; www.watersedgehotel.com; 25 Main St; r incl breakfast $169-499;) This hotel, with its deck extending over the bay, is exemplary for its tasteful modernity. Rooms have an elegant minimalism that combines comfort and style, and all afford an immediate view of the bay. The rooms with rustic, high wood ceilings are quite romantic.

Lodge at Tiburon HOTEL $$
(☎415-435-3133; www.larkspurhotels.com/collection/tiburon; 1651 Tiburon Blvd; r from $135;) Now a stylish and comfortable contemporary hotel with a grill restaurant, the concrete hallways and staircases testify to the more basic motel it once was. The best value in town, it's a short stroll to anywhere – including the ferry – and there's a pool, DVD library, free parking and a rooftop deck with fireplace and heady Mt Tamalpais views.

Eating

Sam's Anchor Cafe SEAFOOD $$
(www.samscafe.com; 27 Main St; mains $17-28; ⊙11am-10pm Mon-Fri, from 9:30am Sat & Sun) Sam's has been slinging seafood and burgers since 1920, and though the entrance looks like a shambling little shack, the area out back has unbeatable views. On a warm afternoon, you can't beat a cocktail or a tasty plate of sautéed prawns on the deck.

Caprice AMERICAN $$$
(☎415-435-3400; www.thecaprice.com; 2000 Paradise Dr; mains $18-49; ⊙5-10pm Tue-Sun, plus 11am-3pm Sun) Splurge-worthy and romantic, book a table here at sunset for riveting views of Angel Island, the Golden Gate Bridge and San Francisco. Caprice mostly features seafood, though other standouts include the artichoke bisque and the filet mignon. Take a peek at the fireplace downstairs – it's constructed into the coast bedrock. A three-course midweek dinner ($25) is easier on the wallet.

Guaymas MEXICAN $$
(www.guaymasrestaurant.com; 5 Main St; mains $15-25; ⊙11am-9pm Sun-Thu, 11am-10pm Fri & Sat) Steps from the ferry, noisy Guaymas packs in a fun, boisterous crowd. Margaritas energize the place, and solid Mexican seafood dishes help keep people upright.

Information

The **Tiburon Peninsula Chamber of Commerce** (☎415-435-5633; www.tiburonchamber.org; 96b Main St) can provide information about the area.

Getting There & Away

Golden Gate Transit (☎415-455-2000; www.goldengatetransit.org) commute bus 8 runs direct between San Francisco and Tiburon ($4.25) during the week.

On Hwy 101, look for the off-ramp for Tiburon Blvd, E Blithedale Ave and Hwy 131; driving east, it leads into town and intersects with Juanita Lane and Main St.

Blue & Gold Fleet (☎415-705-8200; one-way $10.50) sails daily from either Pier 41 or the Ferry Building in San Francisco to Tiburon; ferries dock right in front of the Guaymas restaurant on Main St. You can transport bicycles for free. From Tiburon, ferries also connect regularly to Angel Island.

Mill Valley

Nestled under the redwoods at the base of Mt Tamalpais, tiny Mill Valley is one of the Bay Area's most picturesque hamlets. Mill Valley was originally a logging town, its name stemming from an 1830s sawmill – the first in the Bay Area to provide lumber. Though the 1892 Mill Valley Lumber Company still greets motorists on Miller Ave, the town's a vastly different place today, packed with wildly expensive homes, fancy cars and pricey boutiques.

DON'T MISS

ANGEL ISLAND

Angel Island (☎415-435-5390; www.parks.ca.gov/?page_id=468), in San Francisco Bay, has a mild climate with fresh bay breezes, which make it pleasant for hiking and cycling. For a unique treat, picnic in a protected cove overlooking the close but distant urban surroundings. The island's varied history – it was a hunting and fishing ground for the Miwok people, served as a military base, an immigration station, a WWII Japanese internment camp and a Nike missile site – has left it with some evocative old forts and bunkers to poke around in. There are 12 miles of roads and trails around the island, including a hike to the summit of 781ft **Mt Livermore** (no bicycles) and a 5-mile perimeter trail.

The **Immigration Station**, which operated from 1910 to 1940, was the Ellis Island of the west coast. But this facility was primarily a screening and detention center for Chinese immigrants, who were at that time restricted from entering the US under the Chinese Exclusion Act. Many detainees were held here for long periods before ultimately being returned home, and one of the most unusual sights on the island is the sad and longing Chinese poetry etched into the barrack walls. A **visitor center** (www.aiisf.org/visit; ⊙usually 11am-3pm Wed-Sun) contains interpretive exhibits, and more extensive **tours** (☎415-435-3522, adult/child $7/5) can be reserved ahead or purchased at the cafe near the ferry dock.

Sea Trek (see p105) runs **kayaking** excursions around the island. You can rent **bicycles** at Ayala Cove (per hour/day $10/35), and there are **tram tours** ($13.50) around the island. Schedules vary seasonally; go to www.angelisland.com for more information.

You can camp on the island, and when the last ferry sails off for the night, the place is your own – except for the very persistent raccoons. The dozen hike-, bicycle- or kayak-in **campsites** (☎800-444-7275; www.reserveamerica.com; tent sites $30) are usually reserved months in advance. Near the ferry dock, there's a **cafe** that specializes in barbecued oysters.

From San Francisco, take a **Blue & Gold Fleet** (☎415-705-8200; www.blueandgoldfleet.com) ferry from Pier 41 or the Ferry Building. From May to September there are three ferries a day on weekends and two on weekdays; during the rest of the year the schedule is reduced. Round-trip tickets cost $16 for adults and $9 for children.

From Tiburon, take the **Angel Island–Tiburon Ferry** (☎415-435-2131; www.angelislandferry.com; round trip $13.50, plus $1 for bicycles).

Mill Valley also served as the starting point for the scenic railway that carried visitors up Mt Tamalpais (see p114). The tracks were removed in 1940, and today the Depot Bookstore & Cafe occupies the space of the former station.

Sights & Activities

Old Mill Park PARK

Several blocks west of downtown along Throckmorton Ave is Old Mill Park, perfect for a picnic. Here you'll also find a replica of the town's namesake sawmill. Just past the bridge at Old Mill Creek, the **Dipsea Steps** mark the start of the Dipsea Trail.

Mill Valley Film Festival FILM FESTIVAL

(www.mvff.com) Each October the Mill Valley Film Festival presents an innovative, internationally regarded program of independent films.

Tennessee Valley Trail HIKING

In the Marin Headlands, this trail offers beautiful views of the rugged coastline and is one of the most popular hikes in Marin (expect crowds on weekends), especially for families. It has easy, level access to the cove beach and ocean, and is a short 3.8-mile round trip. From Hwy 101, take the Mill Valley–Stinson Beach–Hwy 1 exit and turn left onto Tennessee Valley Rd from the Shoreline Hwy; follow it to the parking lot and trailhead.

TOP CHOICE **Dipsea Trail** HIKING

A beloved though more demanding hike is the 7-mile Dipsea Trail, which climbs over the coastal range and down to Stinson Beach, cutting through a corner of Muir Woods. This classic trail starts at Old Mill Park with a climb up 676 steps in three separate flights, and includes a few more ups and downs before reaching the ocean. **West Marin Stagecoach** (www.marintransit.org/stage.html) route 61 runs from Stinson Beach to Mill Valley, making it a doable one-way day hike.

Outdoor Art Club HISTORIC SITE
(www.outdoorartclub.org; cnr W Blithedale & Throckmorton Aves) Said to have been founded by 35 Mill Valley women determined to preserve the local environment, this private club is housed in a landmark 1904 building designed by prominent architect Bernard Maybeck.

Sleeping

Mountain Home Inn INN $$$
(415-381-9000; www.mtnhomeinn.com; 810 Panoramic Hwy; r incl breakfast $195-345;) Set amid redwood, spruce and pine trees on a ridge of Mt Tamalpais, this retreat is both modern and rustic. The larger (more expensive) rooms are rugged beauties, with unfinished timbers forming columns from floor to ceiling, as though the forest is shooting up through the floor. Smaller rooms are cozy dens for two. A lack of TVs and the positioning of a good local trail map on the dresser make it clear that it's a place to breathe and unwind.

Acqua Hotel BOUTIQUE HOTEL $$
(415-380-0400, 888-662-9555; www.marinhotels.com; 555 Redwood Hwy; r incl breakfast from $169;) With views of the bay and Mt Tamalpais, and a lobby with a soothing fireplace and fountain, the Acqua doesn't lack for pleasant eye candy. Contemporary rooms are sleekly designed with beautiful fabrics.

Eating & Drinking

Depot Bookstore & Cafe CAFE $
(www.depotbookstore.com; 87 Throckmorton Ave; meals under $10; 7am-7pm;) Smack in the town center, Depot serves cappuccinos, sandwiches and light meals. The bookstore sells lots of local publications, including trail guides.

Buckeye Roadhouse AMERICAN $$
(415-331-2600; www.buckeyeroadhouse.com; 15 Shoreline Hwy; mains $15-33; 11:30am-10:30pm Mon-Sat, 10:30am-10pm Sun) Originally opened as a roadside stop in 1932, the Buckeye is a Marin County gem, and its upscale American cuisine is in no danger of being compared to truck-stop fare. Stop off for chili-lime 'brick' chicken, baby back ribs or oysters Bingo and a devilish wedge of s'more pie before getting back on the highway.

Mill Valley Beerworks PUB
(www.millvalleybeerworks.com; 173 Throckmorton Ave; sandwiches & small plates $9-14; 11am-midnight) With 100 bottled varieties of brew and a few of its own on tap, beer lovers can giddily explore new frontiers while chewing on house-made pretzels. The setting is stark and stylish, with unfinished wood tables and a pressed-tin wall.

Avatar's Punjabi Burritos INDIAN $
(www.enjoyavatars.com; 15 Madrona St; mains $6.50-9; 11am-8pm Mon-Sat, to 7pm Sun;) For a quick bite, try a tasty burrito of lamb and curry or spicy veggies.

Information

Visitor information is available from the **Mill Valley Chamber of Commerce** (415-388-9700; www.millvalley.org; 85 Throckmorton Ave; 9am-5pm Mon-Fri).

Getting There & Away

From San Francisco or Sausalito, take Hwy 101 north to the Mill Valley–Stinson Beach–Hwy 1 exit. Follow Hwy 1 (also called the Shoreline Hwy) to Almonte Blvd (which becomes Miller Ave), then follow Miller Ave into downtown Mill Valley.

From the north, take the E Blithedale Ave exit from Hwy 101, then head west into downtown Mill Valley.

Golden Gate Transit (415-455-2000; www.goldengatetranist.org) bus 4 runs directly from San Francisco to Mill Valley ($4.25) on weekdays.

Sir Francis Drake Blvd & Around

The towns along and nearby the Sir Francis Drake Blvd corridor – including Larkspur, Corte Madera, Ross, San Anselmo and Fairfax – evoke charmed small-town life, even though things get busy around Hwy 101.

Starting from the eastern section in **Larkspur**, window-shop along Magnolia Ave or explore the redwoods in nearby Baltimore Canyon. On the east side of the freeway is the hulking mass of **San Quentin State Penitentiary**, California's oldest and most notorious prison, founded in 1852. Johnny Cash recorded an album here in 1969 after scoring a big hit with his live *Folsom Prison* album a few years earlier.

Take the bicycle and pedestrian bridge from the ferry terminal across the road to the **Marin Brewing Company** (www.marinbrewing.com; 1809 Larkspur Landing Cir, Marin Country Mart, Bldg 2, Larkspur; mains $10-15; 11:30am-midnight Sun-Thu, to 1am Fri & Sat) brewpub, where you can see the glassed-in kettles behind the bar. The head brewer, Arne Johnson, has won many awards, and the Mt Tam Pale Ale complements the menu of pizza, burgers and hearty sandwiches.

The **Tavern at Lark Creek** (415-924-7766; 234 Magnolia Ave, Larkspur; mains $13-29; 5:30-9:30pm Mon-Thu, to 10pm Fri & Sat, 10am-2pm & 5-9:30pm Sun;) is in a lovely spot and offers a fine-dining experience. It's housed in an 1888 Victorian house tucked away in a redwood canyon, and the rotating farm-fresh American food (like the macaroni-and-cheese croquettes, pork loin chop and rainbow trout in brown butter) is gratifying.

Just south, **Corte Madera** is home to one of the Bay Area's best bookstores, **Book Passage** (415-927-0960; www.bookpassage.com; 51 Tamal Vista Blvd), in the Marketplace shopping center. It has a strong travel section, plus frequent author appearances.

Continuing west along Sir Francis Drake, **San Anselmo** has a cute, small downtown area along San Anselmo Ave, including several antique shops. The attractive center of neighboring **Fairfax** has ample dining and shopping options, and cyclists congregate at **Gestalt Haus Fairfax** (28 Bolinas Rd, Fairfax) for the indoor bicycle parking, board games, European draft beers and sausages of the meaty or vegan persuasion.

Arti (www.articafe.com; 7282 Sir Francis Drake Blvd, Lagunitas; mains $9-14; noon-9:30pm Tue-Sun;), between Hwys 1 and 101 in the tiny hamlet of Lagunitas, is a tempting stop for organic Indian fare. There's a cozy casual dining room and an outdoor patio for warm days, and folks from miles around adore its sizzling chicken tikka platter.

Golden Gate Ferry (415-455-2000; www.goldengateferry.org) runs a daily ferry service ($8.75, 50 minutes) from the Ferry Building in San Francisco to Larkspur Landing on E Sir Francis Drake Blvd, directly east of Hwy 101. You can take bicycles on the ferry.

San Rafael

The oldest and largest town in Marin, San Rafael is slightly less upscale than most of its neighbors but doesn't lack atmosphere. It's a common stop for travelers on their way to Point Reyes. Just north of San Rafael, Lucas Valley Rd heads west to Point Reyes Station, passing George Lucas' Skywalker Ranch. Fourth St, San Rafael's main drag, is lined with cafes and shops. If you follow it west out of downtown San Rafael, it meets Sir Francis Drake Blvd and continues west to the coast.

Sights & Activities

Mission San Rafael Arcángel MISSION
(1104 5th Ave) The town began with this mission, founded in 1817, which served as a sanitarium for Native Americans suffering from European diseases. The present building is a replica dating from 1949.

China Camp State Park PARK
(415-456-0766; parking $5) About 4 miles east of San Rafael, this is a pleasant place to stop for a picnic or short hike. From Hwy 101, take the N San Pedro Rd exit and continue 3 miles east. A Chinese fishing village once stood here, and a small museum exhibits interesting artifacts from the settlement. At press time, the future of this state park was uncertain.

Rafael Film Center CINEMA
(415-454-1222; www.cafilm.org/rfc; 1118 4th St) A restored downtown cinema offering innovative art-house programming on three screens in state-of-the-art surroundings.

Sleeping & Eating

Panama Hotel B&B **$$**
(415-457-3993; www.panamahotel.com; 4 Bayview St; r $120-195;) The 10 artsy rooms at this B&B, in a building dating from 1910, each have their own unique style and charming decor – like crazy quilts and vibrant accent walls. The hotel restaurant has an inviting courtyard patio.

TOP CHOICE **Sol Food Puerto Rican Cuisine** PUERTO RICAN **$$**
(415-451-4765; www.solfoodrestaurant.com; Lincoln Ave & 3rd St; mains $7.50-16; 7am-midnight Mon-Thu, to 2am Fri, 8am-2am Sat, to midnight Sun) Lazy ceiling fans, a profusion of tropical plants and the pulse of Latin rhythms create a soothing atmosphere for delicious dishes like a *jíbaro* sandwich (thinly sliced steak served on green plantains) and other island-inspired meals concocted with *plátanos,* organic veggies and free range meats.

WORTH A TRIP

GERMAN TOURIST CLUB

A private club that occasionally shares its sudsy love, the **German Tourist Club** (☎415-388-9987; www.touristclubsf.org; ⏱1-5pm 1st, 3rd & 4th weekends of the month), or Nature Friends (*Die Naturefreunde*), has a gorgeous beer garden patio overlooking Muir Woods and Mt Tamalpais that's a favored spot for parched Marin hikers. By car, turn onto Ridge Ave from Panoramic Hwy, park in the gravel driveway at the end of the road and start the 0.3-mile walk downhill. You can also hike in on the Sun Trail from Panoramic – a half-hour of mostly flat trail with views of the ocean and Muir Woods.

China Camp State Park CAMPGROUND $
(☎800-444-7275; www.reserveamerica.com; tent sites $35; 🐾) The park has 30 walk-in campsites with pleasant shade.

Getting There & Away

Numerous **Golden Gate Transit** (☎415-455-2000; www.goldengatetransit.org) buses operate between San Francisco and the San Rafael Transit Center at 3rd and Hetherton Sts ($5.25, one hour).

Mt Tamalpais State Park

Standing guard over Marin County, majestic Mt Tamalpais (Mt Tam) has breathtaking 360-degree views of ocean, bay and hills rolling into the distance. The rich, natural beauty of the 2571ft mountain and its surrounding area is inspiring – especially considering it lies within an hour's drive from one of the state's largest metropolitan areas.

Mt Tamalpais State Park was formed in 1930, partly from land donated by congressman and naturalist William Kent (who also donated the land that became Muir Woods National Monument in 1907). Its 6300 acres are home to deer, foxes, bobcats and many miles of hiking and cycling trails.

Mt Tam was a sacred place to the coastal Miwok people for thousands of years before the arrival of European and American settlers. By the late 19th century, San Franciscans were escaping the bustle of the city with all-day outings on the mountain, and in 1896 the 'world's crookedest railroad' (281 turns) was completed from Mill Valley to the summit. Though the railroad was closed in 1930, Old Railroad Grade is today one of Mt Tam's most popular and scenic hiking and cycling paths.

Sights

Panoramic Hwy climbs from Mill Valley through the park to Stinson Beach. From Pantoll Station, it's 4.2 miles by car to **East Peak Summit**; take Pantoll Rd and then panoramic Ridgecrest Blvd to the top. Parking is $8 (good for the entire park) and a 10-minute hike leads to a fire lookout at the very top and awesome sea-to-bay views.

Mountain Theater THEATER
(☎415-383-1100; www.mountainplay.org) The park's natural-stone, 4000-seat theater hosts the annual 'Mountain Play' series on a half dozen weekend afternoons between mid-May and late June. Free shuttles are provided from Mill Valley. Free monthly **astronomy programs** (☎415-455-5370; www.mttam.net/astronomy.html; ⏱Apr-Oct) also take place here on Saturday nights around the new moon.

Activities

Hiking

The park map is a smart investment, as there are a dozen worthwhile hiking trails in the area. From Pantoll Station, the **Steep Ravine Trail** follows a wooded creek on to the coast (about 2.1 miles each way). For a longer hike, veer right (northwest) after 1.5 miles onto the **Dipsea Trail**, which meanders through trees for 1 mile before ending at Stinson Beach. Grab some lunch, then walk north through town and follow signs for the **Matt Davis Trail**, which leads 2.7 miles back to Pantoll Station, making a good loop. The Matt Davis Trail continues on beyond Pantoll Station, wrapping gently around the mountain with superb views.

Another worthy option is **Cataract Trail**, which runs along Cataract Creek from the end of Pantoll Rd; it's approximately 3 miles to Alpine Lake. The last mile is a spectacular rooty staircase as the trail descends alongside **Cataract Falls**.

Mountain-Biking

Cyclists must stay on the fire roads (and off the single-track trails) and keep to speeds under 15mph. Rangers are prickly about these rules, and a ticket can result in a steep fine.

The most popular ride is the **Old Railroad Grade**. For a sweaty, 6-mile, 2280ft climb, start in Mill Valley at the end of W Blithedale Ave and cycle up to East Peak. It takes about an hour to reach the West Point Inn (see below) from Mill Valley. For an easier start, begin partway up at the Mountain Home Inn (see p112) and follow the **Gravity Car Grade** to the Old Railroad Grade and the West Point Inn. From the Inn, it's an easy half-hour ride to the summit.

From just west of Pantoll Station, cyclists can either take the **Deer Park fire road**, which runs close to the Dipsea Trail, through giant redwoods to the main entrance of Muir Woods, or the southeastern extension of the **Coastal Trail**, which has breathtaking views of the coast before joining Hwy 1 about 2 miles north of Muir Beach. Either option requires a return to Mill Valley via Frank Valley/Muir Woods Rd, which climbs steadily (800ft) to Panoramic Hwy and then becomes Sequoia Valley Rd as it drops toward Mill Valley. A left turn on Wildomar and two right turns at Mill Creek Park lead to the center of Mill Valley.

For further information on bicycle routes and rules, contact the **Marin County Bicycle Coalition** (☎415-456-3469; www.marinbike.org), whose Marin Bicycle Map is the gold standard for local cycling.

Sleeping & Eating

TOP CHOICE **Steep Ravine** CABINS, CAMPGROUND $
(☎800-444-7275; www.reserveamerica.com; campsites/cabins $25/100; ⊙closed Oct) Just off Hwy 1, about 1 mile south of Stinson Beach, this jewel has seven beachfront campsites and nine rustic five-person cabins with wood stoves overlooking the ocean. Both options are booked out months in advance and reservations can be made up to seven months ahead.

West Point Inn INN $
(☎inn 415-388-9955, reservations 415-646-0702; www.westpointinn.com; per person r or cabin $50; ⊙closed Sun & Mon night) Load up your sleeping bag and hike in to this rustic 1904 hilltop hideaway built as a stopover for the Mill Valley and Mt Tamalpais Scenic Railway. Rates drop to $35 per person Tuesday through Thursday from mid-September until the end of May. It also hosts monthly pancake breakfasts ($10) on Sundays during the summer.

Pantoll Station Campground CAMPGROUND $
(☎415-388-2070; tent sites $25; 🐾) From the parking lot it's a 100yd walk or bicycle ride to the campground, with 16 first-come, first-served tent sites but no showers.

Information

Pantoll Station (☎415-388-2070; 801 Panoramic Hwy; 📶) is the park headquarters. Detailed park maps are sold here. The **Mt Tamalpais Interpretative Association** (www.mttam.net; ⊙11am-4pm Sat & Sun) staffs a small visitor center at East Peak.

Getting There & Away

To reach Pantoll Station by car, take Hwy 1 to the Panoramic Hwy and look for the Pantoll signs. **West Marin Stagecoach** (☎415-526-3239; www.marintransit.org/stage.html) route 61 runs daily minibuses ($2) from Marin City (via Mill Valley; plus weekend and holiday service from the Sausalito ferry) to both the Pantoll Station and Mountain Home Inn.

Muir Woods National Monument

Walking through an awesome stand of the world's tallest trees is an experience to be had only in Northern California and a small part of southern Oregon. The old-growth redwoods at **Muir Woods** (☎415-388-2595; www.nps.gov/muwo; adult/child under 16 $5/free; ⊙8am-sunset), just 12 miles north of the Golden Gate Bridge, is the closest redwood stand to San Francisco. The trees were initially eyed by loggers, and Redwood Creek, as the area was known, seemed ideal for a dam. Those plans were halted when congressman and naturalist William Kent bought a section of Redwood Creek and, in 1907, donated 295 acres to the federal government. President Theodore Roosevelt made the site a national monument in 1908, the name honoring John Muir, naturalist and founder of environmental organization the Sierra Club.

Muir Woods can become quite crowded, especially on weekends. Try to come midweek, early in the morning or late in the afternoon, when tour buses are less of a problem. Even at busy times, a short hike will get you out of the densest crowds and onto trails with huge trees and stunning vistas. A lovely cafe serves local and organic goodies and hot drinks that hit the spot on foggy days.

Activities

The 1-mile **Main Trail Loop** is a gentle walk alongside Redwood Creek to the 1000-year-old trees at **Cathedral Grove**; it returns via **Bohemian Grove**, where the tallest tree in the park stands 254ft high. The **Dipsea Trail** is a good 2-mile hike up to the top of aptly named **Cardiac Hill**.

You can also walk down into Muir Woods by taking trails from the Panoramic Hwy, such as the **Bootjack Trail** from the Bootjack picnic area, or from Mt Tamalpais' Pantoll Station campground, along the **Ben Johnson Trail**.

Getting There & Away

The parking lot fills up during busy periods, so consider taking the summer shuttle operated by **Marin Transit** (www.marintransit.org; round trip adult/child $3/1; ⏲weekends & holidays late-May–Sep). The 40-minute shuttle connects with four Sausalito ferries arriving from San Francisco.

To get there by car, drive north on Hwy 101, exit at Hwy 1 and continue north along Hwy 1/Shoreline Hwy to the Panoramic Hwy (a right-hand fork). Follow that for about 1 mile to Four Corners, where you turn left onto Muir Woods Rd (there are plenty of signs).

The Coast

MUIR BEACH

The turnoff to Muir Beach from Hwy 1 is marked by the longest row of mailboxes on the North Coast. Muir Beach is a quiet little town with a nice beach, but it has no direct bus service. Just north of Muir Beach there are superb views up and down the coast from the **Muir Beach Overlook**; during WWII, watch was kept from the surrounding concrete lookouts for invading Japanese ships.

Pelican Inn (☎415-383-6000; www.pelicaninn.com; 10 Pacific Way; r incl breakfast $190-265; 📶) is the only commercial establishment in Muir Beach. The downstairs restaurant and pub (mains $9 to $34) is an Anglophile's dream and perfect for pre- or post-hike nourishment.

Green Gulch Farm & Zen Center (☎415-383-3134; www.sfzc.org; 1601 Shoreline Hwy; s $90-135, d $160-205, d cottage $300-350, all with 3 meals; @📶🌶) is a Buddhist retreat in the hills above Muir Beach. The center's accommodations are elegant, restful and modern, and delicious buffet-style vegetarian meals are included. A hilltop retreat cottage is 25 minutes away by foot.

STINSON BEACH

Positively buzzing on warm weekends, Stinson Beach is 5 miles north of Muir Beach. The town flanks Hwy 1 for about three blocks and is densely packed with galleries, shops, eateries and B&Bs. The beach itself is often blanketed with fog, and when the sun's shining it's blanketed with surfers, families and gawkers. There are views of Point Reyes and San Francisco on clear days, and the beach is long enough for a vigorous stroll. From San Francisco it's nearly an hour's drive, though on weekends plan for toe-tapping traffic delays.

Three-mile-long **Stinson Beach** is a popular surf spot, but swimming is advised from late May to mid-September only; for updated weather and surf conditions call ☎415-868-1922. The beach is one block west of Hwy 1.

Around 1 mile south of Stinson Beach is **Red Rock Beach**. It's a clothing-optional beach that attracts smaller crowds, probably because it can only be accessed by a steep trail from Hwy 1.

TOP CHOICE **Audubon Canyon Ranch** (☎415-868-9244; www.egret.org; donations requested; ⏲10am-4pm Sat, Sun & holidays mid-Mar–mid-Jul) is about 3.5 miles north of town on Hwy 1, in the hills above the Bolinas Lagoon. A major nesting ground for great blue herons and great egrets, viewing scopes are set up on hillside blinds where you can watch these magnificent birds congregate to nest and hatch their chicks in tall redwoods. At low tide, harbor seals often doze on sand bars in the lagoon.

Just off Hwy 1 and a quick stroll to the beach, the ten comfortable rooms of the **Sandpiper** (☎415-868-1632; www.sandpiperstinsonbeach.com; 1 Marine Wy; r $140-210; 📶) have gas fireplaces and kitchenettes, and are ensconced in a lush garden and picnic area. Prices dip from November through March.

Parkside Cafe (☎415-868-1272; www.parksidecafe.com; 43 Arenal Ave; mains $9-25; ⏲7:30am-9pm Mon-Fri, from 8am Sat & Sun) is famous for its hearty breakfasts and lunches, and noted far and wide for its excellent coastal cuisine. Reservations are recommended for dinner.

West Marin Stagecoach (☎415-526-3239; www.marintransit.org/stage.html) route 61 runs daily minibuses ($2) from Marin City, and weekend and holiday services to the Sausalito ferry; the 62 route runs three days a week from San Rafael.

BOLINAS

For a town that is so famously unexcited about tourism, Bolinas offers some fairly tempting attractions for the visitor. Known as Jugville during the Gold Rush days, the sleepy beachside community is home to writers, musicians and fisherfolk, and deliberately hard to find. The highway department used to put signs up at the turnoff from Hwy 1; locals kept taking them down, so the highway department finally gave up.

Sights & Activities

FREE Bolinas Museum MUSEUM

(☎415-868-0330; www.bolinasmuseum.org; 48 Wharf Rd; ⏰4-7pm Wed, 1-5pm Fri, noon-5pm Sat & Sun) This courtyard complex of five galleries exhibits local artists and showcases the region's history. Look for the weathered Bolinas highway sign affixed to the wall, since you certainly didn't see one on your way into town.

2 Mile Surf Shop SURFING

(☎415-868-0264; 22 Brighton Ave) Surfing's popular in these parts, and this shop behind the post office rents boards and wet suits and also gives lessons. Call ☎415-868-2412 for the surf report.

Agate Beach BEACH

There are tide pools along some 2 miles of coastline at Agate Beach, around the end of Duxbury Point.

PRBO Conservation Science BIRD-WATCHING

(☎415-868-0655; www.prbo.org) Off Mesa Rd west of downtown and formerly known as the Point Reyes Bird Observatory, the Palomarin Field Station of PRBO has bird-banding and netting demonstrations, a visitors center and nature trail. Banding demonstrations are held in the morning every Tuesday to Sunday from May to late November, and on Wednesday, Saturday and Sunday the rest of the year. Check its website for information on monthly bird walks held throughout the region.

HIKING

Beyond the observatory is the Palomarin parking lot and access to various **walking trails** in the southern part of the Point Reyes National Seashore (see p119), including the easy (and popular) 3-mile trail to lovely **Bass Lake**. A sweet inland spot buffered by tall trees, this small lake is perfect for a pastoral swim on a toasty day. You can dive in wearing your birthday suit (or not), bring an inner tube to float about, or do a long lap all the way across.

If you continue 1.5 miles northwest, you'll reach the unmaintained trail to **Alamere Falls**, a fantastic flume plunging 50ft off a cliff and down to the beach. But sketchy beach access makes it more enjoyable to walk another 1.5 miles to **Wildcat Beach** and then backtrack a mile on sand.

Sleeping & Eating

Smiley's Schooner Saloon & Hotel MOTEL $

(☎415-868-1311; www.smileyssaloon.com; 41 Wharf Rd; r $89-109; 📶) A crusty old place dating back to 1851, Smiley's has simple but decent rooms, and last-minute weekday rates can go down to $60. The bar, which serves some food, has live bands Thursday through Saturday and is frequented by plenty of salty dogs and grizzled deadheads.

Coast Café AMERICAN $$

(www.bolinascafe.com; 46 Wharf Rd; mains $10-22; ⏰11:30am-3pm & 5-8pm Tue & Wed, to 9pm Thu & Fri, 8am-3pm & 5-9pm Sat, to 8pm Sun; 🌿👪🐾) The only 'real' restaurant in town, everyone jockeys for outdoor seats among the flowerboxes for fish and chips, barbecued oysters, or buttermilk pancakes with damn good coffee.

Bolinas People's Store MARKET $

(14 Wharf Rd; ⏰8:30am-6:30pm; 🌿) An awesome little co-op grocery store hidden behind the community center, the People's Store serves Fair Trade coffee and sells organic produce, fresh soup and excellent tamales. Eat at the tables in the shady courtyard, and have a rummage through the Free Box, a shed full of clothes and other waiting-to-be-reused items.

Getting There & Away

Route 61 of the **West Marin Stagecoach** (☎415-526-3239; www.marintransit.org/stage.html) goes daily ($2) from the Marin City transit hub (weekend and holiday service from the Sausalito ferry) to downtown Bolinas; the 62 route runs three days a week from San Rafael. By car, follow Hwy 1 north from Stinson Beach and turn west (left) for Bolinas at the first road north of the lagoon. At the first stop sign, take another left onto Olema-Bolinas Rd and follow it 2 miles to town.

WORTH A TRIP

LOCAL AG ROADTRIP

Along the border of Marin and Sonoma County, make a detour for these two local favorites.

At **Marin French Cheese** (www.marinfrenchcheese.com; 7500 Red Hill Rd, Novato; ⌚8:30am-5pm), stop to picnic beside the languid pond of this 150-year-old cheese producer. Sample its soft cheeses, watch the cheesemaking process at one of its four daily tours, and savor the rolling green hills over a baguette with triple crème brie.

Continue north 9 miles on the Petaluma-Point Reyes Rd to Petaluma Blvd and turn left to the stately **Petaluma Seed Bank** (http://rareseeds.com/petaluma-seed-bank; 199 Petaluma Blvd N, Petaluma; ⌚9:30am-5:30pm Sun-Fri, shorter winter hrs). Formerly the Sonoma County National Bank, the soaring windows and carved ceiling of the 1925 building make it a stately place to peruse the 1200 varieties of heirloom seeds.

OLEMA & NICASIO

About 10 miles north of Stinson Beach near the junction of Hwy 1 and Sir Francis Drake Blvd, **Olema** was the main settlement in West Marin in the 1860s. Back then, there was a stagecoach service to San Rafael and there were *six* saloons. In 1875, when the railroad was built through Point Reyes Station instead of Olema, the town's importance began to fade. In 1906 it gained distinction once again as the epicenter of the Great Quake.

The **Bolinas Ridge Trail**, a 12-mile series of ups and downs for hikers or bikers, starts about 1 mile west of Olema, on Sir Francis Drake Blvd. It has great views.

About a 15-minute drive inland from Olema, at the geographic center of Marin County, is **Nicasio**, a tiny town with a low-key rural flavor and a cool saloon and music venue. It's at the west end of Lucas Valley Rd, 10 miles from Hwy 101.

Olema Inn & Restaurant (☎415-663-9559; www.theolemainn.com; cnr Sir Francis Drake Blvd & Hwy 1; r incl breakfast Mon-Thu $174-198, Fri & Sat $198-222; restaurant ⌚9am-9pm; 📶🐾) is a very stylish and peaceful country retreat. Its six rooms retain some of the building's antiquated charm, but are up to modern standards of comfort. The almost-entirely organic **restaurant** (mains $22-30) can set you up with Hog Island oysters, a small plate meal or something from the extensive list of smaller-scale California wineries.

Six miles east of Olema on Sir Francis Drake Blvd, **Samuel P Taylor State Park** (☎415-488-9897; www.reserveamerica.com; tent & RV sites $35; 📶🐾) has beautiful, secluded campsites in redwood groves. It's also located on the **Cross Marin bike path**, with miles of creekside landscape to explore along a former railroad grade. At press time, the future of this state park was uncertain and subject to closure or reduced services.

In the town center, **Rancho Nicasio** (☎415-662-2219; www.ranchonicasio.com; mains $17-23; ⌚11:30am-3pm & 5-9pm Mon-Thu, to 10pm Fri, 11am-3pm & 5-10pm Sat, to 9pm Sun) is the local fun spot. It's a rustic saloon that regularly attracts local and national blues, rock and country performers.

Route 68 of the **West Marin Stagecoach** (☎415-526-3239; www.marintransit.org/stage.html) runs daily to Olema and Samuel P Taylor State Park from the San Rafael Transit Center ($2).

POINT REYES STATION

Though the railroad stopped coming through in 1933 and the town is small, Point Reyes Station is nevertheless the hub of West Marin. Dominated by dairies and ranches, the region was invaded by artists in the 1960s. Today it's an interesting blend of art galleries and tourist shops. The town has a rowdy saloon and the occasional smell of cattle on the afternoon breeze.

Sleeping & Eating

Cute little cottages, cabins and B&Bs are plentiful in and around Point Reyes. The **West Marin Chamber of Commerce** (☎415-663-9232; www.pointreyes.org) has numerous listings, as does the **Point Reyes Lodging Association** (www.ptreyes.com).

Holly Tree Inn INN, COTTAGES **$$**
(☎415-663-1554, 800-286-4655; www.hollytreeinn.com; Silver Hills Rd; r incl breakfast $130-180, cottages $190-265) The Holly Tree Inn, off Bear Valley Rd, has four rooms and three private cottages in a beautiful country setting. The

Sea Star Cottage is a romantic refuge at the end of a small pier on Tomales Bay.

Bovine Bakery BAKERY **$**
(11315 Hwy 1; ⏲6:30am-5pm Mon-Thu, 7am-5pm Sat & Sun) Don't leave town without sampling something buttery from possibly the best bakery in Marin. A bear claw (a large sweet pastry) and an organic coffee are a good way to kick off your morning.

Pine Cone Diner DINER **$$**
(www.pineconediner.com; 60 4th St; mains $9-13; ⏲8am-2:30pm;) The Pine Cone serves big breakfasts and lunches inside a cute retro dining room and at shaded al fresco picnic tables. Try the buttermilk biscuits, the chorizo or tofu scramble, or the fried oyster sandwich.

Osteria Stellina ITALIAN **$$**
(☎415-663-9988; www.osteriastellina.com; 11285 Hwy 1; mains $15-25; ⏲11:30am-2:30pm & 5-9pm;) This place specializes in rustic Italian cuisine, with pizza and pasta dishes and Niman Ranch meats. Head over Tuesday nights for lasagna and live music, and definitely make reservations for the weekend.

Tomales Bay Foods and Cowgirl Creamery MARKET **$$**
(☎415-663-9335; www.cowgirlcreamery.com; 80 4th St; ⏲10am-6pm Wed-Sun;) A local market in an old barn selling picnic items, including gourmet cheeses and organic produce. Reserve a spot in advance for the small-scale artisanal cheesemaker's demonstration and tasting ($5), where you can watch the curd-making and cutting, then sample a half dozen of the fresh and aged cheeses. All of the milk is local and organic, with vegetarian rennet in all its soft cheeses.

☆ Entertainment

The lively community center, **Dance Palace** (☎415-663-1075; www.dancepalace.org; 503 B St), has weekend events, movies and live music. The **Old Western Saloon** (☎415-663-1661; cnr Shoreline Hwy & 2nd St) is a rustic 1906 saloon with live bands and cool tables emblazoned with horseshoes. Prince Charles stopped in here for an impromptu pint during a local visit in 2006.

Getting There & Away

Hwy 1 becomes Main St in town, running right through the center. Route 68 of the **West Marin Stagecoach** (☎415-526-3239; www.marintransit.org/stage.html) runs here daily from the San Rafael Transit Center ($2), and the 62 route goes south to Bolinas and Stinson Beach on Tuesday, Thursday and Saturday.

INVERNESS

This tiny town, the last outpost on your journey westward, is spread along the west side of Tomales Bay. It's got good places to eat and, among the surrounding hills and picturesque shoreline, multiple rental cottages and quaint B&Bs. Several great beaches are only a short drive north.

Blue Waters Kayaking (☎415-669-2600; www.bwkayak.com; kayak rental 2/4hr $50/60), at the Tomales Bay Resort and across the bay in Marshall (on Hwy 1, eight miles north of Point Reyes Station), offers various Tomales Bay tours, or you can rent a kayak and paddle around secluded beaches and rocky crevices on your own; no experience necessary.

Formerly the Golden Hinde Inn, the bayside **Tomales Bay Resort** (☎415-669-1389; www.tomalesbayresort.com; 12938 Sir Francis Drake Blvd; r $120-225;) has 36 recently renovated motel rooms, a pool (unheated) and a restaurant. When rates drop – Sunday through Thursday and in the winter – it's one of the best bargains around.

Inverness Valley Inn (☎415-669-7250, 800-416-0405; www.invernessvalleyinn.com; 13275 Sir Francis Drake Blvd; r $149-219;) is a family-friendly place hidden away in the woods, just a mile from town. It offers clean, modern kitchenette rooms in A-frame structures, and has a tennis court, horseshoe pitches, barbecue pits and in-room DVD players. There's a large garden and a few farm animals on site, and guests receive free eggs from the inn's chickens. It's past the town, on the way down the Pt Reyes Peninsula.

From Hwy 1, Sir Francis Drake Blvd leads straight into Inverness. Route 68 of the **West Marin Stagecoach** (☎415-526-3239; www.marintransit.org/stage.html) makes daily stops here from San Rafael ($2).

POINT REYES NATIONAL SEASHORE

The windswept peninsula Point Reyes is a rough-hewn beauty that has always lured marine mammals and migratory birds as well as scores of shipwrecks. It was here in 1579 that Sir Francis Drake landed to repair his ship, the *Golden Hind*. During his five-week stay he mounted a brass plaque near the shore claiming this land for England. Historians believe this occurred at **Drakes Beach** and there is a marker there today. In

1595 the first of scores of ships lost in these waters, the *San Augustine,* went down. She was a Spanish treasure ship out of Manila laden with luxury goods, and to this day bits of her cargo wash up on shore. Despite modern navigation, the dangerous waters here continue to claim the odd boat.

Point Reyes National Seashore has 110 sq miles of pristine ocean beaches, and the peninsula offers excellent hiking and camping opportunities. Be sure to bring warm clothing, as even the sunniest days can quickly turn cold and foggy.

Sights & Activities

For an awe-inspiring view, follow the **Earthquake Trail** from the park headquarters at Bear Valley. The trail reaches a 16ft gap between the two halves of a once-connected fence line, a lasting testimonial to the power of the 1906 earthquake that was centered in this area. Another trail leads from the visitors center a short way to **Kule Loklo**, a reproduction of a Miwok village.

Limantour Rd, off Bear Valley Rd about 1 mile north of Bear Valley Visitor Center, leads to the Point Reyes Hostel (p120) and **Limantour Beach**, where a trail runs along Limantour Spit with Estero de Limantour on one side and Drakes Bay on the other. The **Inverness Ridge Trail** heads from Limantour Rd up to Mt Vision (1282ft), from where there are spectacular views of the entire national seashore. You can drive almost to the top of Mt Vision from the other side.

About 2 miles past Inverness, Pierce Point Rd splits off to the right from Sir Francis Drake Blvd. From here you can get to two nice swimming beaches on the bay: Marshall Beach requires a mile-long hike from the parking area, while Hearts Desire, in **Tomales Bay State Park** (whose future was uncertain at press time), is accessible by car.

Pierce Point Rd continues to the huge windswept sand dunes at **Abbotts Lagoon**, full of peeping killdeer and other shorebirds. At the end of the road is Pierce Point Ranch, the trailhead for the 3.5-mile **Tomales Point Trail** through the **Tule Elk Reserve**. The plentiful elk are an amazing sight, standing with their big horns against the backdrop of Tomales Point, with Bodega Bay to the north, Tomales Bay to the east and the Pacific Ocean to the west.

Five Brooks Stables HORSEBACK RIDING
(☎415-663-1570; www.fivebrooks.com; trail rides from $40; 👪) Explore the landscape on horseback with a trail ride. Take a slow amble through a pasture or ascend over 1000ft to Inverness Ridge for views of the Olema Valley. If you can stay in the saddle for six hours, ride along the coastline to Alamere Falls (see p117) via Wildcat Beach.

TOP CHOICE **Point Reyes Lighthouse** LIGHTHOUSE
(☎415-669-1534; ⏰10am-4:30pm Thu-Mon) At the very end of Sir Francis Drake Blvd, with wild terrain and ferocious winds, this spot feels like the ends of the earth and offers the best **whale-watching** along the coast. The lighthouse sits below the headlands; to reach it requires descending over 300 stairs. Nearby **Chimney Rock** is a fine short hike, especially in spring when the wildflowers are blossoming. A nearby viewing area allows you to spy on the park's **elephant seal colony**.

Keep back from the water's edge at the exposed North Beach and South Beach, as people have been dragged in and drowned by frequent rogue waves.

Sleeping & Eating

Wake up to deer nibbling under a blanket of fog at one of Point Reyes' four very popular hike-in **campgrounds** (☎415-663-8054; www.nps.gov/pore/planyourvisit/campgrounds.htm; tent sites $15), each with pit toilets, water and tables. Reservations accepted up to three months in advance, and weekends go fast. Reaching the campgrounds requires a 2- to 6-mile hike or bicycle ride, or you can try for a permit to kayak camp on the beach in Tomales Bay.

Point Reyes Hostel HOSTEL $
(☎415-663-8811; www.norcalhostels.org/reyes; dm/r $24/68; @) Just off Limantour Rd, this rustic HI property has bunkhouses with warm and cozy front rooms, big-view windows and outdoor areas with hill vistas, and a brand new LEED-certified building with four more private rooms in the works. It's in a beautiful secluded valley 2 miles from the ocean and surrounded by lovely hiking trails.

Drakes Bay Oyster Company SEAFOOD $$
(☎415-669-1149; www.drakesbayoyster.com; 17171 Sir Francis Drake Blvd, Inverness; 1 dozen oysters to go/on the half shell $15/24; ⏰8:30am-4:30pm) Drakes Bay and nearby Tomales Bay are famous for excellent oysters. Stop by to do some on-the-spot shucking and slurping, or pick some up to grill later.

Information

The park headquarters, **Bear Valley Visitor Center** (☎415-464-5100; Bear Valley Rd; ⌚9am-5pm Mon-Fri, from 8am Sat & Sun), is near Olema and has information and maps. You can also get information at the Point Reyes Lighthouse and the **Ken Patrick Center** (☎415-669-1250; ⌚10am-5pm Sat, Sun & holidays) at Drakes Beach. All visitor centers have slightly longer hours in summer.

Getting There & Away

By car you can get to Point Reyes a few different ways. The curviest is along Hwy 1, through Stinson Beach and Olema. More direct is to exit Hwy 101 in San Rafael and follow Sir Francis Drake Blvd all the way to the tip of Point Reyes. For the latter route, take the Central San Rafael exit and head west on 4th St, which turns into Sir Francis Drake Blvd. By either route, it's about 1½ hours to Olema from San Francisco.

Just north of Olema, where Hwy 1 and Sir Francis Drake Blvd come together, is Bear Valley Rd; turn left to reach the Bear Valley Visitor Center. If you're heading to the further reaches of Point Reyes, follow Sir Francis Drake Blvd through Point Reyes Station and out onto the peninsula (about an hour's drive).

West Marin Stagecoach (☎415-526-3239; www.marintransit.org/stage.html) route 68 makes daily stops at the Bear Valley Visitor Center from San Rafael ($2).

POINT REYES SHUTTLE

On good-weather weekends and holidays from late December through mid-April, the road to Chimney Rock and the lighthouse is closed to private vehicles. Instead you must take a shuttle ($5, children under 17 free) from Drakes Beach.

EAST BAY

Berkeley and Oakland, collectively and affectionately called the 'five and dime,' after their 510 area code, are what most San Franciscans think of as the East Bay, though the area includes numerous other suburbs that swoop up from the bayside flats into exclusive enclaves in the hills. While many residents of the 'West Bay' would like to think they needn't ever cross the Bay Bridge or take a BART train under water, a wealth of museums, universities, excellent restaurants, woodsy parklands and better weather are just some of attractions that lure travelers from San Francisco.

Oakland

Named for the grand oak trees that once lined its streets, Oakland is to San Francisco what Brooklyn is to Manhattan. To some degree a less expensive alternative to the nearby city of hills, it's often where bohemian refugees have fled to escape pricey San Francisco housing costs. An ethnically diverse city, Oakland has a strong African American community and a long labor union history. Urban farmers raise chickens in their backyard or occupy abandoned lots to start community gardens, families find more room to stretch out, and self-satisfied residents thumb their noses at San Francisco's fog while basking in a sunnier Mediterranean climate.

Sights & Activities

Broadway is the backbone of downtown Oakland, running from Jack London Sq at the waterfront all the way north to Piedmont and Rockridge. Telegraph Ave branches off Broadway at 15th St and heads north straight to Berkeley via the Temescal neighborhood (located between 40th St and 51st St). San Pablo Ave also heads north from downtown into Berkeley. Running east from Broadway is Grand Ave, leading to the Lake Merritt commercial district.

Downtown BART stations are on Broadway at both 12th and 19th Sts; other stations are near Lake Merritt, Rockridge and Temescal (MacArthur station).

DOWNTOWN

Oakland's downtown is full of historic buildings and a growing number of colorful local businesses. With such easy access from San Francisco via BART and the ferry, it's worth spending part of a day exploring here – and nearby Chinatown and Jack London Sq – on foot or by bicycle.

The pedestrianized **City Center**, between Broadway and Clay St, 12th and 14th Sts, forms the heart of downtown Oakland. The twin towers of the **Ronald Dellums Federal Building** are on Clay St, just behind it. **City Hall**, at 14th & Clay Sts, is a beautifully refurbished 1914 beaux arts hall.

Continuing north of the City Center, the **Uptown** district contains many of the city's art deco beauties and a proliferating arts

Oakland

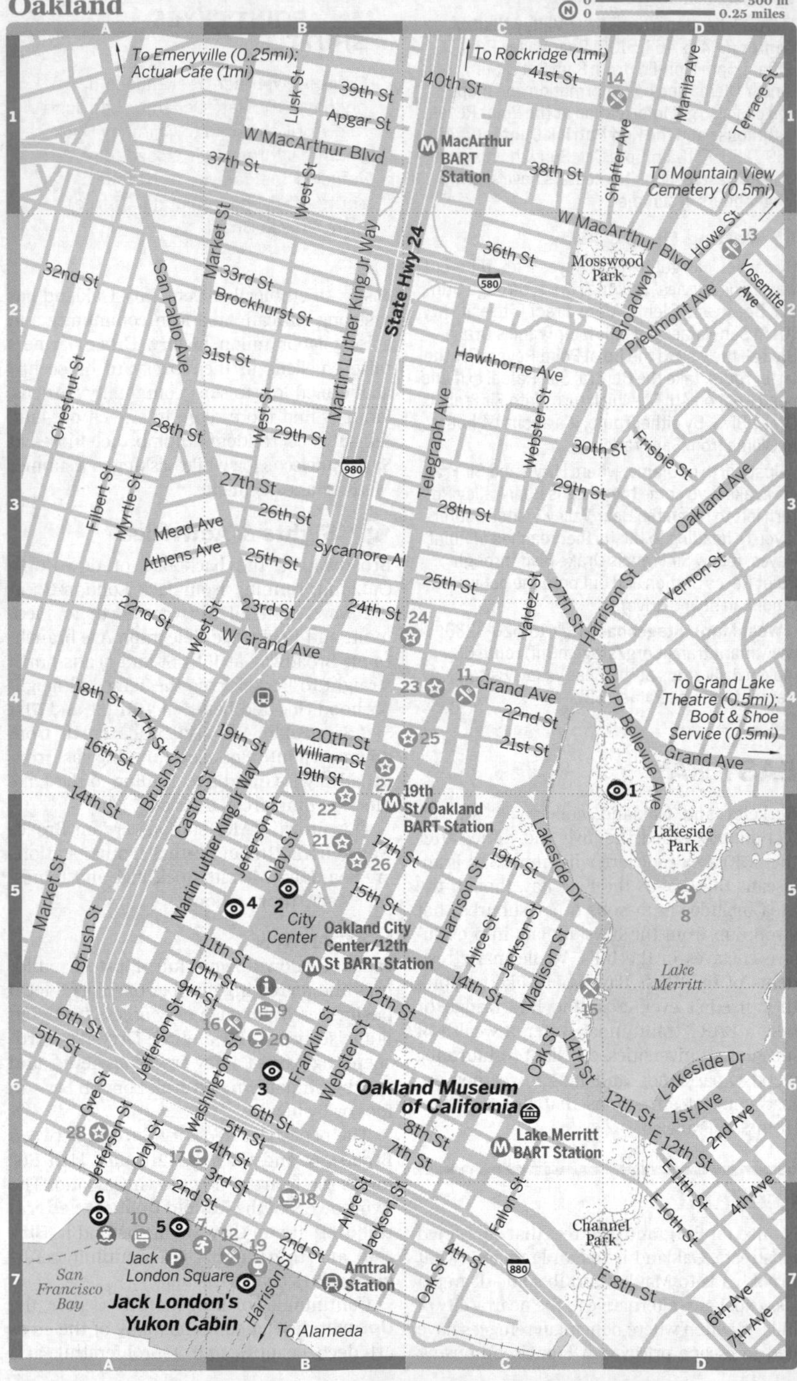

0 500 m
0 0.25 miles
To Emeryville (0.25mi); Actual Cafe (1mi)
To Rockridge (1mi)
To Mountain View Cemetery (0.5mi)
To Grand Lake Theatre (0.5mi); Boot & Shoe Service (0.5mi)
To Alameda
MacArthur BART Station
19th St/Oakland BART Station
Oakland City Center/12th St BART Station
Lake Merritt BART Station
Amtrak Station
Oakland Museum of California
Jack London's Yukon Cabin
Jack London Square
City Center
Mosswood Park
Lakeside Park
Lake Merritt
Channel Park
San Francisco Bay
State Hwy 24
W MacArthur Blvd
Martin Luther King Jr Way
Telegraph Ave
Broadway
Piedmont Ave
San Pablo Ave
Grand Ave
W Grand Ave
Lakeside Dr

and restaurant scene. The area stretches roughly between Telegraph and Broadway, bounded by Grand Ave to the north.

Old Oakland, along Washington St between 8th and 10th Sts, is lined with historic buildings dating from the 1860s to the 1880s. The buildings have been restored and the area has a lively restaurant and after-work scene. The area also hosts a lively **farmers market** every Friday morning.

East of Broadway and bustling with commerce, **Chinatown** centers on Franklin and Webster Sts, as it has since the 1870s. It's much smaller than the San Francisco version.

JACK LONDON SQUARE

The area where writer and adventurer Jack London once raised hell now bears his name, and recent spasms of redevelopment have added a new cinema complex, condo development, excellent restaurants and some eclectic watering holes. The pretty waterfront location is worth a stroll, especially when the Sunday **farmers market** (⏰10am-2pm) takes over, or get off your feet and kayak around the harbor. Catch a ferry from San Francisco – a worthwhile excursion in and of itself – and you'll land just paces away.

Jack London's Yukon Cabin LANDMARK

A replica of Jack London's Yukon cabin stands at the eastern end of the square. It's partially built from the timbers of a cabin London lived in during the Yukon gold rush. Oddly, people throw coins inside as if it's a fountain. Another interesting stop, adjacent to the tiny cabin, is Heinold's First & Last Chance Saloon (see p127).

USS Potomac HISTORIC SHIP

(☎510-627-1215; www.usspotomac.org; admission $10; ⏰11am-3pm Wed, Fri & Sun) Franklin D Roosevelt's 'floating White House,' the 165ft USS Potomac, is moored at Clay and Water Sts by the ferry dock, and is open for dockside tours. Two-hour history cruises (adult/child $45/25) are also held several times a month from May through October.

LAKE MERRITT

An urban respite, Lake Merritt is a popular place to stroll or go running (a 3.5-mile track circles the lake). The two main commercial streets skirting Lake Merritt are Lakeshore Ave on the eastern edge of the lake and Grand Ave, running along the north shore.

TOP CHOICE **Oakland Museum of California** MUSEUM

(☎510-238-2200; www.museumca.org; 1000 Oak St; adult/child 9-17/child under 9 $12/6/free, 1st Sun each month free; ⏰11am-5pm Wed-Sun, to 9pm Fri; 👪) Near the southern end of the lake and one block from the Lake Merritt BART sta-

Oakland

Top Sights
- Jack London's Yukon Cabin B7
- Oakland Museum of California C6

Sights
1. Children's Fairyland D4
2. City Hall B5
3. Friday farmers market B6
4. Ronald Dellums Federal Building B5
5. Sunday farmers market A7
6. USS Potomac A7

Activities, Courses & Tours
7. California Canoe & Kayak A7
8. Lake Merritt Boating Center D5

Sleeping
9. Washington Inn B6
10. Waterfront Hotel A7

Eating
11. Bakesale Betty C4
12. Bocanova B7
13. Commis D2
14. Homeroom D1
15. Lake Chalet C6
- Plum ..... (see 11)
16. Ratto's B6

Drinking
17. Beer Revolution A6
18. Blue Bottle Coffee Company B7
19. Heinold's First & Last Chance Saloon B7
- Punchdown ..... (see 11)
20. Trappist B6

Entertainment
21. Café Van Kleef B5
22. Fox Theater B5
23. Luka's Taproom & Lounge C4
24. Mama Buzz Café C4
25. Paramount Theatre C4
26. Rock Paper Scissors Collective B5
27. Uptown B4
28. Yoshi's A6

tion, this museum has rotating exhibitions on artistic and scientific themes, and excellent permanent galleries dedicated to the state's diverse ecology and history, as well as California art.

Children's Fairyland AMUSEMENT PARK
(☎510-238-6876; www.fairyland.org; admission $8; ⏱10am-4pm Mon-Fri, to 5pm Sat & Sun summer, 10am-4pm Wed-Sun spring & fall, Fri-Sun winter; 👪) Lakeside Park, at the northern end of the saltwater lake, includes this 10-acre attraction, which dates from 1950 and has charming fairy-tale-themed train, carousel and mini Ferris-wheel rides.

Lake Merritt Boating Center BOAT HIRE
(☎510-238-2196; ⏱Sat & Sun Nov-Feb, daily Mar-Oct; 👪) Rents canoes, rowboats, kayaks, pedal boats and sailboats for $10 to $18 per hour.

PIEDMONT AVE & ROCKRIDGE

North of downtown Oakland, Broadway becomes a lengthy strip of car dealerships called Broadway Auto Row. Just past that is **Piedmont Ave**, wall-to-wall with antique stores, coffeehouses, fine restaurants and an art cinema.

One of Oakland's most popular shopping areas is **Rockridge**, a lively, upscale neighborhood. It is centered on College Ave, which runs from Broadway all the way to the UC Berkeley Campus. College Ave is lined with clothing boutiques, good bookstores, a vintage record shop, several pubs and cafes, and quite a few upscale restaurants – maybe the largest concentration in the Bay Area. BART at the Rockridge station puts you in the thick of things.

Mountain View Cemetery CEMETERY
(www.mountainviewcemetery.org; 5000 Piedmont Ave) At the end of Piedmont Ave; perhaps the most serene and lovely artificial landscape in all the East Bay. Designed by Frederic Law Olmstead, the architect of New York City's Central Park, it's great for walking and the views are stupendous.

OAKLAND HILLS

The large parks of the Oakland Hills are ideal for day hiking and challenging cycling, and the **East Bay Regional Parks District** (www.ebparks.org) manages over 1200 miles of trails in 65 regional parks, preserves and recreation areas in the Alameda and Contra Costa counties.

Off Hwy 24, **Robert Sibley Volcanic Regional Preserve** is the northernmost of the Oakland Hills parks. It has great views of the Bay Area from its Round Top Peak (1761ft). From Sibley, Skyline Blvd runs south past **Redwood Regional Park** and adjacent **Joaquin Miller Park** to **Anthony Chabot Regional Park**. A hike or mountain-bike ride through the groves and along the hilltops of any of these sizable parks will make you forget you're in an urban area. At the southern end of Chabot Park is the enormous **Lake Chabot**, with an easy trail along its shore and canoes, kayaks and other boats for rent from the **Lake Chabot marina** (☎510-247-2526; www.norcalfishing.com/chabot).

Chabot Space & Science Center SCIENCE CENTER
(☎510-336-7300; www.chabotspace.org; 10000 Skyline Blvd, Oakland; adult/child $15/11; ⏱10am-5pm Wed & Thu, to 10pm Fri & Sat, 11am-5pm Sun, plus 10am-5pm Tue summer; 👪) Stargazers will go gaga over this science and technology center in the Oakland Hills with loads of exhibits on subjects such as space travel and eclipses, as well as cool planetarium shows. When the weather's good, check out the free Friday and Saturday evening viewings using a 20in refractor telescope.

Sleeping

If you like B&Bs, the **Berkeley and Oakland Bed & Breakfast Network** (www.bbonline.com/ca/berkeley-oakland) lists private homes that rent rooms, suites and cottages; prices start from $100 per night and many have a two-night-minimum stay. Reservations recommended.

Claremont Resort and Spa RESORT $$$
(☎510-843-3000, 800-551-7266; www.claremontresort.com; 41 Tunnel Rd; r $189-309; ❄🏊@📶) Oakland's classy crème de la crème, the Claremont is a glamorous white 1915 building with elegant restaurants, a fitness center, swimming pools, tennis courts and a full-service spa (room/spa packages are available). The bay view rooms are superb. It's located at the foot of the Oakland Hills, off Hwy 13 (Tunnel Rd) near Claremont Ave.

Waterfront Hotel BOUTIQUE HOTEL $$
(☎510-836-3800; www.waterfronthoteloakland.com; 10 Washington; r $149-269; ❄🏊@📶🐾) Paddle-printed wallpaper and lamps fashioned from faux lanterns round out the playful nautical theme of this bright and cheerful hotel at

harbor's edge. A huge brass-topped fireplace warms the foyer, and comfy rooms include MP3-player docking stations and coffeemakers, plus microwaves and fridges upon request. Unless you're an avid trainspotter, water-view rooms are preferred, as freight trains rattle by on the city side.

Washington Inn HISTORIC HOTEL $$
(510-452-1776; www.thewashingtoninn.com; 495 10th St; r incl breakfast $89-149;) Small and modern with a boutique feel, this historic downtown lodging offers updated comfort and character, with a lobby and guest rooms that project snazz and efficient sophistication. The carved lobby bar is perfect for a predinner cocktail, and you're spoiled for choice with several fine restaurants within a few block radius.

Anthony Chabot Regional Park CAMPGROUND $
(510-639-4751; www.ebparks.org/parks/anthony_chabot; tent sites $22, RV sites with hookups $22-28;) This 5000-acre park has 75 campsites open year-round and hot showers. Reservations ($8 service charge) at 888-327-2757 or www.reserveamerica.com.

Eating

Oakland has seen a restaurant renaissance, with scores of fun and sophisticated new eateries opening up all over town.

DOWNTOWN & JACK LONDON SQUARE

TOP CHOICE **Bakesale Betty** BAKERY $
(www.bakesalebetty.com; 2228 Broadway; pastries from $2, sandwiches $6.50-9; 11am-2pm Tue-Fri;) An Aussie expat and Chez Panisse alum, Betty Barakat (in signature blue wig) has patrons licking their lips and lining up out the door for her heavenly scones, strawberry shortcake and scrumptious fried chicken sandwiches. Rolling pins dangle from the ceiling, and blissed-out locals sit down at ironing-board sidewalk tables to savor buttery baked goods and seasonal specialties like sticky date pudding. Free cookie if there's a line!

Bocanova LATIN AMERICAN $$
(510-444-1233; www.bocanova.com; 55 Webster St; mains $12-28; 11:30am-10pm Mon-Thu, 11am-11pm Fri & Sat, to 10pm Sun) A new addition to Jack London Square, you can people-watch from the outdoor patio or eat in a chic industrial dining room lit by hanging glass lamps. The focus here is Pan-American cuisine, and standouts include the Dungeness crab deviled eggs, scallops in Brazilian curry sauce, and the sweet potato and chipotle gratin. Reservations recommended on Wednesday – when wine bottles are half-price – and weekends.

Ratto's DELI $
(www.rattos.com; 821 Washington St; sandwiches from $6; 9am-5:30pm Mon-Fri, 10am-3pm Sat;) If you want to eat outside on a sunny day, grab a sandwich from Ratto's, a vintage Oakland grocery (since 1897) with a deli counter that attracts a devoted lunch crowd.

Plum ORGANIC $$
(510-444-7586; www.plumoakland.com; 2214 Broadway; dishes $10-22; 11:30am-2pm & 5:30pm-1am Mon-Fri, 10am-2pm & 5pm-1am Sat & Sun;) Foodies and design fans pack the communal tables at this minimalist gallery-like space with bruise-black walls and sustainable entrees.

LAKE MERRITT

Lake Chalet SEAFOOD $$
(510-208-5253; www.thelakechalet.com; 1520 Lakeside Dr; mains $13-28; 11am-10pm Mon-Thu, to 11pm Fri, 10am-11pm Sat, to 10pm Sun) Whether you stop by the long pump house view bar for a martini and oysters during the buzzing happy hour (3pm to 6pm and 9pm to close), feast on a whole roasted crab by a window seat in the formal dining room, or cruise Lake Merritt on a Venetian-style **gondola** (www.gondolaservizio.com; per couple from $40), this 100-year-old former park office and boathouse is an enjoyable destination restaurant. Weekend reservations recommended.

Boot & Shoe Service PIZZERIA $$
(510-763-2668; www.bootandshoeservice.com; 3308 Grand Ave; pizza from $10; 5:30-10pm Tue-Thu, 5-10:30pm Fri & Sat, to 10pm Sun) The occasional old-timer comes in looking for the long-gone cobbler shop, but the current patrons pack this place for its wood-fired pizzas, original cocktails and creative antipasti made from sustainably sourced fresh ingredients. Seating is mostly at shared tables, under the watch of anthropomorphic footwear paintings.

Arizmendi BAKERY $
(http://lakeshore.arizmendi.coop; 3265 Lakeshore Ave; pizza slices $2.50; 7am-7pm Tue-Sat, to 6pm Sun, to 3pm Mon;) Great for breakfast or

lunch but beware – this bakery co-op is not for the weak-willed. The gourmet vegetarian pizza, yummy fresh breads and amazing scones are mouthwateringly addictive.

PIEDMONT AVE & ROCKRIDGE

Wood Tavern — AMERICAN $$$

(510-654-6607; www.woodtavern.net; 6317 College Ave; lunch mains $10-19, dinner mains $19-32; 11:30am-10pm Mon-Thu, to 10:30pm Fri & Sat, 5-9pm Sun) With a knock-out cheese board and charcuterie – the restaurant cures meats and makes its own salami – and a constantly changing menu of local and organic California cuisine featuring fish, pork and beef dishes with French and Italian influences, Wood Tavern has established itself as the local favorite for upscale food in a comfortable environment. The formal wood bar serves absinthe drinks and other elegant cocktails and the high-ceiling dining room is cozy enough that weekend dinner reservations are recommended.

À Côté — MEDITERRANEAN $$

(510-655-6469; www.acoterestaurant.com; 5478 College Ave; dishes $8-18; 5:30-10pm Sun-Tue, to 11pm Wed & Thu, to midnight Fri & Sat) This small plates eatery with individual and friendly communal tables is one of the best restaurants along College Ave. What the menu calls 'flatbread' is actually pizza for the gods. Mussels with Pernod is a signature dish.

Commis — CALIFORNIAN $$$

(510-653-3902; www.commisrestaurant.com; 3859 Piedmont Ave; 5-course dinner $68; from 5:30pm Wed-Sat, from 5pm Sun;) The only Michelin-starred restaurant in the East Bay, the signless and discreet dining room counts a minimalist decor and some coveted counter real estate (reservable by phone only) where patrons can watch chef James Syhabout and his team piece together creative and innovative dishes. Reservations highly recommended.

TEMESCAL & EMERYVILLE

Emeryville is a separate bite-sized city, wedged between Oakland and south Berkeley on I-80.

Homeroom — AMERICAN $

(510-597-0400; www.homeroom510.com; 400 40th St; mains $7.50-10; 11am-2pm Tue-Sat, plus 5-9pm Sun-Thu & 5-10pm Fri & Sat;) Follow the instructions to fold your menu into a paper airplane at this quirky mac-n-cheese restaurant modeled after a school. A handy chalkboard caricature of California pinpoints the source of its regionally focused food, and the cheese choices – including cheddar, chêvre, vegan and firehouse jack – are more gourmet than anything Mom packed for your lunchbox.

Emeryville Public Market — INTERNATIONAL $

(www.emerymarket.com; 5959 Shellmound St, Emeryville; mains under $10; 7am-9pm Mon-Thu, from 9am Fri & Sat, 9am-8pm Sun) To satisfy a group of finicky eaters, cross the Amtrak tracks to the indoor and choose from dozens of ethnic food stalls dishing out a huge range of international cuisines.

Drinking

TOP CHOICE Beer Revolution — BEER HALL

(www.beer-revolution.com; 464 3rd St) Go ahead and drool. With almost 50 beers on tap, and over 500 in the bottle, there's a lifetime of discovery ahead, so kick back on the sunny deck or park yourself at that barrel table embedded with bottle caps. Bonuses include no distracting TVs and a punk soundtrack played at conversation-friendly levels. Check the website for special events like the Wednesday night meet-the-brewer sessions and Sunday barbecues.

Actual Café — CAFE

(www.actualcafe.com; 6334 San Pablo Ave; mains $4-7; 7am-8pm Mon-Thu, to 10pm Fri, 8am-10pm Sat, to 8pm Sun;) Known for its wi-fi-free weekends and inside bicycle parking, the Actual promotes sustainability and face-to-face community while keeping folks well fed with its housemade baked goods and sandwiches. Weekly movies (with free popcorn!) and live music promote mingling at its long wooden tables.

Blue Bottle Coffee Company — CAFE

(www.bluebottlecoffee.net; 300 Webster St; pastries $2-3; 7am-5pm Mon-Fri, from 8am Sat & Sun) The java gourmands queue up here for single-origin espressos and what some consider the best coffee in the country. The all-organic and very origin-specific beans are roasted on site, with compostable cups if you're taking your drink to go.

Trappist — PUB

(www.thetrappist.com; 460 8th St) So popular that it busted out of its original brick-and-wood-paneled shoebox and expanded into a second storefront and back terrace, the specialty here is Belgian ales. More than two dozen drafts rotate through the taps – with serving sizes varying based on alcohol content and special glasses for each brew – and tasty stews and sandwiches ($8 to $14) make it easy to linger.

Punchdown WINE BAR
(www.punchdownwine.com; 2212 Broadway; ⏲4-9pm Tue-Thu, to 10pm Fri, 5-1pm Sat) A super-new 'natural' wine bar, Punchdown seeks out organic, sustainably created and biodynamic producers. Playful flights include an 'adventurous orange' – whites with extended grape skin contact – and a blind flight that's free if you guess the three selections. There's an attractive outdoor area plus charcuterie and cheese board options.

Heinold's First & Last Chance Saloon BAR
(48 Webster St) An 1883 bar constructed from wood scavenged from an old whaling ship, you really have to hold on to your beer here. Keeled to a severe slant during the 1906 earthquake, the building's 20% grade might make you feel self-conscious about stumbling before you even order. Its big claim to fame is that author Jack London was a regular patron.

☆ Entertainment

Art

On the first Friday evening of the month, gallery-hop through downtown and Temescal as part of the **Oakland Art Murmur** (www.oaklandartmurmur.com; ⏲6-10pm). One fun place to check out is the crafty DIY art space of the **Rock Paper Scissors Collective** (www.rpscollective.com; 2278 Telegraph Ave).

Music

TOP CHOICE **Café Van Kleef** LIVE MUSIC, BAR
(www.cafevankleef.com; 1621 Telegraph Ave) Order a greyhound (with fresh-squeezed grapefruit juice) and take a gander at the profusion of antique musical instruments, fake taxidermy heads, sprawling formal chandeliers and bizarro ephemera clinging to every surface possible here. Quirky, kitschy and evocative even *before* you get lit, the decade-old Café Van Kleef features live blues, jazz and the occasional rock band from Thursday through Saturday ($5 cover).

Uptown LIVE MUSIC
(www.uptownnightclub.com; 1928 Telegraph Ave) For an eclectic calendar of indie, punk and experimental sounds, a weekly burlesque show and fun DJ dance parties, this club hits the spot. Come for a good mix of national acts and local talent, and the easy two-block walk to BART.

Yoshi's JAZZ
(☎510-238-9200; www.yoshis.com/oakland; 510 Embarcadero W; shows $12-40) Yoshi's has a solid jazz calendar, with talent from around the world passing through on a near-nightly basis. Often, touring artists will stop in for a stand of two or three nights. It's also a Japanese restaurant, so you might enjoy a sushi plate before the show.

Mama Buzz Café LIVE MUSIC
(www.mamabuzzcafe.com; 2318 Telegraph Ave; 📶🖉) This low-key hipster cafe and alternative arts space has an eclectic roster of free music shows most nights. It serves simple vegetarian fare as well as beer.

Luka's Taproom & Lounge DJ
(www.lukasoakland.com; 2221 Broadway) Go Uptown to get down. DJs spin nightly at this popular restaurant and lounge, with a soulful mix of hip-hop, reggae, funk and house. There's generally a $10 cover on Fridays and Saturdays after 11pm.

Theaters & Cinemas

The 2009 reopening of the Fox Theater has contributed to a groundswell of new restaurants and evening activity in the Uptown district.

Fox Theater THEATER
(www.thefoxoakland.com; 1807 Telegraph Ave) A phoenix arisen from the urban ashes, this 1928 art deco stunner was recently restored, adding dazzle to downtown and a corner-

PINBALL WIZARDS, UNITE!

Put down that video game console, cast aside your latest phone app, and return to the bygone days of pinball play. Lose yourself in bells and flashing lights at **Pacific Pinball Museum** (☎510-769-1349; www.pacificpinball.org; 1510 Webster St, Alameda; adult/child $15/7.50; ⏲2-9pm Tue-Thu, to midnight Fri, 11am-midnight Sat, to 9pm Sun; 👪), a pinball parlor with almost 100 games dating from the 1930s to the present, and vintage jukeboxes playing hits from the past. Take AC Transit bus 51A from downtown Oakland.

stone to the happening Uptown theater district. It's now a popular concert venue.

Paramount Theatre THEATER
(☎510-465-6400; www.paramounttheatre.com; 2025 Broadway) This massive 1931 art deco masterpiece shows classic films a few times each month and is also home to the Oakland East Bay Symphony (www.oebs.org) and Oakland Ballet (www.oaklandballet.org). It periodically books big-name concerts. Tours ($5) are given at 10am on the first and third Saturdays of the month.

Grand Lake Theatre CINEMA
(☎510-452-3556; www.renaissancerialto.com; 3200 Grand Ave) In Lake Merritt, this 1926 beauty lures you in with its huge corner marquee (which sometimes displays left-leaning political messages) and keeps you coming with a fun balcony and a Wurlitzer organ playing the pipes on weekends.

Sports

Sports teams play at **Overstock.com Coliseum** or the **Oracle Arena** off I-880 (Coliseum/Oakland Airport BART station). Cheer on the **Golden State Warriors**, the Bay Area's NBA basketball team, the **Oakland A's**, the Bay Area's American League baseball team, and the **Raiders**, Oakland's NFL team.

Information

Oakland's daily newspaper is the *Oakland Tribune*. The free weekly *East Bay Express* (www.eastbayexpress.com) has good Oakland and Berkeley listings.

Oakland Convention & Visitors Bureau (☎510-839-9000; www.visitoakland.org; 463 11th St; ⌚9am-5pm Mon-Fri) Between Broadway and Clay St.

Getting There & Away

Air

Oakland International Airport (www.flyoakland.com) is directly across the bay from San Francisco International Airport, and it's usually less crowded and less expensive to fly here. Southwest Airlines has a large presence.

BART

Within the Bay Area, the most convenient way to get to Oakland and back is by **BART** (☎510-465-2278, 511; www.bart.gov). Trains run on a set schedule from 4am to midnight on weekdays, 6am to midnight on Saturday and 8am to midnight on Sunday, and operate at 15- or 20-minute intervals on average.

To get to downtown Oakland, catch a Richmond or Pittsburg/Bay Point train. Fares to the 12th or 19th St stations from downtown San Francisco are $3.10. From San Francisco to Lake Merritt ($3.10) or the Oakland Coliseum/Airport station ($3.80), catch a BART train that is heading for Fremont or Dublin/Pleasanton. Rockridge ($3.50) is on the Pittsburg/Bay Point line. Between Oakland and downtown Berkeley you can catch a Fremont-Richmond train ($1.75).

For AC Transit connections, take a transfer from the white AC Transit machines in the BART station to save 25¢ off the bus fare.

Bus

Regional company **AC Transit** (☎510-817-1717, 511; www.actransit.org) runs convenient buses from San Francisco's Transbay Temporary Terminal at Howard and Main Streets to downtown Oakland and Berkeley, and between the two East Bay cities. Scores of buses go to Oakland from San Francisco during commute hours ($4.20), but only the 'O' line runs both ways all day and on weekends; you can catch the 'O' line at the corner of 5th and Washington Sts in downtown Oakland.

After BART trains stop, late-night transportation between San Francisco and Oakland is with the 800 line, which runs hourly from downtown Market St and the Transbay Temporary Terminal in San Francisco to the corner of 14th St and Broadway.

Between Berkeley and downtown Oakland ($2.10) on weekdays, take the fast and frequent 1R bus along Telegraph Ave between the two city centers. Alternatively, take bus 18 that runs via Martin Luther King Jr Way daily.

Greyhound (☎510-832-4730; www.greyhound.com; 2103 San Pablo Ave) operates direct buses from Oakland to Vallejo, San Jose, Santa Rosa and Sacramento. The station is pretty seedy.

Car & Motorcycle

From San Francisco by car, cross the Bay Bridge and enter Oakland via one of two ways: I-580, which leads to I-980 and drops you near the City Center; or I-880, which curves through West Oakland and lets you off near the south end of Broadway. I-880 then continues to the Coliseum, the Oakland International Airport and, eventually, San Jose.

Driving to San Francisco, the bridge toll is $4 to $6, depending on the time and day of the week.

Ferry

With splendid bay views, ferries are the most enjoyable way of traveling between San Francisco and Oakland, though also the slowest and most expensive. From San Francisco's Ferry Building, the **Alameda–Oakland ferry** (☎510-522-3300; www.eastbayferry.com) sails to Jack London Sq (one-way $6.25, 30 minutes, about 12 times a day on weekdays and six to nine times a day on weekends). Ferry tickets include a free transfer, which you can use on AC Transit buses from Jack London Sq.

Train

Oakland is a regular stop for Amtrak trains operating up and down the coast. From Oakland's **Amtrak station** (☎800-872-7245; www.amtrak.com; 245 2nd St) in Jack London Sq, you can catch AC Transit bus 72 to downtown Oakland (and on weekdays the free Broadway Shuttle), or take a ferry across the bay to San Francisco.

Amtrak passengers with reservations on to San Francisco need to disembark at the **Emeryville Amtrak station** (5885 Horton St), one stop away from Oakland. From there, an Amtrak bus shuttles you to San Francisco's Ferry Building stop. The free **Emery Go Round** (www.emerygoround.com) shuttle runs a circuit that includes the Emeryville Amtrak station and MacArthur BART.

Getting Around

To/From the Airport

BART is the cheapest and easiest transportation option. AirBART buses connect between the airport and the Coliseum/Oakland Airport BART station every 10 minutes until midnight. Tickets cost $3 with exact change or a BART ticket of that value.

SuperShuttle (☎800-258-3826; www.supershuttle.com) is one of many door-to-door shuttle services operating out of Oakland International Airport. One-way service to San Francisco destinations costs about $27 for the first person and $10 for the second. East Bay service destinations are also served. Reserve ahead.

A taxi from Oakland International Airport to downtown Oakland costs about $30; to downtown San Francisco about $60.

Bus

AC Transit (☎510-817-1717, 511; www.actransit.org) has a comprehensive bus network within Oakland. Fares are $2.10 and exact change is required.

On weekdays, the free new **Broadway Shuttle** (www.meetdowntownoak.com/shuttle.php; ⏲7am-7pm Mon-Fri) runs down Broadway between Jack London Square and Lake Merritt, stopping at Old Oakland/Chinatown, the downtown BART stations and the Uptown district. The lime-green buses arrive every 10 to 15 minutes.

Berkeley

As the birthplace of the Free Speech and disability rights movements, and the home of the hallowed halls of the University of California, Berkeley is no bashful wallflower. A national hotspot of (mostly left-of-center) intellectual discourse and one of the most vocal activist populations in the country, this infamous college town has an interesting mix of graying progressives and idealistic undergrads. It's easy to stereotype 'Beserkeley' for some of its recycle-or-else PC crankiness, but the city is often on the forefront of environmental and political issues that eventually go mainstream.

WATERSPORTS ON THE BAY

The San Francisco Bay makes a lovely postcard or snapshot, and there are myriad outfits to help you play in it.

California Canoe & Kayak (☎510-893-7833; www.calkayak.com; 409 Water St; rental per hr s/d kayak $15/25, canoe $25, stand-up paddleboard $15) Rents kayaks, canoes and stand-up paddleboards at Oakland's Jack London Square.

Cal Adventures (☎510-642-4000; www.recsports.berkeley.edu; 124 University Ave; 👪) Run by the UC Berkeley Aquatic Center and located at the Berkeley Marina, Cal offers sailing, surfing and sea kayaking classes and rentals for adults and youth.

Cal Sailing Club (www.cal-sailing.org) An affordable membership-based and volunteer-run nonprofit with sailing and windsurfing programs. Also based at the Berkeley Marina.

Boardsports School & Shop (http://boardsportsschool.com) Offers lessons and rentals for kiteboarding, windsurfing and stand-up paddleboarding from its three locations in San Francisco, Alameda (East Bay) and Coyote Point (p140).

Sea Trek (p105) Has kayaking and stand-up paddleboards, and a fabulous full moon paddle tour. Located in Sausalito.

Berkeley is also home to a large South Asian community, as evidenced by an abundance of sari shops on University Ave and a large number of excellent Indian restaurants.

Sights & Activities

Approximately 13 miles east of San Francisco, Berkeley is bordered by the bay to the west, the hills to the east and Oakland to the south. I-80 runs along the town's western edge, next to the marina; from here University Ave heads east to downtown and the campus.

Shattuck Ave crosses University Ave one block west of campus, forming the main crossroads of the downtown area. Immediately to the south is the downtown shopping strip and the downtown Berkeley BART station.

UNIVERSITY OF CALIFORNIA, BERKELEY

The Berkeley campus of the University of California (UCB, called 'Cal' by both students and locals) is the oldest university in the state. The decision to found the college was made in 1866, and the first students arrived in 1873. Today UCB has over 35,000 students, more than 1500 professors and more Nobel laureates than you could point a particle accelerator at.

From Telegraph Ave, enter the campus via Sproul Plaza and Sather Gate, a center for people-watching, soapbox oration and pseudotribal drumming. Or you can enter from Center St and Oxford Lane, near the downtown BART station.

UC Berkeley Art Museum MUSEUM

(☎510-642-0808; www.bampfa.berkeley.edu; 2626 Bancroft Way; adult/student $10/7, 1st Thu each month free; ⏰11am-5pm Wed-Sun) The museum has 11 galleries showcasing a huge range of works, from ancient Chinese to cutting-edge contemporary. The complex also houses a bookstore, cafe and sculpture garden. The museum and the much-loved Pacific Film Archive (see p136) are scheduled to move to a new home on Oxford St between Addison and Center Streets by 2014.

Campanile TOWER

(elevator rides $2; ⏰10am-4pm Mon-Fri, to 5pm Sat, to 1:30pm & 3-5pm Sun) Officially called Sather Tower, the Campanile was modeled on St Mark's Basilica in Venice. The 328ft spire offers fine views of the Bay Area, and at the top you can stare up into the carillon of 61 bells, ranging from the size of a cereal bowl to that of a Volkswagen. Recitals take place daily at 7:50am, noon and 6pm, with a longer piece performed at 2pm on Sunday.

FREE **Museum of Paleontology** MUSEUM

(☎510-642-1821; www.ucmp.berkeley.edu; ⏰8am-10pm Mon-Thu, to 5pm Fri, 10am-5pm Sat, 1-10pm Sun) Housed in the ornate Valley Life Sciences Building (and primarily a research facility that's closed to the public), you can see a number of fossil exhibits in the atrium, including a *Tyrannosaurus rex* skeleton.

Bancroft Library LIBRARY

(☎510-642-3781; http://bancroft.berkeley.edu; ⏰10am-5pm Mon-Fri) The Bancroft houses, among other gems, the papers of Mark Twain, a copy of Shakespeare's First Folio and the records of the Donner Party. Its small public exhibits of historical Californiana include the surprisingly small gold nugget that sparked the 1849 Gold Rush. You must register to use the library and, to do so, you need to be 18 years of age (or to have graduated from high school) and present two forms of identification (one with a photo). Stop by the registration desk on your way in.

FREE **Phoebe Hearst Museum of Anthropology** MUSEUM

(☎510-643-7649; http://hearstmuseum.berkeley.edu; ⏰10am-4:30pm Wed-Sat, noon-4pm Sun) South of the Campanile in Kroeber Hall, this museum includes exhibits from indigenous cultures around the world, including ancient Peruvian, Egyptian and African items. There's also a large collection highlighting native Californian cultures.

SOUTH OF CAMPUS

Telegraph Ave STREET

Telegraph Ave has traditionally been the throbbing heart of studentville in Berkeley, the sidewalks crowded with undergrads, postdocs and youthful shoppers squeezing their way past throngs of vendors, buskers and homeless people. Numerous cafes and budget food options cater to students, and most of them are very good.

The frenetic energy buzzing from the university's Sather Gate on any given day is a mixture of youthful posthippies reminiscing about days before their time and young hipsters and punk rockers who sneer at tie-dyed nostalgia. Panhandlers press you for change, and street stalls hawk everything from crystals to bumper stickers to self-published tracts.

People's Park PARK

This park, just east of Telegraph, between Haste St and Dwight Way, is a marker in local history as a political battleground between residents and the city and state government in the late 1960s. The park has since served mostly as a gathering spot for Berkeley's homeless. A publicly funded restoration spruced it up a bit, and occasional festivals do still happen here, but it's rather run-down.

Elmwood District DISTRICT

South along College Ave is the Elmwood District, a charming nook of shops and restaurants that offers a calming alternative to the frenetic buzz around Telegraph Ave. Continue further south and you'll be in Rockridge.

First Church of Christ Scientist CHURCH

(www.friendsoffirstchurch.org; 2619 Dwight Way; ⏲services Sun) Bernard Maybeck's impressive 1910 church uses concrete and wood in its blend of Arts and Crafts, Asian and Gothic influences. Maybeck was a professor of architecture at UC Berkeley and designed San Francisco's Palace of Fine Arts, plus many landmark homes in the Berkeley Hills. Free tours happen the first Sunday of every month at 12:15pm.

Julia Morgan Theatre THEATER

(☎510-845-8542; 2640 College Ave) To the southeast of People's Park is this beautifully understated, redwood-infused 1910 theater, a performance space (formerly a church) created by Bay Area architect Julia Morgan. She designed numerous Bay Area buildings and, most famously, the Hearst Castle (see p299).

DOWNTOWN

Berkeley's downtown, centered on Shattuck Ave between University Ave and Dwight Way, has far fewer traces of the city's tie-dyed reputation. The area has emerged as an exciting arts district with numerous shops and restaurants and restored public buildings. At the center are the acclaimed thespian stomping grounds of the Berkeley Repertory Theatre (see p136) and the Aurora Theatre Company (see p137) and live music at the Freight & Salvage Coffeehouse (see p136); a few good movie houses are also nearby.

NORTH BERKELEY

Not too far north of campus is a neighborhood filled with lovely garden-front homes, parks and some of the best restaurants in California. The popular **Gourmet Ghetto** stretches along Shattuck Ave north of University Ave for several blocks, anchored by Chez Panisse (see p135). Northwest of here, **Solano Ave**, which crosses from Berkeley into Albany, is lined with lots of funky shops and more good restaurants.

On Euclid Ave just south of Eunice St is the **Berkeley Rose Garden** and its eight terraces of colourful explosions. Here you'll find quiet benches and a plethora of almost perpetually blooming roses arranged by hue. Across the street is a picturesque park with a children's playground (including a very fun concrete slide, about 100ft long).

THE BERKELEY HILLS

Tilden Regional Park PARK

(www.ebparks.org/parks/tilden) This 2079-acre park, in the hills east of town, is Berkeley's crown jewel. It has more than 30 miles of trails of varying difficulty, from paved paths to hilly scrambles, including part of the magnificent Bay Area Ridge Trail. Other attractions include a miniature steam train ($2), a children's farm, a wonderfully wild-looking botanical garden, an 18-hole **golf course** (☎510-848-7373) and environmental education center. **Lake Anza** is a favorite area for picnics, and from spring through late fall you can swim here for $3.50. AC Transit bus 67 runs to the park on weekends and holidays from the downtown BART station, but only stops at the entrances on weekdays.

UC Botanical Garden GARDENS

(☎510-643-2755; http://botanicalgarden.berkeley.edu; 200 Centennial Dr; adult/child 13-17/child 5-12 $9/5/2, 1st Thu of month free; ⏲9am-5pm, closed 1st Tue of month) This is another great find in the hills, in Strawberry Canyon. With 34 acres and more than 12,000 species of plants, the garden is one of the most varied collections in the USA. It can be reached via the Bear Transit shuttle H line.

The nearby fire trail is a woodsy walking loop around Strawberry Canyon that has great views of town and the off-limits Lawrence Berkeley National Laboratory. Enter at the trailhead at the parking lot on Centennial Dr just southwest of the Botanical Garden; you'll emerge near the Lawrence Hall of Science.

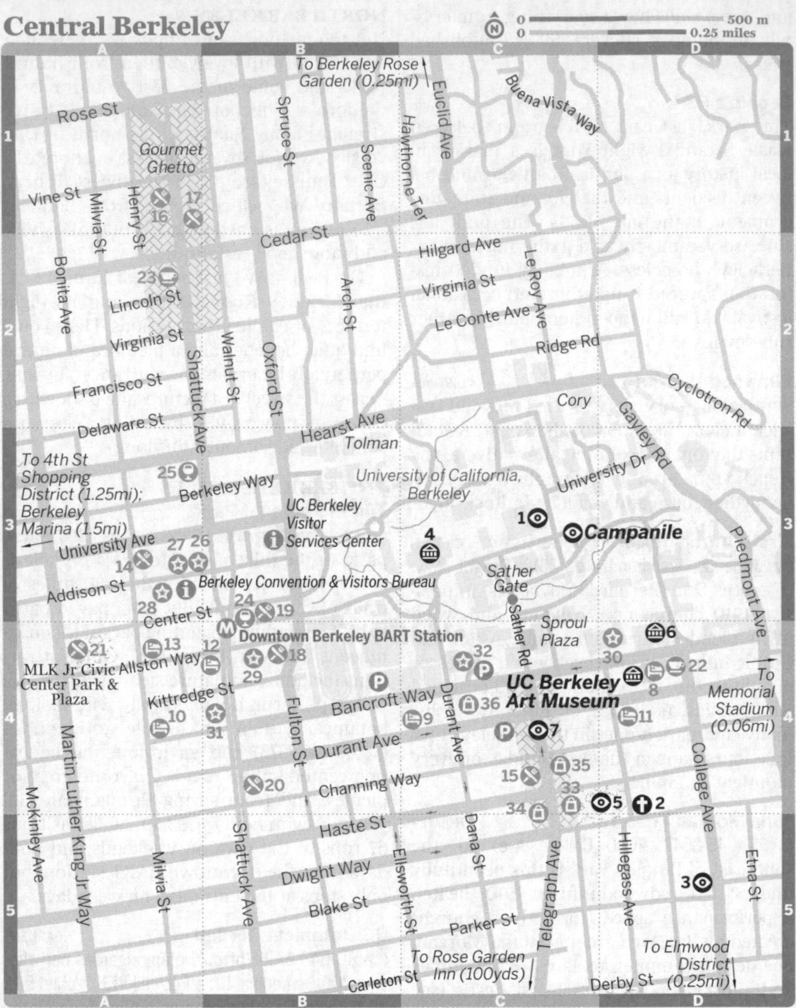

Lawrence Hall of Science
SCIENCE CENTER

(☎510-642-5132; www.lawrencehallofscience.org; Centennial Dr; adult/senior & child 7-8/child 3-6 $12/9/6; ⊙10am-5pm daily;) Near Grizzly Peak Blvd, the science hall is named after Ernest Lawrence, who won the Nobel Prize for his invention of the cyclotron particle accelerator. He was a key member of the WWII Manhattan Project, and he's also the name behind the Lawrence Berkeley and Lawrence Livermore laboratories. The Hall of Science has a huge collection of interactive exhibits for kids and adults on subjects ranging from earthquakes to nanotechnology, and outside there's a 60ft model of a DNA molecule. AC Transit bus 65 runs to the hall from the downtown BART station. You can also catch the university's Bear Transit shuttle (H line) from the Hearst Mining Circle.

WEST BERKELEY

San Pablo Ave
STREET

Formerly US Rte 40, this was the main thoroughfare from the east before I-80 came along. The area north of University Ave is still lined with a few older motels, diners and atmospheric dive bars with neon signs. South of University Ave are pockets of trend-

Central Berkeley

Top Sights

Campanile ... C3
UC Berkeley Art Museum ... D4

Sights

1 Bancroft Library ... C3
2 First Church of Christ Scientist ... D4
3 Julia Morgan Theatre ... D5
4 Museum of Paleontology ... C3
5 People's Park ... D4
6 Phoebe Hearst Museum of Anthropology ... D4
7 Telegraph Avenue ... C4

Sleeping

8 Bancroft Hotel ... D4
9 Berkeley City Club ... C4
10 Downtown Berkeley Inn ... A4
11 Hotel Durant ... D4
12 Hotel Shattuck Plaza ... B4
13 YMCA ... A4

Eating

14 Au Coquelet Café ... A3
15 Café Intermezzo ... C4
16 Cheese Board Collective ... A1
17 Chez Panisse ... A1
18 Gather ... B4
19 Ippuku ... B3
20 La Note ... B4
21 Saturday Berkeley Farmers Market ... A4

Drinking

22 Caffe Strada ... D4
23 Guerilla Café ... A2
24 Jupiter ... B3
25 Triple Rock Brewery & Ale House ... A3

Entertainment

26 Aurora Theatre Company ... A3
27 Berkeley Repertory Theatre ... A3
28 Freight & Salvage Coffeehouse ... A3
29 Marsh ... B4
30 Pacific Film Archive ... D4
31 Shattuck Down Low ... B4
32 Zellerbach Hall ... C4

Shopping

33 Amoeba Music ... C4
34 Moe's ... C4
35 Rasputin ... C4
36 University Press Books ... C4

iness, such as the short stretch of gift shops and cafes around Dwight Way.

4th St Shopping District DISTRICT
Hidden within an industrial area near I-80 lies a three-block area offering shaded sidewalks for upscale shopping or just strolling, and a few good restaurants.

Berkeley Marina MARINA
At the west end of University Ave is the marina, frequented by squawking seagulls, silent types fishing from the pier, unleashed dogs and, especially on windy weekends, lots of colorful kites. Construction of the marina began in 1936, though the pier has much older origins. It was originally built in the 1870s, then replaced by a 3-mile-long ferry pier in 1920 (its length was dictated by the extreme shallowness of the bay). Part of the original pier is now rebuilt, affording visitors sweeping bay views.

Adventure Playground PLAYGROUND
(510-981-6720; www.cityofberkeley.info/marina; 11am-4pm Sat & Sun, closed last week of year;) At the marina is one of the coolest play spaces in the country – a free outdoor park encouraging creativity and cooperation where supervised kids of any age can help build and paint their own structures. Dress the tykes in play clothes, because they *will* get dirty.

FREE **Takara Sake** MUSEUM
(www.takarasake.com; 708 Addison St; noon-6pm) Stop in to see the traditional wooden tools used for making sake and a short video of the brewing process. Tours of the factory aren't offered, but you can view elements of modern production and bottling through a window. Flights ($5) are available in a spacious tasting room constructed with reclaimed wood and floor tiles fashioned from recycled glass.

Sleeping

Lodging rates spike during special university events like graduation (mid-May) and home football games. A number of older motels along University Ave can be handy during peak demand. For B&B options, see the Berkeley & Oakland Bed & Breakfast Network (p124).

TOP CHOICE **Hotel Shattuck Plaza** BOUTIQUE HOTEL **$$$**
(☎510-845-7300; www.hotelshattuckplaza.com; 2086 Allston Way; r $219-59; ❄@📶) Peace is quite posh following a $15 million renovation and greening of this 100-year-old downtown jewel. A foyer of red Italian glass lighting, flocked Victorian-style wallpaper – and yes, a peace sign tiled into the floor – leads to comfortable rooms with down comforters, and an airy and columned restaurant serving all meals. Accommodations off Shattuck are the quietest, and Cityscape rooms boast bay views.

Hotel Durant BOUTIQUE HOTEL **$$**
(☎510-845-8981; www.hoteldurant.com; 2600 Durant Ave; r from $134; @📶🐾) Located a block from campus, this classic 1928 hotel has been cheekily renovated to highlight the connection to the university. The lobby is adorned with embarrassing yearbook photos and a ceiling mobile of exam books, and smallish rooms have dictionary-covered shower curtains and bongs repurposed into bedside lamps.

Berkeley City Club HISTORIC HOTEL **$$**
(☎510-848-7800; www.berkeleycityclub.com; 2315 Durant Ave; r/ste incl breakfast from $145/235; 🏊@📶) Designed by Julia Morgan, the architect of Hearst Castle (see p299), the 36 rooms and dazzling common areas of this refurbished 1929 historic landmark building (which is also a private club) feel like a glorious time warp into a more refined era. The hotel contains lush and serene Italianate courtyards, gardens and terraces, and a stunning indoor pool. Elegant Old-World rooms contain no TVs, and those with numbers ending in 4 and 8 have to-die-for views of the bay and the Golden Gate Bridge.

Bancroft Hotel HISTORIC HOTEL **$$**
(☎510-549-1000, 800-549-1002; www.bancrofthotel.com; 2680 Bancroft Way; r incl breakfast $129-149; @📶) A gorgeous 1928 Arts and Crafts building that was originally a women's club, the Bancroft is just across the street from campus and two blocks from Telegraph Ave. It has 22 comfortable, beautifully furnished rooms (number 302 boasts a lovely balcony) and a spectacular bay-view rooftop, though no elevator.

YMCA HOSTEL **$**
(☎510-848-6800; www.ymca-cba.org/downtown-berkeley; 2001 Allston Way; s/d $49/81; 🏊@📶) Recently remodeled with new bedding and carpet, the 100-year-old downtown Y building is still the best budget option in town. Rates for the austere private rooms (all with shared bathroom) include use of the sauna, pool and fitness center, and kitchen facilities, and wheelchair accessible rooms are available as well. Corner rooms 310 and 410 boast enviable bay views. Entrance on Milvia St.

Downtown Berkeley Inn MOTEL **$**
(☎510-843-4043; www.downtownberkeleyinn.com; 2001 Bancroft Way; r $89-109; ❄📶) A 27-room budget boutique-style motel with good-sized rooms and correspondingly ample flat-screen TVs.

Rose Garden Inn INN **$$**
(☎510-549-2145, 800-922-9005; www.rosegardeninn.com; 2740 Telegraph Ave; r incl breakfast $98-185; @📶) The decor flirting with flowery, this cute place is a few blocks south from the Telegraph Ave action and very peaceful, with two old houses surrounded by pretty gardens.

Eating

Telegraph Ave is packed with cafes, pizza counters and cheap restaurants, and Berkeley's Little India runs along the University Ave corridor. Many more restaurants can be found downtown along Shattuck Ave near the BART station. The section of Shattuck Ave north of University Ave is the 'Gourmet Ghetto,' home to lots of excellent eating establishments.

DOWNTOWN & AROUND CAMPUS

Gather AMERICAN **$$**
(☎510-809-0400; www.gatherrestaurant.com; 2200 Oxford St; lunch mains $10-17, dinner mains $14-19; ⏰11:30am-2pm Mon-Fri, 10am-2:30pm Sat & Sun, & 5-10pm daily; 🌱) When vegan foodies and passionate farm-to-table types dine out together, they often end up here. Inside a salvaged wood interior punctuated by green vines streaking down over an open kitchen, patrons swoon over dishes created from locally sourced ingredients and sustainably raised meats. Reserve for dinner.

TOP CHOICE **Ippuku** JAPANESE **$$**
(☎510-665-1969; www.ippukuberkeley.com; 2130 Center St; small plates $5-18; ⏰5-11pm) Specializing in *shochu* (flights $12), a distilled alcohol made from rice, barley or sweet potato, Japanese expats gush that Ippuku reminds

them of *izakayas* (pub-style restaurants) back in Tokyo. Choose from a menu of skewered meats and settle in at one of the traditional wood platform tables (no shoes, please) or cozy booth perches. Reservations essential.

La Note FRENCH $$
(☎510-843-1535; www.lanoterestaurant.com; 2377 Shattuck Ave; mains $10-17; ⏰8am-2:30pm Mon-Fri, to 3pm Sat & Sun, & 6-10pm Thu-Sat) A rustic country-French bistro downtown, La Note serves excellent breakfasts. Wake up to a big bowl of café au lait, paired with oatmeal raspberry pancakes or lemon gingerbread pancakes with poached pears. Anticipate a wait on weekends.

Café Intermezzo CAFETERIA $
(2442 Telegraph Ave; sandwiches & salads $6.50) Mammoth salads draw a constant crowd, and we're not talking about delicate little rabbit food plates. Bring a friend, or you might drown while trying to polish off a Veggie Delight heaped with beans, hard-boiled egg and avocado.

Au Coquelet Café CAFE $
(www.aucoquelet.com; 2000 University Ave; mains $6-9; ⏰6am-1am Sun-Thu, to 1:30am Sat & Sun; 📶) Open till late, Au Coquelet is a popular stop for postmovie meals or late-night studying. The front section serves coffee and pastries while the skylit and spacious back room does a big range of omelets, pastas, sandwiches, burgers and salads.

Berkeley Farmers Market MARKET $
(⏰10am-3pm Sat) Pick up some organic produce or tasty prepared food at the downtown farmers market, operating year-round, at Center St and MLK Way, and sit down to munch at MLK Park across from city hall.

NORTH BERKELEY

TOP CHOICE **Chez Panisse** AMERICAN $$$
(☎restaurant 510-548-5525, cafe 510-548-5049; www.chezpanisse.com; 1517 Shattuck Ave; restaurant mains $60-95, cafe mains $18-29; ⏰restaurant dinner Mon-Sat, cafe lunch & dinner Mon-Sat) Foodies come to worship here at the church of Alice Waters, the inventor of California cuisine. The restaurant is as good and popular as it ever was, and despite its fame the place has retained a welcoming atmosphere. It's in a lovely Arts and Crafts house in the Gourmet Ghetto, and you can choose to pull all the stops with a prix-fixe meal downstairs, or go less expensive and a tad less formal in the cafe upstairs. Reserve weeks ahead.

Cheese Board Collective PIZZERIA $
(☎510-549-3183; www.cheeseboardcollective.coop; 1504 & 1512 Shattuck Ave; pizza slice $2.50; 🖉) Stop in to take stock of the over 300 cheeses available at this worker-owned business, and scoop up some fresh bread to make a picnic lunch. Or sit down for a slice of the fabulously crispy one-option-per-day veggie pizza just next door, where live music's often featured.

WEST BERKELEY

🍃 **Vik's Chaat Corner** INDIAN $
(www.vikschaatcorner.com; 2390 4th St; dishes $5-7; ⏰11am-6pm Mon-Thu, to 8pm Fri-Sun; 🖉) This longtime and very popular *chaat* house has moved to a larger space but still gets mobbed at lunchtime by regulars that include an equal number of hungry office workers and Indian families. Try a *cholle* (spicy garbanzo curry) or one of the many filling *dosas* (savory crepes) from the weekend menu. It's on the corner of Channing Way, one block east of the waterfront.

Bette's Oceanview Diner DINER $
(☎510-644-3230; www.bettesdiner.com; 1807 4th St; mains $7-11; ⏰6:30am-2:30pm Mon-Fri, to 4pm Sat & Sun) A buzzing breakfast spot, especially on the weekends, serving yummy baked soufflé pancakes and German-style potato pancakes with applesauce, plus eggs and sandwiches. Superfresh food and a nifty diner interior make it worth the wait. It's about a block north of University Ave.

🍷 Drinking

🍃 **Guerilla Café** CAFE
(☎510-845-2233; www.guerillacafe.com; 1620 Shattuck Ave) Exuding a 1970s flavor, this small and sparkling cafe has a creative political vibe, with polka-dot tiles on the counter handmade by one of the artist-owners, and order numbers spotlighting guerillas and liberation revolutionaries. Organic and Fair Trade ingredients feature in the breakfasts and panini sandwiches, and locally roasted Blue Bottle coffee is served. Occasional film screenings and pop-up cuisine nights pack the place.

Caffe Strada CAFE
(2300 College Ave; 📶) A popular, student-saturated hangout with an inviting shaded patio and strong espressos. Try the signature white chocolate mocha.

Jupiter PUB
(www.jupiterbeer.com; 2181 Shattuck Ave) This downtown pub has loads of regional microbrews, a beer garden, good pizza and live bands most nights. Sit upstairs for a bird's-eye view of bustling Shattuck Ave.

Casa Vino WINE BAR
(www.casavinobistro.com; 3136 Sacramento St) A few blocks west of Ashby BART, this unpretentious and somewhat nondescript wine bar serves an eyebrow-raising 95 wines by the glass. Relax on the outdoor patio during warm nights.

Albatross PUB
(www.albatrosspub.com; 1822 San Pablo Ave; 🐾) A block north of University Ave, Berkeley's oldest pub is one of the most inviting and friendly in the entire Bay Area. Some serious darts are played here, and boardgames will be going on around many of the worn-out tables. Sunday is Pub Quiz night.

Triple Rock Brewery & Ale House BREWERY
(1920 Shattuck Ave) Opened in 1986, Triple Rock was one of the country's first brewpubs. The house beers and pub grub are quite good, and the antique wooden bar and rooftop sun deck are delightful.

☆ Entertainment

The arts corridor on Addison St between Milvia and Shattuck Sts anchors a lively downtown entertainment scene.

Live Music

Berkeley has plenty of intimate live music venues. Cover charges range from $5 to $20, and a number of venues are all-ages or 18-and-over.

924 Gilman PUNK ROCK
(www.924gilman.org; 924 Gilman St; ⏲Fri-Sun) This volunteer-run and booze-free all-ages space is a West Coast punk rock institution. Take AC Transit bus 9 from Berkeley BART.

Freight & Salvage Coffeehouse FOLK, WORLD
(☎510-644-2020; www.thefreight.org; 2020 Addison St; 👪) This legendary club has over 40 years of history and recently relocated to the downtown arts district. It still features great traditional folk and world music and welcomes all ages, with half price tickets for patrons under 21.

Shattuck Down Low CLUB
(☎510-548-1159; www.shattuckdownlow.com; 2284 Shattuck Ave) A fun multiethnic crowd fills this basement space that sometimes books big-name bands. Locals love the Tuesday karaoke nights and the smokin' all-levels-welcome salsa on Wednesdays.

La Peña Cultural Center WORLD
(☎510-849-2568; www.lapena.org; 3105 Shattuck Ave) A few blocks east of the Ashby BART station, this cultural center and Chilean cafe presents dynamic musical and visual arts programming with a peace and justice bent. Look for the vibrant mural on its facade.

Ashkenaz FOLK, WORLD
(☎510-525-5054; www.ashkenaz.com; 1317 San Pablo Ave; 👪) Ashkenaz is a 'music and dance community center' attracting activists, hippies and fans of folk, swing and world music who love to dance (lessons offered).

Cinemas

Pacific Film Archive CINEMA
(☎510-642-1124; www.bampfa.berkeley.edu; 2575 Bancroft Way; adult/student & senior $9.50/6.50) A world-renowned film center with an ever-changing schedule of international and classic films, cineastes should seek this place out. The spacious theater has seats that are comfy enough for hours-long movie marathons.

Theater & Dance

Zellerbach Hall PERFORMING ARTS
(☎510-642-9988; http://tickets.berkeley.edu) On the south end of campus near Bancroft Way and Dana St, Zellerbach Hall features dance events, concerts and performances of all types by national and international artists. The onsite **Cal Performances Ticket Office** sells tickets without a handling fee.

Berkeley Repertory Theatre THEATER
(☎510-647-2949; www.berkeleyrep.org; 2025 Addison St) This highly respected company has produced bold versions of classical and modern plays since 1968.

California Shakespeare Theater THEATER
(☎510-548-9666; www.calshakes.org; box office 701 Heinz Ave) Headquartered in Berkeley, with a fantastic outdoor amphitheater further east in Orinda, 'Cal Shakes' is a warm-weather tradition of al fresco Shakespeare (and other classic) productions, with a season that lasts from about June through September.

Aurora Theatre Company THEATER
(☎510-843-4822; www.auroratheatre.org; 2081 Addison St) An intimate downtown theater, it performs contemporary and thought-provoking plays staged with a subtle chamber-theater aesthetic.

Marsh PERFORMING ARTS
(☎510-704-8291; www.themarsh.org; 2120 Allston Way) The 'breeding ground for new performance' now has a Berkeley toehold for eclectic solo and comedy acts.

Shotgun Players THEATER
(☎510-841-6500; www.shotgunplayers.org; 1901 Ashby Avenue) The country's first all-solar-powered theater company stages exciting and provocative work in an intimate space. Across from the Ashby BART station.

Sports

Memorial Stadium, which dates from 1923, is the university's 71,000-seat sporting venue, and the Hayward Fault runs just beneath it. On alternate years, it's the site of the famous football frenzy between the UC Berkeley and Stanford teams.

The **Cal Athletic Ticket Office** (☎800-462-3277; www.calbears.com) has ticket information on all UC Berkeley sports events. Keep in mind that some sell out weeks in advance.

Shopping

Branching off the UC campus, Telegraph Ave caters mostly to students, hawking a steady dose of urban hippie gear, handmade sidewalk-vendor jewelry and head-shop paraphernalia. Audiophiles will swoon over the music stores. Other shopping corridors include College Ave in the Elmwood District, 4th St (north of University Ave) and Solano Ave.

Amoeba Music MUSIC
(☎510-549-1125; 2455 Telegraph Ave) If you're a music junkie, you might plan on spending a few hours at the original Berkeley branch of Amoeba Music, packed with massive quantities of new and used CDs, DVDs, tapes and records (yes, lots of vinyl).

Moe's BOOKS
(☎510-849-2087; 2476 Telegraph Ave) A long-standing local favorite, Moe's offers four floors of new, used and remaindered books for hours of browsing.

University Press Books BOOKS
(☎510-548-0585; 2430 Bancroft Way) Across the street from campus, this academic and scholarly bookstore stocks works by UC Berkeley professors and other academic and museum publishers.

Down Home Music MUSIC
(☎510-525-2129; 10341 San Pablo Ave, El Cerrito) North of Berkeley in El Cerrito, this world-class store for roots, blues, folk, Latin and world music is affiliated with the Arhoolie record label, which has been issuing landmark recordings since the early 1960s.

Rasputin MUSIC
(☎800-350-8700; 2401 Telegraph Ave) Another large music store full of new and used releases.

Marmot Mountain Works OUTDOOR EQUIPMENT
(☎510-849-0735; 3049 Adeline St) Has climbing, ski and backpacking equipment for sale and for rent. Located one block north of Ashby BART station.

North Face Outlet OUTDOOR EQUIPMENT
(☎510-526-3530; cnr 5th & Gilman Sts) Discount store for the well-respected Bay Area-based brand of outdoor gear. It's a few blocks west of San Pablo Ave.

REI OUTDOOR EQUIPMENT
(☎510-527-4140; 1338 San Pablo Ave) This large and busy co-op lures in active folks for camping and mountaineering rentals, sports clothing and all kinds of nifty outdoor gear.

Information

Alta Bates Summit Medical Center (☎510-204-4444; 2450 Ashby Ave) 24-hour emergency services.

Berkeley Convention & Visitors Bureau (☎510-549-7040, 800-847-4823; www.visitberkeley.com; 2030 Addison St; ⊙9am-1pm & 2-5pm Mon-Fri) This helpful bureau has a free visitors guide.

UC Berkeley Visitor Services Center (☎510-642-5215; http://visitors.berkeley.edu; 101 Sproul Hall) Campus maps and information available. Free 90-minute campus tours are given at 10am Monday to Saturday and 1pm Sunday; reservations required.

Getting There & Away

BART

The easiest way to travel between San Francisco, Berkeley, Oakland and other East Bay points is on **BART** (☎510-465-2278, 511; www.bart.gov). Trains run approximately every 10 minutes

SHAKE, RATTLE & ROLL

Curious to find a few places where the earth shook? Visit these notorious spots in and around the Bay Area:

» **Earthquake Trail** (p120) at Point Reyes National Seashore shows the effects of the big one in 1906.

» Forty-two people died when the Cypress Freeway collapsed in West Oakland, one of the most horrifying and enduring images of the 1989 Loma Prieta quake. The **Cypress Freeway Memorial Park** at 14th St and Mandela Parkway commemorates those who perished and those who helped rescue survivors.

» Near Aptos in Santa Cruz County, a sign on the Aptos Creek Trail in the **Forest of Nisene Marks State Park** (☎831-763-7062; www.parks.ca.gov) marks the actual epicenter of the Loma Prieta quake, and on the Big Slide Trail a number of fissures can be spotted.

» The Hayward Fault runs just beneath **Memorial Stadium** (p137) at UC Berkeley.

from 4am to midnight on weekdays, with limited service from 6am on Saturday and from 8am on Sunday.

To get to Berkeley, catch a Richmond-bound train to one of three BART stations: Ashby (Adeline St and Ashby Ave), Downtown Berkeley (Shattuck Ave and Center St) or North Berkeley (Sacramento and Delaware Sts). The fare ranges from $3.50 to $3.85 between Berkeley and San Francisco; $1.75 between Berkeley and downtown Oakland. After 8pm on weekdays, 7pm on Saturday and all day Sunday, there is no direct service operating from San Francisco to Berkeley; instead, catch a Pittsburg/Bay Point train and transfer at 19th St station in Oakland.

A **BART-to-Bus** transfer ticket, available from white AC Transit machines near the BART turnstiles, reduces the connecting bus fare by 25¢.

Bus

The regional company **AC Transit** (☎510-817-1717, 511; www.actransit.org) operates a number of buses from San Francisco's **Transbay Temporary Terminal** (Howard & Main Sts) to the East Bay. The F line leaves from the Transbay Temporary Terminal to the corner of University and Shattuck Aves approximately every half-hour ($4.20, 30 minutes).

Between Berkeley and downtown Oakland ($2.10) on weekdays, take the fast and frequent 1R bus along Telegraph Ave between the two city centers, or bus 18 that runs daily via Martin Luther King Jr Way. Bus 51B travels along University Ave from Berkeley BART to the Berkeley Marina.

Car & Motorcycle

With your own wheels you can approach Berkeley from San Francisco by taking the Bay Bridge and then following either I-80 (for University Ave, downtown Berkeley and the UCB campus) or Hwy 24 (for College Ave and the Berkeley Hills).

Driving to San Francisco, the bridge toll is $4 to $6, depending on the time and day of the week.

Train

Amtrak does stop in Berkeley, but the shelter is not staffed and direct connections are few. More convenient is the nearby **Emeryville Amtrak station** (☎800-872-7245; www.amtrak.com; 5885 Horton St), a few miles south.

To reach the Emeryville station from downtown Berkeley, take a Transbay F bus or ride BART to the MacArthur station and then take the free Emery Go Round bus (Hollis route) to Amtrak.

ℹ Getting Around

Public transportation, cycling and walking are the best options for getting around central Berkeley.

BICYCLE Cycling is a popular means of transportation, and safe and well-marked 'bicycle boulevards' with signed distance information to landmarks make crosstown journeys very easy. Just north of Berkeley, **Solano Avenue Cyclery** (☎510-524-1094; 1554 Solano Ave, Albany; ⊙Mon-Sat) has 24-hour mountain- and road-bike rentals for $35 to $45.

BUS AC Transit operates public buses in and around Berkeley, and UC Berkeley's **Bear Transit** (http://pt.berkeley.edu/around/transit/routes) runs a shuttle from the downtown BART station to various points on campus ($1). From its stop at the Hearst Mining Circle, the H Line runs along Centennial Dr to the higher parts of the campus.

CAR & MOTORCYCLE Drivers should note that numerous barriers have been set up to prevent car traffic from traversing residential streets at high speeds, so zigzagging is necessary in some neighborhoods.

Mt Diablo State Park

Collecting a light dusting of snowflakes on the coldest days of winter, at 3849ft Mt Diablo is more than 1000ft higher than Mt Tamalpais in Marin County. On a clear day (early on a winter morning is a good bet) the views from Diablo's summit are vast and sweeping. To the west you can see over the bay and out to the Farallon Islands; to the east you can see over the Central Valley to the Sierra Nevada.

The **Mt Diablo State Park** (925-837-2525; www.mdia.org; per vehicle $6-10; 8am-sunset) has 50 miles of hiking trails, and can be reached from Walnut Creek, Danville or Clayton. You can also drive to the top, where there's a **visitors center** (10am-4pm). The park office is at the junction of the two entry roads. Of the three **campgrounds** (800-444-7275; www.reserveamerica.com; tent & RV sites $30), Juniper has showers, though all can be closed during high fire danger.

John Muir National Historic Site

Less than 15 miles north of Walnut Creek, the **John Muir residence** (925-228-8860; www.nps.gov/jomu; 4202 Alhambra Ave, Martinez; adult/child $3/free; 10am-5pm Wed-Sun) sits in a pastoral patch of farmland in bustling, modern Martinez. Though he wrote of sauntering the High Sierra with a sack of tea and bread, it may be a shock for those familiar with the iconic Sierra Club founder's ascetic weather-beaten appearance that the house (built by his father-in-law) is a model of Victorian Italianate refinement, with a tower cupola, a daintily upholstered parlor and splashes of fussy white lace. His 'scribble den' has been left as it was during his life, with crumbled papers overflowing from wire wastebaskets and dried bread balls – his preferred snack – resting on the mantelpiece. Acres of his fruit orchard still stand, and visitors can enjoy seasonal samples. The grounds include the 1849 **Martinez Adobe**, part of the rancho on which the house was built.

The park is just north of Hwy 4, and accessible by **County Connection** (http://cccta.org) buses from Amtrak and BART.

Vallejo

For one week in 1852 Vallejo was officially the California state capital – but the fickle legislature changed its mind. It tried Vallejo a second time in 1853, but after a month moved on again (to Benicia). That same year, Vallejo became the site of the first US naval installation on the West Coast (Mare Island Naval Shipyard, now closed). **Vallejo Naval & Historical Museum** (707-643-0077; www.vallejomuseum.org; 734 Marin St; admission $5; noon-4pm Tue-Sat) tells the story.

The town's biggest tourist draw, though, is **Six Flags Discovery Kingdom** (707-643-6722; www.sixflags.com/discoverykingdom; adult/child under 4ft $50/36; approx 10:30am-6pm Fri-Sun spring & fall, to 8pm or 9pm daily summer, variable weekend & holiday hr Dec), a modern wildlife and theme park offering mighty coasters and other rides alongside animal shows featuring sharks and a killer whale. Significant discounts are available on the park's website. Exit I-80 at Hwy 37 westbound, 5 miles north of downtown Vallejo. Parking is $15.

Operated by Blue & Gold Fleet, **Vallejo Baylink Ferry** (877-643-3779; www.baylinkferry.com; one way adult/child $13/6.50) runs ferries from San Francisco's Pier 41 at Fisherman's Wharf and the Ferry Building to Vallejo; the

WORTH A TRIP

EAST BROTHER LIGHT STATION

Most Bay Area residents have never heard of this speck of an island off the East Bay city of Richmond, and even fewer know that the **East Brother Light Station** (510-233-2385; www.ebls.org; d incl breakfast & dinner $355-415; Thu-Sun) is a extraordinary five-room Victorian B&B. Spend the night in the romantic lighthouse or fog signal building (the foghorn is used from October through March), where every window has stupendous bay views and harbor seals frolic in the frigid currents. Resident innkeepers serve afternoon hors d'oeuvres and champagne, and between gourmet meals you can stroll around the breezy one-acre islet and rummage through historical photos and artifacts journey takes one hour. Discount admission and transportation packages for Six Flags are available from San Francisco.

Vallejo is also somewhat of a gateway to the Wine Country. See p161 and p167.

THE PENINSULA

South of San Francisco, squeezed tightly between the bay and the coastal foothills, a vast swath of suburbia continues to San Jose and beyond. Dotted within this area are Palo Alto, Stanford University and Silicon Valley, the center of the Bay Area's immense tech industry. West of the foothills, Hwy 1 runs down the Pacific coast via Half Moon Bay and a string of beaches to Santa Cruz. Hwy 101 and I-280 both run to San Jose, where they connect with Hwy 17, the quickest route to Santa Cruz. Any of these routes can be combined into an interesting loop or extended to the Monterey Peninsula.

And don't bother looking for Silicon Valley on the map – you won't find it. Because silicon chips form the basis of modern microcomputers, and the Santa Clara Valley – stretching from Palo Alto down through Mountain View, Sunnyvale, Cupertino and Santa Clara to San Jose – is thought of as the birthplace of the microcomputer, it's been dubbed 'Silicon Valley.' The Santa Clara Valley is wide and flat, and its towns are essentially a string of shopping centers and industrial parks linked by a maze of freeways. It's hard to imagine that even after WWII this area was still a wide expanse of orchards and farms.

San Francisco to San Jose

South of the San Francisco peninsula, I-280 is the dividing line between the densely populated South Bay area and the rugged and lightly populated Pacific Coast. With sweeping views of hills and reservoirs, I-280 is a more scenic choice than crowded Hwy 101, which runs through miles of boring business parks. Unfortunately, these parallel north-south arteries are both clogged with traffic during commute times and often on weekends.

A historic site where European explorers first set eyes on San Francisco Bay, **Sweeney Ridge** (www.nps.gov/goga/planyourvisit/upload/sb-sweeney-2008.pdf), straddles a prime spot between Pacifica and San Bruno, and offers hikers unparalleled ocean and bay views. From I-280, exit at Sneath Lane and follow it 2 miles west until it dead ends at the trailhead.

Right on the bay at the northern edge of San Mateo, 4 miles south of San Francisco International Airport, is **Coyote Point Recreation Area** (per vehicle $5;), a popular park and windsurfing destination. The main attraction – formerly known as the Coyote Point Museum – is **CuriOdyssey** (650-342-7755; www.curiodyssey.org; adult/child $8/4; 10am-5pm Tue-Sat, noon-5pm Sun, free 1st Sun of month;), with innovative exhibits for kids and adults concentrating on ecological and environmental issues. Exit Hwy 101 at Coyote Point Dr.

San Jose

Though culturally diverse and historic, San Jose has always been in San Francisco's shadow, awash in Silicon Valley's suburbia. Founded in 1777 as El Pueblo de San José de Guadalupe, San Jose is California's oldest Spanish civilian settlement. Its downtown is small and scarcely used for a city of its size, though it does bustle with 20-something clubgoers on the weekends. Industrial parks, high-tech computer firms and look-alike housing developments have sprawled across the city's landscape, taking over where farms, ranches and open spaces once spread between the bay and the surrounding hills.

Sights

Downtown San Jose is at the junction of Hwy 87 and I-280. Hwy 101 and I-880 complete the box. Running roughly north-south along the length of the city, from the old port town of Alviso on the San Francisco Bay all the way downtown, is 1st St; south of I-280, its name changes to Monterey Hwy.

San Jose State University is immediately east of downtown, and the SoFA district, with numerous nightclubs, restaurants and galleries, is on a stretch of S 1st St south of San Carlos St.

TOP CHOICE **History Park** PARK
(408-287-2290; www.historysanjose.org; cnr Senter Rd & Phelan Ave; 11am-5pm Tue-Sun) Historic buildings from all over San Jose have been brought together in this open-air history museum, southeast of the city center in Kelley Park. The centerpiece is a dramatic half-scale

WORTH A TRIP

STANFORD UNIVERSITY

Sprawled over 8200 leafy acres in Palo Alto, **Stanford University** (www.stanford.edu) was founded by Leland Stanford, one of the Central Pacific Railroad's 'Big Four' founders and a former governor of California. When the Stanfords' only child died of typhoid during a European tour in 1884, they decided to build a university in his memory. Stanford University was opened in 1891, just two years before Leland Stanford's death, but the university grew to become a prestigious and wealthy institution. The campus was built on the site of the Stanfords' horse-breeding farm and, as a result, Stanford is still known as 'The Farm.'

Auguste Rodin's *Burghers of Calais* bronze sculpture marks the entrance to the **Main Quad**, an open plaza where the original 12 campus buildings, a mix of Romanesque and Mission revival styles, were joined by the **Memorial Church** (also called MemChu) in 1903. The church is noted for its beautiful mosaic-tiled frontage, stained-glass windows and four organs with over 8000 pipes.

A campus landmark at the east of the Main Quad, the 285ft-high **Hoover Tower** (adult/child $2/1; ⏲10am-4pm, closed during final exams, breaks btwn sessions & some holidays) offers superb views. The tower houses the university library, offices and part of the right-wing Hoover Institution on War, Revolution & Peace (where Donald Rumsfeld caused a university-wide stir by accepting a position after he resigned as Secretary of Defense).

The **Cantor Center for Visual Arts** (http://museum.stanford.edu; 328 Lomita Dr; admission free; ⏲11am-5pm Wed & Fri-Sun, to 8pm Thu) is a large museum originally dating from 1894. Its collection spans works from ancient civilizations to contemporary art, sculpture and photography, and rotating exhibits are eclectic in scope.

Immediately south is the open-air **Rodin Sculpture Garden**, which boasts the largest collection of bronze sculptures by Auguste Rodin outside of Paris, including reproductions of his towering *Gates of Hell.* More sculpture can be found around campus, including pieces by Andy Goldsworthy and Maya Lin.

The **Stanford Visitor Center** (www.stanford.edu/dept/visitorinfo; 295 Galvez St) offers free one-hour walking tours of the campus daily at 11am and 3.15pm, except during the winter break (mid-December through early January) and some holidays. Specialized tours are also available.

Stanford University's free public shuttle, **Marguerite** (http://transportation.stanford.edu/marguerite), provides service from Caltrain's Palo Alto and California Ave stations to the campus, and has bicycle racks. Parking on campus is expensive and trying.

replica of the 237ft-high 1881 **Electric Light Tower**. The original tower was a pioneering attempt at street lighting, intended to illuminate the entire town center. It was a complete failure but was left standing as a central landmark until it toppled over in 1915 because of rust and wind. Other buildings include an 1888 **Chinese temple** and the **Pacific Hotel**, which has rotating exhibits inside. The **Trolley Restoration Barn** restores historic trolley cars to operate on San José's light-rail line. Check the website for when you can ride a trolley along the park's own short line.

Tech Museum MUSEUM
(☎408-294-8324; www.thetech.org; 201 S Market St; museum & 1 IMAX theater admission $10; ⏲10am-5pm Mon-Wed, to 8pm Thu-Sun; ♿) This excellent technology museum, opposite Plaza de Cesar Chavez, examines subjects from robotics to space exploration to genetics. The museum also includes an IMAX dome theater, which screens different films throughout the day.

San Jose Museum of Art MUSEUM
(☎408-271-6840; www.sjmusart.org; 110 S Market St; adult/student & senior $8/5; ⏲11am-5pm Tue-Sun) With a strong permanent collection of 20th-century works and a variety of imaginative changing exhibits, the city's central art museum is one of the Bay Area's finest. The main building started life as the post office in 1892, was damaged by the 1906 earthquake and became an art gallery in 1933. A modern wing was added in 1991.

Rosicrucian Egyptian Museum MUSEUM
(☎408-947-3635; www.egyptianmuseum.org; 1342 Naglee Ave; adult/child/student $9/5/7; ⏱9am-5pm Wed-Fri, 10am-6pm Sat & Sun) West of downtown, this unusual and educational Egyptian Museum is one of San Jose's more interesting attractions, with an extensive collection that includes statues, household items and mummies. There's even a two-room, walk-through reproduction of an ancient subterranean tomb. The museum is the centerpiece of **Rosicrucian Park** (cnr Naglee & Park Aves), west of downtown San Jose.

FREE **MACLA** GALLERY
(Movimiento de Arte y Cultura Latino Americana; ☎408-998-2783; www.maclaarte.org; 510 S 1st St; ⏱noon-7pm Wed & Thu, noon-5pm Fri & Sat) A cutting-edge gallery highlighting themes by both established and emerging Latino artists, MACLA is one of the best community arts spaces in the Bay Area, with open-mic performances, hip-hop and other live music shows, experimental theater and well-curated and thought-provoking visual arts exhibits. It's also a hub for the popular **South First Fridays** (www.southfirstfridays.com) art walk and street fair.

Plaza de Cesar Chavez PLAZA
This leafy square in the center of downtown, which was part of the original plaza of El Pueblo de San José de Guadalupe, is the oldest public space in the city. It's named after Cesar Chavez – founder of the United Farm Workers, who lived part of his life in San Jose – and is surrounded by museums, theaters and hotels.

Cathedral Basilica of St Joseph CHURCH
(80 S Market St) At the top of the plaza, the pueblo's first church. Originally constructed of adobe brick in 1803, it was replaced three times due to earthquakes and fire; the present building dates from 1877.

Santana Row MARKET
(www.santanarow.com; Stevens Creek & Winchester Blvds) An upscale Main St-style mall, Santana Row is a mixed-use space west of downtown with shopping, dining and entertainment along with a boutique hotel, lofts and apartments. Restaurants spill out onto sidewalk terraces, and public spaces have been designed to invite loitering and promenading. On warm evenings, the Mediterranean-style area swarms with an energetic crowd.

San Jose for Children

Children's Discovery Museum MUSEUM
(☎408-298-5437; www.cdm.org; 180 Woz Way; admission $10; ⏱10am-5pm Tue-Sat, from noon Sun; 👪) Downtown, this science and creativity museum has hands-on displays incorporating art, technology and the environment, with plenty of toys, and very cool play-and-learn areas. The museum is on Woz Way, which is named after Steve Wozniak, the cofounder of Apple.

Great America AMUSEMENT PARK
(☎408-986-5886; www.cagreatamerica.com; adult/child under 48in $55/35; 4701 Great America Pkwy, Santa Clara; ⏱Apr-Oct; 👪) If you can handle the shameful product placements, kids love the roller coasters and other thrill rides. Note that online tickets cost much less than walk-up prices listed here; parking costs $12 but it's also accessible by public transportation.

Raging Waters AMUSEMENT PARK
(☎408-238-9900; www.rwsplash.com; 2333 South White Rd; adult/child under 48in $34/24, parking $6; ⏱May-Sep; 👪) A water park inside Lake Cunningham Regional Park, Raging Waters has fast water slides, a tidal pool and a nifty water fort.

Sleeping

Conventions and trade shows keep the downtown hotels busy year-round, and midweek rates are usually higher than weekends.

TOP CHOICE **Sainte Claire Hotel** HISTORIC HOTEL $$
(☎408-295-2000, 866-870-0726; www.thesainteclaire.com; 302 S Market St; r weekend/midweek from $95/169; ❄@📶🐾) Stretched leather ceilings top off the drop-dead beautiful lobby at this 1926 landmark hotel overlooking Plaza de Cesar Chavez. Guest rooms, while smallish, are modern and smartly designed, and bathrooms have hand-painted sky murals, dark wood vanities and restored tile floors.

Hotel De Anza HOTEL $$
(☎408-286-1000, 800-843-3700; www.hoteldeanza.com; 233 W Santa Clara St; r $149-229; ❄@📶🐾) This downtown hotel is a restored art deco beauty, although contemporary stylings overwhelm the place's history. Guest rooms offer plush comforts (the ones facing south are a tad larger) and full concierge service is available.

WHAT THE...?

An odd structure purposefully commissioned to be so by the heir to the Winchester rifle fortune, the **Winchester Mystery House** (☎408-247-2101; www.winchestermysteryhouse.com; 525 S Winchester Blvd; adult/senior/child 6-12 $30/27/20; ⏰9am-5pm Oct-Mar, 8am-7pm Apr-Sep) is a ridiculous Victorian mansion with 160 rooms of various sizes and little utility, with dead-end hallways and a staircase that runs up to a ceiling all jammed together like a toddler playing architect. Apparently, Sarah Winchester spent 38 years constructing this mammoth white elephant because the spirits of the people killed by Winchester rifles told her to. No expense was spared in the construction and the extreme results sprawl over 4 acres. Tours start every 30 minutes, and the standard hour-long guided mansion tour includes a self-guided romp through the gardens as well as entry to an exhibition of guns and rifles. It's west of central San Jose and just north of I-280, across the street from Santana Row.

Hotel Valencia BOUTIQUE HOTEL **$$$**
(☎408-551-0010, 866-842-0100; www.hotelvalencia-santanarow.com; 355 Santana Row; r incl breakfast $199-309;) A burbly lobby fountain and deep-red corridor carpeting set the tone for this tranquil 212-room contemporary hotel in the Santana Row shopping complex. In-room minibars and bathrobes and an outdoor pool and hot tub create an oasis of luxury with European and Asian design accents.

Henry Coe State Park CAMPGROUND **$**
(☎408-779-2728, reservations 800-444-7275 or www.reserveamerica.com; www.coepark.org; sites $20) southeast of San Jose near Morgan Hill, this huge state park has 20 drive-in campsites at the top of an open ridge overlooking the hills and canyons of the park's backcountry. There are no showers. You can't make reservations less than two days in advance, though it rarely fills up except on spring and summer holidays and weekends.

Eating

Original Joe's ITALIAN **$$**
(www.originaljoes.com; 301 S 1st St; mains $14-34; ⏰11am-1am) Waiters in bow ties flit about this busy 1950s San Jose landmark, serving standard Italian dishes to locals and conventioneers. The dining room is a curious but tasteful hodgepodge of '50s brick, contemporary wood paneling and 5ft-tall Asian vases. Expect a wait.

Amber India INDIAN **$$**
(☎408-248-5400; www.amber-india.com; No 1140, 377 Santana Row; dinner mains $14-24) The cooking at this upscale Indian restaurant is superb, offering a full complement of kebabs, curries and tandooris. Presentation is highly styled, with artsy china and groovy paintings on the walls. Whet your whistle with an exotic cocktail as you feast on the delectable butter chicken.

Arcadia STEAKHOUSE **$$$**
(☎408-278-4555; www.michaelmina.net/restaurants; 100 W San Carlos St; lunch mains $11-16, dinner mains $24-42) This fine New American steakhouse restaurant in the Marriott Hotel is run by Chef Michael Mina, one of San Francisco's biggest celebrity chefs. It's not the daring, cutting-edge style Mina is known for, but it's slick, expensive and, of course, very good.

Tofoo Com Chay VEGETARIAN **$**
(www.tofoocomchay.com; 388 E Santa Clara St; mains $6.50; ⏰9am-9pm Mon-Fri, 10am-6pm Sat;) Conveniently located on the border of the San Jose State University campus, students and vegetarians queue up for the Vietnamese dishes like the fake-meat *pho* and the heaped combo plates.

Drinking

TOP CHOICE **singlebarrel** COCKTAIL BAR
(www.singlebarrelsj.com; 43 W San Salvador St; ⏰Tue-Sun) A new speakeasy-style lounge, where bartenders sheathed in tweed vests artfully mix custom cocktails ($10 to $11) tailored to customer's preferences, with some recipes dating back to before Prohibition. There's often a line out the door, but you'll be whisked downstairs as soon as they're ready to craft you a drink.

Caffe Trieste CAFE
(www.caffetrieste.com; 315 S 1st St; ⏰7am-10pm Mon-Thu, to midnight Fri, 8am-midnight Sat, to 9pm Sun;) Photos of local theater folks line the

PSYCHO DONUTS? QU'EST QUE C'EST?

Who knew that a sugary confection with a hole could induce such devious giggles and fiendish delight? Saunter on over to **Psycho Donuts** (www.psycho-donuts.com; 288 S 2nd St; ⌚7am-10pm Mon-Thu, to midnight Fri, 8am-11pm Sat, to 10pm Sun; ✎), where counter staff dressed in saucy medical garb hand out bubble wrap to pop as patrons choose from twisted flavors like Cereal Killer (topped with marshmallows and Cap'n Crunch breakfast cereal), Headbanger (death-metal visage oozing red jelly) and the too-true-to-life Hamburger (sesame seed donut with bacon strips).

walls at this high-ceilinged outpost of San Francisco's North Beach treasure (p89). Linger over a cappuccino with a pastry or panini, and stop by for live music on Thursday, Friday and Saturday nights. Opera performances rattle the cups the first Friday of each month.

Trials Pub PUB
(www.trialspub.com; 265 N 1st St) If you seek a well-poured pint in a supremely comfortable atmosphere, Trials Pub, north of San Pedro Sq, has many excellent ales on tap (try a Fat Lip), all served in a warm and friendly room with no TVs. There's good pub food and a fireplace in the back room.

Hedley Club Lounge LOUNGE
(www.hoteldeanza.com/hedley_club.asp; 233 W Santa Clara St) Also downtown, inside the elegant 1931 Hotel De Anza, Hedley Club is a good place for a quiet drink in swanky art deco surroundings. Jazz combos play Thursday through Saturday night.

☆ Entertainment

Clubs

The biggest conglomeration of clubs is on S 1st St, aka SoFA, and around S 2nd at San Fernando. Raucous young clubgoers pack the streets on Friday and Saturday nights.

South First Billiards POOL HALL
(420 S 1st St; www.sofapool.com) It's a great place to shoot some stick, and a welcoming club to boot. Free rock shows on Friday and Saturday always draw a fun crowd.

Blank Club LIVE MUSIC
(44 S Almaden; www.theblankclub.com; ⌚Tue-Sat) A small club near the Greyhound station and off the main party streets. Live bands jam on a stage cascading with silver tinsel, and a glittering disco ball presides over fun retro dance parties.

Fahrenheit Ultra Lounge LOUNGE
(☎408-998-9998; www.fahrenheitsj.com; 99 E San Fernando St) Expect short party dresses, velvet ropes and clubbers enjoying bottle service and small-plates menu at this buzzing dance club. DJs play a mix and mash-ups of top 40, house and hip-hop, and bartenders pour drinks with flair.

Theaters

California Theatre THEATER
(☎408-792-4111; http://californiatheatre.sanjose.org; 345 S 1st St) The absolutely stunning Spanish interior of this landmark entertainment venue is cathedral-worthy. The theater is home to Opera San José, Symphony Silicon Valley, and is a venue for the city's annual film festival, **Cinequest** (www.cinequest.org), held in late February or early March.

San Jose Repertory Theatre THEATER
(☎408-367-7255; www.sjrep.com; 101 Paseo de San Antonio) Steaming ahead into its third decade, this company offers a full season of top-rated productions in a contemporary 525-seat venue downtown.

Sports

HP Pavilion STADIUM
(☎408-287-9200; www.hppsj.com; cnr Santa Clara & N Autumn Sts) The fanatically popular San Jose Sharks, the city's NHL (National Hockey League) team, plays at the HP Pavilion, a massive glass-and-metal stadium. The NHL season runs from September to April.

Buck Shaw Stadium STADIUM
(www.sjearthquakes.com; 500 El Camino Real, Santa Clara) Located at Santa Clara University, this is the home of the San Jose Earthquakes Major League Soccer team; games run from February through October.

Information

To find out what's happening and where, check out the free weekly *Metro* (www.metroactive.com) newspaper or the Friday 'eye' section of the daily *San Jose Mercury News* (www.mercurynews.com).

San Jose Convention & Visitors Bureau (☎408-295-9600, 800-726-5673; www.sanjose.org; 150 W San Carlos St; ⏰8am-5pm Mon-Fri) Inside the San Jose Convention Center.

Santa Clara Valley Medical Center (☎408-885-5000; 751 S Bascom Ave; ⏰24hr)

Getting There & Away

Air

Two miles north of downtown, between Hwy 101 and I-880, is **Mineta San José International Airport** (www.flysanjose.com). The airport has grown busier as the South Bay gets more crowded, with numerous domestic flights at two terminals and free wi-fi.

BART

To access the BART system in the East Bay, **VTA** (☎408-321-2300; www.vta.org) bus 181 runs daily between the Fremont BART station and downtown ($4).

Bus

Greyhound buses to San Francisco ($10, 90 minutes) and Los Angeles ($42 to $60, seven to 10 hours) leave from the **Greyhound station** (☎408-295-4151; www.greyhound.com; 70 Almaden Ave).

The VTA Hwy 17 Express bus (route 970) plies a handy daily route between Diridon Station and Santa Cruz ($5, one hour).

Car & Motorcycle

San Jose is right at the bottom end of the San Francisco Bay, about 40 miles from Oakland (via I-880) or San Francisco (via Hwy 101 or I-280). Expect lots of traffic at all times of the day on Hwy 101. Although I-280 is slightly longer, it's much prettier and usually less congested. Heading south, Hwy 17 leads over the hill to Santa Cruz.

Many downtown retailers offer two-hour parking validation, and on weekends until 6pm parking is free in city-owned lots and garages downtown. Check www.sjdowntownparking.com for details.

Train

A double-decker commuter rail service that operates up and down the Peninsula between San Jose and San Francisco, **Caltrain** (☎800-660-4287; www.caltrain.com) makes over three dozen trips daily (fewer on weekends); the 60-minute (on the Baby Bullet commuter trains) to 90-minute journey costs $8.50 each way and bicycles can be brought on designated cars. It's definitely your best bet, as traffic can be crazy any day of the week. San Jose's terminal, **Diridon Station** (off 65 Cahill St) is just south of the Alameda.

Diridon Station also serves as the terminal for **Amtrak** (☎408-287-7462; www.amtrak.com), serving Seattle, Los Angeles and Sacramento, and **Altamont Commuter Express** (ACE; www.acerail.com), which runs to Great America, Livermore and Stockton.

VTA runs a free weekday shuttle (known as the Downtown Area Shuttle or DASH) from the station to downtown.

Getting Around

VTA buses run all over Silicon Valley. From the airport, VTA Airport Flyer shuttles (route 10) run every 10 to 15 minutes to the Metro/Airport Light Rail station, where you can catch the San Jose light rail to downtown San Jose. The route also goes to the Santa Clara Caltrain station. Fares for buses (except express lines) and light-rail trains are $2 for a single ride and $6 for a day pass.

The main San Jose light-rail line runs 20 miles north-south from the city center. Heading south gets you as far as Almaden and Santa Teresa. The northern route runs to the Civic Center, the airport and Tasman, where it connects with another line that heads west past Great America to downtown Mountain View.

San Francisco to Half Moon Bay

One of the real surprises of the Bay Area is how fast the urban landscape disappears along the rugged and largely undeveloped coast. The 70-mile stretch of coastal Hwy 1 from San Francisco to Santa Cruz is one of the most beautiful motorways anywhere. For the most part a winding two-lane blacktop, it passes small farmstands and beach after beach, many of them little sandy coves hidden from the highway. Most beaches along Hwy 1 are buffeted by wild and unpredictable surf, making them more suitable for sunbathing (weather permitting) than swimming. The state beaches along the coast don't charge an access fee, but parking can cost a few dollars.

A cluster of isolated and supremely scenic HI hostels, at Point Montara (22 miles south of San Francisco) and Pigeon Point (36 miles), make this an interesting route for cyclists, though narrow Hwy 1 itself can be stressful, if not downright dangerous, for the inexperienced.

WORTH A TRIP

NERDS' NIRVANA

Now touted as the largest computer history exhibition in the world, a $19 million remodel has launched the **Computer History Museum** (650-810-1010; www.computerhistory.org; 1401 N Shoreline Blvd, Mountain View; adult/student & senior $15/12; 10am-5pm Wed-Sun) into a new league. Artifacts range from the abacus to the iPod, including Cray-1 supercomputers and the first Google server. Rotating exhibits draw from its 100,000-item collection and will keep you exploring this place for hours.

PACIFICA & DEVIL'S SLIDE

Pacifica and Point San Pedro, 15 miles from downtown San Francisco, signal the end of the urban sprawl. South of Pacifica is Devil's Slide, an unstable cliff area through which Hwy 1 winds and curves. Drive carefully, especially at night and when it is raining, as rock and mud slides are frequent. Heavy winter storms often lead to the road's temporary closure. A tunnel will soon bypass this dramatic stretch of the highway.

In Pacifica, collecting a suntan or catching a wave are the main attractions at **Rockaway Beach** and the more popular **Pacifica State Beach** (also known as Linda Mar Beach), where the nearby **Nor-Cal Surf Shop** (650-738-9283; 5460 Coast Hwy) rents surfboards ($18 per day) and wet suits ($16).

GRAY WHALE COVE TO MAVERICKS

One of the coast's popular 'clothing-optional' beaches is **Gray Whale Cove State Beach** (650-726-8819), just south of Point San Pedro. Park across the road and cross Hwy 1 to the beach *very* carefully. **Montara State Beach** is just a half-mile south. From the town of Montara, 22 miles from San Francisco, trails climb up from the Martini Creek parking lot into **McNee Ranch State Park**, which has hiking and cycling trails aplenty, including a strenuous ascent to the panoramic viewpoint of Montara Mountain.

Point Montara Lighthouse Hostel (650-728-7177; www.norcalhostels.org/montara; cnr Hwy 1 & 16th St; dm $29, r $78;) started life as a fog station in 1875. The hostel is adjacent to the current lighthouse, which dates from 1928. This very popular hostel has a living room, kitchen facilities and an international clientele. There are a few private rooms for couples or families. Reservations are a good idea anytime, but especially on weekends during summer. From Monday through Friday, SamTrans bus 294 will let you off at the hostel if you ask nicely; bus 17 runs daily and stops across the highway (a ten minute walk).

Montara has a few B&Bs, including the historic **Goose & Turrets B&B** (650-728-5451; www.gooseandturretsbandb.com; 835 George St; r $145-190;), with a lovely garden area, afternoon tea and bright red cannons out front to greet you.

TOP CHOICE **Fitzgerald Marine Reserve** (650-728-3584;), south of the lighthouse at Moss Beach, is an extensive area of natural tidal pools and a habitat for harbor seals. Walk out among the pools at low tide – wearing shoes that you can get wet – and explore the myriad crabs, sea stars, mollusks and rainbow-colored sea anemone. Note that it's illegal to remove any creatures, shells or even rocks from the marine reserve. From Hwy 1 in Moss Beach, turn west onto California Ave and drive to the end. SamTrans buses 294 and 17 stop along Hwy 1.

Moss Beach Distillery (650-728-5595; www.mossbeachdistillery.com; cnr Beach Way & Ocean Blvd; mains $15-33; noon-9pm Mon-Sat, from 11am Sun;) is a 1927 landmark overlooking the ocean. In fair weather the deck here is the best place for miles around to have a leisurely cocktail or glass of vino. Reservations recommended.

South of here is a hamlet named Princeton, with a stretch of coast called Pillar Point. Fishing boats bring in their catch at the Pillar Point Harbor, some of which gets cooked up in a bevy of seafront restaurants. In the harbor, **Half Moon Bay Kayak** (650-773-6101; www.hmbkayak.com) rents kayaks and offers guided trips of Pillar Point and the Fitzgerald Marine Reserve. **Half Moon Bay Brewing Company** (www.hmbbrewinco.com; 390 Capistrano Rd; mains $11-21; 11:30am-8:30pm, longer hr on weekends) serves seafood, burgers and a tantalizing menu of local brews from a sheltered and heated outdoor patio looking out over the bay, complemented by live music on the weekends.

At the western end of Pillar Point is **Mavericks**, a serious surf break that attracts the world's top big-wave riders to battle its huge, steep and very dangerous waves. The annual Mavericks surf contest, called on a few days' notice when the swells get huge, is usually held between December and March.

Half Moon Bay

Developed as a beach resort back in the Victorian era, Half Moon Bay is the main coastal town between San Francisco (28 miles north) and Santa Cruz (40 miles south). Its long stretches of beach still attract rambling weekenders and hearty surfers. Half Moon Bay spreads out along Hwy 1 (called Cabrillo Hwy in town), but despite the development it's still relatively small. The main drag is a five-block stretch called Main St lined with shops, cafes, restaurants and a few upscale B&Bs. Visitor information is available from the **Half Moon Bay Coastside Chamber of Commerce** (☎650-726-8380; www.halfmoonbaychamber.org; 235 Main St; ⊙9am-5pm Mon-Fri).

Pumpkins are a major deal around Half Moon Bay, and the pre-Halloween harvest is celebrated in the annual **Art & Pumpkin Festival** (www.miramarevents.com/pumpkinfest). The mid-October event kicks off with the World Championship Pumpkin Weigh-Off, where the bulbous beasts can bust the scales at more than 1000lb.

Around 1 mile north of the Hwy 92 junction, **Sea Horse Ranch** (☎650-726-9903; www.seahorseranch.org) offers daily horseback rides along the beach. A two-hour ride is $75; an early-bird special leaves at 8am and cost just $50.

Sleeping & Eating

San Benito House HISTORIC HOTEL **$$$**
(☎650-726-3425; www.sanbenitohouse.com; 356 Main St; r incl breakfast with shared bath $80-100, r incl breakfast $130-200;) Supposedly a former bordello, this traditional Victorian inn has creaky wood floors and 11 neatly antiquated rooms without TVs. The saloon downstairs has live music a few nights a week, but doesn't stay open too late.

Pasta Moon ITALIAN **$$**
(☎650-726-5125; www.pastamoon.com; 315 Main St; mains $12-32; ⊙11:30am-2:30pm & 5:30-9pm) If you're in the mood for romantic Italian, come here for yummy housemade pasta, organic produce, locally sourced ingredients and all-Italian wine list. Reservations recommended on weekends.

Getting There & Away

SamTrans (☎800-660-4287; www.samtrans.com) bus 294 operates from the Hillsdale Caltrain station to Half Moon Bay, and up the coast to Moss Beach and Pacifica, weekdays until about 7:30pm ($2).

Half Moon Bay to Santa Cruz

With its long coastline, mild weather and abundant fresh water, this area has always been prime real estate. When Spanish missionaries set up shop along the California coast in the late 1700s, it had been Ohlone

SCENIC DRIVE: HIGHWAY 84

Inland, large stretches of the hills are protected in a patchwork of parks that, just like the coast, remain remarkably untouched despite the huge urban populations only a short drive to the north and east. Heading east toward Palo Alto, Hwy 84 winds its way through thick stands of redwood trees and several local parks with mountain biking and hiking opportunities.

A mile in from San Gregorio State Beach on Hwy 1, kick off your shoes and stomp your feet to live bluegrass, Celtic and folk music on the weekends at the landmark **San Gregorio General Store** (www.sangregoriostore.com), and check out the wooden bar singed by area branding irons.

Eight miles east is the tiny township of **La Honda**, former home to *One Flew Over the Cuckoo's Nest* author Ken Kesey, and the launching spot for his 1964 psychedelic bus trip immortalized in Tom Wolfe's *The Electric Kool-Aid Acid Test*. Housed in an old blacksmith's shop, **Apple Jack's Inn** (☎650-747-0331) is a rustic, down-home bar offering live music on weekends and lots of local color.

Indian territory for thousands of years. Pescadero was formally established in 1856, when it was mostly a farming and dairy settlement, although its location along the stagecoach route – now called Stage Rd – transformed it into a popular vacation destination. The Pigeon Point promontory was an active whaling station until 1900, when Prohibition-era bootleggers favored the isolated regional beaches for smuggling booze.

PESCADERO

A foggy speck of coastside crossroads between the cities of San Francisco and Santa Cruz, 150-year-old Pescadero is a close-knit rural town of sugar-lending neighbors and community pancake breakfasts. But on weekends the tiny downtown strains its seams with long-distance cyclists panting for carbohydrates and day trippers dive-bombing in from the ocean-front highway. They're all drawn to the winter vistas of emerald-green hills parched to burlap brown in summer, the wild Pacific beaches populated by seals and pelicans, and the food at a revered destination restaurant. With its cornucopia of tide-pool coves and parks of sky-blotting redwood canopy, city dwellers come here to slow down and smell the sea breeze wafting over fields of bushy artichokes.

Sights & Activities

A number of pretty sand beaches speckle the coast, though one of the most interesting places to stop is **Pebble Beach**, a tide pool jewel a mile and a half south of Pescadero Creek Rd. As the name implies, the shore is awash in bite-sized eye candy of agate, jade and carnelians, and sandstone troughs are pockmarked by groovy honeycombed formations called tafoni. Bird-watchers enjoy **Pescadero Marsh Reserve**, across the highway from Pescadero State Beach, where numerous species feed year-round.

TOP CHOICE **Pigeon Point Light Station** LIGHTHOUSE
(☎650-879-2120; www.parks.ca.gov/?page_id=533) Five miles south along the coast, the 115ft Light Station is one of the tallest lighthouses on the West Coast. The 1872 landmark had to close access to the Fresnel lens when chunks of its cornice began to rain from the sky, but the beam still flashes brightly and the bluff is a prime though blustery spot to scan for breaching gray whales. The hostel here is one of the best in the state.

Butano State Park PARK
(☎650-879-2040; parking fee $10) About 5 miles south of Pescadero, bobcats and full-throated coyotes reside discreetly in a dense redwood canyon. The hiking is also excellent further down the coast at Big Basin Redwoods State Park (p277), with the easiest access from Santa Cruz. Camping ($35 per site) is available at both parks.

Sleeping & Eating

Pescadero Creek Inn B&B B&B $$
(☎888-307-1898; www.pescaderocreekinn.com; 393 Stage Rd; r $170-255;) Unwind in the private two-room cottage or one of the spotless Victorian rooms in a restored 100-year-old farmhouse. Afternoon wine and cheese features wine bottled by the owners, and organic ingredients from the creekside garden spice up a hot breakfast.

Pigeon Point Lighthouse Hostel HOSTEL $
(☎650-879-0633; www.norcalhostels.org/pigeon; dm $24-26, r $72-98; @) Not your workaday HI outpost, this highly coveted coastside hostel is all about location. Check in early to snag a spot in the outdoor hot tub, and contemplate roaring waves as the lighthouse beacon races through a starburst sky.

Costanoa Lodge RESORT $$
(☎650-879-1100, 877-262-7848; www.costanoa.com; 2001 Rossi Rd; tent cabin $89-145, cabin $189-199, lodge r $179-279;) Even though the resort includes a **campground** (☎800-562-9867; www.koa.com/campgrounds/santa-cruz-north; tent site $22-52, RV site from $65), no one can pull a straight face to declare they're actually roughing it here. Down bedding swaddles guests in cushy canvas tent cabins, and chill-averse tent campers can use communal 'comfort stations' with 24-hour dry saunas, fireside patio seating, heated floors and hot showers. Lodge rooms with private fireplaces and hot tub access fulfill the whims of those without such spartan delusions. There's a **restaurant** (dinner mains $15-27) and spa on site; bicycle rentals and horseback riding are available as well.

TOP CHOICE **Duarte's Tavern** AMERICAN $$
(☎650-879-0464; www.duartestavern.com; 202 Stage Rd; mains $11-40) You'll rub shoulders with fancy-pants foodies, spandex-swathed cyclists and dusty cowboys in spurs at this casual and surprisingly unpretentious

THE CULINARY COAST

Pescadero is renowned for Duarte's Tavern (see opposite page), but loads of other scrumptious tidbits are very close by.

Phipps Country Store (2700 Pescadero Creek Rd;) Peek inside the shop, known universally as 'the bean store,' to marvel at whitewashed bins overflowing with dried heirloom varieties with names like Eye of the Goat, Painted Lady and Desert Pebble.

Arcangeli Grocery/Norm's Market (287 Stage Rd; sandwiches $6-8.50) Create a picnic with made-to-order deli sandwiches, homemade artichoke salsa and a chilled bottle of California wine. And don't go breezing out the door without nabbing a crusty loaf of the famous artichoke garlic herb bread, fresh-baked almost hourly.

Harley Farms Cheese Shop (650-879-0480; www.harleyfarms.com; 250 North St;) Follow the cool wooden cut-outs of the goat and the Wellington-shod girl with the faraway eyes. Another local food treasure with creamy artisanal goat cheeses festooned with fruit, nuts and a rainbow of edible flowers. Weekend farm tours by reservation. Splurge for a seat at one of the monthly five-course farm dinners in the restored barn's airy hayloft.

Pie Ranch (www.pieranch.org; 2080 Cabrillo Hwy; noon-6pm Sat & Sun Mar-Oct;) Hit the brakes for this roadside farmstand in a wooden barn, and pick up fresh produce, eggs and coffee, plus amazing pies made with the fruit grown here. The historic pie-shaped farm is a nonprofit dedicated to leadership development and food education for urban youth. Check the website for details on its monthly farm tours and barn dances. Located 11 miles south of Pescadero Creek Rd.

Swanton Berry Farm (650-469-8804; www.swantonberryfarm.com; Coastways Ranch, 640 Cabrillo Hwy) To get a better appreciation of the rigors and rewards of farm life, smoosh up your shirtsleeves and harvest some fruit at this organic pick-your-own farm near Año Nuevo. It's a union outfit (operated by Cesar Chavez's United Farm Workers), with buckets of seasonal kiwis and olallieberries ripe for the plucking. Its farm stand and strawberry u-pick is 8.5 miles further south near Davenport.

fourth-generation family restaurant. Duarte's (pronounced DOO-arts) is the culinary magnet of Pescadero, and for many the town and eatery are synonymous. Feast on crab cioppino and a half-and-half split of the cream of artichoke and green chili soups, and bring it home with a wedge of olallieberry pie. Except for the unfortunate lull of Prohibition, the wood-paneled bar has been hosting the locals and their honored guests since 1894. Reservations recommended.

Getting There & Away

By car, the town is 3 miles east from Hwy 1 on Pescadero Creek Rd, south of San Gregorio State Beach. On weekdays, **SamTrans** bus 17 runs to/from Half Moon Bay twice a day.

AÑO NUEVO STATE RESERVE

More raucous than a full-moon beach rave, thousands of boisterous elephant seals party down year-round on the dunes of Año Nuevo point, their squeals and barks reaching fever pitch during the winter pupping season. The beach is 5 miles south of Pigeon Point and 27 miles north of Santa Cruz. Check out the park's live **SealCam** (www.parks.ca.gov/popup/main.asp).

Elephant seals were just as fearless two centuries ago as they are today, but unfortunately, club-toting seal trappers were not in the same seal-friendly category as camera-toting tourists. Between 1800 and 1850, the elephant seal was driven to the edge of extinction. Only a handful survived around the Guadalupe Islands off the Mexican state of Baja California. With the availability of substitutes for seal oil and the conservationist attitudes of more recent times, the elephant seal has made a comeback, reappearing on the Southern California coast from around 1920. In 1955 they returned to Año Nuevo Beach.

In the midwinter peak season, during the mating and birthing time from December 15 to the end of March, you must plan well ahead if you want to visit the reserve, because visitors are only permitted access through heavily booked guided tours. For the busiest period, mid-January to mid-February, it's recommended you book eight weeks ahead. If you haven't booked, bad weather can sometimes lead to last-minute cancellations.

The rest of the year, advance reservations aren't necessary, but visitor permits from the entrance station are required; arrive before 3pm from September through November and by 3:30pm from April through August.

Although the **park office** (☎650-879-2025, recorded information 650-879-0227; www.parks.ca.gov/?page_id=523) can answer general questions, high season tour bookings must be made at ☎800-444-4445 or http://anonuevo.reserveamerica.com. When required, these tours cost $7, and parking is $10 per car year-round. From the ranger station it's a 3- to 5-mile round-trip hike on sand, and a visit takes two to three hours. No dogs are allowed on-site, and visitors aren't permitted for the first two weeks of December.

There's another, more convenient viewing site further south in Piedras Blancas.

Pacific Coast Highway

Make your escape from those tangled, traffic-jammed freeways and cruise in the slow lane. Snaking for more than 1000 miles along dizzying sea cliffs, California's legendary coastal highways connect the dots between perpetually sunny San Diego, star-powered Los Angeles and bohemian San Francisco. In between, you'll uncover hidden beaches and surf breaks, rustic seafood shacks and wooden piers for catching sunsets over boundless Pacific horizons.

Pacific Coast Highway

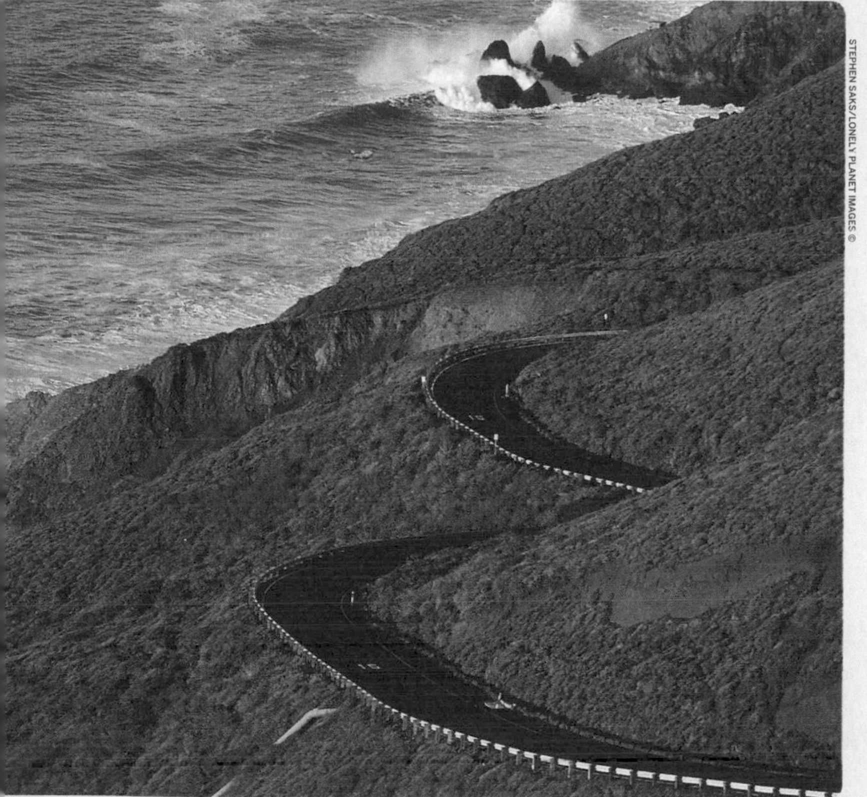

STEPHEN SAKS/LONELY PLANET IMAGES ©

A Beautiful Devil of a Road

In pop culture, the Pacific Coast Highway (PCH) refers to California's entire coastal highway. But officially it's only the short, sun-loving stretch of Hwy 1 along Southern California's Orange County coast that can legally call itself PCH. But never mind those technicalities because equally scenic ribbons of Hwys 1 and 101 await further north, most famously along the Big Sur coast.

Both highways are known for their hairpin turns, steep drop-offs and rocky, muddy landslides, especially when winter storms drench the coast or if late-summer wildfires wreak havoc. Some of the riskiest (and most thrilling!) sections of California's coastal highways regularly close for seemingly never-ending road work and repairs (see p518).

BEST TIMES TO GO

» **Apr–May** After winter rains end, wildflowers bloom and waterfalls peak, but be prepared for 'May gray' weather.

» **Jul–Aug** Summer vacationers crowd the beaches; 'June gloom' fog may linger into July.

» **Sep–Oct** Mostly sunny skies, crisp cool days and far fewer crowds.

Clockwise from top left
1. Stout Grove, Jedediah Smith Redwoods State Park (p265) **2.** Malibu (p360) **3.** Surfer, Del Mar (p457)

JOHN ELK III/LONELY PLANET IMAGES ©

2

SCOTT TUCKER/ALAMY ©

San Francisco to Oregon

A One-Week Itinerary

Northern California's forests and fishing villages sprawl along the continent's edge. Political radicals, maverick artists, pot farmers and nature lovers gravitate here.

JUDY BELLAH/LONELY PLANET IMAGES ©

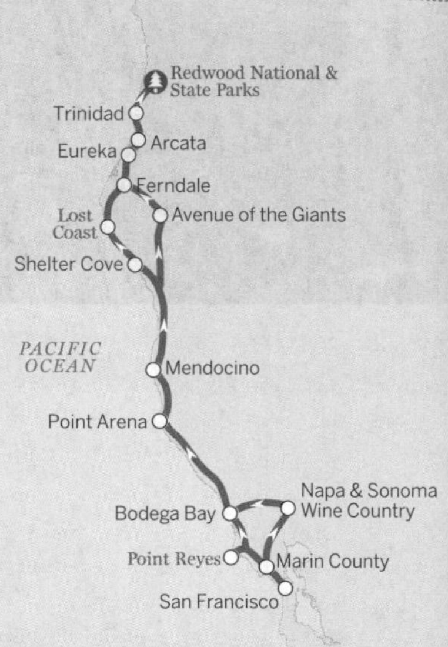

» Get a primer on NorCal's left-leaning beatnik scene starting in **San Francisco** (p48).

» North of the Golden Gate Bridge, outdoorsy **Marin County** (p101) has gorgeous beaches and grassy headlands for exploring.

» Go hiking at **Point Reyes** (p119), devour some fresh oysters or detour inland to **Napa & Sonoma wine country** (p159).

» Made famous by Hitchcock's thriller *The Birds*, **Bodega Bay** (p215) is a gateway to the Sonoma Coast, an eco-haven.

» Keep going north past **Point Arena's lighthouse** (p221) to the fairytale Victorian village of **Mendocino** (p223).

» At Leggett, Hwy 1 rejoins Hwy 101 and the Redwood Empire begins, trundling north to the **Avenue of the Giants** (p247).

» To really get away from it all, detour west to Shelter Cove and the **Lost Coast** (p245).

» When you crave civilization again, visit the farm town of **Ferndale** (p249); the salty sea-dogs' lair of **Eureka** (p251); the trippy, hippie-dippy university town of **Arcata** (p254); or postcard-perfect bayside **Trinidad** (p257).

» Then it's onward into the heart of redwood country. In **Redwood National & State Parks** (p260), take time out for Tall Trees Grove, Fern Canyon, Gold Bluffs Beach and the winding Newton B Drury Scenic Parkway.

Clockwise from top left

1. Golden Gate Bridge (p51), San Francisco **2.** Motorcycling, Humboldt Redwoods State Park (p247) **3.** Wine tasting, Iron Horse Vineyards (p195), Russian River Valley **4.** Point Reyes Lighthouse (p120), Marin County

2

3

San Francisco to Los Angeles

A One-Week Itinerary

Wrongly considered 'flyover' country between San Francisco and LA, the Central Coast is a natural wonderland, from Monterey Bay's underwater canyons and Big Sur's sea cliffs to the beaches of Santa Barbara.

1

4

JUDY BELLAH/LONELY PLANET IMAGES ©

» Just driving Hwy 1 south of **San Francisco** (p48) via **Half Moon Bay** (p147) feels like you're dangling off the edge of the world.

» If you love San Francisco's bohemian side, spend an afternoon in wacky **Santa Cruz** (p269).

» **Monterey** (p278) has the rough-and-ready seafaring atmosphere of a John Steinbeck novel.

» Heading south, Hwy 1 plunges into **Big Sur** (p291), where modern-day beatniks gather.

» Emerging from redwood forests, Hwy 1 passes **Hearst Castle** (p299), a monumental hilltop mansion.

» Slow down for the university town of **San Luis Obispo** (p312), with sea kayaking, lazy beaches and volcanic peaks to climb.

Clockwise from top left

1. Pacific Coast Highway, near Montara (p146) **2.** Pigeon Point Light Station (p148) **3.** Beachfront, Santa Cruz (p269) **4.** Street art, San Luis Obispo (p312)

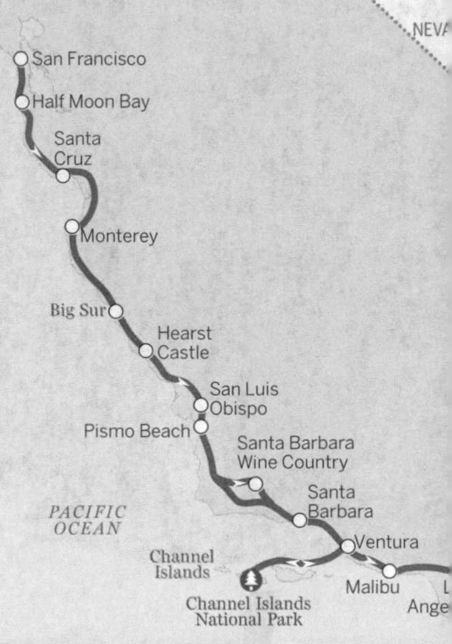

» From retro **Pismo Beach** (p320), Hwy 1 detours out to the monumental sand dunes of Guadalupe.

» Veer off Hwy 101 to taste the fruits of **Santa Barbara wine country** (p322).

» Fall under the spell of a sunny Mediterranean climate, red-tiled roofs and golden beaches in **Santa Barbara** (p327).

» From **Ventura** (p338), sail out to **Chann Islands National Park** (p336) to get truly wet and wild.

» Cruise south on Hwy 1 through star-studded **Malibu** (p360), where celebrity sightings are as predictable as the tides, before heading to **LA** (p341).

2

EDDIE BRADY/LONELY PLANET IMAGES ©

3

JOHN ELK III/LONELY PLANET IMAGES ©

Los Angeles to San Diego

A Five-Day Itinerary

On this short stretch of coastal highway from LA south to San Diego, dive headfirst into a dreamscape of beautiful beaches, epic waves and surfside towns.

RICHARD CUMMINS/LONELY PLANET IMAGES ©

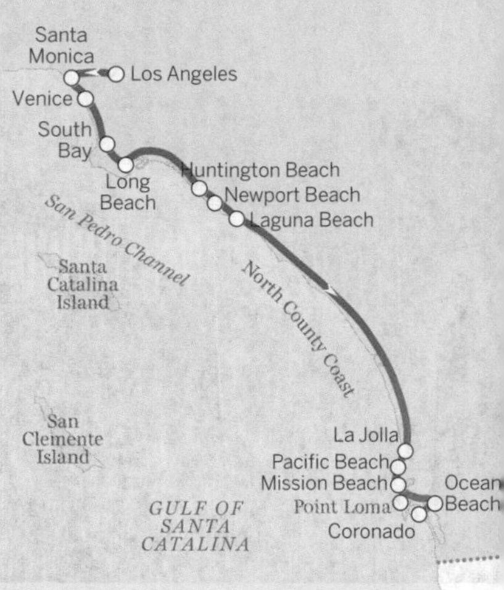

» Starting in **LA** (p341) take a spin on the solar-powered Ferris wheel on the pier at **Santa Monica** (p361) and rollerblade along the beach boardwalk in oddball **Venice** (p361).

» Fashionistas, surfers and beach-volleyball stars head to LA's **South Bay** (p362), with flirty Manhattan Beach, funky Hermosa Beach and touristy Redondo Beach.

» Follow Hwy 1 around the Palos Verdes Peninsula for mesmerizing sea views, then visit the aquarium and HMS *Queen Mary* in **Long Beach** (p363).

» Party-animal **Huntington Beach** (p409) in Orange County claims the title of 'Surf City USA.'

» Don your strappy sandals and Gucci sunglasses for the white sands of **Newport Beach** (p411).

» A former artists' colony, ritzy **Laguna Beach** is another movie-star beautiful hamlet you may never want to leave (p415).

» Easy does it along San Diego's **North County Coast** (p457), rolling south to fancy-pants **La Jolla** (p440), with its wilder nature reserves.

» Join the regular people at **Pacific Beach** (p439), ride the roller coaster at **Mission Beach** (p439) or take a pretty pier walk at **Ocean Beach** (p437) in San Diego.

» Visit the lighthouse at **Point Loma** (p437) and finish up your road trip with a cocktail at the swanky 'Hotel Del' in **Coronado** (p436).

Above
1. Bodybuilders, Venice (p368) **2.** Seagrove Park (p459), San Diego

Napa & Sonoma Wine Country

Includes »

Best Places to Eat

- Zazu (p207)
- Oxbow Public Market (p171)
- Fremont Diner (p189)
- Madrona Manor (p210)

Best Places to Stay

- Beltane Ranch (p192)
- Cottages of Napa Valley (p170)
- Mountain Home Ranch (p178)
- El Bonita Motel (p175)
- Auberge du Soleil (p174)

Why Go?

America's premier viticulture region has earned its reputation among the world's best. Despite hype about Wine Country style, it's from the land that all Wine Country lore springs. Rolling hills, dotted with century-old oaks, turn the color of lion's fur under the summer sun and swaths of vineyards carpet hillsides as far as the eye can see. Where they end, lush redwood forests follow serpentine rivers to the sea.

There are over 600 wineries in Napa and Sonoma Counties, but it's quality, not quantity, that sets the region apart – especially in Napa, which competes with France and doubles as an outpost of San Francisco's top-end culinary scene. Sonoma prides itself on agricultural diversity, with goat-cheese farms, you-pick-em orchards and roadside fruit stands. Plan to get lost on back roads, and, as you picnic atop sun-dappled hillsides, grab a hunk of earth and know firsthand the thing of greatest meaning in Wine Country.

When to Go

Napa

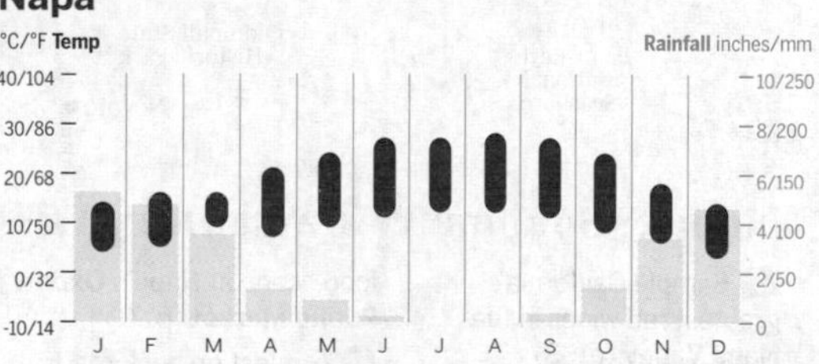

Jan Bright-yellow flowers carpet the valleys during the off-season; room rates plummet.

May Before summer holidays, the weather is perfect for touring, with long days and hot sun.

Sep–Oct 'Crush' time is peak season, when winemaking operations are in full force.

Wine Tasting

To help you discover the real Wine Country, we've mostly avoided factories and listed family-owned boutique houses (producing fewer than 20,000-annual cases) and midsized houses (20,000- to 60,000-annual cases). Why does it matter? Think of it. If you were to attend two dinner parties, one for 10 people, one for 1000, which would have the better food? Small wineries maintain tighter control. Also, you won't easily find these wines elsewhere.

Tastings are called 'flights' and include four-to-six different wines. Napa wineries charge $10 to $50. In Sonoma Valley, tastings cost $5 to $15, refundable with purchase. In Sonoma County, tastings are free or $5 to $10. You must be 21 to taste.

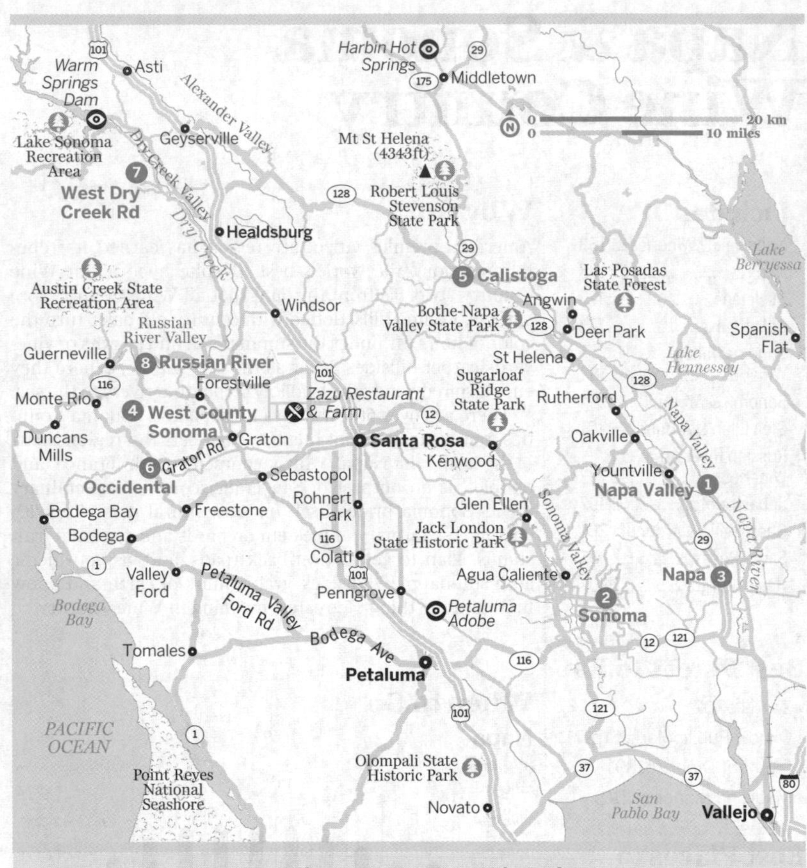

Napa & Sonoma Wine Country Highlights

1. Sample California's greatest red wines in the **Napa Valley** (p163)
2. Picnic in sun-dappled shade on the state's largest town square, **Sonoma Plaza** (p185)
3. Bite into the artisinal food scene at Napa's **Oxbow Public Market** (p171)
4. Get lost on back roads in **West County Sonoma** (p193)
5. Submerge yourself in a volcanic-ash mud bath in **Calistoga** (p177)
6. Chill with locals at the **Occidental Farmers Market** (p199)
7. Pedal between wineries along pastoral **West Dry Creek Rd** (p196)
8. Float in a canoe or kayak down the **Russian River** (p194)

Do not drink and drive. The curvy roads are dangerous, and police monitor traffic, especially on Napa's Hwy 29.

To avoid burnout, visit no more than three wineries per day. Most open daily from 10am or 11am to 4pm or 5pm, but call ahead if you've got your heart set, or absolutely want a tour, especially in Napa, where law requires that some wineries accept visitors only by appointment. If you're buying, ask if the winery has a wine club, which is often free to join and provides discounts, but you'll have to agree to buy a certain amount annually.

High Season vs Low

Many Wine Country restaurants and hotels diminish operations in wintertime. We list high-season hours and rates. Make reservations, especially in summer, or you may not eat. Hotel rates increase during September and October's grape-crushing season – the most popular time to come.

Getting There & Away

Napa and Sonoma counties each have an eponymous city and valley. So, the town of Sonoma is in Sonoma County, at the southern end of Sonoma Valley. The same goes for the city, county and valley of Napa.

From San Francisco, public transportation gets you to the valleys, but it's insufficient for vineyard-hopping. For public-transit information, dial ☎511 from Bay Area telephones, or look online at www.transit.511.org.

Both valleys are 90 minutes' drive from San Francisco. Napa, the farther inland, has over 400 wineries and attracts the most visitors (expect heavy traffic summer weekends). Sonoma County has 260 wineries, 40 in Sonoma Valley, which is less commercial and less congested than Napa. If you have time to visit only one, choose Sonoma for ease.

Bus

Evans Transportation (☎707-255-1559; www.evanstransportation.com) Shuttles ($29) to Napa from San Francisco and Oakland Airports.

Golden Gate Transit (☎415-923-2000; www.goldengate.org) Bus 70/80 from San Francisco to Petaluma ($9.25) and Santa Rosa ($10.25); board at 1st and Mission Sts. Connect with Sonoma County Transit buses (p161).

Greyhound (☎800-231-2222; www.greyhound.com) San Francisco to Santa Rosa ($22 to $30) and Vallejo ($17 to $23); transfer for local buses.

Napa Valley Vine (☎800-696-6443, 707-251-2800; www.nctpa.net) Operates bus 10 from the Vallejo Ferry Terminal and Vallejo Transit bus station, via Napa, to Calistoga ($2.90).

Sonoma County Airport Express (☎707-837-8700, 800-327-2024; www.airportexpressinc.com) Shuttles ($34) between Sonoma County Airport (Santa Rosa) and San Francisco and Oakland Airports.

Sonoma County Transit (☎707-576-7433, 800-345-7433; www.sctransit.com) Buses from Santa Rosa to Petaluma ($2.35, 70 minutes), Sonoma ($2.90, 1¼ hours) and western Sonoma County, including Russian River Valley towns ($2.90, 30 minutes).

Car

From San Francisco, take Hwy 101 north over the Golden Gate Bridge, then Hwy 37 east to Hwy 121 north; continue to the junction of Hwys 12/121. For Sonoma Valley, take Hwy 12 north; for Napa Valley, take Hwy 12/121 east. Plan 70 minutes in light traffic, two hours during weekday commute times.

Hwy 12/121 splits south of Napa: Hwy 121 turns north and joins with Hwy 29 (aka St Helena Hwy); Hwy 12 merges with southbound Hwy 29 toward Vallejo. Hwy 29 backs up weekdays 3pm to 7pm, slowing returns to San Francisco.

From the East Bay (or from downtown San Francisco), take I-80 east to Hwy 37 west (north of Vallejo), then northbound Hwy 29.

From Santa Rosa, take Hwy 12 east to access the northern end of Sonoma Valley. From Petaluma and Hwy 101, take Hwy 116 east.

Ferry

Baylink Ferry (☎877-643-3779; www.baylinkferry.com) Downtown San Francisco to Vallejo (adult/child $13/6.50, 60 minutes); connect with Napa Valley Vine Bus 10 (p161).

Trains

Amtrak (☎800-872-7245; www.amtrak.com) trains travel to Martinez (south of Vallejo), with connecting buses to Napa (45 minutes), Santa Rosa (1¼ hours) and Healdsburg (1¾ hours).

BART trains (☎415 989-2278; www.bart.gov) run from San Francisco to El Cerrito del Norte ($4.05, 30 minutes). Transfer to **Vallejo Transit** (☎707-648-4666; www.vallejotransit.com) for Vallejo ($5, 30 minutes), then take Napa Valley Vine buses to Napa and Calistoga.

Getting Around

You'll need a car to winery-hop. Alternatively visit tasting rooms in downtown Napa or downtown Sonoma.

Bicycle

Touring Wine Country by bicycle is unforgettable. Stick to back roads. We most love pastoral West Dry Creek Rd, northwest of Healdsburg, in

NAPA OR SONOMA?

Napa and Sonoma valleys run parallel, a few miles apart, separated by the narrow, imposing Mayacamas Mountains. The two couldn't be more different. It's easy to mock aggressively sophisticated Napa, its monuments to ego, trophy homes and trophy wives, $1000-a-night inns, $40+ tastings and wine-snob visitors, but Napa makes some of the world's best wines. Constrained by its geography, it stretches along a single valley, so it's easy to visit. Drawbacks are high prices and heavy traffic, but there are 400 nearly side-by-side wineries. And the valley is gorgeous.

Sonoma County is much more down-to-earth and politically left leaning. You'll see lots more rusted-out pick-ups. Though becoming gentrified, Sonoma lacks Napa's chic factor (Healdsburg notwithstanding), and locals like it that way. The wines are more approachable, but the county's 260 wineries are spread out (see boxed text p186). If you're here on a weekend, head to Sonoma (County or Valley), which gets less traffic, but on a weekday, see Napa, too. Ideally schedule two to four days: one for each valley, and one or two additional for western Sonoma County.

Spring and fall are the best times to visit. Summers are hot, dusty and crowded. Fall brings fine weather, harvest time and the 'crush,' the pressing of the grapes, but lodging prices skyrocket. For cost-saving tips on lodging in Napa, see p167.

Sonoma County. Through Sonoma Valley, take Arnold Dr instead of Hwy 12; through Napa Valley, take the Silverado Trail instead of Hwy 29.

Cycling between wineries isn't demanding – the valleys are mostly flat – but crossing between Napa and Sonoma Valleys is intense, particularly via steep Oakville Grade and Trinity Rd (between Oakville and Glen Ellen).

Bicycles, in boxes, can be checked on Greyhound buses for $30 to $40; bike boxes cost $10 (call ahead). You can transport bicycles on Golden Gate Transit buses, which usually have free racks available (first-come, first-served). For rentals, see Tours (this page).

Car

Napa Valley is 30-miles long and 5-miles wide at its widest point (the city of Napa), 1 mile at its narrowest (Calistoga). Two roads run north–south: Hwy 29 (St Helena Hwy) and the more scenic Silverado Trail, a mile east. Drive up one, down the other.

The American Automobile Association determined Napa Valley to be America's 8th most congested rural vacation destination. Summer and fall weekend traffic is unbearable, especially on Hwy 29 between Napa and St Helena. Plan accordingly.

Cross-valley roads that link Silverado Trail with Hwy 29 – including Yountville, Oakville and Rutherford crossroads – are bucolic and get less traffic. For scenery, the Oakville Grade and rural Trinity Rd (which leads southwest to Hwy 12 in Sonoma Valley) are narrow, curvy and beautiful – but treacherous in rainstorms. Mt Veeder Rd leads through pristine countryside west of Yountville.

Note: Police watch like hawks for traffic violators. *Don't drink and drive*.

Shortcuts between Napa and Sonoma Valleys: from Oakville, take Oakville Grade to Trinity Rd; from St Helena, take Spring Mountain Rd into Calistoga Rd; from Calistoga, take Petrified Forest Rd to Calistoga Rd.

Public Transportation

Napa Valley Vine (☎800-696-6443, 707-251-2800; www.nctpa.net) Bus 10 from downtown Napa to Calistoga ($2.15, 1¼ hours).

Sonoma County Transit (☎707-576-7433, 800-345-7433; www.sctransit.com) Buses from Santa Rosa to Petaluma ($2.35, 70 minutes), Sonoma ($2.90, 1¼ hours) and western Sonoma County, including Russian River Valley towns ($2.90, 30 minutes).

Train

A cushy, if touristy, way to see Wine Country, the **Napa Valley Wine Train** (☎707-253-2111, 800-427-4124; www.winetrain.com; adult/child from $89/55) offers three-hour daily trips in vintage Pullman dining cars, from Napa to St Helena and back, with an optional winery tour. Trains depart from McKinstry St near 1st St.

Tours

For balloons and airplane rides, see the boxed text, p173.

Bicycle

Guided tours start around $90 per day including bikes, tastings and lunch. Daily rentals cost $25 to $85; make reservations.

Backroads (☎800-462-2848; www.backroads.com) All-inclusive guided biking and walking.

Calistoga Bike Shop (☎707-942-9687, 866-942-2453; www.calistogabikeshop.com; 1318 Lincoln Ave, Calistoga) Wine-tour rental package ($80) includes wine pickup.

Getaway Adventures (☎707-568-3040, 800-499-2453; www.getawayadventures.com) Great guided tours, some combined with kayaking, of Napa, Sonoma, Calistoga, Healdsburg and Russian River. Single- and multi-day trips.

Good Time Touring (☎707-938-0453, 888-525-0453; www.goodtimetouring.com) Tours of Sonoma Valley, Dry Creek and West County Sonoma.

Napa River Vélo (☎707-258-8729; www.naparivervelo.com; 680 Main St, rear of Bldg, Napa) Daily rentals and weekend tours with wine pickup.

Napa Valley Adventure Tours (☎707-259-1833, 877-548-6877; www.napavalleyadventuretours.com; Oxbow Public Market, 610 1st St, Napa) Guides tours between wineries, off-road trips, hiking and kayaking. Daily rentals.

Napa Valley Bike Tours (☎707-944-2953, 800-707-2453; www.napavalleybiketours.com; 6488 Washington St, Yountville) Daily rentals; easy and moderately difficult tours.

Sonoma Valley Cyclery (Map p184; ☎707-935-3377; www.sonomacyclery.com; 20093 Broadway, Sonoma) Daily rentals; Sonoma Valley tours.

Spoke Folk Cyclery (☎707-433-7171; www.spokefolk.com; 201 Center St, Healdsburg) Daily rentals near Dry Creek Valley.

Jeeps

Wine Country Jeep Tours (☎707-546-1822, 800-539-5337; www.jeeptours.com; 3hr tour $75) Tour Wine Country's back roads and boutique wineries by Jeep, year-round at 10am and 1pm. Also operates tours of Sonoma Coast.

Limousine

Antique Tours Limousine (☎707-226-9227; www.antiquetours.net) Hit the road in style in a 1947 Packard convertible; tours cost $130 per hour (minimum five hours).

Beau Wine Tours (☎707-938-8001, 800-387-2328; www.beauwinetours.com) Winery tours in sedans and stretch limos; charges $60 to $95 per hour (3-hour minimum weekdays, 6 hours weekends).

Beyond the Label (☎707-363-4023; www.btlnv.com; per person $299) Personalized tours, including lunch at home with a vintner, guided by a Napa native.

Flying Horse Carriage Company (☎707-849-8989; www.flyinghorse.org; 4hr tours per person $145) Clippety-clop through Alexander Valley by horse-drawn carriage. Includes picnic.

Magnum Tours (☎707-753-0088; www.magnumwinetours.com) Sedans and specialty limousines from $65 to $125 per hour (four-hour minimum, five hours Saturdays). Exceptional service.

NAPA VALLEY

The birthplace of modern-day Wine Country is famous for regal cabernet sauvignons, château-like wineries and fabulous food. Napa Valley attracts more than four million visitors a year, each expecting to be wined, dined, soaked in hot-springs spas and tucked between crisp linens.

Just a few decades ago, this 5 by 35 mile strip of former stagecoach stops seemed forgotten by time. Grapes had grown here since the Gold Rush, but grape-sucking phylloxera bugs, Prohibition and the Great Depression reduced 140 wineries, in the 1890s, to around 25 by the 1960s.

In 1968, Napa was declared the 'Napa Valley Agricultural Preserve', effectively blocking future valley development for non-agricultural purposes. The law stipulated no subdivision of valley-floor land under 40 acres. This succeeded in preserving the valley's natural beauty, but when Napa wines earned top honors at a 1976 blind tasting in Paris, the wine-drinking world took note and land values shot through the roof. Only the very rich could afford to build. Hence, so many architecturally jaw-dropping wineries. Independent, family-owned wineries still exist – we highlight a number of them – but much of Napa Valley is now owned by global conglomerates.

The city of Napa anchors the valley, but the real work happens up-valley. Napa isn't as pretty as other towns, but has some noteworthy sights, among them Oxbow Public Market (p168). Scenic towns include St Helena, Yountville and Calistoga – the latter more famous for water than wine.

Napa Valley Wineries

Cab is king in Napa. No varietal captures imaginations like the fruit of the cabernet sauvignon vine – Bordeaux is the French equivalent – and no wine fetches a higher price. Napa farmers can't afford *not* to grow cabernet. Other heat-loving varietals, such as sangiovese and merlot, also thrive here.

Napa's wines merit their reputation among the world's finest – complex, with luxurious finishes. Napa wineries sell many 'buy-and-hold' wines, versus Sonoma's 'drink-now' wines.

Artesa Winery WINERY

(Map p164; ☎707-224-1668; www.artesawinery.com; 1345 Henry Rd; nonreserve/reserve tastings $10/15; ⊙10am-4:30pm) Begin or end the day with a glass of bubbly or pinot at Artesa, southwest of Napa. Built into a mountainside, the ultramodern Barcelona-style architecture is stunning, and you can't beat the top-of-the-world vistas over San Pablo Bay. Free tours leave 11am and 2pm. Bottles cost $20 to $60.

Vintners' Collective TASTING ROOM

(Map p169; ☎707-255-7150; www.vintnerscollective.com; 1245 Main St; Napa tasting $25; ⊙11am-6pm) Ditch the car and chill in downtown Napa at this super-cool tasting bar – inside a former 19th-century brothel – that represents 20 high-end boutique wineries too small to have their own tasting rooms.

Ceja WINERY

(Map p164; ☎707-226-6445; www.cejavineyards.com; 1248 First St; tasting $10; ⊙11am-6pm Sun-Wed, 11am-8pm Thu-Sat; 🐾) Ceja was founded by former vineyard workers, who now craft superb pinot noir and unusual blends, including a great pinot-syrah-cabernet for $20. The tasting room stays open late, and features interesting art, including Maceo Montoya's mural celebrating winemaking's roots. Bottles cost $20 to $50.

Twenty Rows WINERY

(off Map p169; ☎707-287-1063; www.vinoce.com; 880 Vallejo St, Napa; tasting $10; ⊙11am-5pm Tue-Sat) Downtown Napa's only working winery crafts light-on-the-palate cabernet sauvignon for a mere $20 a bottle. Taste in the barrel room – a chilly garage with plastic furniture – with fun dudes who know wine. Good sauvignon blanc, too.

Hess Collection WINERY

(Map p164; ☎707-255-1144; www.hesscollection.com; 4411 Redwood Rd; tastings $10; ⊙10am-4pm; 🐾) Art lovers: don't miss Hess Collection, whose galleries display mixed-media and large-canvas works, including pieces by Francis Bacon and Louis Soutter. In the cave-like tasting room, you can find well-known cabernet and chardonnay, but also try the viognier. Hess overlooks the valley, so be prepared to drive a winding road. (NB: Hess Collection is not be be confused

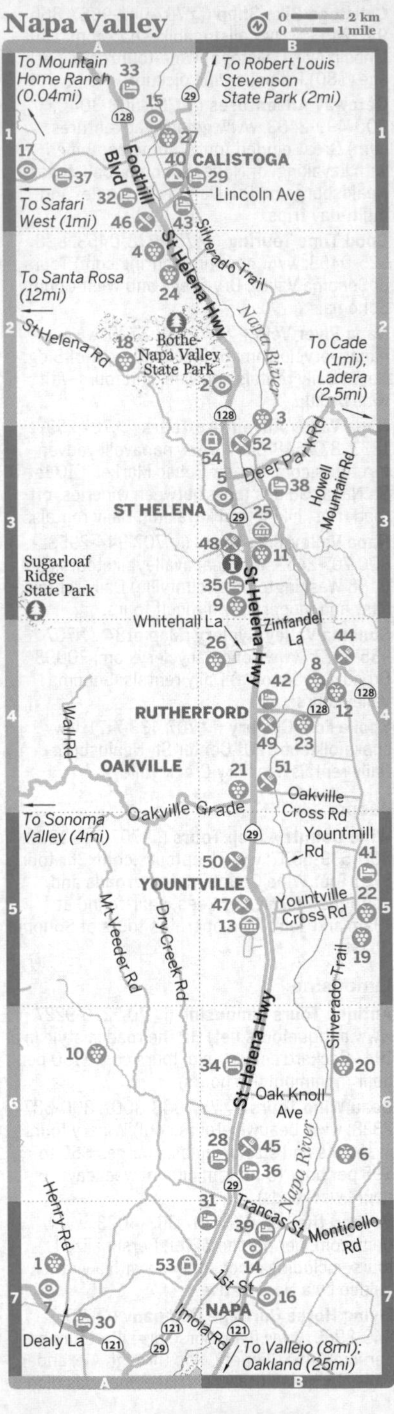

Napa Valley

Sights

1 Artesa Winery A7
2 Bale Grist Mill State Historic Park B2
3 Casa Nuestra B2
4 Castello di Amorosa A2
5 Culinary Institute of America at Greystone B3
6 Darioush B6
7 Di Rosa Preserve A7
Elizabeth Spencer (see 49)
8 Frog's Leap B4
9 Hall B3
10 Hess Collection A6
Lava Vine (see 43)
11 Long Meadow Ranch B3
12 Mumm Napa B4
13 Napa Valley Museum B5
14 Napa Valley Wine Train Depot B7
Oat Hill Mine MTB Trail (see 29)
15 Old Faithful Geyser A1
16 Oxbow Public Market B7
17 Petrified Forest A1
18 Pride Mountain A2
19 Quixote B5
20 Regusci B6
21 Robert Mondavi B4
22 Robert Sinskey B5
23 Round Pond B4
24 Schramsberg A2
25 Silverado Museum B3
26 Tres Sabores B4
27 Vincent Arroyo A1

Activities, Courses & Tours

Calistoga Spa Hot Springs (see 29)
Lavender Hill Spa (see 46)
Spa Solage (see 43)

Sleeping

Auberge de Soleil (see 44)
Aurora Park Cottage (see 32)
28 Best Western Ivy Hotel B6
29 Calistoga Spa Hot Springs B1
30 Carneros Inn A7
31 Chablis Inn B7
32 Chanric Inn A1
33 Chateau de Vie A1
34 Cottages of Napa Valley B6
35 El Bonita Motel B3
36 John Muir Inn B6
37 Meadowlark Country House A1
38 Meadowood B3
39 Milliken Creek Inn B7
40 Napa County Fairgrounds & RV Park A1
Napa Valley Redwood Inn (see 31)
41 Poetry Inn B5
42 Rancho Caymus B4
43 Solage A1
Wine Way Inn (see 46)

Eating

44 Auberge de Soleil B4
45 Bistro Don Giovanni B6
Boon Fly Café (see 30)
46 Buster's Southern BBQ A1
47 Étoile B5
Farmstead (see 11)
48 Gott's Roadside B3
49 La Luna Market & Taqueria B4
50 Mustards Grill B5
51 Oakville Grocery & Cafe B4
Oxbow Public Market (see 16)
Pica-Pica Maize Kitchen (see 16)
Restaurant at Meadowood (see 38)
52 Silverado Brewing Co. B3
Solbar (see 43)
Wine Spectator Restaurant at Greystone (see 5)

Entertainment

Lincoln Theater (see 13)

Shopping

53 Napa Premium Outlets A7
54 St Helena Marketplace B3

with Hess Select, the grocery-store brand.) Bottles cost $15 to $60. Reservations are recommended.

Darioush WINERY

(Map p164; ☎707-257-2345; www.darioush.com; 4240 Silverado Trail; tastings $18-35; ⏰10:30am-5pm) Like a modern-day Persian palace, Darioush ranks high on the fabulosity scale, with towering columns, Le Corbusier furniture, Persian rugs and travertine walls. Though known for cabernet, Darioush also bottles chardonnay, merlot and shiraz, all made with 100% of their respective varietals. Call about wine-and-cheese pairings. Bottles cost $40 to $80.

BOOKING APPOINTMENTS

Because of strict county zoning laws, many Napa wineries cannot legally receive drop-in visitors; unless you've come strictly to buy, you'll have to call ahead. This is *not* the case with all wineries. We recommend booking one appointment and planning your day around it.

Regusci WINERY

(Map p164; ☎707-254-0403; www.regusciwinery.com; 5584 Silverado Trail, Napa; tasting $15-25; ⊙10am-5pm; 🐾) One of Napa's oldest, unfussy Regusci dates to the late 1800s, with 173 acres of vineyards unfurling around a century-old stone winery that makes Bordeaux-style blends on the valley's quieter eastern side – good when traffic up-valley is bad. No appointment necessary; lovely oak-shaded picnic area. Bottles run $36 to $125.

Robert Sinskey WINERY

(Map p164; ☎707-944-9090; www.robertsinskey.com; 6320 Silverado Trail; tastings $25; ⊙10am-4:30pm) For hilltop views and food-friendly wines, visit chef-owned Robert Sinskey, whose discreetly dramatic tasting room of stone, redwood and teak resembles a small cathedral. The winery specializes in organically grown pinot, merlot and cabernet, great Alsatian varietals, *vin gris,* cabernet franc and dry rosé. Small bites accompany the vino. Tasting fees are discounted with a two-bottle purchase – a rarity in Napa. Call about special culinary tours. Bottles cost $22 to $95.

Quixote WINERY

(Map p164; ☎707-944-2659; www.quixotewinery.com; 6126 Silverado Trail; tastings $25; ⊙by appointment) Famed architect Friedensreich Hundertwasser (1928–2000) designed whimsical Quixote. The exterior is a riot of color, with the architect's signature gold-leaf onion dome crowning the building. No two windows are alike, no lines straight, no surfaces perfectly level. Tour it, by appointment only, on weekdays. Weekends, you can only glimpse it while sampling pretty-good, 100% organic petite sirah and cabernet. Bottles cost $40 to $60.

Robert Mondavi WINERY

(Map p164; ☎888-766-6328; www.robertmondavi.com; 7801 Hwy 29, Oakville; tour $25) This huge, corporate-owned winery draws oppressive crowds, but if you know nothing about wine, the worthwhile tours provide excellent insight into wine-making. Otherwise, skip it – unless you're here for one of the wonderful summer **concerts**, ranging from classical and jazz to R&B and Latin; call for schedules. Bottles run $19 to $150.

Tres Sabores WINERY

(Map p164; ☎707-967-8027; www.tressabores.com; 1620 South Whitehall Lane, St Helena; tour/tasting $20; ⊙by appointment; 🐾) At the valley's westernmost edge, where sloping vineyards meet wooded hillsides, Tres Sabores is a portal to old Napa – no fancy tasting room, no snobbery, just great wine in a spectacular setting. Bucking the cabernet custom, Tres Sabores crafts elegantly structured, Burgundian-style zinfandel, and spritely sauvignon blanc, which the *New York Times* dubbed a Top 10. Guinea fowl and sheep control pests on the 35-acre estate, while golden labs chase butterflies through gnarled old vines. Reservations essential, and include a tour. Afterward, linger at olive-shaded picnic tables and drink in gorgeous valley views. Bottles cost $22 to $80.

Mumm Napa WINERY

(Map p164; ☎800-686-6272; www.mummnapa.com; 8445 Silverado Trail, Rutherford; tasting $7-25; ⊙10am-4:45pm; 🐾) The valley views are spectacular at Mumm, which makes respectable sparkling wines that you can sample while seated on a vineyard-view terrace – ideal when you want to impress conservative parents-in-law. No appointment necessary; dodge crowds by paying $5 extra for the reserve-tasting terrace. Check website for discounted-tasting coupons.

Round Pond WINERY

(Map p164; ☎888-302-2575; www.roundpond.com; 875 Rutherford Rd, Rutherford; tastings $25; ⊙by appointment) Fantastic food pairings on a vineyard-view stone patio. We especially love the olive-oil and wine-vinegar tastings, included with guided tours of the olive mill ($25). Bottles $24 to $95.

TOP CHOICE **Frog's Leap** WINERY

(Map p164; ☎707-963-4704, 800-959-4704; www.frogsleap.com; 8815 Conn Creek Rd; tours & tastings $20, ⊙by appointment; 👪🐾) Meandering paths wind through magical gardens and fruit-bearing orchards – pick peaches in July – surrounding an 1884 barn and farmstead with cats and chickens. But more than anything, it's the vibe that's wonderful: casual and down-to-earth, with a major emphasis on *fun*. Sauvignon blanc is its best-known wine, but the merlot merits attention. There's also a dry, restrained cabernet, atypical in Napa. All are organic. Appointments required. Bottles cost $18 to $42.

Hall WINERY
(Map p164; 707-967-2626; www.hallwines.com; 401 St Helena Hwy, St Helena; tastings $15-25; 10am-5:30pm;) Owned by Clinton's former ambassador to Austria, Hall specializes in cabernet franc, sauvignon blanc, merlot and cabernet sauvignon. There's a cool abstract-sculpture garden, a lovely picnic area shaded by mulberry trees (with wines by the glass), and a LEED-gold-certified winery – California's first (tours $45, including barrel tastings). Bottles cost $22 to $80.

Elizabeth Spencer TASTING ROOM
(Map p164; 707-963-6067; www.elizabethspencerwines.com; 1165 Rutherford Rd, Rutherford; tastings $20; 10am-6pm;) Taste inside an 1872 railroad depot or an outdoor garden. Small-lot wines include monster-sized pinot noir, and a well-priced grapefruity sauvignon blanc. Bottles $20 to $85.

Long Meadow Ranch TASTING ROOM
(Map p164; 707-963-4555; www.longmeadowranch.com; 738 Main St, St Helena; tastings $10-30; 11am-6pm) Excellent olive-oil tastings (free) and fine cabernet and sauvignon blanc (bottles $19-35), served inside an 1874 farmhouse surrounded by lovely gardens.

Pride Mountain WINERY
(Map p164; 707-963-4949; www.pridewines.com; 4026 Spring Mountain Rd, St Helena; tastings $10; by appointment;) High atop Spring Mountain, cult-favorite Pride straddles the Napa-Sonoma border and bottles vintages under both appellations. The well-structured cabernet sauvignon and heavy-hitting merlot are the best-known wines, but there are also elegant viognier (perfect with oysters) and standout cab franc, available only at the winery. Picnicking here is spectacular (choose Viewpoint for drop-dead vistas, or Ghost Winery for shade and historic ruins of a 19th-century winery), but you *must* first reserve a tasting appointment. Bottles cost $37 to $85.

Cade WINERY
(Map p164; 707-965-2746; www.cadewinery.com; 360 Howell Mtn Rd, Angwin; tasting $20; by appointment) Ascend Mt Veeder for drop-dead vistas, 1800ft above the valley floor, at Napa's oh-so-swank, first-ever organically farmed, LEED gold-certified winery, owned in part by former San Francisco Mayor Gavin Newsom. Hawks ride thermals at eye level as you sample bright sauvignon blanc and luscious cabernet sauvignon that's more Bordelaise in style than Californian. Reservations required. Bring your camera.

Casa Nuestra WINERY
(Map p164; 707-963-5783; www.casanuestra.com; 3451 Silverado Trail, St Helena; tastings $10, refundable with purchase; by appointment;) A peace flag and a portrait of Elvis greet you in the tasting barn at this old-school, '70s-vintage, mom-and-pop winery, which produces unusual blends and interesting varietals (including good chenin blanc) and 100% cabernet franc. Vineyards are all-organic and the sun provides the power. Best of all, you can picnic free (call ahead and buy a bottle) beneath weeping willows, beside two happy goats. Bottles cost $20 to $55.

Ladera WINERY
(Map p164; 707-965-2445, 866-523-3728; www.laderavineyards.com; 150 White Cottage Rd S, Angwin; tastings $15; by appointment) High atop Howell Mountain, Ladera makes wonderful,

CUTTING COSTS IN NAPA

To avoid overspending on tasting fees, it's perfectly acceptable to pay for one tasting to share between two people. Ask in advance if fees are applicable to purchase (they usually aren't). Tour fees, by contrast, cannot be split. Ask at your hotel for free- or discounted-tasting coupons. If you can't afford the valley's hotels, try western Sonoma County, but if you want to be nearer Napa, try the suburban towns of Vallejo and American Canyon, about 20 minutes from downtown Napa. Both have motels for about $75 to $125 in high season. Also find chains 30 minutes away in Fairfield, off I-80 exits 41 (Pittman Rd) and 45 (Travis Blvd).

little-known, estate-grown cabernet sauvignon and sauvignon blanc. Make an appointment to visit this well-off-the-beaten-path 1886 stone-walled winery, one of Napa's oldest. Tasting fees refunded with two-bottle purchase. Bottles run $25 to $70.

Schramsberg WINERY

(Map p164; ☎707-942-4558; www.schramsberg.com; 1400 Schramsberg Rd; tastings $45; ⊙by appointment) Napa's second-oldest winery, Schramsberg makes some of California's best brut sparkling wines, and in 1972 was the first domestic wine served at the White House. Blanc de blancs is the signature. The appointment-only tasting and tour (book well ahead) is expensive, but you'll sample all the *tête de cuvées,* not just the low-end wines. Tours include a walk through the caves; bring a sweater. Located off Peterson Dr. Bottles cost $22 to $100.

Castello di Amorosa WINERY

(Map p164; ☎707-967-6272; www.castellodiamorosa.com; 4045 Hwy 29, Calistoga; tasting $10-15, tour adult/child $32/22; ⊙by appointment;) It took 14 years to build this perfectly replicated 12th-century Italian castle, complete with moat, hand-cut stone walls, ceiling frescoes by Italian artisans, Roman-style cross-vault brick catacombs, and a torture chamber with period equipment. You can taste without an appointment, but this is one tour worth taking. Oh, the wine? Some respectable Italian varietals, including a velvety Tuscan blend, and a merlot blend that goes great with pizza. Bottles cost $20 to $125.

Vincent Arroyo WINERY

(Map p164; ☎707-942-6995; www.vincentarroyo.com; 2361 Greenwood Ave, Calistoga; tastings free; ⊙by appointment;) The tasting room at Vincent Arroyo is a garage, where you may even meet Mr Arroyo, known for his all-estate-grown petite sirah and cabernet sauvignon. These wines are distributed nowhere else and are so consistently good that 75% of production is sold before it's bottled. Tastings are free, but appointments required. Bottles cost $22 to $45.

Lava Vine TASTING ROOM

(Map p164; ☎707-942-9500; www.lavavine.com; 965 Silverado Trail, Calistoga; tasting $10 waived with purchase; ⊙10am-5pm, appointment suggested;) Breaking ranks with Napa snobbery, the party kids at Lava Vine take a lighthearted approach to their seriously good wines, all paired with small bites, including some hot off the barbecue. Children and dogs play outside, while you let your guard down in the tiny tasting room and tap your toe to James Brown. Bring a picnic. Reservations recommended.

Napa

The valley's workaday hub was once a nothing-special city of storefronts, Victorian cottages and riverfront warehouses, but booming real-estate values caused an influx of new money that has transformed Napa into a growing city of arts and food.

Sights & Activities

Napa lies between Silverado Trail and St Helena Hwy/Hwy 29. For downtown, exit Hwy 29 at 1st St and drive east. Napa's main drag, 1st St, is lined with shops and restaurants.

Oxbow Public Market COVERED MARKET

(Map p169; ☎707-226-6529; www.oxbowpublicmarket.com; 610 1st St; ⊙9am-7pm Mon-Sat, to 8pm Tue, 10am-6pm Sun;) Showcasing all things culinary – from produce stalls to kitchen stores to fantastic edibles – Oxbow is foodie central, with an emphasis on seasonal-regional ingredients, grown sustainably. For more, see p171.

di Rosa Art & Nature Preserve GALLERY, NATURE RESERVE

(Map p164; ☎707-226-5991; www.dirosapreserve.org; 5200 Carneros Hwy 121; ⊙gallery 9:30am-3pm Wed-Fri, by appointment Sat) West of downtown, scrap-metal sheep graze Carneros vineyards at 217-acre di Rosa Preserve, a stunning collection of Northern California art, displayed indoors in galleries and outdoors in sculpture gardens. Reservations recommended for tours.

Sleeping

Summer demand exceeds supply. Weekend rates skyrocket. Also try Calistoga (p178).

TOP CHOICE **Carneros Inn** RESORT $$$

(Map p164; ☎707-299-4900; www.thecarnerosinn.com; 4048 Sonoma Hwy; r Mon-Fri $485-570, Sat & Sun $650-900;) Carneros Inn's snappy aesthetic and retro small-town agricultural theme shatters the predictable Wine Country mold. The semidetached, corrugated-metal cottages look like itinerant housing, but

Napa

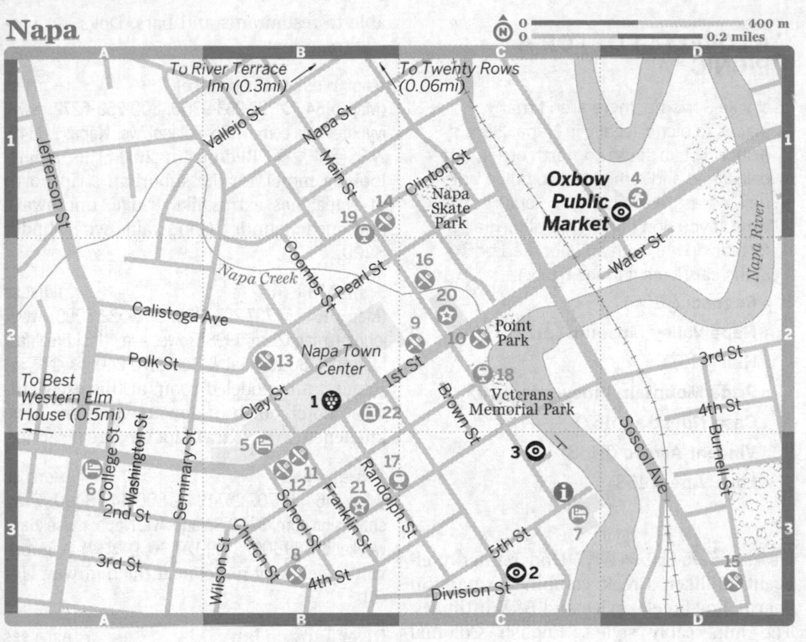

Napa

inside they're snappy and chic, with cherry-wood floors, ultrasuede headboards, wood-burning fireplaces, heated-tile bathroom floors, giant tubs and indoor-outdoor showers. Splurge on a vineyard-view room. Linger by day at the hilltop swimming pool, and by night at the bar's outdoor fireplaces. Two excellent onsite restaurants.

Milliken Creek Inn INN **$$$**
(Map p164; ☎707-255-1197, 888-622-5775; www.millikencreekinn.com; 1815 Silverado Trail; r incl

A LOVELY SPOT FOR A PICNIC

Unlike Sonoma, there aren't many places to picnic legally in Napa. Here's a short list, in south-to-north order, but call ahead and remember to buy a bottle (or glass, if available) of your host's wine. If you don't finish it, California law forbids driving with an uncorked bottle in the car (keep it in the trunk).

» **Regusci** (p166)
» **Napa Valley Museum** (p172)
» **Hall** (p167)
» **Pride Mountain Vineyards** (p167)
» **Casa Nuestra** (p167)
» **Vincent Arroyo** (p168)
» **Lava Vine** (p168)

breakfast $275-650; ❄@📶) Understatedly elegant Milliken Creek combines small-inn charm, fine-hotel service and B&B intimacy. The impeccably styled, English Colonial rooms have top-flight amenities, fireplaces, ultrahigh-thread-count linens, and breakfast in bed. Book a river-view room.

Cottages of Napa Valley BUNGALOWS **$$$**
(Map p164; ☎707-252-7810; www.napacottages.com; 1012 Darns Lane; d $395-500, q $475-575; ❄📶) Originally constructed in the 1940s and rebuilt with top-end amenities in 2005, these eight cottages are ideal for a romantic hideaway, with extra-long soaking tubs, gas fireplaces, and outdoor fire pits beneath towering pines. Cottages 4 and 8 have private porches and swinging chairs. The only drawback is traffic noise, but interiors are silent.

Avia Hotel HOTEL **$$**
(Map p169; ☎707-224-3900; www.aviahotels.com; 1450 1st St, Napa; r $149-249; ❄@📶) Downtown Napa's newest hotel opened in 2009 and feels like a big-city hotel, with business-class-fancy rooms, styled in sexy retro-70s chic. Walkable to restaurants and bars.

Napa River Inn HOTEL **$$$**
(Map p169; ☎707-251-8500, 877-251-8500; www.napariverinn.com; 500 Main St; r include breakfast $229-349; ❄@📶🐾) Beside the river, in the 1884 Hatt Building, the inn has upper-midrange rooms in three satellite buildings, ranging from Victoriana to modern. Walkable to restaurants and bars. Dogs get special treatment.

Best Western Ivy Hotel HOTEL **$$**
(Map p164; ☎707-253-9300, 800-253-6272; www.ivyhotelnapa.com; 4195 Solano Ave, Napa; r $149-249; ❄@📶🏊) Redone in 2011, this smart-looking motel, on the suburban strip north of Napa, has extras like fridge, microwave and onsite laundry. Good value when under $200.

John Muir Inn HOTEL **$$**
(Map p164; ☎707-257-7220, 800-522-8999; www.johnmuirnapa.com; 1998 Trower Ave; r incl breakfast Mon-Fri $130-155, Sat & Sun $170-240; ❄@📶🏊) Request a remodeled room at this excellent-value hotel, north of downtown. Some have kitchenettes ($5 extra). Hot tub, great service.

Chablis Inn MOTEL **$$**
(Map p164; ☎707-257-1944, 800-443-3490; www.chablisinn.com; 3360 Solano Ave, Napa; r weekday/weekend $89-109/$159-179; ❄@📶🏊) A good-value, well-kept motel near the highway. Hot tub.

River Terrace Inn HOTEL **$$$**
(☎7070-320-9000, 866-627-2386; www.riverterraceinn.com; 1600 Soscol Ave; r $189-289; ❄📶🏊) An upmarket chain-style hotel, fronting on the Napa River. Heated outdoor pool.

Casita Bonita BUNGALOW **$$$**
(☎707-259-1980, 707-738-5587; www.lacasitabonita.com; q $375; ❄📶👪) Smartly decorated two-bedroom cottage with full kitchen and veggie garden – kids love the chickens. Perfect for two couples or a family.

Best Western Elm House INN **$$**
(off Map p169; ☎707-255-1831; www.bestwesternelmhouseinn.com; 800 California Blvd; r include breakfast $149-229; ❄@📶) Impeccably kept rooms with generic furnishings in soft pastels. Ideal for conservative travelers. Ten minute walk to downtown; easy highway access. Hot tub.

Blackbird Inn B&B **$$$**
(Map p169; ☎707-226-2450, 888-567-9811; www.blackbirdinnnapa.com; 1775 1st St; r incl breakfast $185-300; ❄📶) Gorgeous, eight-room Arts and Crafts–style B&B, but anticipate traffic noise.

Napa Valley Redwood Inn MOTEL **$$**
(☎707-257-6111, 877-872-6272; www.napavalleyredwoodinn.com; 3380 Solano Ave; r Mon-Fri $90-110,

Sat & Sun $140-150; ❄📶🏊) Generic freeway-side motel.

Eating

Make reservations when possible. July to mid-August, look for the peach stand at Deer Park Rd and Silverado Trail (across Deer Park Rd from Stewart's farmstand) for juicy-delicious heirloom varieties.

Oxbow Public Market COVERED MARKET $
(Map p169; www.oxbowpublicmarket.com; 610 & 644 First St, Napa; ⏲9am-7pm Mon-Sat, 10am-5pm Sun; 👪🌿) Graze your way through this gourmet market and plug into the Northern California food scene. Look for Hog Island oysters (six for $15); comfort cooking at celeb-chef Todd Humphries' Kitchen Door (mains $13 to $20); Pica Pica's Venezuelan cornbread sandwiches ($8); standout Cal-Mexican at Casa (tacos $4 to $8); pastries at Ca'Momi ($1.50); and Three Twins certified-organic ice cream ($3.65 single cone). Tuesday is locals night, with many discounts. Tuesday and Saturday mornings, there's a farmers market. Friday nights bring live music. Some stalls remain open till 9pm, even on Sundays, but many close earlier.

Ubuntu VEGETARIAN $$
(Map p169; ☎707-251-5656; www.ubuntunapa.com; 1140 Main St, Napa; dishes $14-18; ⏲dinner nightly, lunch Sat & Sun; 🌿) The Michelin-starred, seasonal, vegetarian menu features artfully presented natural wonders from the biodynamic kitchen garden, satisfying hearty eaters with four-to-five inspired small plates, and eco-savvy drinkers with 100-plus sustainably produced wines.

Boon Fly Café AMERICAN $$
(Map p164; ☎707-299-4870; www.theboonflycafe.com; 4048 Sonoma Hwy; mains $10-20; ⏲7am-9pm) For New American comfort food done well, make a beeline to Boon Fly – but avoid peak meal times unless you've made reservations. At breakfast, try homemade doughnuts or brioche French toast; at lunch and dinner, grilled Reubens, roasted chicken, and spinach salads. Save room for warm chocolate-chip cookies.

Pearl Restaurant NEW AMERICAN $$
(Map p169; ☎707-224-9161; www.therestaurantpearl.com; 1339 Pearl St; mains $14-19; ⏲Tue-Sat 5:30-9pm; 🐾) Meet locals at this dog-friendly bistro with red-painted concrete floors, pinewood tables and open-rafter ceilings. The winning down-to-earth cooking includes double-cut pork chops, chicken verde with polenta, steak tacos and the specialty, oysters.

Oenotri ITALIAN $$
(☎707-252-1022; www.oenotri.com; 1425 First St, Napa; mains $15-25; ⏲dinner, lunch hours vary) Housemade salumi and pastas, and wood-fired Naples-style pizzas are the stars at always-busy Oenotri, which draws bon vivants for its daily-changing lineup of locally sourced, rustic-Italian cooking, served in a cavernous brick-walled space.

Bistro Don Giovanni ITALIAN $$$
(Map p164; ☎707-224-3300; www.bistrodongiovanni.com; 4110 Howard Lane at Hwy 29; mains $19-26) This long-running favorite roadhouse cooks up modern-Italian pastas, crispy pizzas and wood-roasted meats. Reservations essential. Weekends get packed – and loud. Request a vineyard-view table (good luck).

Bounty Hunter Wine Bar AMERICAN $$
(Map p169; www.bountyhunterwine.com; 975 1st St; dishes $14-24; ⏲11am-10pm; 👪) Inside an 1888 grocery store, Bounty Hunter has an old West vibe and superb barbecue, made with house-smoked meats. The standout whole chicken is roasted over a can of Tecate. Ten local beers and 40 wines by the glass.

Bistro Sabor LATIN AMERICAN $
(Map p169; ☎707-252-0555; www.bistrosabor.com; 1126 1st St; dishes $8-11; ⏲11:30am-11pm Tue-Thu, 11:30am-1:30am Fri & Sat; 👪) Not your typical Mexican joint, this order-at-the-counter downtowner makes super-fresh Latin American street foods, including ceviches, papusas and chile rellenos. Save room for churros.

Alexis Baking Co CAFE $
(Map p169; ☎707-258-1827; www.alexisbakingcompany.com; 1517 3rd St; dishes $6-10; ⏲Mon-Fri 7:30am-3pm, Sat 7am-3pm, Sun 8am-2pm; 👪🌿) Our fave spot for scrambles, granola, focaccia sandwiches, big cups of joe and boxed lunches to go.

Pizza Azzuro PIZZERIA $$
(Map p169; ☎707-255-5552; www.azzurropizzeria.com; 1260 Main St; mains $12-16; 👪🌿) This Napa classic gets deafeningly loud, but the tender-crusted pizzas and salad-topped 'manciata'

bread make the noise worth bearing. Good Caesar salad and pastas.

Norman Rose Tavern PUB $$
(707-258-1516; normanrosenapa.com; 1401 1st St; mains $10-20; 11:30am-10pm) This happening gastropub, styled with reclaimed wood and tufted-leather banquettes, is good for a burger and beer. Great fries. Beer and wine only.

Soscol Café DINER $
(Map p169; 707-252-0651; 632 Soscol Av; dishes $6-9; 6am-2pm Mon-Sat, 7am-1pm Sun) The ultimate greasy-spoon diner, Soscol makes massive huevos rancheros, and chicken-fried steak and eggs. Not a high heel in sight.

Drinking & Entertainment

Silo's Jazz Club LIVE MUSIC
(Map p169; 707-251-5833; www.silosjazzclub.com; 530 Main St; cover varies; Wed-Thu 4-10pm, Fri & Sat to midnight) A cabaret-style wine-and-beer bar, Silo's hosts jazz and rock acts Friday and Saturday nights; Wednesday and Thursdays it's good for drinks. Reservations recommended weekends.

Salsa Saturdays at Bistro Sabor DANCE
(Map p169; www.bistrosabor.com; 1126 1st St; admission free; 10pm-1:30am Sat) DJs spin salsa and merengue at this happening Saturday-night restaurant dance party.

Billco's Billiards & Darts SPORTS BAR
(Map p169; www.billcos.com; 1234 3rd St; noon-1am) Dudes in khakis swill craft beers, shoot pool and throw darts.

Downtown Joe's SPORTS BAR, BREWERY
(Map p169; www.downtownjoes.com; 902 Main St at 2nd St;) Live music Thursday to Sunday, TV sports nightly. Often packed, sometimes messy.

Napa Valley Opera House THEATER
(Map p169; 707-226-7372; www.nvoh.org; 1030 Main St) Restored vintage-1880s opera house; straight plays, comedy and major acts.

Uptown Theatre THEATER
(Map p169; 707-259-0333; www.uptowntheatrenapa.com; 1350 3rd St) Big name acts play this restored 1937 theater.

Shopping

Betty's Girl WOMEN'S CLOTHING, VINTAGE
(707-254-7560; 1144 Main St) Hollywood costume designer Kim Northrup fits women with fabulous vintage cocktail dresses, altering and shipping for no additional charge.

Napa General Store GIFTS
(707-259-0762; www.napageneralstore.com; 540 Main St) Finally, clever Wine Country souvenirs that are reasonably priced. The on-site wine bar is convenient for non-shopping husbands.

Information

Napa Valley Welcome Center (707-260-0107; www.legendarynapavalley.com; 600 Main St; 9am-5pm) Spa deals, wine-tasting passes and comprehensive winery maps.

Napa Library (707-253-4241; www.countyofnapa.org/Library; 580 Coombs St; 10am-9pm Mon-Thu, 10am-6pm Fri & Sat;) Email connections.

Queen of the Valley Medical Center (707-252-4411; 1000 Trancas St) Emergency medical.

Getting Around

Pedi cabs park outside downtown restaurants – especially at the foot of Main St, near the NV Welcome Center – in summertime.

Yountville

This onetime stagecoach stop, 9 miles north of Napa, is now a major foodie destination, with more Michelin stars per capita than any other American town. There are some good inns here, but it's deathly boring at night. You stay in Yountville to drink with dinner without having to drive afterward. St Helena and Calistoga make better bases. Most businesses are on Washington St.

Ma(i)sonry (707-944-0889; www.maisonry.com; 6711 Washington St; 9am-10pm) occupies a 1904 stone house, now transformed into a rustic-modern showplace for furniture, art and wine; the garden is a swank post-dinner fireside gathering spot for vino.

Yountville's modernist 40,000-sq-ft **Napa Valley Museum** (707-944-0500; www.napavalleymuseum.org; 55 Presidents Circle; adult/child $5/2.50; 10am-5pm Wed-Mon), off California Dr, chronicles cultural history and showcases local paintings. Good picnicking outside.

The only worthwhile shop at V Marketplace is TV-chef Michael Chiarello's **Napa Style** (www.napastyle.com; 6525 Washington St), but it's overpriced.

FLYING & BALLOONING

Wine Country is stunning from the air – a multihued tapestry of undulating hills, deep valleys and rambling vineyards. Make reservations.

The **Vintage Aircraft Company** (Map p184; ☎707-938-2444; www.vintageaircraft.com; 23982 Arnold Dr) flies over Sonoma in a vintage biplane with an awesome pilot who'll do loop-de-loops on request (add $50). Twenty-minute tours cost $175/270 for one/two adults.

Napa Valley's signature hot-air balloon flights leave early, around 6am or 7am, when the air is coolest; they usually include a champagne breakfast on landing. Adults pay about $200 to $250, and kids $130 to $150. Call **Balloons above the Valley** (☎707-253-2222, 800-464-6824; www.balloonrides.com) or **Napa Valley Balloons** (☎707-944-0228, 800-253-2224; www.napavalleyballoons.com), both in Yountville.

Sleeping

Bardessono LUXURY HOTEL **$$$**
(☎707-204-6000, 877-932-5333; www.bardessono.com; 6524 Yount St; r $600-800, ste from $800;) The outdoors flows indoors at California's first-ever LEED-platinum-certified green hotel, made of recycled everything, styled in Japanese-led austerity, with neutral tones and hard angles that feel exceptionally urban for farm country. Glam pool deck and onsite spa. Tops for a splurge.

Poetry Inn INN **$$$**
(☎707-944-0646; www.poetryinn.com; 6380 Silverado Trail; r incl breakfast $650-1400;) There's no better view of Napa Valley than from this understatedly chic, three-room inn, high on the hills east of Yountville. Rooms are decorated in Arts and Crafts-inspired style, and have private balconies, wood-burning fireplaces, 1000-thread-count linens and enormous baths with indoor-outdoor showers. Bring a ring.

Maison Fleurie B&B **$$$**
(☎707-944-2056, 800-788-0369; www.maisonfleurienapa.com; 6529 Yount St; r incl breakfast $145-295;) Rooms at this ivy-covered country inn are in a century-old home and carriage house, decorated in French-provincial style. There's a big breakfast, and afternoon wine and *hors d'oeuvres*. Hot tub.

Napa Valley Lodge HOTEL **$$$**
(☎707-944-2468, 888-944-3545; www.napavalleylodge.com; 2230 Madison St; r $300-455;) It looks like a condo complex, but rooms are spacious and modern, some with fireplaces. Hot tub, sauna and exercise room.

Petit Logis INN **$$$**
(☎707-944-2332, 877-944-2332; www.petitlogis.com; 6527 Yount St; r Mon-Fri $195-255, Sat & Sun $235-285;) This cedar-sided inn has five individually decorated rooms. Think white wicker furniture and dusty-rose fabric. Add $20 for breakfast for two.

Napa Valley Railway Inn THEME INN **$$**
(☎707-944-2000; www.napavalleyrailwayinn.com; 6523 Washington St, Yountville; r $125-260;) Sleep in a converted railroad car, part of two short trains parked at a central platform. They've little privacy, but are moderately priced. Bring earplugs.

Eating

Make reservations or you might not eat. **Yountville Park** (cnr Washington & Madison Sts) has picnic tables and barbecue grills, you'll find groceries across from the post office, and there's a great **taco truck** (6764 Washington St).

French Laundry CALIFORNIAN **$$$**
(☎707-944-2380; www.frenchlaundry.com; 6640 Washington St; prix fixe incl service charge $270; dinner, lunch Sat & Sun) The pinnacle of California dining, Thomas Keller's French Laundry is epic, a high-wattage culinary experience on par with the world's best. Book two months ahead at 10am sharp, or log onto OpenTable.com precisely at midnight. Avoid tables before 7pm; first-service seating moves faster than the second – sometimes too fast.

Bouchon FRENCH **$$$**
(☎707-944-8037; www.bouchonbistro.com; 6534 Washington St; mains $17-36; 11:30am-12:30am) At celeb-chef Thomas Keller's French brasserie, everything from food to decor is so authentic, from zinc bar to white-aproned

waiters, you'd swear you were in Paris – even the Bermuda-shorts-clad Americans look out of place. On the menu: oysters, onion soup, roasted chicken, leg of lamb, trout with almonds, runny cheeses and profiteroles for dessert, impeccably prepared.

TOP CHOICE **Ad Hoc** NEW AMERICAN $$$
(☎707-944-2487; www.adhocrestaurant.com; 6476 Washington St, Yountville; menu $48; ⏰Wed-Mon dinner, Sun 10:30am-2pm) Another winning formula by Yountville's culinary oligarch, Thomas Keller, Ad Hoc serves the master's favorite American home cooking in four-course family-style menus, with no variations except for dietary restrictions. Monday is fried-chicken night, which you can also sample weekend lunchtime, take-out only, behind the restaurant at Keller's latest venture, **Addendum** (⏰11am-2pm Thu-Sat), which also serves barbecue; get the daily menu on Twitter at @AddendumatAdHoc.

Étoile CALIFORNIAN $$$
(Map p164; ☎707-944-8844; www.chandon.com; 1 California Dr; lunch/dinner mains $26-31/$32-36; ⏰11:30am-2:30pm & 6-9pm Thu-Mon) Within Chandon winery, Michelin-starred Étoile's is perfect for a lingering white-tablecloth lunch in the vines; ideal when you want to visit a winery and eat a good meal with minimal driving.

Bistro Jeanty FRENCH $$$
(☎707-944-0103; www.bistrojeanty.com; 6510 Washington St; mains $18-29) A true French bistro serves comfort food to weary travelers, and that's exactly what French-born chef-owner Philippe Jeanty does, with succulent cassoulet, coq au vin, *steak-frites,* braised pork with lentils, and scrumptious tomato soup.

Paninoteca Ottimo SANDWICHES, CAFE $
(☎707-945-1229; www.napastyleottimocafe.com; 6525 Washington St; dishes $8-10; ⏰10am-6pm Mon-Sat, 10am-5pm Sat) TV-chef Michael Chiarello's cafe makes stellar salads and delish paninos (try the slow-roasted pork) that pair well with his organically produced wines. Tops for picnic supplies.

Bouchon Bakery BAKERY $
(☎707-944-2253; www.bouchonbakery.com; 6528 Washington St; dishes $3-9; ⏰7am-7pm) Bouchon makes perfect French pastries and strong coffee. Order at the counter and sit outside, or pack a bag to go.

Mustards Grill CALIFORNIAN $$$
(Map p164; ☎707-944-2424; www.mustardsgrill.com; 7399 St Helena Hwy; mains $22-27; 🚸) The valley's original roadhouse whips up wood-fired California comfort food – roasted meats, lamb shanks, pork chops, hearty salads and sandwiches. Great crowd-pleaser.

Drinking & Entertainment

Pancha's DIVE BAR
(6764 Washington St) Swill tequila with vineyard workers early, restaurant waiters late.

Lincoln Theater THEATER
(Map p164; ☎707-944-1300, 866-944-9199; www.lincolntheater.org; 100 California Dr) Various artists play this 1200-seat theater, including the Napa Valley Symphony.

Oakville & Rutherford

But for its famous grocery, you'd drive through Oakville (pop 71) and never know you'd missed it. This is the middle of the grapes – vineyards sprawl in every direction. Rutherford (pop 164) is more conspicuous, but the wineries put these towns on the map.

Sleeping & Eating

There's no budget lodging here.

Auberge du Soleil LUXURY HOTEL $$$
(Map p164; ☎707-963-1211, 800-348-5406; www.aubergedusoleil.com; 180 Rutherford Hill Rd; r $650-975, ste $1400-2200; ❄📶🏊) The top splurge for a no-holds-barred romantic weekend, Auberge's hillside cottages are second to none. Less-expensive rooms feel comparatively cramped; book a suite. Excellent guests-only spa. Auberge's **dining room** (mains breakfast $16-19, lunch $29-42, 3-/4-/6-course prix-fixe dinner $98/115/140) showcases an expertly prepared Euro-Cal menu, among the valley's best. Come for a fancy breakfast, lazy lunch or will-you-wear-my-ring dinner. Valley views are mesmerizing from the terrace – *don't* sit inside. Make reservations; arrive before sunset.

Rancho Caymus HOTEL $$$
(☎707-963-1777, 800-845-1777; www.ranchocaymus.com; 1140 Rutherford Rd, Rutherford; r $175-285; ❄📶🐾) Styled after California's missions, this hacienda-style inn scores high marks for its tiled fountain courtyard, and rooms' kiva-style fireplaces, oak-beamed

ceilings and wood floors, but the furniture looks tired.

La Luna Market & Taqueria MARKET $
(Map p164; ☎707-963-3211; 1153 Rutherford Rd, Rutherford; dishes $4-6; ⏰9am-5pm May-Nov) Look no further for honest burritos with homemade hot sauce.

Rutherford Grill AMERICAN $$
(☎707-963-1792; www.hillstone.com; 1180 Rutherford Rd, Rutherford; mains $15-30) Yes, it's a chain (Houston's), but to rub shoulders with winemakers, snag a stool for lunch at the bar. The food is consistent – ribs, rotisserie chicken, outstanding grilled artichokes – and there's no corkage, so bring that bottle you just bought down the road.

Oakville Grocery & Cafe DELI $$
(Map p164; ☎707-944-8802; www.oakvillegrocery.com; 7856 Hwy 29, Oakville; ⏰8am-5:30pm) The once-definitive Wine Country deli has gotten ridiculously overpriced, with less variety than in previous years, but still carries excellent cheeses, charcuterie, bread, olives and wine. There are tables outside, but ask where to picnic nearby.

St Helena

You'll know you're arriving when traffic halts. St Helena (ha-*lee*-na) is the Rodeo Dr of Napa, with fancy boutiques lining Main St (Hwy 29). The historic downtown is good for a stroll, with great window-shopping, but parking is next-to-impossible summer weekends.

The **St Helena Welcome Center** (☎707-963-4456, 800-799-6456; www.sthelena.com; 657 Main St; ⏰9am-5pm Mon-Fri) has information and lodging assistance.

Sights & Activities

FREE **Silverado Museum** MUSEUM
(Map p164; ☎707-963-3757; www.silveradomuseum.org; 1490 Library Lane; ⏰noon-4pm Tue-Sat) Contains a fascinating collection of Robert Louis Stevenson memorabilia. In 1880, the author – then sick, penniless and unknown – stayed in an abandoned bunkhouse at the old Silverado Mine on Mt St Helena (p181) with his wife, Fanny Osbourne; his novel *The Silverado Squatters* is based on his time there. To reach Library Lane, turn east off Hwy 29 at the Adams St traffic light and cross the railroad tracks.

Culinary Institute of America at Greystone COOKING SCHOOL
(Map p164; ☎707-967-2320; www.ciachef.edu/california; 2555 Main St; mains $25-29, cooking demonstration $20; ⏰restaurant 11:30am-9pm, cooking demonstrations 1:30pm Sat & Sun) An 1889 stone chateau houses a gadget- and cookbook-filled **culinary shop**; fine **restaurant**; weekend **cooking demonstrations**; and **wine-tasting classes** by luminaries in the field, including Karen MacNeil, author of *The Wine Bible*.

Farmers market MARKET
(www.sthelenafarmersmkt.org; ⏰7:30am-noon Fri May-Oct) Meets at Crane Park, half a mile south of downtown.

Sleeping

Meadowood RESORT $$$
(Map p164; ☎707-963-3646, 800-458-8080; www.meadowood.com; 900 Meadowood Lane; r from $600; ❄@🛜≋👪) Hidden in a wooded dell with towering pines and miles of hiking, Napa's grandest resort has cottages and rooms in satellite buildings surrounding a croquet lawn. We most like the hillside fireplace cottages; lawn-view rooms lack privacy but are good for families, with room to play outside. The vibe is country club, with white-clapboard buildings reminiscent of New England. Wear linen and play *Great Gatsby*. Kids love the mammoth pool.

🍃 **Harvest Inn** INN $$$
(☎707-963-9463, 800-950-8466; www.harvestinn.com; 1 Main St; r incl breakfast $329-549; ❄🛜≋) If you can't swing Meadowood, this former estate, with sprawling gardens and rooms in satellite buildings, is a lovely backup. The new building is generic; book the vineyard-view rooms, with their private hot tubs.

El Bonita Motel MOTEL $$
(Map p164; ☎707-963-3216, 800-541-3284; www.elbonita.com; 195 Main St, St Helena; $119-179; ❄@🛜≋🐾) Book in advance to secure a room at this sought-after motel, with up-to-date rooms (quietest are in back), attractive grounds, hot tub and sauna.

Hotel St Helena HISTORIC HOTEL $$
(☎707-963-4388; www.hotelsthelena.net; 1309 Main St; r with/without bath $125-235/$105-165; ❄🛜) Decorated with period furnishings, this frayed-at-the-edges 1881 hotel sits right downtown. Rooms are tiny, but good value, especially those with shared bathroom. No elevator.

Eating

Make reservations where possible. If you're just after something quick, consider **Gillwood's Cafe** (www.gillwoodscafe.com; 1313 Main St; dishes $8-12; ⏲7am-3pm) for an all-day breakfast; **Sunshine Foods** (www.sunshinefoodsmarket.com; 1115 Main St; ⏲7:30am-8:30pm), the town's best grocery and deli; **Model Bakery** (www.themodelbakery.com; 1357 Main St; dishes $5-10; ⏲7am-6pm Tue-Sun, 8am-4pm Sun) for great scones, muffins, salads, gelato, pizzas, sandwiches and strong coffee; or **Armadillo's** (1304 Main St; mains $8-12) for respectable and reasonable Mexican eats.

Gott's Roadside (Taylor's Auto Refresher) BURGERS **$$**
(☎707-963-3486; www.gottsroadside.com; 933 Main St; dishes $8-15; ⏲10:30am-9pm; 👪) Wiggle your toes in the grass and feast on all-natural burgers, Cobb salads and fried calamari at this classic roadside drive-in, whose original name, 'Taylor's Auto Refresher,' is still listed on the roadside sign. Avoid big weekend waits by calling in your order. There's another branch at **Oxbow Public Market** (p171).

Napa Valley Olive Oil Mfg Co MARKET **$**
(☎707-963-4173; www.oliveoilsainthelena.com; 835 Charter Oak St; ⏲8am-5:30pm) Before the advent of fancy-food stores, this ramshackle Italian market introduced Napa to Italian delicacies – succulent prosciutto and salami, meaty olives, fresh bread, nutty cheeses and, of course, olive oil. Yellowed business cards from 50 years ago adorn the walls, and the owner knows everyone in town. He'll lend you a knife and a board to make a picnic at the rickety wooden tables outside in the grass. Cash only.

Cook CAL-ITALIAN **$$**
(☎707-963-7088; www.cooksthelena.com; 1310 Main St; lunch mains $12-21, dinner mains $17-25; ⏲11:30am-10pm Mon-Sat, 5-10pm Sun) Locals crowd the counter at this tiny storefront bistro, much loved for its earthy cooking – homemade pasta, melt-off-the-bone ribs and simple-delicious burgers. Try the butter-braised Brussels sprouts – fantastic. Expect a wait, even with reservations.

Market NEW AMERICAN **$$**
(☎707-963-3799; www.marketsthelena.com; 1347 Main St; mains $13-24; ⏲11:30am-9pm) We love the big portions of simple, fresh American cooking at Market. Maximizing the season's best produce, the chef creates enormous, inventive salads and soul-satisfying mains like buttermilk fried chicken. The stone-walled dining room dates to the 19th century, as does the ornate backbar, where cocktails are muddled to order.

Cindy's Backstreet Kitchen NEW AMERICAN **$$**
(☎707-963-1200; www.cindysbackstreetkitchen.com; 1327 Railroad Ave; mains $17-25) The inviting retro-homey decor complements the menu's Cal-American comfort food, like avocado-and-papaya salad, wood-fired duck, steak with French fries, and the simple grilled burger. The bar makes a mean mojito.

Farmstead NEW AMERICAN **$$$**
(☎707-963-9181; www.farmsteadnapa.com; 738 Main St; mains $16-26; ⏲11:30am-9pm) A cavernous open-truss barn with big leather booths and rocking-chair porch, Farmstead grows many of its own ingredients – including grass-fed beef – for its earthy menu that highlights wood-fired cooking.

Terra CALIFORNIAN **$$$**
(☎707-963-8931; www.terrarestaurant.com; 1345 Railroad Ave; 3-/4-/5-/6-course menus $57/66/81/92; ⏲6-9pm Wed-Sun) Inside an 1884 stone building, Terra wows diners with seamlessly blended Japanese, French and Italian culinary styles. The signature is broiled sake-marinated black cod with shrimp dumplings in shiso broth. Perfect. The bar serves small bites, but the dining room's the thing.

Restaurant at Meadowood CALIFORNIAN **$$$**
(Map p164; ☎707-967-1205; www.meadowood.com; 900 Meadowood Lane; 4-/9-course menu $125/225; ⏲5:30-10pm Mon-Sat) If you couldn't score reservations at French Laundry, fear not: the clubby Restaurant at Meadowood – the valley's only other Michelin-three-star restaurant – has a more sensibly priced menu, elegant but unfussy forest-view dining room, and lavish haute cuisine that's never too esoteric. Auberge has better views, but Meadowood's food and service far surpass the former.

Silverado Brewing Co BREWPUB **$$**
(Map p164; ☎707-967-9876; www.silveradobrewingcompany.com; 3020 Hwy 29; mains $12-18; ⏲11:30am-1am; 👪) Silverados' microbrews

measure up to Napa's wines – Brewmaster Ken Mee's Certifiable Blonde has organic ingredients and crazy-tasty malts, and competes for top choice with the hopped-up Amber Ale. Food is typical pub grub that keeps your buzz in check.

Shopping

Main St is lined with high-end boutiques (think $100 socks), but some mom-and-pop shops remain. Also see p182.

Woodhouse Chocolates FOOD
(www.woodhousechocolate.com; 1367 Main St) Woodhouse looks more like Tiffany & Co than a candy shop, with chocolates similarly priced, but they're made in town and their quality is beyond reproach.

Napa Soap Company BEAUTY
(www.napasoap.com; 651 Main St) Hand-crafted eco-friendly bath products, locally produced.

Lolo's Consignment VINTAGE
(www.lolosconsignment.com; 1120 Main St) Groovy dresses and cast-off cashmere.

Main Street Books BOOKS
(1315 Main St; Mon-Sat) Good used books.

Calistoga

The least gentrified town in Napa Valley feels refreshingly simple, with an old-fashioned main street lined with shops, not boutiques, and diverse characters wandering the sidewalks. Bad hair? No problem. Fancy-pants St Helena couldn't feel farther away. Most tourists don't make it this far north. You should.

Famed 19th-century author Robert Louis Stevenson said of Calistoga: 'the whole neighborhood of Mt St Helena is full of sulfur and boiling springs…Calistoga itself seems to repose on a mere film above a boiling, subterranean lake.'

Indeed, it does. Calistoga is synonymous with the mineral water bearing its name, bottled here since 1924. Its springs and geysers have earned it the nickname the 'hot springs of the West.' Plan to visit one of the town's spas, where you can indulge in the local specialty: a hot-mud bath, made of the volcanic ash from nearby volcanic Mt St Helena.

The town's odd name comes from Sam Brannan, who founded Calistoga in 1859, believing it would develop like the New York spa town of Saratoga. Apparently Sam liked his drink and at the founding ceremony tripped on his tongue, proclaiming it the 'Cali-stoga' of 'Sara-fornia.' The name stuck.

Sights

Hwys 128 and 29 run together from Rutherford through St Helena; in Calistoga, they split. Hwy 29 turns east and becomes Lincoln Ave, continuing across Silverado Trail, toward Clear Lake. Hwy 128 continues north as Foothill Blvd (not St Helena Hwy). Calistoga's shops and restaurants line Lincoln Ave.

Old Faithful Geyser GEYSER
(Map p164; 707-942-6463; www.oldfaithfulgeyser.com; 1299 Tubbs Lane; adult/child $10/free; 9am-6pm summer, to 5pm winter;) Calistoga's mini-version of Yellowstone's Old Faithful shoots boiling water 60ft to 100ft into the air, every 30 minutes. The vibe is pure roadside Americana, with folksy hand-painted interpretive exhibits, picnicking and a little petting zoo, where you can come nose-to-nose with llamas. It's 2 miles north of town, off Silverado Trail. Look for discount coupons around town.

Sharpsteen Museum MUSEUM
(707-942-5911; www.sharpsteen-museum.org; 1311 Washington St; adult/child $3/free; 11am-4pm;) Across from the picturesque 1902 City Hall (which was originally an opera house), the Sharpsteen Museum was created by an ex-Disney animator (whose Oscar is on display) and houses a fabulous diorama of the town in the 1860s, big Victorian dollhouse, full-size horse-drawn carriage, cool taxidermy and a restored cottage from Brannan's original resort. (The only Brannan cottage still at its

TOP KID-FRIENDLY WINERIES

» **Kaz** (p184) Play-Doh, playground and grape juice
» **Benziger** (p183) Open-air tram ride and peacocks
» **Frog's Leap** (p166) Cats, chickens and croquet.
» **Casa Nuestra** (p167) Playful goats.
» **Castello di Amorosa** (p168) Historical-imagination sparker.
» **Lava Vine** (p168) Mellow vibe, grassy play area.

original site is at 106 Wapoo Ave, near the Brannan Cottage Inn.)

Activities

Hardcore mountain bikers can tackle **Oat Hill Mine Trail**, one of Northern California's most technically challenging trails, just outside town. Find information and rentals at **Calistoga Bike Shop** (707-942-9687, 866-942-2453; www.calistogabikeshop.com; 1318 Lincoln Ave), which rents full-suspension mountain bikes (per day $75) and hybrids (per hour/day $10/35). Wine-touring packages (per day $80) include wine-rack baskets and free wine pickup.

SPAS

Calistoga is famous for hot-spring spas and mud-bath emporiums, where you're buried in hot mud and emerge feeling supple, detoxified and enlivened. (The mud is made with volcanic ash and peat; the higher the ash content, the better the bath.)

Packages take 60 to 90 minutes and cost $70 to $90. You start semi-submerged in hot mud, then soak in hot mineral water. A steam bath and blanket-wrap follow. The treatment can be extended with a massage, increasing the cost to $130 and up.

Baths can be taken solo or, at some spas, as couples. Variations include thin, painted-on clay-mud wraps (called 'fango' baths, good for those uncomfortable sitting in mud), herbal wraps, seaweed baths and various massage treatments. Discount coupons are sometimes available from the visitors center. Book ahead, especially on summer weekends. Reservations essential at all spas.

The following spas in downtown Calistoga offer one-day packages. Some also offer discounted spa-lodging packages.

TOP CHOICE **Indian Springs** SPA
(707-942-4913; www.indianspringscalistoga.com; 1712 Lincoln Ave; 8am-9pm) The longest continually operating spa and original Calistoga resort has concrete mud tubs and mines its own ash. Treatments include use of the huge, hot-spring-fed pool. Great cucumber body lotion.

Spa Solage SPA
(Map p164; 707-226-0825; www.solagecalistoga.com; 755 Silverado Trail; 8am-8pm) Chichi, austere, top-end spa, with couples' rooms and a fango-mud bar for DIY paint-on treatments. Also has zero-gravity chairs for blanket wraps, and a clothing-optional pool.

Dr Wilkinson's Hot Springs SPA
(707-942-4102; www.drwilkinson.com; 1507 Lincoln Ave; 8:30am-5:30pm) Fifty years running; 'the doc' uses more peat in its mud.

Mount View Spa SPA
(707-942-6877, 800-816-6877; www.mountviewhotel.com; 1457 Lincoln Ave; 9am-9pm) Traditional full-service, 12-room spa, good for clean-hands gals who prefer painted-on mud to submersion.

Lavender Hill Spa SPA
(Map p164; 707-942-4495; www.lavenderhillspa.com; 1015 Foothill Blvd; 10am-6pm, to 8pm Fri & Sat) Small, cute, two-room spa that uses much-lighter, less-icky lavender-infused mud; offers couples' treatments.

Golden Haven Hot Springs SPA
(707-942-8000; www.goldenhaven.com; 1713 Lake St; 8am-8pm) Old-school and unfussy; offers couples' mud baths and couples' massage.

Calistoga Spa Hot Springs SPA
(707-942-6269, 866-822-5772; www.calistogaspa.com; 1006 Washington St; appointments 8:30am-4:30pm Tue-Thu, to 9pm Fri-Mon;) Traditional mud baths and massage at a motel complex with two huge **swimming pools** (10am-9pm) where kids can play while you soak (pool passes $25).

Sleeping

Also see Safari West (p182).

TOP CHOICE **Mountain Home Ranch** LODGE, B&B $$
(off Map p164; 707-942-6616; www.mountainhomeranch.com; 3400 Mountain Home Ranch Rd; r $109-119, cabin with/without bath $119-144/$69; @) In continuous operation since 1913, this 340-acre homestead ranch is a flashback to old California. Doubling as a retreat center, the ranch has simple lodge rooms and rustic freestanding cabins, some with kitchens and fireplaces, ideal for families, but you may be here during someone else's family reunion or spiritual quest. No matter. With miles of oak-woodland trails, a hilltop swimming pool, private lake with canoeing and fishing, and hike-to warm springs in a magical fault-line canyon, you may hardly notice – and you may never make it to a single winery. Breakfast included, but you'll have to drive 15 minutes to town for dinner. Pack hiking boots, not high heels.

Solage RESORT $$$
(Map p164; ☎707-226-0800, 866-942-7442; www.solagecalistoga.com; 755 Silverado Trail; r $510-625; ❄📶🏊🐾) The latest addition to Calistoga's spa-hotels ups the style factor, with Cali-chic semidetached cottages and a glam palm-tree-lined pool. Rooms are austere, with vaulted ceilings, zillion-thread-count linens and pebble-floor showers. Cruiser bikes included.

Indian Springs Resort RESORT $$$
(☎707-942-4913; www.indianspringscalistoga.com; 1712 Lincoln Ave; motel r $229-299, bungalow $259-349, 2-bedroom bungalow $359-419; ❄📶🏊👪) The definitive old-school Calistoga resort, Indian Springs has bungalows facing a central lawn with palm trees, shuffleboard, bocce, hammocks and Weber grills – not unlike a vintage Florida resort. Some bungalows sleep six. There are also top-end motel-style rooms. Huge hot-springs-fed swimming pool.

Chateau De Vie B&B $$$
(Map p164; ☎707-942-6446, 877-558-2513; www.cdvnapavalley.com; 3250 Hwy 128; r incl breakfast $229-429; ❄📶🏊🐾) Surrounded by vineyards, with gorgeous views of Mt St Helena, CDV has five modern B&B rooms with top-end amenities. The house is elegantly decorated, with zero froufrou. Charming owners serve wine every afternoon on the sun-dappled patio, then leave you alone. Hot tub, big pool. Gay-friendly.

Meadowlark Country House B&B $$$
(Map p164; ☎707-942-5651, 800-942-5651; www.meadowlarkinn.com; 601 Petrified Forest Rd; r incl breakfast $195-275, ste $285; ❄📶🏊🐾) On 20 acres west of town, Meadowlark has luxury rooms decorated in contemporary style, most with decks and Jacuzzis. Outside there's a hot tub, sauna and clothing-optional pool. The truth-telling innkeeper lives in another house, offers helpful advice, then vanishes when you want privacy. There's a fabulous cottage for $450. Gay-friendly.

Mount View Hotel & Spa HISTORIC HOTEL $$$
(☎707-942-6877, 800-816-6877; www.mountviewhotel.com; 1457 Lincoln Ave; r $179-329; ❄📶🏊) Smack in the middle of town, this 1917 Mission Revival hotel was redone in 2009 in vaguely mod-Italian style, sometimes at odds with the vintage building, but clean and fresh-looking nonetheless. Gleaming bathrooms, on-site spa, year-round heated pool, but no elevator.

Eurospa Inn MOTEL $$
(☎707-942-6829; www.eurospa.com; 1202 Pine St, Calistoga; r $139-189; ❄📶🏊) Immaculate single-story motel on a quiet side street, with extras like gas-burning fireplaces, afternoon wine and small on-site spa. Wonderful service, but tiny pool.

Brannan Cottage Inn B&B $$$
(☎707-942-4200; www.brannancottageinn.com; 109 Wapoo Ave; r incl breakfast $195-230, ste $230-270; ❄📶🐾) Sam Brannan built this 1860 cottage, listed on the National Register of Historic Places. Long on folksy charm and friendly service, it's decorated with floral-print fabrics and simple country furnishings, but walls are thin and floors creak. Suites sleep four. Guests use the pool at Golden Haven motel.

Dr Wilkinson's Motel & Hideaway Cottages MOTEL, COTTAGES $$
(☎707-942-4102; www.drwilkinson.com; 1507 Lincoln Ave; r $149-255, cottages w/kitchens $165-270; ❄📶🏊) This good-value vintage-1950s motel has well-kept rooms facing a swimming-pool courtyard. No hot tub, but three pools (one indoors) and mud baths. Doc Wilkinson's also rents simple stand-alone cottages, with kitchens, at the affiliated Hideaway Cottages.

Chanric B&B $$$
(Map p164; ☎707-942-4535; www.thechanric.com; 1805 Foothill Blvd; r incl breakfast $229-349; ❄📶🏊) A converted Victorian close to the road, this B&B has smallish rooms with modern furnishings, but the affable owners compensate with a lavish three-course breakfast. Gay-friendly.

Aurora Park Cottages COTTAGES $$$
(Map p164; ☎707-942-6733, 877-942-7700; www.aurorapark.com; 1807 Foothill Blvd; cottages incl breakfast $259-289; ❄📶) Six immaculately kept, sunny-yellow cottages – with polished-wood floors, featherbeds and sundeck – stand in a row beside flowering gardens, and though close to the road, they're quiet by night. The innkeeper couldn't be nicer.

Calistoga Spa Hot Springs MOTEL $$
(Map p164; ☎707-942-6269, 866-822-5772; www.calistogaspa.com; 1006 Washington St; r $132-252; ❄📶🏊👪) Great for families, who jam the place weekends, this motel-resort has slightly scuffed generic rooms, with kitchenettes, and fantastic pools – two full-size, a kiddie-pool with miniwaterfall and a huge

adults-only Jacuzzi. Outside are barbecues and snack bar. Wi-fi in lobby.

Golden Haven Hot Springs MOTEL $$
(707-942-8000; www.goldenhaven.com; 1713 Lake St; r $149-219;) This motel-spa has mudbath-lodging packages and well-kept rooms; some have Jacuzzis.

Calistoga Inn & Brewery INN $
(707-942-4101; www.calistogainn.com; 1250 Lincoln Ave; r Mon-Fri/Sat & Sun $69/$119;) For no-fuss bargain-hunters, this inn, upstairs from a busy bar, has 18 clean, basic rooms with shared bath. No TVs. Bring earplugs.

Bothe-Napa Valley State Park CAMPGROUND $
(707-942-4575, reservations 800-444-7275; www.reserveamerica.com; tent & RV sites $35;) Three miles south, Bothe has shady camping near redwoods, coin-operated showers, and gorgeous hiking, but call ahead to confirm it's open. Sites 28 to 36 are most secluded.

Napa County Fairgrounds & RV Park CAMPGROUND $
(Map p164; 707-942-5221; www.napacountyfair.org; 1435 Oak St; tent sites $20, RV sites w/hookups $33-36;) A dusty RV park northwest of downtown.

Cottage Grove Inn BUNGALOWS $$$
(707-942-8400, 800-799-2284; www.cottagegrove.com; 1711 Lincoln Ave; cottages $250-425;) Romantic cottages for over-40s, with wood-burning fireplaces, two-person tubs and rocking-chair front porches.

Chelsea Garden Inn B&B $$$
(707-942-0948; www.chelseagardeninn.com; 1443 2nd St; r incl breakfast $195-275;) On a quiet street, five floral-print rooms with private entrances. Pretty gardens, but the pool looked dingy at our last inspection.

Wine Way Inn B&B $$
(Map p164; 707-942-0680, 800-572-0679; www.winewayinn.com; 1019 Foothill Blvd; r $180-220;) A small B&B, in a 1910-era house, close to the road; friendly owners.

Eating

Jolé CALIFORNIAN $$
(707-942-5938; www.jolerestaurant.com; 1457 Lincoln Ave, Calistoga; mains $15-20; 5-9pm Sun-Thu, to 10pm Fri & Sat) The earthy and inventive farm-to-table small plates at chef-owned Jolé evolve seasonally, and may include such dishes as local sole with tangy miniature Napa grapes, caramelized Brussels sprouts with capers, and organic Baldwin apple strudel with burnt-caramel ice cream. Four courses cost $50. Reservations essential.

Solbar CALIFORNIAN $$$
(Map p164; 707-226-0850; www.solagecalistoga.com; 755 Silverado Trail; lunch/dinner mains $15-19/$30-37; 7am-11am, 11:30am-3pm, 5:30-9pm) The ag-chic look at this superb restaurant is spare, with concrete floors, exposed-wood tables and soaring ceilings. Maximizing seasonal produce, each dish is elegantly composed, some with tongue-in-cheek playfulness. The menu is divided into light and hearty, so you can mind calories. Reservations essential.

All Seasons Bistro NEW AMERICAN $$$
(707-942-9111; www.allseasonsnapavalley.net; 1400 Lincoln Ave; lunch mains $10-15, dinner mains $16-22; noon-2pm & 5:30-8:30pm Tue-Sun) The dining room looks like a white-tablecloth soda fountain, but All Seasons makes some very fine meals, from simple steak-*frites* to composed dishes like cornmeal-crusted scallops with summer succotash. Good lobster bisque.

Buster's Southern BBQ BARBECUE $
(Map p164; 707-942-5605; www.busterssouthernbbq.com; 1207 Foothill Blvd; dishes $8-11; 10am-7:30pm Mon-Sat, 10:30am-6:30pm Sun;) The sheriff eats lunch at this indoor-outdoor barbecue joint, which serves smoky ribs, chicken, tri-tip steak and burgers, but closes early at dinnertime. Beer and wine.

Calistoga Inn & Brewery AMERICAN $$
(707-942-4101; www.calistogainn.com; 1250 Lincoln Ave; lunch/dinner mains $9-13/$14-26; 11:30am-3pm & 5:30-9pm) Locals crowd the outdoor beer garden Sundays. Midweek we prefer the country dining room and its big oakwood tables, a homey spot for pot roast and other simple American dishes. There's live music summer weekends.

Drinking

Yo El Rey CAFE
(707-942-1180; www.yoelrey.com; 1217 Washington St; 6:30am-8pm) Meet the hip kids at this micro-roastery cafe and living room, which brews superb small-batch fair-trade coffee.

Hydro Grill BAR
(707-942-9777; 1403 Lincoln Ave) Live music plays weekend evenings at this hoppin' corner bar-restaurant.

Solbar BAR
(Map p164; ☎707-226-0850; www.solagecalistoga.com; 755 Silverado Trail) Sip cocktails and wine on cane sofas beside outdoor fireplaces and a palm-lined pool. Wear white.

Brannan's Grill BAR
(☎707-942-2233; www.brannansgrill.com; 1374 Lincoln Ave) Calistoga's most handsome restaurant; the mahogany bar is great for martinis and microbrews, especially weekends, when jazz combos sometimes play.

Susie's Bar DIVE BAR
(☎707-942-6710; 1365 Lincoln Ave) Turn your baseball cap sideways, do shots and play pool while the juke box blares classic rock and country and western.

Shopping

Wine Garage WINE
(☎707-942-5332; www.winegarage.net; 1020 Foothill Blvd) Every bottle costs under $25 at this winning wine store, formerly a service station.

Mudd Hens BEAUTY
(☎707-942-0210; www.muddhens.com; 1348 Lincoln Ave) Recreate mud baths at home with mineral-rich Calistoga Mud ($27/pound) and volcanic-ash soap from this cute bath shop.

Calistoga Pottery CERAMICS
(☎707-942-0216; www.calistogapottery.com; 1001 Foothill Blvd) Winemakers aren't the only artisans in Napa. Watch potters throw vases, bowls and plates, all for sale.

Coperfield's Bookshop BOOKS
(☎707-942-1616; 1330 Lincoln Ave) Great indie bookshop, with local maps and guides.

Information

Chamber of Commerce & Visitors Center
(☎707-942-6333, 866-306-5588; www.calistogavisitors.com; 1133 Washington St; ⏲9am-5pm)

Around Calistoga

Sights & Activities

Bale Grist Mill & Bothe-Napa Valley State Parks HISTORIC PARK $
There's good weekend picnicking at **Bale Grist Mill State Historic Park** (☎707-963-2236; adult/child $3/2; ⏲10am-5pm Sat & Sun 👪), which features a 36ft water-powered mill wheel dating from 1846 – the largest still operating in North America. Watch it grind corn and wheat into flour Saturdays and Sundays; call for times. In early October, look for the living-history festival, **Old Mill Days**.

A mile-long trail leads to adjacent **Bothe-Napa Valley State Park** (Map p164; ☎707-942-4575; parking $8; ⏲8am-sunset; 👪), where there's a **swimming pool** (adult/child $5/2; ⏲summer only) and lovely hiking through redwood groves.

Admission to one park includes the other. If you're more than three, go to Bothe first, and pay $8 instead of the per-head charge at Bale Grist Mill.

The mill and both parks are on Hwy 29/128, midway between St Helena and Calistoga.

FREE **Robert Louis Stevenson State Park** MOUNTAIN
(off Map p164; ☎707-942-4575; www.parks.ca.gov) The long-extinct volcanic cone of Mt St Helena marks the valley's end, 8 miles north of Calistoga. The undeveloped state park on Hwy 29 often gets snow in winter.

It's a strenuous 5-mile climb to the peak's 4343ft summit, but what a view – 200 miles on a clear winter's day. Check conditions before setting out. Also consider 2.2-mile one-way Table Rock Trail (go south from the summit parking arca) for drop-dead valley views. Temperatures are best in wildflower season, February to May; fall is prettiest, when the vineyards change colors.

The park includes the site of the Silverado Mine where Stevenson and his wife honeymooned in 1880.

Petrified Forest FOREST
(Map p164; ☎707-942-6667; www.petrifiedforest.org; 4100 Petrified Forest Rd; adult/child $10/5; ⏲9am-7pm summer, to 5pm winter) Three million years ago, a volcanic eruption at nearby Mt St Helena blew down a stand of redwoods between Calistoga and Santa Rosa. The trees fell in the same direction, away from the blast, and were covered in ash and mud. Over the millennia, the mighty giants' trunks turned to stone; gradually the overlay eroded, exposing them. The first stumps were discovered in 1870. A monument marks Robert Louis Stevenson's 1880 visit. He describes it in *The Silverado Squatters*.

It's 5 miles northwest of town, off Hwy 128. Check online for 10%-off coupons.

OUTLET SHOPPING

Max out your credit cards on last season's close-outs.

Napa Premium Outlets (Map p164; ☎707-226-9876; www.premiumoutlets.com; 629 Factory Stores Dr, Napa) 50 stores

Petaluma Village Premium Outlets (☎707-778-9300; www.premiumoutlets.com; 2200 Petaluma Blvd North, Petaluma) 60 stores, Sonoma County

Vacaville Premium Outlets (☎707-447-5755; www.premiumoutlets.com/vacaville; 321 Nut Tree Rd, Vacaville) 120 stores, northeast of the Wine Country on I-80

Safari West WILDLIFE RESERVE
(off Map p164; ☎707-579-2551, 800-616-2695; www.safariwest.com; 3115 Porter Creek Rd; adult/child $68/30; 👪) Giraffes in Wine Country? Whadya know! Safari West covers 400 acres and protects zebras, cheetahs and other exotic animals, which mostly roam free. See them on a guided three-hour safari in open-sided jeeps; reservations required. You'll also walk through an aviary and lemur condo. The reservations-only cafe serves lunch and dinner. If you're feeling adventurous, stay overnight in nifty canvas-sided **tent cabins** (cabins incl breakfast $200-295), right in the preserve.

SONOMA VALLEY

We have a soft spot for Sonoma's folksy ways. Unlike in fancy Napa, nobody cares if you drive a clunker and vote Green. Locals call it 'Slow-noma.' Anchoring the bucolic 17-mile-long Sonoma Valley, the town of Sonoma makes a great jumping-off point for exploring Wine Country – it's only an hour from San Francisco – and has a marvelous sense of place, with storied 19th-century historical sights surrounding the state's largest town square. Halfway up-valley, tiny Glen Ellen is right out of a Norman Rockwell painting, in stark contrast to the valley's northernmost town, Santa Rosa, the workaday urban center best known for its traffic. If you have more than a day, explore Sonoma's quiet, rustic side along the Russian River Valley (p194) and work your way to the sea.

Sonoma Hwy/Hwy 12 is lined with wineries and runs from Sonoma to Santa Rosa, then to western Sonoma County; Arnold Dr has less traffic (but few wineries) and runs parallel, up the valley's western side to Glen Ellen.

Sonoma Valley Wineries

Rolling grass-covered hills rise from 17-mile-long Sonoma Valley. Its 40 wineries get less attention than Napa's, but many are equally good. If you love zinfandel and syrah, you're in for a treat.

Picnicking is allowed at Sonoma wineries. Get maps and discount coupons in the town of Sonoma (p191) or, if you're approaching from the south, the **Sonoma Valley Visitors Bureau** (Map p184; ☎707-935-4747; www.sonomavalley.com; Cornerstone Gardens, 23570 Hwy 121; ⏰10am-4pm) at Cornerstone Gardens (p187).

Plan at least five hours to visit the valley from bottom to top. For other Sonoma County wineries, see the Russian River Valley section.

Homewood WINERY
(Map p184; ☎707-996-6353; www.homewoodwinery.com; 23120 Burndale Rd at Hwy 121/12; tastings free; ⏰10am-4pm; 🐾) A stripy rooster named Steve chases dogs in the parking lot of this down-home winery, where the tasting room is a garage, and the winemaker crafts standout ports and Rhône-style grenache, mourvèdre and syrah – 'Da redder, da better.' Ask about 'vertical tastings,' and sample wines from the same vineyards, but different years. Dogs welcome, but you've been warned. Bottles cost $18 to $32.

Nicholson Ranch WINERY
(☎707-938-8822; www.nicholsonranch.com; 4200 Napa Rd; tastings $10; ⏰10am-6pm) Unfiltered pinot noir and non-buttery chardonnay in a hilltop tasting room; lovely for picnicking.

Robledo WINERY
(Map p184; ☎707-939-6903; www.robledofamilywinery.com; 21901 Bonness Rd, of Hwy 116; tastings $5-10; ⏰by appointment only) Sonoma Valley's feel-good winery, Robledo was founded by a former grape-picker from Mexico who worked his way up to vineyard manager, then land owner, now vintner. His kids run the place. The wines – served at hand-carved Mexican furniture in a windowless tasting room – include a no-oak sauvignon blanc,

jammy syrah, spicy cabernet, and bright-fruit pinot noir. Bottles cost $18 to $45.

Gundlach-Bundschu WINERY
(Map p184; ☎707-938-5277; www.gunbun.com; 2000 Denmark St; tastings $10; ⏱11am-4:30pm) One of Sonoma Valley's oldest and prettiest, Gundlach-Bundschu looks like a storybook castle. Founded in 1858 by Bavarian immigrant Jacob Gundlach, it's now at the cutting edge of sustainability. Signature wines are rieslings and gewürztraminers, but 'Gun-Bun' was the first American winery to produce 100% merlot. Tours of the 2000-barrel cave ($20) are available by reservation. Down a winding lane, it's a good bike-to winery, with picnicking, hiking and a small lake. Bottles cost $22 to $40.

Bartholomew Park Winery WINERY, MUSEUM
(Map p184; ☎707-939-3026; www.bartpark.com; 1000 Vineyard Lane; tasting $5-10, museum & park entry free; ⏱tasting room & museum 11am-4:30pm) Gundlach-Bundschu also runs nearby Bartholomew Park Winery (another good bike-to destination), a 400-acre preserve with vineyards originally cultivated in 1857 and now certified-organic, yielding citrusy sauvignon blanc and smoky merlot. Bottles cost $22 to $40.

Hawkes TASTING ROOM
(Map p188; ☎707-938-7620; www.hawkeswine.com; 383 1st St W; tasting $10, waived with purchase over $30; ⏱noon-6pm) When you're in downtown Sonoma and don't feel like fighting traffic, Hawke's refreshingly unfussy tasting room showcases meaty merlot and cabernet sauvignon, never blended with other grape varietals. Bottles cost $20 to $60.

Little Vineyards WINERY
(Map p184; ☎707-996-2750; www.littlevineyards.com; 15188 Sonoma Hwy, Glen Ellen; tastings $5; ⏱11am-4:30pm Thu-Mon; 👪) The name fits at this family-owned small-scale winery, long on atmosphere, with a lazy dog to greet you and a weathered, cigarette-burned tasting bar, which Jack London drank at (before it was moved here). The tiny tasting room is good for shy folks who dislike crowds. If you're new to wine, consider the $20 introductory class (call ahead). Good picnicking on the vineyard-view terrace. The big reds include syrah, petite sirah, zin, cab and several delish blends. Bottles cost $17 to $35. Also rents a cottage in the vines.

BR Cohn WINERY
(Map p184; ☎707-938-4064; www.brcohn.com; 15000 Sonoma Hwy, Glen Ellen; tasting $10, applicable to purchase; ⏱10am-5pm) Picnic like a rock star at always-busy BR Cohn, whose founder managed '70s superband the Doobie Brothers before moving on to make outstanding organic olive oils and fine wines – including excellent cabernet sauvignon, unusual in Sonoma. In autumn, he throws benefit concerts, amid the olives, by the likes of Skynyrd and the Doobies. Bottles cost $16 to $55.

Arrowood WINERY
(Map p184; ☎707-935-2600; www.arrowoodvineyards.com; 14347 Sonoma Hwy; tastings $5-10; ⏱10am-4:30pm) Excellent cabernet and chardonnay; stunning views.

Benziger WINERY
(Map p184; ☎888-490-2739; www.benziger.com; 1883 London Ranch Rd, Glen Ellen; tasting $10-20, tram tour adult incl tasting/child $15/5; ⏱10am-5pm; 👪) If you're new to wine, make Benziger your first stop for Sonoma's best crash course in wine-making. The worthwhile, non-reservable tour includes an open-air tram ride through biodynamic vineyards, and a four-wine tasting. Kids love the peacocks. The large-production wine's OK (head for the reserves); the tour's the thing. Bottles cost $15 to $80.

Imagery Estate WINERY
(Map p184; ☎877-550-4278; www.imagerywinery.com; 14355 Sonoma Hwy; tastings $10-15; ⏱10am-4:30pm) Obscure varietals, biodynamically grown, with artist-designed labels.

Loxton WINERY
(Map p184; ☎707-935-7221; www.loxtonwines.com; 11466 Dunbar Rd, Glen Ellen; tastings free) Say g'day to Chris, the Aussie winemaker, at Loxton, a no-frills winery with million-dollar views. The 'tasting room' is actually a small warehouse, where you can taste wonderful syrah and zinfandel; non-oaky, fruit-forward chardonnay; and good port. Bottles cost $15 to $25.

Wellington WINERY
(Map p184; ☎707-939-0708; www.wellingtonvineyards.com; 11600 Dunbar Rd, Glen Ellen; tastings $5) Known for port (including a white) and meaty reds, Wellington makes great zinfandel, one from vines planted in 1892 – wow, what color! The noir de noir is a cult

favorite. Alas, servers have vineyard views, while you face the warehouse. Bottles cost $15 to $30.

Family Wineries TASTING ROOM
(Map p184; ☎707-433-0100; www.familywines.com; 9300 Sonoma Hwy at Laurel Ave; tastings $5-10; ⊙10:30am-5pm) Several labels under one roof. Standout: David Noyes pinot noir.

TOP CHOICE **Kaz** WINERY
(Map p184; ☎707-833-2536; www.kazwinery.com; 233 Adobe Canyon Rd, Kenwood; tastings $5; ⊙11am-5pm Fri-Mon;) Sonoma's cult favorite, supercool Kaz is about blends: whatever's in the organic vineyards goes into the wine – and they're blended at crush, not during fermentation. Expect lesser-known varietals like Alicante Bouchet and Lenoir, and a worthwhile cabernet-merlot blend. Kids can sample grape juice, then run around the playground out back, while you sift through LPs and pop your favorites onto the turntable. Crazy fun. Dogs welcome. Bottles cost $20 to $48.

Sonoma & Around

Fancy boutiques may lately be replacing hardware stores, but Sonoma still retains an old-fashioned charm, thanks to the plaza – California's largest town square – and its surrounding frozen-in-time historic buildings. You can legally drink on the plaza, a rarity in California parks.

Sonoma has rich history. In 1846 it was the site of a second American revolution, this time against Mexico, when General Mariano Guadalupe Vallejo deported all foreigners from California, prompting outraged American frontiersmen to occupy the Sonoma Presidio and declare independence. They dubbed California the Bear Flag Republic after the battle flag they'd fashioned.

The republic was short-lived. The Mexican-American War broke out a month later, and California was annexed by the US. The revolt gave California its flag, which remains emblazoned with the words 'California Republic' beneath a muscular brown bear. Vallejo was initially imprisoned, but ultimately returned to Sonoma and played a major role in the region's development.

Sights

Sonoma Hwy (Hwy 12) runs through town. Sonoma Plaza, laid out by General Vallejo

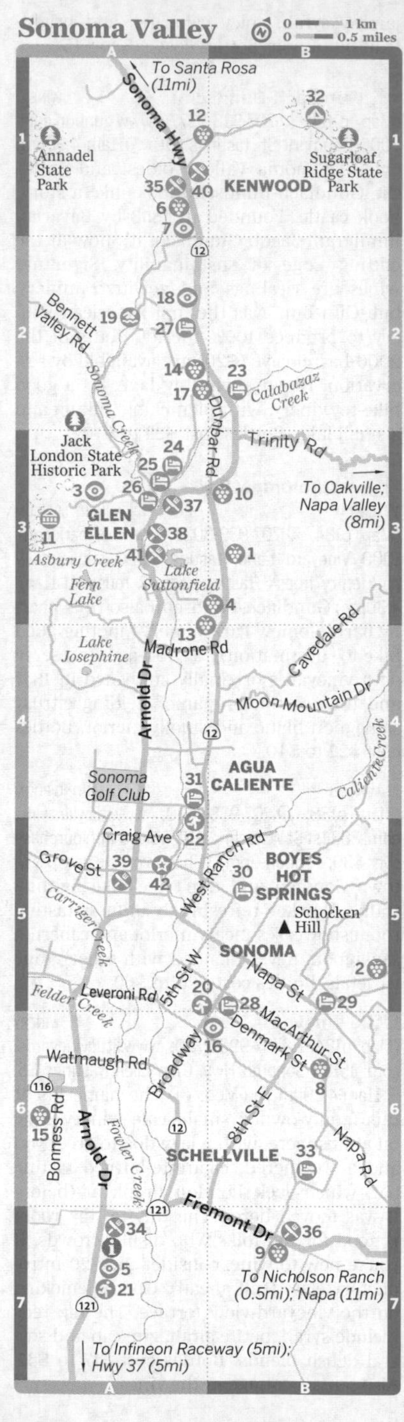

Sonoma Valley

in 1834, is the heart of downtown, lined with hotels, restaurants and shops. Pick up a walking-tour brochure from the visitors bureau. Immediately north along Hwy 12, expect a brief suburban landscape before the valley's pastoral gorgeousness begins, outside town.

SONOMA PLAZA & AROUND

Sonoma Plaza SQUARE

(Map p188) Smack in the center of the plaza, the Mission-revival-style **city hall**, built 1906–08, has identical facades on four sides, reportedly because plaza businesses all demanded City Hall face their direction. At the plaza's northeast corner, the **Bear Flag Monument** marks Sonoma's moment of revolutionary glory. The town shows up for the **farmers market** (5:30-8pm Tue, Apr-Oct), where you can sample Sonoma's exquisite produce.

Sonoma State Historic Park HISTORIC BUILDINGS

(707-938-1519; www.parks.ca.gov; adult/child $3/2; 10am-5pm Tue-Sun) The park is comprised of multiple sites. The **Mission San Francisco Solano de Sonoma** (Map p188; E Spain St), at the plaza's northeast corner, was built in 1823, in part to forestall the Russian coastal colony at Fort Ross from moving inland. The mission was the 21st and final California mission, and the only one built during the Mexican period (the rest were founded by the Spanish). It marks the northernmost point on El Camino Real. Five of the mission's original rooms remain. The not-to-be-missed chapel dates from 1841.

The adobe **Sonoma Barracks** (Map p188; E Spain St; daily) was built by Vallejo between 1836 and 1840 to house Mexican troops, but it became the capital of a rogue nation on June 14, 1846, when American settlers, of

A WINE COUNTRY PRIMER

When people talk about Sonoma, they're referring to the *whole* county, which unlike Napa is huge. It extends all the way from the coast, up the Russian River Valley, into Sonoma Valley and eastward to Napa Valley; in the south it stretches from San Pablo Bay (an extension of San Francisco Bay) to Healdsburg in the north. It's essential to break Sonoma down by district.

West County refers to everything west of Hwy 101 and includes the **Russian River Valley** and the coast. **Sonoma Valley** stretches north-south along Hwy 12. In northern Sonoma County, **Alexander Valley** lies east of Healdsburg, and **Dry Creek Valley** lies north of Healdsburg. In the south, **Carneros** straddles the Sonoma–Napa border, north of San Pablo Bay. Each region has its own particular wines; what grows where depends upon the weather.

Inland valleys get hot; coastal regions stay cool. In West County and Carneros, nighttime fog blankets the vineyards. Burgundy-style wines do best, particularly pinot noir and chardonnay. Further inland, Alexander, Sonoma and much of Dry Creek Valleys (as well as Napa Valley) are fog-protected. Here, Bordeaux-style wines thrive, especially cabernet sauvignon, sauvignon blanc, merlot and other heat-loving varieties. For California's famous cabernets, head to Napa. Zinfandel and Rhône-style varieties, such as syrah and viognier, grow in both regions, warm and cool. In cooler climes, resultant wines are lighter, more elegant; in warmer areas they are heavier and more rustic.

For a handy-dandy reference on the road, pick up a copy of Karen MacNeil's *The Wine Bible* (2001, Workman Publishing) or Jancis Robinson's *Concise Wine Companion* (2001, Oxford University Press) to carry in the car.

varying sobriety, surprised the guards and declared an independent 'California Republc' [sic] with a homemade flag featuring a blotchy bear. The US took over the republic a month later, but abandoned the barracks during the Gold Rush, leaving Vallejo to turn then into (what else?) a winery in 1860. Today, displays describe life during the Mexican and American periods.

Next to the Sonoma Barracks, **Toscano Hotel** (Map p188; 20 E Spain St) opened as a store and library in the 1850s, then became a hotel in 1886. Peek into the lobby from 10am to 5pm; except for the traffic outside, you'd swear you'd stepped back in time. Free tours 1pm through 4pm, weekends and Mondays.

A half-mile northwest, the lovely **Vallejo Home** (Map p188; 363 3rd St W), otherwise known as Lachryma Montis (Latin for 'Tears of the Mountain'), was built 1851–52 for General Vallejo. It's named for the spring on the property; the Vallejo family later made a handy income piping water to town. The property remained in the family until 1933, when the state of California purchased it, retaining much of its original furnishings. A bike path leads to the house from downtown.

Admission here includes entry to the **Petaluma Adobe** (Map p160; ☎707-762-4871; www.petalumaadobe.com; 3325 Adobe Rd, Petaluma; ⏲10am-5pm Sat & Sun), a historic ranch 15 miles northwest in suburban Petaluma.

La Haye Art Center ARTS CENTER
(Map p188; ☎707-996-9665; www.lahayeartcenter.com; 148 E Napa St; ⏲11am-5pm) At this collective in a converted foundry, you can tour a storefront gallery and meet the artists – sculptor, potter and painters – in their garden studios. Beverly Prevost's asymmetrical ceramic dinnerware is featured next door at Café La Haye (p189).

Sonoma Valley Museum of Art MUSEUM
(Map p188; ☎707-939-7862; www.svma.org; 551 Broadway; adult/family $5/8; ⏲11am-5pm Wed-Sun) Though this 8000-sq-ft museum presents compelling work by local and international artists, such as David Hockney, the annual standout is October's Día de los Muertos exhibition.

BEYOND SONOMA PLAZA

FREE **Bartholomew Park** PARK
(Map p184; ☎707-935-9511; www.bartholomewparkwinery.com; 1000 Vineyard Lane) The top close-to-town outdoors destination is 375-acre Bartholomew Park, off Castle Rd, where you can picnic beneath giant oaks and hike three miles of trails, with hilltop vistas to San Francisco. There's also a good winery

(p186) and small museum. The Palladian Villa, at the park's entrance, is a turn-of-the-20th-century replica of Count Haraszthy's original residence, open noon to 3pm, Saturdays and Sundays, operated by the **Bartholomew Foundation** (☎707-938-2244).

FREE **Cornerstone Gardens** GARDENS
(Map p184; ☎707-933-3010; www.cornerstongardens.com; 23570 Arnold Dr; ⊙10am-4pm;) There's nothing traditional about Cornerstone Gardens, which showcase the work of 19 renowned avant-garde landscape designers. We especially love Pamela Burton's 'Earth Walk,' which descends into the ground; and Planet Horticulture's 'Rise,' which exaggerates space. Let the kids run around while you explore top-notch garden shops and gather information from the onsite **Sonoma Valley Visitors Bureau** (☎707-935-4747; www.sonomavalley.com; ⊙10am-4pm), then refuel at the on-site cafe. Look for the enormous blue chair at road's edge.

Traintown AMUSEMENT PARK
(Map p184; ☎707-938-3912; www.traintown.com; 20264 Broadway; ⊙10am-5pm daily summer, Fri-Sun only mid-Sep-late May) Little kids adore Traintown, one mile south of the plaza. A miniature steam engine makes 20-minute loops ($4.75), and there are vintage amusement-park rides ($2.75 per ride), including a carousel and a Ferris wheel.

Activities

Many local inns provide bicycles.

Sonoma Valley Cyclery BICYCLE RENTAL
(Map p184; ☎707-935-3377; www.sonomacyclery.com; 20091 Broadway/Hwy 12; bikes from $25 per day; ⊙10am-6pm Mon-Sat, to 4pm Sun;) Sonoma is ideal for cycling – not too hilly – with multiple wineries near downtown. Book ahead weekends.

Willow Stream Spa at Sonoma Mission Inn SPA
(Map p184; ☎707-938-9000; www.fairmont.com/sonoma; 100 Boyes Blvd; ⊙7:30am-8pm) Few Wine Country spas compare with glitzy Sonoma Mission Inn, where two treatments – or $89 – allows use of three outdoor and two indoor mineral pools, gym, sauna, and herbal steam room at the Romanesque bathhouse. No children.

Triple Creek Horse Outfit HORSEBACK RIDING
(☎707-887-8700; www.triplecreekhorseoutfit.com; 1-/2hr rides $60/100; ⊙Wed-Mon) Hit the trail for stunning vistas of Sonoma Valley. Reservations required.

Courses

Ramekins Sonoma Valley Culinary School COOKING SCHOOL
(Map p188; ☎707-933-0450; www.ramekins.com; 450 W Spain St;) Offers excellent demonstrations and hands-on classes for home chefs. Also runs weekend 'culinary camps' for both adults and kids.

Sleeping

Off-season rates plummet. Reserve ahead. Ask about parking; some historic inns have no lots. Also consider Glen Ellen (p192) and, if counting pennies, Santa Rosa (p206).

Sonoma Chalet B&B, COTTAGES $$
(Map p184; ☎707-938-3129; www.sonomachalet.com; 18935 5th St W; r without bath $125, r with bath $140-180, cottages $190-225;) An old farmstead surrounded by rolling hills, Sonoma Chalet has rooms in a Swiss chalet-style house adorned with little balconies and country-style bric-a-brac. We love the free-standing cottages; Laura's has a wood-burning fireplace. Breakfast is served on a deck overlooking a nature preserve. No air-con in rooms with shared bath. No phones, no internet.

Sonoma Hotel HISTORIC HOTEL $$
(Map p188; ☎707-996-2996; www.sonomahotel.com; 110 W Spain St; r incl breakfast $170-200;) Long on charm, this spiffy vintage-1880s hotel is decked with Spanish-colonial and American-country-crafts furnishings. No elevator or parking lot.

El Dorado Hotel HOTEL $$$
(Map p188; ☎707-996-3030, 800-289-3031; www.eldoradosonoma.com; 405 1st St W; r weekday/weekend $195/225;) Stylish touches like high-end linens make up for the rooms' compact size, as do private balconies overlooking the plaza or the rear courtyard (we prefer the plaza view, despite the noise). No elevator.

Swiss Hotel HISTORIC HOTEL $$
(Map p188; ☎707-938-2884; www.swisshotelsonoma.com; 18 W Spain St; r incl breakfast Mon-Fri $150-170, Sat & Sun $200-240;) It opened in 1905, so you'll forgive the wavy floors. Think knotty pine and wicker. In the morning sip coffee on the shared plaza-view balcony. Downstairs there's a raucous bar and restaurant. No parking lot or elevator.

Sonoma

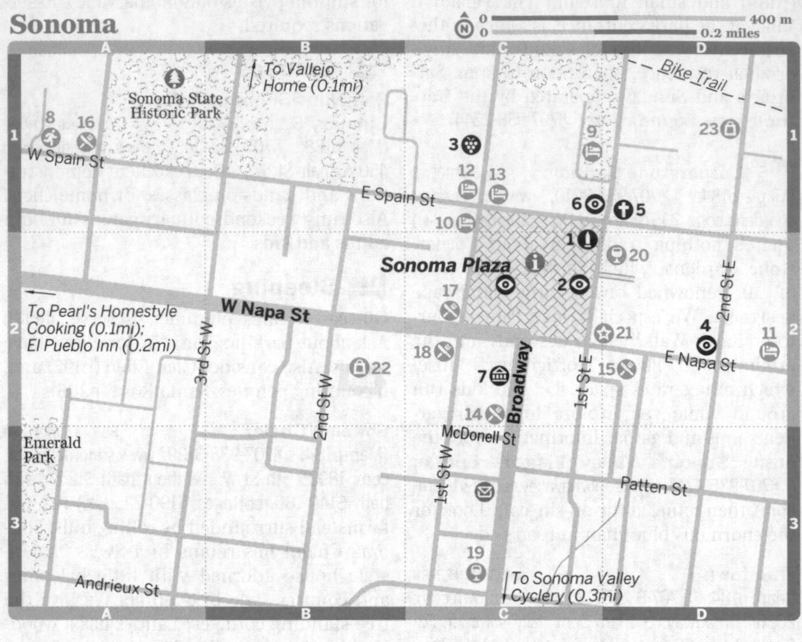

Sonoma

Top Sights

Sonoma Plaza C2

Sights

1 Bear Flag Monument C2
2 City Hall C2
3 Hawkes C1
4 La Haye Art Center D2
5 Mission San Francisco Solano de Sonoma D1
6 Sonoma Barracks C1
7 Sonoma Valley Museum of Art C2
Toscano Hotel .... (see 6)

Activities, Courses & Tours

8 Ramekins Sonoma Valley Culinary School A1

Sleeping

9 Bungalows 313 .... C1
10 El Dorado Hotel C1
11 Hidden Oak Inn D2
12 Sonoma Hotel C1
13 Swiss Hotel C1

Eating

14 599 Thai Cafe C2
Café la Haye .... (see 4)
15 Della Santina's D2
El Dorado Corner Cafe .... (see 10)
16 Estate A1
girl & the fig .... (see 12)
17 Harvest Moon Cafe C2
18 Red Grape C2
Taste of the Himalayas .... (see 20)

Drinking

Enoteca Della Santina .... (see 15)
19 Hopmonk Tavern C3
20 Murphy's Irish Pub D2
Steiner's .... (see 17)
Sunflower Caffé & Wine Bar .... (see 10)
Swiss Hotel .... (see 13)

Entertainment

21 Sebastiani Theater D2

Shopping

Chanticleer Books & Prints .... (see 4)
22 Chateau Sonoma B2
Readers' Books .... (see 4)
Sign of the Bear .... (see 17)
Tiddle E Winks .... (see 15)
23 Vella Cheese Co D1

El Pueblo Inn MOTEL $$
(Off Map p188; 707-996-3651, 800-900-8844; www.elpuebloinn.com; 896 W Napa St; r incl breakfast $169-289;) One mile west of downtown, family-owned El Pueblo has surprisingly cushy rooms with great beds. The big lawns and the heated pool are perfect for kids; parents appreciate the 24-hour hot tub.

Sonoma Creek Inn MOTEL $$
(Map p184; 707-939-9463, 888-712-1289; www.sonomacreekinn.com; 239 Boyes Blvd; r $139-199;) This cute-as-a-button motel has cheery, retro-Americana rooms, with primary colors and country quilts. It's not downtown; valley wineries are a short drive.

Les Petites Maisons COTTAGES $$$
(Map p184; 707-933-0340, 800-291-8962; www.lespetitesmaisons.com; 1190 E Napa St;cottages $165-295;) A mile east of the plaza, each of these four colorful, inviting cottages has a bedroom, living room, kitchen and barbecue, with comfy furniture, stereos, DVDs and bicycles.

Windhaven Cottage COTTAGE $$
(Map p184; 707-938-2175, 707-483-1856; www.windhavencottage.com; 21700 Pearson Ave; cottage $155-165;) Great-bargain Windhaven has two units: a hideaway cottage with vaulted wooden ceilings and a fireplace, and a handsome 800-sq-ft studio. We prefer the romantic cottage. Both have hot tubs. Tennis facilities, bicycles and barbecues sweeten the deal.

Bungalows 313 BUNGALOWS $$$
(Map p188; 707-996-8091; www.bungalows313.com; 313 1st St E; d $229-329, q $379-469;) Century-old brick farmhouse and bungalows with kitchens. Gorgeous gardens. Perfect for couples.

MacArthur Place INN $$$
(Map p184; 707-938-2929, 800-722-1866; www.macarthurplace.com; 29 E MacArthur St; r from $350, ste from $425;) Sonoma's top full-service inn; built on a former estate, with century-old gardens.

Hidden Oak Inn B&B $$$
(Map p184; 707-996-9863, 877-996-9863; www.hiddenoakinn.com; 214 E Napa St; r incl breakfast $195-245;) A B&B built c 1914.

Sugarloaf Ridge State Park CAMPGROUND $
(Map p184; 707-833-5712, reservations 800-444-7275; www.reserveamerica.com; 2605 Adobe Canyon Rd; sites $30) Sonoma's nearest camping is north of Kenwood at this lovely hilltop park, with 50 drive-in sites, clean coin-operated showers, and great hiking.

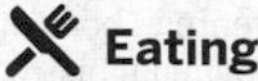

Eating

Also see Glen Ellen, p192. There's creek-side picnicking, with barbecue grills, up-valley at **Sugarloaf Ridge State Park** (2605 Adobe Canyon Rd; per car $8). Find late-night taco trucks on Hwy 12, between Boyes Blvd and Aqua Caliente.

Fremont Diner AMERICAN $
(Map p184; 707-938-7370; 2698 Fremont Dr/Hwy 121; mains $8-11; 8am-3pm Mon-Fri, 7am-4pm Sat & Sun;) Lines snake out the door weekends at this order-at-the-counter, farm-to-table roadside diner. Snag a table indoors or out and feast on ricotta pancakes with real maple syrup, chicken and waffles, oyster po' boys and finger-licking barbecue. Arrive early to beat the line.

Café La Haye NEW AMERICAN $$$
(Map p188; 707-935-5994; www.cafelahaye.com; 140 E Napa St; mains $15-25; 5:30-9pm Tue-Sat) One of Sonoma's top tables for earthy New American cooking, made with produce sourced from within 60 miles, La Haye's tiny dining room gets packed cheek-by-jowl and service can border on perfunctory, but the clean simplicity and flavor-packed cooking make it many foodies' first choice. Reserve well ahead.

Harvest Moon Cafe NEW AMERICAN $$
(Map p188; 707-933-8160; www.harvestmooncafesonoma.com; 487 1st St W; dinner/brunch mains $18-25/$10-15; 5:30-9pm Wed-Mon, 10am-2pm Sun) Inside a cozy 1836 adobe, this casual bistro uses local ingredients in its changing menu, with simple soul-satisfying dishes like duck risotto with Bellwether Farms ricotta. Book a garden table.

Estate ITALIAN-CALIFORNIAN $$
(Map p188; 707-933-3633; www.estate-sonoma.com; 400 W Spain St; pizzas $10-14, dinner/brunch mains $21-24/$11-14; from 5pm nightly, 10am-3pm Sun) Sonoma's landmark mansion features earthy Cal-Italian cooking, on-site produce garden and lovely outdoor porch. Come before 6:30pm (6:15 Fri & Sat) for pizza and a glass of pinot noir for $15. Nightly four-course dinners cost $26. Great Sunday brunch. Make reservations.

girl & the fig FRENCH-CALIFORNIAN $$$
(Map p188; ☎707-938-3634; www.thegirlandthefig.com; 110 W Spain St; lunch mains $10-15, dinner mains $18-26) For a festive evening, book a garden table at this French-provincial bistro. We like the small plates ($11 to $14), especially the steamed mussels with matchstick fries, and duck confit with lentils. Weekday three-course prix-fixe costs $34; add $10 for wine. Stellar cheeses. Reservations essential.

Della Santina's ITALIAN $$
(Map p188; ☎707-935-0576; www.dellasantinas.com; 135 E Napa St; mains $11-17) The waiters have been here forever, and the 'specials' never change, but Della Santina's Italian-American cooking – linguini pesto, veal parmigiana, rotisserie chickens – is consistently good. The brick courtyard is charming on warm evenings.

El Dorado Corner Cafe CAFE $$
(Map p188; ☎707-996-3030; www.eldoradosonoma.com; 405 1st St W; dishes $9-15; 7am-10pm) Little sister to El Dorado Kitchen (whose chef had just left at the time of writing, hence the non-review of this noteworthy restaurant), the Corner Cafe has more affordable cooking – pizzas, sandwiches, and salads – all made with artisinal local produce and served continuously throughout the day. Save room for house-made ice cream.

Juanita Juanita MEXICAN $$
(Map p188; ☎707-935-3981; 19114 Arnold Dr; mains $8-15; Wed-Mon 11am-8pm;) Dig the crazy mural outside this drive-in Mexican, which makes winning tostadas, garlic-garlic burritos and fiery *chile verde* (green chili stew with pork or chicken). Dog-friendly patio. Beer and wine.

Red Grape PIZZA $$
(Map p188; ☎707-996-4103; www.theredgrape.com; 529 1st St W; mains $11-15; 11:30am-8:30pm;) A reliable spot for an easy meal, Red Grape serves good thin-crust pizzas and big salads in a cavernous, echoey space. Good for takeout, too.

Pearl's Homestyle Cooking DINER $
(Map p188; ☎707-996-1783; 561 5th St W; mains $7-10; 7am-2:30pm;) Across from Safeway's west-facing wall, Pearl's serves giant American breakfasts, including succulent bacon and waffles (the secret is melted vanilla ice cream in the batter).

Angelo's Wine Country Deli DELI $
(Map p184; ☎707-938-3688; 23400 Arnold Dr; sandwiches $6; 9am-5pm Tue-Sun) Look for the cow on the roof of this roadside deli, south of town, a fave for fat sandwiches and homemade jerky. In springtime, little lambs graze outside.

Taste of the Himalayas INDIAN, NEPALESE $$
(Map p188; ☎707-996-1161; 464 1st St E; mains $10-20; 11am-10pm) Spicy curries, luscious lentil soup and sizzle-platter meats – a refreshing break from the usual French-Italian Wine Country fare.

599 Thai Cafe THAI $
(Map p188; ☎707-938-8477; 599 Broadway; mains $7-10; 11am-9pm Mon-Sat;) Reliably good, tiny Thai cafe.

Sonoma Market DELI, MARKET $
(Map p188; ☎707-996-3411; www.sonoma-glenellenmkt.com; 500 W Napa St; sandwiches $7) Sonoma's best groceries and deli sandwiches.

Drinking

Murphy's Irish Pub PUB
(Map p188; ☎707-935-0660; www.sonomapub.com; 464 1st St E) Don't ask for Bud – only *real* brews here. Good hand-cut fries and shepherd's pie, too. Live music Thursday through Sunday evenings.

Swiss Hotel BAR
(Map p188; 18 W Spain St) Locals and tourists crowd the 1909 Swiss Hotel for afternoon cocktails. There's OK food, but the bar's the thing.

Hopmonk Tavern BREWERY
(Map p188; ☎707-935-9100; www.hopmonk.com; 691 Broadway; dishes $12-22; 11:30am-10pm) This happening gastro-pub and beer garden takes its brews seriously, with 16 on tap, served in type-appropriate glassware. Live music Friday through Sunday.

Enoteca Della Santina WINE BAR
(Map p188; www.enotecadellasantina.com; 127 E Napa St; 2-10pm Wed-Fri, noon-11pm Sat, 4-10pm Tue & Sun) Thirty global vintages by the glass let you compare what you're tasting in California with the rest of the world's wines.

Steiner's BAR
(Map p188; 456 1st St W) Sonoma's oldest bar gets crowded Sunday afternoons with cyclists and motorcyclists. Dig the taxidermy mountain lions.

Sunflower Caffé & Wine Bar CAFE $$
(☎707-996-6845; www.sonomasunflower.com; 421 1st St W; dishes $9-14; ⏰7am-8pm; 📶) The big back garden at this local hangout is a good spot for breakfast, a no-fuss lunch, or an afternoon glass of wine.

☆ Entertainment

Free jazz concerts happen on the plaza every second Tuesday, June to September, 6pm to 8:30pm; arrive early and bring a picnic.

Little Switzerland BEER HALL
(Map p184; ☎707-938-9990; www.lilswiss.com; 401 Grove St; ⏰Wed-Sun) Long before Sonoma became 'Wine Country,' locals drank and shot pool at this old-fashioned beer garden and dance hall, open continuously since 1906 – dig the vintage 1936 murals of Switzerland. Latin bands play Friday evenings; Saturday it's jazz, swing or zydeco; Sundays the great tradition is polka parties (⏰5-9pm), when you can bring kids. There's barbecue Friday through Sunday.

Sebastiani Theatre CINEMA
(Map p188; ☎707-996-2020; sebastianitheatre.com; 476 1st St E) The plaza's gorgeous 1934 Mission-revival cinema screens art house and revival films, and sometimes live theater.

Shopping

Vella Cheese Co FOOD
(Map p188; ☎707-928-3232; www.vellacheese.com; 315 2nd St E) Known for its dry-jack cheeses (made here since the 1930s), Vella also makes good Mezzo Secco with cocoa powder–dusted rind. Staff will vacuum-pack for shipping.

Tiddle E Winks TOYS
(Map p188; ☎7070-939-6993; www.tiddleewinks.com; 115 E Napa St; 👪) Vintage five-and-dime, with classic, mid-20th-century toys.

Sign of the Bear HOMEWARES
(Map p188; ☎707-996-3722; 435 1st St W) Kitchen-gadget freaks: make a beeline to this indie cookware store.

Chateau Sonoma HOMEWARES, GIFTS
(Map p188; ☎707-935-8553; www.chateausonoma.com; 153 W Napa St) Provence meets Sonoma in a one-of-a-kind gifts and arty home decor.

Chanticleer Books & Prints BOOKS
(Map p188; ☎707-996-7613; chanticleerbooks.com; 127 E Napa St; ⏰Wed-Sun) Rare books, first editions and California history.

Readers' Books BOOKS
(Map p188; ☎707-939-1779; readers.indiebound.com; 130 E Napa St) Independent bookseller.

ℹ Information

Sonoma Post Office (☎800-275-8777; www.usps.com; 617 Broadway; ⏰Mon-Fri)

Sonoma Valley Hospital (☎707-935-5000; 347 Andrieux St)

Sonoma Valley Visitors Bureau (☎707-996-1090; www.sonomavalley.com; 453 1st St E; ⏰9am-6pm Jul-Sep, to 5pm Oct-Jun) Arranges accommodations; has a good walking-tour pamphlet and information on events. There's another location at Cornerstone Gardens (p187).

Glen Ellen & Around

Sleepy Glen Ellen is a snapshot of old Sonoma, with white picket fences, tiny cottages and 19th-century brick buildings beside a poplar-lined creek. When downtown Sonoma is jammed, you can wander quiet Glen Ellen and feel far away. It's ideal for a leg-stretching stopover between wineries or a romantic overnight – the nighttime sky blazes with stars.

Arnold Dr is the main drag and the valley's back-way route. Kenwood is just north, along Hwy 12, but has no town center like Glen Ellen's. For services, drive 8 miles south to Sonoma.

Glen Ellen's biggest draws are Jack London State Historic Park (p193) and Benziger winery (p183); several interesting shops line Arnold Dr.

Two family-friendly alternatives to wine tasting: **Figone's Olive Oil** (Map p184; ☎707-282-9092; www.figoneoliveoil.com; 9580 Sonoma Hwy), in Kenwood, presses its own extra-virgin olive oil – including lovely Meyer lemon-infused oil – which you can taste; in Glen Ellen, compare chocolates of varying percentages of cacao at **Wine Country Chocolates Tasting Bar** (Map p184; ☎707-996-1010; www.winecountrychocolates.com; 14301 Arnold Dr).

Gardeners: don't miss **Wildwood Farm and Sculpture Garden** (Map p184; ☎707-833-1161, 888-833-4181; www.wildwoodmaples.com; 10300 Sonoma Hwy, Kenwood; ⏰10am-4pm Wed-Sun, 10am-3pm Tue), where abstract outdoor sits between exotic plants and Japanese maples.

There's fantastic hiking (when it's not blazingly hot) at **Sugarloaf Ridge State Park** (Map p184; ☎707-833-5712; www.parks.ca.gov; 2605 Adobe Canyon Rd, Kenwood; per car

$8). On clear days, Bald Mountain has drop-dead views to the sea, while Bushy Peak Trail peers into Napa Valley. Both are moderately strenuous; plan four hours round-trip.

On hot days, families cool off in mineral-spring-fed swimming pools at **Morton's Warm Springs Resort** (Map p184; ☎707-833-5511; www.mortonswarmsprings.com; 1651 Warm Springs Rd; adult/child $8/7, reserved picnic & BBQ sites per person $11; ⊙10am-6pm Sat & Sun May & Sep, Tue-Sun Jun-Aug, closed Oct-Apr). From Sonoma Hwy in Kenwood, turn west on Warm Springs Rd.

For shopping, stop by **Kenwood Farmhouse** (Map p184; 9255 Sonoma Hwy, Kenwood; ⊙10:30am-7pm), a co-op of vendors selling artisinal crafts and gifts.

Sleeping

Jack London Lodge MOTEL $$
(Map p184; ☎707-938-8510; http://jacklondonlodge.com; 13740 Arnold Dr; r Mon-Fri/Sat & Sun $120/180) An old-fashioned wood-sided motel, with well-kept rooms decorated with a few antiques, this is a weekday bargain – and the manager will sometimes negotiate rates. Outside there's a hot tub; next door there's a saloon.

TOP CHOICE **Beltane Ranch** INN $$
(Map p184; ☎707-996-6501; www.beltaneranch.com; 11775 Hwy 12; r incl breakfast $150-240) Surrounded by horse pastures, Beltane is a throwback to 19th-century Sonoma. The cheerful, lemon-yellow 1890s ranch house occupies 100 acres and has double porches lined with swinging chairs and white wicker. Though technically a B&B, each unfussy, country-Americana-style room has a private entrance – nobody will make you pet the cat. Breakfast in bed. No phones or TVs mean zero distraction from pastoral bliss.

WHAT'S CRUSH?

Crush is harvest, the most atmospheric time of year, when the vine's leaves turn brilliant colors, and you can smell fermenting fruit on the breeze. Farmers throw big parties for the vineyard workers to celebrate their work. Everyone wants to be here. That's why room rates skyrocket. If you can afford it, come during autumn. To score party invitations, join your favorite winery's wine club.

Gaige House INN $$$
(Map p184; ☎707-935-0237, 800-935-0237; www.gaige.com; 13540 Arnold Dr, Glen Ellen; r $249-299, ste $299-599) Sonoma's chicest inn serves lavish breakfasts. An 1890 house contains five of the 22 rooms, decked out in Euro-Asian style. But best are the Japanese-style 'spa suites,' with requisite high-end bells and whistles, including freestanding tubs made from hollowed-out granite boulders. Fabulous.

Kenwood Inn & Spa INN $$$
(Map p184; ☎707-833-1293, 800-353-6966; www.kenwoodinn.com; 10400 Sonoma Hwy, Kenwood; r incl breakfast $425-850, ste $850-1375) Lush gardens surround ivy-covered bungalows at this gorgeous inn, which feels like a Mediterranean château. Two hot tubs (one with a waterfall) and an on-site spa make this ideal for lovers: leave the kids home. Book an upstairs balcony room.

Glen Ellen Cottages BUNGALOWS $$
(Map p184; ☎707-996-1174; www.glenelleninn.com; 13670 Arnold Dr; cottage Mon-Fri/Sat & Sun $149/239) Hidden behind Glen Ellen Inn, these five creek-side cottages are designed for romance, with oversized jetted tubs, steam showers and gas fireplaces.

Eating

fig café & winebar CALIFORNIAN, FRENCH $$
(☎707-938-2130; www.thefigcafe.com; 13690 Arnold Dr, Glen Ellen; mains $15-20; ⊙5:30-9pm daily, 10am-2:30pm Sat & Sun) It's worth a trip to Glen Ellen for the fig's earthy California-Provençal comfort food, like flash-fried calamari with spicy-lemon aioli, duck confit and *moules-frites* (mussels and French fries). Good wine prices and weekend brunch give reason to return.

Vineyards Inn Bar & Grill SPANISH, TAPAS $$
(Map p184; ☎707-833-4500; www.vineyardsinn.com; 8445 Sonoma Hwy 12, Kenwood; mains $8-20; ⊙11:30am-9:30pm) Though nothing fancy, this roadside tavern's food is terrific – succulent organic burgers, line-caught seafood, paella, ceviche, and biodynamic produce from the chef's ranch. Full bar.

Cafe Citti ITALIAN $$
(☎707-833-2690; www.cafecitti.com; 9049 Sonoma Hwy; mains $8-15; ⊙11am-3:30pm, 5-9pm) Locals flock to this mom-and-pop Italian-

American deli-trattoria, where you order at the counter then snag a seat on the deck. Standouts include roasted chicken, homemade gnocchi and ravioli; at lunchtime, there's also pizza and housebaked focaccia-bread sandwiches.

Glen Ellen Village Market MARKET $
(Map p184; www.sonoma-glenellenmkt.com; 13751 Arnold Dr; ⏲6am-9pm) Fantastic market, perfect for picnics.

Olive & Vine NEW AMERICAN $$$
(Map p184; ☎707-996-9152; oliveandvinerestaurant.com; 14301 Arnold Dr; mains $17-28; ⏲5:30-9pm Wed-Sat) Part catering kitchen, part restaurant, with great seasonal flavors; make reservations.

Yeti INDIAN $$
(Map p184; ☎707-996-9930; www.yetirestaurant.com; 14301 Arnold Dr; mains $10-18; ⏲11:30am-2:30pm & 5-9pm) Indian on a creek-side patio. Great naan.

Glen Ellen Inn AMERICAN $$
(Map p184; ☎707-996-6409; www.glenelleninn.com; 13670 Arnold Dr; mains $13-23; ⏲11:30am-9pm) Oysters, martinis and grilled steaks. Lovely garden, full bar.

Garden Court Cafe CAFE $
(Map p184; ☎707-935-1565; www.gardencourtcafe.com; 13647 Arnold Dr; mains $9-12; ⏲7:30am-2pm Wed-Mon) Basic breakfasts, sandwiches and salads.

Mayo Winery Reserve Room WINERY $$
(Map p184; ☎707-833-5544; www.mayofamilywinery.com; 9200 Sonoma Hwy, Kenwood; 7-course menu $35; ⏲11am-5pm, by reservation) Snag a seven-course small-plates menu, paired with seven wines, for just $35 at this roadside wine-tasting room.

Jack London State Historic Park

Napa has Robert Louis Stevenson, but Sonoma's got Jack London. This 1400-acre **park** (Map p184; ☎707-938-5216; www.jacklondonpark.com; 2400 London Ranch Rd, Glen Ellen; parking $8; ⏲10am-5pm Thu-Mon; 👪) traces the last years of the author's life.

Changing occupations from Oakland fisherman to Alaska gold prospector to Pacific yachtsman – and novelist on the side – London (1876–1916) ultimately took up farming. He bought Beauty Ranch in 1905 and moved there in 1910. With his second wife, Charmian, he lived and wrote in a small cottage while his mansion, Wolf House, was under construction. On the eve of its completion in 1913, it burned down. The disaster devastated London, and although he toyed with rebuilding, he died before construction got underway. His widow, Charmian, built the House of Happy Walls, which has been preserved as a museum. It's a half-mile walk from there to the remains of Wolf House, passing London's grave along the way. Other paths wind around the farm to the cottage where he lived and worked. Miles of hiking trails (some open to mountain bikes) weave through oak-dotted woodlands, between 600ft and 2300ft elevation. Watch for poison oak. NB: State budget cuts may temporarily close this park; call ahead.

RUSSIAN RIVER AREA

Lesser-known West Sonoma County was formerly famous for its apple farms and vacation cottages. Lately vineyards are replacing the orchards, and the Russian River has now taken its place among California's important wine appellations for superb pinot noir.

'The River,' as locals call it, has long been a summertime weekend destination for Northern Californians, who come to canoe, wander country lanes, taste wine, hike redwood forests and live at a lazy pace. In winter the river floods, and nobody's here.

The Russian River begins in the mountains north of Ukiah, in Mendocino County, but the most famous sections lie southwest of Healdsburg, where it cuts a serpentine course toward the sea. Just north of Santa Rosa, River Rd, the lower valley's main artery, connects Hwy 101 with coastal Hwy 1 at Jenner. Hwy 116 heads northwest from Cotati through Sebastopol and on to Guerneville. Westside Rd connects Guerneville and Healdsburg. West County's winding roads get confusing; carry a map.

Russian River Area Wineries

Outside Sonoma Valley, Sonoma County's wine-growing regions encompass several diverse areas, each famous for different reasons (see A Wine Country Primer, p186). Pick up the free, useful *Russian River Wine*

Russian River Area

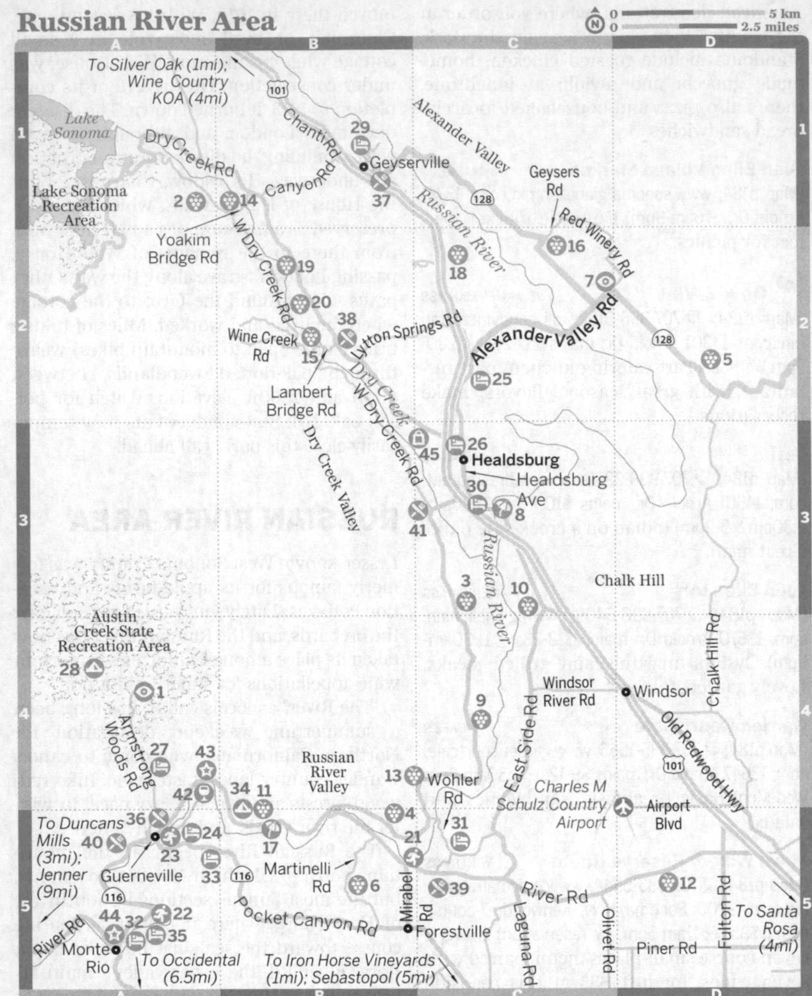

Road map (www.wineroad.com) in tourist-brochure racks.

RUSSIAN RIVER VALLEY

Nighttime coastal fog drifts up the Russian River Valley, then usually clears by midday. Pinot noir does beautifully here, as does chardonnay, which also grows in hotter regions, but prefers the longer 'hang time' of cooler climes. The highest concentration of wineries is along **Westside Rd**, between Guerneville and Healdsburg.

Hartford Family Winery WINERY

(Map p194; ☎707-887-8030; www.hartfordwines.com; 8075 Martinelli Rd, Forestville; tastings $5-15, applicable to purchase; ⏲10am-4:30pm; 🐾) Surprisingly upscale for West County, Hartford sits in a pastoral valley surrounded by redwood-forested hills, on one of the area's prettiest back roads. It specializes in fine single-vineyard pinot (eight kinds), chardonnay and zinfandel, some from old-vine fruit. Umbrella-shaded picnic tables dot the garden. Bottles cost $35 to $70.

Russian River Area

Sights

1 Armstrong Redwoods State Reserve A4
2 Bella Vineyards A1
3 De la Montanya C3
4 Gary Farrell B5
5 Hanna D2
6 Hartford Family Winery B5
7 Hawkes C2
8 Healdsburg Veterans Memorial Beach C3
9 Hop Kiln Winery C4
10 J Winery C3
11 Korbel B4
Locals Tasting Room .... (see 37)
12 Martinelli D5
13 Porter Creek B4
14 Preston Vineyards B1
15 Quivira B2
Sophie's Cellars .... (see 32)
16 Stryker Sonoma C2
17 Sunset Beach B5
18 Trentadue C2
19 Truett-Hurst B2
20 Unti Vineyards B2

Activities, Courses & Tours

21 Burke's Canoe Trips B5
22 Northwood Golf Course A5
23 Pee Wee Golf & Arcade A5
River's Edge Kayak & Canoe Trips .... (see 8)
Russian River Adventures .... (see 8)

Sleeping

24 Applewood Inn A5
25 Belle de Jour Inn C2
26 Best Western Dry Creek Inn C3
27 Boon Hotel & Spa A4
28 Bullfrog Pond A4
Farmhouse Inn .... (see 39)
29 Geyserville Inn B1
Highland Dell .... (see 35)
30 L&M Motel C3
Madrona Manor .... (see 41)
31 Raford Inn C5
32 Rio Villa Beach Resort A5
33 Santa Nella House A5
34 Schoolhouse Canyon Campground B4
35 Village Inn A5

Eating

Applewood Inn Restaurant .... (see 24)
36 Coffee Bazaar A5
37 Diavola B1
Don's Dogs .... (see 44)
38 Dry Creek General Store B2
39 Farmhouse Inn C5
40 Garden Grill A5
Highland Dell .... (see 35)
Jimtown Store .... (see 7)
41 Madrona Manor C3
Village Inn .... (see 35)

Drinking

42 Stumptown Brewery A4

Entertainment

43 Rio Nido Roadhouse A4
44 Rio Theater A5

Shopping

45 Gardener C3

Sophie's Cellars WINE SHOP $

(Map p194; ☎707-865-1122; www.sophiescellars.com; 20293 Hwy 116; ⏰11am-7pm Thu-Tue) Stellar wine shop, with many hard-to-find local cult labels; the owner-connoisseur can help direct you to good wineries. Also stocks Sonoma cheeses, good for picnics. Find it across the road from Rio Villa Beach Resort.

Korbel WINERY

(Map p194; ☎707-824-7316, 707-824-7000; www.korbel.com; 13250 River Rd; tastings free; ⏰10am-5pm; 🐾) Gorgeous rose gardens (April to October) and stellar on-site deli make Korbel worth a stop, but the champagne's just OK.

Iron Horse Vineyards WINERY

(Map p160; ☎707-887-1507; www.ironhorsevineyards.com; 9786 Ross Station Rd, Sebastopol; tastings $10-20, refundable with purchase; ⏰10am-4:30pm; 🐾) Atop a hill with drop-dead views over the county, Iron Horse is known for pinot noir and sparkling wines, which the White House often pours. The outdoor tasting room is refreshingly unfussy; when you're done with your wine, pour it in the grass. Located off Hwy 116. Bottles cost $20 to $85.

Marimar WINERY

(Map p160; ☎707-823-4365; www.marimarestate.com; 11400 Graton Rd, Sebastopol; tastings $10;

11am-4pm;) Middle-of-nowhere Marimar specializes in all-organic pinot – seven different kinds – and chardonnay. The Spanish-style hilltop tasting room has a knockout vineyard-view terrace, lovely for picnics. Also consider tapas-and-wine pairings ($35). Bottles cost $29 to $52.

Gary Farrell WINERY

(Map p194; 707-473-2900; www.garyfarrellwines.com; 10701 Westside Rd; tastings $10-15; 10:30am-4:30pm;) High on a hilltop, overlooking the Russian River, Gary Farrell's tasting room sits perched among second-growth redwoods. The elegant chardonnay and long-finish pinot, made by a big-name winemaker, score high marks for consistency. Bottles cost $32 to $60.

Porter Creek WINERY

(Map p194; 707-433-6321; www.portercreekvineyards.com; 8735 Westside Rd; tastings free;) Inside a vintage 1920s garage, Porter Creek's tasting bar is a former bowling-alley lane, plunked atop barrels. Porter is old-school Northern California and an early pioneer in biodynamic farming. High-acid, food-friendly pinot noir and chardonnay are specialties, but there's silky zinfandel and other Burgundian- and Rhône-style wines, too. Check out the aviary and yurt. Bottles cost $24 to $65.

Hop Kiln Winery WINERY

(Map p194; 707-433-6491; www.hopkilnwinery.com; 6050 Westside Rd; tastings $5-7; 10am-5pm) Photogenic, historic landmark, with busy redwood tasting barn; the excellent artisinal vinegars make great $10 gifts.

De La Montanya WINERY

(Map p194; 707-433-3711; www.dlmwine.com; 2651 Westside Rd at Foreman Lane; tastings $5, refundable with purchase; Mon-Thu call ahead, Fri-Sun 11am-4:30pm;) On weekends, meet the practical-joker winemaker at this tiny winery, known for 17 small-batch varieties made with estate-grown fruit. Viognier, primitivo, pinot and cabernet are signatures; the 'summer white' and gewürztraminer are great back-porch wines. Apple-shaded picnic area and bocce ball, too. Bottles $20 to $60.

Martinelli WINERY

(Map p194; 707-525-0570; www.martinelliwinery.com; 3360 River Rd, Windsor; tastings $5-15; 10am-5pm;) Celeb winemaker Helen Turley makes the top-end pinot; there's also good syrah, sauvignon blanc and chardonnay in the gift shop-tasting barn.

J Winery WINERY

(Map p194; 707-431-3646; www.jwine.com; 11447 Old Redwood Hwy; tastings $20; 11am-5pm) Crafts crisp sparkling wines – some of Wine Country's best – but tastings are overpriced. Buy it in local shops.

DRY CREEK VALLEY

Hemmed in by 2000ft-high mountains, Dry Creek Valley is relatively warm, ideal for sauvignon blanc and zinfandel, and in some places cabernet sauvignon. It's west of Hwy 101, between Healdsburg and Lake Sonoma. Dry Creek Rd is the fast-moving main thoroughfare. Parallel-running West Dry Creek Rd is an undulating country lane with no center stripe – one of Sonoma's great back roads, ideal for cycling.

Bella Vineyards WINERY

(Map p194; 707-473-9171; www.bellawinery.com; 9711 W Dry Creek Rd; tasting $5-10; 11am-4:30pm;) Atop the valley's north end, always-fun Bella has caves built into the hillside. The estate-grown grapes include 110-year-old vines from the Alexander Valley. The focus is on big reds – zin and syrah – but there's terrific rosé (good for barbecues), and late-harvest zin (great with brownies). The wonderful vibe and dynamic staff make Bella special. Bottles cost $25 to $40.

Preston Vineyards WINERY

(Map p194; 707-433-3372; www.prestonvineyards.com; 9282 W Dry Creek Rd; tasting $10, refundable with purchase; 11am-4:30pm;) An early leader in organics, Lou Preston's 19th-century farm feels like old Sonoma County. Weathered picket fencing frames the 19th-century farmhouse-turned-tasting room, with candy-colored walls and tongue-in-groove ceilings setting a country mood. The signature is citrusy sauvignon blanc, but try the Rhône varietals and small-lot wines: mourvèdre, viognier, cinsault and cult-favorite barbera. Preston also bakes good bread; have a picnic in the shade of the walnut tree. Monday to Friday there's bocce ball. Bottles cost $24 to $38.

Truett-Hurst WINERY

(Map p194; 707-433-9545; www.truetthurst.com; 5610 Dry Creek Rd; tastings $5, refundable with purchase; 10am-5pm;) Pull up an Adirondack chair and picnic creekside at Truett-Hurst, Dry Creek's newest biodynamic winery.

Sample terrific old-vine zins, standout petite sirah and Russian River pinots at the handsome contemporary tasting room, then meander through fragrant butterfly gardens to the creek, where salmon spawn in autumn. Ever-fun weekends, with food-and-wine pairings and **live music** (⏲1-5pm Sat & Sun).

Unti Vineyards WINERY

(Map p194; ☎707-433-5590; www.untivineyards.com; 4202 Dry Creek Rd; tastings $5, waived with purchase; ⏲by appointment 10am-4pm; 🐾) Inside a fluorescent-lit windowless garage, Unti makes all estate-grown reds – Châteauneuf-du-Pape–style grenache, compelling syrah, and superb sangiovese – favored by oenophiles for their structured tannins and concentrated fruit. If you love artisinal wines, don't miss Unti. Bottles cost $22 to $35.

Quivira WINERY

(Map p194; ☎707-431-8333; www.quivirawine.com; 4900 W Dry Creek Rd; tastings $5, waived with purchase; ⏲11am-5pm; 👪🐾) Sunflowers, lavender and crowing roosters greet your arrival at this winery and biodynamic farm, with self-guided garden tours and picnic grove beside the vineyards. The kids can scan the grapes for the football-sized feral sow – the winery's mascot – while you sample Rhône varietals and unusual blends, including lip-smacking sauvignon blanc-gewürztraminer. Bottles cost $18 to $45.

ALEXANDER VALLEY

Bucolic Alexander Valley flanks the Mayacamas Mountains, with postcard-perfect vistas and wide-open vineyards. Summers are hot, ideal for cabernet sauvignon, merlot and warm-weather chardonnays, but there's also fine sauvignon blanc and zinfandel. For events info, visit www.alexandervalley.org.

Stryker Sonoma WINERY

(Map p194; ☎707-433-1944; www.strykersonoma.com; 5110 Hwy 128; tastings $10, refundable with purchase; ⏲10:30am-5pm; 🐾) Wow, what a view from the hilltop concrete-and-glass tasting room at Stryker Sonoma. The standouts are fruit-forward zinfandel and sangiovese, which you can't buy anywhere else. Good picnicking. Bottles cost $20 to $50.

Hawkes TASTING ROOM

(Map p194; ☎707-433-4295; www.hawkeswine.com; 6734 Hwy 128; tastings $10, refundable with purchase; ⏲10am-5pm; 🐾) Funky teapots grace the walls at friendly Hawkes', an easy roadside stopover while you're exploring the valley. The single-vineyard cab is damn good, as is the blend; there's also a clean-and-crisp, non-malolactic chardonnay. Bottles cost $20 to $70.

Hanna WINERY

(Map p194; ☎707-431-4310, 800-854-3987; http://hannawinery.com; 9280 Hwy 128; tastings $10; ⏲10am-4pm; 🐾) Abutting oak-studded hills, Hanna's tasting room has lovely vineyard views and good picnicking. At the bar, find estate-grown merlot and cabernet, and big-fruit zins and syrah. Sit-down wine-and-cheese tastings available ($25). Bottles cost $15 to $48.

Silver Oak WINERY

(off Map p194; ☎800-273-8809; www.silveroak.com; 24625 Chianti Rd; tastings $20, partially applicable to purchase; ⏲9am-4pm Mon-Sat) Sister to the legendary Napa winery; the Alexander Valley cabernet is similarly luxurious. Bottles start at $70.

Trentadue WINERY

(Map p194; ☎707-433-3104, 888-332-3032; www.trentadue.com; 19170 Geyserville Ave; port tastings $5; ⏲10am-5pm) Specializes in ports (ruby, not tawny); the chocolate port makes a great gift.

Sebastopol

Grapes have replaced apples as the new cash crop, but Sebastopol's farm-town identity remains rooted in the apple – evidence the much-heralded summertime Gravenstein Apple Fair. The town center feels suburban because of traffic, but a hippie tinge gives it color. This is the refreshingly unfussy side of Wine Country, and makes a good-value home base for exploring the area.

Hwy 116 splits downtown; southbound traffic uses Main St, northbound traffic Petaluma Ave. North of town, it's called Gravenstein Hwy N and continues toward Guerneville; south of downtown, it's Gravenstein Hwy S, which heads toward Hwy 101 and Sonoma.

Sights & Activities

Around Sebastopol, look for family-friendly farms, gardens, animal sanctuaries and pick-your-own orchards. For a countywide list, check out the **Sonoma County Farm Trails Guide** (www.farmtrails.org).

Farmers market MARKET
(cnr Petaluma & McKinley Aves; ⏲10am-1:30pm Sun Apr–mid-Dec) Meets at the downtown plaza.

Sturgeon's Mill MILL
(www.sturgeonsmill.com; 2150 Green Hill Rd; 👪) A historic steam-powered sawmill, open for demonstrations several weekends a year; check the website.

Festivals & Events

Apple Blossom Festival CULTURAL
(www.sebastopol.org) April

Gravenstein Apple Fair FOOD
(www.farmtrails.org/gravenstein-apple-fair) August

Sleeping

Sebastopol is good for get-up-and-go travelers exploring Russian River Valley and the coast.

Sebastopol Inn MOTEL $$
(☎707-829-2500, 800-653-1082; www.sebastopolinn.com; 6751 Sebastopol Ave; r $119-179; ❄📶🏊👪) We like this independent, *non-*cookie-cutter motel for its quiet, off-street location, usually reasonable rates and good-looking if basic rooms. Outside are grassy areas for kids and a hot tub.

Vine Hill Inn B&B $$
(☎707-823-8832; www.vine-hill-inn.com; 3949 Vine Hill Rd; r incl breakfast $170; ❄📶🏊🐾) Mature landscaping surrounds this four-room 1897 Victorian farmhouse, with gorgeous vineyard views, just north of town off Hwy 116. Breakfast is made with eggs from the barn's chickens. Two rooms have Jacuzzis.

Raccoon Cottage COTTAGE $$
(☎707-545-5466; www.raccooncottage.com; 2685 Elizabeth Ct; cottage incl breakfast $130-150) A small B&B cottage, off Vine Hill Rd, amid oaks, fruit trees and gardens.

Fairfield Inn & Suites HOTEL $$
(☎707-829-6677, 800-465-4329; www.winecountryhi.com; 1101 Gravenstein Hwy S; r $129-209; ❄@📶🏊👪) Generic, but modern, with in-room refrigerators, coffee makers and hot tub.

Eating

Gourmet **food trucks** (⏲11:30am-2:30pm Thu) gather in the parking lot at **O'Reilly Media** (1050 Gravenstein Hwy N).

K&L Bistro FRENCH $$$
(☎707-823-6614; www.klbistro.com; 119 S Main St; lunch $14-20, dinner $19-29; ⏲11:30am-2:30pm & 5:30-9pm Mon-Sat) Sebastopol's top restaurant serves down-to-earth provincial Cal-French bistro cooking in a convivial – if loud – room, with classics like mussels and French fries, and grilled steaks with red-wine reduction. Tables are tight, but the crowd is friendly. Reservations essential.

Hopmonk Tavern PUB $$
(☎707-829-7300; www.hopmonk.com; 230 Petaluma Ave; mains $10-20; ⏲11:30am-9pm) Inside a converted 1903 railroad station, Hopmonk's competent cooking is designed to pair with beer – 76 varieties – served in type-specific glassware. Good burgers, fried calamari, charcuterie platters and salads.

East-West Cafe MEDITERRANEAN $
(☎707-829-2822; www.eastwestcafesebastopol.com; 128 N Main St; meals $9-12; ⏲8am-9pm Mon-Sat, 8am-8pm Sun; 🥬👪) This unfussy cafe serves everything from grass-fed burgers to macrobiotic wraps, stir-fries to *huevos rancheros* (corn tortilla with fried egg and chili-tomato sauce). Good blue-corn pancakes at breakfast.

Slice of Life VEGETARIAN $
(☎707-829-6627; www.thesliceoflife.com; 6970 McKinley St; mains under $10; ⏲11am-9pm Tue-Fri, 9am-9pm Sat & Sun; 🥬) This terrific vegan-vegetarian kitchen doubles as a pizzeria. Breakfast all day. Great smoothies and date shakes.

Mom's Apple Pie DESSERTS $
(☎707-823-8330; www.momsapplepieusa.com; 4550 Gravenstein Hwy N; whole pies $7-15; ⏲10am-6pm; 🥬👪) Pie's the thing here – and yum, that flaky crust. Apple is predictably good, especially in autumn, but the blueberry is our fave, made better with vanilla ice cream.

Viva Mexicana MEXICAN $
(☎707-823-5555, 707-829-5555; 841 Gravenstein Hwy S; mains $8-10; ⏲8am-8pm; 🥬) A tiny roadside *taquería* with outdoor tables and good vegetarian choices.

Fiesta Market MARKET $
(☎707-823-9735; fiestamkt.com; 550 Gravenstein Hwy N; ⏲8am-8pm) The town's best groceries and picnics.

Screamin' Mimi DESSERT $
(☎707-823-5902; www.screaminmimisicecream.com; 6902 Sebastopol Ave; ⏲11am-10pm) Delish homemade ice cream.

Drinking & Entertainment

Hardcore Espresso CAFE
(☎707-823-7588; 1798 Gravenstein Hwy S; ⊙6am-7pm; 📶) Meet local hippies and art freaks over coffee and smoothies at this classic Nor-Cal off-the-grid, indoor-outdoor coffeehouse that's essentially a corrugated-metal-roofed shack surrounded by umbrella tables. The organic coffee is the town's best.

Hopmonk Tavern PUB
(☎707-829-7300; www.hopmonk.com; 230 Petaluma Ave; ⊙11:30am-10pm, later weekends) Always-fun beer garden with 76 craft brews, several housemade. Live music most nights; Tuesday is open mic.

Aubergine After Dark CABARET
(☎707-861-9190; auberginеafterdark.com; 755 Petaluma Ave; ⊙4pm-midnight Sun-Thu, to 1am Sat & Sun) Various acts play weekends at this cool cafe with a bohemian bent, adjoining a vintage-thrift shop; full bar, snacks, and coffee drinks.

Jasper O'Farrell's BAR
(☎707-823-1389; 6957 Sebastopol Ave; ⊙Tue-Sun) Busy bar with billiards and live bands Wednesday nights; good drink specials.

Coffee Catz CAFE
(☎707-829-6600; www.coffeecatz.com; 6761 Sebastopol Ave; ⊙7am-10pm Fri & Sat, to 6pm Sun-Thu) Early-evening and afternoon acoustic music, Thursday to Sunday, at a cafe in an historic rail barn (Gravenstein Station).

Shopping

Antique shops line Gravenstein Hwy S toward Hwy 101.

Renga Arts ARTS & CRAFTS, GIFTS
(☎707-823-9407; www.rengaarts.com; ⊙11am-5pm Thu-Mon) Reduce, reuse, rejoice at Renga Arts, a functional-art shop, where every ingenious item is made with repurposed, reclaimed goods, from bottle-cap necklaces to birdhouses. Owner Joe is an excellent resource on all things West County Sonoma. Say hello.

Aubergine VINTAGE CLOTHING
(☎707-827-3460; www.auberginеafterdark.com; 755 Petaluma Ave, Sebastopol) Vast vintage emporium, specializing in cast-off European thrift-shop clothing.

Sumbody BEAUTY
(☎707-823-2053; www.sumbody.com; 118 N Main St; ⊙10am-7pm Mon-Sat, 10am-5pm Sun) Eco-friendly bath products made with all-natural ingredients. Also offers well-priced facials ($49) and massages ($75) at small on-site spa.

Toyworks TOYS
(☎707-829-2003; www.sonomatoyworks.com; 6940 Sebastopol Ave; 👪) Indie toy-seller with phenomenal selection of quality games for kids.

Antique Society ANTIQUES
(☎707-829-1733; www.antiquesociety.com; 2661 Gravenstein Hwy S) Antiques vendors, 125 of them, under one roof.

Beekind FOOD, HOMEWARES
(☎707-824-2905; www.beekind.com; 921 Gravenstein Hwy S) Local honey and beeswax candles.

Copperfield's Books BOOKS
(☎707-823-2618; www.copperfields.net; 138 N Main St) Indie bookshop with literary events.

Incredible Records MUSIC
(☎707-824-8099; 112 N Main St) A legendary record store.

Midgley's Country Flea Market MARKET
(☎707-823-7874; mfleamarket.com; 2200 Gravenstein Hwy S; ⊙6:30am-4:30pm Sat & Sun) The region's largest flea market.

Information

Sebastopol Area Chamber of Commerce & Visitors Center (☎707-823-3032, 877-828-4748; www.visitsebastopol.org; 265 S Main St; ⊙10am-4pm Mon-Fri) Maps, information and exhibits.

Occidental

Our favorite West County town is a haven of artists, back-to-the-landers and counterculturalists. Historic 19th-century buildings line a single main street, easy to explore in an hour; continue north by car and you'll hit the Russian River, in Monte Rio. Check out **Bohemian Connection** (www.bohemianconnection.com) for information. At Christmastime, Bay Area families flock to Occidental to buy trees. The town decorates to the nines, and there's weekend cookie-decorating and caroling at the Union Hotel's Bocce Ballroom.

Sights & Activities

Meet the whole community at the detour-worthy **farmers market** (www.occidentalfarmersmarket.com; 4pm-dusk Fridays, Jun-Oct), with musicians, craftspeople and – the star attraction – **Gerard's Paella** (www.gerardspaella.com) of TV-cooking-show fame.

Sonoma Canopy Tours ECOTOUR
(888-494-7868; www.sonomacanopytours.com; 6250 Bohemian Hwy; adult $79-89, child $49) North of town, fly through the redwood canopy on seven interconnected ziplines, ending with an 80ft-rappel descent; reservations required.

Osmosis Enzyme Bath & Massage BATH HOUSE
(707-823-8231; www.osmosis.com; 209 Bohemian Hwy; 9am-9pm) Three miles south in Freestone, tranquility prevails at this Japanese-inspired place, which indulges patrons with dry-enzyme baths of aromatic cedar fibers (bath-and-blanket wrap $85), lovely tea-and-meditation gardens, plus outdoor massages. Make reservations.

Sleeping

Inn at Occidental INN $$$
(707-874-1047, 800-522-6324; www.innatoccidental.com; 3657 Church St; r incl breakfast $229-339;) This beautifully restored 18-room Victorian inn – one of Sonoma's finest – is filled with collectible antiques; rooms have gas fireplaces and cozy feather beds.

Valley Ford Hotel INN $$
(707-876-1983; www.vfordhotel.com; r $115-165) Surrounded by pastureland in the nearby tiny town of Valley Ford, this 19th-century six-room inn has good beds, soft linens, and great rates. Downstairs there's a terrific roadhouse restaurant.

Occidental Hotel MOTEL $$
(707-874-3623, 877-867-6084; www.occidentalhotel.com; 3610 Bohemian Hwy; r $130-160, 2-bedroom q $180-200;) Fresh-looking motel rooms.

Eating

Bohemian Market (707-874-3312; 3633 Main St; 8am-9pm) has the best groceries. In Freestone, **Wild Flour Bakery** (707-874-3928; www.wildflourbread.coml 140 Bohemian Hwy; 8:30am-6pm Fri-Mon) makes hearty artisinal brick-oven breads, scones and coffee.

Bistro des Copains FRENCH-CALIFORNIAN $$$
(707-874-2436; www.bistrodescopains.com; 3728 Bohemian Hwy; mains $23-25, 3-course menu $38-42; 5-9pm Wed-Mon) Worth a special trip, this bistro draws bon vivants for its Cal-French country cooking, like steak-*frites* and roast duck. Great wines; $10 corkage for Sonoma vintages. Make reservations.

Howard Station Cafe CAFE $
(707-874-2838; www.howardstationcafe.com; 3811 Bohemian Hwy; mains $8-11; 7am-2:30pm;) Makes big plates of comfort cooking and fresh-squeezed juices.

Barley & Hops PUB $$
(707-874-9037; barleyandhopstavern.blogspot.com; 3688 Bohemian Hwy; mains $10-15; 4-9:30pm Mon-Fri, from 11am Sat & Sun;) Serves over 100 beers, sandwiches, giant salads and lamb stew.

Union Hotel ITALIAN $$
(707-874-3555; www.unionhoteloccidental.com; 3703 Bohemian Hwy; meals $15-25;) Occidental has two old-school American Italian restaurants that serve family-style meals. Of the two, the Union is slightly better than

SCENIC DRIVE: COLEMAN VALLEY ROAD

Wine Country's most scenic drive isn't through the grapes, but along these 10 miles of winding West County byway, from Occidental to the sea. It's best late morning, after the fog has cleared. Drive west, not east, with the sun behind you and the ocean ahead. First you'll pass through redwood forests and lush valleys where Douglas firs stand draped in sphagnum moss – an eerie sight in the fog. The real beauty shots lie further ahead, when the road ascends 1000ft hills, dotted with gnarled oaks and craggy rock formations, with the vast blue Pacific unfurling below. The road ends at coastal Hwy 1, where you can explore Sonoma Coast State Beach, then turn left and find your way to the tiny town of Bodega (not Bodega Bay) to see locales where Hitchcock shot his 1963 classic, *The Birds*.

WORTH A TRIP

VALLEY FORD

Valley Ford (population 147) is a tableau of rural California, with rolling hills dotted with grazing cows and manure lingering on the breeze – the forced sophistication of other Wine Country locales couldn't feel further away. It's ideal for an affordable one-nighter, or a lazy meal while exploring back roads.

West County Design (☎707-875-9140; 14390 Hwy 1; ⊙Thu-Sun) houses a stonemason's and custom furniture–builder's shops, giving a glimpse of contemporary California home-furnishings styles. 'Round back there's a man who builds birdhouses.

We love the flavor-rich cooking at **Rocker Oysterfeller's** (☎707-876-1983; www.rockeroysterfellers.com; 14415 Hwy 1; mains $14-22; ⊙Wed-Fri 4:30pm-8:30pm, 10am-8:30pm Sat & Sun), with its barbecued oysters, local crab cakes, steaks and fried chicken. Great wine bar, too. Or snag a picnic table at **Fish Bank** (☎707-876-3473; www.sonomacoastfishbank.com; 14435 Hwy 1; ⊙Wed-Sun 11:30am-6pm) for crab rolls, fish salads, chowder, cheese and bread – good picnic fixings if you're continuing to the coast. Stay the night at the Valley Ford Hotel (p200), with simple country B&B rooms.

Negri's (neither is great), and has a hard-to-beat lunch special in its 1869 saloon – whole pizza, salad and soda for $12. At dinner, sit in the fabulous Bocce Ballroom.

Negri's ITALIAN $$
(☎707-823-5301; www.negrisrestaurant.com; 3700 Bohemian Hwy; meals $15-25; 👪) Serves multi-course family-style dinners.

Shopping

Verdigris HOMEWARES
(☎707-874-9018; www.1lightartlamps.com; 72 Main St; ⊙Thu-Mon) Crafts gorgeous art lamps.

Hand Goods CERAMICS
(☎707-874-2161; www.handgoods.net; 3627 Main St) A collective of ceramicists and potters.

Guerneville & Around

The Russian River's biggest vacation-resort town, Guerneville gets busy summer weekends with party hardy gay boys, sun-worshipping lesbians and long-haired beer-drinking Harley riders, earning it the nickname 'Groin-ville.' The gay scene has died back since the unfortunate closure of Fife's, the world's first gay resort, but fun-seeking crowds still come to canoe, hike redwoods and hammer cocktails poolside.

Downriver, some areas are sketchy (due to drugs). The local chamber of commerce has chased most of the tweakers from Main St in Guerneville, but if some off-the-beaten-path areas feel creepy – especially campgrounds – they probably are.

Four miles downriver, tiny Monte Rio has a sign over Hwy 116 declaring it 'Vacation Wonderland' – an overstatement, but the dog-friendly beach is a hit with families. Further west, idyllic Duncans Mills is home to a few dozen souls, but has picture-ready historic buildings. Upriver, east of Guerneville, Forestville is where agricultural country resumes.

Sights & Activities

Look for sandy beaches and swimming holes along the river; there's good river access east of town at **Sunset Beach** (Map p194; www.sonoma-county.org/parks; 11403 River Rd, Forestville; per car $6). Fishing and watercraft outfitters operate mid-May to early October, after which winter rains dangerously swell the river. A **farmers market** meets downtown on Wednesdays June through September, from 4pm to 7pm. On summer Saturdays, there's also one at Monte Rio Beach, 11am to 2pm.

Armstrong Redwoods State Reserve NATURE RESERVE
(Map p194; www.parks.ca.gov; 17000 Armstrong Woods Rd; day use per vehicle $8) A magnificent redwood forest 2 miles north of Guerneville, the 805-acre Armstrong Redwoods State Reserve was set aside by a 19th-century lumber magnate. Walk or cycle in for free; you pay only to park. Short interpretive trails lead into magical forests; beyond lie 20 miles of backcountry trails, through oak woodlands, in adjoining **Austin Creek State Recreation Area**, one of Sonoma County's

few-remaining wilderness areas (although State budget cuts may temporarily close this park).

Burke's Canoe Trips CANOEING, KAYAKING
(Map p194; ☎707-887-1222; www.burkescanoetrips.com; 8600 River Rd, Forestville; canoes $60;) You can't beat Burke's for a day on the river. Self-guided canoe and kayak trips include shuttle back to your car. Make reservations; plan four hours. Camping in its riverside redwood grove costs $10 per person.

Pee Wee Golf & Arcade GOLF, BICYCLING
(Map p194; ☎707-869-9321; 16155 Drake Rd at Hwy 116; 18/36 holes $8/12; 11am-10pm Memorial Day-Labor Day, Sat & Sun Sep;) Flashback to 1948 at this impeccably kept retro-kitsch 36-hole miniature golf course, just south of the Hwy 116 bridge, with brilliantly painted obstacles, including T Rex and Yogi Bear. Bring your own cocktails; also rents gas barbecue grills ($20) and bicycles ($30).

Armstrong Woods Pack Station HORSEBACK RIDING
(☎707-887-2939; www.redwoodhorses.com) Leads year-round 2½-hour trail rides ($80), full-day rides and overnight treks. Reservations required.

Johnson's Beach BOATING
(☎707-869-2022; www.johnsonsbeach.com; end of Church St, Guerneville) Canoe, paddleboat and watercraft rental (from $30).

King's Sport & Tackle FISHING, KAYAKING, CANOEING
(☎707-869-2156; www.kingsrussianriver.com; www.guernevillesport.com; 16258 Main St, Guerneville) *The* local source for fishing and river-condition information. Also rents kayaks ($35 to $55) and canoes ($55).

Northwood Golf Course GOLF
(Map p194; ☎707-865-1116; www.northwoodgolf.com; 19400 Hwy 116, Monte Rio) Vintage-1920s Alistair MacKenzie-designed, par-36, nine-hole course.

Festivals & Events

Monte Rio Variety Show MUSIC
(www.monterioshow.org) Members of the elite, secretive Bohemian Grove (Google it) perform publicly, sometimes showcasing unannounced celebrities; July.

Lazy Bear Weekend CULTURAL
(www.lazybearweekend.com) Read: heavy, furry gay men; August.

Russian River Jazz & Blues Festival MUSIC
(www.omegaevents.com/russianriver) September. A day of jazz, followed by a day of blues, with occasional luminaries like BB King.

Sleeping

Russian River has few budget sleeps, although prices drop midweek. On weekends and holidays, book ahead. Many places have no TVs. Because the river sometimes floods, some lodgings have cold linoleum floors, so pack slippers.

GUERNVILLE

The advantage of staying downtown is you can walk to dinner and bars. At this writing, the long-running gay hotel and disco, Russian River Resort (aka Triple R), had closed, but may re-open. Check with the chamber of commerce.

Applewood Inn INN $$$
(Map p194; ☎707-869-9093, 800-555-8509; www.applewoodinn.com; 13555 Hwy 116; r incl breakfast $195-345;) A former estate on a wooded hilltop south of town, cushy Applewood has marvelous Arts and Crafts-era detail, with dark wood and heavy furniture. Rooms sport Jacuzzis, couples' showers and top-end linens; some have fireplaces. Great hideaway. Small onsite spa.

Fern Grove Cottages CABINS $$
(☎707-869-8105; www.ferngrove.com; 16650 River Rd; cabins incl breakfast $159-219, with kitchen $199-269;) Downtown Guerneville's cheeriest resort, Fern Grove has vintage-1930s pine-paneled cabins, tucked beneath redwoods and surrounded by lush flowering gardens. Some have Jacuzzis and fireplaces. The pool uses salt, not chlorine; the lovely English innkeeper provides concierge service; and breakfast includes homemade scones.

Boon Hotel & Spa INN $$$
(Map p194; ☎707-869-2721; www.boonhotels.com; 14711 Armstrong Woods Rd; r $180-225;) Rooms surround a swimming-pool courtyard (with Jacuzzi) at this mid-century-modern, 14-room motel, gussied up in minimalist style. The look is austere but fresh, with organic-cotton linens and spacious rooms; most have wood-burning fireplaces. Drive to town, or ride the free bicycles.

Santa Nella House B&B $$
(Map p194; 707-869-9448; www.santanellahouse.com; 12130 Hwy 116; r incl breakfast $179-199;) All four spotless rooms at this 1871 Victorian, south of town, have wood-burning fireplaces and frilly Victorian furnishings. Upstairs rooms are biggest. Outside there's a hot tub and sauna. Best for travelers who appreciate the B&B aesthetic.

Highlands Resort CABINS, CAMPGROUND $$
(707-869-0333; www.highlandsresort.com; 14000 Woodland Dr; tent sites $20-25; r with/without bathroom $90-100/70-80, cabins $120-205;) Guerneville's mellowest all-gay resort sits on a wooded hillside, walkable to town, and has simply furnished rooms and little cottages with porches. The large pool and hot tub are clothing-optional (weekday/weekend day use $5/10). There's camping, too.

Riverlane Resort CABINS $$
(707-869-2323, 800-201-2324; www.riverlaneresort.com; 16320 1st St; cabins $90-150;) Right downtown, Riverlane has cabins with kitchens, decorated with mismatched furniture, but they're very clean and all have decks with barbecues. Best for no-frills travelers or campers wanting an upgrade. Friendly service, heated pool, private beach and hot tub.

Johnson's Beach Resort CABINS, CAMPGROUND $
(707-869-2022; www.johnsonsbeach.com; 16241 1st St; tent sites $25, RV sites from $25-35, cabins $50, per week $300) On the river in Guerneville, Johnson's has rustic, but clean, thin-walled cabins on stilts; all have kitchens. Bring earplugs. There's camping, too, but it's loud. No credit cards.

Bullfrog Pond CAMPGROUND $
(Map p194; www.parks.ca.gov; tent sites $25) Reached via a steep road from Armstrong Redwoods, Bullfrog Pond has forested campsites, with cold water, and primitive hike-in and equestrian backcountry campsites. All are first-come, first-served. Budget cuts may limit operation to summer only.

Schoolhouse Canyon Campground CAMPGROUND $
(Map p194; 707-869-2311; www.schoolhousecanyon.com; 12600 River Rd; tent sites $30;) Two miles east of Guerneville, Schoolhouse's tent sites lie beneath tall trees, across the road from the river. Coin-operated hot showers, clean bathrooms, quiet location.

FORESTVILLE

Raford Inn B&B $$
(Map p194; 707-887-9573, 800-887-9503; www.rafordhouse.com; 10630 Wohler Rd, Healdsburg; r $160-260;) We love this 1880 Victorian B&B's secluded hilltop location, surrounded by tall palms and rambling vineyards. Rooms are big and airy, done with lace and antiques; some have fireplaces. And wow, those sunset views.

Farmhouse Inn INN $$$
(Map p194; 707-887-3300, 800-464-6642; www.farmhouseinn.com; 7871 River Rd; r $325-695;) Think love nest. The area's premier inn has spacious rooms and cottages, styled with cushy amenities like saunas, steam-showers and wood-burning fireplaces. Small on-site spa and top-notch restaurant (p204). Check in early to maximize time.

MONTE RIO

Village Inn INN $$
(Map p194; 707-865-2304; www.villageinn-ca.com; 20822 River Blvd; r $145-235;) A retired concierge owns this cute, old-fashioned 11-room inn, beneath towering trees, right on the river. Some rooms have river views; all have fridge and microwave.

Rio Villa Beach Resort INN $$
(Map p194; 707-865-1143, 877-746-8455; www.riovilla.com; 20292 Hwy 116; r with kitchen $149-209, r without kitchen $139-189;) Landscaping is lush at this small riverside resort with excellent sun exposure (you see redwoods, but you're not under them). Rooms are well kept but simple (request a quiet room, not by the road); the emphasis is on the outdoors, evident by the large riverside terrace, outdoor fireplace and barbecues.

Highland Dell INN $$
(Map p194; 707-865-2300; highlanddell.com; 21050 River Blvd; r $109-179;) Built in 1906 in grand lodge style, redone in 2007, the inn fronts right on the river. Above the giant dining room are 12 bright, fresh-looking rooms (carpet stains notwithstanding) with comfy beds.

DUNCANS MILLS

Casini Ranch CAMPGROUND $
(707-865-2255, 800-451-8400; www.casiniranch.com; 22855 Moscow Rd, Duncans Mills; tent sites $38-45, RV sites partial/full hookups $40-51/46-49;

) In quiet Duncans Mills, beautifully set on riverfront ranchlands, Casini is an enormous, well-run campground. Amenities include kayaks and paddleboats (day use $3); bathrooms are spotless.

Eating

GUERNEVILLE

There's a good **taco truck** (16451 Main St), in the Safeway parking lot.

Boon Eat + Drink NEW AMERICAN $$$
(707-869-0780; www.eatatboon.com; 16248 Main St; lunch/dinner mains $10-12/$20-24; 11am-3pm & 5-9pm) Locally sourced ingredients inform the seasonal, Cali-smart cooking at this tiny, always-packed New American bistro, with cheek-by-jowl tables that fill every night. Make reservations or expect to wait.

Applewood Inn Restaurant CALIFORNIAN $$$
(Map p194; 707-869-9093, www.dineatapplewood.com; 13555 Hwy 116; mains $20-28; 5:30-8:30pm Wed-Sun) Cozy by the fire in the treetop-level dining room and sup on Michelin-starred Euro-Cal cooking that maximizes seasonal produce, with dishes like rack of lamb with minted *chimichuri* (garlic-parsley vinaigrette) and smoked trout with corn and crayfish. Reservations essential.

Coffee Bazaar CAFE $
(707-869-9706; www.mycoffeeb.com; 14045 Armstrong Woods Rd; dishes $5-9; 6am-8pm;) Happening cafe with salads, sandwiches and all-day breakfasts; adjoins a good used bookstore.

Garden Grill BARBECUE $
(707-869-3922; www.gardengrillbbq.com; 17132 Hwy 116, Guernewood Park; mains $6-12; 8am-8pm) The Garden Grill is a roadhouse barbecue joint, with a redwood-shaded patio, one mile west of Guerneville; good house-smoked meats, but the fries could be better. Breakfast till 3pm.

Andorno's Pizza PIZZERIA $
(707-869-0651; www.andornospizza.com; 16205 1st St; 11:30am-9pm;) Downtown pizzeria with river-view terrace.

Taqueria La Tapatia MEXICAN $
(707-869-1821; 16632 Main St; mains $7-14; 11am-9pm) Reasonable choice for traditional Mexican.

Big Bottom Market MARKET $
(707-604-7295; www.bigbottommarket.com; 16228 Main St) Gourmet deli and wine shop, with grab-and-go picnic supplies.

Food for Humans MARKET $
(707-869-3612; 16385 1st St; 9am-8pm;) Organic groceries; better alternative than neighboring Safeway, but no meat.

FORESTVILLE

Farmhouse Inn NEW AMERICAN $$$
(Map p194; 707-887-3300; www.farmhouseinn.com; 7871 River Rd; 3-/4-course dinner $69/89; dinner Thu-Sun) Special-occasion worthy, Michelin-starred Farmhouse changes its seasonal Euro-Cal menu daily, using locally raised, organic ingredients like Sonoma lamb, wild salmon and rabbit – the latter is the house specialty. Details are impeccable, from aperitifs in the garden to tableside cheese service. Make reservations.

MONTE RIO

Highland Dell GERMAN $$
(Map p194; 707-865-2300; http://highlanddell.com; 21050 River Blvd; lunch mains $9-15, dinner mains $16-26; 5-9pm Mon, Tue, Fri & Sat, 1-7pm Sun; closed Oct-May) A dramatic three-story-high chalet-style dining room with a river-view deck, Highland Dell makes pretty good German food – steaks, schnitzel, sauerbraten and sausage. Full bar.

Village Inn AMERICAN $$$
(Map p194; 707-865-2304; www.villageinn-ca.com; 20822 River Blvd; mains $19-26; 5-8:30pm Wed-Sun) The straightforward steaks-and-seafood menu is basic American and doesn't distract from the wonderful river views. Great local wine list, full bar.

Don's Dogs SNACK BAR $
(Map p194; 707-865-4190; cnr Bohemian Hwy & Hwy 116; 9am-5pm Wed-Sun) Gourmet hot dogs and coffee, behind the Rio Theater.

Drinking & Entertainment

Stumptown Brewery BREWERY
(Map p194; www.stumptown.com; 15045 River Rd; 11am-midnight Sun-Thu, 11-2am Fri & Sat) Guerneville's best straight bar is gay-friendly and has a foot-stompin' jukebox, billiards, riverside beer garden, and several homemade brews. Pretty good pub grub, including house-smoked barbecue.

Rio Theater CINEMA
(Map p194; ☎707-865-0913; www.riotheater.com; cnr Bohemian Hwy & Hwy 116, Monte Rio; adult/child $7/5; ⊙Fri-Sun) Dinner and a movie take on new meaning at this vintage-WWII Quonset hut converted to a cinema in 1950, with a concession stand serving gourmet hot dogs ($7). It's freezing inside on cool nights, but they supply blankets. Charming. Call to confirm showtimes, especially off-season.

Rainbow Cattle Company GAY
(www.queersteer.com; 16220 Main St) The stalwart gay watering hole.

Guerneville River Theater LIVE MUSIC, DJS
(www.rivertheater.biz; 16135 Main St; ⊙Wed, Fri & Sat) Former movie theater, now a honky-tonk club, with town's biggest dance floor. Live bands weekends, open mic Wednesdays. Very DIY feeling. Beer and wine only.

Rio Nido Roadhouse BAR, LIVE MUSIC
(www.rionidoroadhouse.com; 14540 Canyon Two, off River Rd) Raucous roadhouse bar with eclectic lineup of live bands. Shows start 6pm Saturdays and sometimes Fridays and Sundays, too; check website.

Main Street Station CABARET
(☎707-869-0501; www.mainststation.com; 16280 Main, Guerneville; cover $3-6) Live acoustic-only jazz, blues and cabaret nightly in summer, weekends in winter. Suggest reservations, but you can normally walk in. Also an Italian-American restaurant.

Kaya Organic Espresso CAFE
(16626 Main St, Guerneville; ⊙7am-2pm) Hippie kids strum guitars and play hackie sack outside this coffee shack.

Wine Tasting of Sonoma County WINE BAR $
(☎707-865-0565; winetastingofsonomacounty.com; 25179 Hwy 116, Duncans Mills; wine tastings $5; ⊙noon-5pm Fri-Mon) Local vino and cheeses alfresco.

Information

Get information and lodging referrals:

Russian River Chamber of Commerce & Visitor Center (☎707-869-9000, 877-644-9001; www.russianriver.com; 16209 1st St, Guerneville; ⊙10am-5pm Mon-Sat, to 4pm Sun)

Russian River Visitor Information Center (☎707-869-4096; ⊙10am-3:45pm) At Korbel Cellars.

Santa Rosa

Wine Country's biggest city, and the Sonoma County seat, Santa Rosa is known for traffic and suburban sprawl. It lacks small-town charm, but has reasonably priced accommodations and easy access to Sonoma County and Valley.

Santa Rosa claims two famous native sons – a world-renowned cartoonist and a celebrated horticulturalist – and you'll find enough museums, gardens and shopping for an afternoon. Otherwise, there ain't much to do, unless you're here in July during the **Sonoma County Fair** (www.sonomacountyfair.com), at the fairgrounds on Bennett Valley Rd.

Sights & Activities

The main shopping stretch is 4th St, which abruptly ends at Hwy 101 but reemerges on the other side at historic Railroad Sq. Downtown parking garages ($0.75/hour, $8 max) are cheaper than street parking. East of town, 4th St turns into Hwy 12 to Sonoma Valley.

FREE **Luther Burbank Home & Gardens** GARDENS
(☎707-524-5445; www.lutherburbank.org; ☎8am-dusk) Pioneering horticulturist Luther Burbank (1849–1926) developed many hybrid plant species at his 19th-century Greek-revival home, at Santa Rosa and Sonoma Aves, including the Shasta daisy. The extensive gardens are lovely. The house and adjacent **Carriage Museum** (guided tour adult/child $7/free, self-guided cell-phone tour free ⊙10am-3:30pm Tue-Sun Apr-Oct) have displays on Burbank's life and work. Across the street from Burbank's home, Julliard Park has a playground.

OLIVE-OIL TASTING

When you weary of wine tasting, pop in to one of the following olive-oil mills (all free except Round Pond) and dip some crusty bread. The harvest and pressing happen in November.

» **BR Cohn** (p205)

» **Long Meadow Ranch** (p167)

» **Round Pond** (p166) Ninety-minute mill tour and tasting $25.

» **Figone's Olive Oil** (p191)

Charles M Schulz Museum MUSEUM
(707-579-4452; www.schulzmuseum.org; 2301 Hardies Lane; adult/child $10/5; 11am-5pm Mon-Fri, 10am-5pm Sat & Sun, closed Tue Sep-May;) Charles Schulz, creator of *Peanuts* cartoons, was a long-term Santa Rosa resident. Born in 1922, he published his first drawing in 1937, introduced the world to Snoopy and Charlie Brown in 1950, and produced Peanuts cartoons until just before his death in 2000.

At the museum a glass wall overlooks a courtyard with a Snoopy labyrinth. Exhibits include Peanuts-related art and Schulz's actual studio. Skip Snoopy's Gallery gift shop; the museum has the good stuff.

Redwood Empire Ice Arena SKATING
(707-546-7147; www.snoopyshomeice.com; adult/child incl skates $12/10;) This skating rink was formerly owned and deeply loved by Schulz. It's open most afternoons (call for schedules). Bring a sweater.

Farmers Markets MARKET
Sonoma County's largest farmers market meets Wednesday, 5pm to 8:30pm, mid-May through August, at 4th and B Sts. A year-round market meets Saturdays at the Santa Rosa Veterans Building, 8:30am to 1pm, 1351 Maple Ave.

Sleeping

Look for hotels near Railroad Square. Nothing-special motels line Cleveland Ave, fronting Hwy 101's western side, between Steele Lane and Bicentennial Lane exits; skip the Motel 6. Also consider nearby Windsor, which has two chain hotels off Hwy 101 at the Central Windsor exit.

Hotel La Rose HISTORIC HOTEL $$
(707-579-3200; www.hotellarose.com; 308 Wilson St; r weekday/weekend $129-189/$199-219;) At Railroad Sq, this charming 1907 hotel has rooms with marble baths, sitting areas with thick carpeting and wing chairs, and supercomfy mattresses with feather beds. Great for a moderate splurge. Rooftop hot tub.

Vintners Inn INN $$$
(707-575-7350, 800-421-2584; www.vintnersinn.com; 4350 Barnes Rd; r $225-495;) Built in the 1980s, Vintners Inn sits on the rural outskirts of town (near River Rd) and appeals to the gated-community crowd. Rooms' amenities are business-class fancy. Jacuzzi, but no pool. Check for last-minute specials.

Flamingo Resort Hotel HOTEL $$
(707-545-8530, 800-848-8300; www.flamingoresort.com; 2777 4th St; r $99-219;) Sprawling over 11 acres, this mid-century modern hotel doubles as a conference center. Rooms are motel-generic, but what a gigantic pool – and it's 82 degrees year-round. Kids love it. On-site health-club and gym. Prices double summer weekends.

Hillside Inn MOTEL $
(707-546-9353; www.hillside-inn.com; 2901 4th St, Santa Rosa; s/d Nov-Mar $70/82, Apr-Oct $74/86;) One of Santa Rosa's best-kept motels, Hillside is close to Sonoma Valley; add $4 for kitchens. Furnishings are dated, but everything is scrupulously maintained. Adjoins an excellent breakfast cafe.

Best Western Garden Inn MOTEL $$
(707-546-4031, 888-256-8004; www.thegardeninn.com; 1500 Santa Rosa Ave; r $119-149;) Book a room in back for quiet, up front for privacy, at this well-kept cookie-cutter motel, south of downtown. The street gets seedy by night, but the hotel is secure, clean and comfortable.

Spring Lake Park CAMPGROUND $
(707-539-8092, reservations 707-565-2267; www.sonoma-county.org/parks; 5585 Newanga Ave; sites $28; daily May-Sep, weekends only Oct-Apr;) Lovely lakeside park, 4 miles from downtown; make reservations ($7 fee) 10am to 3pm weekdays. The park is open year-round, with **lake swimming** in summer; campground operates May to September, weekends October to April. Take 4th St eastbound, turn right on Farmer's Lane, pass the first Hoen St and turn left on the *second* Hoen St, then left on Newanga Ave.

Best Western Wine Country Inn & Suites HOTEL $$
(707-545-9000, 800-780-7234; www.winecountryhotel.com; 870 Hopper Ave; r weekday/weekends $120/170;) Generic chain hotel, off Cleveland Ave.

Sandman Hotel MOTEL $
(707-544-8570; www.sandmansantarosa.com; 3421 Cleveland Ave; $83-102) Cleveland Ave's reliable budget choice.

Eating

TOP CHOICE **Zazu** CALIFORNIAN, ITALIAN $$
(☎707-523-4814; 3535 Guerneville Rd, Santa Rosa; brunch mains $11-15, dinner mains $18-26; ⊙5:30-8:30pm Wed-Mon, 9am-2pm Sun) The cooking at Zazu is an expression of the land: if it's in the garden, it's on the plate. Husband-and-wife team Duske Estes and John Stewart use only local ingredients from within 30 miles of their little roadhouse restaurant, 10 miles west of downtown Santa Rosa. John raises heirloom pigs, which he transforms into gorgeous salumi. Duske fashions homemade pasta, using eggs from their own hens. Dishes skew Italian-country, using few ingredients that let the dynamic flavors sparkle. One of Sonoma's top tables for seasonal-regional cooking. Great brunch, too. Wednesday, Thursday and Sunday are pizza-and-pinot nights, with wine flights paired for pizza. For true farm-to-table cooking, don't miss Zazu.

Rosso Pizzeria & Wine Bar PIZZERIA $$
(☎707-544-3221; 53 Montgomery St, Creekside Shopping Centre; pizzas $12-15; ⊙11am-10pm;) Crispy brick-oven pizzas – some of NorCal's best – along with inventive salads and a standout wine list make Rosso worth seeking out.

Jeffrey's Hillside Cafe AMERICAN $
(www.jeffreyshillsidecafe.com; 2901 4th St; dishes $8-12; ⊙7am-2pm;) East of downtown, near the top of Sonoma Valley, chef-owned Jeffrey's is excellent for breakfast or brunch before wine tasting.

Taqueria Las Palmas MEXICAN $
(☎707-546-3091; 415 Santa Rosa Ave; dishes $4-7; ⊙9am-9pm;) For Mexican, this is the real deal, with standout *carnitas* (barbecued pork), homemade salsas and veggie burritos.

Pho Vietnam VIETNAMESE $
(☎707-571-7687; No 8, 711 Stony Point Rd; dishes $6-8; ⊙10am-8:30pm Mon-Sat, to 7:30pm Sun) Fantastic noodle bowls and rice plates at a hole-in-the-wall shopping-center restaurant, just off Hwy 12, west of downtown.

Willi's Wine Bar TAPAS $$$
(☎707-526-3096; www.williswinebar.net; dishes $10-15; ⊙11am-9:30pm Wed-Sat, 5-9pm Sun & Mon) Stellar small plates.

Traverso's Gourmet Foods DELI $
(☎707-542-2530; www.traversos.com; 2097 Stagecoach Rd; ⊙10am-6pm Mon-Sat) Excellent Italian deli and wine shop.

Mac's Delicatessen DELI $
(☎707-545-3785; 630 4th St; dishes under $10; ⊙7am-5pm Mon-Fri, 7am-4pm Sat) Downtown Kosher-style deli.

Drinking

Third Street Aleworks BREWERY
(thirdstreetaleworks.com; 610 3rd St;) This giant brew pub gets packed weekends and game days. Great garlic fries and half-a-dozen pool tables.

Aroma Roasters CAFE
(www.aromaroasters.com; 95 5th St, Railroad Sq;) Town's hippest café; serves no booze; acoustic music Friday and Saturday evenings.

Russian River Brewing Co BREWERY
(www.russianriverbrewing.com; 729 4th St) Locally crafted brews.

Information

Aroma Roasters (☎707-576-7765; 95 5th St, Railroad Sq; per 15min $1.50; ⊙6am-11pm Mon-Thu, 7am-midnight Fri & Sat, 7am-10pm Sun; @) Internet access. No electrical outlets for laptops.

California Welcome Center & Santa Rosa Visitors Bureau (☎707-577-8674, 800-404-7673; www.visitsantarosa.com; 9 4th St; ⊙9am-5pm Mon-Sat, 10am-5pm Sun) At Railroad Sq, west of Hwy 101; take the downtown Santa Rosa exit off Hwy 12 or Hwy 101.

Santa Rosa Memorial Hospital (☎707-935-5000; 347 Andrieux St)

Healdsburg

Once a sleepy ag town best known for its Future Farmers of America parade, Healdsburg has emerged as northern Sonoma County's culinary capital. Foodie-scenester restaurants and cafes, wine-tasting rooms and fancy boutiques line Healdsburg Plaza, the town's sun-dappled central square (bordered by Healdsburg Ave and Center, Matheson and Plaza Sts). Traffic grinds to a halt summer weekends, when second-home-owners and tourists jam downtown. Old-timers aren't happy with the Napa-style gentrification, but at least Healdsburg retains its historic look, if not its once-quiet summers. It's best visited weekdays – stroll tree-lined streets, sample locavore cooking and soak up the NorCal flavor.

Sights

Tasting rooms surround the plaza. Free summer concerts play Tuesday afternoons.

Healdsburg Museum MUSEUM
(☎707-431-3325; www.healdsburgmuseum.org; 221 Matheson St; donation requested; ⏲11am-4pm Thu-Sun) East of the plaza, worth a visit for a glimpse of Healdsburg's past. Exhibits include compelling installations on northern Sonoma County history. Pick up a walking-tour pamphlet.

Locals Tasting Room TASTING ROOM
(Map p194; ☎707-857-4900; www.tastelocalwines.com; tastings free; Geyserville Ave & Hwy 128; ⏲10am-6pm) Eight miles north, photo-ready one-block-long Geyserville is home to this indie tasting room, which represents ten small-production wineries.

Farmers Markets MARKET
(www.healdsburgfarmersmarket.org) Meet locals and discover the region's agricultural abundance at the **Tuesday market** (cnr Vine & North Sts; ⏲4-7pm Tue Jun-Oct) and **Saturday market** (one block west of the plaza; ⏲9am-noon Sat May-Nov).

Activities

The more active you are in Healdsburg, the more you can eat. After you've walked around the plaza, there isn't much to do in town. Go wine tasting in Dry Creek Valley (p196) or Russian River Valley (p194). Bicycling on winding West Dry Creek Rd is brilliant, as is paddling the Russian River, which runs through town. You can swim at **Healdsburg Veterans Memorial Beach** (Map p194; ☎707-433-1625; www.sonoma-county.org/parks; 13839 Healdsburg Ave; parking $7; ♿); lifeguards are on duty daily in summer (call ahead). If you're squeamish, confirm current water quality online (www.sonoma-county.org/health/eh/russian_river.htm).

Russian River Adventures CANOEING
(Map p194; ☎707-433-5599; www.rradventures.info; 20 Healdsburg Ave; adult/child $50/25; 👪🐾) Paddle a secluded stretch of river, in quiet inflatable canoes, stopping for rope swings, swimming holes, gravel beaches, and bird-watching. This ecotourism outfit points you in the right direction and shuttles you back at day's end. Or they'll guide your kids downriver while you go wine-tasting (guides $120/day). Self-guided departures leave 10am sharp; reservations required.

Getaway Adventures CYCLING, KAYAKING
(☎707-763-3040, 800-499-2453; www.getawayadventures.com) Guides spectacular morning vineyard cycling in Dry Creek Valley, followed by lunch and optional kayaking on Russian River ($150 to $175).

River's Edge Kayak & Canoe Trips BOATING
(Map p194; ☎707-433-7247; www.riversedgekayakandcanoe.com; 13840 Healdsburg Ave) Rents hard-sided canoes ($70/85 per half/full day) and kayaks ($40/55). Self-guided rentals include shuttle. Guided trips – by reservation – originate upriver in Alexander Valley, and end in town.

Healdsburg Spoke Folk Cyclery BICYCLE RENTAL
(☎707-433-7171; www.spokefolk.com; 201 Center St) Rents touring, racing and tandem bicycles. Great service.

Relish Culinary Adventures COOKING COURSE
(☎707-431-9999, 877-759-1004; www.relishculinary.com; 14 Matheson St; ⏲by appointment) Plug into the locavore food scene with culinary day trips, demo-kitchen classes or winemaker dinners.

Festivals & Events

Russian River Wine Road Barrel Tasting WINE
(www.wineroad.com) March

Future Farmers Parade CULTURAL
(www.healdsburgfair.org) May

Wine & Food Affair FOOD
(www.wineroad.com/events) November

Sleeping

Healdsburg is expensive and demand exceeds supply. Rates drop winter to spring, but not by that much. Guerneville (p202) is much less expensive, and only 20 minutes away.

Most Healdsburg inns are within walking distance of the plaza; several B&Bs are in surrounding countryside. Two older motels lie south of the plaza, two to the north at Hwy 101's Dry Creek exit.

Hotel Healdsburg HOTEL $$$
(☎707-431-2800, 800-889-7188; www.hotelhealdsburg.com; 25 Matheson St; r incl breakfast $335-585; ❄@📶🏊) Smack on the plaza, the chic

HH has a coolly minimalist style. Wear Armani and blend in. The ultracushy rooms, all hard angles and muted colors, have delicious beds and extra-deep tubs. Downstairs there's a full-service spa.

H2 Hotel HOTEL $$$
(☎707-431-2202, 707-922-5251; www.h2hotel.com; 219 Healdsburg Ave; r incl breakfast weekday $255-455, weekend $355-555;) Little sister to Hotel Healdsburg, H2 has the same angular concrete style, but was built LEED-gold-certified from the ground up, with a living roof, reclaimed everything, and fresh-looking rooms with cush organic linens. Tiny pool, free bikes.

Madrona Manor HISTORIC INN $$$
(Map p194; ☎707-433-4231, 800-258-4003; www.madronamanor.com; 1001 Westside Rd; r & ste $270-390;) The first choice of lovers of country inns and stately manor homes, the regal 1881 Madrona Manor exudes Victorian elegance. Surrounded by eight acres of woods and gorgeous century-old gardens, the hilltop mansion is decked out with many original furnishings. A mile west of downtown, it's convenient to Westside Rd wineries.

Belle de Jour Inn B&B $$$
(Map p194; ☎707-431-9777; www.belledejourinn.com; 16276 Healdsburg Ave; r $225-295, ste $355;) Belle de Jour's sunny, uncomplicated, lovely rooms have American-country furnishings, with extras like sun-dried sheets, hammocks and CD players. The manicured gardens are perfect for a moonlight tryst.

Healdsburg Inn on the Plaza INN $$$
(☎707-433-6991, 800-431-8663; www.healdsburginn.com; 110 Matheson St; r $295-375;) The spiffy, clean-lined rooms, conservatively styled in khaki and beige, feel bourgeois summer-house casual, with fine linens and gas fireplaces; some have jetted double tubs. The plaza-front location explains the price.

Best Western Dry Creek Inn MOTEL $$
(Map p194; ☎707-433-0300, 800-222-5784; www.drycreekinn.com; 198 Dry Creek Rd, Healdsburg; weekday/weekend r $59-129/199-259;) Town's top motel has good service and an outdoor hot tub. New rooms have jetted tubs and gas fireplaces. Check for weekday discounts.

Geyserville Inn MOTEL $$
(Map p194; ☎707-857-4343, 877-857-4343; www.geyservilleinn.com; 21714 Geyserville Ave, Geyserville; r weekday $119-169, weekend $189-249;) Eight miles north of Healdsburg, this immaculately kept upmarket motel is surrounded by vineyards. Rooms have unexpectedly smart furnishings, like overstuffed side chairs and fluffy feather pillows. Request a remodeled room. Hot tub.

Honor Mansion INN $$$
(☎707-433-4277, 800-554-4667; www.honormansion.com; 891 Grove St; r incl breakfast $300-550;) Victorian mansion c 1883; spectacular grounds.

Camellia Inn B&B $$$
(☎707-433-8182, 800-727-8182; www.camelliainn.com; 211 North St; r $139-329;) Italianate 1869 house; one room accommodates families.

George Alexander House B&B $$$
(☎707-433-1358, 800-310-1358; www.georgealexanderhouse.com; 423 Matheson St; r $180-350;) Queen Anne c 1905, with Victorian and Asian antiques; also a sauna.

Haydon Street Inn B&B $$$
(☎707-433-5228, 800-528-3703; www.haydon.com; 321 Haydon St; r $195-325, cottage $425;) Two-story Queen Anne with big front porch and cottage out back.

Piper Street Inn INN $$$
(☎707-433-8721, 877-703-0370; www.piperstreetinn.com; 402 Piper St; r $195-265;) Two rooms: homey bedroom, garden cottage.

L&M Motel MOTEL $$
(Map p194; ☎707-433-6528; www.landmmotel.com; 70 Healdsburg Ave, Healdsburg; r incl breakfast $100-140;) Simple, clean old-fashioned motel; big lawns and barbecue grills, great for families. Dry sauna and Jacuzzi.

Cloverdale Wine Country KOA CAMPGROUND $
(☎707-894-3337, 800-368-4558; www.winecountrykoa.com; 1166 Asti Ridge Rd, Cloverdale; tent/RV sites from $42/60, 1-/2-bedroom cabins $80/90;) Six miles from Central Cloverdale exit off Hwy 101; hot showers, pool, hot tub, laundry, paddleboats and bicycles.

Eating

Healdsburg is the gastronomic capital of Sonoma County. Your hardest decision will be choosing where to eat. Reservations essential.

Cyrus FRENCH-CALIFORNIAN $$$
(☎707-433-3311; www.cyrusrestaurant.com; 29 North St, Healdsburg; fixed-price menu $102-130; ⊙dinner Thu-Mon, lunch Sat) Napa's venerable French Laundry has stiff competition in swanky Cyrus, an ultrachic dining room in the great tradition of the French country auberge. The emphasis is on luxury foods, expertly prepared with a French sensibility and flavored with global spices, as in the signature Thai marinated lobster. The staff moves as if in a ballet, ever intuitive of your pace and tastes. From the caviar cart to the cheese course, Cyrus is a meal to remember.

TOP CHOICE **Madrona Manor** CALIFORNIAN $$$
(Map p194; ☎707-433-4231, 800-258-4003; www.madronamanor.com; 1001 Westside Rd; 4-/5-/6-course menu $73/82/91; ⊙6-9pm Wed-Sun) You'd be hard-pressed to find a lovelier place to pop the question than this retro-formal Victorian mansion's garden-view veranda – though there's nothing old-fashioned about the artful Californian haute cuisine: the kitchen churns its own butter, each course comes with a different variety of still-warm house-baked bread, lamb and cheese originate down the road, and deserts include ice cream flash-frozen tableside. Reserve a pre-sunset table.

Scopa ITALIAN $$
(☎707-433-5282; www.scopahealdsburg.com; 109-A Plaza St, Healdsburg; mains $12-26; ⊙5:30-10pm Tue-Sun) Space is tight inside this converted barbershop, but it's worth cramming in for perfect thin-crust pizza and rustic Italian home cooking, like Nonna's slow-braised chicken, with sautéed greens, melting into toasty polenta. A lively crowd and good wine prices create a convivial atmosphere.

Bovolo ITALIAN, CAFE $$
(☎707-431-2962; www.bovolorestaurant.com; 106 Matheson St, Healdsburg; dishes $6-14; [⊙9am-4pm Mon, Weds, Thu, 9am-8pm Tue, Fri, Sat, 9am-6pm Sun;) Fast food gets a slow-food spin at this order-at-the-counter Cal-Ital bistro – little sister to Zazu (p207) – that serves farm-fresh egg breakfasts, just-picked salads, and hand-thrown pizzas topped with house-cured meats from heirloom pigs. Sit outside and save room for hand-turned gelato. Enter through the bookstore.

Healdsburg Bar & Grill PUB $$
(☎707-433-3333; www.healdsburgbarandgrill.com; 245 Healdsburg Ave; mains $9-15; ⊙11:30am-9pm) Great when you're famished but don't want to fuss, HBG does gastropub cooking right – mac-n-cheese, pulled-pork sandwiches, top-end burgers and truffle-parmesan fries. Sit in the garden, or watch the game at the bar.

Zin NEW AMERICAN $$
(☎707-473-0946; www.zinrestaurant.com; 344 Center St; lunch mains $10-20, dinner mains $76-27; ⊙11:30am-2:30pm Mon-Fri, dinner nightly;) Reliable zin makes hearty Cal-American comfort food, designed to pair with zinfandel and other local varietals. Think pot roast and apple pie. Fun wine bar, good service.

Oakville Grocery DELI $$
(☎707-433-3200; www.oakvillegrocery.com; 124 Matheson St; sandwiches $10; ⊙8am-7pm) Luxurious smoked fish and caviar, fancy sandwiches and grab-and-go gourmet picnics. It's overpriced, but the plaza-view fireside terrace is ever-fun for scouting Botox blonds, while nibbling cheese and sipping vino.

Diavola ITALIAN $$
(Map p194; ☎707-814-0111; www.diavolapizzera.com; 21021 Geyserville Ave, Geyserville; pizzas $12-15; ⊙11:30am-9pm Wed-Mon;) Ideal for lunch while wine tasting in Alexander Valley, Diavola makes excellent salumi and thin-crust pizzas, served in an Old West brick-walled space, loud enough to drown out the kids.

Barndiva CALIFORNIAN $$$
(☎707-431-0100; www.barndiva.com; 231 Center St; brunch mains $16-22, dinner mains $25-34; ⊙noon-11pm Wed-Sun) Impeccable seasonal-regional cooking, happening bar, beautiful garden, but service sometimes misses.

Ravenous NEW AMERICAN $$
(☎707-431-1770; www.theravenous.com; 420 Center St; mains $13-17) Chalkboard-scrawled menu, with California comfort cooking and excellent burgers, served (s-l-o-w-l-y) inside a former cottage. Sit outside with Healdsburg's hipper half. $10 corkage.

Flaky Cream Coffee Shop DINER $
(☎707-433-3895; Healdsburg Shopping Center, 441 Center St; dishes $5-9; ⊙6am-2pm) Bacon-and-egg breakfasts, yummy doughnuts.

Self-Catering

Dry Creek General Store DELI $
(Map p194; ☎707-433-4171; www.dcgstore.com; 3495 Dry Creek Rd; sandwiches $8-10; ⊙6am-6pm) Before wine tasting in Dry Creek Valley, make

a pit stop at this vintage general store, where locals and bicyclists gather for coffee on the creaky front porch. Perfect picnics supplies include Toscano-salami-and-manchego sandwiches on chewy-dense ciabatta.

Jimtown Store DELI $
(Map p194; ☎707-433-1212; www.jimtown.com; sandwiches $8-11; 6706 Hwy 128; ⏲7:30am-4pm) One of our favorite Alexander Valley stopovers, Jimtown is great for picnic supplies and sandwiches made with housemade condiment spreads.

Downtown Bakery & Creamery BAKERY $
(☎707-431-2719; www.downtownbakery.net; 308a Center St; ⏲7am-5:30pm) Healdsburg's finest bakery makes scrumptious pastries.

Costeaux French Bakery & Cafe BAKERY $
(☎707-433-1913; www.costeaux.com; 417 Healdsburg Ave; ⏲7am-4pm Mon-Sat, to 1pm Sun) Fresh bread and good boxed lunches.

Cheese Shop CHEESE $
(☎707-433-4998; www.doraliceimports.com; 423 Center St; ⏲Mon-Fri 11am-6pm, Sat 10am-6pm) Top-notch imported and local cheeses.

Shelton's Natural Foods MARKET, DELI $
(☎707-431-0530; www.sheltonsmarket.com; 428 Center S; ⏲8am-8pm) Indie alternative for groceries and picnic supplies more reasonably priced than Oakville Grocery.

Drinking & Entertainment

Flying Goat Coffee CAFE
(www.flyinggoatcoffee.com; 324 Center St; ⏲7am-6pm) See ya later, Starbucks. Flying Goat is what coffee should be - fair-trade and house-roasted - and locals line up for it every morning.

Bear Republic Brewing Company BREWERY
(www.bearrepublic.com; 345 Healdsburg Ave; ⏲11:30am-late) Bear Republic features handcrafted award-winning ales, non-award-winning pub grub and live music weekends.

Barndiva COCKTAIL BAR
(☎707-431-0100; www.barndiva.com; 231 Center St; ⏲noon-11pm Wed-Sun) Swanky seasonal cocktails, like blood-orange margaritas, with a pretty crowd.

Raven Theater & Film Center THEATER
(☎707-433-5448; www.raventheater.com; 115 N Main St) Hosts concerts, events and first-run art-house films.

Shopping

Arboretum CLOTHING
(☎707-433-7033; www.arboretumapparel.com; 332 Healdsburg Ave; ⏲Wed-Mon) Lending fresh meaning to 'fashion-conscious,' this eco-boutique features fair trade and US designers, with great finds like organic-cotton pants for men and ultra-soft bamboo-fiber cardigans for gals.

Jimtown Store GIFTS
(Map p194; ☎707-433-1212; www.jimtown.com; 6706 Hwy 128) Forage antique bric-a-brac, candles and Mexican oilcloths at this roadside deli and store in Alexander Valley.

Baksheesh GIFTS, HOMEWARES
(☎707-473-0880; www.baksheeshfairtrade.com; 106B Matheson St) Household goods with a global outlook: everything sourced from fair-trade collectives, from Alpaca shawls to Vietnamese trivets.

Gardener HOMEWARES
(Map p194; ☎707-431-1063; www.thegardener.com; 516 Dry Creek Rd) Garden-shop lovers: don't miss this rural beauty.

Studio Barndiva GIFTS, HOMEWARES
(☎707-431-7404; www.studiobarndiva; 237 Center St) Reclaimed ephemera never looked so chic: thousand-dollar *objets d'art*.

Copperfield's Books BOOKS
(☎707-433-9270; copperfieldsbooks.com; 104 Matheson St) Good general-interest books.

Levin & Company BOOKS, MUSIC
(☎707-433-1118; 306 Center St) Fiction and CDs; co-op art gallery.

Information

Healdsburg Chamber of Commerce & Visitors Bureau (☎707-433-6935, 800-648-9922; www.healdsburg.org; 217 Healdsburg Ave; ⏲9am-5pm Mon-Fri, to 3pm Sat, 10am-2pm Sun) A block south of the plaza. Has winery maps and information on hot-air ballooning, golf, tennis, spas and nearby farms (get the *Farm Trails* brochure); 24-hour walk-up booth.

Healdsburg Public Library (☎707-433-3772; www.sonoma.lib.ca.us; cnr Piper & Center Sts; ⏲10am-6pm Mon & Wed, to 8pm Tue & Thu-Sat; @📶) One-hour free internet access (bring ID). Wine Country's leading oenology-reference library.

North Coast & Redwoods

Includes »

Best Places to Eat

» Café Beaujolais (p227)
» Six Rivers Brewery (p256)
» Ravens (p227)
» Franny's Cup & Saucer (p222)
» Table 128 (p237)

Best Places to Stay

» Mar Vista (p220)
» Victorian Gardens (p222)
» Apple Farm (p236)
» Andiron (p225)
» Redwood National Park (p260)

Why Go?

The craggy cliffs, towering redwoods and windswept bluffs of the north have little in common with California's other coastline. This is no Beach Boys' song; there are no bikinis and few surfboards. The jagged edge of the continent is wild, scenic and even slightly foreboding, where spectral fog and outsider spirit have fostered the world's tallest trees, most potent weed and a string of idiosyncratic two-stoplight towns. Visitors explore hidden coves with a blanket and bottle of local wine, scan the horizon for migrating whales and retreat at night to fire-warmed Victorians. The further north you travel on the region's winding two-lane blacktop, the more dominant the landscape becomes, with valleys of redwood, wide rivers and mossy, overgrown forests. Befitting this dramatic clash of land and water are its unlikely mélange of residents: timber barons and tree huggers, pot farmers and political radicals of every stripe.

When to Go

Eureka

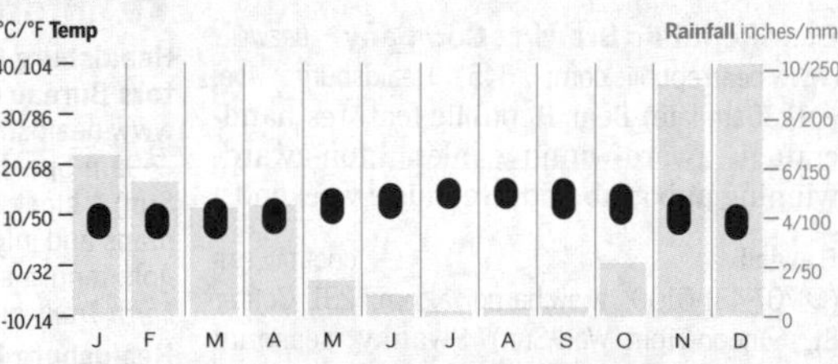

Jun–Jul The driest season in the Redwoods is spectacular for day hikes and big views.

Aug–Oct Warm weather and clear (or clearer) skies are the best for hiking the Lost Coast.

Dec–Apr Whales migrate off the coast. In early spring look for mothers and calves.

Getting Around

Although Hwy 1 is popular with cyclists and there are bus connections, you will almost certainly need a car to explore this region. Those headed to the far north and on a schedule should take Hwy 101, the faster, inland route and then cut over to the coast. Windy Hwy 1 hugs the coast, then cuts inland and ends at Leggett, where it joins Hwy 101. Neither Amtrak nor Greyhound serve cities on coastal Hwy 1.

Amtrak (☎800-872-7245; www.amtrakcalifornia.com) operates the *Coast Starlight* between Los Angeles and Seattle (see p519). From LA, buses connect to several North Coast towns including Leggett ($82, 11 hours, two daily) and Garberville ($84, 11½ hours, two daily).

Brave souls willing to piece together bus travel through the region will face a time-consuming headache, but connections are possible to almost every town in the region. **Greyhound** (☎800-231-2222; www.greyhound.com) runs buses from San Francisco to Santa Rosa ($22, 1¾ hours, one daily), Ukiah, ($40, three hours, one daily) Willits ($40, 3½ hours, one daily), Rio Dell (near Fortuna, $52.50, six hours, one daily), Eureka ($52.50, 6¾ hours, one daily) and Arcata ($52.20, seven hours, one daily). In Santa Rosa, **Golden Gate Transit** (☎707-541-2000; www.goldengatetransit.org) bus 80 serves San Rafael ($5.55, 1½ hours) and San Francisco ($8.80, 1¼ hours, 19 times daily), **Sonoma County Transit** (☎800-345-7433; www.sctransit.com) serves Sonoma County, and **Sonoma County Airport Express** (☎707 837 8700, 800 327-2024; www.airportexpressinc.com) operates buses to San Francisco ($32, 2¼ hours, 15 daily) and Oakland ($34, 2¼ hours, 10 daily) airports.

The **Mendocino Transit Authority** (MTA; ☎707-462-1422, 800-696-4682; www.4mta.org; fares $3.25-7.75) operates bus 65, which travels between Mendocino, Fort Bragg, Willits, Ukiah and Santa Rosa daily, with an afternoon return. Bus 95 runs between Point Arena and Santa Rosa, via Jenner, Bodega Bay and Sebastopol. Bus 54 connects Ukiah and Hopland on weekdays. Bus 75 heads north every weekday from Gualala to the Navarro River junction at Hwy 128, then runs inland through the Anderson Valley to Ukiah, returning in the afternoon. The North Coast route goes north from Navarro River junction to Albion, Little River, Mendocino and Fort Bragg, Monday to Friday. The best long distance option is a daily ride from Fort Bragg south to Santa Rosa via Willits and Ukiah ($21, three hours).

North of Mendocino County, the **Redwood Transit System** (☎707-443-0826; www.hta.org) operates buses ($2.75) Monday through Saturday between Scotia and Trinidad (2½ hours), stopping en route at Eureka (1¼ hours) and Arcata (1½ hours). **Redwood Coast Transit** (☎707-464-9314; www.redwoodcoasttransit.org) runs buses Monday to Saturday between Crescent City, Klamath ($1.50, one hour, five daily) and Arcata ($25, two hours, three time daily), with numerous stops along the way.

FAST FACTS

» **Population of Mendocino** 1000

» **Average temperature low/high in Mendocino** Jan 47/60°F, Jul 50/71°F

» **Mendocino to San Francisco** 155 miles, 3¼ hours

» **Mendocino to Los Angeles** 530 miles, nine hours

» **Mendocino to Eureka** 145 miles, three hours

COASTAL HIGHWAY 1

Down south it's called the 'PCH,' or Pacific Coast Hwy, but North Coast locals simply call it 'Hwy 1.' However you label it, get ready for a fabulous coastal drive, which cuts a winding course on isolated cliffs high above the crashing surf. Compared to the famous Big Sur coast, the serpentine stretch of Hwy 1 up the North Coast is more challenging, more remote and more *real*; passing farms, fishing towns and hidden beaches. Drivers use roadside pull-outs to scan the hazy Pacific horizon for migrating whales and explore a coastline dotted with rock formations that are relentlessly pounded by the surf. The drive between Bodega Bay and Fort Bragg takes four hours of daylight driving without stops. At night in the fog, it takes steely nerves and much, much longer. The most popular destination is the cliffside charmer of Mendocino.

Considering their proximity to the Bay Area, Sonoma and Mendocino counties remain unspoiled, and the austere coastal bluffs are some of the most spectacular in the country. But the trip north gets more rewarding and remote with every mile. By the time Hwy 1 cuts inland to join Hwy 101, the land along the Pacific – called the Lost Coast – the highway disappears and offers the state's best-preserved natural gifts.

Coastal accommodations (including campgrounds) can fill from Memorial Day to Labor Day and on fall weekends, and often require two-night stays, so reserve ahead. Try to visit

North Coast & Redwoods Highlights

1. Explore the largest stands of old growth redwood in **Humboldt Redwoods State Park** (p247)
2. Hike the remote and wild **Lost Coast** (p245)
3. Backpack under giants along **Redwood Creek** (p260)
4. Find a hidden cove on the **Sonoma Coast** (p217)
5. Get pampered at **Mendocino's B&Bs** (p225)
6. Drink the sampler at **Six Rivers Brewery** (p256), NorCal's best brewpub
7. Rent a canoe to float down the **Big River** (p225)
8. Visit immaculate botanical gardens in **Fort Bragg** (p229)
9. Tour the vineyards of the **Anderson Valley** (p236)
10. Stay at **Mar Vista** (p220), a plush and sustainable retreat

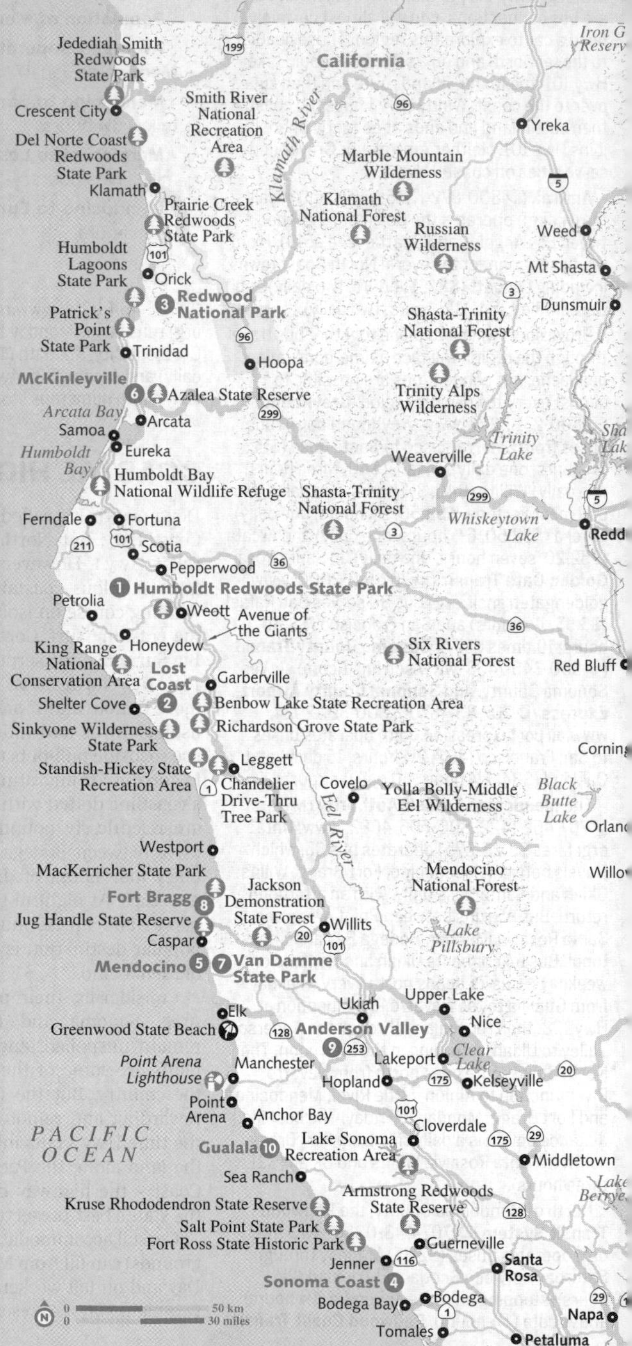

during spring or fall, especially in September and October; when the fog lifts, the ocean sparkles and most other visitors have gone home.

Bodega Bay

Bodega Bay is the first pearl in a string of sleepy fishing towns that line the North Coast and was the setting of Hitchcock's terrifying 1963 avian psycho-horror flick *The Birds*. The skies are free from bloodthirsty gulls today (though you best keep an eye on the picnic); it's Bay Area weekenders who descend en masse for extraordinary beaches, tide pools, whale-watching, fishing, surfing and seafood. Mostly a few restaurants, hotels and shops on both sides of Hwy 1, the downtown is not made for strolling, but it is a great base for exploring the endless nearby coves of the Sonoma Coast State Beach (p217).

Originally inhabited by the Pomo people, the bay takes its name from Juan Francisco de la Bodega y Quadra, captain of the Spanish sloop *Sonora,* which entered the bay in 1775. The area was then settled by Russians in the early 19th century, and farms were established to grow wheat for the Russian fur-trapping empire, which stretched from Alaska all the way down the coast to Fort Ross. The Russians pulled out in 1842, abandoning fort and farms, and American settlers moved in.

Hwy 1 runs through town and along the east side of Bodega Bay. On the west side, a peninsula resembling a crooked finger juts out to sea, forming the entrance to Bodega Harbor.

Sights & Activities

Surfing, beach combing and sportfishing are the main activities here – the latter requires advance booking. From December to April, the fishing boats host whale-watching trips, which are also good to book ahead. The excellent *Farm Trails* (www.farmtrails.org) guide at the Sonoma Coast Visitor Center has suggestions for tours of local ranches, orchards, farms and apiaries.

Bodega Head LOOKOUT

At the peninsula's tip, Bodega Head rises 265ft above sea level. To get there (and see the open ocean), head west from Hwy 1 onto Eastshore Rd, then turn right at the stop sign onto Bay Flat Rd. It's great for whale-watching. Landlubbers enjoy **hiking** above the surf, where several good trails include a 3.75-mile trek to Bodega Dunes Campground and a 2.2-mile walk to Salmon Creek Ranch. **Candy & Kites** (☎10am-5pm) is right along Hwy 1 in the middle of town – you can't miss it – selling kites to take advantage of all that wind.

Bodega Marine Laboratory & Reserve SCIENCE CENTER

(☎707-875-2211; www.bml.ucdavis.edu; 2099 Westside Rd; admission free; ⏲2-4pm Fri) Run by University of California (UC) Davis, this spectacularly diverse teaching and research reserve surrounds the functioning research lab, which has studied Bodega Bay since the 1920s. The 263-acre reserve hosts many marine environments, including rocky intertidal coastal areas, mudflats and sandflats, salt marsh, sand dunes and freshwater wetlands. On most Friday afternoons docents give tours of the lab and its aquaria.

Ren Brown Collection Gallery GALLERY

(www.renbrown.com; 1781 Hwy 1; ⏲10am-5pm Wed-Sun) The renowned collection of modern Japanese prints and California works at this small gallery is a tranquil escape from the elements.

Chanslor Riding Stables HORSEBACK RIDING

(☎707-875-3333; www.chanslor.com; 2660 Hwy 1, group rides $40-125) Just north of town, this friendly outfit leads horseback expeditions along the coastline and the rolling inland hills. Ron, the trip leader, is an amiable, sun-weathered cowboy straight from central casting; he recommends taking the Salmon Creek ride or calling ahead for weather-permitting moonlight rides. The 90-minute beach rides are donation based, and support a horse rescue program. Overnight trips in simple platform tents, which are excellent for families, can also be arranged. If you book a ride, you can park your RV at the ranch for free.

Bodega Bay Sportfishing Center FISHING, WHALE-WATCHING

(☎707-875-3344; www.bodegacharters.com; 1410 Bay Flat Rd) Beside the Sandpiper Cafe, this outfit organizes full-day fishing trips ($135) and whale-watching excursions (three hours adult/child $35/25). It also sells bait, tackle and fishing licenses. Call ahead to ask about recent sightings.

BLOODTHIRSTY BIRDS OF BODEGA BAY

Bodega Bay has the enduring claim to fame as the setting for Alfred Hitchcock's *The Birds*. Although special effects radically altered the actual layout of the town, you still get a good feel for the supposed site of the farm owned by Mitch Brenner (played by Rod Taylor). The once-cozy Tides Restaurant, where much avian-caused havoc occurs in the movie, is still there but since 1962 it has been transformed into a vast restaurant complex. Venture 5 miles inland to the tiny town of Bodega and you'll find two icons from the film: the schoolhouse and the church. Both stand just as they did in the movie – a crow overhead may make the hair rise on your neck.

Coincidentally, right after production of *The Birds* began, a real-life bird attack occurred in Capitola, the sleepy seaside town south of Santa Cruz. Thousands of seagulls ran amok, destroying property and attacking people.

Bodega Bay Surf Shack SURFING, KAYAKING
(www.bodegabaysurf.com; 1400 N Hwy 1; surfboards per day $15, kayaks per 4hr single/double $45/65 ⏲10am-6pm Mon-Fri, 9am-7pm Sat & Sun) If you want to get on the water, this easygoing one-stop shop has all kinds of rentals, lessons and good local information.

Festivals & Events

Bodega Seafood, Art & Wine Festival FOOD, WINE
(www.winecountryfestivals.com) In late August, this festival of food and drink brings together the best beer- and wine-makers of the area, tons of seafood and activities for kids.

Bodega Bay Fishermen's Festival CULTURAL
(www.bbfishfest.org) At the end of April, this festival culminates in a blessing of the fleet, a flamboyant parade of vessels, an arts-and-crafts fair, kite-flying and feasting.

Sleeping

There's a wide spread of options – RV and tent camping, quaint motels and fancy hotels. All fill up early during peak seasons. Campers should consider heading just north of town to the state-operated sites.

Bodega Bay Lodge & Spa LODGE $$$
(☎707-875-3525, 888-875-2250; www.bodegabaylodge.com; 103 Hwy 1; r $300-470; @🛜🏊) Bodega's plushest, this small oceanfront resort has indulgent accommodations and a price tag to match. There is an ocean-view swimming pool, a whirlpool and a state-of-the-art fitness club. In the evenings it hosts wine tastings. The more expensive rooms have commanding views, but all have balconies, high-thread-count sheets, feather pillows and the usual amenities of a full-service hotel. The other pluses on-site include a golf course, Bodega Bay's best spa and a fine-dining restaurant, the **Duck Club** (☎707-875-3525; mains $16-37; ⏲7:30-11am & 6-9pm), which is the fanciest dining in town.

Bodega Harbor Inn MOTEL $$
(☎707-875-3594; www.bodegaharborinn.com; 1345 Bodega Ave; r $90-155; 🛜🐾) Half a block inland from Hwy 1, surrounded by grassy lawns and furnished with both real and faux antiques, this modest blue-and-white shingled motel is the town's most economical option. Pets are allowed in some rooms for a fee of $15 plus a security deposit of $50. Freestanding cottages have BBQs.

Chanslor Guest Ranch RANCH $$
(☎707-875-2721; www.chanslorranch.com; 2660 Hwy 1; furnished tents & eco-cabins $75-125, r $350) A mile north of town, this working horse ranch has three rooms and options for upscale camping. Wildlife programs and guided horse tours make this one sweet place, with sweeping vistas across open grasslands to the sea. If you take a horse ride, you can negotiate a great deal for camping in your own tent.

Sonoma County Regional Parks CAMPGROUND $
(☎707-565-2267; www.sonoma-county.org/parks; tent 7 RV sites without hookups $30) There are a few walk-in sites at the **Doran Regional Park** (201 Doran Beach Rd), at the quiet Miwok Tent Campground, and **Westside Regional Park** (2400 Westshore Rd), which is best for RVs. It caters primarily to boaters and has windy exposures, beaches, hot showers, fishing and boat ramps. Both are heavily used. Excellent camping is also available at the Sonoma Coast State Beach (p217).

Eating & Drinking

For the old-fashioned thrill of seafood by the docks there are two options: **Tides Wharf & Restaurant** (835 Hwy 1; breakfast $6-12, lunch $12-22, dinner $15-25; 7:30am-9:30pm Mon-Thu, 7:30am-10pm Fri, 7am-10pm Sat, 7am-9:30pm Sun;) and **Lucas Wharf Restaurant & Bar** (595 Hwy 1; mains $14-25; 11:30am- 9pm Mon-Fri, 11am-10pm Sat;). Both have views and similar menus of clam chowder, fried fish and coleslaw and markets for picnic supplies. Tides boasts a great fish market, though Lucas Wharf feels less like a factory. Don't be surprised if a bus pulls up outside either of them.

Spud Point Crab Company SEAFOOD $
(www.spudpointcrab.com; 1860 Bay Flat Rd; mains $4-10; 9am-5pm Thu-Tue;) In the classic tradition of dockside crab shacks, Spud Point serves salty-sweet crab cocktails and *real* clam chowder, served at picnic tables overlooking the marina. Take Bay Flat Rd to get here.

Terrapin Creek Cafe & Restaurant CALIFORNIAN $$
(707-875-2700; www.terrapincreekcafe.com; 1580 Eastshore Dr; mains $18-20; 11am-2pm & 4:30-9pm Thu-Sun;) Bodega Bay's most exciting upscale restaurant is run by a husband-wife team who espouse the slow food movement and serve local dishes sourced from the surrounding area. Modest comfort-food offerings like the pulled pork sandwich are artfully executed, while the Dungeness crab salad is fresh, briny and perfect. Jazz and warm light complete the atmosphere.

Sandpiper Restaurant SEAFOOD $$
(www.sandpiperrestaurant.com; 1410 Bay Flat Rd; mains $13-26; 8am-8pm Sun-Thu, to 8:30pm Fri & Sat) Popular with the locals, Sandpiper serves breakfast, straightforward seafood and chowder that can be ordered in a formidable 'Viking Bowl' (downing two of these wins you a free t-shirt).

Dog House AMERICAN $
(573 Hwy 1; dishes $5-9; 11am-6pm) Load up on Vienna beef dogs, hand-cut fries and shakes made with hand-scooped ice cream. There's even a view.

Gourmet Au Bay WINE BAR $$
(11am-6pm Thu-Tue) The back deck of this wine bar offers a salty breeze with local zinfandel.

Information

Sonoma Coast Visitor Center (707-875-3866; www.bodegabay.com; 850 Hwy 1; 9am-5pm Mon-Thu & Sat, 9am-6pm Fri, 10am-5pm Sun) Opposite the Tides Wharf. The best reason to stop by is for a copy of the *North Coaster*, a small-press indie newspaper of essays and brilliant insight on local culture.

Sonoma Coast State Beach

Stretching 17 miles north from Bodega Head to Vista Trail, the glorious **Sonoma Coast State Beach** (707-875-3483) is actually a series of beaches separated by several beautiful rocky headlands. Some beaches are tiny, hidden in little coves, while others stretch far and wide. Most of the beaches are connected by vista-studded coastal hiking trails that wind along the bluffs. Exploring this area makes an excellent day-long adventure, so bring a picnic. Be advised however: the surf is often too treacherous to wade, so keep an eye on children. While this system of beaches and parks has some camping, you can't just pitch a tent anywhere; most are for day-use only.

Sights & Activities

Beaches

The following beaches are listed from south to north.

Salmon Creek Beach BEACH
Situated around a lagoon, this has 2 miles of hiking and good waves for surfing.

Portuguese Beach & Schoolhouse Beach BEACH
Both are very easy to access and have sheltered coves between rocky outcroppings.

Duncan's Landing BEACH
Small boats unload near this rocky headland in the morning. A good place to spot wild flowers in the spring.

Shell Beach BEACH
A boardwalk and trail leads out to a stretch perfect for tide-pooling and beachcombing.

Goat Rock BEACH
Famous for its colony of harbor seals, lazing in the sun at the mouth of the Russian River.

Sleeping

Bodega Dunes CAMPGROUND $
(800-444-7275; www.reserveamerica.com; 3095 Hwy 1, Bodega Bay; tent & RV sites $35, $8

day use) The largest campground in the Sonoma Coast State Beach system of parks, it is also closest to Bodega Bay. It gets a lot of use. Sites are in high dunes and have hot showers but be warned – the fog horn sounds all night.

Wright's Beach Campground CAMPGROUND $
(☎800-444-7275; www.reserveamerica.com; tent & RV sites $35, $8 day use) Of the few parks that allow camping along Sonoma Coast State Beach, this is the best, even though sites lack privacy. Sites can be booked six months in advance, and numbers 1–12 are right on the beach. There are BBQ pits for day use and it's a perfect launch for sea kayakers. Everyone else, stay out of the water; according to camp hosts the treacherous rip tides claim a life every season.

Willow Creek Environmental Campground CAMPGROUND $
(tent sites $20) The beautiful environmental campground is under a cathedral-like grove of second-growth redwoods on Willow Creek Rd, inland from Hwy 1 on the southern side of the Russian River Bridge. To reach the sites, walk the **Pomo Canyon trail** and emerge into wildflower-studded meadows with exquisite views of the Russian River and vistas that extend south as far as Pt Reyes on a clear day. Note that Willow Creek has no running water, though it is possible to filter water from the river. It is usually open April to November.

Jenner

Perched on the hills looking out to the Pacific and above the mouth of the Russian River, tiny Jenner offers access to the coast and the Russian River wine region (see p193). A **harbor-seal colony** sits at the river's mouth and pups are born here from March to August. There are restrictions about getting too close to the chubby, adorable pups – handling them can be dangerous and cause the pups to be abandoned by their mothers. Volunteers answer questions along the roped-off area where day trippers can look on at a distance. The best way to see them is by kayak and most of the year you will find a truck renting kayaks at the rivers edge. Heading north on Hwy 1 you will begin driving on one of the most beautiful, windy stretches of California highway. You'll also probably lose cell-phone service – possibly a blessing.

Sleeping & Eating

Jenner Inn & Cottages INN $$
(☎707-865-2377; www.jennerinn.com; 10400 Hwy 1; r incl breakfast creekside $118-178, ocean-view $178-278, cottages $228-278; @) It's difficult to sum up this collection of properties dispersed throughout Jenner – some are in fairly deluxe ocean-view cottages with kitchen and ready-to-light fireplaces, others are small upland near a creek. All have the furnishings of a stylish auntie from the early 1990s.

TOP CHOICE **River's End** CALIFORNIAN $$$
(☎707-865-2484; www.rivers-end.com; 11048 Hwy 1; lunch mains $13-26, dinner mains $25-39; ⏲noon-3pm & 5-8:30pm Thu-Mon; ✎) Unwind in style at this picture-perfect restaurant, perched on a cliff overlooking the river's mouth and the grand sweep of the Pacific Ocean. It serves world-class meals at world-class prices, but the real reward is the view. Its ocean-view **cottages** (r & cottages $120-200) are wood paneled and have no TVs, wi-fi or phones. Children under 12 are not recommended.

Café Aquatica CAFE $
(www.cafeaquatica.com; 11048 Hwy 1; sandwiches $10-13; 📶) This is the kind of North Coast coffee shop you've been dreaming of: fresh pastries, fog-lifting coffee and chatty locals. The expansive view of the Russian River from the patio and strangely appropriate new-age tunes are bonuses.

Fort Ross State Historic Park

A curious glimpse into Tsarist Russia's exploration of the California coast, the salt-washed buildings of Fort Ross State Historic Park offer a fascinating insight into the pre-American Wild West. It's a quiet, picturesque place with a riveting past.

In March 1812, a group of 25 Russians and 80 Alaskans (including members of the Kodiak and Aleutian tribes) built a wooden fort here, near a Kashaya Pomo village. The southernmost outpost of the 19th-century Russian fur trade on America's Pacific coast, Fort Ross was established as a base for sea-otter hunting operations and trade with Alta California, and for growing crops for Russian settlements in Alaska. The Russians dedicated the fort in August 1812 and occupied it until 1842, when it was abandoned because the sea otter population had been decimated and agricultural production had never taken off.

Fort Ross State Historic Park (☎707-847-3286; www.fortrossstatepark.org; 19005 Hwy 1; per car $8; ☉10am-4:30pm), an accurate reconstruction of the fort, is 11 miles north of Jenner on a beautiful point. The original buildings were sold, dismantled and carried off to Sutter's Fort during the Gold Rush. The **visitor center** (☎707-847-3437) has a great museum with historical displays and an excellent bookshop on Californian and Russian history. Ask about hikes to the Russian cemetery.

On **Fort Ross Heritage Day**, the last Saturday in July, costumed volunteers bring the fort's history to life; check the website www.parks.ca.gov or call the visitor center for other special events.

Timber Cove Inn (☎707-847-3231, 800-987-8319; www.timbercoveinn.com; 21780 N Hwy 1; r from $155, ocean-view from $183) is a dramatic and quirky '60s-modern seaside inn that was once a top-of-the-line luxury lodge. Though the price remains high, it has slipped a bit. The rustic architectural shell is still stunning, though, and a duet of tinkling piano and crackling fire fills the lobby. The quirky rooms facing the ocean have a tree house feel, with rustic redwood details, balconies, fireplaces and lofted beds. Even those who don't bunk here should wander agape in the shadow of Benny Bufano's 93ft peace statue, a spectacular totem on the edge of the sea. The expensive restaurant on-site is nothing to write home about.

Stillwater Cove Regional Park (☎reservations 707-565-2267; www.sonoma-county.org/parks; 22455 N Hwy 1; tent & RV sites $28), 2 miles north of Timber Cove, has hot showers and hiking under Monterey pines. Sites 1, 2, 4, 6, 9 and 10 have ocean views.

Salt Point State Park

If you stop at only one park along the Sonoma Coast, make it 6000-acre **Salt Point State Park** (☎707-847-3221; per car $8), where sandstone cliffs drop dramatically into the kelp-strewn sea and hiking trails crisscross windswept prairies and wooded hills, connecting pygmy forests and coastal coves rich with tidepools. The 6-mile-wide park is bisected by the San Andreas Fault – the rock on the east side is vastly different from that on the west. Check out the eerily beautiful *tafonis*, honeycombed-sandstone formations, near Gerstle Cove. For a good roadside photo op, there's a pullout at mile-marker 45, with views of decaying redwood shacks, grazing goats and headlands jutting out to the sea.

Though many of the day use areas have been closed off due to budget cuts, trails lead off Hwy 1 pull-outs to views of the pristine coastline. The platform overlooking **Sentinel Rock** is just a short stroll from the Fisk Mill Cove parking lot at the park's north end. Further south, seals laze at **Gerstle Cove Marine Reserve**, one of California's first underwater parks. Tread lightly around tidepools and don't lift the rocks: even a glimpse of sunlight can kill some critters. If it's springtime, you *must* see **Kruse Rhododendron State Reserve**. Growing abundantly in the forest's filtered light, magnificent, pink rhododendrons reach heights of over 30ft, making them the tallest species in the world; turn east from Hwy 1 onto Kruse Ranch Rd and follow the signs.

Two campgrounds, **Woodside** and **Gerstle Cove** (☎800-444-7275; www.reserveamerica.com; tent & RV sites $35), both signposted off Hwy 1, have campsites with cold water. Inland Woodside is well protected by Monterey pines. Gerstle Cove's trees burned over a decade ago and have only grown halfway back, giving the gnarled, blackened trunks a ghostly look when the fog twirls between the branches.

Sea Ranch

Though not without its fans, the exclusive community of Sea Ranch might well be termed Stepford-by-the-Sea. The ritzy subdivision that sprawls 10 miles along the coast is connected with a well-watched network of private roads. Approved for construction prior to the existence of the watchdog Coastal Commission, the community was a precursor to the concept of 'slow growth,' with strict zoning laws requiring that houses be constructed of weathered wood only. According to *The Sea Ranch Design Manual:* 'This is not a place for the grand architectural statement; it's a place to explore the subtle nuances of fitting in...' Indeed. Though there are some lovely and recommended short-term rentals here, don't break any community rules – like throwing wild parties – or security will come knockin'. For supplies and gasoline, go to Gualala.

After years of litigation, public throughways onto private beaches have been legally mandated and are now well marked. Hiking trails lead from roadside parking lots to the sea and along the bluffs, but don't dare trespass on adjacent lands. **Stengel Beach** (Hwy 1 Mile 53.96) has a beach-access staircase, **Walk-On Beach** (Hwy 1 Mile 56.53) provides wheelchair access and **Shell Beach** (Hwy 1 Mile 55.24) also has beach-access stairs; parking at all three areas costs $6. For hiking details, including maps, contact the **Sea Ranch Association** (www.tsra.org).

Sea Ranch Lodge (707-785-2371, www.searanchlodge.com; 60 Sea Walk Dr; r incl breakfast from $212;), a marvel of '60s-modern California architecture, has spacious, luxurious, minimalist rooms, many with dramatic views to the ocean; some have hot tubs and fireplaces. For the past few years the entire lodge was slated for a decadent stem-to-stern renovation, but the last update was that they couldn't find a bank to float the loan. The fine contemporary **restaurant** (lunch mains $12-16, dinner mains $22-35; 8am-9pm) has a menu for discerning guests; expect everything from duck breast to local fish tacos. North of the lodge you'll see Sea Ranch's iconic nondenominational **chapel**; it's on the inland side of Hwy 1, mileage marker 55.66. For those short on time or on a budget, this is the best reason to pull over in Sea Ranch.

Depending on the season, it can be surprisingly affordable to rent a house in Sea Ranch; contact **Rams Head Realty** (www.ramshead-realty.com), **Sea Ranch Rentals** (www.searanchrentals.com), or **Sea Ranch Escape** (www.searanchescape.com).

Gualala & Anchor Bay

At just 2½ hours north of San Francisco, Gualala – pronounced by most locals as 'Wah-*la*-la' – is northern Sonoma coast's hub for a weekend getaway as it sits square in the middle of the 'Banana Belt,' a stretch of coast known for unusually sunny weather. Founded as a lumber town in the 1860s, the downtown stretches along Hwy 1 with a bustling commercial district that has a great grocery store and some cute, slightly upscale shops. Just north, quiet Anchor Bay has several inns, a tiny shopping center and, heading north, a string of secluded, hard-to-find beaches. Both are excellent jumping-off points for exploring the area.

Sights & Activities

Gualala Arts Center ARTS CENTER

(707-884-1138; www.gualalaarts.org; 9am-4pm Mon-Fri, noon-4pm Sat & Sun) Inland along Old State Rd, at the south end of town and beautifully built entirely by volunteers, this center hosts changing exhibitions, organizes the Art in the Redwoods Festival in late August and has loads of info on local art.

Adventure Rents CANOEING, KAYAKING

(707-884-4386, 888-881-4386; www.adventurerents.com) In the summer, a sand spit forms at the mouth of the river, cutting it off from the ocean and turning it into a warm-water lake. This outfit rents **canoes** (2 hours/half-day/full day $70/80/90) and **kayaks** (2 hours/half-day/full day $35/40/45) and provides instruction.

Seven miles north of Anchor Bay, pull off at mileage marker 11.41 for **Schooner Gulch**. A trail into the forest leads down cliffs to a sandy beach with tidepools. Bear right at the fork in the trail to reach iconic **Bowling Ball Beach**, where low tide reveals rows of big, round rocks resembling bowling balls. Consult tide tables for Arena Cove. The forecast low tide must be lower than +1.5ft on the tide chart for the rocks to be visible.

Sleeping & Eating

Of the two towns, Gualala has more services and is a more practical hub for exploring – there are a bunch of good motels and a pair of nice grocery stores. Get fresh veggies at the **farmers market** (Gualala Community Center; 10am-12:30pm Sat Jun-Oct) and organic supplies and local wine at the **Anchor Bay Village Market** (35513 S Hwy 1).

TOP CHOICE **Mar Vista Cottages** COTTAGES $$$

(707-884-3522, 877-855-3522; www.marvistamendocino.com; 35101 S Hwy 1, Anchor Bay; cottages from $155;) The elegantly renovated 1930s fishing cabins of Mar Vista is a simple, stylish seaside escape with a vanguard commitment to sustainability. The harmonious environment, situated in the sunny 'Banana Belt' of the North Coast, is the result of pitch perfect details: linens are line-dried over lavender, guests browse the organic vegetable garden to harvest their own dinner and chickens cluck around the grounds laying the next morning's breakfast. It often requires two-night stays.

North Coast Country Inn B&B $$
(☎707-884-4537, 800-959-4537; www.northcoastcountryinn.com; 34591 S Hwy 1; r incl breakfast $195-225; @🐾) Perched on an inland hillside beneath towering trees, surrounded by lovely gardens, the perks of this place begin with the gregarious owner and a hot tub. The six spacious country-style rooms are decorated with lovely prints and boast exposed beams, fireplaces, board games and private entrances.

Gualala Point Regional Park CAMPGROUND $
(www.sonoma-county.org/parks; 42401 S Hwy 1, Gualala; tent & RV sites $28) Shaded by a stand of redwoods and fragrant California Bay Laurel trees, a short trail connects this creekside campground to the windswept beach. The quality of sites, including several secluded hike-in spots, makes it the best drive-in camping on this part of the coast.

St Orres Inn INN $$
(☎707-884-3303; www.saintorres.com; 36601 Hwy 1; B&B $95-135, cottages from $140; 🐾) Famous for its unusual Russian-inspired architecture: dramatic rough-hewn timbers and copper domes, there's no place quite like St Orres. On the property's 90 acres, hand-built cottages range from rustic to luxurious. The inn's fine **restaurant** (☎707 884 3335; dinner mains $40-50) serves inspired Californian cuisine in one of the coast's most romantic rooms. Decidedly spendy, sure, but the Andouille-stuffed pheasant with mushroom risotto is *so* worth it.

Gualala River Redwood Park COUNTY CAMPGROUND $
(☎707-884-3533; www.gualalapark.com; day use $6, tent & RV sites $22-42; ☐Memorial Day-Labor Day) Another excellent Sonoma County Park. Inland along Old State Rd, you can camp and do short hikes along the river.

Laura's Bakery & Taqueria MEXICAN $
(☎707-884-3175; 38411 Robinson Reef Rd at Hwy 1; mains $7-12; ☐7am-7pm Mon-Sat; ☐) Laura's is a refreshing, low-key break from Hwy 1 upscale dining. The menu's taqueria staples are fantastic (the Baja style fish tacos are a steal) but the fresh *mole* dishes and distant ocean view are the real surprises.

Bones Roadhouse BBQ $$
(www.bonesroadhouse.com; 39350 S Hwy 1, Gualala; mains $10-20; ⏲11:30am-9pm Sun-Thu, to 10pm Fri & Sat) Savory smoked meats make this Gualala's best lunch. On weekends, a codgerly blues outfit may be growling out 'Mustang Sally.'

ℹ Information

Redwood Coast Chamber of Commerce
(www.redwoodcoastchamber.com) In Gualala; has local information.

Point Arena

This laid-back little town combines creature comforts with relaxed, eclectic California living and is the first town up the coast where the majority of residents don't seem to be retired Bay Area refugees. Sit by the docks a mile west of town at Arena Cove and watch surfers mingle with fishermen and hippies.

Point Arena Lighthouse LIGHTHOUSE
(www.pointarenalighthouse.com; adult/child $7.50/1; ☐10am-3:30pm winter, to 4:30pm summer) Two miles north of town, this 1908 lighthouse stands 10 stories high and is the only lighthouse in California you can ascend. Check in at the museum, then climb the 145 steps to the top and see the Fresnel lens and the jaw-dropping view. After $1.5-million renovations, the building and adjoining fog signal building are looking fantastic. True light house buffs should look into staying at the plain three-bedroom former **Coast Guard homes** (☎707-882-2777; houses $125-300) onsite. They're a quiet, wind-swept retreat.

Stornetta Public Lands NATURE AREA
For fabulous bird-watching, hiking on terraced rock past sea caves and access to hid-

TOP WHALE-WATCHING SPOTS

Watch for spouts, sounding and breaching whales and pods. Anywhere coastal will do, but the following are some of the north coast's best:

» Bodega Head (p215)

» Mendocino Headlands State Park (p225)

» Jug Handle State Reserve (p228)

» MacKerricher State Park (p232)

» Shelter Cove & The Lost Coast (p246)

» Trinidad Head Trail (p257)

» Klamath River Overlook (p261)

den coves, head 1 mile down Lighthouse Rd from Hwy 1 and look for the Bureau of Land Management (BLM) signs on the left indicating these 1132-acre public lands.

Sleeping & Eating

Wharf Master's Inn HOTEL **$$$**
(707-882-3171, 800-932-4031; www.wharfmasters.com; 785 Port Rd; r $105-255;) This is a cluster of small, modern rooms on a cliff overlooking fishing boats and a stilting pier. Tidy and very clean, rooms have the character of a chain hotel.

Coast Guard House Inn INN **$$**
(707-882-2442; www.coastguardhouse.com; 695 Arena Cove; r $105-225) Come here if you want to soak up old-world ocean side charm and are willing to deal with historic plumbing. It's a 1901 Cape Cod–style house and cottage, with water-view rooms.

TOP CHOICE **Franny's Cup & Saucer** PATISSERIE **$**
(707-882-2500; www.frannyscupandsaucer.com; 213 Main St; pastries $1-5; 8am-4pm Wed-Sat;) The cutest patisserie on this stretch of coast is run by Franny and her mother, Barbara (a veteran of Chez Panisse). The fresh berry tarts and rich chocolaty desserts seem too beautiful to eat, until you take the first bite and immediately want to order another. Several times a year they pull out all the stops for a Sunday garden brunch ($28).

Pizzas N Cream PIZZA **$**
(www.pizzasandcream.com; 790 Port Rd; pizzas $10-18; 11:30am-9pm;) In Arena Cove, this friendly place whips up exquisite pizzas and fresh salads, and serves beer and ice cream.

Arena Market ORGANIC DELI **$**
(www.arenaorganics.org; 183 Main St; 7:30am-7pm Mon-Sat, 8:30am-6pm Sun;) The deli in front of this fully stocked organic grocer makes excellent to-go veg options, often sourced from local farms.

Drinking & Entertainment

215 Main BAR
(www.facebook.com/215Main; 215 Main; 2pm-2am Tue-Sun) Head to this open, renovated historic building to drink local beer and wine. There's jazz on the weekends.

Arena Cinema CINEMA
(www.arenatheater.org; 214 Main St) shows mainstream, foreign and art films in a beautifully restored movie house. Sue, the ticket seller, has been in that booth for 40 years. Got a question about Point Arena? Ask Sue.

Information

Public library (707-882-3114; 225 Main St; noon-6pm Mon-Fri, to 3pm Sat) Free internet access.

Manchester

Follow Hwy 1 for about 7 miles north of Point Arena, through gorgeous rolling fields dropping down from the hills to the blue ocean, and a turnoff leads to **Manchester State Beach**, a long, wild stretch of sand. The area around here is remote and beautiful (only one grocery store), but it's a quick drive to Point Arena for more elaborate provisions.

Ross Ranch (707-877-1834; www.elkcoast.com/rossranch) at Irish Beach, another 5 miles to the north, arranges two-hour horseback beach ($60) and mountain ($50) rides; reservations recommended.

TOP CHOICE **Victorian Gardens** (707-882-3606; www.innatvictoriangardens.com; 14409 S Hwy 1; r $240-310) is wihout doubt the finest B&B on the coast. This lovingly restored 1904 farmhouse (smartly expanded by the owner, an architect) sits on 92 exquisitely situated acres just north of Manchester. Every detail here is picture perfect: the spacious gardens that provide fresh flowers and vegetables for gourmet meals, the rustic green house dining room which opens to the sea breeze and comfortable common spaces, decorated with a discerningly elegant mix of antique pieces and modern furniture. There's even a Picasso. For larger groups, the owners can prepare five-course authentic Italian dinners with carefully paired wines.

Mendocino Coast KOA (707-882-2375, www.manchesterbeachkoa.com; tent/RV sites from $35/50, cabins $68-78;) is an impressive private campground with tightly packed campsites beneath enormous Monterey pines, a cooking pavilion, hot showers, a hot tub and bicycles. The cabins are a great option for families who want to get the camping experience without roughing it.

A quarter-mile west, the sunny, exposed campground at **Manchester State Park** (tent & RV sites $25-35) has cold water and quiet right by the ocean. Sites are nonreservable. Budget cuts have all but eliminated ranger service.

Elk

Thirty minutes north of Point Arena, itty-bitty Elk is famous for its stunning cliff-top views of 'sea stacks,' towering rock formations jutting out of the water. There is *nothing* to do after dinner, so bring a book – and sleeping pills if you're a night owl. And you can forget about the cell phone, too; reception here is nonexistent. Elk's **visitor center** (5980 Hwy 1; ⌚11am-1pm Sat & Sun mid-Mar–Oct) has exhibits on the town's logging past. At the southern end of town, **Greenwood State Beach** sits where Greenwood Creek meets the sea. **Force 10** (☎707-877-3505; www.force10tours.com) guides ocean-kayaking tours ($115).

Tucked into a tiny clapboard house looking across the road to the ocean, the **Elk Studio Gallery & Artist's Collective** (www.artists-collective.net; 6031 S Hwy 1; ☎10am-5pm) is cluttered with tons of local art – everything from carvings and pottery to photography and jewelry.

Several upmarket B&Bs take advantage of the views. **Harbor House Inn** (☎707-877-3203, 800-720-7474; www.theharborhouseinn.com; 5600 S Hwy 1; r & cottages incl breakfast & dinner $360-490; 📶), located in a 1915 Arts and Crafts–style mansion built by the town's lumber baron, has gorgeous cliff-top gardens and a private beach. The view from the Lookout, Oceansong and Shorepine rooms are the best. Rates include a superb four-course dinner for two in the ocean view room with a lauded wine list.

Griffin House (☎707-877-3422; www.griffinn.com; 5910 S Hwy 1; cottages $130-160, ocean-view cottages $145-325; @📶) is an unpretentious cluster of simple, powder-blue bluffside cottages with wood-burning stoves.

A new-agey feel pervades the Buddha-dotted grounds and ocean-view cottages at **Greenwood Pier Inn** (☎707-877-9997; www.greenwoodpierinn.com; 5928 S Hwy 1; d incl breakfast $185-335; 📶🐾). If you can look past the trippy art work, the rooms have fireplaces and private decks. Its cafe is open for lunch and dinner.

Everyone swears by excellent **Queenie's Roadhouse Cafe** (☎707-877-3285; 6061 S Hwy 1; dishes $6-10; ☎8am-3pm Thu-Mon; 🖉) for a creative range of breakfast (try the wild rice waffles) and lunch treats. Sweet, little **Bridget Dolan's** (☎707-877-1820; 5910 S Hwy 1; mains $10-15; ⌚4:30-8pm) serves straight-forward cookin' like pot pies, and bangers and mash.

Van Damme State Park

Three miles south of Mendocino, this gorgeous 1831-acre **park** (☎707-937-5804; www.parks.ca.gov; day use $6) draws divers, beach-combers and kayakers to its easy-access beach. It's also known for its **pygmy forest**, where the acidic soil and an impenetrable layer of hardpan just below the surface create a bonsai forest with decades-old trees growing only several feet high. A wheelchair-accessible boardwalk provides access to the forest. To get there, turn east off Hwy 1 onto Little River Airport Rd, a half-mile south of Van Damme State Park, and drive for 3 miles. Alternatively, hike or bike up from the campground on the 3.5-mile **Fern Canyon Scenic Trail**, which crosses back and forth over Little River.

The **visitor center** (☎707-937-4016; ⌚10am-3pm Fri-Sun) has nature exhibits, videos and programs; a half-hour marsh loop trail starts nearby.

Two pretty **campgrounds** (☎800-444-7275; www.reserveamerica.com; tent & RV sites $35; 📶) are excellent for family car camping. They both have hot showers: one is just off Hwy 1, the other is in a highland meadow, which has lots of space for kids to run around. Nine **environmental campsites** (tent sites $25) lie just a 1¼-mile hike up Fern Canyon; there's untreated creek water.

For sea-cave kayaking tours ($50), contact **Lost Coast Kayaking** (☎707-937-2434; www.lostcoastkayaking.com).

Mendocino

Leading out to a gorgeous headland, Mendocino is the North Coast's salt-washed gem, with B&Bs surrounded by rose gardens, white-picket fences and New England–style redwood water towers. Bay Area weekenders walk along the headland among berry bramble and wildflowers, where cypress trees stand over dizzying cliffs. Nature's power is evident everywhere, from drift-wood-littered fields and cave tunnels to the raging surf. The town itself is full of cute shops – no chains – and has earned the nickname 'Spendocino,' for its upscale goods. In summer, fragrant bursts of lavender and jasmine permeate the foggy wind, tempered by salt air from the churning surf, which is never out of earshot.

Built by transplanted New Englanders in the 1850s, Mendocino thrived late into the

Mendocino

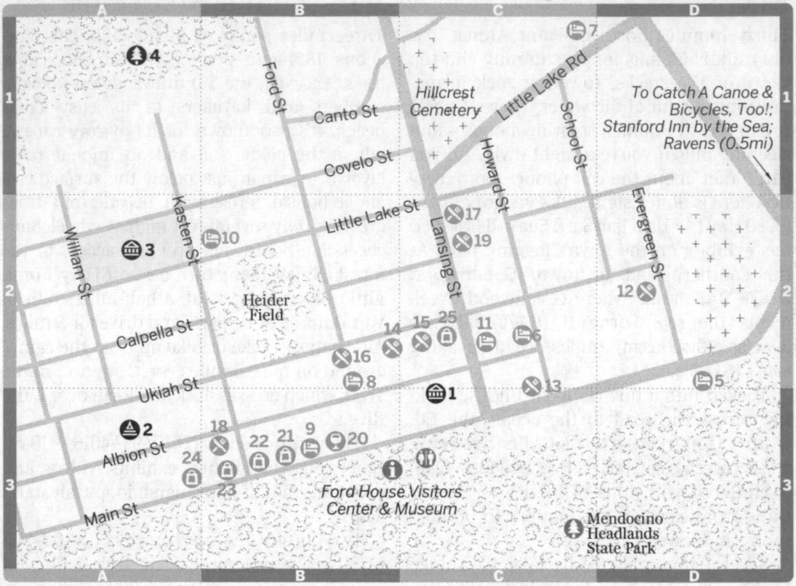

0 — 200 m
0 — 0.1 miles

Canto St
Covelo St
Little Lake St
Calpella St
Ukiah St
Albion St
Main St
Ford St
Kasten St
William St
Lansing St
Howard St
School St
Evergreen St
Little Lake Rd
Hillcrest Cemetery
Heider Field
To Catch A Canoe & Bicycles, Too!; Stanford Inn by the Sea; Ravens (0.5mi)
Ford House Visitors Center & Museum
Mendocino Headlands State Park

19th century, with ships transporting redwood timber from here to San Francisco. The mills shut down in the 1930s, and the town fell into disrepair until it was rediscovered in the 1950s by artists and bohemians. Today the culturally savvy, politically aware, well-traveled citizens welcome visitors, but eschew corporate interlopers – don't look for a Big Mac or try to use your cell phone. To avoid crowds, come midweek or in the low season, when the vibe is mellower – and prices more reasonable.

Sights

Mendocino is lined with all kinds of interesting galleries, which hold openings on the second Saturday of each month from 5pm to 8pm.

Mendocino Art Center GALLERY
(www.mendocinoartcenter.org; 45200 Little Lake St; ⏲10am-5pm Apr-Oct, to 4pm Tue-Sat Nov-Mar) Behind a yard of twisting iron sculpture, the city's art center takes up a whole tree-filled block, hosting exhibitions, the 81-seat Helen Schonei Theatre and nationally renowned art classes. This is also where to pick up the *Mendocino Arts Showcase* brochure, a quarterly publication listing all the happenings and festivals in town.

Kelley House Museum MUSEUM
(www.mendocinohistory.org; 45007 Albion St; admission $2; ⏲11am-3pm Thu-Tue Jun-Sep, Fri-Mon Oct-May) With a research library and changing exhibits on early California and Mendocino, the 1861 museum hosts seasonal, two-hour walking tours for $10; call for times.

Point Cabrillo Lighthouse LIGHTHOUSE
(www.pointcabrillo.org; Point Cabrillo Dr; admission free; ⏲11am-4pm Sat & Sun Jan & Feb, daily Mar-Oct, Fri-Mon Nov & Dec) Restored in 1909, this lighthouse stands on a 300-acre wildlife preserve north of town, between Russian Gulch and Caspar Beach. The head lighthouse keeper's home is now a simple lodging (p226). Guided walks of the preserve leave at 11am on Sundays from May to September.

Kwan Tai Temple TEMPLE
(www.kwantaitemple.org; 45160 Albion St) Peering in the window of this 1852 temple reveals an old altar dedicated to the Chinese god of war. Tours are available by appointment.

Activities

Wine tours, whale watching, shopping, hiking, cycling: there's more to do in the area than a thousand long weekends could accom-

Mendocino

plish. For navigable river and ocean kayaking, launch from tiny Albion, which hugs the north side of the Albion River mouth, 5 miles south of Mendocino.

TOP CHOICE Catch A Canoe & Bicycles, Too! BICYCLE & CANOE RENTAL
(www.stanfordinn.com; Comptche-Ukiah Rd & Hwy 1; 9am-5pm) This friendly riverside outfit south of town rents bikes, kayaks and stable outrigger canoes for trips up the 8-mile Big River tidal estuary, the longest undeveloped estuary in Northern California. No highways or buildings, only beaches, forests, marshes, streams, abundant wildlife and historic logging sites. Bring a picnic and a camera to enjoy the ramshackle remnants of century-old train trestles and majestic blue herons.

Mendocino Headlands State Park COASTAL PARK
A spectacular park surrounds the village, with trails crisscrossing the bluffs and rocky coves. Ask at the visitor center about guided weekend walks, including spring wildflower walks and whale-watching.

Festivals & Events

For a complete list of Mendocino's many festivals, check with the visitor center or www.gomendo.com.

Mendocino Whale Festival WHALE-WATCHING
(www.mendowhale.com) Early March, with wine and chowder tastings, whale-watching and music.

Mendocino Music Festival MUSIC
(www.mendocinomusic.com) Mid-July, with orchestral and chamber music concerts on the headlands, children's matinees and open rehearsals.

Mendocino Wine & Mushroom Festival FOOD, WINE
(www.mendocino.com) Early November, guided mushroom tours and symposia.

Sleeping

Standards are high and so are prices; two-day minimums often crop up on weekends. Fort Bragg, 10 miles north, has cheaper lodgings (see p230). All B&B rates include breakfast; only a few places have TVs. For a range of cottages and B&Bs, contact **Mendocino Coast Reservations** (707-937-5033, 800-262-7801; www.mendocinovacations.com; 45084 Little Lake St; 9am-5pm).

TOP CHOICE Andiron COTTAGES $$
(800-955-6478; www.theandiorn.com; 6051 N Hwy 1, Mendocino; r $99-149;) Styled with hip vintage decor, this cluster of 1950s roadside cottages is a refreshingly playful option amid the stuffy cabbage-rose and

lace aesthetic of Mendocino. Each cabin houses two rooms with complementing themes: 'Read' has old books, comfy vintage chairs, and hip retro eyeglasses while the adjoining 'Write' features a huge chalkboard and ribbon typewriter. A favorite for travelers? 'Here' and 'There,' themed with old maps, 1960s airline paraphernalia and collectables from North Coast's yesteryear.

MacCallum House Inn B&B $$$
(707-937-0289, 800-609-0492; www.maccallumhouse.com; 45020 Albion St; r from $204;) The finest B&B option in the center of town. When the weather is warm, the gardens surrounding the refurbished 1882 barn are a riot of color. There are bright and cheerful cottages, and a modern luxury home, but the most memorable space here is within one of Mendocino's iconic historic water towers – where living quarters fill the ground floor, a sauna is on the second and there's a view of the coast from the top. All accommodations have cushy extras like robes, DVD players, stereos and plush linens.

Stanford Inn by the Sea INN $$
(707-937-5615, 800-331-8884; www.stanfordinn.com; cnr Hwy 1 & Comptche-Ukiah Rd; r $195-305;) This masterpiece of a lodge standing on 10 lush acres has wood-burning fireplaces, original art, stereos and top-quality mattresses in every room. Figure in a stroll in the organic gardens, where they harvest food for the excellent on-site restaurant, the solarium-enclosed pool and the hot tub, and it's a sublime getaway.

Brewery Gulch Inn B&B $$$
(800-578-4454; www.brewerygulchinn.com; 9401 N Hwy 1, Mendocino; r $210-450;) Just south of Mendocino, this fresh place has 10 modern rooms (all with flat-screen televisions, iPod docs, gas fireplaces and spa bathtubs), and guests enjoy luxury touches like feather beds and leather reading chairs. The hosts pour heavily at the complimentary wine hour and leave out sweets for midnight snacking. Made-to-order breakfast is served in a small dining room overlooking the distant water.

Sea Gull Inn B&B $$
(707-937-5204, 888-937-5204; www.seagullbb.com; 44960 Albion St; r $130-165, barn $185;) With pristine white bedspreads, organic breakfasts and a flowering garden, this cute, converted motel is extremely comfortable, fairly priced, and right in the thick of the action.

Mendocino Hotel HISTORIC HOTEL $$
(707-937-0511, 800-548-0513; www.mendocinohotel.com; 45080 Main St; r with bath $135-295, without bath $95-125, ste $325-395; P) Built in 1878 as the town's first hotel, this is like a piece of the Old West. The modern garden suites sit behind the main building and don't have a shade of old-school class, but are modern and serviceable. Some wheelchair accessible.

Packard House B&B $$$
(707-937-2677, 888-453-2677; www.packardhouse.com; 45170 Little Lake St; r $190-275) Decked out in contemporary style, this place is Mendocino's sleekest B&B choice – chic and elegant, with beautiful fabrics, colorful minimalist paintings and limestone bathrooms.

Alegria B&B $$
(707-937-5150, 800-780-7905; www.oceanfrontmagic.com; 44781 Main St; r $159-189, r with ocean view $239, cottages $179-269) Perfect for a romantic hideaway, rooms have ocean-view decks and wood-burning fireplaces; outside a gorgeous path leads to a private beach. Ever-so-friendly innkeepers rent simpler rooms in a 1900s Arts and Crafts place across the street.

Headlands Inn B&B $$$
(707-937-4431; www.headlandsinn.com; cnr Albion & Howard Sts; r $139-249) Homey saltbox with featherbeds and fireplaces. Quiet dorm rooms have sea views and staff will bring you the gourmet breakfast in bed.

Lighthouse Inn at Point Cabrillo HISTORIC B&B $$
(707-937-6124; 866-937-6124; www.pointcabrillo.org; Point Cabrillo Dr; r $152-279) On 300 acres, in the shadow of Point Cabrillo Lighthouse, the lightkeeper's house and several cottages have been turned into B&B rooms. Rates include a private night tour of the lighthouse and a five-course breakfast.

Joshua Grindle Inn B&B $$$
(707-937-4143, 800-474-6353; www.joshgrin.com; 44800 Little Lake Rd; r $189-299) Mendocino's oldest B&B has bright, airy, uncluttered rooms in an 1869 house, a weathered saltbox cottage and water tower. Enjoy goodies like fluffy muffins, warm hospitality and gorgeous gardens.

Glendeven B&B $$$
(☎707-937-0083; www.glendeven.com; 8205 N Hwy 1; r $135-320;) Elegant estate 2 miles south of town with organic gardens.

Russian Gulch State Park CAMPGROUND $
(☎reservations 800-444-7275; www.reserveamerica.com; tent & RV sites $35) In a wooded canyon 2 miles north of town, with secluded drive-in sites, hot showers, a small waterfall and the Devil's Punch Bowl (a collapsed sea arch).

Eating

With quality to rival Napa Valley, the influx of Bay Area weekenders have fostered an excellent dining scene that enthusiastically espouses organic, sustainable principles. Make reservations. Gathering picnic supplies is easy at the central markets and the **farmers market** (Howard & Main St; ☎noon-2pm Fri May-Oct).

TOP CHOICE **Café Beaujolais** CALIFORNIAN, FUSION $$
(☎707-937-5614; www.cafebeaujolais.com; 961 Ukiah St; mains lunch $9-16, dinner $24-36; 11:30am-2:30pm Wed-Sun, dinner from 5:30pm nightly) Mendocino's iconic, beloved country-Cal–French restaurant occupies an 1896 house restyled into a monochromatic urban-chic dining room, perfect for holding hands by candlelight. The refined, inspired cooking draws diners from San Francisco, who make this the centerpiece of their trip. The locally sourced menu changes with the seasons, but the Petaluma duck breast served with crispy skin is a gourmand's delight.

Ravens CALIFORNIAN $$$
(☎707-937-5615; www.ravensrestaurant.com; Stanford Inn, Comptche-Ukiah Rd; breakfast $11-15, mains $22-35; 8-10:30am Mon-Sat, to noon Sun, dinner 5:30-10pm;) Ravens brings haute-contemporary concepts to a completely vegetarian and vegan menu. Produce comes from the inn's own idyllic organic gardens, and the bold menu takes on everything from sea-palm strudel and portabella sliders to decadent (guilt-free) deserts.

MacCallum House Restaurant CALIFORNIAN $$$
(☎707-937-0289; www.maccallumhouse.com; 45020 Albion St; cafe dishes $12-16, mains $25-42; 8:15-10am Mon-Fri, to 11am Sat & Sun, 5:30-9pm daily;) Sit on the veranda or fireside for a romantic dinner of all-organic game, fish or risotto primavera. Chef Alan Kantor makes *everything* from scratch and his commitment to sustainability and organic ingredients is nearly as visionary as his menu. The cafe menu, served at the Grey Whale Bar, is one of Mendocino's few four-star bargains.

Garden Bakery BAKERY $
(☎707-937-0282; 10450 Lansing; baked goods $3-6; 9am-4pm) Nearly every corner of Mendocino gets explored by hordes, but this little garden-side bakery still feels like a hidden gem. To describe the quality of the baked goods would invite hyperbole: they are *a-ma-zing*. The menu changes with the seasons and the baker's whim; one day, you're trying not to inhale the savory, cabbage-stuffed German pastry (a family recipe), on another you'll find apple cheddar croissants. If you show up early enough you'll get a taste of their renowned bear claw. If you don't find this place at first, keep looking: the bakery is located off the street, accessible by sidewalks that cut through the block.

Mendocino Cafe CALIFORNIAN, FUSION $$
(www.mendocinocafe.com; 10451 Lansing St; lunch mains $12-15, dinner mains $12-24; 11:30am-8pm;) One of Mendocino's few midpriced dinner spots also serves lovely alfresco lunches on its ocean-view deck surrounded by roses. Try the fish tacos or the Thai burrito. At dinner there's grilled steak and seafood.

Patterson's Pub PUB $$
(www.pattersonspub.com; 10485 Lansing St; mains $10-15 11am-11pm Mon-Fri, brunch 10am-2pm Sat & Sun) If you pull into town late and you're hungry, you'll thank your lucky stars for this place; it serves quality pub grub – fish and chips, huge burgers and dinner salads – with cold beer. The only spoiler to the traditional Irish pub ambience is the plethora of flat-screen TVs.

Moosse Cafe CALIFORNIAN $$
(☎707-937-4323; www.themoosse.com; 390 Kasten St; lunch mains $12-16, dinner mains $22-28; noon-2:30pm & 5:30-8:30pm;) The blond woodwork and starched linen napkins set a relaxed yet elegant tone for top-notch Cal-French cooking. Try the cioppino in saffron-fennel-tomato broth at dinner; lunch is more casual. Note that it keeps variable hours in the winter and on slow weekdays.

Ledford House MEDITERRANEAN $$
(☎707-937-0282; www.ledfordhouse.com; 3000 N Hwy 1, Albion; mains $19-30; 5-8pm Wed-Sun;

) Watch the water pound the rocks and the sun set out of the Mendocino hubbub (8 miles south) at this friendly Cal-Med bistro. Try the cassoulet or the gnocchi. It's a local hangout and gets hoppin' with live jazz most nights.

Mendosa's MARKET $
(www.harvestmarket.com; 10501 Lansing St; 8am-9pm) The town's biggest grocery store has legit organic credentials, an excellent cold food bar and great cheese and meat.

Mendocino Market DELI $
(45051 Ukiah St; sandwiches $6-9; 11am-5pm Mon-Fri, to 4pm Sat & Sun;) Pick up huge deli sandwiches and picnics here.

Lu's Kitchen INTERNATIONAL $
(707-937-4939; 45013 Ukiah St; mains $8-10; 11:30am-5:30pm;) Rustles up fab organic veggie burritos in a tiny shack; outdoor-only tables.

Drinking

Have cocktails at the **Mendocino Hotel** (45080 Main St) or the **Grey Whale Bar** (45020 Albion St)at the MacCallum House Inn.

Patterson's Pub PUB
(www.pattersonspub.com; 10485 Lansing St) This boisterous, inviting, Irish-style bar has a friendly staff and a good vibe.

Dick's Place DIVE BAR
(45080 Main St) A bit out of place among the fancy-pants shops downtown, but an excellent spot to check out the *other* Mendocino and do shots with rowdy locals.

Moody's Coffee Bar COFFEE SHOP
(10450 Lansing St; 6am-8pm;) Moody's covers the essentials: strong coffee, wi-fi and the *New York Times*.

Shopping

Mendocino's walkable streets are great for shopping, and the ban on chain stores ensures unique, often upscale gifts. There are many small galleries in town where one-of-a-kind artwork is for sale.

Compass Rose Leather LEATHER GOODS
(45150 Main St) From hand-tooled belts and leather bound journals to purses and peg-secured storage boxes, the craftsmanship here is unquestionable.

Out Of This World OUTDOOR & SCIENCE SUPPLIES
(45100 Main St) Birders, astronomy buffs and science geeks head directly to this telescope, binocular and science-toy shop.

Village Toy Store TOYS
(10450 Lansing St) Get a kite to fly on Bodega head or browse the old-world selection of wooden toys and games that you won't find in the chains – hardly anything requires batteries.

Gallery Bookshop BOOKS
(www.gallerybookshop.com; 319 Kasten St) Stocks a great selection of books on local topics, titles from California's small presses and specialized outdoor guides.

Twist CLOTHING
(45140 Main St) Twist stocks ecofriendly, natural-fiber clothing and lots of locally made clothing and toys.

Moore Used Books SECONDHAND BOOKS
(990 Main St) An excellent bad weather hideout, the stacks here have over 10,000 used titles. The shop is in an old house at the far east end of Main Street.

Information

Ford House Visitor Center & Museum (707-937-5397; www.gomendo.com; 735 Main St; suggested donation $2; 11am-4pm) Maps, books, information and exhibits, including a scale model of 1890 Mendocino.

Mendocino Coast Clinics (707-964-1251; 205 South St; 9am-5pm Mon-Fri, to 8pm Wed, 9am-1pm Sat) Nonemergencies.

Jug Handle State Reserve

Between Mendocino and Fort Bragg, Jug Handle preserves an **ecological staircase** that you can view on a 5-mile (round-trip) self-guided nature trail. Five wave-cut terraces ascend in steps from the seashore, each 100ft and 100,000 years removed from the previous one, and each with its own distinct geology and vegetation. One of the terraces has a pygmy forest, similar to the better-known example at Van Damme State Park (p223). Pick up a printed guide detailing the area's geology, flora and fauna from the parking lot. The reserve is also a good spot to stroll the headlands, whale-watch or lounge on the beach. It's easy to miss the entrance; watch for the turnoff, just north of Caspar.

Jug Handle Creek Farm & Nature Center (☎707-964-4630; www.jughandlecreekfarm.com; tent sites $12, r & cabins adult $40-50, child $15, student $28-33; 🐾) is a nonprofit 39-acre farm with rustic cabins and hostel rooms in a 19th-century farmhouse. Call ahead about work-stay discounts. Drive 5 miles north of Mendocino to Caspar; the farm is on the east side of Hwy 1. Take the second driveway after Fern Creek Rd.

Fort Bragg

In the past, Fort Bragg was Mendocino's ugly stepsister, home to a lumber mill, a scrappy downtown and blue-collar locals who gave a cold welcome to outsiders. Since the mill closure in 2002, the town has started to reinvent itself, slowly warming to a tourism-based economy. What to do with the seaside mill site is the talk of the town, running the gamut from progressive ideas like a marine research center or university to disastrous ones like a condo development, a world-class golf course or (gasp!) another mill. Regardless, the effect on Fort Bragg is likely to be profound. Follow the progress at www.fortbraggmillsite.com.

In the meantime, Fort Bragg's downtown continues to develop as an unpretentious alternative to Mendocino, even if the southern end of town is hideous. Unlike the *entire* franchise-free 180-mile stretch of Coastal Hwy 1 between here and the Golden Gate, southern Fort Bragg is blighted by McDonalds, Starbucks and other Anywhere, USA chain stores polluting the coastal aesthetic. Put on blinkers and don't stop till you're downtown, where you'll find better hamburgers and coffee, old-school architecture and residents eager to show off their little town.

Twisting Hwy 20 provides the main access to Fort Bragg from the east, and most facilities are near Main St, a 2-mile stretch of Hwy 1. Franklin St runs parallel, one block east.

Sights & Activities

Fort Bragg has the same banner North Coast activities as Mendocino – beach combing, surfing, hiking – but basing yourself here is much cheaper and a little less quaint. The wharf lies at Noyo Harbor – the mouth of the Noyo River – south of downtown where you can find whale-watching cruises and deep-sea fishing trips.

NORTH COAST BEER TOUR

The craft breweries of the North Coast don't mess around – bold hop profiles, Belgium-style ales and smooth lagers are regional specialties, and they're produced with style. Some breweries are better than others, but the following tour makes for an excellent long weekend of beer tasting in the region.

» Ukiah Brewing Company (p238), Ukiah

» Anderson Valley Brewing Company (p236), Boonville.

» North Coast Brewing Company (p231), Fort Bragg

» Six Rivers Brewery (p256), McKinleyville

» Eel River Brewing (p248), Fortuna

TOP CHOICE Skunk Train HISTORIC TRAIN
(☎707-964-6371, 866-866-1690; www.skunktrain.com; adult/child $49/24) Fort Bragg's pride and joy, the vintage train got its nickname in 1925 for its stinky gas-powered steam engines, but today the historic steam and diesel locomotives are odorless. Passing through redwood-forested mountains, along rivers, over bridges and through deep mountain tunnels, the trains run from both Fort Bragg and Willits (p240) to the midway point of Northspur, where they turn around (if you want to go to Willits, plan to spend the night). The depot is downtown at the foot of Laurel St, one block west of Main St.

Mendocino Coast Botanical Gardens GARDENS
(☎707-964-4352; www.gardenbythesea.org; 18220 N Hwy 1; adult/child/senior $14/5/10; ⏰9am-5pm Mar-Oct, to 4pm Nov-Feb; 🐾) This gem of Northern California displays native flora, rhododendrons and heritage roses. The succulent display alone is amazing and the organic garden is harvested by volunteers to feed area residents in need. The serpentine paths wander along 47 seafront acres south of town. Primary trails are wheelchair-accessible.

Glass Beach BEACH
Named for (what's left of) the sea-polished glass in the sand, remnants of its days as a city dump, this beach is now part of MacKerricher State Park where visitors comb

the sand for multicolored glass. Take the headlands trail from Elm St, off Main St, but leave the glass; as a part of the park system, visitors are not supposed to pocket souvenirs.

All-Aboard Adventures FISHING, WHALE-WATCHING
(☎707-964-1881; www.allaboardadventures.com; 32400 N Harbor Dr) Captain Tim leads crabbing and salmon fishing trips (five hours, $80) and whale watching during the whale migration (two hours, $35).

Northcoast Artists Gallery GALLERY
(www.northcoastartists.org; 362 N Main St; ⏲10am-6pm) An excellent local arts cooperative that has the useful *Fort Bragg Gallery & Exhibition Guide,* which directs you to other galleries around town. Openings are the first Fridays of the month. Antique and book stores line Franklin St, one block east.

FREE **Triangle Tattoo & Museum** MUSEUM
(www.triangletattoo.com; 356B N Main St; admission free; ☎noon-7pm) Shows multicultural, international tattoo art.

Guest House Museum MUSEUM
(☎707-964-4251; www.fortbragghistory.org; 343 N Main St; admission $2; ⏲1-3pm Mon, 11am-2pm Tue-Fri, 10am-4pm Sat-Sun May-Oct, 11am-2pm Thu-Sun) A majestic Victorian structure built in 1892, displays historical photos and relics of Fort Bragg's history. As hours vary, call ahead.

Pudding Creek Trestle BOARDWALK
The walk along the Pudding Creek Trestle, north of downtown, is fun for the whole family.

Festivals & Events

Fort Bragg Whale Festival WILDLIFE
(www.mendowhale.com) Held on the third weekend in March, with microbrew tastings, crafts fairs and whale-watching trips.

Paul Bunyan Days COMMUNITY FESTIVAL
(www.paulbunyandays.com) Held on Labor Day weekend in September, celebrate California's logging history with a logging show, square dancing, parade and fair.

Sleeping

Fort Bragg's lodging is cheaper than Mendocino's, but most of the motels along noisy Hwy 1 don't have air-conditioning, so you'll hear traffic through your windows. Most B&Bs do not have TVs and they all include breakfast. The usual chains abound.

Shoreline Cottages COTTAGES $$
(☎707-964-2977; www.shoreline-cottage.com; 18725 N Hwy 1; r $120-155;) Low-key and pet-friendly four-person rooms and cottages with kitchens surround a central tree-filled lawn. The family rooms are a good bargain, and suites feature modern art work and clean sight lines. All rooms have docks for your iPod, snacks and access to a library of DVDs.

Country Inn B&B $
(☎707-964-3737; www.beourguests.com; 18725 N Hwy 1; r $90-145;) This unpretentious bed & breakfast is right in the middle of town and is an excellent way to dodge the chain motels for a good value stay. The lovely family hosts are welcoming and easy going, and can offer good local tips. Breakfast can be delivered to your room and at night you can soak in a hot tub out back.

Weller House Inn B&B $$
(☎707-964-4415, 877-893-5537; www.wellerhouse.com; 524 Stewart St; r $130-195;) Rooms in this beautifully restored 1886 mansion have down comforters, good mattresses and fine linens. The water tower is the tallest structure in town – and it has a hot tub at the top! Breakfast is in the massive redwood ballroom.

Grey Whale Inn B&B $$
(☎707-964-0640, 800-382-7244; www.greywhaleinn.com; 615 N Main St; r $100-195;) Situated in a historic building on the north side of town, this comfortable, family-run inn has simple, straightforward rooms that are good value – especially for families.

California Department of Forestry CAMPING $
(☎707-964-5674; 802 N Main St; ⏲8am-4:30pm Mon, to noon Tue-Thu) Come here for maps, permits and camping information for the Jackson State Forest, east of Fort Bragg, where camping is free.

Eating

Similar to the lodging scene, the food in Fort Bragg is less spendy than Mendocino, and there are a number of good options. Self-caterers should try the **farmers market** (cnr Laurel & Franklin Sts; ⏲3:30-6pm Wed May-Oct) downtown or the **Harvest Market** (☎707-

964-7000; cnr Hwys 1 & 20; ⏱5am-11pm) for the best groceries.

TOP CHOICE **Piaci Pub & Pizzeria** PIZZA $
(www.piacipizza.com; 120 W Redwood Ave; pizza $8-12; ⏱11am-4pm Mon-Fri, 4-9pm Sun-Thu, 4-10pm Fri & Sat) Fort Bragg's must-visit pizzeria is the place to chat up locals while enjoying microbrews and a menu of fantastic wood-fired, brick-oven, 'adult' pizzas (a sight more sophisticated than your average Dominos pie). The 'Gustoso' – an immaculate selection with Chevre, pesto and seasonal pears – speaks to the carefully orchestrated thin-crust pies. It's tiny, loud and fun, but expect to wait at peak times.

Mendo Bistro AMERICAN $$
(☎707-964-4974; www.mendobistro.com; 301 N Main St; mains $14-25; ⏱5-9pm; 👪) This dining option gets packed with a young crowd on the weekend, offering a choose-your-own-adventure menu, where you select a meat, a preparation and an accompanying sauce from a litany of options. The loud, bustling 2nd-story room is big enough for kids to run around and nobody will notice.

Chapter & Moon AMERICAN $
(32150 N Harbor Dr; mains $8-18; ☎8am-8pm) Overlooking Noyo Harbor, this small cafe serves blue-plate American cooking: chicken and dumplings, meatloaf melts, and fish with yam chips. Save room for fruit cobbler.

North Coast Brewing Company BREWPUB $$
(www.northcoastbrewing.com; 444 N Main St; mains $8-25; ⏱7am-9:30pm Sun-Thu, to 10pm Fri & Sat) Though thick, rare slabs of steak and a list of specials demonstrate that they take the food as seriously as the bevvies, it's burgers and garlic fries that soak up the fantastic selection of handcrafted brews.

Headlands Coffeehouse DELI $
(www.headlandscoffeehouse.com; 120 E Laurel St; dishes $4-8; ⏱7am-10pm Mon-Sat, to 7pm Sun; 📶🥗) The town's best cafe is in the middle of the historic downtown, with high ceilings and lots of atmosphere. The menu gets raves for the Belgian waffles, homemade soups, veggie-friendly salads, panini and lasagna.

🍃 **Living Light Café** VEGAN, RAW $
(☎707-964-2420; 444 N Main St; mains $5-11; ⏱8am-5:30pm Mon-Sat, to 4pm Sun; 🥗) As an extension of the renowned Living Light Culinary Institute, one of the nation's leading raw food schools, this bright cafe serves a tasty to-go menu that's a sight better than bland crudités, like the Sicilian-style pizza on a spouted seed crust, raw desserts and tangy cold soups.

Eggheads BREAKFAST $
(www.eggheadsrestaurant.com; 326 N Main St; mains $8-13; ⏱7am-2pm) Enjoy the *Wizard of Oz* theme as you tuck into one of 50 varieties of omelet, crepe or burrito, some with local Dungeness crab.

La Playa MEXICAN $
(542 N Main St; mains $6-12; ⏱10am-9pm Mon-Sat) Down-home, no-frills Mexican cookin' right by the train tracks – try the *carne asada* (seasoned, roasted beef).

Cap'n Flint's SEAFOOD $$
(32250 N Harbor Dr; mains $11; ⏱11am-9pm) Skip the overpriced Wharf Restaurant (aka Silver's), and head next door to this unpretentious place to eat the same fried fish for less.

Drinking & Entertainment

Caspar Inn LIVE MUSIC
(www.casparinn.com; 14957 Caspar Rd; cover $3-25 Tue-Sat) Square in the middle of Mendocino and Fort Bragg, off Hwy 1, this jumpin' roadhouse rocks out the reggae, hip-hop, rockabilly, jam bands and international acts. The best live music venue on this stretch of the coast, it's worth checking out the calendar, which is posted on bulletin boards and public spaces throughout the area. Hours vary according to the events and the season.

North Coast Brewing Company BREWERY
(www.northcoastbrewing.com; 444 N Main St) Of all the many breweries up the coast, this might be the most *serious*, with an arsenal of handcrafted, bold brews. If you order the sampler, designate a driver.

Gloriana Opera Company THEATER COMPANY
(www.gloriana.org; 721 N Franklin St) Stages musical theater and operettas.

Shopping

There's plenty of window-shopping in Fort Bragg's compact downtown, including a string of antique shops along Franklin St.

Outdoor Store OUTDOOR EQUIPMENT
(www.mendooutdoors.com; 247 N Main St) If you're planning on camping on the coast or

exploring the Lost Coast, this is the best outfitter in the region, stocking detailed maps of the region's wilderness areas, fuel for stoves and high-quality gear.

Mendocino Vintage ANTIQUES
(www.mendocinovintage.com; 344 N Franklin St) Of the antique shops on Franklin, this is the hippest by a long shot, with a case full of vintage estate jewelry, antique glassware and old local oddities.

Information

Fort Bragg-Mendocino Coast Chamber of Commerce (www.fortbragg.com, www.mendocinocoast.com; 332 N Main St; per 15min $1; ⌚9am-5pm Mon-Fri, to 3pm Sat) Internet access.

Mendocino Coast District Hospital (☎707-961-1234; 700 River Dr; ⌚24hr) Emergency room.

Getting There & Around

Fort Bragg Cyclery (☎707-964-3509; www.fortbraggcyclery.com; 221a N Main St) Rents bicycles.

Mendocino Transit Authority (MTA; ☎707-462-1422, 800-696-4682; www.4mta.org) Runs local route 5 'BraggAbout' buses between Noyo Harbor and Elm St, north of downtown ($1). Service runs throughout the day.

Mackerricher State Park

Three miles north of Fort Bragg, the **MacKerricher State Park** (☎707-964-9112; www.parks.ca.gov) preserves 9 miles of pristine rocky headlands, sandy beaches, dunes and tidepools.

The **visitor center** (⌚10am-4pm Mon-Fri & 9am-6pm Sat & Sun summer, 9am-3pm rest of year) sits next to the whale skeleton at the park entrance. Hike the **Coastal Trail** along dark-sand beaches and see rare and endangered plant species (tread lightly). **Lake Cleone** is a 30-acre freshwater lake stocked with trout and visited by over 90 species of birds. At nearby **Laguna Point** an interpretive disabled-accessible boardwalk overlooks harbor seals and, from December to April, migrating whales. **Ricochet Ridge Ranch** (☎707-964-7669; www.horse-vacation.com; 24201 N Hwy 1) offers horseback-riding trips through redwoods or along the beach ($45 for 90 minutes).

Popular **campgrounds** (☎800-444-2725; www.reserveamerica.com; tent & RV sites $35), nestled in pine forest, have hot showers and water; the first-choice reservable tent sites are numbers 21 to 59. Ten superb, secluded walk-in tent sites (numbers 1 to 10) are first-come, first-served.

Westport

If sleepy Westport feels like the peaceful edge of nowhere, that's because it is. The last hamlet before the Lost Coast, on a twisting 15-mile drive north of Fort Bragg, it is the last town before Hwy 1 veers inland on the 22-mile ascent to meet Hwy 101 in Leggett. For details on accessing the Lost Coast's southernmost reaches from Westport, see p246.

Head 1.5 miles north of town for the ruggedly beautiful **Westport-Union Landing State Beach** (☎707-937-5804; tent sites $25), which extends for 3 miles on coastal bluffs. A rough hiking trail leaves the primitive campground and passes by tidepools and streams, accessible at low tide. Bring your own water.

Simple accommodations in town include the blue-and-red, plastic-flower-festooned **Westport Inn** (☎707-964-5135; 37040 N Hwy 1; r incl breakfast from $77).

TOP CHOICE **Westport Hotel & Old Abalone Pub** (☎877-964-3688; www.westporthotel.us; Hwy 1; r $90-165, ste $125-200, cabins $140-195; wi-fi) has been elegantly refashioned under new proprietors; the place is quiet enough to have a motto which brags 'You've finally found nowhere.' The rooms are bright and beautiful – feather duvets, hardwood furniture, simple patterns – and enjoy excellent views. The classy historic pub downstairs is the only option for dinner, so be thankful it's a delicious sampling of whimsical California fusions (like turduken sausage and buttermilk potatoes and rock shrimp mac and cheese) and hearty, expertly presented pub food.

Howard Creek Ranch (☎707-964-6725; www.howardcreekranch.com; 40501 N Hwy 1; r $90-165, ste $125-200, cabins $75-200; wi-fi), sitting on 60 stunning acres of forest and farmland abutting the wilderness, has accommodations in an 1880s farmhouse or a carriage barn, whose way-cool redwood rooms have been expertly handcrafted by the owner. Rates include full breakfast. Bring hiking boots, not high heels.

ALONG HIGHWAY 101

To get into the most remote and wild parts of the North Coast on the quick, eschew winding Hwy 1 for inland Hwy 101, which runs north from San Francisco as a freeway, then as a two- or four-lane highway north of Sonoma County, occasionally pausing under the traffic lights of small towns.

Know that escaping the Bay Area at rush hour (weekdays between 4pm and 7pm) ain't easy. You might sit bumper-to-bumper through Santa Rosa or Willits, where trucks bound for the coast turn onto Hwy 20.

Although Hwy 101 may not look as enticing as the coastal route, it's faster and less winding, leaving you time along the way to detour into Sonoma and Mendocino counties' wine regions (Mendocino claims to be the greenest wine region in the country), explore pastoral Anderson Valley, splash about Clear Lake or soak at hot-springs resorts outside Ukiah – time well spent indeed!

Hopland

Cute Hopland is the gateway to Mendocino County's wine country. Hops were first grown here in 1866, but Prohibition brought the industry temporarily to a halt. Today, booze drives the local economy again with wine tasting as the primary draw.

Sights & Activities

For an excellent weekend trip, use Hopland as a base for exploring the regional wineries. More information about the constantly growing roster of wineries is available at www.destinationhopland.com. Find a map to the wine region at www.visitmendocino.com.

Real Goods Solar Living Center SOLAR ENERGY CENTER
(www.solarliving.org; 13771 S Hwy 101; 9am-5pm;) The progressive, futuristic 12-acre campus at the south end of town is largely responsible for the areas bold green initiates. There's no charge but the suggested donation is $3 to $5.

SIP! Mendocino TASTING ROOM
(www.sipmendocino.com; 13420 S Hwy 101; 11am-6pm) In central Hopland, this is a friendly place to get your bearings, pick up a map to the region and taste several wines without navigating all the back roads. Amiable proprietors guide you through a tour of 18 wines with delectable appetizer pairings and a blossom-filled courtyard.

Saracina WINERY
(www.saracina.com; 11684 S Hwy 101; 10am-5pm) The highlight of a tour here is the descent into the cool caves. Sensuous whites are all biodynamcially and sustainably farmed.

Fetzer Vineyards Organic Gardens WINERY
(www.fetzer.com; 13601 Eastside Rd; 9am-5pm) Fetzer's sustainable practices have raised the bar, and their gardens are lovely. The wines are excellent value.

Brutocao Schoolhouse Plaza TASTING ROOM
(www.brutocaoschoolhouseplaza.com; 13500 S Hwy 101; 11am-8pm) In central Hopland, this place has bocce courts and bold reds – a perfect combo.

Graziano Family of Wines WINERY
(www.grazianofamilyofwines.com; 13251 S Hwy 101; 10am-5pm) Specializes in 'Cal-Ital' wines – nebbiolo, dolcetto, barbera and sangiovese – at some great prices.

Sleeping & Eating

Hopland Inn HISTORIC HOTEL $$
(707-744-1890, 800-266-1891; www.hoplandinn.com; 13401 S Hwy 101; r $180;) If you're spending the night in town, your only choice is a good one: the 1890 inn in the middle of town. Enjoy bevvies from the full bar downstairs in the cozy, wood-paneled library.

Bluebird Cafe AMERICAN $
(707-744-1633; 13340 S Hwy 101; breakfast & lunch $5-12, dinner $12-17; 7am-2pm Mon-Thu, to 7pm Fri-Sun;) For conservative tastes, this classic American diner serves hearty breakfasts, giant burgers and homemade pie (the summer selection of peach-blueberry pie is dreamy). For a more exciting culinary adventure, try the wild game burgers, including boar with apple chutney and elk with a bite of horseradish.

Clear Lake

With over 100 miles of shoreline, Clear Lake is the largest naturally occurring freshwater lake in California (Tahoe is bigger, but crosses the Nevada state line). In summer the warm water thrives with algae, giving it a murky green appearance and creating a

TOP CLEAR LAKE WINERIES

From north to south, the following four wineries are the best; some offer tours by appointment.

» **Ceago Vinegarden** (www.ceago.com; 5115 E Hwy 20, Nice; ⏲10am-6pm) Ceago (cee-*ay*-go) occupies a spectacular spot on the north shore, and pours biodynamic, fruit-forward wines.

» **Wildhurst Vineyards** (www.wildhurst.com; 3855 Main St, Kelseyville; ⏲10am-5pm) The best wine on the lake, but lacks atmosphere. Try the sauvignon blanc.

» **Ployez Winery** (1171 S Hwy 29, Lower Lake; ⏲11am-5pm) Above-average *méthode champenoise* sparkling wines; surrounded by farmland.

» **Langtry Estate Vineyards** (21000 Butts Canyon Rd, Middletown; ⏲11am-5pm) The most beautiful vineyard. Try the port.

fabulous habitat for fish – especially bass – and tens of thousands of birds. Mt Konocti, a 4200ft-tall dormant volcano, lords over the scene. Alas, the human settlements don't always live up to the grandeur and thousands of acres near the lake remain scarred from wildfires in 2008.

Sights & Activities

Locals refer to the northwest portion as 'upper lake' and the southeast portion as 'lower lake.' **Lakeport** (population 5240) sits on the northwest shore, a 45-minute drive east of Hopland along Hwy 175 (off Hwy 101); **Kelseyville** (population 3000) is 7 miles south. **Clearlake**, off the southeastern shore, is the biggest (and ugliest) town.

Hwy 20 links the north-shore hamlets of **Nice** (the northernmost town) and **Lucerne**, 4 miles southeast. **Middletown**, a cute village, lies 20 miles south of Clearlake at the junction of Hwys 175 and 129, 40 minutes north of Calistoga.

Many outfits rent boats, including **On the Waterfront** (☎707-263-6789; 60 3rd St, Lakeport, six person boats per 3hr/day $185/350) and Konocti Harbor Resort & Spa in Kelseyville (p234).

Clear Lake State Park STATE PARK

(☎707-279-4293; 5300 Soda Bay Rd, Kelseyville; per car $8) Six miles from Lakeport, on the lake's west shore, the park is idyllic and gorgeous, with hiking trails, fishing, boating and camping. The **bird-watching** is extraordinary. The **visitor center** has geological and historical exhibits.

Redbud Audubon Society BIRD WATCHING

(www.redbudaudubon.org) In Lower Lake, this conservation group leads birding walks.

Sleeping & Eating

Make reservations on weekends and during summer, when people flock to the cool water.

LAKEPORT & KELSEYVILLE

There are a number of motels along the main drag in Keleysville and Lakeport, but if you want fresh air, Clear Lake State Park has four **campgrounds** (☎800-444-7275; www.reserveamerica.com; tent & RV sites $35) with showers. The weekly **farmers market** (Hwy 29 & Thomas Rd; ⏲8:30am-noon Sat May-Oct) is in Kelseyville.

TOP CHOICE **Lakeport English Inn** B&B $$

(☎707-263-4317; www.lakeportenglishinn.com; 675 N Main St, Lakeport; r $159-210, cottages $210; ❄📶) The finest B&B at Clear Lake is an 1875 Carpenter Gothic with 10 impeccably furnished rooms, styled with a nod to the English countryside. Weekends take high tea (public welcome by reservation) – with real Devonshire cream.

Konocti Harbor Resort & Spa RESORT $$

(☎707-279-4281, 800-660-5253; www.konoctiharbor.com; 8727 Soda Bay Rd, Konocti Bay; r $89-199, apt & beach cottages $199-349, ste $259-399; 📶🏊) On Konocti Bay, 4 miles from Kelseyville, this gargantuan resort, famous for huge concerts, includes four pools, a fitness center, tennis, golf, marina and spa. Rates spike on concert nights.

Mallard House MOTEL $

(☎707-262-1601; www.mallardhouse.com; 970 N Main St, Lakeport; r with kitchen $69-149, without $49-99; ❄📶) Waterfront motels with boat slips include this cottage-style place, which is a fantastic value during the week.

TOP CHOICE **Saw Shop Gallery Bistro** CALIFORNIAN $$$
(☎707-278-0129; www.sawshopbistro.com; 3825 Main St, Kelseyville; small plates $10-12, mains $18-30; ☎dinner Tue-Sat) The best restaurant in Lake County serves a Californian-cuisine menu of wild salmon and rack of lamb, as well as a small plates menu of sushi, lobster tacos, Kobe-beef burgers and flatbread pizzas. Laid-back atmosphere, too.

Molly Brennan's PUB $
(www.mollybrennans.com; 175 Main St, Lakeport; mains $9-20; ⌚11am-11pm Mon, Wed & Thu, to 2am Fri-Sun) Big mirrors and dark wood, pints of Guinness and bangers and mash make Molly Brennan's a quality pub. You'd be remiss to leave without trying the more ambitious menu items, like the lamb stew or pistachio-crusted salmon.

Bigg's 155 DINER $
(155 Park St, Lakeport; mains $5-12) It may look like a humble diner, but the menu is adventuresome (Shrimp Po' Boys?) and the ice cream treats are enormous.

NORTH SHORE

Tallman Hotel HISTORIC HOTEL $$
(☎707-274-0200, 888-880-5253; www.tallmanhotel.com; 4057 E Hwy 20, Nice; cottages $159-229; ❄📶🏊) The centerpiece may be the smartly renovated historic hotel – tile bathrooms, warm lighting, thick linens – but the rest of the property's lodging, including several modern, sustainably built cottages, are equally peaceful. The shaded garden, walled-in swimming pool, brick patios and big porches exude a timeless elegance. Garden rooms come with Japanese soaking tubs, all heated and cooled by an energy-efficient geothermal-solar system.

Featherbed Railroad Co HOTEL $$
(☎707-274-8378, 800-966-6322; www.featherbedrailroad.com; 2870 Lakeshore Blvd, Nice; cabooses incl breakfast $140-190; ❄🏊) A treat for train buffs and kids, Featherbed has 10 comfy, real cabooses on a grassy lawn. Some of the cabooses straddle the border between kitschy and tacky (the 'Easy Rider' has a Harley Davidson headboard and a mirrored ceiling), but they're great fun if you keep a sense of humor. There's a tiny beach across the road.

Sea Breeze Resort COTTAGES $$
(☎707-998-3327; www.seabreezeresort.net; 9595 Harbor Dr, Glenhaven; cottages with kitchen $130-150, without $100; ☎Apr-Oct; ❄📶) Just south of Lucerne on a small peninsula, gardens surround seven spotless lakeside cottages. All have barbecues.

MIDDLETOWN

Harbin Hot Springs SPA $$
(☎707-987-2377, 800-622-2477; www.harbin.org; Harbin Hot Springs Rd; tent & RV sites midweek/weekend $25/35, dm $35/50, s midweek $60-75, weekend $95-120, d midweek $90-190, weekend $140-260) Harbin is classic Northern California. Originally a 19th-century health spa and resort, it now has a retreat-center vibe and people come to unwind in silent, clothing-optional hot- and cold-spring pools. This is the birthplace of Watsu (floating massage) and there are wonderful body therapies as well as yoga, holistic-health workshops and 1160 acres of hiking. Accommodations are in Victorian buildings (which could use sprucing up) and share a common vegetarian-only kitchen. Food is available at the market, cafe and restaurant. Day-trippers are welcome; day rates are $25 and require one member of your group to purchase a membership (one month $10).

The springs are 3 miles off Hwy 175. From Middletown, take Barnes St, which becomes Big Canyon Rd, and head left at the fork.

☆ Entertainment

Library Park, in Lakeport, has free lakeside Friday-evening **summer concerts**, with blues and rockabilly tunes to appeal to middle-aged roadtrippers. Harbin Hot Springs (p235) presents a surprising lineup of world music and dances. The Konocti Harbor Resort & Spa (p234) hosts national acts (recent guests include Los Lonely Boys and Lyle Lovett) in an outdoor amphitheater and indoor concert hall.

ℹ Information

Lake County Visitor Information Center (www.lakecounty.com; 6110 E Hwy 120, Lucerne; ⌚9am-5pm Mon-Sat, noon-4pm Sun) Has complete information and an excellent website, which allows potential visitors to narrow their focus by interests.

ℹ Getting Around

Lake Transit (☎707-263-3334, 707-994 3334; www.laketransit.org) operates weekday routes between Middletown and Calistoga ($3.50, 35 minutes, three daily); on Thursday it connects through to Santa Rosa. Buses serve Ukiah ($3.50, two hours, four daily), from Clearlake via

TOP ANDERSON VALLEY WINERIES

The valley's cool nights yield high-acid, fruit-forward, food-friendly wines. Pinot noir, chardonnay and dry gewürztraminer flourish. Most **wineries** (www.avwines.com) sit outside Philo. Many are family-owned and offer tastings, some give tours. The following are particularly noteworthy.

» **Navarro** (www.navarrowine.com; 5601 Hwy 128; ⏲10am-6pm) The best option, and picnicking is encouraged.

» **Esterlina** (www.esterlinavineyards.com) For big reds, pack a picnic and head high up the rolling hills; call ahead.

» **Husch** (www.huschvineyards.com; 4400 Hwy 128; ⏲10am-5pm) Husch serves exquisite tastings inside a rose-covered cottage.

Lakeport ($2.25, 1¼ hours, seven daily). Since piecing together routes and times can be difficult, it's best to phone ahead.

Anderson Valley

Rolling hills surround pastoral Anderson Valley, famous for apple orchards, vineyards, pastures and quiet. Visitors come primarily to winery-hop, but there's good hiking and bicycling in the hills, and the chance to escape civilization. Traveling through the valley is the most common route to Mendocino from San Francisco.

Sights & Activities

Boonville (population 1370) and **Philo** (population 1000) are the valley's principal towns. From Ukiah, winding Hwy 253 heads 20 miles south to Boonville. Equally scenic Hwy 128 twists and turns 60 miles between Cloverdale on Hwy 101, south of Hopland, and Albion on coastal Hwy 1.

Apple Farm ORCHARD
(☎707-895-2333; www.philoapplefarm.com; 18501 Greenwood Rd, Philo; ⏲daylight) For the best fruit, skip the obvious roadside stands and head to this gorgeous farm for organic preserves, chutneys, heirloom apples and pears. It also hosts **cooking classes** with some of the Wine Country's best chefs. You can make a weekend out of it by staying in one of the orchard cottages (p236).

Anderson Valley Brewing Company BREWERY, FRISBEE GOLF
(☎707-895-2337; www.avbc.com; 17700 Hwy 253; tours $5; ⏲11am-6pm) East of the Hwy 128 crossroads, this solar-powered brewery crafts award-winning beers in a Bavarian-style brewhouse. You can also toss around a disc on the course while enjoying the brews, but, be warned, the sun can take its toll. Tours leave at 1:30pm and 3pm daily (only Tuesday and Wednesday in winter); call ahead.

Anderson Valley Historical Society Museum MUSEUM
(www.andersonvalleymuseum.org; 12340 Hwy 128; ⏲1-4pm Fri-Sun Feb-Nov) In a recently renovated little red schoolhouse west of Boonville, this museum displays historical artifacts.

Festivals & Events

Pinot Noir Festival WINE
(www.avwines.com) One of Anderson Valley's many wine celebrations.

Sierra Nevada World Music Festival MUSIC
(www.snwmf.com) In June, the sounds of reggae and roots fill the air, co-mingling with the scent of Mendocino county's *other* cash crop.

California Wool & Fiber Festival CRAFT
(www.fiberfestival.com) Events with names like 'Angora Rabbit Demonstration' bring out the natural-fiber fanatics from around the state.

Mendocino County Fair FAIR
(www.mendocountyfair.com) A county classic in mid-September.

Sleeping

Accommodations fill on weekends.

TOP CHOICE **Apple Farm** COTTAGES $$$
(☎707-895-2333; www.philoapplefarm.com; 18501 Greenwood Rd, Philo; r midweek/weekend $175/250) Set within the orchard, guests of Philo's bucolic Apple Farm choose from four exquisite cottages, each built with reclaimed materials. With bright, airy spaces, polished

plank floors, simple furnishings and views of the surrounding trees, each one is an absolute dream. Red Door cottage is a favorite because of the bathroom – you can soak in the slipper tub, or shower on the private deck under the open sky. The cottages often get booked with participants of the farm's **cooking classes**, so book well in advance. For a swim, the Navarro River is within walking distance.

Boonville Hotel BOUTIQUE HOTEL **$$**
(☎707-895-2210; www.boonvillehotel.com; 14040 Hwy 128; r $125-200, ste $225) Decked out in a contemporary American-country style with sea-grass flooring, pastel colors and fine linens that would make Martha Stewart proud, this historic hotel's rooms are safe for urbanites who refuse to abandon style just because they've gone to the country.

Hendy Woods State Park CAMPGROUND **$**
(☎707-937-5804, reservations 800-444-7275; www.reserveamerica.com; tent & RV sites $35, cabins $50) Bordered by the Navarro River on Hwy 128, west of Philo, the park has hiking, picnicking and a forested campground with hot showers.

Other Place COTTAGES **$$**
(☎707-895-3979; www.sheepdung.com; cottages $140-200;) Outside of town, 500 acres of ranch land surrounds private hilltop cottages.

Eating & Drinking

Boonville restaurants seem to open and close as they please, so expect variations in the hours listed below based on season and whimsy. There are several places along Hwy 128 which can supply a picnic with fancy local cheese and fresh bread.

Table 128 NEW AMERICAN **$$**
(☎707-895-2210; www.boonvillehotel.com; 14040 Hwy 128; 3-/4-course prixe fixe $40/50; 5-9pm Thu-Mon) Food-savvy travelers love the constantly changing New American menu here, featuring simple dishes done well, like roasted chicken, grilled local lamb and strawberry shortcake. The family-style service makes dinner here a freewheeling, elegant social affair, with big farm tables and soft lighting.

Paysenne ICE CREAM **$**
(14111 Hwy 128; ice cream cone $3; 10am-3pm Thu-Mon) Booneville's new ice-cream shop serves the innovative flavors of Three Twins Ice Cream, whose delightful flavors include Lemon Cookie and Strawberry Je Ne Sais Quoi (which has a hint of balsamic vinegar).

Boonville General Store DELI **$**
(17810 Farrer Lane; dishes $5-8; 7:30am-3pm Mon-Fri from 8:30am Sat & Sun, pizza night Fri 5:30-8pm) Opposite the Boonville Hotel, this deli is good to stock up for picnics, offering sandwiches on homemade bread, thin-crust pizzas and organic cheeses.

Lauren's AMERICAN **$$**
(www.laurensgoodfood.com; 14211 Hwy 128, Boonville; mains $8-14; 5-9pm Tue-Sat;) Locals pack Lauren's for eclectic homemade cookin' and a good wine list. Musicians sometimes jam on the stage by the front window.

Information

Anderson Valley Chamber of Commerce
(☎707-895-2379; www.andersonvalleychamber.com) Has tourist information and a complete schedule of annual events.

Ukiah

As the county seat and Mendocino's largest city, Ukiah is mostly a utilitarian stop for travelers to refuel the car and get a bite. But, if you have to stop here for the night, you could do much worse: the town is a friendly place, there are a plethora of cookie-cutter hotel chains, some cheaper midcentury motels and a handful of good dining options. The coolest attractions, a pair of thermal springs and a sprawling campus for Buddhist studies, lie outside the city limits.

BOONTLING

Boonville is famous for its unique language, 'Boontling,' which evolved about the turn of the 20th century when Boonville was very remote. Locals developed the language to *shark* (stump) outsiders and amuse themselves. You may hear *codgie kimmies* (old men) asking for a horn of *zeese* (a cup of coffee) or some *bahl gorms* (good food). If you are really lucky, you'll spot the tow truck called Boont Region De-arkin' Moshe (literally 'Anderson Valley Unwrecking Machine').

Sights

Grace Hudson Museum-Sun House MUSEUM
(www.gracehudsonmuseum.org; 431 S Main St; donation $2; ⏲10am-4:30pm Wed-Sat, from noon Sun) One block east of State St, the collection's mainstays are paintings by Grace Hudson (1865–1937). Her sensitive depictions of Pomo people complement the ethnological work and Native American baskets collected by her husband, John Hudson.

Festivals & Events

Redwood Empire Fair COUNTY FAIR
(www.redwoodempirefair.com) On the second weekend of August.

Ukiah Country PumpkinFest CULTURAL
(www.cityofukiah.com) In late October, with an arts-and-crafts fair, children's carnival and fiddle contest.

Sleeping

Every imaginable chain resort is here, just off the highway. For something with more personality, resorts and campgrounds cluster around Ukiah (see p239).

Sanford House B&B B&B $$
(☎707-462-1653; www.sanfordhouse.com; 306 S Pine St; s/d $95/175; ❄) This well-preserved Victorian is situated among a lovely garden. The rooms fit the standard of northern California's other Victorian B&Bs – lace curtains, wicker chairs, floral wallpaper and brass beds. The sweet owners offer an organic breakfast.

Sunrise Inn MOTEL $
(☎707-462-6601; www.sunriseinn.net; 650 S State St; r $58-78; ❄📶) Request one of the remodeled rooms at Ukiah's best budget motel. All have microwaves and refrigerators.

Discovery Inn Motel MOTEL $
(☎707-462-8873; www.discoveryinnukiahca.com; 1340 N State St; r $55-95; ❄📶🏊) Clean, but dated with a 75ft pool and several Jacuzzis.

Eating

It'd be a crime to eat the fast food junk located off the highway; Ukiah has a lot of affordable, excellent eateries.

TOP CHOICE **Oco Time** JAPANESE $$
(☎707-462-2422; www.ocotime.com; 111 W Church St; lunch mains $7-10, dinner mains $8-16; ⏲11:15am-2:30pm Tue-Fri, 5:30-8:30pm Mon-Sat; 🖉) Shoulder your way through the locals to get Ukiah's best sushi, noodle bowls and *oco* (a delicious mess of seaweed, grilled cabbage, egg and noodles). The 'Peace Café' has a great vibe, a friendly staff and interesting special rolls. Downside? The place gets mobbed, so reservations are a good idea.

Patrona NEW AMERICAN $$
(☎707-462-9181; www.patronarestaurant.com; 130 W Standley St; lunch mains $10-15, dinner mains $15-28; ⏲11am-3pm & 5-9pm Tue-Sat; 🖉) Foodies flock to excellent Patrona for earthy, flavor-packed, seasonal and regional organic cooking. The unfussy menu includes dishes like roasted chicken, brined-and-roasted pork chops, housemade pasta and local wines. Make reservations and ask about the prix fixe.

Ukiah Brewing Company BREWPUB $$
(www.ukiahbrewingco.com; 102 S State St, Ukiah; dinner mains $15-25; ⏲11:30am-9pm Sun-Thu, to 10pm Fri-Sat; 📶) The brews might outshine the food – barely – but there's no question that the dance floor is the most happening spot downtown. When it gets rowdy to live music on the weekend, this place is a blast. The menu has a strong organic and sustainable bent, with plenty of vegan and raw options.

Schat's Courthouse Bakery & Cafe CAFE $
(www.schats.com; 113 W Perkins St; lunch mains $3-7, dinner mains $8-14; ⏲5:30am-6pm Mon-Fri, to 5pm Sat) Founded by Dutch bakers, Schat's makes a dazzling array of chewy, dense breads, sandwiches, wraps, big salads, dee-lish hot mains and homemade pastries.

Kilkenny Kitchen CAFE $
(www.kilkennykitchen.com; 1093 S Dora St; lunch $7-10; ⏲10am-3pm Mon-Fri; 🖉) Tucked into a neighborhood south of downtown, county workers love this chipper yellow place for the fresh rotation of daily soups and sandwich specials (a recent visit on a blazing hot day found a heavenly, cold cucumber dill soup). The salads – like the pear, walnut and blue cheese – are also fantastic.

Himalayan Cafe HIMALAYAN $
(www.thehimalayancafe.com; 1639 S State St; mains lunch $9-13, dinner $10-17; 🖉) South of

downtown, find delicately spiced Nepalese cooking – tandoori breads and curries.

Ukiah farmers market MARKET
(cnr School & Clay Sts; 8:30am-noon Sat May-Oct, 3-6pm Tue Jun-Oct) The market offers farm-fresh produce, crafts and entertainment.

Drinking & Entertainment

Dive bars and scruffy cocktail lounges line State St. Ask at the chamber of commerce about cultural events, including Sunday summer concerts at Todd Grove Park, which have a delightfully festive atmosphere, and local square dances.

Ukiah Brewing Co BREWERY
(www.ukiahbrewingco.com; 102 S State St;) A great place to drink, this local brewpub makes organic beer and draws weekend crowds.

Coffee Critic COFFEE SHOP
(www.thecoffeecritic.com; 476 N State St;) Drop in for fair trade espresso, ice cream and occasional live music.

Shopping

Ukiah has a pleasant, walkable shopping district along School St near the courthouse.

Nomad's World JEWELRY, HOMEWARES
(www.nomads-world.com; 111 S School St; Mon-Sat) Step inside for cool jewelry and home furnishings.

Ruby Slippers VINTAGE
(110 N School St; Wed-Sat) Take turns trying on vintage drag.

Mendocino Book Co BOOKS
(www.mendocinobookcompany.com; 102 S School St; Mon-Sat) The best bookstore in town.

Information

Running north–south, west of Hwy 101, State St is Ukiah's main drag. School St, near Perkins St, is also good for strolling.

Bureau of Land Management (707-468-4000; 2550 N State St) Maps and information on backcountry camping, hiking and biking in wilderness areas.

Greater Ukiah Chamber of Commerce (707-462-4705; www.gomendo.com; 200 S School St; 9am-5pm Mon-Fri) One block west of State St; information on Ukiah, Hopland and Anderson Valley.

Around Ukiah

UKIAH WINERIES

You'll notice the acres of grapes stretching out in every direction on your way into town. Winemakers around Ukiah enjoy much of the same climatic conditions that made Napa so famous. Pick up a wineries map from the Ukiah chamber of commerce (p239).

Parducci Wine Cellars WINERY
(www.parducci.com; 501 Parducci Rd, Ukiah; 10am-5pm) Sustainably grown, harvested and produced, 'America's Greenest Winery' produces affordable, bold, earthy reds. The tasting room, lined in brick and soft light, is a perfect little cave-like environment to get out of the summer heat, sip wine and chat about sustainability practices.

Fife WINERY
(707-485-0323; www.fifevineyards.com; 3621 Ricetti Lane, Redwood Valley; 10am-5pm) Fruit-forward reds include a peppery zinfandel and petite sirah, both affordable and food-friendly. And oh, the hilltop views! Bring a picnic.

Germain-Robin DISTILLERY
(707-462-0314; Unit 35, 3001 S State St; by appointment) Makes some of the world's best brandy, which is handcrafted by a fifth-generation brandy-maker from the Cognac region of France. It's just a freeway-side warehouse, but if you're into cognac, you gotta come.

VICHY HOT SPRINGS RESORT

Opened in 1854, Vichy is the oldest continuously operating mineral-springs spa in California. The water's composition perfectly matches that of its famous namesake in Vichy, France. A century ago, Mark Twain, Jack London and Robert Louis Stevenson traveled here for the water's restorative properties, which ameliorate everything from arthritis to poison oak.

Today, the beautifully maintained historic **resort** (707-462-9515; www.vichysprings.com; 2605 Vichy Springs Rd, Ukiah; lodge s/d $135/195, creekside r $195/245, cottages from $280;) has the only warm-water, naturally carbonated mineral baths in North America. Unlike others, Vichy requires swimsuits (rentals $2). Day use costs $30 for two hours, $50 for a full day.

Facilities include a swimming pool, outdoor mineral hot tub, 10 indoor and outdoor tubs with natural 100°F waters, and a grotto for sipping the effervescent waters. Massages and facials are available. Entry includes use of the 700-acre grounds, abutting Bureau of Land Management (BLM) lands; hiking trails lead to a 40ft waterfall, an old cinnabar mine and 1100ft peaks – great for sunset views.

The resort's suite and two cottages, built in 1854, are Mendocino County's three oldest structures. The cozy rooms have wooden floors, top-quality beds, breakfast and spa privileges, and no TVs.

From Hwy 101, exit at Vichy Springs Rd and follow the state-landmark signs east for 3 miles. Ukiah is five minutes, but a world, away.

ORR HOT SPRINGS

A clothing-optional resort that's beloved by locals, back-to-the-land hipsters, backpackers and liberal-minded tourists, **springs** (707-462-6277; tent sites $45-50, d $140-160, cottages $195-230; 10am-10pm) has private tubs, a sauna, spring-fed rock-bottomed swimming pool, steam, massage and magical gardens. Day use costs $25, $20 on Mondays.

Accommodation includes use of the spa and communal kitchen; some cottages have kitchens. Reservations are essential.

To get there from Hwy 101, take N State St exit, go north a quarter of a mile to Orr Springs Rd, then 9 miles west. The steep, winding mountain road takes 30 minutes to drive.

MONTGOMERY WOODS STATE RESERVE

Two miles west of Orr, this 1140-acre **reserve** (Orr Springs Rd) protects five old-growth redwood groves, and some of the best groves within a day's drive from San Francisco. A 2-mile loop trail crosses the creek, winding through the serene groves, starting near the picnic tables and toilets. It's out of the way, so visitors are likely to have it mostly to themselves. Day use only; no camping.

LAKE MENDOCINO

Amid rolling hills, 5 miles northeast of Ukiah, this tranquil 1822-acre artificial lake fills a valley, once the ancestral home of the Pomo people. On the lake's north side, **Pomo Visitor Center** (707-467-4200) is modeled after a Pomo roundhouse, with exhibits on tribal culture and the dam. The center was closed indefinitely for upgrades at the time of update, but was still offering information via phone about camping.

Coyote Dam, 3500ft long and 160ft high, marks the lake's southwest corner; the lake's eastern part is a 689-acre protected wildlife habitat. The **Army Corps of Engineers** (www.spn.usace.army.mil/mendocino; 1160 Lake Mendocino Dr; 8am-4pm Mon-Fri) built the dam, manages the lake and provides recreation information. Its office is inconveniently located on the lower lake.

There are 300 **tent and RV sites** (877-444-6777; www.reserveusa.com; $20-22), most with hot showers and primitive boat-in sites ($8).

CITY OF TEN THOUSAND BUDDHAS

Three miles east of Ukiah, via Talmage Rd, the **site** (707-462-0939; www.cttbusa.org; 2001 Talmage Rd; 8am-6pm) used to be a state mental hospital. Since 1976 it has been a lush, quiet 488-acre Chinese-Buddhist community. Don't miss the temple hall, which really does have 10,000 Buddhas. As this is a place of worship, please be respectful of those who use the grounds for meditating. Stay for lunch in the vegetarian Chinese **restaurant** (4951 Bodhi Way; mains $10; noon-3pm).

Willits

Twenty miles north of Ukiah, Willits mixes NorCal dropouts with loggers and ranchers (the high school has a bull-riding team). Lamp posts of the main drag are decorated with bucking broncos and cowboys, but the heart of the place is just as boho. Though ranching, timber and manufacturing may be its mainstays, tie-dye is de rigueur. For visitors, Willits' greatest claim to fame is as the eastern terminus of the Skunk Train. Fort Bragg is 35 miles away on the coast; allow an hour to navigate twisty Hwy 20.

Sights & Activities

Ten miles north of Willits, **Hwy 162/Covelo Rd** makes for a superb drive following the route of the Northwestern Pacific Railroad along the Eel River and through the Mendocino National Forest. The trip is only about 30 miles, but plan on taking at least an hour on the winding road, passing exquisite river canyons and rolling hills. Eventually, you'll reach **Covelo**, known for its unusual round valley.

Skunk Train HISTORIC TRAIN
(☎707 964-6371, 866-866-1690; www.skunktrain.com; adult/child $49/24) The depot is on E Commercial St, three blocks east of Hwy 101. Trains run between Willits and Fort Bragg (p229).

Mendocino County Museum MUSEUM
(www.mendocinomuseum.org; 400 E Commercial St; adult/child $4/1; ⏲10am-4:30pm Wed-Sun) Among the best community museum's in the northern half of the state, this puts the lives of early settlers in excellent historical context – much drawn from old letters – and there's an entire 1920s soda fountain and barber shop inside. You could spend an hour perusing Pomo and Yuki basketry and artifacts, or reading about local scandals and countercultural movements. Outside, the **Roots of Motive Power** (www.rootsofmotivepower.com) exhibit occasionally demonstrates steam logging and machinery.

Ridgewood Ranch RANCH
(☎reservations 707-459-7910; www.seabiscuitheritage.com; 16200 N Hwy 101; tours $15-25) Willits' most famous resident was the horse Seabiscuit, which grew up here. Ninety-minute tours operate on Monday, Wednesday and Friday (June to September); once a month on Saturday there's a three-hour tour by reservation.

Jackson Demonstration State Forest HIKING
Fifteen miles west of Willits on Hwy 20, the forest offers day-use recreational activities, including educational hiking trails and mountain-biking. You can also camp here (see p241).

Festivals & Events

Willits Frontier Days & Rodeo RODEO
(www.willitsfrontierdays.com) Dating from 1926, Willits has the oldest continuous rodeo in California, occurring the first week in July.

Willits Renaissance Faire CULTURAL
(www.willitsfaire.com) Held in August, featuring Highland Scottish games, food, music, jugglers, arts and crafts.

Sleeping

Some of the in-town motels – and there seems to be about a hundred of them – are dumps, so absolutely check out the room before checking in. Ask about Skunk Train packages. There are a couple crowded, loud RV parks on the edges of town for only the most desperate campers.

Baechtel Creek Inn & Spa BOUTIQUE HOTEL $$
(☎707-459-9063, 800-459-9911; www.baechtelcreekinn.com; 101 Gregory Lane; d incl breakfast $100-130; ❄@≋) As Willits' only upscale option, this place draws an interesting mix: Japanese bus tours, business travelers and wine trippers. The standard rooms are nothing too flashy, but they have top knotch linens, iPod docks and tasteful art. Custom rooms come with local wine and more space. The immaculate pool and lovely egg breakfast on the patio are perks.

Best Value Inn Holiday Lodge MOTEL $
(☎707-459-5361, 800-835-3972; www.bestvalueinn.com; 1540 S Main St; d from $63; ❄≋) It's a bit of a draw between the 1950s motels that line Willits' main drag, but this is our favorite because of the kind staff and relatively quiet rooms.

Jackson Demonstration State Forest CAMPGROUND $
(☎707-964-5674; sites free) Campsites have barbecue pits and pit toilets, but no water. Get a permit from the on-site host, or from a self-registration kiosk.

Eating

TOP CHOICE **Zaza's Bakery, Bistro & Gallery** BAKERY, CAFE $
(35 E Commercial St; pastries $2-4, sandwiches $8; ⏲9am-2pm) So far, little Zaza's is the only bakery in California to sell a bagel that could be mistaken for one baked in New York. And that's only where the delightful surprises begin: a delicious, delicate soup menu that changes every day (last visit it was red snapper, corn and coconut chowder), a bright atmosphere completed by good artwork, jazz on the radio and hearty sandwiches on nutty, multigrain bread.

Purple Thistle FUSION $$
(☎707-459-4750; 50 S Main St; mains $13-25; ⏲5-9pm) Willits' best fine dining; cooks up Cajun- and Japanese-inspired 'Mendonesian' cuisine, using fresh organic ingredients. Make reservations, and expect it to be a bit crowded.

Loose Caboose Cafe SANDWICHES $
(10 Woods St; sandwiches $7-10; ⏲7:30am-3pm) People tend to get a bit flushed when talking about the sandwiches at the Loose Caboose,

which gets jammed at lunch. The Reuben and Sante Fe Chicken sandwiches are two savory delights.

Burrito Exquisito MEXICAN $
(42 S Hain St; mains $7; ⏲11am-7pm) A cute hippie burrito shop dishes out big burritos, which you can eat in the back garden.

Ardella's Kitchen DINER $$
(35 E Commercial St; mains $5-11; ⏲6am-noon Tue-Sat) For quick eats, this tiny place is tops for breakfast – and is *the* place for gossip.

Mariposa Market GROCERIES $
(600 S Main St) Willits natural food outlet.

Drinking & Entertainment

Shanachie Pub BAR
(50B S Main St; ⏲Mon-Sat) Sharing the garden with Burrito Exquisito, this is a friendly little dive with tons on tap.

Willits Community Theatre THEATER
(www.willitstheatre.org; 212 S Main St) Stages award-winning plays, poetry readings and comedy.

Shopping

JD Redhouse & Co CLOTHING, HOMEWARES
(212 S Main St; ⏲10am-6pm) Family-owned and operated, this central mercantile is a good reflection of Willits itself, balancing cowboy essentials – boots and grain, tools and denim – with treats for the weekend tourist. The ice cream counter is a good place to cool off when the heat on the sidewalk gets intense.

Book Juggler BOOKS
(50B S Main St; ⏲10am-7pm Mon-Thu, to 8pm Fri, 10am-6pm Sat, noon-5pm Sun) Has dense rows of new and used books, music books and local papers (pick up the weird, locally printed *Anderson Valley Advertiser* here).

SOUTHERN REDWOOD COAST

There's some real magic in the loamy soil and misty air 'beyond the redwood curtain'; it yields the tallest trees and most potent herb on the planet. North of Fort Bragg, Bay Area weekenders and antique-stuffed B&Bs give way to lumber wars, pot farmers and an army of carved bears. The 'growing' culture here is palpable and the huge profit it brings to the region has evident cultural side effects – an omnipresent population of transients who work the harvests, a chilling respect for 'No Trespassing' signs and a political culture that is an uneasy balance between gun-toting libertarians, ultra-left progressives and typical college-town chaos. Nevertheless, the reason to visit is to soak in the magnificent landscape, which runs through a number of pristine, ancient redwood forests.

Information

Redwood Coast Heritage Trails (www.redwoods.info) Gives a nuanced slant on the region with itineraries based around lighthouses, Native American culture, the timber and rail industries, and maritime life.

Leggett

Leggett marks the redwood country's beginning and Hwy 1's end. There ain't much but an expensive gas station, pizza joint and two markets.

Visit 1000-acre **Standish-Hickey State Recreation Area** (69350 Hwy 101; day use $8), 1.5 miles to the north, for picnicking, swimming and fishing in the Eel River and hiking trails among virgin and second-growth redwoods. Year-round **campgrounds** (☎800-444-7275; www.reserveamerica.com; tent & RV sites $35) with hot showers book up in summer. Avoid highway-side sites.

Chandelier Drive-Thru Tree Park (www.drivethrutree.com; Drive-Thru Tree Rd; per car $5; ⏲8am-dusk) has 200 private acres of virgin redwoods with picnicking and nature walks. And yes, there's a redwood with a square hole carved out, which cars can drive through. Only in America.

The 1949 tourist trap of **Confusion Hill** (www.confusionhill.com; 75001 N Hwy 101; adult/child Gravity House $5/4, train rides $8.50/6.50; ⏲9am-6pm May-Sep, 10am-5pm Oct-Apr; 👪) is an enduring curiosity and the most elaborate of the old-fashioned stops that line the route north. The Gravity House challenges queasy visitors to keep their balance while standing at a 40-degree angle (a rad photo op). Kids and fans of kitsch go nuts for the playhouse quality of the space and the narrow-gauge train rides are exciting for toddlers.

For basic supplies, visit **Price's Peg House** (☎707-925-6444; 69501 Hwy 101; ⏲8am-9pm).

Richardson Grove State Park

Fifteen miles to the north, and bisected by the Eel River, serene **Richardson Grove** (Hwy 101; per car $8) occupies 1400 acres of virgin forest. Many trees are over 1000 years old and 300ft tall, but there aren't many hiking trails. In winter, there's good fishing for silver and king salmon. At the time of research, CalTrans was considering widening the road through Richardson Grove, which sparked an intense protest.

The **visitor center** (☎707-247-3318; ⏰9am-2pm) sells books inside a 1930s lodge, which often has a fire going during cool weather. The park is primarily a **campground** (☎reservations 800-444-7275; www.reserveamerica.com; tent & RV sites $35) with three separate areas with hot showers; some remain open year-round. Summer-only Oak Flat on the east side of the river is shady and has a sandy beach.

Benbow Lake

On the Eel River, 2 miles south of Garberville, the 1200-acre **Benbow Lake State Recreation Area** (☎summer 707-923-3238, winter 707-923-3318, per car $8) exists when a seasonal dam forms the 26-acre Benbow Lake, mid-June to mid-September. In mid-August, avoid swimming in the lake or river until two weeks after the Reggae on the River festival (p244), when 25,000 people use the river as a bathtub. The water is cleanest in early summer. The year-round riverside **campground** (☎reservations 800-444- 7275; www.reserveamerica.com; tent & RV sites $35) is subject to wintertime bridge closures due to flooding. This part of the Eel has wide banks and is also excellent for swimming and sunbathing. You can avoid the day use fee by parking near the bridge and walking down to the river. According to a ranger, you can float from here all the way through the redwood groves along the Avenue of the Giants.

Benbow Inn (☎707-923-2124, 800-355-3301; www.benbowinn.com; 445 Lake Benbow Dr; r $90-305, cottage $395-595; ❄📶🏊) is a monument to 1920s rustic elegance; the Redwood Empire's first luxury resort is a national historic landmark. Hollywood's elite once frolicked in the Tudor-style resort's lobby, where you can play chess by the crackling fire, and enjoy complimentary afternoon tea and evening hors d'oeuvres. Rooms have top-quality beds and antique furniture. The window-lined dining room (br eakfast and lunch $10 to $15, dinner mains $22 to $32) serves excellent meals and the rib eye earns raves.

Southern Redwood Coast

Garberville

The main supply center for southern Humboldt County is the primary jumping-off point for both the Lost Coast, to the west, and the Avenue of the Giants, to the north. There's an uneasy relationship between the old-guard loggers and the hippies, many of whom came in the 1970s to grow sinsemilla (potent, seedless marijuana) after the feds chased them out of Santa Cruz. At last count, the hippies were winning the culture wars, but it rages on: a sign on the door of a local bar reads simply: 'Absolutely NO patchouli oil!!!' Two miles west, Garberville's ragtag sister, Redway, has fewer services. Garberville is about four hours north of San Francisco, one hour south of Eureka.

Festivals & Events

The **Mateel Community Center** (www.mateel.org), in Redway, is the nerve center for many of the area's long-running annual festivals, which celebrate everything from hemp to miming.

Reggae on the River/Reggae Rising MUSIC
(www.reggaeontheriver.com) In mid-July, drawing huge crowds for reggae, world music, arts and craft fairs, camping and swimming in the river.

Avenue of the Giants Marathon MARATHON
(www.theave.org) Among the nation's most picturesque marathons, held in May.

Harley-Davidson Redwood Run MOTORCYCLE RALLY
(www.redwoodrun.com) The redwoods rumble with the sound of hundreds of shiny bikes in June.

Sleeping

Garberville is lined with motels, and many of them are serviceable, if uninspiring. South of town, Benbow Inn (p243) blows away the competition. For cheaper lodging, there are two satisfactory motels. First try **Sherwood Forest** (707-923-2721; www.sherwoodforestmotel.com; 814 Redwood Dr; r $66-84;), then **Humboldt Redwoods Inn** (707-923-2451; www.humboldtredwoodsinn.com; 987 Redwood Dr; r $59-95;), though the desk clerks are hardly ever there, so call ahead.

Eating & Drinking

Woodrose Café BREAKFAST $
(www.woodrosecafe.com; 911 Redwood Dr; meals $7-11; 7am-1pm;) Garberville's beloved cafe serves organic omelettes, veggie scrambles and buckwheat pancakes with *real* maple syrup in a cozy room. Lunch brings crunchy salads, sandwiches with all-natural meats and good burritos. No credit cards.

Cecil's New Orleans Bistro CAJUN $$$
(www.cecilsrestaurant.com; 733 Redwood Dr; dinner mains $20-26; 6-10pm Thu-Mon) This 2nd story eatery overlooks Main St and serves ambitious dishes that may have minted the California-Cajun style. Start with fried green tomatoes before launching into the smoked boar gumbo.

Mateel Café AMERICAN $$
(3342-3344 Redwood Dr, Redway; mains lunch $8-12, dinner $20-26; 11:30am-9pm Mon-Sat) The big, diverse menu of this Redway joint includes a rack of lamb, stone-baked pizzas and terrific salads. There's pleasant patio seating out back.

Chautauqua Natural Foods HEALTH FOOD $
(436 Church St; sandwiches & lunch plates $5-10; 10am-6pm Mon-Sat) Sells natural groceries. It has a small dining area and a great bulletin board.

Nacho Mama MEXICAN $
(375 Sprowel Creek Rd; meals under $6; 11am-7pm Mon-Sat) A tiny shack on the corner of Redwood Dr with organic fast-food Mexican.

Calico's Deli & Pasta ITALIAN $
(808 Redwood Dr; dishes $6-13; 11am-9pm;) Calico's has house-made pasta and sandwiches, and is good for kids.

Branding Iron Saloon BAR $
(744 Redwood Dr) Craft beer, nice locals and a hopping pool table. We'll forgive the stripper pole in the middle of the room.

Information

Garberville-Redway Area Chamber of Commerce (www.garberville.org; 784 Redwood Dr; 10am-4pm May-Aug, Mon-Fri Sep-Apr) Inside the Redwood Dr Center.

KMUD FM91 (www.kmud.org) Find out what's really happening by tuning in to community radio.

Lost Coast

The North Coast's superlative backpacking destination is a rugged, mystifying stretch of coast where narrow dirt trails ascend rugged coastal peaks and volcanic beaches of black sand and ethereal mist hovers above the roaring surf as majestic Roosevelt elk graze the forests. Here, the rugged King Range boldly rises 4000ft within 3 miles of the coast between where Hwy 1 cuts inland north of Westport to just south of Ferndale. The coast became 'lost' when the state's highway system deemed the region impassable in the early 20th century.

The best hiking and camping is within the King Range National Conservation Area and the Sinkyone Wilderness State Park, which make up the central and southern stretch of the region. The area north of the King Range is more accessible, if less dramatic.

In autumn, the weather is clear and cool. Wildflowers bloom from April through May and gray whales migrate from December through April. The warmest, driest months are June to August, but days are foggy. Note that the weather can quickly change.

Hiking

The best way to see the Lost Coast is to hike, and the best hiking is through the southern regions within the Sinkyone and Kings Range Wilderness areas. Some of the best trails start from Mattole Campground, just south Petrolia, which is on the northern border of the Kings Range. It's at the ocean end of Lighthouse Rd, 4 miles from Mattole Rd (sometimes marked as Hwy 211), southeast of Petrolia.

The **Lost Coast Trail** follows 24.7 miles of coastline from Mattole Campground in the north to Black Sands Beach at Shelter Cove in the south. The prevailing northerly winds make it best to hike from north to south; plan for three or four days. In October and November, and April and May, the weather is iffy and winds can blow south to north, depending on whether there's a low-pressure system overhead. The best times to come are summer weekdays in early June, at the end of August, September and October. The trail will often have hikers; busiest times are Memorial Day, Labor Day and summer weekends. Only two shuttles have permits to transport backpackers through the area, **Lost Coast Trail Transport Services** (☎707-986-9909; www.lostcoasttrail.com) or the more reliable **Lost Coast Shuttle** (☎707-223-1547; www.lostcoastshuttle.com). Neither is cheap; prices for the ride between Mattole and Black Sands Beach start at $100 per person with a two-person minimum.

Highlights include an abandoned lighthouse at Punta Gorda, remnants of early shipwrecks, tidepools and abundant wildlife including sea lions, seals and some 300 bird species. The trail is mostly level, passing beaches and crossing over rocky outcrops. Along the Lost Coast Trail, **Big Flat** is the most popular backcountry destination. Carry a tide table, lest you get trapped: from Buck Creek to Miller Creek, you can only hike during an outgoing tide.

A good **day hike** starts at the Mattole Campground trailhead and travels 3 miles south along the coast to the Punta Gorda lighthouse (return against the wind).

People have discovered the Lost Coast Trail. To ditch the crowds, take any of the (strenuous) upland trails off the beach toward the ridgeline. For a satisfying, hard 21-mile-long hike originating at the Lost Coast Trail, take Buck Creek Trail to King Crest Trail to Rattlesnake Ridge Trail. The 360 degree views from **King Peak** are stupendous, particularly with a full moon or during a meteor shower. Note that if you hike up, it can be hellishly hot on the ridges, though the coast remains cool and foggy; wear removable layers. Carry a topographical map and a compass: signage is limited.

Both Wailaki and Nadelos have developed **campgrounds** (tent sites $8) with toilets and water. There are another four developed campgrounds around the range, with toilets but no water (except Honeydew, which has purifiable creek water). There are multiple primitive walk-in sites. You'll need a bear canister and backcountry permit, both available from BLM offices.

ℹ Information

Aside from a few one-horse villages, Shelter Cove, the isolated unincorporated town 25 long miles west of Garberville, is the option for services. Get supplies in Garberville, Fort Bragg, Eureka or Arcata. The area is a patchwork of government-owned land and private property; visit the Bureau of Land Management office (p257) for information, permits and maps. There are few circuitous routes for hikers, and rangers can advise on reliable (if expensive) shuttle services in the area. A few words of caution: lots of weed is grown around here and it's wise to stay on trail to and respect no trespassing signs, lest you find yourself at the business end of someone's right to bear arms. And pot farmers don't pose the only threat: you'll want to check for ticks (Lyme disease is common) and keep food in bear-proof containers, which are required for camping.

SINKYONE WILDERNESS STATE PARK

Named for the Sinkyone people who once lived here, this 7367-acre wilderness extends south of Shelter Cove along pristine coastline. The **Lost Coast Trail** continues here for another 22 miles, from Whale Gulch south to Usal Beach Campground, taking at least three days to walk as it meanders along high ridges, providing bird's-eye views down to deserted beaches and the crashing surf (side trails descend to water level). Near the park's northern end, the (haunted!) **Needle Rock Ranch** (☎707-986-7711; tent sites $35) serves as a remote visitor center. Register here for the adjacent campsites ($25 to $35). This is the only source of potable water. For information on when the ranch is closed (most of the time), call **Richardson Grove State Park** (☎707-247-3318).

To get to Sinkyone, drive west from Garberville and Redway on Briceland-Thorn Rd, 21 miles through Whitethorn to Four Corners. Turn left (south) and continue for 3.5 miles down a very rugged road to the ranch house; it takes 1½ hours.

There's access to the **Usal Beach Campground** (tent sites $25) at the south end of the park from Hwy 1 (you can't make reservations). North of Westport, take the unpaved County Rd 431 beginning from Hwy 1's Mile 90.88 and travel 6 miles up the coast to the campground. The road is graded yearly in late spring and is passable in summer via two-wheel-drive vehicles. Most sites are past the message board by the beach. Use bear canisters or keep food in your trunk. Look for giant elk feeding on the tall grass – they live behind sites No 1 and 2 – and osprey by the creek's mouth.

North of the campground, Usal Rd (County Rd 431) is much rougher and recommended only if you have a high-clearance 4WD and a chainsaw. Seriously.

KING RANGE NATIONAL CONSERVATION AREA

Stretching over 35 miles of virgin coastline, with ridge after ridge of mountainous terrain plunging to the surf, the 60,000-acre area tops out at namesake King's Peak (4087ft). The wettest spot in California, the range receives over 120 inches – and sometimes as much as 240 inches – of annual rainfall, causing frequent landslides; in winter, snow falls on the ridges. (By contrast, nearby sea-level Shelter Cove gets only 69 inches of rain and no snow.) Two-thirds of the area is awaiting wilderness designation.

Nine miles east of Shelter Cove, the **Bureau of Land Management** (BLM; ☎707-986-5400, 707-825-2300; 768 Shelter Cove Rd; ⌚8am-4:30pm Mon-Sat Memorial Day-Labor Day, 8am-4:30pm Mon-Fri May-Sep) has maps and directions for trails and campsites; they're posted outside after hours. For overnight hikes, you'll need a backcountry-use permit. Don't turn left onto Briceland-Thorn Rd to try to find the 'town' of Whitethorn; it doesn't exist. Whitethorn is the BLM's name for the *general* area. To reach the BLM office from Garberville/Redway, follow signs to Shelter Cove; look for the roadside information panel, 0.25 miles past the post office. Information and permits are also available from the BLM in Arcata (p257).

Fire restrictions begin July 1 and last until the first soaking rain, usually in November. During this time, there are no campfires allowed outside developed campgrounds.

NORTH OF THE KING RANGE

Though it's less of an adventure, you can reach the Lost Coast's northern section year-round via paved, narrow Mattole Rd. Plan three hours to navigate the sinuous 68 miles from Ferndale in the north to the coast at Cape Mendocino, then inland to Humboldt Redwoods State Park and Hwy 101. Don't expect redwoods; the vegetation is grassland and pasture. It's beautiful in spots – lined sweeping vistas and wildflowers that are prettiest in spring.

You'll pass two tiny settlements, both 19th-century stage-coach stops. **Petrolia** has an all-in-one **store** (☎707-629-3455; ⌚9am-5pm) which rents bear canisters and sells supplies for the trail, good beer and gasoline. **Honeydew** also has a **general store**. The drive is enjoyable, but the Lost Coast's wild, spectacular scenery lies further south in the more remote regions.

SHELTER COVE

The only sizable community on the Lost Coast, Shelter Cove is surrounded by the King Range National Conservation Area and abuts a large south-facing cove. It's a tiny

DRIVE-THRU TREES

Three carved-out (but living) redwoods await along Hwy 101, a bizarre holdover from a yesteryear road trip.

Chandelier Drive-Thru Tree Fold in your mirrors and inch forward, then cool off in the uberkitschy gift shop; in Leggett.

Shrine Drive-Thru Tree Look up to the sky as you roll through, on the Ave of the Giants in Myers Flat. The least impressive of the three.

Tour Thru Tree Take exit 769 in Klamath, squeeze through a tree and check out an emu.

seaside subdivision with an airstrip in the middle – indeed, many visitors are private pilots. Fifty years ago, Southern California swindlers subdivided the land, built the airstrip and flew in potential investors, fast-talking them into buying seaside land for retirement. But they didn't tell buyers that a steep, winding, one-lane dirt road provided the *only* access and that the seaside plots were eroding into the sea.

Today, there's still only one route, but now it's paved. Cell phones don't work here: this is a good place to disappear. The town is a mild disappointment, with not much to do, but stunning **Black Sands Beach** stretches for miles northward.

Sleeping

Shelter Cove has some plain motels and decent inns, but camping is far and away the best way to spend the night here.

TOP CHOICE Tides Inn INN $$
(707-986-7900, 888-998-4377; www.sheltercovetidesinn.com; 59 Surf Point Rd; r from $155;) Perched above tidepools teeming with starfish and sea urchins, this is the top-choice indoor sleeping in Shelter Cove. The squeaky clean rooms offer excellent views (go for the mini suites on the 3rd floor). The suite options are good for families, and kids are greeted warmly by the innkeeper with an activity kit.

Inn of the Lost Coast INN $$
(707-986-7521, 888-570-9676; www.innofthelostcoast.com; 205 Wave Dr; r $160-250;) After a big overhaul, this renovated inn has breathtaking ocean views and clean, fireplace rooms. Downstairs there's a serviceable take-out pizza place and Shelter Cove's only breakfast joint, an espresso stand named Fish Tanks.

Oceanfront Inn & Lighthouse INN $$
(707-986-7002; www.sheltercoveoceanfrontinn.com; 10 Seal Court; r $135-165, ste $195) The tidy, modern rooms here have microwaves, refrigerators and balconies overlooking the sea. The decor is spartan so as not to detract from the view. Splurge on a kitchen suite; the best is upstairs, with its peaked ceiling and giant windows.

Shelter Cove RV Park, Campground & Deli CAMPGROUND $
(707-986-7474; 492 Machi Rd; tent/RV sites $33/43) The services may be basic, but the fresh gusts of ocean air can't be beat – the deli has good fish and chips.

Eating

The first-choice place to eat, **Cove Restaurant** (707-986-1197; 10 Seal Court; mains $6-19; 5-9pm Thu-Sun), has everything from veggie stir-fries to New York steaks. For those who are self-catering, **Shelter Cove General Store** (707-986-7733; 7272 Shelter Cove Rd) is 2 miles beyond town. Get groceries and gasoline here.

Humboldt Redwoods State Park & Avenue of the Giants

Don't miss this magical drive through California's largest redwood park, **Humboldt Redwoods State Park** (www.humboldtredwoods.org), which covers 53,000 acres – 17,000 of which are old-growth – and contains some of the world's most magnificent trees. It also boasts three-quarters of the world's tallest 100 trees. Tree huggers take note: these groves rival (and many say surpass) those in Redwood National Park, which is a long drive further north.

Exit Hwy 101 when you see the 'Avenue of the Giants' sign, take this smaller alternative to the interstate; it's an incredible, 32-mile, two-lane stretch. You'll find free driving guides at roadside signboards at both the avenue's southern entrance, 6 miles north of Garberville, near Phillipsville, and at the northern entrance, south of Scotia, at Pepperwood; there are access points off Hwy 101.

South of Weott, a volunteer-staffed **visitor center** (☎707-946-2263; ⌚9am-5pm May-Sep, 10am-4pm Oct-Apr) shows videos and sells maps.

Three miles north, the **California Federation of Women's Clubs Grove** is home to an interesting four-sided hearth designed by renowned San Franciscan architect Julia Morgan in 1931 to commemorate 'the untouched nature of the forest.'

Primeval **Rockefeller Forest**, 4.5 miles west of the avenue via Mattole Rd, appears as it did a century ago. You quickly walk out of sight of cars and feel like you have fallen into the time of dinosaurs. It's the world's largest contiguous old-growth redwood forest, and contains about 20% of all such remaining trees. Check out the subtly variegated rings (count one for each year) on the cross sections of some of the downed giants that are left to mulch back into the earth over the next few hundred years.

In **Founders Grove**, north of the visitor center, the **Dyerville Giant** was knocked over in 1991 by another falling tree. A walk along its gargantuan 370ft length, with its wide trunk towering above, helps you appreciate how huge these ancient trees are.

The park has over 100 miles of trails for hiking, mountain-biking and horseback riding. Easy walks include short nature trails in Founders Grove and Rockefeller Forest and **Drury-Chaney Loop Trail** (with berry picking in summer). Challenging treks include popular **Grasshopper Peak Trail**, south of the visitor center, which climbs to the 3379ft fire lookout.

Sleeping & Eating

If you want to stay along the avenue, several towns have simple lodgings of varying calibers and levels of hospitality, but camping at Humboldt Redwoods is by far the best option.

Humboldt Redwoods State Park Campgrounds CAMPGROUND $
(☎reservations 800-444-7275; www.reserveamerica.com; tent & RV sites $20-35) The park runs three campgrounds, with hot showers, two environmental camps, five trail camps, a hike/bike camp and an equestrian camp. Of the developed spots, **Burlington Campground** is open year-round beside the visitor center and near a number of trailheads. **Hidden Springs Campground**, 5 miles south, and **Albee Creek Campground**, on Mattole Rd past Rockefeller Forest, are open mid-May to early fall.

Miranda Gardens Resort RESORT $$
(☎707-943-3011; www.mirandagardens.com; 6766 Ave of the Giants, Miranda; cottages with kitchen $165-275, without $115-175;) The best indoor stay along the avenue. The cozy, slightly rustic cottages have redwood paneling, some with fireplaces, and are spotlessly clean. The grounds – replete with outdoor ping pong and a play area for kids and swaying redwoods – have wholesome appeal for families.

Riverbend Cellars TASTING ROOM $$
(www.riverbendcellars.com; 12990 Ave of the Giants, Myers Flat; ⌚11am-5pm) For something a bit more posh, pull over here. The El Centauro red – named for Pancho Villa – is an excellent estate-grown blend.

Groves NEW AMERICAN $$
(13065 Ave of the Giants, Myers Flat; ⌚5-9pm) This is the most refined eating option within miles, despite an aloof staff. The menu turns out simple, brick oven pizzas, but spicy prawns and fresh salads are all artfully plated.

Chimney Tree AMERICAN $
(1111 Ave of the Giants, Phillipsville; burgers $7-11; ⌚10am-7pm May-Sep) If you're just passing through and want something quick, come here. It raises its own grass-fed beef. Alas, the fries are frozen, but those burgers... mmm-mmm!

Scotia

For years, Scotia was California's last 'company town,' entirely owned and operated by the Pacific Lumber Company, which built cookie-cut houses and had an open contempt for long-haired outsiders who liked to get between their saws and the big trees. The company recently went belly up, sold the mill to another redwood company and, though the town still has a creepy *Twilight Zone* vibe, you no longer have to operate by the company's posted 'Code of Conduct.' A history of the town awaits at the **Scotia Museum & Visitor Center** (www.townofscotia.com; cnr Main & Bridge Sts; ⌚8am-4:30pm Mon-Fri Jun-Sep), at the town's south end. The museum's **fisheries center** (admission free) is remarkably informative – ironic, considering that logging destroys fish habitats – and houses the largest freshwater aquarium on the North Coast.

There are dingy motels and diners in **Rio Dell** (aka 'Real Dull'), across the river. Back in the day, this is where the debauchery happened: because it wasn't a company town, Rio Dell had bars and hookers. In 1969, the freeway bypassed the town and it withered.

As you drive along Hwy 101 and see what appears to be a never-ending redwood forest, understand that this 'forest' sometimes consists of trees only a few rows deep – called a 'beauty strip' – a carefully crafted illusion for tourists. Most old-growth trees have been cut. **Bay Area Coalition for Headwaters Forest** (www.headwaterspreserve.org) helped preserve over 7000 acres of land with public funds through provisions in a long-negotiated agreement between the Pacific Lumber Company and state and federal agencies.

Up Hwy 101 there's a great pit stop at **Eel River Brewing** (www.eelriverbrewing.com; 1777 Alamar Way, Fortuna; ⏲11am-11pm Mon-Sun), where a breezy beer garden and excellent burgers accompany all-organic brews.

Ferndale

The North Coast's most charming town is stuffed with impeccable Victorians – known locally as 'butterfat palaces' because of the dairy wealth that built them. There are so many, in fact, that the entire place is a state and federal historical landmark. Dairy farmers built the town in the 19th century and it's still run by the 'milk mafia': you're not a local till you've lived here 40 years. A stroll down Main St offers galleries, old-world emporiums and soda fountains. Although Ferndale relies on tourism, it has avoided becoming a tourist trap – and has no chain stores. Though a lovely place to spend a summer night, it's dead as a doornail in winter.

Sights & Activities

Half a mile from downtown via Bluff St, enjoy short tramps through fields of wildflowers, beside ponds, past redwood groves and eucalyptus trees at 110-acre **Russ Park**. The **cemetery**, also on Bluff St, is amazingly cool with graves dating to the 1800s and expansive views to the ocean. Five miles down Centerville Rd, **Centerville Beach** is one of the few off-leash dog beaches in Humboldt County.

FREE **Kinetic Sculpture Museum** MUSEUM, GALLERY
(580 Main St; ⏲10am-5pm Mon-Sat, noon-4pm Sun; 👪) This warehouse holds the fanciful, astounding, human-powered contraptions used in the town's annual Kinetic Grand Championship. Shaped like giant fish and UFOs, these colorful piles of junk propel racers over roads, water and marsh in the May event.

Fern Cottage HISTORIC BUILDING
(☎707-786-4835; www.ferncottage.org; Centerville Rd; group tours $10 per person; ⏲by appointment) This 1866 Carpenter Gothic grew to a 32-room mansion. Only one family ever lived here, so the interior is completely preserved.

Gingerbread Mansion HISTORIC BUILDING
(400 Berding St) An 1898 Queen Anne-Eastlake, this is the town's most photographed building. It held guests as a B&B for years, but has recently closed.

Festivals & Events

This wee town has a packed social calendar, especially in the summer. If you're planning a visit, check the events page at www.victorianferndale.com.

Tour of the Unknown Coast BICYCLE RACE
(www.tuccycle.org) A challenging event in May, in which participants of the 100 mile race climb nearly 10,000 feet.

Humboldt County Fair FAIR
(www.humboldtcountyfair.org) Held in mid-August, the longest running county fair in California.

Sleeping

Shaw House B&B $$
(☎707-786-9958, 800-557-7429; www.shawhouse.com; 703 Main St; r $145-175, ste $225-275; 📶) Shaw House, an emblematic 'butterfat palace,' was the first permanent structure in Ferndale, completed by founding father Seth Shaw in 1866. Today, it's California's oldest B&B, set back on extensive grounds. Original details remain, including painted wooden ceilings. Most of the rooms have private entrances, and three have private balconies over a large garden.

Francis Creek Inn MOTEL $
(☎707-786-9611; www.franciscreekinn.com; 577 Main St; r from $85; 📶) White picket balconies stand in front of this sweet little downtown motel, which is family owned and operated

(you check in at the Red Front convenience store, right around the corner). Spartan rooms are basic, clean and furnished simply, and the value is outstanding.

Hotel Ivanhoe HISTORIC HOTEL **$$**
(☎707-786-9000; www.ivanhoe-hotel.com; 315 Main St; r $95-145) Ferndale's oldest hostelry opened in 1875. It has four antique-laden rooms and an Old West–style 2nd-floor gallery, perfect for morning coffee. The adjoining saloon, with dark wood and lots of brass, is an atmospheric place for a nightcap.

Victorian Inn HISTORIC HOTEL **$$**
(☎707-786-4949, 888-589-1808; www.victorianvillageinn.com; 400 Ocean Ave; r $105-225;) The bright, sunny rooms inside this venerable 1890 two-story, former bank building, are comfortably furnished with thick carpeting, good linens and antiques.

Humboldt County Fairgrounds CAMPGROUND **$**
(☎707-786-9511; www.humboldtcountyfair.org; 1250 5th St; tent/RV sites $10/20) Turn west onto Van Ness St and go a few blocks for lawn camping with showers.

Eating

A **farmers market** (400 Ocean Ave; ⏰10:30am-2pm Sat May-Oct) has locally grown veggies and locally produced dairy – including the freshest cheese you'll find anywhere. Main St has lots of cafe options for eating, as well as white table cloth spots in both historic hotels.

Lotus Asian Bistro & Tea Room PAN-ASIAN **$**
(www.lotusasianbistro.com; 619 Main St; mains $7-14; ⏰11:30am-9pm Sat, Sun & Tue, 4-9pm Mon & Fri) Cherry glazed beef, crispy scallion pancakes with pulled duck and udon bowls spiced with a ginger broth – the menu at this excellent Asian fusion bistro offers welcome diversity to Ferndale's lunch and dinner options.

No Brand Burger Stand BURGERS **$**
(989 Milton St; burgers $7; ⏰11am-5pm) Sitting near the entrance to town, this hole-in-the-wall turns out a juicy jalpeño double cheese burger that ranks easily as the North Coast's best burger. The shakes – so thick your cheeks hurt from pulling on the straw – are about the only other thing on the menu.

Poppa Joe's AMERICAN **$**
(409 Main St; mains $5-7; ⏰11am-8:30pm Mon-Fri, 6am-noon Sat & Sun) You can't beat the atmosphere at this diner, where trophy heads hang from the wall, the floors slant at a precarious angle and old men play poker all day. The American-style breakfasts are good, too – especially the pancakes.

Sweetness & Light CANDY **$**
(554 Main St; confections $2-3) The housemade, gooey Moo bars are this antique candy shop's flagship. It also serves great ice cream and espresso.

Entertainment

Ferndale Repertory Theatre THEATER
(☎707-786-5483; www.ferndale-rep.org; 447 Main St) This top-shelf community company produces excellent contemporary theatre in the historic Hart Theatre Building.

Shopping

Blacksmith Shop & Gallery METAL GOODS
(☎707-786-4216; www.ferndaleblacksmith.com; 455 & 491 Main St) From wrought-iron art to hand-forged furniture, this is the largest collection of contemporary blacksmithing in America.

Abraxas Jewelry & Leather Goods JEWELRY
(505 Main St) The pieces of locally forged jewelry here are extremely cool and moderately priced. The back room is filled with tons of hats.

Farmer's Daughter CLOTHING
(358 Main; ⏰11am-5pm Tue-Sat, noon-4pm Sun) An actual dairy farmer's daughter owns this cute Western boutique.

Humboldt Bay National Wildlife Refuge

This pristine **wildlife refuge** (☎707-733-5406; ⏰sunrise-sunset) protects wetland habitats for more than 200 species of birds migrating annually along the Pacific Flyway. Between the fall and early spring, when Aleutian geese descend en masse to the area, more than 25,000 geese might be seen in a cackling gaggle outside the visitor center.

The peak season for waterbirds and raptors runs September to March; for black brant geese and migratory shorebirds mid-March to late April. Gulls, terns, cormorants, pelicans, egrets and herons come year-round. Look for harbor seals offshore; bring binoculars. If it's open, drive out South Jetty Rd to the mouth of Humboldt Bay for a stunning perspective.

Pick up a map from the **visitor center** (1020 Ranch Rd; 8am-5pm). Exit Hwy 101 at Hookton Rd, 11 miles south of Eureka, turn north along the frontage road, on the freeway's west side. In April, look for the **Godwit Days** festival.

Eureka

One hour north of Garberville, on the edge of the giant Humboldt Bay, lies Eureka, the largest bay north of San Francisco. With strip-mall sprawl surrounding a lovely historic downtown, it wears its role as the county seat a bit clumsily. Despite a diverse and interesting community of artists, writers, pagans and other free-thinkers, Eureka's wild side slips out only occasionally – the **Redwood Coast Dixieland Jazz Festival** (www.redwoodcoastmusicfestivals.org) is a rollicking festival with events all over town, and summer concerts rock out the F Street Pier – but mostly, it goes to bed early. Make for Old Town, a small district with colorful Victorians, good shopping and a revitalized waterfront. For night life, head to Eureka's trippy sister up the road, Arcata.

Sights

The free *Eureka Visitors Map*, available at tourist offices, details walking tours and scenic drives, focusing on architecture and history. **Old Town**, along 2nd and 3rd Sts from C St to M St, was once down-and-out, but has been refurbished into a buzzing pedestrian district. The F Street Plaza and Boardwalk run along the waterfront at the foot of F St. Gallery openings fall on the first Saturday of every month.

Blue Ox Millworks & Historic Park MILL
(www.blueoxmill.com; adult/child 6-12yr $7.50/3.50; 9am-4pm Mon-Sat;) One of only seven of its kind in America, antique tools and mills are used to produce authentic gingerbread trim for Victorian buildings; one-hour self-guided tours take you through the mill and historical buildings, including a blacksmith shop and 19th-century skid camp. Kids love the oxen.

Romano Gabriel Wooden Sculpture Garden ART INSTALLATION
(315 2nd St) The coolest thing to gawk at downtown is this collection of whimsical outsider art that's enclosed by glass. For 30 years, wooden characters in Gabriel's front yard delighted locals. After he died in 1977, the city moved the collection here.

Clarke Historical Museum MUSEUM
(www.clarkemuseum.org; 240 E St; admission $1; 11am-4pm Wed-Sat) The best community historical museum on this stretch of the coast houses a set of typically musty relics – needlework hankies and paintings of the area's history-making notables (in this case Ulysses Grant, who was once dismissed from his post at Fort Humboldt for drunkenness). Its best collection is that of intricately woven baskets from local tribes. One look at the scenes of animals and warriors that unfold in the weave and you'll quickly understand the Pomo saying that 'every basket tells a story.'

Carson Mansion HISTORIC BUILDING
(134 M St) Of Eureka's fine Victorian buildings the most famous is the ornate 1880s home of lumber baron William Carson. It took 100 men a full year to build. Today it's a private men's club. The **pink house** opposite, at 202 M St, is an 1884 Queen Anne Victorian designed by the same architects and built as a wedding gift for Carson's son.

Sequoia Park PARK
(www.sequoiaparkzoo.net; 3414 W St; park free, zoo adult/child $5.50/3.50; zoo 10am-5pm May-Sep, Tue-Sun Oct-Apr;) A 77-acre old-growth redwood grove is a surprising green gem in the middle of a residential neighborhood. It has biking and hiking trails, a children's playground and picnic areas, and a small zoo.

Morris Graves Museum of Art MUSEUM
(www.humboldtarts.org; 636 F St; suggested donation $4; noon-5pm Thu-Sun) Across Hwy 101, the excellent museum shows rotating Californian artists and hosts performances inside the 1904 Carnegie library, the state's first public library.

Discovery Museum MUSEUM
(www.discovery-museum.org; 517 3rd St; admission $4; 10am-4pm Tue-Sat, from noon Sun;) A hands-on kids' museum.

Activities

Harbor Cruise HARBOR CRUISE
(www.humboldtbaymaritimemuseum.com; 75-minute narrated cruise adult/child $18/10, 1-hour cocktail cruise $10) Board the 1910 *Madaket*, America's oldest continuously operating passenger vessel, and learn the history of Humboldt Bay. Located at the foot of C St, it originally ferried

mill workers and passengers until the Samoa Bridge was built in 1972. The $10 sunset cocktail cruise serves from the smallest licensed bar in the state.

Hum-Boats Sail, Canoe & Kayak Center BOAT RENTAL
(www.humboats.com; Startare Dr; 9am-5pm Mon-Fri, 9am-6pm Sat & Sun Apr-Oct, 9am-2:30pm Nov-Mar) At Woodley Island Marina, this outfit rents kayaks and sailboats, offering lessons, tours, charters, sunset sails and full-moon paddles.

Sleeping

Every brand of chain hotel is along Hwy 101. Room rates run high midsummer; you can sometimes find cheaper in Arcata, to the north, or Fortuna, to the south. There are also a handful of motels which cost from $60 to $100 and have no air-conditioning; choose places set back from the road. The cheapest are south of downtown on the suburban strip.

Hotel Carter & Carter House Victorians HOTEL, B&B $$$
(707-444-8067, 800-404-1390; www.carterhouse.com; 301 L St; r incl breakfast $159-225, ste incl breakfast $304-385;) For those with a few extra bucks, the Hotel Carter and its associated Victorian rentals bear the standard for North Coast luxury. Recently constructed in period style, the hotel is a Victorian look-alike, holding rooms with top-quality linens and modern amenities; suites have in-room whirlpools and marble fireplaces. The same owners operate three sumptuously decorated houses: a single-level 1900 house, a honeymoon-hideaway cottage and a replica of an 1880s San Francisco mansion, which the owner built himself, entirely by hand. Unlike elsewhere, you won't see the innkeeper unless you want to. Guests have an in-room breakfast or can eat at the understated, elegant restaurant.

Eagle House Inn HISTORIC INN $$
(707-444-3344; www.eaglehouseinn.com; 139 2nd St; r $105-205;) This hulking Victorian hotel in Old Town has 24 rooms above a turn-of-the-century ballroom perfect for hide-and-seek. Rooms aren't overly stuffed with precious period furniture – carved headboards, floral-print carpeting and antique armoires – but some have bizarre touches (like the bright red spa tub that would fit in on an '80s adult film set). The coolest rooms are in the corner and have sitting areas in turrets looking over the street.

Abigail's Elegant Victorian Mansion B&B $$
(707-444-3144; www.eureka-california.com; 1406 C St; r $145-215) Inside this National Historic Landmark that's practically a living-history museum, the sweet-as-could-be innkeepers lavish guests with warm hospitality.

Daly Inn B&B $$
(707-445-3638, 800-321-9656; www.dalyinn.com; 1125 H St; r with bathroom $170-185, without bathroom $130) This impeccably maintained 1905 Colonial Revival mansion has individually decorated rooms with turn-of-the-20th-century European and American antiques. Guest parlors are trimmed with rare woods; outside are century-old flowering trees.

Bayview Motel MOTEL $
(707-442-1673, 866-725-6813; www.bayviewmotel.com; 2844 Fairfield St; r $109;) Spotless rooms are of the chain motel standard; some have patios overlooking Humboldt Bay.

Eureka Inn HISTORIC HOTEL $
(707-497-6903, 877-552-3985; www.eurekainn.com; cnr 7th & F St; r $65-90, ste $85-130;) This enormous historic hotel, long dormant, has found a new owner. While rooms are bland, they're cheap and the structure itself is magnificent.

Ship's Inn B&B $$
(707-443-7583, 877-443-7583; www.shipsinn.net; 821 D St; r $130-175, cottages $160;) Warmly modern furnishings with nautical themes, kind hosts and a full breakfast make this three-room inn a favorite for return guests.

Eating

Eureka is blessed with two excellent natural food grocery stores – **Eureka Co-op** (cnr 5th & L Sts) and **Eureka Natural Foods** (1626 Broadway) – and two weekly farmers markets – at the corner of **2nd & F Sts** (10am-1pm Tue Jun-Oct) and the **Henderson Center** (10am-1pm Thu Jun-Oct). The vibrant dining scene is focused in the Old Town district.

Kyoto JAPANESE $$
(707-443-7777; 320 F St; sushi $4-6, mains $15-25; 5:30-9:30pm Wed-Sat) New owners have had big shoes to fill by taking over a place renowned as the best sushi in Humboldt County, but the quality has not slipped and the atmosphere – in a tiny, packed room,

where conversation with the neighboring table is inevitable – is as fun as ever. A menu of sushi and sashimi is rounded out by grilled scallops and fern tip salad. North coast travelers who absolutely need sushi should phone ahead for a reservation.

Hurricane Kate's TAPAS $$
(www.hurricanekates.com; 511 2nd St; lunch mains $9-15, dinner mains $16-26; ⊙11am-2:30pm & 5-9pm; ☑) The favorite spot of local *bon vivants,* Kate's open kitchen pumps out pretty good, eclectic, tapas-style dishes and roast meats, but the wood-fired pizzas are the standout option. There is a full bar.

Restaurant 301 CALIFORNIAN $$$
(☎707-444-8062; www.carterhouse.com; 301 L St; breakfast $11, dinner mains $20-35, 4-course menu $62; ⊙7:30-10am & 6-9pm) Eureka's top table, romantic, sophisticated 301 serves a contemporary Californian menu, using produce from its organic gardens (tours available). Mains are pricey, but the prix-fixe menu is a good way to taste local food in its finest presentation. The eight-course Chef's Grand Menu ($92) is only worthy of *really* special occasions.

Waterfront Café Oyster Bar SEAFOOD $$
(102 F St; mains lunch $8-13, dinner $13-20; ⊙9am-9pm) With a nice bay view and baskets of steamed clams, fish and chips, oysters and chowder, this is a solid bay-side lunch. A top spot for Sunday brunch, with jazz and Ramos fizzes.

La Chapala MEXICAN $
(201 2nd St; mains $6-14; ⊙11am-8pm) For Mexican, family-owned La Chapala makes strong margaritas and homemade flan.

Ramone's BAKERY, DELI $
(2223 Harrison St; mains $6-10; ⊙7am-6pm Mon-Sat, 8am-4pm Sun) For grab-and-go sandwiches, fresh soups and wraps.

Drinking

Lost Coast Brewery BREWERY
(☎707-445-4480; 617 4th St;) The roster of the regular brews at Eureka's colorful brewery might not knock the socks off a serious beer snob (and can't hold a candle to some of the others on the coast), but highlights include the Downtown Brown Ale, Great White and Lost Coast Pale Ale. After downing a few pints, the fried pub grub starts to look pretty tasty.

Shanty DIVE BAR
(213 2nd St; ⊙noon-2am;) The coolest spot in town is grungy and fun. Play pool, Donkey Kong, Ms Pac Man or Ping Pong, or kick it on the back patio with local 20- and 30-something hipsters.

321 Coffee COFFEE SHOP
(321 3rd St; ⊙8am-9pm;) Students sip French-press coffee and play chess at this living-room-like coffeehouse. Good soup.

Shopping

Eureka's streets lie on a grid; numbered streets cross lettered streets. For the best window-shopping, head to the 300, 400 and 500 blocks of 2nd St, between D and G Sts. The town's low rents and cool old spaces harbor lots of indie boutiques.

Shipwreck VINTAGE
(430 3rd St) The quality of vintage goods here – *genuinely* distressed jeans and leather jackets, 1940s housedresses and hats – is complimented by hand-made local jewelry and paper products.

Going Places TRAVELGOODS, BOOKS
(www.goingplacesworld.com; 1328 2nd St) Guidebooks, travel gear and international goods are certain to give a thrill to any vagabond. It's one of three excellent book shops in Old Town.

Entertainment

Morris Graves Museum of Art PERFORMANCE SPACE
(www.humboldtarts.org; 636 F St; suggested donation $4; ⊙noon-5pm Thu-Sun) Hosts performing-arts events between September and May, usually on Saturday evenings and Sunday afternoons.

Arkley Center for the Performing Arts ARTS CENTER
(www.arkleycenter.com; 412 G St) Home to the Eureka Symphony and North Coast Dance, and stages musicals and plays.

Club Triangle at The Alibi CLUB
(535 5th St) On Sunday nights this place becomes the North Coast's gay dance club. For gay events, log onto www.queerhumboldt.com.

Information

Eureka Chamber of Commerce (☎707-442-3738, 800-356-6381, www.eurekachamber.com; 2112 Broadway; ⊙8:30am-5pm Mon-Fri)

The main visitor information center is on Hwy 101.

Pride Enterprises Tours (☎707-445-2117, 800-400-1849) Local historian Ray Hillman leads outstanding history tours. He's also licensed to guide in the national parks.

Six Rivers National Forest Headquarters (☎707-442-1721; 1330 Bayshore Way; ⌚8am-4:30pm Mon-Fri) Maps and information.

Getting There & Around

The Arcata/Eureka airport (ACV) is a small, expensive airport which connects regionally. See p257 for more information. The Greyhound station is in Arcata; see p257).

Eureka Transit Service (☎707-443-0826; www.eurekatransit.org) operates local buses ($1.30), Monday to Saturday.

Samoa Peninsula

Grassy dunes and windswept beaches extend along the half-mile-wide, 7-mile long Samoa Peninsula, Humboldt Bay's western boundary. Stretches of it are spectacular, particularly the dunes, which are part of a 34-mile-long dune system – the largest in Northern California – and the wildlife viewing is excellent. The shoreline road (Hwy 255) is a backdoor route between Arcata and Eureka.

At the peninsula's south end, **Samoa Dunes Recreation Area** (⌚sunrise-sunset) is good for picnicking and fishing. For wildlife, head to **Mad River Slough & Dunes**; from Arcata, take Samoa Blvd west for 3 miles, then turn right at Young St, the Manila turn-off. Park at the community center lot, from where a trail passes mudflats, salt marsh and tidal channels. There are over 200 species of birds: migrating waterfowl in spring and fall, songbirds in spring and summer, shorebirds in fall and winter, and waders year-round.

These undisturbed dunes reach heights of over 80ft. Because of the environment's fragility, access is by guided tour only. **Friends of the Dunes** (www.friendsofthedunes.org) leads free guided walks; register via email through the website. Check online for departure locations and information.

The lunch place on the peninsula is the **Samoa Cookhouse** (☎707-442-1659; www.samoacookhouse.net; off Samoa Blvd; breakfast/lunch/dinner $12/13/16; 👪), the last surviving lumber camp cookhouse in the West, where you can shovel down all-you-can-eat family meals at long red-checkered tables. Kids eat for half-price. The cookhouse is five minutes northwest of Eureka, across the Samoa Bridge; follow the signs. From Arcata, take Samoa Blvd (Hwy 255).

Arcata

The North Coast's most progressive town, Arcata surrounds a tidy central square that fills with college students, campers, transients and tourists. Sure, it occasionally reeks of patchouli and its politics lean far left (in 2003, the city outlawed voluntary compliance with the USA Patriot Act, in 2006 it spearheaded a coalition of cities to impeach conservative president George W Bush), but its earnest embrace of sustainability has fostered some of the most progressive civic action in America. Here, garbage trucks run on biodiesel, recycling gets picked up by tandem bicycle, wastewater gets filtered clean in marshlands and almost every street has a bike lane.

Founded in 1850 as a base for lumber camps, today Arcata is defined as a magnate for 20-somethings looking to expand their minds: either at Humboldt State University (HSU), and/or on the highly potent marijuana which grows around here like, um, weeds. After a 1996 state proposition legalized marijuana for medical purposes, Arcata became what one *New Yorker* article referred to as the 'heartland of high grade marijuana.' The economy of the regions has become inexorably tied to the crop since.

Roads run on a grid, with numbered streets traveling east–west and lettered streets going north–south. G and H Sts run north and south (respectively) to HSU and Hwy 101. The plaza is bordered by G and H and 8th and 9th Sts.

Sights

Around **Arcata Plaza** are two National Historic Landmarks: the 1857 **Jacoby's Storehouse** (cnr H & 8th Sts) and the 1915 **Hotel Arcata** (cnr G & 9th Sts). Another great historic building is the 1914 **Minor Theatre** (1013 10th St), which some local historians claim is the oldest theater in the US built specifically for showing film.

Humboldt State University UNIVERSITY
(HSU; www.humboldt.edu) The University on the northeastern side of town holds the Campus Center for Appropriate Technology (CCAT), a

world leader in developing sustainable technologies; on Fridays at 2pm you can take a self-guided tour of the **CCAT House**, a converted residence that uses only 4% of the energy of a comparably sized dwelling.

Arcata Marsh & Wildlife Sanctuary WILDLIFE SANCTUARY
On the shores of Humboldt Bay, this has 5 miles of walking trails and outstanding birding. The **Redwood Region Audubon Society** (www.rras.org; donation welcome) offers guided walks Saturdays at 8:30am, rain or shine, from the parking lot at I St's south end. Friends of Arcata Marsh offer guided tours Saturdays at 2pm from the **Arcata Marsh Interpretive Center** (707 826 2359; 569 South G St; tours free; 9am-5pm).

Activities

TOP CHOICE **Finnish Country Sauna & Tubs** HOT TUBS, SAUNA
(707-822-2228, www.cafemokkaarcata.com; cnr 5th & J Sts; noon-11pm Sun-Thu, to 1am Fri & Sat) Like some kind of Euro-crunchy bohemian dream, these private, open-air redwood hot tubs (half-hour/hour $9/17) and sauna are situated around a small frog pond, perfect for the sore legs of hikers or weary travelers up Hwy 101. The rates are reasonable, the staff is easygoing, and the facility is relaxing, simple and clean. Reserve ahead, especially on weekends.

HSU Center Activities OUTDOOR ACTIVITIES
(www.humboldt.edu/centeractivities) An office on the 2nd floor of the University Center, beside the campus clock tower, sponsors myriad workshops, outings and sporting-gear rentals; nonstudents welcome.

Arcata Community Pool SWIMMING
(ww.arcatapool.com; 1150 16th St; adult/child $7/5.25; 5:30am-9pm Mon-Fri, 9am-6pm Sat, 1-4pm Sun;) Has a coed hot tub, sauna and exercise room.

Adventure's Edge OUTDOOR GEAR RENTAL
(www.adventuresedge.com; 650 10th St; 9am-6pm Mon-Sat, 10am-5pm Sun) Rents, sells and services outdoor equipment.

Festivals & Events

Kinetic Grand Championship RACE
(www.kineticgrandchampionship.com) Arcata's most famous event is held Memorial Day weekend: people on amazing self-propelled contraptions travel 38 miles from Arcata to Ferndale.

Arcata Bay Oyster Festival FOOD FESTIVAL
(www.oysterfestival.net) A magical celebration of oysters and beer happens in June.

North Country Fair FAIR
(www.sameoldpeopl.org) A fun September street fair, where bands with names like The Fickle Hillbillies jam.

Sleeping

Arcata has affordable but limited lodgings. A cluster of hotels – Comfort Inn, Hamption Inn, etc – is just north of town, off Hwy 101's Giuntoli Lane. There's cheap camping further north at Clam Beach (p258).

Hotel Arcata HISTORIC HOTEL $$
(707-826-0217, 800-344-1221; www.hotelarcata.com; 708 9th St; r $96-156;) Anchoring the plaza, the renovated 1915 brick landmark has friendly staff, high ceilings and comfortable, old-world rooms of mixed quality. The rooms in front are an excellent perch for people-watching on the square, but the quietest face the back.

Lady Anne Inn B&B $$
(707-822-2797; www.ladyanneinn.com; 902 14th St; r $125-140) Roses line the walkway to this 1888 mansion full of Victorian bric-a-brac. The frilly rooms are pretty, but there's no breakfast.

Arcata Stay VACATION RENTALS $$
(707-822-0935, 877-822-0935; www.arcatastay.com; apt from $165) A network of excellent

MONEY TREES: ECONOMICS OF HUMBOLDT HERB

» Estimated percentage of Humboldt residents (18–65) with income partially tied to cultivating marijuana: 50

» Estimated wholesale value of one pound of 'Humboldt Kush': $3000

» Number of plants allowed per Proposition 215 card holder: 99

» Number of pounds produced by one high-yield plant: 1

» Estimated cost of production, one ounce: $100–180

» Estimated street value, one ounce: $300–600

apartment and cottage rentals. There is a two-night minimum.

Fairwinds Motel MOTEL $
(☎707-822-4824; www.fairwindsmotelarcata.com; 1674 G St; s $70-75, d $80-90;) Serviceable rooms in this standard-issue motel, with some noise from Hwy 101.

Eating

Great food abounds in restaurants throughout Arcata, almost all casual.

There are fantastic **farmers markets**, at the **Arcata Plaza** (9am-2pm Sat Apr-Nov) and in the parking lot of **Wildberries Market** (3:30-6:30pm Tue Jun-Oct). Even at other times, **Wildberries Marketplace** (www.wildberries.com; 747 13th St; 7am-11pm), has a deli counter and a great selection of natural foods. The gigantic **North Coast Co-op** (cnr 8th & I Sts; 6am-9pm) carries organic foods and is a community staple; check the kiosk out front. Just a few blocks north of downtown, there is a cluster of the town's best restaurants on G St.

Folie Douce NEW AMERICAN $$$
(☎707-822-1042; www.holyfolie.com; 1551 G St; dinner mains $27-36; 5:30-9pm Tue-Thu, to 10pm Fri-Sat;) Just a slip of a place, but with an enormous reputation. The short but inventive menu features seasonally inspired bistro cooking, from Asian to Mediterranean, with an emphasis on local organics. Wood-fired pizzas ($14 to $19) are renowned. Sunday brunch, too. Reservations essential.

Jambalaya LATIN AMERICAN FUSION $$
(915 H St; mains lunch $7-9, dinner $15-20; 5pm-2am Mon-Tue & Thu-Fri, from 9pm Wed, from 10am Sat-Sun) Probably the most vibrant dining option on the square, Jambalaya serves a mishmash of Caribbean-influenced dishes – at lunch Cuban sandwiches, at dinner wild salmon and (of course) jambalaya. The drink menu also shines, with fresh fruit cocktails and a great beer selection. As if this wasn't fun enough, it also hosts Arcata's best live music scene.

3 Foods Cafe FUSION $$
(www.cafeattheendoftheuniverse.com; 835 J St; mains brunch $8-14, dinner $10-30; 5:30am-10pm Tue-Thu, to 11pm Fri & Sat, to 9pm Sun;) A perfect fit with the Arcata dining scene: whimsical, creative, worldly dishes (think Korean beef in a spicy chili sauce) at moderate prices (a prix fixe is sometimes available for $20). The lavender-infused cocktails start things off on the right foot. The mac and cheese is the crowd favorite.

Wildflower Cafe & Bakery CAFE $$
(☎707-822-0360; 1604 G St; breakfast & lunch $5-8, dinner mains $15-16; 8am-8pm Sun-Wed;) Tops for vegetarians, this tiny storefront serves fab frittatas, pancakes and curries, and big crunchy salads.

Japhy's Soup & Noodles NOODLES $
(1563 G St; mains $5-8; 11:30am-8pm Mon-Fri) Big salads, tasty coconut curry, cold noodle salads and homemade soups – and cheap!

Stars Hamburgers BURGERS $
(1535 G St; burgers $3-5; 11am-8pm Mon-Thu, to 9pm Fri, to 7pm Sat, noon-6pm Sun;) Uses grass-fed beef to make fantastic burgers.

Don's Donuts FAST FOOD $
(933 HSt; donuts $0.80-1.35, sandwiches from $6; 24hr) Get a southeast-Asian sandwich.

Drinking

Dive bars and cocktail lounges line the plaza's northern side. Arcata is awash in coffeehouses.

TOP CHOICE **Six Rivers Brewery** BREWPUB
(www.sixriversbrewery.com; 1300 Central Ave, McKinleyville; mains $11-18; 11:30am-midnight Tue-Sun, from 4pm Mon) One of the first female-owned breweries in California, the 'brew with a view' kills it in every category: great beer, amazing community vibe, occasional live music and delicious hot wings. The spicy chili pepper ale is amazing. At first glance the menu might seem like ho-hum pub grub, but the batter crusted halibut is a golden treat and the salads are fresh and huge. They also make a helluva pizza.

Humboldt Brews BAR
(www.humbrews.com; 856 10th St; pub grub $5-10) This popular beer house has been elegantly remodeled and has a huge selection of carefully selected beer taps, fish tacos and buffalo wings. Live music nightly.

Cafe Mokka COFFEE SHOP
(www.cafemokkaarcata.com; cnr 5th & J Sts; snacks $4) Bohos head to this cafe at Finnish Country Sauna & Tubs (p255) for a mellow, old-world vibe, good coffee drinks and homemade cookies.

Entertainment

Arcata Theatre CINEMA
(www.arcatatheater.com; 1036 G St) An exquisite remodeling has revived this classic movie house, which shows art films, rock documentaries, silent films and more. Plus, it serves beer.

Center Arts ARTS CENTER
(☎tickets 707-826-3928; www.humboldt.edu/centerarts/) Hosts events on campus and you'd be amazed at who shows up: from Diana Krall and Dave Brubeck to Lou Reed and Ani Difranco. The place to buy tickets is at the University Ticket Office in the HSY Bookstore on the 3rd floor of the University Center.

Information

Arcata Eye (www.arcataeye.com) Free newspaper listing local events; the 'Police Log' column is hysterical.

Bureau of Land Management (BLM; ☎707-825-2300; 1695 Heindon Rd) Has information on the Lost Coast.

California Welcome Center (☎707-822-3619; www.arcatachamber.com; 1635 Heindon Rd; ⊙9am-5pm) Two miles north of town, off Giuntoli Lane, Hwy 101's west side. Operated by the Arcata Chamber of Commerce. Provides local and statewide information. Get the free *Official Map Guide to Arcata*.

Tin Can Mailman (www.tincanbooks.com; 1000 HSt) Used volumes on two floors; excellent for hard-to-find books.

Getting There & Around

Horizon Air (www.alaskaair.com) and **United** (www.united.com) make regional connections (which are predictably expensive) to the Arcata/Eureka airport.

Greyhound (www.greyhound.com) serves Arcata; from San Francisco budget $53 and seven hours. **Redwood Transit buses** (www.hta.org) serve Arcata and Eureka on the Trinidad–Scotia routes ($2.50, 2½ hours), which don't run on Sunday.

Arcata city buses (☎707-822-3775; ⊙Mon-Sat) stop at the **Arcata Transit Center** (☎707-825-8934; 925 E St at 9th St). For shared rides, read the bulletin board at the North Coast Co-op (p256).

Revolution Bicycle (www.revolutionbicycle.com; 1360 G St) and **Life Cycle Bike Shop** (www.lifecyclearcata.com; 1593 G St; ⊙Mon-Sat) rent, service and sell bicycles.

Only in Arcata: borrow a bike from **Library Bike** (www.arcata.com/greenbikes; 865 8th St) for a $20 deposit, which gets refunded when you return the bike – up to six months later! They're beaters, but they ride.

Though hitchhiking is still fairly rare and safety concerns should be taken seriously, a culture of hippies of all ages and transient marijuana harvesters makes this the easiest region in California to thumb a ride.

NORTHERN REDWOOD COAST

Congratulations, traveler, you've reached the middle of nowhere, or at least the top of the middle of nowhere. Here, the trees are so large that the tiny towns along the road seem even smaller. The scenery is pure drama: cliffs and rocks, native lore, legendary salmon runs, mammoth trees, redneck towns and RVing retirees. It's certainly the *weirdest* part of the California Coast. Leave time to dawdle and bask in the haunting grandeur of it all and, even though there are scores of mid-century motels, you simply must make an effort to sleep outdoors if possible.

Trinidad

Cheery Trinidad perches prettily on the side of the ocean, combining upscale homes with a mellow surfer vibe. Somehow it feels a bit off-the-beaten-path even though tourism augments fishing to keep the economy going. Trinidad gained its name when Spanish sea captains arrived on Trinity Sunday in 1775 and named the area La Santisima Trinidad (the Holy Trinity). It didn't boom, though, until the 1850s, when it became an important port for miners.

Sights & Activities

Trinidad is small: approach via Hwy 101 or from the north via Patrick's Point Dr (which becomes Scenic Dr further south). To reach town, take Main St.

The free town map at the information kiosk shows several fantastic hiking trails, most notably the **Trinidad Head Trail** with superb coastal views; excellent for whale-watching (December to April). Stroll along an exceptionally beautiful cove at **Trinidad State Beach**; take Main St and bear right at Stagecoach, then take the second turn left (the first is a picnic area) into the small lot.

Scenic Dr twists south along coastal bluffs, passing tiny coves with views back

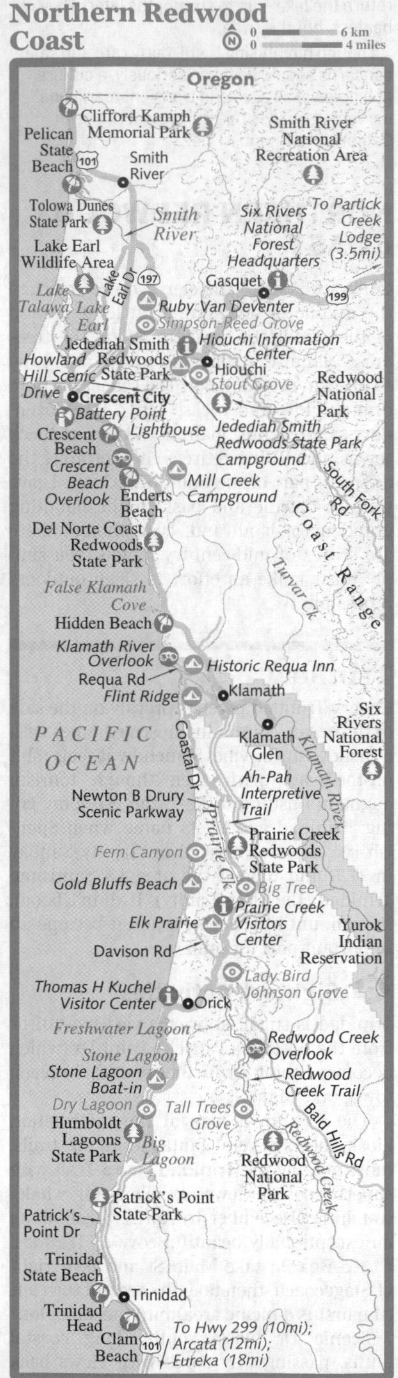

toward the bay. It peters out before reaching the broad expanses of **Luffenholtz Beach** (accessible via the staircase) and serene white-sand **Moonstone Beach**. Exit Hwy 101 at 6th Ave/Westhaven to get there. Further south Moonstone becomes **Clam Beach County Park**.

Surfing is good year-round, but potentially dangerous: unless you know how to judge conditions and get yourself out of trouble – there are no lifeguards here – surf in better-protected Crescent City.

FREE **HSU Telonicher Marine Laboratory** SCIENCE CENTER
(☎707-826-3671; www.humboldt.edu/marinelab; Ewing St; ⏲9am-4:30pm Mon-Fri, noon-4pm Sat Sep–mid-May; 👪) Near Edwards St, has a touch tank, several aquariums (look for the giant Pacific octopus), an enormous whale jaw and a cool three-dimensional map of the ocean floor. You can also join a naturalist on tide pooling expeditions (90 minutes, $3); call ahead to ask about conditions.

Sleeping

Many of the inns line Patrick's Point Dr, north of town. **Trinidad Retreats** (www.trinidadretreats.com) and **Redwood Coast Vacation Rentals** (www.enjoytrinidad.com) handle local property rentals.

TOP CHOICE **Trinidad Bay B&B** B&B $$$
(☎707-677-0840; www.trinidadbaybnb.com; 560 Edwards St; r incl breakfast from $200; 📶) Opposite the lighthouse, this gorgeous light-filled Cape Cod overlooks the harbor and Trinidad Head. Breakfast is delivered to your uniquely styled room and in the afternoon the house fills with the scent of freshly baked cookies. Each room also comes with a loaner iPad to use, loaded up with apps focused on local events and activities.

Clam Beach CAMPGROUND $
(tent sites per vehicle $10) South of town off Hwy 101, has excellent camping, but can get very crowded. Pitch your tent in the dunes (look for natural windbreaks). Facilities include pit toilets, cold water, picnic tables and fire rings.

View Crest Lodge LODGE $$
(☎707-677-3393; www.viewcrestlodge.com; 3415 Patrick's Point Dr; sites $32, 1-bedroom cottages $95-170; 📶) On a hill above the ocean on the inland side, some of the well-maintained, modern cottages have views and Jacuzzis;

most have kitchens. Also a good campground.

Trinidad Inn INN $
(☎707-677-3349; www.trinidadinn.com; 1170 Patrick's Point Dr; r $75-115; 📶) Sparklingly clean and attractively decorated rooms (many with kitchens) fill this upmarket, gray-shingled motel under tall trees.

Bishop Pine Lodge LODGE $$
(☎707-677-3314; www.bishoppinelodge.com; 1481 Patrick's Point Dr; cottages with/without kitchen from $150/110; 🐾) It feels like summer camp: rent free-standing redwood cottages in a grassy meadow. Expect woodsy charm and unintentionally retro-funky furniture.

Lost Whale Inn B&B $$$
(☎707-677-3425; www.lostwhaleinn.com; 3452 Patrick's Point Dr; r all incl breakfast $200-285, ste all incl breakfast $375; 📶👪) Perched atop a grassy cliff, high above crashing waves and braying sea lions, this spacious, modern, light-filled B&B has jaw-dropping views out to the sea. The lovely gardens have a 24-hour hot tub.

Eating & Drinking

TOP CHOICE **Larrupin Cafe** CALIFORNIAN $$$
(☎707-677-0230; www.larrupin.com; 1658 Patrick's Point Dr; mains $20-30; ⏲5-9pm Thu-Tue) Everybody loves Larrupin, where Moroccan rugs, chocolate brown walls, gravity-defying floral arrangements and deep-burgundy Oriental carpets create a moody atmosphere perfect for a lovers' tryst. On the menu, expect consistently good mesquite-grilled seafood and meats. In the summer, book a table on the garden patio. No credit cards.

Kahish's Catch Café FAST FOOD $
(☎707-677-0390; 355 Main St; mains $6-9; ⏲11am-7pm Tue-Sun; 👪) Across from the Chevron, this fun little hippie joint makes good food fast, using mostly organic ingredients – from pizzettas and grass-fed burgers to brown rice and veggies. Order at the counter and then sit outside.

Moonstone Grill SEAFOOD $$$
(Moonstone Beach; mains $20-32; ⏲5:30-8:30pm Wed-Sun) Enjoy drop-dead sunset views over a picture-perfect beach while supping on the likes of oysters on the half-shell, Pacific wild king salmon or spice-rubbed rib eye. If the high price tag is a bit out-of-budget, drop in for a glass of wine.

Katy's Smokehouse & Fishmarket SEAFOOD $
(www.katyssmokehouse.com; 740 Edwards St; ⏲9am-6pm) Makes its own chemical-free smoked and canned fish, using line-caught sushi-grade seafood.

Beachcomber Café CAFE $
(☎707-677-0106; 363 Trinity St; ⏲7am-4pm Mon-Fri, 9am-4pm Sat & Sun) Head here for the best homemade cookies and to meet locals. Friday rocks live music.

Information

Beachcomber Cafe (☎707-677-0106; 363 Trinity St; per hr $5; ⏲7am-4pm Mon-Thu, to 9pm Fri, 9am-4pm Sat & Sun) Internet access.

Information kiosk (cnr Patrick's Point Dr & Main St) Just west of the freeway. The pamphlet *Discover Trinidad* has an excellent map.

Trinidad Chamber of Commerce (☎707-667-1610; www.trinidadcalif.com) Information on the web, but no visitor center.

Patrick's Point State Park

Coastal bluffs jut out to sea at 640-acre **Patrick's Point** (☎707-677-3570; 4150 Patrick's Point Dr; day use $8; 👪), where sandy beaches abut rocky headlands. Five miles north of Trinidad, with supereasy access to dramatic coastal bluffs, it's a best-bet for families. Stroll scenic overlooks, climb giant rock formations, watch whales breach, gaze into tidepools, or listen to barking sea lions and singing birds from this manicured park.

Sumêg is an authentic reproduction of a Yurok village, with hand-hewn redwood buildings where Native Americans gather for traditional ceremonies. In the native plant garden you'll find species for making traditional baskets and medicines.

On **Agate Beach** look for stray bits of jade and sea-polished agate. Follow the signs to tidepools, but tread lightly and obey regulations. The 2-mile **Rim Trail**, a former Yurok trail around the bluffs, circles the point with access to huge rocky outcroppings. Don't miss **Wedding Rock**, one of the park's most romantic spots. Other trails lead around unusual formations like **Ceremonial Rock** and **Lookout Rock**.

The park's three well-tended **campgrounds** (☎reservations 800-444-7275; www.reserveamerica.com; tent & RV sites $35) have coin-operated hot showers and very clean bathrooms. Penn Creek and Abalone campgrounds are more sheltered than Agate Beach.

Humboldt Lagoons State Park

Stretching out for miles along the coast, **Humboldt Lagoons** has long, sandy beaches and a string of coastal lagoons. **Big Lagoon** and the even prettier **Stone Lagoon** are both excellent for kayaking and bird-watching. Sunsets are spectacular, with no manmade structures in sight. Picnic at Stone Lagoon's north end. The Stone Lagoon Visitor Center, on Hwy 101, has closed due to staffing shortages, but there's a toilet and a bulletin board displaying information.

A mile north, **Freshwater Lagoon** is also great for birding. South of Stone Lagoon, tiny **Dry Lagoon** (a freshwater marsh) has a fantastic day hike. Park at Dry Lagoon's picnic area and hike north on the unmarked trail to Stone Lagoon; the trail skirts the southwestern shore and ends up at the ocean, passing through woods and marshland rich with wildlife. Mostly flat, it's about 2.5 miles one way – and nobody takes it because it's unmarked.

All campsites are first-come, first-served. The park runs two **environmental campgrounds** (tent sites $20; ⏲Apr-Oct); bring water. Stone Lagoon has six boat-in environmental campsites; Dry Lagoon has six walk-in campsites. Check in at Patrick's Point State Park, at least 30 minutes before sunset.

Humboldt County Parks (☎707-445-7651; tent sites $20) operates a lovely cypress-grove picnic area and campground beside Big Lagoon, a mile off Hwy 101, with flush toilets and cold water, but no showers.

Redwood National & State Parks

A patchwork of public lands jointly administered by the state and federal governments, the **Redwood National & State Parks** include Redwood National Park, Prairie Creek Redwoods State Park (p261), Del Norte Coast Redwoods State Park (p262) and Jedediah Smith Redwoods State Park (p265). A smattering of small towns break up the forested area, making it a bit confusing to get a sense of the parks as a whole. Prairie Creek and Jedediah Smith parks were originally land slated for clear-cutting, but in the '60s activists successfully protected them and today all these parks are an International Biosphere Reserve and World Heritage Site. At one time the national park was to absorb at least two of the state parks, but that did not happen, and so the cooperative structure remains.

Little-visited compared to their southern brethren, the world's tallest living trees have been standing here for time immemorial, predating the Roman Empire by over 500 years. Prepare to be impressed.

The small town of **Orick** (population 650), at the southern tip of the park, in a lush valley, is barely more than a few storefronts and a vast conglomeration of woodcarving.

Sights & Activities

Just north of the southern visitor center, turn east onto Bald Hills Rd and travel 2 miles to **Lady Bird Johnson Grove**, one of the park's most spectacular groves, accessible via a gentle 1-mile loop trail. Continue for another 5 miles up Bald Hills to **Redwood Creek Overlook**. On the top of the ridgeline at 2100ft get views over the forest and the entire watershed – provided it's not foggy. Just past the overlook lies the gated turnoff for **Tall Trees Grove**, the location of several of the world's tallest trees. Rangers issue only 50 vehicle permits per day, but they rarely run out. Pick one up, along with the gate-lock combination, from the visitor centers. Allow four hours for the round-trip, which includes a 6-mile drive down a rough dirt road (speed limit 15mph) and a steep 1.3-mile one-way hike, which descends 800ft to the grove.

Several longer trails include the awe-inspiring **Redwood Creek Trail**, which also reaches Tall Trees Grove. You'll need a free backcountry permit to hike and camp (highly recommended, as the best backcountry camping in on the North Coast), but the area is most accessible from Memorial Day to Labor Day, when summer footbridges are up. Otherwise, getting across the creek can be perilous or impossible.

Information

Unlike most national parks, there are no fees and no highway entrance stations at Redwood National Park, so it's imperative to pick up the free map at the park headquarters (p264) in Crescent City or at the **Redwood Information Center** (Kuchel Visitor Center;

(☎707-464-6101; www.nps.gov/redw; Hwy 101; ⌚9am-6pm June-Aug, to 5pm Sept-Oct & March-May, to 4pm Nov-Feb) in Orick. Rangers here issue permits to visit Tall Trees Grove and loan bear-proof containers for backpackers. For in-depth redwood ecology, buy the excellent official park handbook. The **Redwood Parks Association** (www.redwoodparksassociation.org) provides good information on its website, including detailed descriptions of all the parks hikes.

Prairie Creek Redwoods State Park

Famous for virgin redwood and unspoiled coastline, this 14,000-acre section of Redwood National & State Parks has spectacular scenic drives and 70 miles of hiking trails, many of which are excellent for children. Pick up maps and information and sit by the river-rock fireplace at **Prairie Creek Visitor Center** (☎707-464-6101; ⌚9am-5pm Mar-Oct, 10am-4pm Nov-Feb; 👪). Kids will love the taxidermy dioramas with push-button, light-up displays. Outside, elk roam grassy flats.

Sights & Activities

Newton B Drury Scenic Parkway SCENIC DRIVE

Just north of Orick is the turn off for the 8-mile parkway, which runs parallel to Hwy 101 through untouched ancient redwood forests. It's worth the short detour off the freeway to view the magnificence of these trees. Numerous trails branch off from roadside pullouts, including family- and ADA (American Disabilities Act) -friendly trails including Big Tree and Revelation Trail.

Hiking & Mountain-Biking

There are 28 mountain-biking and hiking trails through the park, from simple to strenuous. Only a few of these will appeal to hard core hikers, who should take on the Del Norte Coast Redwoods. Those tight on time or with mobility impairments should stop at **Big Tree**, an easy 100yd walk from the car park. Several other easy nature trails start near the visitor center, including **Revelation Trail** and **Elk Prairie Trail**. Stroll the recently reforested logging road on the **Ah-Pah Interpretive Trail** at the park's north end. The most challenging hike in this corner of the park is the truly spectacular 11.5-mile **Coastal Trail** which goes through primordial redwoods.

Just past the **Gold Bluffs Beach Campground** the road dead ends at **Fern Canyon**, where 60ft fern-covered sheer-rock walls can be seen from Steven Spielberg's *Jurassic Park 2: The Lost World*. This is one of the most photographed spots on the North Coast – damp and lush, all emerald green – and *totally* worth getting your toes wet to see.

Sleeping

Welcome to the great outdoors: without any motels or cabins, the only choice here is to pitch a tent in the campgrounds at the southern end of the park.

Gold Bluffs Beach CAMPGROUND $

(no reservations; tent sites $35) This campground sits between 100ft cliffs and wide-open ocean, but there are some windbreaks and solar-heated showers. Look for sites up the cliff under the trees.

Elk Prairie Campground CAMPGROUND $

(☎reservations 800-444-7275; www.reserveamerica.com; tent & RV sites $35) Elk roam this popular campground, where you can sleep under redwoods or at the prairie's edge. There are hot showers, some hike-in sites and a shallow creek to splash in. Sites 1–7 and 69–76 are on grassy prairies and get full sun; sites 8–68 are wooded. To camp in a mixed redwood forest, book sites 20–27.

Klamath

Giant metal-cast golden bears stand sentry at the bridge across the Klamath River, announcing Klamath, one of the tiny settlements that break up Redwood National & State Parks. With a gas station/market, a great diner and a casino, Klamath is basically a wide spot in the road. The Yurok Tribal Headquarters is here and the entire town and much of the surrounding area is the tribe's ancestral land. Klamath is roughly an hour north of Eureka.

Sights & Activities

The mouth of the **Klamath River** is a dramatic sight. Marine, riparian, forest and meadow ecological zones all converge and the birding is exceptional. For the best views, head north of town to Requa Rd and the **Klamath River Overlook** and picnic on high bluffs above driftwood-strewn beaches. On a clear day, this is one of the most spectacular viewpoints on the North Coast, and one of the best whale-watching spots in California. For a good hike, head north along the Coastal Trail. You'll have the sand to yourself at **Hidden Beach**; access the trail at the northern end of Motel Trees.

Just south of the river, on Hwy 101, follow signs for the scenic **Coastal Drive**, a narrow, winding country road (unsuitable for RVs and trailers) atop extremely high cliffs over the ocean. Come when it's not foggy, and mind your driving. Though technically in Redwood National Park, it's much closer to Klamath.

Klamath Jet Boat Tours BOAT TOURS
(www.jetboattours.com; 2hr tours adult/child $42/22) Book jet-boat excursions and fishing trips.

Sleeping & Eating

Woodsy Klamath is cheaper than Crescent City, but there aren't as many places to eat or buy groceries, and there's nothing to do at night but play cards. There are ample private RV parks in the area.

TOP CHOICE **Historic Requa Inn** HISTORIC HOTEL $
(707-482-1425; www.requainn.com; 451 Requa Rd, Klamath; r $85-155;) A woodsy country lodge on bluffs overlooking the mouth of the Klamath, the 1914 Requa Inn is one of our North Coast favorites and – a cherry on top – it's a carbon neutral facility. Many of the charming country-style rooms have mesmerizing views over the misty river, as does the dining room, where guests have breakfast.

Ravenwood Motel MOTEL $$
(707-482-5911, 866-520-9875; www.ravenwoodmotel.com; 131 Klamath Blvd; r/ste with kitchen $75/115) The spotlessly clean rooms are better than anything in Crescent City and individually decorated with furnishings and flair you'd expect in a city hotel, not a small-town motel.

FREE **Flint Ridge Campground** CAMPGROUND
(707-464-6101) Four miles from the Klamath River Bridge via Coastal Dr, this tent-only, hike-in campground sits among a wild, overgrown meadow of ghostly, overgrown ferns and moss. It's a 10-minute walk east, uphill from the dirt parking area. There's no water, plenty of bear sightings (bear boxes on site) and you have to pack out trash. But, hey, it's free.

Klamath River Cafe AMERICAN $
(707-482-1000;mains $8-12; 7:30am-2pm) With excellent homemade baked goods, a daily pie special and excellent breakfast food, this shiny new place is the best diner food within miles. The breakfasts are killer. Seasonal hours vary, so call ahead. If you arrive around dinner time, cross your fingers – it's open sporadically for dinner.

WHAT THE...?

It's hard to miss the giant statues of Paul Bunyan and Babe the Blue Ox towering over the parking lot at **Trees of Mystery** (707-482-2251; www.treesofmystery.net; 15500 Hwy 101; adult/child & senior $14/7; 8am-7pm Jun-Aug, 9am-4pm Sep-May;), a shameless tourist trap with a gondola running through the redwood canopy. The **End of the Trail Museum** located behind the Trees of Mystery gift shop has an outstanding collection of Native American arts and artifacts, and it's *free*.

Del Norte Coast Redwoods State Park

Marked by steep canyons and dense woods, half the 6400 acres of this **park** (vehicle day-use $8) are virgin redwood forest, crisscrossed by 15 miles of hiking trails. Even the most cynical of redwood-watchers can't help but be moved.

Pick up maps and inquire about guided walks at the Redwood National & State Parks Headquarters (p264) in Crescent City or the Redwood Information Center in Orick (p260).

Hwy 1 winds in from the coast at rugged, dramatic **Wilson Beach**, and traverses the dense forest, with groves stretching off as far as you can see.

Picnic on the sand at **False Klamath Cove**. Heading north, tall trees cling precipitously to canyon walls that drop to the rocky, timber-strewn coastline, and it's almost impossible to get to the water, except via gorgeous but steep **Damnation Creek Trail** or **Footsteps Rock Trail**.

Between these two, serious hikers will be most greatly rewarded by the Damnation Creek Trail. It's only 4 miles long, but the 1100-foot elevation change and cliff-side redwood makes it the park's best hike. The

WORTH A TRIP

SMITH RIVER NATIONAL RECREATION AREA

West of Jedediah Smith Redwoods, the Smith River, the state's last remaining undammed waterway, runs right beside Hwy 199. Originating high in the Siskiyou Mountains, its serpentine course cuts through deep canyons beneath thick forests. Chinook salmon and steelhead trout annually migrate up its clear waters. Camp, hike, raft and kayak here, but check regulations if you want to fish. Stop by the **Six Rivers National Forest Headquarters** (707-457-3131; www.fs.fed.us/r5/sixrivers; 10600 Hwy 199, Gasquet; 8am-4:30pm daily May-Sep, 8am-4:30pm Mon-Fri Oct-Apr) to get your bearings. Pick up pamphlets for the **Darlingtonia Trail** and **Myrtle Creek Botanical Area**, both easy jaunts into the woods, where you can see rare plants and learn about the area's geology.

unmarked trailhead starts from a parking area off Hwy 101 at mile mark 16.

Crescent Beach Overlook and picnic area has superb wintertime whale-watching. At the park's north end, watch the surf pound at **Crescent Beach**, just south of Crescent City via Enderts Beach Rd.

Mill Creek Campground (800-444-7275; www.reserveamerica.com; tent & RV sites $35) has hot showers and 145 sites in a redwood grove, 2 miles east of Hwy 101 and 7 miles south of Crescent City. Sites 1-74 are woodsier; sites 75-145 sunnier. Hike-in sites are prettiest.

Crescent City

Though Crescent City was founded as a thriving 1853 seaport and supply center for inland gold mines, the town's history was quite literally washed away in 1964, when half the town was swallowed by a tsunami. Of course, it was rebuilt (though mostly with the utilitarian ugliness of ticky-tacky buildings), but its marina was devastated by the 2011 Japan earthquake and tsunami, when the city was evacuated. Crescent City remains California's last big town north of Arcata, though the constant fog (and sounding fog horn) and damp, '60s sprawl makes it about as charming as a wet bag of dirty laundry. The economy depends heavily on shrimp and crab fishing, hotel tax and on Pelican Bay maximum-security prison, just north of town, which adds tension to the air and lots of cops on the streets.

Sights & Activities

Hwy 101 splits into two parallel one-way streets, with the southbound traffic on L St, northbound on M St. To see the major sights, turn west on Front St toward the lighthouse. Downtown is centered along 3rd St.

If you're in town in August, the **Del Norte County Fair** features a rodeo, and lots of characters.

North Coast Marine Mammal Center SCIENCE CENTER
(707-465-6265; www.northcoastmmc.org; 424 Howe Dr; by donation; 10am-5pm;) Just east of Battery Point, this is the ecologically minded foil to the garish Ocean World: the clinic treats injured seals, sea lions and dolphins and releases them back into the wild (donation requested).

Battery Point Lighthouse LIGHTHOUSE
(www.delnortehistory.org/lighthouse) The 1856 lighthouse, at the south end of A St, still operates on a tiny, rocky island that you can easily reach at low tide. From April to September, tour the **museum** (adult/child $3/1; 10am-4pm Mon-Sat May Sep); hours vary with tides and weather.

Beachfront Park PARK
(Howe Dr;) Between B and H Sts, this park has a harborside beach with no large waves, making it perfect for little ones. Further east on Howe Dr, near J St, you'll come to **Kidtown**, with slides and swings and a make-believe castle.

Sleeping

Most people stop here for one night while traveling; motels are overpriced, but you'll pass a slew of hotels on the main arteries leading into and out of town. The county operates two excellent reservable **campgrounds** (707-464-7230; tent & RV sites $10) just outside of town. **Florence Keller Park** (3400 Cunningham Lane) has 50 sites in a beautiful grove of young redwoods (take Hwy 101 north to Elk Valley Cross Rd and follow the signs). **Ruby Van Deventer Park** (4705 N Bank Rd) has 18 sites along the Smith River, off Hwy 197. Both of these are an excellent bargain.

TOP CHOICE **Curly Redwood Lodge** MOTEL $
(707-464-2137; www.curlyredwoodlodge.com; 701 Hwy 101 S; r $68-73;) The Redwood Lodge is a marvel: it's entirely built and paneled from a single curly redwood tree which measured over 18-in thick in diameter. Progressively restored and polished into a gem of mid-century kitsch, the inn is a delight for retro junkies. Rooms are clean, large and comfortable (request one away from the road). For truly modern accommodations, look elsewhere.

Bay View Inn HOTEL $
(800-742-8439; www.bayviewinn.net; 2844 Fairfield; r $74-89;) Bright, modern, updated rooms with microwaves and refrigerators fill this centrally located independent hotel. It may seem a bit like better-than-average highway exit chain, but colorful bead spreads and warm hosts add necessary homespun appeal. The rooms upstairs in the back have views of the lighthouse and the harbor.

Crescent Beach Motel MOTEL $
(707-464-5436; www.crescentbeachmotel.com; 1455 Hwy 101 S; r $70-100;) Just south of town, this basic, old-fashioned motel is the only place in town to stay right on the beach, offering views that distract you from the somewhat plain indoor environs. Try here first, but skip rooms without a view.

Anchor Beach Inn HOTEL $
(707-464-2600; www.anchorbeachinn.com; 880 Hwy 101 S; r $85-105;) Microwave, DSL, soundproof walls and personality-free.

Eating & Drinking

Beacon Burger BURGERS $
(160 Anchor Way; burgers $6-10; 11:30am-8:30pm Mon-Sat) This scrappy little one-room burger joint has been here forever, square in the middle of a parking lot overlooking the South Bay. It looks like it might invite a health inspector's scorn, but you'll quickly forgive it after ordering a burger – perfectly greasy and mysteriously wonderful. They come sided with potato gems and a menu of thick shakes.

Wing Wah Restaurant CHINESE $
(383 M St; mains $7-11; 11:30am-9pm Sun-Thu, to 9:30 Fri & Sat) Tucked into a shopping center, Wing Wah serves Crescent City's best Chinese food; savory pork and beef dishes are fresh and come quickly to the table.

Good Harvest Café AMERICAN $
(575 Hwy 101 S; mains $7-10; 7am-9pm Mon-Sat, from 8am Sun;) This popular local cafe recently moved into a spacious new location across from the harbor. It also added a dinner menu on par with the quality salads, smoothies and sandwiches that made it so popular in the first place. Good beers, a crackling fire and loads of vegetarian options make this the best dining spot in town.

Chart Room SEAFOOD $
(130 Anchor Way; dinner mains $9-23; 6:30am-7pm Sun-Thu, to 8pm Fri & Sat;) At the tip of the South Harbor pier, this joint is renowned far and wide for its fish and chips: batter-caked golden beauties which deliver on their reputation. It's often a hive of families, retirees, Harley riders and local businessmen, so grab a beer at the small bar and wait for a table.

Tomasini's CAFE $
(960 3rd St; mains $4-8; 7:30am-2pm;) Stop in for salads, sandwiches or jazz on weekend nights. Hands down the most happening place downtown.

Information

Crescent City-Del Norte Chamber of Commerce (707-464-3174, 800-343-8300; www.northerncalifornia.net; 1001 Front St; 9am-5pm May-Aug, 9am-5pm Mon-Fri Sep-Apr) Local information.

Redwood National & State Parks Headquarters (707-464-6101; 1111 2nd St; 9am-5pm Oct-May, to 6pm Jun-Sep) On the corner of K St; rangers and information about all four parks under its jurisdiction.

Getting There & Around

United Express (800-241-6522) flies into tiny **Crescent City Airport** (CEC), north of town. **Redwood Coast Transit** (www.redwoodcoasttransit.org) serves Crescent City with local buses ($1), and runs buses Monday to Saturday to Klamath ($1.50, one hour, two daily) and Arcata ($20, two hours, two daily) with stops in between.

Tolowa Dunes State Park & Lake Earl Wildlife Area

Two miles north of Crescent City, this **state park and wildlife area** (707-464-6101, ext 5112; sunrise-sunset) encompasses 10,000 acres of wetlands, dunes, meadows and two lakes, **Lake Earl** and **Lake Tolowa**. This major stopover on the Pacific Flyway route brings over 250 species of birds. Listen for the whistling, warbling chorus. On land, look for coyotes and deer. Angle for trout, or hike or ride 20 miles of trails; at sea, spot whales, seals and sea lions.

The park and wildlife area is a patchwork of lands administered by California State Parks and the Department of Fish and Game (DFG). The DFG focuses on single-species management, hunting and fishing; the State Parks' focus is on ecodiversity and recreation. You might be hiking a vast expanse of pristine dunes, then suddenly hear a shotgun or a whining 4WD. Strict regulations limit where and when you can hunt and drive; trails are clearly marked.

Register for two primitive, nonreservable **campgrounds** (tent sites $20) at Jedediah Smith or Del Norte Coast Redwoods State Park campgrounds. The mosquitoes are plentiful in the spring and early summer.

Jedediah Smith Redwoods State Park

The northern-most park in the system of Redwood National & State Parks, the dense stands at **Jedediah Smith** (day use $8) are 10 miles northeast of Crescent City (via Hwy 101 east to Hwy 197). The redwood stands are so thick that few trails penetrate the park, but the outstanding 11-mile **Howland Hill scenic drive** cuts through otherwise inaccessible areas (take Hwy 199 to South Fork Rd; turn right after crossing two bridges). It's a rough road, impassable for RVs, but if you can't hike, it's the best way to see the forest.

Stop for a stroll under enormous trees in **Simpson-Reed Grove**. If it's foggy at the coast it may be sunny here. There's a **swimming hole** and picnic area near the park entrance. An easy half-mile trail, departing from the far side of the campground, crosses the **Smith River** via a summer-only footbridge, leading to **Stout Grove**, the park's most famous grove. The **visitor center** (707-464-6101; 10am-4pm daily Jun-Aug, 10am-4pm Sat & Sun Sep-Oct & Apr-May) sells hiking maps and nature guides. If you wade in the river, be careful in the spring when currents are swift and the water cold.

The popular **campground** (reservations 800-444-7275; www.reserveamerica.com; tent & RV sites $35) has gorgeous sites tucked through the redwoods beside the Smith River.

If you don't camp, try the renovated **Hiouchi Motel** (707-458-3041, 888-881-0819; www.hiouchimotel.com; 2097 Hwy 199; s $50, d $65-70; @) offering clean, straightforward motel rooms.

Pelican Beach State Park

Never-crowded **Pelican State Beach** (707-464-6101, ext 5151) occupies five coastal acres on the Oregon border. There are no facilities, but it's great for kite flying; pick one up at the shop just over the border in Oregon.

The best reason to visit is to stay at secluded, charming **Casa Rubio** (707-487-4313; www.casarubio.com; 17285 Crissey Rd; r $108-168; @), where three of the four ocean-view rooms have kitchens.

Pitch a tent by the ocean (no windbreaks) at **Clifford Kamph Memorial Park** (707-464-7230; 15100 Hwy 101; tent sites $10); no RVs. It's a steal for the beachside location and, even though sites are exposed in a grassy area and there isn't much privacy, all have BBQs.

Central Coast

Includes »

Best Places to Eat

- Passionfish (p288)
- Cracked Crab (p321)
- Cass House Restaurant (p303)
- San Luis Obispo Farmers Market (p313)
- Bouchon (p333)

Best Places to Stay

- Post Ranch Inn (p296)
- Inn of the Spanish Garden (p332)
- Cass House Inn (p302)
- El Capitan Canyon (p332)
- Dream Inn (p271)

Why Go?

Too often forgotten or dismissed as 'flyover' country between San Francisco and LA, this fairytale stretch of California coast is packed with wild Pacific beaches, misty redwood forests where hot springs hide, and rolling golden hills of fertile vineyards and farm fields.

Here Hwy 1 pulls out all the stops, scenery-wise. Flower-power Santa Cruz and the historic port town of Monterey are gateways to the rugged wild lands of the bohemian Big Sur coast. It's an epic journey snaking down to vainglorious Hearst Castle, past lighthouses and cliffs over which condors soar.

Or get acquainted with California's agricultural heartland along inland Hwy 101, called El Camino Real (the King's Highway) by Spanish conquistadors and Franciscan friars. Then soothe your nature-loving soul between laid-back San Luis Obispo and idyllic seaside Santa Barbara, just a short hop from the Channel Islands.

When to Go

Santa Barbara

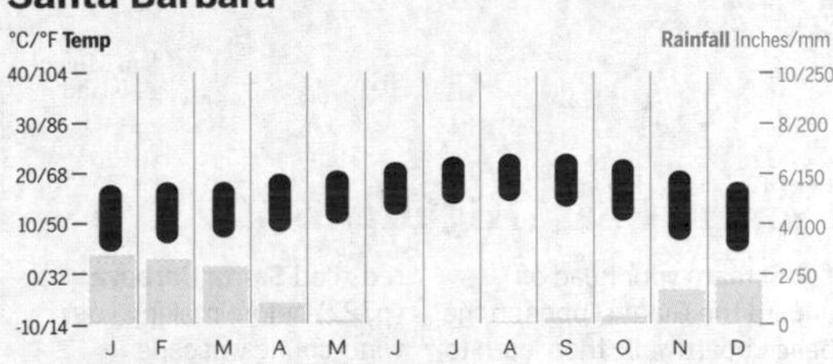

Apr Balmy temperatures and fewer tourists than summer. Wildflowers bloom.

Jul Summer vacation and beach season kick off; SoCal ocean waters warm up.

Oct Sunny blue skies, yet smaller crowds. Wine country harvests celebrated.

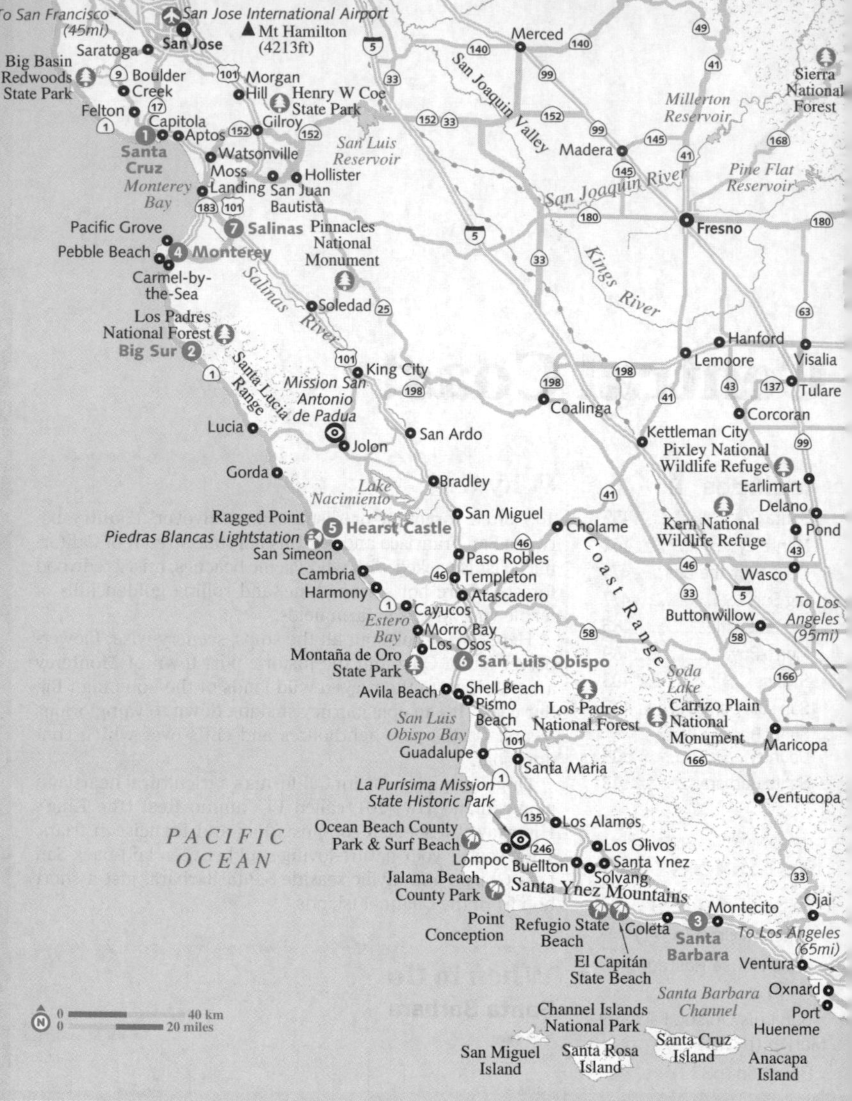

Central Coast Highlights

1. Scream your head off aboard the Giant Dipper on the beach boardwalk, then learn to surf in **Santa Cruz** (p269)

2. Cruise Hwy 1, where the sky touches the sea, along the rocky coastline of fairytale **Big Sur** (p291)

3. Soak up the chic atmosphere of whitewashed, red-tiled **Santa Barbara** (p327) before making your wine-country escape

4. Brings the kids to gawk at the aquatic denizens of the 'indoor ocean' at the **Monterey Bay Aquarium** (p278)

5. Marvel in disbelief at the grandiosity of **Hearst Castle** (p299) after meeting the neighbors: ginormous elephant seals

6. Hang loose in college-town **San Luis Obispo** (p312), surrounded by bodacious beaches and parklands

7. Explore down-to-earth novelist John Steinbeck's blue-collar world in the agricultural valley town of **Salinas** (p307)

ALONG HIGHWAY 1

Teeming with richly varied marine life, lined with often deserted beaches, and home to towns full of character and idiosyncratic charm all along its half-moon shore, Monterey Bay is anchored by Santa Cruz to the north. On the 125-mile stretch south of the Monterey Peninsula, you'll snake along an unbelievably picturesque coast until Hwy 1 joins with Hwy 101 at San Luis Obispo.

Santa Cruz

Santa Cruz has marched to its own beat since long before the Beat Generation. It's counterculture central, a touchy-feely, new-agey city famous for its leftie-liberal politics and live-and-let-live ideology – except when it comes to dogs (rarely allowed off-leash), parking (meters run seven days a week) and Republicans (allegedly shot on sight). It's still cool to be a hippie or a stoner here (or better yet, both), although some far-out–looking freaks are just slumming Silicon Valley millionaires and trust-fund babies underneath.

Santa Cruz is a city of madcap fun, with a vibrant but chaotic downtown. On the waterfront is the famous beach boardwalk, and in the hills redwood groves embrace the University of California, Santa Cruz (UCSC) campus. Plan to spend at least half a day here, but to appreciate the aesthetic of jangly skirts, crystal pendants and Rastafarian dreadlocks, stay longer and plunge headlong into the rich local brew of surfers, students, punks and eccentric characters.

Sights

One of the best things to do in Santa Cruz is simply stroll, shop and people-watch along **Pacific Ave** downtown. A 15-minute walk away is the beach and the **Municipal Wharf**, where seafood restaurants, gift shops and barking sea lions compete for attention. Ocean-view **West Cliff Dr** follows the waterfront southwest of the wharf, paralleled by a paved recreational path.

Santa Cruz Beach Boardwalk — AMUSEMENT PARK

(Map p272; ☎831-423-5590; www.beachboardwalk.com; 400 Beach St; per ride $3-5, all-day pass $30; ⏰from 10am or 11am daily May-Sep; 🚸) The West Coast's oldest beachfront amusement park, this 1907 boardwalk has a glorious old-school Americana vibe, with the smell of cotton candy mixing with the salt air, punctuated by the squeals of kids hanging upside down on carnival rides. Famous thrills include the Giant Dipper, a 1924 wooden roller coaster, and the 1911 Looff carousel, both National Historic Landmarks. On summer Friday nights, catch free concerts by rock veterans you may have thought were already dead. For kid-friendly train rides up into the redwoods, see p277. Closing times and off-season hours vary.

Seymour Marine Discovery Center — MUSEUM

(Map p276; www2.ucsc.edu/seymourcenter; end of Delaware Ave; adult/child 4-16yr $6/4; ⏰10am-5pm Tue-Sat, noon-5pm Sun, also 10am-5pm Mon Jul & Aug; 🚸) Near Natural Bridges State Beach, this kids' educational center is part of UCSC's Long Marine Laboratory. Interactive natural-science exhibits include tidal touch pools and aquariums, while outside you can gawk at the world's largest blue-whale skeleton. Guided tours are usually given at 1pm, 2pm and 3pm daily; sign up in person an hour in advance (no reservations).

Santa Cruz Surfing Museum — MUSEUM

(Map p276; www.santacruzsurfingmuseum.org; 701 W Cliff Dr; admission by donation; ⏰noon-4pm Thu-Mon Sep-Jun, 10am-5pm Wed-Mon Jul & Aug) A mile south of the wharf along the coast, the old lighthouse is packed with memorabilia, including vintage redwood surfboards. Fittingly, Lighthouse Point overlooks two popular surf breaks.

University of California, Santa Cruz — UNIVERSITY

(UCSC; Map p276; www.ucsc.edu) Check it: the school mascot is a banana slug! Established

> **FAST FACTS**
>
> » **Population of Santa Barbara** 88,410
>
> » **Average temperature low/high in Santa Barbara** Jan 42/65°F, Jul 57/77°F
>
> » **Los Angeles to Santa Barbara** 95 miles, 1¾ to 2½ hours
>
> » **Monterey to San Luis Obispo** 140 miles, 2½ to three hours
>
> » **San Francisco to Santa Cruz** 75 miles, 1½ to two hours

MYSTERY SPOT

A kitschy, old-fashioned tourist trap, Santa Cruz's **Mystery Spot** (☎831-423-8897; www.mysteryspot.com; 465 Mystery Spot Rd; admission $5, parking $5; ⏰10am-6pm Sun-Thu & 9am-7pm Fri & Sat late May-early Sep, 10am-4pm Sun-Thu & 10am-5pm Fri & Sat early Sep-late May; 👪) has scarcely changed since it opened in 1940. On a steeply sloping hillside, compasses seem to point crazily, mysterious forces push you around and buildings lean at odd angles. Make reservations, or risk being stuck waiting for a tour. It's 3 miles north of downtown: take Water St to Market St, turn left and continue on Branciforte Dr into the hills.

in 1965 in the hills above town, this youthful university is known for its creative, liberal bent. The rural campus has fine stands of redwoods and architecturally interesting buildings – some made with recycled materials – designed to blend in with rolling pastureland. Peruse two top-notch art galleries, a peaceful **arboretum** (http://arboretum.ucsc.edu/; 1156 High St; adult/child 6-17yr $5/2, free 1st Tue of the month; ⏰9am-5pm) and picturesquely decaying 19th-century structures from Cowell Ranch, upon which the campus was built.

Santa Cruz Museum of Natural History MUSEUM
(Map p276; www.santacruzmuseums.org; 1305 E Cliff Dr; adult/child under 18yr $4/free; ⏰10am-5pm Wed-Sun late May-early Sep, 10am-5pm Tue-Sat early Sep-late May; 👪) The collections at this pint-sized museum include cultural artifacts from Ohlone tribespeople and a touch-friendly tidepool that shows off sea critters living along the beach right across the street.

Museum of Art & History MUSEUM
(Map p272; www.santacruzmah.org; McPherson Center, 705 Front St; adult/child 12-17yr $5/2; ⏰11am-5pm Tue-Sun, to 9pm 1st Fri of the month) Downtown, this smart little museum is worth a look for its rotating displays by contemporary California artists and exhibits exploring offbeat local history.

Beaches

Sun-kissed Santa Cruz has warmer beaches than often-foggy Monterey. *Baywatch* it isn't, but 29 miles of coastline reveal a few Hawaii-worthy beaches, craggy coves, some primo surf spots and big sandy stretches where your kids will have a blast. Too bad fog ruins many a summer morning; it often burns off by the afternoon.

West Cliff Dr is lined with scramble-down-to coves and plentiful parking. If you don't want sand in your shoes, park yourself on a bench and watch enormous pelicans dive for fish. You'll find bathrooms and showers at the lighthouse parking lot.

Locals favor less-trampled **East Cliff Dr** beaches, which are bigger and more protected from the wind, meaning calmer waters. Except at a small metered lot at 26th Ave, parking is by permit only on weekends (buy a $7 per day permit at 9th Ave).

Less crowded **state beaches** (www.parks.ca.gov; per car $10; ⏰8am-sunset) await off Hwy 1 southbound. In Aptos, **Seacliff State Beach** (☎831-685-6442) harbors a 'cement boat,' a quixotic freighter built of concrete that floated OK, but ended up here as a coastal fishing pier. Further south near Watsonville, the La Selva Beach exit off Hwy 1 leads to **Manresa State Beach** (☎831-761-1975) and **Sunset State Beach** (☎831-763-7062), for miles of sand and surf practically all to yourself.

Activities

Surfing

Year-round, water temperatures average less than 60°F, meaning that without a wetsuit, body parts quickly turn blue. Surfing is incredibly popular, especially at experts-only **Steamer Lane** and beginners' **Cowell's**, both off West Cliff Dr. Other favorite surf spots include **Pleasure Point Beach**, on East Cliff Dr toward Capitola, and South County's **Manresa State Beach** off Hwy 1.

Santa Cruz Surf School SURFING
(Map p272; ☎831-426-7072; www.santacruzsurfschool.com; 322 Pacific Ave; 2hr lesson incl equipment rental $80-90) Wanna learn to surf? Near the wharf, friendly male and female instructors will have you standing and surfing on your first day out.

O'Neill Surf Shop SURFING
(Map p276; ☎831-475-4151; www.oneill.com; 1115 41st Ave; wetsuit/surfboard rental from $10/20; ⏰9am-8pm Mon-Fri, 8am-8pm Sat & Sun) Head east to Capitola to worship at this internationally renowned surfboard maker's flagship store. Also on the beach boardwalk and downtown.

Cowell's Beach Surf Shop SURFING
(Map p272; 831-427 2355; 30 Front St; 2hr lesson $80; 8am-6pm;) Rent surfboards, boogie boards, wetsuits and other beach gear near the wharf, where veteran staff offer heaps of local tips and teach surfing too.

Kayaking

Kayaking lets you discover the craggy coastline and kelp beds where sea otters float.

Venture Quest KAYAKING
(Map p272; 831-427-2267; www.kayaksantacruz.com; Municipal Wharf; kayak rentals $30-100, tours $30-70;) Convenient rentals on the wharf, with whale-watching and sea-cave tours, including moonlight paddles.

Kayak Connection KAYAKING
(Map p276; 831-479-1121; www.kayakconnection.com; Santa Cruz Harbor, 413 Lake Ave; kayak rentals $35-50, tours & lessons $50-100;) Rents kayaks and offers lessons and tours, including sunrise, sunset and full-moon trips on Monterey Bay.

Whale-Watching & Fishing

Winter whale-watching trips run from December to April, though there's plenty of marine life to see on a summer bay cruise, too. Many fishing trips depart from the wharf, where a few shops rent fishing tackle and poles, if you're keen to join locals waiting patiently for a bite.

Stagnaro's CRUISES, TOURS
(800-979-3370; www.stagnaros.com) This longstanding tour operator offers scenic and sunset cruises around Monterey Bay (adult/child under 14 years from $20/13), whale-watching tours (adult/child under 14 years $45/31) and fishing trips (adult/child under 16 years from $50/40).

Festivals & Events

Woodies on the Wharf CULTURAL
(www.santacruzwoodies.com) A classic car show featuring vintage surf-style station wagons in late June.

Shakespeare Santa Cruz THEATER
(www.shakespearesantacruz.org) Damn good productions of the Bard at UCSC and in a redwood grove during July, August and September.

Open Studio Art Tour CULTURAL
(www.ccscc.org) Explore local artists' creative workshops over three weekends in October.

Sleeping

Santa Cruz does not have not enough beds to satisfy demand: expect outrageous prices at peak times for nothing-special rooms. Places near the boardwalk run the gamut from friendly to frightening. If you're looking for a straightforward motel, check out Ocean St further inland or Mission St (Hwy 1) near the UCSC campus.

TOP CHOICE **Dream Inn** BOUTIQUE HOTEL $$$
(Map p272; 831-426-4330, 866-774-7735; www.dreaminnsantacruz.com; 175 W Cliff Dr; r $200-380;) Overlooking the wharf from a spectacular hillside perch, this retro-chic boutique-on-the-cheap hotel is as stylish as Santa Cruz gets. Rooms have all mod cons, while the beach is just steps away. Don't miss happy hour at Aquarius restaurant's ocean-view bar.

DON'T MISS

TOP SANTA CRUZ BEACHES

» **Main Beach** *The* scene, with a huge sandy stretch, volleyball courts and swarms of people. Park on East Cliff Dr and walk across the *Lost Boys* trestle to the boardwalk.

» **Its Beach** The only official off-leash beach for dogs (before 10am and after 4pm) is just west of the lighthouse. The field across the street is another good romping ground.

» **Natural Bridges State Beach** Best for sunsets, this family favorite has lots of sand, tidepools and monarch butterflies from mid-October through late February. It's at the far end of West Cliff Dr; parking costs $10.

» **Twin Lakes State Beach** Big beach with bonfire pits and a lagoon, good for kids and often fairly empty. It's off East Cliff Dr around 7th Ave.

» **Moran Lake County Park** With a good surf break and bathrooms, this pretty all-around sandy spot is further east at 26th Ave off East Cliff Dr.

Santa Cruz

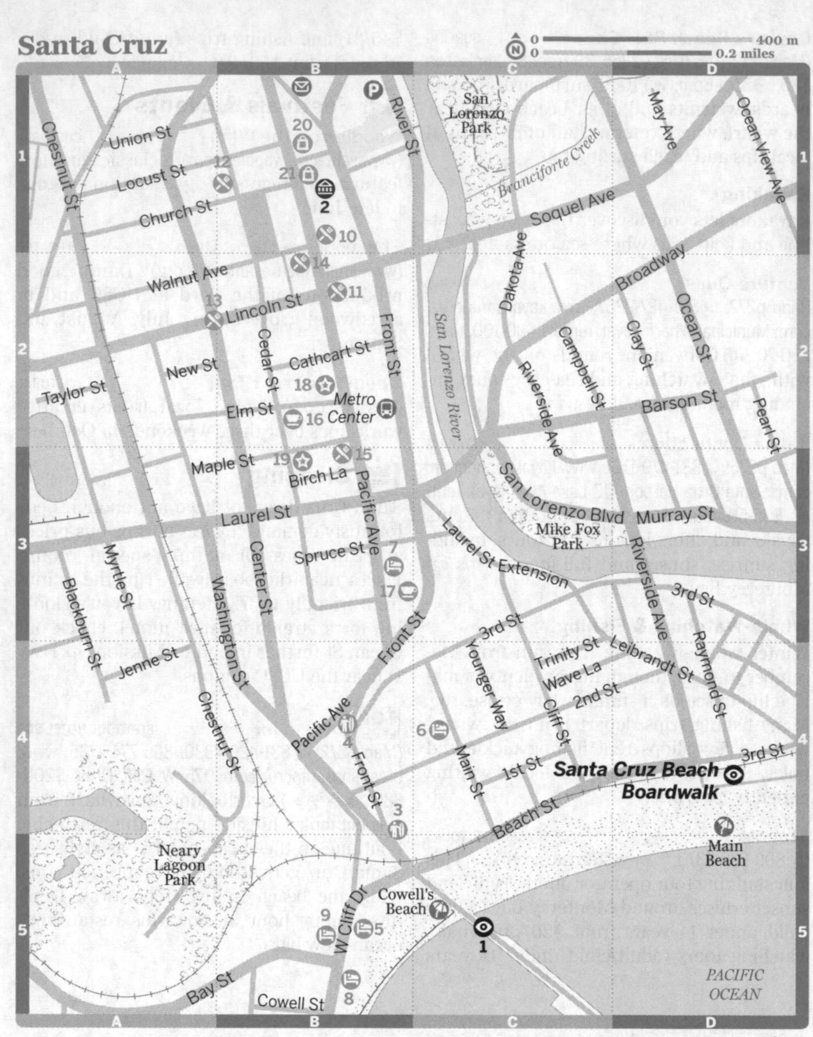

Adobe on Green B&B B&B **$$**
(Map p276; ☎831-469-9866; www.adobeongreen.com; 103 Green St; r incl breakfast $149-199; 📶) Peace and quiet are the mantras at this place, a short walk from Pacific Ave. The hosts are practically invisible, but their thoughtful touches are everywhere, from boutique-hotel amenities in spacious, stylish and solar-powered rooms to breakfast spreads from their organic gardens.

Pleasure Point Inn INN **$$$**
(Map p276; ☎831-475-4657; www.pleasurepointinn.com; 23665 E Cliff Dr; r incl breakfast $225-295; 📶) Live out your fantasy of California beachfront living in four clean-lined, contemporary rooms with hardwood floors, tiled bathrooms with Jacuzzi tubs, kitchenettes and private patios. Climb to the rooftop hot-tub deck for drop-dead ocean views.

Pacific Blue Inn B&B **$$**
(Map p272; ☎831-600-8880; http://pacificblueinn.com; 636 Pacific Ave; r incl breakfast $170-240; 📶) This downtown courtyard B&B is an eco-conscious gem, with water-saving fixtures and both renewable and recycled building materials. Refreshingly sleek rooms have

Santa Cruz

pillowtop beds, fireplaces and flat-screen TVs with DVD players. Free loaner bikes.

West Cliff Inn INN $$$
(Map p272; 831-457-2200; www.westcliffinn.com; 174 W Cliff Dr; r incl breakfast $175-400;) In a classy Victorian house west of the wharf, this boutique inn's quaint rooms mix sea-grass wicker, dark wood and jaunty striped curtains. The most romantic suites have gas fireplaces and let you spy on the breaking surf.

Sea & Sand Inn MOTEL $$$
(Map p272; 831-427-3400; www.santacruzmotels.com; 201 W Cliff Dr; r $109-429;) With a grassy lawn at the cliff's edge, this spiffy, if overpriced motel overlooks Main Beach and the wharf. Fall asleep to braying sea lions! Rooms are smallish, but ocean views can be stellar.

Pelican Point Inn INN $$
(Map p276; 831-475-3381; www.pelicanpointinn-santacruz.com; 21345 E Cliff Dr; ste $99-199;) Ideal for families, these roomy apartments near a kid-friendly beach are equipped with everything you'll need for a lazy vacation, from kitchenettes to high-speed internet. Weekly rates available.

Sunny Cove Motel MOTEL $$
(Map p276; 831-475-1741; www.sunnycovemotel.com; 21610 E Cliff Dr; r $90-200;) It's nothing fancy, but this tidy little hideaway east of downtown is a staunch budget fave. The long-time Santa Cruzian owner rents retro beach-house rooms and kitchenette suites.

HI Santa Cruz Hostel HOSTEL $
(Map p272; 831-423-8304; www.hi-santacruz.org; 321 Main St; dm $25-28, r $55-105, all with shared bath; check-in 5-10pm; @) Budget overnighters dig this cute hostel at the century-old Carmelita Cottages surrounded by flowering gardens, just two blocks from the beach. Cons: 11pm curfew, three-night maximum stay. Reservations essential.

State Park Campgrounds CAMPGROUND $
(reservations 800-444-7275; www.reserveamerica.com; tent & RV sites $35-50) Book well ahead to camp by the beaches and in the cool Santa Cruz Mountains. Terrific spots include Henry Cowell Redwoods and Big Basin Redwoods State Parks, in the redwood forests off Hwy 9 (see p277); New Brighton State Beach, near Capitola; and Manresa and Sunset State Beaches farther south off Hwy 1 (see p330).

Best Western Plus Capitola By-the-Sea Inn & Suites MOTEL $$
(Map p276; 831-477-0607; www.bestwesterncapitola.com; 1435 41st Ave; r incl breakfast $90-240; @) Dependable motel away from the beach. Impeccably clean rooms, spacious enough for families.

Mission Inn MOTEL $$
(Map p276; ☎831-425-5455, 800-895-5455; www.mission-inn.com; 2250 Mission St (Hwy 1); r incl breakfast $80-140;) Serviceable motel with a sauna and garden courtyard, near UCSC. Away from the beach.

Eating

Alas, Santa Cruz's food scene lacks luster. Downtown is chockablock with just-okay cafes. If you're looking for seafood, wander among the wharf's takeout counter joints. Mission St near UCSC and neighboring Capitola offer cheap, casual eats.

Soif BISTRO $$$
(Map p272; ☎831-423-2020; www.soifwine.com; 105 Walnut Ave; small plates $5-17, mains $19-28; ⊙5-10pm Sun-Thu, to 11pm Fri & Sat) Downtown is where bon vivants flock for a heady selection of 50 international wines by the glass, paired with a sophisticated, seasonally driven Euro-Cal menu. Expect tastebud-ticklers like wild arugula salad with roasted apricot and curry-honey vinaigrette or baby back ribs with coffee-barbecue sauce. Live music some nights.

Cellar Door CALIFORNIAN $$$
(Map p276; ☎831-425-6771; www.bonnydoonvineyard.com; 328 Ingalls St; small plates $5-22, prix-fixe dinner $25-40; ⊙noon-2pm Sat & Sun, 5:30-9pm Thu-Sun, community dinner 6:30pm Wed) At Bonny Doon Vineyard's tasting room, this hideaway cafe packs organic, biodynamic and seasonal farm-to-table goodness into tidy tapas plates and hosts barrel-tasting winemakers' dinners. Linger over a glass of whimsically named *Le Cigare Volant*, a wicked Rhone blend.

Engfer Pizza Works PIZZERIA $$
(Map p276; www.engferpizzaworks.com; 537 Seabright Ave; pizzas $8-23; ⊙4-9:30pm Tue-Sun;) Detour to find this old factory, where wood-fired oven pizzas are made from scratch with love – the no-name specialty is like a giant salad on roasted bread. Play ping-pong and down draft microbrews while you wait.

El Palomar MEXICAN $$
(Map p272; ☎831-425-7575; 1336 Pacific Ave; mains $7-27; ⊙11am-11pm;) Always packed and consistently good (if not great), El Palomar serves tasty Mexican staples – try the seafood *ceviches* – and fruity margaritas. Tortillas are made fresh by charming women in the covered courtyard.

Zachary's AMERICAN $
(Map p272; 819 Pacific Ave; mains $6-11; ⊙7am-2:30pm Tue-Sun) At the scruffy brunch spot that locals don't want you to know about, huge portions of sourdough pancakes and blueberry cream-cheese coffee cake will keep you going all day. 'Mike's Mess' is the kitchen-sink standout.

Tacos Moreno MEXICAN $
(Map p276; www.tacosmoreno.com; 1053 Water St; dishes $2-6; ⊙11am-8pm) Who cares how long the line is at lunchtime when every hungry surfer in town is here? Aficionados find taquería heaven, from marinated pork, chicken and beef soft tacos and quesadillas to supremely stuffed burritos.

Buttery BAKERY $
(Map p276; http://butterybakery.com; 702 Soquel Ave; snacks $4-8; ⊙7am-7pm;) For more than two decades, this bustling bakery has been baking such old-world confections as chocolate croissants and fruit tarts. Squeeze yourself into the corner cafe for deli sandwiches and soups.

Bagelry DELI $
(Map p272; 320a Cedar St; items $3-6; ⊙6:30am-5:30pm Mon-Fri, 7:30am-4:30pm Sat, 6:30am-4pm Sun;) The bagels here are twice-cooked (boiled, then baked), and come with fantastic crunchy spreads, like hummus and egg salad. Check out the bulletin board for community goings-on.

Penny Ice Creamery ICE CREAM $
(Map p272; http://thepennyicecreamery.com; 913 Cedar St; ice cream $2-4; ⊙noon-9pm Sun-Wed, to 11pm Thu-Sat) With a cult following, this artisan ice-cream shop makes its zany flavors, like avocado, cherry-balsamic or roasted barley, from scratch using local, organic and even wild ingredients.

Donnelly Fine Chocolates CANDY $
(Map p276; www.donnellychocolates.com; 1509 Mission St; candy $2-5; ⊙10:30am-6pm Tue-Fri, noon-6pm Sat & Sun) The Willy Wonka of Santa Cruz makes stratospherically priced chocolates on par with the big city. This guy is an alchemist! Try the cardamom truffles.

New Leaf Community Market GROCERIES $
(Map p272; www.newleaf.com; 1134 Pacific Ave; ⊙9am-9pm) Organic local produce, natural-foods groceries and deli take-out downtown.

Santa Cruz Farmers Market MARKET $
(Map p272; www.santacruzfarmersmarket.org; cnr Lincoln & Center Sts; ⌚2:30-6:30pm Wed) For organic produce and an authentic taste of the local vibe.

Drinking

Downtown overflows with bars, hookah lounges and coffee shops.

Caffe Pergolesi CAFE
(Map p272; www.theperg.com; 418 Cedar St; ⌚7am-11pm; 📶) Discuss conspiracy theories over stalwart coffee, tea or beer at this way-popular landmark cafe in a Victorian house with a big ol' tree-shaded veranda overlooking the street. Local art hangs on the walls, with live musicians some evenings.

Santa Cruz Mountain Brewing BREWPUB
(Map p276; www.santacruzmountainbrewing.com; Swift Street Courtyard, 402 Ingalls St; ⌚noon-10pm) Bold organic brews are poured at this tiny brewpub, squeezed between Santa Cruz Mountains wine-tasting rooms just west of town off Mission St (Hwy 1). Oddest flavor? Olallieberry cream ale.

Vino Prima WINE BAR
(Map p272; www.vinoprimawines.com; Municipal Wharf; ⌚2-8pm Mon-Tue, 2-10pm Wed-Fri, noon-10pm Sat, noon-8pm Sun) Near the far end of the wharf, with dreamy ocean views, this spot pours California boutique wines, including hard-to-find bottles from Santa Cruz and Monterey Counties.

Surf City Billiards & Cafe BAR
(Map p272; www.surfcitybilliards.com; 931 Pacific Ave; ⌚4-11pm Mon-Thu, 4pm-1am Fri & Sat, 10am-11pm Sun) A relief from downtown's dive bars, this upstairs pool hall has Brunswick Gold Crown tables for shooting stick, pro dartboards, big-screen TVs and pretty good pub grub.

Verve Coffee Roasters CAFE
(Map p276; www.vervecoffeeroasters.com; 816 41st Ave; ⌚6am-7:30pm Mon-Fri, 7am-8:30pm Sat, 7am-7:30pm Sun; 📶) To sip freshly roasted artisan espresso, join the surfers and internet hipsters at this industrial-zen cafe. Single-origin brews and house-made blends rule.

Firefly Coffee House CAFE
(Map p272; 131 Front St; ⌚5:30am-6pm Mon-Sat, 7am-2pm Sun; 📶) Bohemian indoor/outdoor people's coffeeshop brews organic, fair-trade java and delish chai flavored with orange zest and an Indian bazaar's worth of spices.

Entertainment

Free weeklies *Metro Santa Cruz* (www.metrosantacruz.com) and *Good Times* (www.gtweekly.com) cover the music, arts and nightlife scenes.

Catalyst LIVE MUSIC
(Map p272; ☎831-423-1336; www.catalystclub.com; 1011 Pacific Ave) Over the years, this venue for local bands has seen big-time national acts perform, from Queens of the Stone Age to Snoop Dogg. When there's no music, hang in the upstairs bar and pool room.

Moe's Alley LIVE MUSIC
(Map p276; ☎831-479-1854; www.moesalley.com; 1535 Commercial Way; ⌚Tue-Sun) Hidden in an industrial wasteland, this casual place puts on live sounds almost every night, from jazz and blues to reggae, roots, salsa and acoustic world-music jams.

Kuumbwa Jazz Center LIVE MUSIC
(Map p272; ☎831-427-2227; www.kuumbwajazz.org; 320 Cedar St) Hosting jazz luminaries since 1975, this nonprofit theater is for serious jazz cats who come for the famous-name performers in an electrically intimate room.

Shopping

Wander Pacific Ave and downtown's side streets to find one-of-a-kind, locally owned boutiques (not just head shops, we promise).

Annieglass ART
(Map p272; www.annieglass.com; 110 Cooper St; ⌚11am-6pm Mon-Sat, to 5pm Sun) Handcrafted sculptural glassware sold in ultrachic New York department stores and displayed in the Smithsonian American Art Museum are made right here in wackadoodle Santa Cruz. Go figure.

O'Neill Surf Shop SURFBOARDS, CLOTHING
(Map p272; www.oneills.com; 110 Cooper St; ⌚10am-6pm) For Santa Cruz' own internationally popular brand of surf wear and gear, from hoodies to board shorts. Also on the beach boardwalk and in Capitola.

Bookshop Santa Cruz BOOKS
(Map p272; www.bookshopsantacruz.com; 1520 Pacific Ave; ⌚9am-10pm Sun-Thu, to 11pm Fri & Sat) Vast selection of new books, a few used ones, and popular and unusual magazines. Buy 'Keep Santa Cruz Weird' bumper stickers here.

Around Santa Cruz

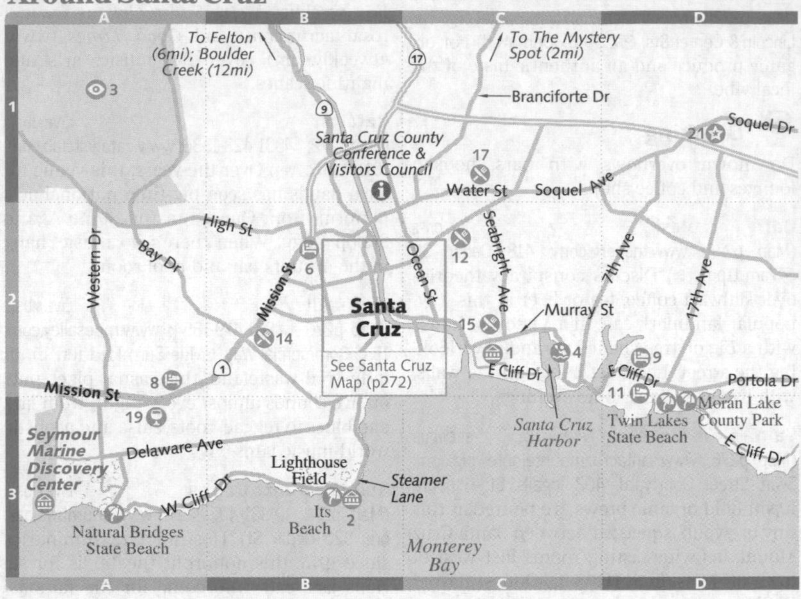

Around Santa Cruz

Top Sights

Seymour Marine Discovery Center....... A3

Sights

1 Santa Cruz Museum of Natural History....... C2
2 Santa Cruz Surfing Museum....... B3
3 University of California, Santa Cruz....... A1

Activities, Courses & Tours

4 Kayak Connection....... C2
5 O'Neill Surf Shop....... E2

Sleeping

6 Adobe on Green B&B....... B2
7 Best Western Plus Capitola By-the-Sea Inn & Suites....... E2
8 Mission Inn....... A2
9 Pelican Point Inn....... D2
10 Pleasure Point Inn....... E3
11 Sunny Cove Motel....... D2

Eating

12 Buttery....... C2
13 Dharma's....... E2
14 Donnelly Fine Chocolate....... B2
15 Engfer Pizza Works....... C2
16 Gayle's Bakery & Rosticceria....... E2
17 Tacos Moreno....... C1

Drinking

18 Mr Toots Coffeehouse....... E2
19 Santa Cruz Mountain Brewing....... A3
20 Verve Coffee Roasters....... E2

Entertainment

Cellar Door....... (see 19)
21 Moe's Alley....... D1

Information

FedEx Office (Map p272; 712 Front St; per min 20-30¢; 24hr Mon-Thu, midnight-11pm Fri, 9am-9pm Sat, 9am-midnight Sun; @) Pay-as-you-go internet workstations and free wi-fi.

KPIG 107.5FM Plays the classic Santa Cruz soundtrack (think Bob Marley, Janis Joplin and Willie Nelson).

Post office (Map p272; www.usps.com; 850 Front St; 9am-5pm Mon-Fri)

Public library (Map p272; www.santacruzpl.org; 224 Church St; 10am-7pm Mon-Thu, 10am-5pm Sat, 1-5pm Sun; @) Free wi-fi and public internet terminals.

Santa Cruz County Conference & Visitors Council (Map p276; 831-425-1234; www.

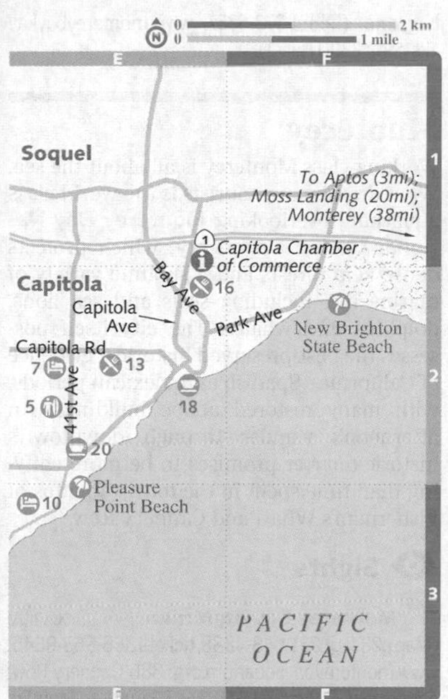

santacruzca.org; 1211 Ocean St; ⏲9am-5pm Mon-Fri, 10am-4pm Sat & Sun; @) Free brochures, maps and internet-terminal access.

Getting There & Around

Santa Cruz is 75 miles south of San Francisco via Hwy 17, a nail-bitingly narrow, winding mountain road. Monterey is about an hour's drive further south via Hwy 1.

Greyhound (www.greyhound.com; Metro Center, 920 Pacific St) has a few daily buses to San Francisco ($16, three hours), Salinas ($14, 65 minutes), Santa Barbara ($50, six hours) and Los Angeles ($57, nine hours).

Santa Cruz Metro (☎831-425-8600; www.scmtd.com; single-ride/day pass $1.50/4.50) operates local and countywide bus routes that converge on downtown's **Metro Center** (Map p272; 920 Pacific Ave). Frequent Hwy 17 express buses link Santa Cruz with San Jose's Amtrak/CalTrain station ($5, 50 minutes).

Santa Cruz Airport Shuttles (☎831-421-9883; http://santacruzshuttles.com) runs shared shuttles to/from the airports at San Jose ($45), San Francisco ($75) and Oakland ($75); prices are the same for one or two passengers (credit-card surcharge $5).

Around Santa Cruz

SANTA CRUZ MOUNTAINS

Winding between Santa Cruz and Silicon Valley, Hwy 9 is a 40-mile backwoods byway through the Santa Cruz Mountains, passing tiny towns, towering redwood forests and fog-kissed vineyards (estate-bottled pinot noir is a specialty). Many wineries are only open on 'Passport Days' on the third Saturday of January, April, July and November. The **Santa Cruz Mountains Winegrowers Association** (www.scmwa.com) publishes a free winery map, available at tasting rooms, including those that have relocated to Santa Cruz itself, west of downtown off Hwy 1.

Heading north from Santa Cruz, it's 7 miles to Felton, passing **Henry Cowell Redwoods State Park** (☎831-335-4598; www.parks.ca.gov; 101 N Big Trees Park Rd; per car $10; ⏲sunrise-sunset), which has miles of hiking trails through old-growth redwood groves and camping along the San Lorenzo River. In Felton, **Roaring Camp Railroads** (☎831-335-4484; www.roaringcamp.com; 5401 Graham Hill Rd; tours adult/child 2-12yr from $24/17, parking $8; ⏲call for schedules) operates narrow-gauge steam trains up into the redwoods and a standard-gauge train down to the Santa Cruz Beach Boardwalk (p269).

Seven miles further north on Hwy 9, you'll drive through the pretty town of **Boulder Creek**, a good place to grab a bite. Roadside **Boulder Creek Brewery & Cafe Company** (www.bouldercreekbrewery.net; 13040 Hwy 9; mains $7-15; ⏲11:30am-10pm Sun-Thu, to 10:30pm Fri & Sat) is a local institution.

Follow Hwy 236 northwest for nine twisting miles to **Big Basin Redwoods State Park** (☎831-338-8860; www.bigbasin.org, www.parks.ca.gov; 21600 Big Basin Way; per car $10), where nature trails loop past giant old-growth redwoods. A 12.5-mile one-way section of the exhilarating **Skyline to the Sea Trail** ends at Waddell Beach on the coast, almost 20 miles northwest of Santa Cruz. On weekends, if you check Santa Cruz Metro schedules carefully, you may be able to ride up to Big Basin on bus 35A in the morning and get picked up by bus 40 at the beach in the afternoon.

CAPITOLA

Six miles east of Santa Cruz, the little seaside town of Capitola, nestled quaintly between ocean bluffs, attracts affluent crowds and families. Downtown is laid out for strolling, with arty shops and touristy restaurants inside seaside houses. Show up for mid-September's **Capitola Art & Wine Festival**, or the famous **Begonia Festival**, held over Labor Day weekend, with a flotilla of floral floats along Soquel Creek.

Catch an organic, shade-grown and fairly traded caffeine buzz at **Mr Toots Coffeehouse** (Map p276; http://tootscoffee.com; 2nd fl, 231 Esplanade; ⌚7am-10pm; 📶), which has an art gallery and live music. Head inland to **Gayle's Bakery & Rosticceria** (Map p276; www.gaylesbakery.com; 504 Bay Ave; ⌚6:30am-8:30pm; 👪), with its fresh deli where you can assemble beach picnics, or **Dharma's** (Map p276; www.dharmaland.com; 4250 Capitola Rd; mains $7-14; ⌚8am-9pm; 🌿), a global-fusion fast-food vegetarian and vegan restaurant.

The **Capitola Chamber of Commerce** (Map p276; ☎800-474-6522; www.capitolachamber.com; 716g Capitola Ave; ⌚10am-4pm) offers travel tips. Driving downtown can be a nightmare in summer and on weekends; try the parking lot behind City Hall, off Capitola Ave by Riverview Dr.

MOSS LANDING & ELKHORN SLOUGH

Hwy 1 swings back toward the coast at Moss Landing, just south of the Santa Cruz County line, and almost 20 miles north of Monterey. From the working fishing harbor, **Sanctuary Cruises** (☎831-917-1042; www.sanctuarycruises.com; tours adult/child under 3yr/child 3-12yr $48/10/38) operates year-round whale-watching and dolphin-spotting cruises aboard biodiesel-fueled boats (reservations essential). Devour dock-fresh seafood down at warehouse-sized **Phil's Fish Market** (www.philsfishmarket.com; 7600 Sandholdt Rd; mains $10-20; ⌚10am-8pm Sun-Thu, to 9pm Fri & Sat) or, after browsing the antiques shops, lunch at the **Haute Enchilada** (www.hauteenchilada.com; 7902 Moss Landing Rd; mains $11-26; ⌚10am-8pm), an inspired Mexican restaurant inside a Frida Kahlo–esque art gallery.

Just east, **Elkhorn Slough National Estuarine Research Reserve** (☎831-728-2822; www.elkhornslough.org; 1700 Elkhorn Rd; adult/child under 16yr $2.50/free; 1700 Elkhorn Rd, Watsonville; ⌚9am-5pm Wed-Sun) is popular with bird-watchers and hikers. Docent-led tours are typically offered at 10am and 1pm on Saturday and Sunday. Kayaking is a fantastic way to see the slough, though not on a windy day or when the tide is against you. Reserve ahead for kayak rentals ($35 to $70) or guided tours ($30 to $120) with **Kayak Connection** (☎831-724-5692; www.kayakconnection.com; 2370 Hwy 1) or **Monterey Bay Kayaks** (☎831-373-5357; www.montereybaykayaks.com; 2390 Hwy 1).

Monterey

Working-class Monterey is all about the sea. What draws many tourists is the world-class aquarium, overlooking **Monterey Bay National Marine Sanctuary**, which protects dense kelp forests and a sublime variety of marine life, including seals and sea lions, dolphins and whales. The city itself possesses the best-preserved historical evidence of California's Spanish and Mexican periods, with many restored adobe buildings. An afternoon's wander through downtown's historic quarter promises to be more edifying than time spent in the tourist ghettos of Fisherman's Wharf and Cannery Row.

Sights

Monterey Bay Aquarium AQUARIUM
(Map p284; ☎831-648-4888, tickets 866-963-9645; www.montereybayaquarium.org; 886 Cannery Row; adult/child 3-12yr $30/20; ⌚9:30am-6pm Mon-Fri, 9:30am-8pm Sat & Sun Jun-Aug, 10am-5pm or 6pm daily Sep-May; 📶👪) Monterey's most mesmerizing experience is its enormous aquarium, built on the former site of the city's largest sardine cannery. All kinds of aquatic creatures are on proud display, from kid-tolerant sea stars and slimy sea slugs to animated sea otters and surprisingly nimble 800lb tuna. The aquarium is much more than an impressive collection of glass tanks – thoughtful placards underscore the bay's cultural and historical contexts.

Every minute, upwards of 2000 gallons of seawater is pumped into the three-story **kelp forest**, re-creating as closely as possible the natural conditions you see out the windows to the east. The large fish of prey are at their charismatic best during mealtimes; divers hand-feed at 11:30am and 4pm. More entertaining are the sea otters, which may be seen basking in the **Great Tide Pool** outside the aquarium, where they are readied for reintroduction to the wild.

Even new-agey music and the occasional infinity-mirror illusion don't detract from the astounding beauty of jellyfish in the **Jellies Gallery**. To see fish – including hammerhead sharks and green sea turtles – that outweigh kids many times over, ponder the awesome **Open Sea** tank. Upstairs and downstairs you'll find **touch pools**, where you can get close to sea cucumbers, bat rays and tidepool creatures. Younger kids will love the interactive, bilingual **Splash Zone**, with penguin feedings at 10:30am and 3pm.

A visit can easily become a full-day affair, so get your hand stamped and break for lunch. To avoid long lines in summer and on weekends and holidays, buy tickets in advance. Metered on-street parking is limited, but parking lots and garages offering daily rates are plentiful uphill from Cannery Row.

Cannery Row HISTORIC SITE

(Map p284) John Steinbeck's novel *Cannery Row* immortalized the sardine-canning business that was Monterey's lifeblood for the first half of the 20th century. Back in Steinbeck's day, it was a stinky, hardscrabble, working-class melting pot, which the novelist described as 'a poem, a stink, a grating noise, a quality of light, a tone, a habit, a nostalgia, a dream.' Sadly, there's precious little evidence of that era now. Overfishing and climatic changes caused the industry's collapse in the 1950s.

A bronze **bust** of the Pulitzer Prize–winning writer sits at the bottom of Prescott Ave, just steps from the unabashedly commercial experience his row has devolved into, chockablock with chain restaurants and souvenir shops hawking saltwater taffy. Check out the **Cannery Workers Shacks** at the base of flowery Bruce Ariss Way, which have sobering explanations of the hard lives led by the Filipino, Japanese, Spanish and other immigrant laborers.

Monterey State Historic Park HISTORIC SITE

(☎cellphone audiotour 831-998-9458; www.parks.ca.gov) Old Monterey is home to an extraordinary assemblage of 19th-century brick and adobe buildings, administered as Monterey State Historic Park, all found along a 2-mile self-guided walking tour portentously called the Path of History. You can inspect dozens of buildings, many with charming gardens; expect some to be open while others aren't, according to a capricious schedule dictated by severe state-park budget cutbacks.

Pacific House Museum

(Map p284; ☎831-649-7118; 20 Custom House Plaza; donations welcome; ⏲10am-4:30pm) Grab a free map, find out what's currently open and buy guided tour tickets for individual historic houses inside this 1847 adobe building, which has in-depth exhibits covering the state's multinational history. Nearby are a few more of the park's highlights, including an **old whaling station**, California's first **theater** and a short walk further afield, the **old Monterey jail** featured in John Steinbeck's novel *Tortilla Flat*.

Custom House

(Map p284; Custom House Plaza; ⏲10am-4pm Sat & Sun) In 1822 newly independent Mexico ended the Spanish trade monopoly and stipulated that any traders bringing goods to Alta California must first unload their cargoes here for duty to be assessed. In 1846 when the US flag was raised over the Custom House, *voilà!* California was formally annexed from Mexico. Restored to its 1840s appearance, today the house displays an exotic selection of goods that traders brought to exchange for California cowhides.

Casa Soberanes

(Map p284; 336 Pacific St) A beautiful garden with meandering walkways paved with abalone shells, bottle glass and even whalebones fronts, this adobe house was built in the 1840s during the late Mexican period. The interior is adorned with an eclectic mix of New England antiques, 19th-century goods imported on Chinese trading ships and modern Mexican folk art. Opening hours vary.

Across Pacific St, the large and colorful **Monterey Mural**, a contemporary mosaic on the exterior of the Monterey Conference Center, illustrates the city's history.

Stevenson House

(Map p284; 530 Houston St; ⏲1-4pm Sat) Scottish writer Robert Louis Stevenson came to Monterey in 1879 to court his wife-to-be, Fanny Osbourne. This building, then the French Hotel, was where he stayed while reputedly devising his novel *Treasure Island*. The boarding-house rooms were primitive and Stevenson was still a penniless unknown. Today the house displays a superb collection of the writer's memorabilia.

Cooper-Molera Adobe

(Map p284; 525 Polk St; ⏲store 10am-4pm daily, to 5pm May-Sep, tour schedules vary) In 1827, this stately adobe home was built by John Rogers Cooper, a New England sea captain, and three generations of his family resided here until 1968. Over time, the adobe buildings were partitioned and expanded, gardens were added, and it was later willed to the National Trust. Worth a browse, the bookshop also sells nostalgic toys and household goods.

Monterey Peninsula

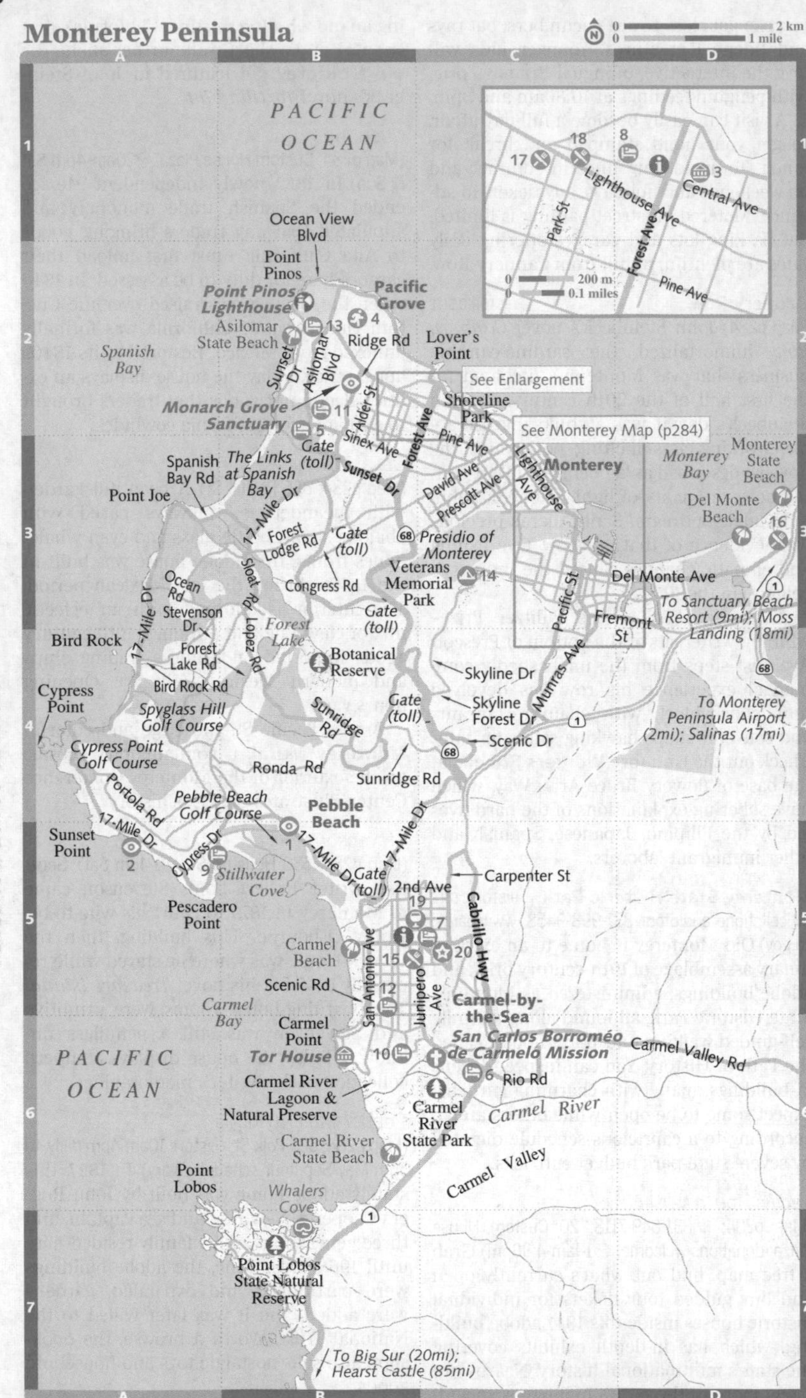

Monterey Peninsula

Top Sights
- Monarch Grove Sanctuary B2
- Point Pinos Lighthouse B2
- San Carlos Borroméo de Carmelo Mission C6
- Tor House B6

Sights
- 1 17-Mile Drive B5
- 2 Lone Cypress A5
- 3 Museum of Natural History D1

Activities, Courses & Tours
- 4 Pacific Grove Golf Links B2

Sleeping
- 5 Asilomar Conference Grounds B2
- 6 Carmel River Inn C6
- 7 Carmel Village Inn C5
- 8 Centrella Inn D1
- 9 Lodge at Pebble Beach A5
- 10 Mission Ranch B6
- 11 Pacific Gardens Inn B2
- 12 Sea View Inn B5
- 13 Sunset Inn Hotel B2
- 14 Veterans Memorial Park Campground C3

Eating
- Bruno's Market & Deli .... (see 7)
- Carmel Belle .... (see 15)
- 15 La Bicyclette B5
- 16 Monterey's Fish House D3
- Mundaka .... (see 15)
- 17 Passionfish C1
- 18 Red House Cafe C1

Drinking
- 19 Jack London's B5

Entertainment
- 20 Forest Theater C5

Monterey History & Maritime Museum MUSEUM
(Map p284; ☎831-372-2608; http://montereyhistory.org; 5 Custom House Plaza; admission $5, free after 3pm on 1st Tue of the month; ⏲10am-5pm Tue-Sun) Near the waterfront, this voluminous modern exhibition hall illuminates Monterey's salty past, from early Spanish explorers to the roller-coaster–like rise and fall of the local sardine industry that brought Cannery Row to life in the mid-20th century. Highlights include a ship-in-a-bottle collection and the historic Fresnel lens from Point Sur Lightstation.

Monterey Museum of Art MUSEUM
(MMA; www.montereyart.org; adult/child under 13 $10/free; ⏲11am-5pm Wed-Sat & 1-4pm Sun) Downtown, **MMA Pacific Street** (Map p284; ☎831-372-5477; 559 Pacific St) is particularly strong in California contemporary art and modern landscape painters and photographers, including Ansel Adams and Edward Weston. Temporary exhibits fill **MMA La Mirada** (Map p284; ☎831-372-3689; 720 Via Mirada), a silent-film-star's villa, whose humble adobe origins are exquisitely concealed. Visit both locations on the same ticket.

Royal Presidio Chapel CHURCH
(Map p284; www.sancarloscathedral.net; San Carlos Cathedral, 500 Church St; admission by donation; ⏲10am-noon Wed, 10am-3pm Fri, 10am-2pm Sat, 1-3pm Sun, also 10am-noon & 1:15-3:15pm 2nd & 4th Mon of the month) Built of sandstone in 1794, this graceful chapel is California's oldest continuously functioning church. The original 1770 mission church stood here before being moved to Carmel. As Monterey expanded under Mexican rule in the 1820s, older buildings were gradually destroyed, leaving behind this National Historic Landmark as the strongest reminder of the defeated Spanish colonial presence.

FREE **Presidio of Monterey Museum** MUSEUM
(Map p284; www.monterey.org; Bldg 113, Corporal Ewing Rd; ⏲10am-1pm Mon, 10am-4pm Thu-Sat, 1-4pm Sun) On the grounds of the original Spanish fort, this minor museum treats Monterey's history from a military perspective, looking at the Native American, Mexican and American periods.

Activities

Like its larger namesake in San Francisco, **Fisherman's Wharf** is a tacky tourist trap at heart, and a jumping-off point for deep-sea fishing trips. On the flip side, the authentic **Municipal Wharf II** is a short walk east. There fishing boats bob and sway, painters work on their canvases and seafood purveyors hawk fresh catches.

FREE **Dennis the Menace Park** PLAYGROUND
(Map p284; 777 Pearl St; ⊙10am-dusk, closed Tue Sep-May;) A must for fans of kick-ass playgrounds, this park was the brainchild of Hank Ketcham, the creator of the classic comic strip. This ain't your standard dumbed-down playground, suffocated by Big Brother's safety regulations. With lightning-fast slides, a hedge maze and towering climbing walls, even some adults can't resist playing here.

Cycling & Mountain-Biking

Along a former railway line, the **Monterey Peninsula Recreational Trail** travels 18 car-free miles along the waterfront, passing Cannery Row en route to Lovers Point in Pacific Grove. Road-cycling enthusiasts with nerves of steel can make the round trip to Carmel along the **17-Mile Drive** (see the boxed text, p289). Mountain-bikers head to **Fort Ord** for 50 miles of single-track and fire roads; the **Sea Otter Classic** (www.seaotterclassic.com) races there in mid-April.

Adventures by the Sea CYCLING
(Map p284; ☎831-372-1807; www.adventuresbythesea.com; 299 Cannery Row; rental per hr/day $7/25) Beach cruiser and hybrid mountain-bike rentals on Cannery Row and **downtown** (210 Alvarado St).

Bay Bikes CYCLING
(Map p284; ☎831-655-2453; www.baybikes.com; 585 Cannery Row; per hr/day from $8/32) Cruiser, tandem, hybrid and mountain bike rentals near the aquarium.

Whale-Watching

You can spot whales off the coast of Monterey Bay year-round. The season for blue and humpback whales runs from late April to early December, while gray whales pass by from mid-December to mid-April. Tour boats depart from downtown's Fisherman's Wharf and also Moss Landing (see p278). Reserve trips at least a day in advance; be prepared for a bumpy, cold ride.

Monterey Whale Watching BOAT TOURS
(Map p284; ☎831-372-2203, tickets 800-979-3370; www.montereywhalewatching.com; 96 Fisherman's Wharf; 2½hr tour adult/child 3-12yr $40/30) Several daily departures.

Monterey Bay Whale Watch BOAT TOURS
(Map p284; ☎831-375-4658; www.montereybaywhalewatch.com; 84 Fisherman's Wharf; 2½hr tour adult/child 4-12yr from $38/27) Morning and afternoon departures.

Diving & Snorkeling

Monterey Bay offers world-renowned diving and snorkeling, including off **Lovers Point** in Pacific Grove and at **Point Lobos State Natural Reserve** near Carmel-by-the-Sea. You'll want a wetsuit year-round. In summer upwelling currents carry cold water from the deep canyon below the bay, sending a rich supply of nutrients up toward the surface level to feed the bay's diverse marine life. These frigid currents also account for the bay's chilly water temperatures and summer fog that blankets the peninsula.

Monterey Bay Dive Charters SCUBA DIVING
(☎831-383-9276; www.mbdcscuba.com; scuba rental per day $79-89, shore/boat dive from $49/199) Rent a full scuba kit with wetsuit, arrange small-group shore or boat dives or take a virgin undersea plunge by booking a three-hour beginners' dive experience ($159, no PADI certification required).

Kayaking & Surfing

Monterey Bay Kayaks KAYAKING
(Map p284; ☎800-649-5357; www.montereybaykayaks.com; 693 Del Monte Ave; rental per day $30-50, tours adult/child from $50/40;) Rents kayaks and stand-up paddle boarding (SUP) equipment and leads kayaking lessons and guided tours of Monterey Bay, including full-moon, sunrise and sunset trips, and family adventures.

Sunshine Freestyle Surf SURFING
(Map p284; ☎831-375-5015; http://sunshinefreestyle.com; 443 Lighthouse Ave; rental per half/full day surfboard $20/30, wetsuit $10/15, boogie board $7/10) Monterey's oldest surf shop rents and sells all the gear you'll need. Staff grudgingly dole out tips.

Festivals & Events

AT&T Pebble Beach National Pro-Am GOLF
(www.attpbgolf.com) Famous golf tournament mixes pros with celebrities; in early February.

Castroville Artichoke Festival FOOD
(www.artichoke-festival.org) North of Monterey, features 3D 'agro art' sculptures, cooking demos, a farmers market and field tours; in mid-May.

Strawberry Festival at Monterey Bay FOOD
(www.mbsf.com) Berry-licious pie-eating contests and live bands in Watsonville, north of Monterey, in early August.

Concours d'Elegance STREET
(www.pebblebeachconcours.net) Classic cars roll onto the fairways at Pebble Beach in mid-August.

Monterey County Fair CULTURE
(www.montereycountyfair.com) Old-fashioned fun, carnival rides, horse-riding and livestock competitions, wine tasting and live music in late August and early September.

TOP CHOICE **Monterey Jazz Festival** MUSIC
(www.montereyjazzfestival.org) One of the world's longest-running jazz festivals (since 1958), held in mid-September.

Sleeping

Book ahead for special events and summer visits. To avoid the tourist congestion and jacked-up prices of Cannery Row, consider staying in Pacific Grove (p288). Cheaper chain and indie motels line Munras Ave, south of downtown, and N Fremont St, east of Hwy 1.

InterContinental–The Clement HOTEL $$$
(Map p284; ☎831-375-4500, 888-424-6835; www.intercontinental.com; 750 Cannery Row; r $200-455;) Like an upscale version of a New England millionaire's seaside compound, this all-encompassing resort presides over Cannery Row. For the utmost luxury and romance, book an ocean-view suite with a balcony and private fireplace, then breakfast in bayfront C Restaurant downstairs. Parking $18.

Sanctuary Beach Resort HOTEL $$$
(☎831-883-9478, 877-944-3863; www.thesanctuarybeachresort.com; 3295 Dunes Dr, Marina; r $179-329;) Be lulled to sleep by the surf at this low-lying retreat hidden in the sand dunes north of Monterey. Townhouses harbor petite rooms with gas fireplaces and binoculars to borrow for whale-watching. The beach is an off-limits nature preserve, but there are plenty of other beaches and walking trails nearby.

Jabberwock B&B $$$
(Map p284; ☎831-372-4777, 888-428-7253; www.jabberwockinn.com; 598 Laine St; r incl breakfast $169-309;) High atop a hill and barely visible through a shroud of foliage, this 1911 Arts and Crafts house hums a playful *Alice in Wonderland* tune through its seven immaculate rooms. Over afternoon tea and cookies or evening wine and hors d'oeuvres, ask the genial hosts about the house's many salvaged architectural elements.

Casa Munras BOUTIQUE HOTEL $$
(Map p284; ☎831-375-2411; www.hotelcasamunras.com; 700 Munras Ave; r $185-279;) Built around an adobe hacienda once owned by a 19th-century Spanish colonial don, chic modern rooms come with lofty beds and some gas fireplaces, all inside two-story motel-esque buildings. Splash in a heated outdoor pool, unwind at the tapas bar or take a sea-salt scrub in the tiny spa. Pet fee $50.

Hotel Abrego BOUTIQUE HOTEL $$
(Map p284; ☎831-372-7551; www.hotelabrego.com; 755 Abrego St; r $140-270;) Another downtown boutique hotel, albeit with slightly fewer amenities, where most of the spacious, clean-lined contemporary rooms have gas fireplaces and chaise longues. Take a dip in the outdoor pool or warm up in the hot tub. Pet fee $30.

Monterey Hotel HISTORIC HOTEL $$
(Map p284; ☎831-375-3184, 800-966-6490; www.montereyhotel.com; 406 Alvarado St; r $70-310;) In the heart of downtown and a short walk from Fisherman's Wharf, this 1904 edifice harbors five dozen small, somewhat noisy, but freshly renovated rooms with Victorian-styled furniture and plantation shutters. No elevator. Parking $17.

Colton Inn MOTEL $$
(Map p284; ☎831-649-6500; www.coltoninn.com; 707 Pacific St; r $109-199;) Downtown, this champ of a motel prides itself on cleanliness and friendliness. There's no pool and zero view, but staff loan out DVDs, some rooms have real log-burning fireplaces, hot tubs or kitchenettes, and there's even a dry sauna for guests.

HI Monterey Hostel HOSTEL $
(Map p284; ☎831-649-0375; www.montereyhostel.org; 778 Hawthorne St; dm $25-28, r $59-75, all with shared bath; check-in 4-10pm;) Four blocks from Cannery Row and the aquarium, this simple, clean hostel lets budget backpackers stuff themselves silly with make-your-own waffle breakfasts. Reservations strongly

Monterey

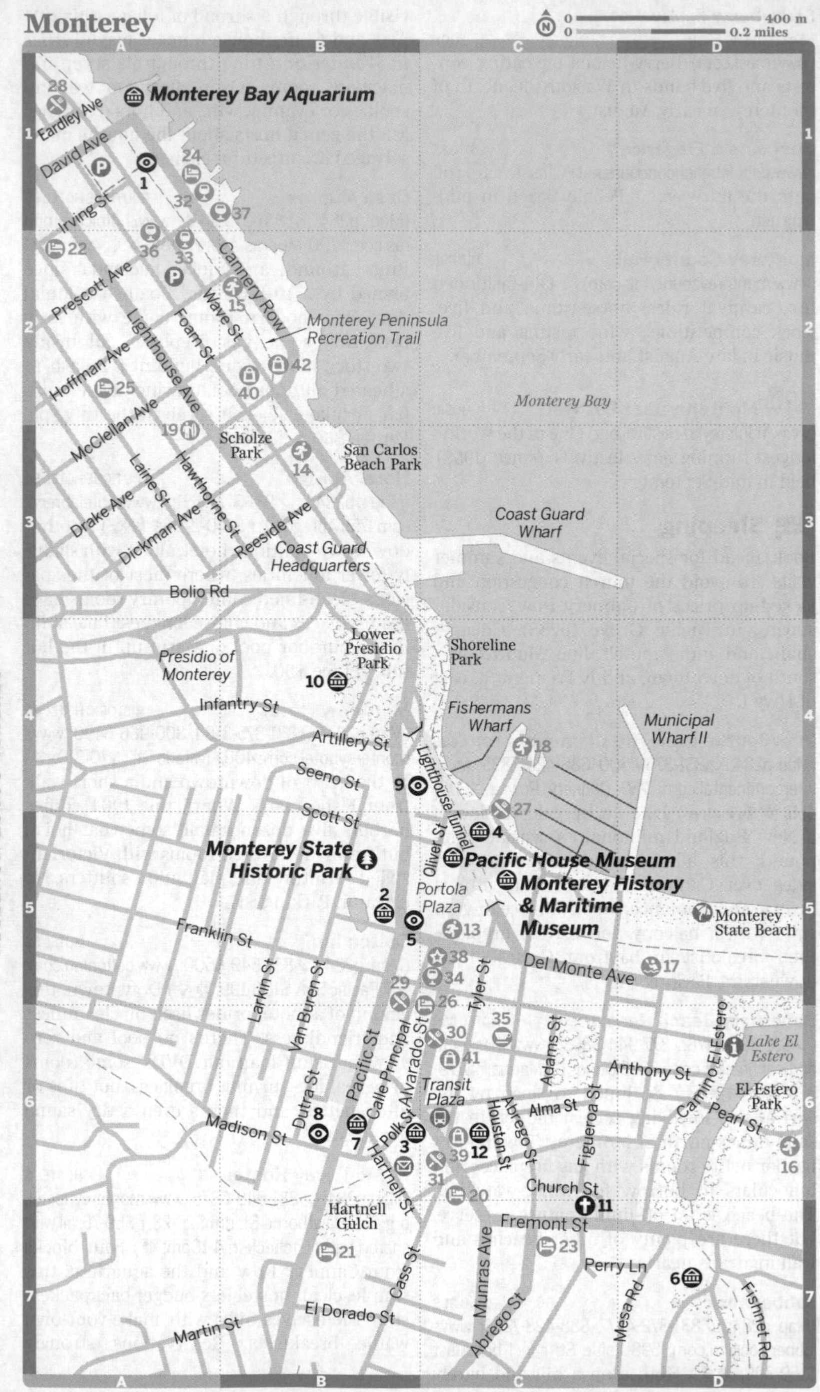

Monterey Bay Aquarium
Monterey Peninsula Recreation Trail
Monterey Bay
Scholze Park
San Carlos Beach Park
Coast Guard Wharf
Coast Guard Headquarters
Presidio of Monterey
Lower Presidio Park
Shoreline Park
Fishermans Wharf
Municipal Wharf II
Monterey State Historic Park
Pacific House Museum
Monterey History & Maritime Museum
Portola Plaza
Monterey State Beach
Transit Plaza
Lake El Estero
El Estero Park
Hartnell Gulch
Cannery Row
Lighthouse Ave
Del Monte Ave
Lighthouse Tunnel
0 400 m
0 0.2 miles

Monterey

Top Sights

	Monterey Bay Aquarium	A1
	Monterey History & Maritime Museum	C5
	Monterey State Historic Park	B5
	Pacific House Museum	C5

Sights

1	Cannery Row Workers' Shacks	A1
2	Casa Soberanes	B5
3	Cooper-Molera Adobe	B6
4	Custom House	C5
5	Monterey Conference Center	B5
	Monterey Mural	(see 5)
6	Monterey Museum of Art (MMA) La Mirada	D7
7	Monterey Museum of Art (MMA) Pacific Street	B6
8	Old Monterey Jail	B6
9	Old Whaling Station	B4
10	Presidio of Monterey Museum	B4
11	Royal Presidio Chapel	C7
12	Stevenson House	C6

Activities, Courses & Tours

13	Adventures by the Sea	C5
14	Adventures by the Sea	B3
15	Bay Bikes	B2
16	Dennis the Menace Park	D6
17	Monterey Bay Kayaks	D5
	Monterey Bay Whale Watch	(see 18)
18	Monterey Whale Watching	C4
19	Sunshine Freestyle Surf	A3

Sleeping

20	Casa Munras	C6
21	Colton Inn	B7
22	HI Monterey Hostel	A2
23	Hotel Abrego	C7
24	InterContinental - The Clement	A1
25	Jabberwock	A2
26	Monterey Hotel	C5

Eating

27	Crêpes of Brittany	C4
28	First Awakenings	A1
29	Montrio Bistro	B5
30	Old Monterey Marketplace	C6
31	RG Burgers	C6

Drinking

32	A Taste of Monterey	A1
33	Cannery Row Brewing Co	A2
34	Crown & Anchor	C5
35	East Village Coffee Lounge	C6
36	Sardine Factory	A2
37	Sly McFly's Fueling Station	B1

Entertainment

38	Osio Cinemas	C5

Shopping

39	Book Haven	C6
40	Cannery Row Antique Mall	B2
41	Luna Blu	C6
42	Monterey Peninsula Art Foundation Gallery	B2

recommended. Take MST bus 1 from downtown's Transit Plaza.

Veterans Memorial Park CAMPGROUND $
(Map p280; ☎831-646-3865; www.monterey.org; Veterans Memorial Park, off Skyline Dr; tent & RV sites $25-30) Tucked into the forest, this municipal campground has 40 well-kept, grassy, nonreservable sites near nature-preserve hiking trails. Amenities include coin-op hot showers, flush toilets, drinking water, firepits and BBQ picnic areas. Three-night maximum stay.

Eating

Uphill from Cannery Row, Lighthouse Ave is lined with budget-friendly, multiethnic eateries, from Japanese sushi to Hawaiian barbecue to Middle Eastern kebabs. Alternatively, keep going west to Pacific Grove (p288).

First Awakenings BRUNCH $
(Map p284; www.firstawakenings.net; American Tin Cannery Mall, 125 Oceanview Blvd; mains $5-12; 7am-2pm Mon-Fri, to 2:30pm Sat & Sun;) Sweet and savory, all-American breakfasts and lunches and bottomless pitchers of coffee merrily weigh down outdoor tables at this hideaway cafe. Order creative dishes like 'bluegerm' pancakes or the spicy 'Viva Carnita' egg scramble.

Monterey's Fish House SEAFOOD $$$
(Map p280; ☎831-373-4647; 2114 Del Monte Ave; mains $12-35; 11:30am-2:30pm Mon-Fri, 5-9:30pm daily) Watched over by photos of Sicilian fishermen, dig into dock-fresh seafood with an occasional Asian twist. Reservations are essential (it's *so* crowded), but the vibe is island-casual: Hawaiian shirts seem to be de rigueur for men. Try the barbecued oysters

or, for those stout of heart, the Mexican squid steak.

Montrio Bistro CALIFORNIAN $$$
(Map p284; ☎831-648-8880; www.montrio.com; 414 Calle Principal; mains $14-29; ⏲5-10pm Sun-Thu, to 11pm Fri & Sat; 👪) Inside a 1910 firehouse, Montrio looks dolled up with leather walls and iron trellises, but the tables have butcher paper and crayons for kids. The seasonal New American menu mixes local, organic fare with California flair, including tapas-style small bites.

RG Burgers DINER $
(Map p284; www.rgburgers.com; 570 Munras Ave; items $4-12; ⏲11am-8:30pm Sun-Thu, to 9pm Fri & Sat) Next to Trader Joe's supermarket, where you can stock up on trail mix and take-out salads, this locally owned burger shop slings beef, bison, turkey, chicken and veggie patties, sweet tater fries and thick milkshakes.

Old Monterey Marketplace FARMERS MARKET $
(Map p284; www.oldmonterey.org; Alvarado St, btwn Del Monte Ave & Pearl St; ⏲4-7pm Tue Sep-May, to 8pm Jun-Aug) Rain or shine, head downtown for farm-fresh fruit and veggies, artisan cheeses and baked goods, and multiethnic takeout.

Crêpes of Brittany SNACKS $
(Map p284; www.vivalecrepemonterey.com; 6 Old Fisherman's Wharf; snacks $4-9; ⏲8:30am-7pm Sun-Thu, 8:30am-8pm Sun) Find authentic savory and sweet crepes swirled by a French expat – the homemade caramel is a treat. Expect long lines on weekends. Hours are reduced in winter.

Drinking & Entertainment

Prowl downtown's Alvarado St, touristy Cannery Row and locals-only Lighthouse Ave for more watering holes. For comprehensive entertainment and nightlife listings, check the free tabloid *Monterey County Weekly* (www.montereycountyweekly.com).

A Taste of Monterey WINE BAR
(Map p284; www.atasteofmonterey.com; 700 Cannery Row; tasting fee $5-20; ⏲11am-6pm) Sample medal-winning Monterey County wines from as far away as the Santa Lucia Highlands while soaking up dreamy sea views, then peruse thoughtful exhibits on barrel-making and cork production.

East Village Coffee Lounge CAFE
(Map p284; www.eastvillagecoffeelounge.com; 498 Washington St; ⏲6am-late Mon-Fri, 7am-late Sat & Sun) Sleek coffeehouse on a busy downtown corner brews fair-trade, organic beans. At night, it pulls off a big-city lounge vibe with film, open-mic, live-music and DJ nights and an all-important booze license.

Cannery Row Brewing Co BREWPUB
(Map p284; www.canneryrowbrewingcompany.com; 95 Prescott Ave; ⏲11:30am-midnight Sun-Thu, to 2am Fri & Sat) Brews from around the world bring crowds to Cannery Row's microbrew bar, as does the enticing outdoor deck with roaring firepits. Decent brewpub menu of burgers, fries, salads, BBQ and more.

Crown & Anchor PUB
(Map p284; www.crownandanchor.net; 150 W Franklin St; ⏲11am-2am) Descend into the basement of this British pub and the first thing you'll notice is the red plaid carpeting. At least these blokes know their way around a bar, with plentiful draft beers and single-malt scotch, not to mention damn fine fish and chips.

Sly McFly's Fueling Station LIVE MUSIC
(Map p284; www.slymcflys.net; 700 Cannery Row; ⏲11:30am-2am) Rubbing shoulders with billiards halls, comedy shops and touristy restaurants, this waterfront dive shows live blues, jazz and rock bands nightly. Skip the food, though.

Sardine Factory LOUNGE
(Map p284; www.sardinefactory.com; 701 Wave St; ⏲5pm-midnight) The legendary restaurant's fireplace cocktail lounge pours wines by the glass, delivers filling appetizers to your table and features live piano some nights.

Osio Cinemas CINEMA
(Map p284; ☎831-644-8171; www.osiocinemas.com; 350 Alvarado St) Downtown cinema screens indie dramas, cutting-edge documentaries and offbeat Hollywood films. Drop by Cafe Lumiere for decadent cheesecakes and loose-leaf or bubble teas.

Shopping

Cannery Row is jammed with touristy shops, while downtown side streets hide one-of-a-kind finds.

Monterey Peninsula Art Foundation Gallery ART
(Map p284; www.mpaf.org; 425 Cannery Row; ⏲11am-5pm) Inside a cozy sea-view house, over two dozen local artists sell their plein-

air paintings and sketches, plus contemporary works in all media.

Cannery Row Antique Mall ANTIQUES
(Map p284; http://canneryrowantiquemall.com; 471 Wave St; ⏲10am-5:30pm) Inside a historic 1920s canning company building, two floors are stacked high with beguiling flotsam and jetsam from decades past.

Book Haven BOOKS
(Map p284; 559 Tyler St; ⏲10am-6pm Mon-Sat) Tall shelves of new and used books, including rare first editions and John Steinbeck titles.

Luna Blu CLOTHING
(Map p284; 176 Bonifacio Pl; ⏲11am-7pm Tue-Sat, to 5pm Sun & Mon) Vintage and name-brand consignment clothing, bags, and jaunty hats for women and men.

Information

Doctors on Duty (Map p284; ☎831-649-0770; http://doctorsonduty.com; 501 Lighthouse Ave; ⏲8am-8pm Mon-Sat, 8am-6pm Sun) Walk-in, nonemergency medical clinic.

FedEx Office (Map p284; www.fedex.com; 799 Lighthouse Ave; per min 20-30¢; ⏲7am-11pm Mon-Fri, 9am-9pm Sat & Sun; @ wi-fi) Pay-as-you-go internet workstations and free wi-fi.

Monterey County Convention & Visitors Bureau (Map p284; ☎831-657-6400, 877-666-8373; www.seemonterey.com; 401 Camino El Estero; ⏲9am-6pm Mon-Sat, to 5pm Sun) Ask for a free *Monterey County Film & Literary Map*. Closes one hour earlier November to March.

Post office (Map p284; www.usps.com; 565 Hartnell St; ⏲8:30am-5pm Mon-Fri, 10am-2pm Sat)

Public library (Map p284; www.monterey.org; 625 Pacific St; ⏲noon-8pm Mon-Wed, 10am-6pm Thu-Sat; @ wi-fi) Free wi-fi and public internet terminals.

Getting There & Around

A few miles east of downtown off Hwy 68, **Monterey Peninsula Airport** (MRY; www.montereyairport.com; 200 Fred Kane Dr, off Olmsted Rd) has flights with United (LA, San Francisco and Denver), American (LA), Allegiant Air (Las Vegas) and US Airways (Phoenix).

Monterey Airbus (☎831-373-7777; www.montereyairbus.com) links Monterey with airports in San Jose ($35, 90 minutes) and San Francisco ($45, 2¼ hours) almost a dozen times daily.

If you don't fly or drive to Monterey, first take a Greyhound bus or Amtrak train to Salinas, then catch a local Monterey-Salinas Transit bus (for details, see p308).

Monterey-Salinas Transit (☎888-678-2871; www.mst.org) operates local and regional buses; one-way fares cost $1 to $3 (day pass $8). Routes converge on downtown's **Transit Plaza** (Map p284; cnr Pearl & Alvarado Sts).

From late May until early September, MST's free **trolley** loops around downtown, Fisherman's Wharf and Cannery Row from 10am to 7pm daily.

Pacific Grove

Founded as a tranquil Methodist summer retreat in 1875, PG maintained a quaint, holier-than-thou attitude well into the 20th century – the selling of liquor was illegal up until 1969, making it California's last 'dry' town. Today, leafy streets are lined by stately Victorian homes. The charming, compact downtown orbits Lighthouse Ave.

Sights & Activities

Aptly named **Ocean View Blvd** affords views from Lover's Point west to Point Pinos, where it becomes **Sunset Dr**, offering tempting turnouts where you can stroll by pounding surf, rocky outcrops and teeming tidepools. This seaside route is great for cycling too. Some say it even rivals the famous 17-Mile Drive for beauty, and it's free.

Point Pinos Lighthouse LIGHTHOUSE
(Map p280; www.ci.pg.ca.us/lighthouse; off Asilomar Ave; adult/child $2/1; ⏲1-4pm Thu-Mon) On the tip of the Monterey Peninsula, the West Coast's oldest continuously operating lighthouse has been warning ships off this hazardous point since 1855. Inside are modest exhibits on the lighthouse's history and, alas, its failures – local shipwrecks.

FREE **Monarch Grove Sanctuary** PARK
(Map p280; www.ci.pg.ca.us/monarchs; off Ridge Rd, Pacific Grove; ⏲dawn-dusk) Between October and February, over 25,000 migratory monarch butterflies cluster in this thicket of tall eucalyptus trees, secreted inland from Lighthouse Ave. Volunteers are on hand to answer all of your questions.

Museum of Natural History MUSEUM
(Map p280; www.pgmuseum.org; 165 Forest Ave; suggested donation per person/family $3/5; ⏲10am-5pm Tue-Sat; family-friendly) With a gray whale sculpture out front, this small kids' museum has old-fashioned exhibits about sea otters,

coastal bird life, butterflies, the Big Sur coast and Native American tribes.

Pacific Grove Golf Links GOLF
(Map p280; 831-648-5775; www.pggolflinks.com; 77 Asilomar Blvd; greens fees $42-65) Can't afford to play at famous Pebble Beach? This historic 18-hole municipal course, where black-tailed deer freely range, has impressive sea views, and it's a lot easier (not to mention cheaper) to book a tee time.

Sleeping

B&Bs have taken over many stately Victorian homes around downtown and by the beach. Motels cluster at the peninsula's western end, off Lighthouse and Asilomar Aves.

TOP CHOICE **Asilomar Conference Grounds** LODGE $$
(Map p280; 831-372-8016, 888-635-5310; www.visitasilomar.com; 800 Asilomar Ave, Pacific Grove; r incl breakfast $115-175;) Sprawling over more than 100 acres of sand dunes and pine forests, this state-park lodge is a find. Skip ho-hum motel rooms for historic houses designed by early-20th-century architect Julia Morgan (of Hearst Castle fame) – the thin-walled, hardwood-floored rooms may be small, but share a sociable fireplace lounge. The lobby rec room has ping-pong and pool tables, and wi-fi. Bike rentals available.

Centrella Inn B&B $$$
(Map p280; 831-372-3372, 800-233-3372; www.centrellainn.com; 612 Central Ave; d incl breakfast $119-399; @) For a romantic night inside a Victorian seaside mansion, this turreted National Historic Landmark beckons with enchanting gardens and a player piano. Some of the stately rooms have fireplaces, clawfoot tubs and kitchenettes, while private cottages welcome honeymooners and families. Rates include afternoon fresh-baked cookies and evening wine and hors d'oeuvres.

Sunset Inn Hotel MOTEL $$$
(Map p280; 831-375-3529; www.gosunsetinn.com; 133 Asilomar Blvd; r $139-400;) At this small motor lodge near the golf course and the beach, attentive staff check you into crisply redesigned rooms that have hardwood floors, king-sized beds with cheery floral-print comforters and some hot tubs and fireplaces. Ask about guest access to the top-notch Spa at Pebble Beach.

Pacific Gardens Inn MOTEL $$
(Map p280; 831-646-9414, 800-262-1566; www.pacificgardensinn.com; 701 Asilomar Blvd; d $105-225; @) A hospitable owner and a communal lobby make all the difference at this welcoming, wood-shingled motor lodge sheltered among tall oak trees. For chilly nights, some comfy rooms have wood-burning fireplaces. It's an easy stroll over to the beach.

Eating

Make reservations for these popular downtown eateries.

TOP CHOICE **Passionfish** SEAFOOD $$$
(Map p280; 831-655-3311; www.passionfish.net; 701 Lighthouse Ave; mains $16-28; 5-10pm) Fresh, sustainable seafood is artfully presented in any number of inventive ways, and the seasonally inspired menu also carries slow-cooked meats and vegetarian dishes. The earth-tone decor is spare, with tables squeezed a tad too close together. But an ambitious world-ranging wine list is priced near retail, and there are twice as many Chinese teas as wines by the glass.

Red House Cafe CAFE $$
(Map p280; 831-643-1060; www.redhousecafe.com; 662 Lighthouse Ave; mains $5-16; 8-11am Sat & Sun, 11am-2:30pm & 5-9pm Tue-Sun;) Crowded with locals, this 1895 shingled house dishes up comfort food with delightful haute touches, from cinnamon-brioche French toast for breakfast to blue-cheese soufflés and roast chicken at dinner. Haute French tea list. Cash only.

Information

Pacific Grove Chamber of Commerce (Map p280; 831-373-3304, 800-656-6650; www.pacificgrove.org; 584 Central Ave; 9:30am-5pm Mon-Fri, 10am-3pm Sat) Tourist information.

Getting There & Around

MST (888-678-2871; www.mst.org) bus 1 connects downtown Monterey, Cannery Row and Pacific Grove every half hour from 6:15am to 10:45pm daily.

Carmel-by-the-Sea

With borderline fanatical devotion to its canine citizens, quaint Carmel-by-the-Sea has the well-manicured feel of a country club. Simply plop down in any cafe and watch

SCENIC DRIVE: 17-MILE DRIVE

What to See

Pacific Grove and Carmel are linked by the spectacularly scenic, if overhyped 17-Mile Drive (Map p280), which meanders through Pebble Beach, a wealthy private resort. It's no chore staying within the 25mph limit – every curve in the road reveals another postcard vista, especially when wildflowers bloom. Cycling the drive is enormously popular, but try to do it during the week, when traffic isn't as heavy, and ride with the flow of traffic, from north to south.

Using the self-guided touring map provided upon entry, you can easily pick out landmarks such as **Spanish Bay**, where explorer Gaspar de Portolá dropped anchor in 1769; treacherously rocky **Point Joe**, which in the past was often mistaken for the entrance to Monterey Bay and thus became the site of several shipwrecks; and **Bird Rock**, also a haven for harbor seals and sea lions. The ostensible pièce de résistance is the trademark **Lone Cypress**, which has perched on a seaward rock for more than 250 years.

Besides the coastal scenery, star attractions at Pebble Beach include world-famous **golf courses**, where a celebrity and pro tournament happens every February – just imagine Tiger Woods driving down the spectacular 18th-hole fairway for a victory. The luxurious **Lodge at Pebble Beach** (☎831-624-3811, 800-654-9300; www.pebblebeach.com; 1700 17-Mile Drive; r $715-995; ❄@📶🏊) embraces a spa and designer shops where the most demanding of tastes are catered to. Even if you're not a trust-fund baby, you can still soak up the rich atmosphere in the resort's art-filled public spaces or at the cocktail bar.

The Route

Operated as a toll road by the **Pebble Beach Company** (www.pebblebeach.com; per vehicle/bicycle $9.50/free), 17-Mile Drive is open from sunrise to sunset. The toll can be refunded later as a discount on a $25 minimum food purchase at Pebble Beach restaurants.

Time & Mileage

There are five separate gates for the 17-Mile Drive; how far you drive and how long you take is up to you. For the most scenery, enter at Pacific Grove (off Sunset Dr) and exit at Carmel.

the parade of behatted ladies toting fancy-label shopping bags to lunch and dapper gents driving top-down convertibles along Ocean Ave, the village's slow-mo main drag. Fairy-tale Comstock cottages, with their characteristic stone chimneys and pitched gable roofs, dot the town. Even payphones, garbage cans and newspaper vending boxes are shingled, and local bylaws forbid neon signs and billboards.

Founded as a seaside resort in the 1880s – fairly odd, given that its beach is often blanketed in fog – Carmel quickly attracted famous artists and writers, such as Sinclair Lewis and Jack London, and their hangers-on. An artistic flavor survives in the more than 100 galleries that line the town's immaculate streets, but sky-high property values have long obliterated any salt-of-the-earth bohemia.

Sights

Escape downtown's harried shopping streets and stroll tree-lined neighborhoods on the lookout for domiciles charming and peculiar. The Hansel and Gretel houses on Torres St, between 5th and 6th Avenues, are just how you'd imagine them. Another wicked cool house in the shape of a ship, made from stone and salvaged ship parts, is near 6th Ave and Guadalupe St, about three blocks east of Torres St.

San Carlos Borroméo de Carmelo Mission CHURCH
(Map p280; www.carmelmission.org; 3080 Rio Rd; adult/child $6.50/2; ⏱9:30am-5pm Mon-Sat, 10:30am-5pm Sun) The original Monterey mission was established by Spanish priest Junípero Serra in 1770, but poor soil and the corrupting influence of Spanish soldiers

forced the move to Carmel two years later. Today this is one of the most strikingly beautiful missions in California, an oasis of solemnity bathed in flowering gardens.

The mission's adobe (formerly wooden) chapel was later replaced with an arched basilica made of stone quarried in the Santa Lucia Mountains. Museum exhibits are scattered throughout the meditative complex. The spartan cell attributed to Serra looks like something out of *The Good, the Bad and the Ugly*, while a separate chapel houses his memorial tomb. Don't overlook the gravestone of 'Old Gabriel,' a Native American convert whom Serra baptized, and whose dates put him at 151 years old when he died. People say he smoked like a chimney and outlived seven wives. There's a lesson in there somewhere.

Tor House HISTORIC BUILDING
(Map p280; ☎831-624-1813; www.torhouse.org; 26304 Ocean View Ave; tour adult/child 12-17yr $10/5; ⏱10am-3pm Fri & Sat) Even if you've never heard of 20th-century poet Robinson Jeffers, a pilgrimage to this house, which was built with his own hands, offers fascinating insights into both the man and the bohemian ethos of Old Carmel. A porthole in the Celtic-inspired **Hawk Tower** reputedly came from the wrecked ship that carried Napoleon from Elba. The only way to visit the property is to reserve space on a tour (children under 12 not allowed), although the tower can be glimpsed from the street.

Activities

Not always sunny, **Carmel Beach** is a gorgeous white-sand crescent, where pampered pups excitedly run off-leash.

TOP CHOICE **Point Lobos State Natural Reserve** PARK
(Map p280; www.parks.ca.gov, www.pointlobos.org; per car $10; ⏱8am-30min after sunset; 👪) They bark, they bathe and they're fun to watch – sea lions are the stars here at Punta de los Lobos Marinos (Point of the Sea Wolves), 4 miles south of Carmel, where a dramatically rocky coastline offers excellent tide-pooling.

The full perimeter hike is 6 miles, but shorter walks take in wild scenery too, including **Bird Island**, shady **Piney Woods**, the historic **Whaler's Cabin** and **Devil's Cauldron**, a whirlpool that gets splashy at high tide. The kelp forest at **Whalers Cove** is popular with snorkelers and divers; reservations for **scuba-diving permits** (☎831-624-8413; per two-person team $10) are required.

Arrive early on weekends; parking is limited. Don't skip paying the entry fee by parking along Hwy 1; California's state parks are chronically underfunded, and need your help!

Festivals & Events

Carmel Art Festival CULTURE
(www.carmelartfestival.org) Meet plein-air painters and local sculptors in Devendorf Park over a long weekend in mid-May.

Carmel Bach Festival MUSIC
(www.bachfestival.org) In July, classical and chamber-music performances and open rehearsals take place around town.

Harvest Farm-to-Table FOOD, WINE
(www.harvestcarmel.com) Chefs' cooking demos, gardening and BBQ workshops, and wine and artisan-cheese tasting in the neighboring Carmel Valley in late September.

Sleeping

Seriously overpriced boutique hotels, inns and B&Bs fill up quickly, especially in summer; expect a two-night minimum on weekends. Ask at the chamber of commerce about last-minute lodging deals. For better-value lodgings, head north to Monterey.

Mission Ranch INN $$$
(Map p280; ☎831-624-6436, 800-538-8221; www.missionranchcarmel.com; 26270 Dolores St; r incl breakfast $135-285; 📶) If woolly sheep grazing on green fields within view of the Pacific don't convince you to stay here, perhaps knowing that actor and director Clint Eastwood restored this historic ranch will. Accommodations range from shabby-chic rooms inside a converted barn to a family-sized 1850s farmhouse.

Sea View Inn B&B $$
(Map p280; ☎831-624-8778; www.seaviewinncarmel.com; Camino Real btwn 11th & 12th Aves; r incl breakfast $135-265; 📶) At the Sea View – an intimate retreat away from downtown's hustle – fireside nooks are tailor-made for reading or taking afternoon tea. The cheapest rooms with slanted ceilings are short on cat-swinging space, but the beach is nearby.

Carmel River Inn INN $$$
(Map p280; ☎831-624-1575, 800-966-6490; www.carmelriverinn.com; 26600 Oliver Rd; d $159-319;) Tucked off Hwy 1, this peaceful garden retreat south of Carmel's mission rents white-picket-fenced honeymooner and family cottages, many with fireplaces and kitchenettes, and simple country-style rooms. Pet fee $20.

Carmel Village Inn MOTEL $$
(Map p280; ☎831-624-3864, 800-346-3864; www.carmelvillageinn.com; cnr Ocean & Junípero Aves; d incl breakfast buffet $80-250;) With cheerful flowers decorating its exterior, this centrally located motel across from Devendorf Park has pleasant rooms, some with gas fireplaces, and nightly quiet hours.

Eating

Carmel's restaurant scene is more about old-world sidewalk atmosphere than sustenance. Most places open early for breakfast, and stop serving dinner before 9pm.

La Bicyclette FRENCH, ITALIAN $$$
(Map p280; www.labicycletterestaurant.com; Dolores St at 7th Ave; lunch mains $7-16, 3-course prix-fixe dinner $28; ⏲11:30am-4pm & 5-10pm) Rustic European comfort food using seasonal local ingredients packs canoodling couples into this bistro, with an open kitchen baking wood fired oven pizzas. Excellent local wines by the glass.

Mundaka TAPAS $$
(Map p280; www.mundakacarmel.com; San Carlos St btwn Ocean & 7th Aves; small plates $4-19; ⏲5:30-10pm Sun-Wed, 5:30-11pm Thu-Sat) This stone courtyard hideaway is a svelte escape from Carmel's stuffy 'newly wed and nearly dead' crowd. Take Spanish tapas plates for a spin and sip the house-made sangria while DJs or flamenco guitars play.

Carmel Belle CALIFORNIAN $$
(Map p280; www.carmelbelle.com; Doud Craft Studios, cnr Ocean Ave & San Carlos St; brunch mains $5-12; ⏲8am-5pm) Fresh, often organic ingredients flow from Carmel Valley farms onto mini-mall tables at this charcuterie, cheese and wine shop.

Bruno's Market & Deli DELI, GROCERIES $
(Map p280; www.brunosmarket.com; cnr 6th & Junípero Aves; sandwiches $5-8; ⏲7am-8pm) This small supermarket deli counter makes a saucy tri-trip beef sandwich and stocks all the accoutrements for a beach picnic, including Sparky's root beer from Pacific Grove.

Drinking & Entertainment

Forest Theater THEATER
(Map p280; ☎831-626-1681; www.foresttheaterguild.org; cnr Mountain View Ave & Santa Rita St; ⏲May-Jul) Founded in 1910 and now the oldest community theater west of the Rockies, here musicals, drama, comedies and film screenings take place under the stars by flickering firepits.

Jack London's PUB
(Map p280; www.jacklondons.com; Su Vecino Court, Dolores St, btwn 5th & 6th Aves; ⏲11am-late) Knock back a few drinks with the caddies from Pebble Beach next to the crackling fireplace at this Carmel institution.

Information

Downtown buildings have no street numbers, so addresses specify the street and nearest intersection only.

Carmel Chamber of Commerce (☎831-624-2522, 800-550-4333; www.carmelcalifornia.org; San Carlos St, btwn 5th & 6th Aves; ⏲10am-5pm) Free maps and information, including about local art galleries.

Carmel Pine Cone (www.pineconearchive.com) Free weekly newspaper packed with local personality and color – the police log is a comedy of manners.

Getting There & Around

Carmel is 5 miles south of Monterey via Hwy 1. Find free unlimited parking in a **municipal lot** (cnr 3rd & Junípero Aves) behind the Vista Lobos building.

MST (☎888-678-2871; www.mst.org) bus 5 ($2, every 30 minutes) and bus 7 ($2, hourly) connect Carmel with Monterey. Bus 4 runs between downtown Carmel and the mission ($1, every 30 minutes). Bus 22 ($3) passes through en route to/from Big Sur three times daily between late May and early September, and twice daily on Saturday and Sunday only the rest of the year.

Big Sur

Big Sur is more a state of mind than a place you can pinpoint on a map. There are no traffic lights, banks or strip malls, and when the sun goes down, the moon and the stars are the only streetlights – if summer's dense fog hasn't extinguished them, that is. Much ink has been spilled extolling the raw beauty

Big Sur

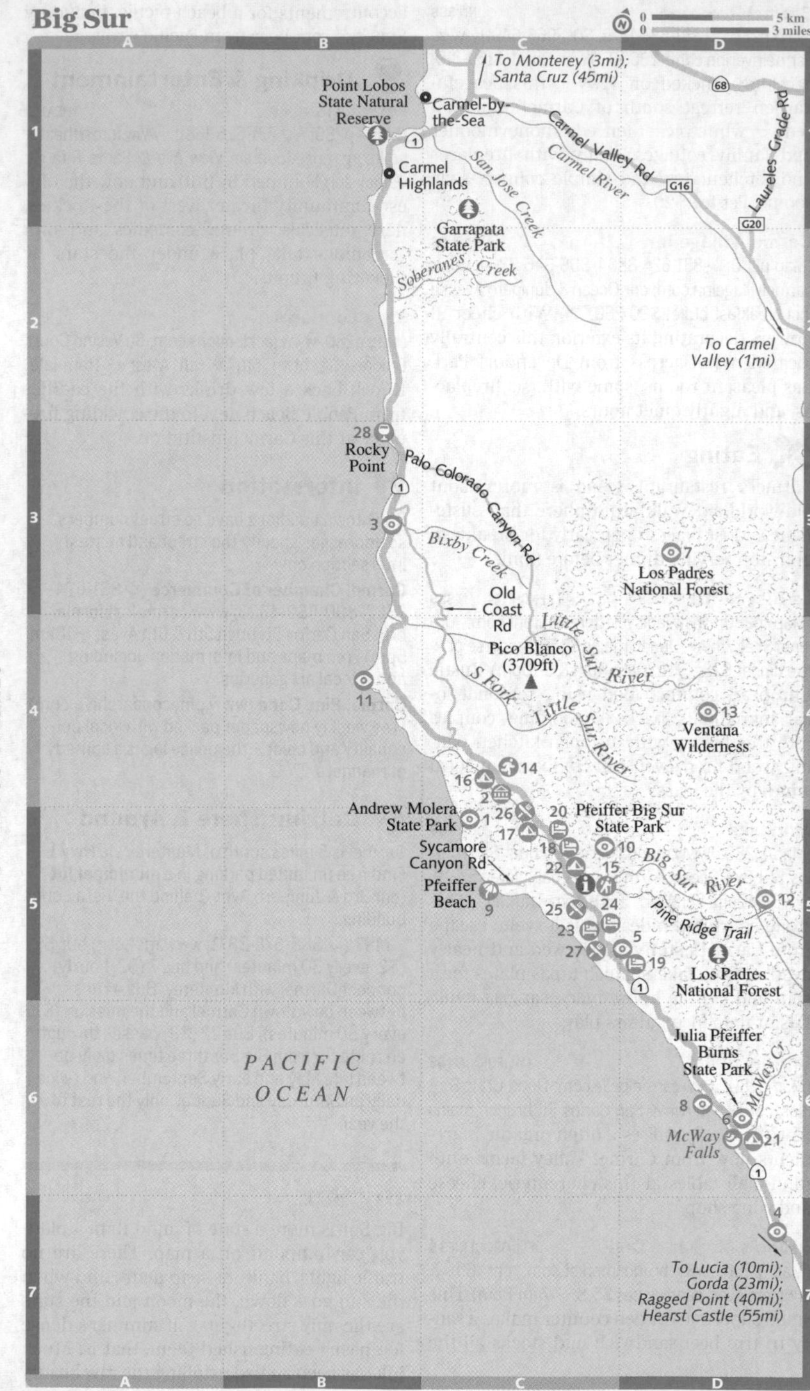
0 5 km
0 3 miles
To Monterey (3mi); Santa Cruz (45mi)
Point Lobos State Natural Reserve
Carmel-by-the-Sea
Carmel Valley Rd
Carmel River
Laureles Grade Rd
Carmel Highlands
San Jose Creek
Garrapata State Park
Soberanes Creek
To Carmel Valley (1mi)
28
Rocky Point
Palo Colorado Canyon Rd
3
Bixby Creek
7
Los Padres National Forest
Old Coast Rd
Little Sur River
Pico Blanco (3709ft)
S Fork
Little Sur River
11
13
Ventana Wilderness
14
16
2
Andrew Molera State Park
1
26
20
Pfeiffer Big Sur State Park
17
18
10
Sycamore Canyon Rd
22
15
Big Sur River
Pfeiffer Beach
9
24
Pine Ridge Trail
12
25
23
5
27
19
Los Padres National Forest
Julia Pfeiffer Burns State Park
McWay Cr
PACIFIC OCEAN
8
6
McWay Falls
21
4
To Lucia (10mi); Gorda (23mi); Ragged Point (40mi); Hearst Castle (55mi)

and energy of this precious piece of land shoehorned between the Santa Lucia Range and the Pacific Ocean, but nothing quite prepares you for your first glimpse of the craggy, unspoiled coastline.

In the 1950s and '60s, Big Sur – so named by Spanish settlers living on the Monterey Peninsula, who referred to the wilderness as *el país grande del sur* ('the big country to the south') – became a retreat for artists and writers, including Henry Miller and Beat Generation visionaries such as Lawrence Ferlinghetti. Today Big Sur attracts self-proclaimed artists, new-age mystics, latter-day hippies and city slickers seeking to unplug and reflect more deeply on this emerald-green edge of the continent.

Sights & Activities

All of the following places are listed north to south. Most parks are open from a half-hour before sunrise until a half-hour after sunset, with 24-hour campground access. At state parks, your parking fee ($10) receipt is valid for same-day entry to all except Limekiln; don't skip paying the entry fee by parking illegally outside along Hwy 1.

Bixby Bridge LANDMARK

Under 15 miles south of Carmel, this landmark spanning Rainbow Canyon is one of the world's highest single-span bridges. Completed in 1932, it was built by prisoners eager to lop time off their sentences. There's a perfect photo-op pull-off on the bridge's north side. Before Bixby Bridge was constructed, travelers had to trek inland on what's now called the **Old Coast Rd**, which heads off opposite the pull-off, reconnecting after 11 miles with Hwy 1 near Andrew Molera State Park. When the weather is dry enough, this route is usually navigable by 4WD or a mountain bike.

Point Sur State Historic Park LIGHTHOUSE

(☎831-625-4419; www.pointsur.org; adult/child 6-17yr $10/5, moonlight tour $15/10; ⊙tour schedules vary) Just over 6 miles south of Bixby Bridge, Point Sur rises like a green velvet fortress. This imposing volcanic rock looks like an island, but is actually connected to land by a sandbar. Atop the rock is the 1889 stone lightstation, which operated until 1974. Ocean views and tales of the lighthouse keepers' family lives are engrossing. Meet your tour guide at the locked gate a ¼-mile north of Point Sur Naval Facility, usually at 10am

Big Sur

Sights

1 Andrew Molera State Park ... C5
2 Big Sur Discovery Center ... C4
3 Bixby Bridge ... B3
4 Esalen Institute ... D7
5 Henry Miller Library ... D5
6 Julia Pfeiffer Burns State Park ... D6
7 Los Padres National Forest ... D3
8 Partington Cove ... D6
9 Pfeiffer Beach ... C5
10 Pfeiffer Big Sur State Park ... C5
11 Point Sur State Historic Park ... B4
12 Sykes Hot Springs ... D5
13 Ventana Wilderness ... D4

Activities, Courses & Tours

14 Molera Horseback Tours ... C4
15 Pine Ridge Trailhead ... C5

Sleeping

16 Andrew Molera State Park Campground ... C4
17 Big Sur Campground & Cabins ... C5
18 Big Sur Lodge ... C5
19 Deetjen's Big Sur Inn ... D5
20 Glen Oaks Motel ... C5
21 Julia Pfeiffer Burns State Park Campground ... D6
22 Pfeiffer Big Sur State Park Campground ... C5
23 Post Ranch Inn ... C5
Ripplewood Resort ... (see 20)
24 Ventana Inn & Spa ... C5

Eating

25 Big Sur Bakery & Restaurant ... C5
Big Sur Lodge ... (see 18)
26 Big Sur River Inn ... C5
Big Sur Roadhouse ... (see 26)
Deetjen's Big Sur Inn ... (see 19)
27 Nepenthe & Café Kevah ... C5
Restaurant at Ventana ... (see 24)

Drinking

Maiden Publick House ... (see 26)
28 Rocky Point ... B3

Entertainment

Henry Miller Library ... (see 5)

Saturday and Sunday year-round, and 1pm Wednesday from November through March. Tours also depart at 2pm Wednesday and Saturday from April to October, when monthly full-moon tours are also available. Call ahead to confirm tour schedules. Arrive early because space is limited (no reservations).

Andrew Molera State Park PARK
(☎831-667-2315; www.parks.ca.gov; per vehicle $10) Named after the farmer who first planted artichokes in California, this oft-overlooked park is a trail-laced pastiche of grassy meadows, waterfalls, ocean bluffs and rugged beaches offering excellent wildlife watching. Look for the turn-off just over 8 miles south of Bixby Bridge.

From the parking lot, a half-mile walk along the beach-bound trail leads to a first-come, first-served campground, from where a gentle quarter-mile spur trail leads past the 1861 redwood **Cooper Cabin**, Big Sur's oldest building. Otherwise, keep hiking on the main trail out toward a beautiful beach where the Big Sur River runs into the ocean and condors can occasionally be spotted circling overhead.

South of the parking lot, learn all about endangered California condors at the park's **Big Sur Discovery Center** (☎831-620-0702; www.ventanaws.org; admission free; ⌚9am-4pm Fri-Sun late May–mid-Sep). At the nearby bird banding lab, inside a small shed which operates when funding allows, the public is welcome to watch naturalists at work carrying out long-term species monitoring programs.

Across Hwy 1 from the park entrance, **Molera Horseback Tours** (☎831-625-5486, 800-942-5486; http://molerahorsebacktours.com; per person $40-70; 👪) offers guided trail rides on the beach. Walk-ins and novices are welcome; children must be at least six years old.

Pfeiffer Big Sur State Park PARK
(☎831-667-2315; www.parks.ca.gov; per vehicle $10) Named after Big Sur's first European settlers, who arrived in 1869, Pfeiffer Big Sur is the largest state park in Big Sur. Hiking trails loop through redwood groves and head into the adjacent Ventana Wilderness. The most popular trail – to 60ft-high **Pfeiffer Falls**, a delicate cascade hidden in the forest, which usually runs from December to May – is an easy 1.4-mile round-trip. Built in the 1930s by the Civilian Conservation Corps (CCC), the rustic Big Sur Lodge is near the park entrance, about 13 miles south of Bixby Bridge.

Pfeiffer Beach BEACH
(www.fs.usda.gov; per vehicle $5; ⌚9am-8pm; 🐾) This phenomenal, crescent-shaped and dog-friendly beach is known for its huge double rock formation, through which waves crash with life-affirming power. It's often windy, and the surf is too dangerous for swimming. But dig down into the wet sand – it's purple! That's because manganese garnet washes down from the craggy hillsides above.

To get here from Hwy 1, make a sharp right onto Sycamore Canyon Rd, marked by a small yellow sign that says 'narrow road' at the top. It's about half a mile south of Big Sur Station, or 2 miles south of Pfeiffer Big Sur State Park. From the turnoff, it's two more narrow, twisting miles (RVs and trailers prohibited) down to the beach.

Henry Miller Library ARTS CENTER
(☎831-667-2574; www.henrymiller.org; admission by donation; ⌚11am-6pm Wed-Mon; @📶) 'It was here in Big Sur I first learned to say Amen!' wrote Henry Miller, a Big Sur denizen for 17 years. More of a living memorial, alt-cultural venue and bookshop, this community gathering spot was never Miller's home. The house belonged to Miller's friend, painter Emil White, until his death and is now run by a nonprofit group. Inside are copies of all of Miller's written works, many of his paintings and a collection of Big Sur and Beat Generation material, including copies of the top 100 books Miller said most influenced him. Stop by to browse and hang out on the front deck. It's about 0.4 miles south of Nepenthe restaurant.

Partington Cove BEACH
A raw and breathtaking spot where crashing surf salts your skin, this hidden cove is named for a settler who built a dock here in the 1880s. Originally used for loading freight, Partington Cove allegedly became a landing spot for Prohibition-era bootleggers. On the steep, half-mile dirt hike down to the cove, you'll cross a cool bridge and go through an even cooler tunnel. The water in the cove is unbelievably aqua and within it grow tangled kelp forests. There's no real beach access and ocean swimming isn't safe, but some people scamper on the rocks and look for tidepools as waves splash ominously.

Look for the unmarked trailhead turnoff inside a large hairpin turn on the west side of Hwy 1, about 6 miles south of Nepenthe restaurant or 2 miles north of Julia Pfeiffer

Burns State Park. The trail starts just beyond the locked vehicle gate.

Julia Pfeiffer Burns State Park PARK
(☎831-667-2315; www.parks.ca.gov; per vehicle $10) Named for another Big Sur pioneer, this park hugs both sides of Hwy 1. The big attraction is California's only coastal waterfall, **McWay Falls**, which drops 80ft straight into the sea – or onto the beach, depending on the tide. This is *the* classic Big Sur postcard shot, with tree-topped rocks jutting above a golden, crescent-shaped beach next to swirling blue pools and crashing white surf. To reach this spectacular viewpoint, take the short Overlook Trail west from the parking lot and cross underneath Hwy 1 via a tunnel. From trailside benches, you might spot migrating gray whales between mid-December and mid-April.

The park entrance is on the east side of Hwy 1, about 8 miles south of Nepenthe restaurant.

Esalen Institute HOT SPRINGS
(☎831-667-3000; www.esalen.org; 55000 Hwy 1; 🛜) Marked only by a lighted sign reading 'Esalen Institute – By Reservation Only,' this infamous spot is like a new-age hippie camp for adults. Esoteric workshops treat anything 'relating to our greater human capacity,' from shapeshifting to Thai massage. Things have sure changed a lot since Hunter S Thompson was the gun-toting caretaker here in the 1960s.

Esalen's famous **baths** (☎831-667-3047; per person $20, credit cards only; ⏲public entry 1-3am nightly, reservations accepted 8am-8pm Mon-Thu & Sat, 8am-noon Fri & Sun) are fed by a natural hot spring and sit on a ledge above the ocean. Dollars to donuts you'll never take another dip that compares panorama-wise with the one here, especially on stormy winter nights. Only two small outdoor pools perch directly over the waves, so once you've stripped down (bathing is clothing-optional) and taken a quick shower, head outside immediately to score the best views. Otherwise, you'll be stuck with a tepid, no-view pool or even worse, a rickety bathtub.

Esalen is just over 11 miles south of Nepenthe restaurant and 10 miles north of Lucia.

Limekiln State Park PARK
(☎831-667-2403; www.parks.ca.gov; per vehicle $8; ⏲8am-sunset) Two miles south of Lucia, this petite park gets its name from the four remaining wood-fired kilns originally built here in the 1870s and '80s to smelt quarried limestone into powder, a key ingredient in cement used to construct buildings from Monterey to San Francisco. Tragically, pioneers chopped down the steep canyon's old-growth redwood forests to fuel the kilns' fires. A one-mile round-trip trail through a redwood grove leads to the historic site, passing a quarter-mile spur trail to a gorgeous 100ft-high waterfall.

At press time, the future of this park was uncertain – it may close in 2012.

DRIVING HIGHWAY 1

Driving this narrow two-lane highway through Big Sur and beyond is very slow going. Allow about three hours to cover the distance between the Monterey Peninsula and San Luis Obispo, much more if you want to explore the coast. Traveling after dark can be risky and more to the point, it's futile, since you'll miss out on the seascapes. Watch out for cyclists and always use signposted roadside pullouts to let faster-moving traffic pass.

Los Padres National Forest FOREST
The tortuously winding 40-mile stretch of Hwy 1 south of Lucia to Hearst Castle is even more sparsely populated, rugged and remote, mostly running through national forest lands. Make sure you've got at least enough fuel in the tank to reach the expensive gas station at Gorda, around 11 miles south of Limekiln State Park.

About 5 miles south of Nacimiento-Fergusson Rd, almost opposite Plaskett Creek Campground, is **Sand Dollar Beach Picnic Area** (www.fs.usda.gov; per vehicle $5; ⏲9am-8pm), from where it's a five-minute walk down to southern Big Sur's longest sandy beach, a crescent-shaped strip of sand protected from winds by high bluffs.

In 1971, in the waters of **Jade Cove**, local divers recovered a 9000lb jade boulder that measured 8ft long and was valued at $180,000. People still comb the beach today. The best time to find jade, which is black or blue-green and looks dull until you dip it in water, is during low tide or after a big storm. Keep an eye out for hang gliders flying in for a dramatic landing on the beach. Trails down to the water start from roadside pulloffs immediately south of Plaskett Creek Campground.

CALIFORNIA'S COMEBACK CONDORS

When it comes to endangered species, one of the state's biggest success stories is the California condor. These gigantic, prehistoric birds weigh over 20lb with a wingspan of up to 10ft, letting them fly great distances in search of carrion. They're easily recognized by their naked pink head and large white patches on the underside of each wing.

This big bird became so rare that in 1987 there were only 27 left in the world – all were removed from the wild to special captive-breeding facilities. There are almost 400 California condors alive today, with increasing numbers of captive birds being released back into the wild, where it's hoped they will begin breeding naturally.

Pinnacles National Monument (p309) and the Big Sur coast both offer excellent opportunities to view this majestic bird.

If you have any sunlight left, keep trucking down the highway to **Salmon Creek Falls**, which usually flows from December through May. Tucked up a forested canyon, the double-drop waterfall can be glimpsed from the hairpin turn on Hwy 1, about 8 miles south of Gorda. Roadside parking gets very crowded, as everyone takes the 10-minute walk up to the falls to splash around in the pools, where kids shriek and dogs happily yip and yap.

Ragged Point LANDMARK

Your last – or first – taste of Big Sur's rocky grandeur comes at this craggy cliff outcropping with fabulous views of the coastline in both directions, about 15 miles north of Hearst Castle. Once part of the Hearst empire, it's now taken over by a sprawling, ho-hum resort with a pricey gas station. Heading south, the land grows increasingly wind-swept as Hwy 1 rolls gently down to the water's edge.

Sleeping

With few exceptions, Big Sur's lodgings do not have TVs and rarely have telephones. This is where you come to escape the world. There aren't a lot of rooms overall, so demand often exceeds supply and prices can be outrageous. Bigger price tags don't necessarily buy you more amenities either. In summer and on weekends, reservations are essential, whether for resort rooms or campsites.

TOP CHOICE **Post Ranch Inn** RESORT **$$$**

(☎831-667-2200, 888-524-4787; www.postranchinn.com; 47900 Hwy 1; d from $595;) The last word in luxurious coastal getaways, the legendary Post Ranch pampers guests with exclusive accommodations featuring slate spa tubs, fireplaces, private decks and walking sticks for coastal hikes. Ocean-view rooms celebrate the sea, while the treehouses without views have a bit of sway. Paddle around the clifftop infinity pool after your shamanic healing session in the spa or a group yoga, meditation or tai chi chuan class. One sour note: disappointing food from the panoramic sea-view restaurant.

Ventana Inn & Spa RESORT **$$$**

(☎831-667-2331, 800-628-6500; www.ventanainn.com; 48123 Hwy 1; d from $450;) Almost at odds with Big Sur's hippie-alternative vibe, Ventana manages to inject a little soul into its luxury digs. Honeymooning couples and paparazzi-fleeing celebs pad from yoga class to the Japanese baths and clothing-optional pool, or hole up all day next to the wood-burning fireplace in their villa or ocean-view cottage.

Glen Oaks Motel MOTEL **$$$**

(☎831-667-2105; www.glenoaksbigsur.com; Hwy 1; d $175-350;) At this 1950s redwood-and-adobe motor lodge, rustic rooms and cabins seem effortlessly chic. Dramatically transformed by eco-conscious design, these snug romantic hideaways all have gas fireplaces. The woodsy studio cottage has a kitchenette and walk-in shower built for two, or retreat to the one-bedroom house equipped with a full kitchen.

Treebones Resort YURTS **$$$**

(☎877-424-4787; www.treebonesresort.com; 71895 Hwy 1; d $170-285;) Don't let the word 'resort' throw you. Yes, they've got an ocean-view hot tub, heated pool and massage treatments available. But noisy yurts with polished pine floors, quilt-covered beds, sink vanities and redwood decks are actually like 'glamping,' with little privacy. Bathrooms and showers are a short stroll away. Rates include a make-your-own waffle breakfast.

Look for the signposted turnoff a mile north of Gorda.

Big Sur Lodge LODGE $$$
(☎831-667-3100, 800-424-4787; www.bigsurlodge.com; 47225 Hwy 1; d $189-369;) What you're really paying for is a peaceful location, right inside Pfeiffer Big Sur State Park. Fairly rustic duplexes each have a deck or balcony looking out into the redwood forest, while family-sized rooms may have kitchens or wood-burning fireplaces. The outdoor swimming pool is usually open from March until October.

Big Sur Campground & Cabins CABINS, CAMPGROUND $$
(☎831-667-2322; www.bigsurcamp.com; 47000 Hwy 1; cabins $90-345, tent/RV sites from $40/50;) Right on the Big Sur River and shaded by redwoods, cozy housekeeping cabins come with full kitchens and fireplaces, while canvas-sided tent cabins are dog-friendly (pet fee $15). The riverside campground is especially popular with RVs. There are hot showers, a coin-op laundry, playground and general store.

Ripplewood Resort CABINS $$
(☎831-667-2242; www.ripplewoodresort.com; 47047 Hwy 1; cabins $95-195;) North of Pfeiffer Big Sur State Park, Ripplewood has struck a blow for fiscal equality by asking the same rates year-round. Throwback Americana cabins all have kitchens and private baths, while some sport fireplaces. Quiet riverside cabins are surrounded by redwoods, but roadside cabins can be noisy. Wi-fi works in the restaurant only.

Deetjen's Big Sur Inn LODGE $$
(☎831-667-2377; www.deetjens.com; 48865 Hwy 1; d $90-250) Nestled among redwoods and wisteria, this creekside conglomeration of rustic, thin-walled rooms and cottages was built by Norwegian immigrant Helmuth Deetjen in the 1930s. Some rooms are warmed by wood-burning fireplaces, while cheaper ones share bathrooms.

Ragged Point Inn MOTEL $$
(☎805-927-4502; www.raggedpointinn.net; 19019 Hwy 1; r $129-269;) Split-level motel rooms are nothing special, except for ocean views; pet fee $50.

Lucia Lodge MOTEL $$
(☎831-688-4884, 866-424-4787; www.lucialodge.com; 62400 Hwy 1; d $150-275;) Dreamy clifftop views from tired 1930s cabin rooms.

Public Campgrounds

Camping is currently available at four of Big Sur's **state parks** (☎reservations 916-638-5883, 800-444-7275; www.reserveamerica.com) and two **United States Forest Service (USFS) campgrounds** (☎reservations 518-885-3639, 877-444-6777; www.recreation.gov) along Hwy 1.

Pfeiffer Big Sur State Park CAMPGROUND $
(www.parks.ca.gov; Hwy 1; tent & RV sites $35-50, hike-and-bike sites $5) Over 200 sites nestle in a redwood-shaded river valley. Facilities include drinking water, coin-op showers and laundry, but no RV hookups.

Andrew Molera State Park CAMPGROUND $
(www.parks.ca.gov; Hwy 1; tent sites $25) Two dozen first-come, first-served primitive walk-in sites with fire pits and drinking water, but no ocean views.

Julia Pfeiffer Burns State Park CAMPGROUND $
(www.parks.ca.gov; Hwy 1; tent sites $30) Two small walk-in campsites on a semi-shaded ocean bluff; register at Big Sur Station (10.5 miles north) or Pfeiffer Big Sur State Park (11 miles north).

Limekiln State Park CAMPGROUND $
(www.parks.ca.gov; Hwy 1; tent & RV sites $35) Near the park entrance, two dozen sites huddle under a Hwy 1 bridge next to the ocean; showers are available.

USFS Kirk Creek Campground CAMPGROUND
(www.campone.com; Hwy 1; tent & RV sites $22) Over 30 beautiful, if exposed ocean-view blufftop campsites with drinking water and BBQ grills, 2 miles south of Limekiln.

USFS Plaskett Creek Campground CAMPGROUND
(www.campone.com; Hwy 1; tent & RV sites $22) Almost 40 spacious, shaded campsites with drinking water in a forested meadow near Sand Dollar Beach, about 5 miles south of Nacimiento-Fergusson Rd.

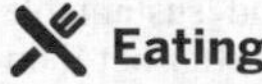

Eating

Like Big Sur's lodgings, restaurants and cafes are often overpriced, overcrowded and underwhelming.

Restaurant at Ventana CALIFORNIAN $$$
(☎831-667-4242; www.ventanainn.com; 48123 Hwy 1; lunch mains $10-18, dinner mains $29-38; ⏲11:30am-9pm;) The old truism about the better the views, the worse the food just doesn't seem to apply here. The resort's

ocean-view terrace restaurant and cocktail bar is hands down the happiest place for foodies anywhere along Hwy 1. Dig into tender bison steaks with truffled mac 'n cheese, curried chicken salad or roasted vegetable pastas flavored with herbs grown in the garden right outside.

Nepenthe & Café Kevah CALIFORNIAN **$$$**
(☎831-667-2345; www.nepenthebigsur.com 48510 Hwy 1; cafe mains $11-17, restaurant mains $15-39; ⊙restaurant 11:30am-10pm, cafe 9am-4pm; 👪) Nepenthe comes from a Greek word meaning 'isle of no sorrow,' and indeed, it's hard to feel blue while sitting by the firepit on this clifftop terrace. Just-okay California bistro cuisine (try the renowned Ambrosia burger) takes a backseat to the views and Nepenthe's history – Orson Welles and Rita Hayworth briefly owned a cabin here in the 1940s. Downstairs, Café Kevah serves light, casual brunches and has head-spinning ocean views from its own outdoor patio (closed in winter and bad weather).

Big Sur Bakery & Restaurant CALIFORNIAN **$$$**
(☎831-667-0520; www.bigsurbakery.com; 47540 Hwy 1; snacks & drinks from $4, mains $14-36; ⊙bakery from 8am daily, restaurant 11am-2:30pm Tue-Fri, 10:30am-2:30pm Sat & Sun, dinner from 5:30pm Tue-Sat) Behind the Shell station, this warmly lit, funky house has seasonally changing menus; wood-fired pizzas share space with more refined dishes like butter-braised halibut. Fronted by a pretty patio, the bakery pours Big Sur's priciest espresso. Expect long waits and standoffish service.

Deetjen's Big Sur Inn CALIFORNIAN **$$$**
(☎831-667-2377; www.deetjens.com; 48865 Hwy 1; breakfast mains $10-12, dinner mains $24-36; ⊙8-11:30am & 6-9pm) This quaint yesteryear lodge has a cozy, candle-lit dining room serving up steaks, cassoulets and other hearty country fare from a daily changing menu, primarily sourced from organic local produce, hormone-free meat and sustainable seafood. Breakfast is a much better bet than dinner.

Big Sur Lodge AMERICAN, GROCERIES **$$$**
(☎831-667-3100; www.bigsurlodge.com; 47225 Hwy 1; breakfast & lunch mains $8-15, dinner mains $8-27; ⊙restaurant 7:30am-9pm, general store 8am-9pm; 👪) Inside Pfeiffer Big Sur State Park, pull up a wooden table in this cabinesque dining room and fill up on rainbow trout, pasta primavera, roast chicken and trail-mix salads, all made with hungry hikers in mind. The lodge's small general store stocks camping supplies, snacks, drinks and ice-cream treats.

Big Sur River Inn AMERICAN, GROCERIES **$$$**
(☎831-667-2700; www.bigsurriverinn.com; Hwy 1; mains $9-29; ⊙restaurant 8am-9pm, general store 11am-7pm; 📶👪) Woodsy old supper club with a deck overlooks a creek teeming with throaty frogs. The wedding reception–quality food is mostly classic American seafood, grilled meats and pastas, but diner-style breakfasts and lunches – from berry pancakes to BLT sandwiches – satisfy. The nearby general store has limited packaged foods and produce, but also a made-to-order fruit smoothie and burrito bar at the back.

Big Sur Roadhouse MEXICAN, AMERICAN **$$**
(☎831-667-2264; www.bigsurroadhouse.com; 47080 Hwy 1; mains $14-26; ⊙5:30-9pm Wed-Mon) This Latin-flavored roadhouse fairly glows with its coppertop bar and corner fireplace. At outdoor riverside tables, fork into hearty adobo-marinated skirt steak, stuffed pasilla peppers or barbecue chicken with jicama salad.

Drinking & Entertainment

Henry Miller Library PERFORMING ARTS
(☎831-667-2574; www.henrymiller.org; Hwy 1) Just south of Nepenthe, this nonprofit performance space hosts a bohemian carnival of live-music concerts, author readings, open-mic nights and indie film screenings outdoors.

Maiden Publick House BAR
(☎831-667-2355; Hwy 1) Near the Big Sur River Inn, this dive has an encyclopedic beer bible and motley local musicians jamming, mostly on weekends.

Rocky Point BAR
(www.rocky-point.com; 36700 Hwy 1; ⊙9am-9pm) Come for the dizzying ocean-view terrace, where Bloody Marys are served all day, 2.5 miles north of Bixy Bridge.

Information

Visitors often wander into businesses along Hwy 1 and ask, 'How much further to Big Sur?' In fact, there is no town of Big Sur as such, though you may see the name on maps. Commercial activity is concentrated along the stretch north of Pfeiffer Big Sur State Park. Sometimes called 'the Village,' this is where you'll find most of the lodging, restaurants and shops, some of which offer free wi-fi, although cellphone reception is rare.

Big Sur Chamber of Commerce (☎831-667-2100; www.bigsurcalifornia.org; ⏲9am-1pm Mon, Wed & Fri) Pick up the free *Big Sur Guide* newspaper (also downloadable online) at local businesses.

Big Sur Station (☎831-667-2315; www.parks.ca.gov; Hwy 1; ⏲8am-4pm, closed Mon & Tue Nov-Mar) About 1.5 miles south of Pfeiffer Big Sur State Park, this multiagency ranger station has information and maps for state parks, Los Padres National Forest and Ventana Wilderness.

Henry Miller Library (www.henrymiller.org; Hwy 1; ⏲11am-6pm Wed-Mon; @) Free wi-fi and public internet terminals (donation requested).

Pacific Valley Station (☎805-927-4211; www.fs.usda.gov; Hwy 1; ⏲8am-4:30pm) South of Nacimiento-Fergusson Rd, USFS ranger station has limited visitor information.

Post office (www.usps.com; 47500 Hwy 1; ⏲10:30am-2:30pm Mon-Fri) Just north of Big Sur Bakery.

Getting There & Around

Big Sur is best explored by car, since you'll be itching to stop frequently and take in the rugged beauty and vistas that reveal themselves after every hairpin turn. Even if your driving skills are up to these narrow switchbacks, others' aren't: expect to average 35mph or less along the route. Parts of Hwy 1 are battle-scarred, evidence of a continual struggle to keep them open after landslides and washouts. Call ☎800-427-7623 to check current highway conditions, and fill up your gas tank beforehand.

MST (☎888-678-2871; www.mst.org) bus 22 ($3, 1¼ hours) travels from Monterey via Carmel as far south as Nepenthe restaurant three times daily between late May and early September, and twice daily on Saturdays and Sundays only the rest of the year.

Point Piedras Blancas

Many lighthouses still stand along California's coast, but few offer such a historically evocative seascape. Federally designated an outstanding natural area, the jutting, windblown grounds of this 1875 **lightstation** (☎805-927-7361; www.piedrasblancas.org; tour adult/child 6-17yr $10/5; ⏲tour schedules vary) – one of the tallest on the West Coast – have been laboriously replanted with native flora. Picturesquely, everything looks much the way it did when the first lighthouse keepers helped ships find safe harbor at the whaling station at San Simeon Bay. Guided tours currently meet at 9:45am on Tuesdays, Thursdays and Saturdays at the old Piedras Blancas Motel, about 1.5 miles north of the lightstation. No reservations are taken, but call ahead to check tour schedules.

At a signposted vista point 4.5 miles north of Hearst Castle, you can observe a colony of elephant seals bigger than the one at Anõ Nuevo State Reserve. During peak winter season, about 16,000 seals seek shelter in the coves and beaches along this stretch of coast. On sunny days the seals usually 'lie around like banana slugs,' in the words of one docent. Interpretative panels and blue-jacketed **Friends of the Elephant Seal** (www.elephantseal.org) docents demystify the behavior of these beasts.

Hearst Castle

The most important thing to know about William Randolph Hearst (1863–1951) is that he did not live like *Citizen Kane*. Not that Hearst wasn't bombastic, conniving and larger than life, but the moody recluse of the movie he was definitely not. Hearst also didn't call his 165-room monstrosity a castle, preferring its official name, *La Cuesta Encantada* ('The Enchanted Hill'), or more often calling it simply 'the ranch.' From the 1920s into the '40s, Hearst and Marion Davies, his longtime mistress (Hearst's wife refused to grant him a divorce), adored entertaining a steady stream of the era's biggest movers and shakers. Invitations were highly coveted, but Hearst had his quirks – he despised drunkenness, and guests were forbidden to speak of death.

Hearst Castle is a wondrous, historic (Winston Churchill penned anti-Nazi essays here in the 1930s), over-the-top homage to material excess, perched high on a hill; a visit is practically a must. Architect Julia Morgan based the main building, Casa Grande, on the design of a Spanish cathedral, and over the decades catered to Hearst's every design whim, deftly integrating the spoils of his fabled European shopping sprees (ancient artifacts, monasteries etc). The estate sprawls across acres of lushly landscaped gardens, accentuated by shimmering pools and fountains, statues from ancient Greece and Moorish Spain and the ruins of what was in Hearst's day the world's largest private zoo (drivers along Hwy 1 can sometimes still spot the remnant zebra herd).

WORTH A TRIP

VENTANA WILDERNESS

The 200,000-acre **Ventana Wilderness** (www.ventanawild.org) is Big Sur's wild backcountry. It lies within the northern Los Padres National Forest, which straddles the Santa Lucia Range and runs parallel to the coast. Most of this wilderness is covered with oak and chaparral, though canyons cut by the Big Sur and Little Sur Rivers support virgin stands of coast redwoods. The endemic Santa Lucia fir grows upslope in rocky outcroppings.

Partly reopened after devastating wildfires in 2008, the wilderness remains popular with adventurous backpackers. A favorite overnight destination is **Sykes Hot Springs**, natural 100°F (35°C) mineral pools framed by redwoods, but don't expect solitude during peak season (April through September). It's a moderately strenuous 10-mile one-way hike along the **Pine Ridge Trail**, starting from **Big Sur Station** (☎831-667-2315; www.parks.ca.gov; Hwy 1; ⊙8am-4pm, closed Mon & Tue Nov-Mar), where you can get free campfire permits and pay for overnight trailhead parking ($5).

Much like Hearst's construction budget, the castle will devour as much of your time and money as you let it. To see anything of this **state historic monument** (☎info 805-927-2020, reservations 800-444-4445; www.hearstcastle.org; tours adult/child from $25/12; ⊙daily, hr vary), you have to take a tour. In peak summer months, show up early enough and you might be able to get a same-day ticket for later that afternoon. For special holiday and evening tours, book at least two weeks in advance.

Tours usually start daily at 8:20am, with the last leaving the visitor center for the 10-minute ride to the hilltop at 3:20pm (later in summer and during December). There are three main tours: the guided portion of each lasts about 45 minutes, after which you're free to wander the gardens and terraces, photograph the iconic Neptune and Roman Pools and soak up views. Tour guides are almost preternaturally knowledgeable – just try and stump 'em. Best of all are Christmas holiday evening tours, featuring living-history reenactors who escort you back in time to the castle's 1930s heyday.

Facilities at the visitor center (no eating or drinking is allowed on the hilltop) are geared for industrial-sized mobs of visitors. It's better to grab lunch at Sebastian's General Store by the beach across Hwy 1, or in Cambria. Before you leave the castle, take a moment to visit the often-overlooked museum area at the back of the visitors center. The center's five-story-high **theater** shows a 40-minute historical film (admission included with tour tickets) about the castle and the Hearst family.

Dress with plenty of layers: gloomy fog at the sea-level visitors center can turn into sunny skies at the castle's hilltop location, and vice versa. **RTA** (☎805-541-2228; www.slorta.org) bus 12 makes three or four daily round-trips to Hearst Castle from San Luis Obispo ($3, two hours) via Morro Bay, Cayucos and Cambria.

San Simeon

Little San Simeon Bay sprang to life as a whaling station in 1852. Shoreline whaling was practiced to catch gray whales migrating between Alaskan feeding grounds and birthing waters in Baja California, while sea otters were hunted here by Russian fur traders. In 1865 Senator George Hearst purchased 45,000 acres of ranch land and established an oceanfront settlement on the western side of Hwy 1. Designed by architect Julia Morgan, the historic 19th-century houses are now rented to employees of the Hearst Corporation's 80,000-acre free-range cattle ranch.

Sights & Activities

FREE William Randolph Hearst Memorial State Beach BEACH
(www.parks.ca.gov; ⊙dawn-dusk) Across Hwy 1 from Hearst Castle, this bayfront beach has a pleasant sandy stretch with rock outcroppings, kelp forests, a rickety wooden pier (fishing permitted) and picnic areas with barbecue grills.

Sea for Yourself Kayak Tours KAYAKING
(☎805-927-1787, 800-717-5225; www.kayakcambria.com; rentals $20-65, tours from $50) Right on the beach, you can rent sea kayaks, wet-

suits, bodyboards and surfboards, or take a guided paddle around San Simeon Cove.

FREE **Coastal Discovery Center** MUSEUM
(805-927-6575; Hwy 1; 11am-5pm Fri-Sun mid-Mar–Oct, 10am-4pm Fri-Sun Nov–mid-Mar;) Educational displays include a talking artificial tidepool that kids can touch and videos of deep-sea diving and a WWII-era shipwreck just offshore.

Sleeping & Eating

A few miles south of the original whaling station, the modern town of San Simeon is nothing more than a strip of unexciting motels and restaurants. There are better places to stay in Cambria and beach towns further south like Cayucos.

San Simeon State Park CAMPGROUND $
(reservations 800-444-7275; www.reserveamerica.com; Hwy 1; tent & RV sites $20-35) About 4.5 miles south of Hearst Castle are two popular campgrounds: **San Simeon Creek**, with hot showers and flush toilets; and undeveloped **Washburn**, located along a dirt road. Drinking water is available at both.

Sebastian's General Store DELI, GROCERIES $
(442 San Simeon Rd, off Hwy 1; mains $7-12; 11am-5pm Tue-Sun, kitchen to 4pm) Down a side road across Hwy 1 from the castle, this tiny historic market sells cold drinks, Hearst Ranch beef burgers, giant deli sandwiches and salads for beach picnics at San Simeon Cove. Hearst Ranch Winery tastings are available at the copper-top bar.

Cambria

With a whopping dose of natural beauty, the coastal idyll of Cambria is a lone pearl cast along the coast. Built on lands that once belonged to Mission San Miguel, one of the village's first nicknames was Slabtown, after the rough pieces of wood pioneer buildings were constructed from. Today, just like at neighboring Hearst Castle, money is no object in this wealthy retirement community, whose motto 'Pines by the Sea' is affixed to the back of BMWs that toodle around town.

Sights & Activities

Although its milky-white moonstones are long gone, **Moonstone Beach** still attracts romantics with its oceanfront boardwalk and truly picturesque rocky shoreline. For solitude, take the Windsor Rd exit off Hwy 1 and drive down to where the road dead-ends, then follow a 2-mile round-trip blufftop hiking trail across **East West Ranch**.

A 10-minute drive south of Cambria, past the Hwy 46 turnoff to Paso Robles' wine country, tiny **Harmony** is a slice of rural Americana, with an 1865 creamery now housing local artists' workshops and a hillside winery, **Harmony Cellars** (www.harmonycellars.com; 3255 Harmony Valley Rd; 10am-5pm).

Sleeping

Cambria's choicest motels and hotels line Moonstone Beach Dr, while quaint B&Bs cluster around the village.

Blue Dolphin Inn HOTEL $$$
(805-927-3300, 800-222-9157; www.cambriainns.com; 6470 Moonstone Beach Dr; d incl breakfast basket $159-239;) This sand-colored two-story, slat-sided building may not look as upscale as other oceanfront motels, but rooms do have romantic fireplaces, pillowtop mattresses and rich linens. Pet fee $25.

Fogcatcher Inn HOTEL $$$
(805-927-1400, 800-425-4121; www.fogcatcherinn.com; 6400 Moonstone Beach Dr; d incl breakfast $129-379;) Motels along Moonstone Beach Dr are nearly identical, but this one is a standout for its hot tub. Faux English Tudor–style cottages harbor luxurious modern rooms, some with fireplaces and ocean views.

Cambria Shores Inn MOTEL $$$
(805-927-8644, 800-433-9179; www.cambriashores.com; 6276 Moonstone Beach Dr; d incl breakfast $150-290;) A stone's throw from Moonstone Beach, this ocean-view motel offers pampering amenities for pooches (pet fee $15), including a welcome doggie basket. Rates include a breakfast basket delivered to your door.

Bluebird Inn MOTEL $$
(805-927-4634, 800-552-5434; http://bluebirdmotel.com; 1880 Main St; d $70-220;) With peaceful gardens, this friendly East Village motel offers basic, budget-conscious rooms, some with fireplaces and private creekside patios or balconies. Wi-fi in lobby only.

HI Cambria Bridge Street Inn HOSTEL $
(805-927-7653; www.bridgestreetinncambria.com; 4314 Bridge St; dm $22-25, r $45-80; check-in

5-9pm;) Inside a 19th-century parsonage, this tiny hostel sleeps more like a grandmotherly B&B. It has floral charm and a communal kitchen, but the shabby-chic rooms are thin-walled. Book ahead.

Eating & Drinking

It's a short walk between several cafes and eateries in the East Village.

Indigo Moon CALIFORNIAN $$

(www.indigomooncafe.com; 1980 Main St; lunch mains $6-13, dinner mains $13-29; 10am-4pm & 5-9pm Mon-Sat, 10am-3pm & 5-9pm Sun) Inside this artisan cheese and wine shop, breezy bistro tables complement market-fresh salads, toasty sandwiches and sweet-potato fries. Local luminaries gossip over lunch on the back patio, while dinner dates order lemon risotto, crab-stuffed trout or coriander-encrusted chicken.

Sow's Ear AMERICAN $$$

(805-927-4865; www.thesowsear.com; 2248 Main St; dinner mains $11-30; 5-9pm) For over a decade, the old-school Sow's Ear has been whipping up haute comfort food inside a cozy house on the East Village's main drag. Make reservations to dine on traditional lobster pot pie, pork tenderloin with olallieberry chutney and fresh bread baked in terracotta flowerpots.

Linn's Easy as Pie Cafe DELI, BAKERY $

(www.linnsfruitbin.com; 4251 Bridge St; items $4-10; 10am-6pm Oct-Apr, to 7pm May-Sep;) If you don't have time to visit Linn's Fruit Bin, the original farm store out on Santa Rosa Creek Rd (a 20-minute drive east via Main St), you can fork into their famous olallieberry pies and preserves at this take-out counter delivering salads, sandwiches and comfort fare to a sunny East Village patio.

Wild Ginger FUSION $$

(www.wildgingercambria.com; 2380 Main St; mains $12-17; 11am-2:30pm Mon-Wed, Fri & Sat & 5-9pm Fri-Wed;) This bright, cheery chef-owned cafe dishes up garden-fresh, pan-Asian fare, perfectly seasoned and presented, plus housemade sorbets in exotic flavors like pomegranate and pineapple-coconut. Expect long waits.

Lily's Coffeehouse CAFE $

(www.lilyscoffee.com; 2028 Main St; coffee & snacks $2-8; 8:30am-5pm Wed-Mon;) Francophilic Lily's has a peaceful garden patio and brews robust coffees and teas. Drop in on Saturday between 11am and 4pm for made-to-order crepes.

Information

Cambria has three distinct parts: the tourist-choked East Village, a half-mile from Hwy 1, where antiques shops, art galleries and coffeehouses line Main St; the newer West Village, further west along Main St, is where you'll find the **chamber of commerce** (805-927-3624; www.cambriachamber.org; 767 Main St; 9am-5pm Mon-Fri, noon-4pm Sat & Sun); and motel-lined Moonstone Beach, off Hwy 1.

Getting There & Around

From San Luis Obispo, **RTA** (805-541-2228; www.slorta.org) bus 12 makes three or four daily round trips via Morro Bay and Cayucos to Cambria ($3, 1¾ hours), running along Moonstone Beach Dr and Main St through the East and West Villages.

Cayucos

With its historic storefronts housing antiques shops and eateries, the main drag of amiable, slow-paced Cayucos calls to mind an Old West frontier town. But just one block west of Ocean Ave, surf's up!

Sights & Activities

At downtown's north end, fronting a broad white-sand beach, Cayucos' long wooden pier is popular with fishers – it's also a sheltered spot for beginning surfers.

Cayucos Surf Company SURFING

(805-995-1000; www.surfcompany.com; 95 Cayucos Dr; board & wetsuit rental $8-38, 2hr lesson $80-100; 9am-6pm) Near the pier, this fun local surf shop rents surfboards, boogie boards and wetsuits. Call ahead for learn-to-surf lessons.

Sleeping

Cayucos doesn't lack for motels or beachfront inns, most higher-priced than in Morro Bay, 6 miles south.

TOP CHOICE **Cass House Inn** B&B $$$

(805-995-3669; www.casshouseinn.com; 222 N Ocean Ave; d incl breakfast $165-325;) Inside a charmingly renovated 1867 Victorian inn, five truly luxurious rooms await, some with ocean views, deep-soaking tubs and antique fireplaces to ward off chilly coastal fog. All have plush beds, flat-screen TVs with DVD players and tasteful, romantic accents. Reservations are essential.

Seaside Motel MOTEL $$
(805-995-3809, 800-549-0900; www.seasidemotel.com; 42 S Ocean Ave; d $80-160;) Expect a warm welcome from the hands-on owners of this vintage motel. Country-kitsch rooms may be on the small side, but some have kitchenettes. Cross your fingers for quiet neighbors.

Cayucos Beach Inn MOTEL $$
(805-995-2828, 800-482-0555; www.cayucosbeachinn.com; 333 S Ocean Ave; d $85-175;) A remarkably pet-friendly motel, where even the doors have special peepholes for your canine (pet fee $10). Spacious rooms are nothing special, but you'll find invitingly grassy picnic areas and BBQ grills out front.

Cypress Tree Motel MOTEL $$
(805-995-3917, 800-241-4289; www.cypresstreemotel.com; 125 S Ocean Ave; d $50-120;) Retro motor court has lovingly cared-for, but kinda hokey theme rooms, like 'Nautical Nellie' with a net of seashells suspended behind the bed. Pet fee $10.

Eating

TOP CHOICE **Cass House Restaurant** EURASIAN $$$
(805-995-3669; www.casshouseinn.com; 222 N Ocean Ave; 4-course prix-fixe dinner $64, incl wine pairings $92; 5-9pm Thu-Mon) The inn's flawless chef-driven restaurant defies expectations. Linger over the locally sourced, seasonally inspired menu that ambitiously ranges from finger-lime snapper ceviche and artisan cheeses to heritage pork loin in cherry jus and black cod with lemongrass beurre blanc, all paired with top-notch regional wines.

Hoppe's Bistro & Wine Bar CALIFORNIAN $$$
(805-995-1006; www.hoppesbistro.com; 78 N Ocean Ave; dinner mains $18-35; 11am-10pm Wed-Sun) This slightly kitschy dining rooms features fresh seafood on its respectable coastal, often organic menu – don't skip the incredible red-abalone dishes. The sommelier really knows local wines.

Ruddell's Smokehouse SEAFOOD $
(www.smokerjim.com; 101 D St; items $5-12; 11am-6pm;) 'Smoker Jim' transforms fresh-off-the-boat seafood into succulently smoked slabs and sandwiches, while fish tacos come slathered in a unique apple-celery relish. Squeeze yourself in the door to order. Dogs allowed at sidewalk tables.

Sea Shanty DINER $
(www.seashantycayucos.com; 296 S Ocean Ave; mains $7-25; 8am-9pm Sep-May, to 10pm Jun-Aug;) At this family joint, where a bazillion baseball caps hang from the ceiling, just-OK breakfasts and fish and chips take a back seat to killer desserts.

Brown Butter Cookie Co BAKERY $
(www.brownbuttercookies.com; 250 N Ocean Ave; snacks from $2; 10am-5pm) Seriously addictive cookies, worth the shocking price.

Schooner's Wharf BAR & GRILL $$
(www.schoonerswharf.com; 171 N Ocean Ave; mains $9-42; 11am-9pm Sun-Thu, to 10pm Fri & Sat) Come for the ocean-view bar, not necessarily the food.

Getting There & Away

From San Luis Obispo, **RTA** (805-541-2228; www.slorta.org) bus 12 travels three or four times daily along Hwy 1 to Cayucos ($2.50, one hour) via Morro Bay, continuing north to Cambria ($2, 25 minutes) and Hearst Castle ($2, 40 minutes).

Morro Bay

Home to a commercial fishing fleet, Morro Bay's biggest claim to fame is Morro Rock, a volcanic peak jutting dramatically from the ocean floor. It's one of the Nine Sisters, a 21-million-year-old chain of rocks stretching all the way south to San Luis Obispo. Morro Bay's less boast-worthy landmark comes courtesy of the power plant, which threw up three cigarette-shaped smokestacks by the bay. Along this humble, working-class stretch of coast are fantastic opportunities for kayaking, hiking and camping, all within easy reach of San Luis Obispo, where Hwy 1 meets Hwy 101.

Sights & Activities

This town harbors natural riches, easily worth a half day's exploration. The bay itself is a deep inlet separated from the ocean by a 5-mile-long sand spit. Leading south from Morro Rock is the Embarcadero, a small waterfront boulevard jam-packed with seafood eateries and souvenir shops that's also a launching point for boat trips.

Morro Rock LANDMARK
Chumash tribespeople are the only people legally allowed to climb this volcanic rock, now the protected nesting ground of peregrine falcons. You can laze at the small beach on the rock's north side, but you

can't drive all the way around – instead, rent a kayak. The waters below are a giant estuary inhabited by two dozen threatened and endangered species, including brown pelicans, snowy plovers and sea otters.

Morro Bay State Park PARK
(☎info 805-772-2560, museum 805-772-2694; www.parks.ca.gov; Morro Bay State Park Rd; park entry free, museum adult/child $2/free; ⏰park sunrise-sunset, museum 10am-5pm; 👪) Inside this woodsy waterfront park, a small natural-history **museum** has cool interactive exhibits geared toward kids that demonstrate how the forces of nature affect us all. Just north of the museum is a eucalyptus grove harboring one of California's last remaining great blue heron rookeries.

Kayak Horizons KAYAKING
(☎805-772-6444; www.kayakhorizons.com; 551 Embarcadero; kayak & canoe rentals $12-44, tours & lessons $65) One of several places on the Embarcadero offering kayak rentals and tours for novices. When paddling out on your own, be aware of the tide schedules. Ideally, you'll want to ride the tide out and then back in. Winds are generally calmest in the mornings.

Morro Bay Golf Course GOLF
(☎805-782-8060; www.slocountyparks.com; green fees $15-50) South of the Embarcadero, adjacent to the state park, this 18-hole golf course boasts tree-lined fairways and ocean views. A driving range and rental clubs and carts are available.

Tours

Sub-Sea Tours BOAT TRIPS
(☎805-772-9463; www.subseatours.com; 699 Embarcadero; 45min tour adult/child 3-12yr $14/7; ⏰hourly departures 10am-4pm Jun-Sep, 11am-3pm Sat & Sun & 1pm Mon-Fri Oct-May; 👪) For pint-sized views of kelp forests and schools of fish, take the kids on a spin on a yellow semi-submersible.

Virg's Landing FISHING
(☎805-772-1222, 800-762-5263; www.morrobaysportfishing.com; 1169 Market St; tours $65-250) Salty dogs ready for a little sportfishing can book half-day or all-day trips with this long-running local outfit.

Central Coast Outdoors OUTDOOR SPORTS
(☎805-528-1080, 888-873-5610; www.centralcoastoutdoors.com; tours $65-150) Leads kayaking tours (including sunset and full-moon paddles), guided hikes and cycling trips along the coast and in nearby wine countries.

Festivals & Events

Morro Bay Winter Bird Festival OUTDOORS
(www.morrobaybirdfestival.org) Every January, bird-watchers flock together for guided hikes, kayaking trips and naturalist-led events, during which over 200 species can be spotted along the Pacific Flyway.

Sleeping

Dozens of motels cluster along Hwy 1 and around Harbor and Main Sts, between downtown and the Embarcadero.

Anderson Inn INN $$$
(☎805-772-3434, 866-950-3434; www.andersoninnmorrobay.com; 897 Embarcadero; d $239-349; 📶) Like a small boutique hotel, this waterfront inn has just a handful of spacious, soothingly earth-toned rooms with flat-screen TVs, mini-fridges and if you're lucky, a gas fireplace, your own hot tub and harbor views.

La Serena Inn MOTEL $$
(☎805-772-5665, 800-248-1511; www.laserenainn.com; 990 Morro Ave; d $89-169; 📶) Large, well-kept rooms at this bland three-story motel each have a microwave and minifridge. If you're feeling flush, request one with views of Morro Rock and a private balcony to hear the gentle clank-clank of boats in the harbor below.

Morro Bay State Park Campground CAMPGROUND $
(☎reservations 800-444-7275; www.reserveamerica.com; tent & RV sites without/with hookups $35/50) Less than 2 miles south of downtown and the Embarcadero, over 115 woodsy sites are fringed by eucalyptus and cypress trees, with trails leading down to the beach. Facilities include fire pits, showers and an RV dump station.

Beach Bungalow Inn & Suites MOTEL $$
(☎805-772-9700; www.morrobaybeachbungalow.com; 1050 Morro Ave; d $100-250; 📶🐾) This butter-yellow motor court's chic, contemporary rooms have mod-cons; pet fee $20.

Inn at Morro Bay MOTEL $$
(☎805-772-5651, 800-321-9566; www.innatmorrobay.com; 60 State Park Rd; d $115-275; 🏊) Dated two-story waterfront lodge inside the state park set for renovations.

Eating & Drinking

More predictable seafood shacks line the Embarcadero.

Taco Temple CALIFORNIAN $$
(2680 Main St, off Hwy 1; mains $7-13; ⏲11am-9pm Mon & Wed-Sat, to 8:30pm Sun;) Overlook the frontage-road location for huge helpings of Cal-Mex fusion flavor. At the next table, there might be fishers talking about the good ole' days or starving surfer buddies. Try one of the specials – they deserve the name. Cash only.

Giovanni's Fish Market & Galley SEAFOOD $$
(www.giovannisfishmarket.com; 1001 Front St; mains $7-13; ⏲9am-6pm;) This family-run joint on the Embarcadero is a classic California seafood shack. Folks line up for batter-fried fish and chips and killer garlic fries. Inside there's a market with all the fixin's for a beach campground fish fry.

Shine Cafe & Sunshine Health Foods VEGETARIAN $
(www.sunshinehealthfoods-shinecafe.com; 415 Morro Bay Blvd; mains $5-14; ⏲11am-5pm Mon-Fri, 9am-5pm Sat, 10am-4pm Sun;) Hidden inside a small natural-foods market, the mostly organic Shine Cafe serves karma-cleansing grub like tempeh tacos, garden-fresh salads and blueberry smoothies.

Stax Wine Bar TAPAS $$
(www.staxwine.com; 1099 Embarcadero; shared plates $6-10; ⏲noon-8pm Sun-Thu, to 10pm Fri & Sat) Perch on barstools in front of the harbor-view windows for a hand-selected tasting flight of local California wines. Tapas-sized bites such as artisan cheese and cured-meat plates keep revelers fueled, especially on live-music nights.

Last Stage West BARBECUE $$
(www.laststagewest.net; 15050 Morro Rd, Atascadero; mains $6-20; ⏲noon-9pm) At this Old West roadhouse and boot-stomping live-music venue, say 'Howdy, pardner!' to smoked tri-tip barbecue, slow-cooked pork ribs and rib-eye steak. To get here, drive Hwy 41 about 10 miles northeast of its intersection with Hwy 1 in Morro Bay.

Information

Morro Bay Chamber of Commerce (☎805-772-4467, 800-231-0592; www.morrobay.org; 845 Embarcadero; ⏲9am-5pm Mon-Fri, 10am-4pm Sat, 10am-2pm Sun) is in the thick of everything. A few blocks uphill, Main St is the less touristy downtown.

Getting There & Around

From San Luis Obispo, **RTA** (☎805-541-2228; www.slorta.org) bus 12b travels hourly on weekdays and a few times daily on weekends along Hwy 1 to Morro Bay ($2.50, 40 minutes). Three or four times daily, bus 12b continues north from Morro Bay to Cayucos ($1.50, 15 minutes), Cambria ($2, 45 minutes) and Hearst Castle ($2, one hour). From late May to early October, a **trolley** (single ride $1.25, day pass $3) loops around the waterfront and downtown, operating varying hours (no service Tuesday to Thursday).

Montaña de Oro State Park

In spring the hillsides are blanketed by bright California native poppies, wild mustard and other wildflowers, giving this park its Spanish name, meaning 'mountain of gold.' Wind-tossed coastal bluffs with wild, wide-open sea views make it a favorite spot with hikers, mountain bikers and horseback riders. The northern half of the park features sand dunes and an ancient marine terrace visible due to seismic uplifting. **Spooner's Cove**, once used by smugglers, is now a postcard-perfect sandy beach and picnic area. If you go tidepooling, remember to only touch the marine creatures like sea stars, limpets and crabs with the back of one hand to avoid disturbing them, and never remove them from their aquatic homes. You can hike along the beach and the grassy ocean bluffs, or drive uphill past the visitors center to the start of the exhilarating 7-mile loop trail tackling **Valencia** and **Oats Peaks**.

Sleeping

Montaña de Oro State Park Campground CAMPGROUND $
(☎reservations 800-444-7275; www.reserveamerica.com; tent & RV sites $20-25, hike-and-bike sites $5) Tucked into a small canyon by the visitor center, this minimally developed campground has pleasantly cool drive-up and environmental walk-in sites. Limited amenities include vault toilets, drinking water and firepits.

Information

Montaña de Oro State Park (☎805-772-7434; www.parks.ca.gov; 3550 Pecho Valley Rd, Los Osos; admission free; ⏲sunrise-sunset)

Getting There & Away

From the north, exit Hwy 1 in Morro Bay at South Bay Blvd; after 4 miles, turn right onto Los Osos Valley Rd (which runs into Pecho Valley Rd) for 6 miles. From the south, exit Hwy 101 in San Luis Obispo at Los Osos Valley Rd, then drive northwest 16 miles.

ALONG HIGHWAY 101

Driving inland along Hwy 101 is a quicker way to travel between the Bay Area and Southern California. Although it lacks the striking scenery of coastal Hwy 1, the historic El Camino Real (the King's Highway), established by Spanish conquistadors and missionaries, has a beauty of its own, ranging from the fertile fields of Salinas, immortalized by novelist John Steinbeck, to the oak-dappled golden hills of San Luis Obispo and beyond to seaside Santa Barbara. Along the way are ghostly missions, jaw-dropping Pinnacles National Monument and standout wineries.

Gilroy

About 30 miles south of San Jose, the self-proclaimed 'garlic capital of the world' puts on the jam-packed **Gilroy Garlic Festival** (www.gilroygarlicfestival.com) over the last full weekend in July. Show up for carnival-quality chow – garlicky fries, garlic-flavored ice cream and more – and for cooking contests under the blazing-hot sun.

Unusual **Gilroy Gardens** (408-840-7100; www.gilroygardens.org; 3050 Hecker Pass Hwy/Hwy 152; adult/child 3-10yr $45/35; 11am-5pm Mon-Fri mid-Jun–mid-Aug, 11am-6pm Sat & Sun late Mar-Nov;) is a nonprofit family-oriented theme park focused on food and plants rather than Disney-esque cartoon characters. You've got to really love flowers, fruit and veggies to get your money's worth. Rides like the 'Mushroom Swing' are mostly tame.

Heading east on Hwy 152 toward I-5, **Casa de Fruta** (408-842-7282; www.casadefruta.com; 10021 Pacheco Pass Hwy, Hollister; admission free;) is a commercialized farm stand with some hokey, old-fashioned rides ($2.50 to $4) for youngsters, including carousels and choo-choo trains. Opening hours vary.

San Juan Bautista

In atmospheric old San Juan Bautista, where you can practically hear the whispers of the past, California's 15th mission is fronted by the only original Spanish plaza remaining in the state. Along 3rd St, evocative historic buildings mostly shelter antiques shops and petite garden restaurants. Hark! That cock you hear crowing is one of the town's roosters, which are allowed by tradition to stroll the streets at will.

Sights

Mission San Juan Bautista MISSION

(www.oldmissionsjb.org; 406 2nd St; adult/child 5-17yr $4/2; 9:30am-4:30pm) Founded in 1797, this mission has the largest church among California's original 21 missions. As it was unknowingly built directly atop the San Andreas Fault, the mission has been rocked by earthquakes. Bells hanging in the tower today include chimes that were salvaged after the 1906 San Francisco earthquake toppled the original mission. Parts of Alfred Hitchcock's thriller *Vertigo* were shot here, although the bell tower in the climactic scene is just a special effect. Below the cemetery, a section of El Camino Real, the Spanish colonial road built to link the missions, can still be seen.

WHAT THE...?

'Oh, my!' is one of the more printable exclamations overheard from visitors at the **Madonna Inn** (805-543-3000, 800-543-9666; www.madonnainn.com; 100 Madonna Rd; r $179-449;), a garish confection visible from Hwy 101. You'd expect outrageous kitsch like this in Las Vegas, not SLO, but here it is, in all its campy extravagance. Japanese tourists, vacationing Midwesterners and hipster, irony-loving urbanites all adore the 110 themed rooms – including Yosemite Rock, Caveman and hot-pink Floral Fantasy. Check out photos of the different rooms online, or wander the halls and spy into the ones being cleaned. The urinal in the men's room is a bizarre waterfall. But the most irresistible reason to stop here? Old-fashioned cookies from the storybook-esque bakery.

San Juan Bautista State Historic Park PARK
(831-623-4881; www.parks.ca.gov; 2nd St, btwn Washington & Mariposa Sts; park entry free, museum adult/child $3/free; 10am-4:30pm) Buildings around the old Spanish plaza opposite the mission anchor this historical park. The large plaza stables hint at San Juan Bautista in its 1860s heyday as a stagecoach stop. In 1876 the railroad bypassed the town, which has been a sleepy backwater ever since.

Across 2nd St is the 1858 **Plaza Hotel**, which started life as a single-story adobe building, and now houses a little historical museum. Next door, the **Castro-Breen Adobe** once belonged to Mexican general José Castro, who led a successful revolt against an unpopular governor. In 1848 it was bought by the Breen family, survivors of the Donner Party disaster.

Sleeping

Fremont Peak State Park CAMPGROUND $
(831-623-4255; www.parks.ca.gov; San Juan Canyon Rd, off Hwy 156; per car $6, tent & RV sites $25; park 8am-30min after sunset, campground 24hr) Eleven miles south of town, this park has a pretty, but primitive, 20-site campground shaded by oak trees on a hilltop with distant views of Monterey Bay. Equipped with a 30in telescope, the park's **astronomical observatory** (831-623-2465) is usually open to the public on moonless Saturday nights between April and October, starting around 8pm.

Eating & Drinking

Jardines de San Juan MEXICAN $$
(www.jardinesrestuarant.com; 115 3rd St; mains $8-18; 11:30am-9pm Sun-Thu, to 10pm Fri & Sat) Here at the longest-running contender in the town's long lineup of touristy Mexican eateries, it's all about the pretty outdoor garden, not necessarily authentic food. Sunday dinner brings out *pollos borrachos* ('drunken chickens').

San Juan Bakery BAKERY $
(319 3rd St; snacks $2-4; 7:30am-3pm) Pick up fresh loaves of cinnamon bread, hot-cross buns and guava turnovers to sustain you during the long drive south. Get there early, as it often sells out.

Vertigo Coffee COFFEESHOP $
(www.vertigocoffee.com; 81 4th St; snacks & drinks $2-5; 6:30am-4pm Mon, 6:30am-5:30pm Tue-Thu, 6:30am-7pm Fri, 8am-7pm Sat, 8am-4pm Sun) Rich espresso, pour-over brews and sticky bear claws make this coffee roaster's cafe a find.

Getting There & Away

San Juan Bautista is on Hwy 156, a 3.5-mile detour east of Hwy 101, south of Gilroy en route to Monterey or Salinas. Further south, Hwy 101 enters the sun-dappled eucalyptus grove that James Stewart and Kim Novak drove through in *Vertigo*.

Salinas

Best known as the birthplace of John Steinbeck and nicknamed the 'Salad Bowl of the World,' Salinas is a working-class agricultural center with down-and-out, even mean streets. It makes a thought-provoking contrast with the affluence of the Monterey Peninsula, a fact of life that helped shape Steinbeck's novel *East of Eden*. The historic center stretches along Main St, with the National Steinbeck Center at its northern end.

Sights

National Steinbeck Center MUSEUM
(831-775-4721; www.steinbeck.org; 1 Main St; adult/child 6-12yr/youth 13-17yr $11/6/8; 10am-5pm) This museum will enthrall almost anyone, even if you don't know a lick about Salinas' Nobel Prize–winning native son, John Steinbeck (1902–68), a Stanford University dropout. Tough, funny and brash, he sensitively portrayed the troubled spirit of rural, working-class Americans in such novels as *The Grapes of Wrath*. Interactive, kid-accessible exhibits and short video clips chronicle the writer's life and works in an engaging way. Gems include Rocinante, the customized camper in which Steinbeck traveled around America while researching *Travels with Charley*. Take a moment and listen to Steinbeck's Nobel acceptance speech – it's grace and power combined.

Admission also includes the small **Rabobank Agricultural Museum**, which takes visitors on a journey through the modern agricultural industry, from water to pesticides to transportation – it's way more interesting than it sounds, trust us.

Steinbeck House HISTORIC BUILDING
(132 Central Ave) Steinbeck was born and spent much of his boyhood in this house, three blocks west of the center. It's now a twee lunch cafe; we're not sure he'd approve.

Garden of Memories Memorial Park CEMETERY
(768 Abbott St, west of Hwy 101 exit Sanborn Rd) Steinbeck is buried in the Hamilton family plot, about 2 miles south of the center via Main, John and Abbott Sts.

Tours

Farm TOURS
(☎831-455-2575; www.thefarm-salinasvalley.com; admission free, tours adult/child 2-15yr $8/6; ⊙10am-5pm early Nov–mid-Mar, to 6pm mid-Mar–early Nov) This family-owned organic fruit-and-veggie stand offers educational 45-minute walking tours of its fields, usually at 1pm on Tuesdays and Thursdays. On the drive in, watch for the kinda-creepy giant sculptures of farm workers by local artist John Cerney, which also stand along Hwy 101. The farm is off Hwy 68 at Spreckels Blvd, about 3.5 miles south of the center.

Ag Venture Tours TOURS
(☎831-761-8463; http://agventuretours.com; half-day minivan tours from adult/child 7-20yr $70/55) Take a more in-depth look at commercial and organic farm fields and vineyards around the Salinas Valley and Monterey County.

Festivals & Events

California Rodeo Salinas RODEO
(www.carodeo.com) Bull riding, calf roping, horse shows and cowboy poetry in late July.

Steinbeck Festival CULTURE
(www.steinbeck.org) Four-day festival in early August features films, lectures, guided bus and walking tours, music and a literary pub crawl.

California International Airshow OUTDOORS
(www.salinasairshow.com) Professional stunt flying and vintage and military aircraft take wing in late September.

Sleeping

Salinas has plenty of budget motels off Hwy 101, including at the Market St exit.

Best Western Plus Salinas Valley Inn & Suites MOTEL $$
(☎831-751-6411, 800-780-7234; www.bestwestern.com; 187 Kern St; r incl breakfast $99-299;) As posh as you can get next to the freeway, this chain has newer, tasteful rooms (pet fee $20) and an outdoor pool and hot tub. Don't confuse it with the less appealing Best Western Salinas Monterey Hotel.

Laurel Inn MOTEL $
(☎831-449-2474, 800-354-9831; www.laurelinnmotel.com; 801 W Laurel Dr; r $60-100;) If chains don't do it for you, this sprawling, family-owned cheapie has predictable motel rooms that are nevertheless spacious. There's a swimming pool, whirlpool tub and dry sauna for relaxing.

Eating & Drinking

Habanero Cocina Mexicana MEXICAN $$
(157 Main St; mains $5-15; ⊙11am-9pm Sun-Thu, to 10pm Fri & Sat) On downtown's Restaurant Row just south of the National Steinbeck Center, this storefront Mexican kitchen gets a stamp of approval for its handmade tortillas, a rainbow of fresh salsas and chile-spiked carne asada tacos.

First Awakenings DINER $$
(www.firstawakenings.net; 171 Main St; mains $5-12; ⊙7am-2pm;) Fork into oversized diner breakfasts of fruity pancakes and egg crepes, or turn up later in the day for hand-crafted deli sandwiches, BBQ bacon burgers and market-fresh salads.

Monterey Coast Brewing Co BREWPUB $$
(165 Main St; mains $8-25; ⊙11am-11pm Tue-Sun, to 9pm Mon) This microbrewery is a welcome sign of life downtown; the nine-beer tasting sampler costs just 10 bucks.

A Taste of Monterey WINE BAR
(www.atasteofmonterey.com; tasting fee $5; 127 Main St; ⊙11am-5pm Mon-Wed, to 6pm Thu-Sat) This downtown tasting room pours Monterey Co wines. Ask for a free map to find local vineyards along Hwy 101.

Information

Salinas Valley Chamber of Commerce (☎831-751-7725; www.salinaschamber.com; 119 E Alisal St; ⊙8am-5pm Mon & Wed-Fri, 9:30am-5pm Tue) Hands out free tourist information and maps, five blocks east of Main St.

Getting There & Away

Amtrak (www.amtrak.com; 11 Station Pl, off W Market St) runs daily trains on the Seattle–LA *Coast Starlight* route via Oakland ($16, three hours), Paso Robles ($24, two hours), San Luis Obispo ($31, 3½ hours) and Santa Barbara ($49, 6½ hours).

Greyhound (www.greyhound.com; 19 W Gabilan St, cnr Salinas St) has a few daily buses to Santa Cruz ($14, 65 minutes), and along Hwy 101 north to San Francisco ($25, four hours) or south to San Luis Obispo ($30, 2½ hours) and Santa Barbara ($50, 4¾ hours).

From the nearby **Salinas Transit Center** (110 Salinas St), **MST** (☎888-678-2871; www.mst.org) buses 20 and 21 leave every 30 to 60 minutes daily for Monterey ($3, one hour).

Pinnacles National Monument

Named for the towering spires that rise abruptly out of the chaparral-covered hills east of Salinas Valley, this off-the-beaten-path **park** (☎831-389-4486; www.nps.gov/pinn; per vehicle $5) protects the remains of an ancient volcano. A study in stunning geological drama, its craggy monoliths, sheer-walled canyons and twisting caves are the result of millions of years of erosion.

Sights & Activities

Besides **rock climbing** (for route information, surf www.pinnacles.org), the park's biggest attractions are its two talus caves, formed by piles of boulders. **Balconies Cave** is always open for exploration. Scrambling through it is not an exercise recommended for claustrophobes, as it's pitch-black inside, making a flashlight essential. Be prepared to get lost a bit, too. The cave is found along a 2.5-mile hiking loop from the west entrance. Nearer the east entrance, **Bear Gulch Cave** is closed seasonally, so as not to disturb a resident colony of Townsend's big-eared bats.

To really appreciate Pinnacles' stark beauty, you need to hike. Moderate loops of varying lengths and difficulty ascend into the **High Peaks** and include thrillingly narrow clifftop sections. In the early morning or late afternoon, you may spot endangered California condors (see p296) soaring overhead. Rangers lead guided full-moon and dark-sky hikes, as well as cool bat-viewing and star-gazing programs, on select Friday and Saturday nights from spring through fall. Reservations are required for these programs; call ☎831-389-4486, ext 243.

Sleeping

Pinnacles Campground CAMPGROUND **$**
(☎info 831-389-4485, reservations 877-444-6777; www.recreation.gov; tent & RV sites without/with hookups $23/36;) On the park's east side, this popular family-oriented campground has over 130 sites (some with shade), plus drinking water, firepits and a seasonal outdoor pool.

Information

The best time to visit Pinnacles National Monument is during spring or fall; summer's heat is extreme. Information, maps, books and bottled water are available on the park's east side from the small **NPS visitor center** (9:30am-5pm) inside the **campground store** (3-6pm Mon-Fri, 9am-6pm Sat & Sun).

Getting There & Away

There is no road connecting the two sides of the park. To reach the less-developed **west entrance** (7:30am-8pm mid-Mar–early Nov, to 6pm early Nov–mid-Mar), exit Hwy 101 at Soledad and follow Hwy 146 northeast for 14 miles. The **east entrance** (24hr), where you'll find the visitor center and campground, is accessed via lonely Hwy 25 in San Benito County, southeast of Hollister and northeast of King City.

Mission San Antonio De Padua

Remote, tranquil and evocative, this **mission** (☎831-385-4478; www.missionsanantonio.net; end of Mission Rd, Jolon; adult/child under 13yr $5/3; 10am-4pm) sits in the Valley of the Oaks, once part of the sprawling Hearst Ranch land holdings. It's now inside the boundaries of active Fort Hunter Liggett.

The mission was founded in 1771 by Franciscan priest Junípero Serra. Built with Native American labor, the church has been restored to its early 19th-century appearance, with a wooden pulpit, canopied altar and decorative flourishes on whitewashed walls. A creaky door leads to a cloistered garden anchored by a fountain. The museum has a small collection of such utilitarian items as an olive press and a weaving loom once used in the mission's workshops. Around the grounds, you can inspect the remains of a grist mill and irrigation system with aqueducts.

It's seldom crowded here, and you may have this vast site all to yourself, except during **Mission Days** in late April and **La Fiesta** on the second Sunday of June. Pick up a visitor's pass from a military checkpoint on the way in; bring photo ID and proof of your vehicle's registration. From the north, take the Jolon Rd exit off Hwy 101 before King City and follow Jolon Rd (County Rte G14) about 18 miles south to Mission Rd. From the south, take the Jolon Rd (County Rte G18) exit off Hwy 101 and drive 22 miles northwest to Mission Rd.

San Miguel

San Miguel is a small farming town right off Hwy 101, where life seems to have remained almost unchanged for decades. **Mission San Miguel Arcángel** (☎805-467-3256; www.missionsanmiguel.org; 775 Mission St; suggested donation per person/family $2/5; ⏱10am-4:30pm) suffered heart-breaking damage during the 2003 Paso Robles earthquake. Although repairs are still underway, the restored mission church, cemetery, museum and gardens have since re-opened. An enormous cactus out front was planted around the same time as the mission was built in 1818.

Hungry? Inside a retro converted gas station downtown, **Station 3** (1199 Mission St; items $2-6; ⏱6am-2:30pm Mon-Fri, 7am-2:30pm Sat & Sun) vends live-wire espresso and cups o' coffee, breakfast burritos, pulled-pork sandwiches and whopping good brownies.

Paso Robles

In northern San Luis Obispo County, Paso Robles is the heart of an agricultural region where grapes are now the biggest money-making crop. Scores of wineries along Hwy 46 produce a brave new world of more-than-respectable bottles. The Mediterranean climate is yielding another bounty, too: a fledging olive-oil industry. Paso's historic downtown centers on Park and 12th Sts, where boutique shops and wine-tasting rooms await.

Sights & Activities

You could spend days wandering country back roads off Hwy 46, both east and west of Hwy 101. Most wineries have tasting rooms and a few offer vineyard tours. For anything else you might want to know, check www.pasowine.com.

EASTSIDE

FREE **Tobin James Cellars** WINERY

(www.tobinjames.com; 8950 Union Rd; ⏱10am-6pm) Boisterous Old West saloon pours bold reds, including an outlaw 'Ballistic' zinfandel and 'Liquid Love' late-harvest dessert wine. No tasting fee.

FREE **Eberle** WINERY

(www.eberlewinery.com; 3810 E Hwy 46; ⏱10am-5pm Oct-Mar, 10am-6pm Apr-Sep) Offers lofty vineyard views, bocce ball courts and daily tours of its wine caves. No-fee tastings run the gamut of white and red varietals and blends, plus port.

Clautiere WINERY

(www.clautiere.com; 1340 Penman Springs Rd; ⏱noon-5pm Thu-Mon) Don't let the fantastical tasting room, where you can try on Dr Seuss-ian hats, fool you: serious Rhône-style blends will delight connoisseurs.

Cass WINERY

(www.casswines.com; 7350 Linne Rd; ⏱noon-5pm Mon-Fri, 11am-6pm Sat & Sun) All that rich Rhône wine-tasting, from Roussanne to Syrah, going straight to your head? Light lunches are served in the market cafe until 4pm daily.

WESTSIDE

Tablas Creek WINERY

(www.tablascreek.com; 9339 Adelaida Rd; ⏱10am-5pm) Breathe easy at this organic estate vineyard in the rolling hillsides. Known for their Rhône varietals, signature blends also rate highly. Tours are usually offered at 10:30am and 2pm daily (reservations advised).

Castoro WINERY

(www.castorocellars.com; 1315 N Bethel Rd; ⏱10am-5:30pm) Husband-and-wife team produces 'dam fine wine' (the mascot is a beaver, get it?), including from custom-crushed and organic grapes. Outdoor vineyard concerts in summer.

Zenaida WINERY

(www.zenaidacellars.com; 1550 W Hwy 46; ⏱11am-5pm) Rustic tasting room that's simply zen for sampling estate zins and a signature 'Fire Sign' blend. Overnight vineyard accommodations (from $250 per night) are tempting too.

Dark Star WINERY

(www.darkstarcellars.com; 2985 Anderson Rd; ⏱10:30am-5pm Fri-Sun) If you're lucky, you might meet the winemaker in this family-run tasting room, pouring big, bold red varietals and blends like 'Left Turn.'

Festivals & Events

Wine Festivals FOOD & WINE

(www.pasowine.com) Oenophiles crowd the Zinfandel Festival in mid-March, Wine Festival in mid-May and Harvest Wine Weekend in mid-October.

California Mid-State Fair CULTURE

(www.midstatefair.com) In late July and early August, 12 days of live rock and country-

and-western concerts, farm exhibits, carnival rides and a rodeo draw huge crowds.

Sleeping

Chain motels and hotels line Hwy 101. B&Bs and vacation rentals are scattered among the vineyards outside town.

Hotel Cheval BOUTIQUE HOTEL $$$
(805-226-9995, 866-522-6999; www.hotelcheval.com; 1021 Pine St; d incl breakfast $300-400;) Cocoon with your lover inside an art-splashed aerie downtown. A dozen stylish, modern rooms all come with California king beds, spa-worthy amenities and plantation shutters; some have gas fireplaces and sundecks with teak furniture. Staff can be snobby. Pet fee $30.

Wild Coyote Estate Winery B&B $$$
(805-610-1311; www.wildcoyote.biz; 3775 Adelaida Rd; d incl breakfast $225-275;) Steal yourself away among the stellar vineyards of Paso Robles' west side, where just five romantic adobe-walled casitas echo the Southwest and a complimentary bottle of wine awaits by your kiva-style fireplace. There's an outdoor hot tub and barbecue grills too.

Inn Paradiso B&B $$
(805-239-2800; www.innparadiso.com; 975 Mojave Ln; d incl breakfast from $265;) At an intimate B&B with only three contemporary rooms, amiable hosts pull out all the luxury stops, with gas fireplace sitting areas, deep soaking tubs, canopy king-sized beds and French balcony doors. Vegetarian breakfasts available.

Melody Ranch Motel MOTEL $
(805-238-3911, 800-909-3911; 939 Spring St; r $63-78;) There's just one story and only 19 basic rooms at this small, family-owned, 1950s motor court downtown, which translates into prices that are almost as small as the outdoor pool.

Courtyard Marriott HOTEL $$
(805-239-9700, 888-236-2427; www.courtyardpasorobles.com; 120 S Vine St, off Hwy 101; r $129-259;) Contemporary hotel with immaculate rooms and full amenities.

Adelaide Inn MOTEL $$
(805-238-2770, 800-549-7276; www.adelaideinn.com; 1215 Ysabel Ave, off Hwy 101; r $85-135;) Fresh-baked cookies and mini golf keep kids happy at this family motel.

JAMES DEAN MEMORIAL

In Cholame, about 25 miles east of Paso Robles via Hwy 46, there's a memorial near the spot where *Rebel Without a Cause* star James Dean fatally crashed his Porsche on September 30, 1955, at the age of 24. Ironically, the actor had recently filmed a public-safety campaign TV spot, in which he said, 'The road is no place to race your car. It's real murder. Remember, drive safely. The life you save might be mine.' Look for the shiny silver memorial wrapped around an oak tree outside the truck-stop Jack Ranch Cafe, which has old photographs and movie-star memorabilia inside.

Eating & Drinking

Restaurants, cafes and bars surround downtown's City Park, a grassy central square off Spring St between 11th and 12th Sts.

Artisan CALIFORNIAN $$$
(805-237-8084; www.artisanpasorobles.com; 1401 Park St; lunch mains $10-22, dinner mains $26-31; 11am-9pm Sun-Thu, to 10pm Fri & Sat) Eco-conscious chef Chris Kobayashi often ducks out of the kitchen just to make sure you're loving his impeccable contemporary renditions of modern American cuisine, featuring sustainably farmed meats, wild-caught seafood and artisan California cheeses. Make reservations and expect long waits.

Thomas Hill Organics Market Bistro ECLECTIC $$$
(805-226-5888; www.thomashillorganics.com; 1305 Park St; mains $18-26; lunch 11am-3pm Mon & Wed-Sat, 10am-3pm Sun, dinner 5-9pm Wed, Thu, Sun & Mon, to 10pm Fri & Sat) Hidden down a side alley, this farm-fresh gourmands' kitchen has only a few tables, so book ahead. On the eclectic fusion menu, which ranges from Vietnamese pork sandwiches to roasted duck breast with harissa sauce, most ingredients are locally sourced. Service is slooow.

Villa Creek CALIFORNIAN $$$
(805-238-3000; 1144 Pine St; mains $22-35; 5:30-10pm) Perch casually at the wine bar and spin tapas plates or dine like a don in the formal restaurant, which marries early Spanish-colonial mission cooking traditions

with sustainable, organic ingredients in shepherd's plates of artisan cheese, sausages and olives, or rancho-style cassoulet with duck. Reservations recommended.

Firestone Walker Brewing Co BREWERY
(www.firestonebeer.com; 1400 Ramada Dr; ⏲noon-7pm) Bring your buddies to the taproom to sample famous brews like Double Barrel Ale.

Vinoteca WINE BAR
(www.vinotecawinebar.com; 835 12th St; ⏲4-9pm Mon-Thu, to 11pm Fri & Sat) Sends you soaring with its wine flights and Wednesday meet-the-winemaker nights.

Information

Paso Robles Chamber of Commerce (☎805-238-0506; www.pasorobleschamber.com; 1225 Park St; ⏲8:30am-4:30pm Mon-Fri, 10am-2pm Sat) Information and free winery maps.

Getting There & Away

With **Amtrak** (www.amtrak.com; 800 Pine St), daily *Coast Starlight* trains head north to Salinas ($19, two hours) and Oakland ($29, five hours) or south to Santa Barbara ($26, 4¾ hours) and Los Angeles ($45, 7½ hours). Several daily Thruway buses link to more-frequent regional trains, including the *Pacific Surfliner*.

From the train station, **Greyhound** (www.greyhound.com; 800 Pine St) runs a few daily buses along Hwy 101 south to Santa Barbara ($40, three hours) and LA ($58, six hours) or north to San Francisco ($54, 6½ hours) via Santa Cruz ($40, 3¼ hours).

RTA (☎805-541-2228; www.slorta.org) bus 9 travels between San Luis Obispo and Paso Robles ($2.50, 70 minutes) hourly on weekdays, and three or four times daily on weekends.

San Luis Obispo

Almost halfway between LA and San Francisco, San Luis Obispo is the classic stopover point for road trippers. With no must-see attractions, SLO might not seem to warrant much of your time. That said, this lively yet low-key town has an enviably high quality of life – in fact, talk-show diva Oprah once deemed it America's happiest city. For travelers, SLO's proximity to beaches, state parks and Hearst Castle make it a convenient coastal hub. CalPoly university students inject a healthy dose of hubbub into the city's streets, pubs and cafes throughout the school year. Nestled at the base of the Santa Lucia foothills, SLO is just a grape's throw from thriving Edna Valley wineries, known for their crisp chardonnays and subtle syrahs and pinot noirs.

Sights

San Luis Obispo Creek, once used to irrigate mission orchards, flows through downtown. Uphill from Higuera St, **Mission Plaza** is a shady oasis with restored adobe buildings and fountains overlooking the creek. Look for the **Moon Tree**, a coast redwood grown from a seed that journeyed on board Apollo 14's lunar mission.

Mission San Luis Obispo de Tolosa MISSION
(www.missionsanluisobispo.org; 751 Palm St; suggested donation $2; ⏲9am-4pm) Those satisfyingly reverberatory bells heard around downtown emanate from this active parish. The fifth California mission, it was established in 1772 and named for a 13th-century French saint. Nicknamed the 'Prince of the Missions,' its modest church has an unusual L-shape and whitewashed walls depicting Stations of the Cross. An adjacent building contains an old-fashioned museum about daily life during the Chumash tribal and Spanish colonial periods.

FREE **San Luis Obispo Museum of Art** MUSEUM
(www.sloma.org; 1010 Broad St; ⏲11am-5pm, closed Tue Sep-Jun) Near the creek, this small gallery showcases local painters, sculptors, printmakers and fine-art photographers, as well as traveling California art exhibitions.

Bubblegum Alley QUIRKY
(off 700 block of Higuera St) SLO's weirdest sight is colorfully plastered with thousands of wads of ABC ('already been chewed') gum. Watch where you step!

Activities

The most popular local hiking trail summits **Bishop Peak** (1546ft), the tallest of the Nine Sisters, a chain of volcanic peaks that stretches north to Morro Bay. The 2.2-mile one-way trail starts in a grove of live oaks (watch out for poison oak, too) and heads uphill along rocky, exposed switchbacks. Scramble up boulders at the tippy-top for panoramic views. To get to the trailhead, drive northwest from downtown on Santa Rosa St (Hwy 1), turn left onto Foothill Dr, then right onto Patricia Dr; after 0.8 miles,

TOP FIVE EDNA VALLEY WINERIES

For a winery map and more vineyards to explore, visit www.slowine.com.

» **Edna Valley Vineyard** (ednavalleyvineyard.com; 2585 Biddle Ranch Rd; ⏲10am-5pm) Sip Paragon Vineyard estate chardonnay by panoramic windows.

» **Kynsi** (www.kynsi.com; 2212 Corbett Canyon Rd; ⏲11am-5pm Thu-Mon) Small, family-run vineyard pours cult-worthy pinot noirs.

» **Niven Family Wine Estates** (www.baileyana.com; 5828 Orcutt Rd; ⏲10am-5pm) Tastings from five premium labels inside an early-20th-century wooden schoolhouse.

» **Talley** (www.talleyvineyards.com; 3031 Lopez Dr; ⏲10:30am-4:30pm) Unpretentious, value-priced wines set among rolling hillsides, with vineyard tours daily.

» **Tolosa** (www.tolosawinery.com; 4910 Edna Rd; ⏲11am-4:45pm) Classic no-oak chardonnay, soft pinot noir and bold red blends; guided tours and barrel tastings by appointment.

look for three black posts with a trailhead sign on your left.

For more peak hikes with ocean views, visit nearby Montaña de Oro State Park (p305).

Festivals & Events

TOP CHOICE San Luis Obispo Farmers Market FOOD, CULTURE
(www.downtownslo.com; ⏲6-9pm Thu) The county's biggest and best weekly farmers market turns downtown's Higuera St into a giant street party, with smokin' barbecues, overflowing fruit and veggie stands, live music of all stripes and free sidewalk entertainment, from salvation peddlers to wackadoodle political activists. It's one of the liveliest evenings out anywhere along the Central Coast.

Concerts in the Plaza MUSIC, FOOD
(www.downtownslo.com) From early June until early September, Friday night concerts in downtown's Mission Plaza rock out with local bands and food vendors.

Savor the Central Coast FOOD, WINE
(www.savorcentralcoast.com) Behind-the-scenes farm and ranch tours, wine-tasting competitions and celebrity chefs' dinners happen in late September and early October.

Sleeping

Motels cluster off Hwy 101, especially at the northeast end of Monterey St and around Santa Rosa St (Hwy 1).

San Luis Creek Lodge HOTEL $$
(☎805-541-1122, 800-593-0333; www.sanluiscreeklodge.com; 1941 Monterey St; r incl breakfast $139-239; ❄@📶♿) Although it rubs shoulders a little too closely with neighboring motels, this boutique inn has fresh, spacious rooms with divine beds (some with gas fireplaces and jetted tubs) in three whimsically mismatched buildings built in Tudor, Arts and Crafts, and Southern Plantation styles. Fluffy robes, DVDs, chess sets and board games are free to borrow.

Peach Tree Inn MOTEL $$
(☎805-543-3170, 800-227-6396; www.peachtreeinn.com; 2001 Monterey St; r incl breakfast $79-200; ❄@📶) The folksy, nothing-fancy motel rooms here are inviting, especially those right by the creek or with rocking chairs on wooden porches overlooking grassy lawns, eucalyptus trees and rose gardens. A hearty breakfast features homemade breads.

Petit Soleil INN $$
(☎805-549-0321; www.petitsoleilslo.com; 1473 Monterey St; r incl breakfast $159-299; 📶) This French-themed, gay-friendly 'bed et breakfast' is a mostly charming retrofit of a courtyard motel. Each room is tastefully decorated with Provençal flair, and breakfast is a gourmet feast. The front rooms catch some street noise, though.

HI Hostel Obispo HOSTEL $
(☎805-544-4678; www.hostelobispo.com; 1617 Santa Rosa St; dm $24-27, r from $45; ⏲check-in 4:30-10pm; @📶) On a tree-lined street near the train station, this solar-empowered, avocado-colored hostel inhabits a converted Victorian, which gives it a bit of a B&B feel. Amenities include a kitchen and bike rentals (from $10 per day); BYOT (bring your own towel). No credit cards.

San Luis Obispo

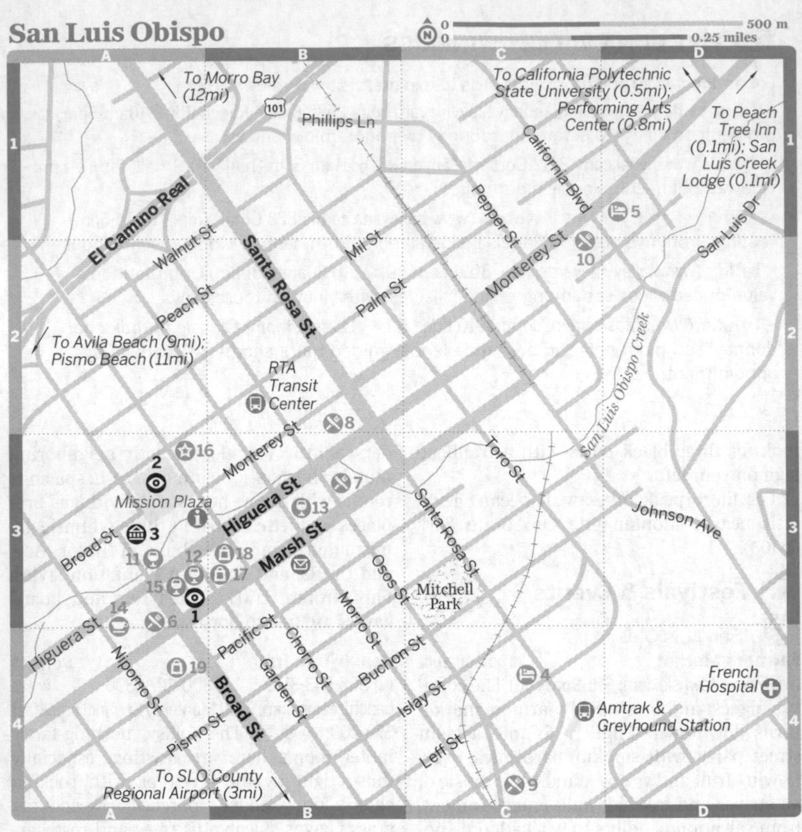

Eating

Luna Red FUSION $$$
(805-540-5243; www.lunaredslo.com; 1009 Monterey St; small plates $4-15, dinner mains $18-26; 11am-9pm Mon-Thu, 11am-10pm Fri, 4-10pm Sat, 5-9pm Sun) An inspired chef spins recherché Californian, Mediterranean and Asian tapas, with a keen eye towards freshness and spice. Local bounty from the land and sea rules the menu, including house-smoked salumi and artisan cheeses. Stiff cocktails enhance the sophisticated ambience, with glowing lanterns and polished parquet floors.

Big Sky Café CALIFORNIAN $$
(www.bigskycafe.com; 1121 Broad St; mains $6-22; 7am-9pm Mon-Wed, 7am-10pm Thu-Fri, 8am-10pm Sat, 8am-9pm Sun;) Big Sky is a big room, and still the wait can be long – its tagline is 'analog food for a digital world.' Vegetarians have almost as many options as carnivores, and many of the ingredients are sourced locally. Big-plate dinners can be bland, but breakfast (until 1pm daily) gets top marks.

Meze Wine Café & Market MEDITERRANEAN $$
(www.mezemarket.com; 1880 Santa Barbara Ave; sandwiches $8-10, shared plates $5-25; 10am-9:30pm Mon-Sat, 11:30am-8:30pm Sun) Hidden downhill from the Amtrak station, this tiny Mediterranean and North African epicurean market, wine shop and tapas bar is an eclectic gem. Gather with friends around the cheese and charcuterie board, or stop in for a hand-crafted sandwich accompanied by couscous salad.

Firestone Grill BARBECUE $
(www.firestonegrill.com 1001 Higuera St; mains $5-12; 11am-10pm Sun-Wed, 11am-11pm Thu-Sun;) If you can stomach huge lines, long waits for

San Luis Obispo

Sights

1 Bubblegum Alley A3
2 Mission San Luis Obispo de Tolosa A3
3 San Luis Obispo Museum of Art A3

Sleeping

4 HI Hostel Obispo C4
5 Petit Soleil D1

Eating

Bel Frites .... (see 12)
6 Big Sky Café A3
7 Firestone Grill B3
8 Luna Red B2
9 Meze Wine Café & Market C4
10 Splash Cafe C2

Drinking

11 Creekside Brewing Co A3
12 Downtown Brewing Co A3
13 Granada Bistro B3
14 Kreuzberg A3
15 Mother's Tavern A3

Entertainment

16 Palm Theatre A3

Shopping

17 Finders Keepers B3
18 Hands Gallery B3
19 Mountain Air Sports A4

a table and sports bar–style service, you'll get to sink your teeth into an authentic Santa Maria–style tri-tip steak sandwich on a toasted garlic roll, or a rack of succulent pork ribs.

Splash Cafe CAFE $
(www.splashbakery.com; 1491 Monterey St; dishes $3-10; 7am-8:30pm Sun-Thu, to 9:30pm Fri & Sat;) Fresh soups and salads, sandwiches on house-made bread and tempting bakery treats are reason enough to kick back inside this airy uptown cafe, not far from motel row. The organic, hand-made Sweet Earth Chocolates shop is nearby.

New Frontiers Natural Marketplace GROCERIES, FAST FOOD $
(http://newfrontiers.com; 1531 Froom Ranch Way, off Hwy 101 exit Los Osos Valley Rd; 8am-9pm) For organic groceries, deli picnic meals and a hot-and-cold salad bar. It's a 15-minute drive from downtown via Hwy 101 southbound.

SLO Donut Company SNACKS $
(www.slodonutcompany.com; 793 E Foothill Blvd; snacks from $2; 24hr;) Home of bizarrely tasty donuts like bacon-maple or PB&J and organic, fair-trade, locally roasted coffee. It's a five-minute drive north of downtown off Santa Rosa St (Hwy 1).

Bel Frites SNACKS $
(www.belfrites.com; 1127 Garden St; snacks $4-8; 3pm-2:30am Tue-Thu, noon-2:30am Fri & Sat, noon-6pm Sun) Belgian fries with New World seasonings and dipping sauces for late-night bar hoppers.

Drinking

Downtown, Higuera St is littered with college student–jammed bars and clubs.

Downtown Brewing Co BREWPUB
(www.slobrew.com; 1119 Garden St) More often called just SLO Brew, this study in rafters and exposed brick has plenty of craft beers to go with filling pub grub. Downstairs, you'll find DJs spinning or live bands with names like 'Atari Teenage Riot' playing most nights.

Creekside Brewing Co BREWPUB
(www.creeksidebrewing.com; 1040 Broad St) Kick back at a breezy patio overhanging the bubbling creek. It has got its own fairly respectable brews on tap, plus bottled Belgian beers. On Mondays, all pints are usually just three bucks.

Kreuzberg COFFEE SHOP
(www.kreuzbergcalifornia.com; 685 Higuera St; 6:30am-midnight;) SLO's newest coffeehouse has earned a fervent following, with comfy couches, sprawling bookshelves, local art splashed on the walls and occasionally live music.

Mother's Tavern BAR
(www.motherstavern.com; 729 Higuera St;) Cavernous two-story 'MoTav' pub that draws in the party-hardy CalPoly student masses with its no-cover DJ-driven dance floor and frequent live-music shows.

Granada Bistro LOUNGE
(www.granadabistro.com; 1126 Morro St; Thu-Sun) Like a celebutante's living room, this swank lounge classes up the downtown scene, with imported wines and beers and live acoustic tunes.

Entertainment

Palm Theatre CINEMA
(805-541-5161; www.thepalmtheatre.com; 817 Palm St) In SLO's blink-and-you'll-miss-it Chinatown, this small-scale movie house showing foreign and indie flicks happens to be the USA's first solar-powered cinema. Look for the San Luis Obispo International Film Festival in mid-March.

Sunset Drive-In CINEMA
(805-544-4475; www.fairoakstheatre.net; 255 Elks Lane, off S Higuera St;) Recline your seat, put your feet up on the dash and munch on bottomless bags of popcorn at this classic Americana drive-in. Sticking around for the second feature (usually a B-list Hollywood blockbuster) doesn't cost extra. It's off Higuera St, about a 10-minute drive south of downtown.

Performing Arts Center PERFORMING ARTS
(PAC; 805-756-2787, 888-233-2787; www.pacslo.org; 1 Grand Ave) On the CalPoly campus, this state-of-the-art theater is SLO's biggest cultural venue, presenting a variety of concerts, theater, dance recitals, stand-up comedy and other shows by big-name performers. Event parking costs $6.

Shopping

Downtown, Higuera and Marsh Sts, along with all of the arcades and cross streets in between, are stuffed full of unique boutiques. Take a wander and find something wonderful.

Hands Gallery ART, JEWELRY
(www.handsgallery.com; 777 Higuera St; 10am-6pm Mon-Wed, 10am-8pm Thu, 10am-7pm Fri & Sat, 11am-5pm Sun) Brightly lit gallery sells fine contemporary craftwork by vibrant California artisans, including jewelry, fiber arts, metal sculptures, ceramics and blown glass, perfect for gifts or souvenirs.

Mountain Air Sports OUTDOORS
(www.mountainairsports.com; 667 Marsh St; 10am-6pm Mon-Sat, to 8pm Thu, 11am-4pm Sun) Almost the only outdoor outfitter between Monterey and Santa Barbara, here you can pick up anything from campstove fuel and tents to brand-name active clothing and hiking boots.

Finders Keepers CLOTHING
(www.finderskeepersconsignment.com; 1124 Garden St; 10am-5pm) Seriously stylish second-hand women's fashions that match SLO's breezy, laid-back coastal lifestyle, plus hand-picked handbags, coats and jewelry.

Information

SLO's compact downtown is bisected by the parallel one-way arteries of Higuera St and Marsh St. Banks with 24-hour ATMs are off Marsh St, near the post office. Most downtown coffee shops offer free wi-fi.

FedEx Office (www.fedex.com; 1127 Chorro St; per min 20-30¢; 7am-11pm Mon-Fri, 9am-9pm Sat & Sun;) Pay-as-you-go internet workstations and free wi-fi.

French Hospital (805-543-5353; www.frenchmedicalcenter.org; 1911 Johnson Ave; 24hr) Emergency room.

Public library (www.slolibrary.org; 995 Palm St; 10am-5pm Wed-Sat, to 8pm Tue;) Free wi-fi and public internet terminals.

San Luis Obispo Chamber of Commerce (805-781-2777; www.visitslo.com; 1039 Chorro St; 10am-5pm Sun-Wed, 10am-7pm Thu-Sat) Free maps and information.

Getting There & Around

Off Broad St, over 3 miles southeast of downtown, **SLO County Regional Airport** (SBP; www.sloairport.com;) offers commuter flights with United (LA and San Francisco) and US Airways (Phoenix).

Amtrak (www.amtrak.com; 1011 Railroad Ave) runs daily Seattle–LA *Coast Starlight* and twice-daily SLO–San Diego *Pacific Surfliner* trains. Both routes head south to Santa Barbara ($29, 2¾ hours) and Los Angeles ($34, 5½ hours). Only the *Coast Starlight* connects north to Salinas ($31, 3½ hours) and Oakland ($34, six hours). Several daily Thruway buses link to more regional trains.

From the train station, about 0.6 miles east of downtown, **Greyhound** (www.greyhound.com; 1023 Railroad Ave) operates a few daily buses along Hwy 101 south to Los Angeles ($38, 5¼ hours) via Santa Barbara ($26, 2¼ hours) and north to San Francisco ($48, 6½ hours) via Santa Cruz ($39, four hours).

San Luis Obispo's **Regional Transit Authority** (RTA; 805-541-2228; www.slorta.org) operates daily county-wide buses with limited weekend services; one-way fares are $1.50 to $3 (day pass $5). All buses are equipped with two-bicycle racks. Lines converge on downtown's **transit center** (cnr Palm & Osos Sts).

SLO Transit (805-541-2877; www.slocity.org) runs local city buses and the downtown trolley (50¢), which loops around every 15 to 20 minutes between 3pm and 10pm on Thursday

WORTH A TRIP

CARRIZO PLAIN NATIONAL MONUMENT

Hidden in eastern SLO County, **Carrizo Plain National Monument** (www.ca.blm.gov/bakersfield; admission free; ⌚24hr) is a geological wonderland, where you can walk or drive atop the San Andreas Fault. This peaceful wildlife preserve also protects a diversity of species including endangered California condors and jewel flowers, tule elk, pronghorn antelope and the San Joaquin kit fox. Pick up 4WD and hiking maps at the **Goodwin Education Center** (☎805-475-2131; ⌚9am-4pm Thu-Sun Dec-May), past the dazzling white salt flats of Soda Lake, near the trailhead for Painted Rock, which displays Native American pictographs. The monument is about 55 winding miles east of Hwy 101, or 55 miles west of the I-5 Freeway, via Hwy 58 and Soda Lake Rd. Two primitive **Bureau of Land Management (BLM) Campgrounds** offer free, first-come, first-served campsites.

year-round, and 3pm to 10pm Friday and 1pm to 10pm Saturday from April through October.

Avila Beach

Quaint, sunny Avila Beach lures crowds with its strand of golden sand and a freshly built seafront commercial district lined by restaurants, shops and cafes. Two miles west of downtown, Port San Luis is a working fishing harbor.

Sights & Activities

For a lazy summer day at the beach, rent beach chairs and umbrellas, surfboards, boogie boards and wetsuits underneath **Avila Pier**, off downtown's waterfront promenade. At the port, the barking of sea lions accompanies you as you stroll **Harford Pier**, one of the Central Coast's most authentic fishing piers.

Point San Luis Lighthouse LIGHTHOUSE
(Map p318; www.sanluislighthouse.org; lighthouse admission adult/family $5/10, trolley tour incl lighthouse admission per person $20; ⌚guided hikes 9am-1pm Wed & Sat, trolley tours noon, 1pm & 2pm on 1st & 3rd Sat of the month) Just getting to this scenic 1890 lighthouse, overshadowed by Diablo Canyon nuclear power plant, is an adventure. The cheapest way to reach the lighthouse is via a rocky, crumbling, 3.75-mile trail. Weather permitting, it's open only for **guided hikes** (☎805-541-8735) led by Pacific Gas & Electric docents. Children under nine years old are not allowed to hike; call for reservations at least two weeks in advance and bring plenty of water. If you'd rather take it easy and ride out to the lighthouse, which harbors an original Fresnel lens and authentic Victorian period furnishings, join a Saturday afternoon **trolley tour** (☎805-540-5771). Reservations are required.

Avila Valley Barn FARM
(Map p318; http://avilavalleybarn.com; 560 Avila Beach Dr; ⌚9am 6pm daily Jun-Oct, 9am-5pm Thu-Mon Nov-May; 👪) At this rural farmstand and pick-your-own berry farm, park alongside the sheep and goat pens, lick an ice-cream cone, then grab a basket and walk out into the fields to harvest jammy olallieberries and strawberries in late spring, midsummer peaches and nectarines or apples and pumpkins in autumn.

Sycamore Mineral Springs HOT SPRINGS
(Map p318; ☎805-595-7302, 800-234-5831; www.sycamoresprings.com; 1215 Avila Beach Dr; per person per hr $12.50-17.50; ⌚8am-midnight, last reservation 10:45pm) Make time for a luxuriant soak, where private redwood hot tubs are discreetly laddered up a woodsy hillside. Call in advance for reservations, as it's often fully booked, especially during summer and on weekends after dark.

Avila Hot Springs HOT SPRINGS
(Map p318; ☎805-595-2359; www.avilahotsprings.com; 250 Avila Beach Dr; adult/child under 16yr $10/8; ⌚8am-9pm Sun-Thu, to 10pm Fri & Sat; 👪) For families, this slightly sulfuric, lukewarm public swimming pool has a pretty cool waterslide (open noon to 5pm daily).

Central Coast Kayaks KAYAKING
(Map p318; ☎805-773-3500; www.centralcoastkayaks.com; 1879 Shell Beach Rd, Shell Beach; kayak or SUP rentals $20-60, 2hr kayaking tour $70) Paddle out among sea otters and seals and through mesmerizing sea caves, arches and kelp forests.

San Luis Obispo Bay

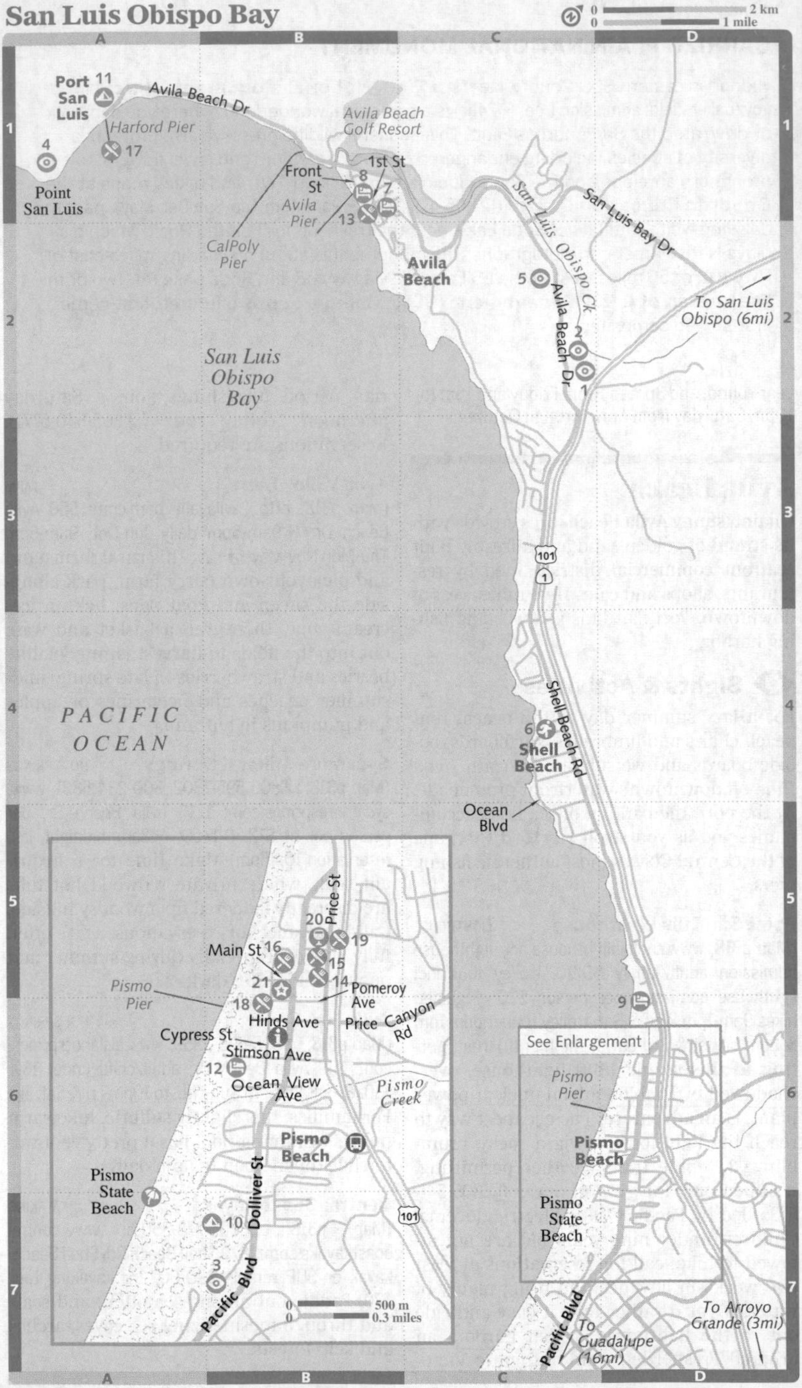

0 — 2 km
0 — 1 mile

Port San Luis 11
Avila Beach Dr
Harford Pier
17
4
Point San Luis
Avila Beach Golf Resort
Front St
1st St
8
7
Avila Pier
13
CalPoly Pier
Avila Beach
San Luis Obispo Ck
San Luis Bay Dr
5
Avila Beach Dr
To San Luis Obispo (6mi)
2
1
San Luis Obispo Bay
101
1
PACIFIC OCEAN
6
Shell Beach
Shell Beach Rd
Ocean Blvd
9
See Enlargement
Pismo Pier
Pismo Beach
Pismo State Beach
Pacific Blvd
To Guadalupe (16mi)
To Arroyo Grande (3mi)

Price St
20
19
Main St
16
15
14
Pismo Pier
21
Pomeroy Ave
18
Hinds Ave
Price Canyon Rd
Cypress St
Stimson Ave
12
Ocean View Ave
Pismo Creek
Pismo Beach
Pismo State Beach
10
Dolliver St
101
3
Pacific Blvd
0 — 500 m
0 — 0.3 miles

San Luis Obispo Bay

Sights

1 Avila Hot Springs C2
2 Avila Valley Barn C2
3 Monarch Butterfly Grove B7
4 Point San Luis Lighthouse A1
5 Sycamore Mineral Springs C2

Activities, Courses & Tours

6 Central Coast Kayaks C4
Patriot Sportfishing ......(see 17)

Sleeping

Avila Hot Springs Campground ......(see 1)
7 Avila La Fonda B1
8 Avila Lighthouse Suites B1
9 Pismo Lighthouse Suites D6
10 Pismo State Beach – North Beach Campground B7
11 Port San Luis A1
12 Sandcastle Inn B6

Eating

Avila Beach Fish & Farmers Market ......(see 13)
13 Avila Grocery & Deli B1
14 Cracked Crab B5
15 Giuseppe's B5
16 Old West Cinnamon Rolls B5
17 Olde Port Inn A1
Pete's Pierside Cafe ......(see 17)
18 Splash Cafe B6
19 Utopia Bakery Cafe B5

Drinking

20 Taste of the Valleys B5

Entertainment

21 Pismo Bowl B5

Patriot Sportfishing BOAT TOURS
(Map p318; ☎805-595-7200, 800-714-3474; www.patriotsportfishing.com; Harford Pier, off Avila Beach Dr; tours adult/child 4-12yr/child under 4yr from $35/15/10) This long-running local biz organizes deep-sea fishing trips and tournaments, as well as whale-spotting cruises between December and April.

Sleeping

Avila La Fonda BOUTIQUE HOTEL $$$
(Map p318; ☎805-595-1700; www.avilalafonda.com; 101 San Miguel St; ste $250-800; @📶🐾) Downtown, this small inn evinces a harmonious mix of Mexican and Spanish colonial styles, with hand-painted tiles, stained-glass windows, wrought iron and rich wood. The deck has barbecue grills, a wet bar and a sociable fireplace for nightly wine and hors d'oeuvres. With vibrant colors, the sprawling rooms and suites have all mod cons (except air-con), plus hot tubs and some kitchens. Pet fee $50.

Avila Lighthouse Suites HOTEL $$$
(Map p318; ☎805-627-1900, 800-372-8452; www.avilalighthousesuites.com; 550 Front St; ste incl breakfast $229-479; ❄@📶🏊👪) Any closer to the ocean, and your bed would actually be sitting on the sand. Made with families in mind, this apartment-style hotel offers suites and villas with kitchenettes. But it's the giant heated outdoor pool, ping-pong tables, putting green and life-sized checkers board that keeps kids amused.

Port San Luis CAMPGROUND $
(Map p318; RV sites without/with hookups from $30/45) First-come, first-served parking spaces by the side of the road have ocean views; RVs only (no tents).

Avila Hot Springs Campground CAMPGROUND $
(Map p318; ☎805-595-2359; www.avilahotsprings.com; 250 Avila Beach Dr; tent & RV sites without/with hookups from $30/45) Crowded campground off Hwy 101 has hot showers and flush toilets; reservations essential in summer.

Eating

At Port San Luis, Harford Pier is home to seafood shops that sell rockfish, sole, salmon and other fresh catch right off the boats.

Avila Beach Fish & Farmers Market MARKET $
(Map p318; www.avilabeachpier.com; ⏰4-8pm Fri Apr–mid-Sep) With finger-lickin' food booths (seafood is a specialty, of course) and live music and entertainment, this outdoor street party takes over downtown's oceanfront promenade weekly in spring and summer.

Avila Grocery & Deli AMERICAN, FAST FOOD $
(Map p318; http://avilagrocery.com; 354 Front St; mains $5-11; ⏰7am-7pm; 👪) Gather everything you'll need for a beach picnic at this family-owned deli and general store on the ocean-front promenade. The chipotle tri-tip steak wrap is a gold-medal winner; so are bang-up breakfasts.

Pete's Pierside Cafe SEAFOOD, FAST FOOD $
(Map p318; www.petespiersidecafe.com; Harford Pier, off Avila Beach Dr; mains $5-12; ⏰11am-5pm) Hit this unpretentious seafood shack for crispy fish and chips, fresh oysters and crab legs, and an excellent salsa bar to doctor your fish taco with.

Olde Port Inn SEAFOOD $$$
(Map p318; ☎805-595-2515; www.oldeportinn.com; Harford Pier, off Avila Beach Dr; mains $10-38; ⏰11:30am-9pm Sun-Thu, to 10pm Fri & Sat) Clam chowder and cioppino are standouts at this seriously old-school seafood restaurant at the tip of Harford Pier. A few tables have glass tops, so lucky diners can peer down into the ocean.

Getting There & Around

From late May through September, a free **trolley** loops around downtown Avila Beach and Port San Luis, and out to Hwy 101. It usually operates hourly from 10am to 8pm on Saturday and 10am to 5pm on Sunday. In Shell Beach, the trolley connects with **South County Regional Transit** (SCAT; ☎805-781-4472; www.slorta.org) bus 21, which runs hourly to Pismo Beach ($1.25, 15 minutes).

Pismo Beach

The largest of San Luis Obispo Bay's 'Five Cities,' this 1950s-retro California beach town fronts a more commercial pier than neighboring Avila, but its beach is invitingly wide and sandy. Backed by a wooden pier that stretches toward the setting sun, here James Dean once trysted with Pier Angeli, and Pismo Beach today still feels like somewhere straight out of *Rebel Without a Cause* or *American Graffiti*. If you're looking for a sand-and-surf respite from road tripping, break your journey here.

Sights & Activities

Pismo likes to call itself the 'Clam Capital of the World,' but these days the **beach** is pretty much clammed out. You'll have better luck catching something fishy off the **pier**, where you can rent rods. To rent a wetsuit, boogie board or surfboard, cruise the nearby surf shops.

FREE **Monarch Butterfly Grove** PARK
(Map p318; www.monarchbutterfly.org; ⏰sunrise-sunset) From late October until February, over 25,000 black-and-orange monarchs make their winter home here. Forming dense clusters in the tops of eucalyptus trees, they might easily be mistaken for leaves. Volunteers can tell you all about the insects' incredible journey, which outlasts any single generation of butterflies. Look for a gravel parking pull-out on the west side of Pacific Blvd (Hwy 1), just south of Pismo State Beach's North Beach Campground.

Festivals & Events

Classic at Pismo Beach CULTURE
(www.thepismobeachclassic.com) Show up in mid-June when hot rods and muscle cars line the main drags off Hwy 1.

Clam Festival FOOD
(www.classiccalifornia.com) In mid-October, celebrate the formerly abundant and still tasty mollusk with a clam dig, chowder cookoff, food vendors and live music.

Sleeping

Pismo Beach has dozens of motels, but rooms fill up quickly and prices skyrocket in summer, especially on weekends. Resort hotels roost on cliffs north of town via Price St and Shell Beach Rd, while motels cluster near the beach and along Hwy 101.

Pismo Lighthouse Suites HOTEL $$$
(Map p318; ☎805-773-2411, 800-245-2411; www.pismolighthousesuites.com; 2411 Price St; ste incl breakfast $149-329; ❄@📶🏊👪) With everything a vacationing family needs – from in-room Nintendo and kitchenettes, to a life-sized outdoor chessboard, a putting green, table tennis and badminton courts – this contemporary all-suites hotel is hard to tear yourself away from.

Sandcastle Inn HOTEL $$$
(Map p318; ☎805-773-2422, 800-822-6606; www.sandcastleinn.com; 100 Stimson Ave; r incl breakfast $169-435; 📶) Many of these Eastern Seaboard–styled rooms are mere steps from the sand. The best suite in the house is perfect for getting engaged after cracking open a bottle of wine at sunset on the ocean-view patio. Wi-fi in lobby only.

WORTH A TRIP

GUADALUPE

Hwy 1 ends its brief relationship with Hwy 101 just south of Pismo Beach, as it veers off toward the coast. Over 15 miles further south, you almost expect to have to dodge Old West tumbleweeds as you drive into the one-road agricultural town of Guadalupe.

In 1923 a huge Hollywood crew descended on this remote outpost for the filming of the silent version of the *Ten Commandments*. Enormous Egyptian sets were constructed in Guadalupe's oceanfront sand dunes, complete with huge sphinxes and more. Afterward, director Cecil B DeMille saved money by leaving the magnificent sets – albeit ones constructed of hay, plaster and paint – in place and simply burying them in the sand. Over the following decades knowledge of the exact location of the vast sets was lost.

In 1983 film and archaeology buffs started looking for the 'Lost City of DeMille.' Many artifacts have been found and the locations of main structures pinpointed. Learn loads more about these oddball archaeological excavations online at www.lostcitydemille.com.

Back in town, inspect some of the recovered movie-set pieces at the tiny **Dunes Visitor Center** (www.dunescenter.org; 1055 Guadalupe St; admission by donation; ⏲10am-4pm Tue-Sat), which has exhibits about the ecology of North America's largest coastal dunes and also about the Dunites, mystical folks who called the dunes home during the 1930s.

The dunes preserve, which is a state-protected archaeological site (no digging or taking away souvenirs, sorry!) is about 5 miles west of town via Hwy 166. More recent movies shot here include *Pirates of the Caribbean: At World's End* (2007).

Pismo State Beach CAMPGROUND $
(Map p318; ☎reservations 800-444-7275; www.reserveamerica.com; tent & RV sites $25-35) About a mile south of downtown, off Dolliver St (Hwy 1), the state park's **North Beach Campground** has over 100 well-spaced, grassy sites, in the shade of eucalyptus trees. The campground offers easy beach access, flush toilets and hot showers.

Eating

TOP CHOICE **Cracked Crab** SEAFOOD $$$
(Map p318; www.crackedcrab.com; 751 Price St; mains $9-50; ⏲11am-9pm Sun-Thu, 11am-10pm Fri & Sat; 👪) Fresh seafood is the staple at this super-casual, family-owned grill. When the famous bucket o'seafood, full of flying bits of fish, Cajun sausage, red potatoes and cob corn, gets dumped on your butcher-paper-covered table, make sure you're wearing one of those silly-looking plastic bibs. Excellent regional wine list.

Giuseppe's ITALIAN $$$
(Map p318; www.guiseppesrestaurant.com; 891 Price St; lunch mains $9-15, dinner mains $12-32; ⏲lunch 11:30am-3pm Mon-Fri, dinner 4:30-10pm Sun-Thu, to 11pm Fri & Sat) Occasionally outstanding Southern Italian fare is served at this date-worthy *cucina,* which brims with the owner's personality – just eyeball the lineup of Vespa scooters parked out front. Safe bets are wood-fired pizzas and traditional pastas like spicy prawn spaghettini. Show up early, or expect a long wait (no reservations).

Splash Cafe SEAFOOD $
(Map p318; www.splashcafe.com; 197 Pomeroy Ave; dishes $4-10; ⏲8am-9pm; 👪) Uphill from the pier, lines go out the door to wrap around this scruffy surf-style hole-in-the-wall, famous for its award-winning clam chowder in a home-baked sourdough bread bowl, and a long lineup of grilled and fried briny fare. It keeps shorter hours in winter.

Klondike Pizza PIZZA $$
(www.klondikepizza.com; 104 Bridge St; pizzas $12-26; ⏲11am-9pm Sun-Thu, to 10pm Fri & Sat; 👪) Across Hwy 101 in small-town Arroyo Grande, this subterranean Alaskan-run pizzeria is littered with peanut shells and has checkers and other board games to play while you wait for your reindeer-sausage pie. Hum along with a kazoo during twice-monthly Saturday-night sing-alongs.

Doc Burnstein's Ice Cream Lab ICE CREAM $
(www.docburnsteins.com; 114 W Branch St; snacks $3-8; ⏲11am-9:30pm Sun-Thu, to 10:30pm Fri & Sat; 👪) On Arroyo Grande's main drag, Doc's scoops up fantastical flavors like Petite Syrah sorbet and the 'Elvis Special' (peanut butter with banana swirls). Live ice-cream lab shows start at 7pm sharp on Wednesday.

Old West Cinnamon Rolls BAKERY $
(Map p318; www.oldwestcinnamon.com; 861 Dolliver St; snacks & drinks $2-5; ⊙6:30am-5:30pm) Really, the name says it all at this gobsmacking bakery by the beach.

Utopia Bakery Cafe BAKERY $
(Map p318; www.utopiabakery.com; 950 Price St; snacks & sandwiches $2-8; ⊙6am-6pm) Corner stop for cookies, croissants, chocolate-chip scones and espresso drinks.

Drinking & Entertainment

Taste of the Valleys WINE BAR
(Map p318; www.pismowineshop.com; 911 Price St; ⊙noon-9pm Mon-Thu, to 10pm Fri & Sat, to 8pm Sun) Inside a quiet wine shop stacked floor to ceiling with California vintages; ask for a taste of anything they've got open today, or sample from the astounding list of 500 wines poured by the glass.

Pismo Bowl BOWLING ALLEY
(Map p318; www.pismobeachbowl.com; 277 Pomeroy Ave; ⊙noon-10pm Sun-Thu, to midnight Fri & Sat;) Epitomizing Pismo Beach's retro vibe, this old-fashioned bowling alley is just a short walk uphill from the pier. Rockin' blacklight 'cosmic bowling' rules on Friday and Saturday nights.

Information

Pismo Beach Visitors Information Center (☎805-773-4382, 800-443-7778; www.classiccalifornia.com; 581 Dolliver St, cnr Hinds Ave; ⊙9am-5pm Mon-Fri, 11am-4pm Sat) Free tourist maps and brochures.

Getting There & Around

Operating hourly on weekdays, and a few times daily on weekends, **RTA** (☎805-541-2228; www.slorta.org) bus 10 links Pismo's Premium Outlets mall, about a mile from the beach, with San Luis Obispo ($2, 25 minutes). **South County Regional Transit** (SCAT; ☎805-781-4472; www.slorta.org) runs hourly local buses ($1.25) connecting Pismo Beach with Shell Beach and Arroyo Grande.

La Purísima Mission State Historic Park

Surrounded by colorful commercial flower fields, this pastoral valley **mission** (www.lapurisimamission.org, www.parks.ca.gov; 2295 Purisima Rd, Lompoc; per car $6; ⊙9am-5pm) was extensively restored by the Civilian Conservation Corps (CCC) in the 1930s. Today it's one of the most evocative of California's original 21 Spanish colonial missions, with atmospheric adobe buildings that include a church, living quarters and shops. The mission's fields still support grazing livestock, while nearby flowering gardens are planted with medicinal plants used by Chumash tribespeople.

The mission is 15 miles west of Hwy 101 via Hwy 246. Past the golf course, take the turnoff for Purisima Rd on the north (right) side of the highway, then drive about another mile.

Santa Barbara Wine Country

Oak-dotted hillsides, winding country lanes, rows of sweetly heavy grapevines stretching as far as the eye can see – it's hard not to gush about the Santa Maria and Santa Ynez Valleys. Maybe you've been inspired to visit by the Oscar-winning film *Sideways*, an ode to the joys and hazards of wine-country living, as seen through the misadventures of middle-aged buddies Miles and Jack. The movie is like real life in one respect: this wine country is ideal for do-it-yourself-exploring with friends.

With more than 100 wineries spread out across the landscape, it can seem daunting at first. But the wine country's five small towns – Buellton, Solvang, Santa Ynez, Ballard and Los Olivos – are all clustered within 10 miles of one another, so it's easy to stop, shop and eat whenever and wherever you happen to feel like it. Don't worry about sticking to a regimented plan or following prescriptive wine guides. Just soak up the scenery and pull over where the signs look welcoming and the vibe feels right.

Sights & Activities

Nearer the coast, pinot noir – a particularly fragile grape – flourishes in the fog. Further inland, sun-loving Rhône varietals like Syrah thrive. Tasting fees average $10, and some wineries give vineyard tours (reservations may be required).

FOXEN CANYON

The pastoral **Foxen Canyon Wine Trail** (www.foxencanyonwinetrail.com) runs north from Hwy 154, just west of Los Olivos, into the rural Santa Maria Valley.

WORTH A TRIP

HIDDEN BEACHES OFF HIGHWAY 1

West of Lompoc lie some truly wild beaches worth the trouble of visiting.

Ocean Beach County Park (www.countyofsb.org/parks; ⏲8am-sunset) and **Surf Beach**, with its remote Amtrak train stop, are really one beach sidling up to Vandenberg Air Force Base. During the 10-mile drive west of Lompoc via Ocean Ave, you'll pass mysterious-looking structures supporting spy and commercial satellite launches. The dunes are untrammeled and interpretive signs explain the estuary's ecology. Because endangered snowy plovers nest here, vast areas of the beach are often closed between March and September.

Leaving Hwy 1 around 5 miles east of Lompoc, Jalama Rd follows 14 miles of twisting tarmac across ranch and farmlands, leading to **Jalama Beach County Park** (www.countyofsb.org/parks; per car/dog $10/3;). Utterly isolated, it's home to a crazy-popular **campground** (☎805-736-3504; www.jalamabeach.com; tent & RV sites without/with hookups from $25/40, cabins $100-220; ⏲campground store & cafe 7am-9pm) that only accepts reservations for its newly built cabins. Otherwise, you should arrive by 8am to get on the waiting list for a campsite – look for the 'campground full' sign, a half-mile south of Hwy 1, to avoid a wasted trip.

Firestone WINERY

(☎805-688-3940; www.firestonewine.com; 5000 Zaca Station Rd; tour $5; ⏲tasting room 10am-5pm, tour schedules vary) Firestone Vineyard is Santa Barbara's oldest estate winery, founded in 1972. Sweeping views of the vineyard from the sleek, wood-paneled tasting room are as impressive as the value-priced Syrah, pinot noir and Bordeaux-style blends.

Foxen WINERY

(www.foxenvineyard.com; 7600 Foxen Canyon Rd; ⏲11am-4pm) Crafts full-fruited pinot noirs, steel-cut chardonnays and Rhône-style reds inside a solar-powered tasting room on a former cattle ranch. Down the road, its rustic tin-roofed 'shack' pours Bordeaux-style and Cal-Ital varietals under the boutique 'Foxen 7200' label.

Zaca Mesa WINERY

(www.zacamesa.com; 6905 Foxen Canyon Rd; ⏲10am-4pm, to 5pm Fri & Sat late May-early Sep) Known not only for its sustainably-grown estate Rhône varietals and signature Z Cuvée red blend, but also a life-sized outdoor chessboard, shady picnic area and walking trails overlooking the vineyards.

Kenneth Volk WINERY

(www.volkwines.com; 5230 Tepusquet Rd; ⏲10:30am-4:30pm) Only an established cult winemaker could convince oenophiles to drive this far out of their way to taste standard-bearing pinot noir and heritage varietals like floral-scented Malvasia or inky Negrette.

SANTA RITA HILLS

The **Santa Rita Hills Wine Trail** (www.santaritahillswinetrail.com) shines brightly when it comes to ecoconscious farming practices and top-notch pinot noir. Country tasting rooms line a scenic loop west of Hwy 101 via Santa Rosa Rd and Hwy 246.

Alma Rosa WINERY

(www.almarosawinery.com; 7250 Santa Rosa Rd; ⏲11am-4:30pm) Cacti and cobblestones welcome you to the ranch, reached via a long, winding gravel driveway. Knock-out vineyard-designated pinot noirs and a fine pinot blanc made with California-certified organic grapes are poured.

Melville WINERY

(www.melvillewinery.com; 5185 E Hwy 146; ⏲11am-4pm) Mediterranean hillside villa offers estate-grown, small-lot bottled pinot noir, Syrah and chardonnay made by folks who believe in talking about pounds per plant, not tons per acre. Over a dozen different clones of pinot noir alone grow here.

Babcock WINERY

(www.babcockwinery.com; 5175 E Hwy 146; ⏲10:30am-4pm, to 5pm Apr-Oct) Family-owned vineyards overflowing with different varietals – chardonnay, sauvignon blanc, pinot noir, Syrah, cabernet sauvignon and more – let an innovative small-lot winemaker be the star. The Fathom red blend is pilgrimage-worthy.

Santa Barbara Wine Country

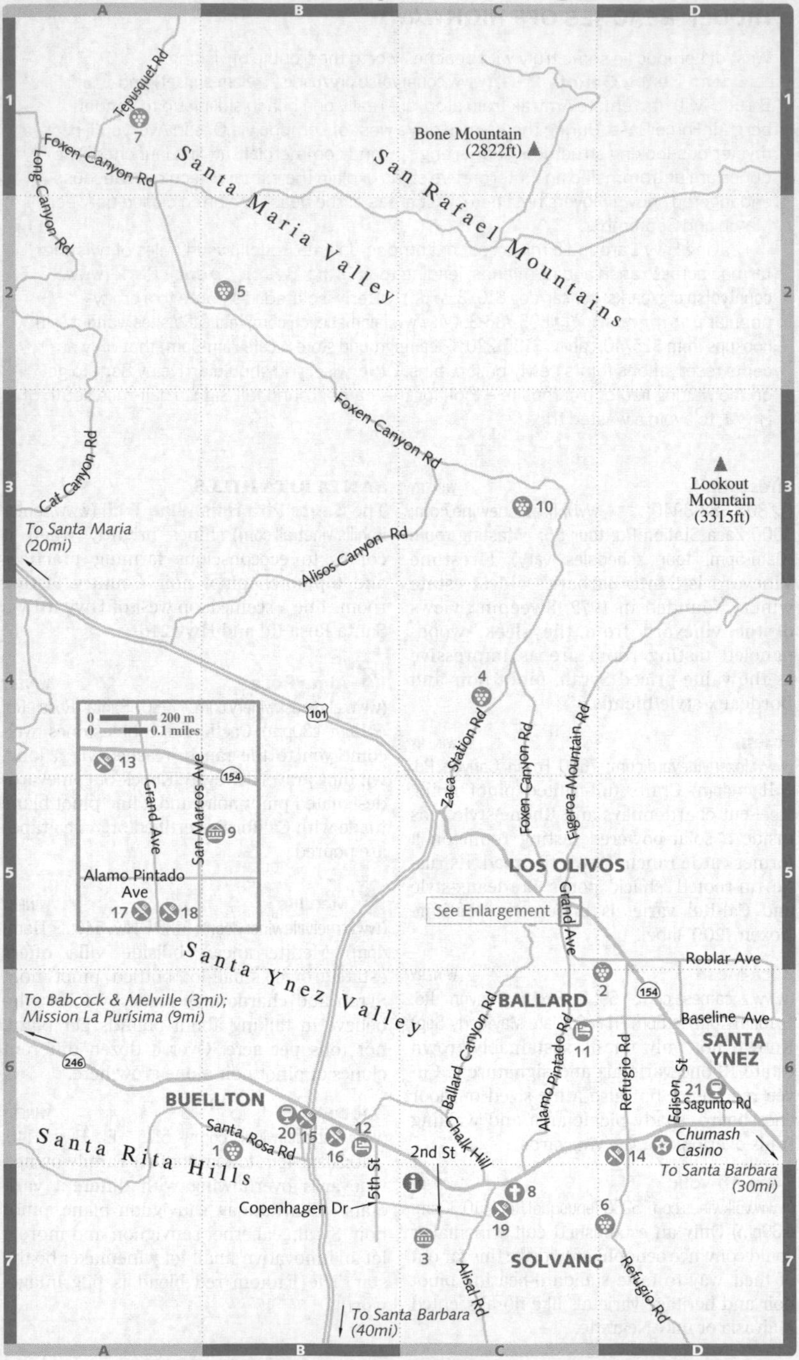

0 — 4 km
0 — 2 miles

Santa Maria Valley
San Rafael Mountains
Bone Mountain (2822ft)
Lookout Mountain (3315ft)
Santa Ynez Valley
Santa Rita Hills
Tepusquet Rd
Foxen Canyon Rd
Long Canyon Rd
Cat Canyon Rd
Alisos Canyon Rd
Zaca Station Rd
Figeroa Mountain Rd
Ballard Canyon Rd
Chalk Hill
Alamo Pintado Rd
Refugio Rd
Edison St
Grand Ave
Roblar Ave
Baseline Ave
Sagunto Rd
Santa Rosa Rd
5th St
2nd St
Copenhagen Dr
Alisal Rd
101
154
246
To Santa Maria (20mi)
To Babcock & Melville (3mi); Mission La Purísima (9mi)
To Santa Barbara (40mi)
To Santa Barbara (30mi)
LOS OLIVOS
BALLARD
SANTA YNEZ
BUELLTON
SOLVANG
Chumash Casino
See Enlargement

0 — 200 m
0 — 0.1 miles
Grand Ave
San Marcos Ave
Alamo Pintado Ave

1 2 3 4 5 6 7 8 9 10 11 12 13 14 15 16 17 18 19 20 21

Santa Barbara Wine Country

Sights

1 Alma Rosa B6
2 Beckmen D6
3 Elverhøj Museum C7
4 Firestone C4
5 Foxen B2
6 Kalyra D7
7 Kenneth Volk A1
8 Mission Santa Inés C7
9 Wildling Art Museum B5
10 Zaca Mesa C3

Sleeping

11 Ballard Inn & Restaurant C6
12 Hadsten House Inn B6

Eating

13 Brothers' Restaurant at Mattei's Tavern A4
14 El Rancho Market D6
15 Ellen's Danish Pancake House B6
16 Hitching Post II B6
17 Los Olivos Café A5
18 Petros A5
19 Solvang Bakery C7

Drinking

20 Avant Tapas & Wine B6
21 Maverick Saloon D6

SANTA YNEZ VALLEY

You'll find dozens of wineries inside the triangle of Hwys 154, 246 and 101, including in downtown Los Olivos and Solvang. Noisy tour groups, harried staff and stingy pours too often disappoint at many popular places, but not at these welcoming wineries.

Beckmen WINERY
(www.beckmenvineyards.com; 2670 Ontiveros Rd; 11am-5pm) Bring a picnic to the duck-pond gazebos at this tranquil winery, where biodynamically farmed, estate-grown Rhône varietals flourish on the unique terroir of Purisima Mountain. Follow Roblar Ave west of Hwy 154.

Kalyra WINERY
(www.kalyrawinery.com; 343 Refugio Rd; 11am-5pm Mon-Fri, 10am-5pm Sat & Sun) An Australian surfer traveled halfway around the world to combine his two loves: surfing and wine making. Try his unique Shiraz–cabernet sauvignon blend made from Australian grapes or more locally grown varietals, all in bottles with Aboriginal art–inspired labels.

AROUND THE WINE COUNTRY TOWNS

Cap'n, we've hit a windmill! **Solvang** is a touristy Danish village founded in 1911 on what was once a 19th-century Spanish colonial mission, later a Mexican *rancho* land grant. With its knickknack stores and cutesy motels, the town is almost as sticky-sweet as the Scandinavian pastries foisted upon the wandering hordes. Solvang's **Elverhøj Museum** (www.elverhoj.org; 1624 Elverhoy Way; adult/child under 13 $3/free; 1-4pm Wed & Thu, noon-4pm Fri-Sun) uncovers the roots of real Danish life in the area, while **Mission Santa Inés** (www.missionsantaines.org; 1760 Mission Dr; adult/child under 12 $5/free; 9am-4:30pm) witnessed an 1824 Chumash revolt against Spanish colonial cruelty.

Farther northwest, the posh ranching town of **Los Olivos** has a four-block-long main street lined with wine-tasting rooms and bars, art galleries, cafes and surprisingly fashionable shops seemingly airlifted straight out of Napa. The petite **Wilding Art Museum** (www.wildingmuseum.org; 2928 San Marcos Ave; admission by donation; 11am-5pm Wed-Sun) exhibits nature-themed California and American Western art.

ALONG HIGHWAY 154 (SAN MARCOS PASS RD)

The **Los Padres National Forest** (www.r5.fs.fed.us/lospadres) offers several good hiking trails off Paradise Rd, which crosses Hwy 154 north of San Marcos Pass. Try the 2-mile round-trip **Red Rock Trail**, where the Santa Ynez River deeply pools among rocks and waterfalls, a tempting spot for swimming and sunbathing. En route to the trailhead, which lies beyond the river crossing, drop by the **ranger station** (805-967-3481; 3505 Paradise Rd; 8:30am-4:30pm Mon-Fri) for posted trail maps and information and a National Forest Adventure Pass for parking ($5 per day).

Just northwest, **Cachuma Lake Recreation Area** (www.cachuma.com; per car $10; sunrise-sunset) is a county-park haven for fishers, canoers and kayakers, with wildlife-watching **cruises** (805-686-5050/5055; adult/child 4-12yr $15/7) and a kid-friendly

nature center (☎805-693-0691; 2265 Hwy 154; ⏱daily Jun-Aug, weekends only Sep-May; 👪).

Tours

Sustainable Vine Wine Tours WINERY TOURS
(☎805-698-3911; www.sustainablevine.com; full-day tour incl lunch $125) Biodiesel van tours of wineries implementing organic and sustainable agricultural practices.

Santa Barbara Wine Country Cycling Tours WINERY TOURS
(☎888-557-8687; www.winecountrycycling.com; bike rentals per day $45-85, half-/full-day tours from $70/135) Cycling tours leave from Santa Ynez; quality road and hybrid mountain bike rentals also available.

Sleeping

Avoid the price-gouging by taking a day trip from Santa Barbara. Otherwise, Buellton has bland chains right off Hwy 101. A few miles east along Hwy 246, Solvang has many more motels and hotels, but don't expect any bargains, especially not on weekends. Smaller wine-country towns offer a handful of historic inns.

Ballard Inn & Restaurant B&B $$$
(☎805-688-7770, 800-638-2466; www.ballardinn.com; 2436 Baseline Ave, Ballard; r incl breakfast $269-345; 📶) For honeymooners and romantics, this contemporary-built inn awaits in the 19th-century stagecoach town of Ballard, flung between Los Olivos and Solvang. Wood-burning fireplaces make private en-suite rooms even more cozy. Rates include wine tastings. Reservations essential.

Hadsten House Inn BOUTIQUE HOTEL $$
(☎805-688-3210, 800-457-5373; www.hadstenhouse.com; 1450 Mission Dr; r incl breakfast $150-255; 📶🏊) This revamped motel has glammed up everything except an uninspiring exterior. Inside, you'll find a heated pool and rooms that are surprisingly plush, with flatscreen TVs, triple-sheeted beds and L'Occitane bath products. Rates include afternoon wine-and-cheese tasting.

Cachuma Lake Recreation Area CAMPGROUND, CABINS $
(☎info 805-686-5055, yurt & cabin reservations 805-686-5050; www.cachuma.com; tent & RV sites without/with hookups from $20/40, yurts $80-105, cabins $100-220) First-come, first-served campsites with access to hot showers fill quickly, especially in summer and on weekends. Book ahead for ecofriendly canvas-sided yurts and knotty pine-paneled cabins (no air-con).

Los Padres National Forest CAMPGROUND $
(☎reservations 877-444-6777; www.recreation.gov; tent & RV sites $19-35) First-come, first-served and reservable sites include Fremont, Paradise and Los Prietos before the ranger station and Upper Oso at the end of Paradise Rd, off Hwy 154.

Eating

Petros MEDITERRANEAN $$$
(☎805-686-5455; www.petrosrestaurant.com; Fess Parker Wine Country Inn & Spa, 2860 Grand Ave, Los Olivos; shared plates $6-18, dinner mains $22-36; ⏱7am-10pm Sun-Thu, to 11pm Fri & Sat) In a sunny, modern clean-lined dining room, sophisticated Greek cuisine makes for a refreshing change from Italianate wine-country kitsch. Grilled pita with sweet-and-savory dips, flatbread pizzas and feta-crusted rack of lamb will satisfy even picky foodies. Reservations recommended.

Los Olivos Café CALIFORNIAN $$$
(☎805-688-7265; www.losolivoscafe.com; 2879 Grand Ave, Los Olivos; mains $12-30; ⏱11:30am-8:30pm) With white canopies and a wisteria-covered trellis, this Cal-Mediterranean bistro swirls up a casual-chic ambience that adds a nice finish to a long day of touring. The menu gets mixed marks; stick with antipasto platters, hearty salads and crispy pizzas, and wine flights at the bar. Reservations essential.

Brothers Restaurant at Mattei's Tavern AMERICAN $$$
(☎805-688-4820; www.matteistavern.com; 2350 Railway Ave, Los Olivos; mains $18-44; ⏱5-9pm) You half expect a stagecoach to come thundering up in time for dinner at this authentic late-19th-century tavern. At checkered-tablecloth tables, dine on bold American country flavors like hickory-smoked salmon and oven-roasted rack of lamb. Get gussied up, pardner! Reservations advisable.

Hitching Post II STEAKHOUSE $$$
(☎805-688-0676; www.hitchingpost2.com; 406 E Hwy 246, Buellton; mains $22-48; ⏱5-9:30pm Mon-Fri, 4-9:30pm Sat & Sun) You'll be hard-pressed to find better steaks and chops than at this legendary, old-guard country steakhouse, which serves oak-grilled steaks and baby back ribs and makes its own pinot noir

(which is damn good, by the way). Reservations essential.

El Rancho Market FAST FOOD, GROCERIES $
(www.elranchomarket.com; 2886 Mission Dr (Hwy 246), Solvang; ⏲6am-10pm) If you want to fill a picnic basket, not to mention reintegrate into society after a day of windmills, clogs and *abelskiver*, this supermarket has a fantastic deli case; take-out barbecue, soups and salads; bargain wine racks; and an espresso bar.

Ellen's Danish Pancake House BREAKFAST $$
(www.ellensdanishpancakehouse.com; 272 Ave of the Flags, Buellton; mains $6-12; ⏲6am-8pm Tue-Sun, to 2pm Mon; 👪) Who needs Solvang? Locals know to come here for the wine country's best Danish pancakes, Danish sausages and not-so-Danish Belgian waffles.

Solvang Bakery BAKERY $
(www.solvangbakery.com; 460 Alisal Rd, Solvang; items from $2; ⏲7am-6pm) Solvang's bakeries prove an irresistible draw, but most aren't especially good. This tasty exception vends Danish cookies, iced almond butter rings and more.

Drinking & Entertainment

Avant Tapas & Wine WINE BAR
(www.avantwines.com; 35 Industrial Way, Buellton; ⏲11am-8pm Thu & Sun, to 10pm Fri & Sat) Hidden upstairs in an industrial-chic space, this under-the-radar gathering spot tempts with hot and cold tapas, pizzas and DIY tastes of over 30 boutique wines barreled on-site.

Maverick Saloon BAR, NIGHTCLUB
(www.mavericksaloon.org; 3687 Sagunto St, Santa Ynez; ⏲noon-2am) In the one-horse town of Santa Ynez, en route to Chumash Casino, this Harley-friendly honky-tonk stages live country-and-western and rock bands, late-night DJs and dancing on weekends.

Information

The **Santa Barbara County Vintners' Association** (www.sbcountywines.com) publishes a self-guided winery touring map, available free at tasting rooms and the **Solvang Visitors Center** (☎805-688-6144, 800-468-6765; www.solvangusa.com; 1639 Copenhagen Dr, Solvang; ⏲9am-5pm).

Getting There & Around

The wine country is northwest of Santa Barbara; drive there in under an hour via Hwy 101 or more scenic, narrow and winding Hwy 154 (San Marcos Pass Rd). Hwy 246 runs east–west across the bottom of the Santa Ynez Valley, passing Solvang (where it's called Mission Dr) between Santa Ynez (off Hwy 154) and Buellton (off Hwy 101).

Santa Barbara

Frankly put, this area is damn pleasant to putter around. Just a 90-minute drive north of Los Angeles, tucked between mountains and the Pacific, Santa Barbara basks smugly in its near-perfection. Founded by a Spanish mission, the city's signature red-tile roofs, white stucco buildings and Mediterranean vibe have long given credence to its claim to the title of the 'American Riviera.' Santa Barbara is blessed with almost freakishly good weather, and no one can deny the appeal of those beaches that line the city tip to toe either. Just ignore those pesky oil derricks out to sea.

History

For hundreds of years before the arrival of the Spanish, the Chumash people thrived here, setting up trading routes over to the Channel Islands, which they reached in redwood canoes called *tomols*. In 1542 explorer Juan Rodríguez Cabrillo sailed into the channel and claimed it for Spain, then quickly met his doom on a nearby island.

The Chumash had little reason for concern until the permanent return of the Spanish in the late 1700s, when priests and soldiers arrived to establish military outposts and to convert the tribe to Christianity. The Spaniards forced the Chumash to evacuate the Channel Islands, construct the missions and presidios and provide subsequent labor. Many Native Americans changed their diet and clothing, and died of European diseases, ill treatment and culture shock.

Mexican ranchers arrived after wining independence from Spain in 1821. Easterners began arriving en masse with the 1849 Gold Rush, and by the late 1890s the city was an established vacation spot for the wealthy. After a massive earthquake in 1925, laws were passed requiring much of the city to be rebuilt in its now characteristic faux-Spanish style of white-stucco buildings with red-tiled roofs.

Sights

Mission Santa Barbara MISSION
(www.sbmission.org; 2201 Laguna St; adult/child 6-15yr $5/1; ⏲9am-4:30pm) Reigning from a hilltop above town, the 'Queen of the Missions' became the 10th California mission

Downtown Santa Barbara

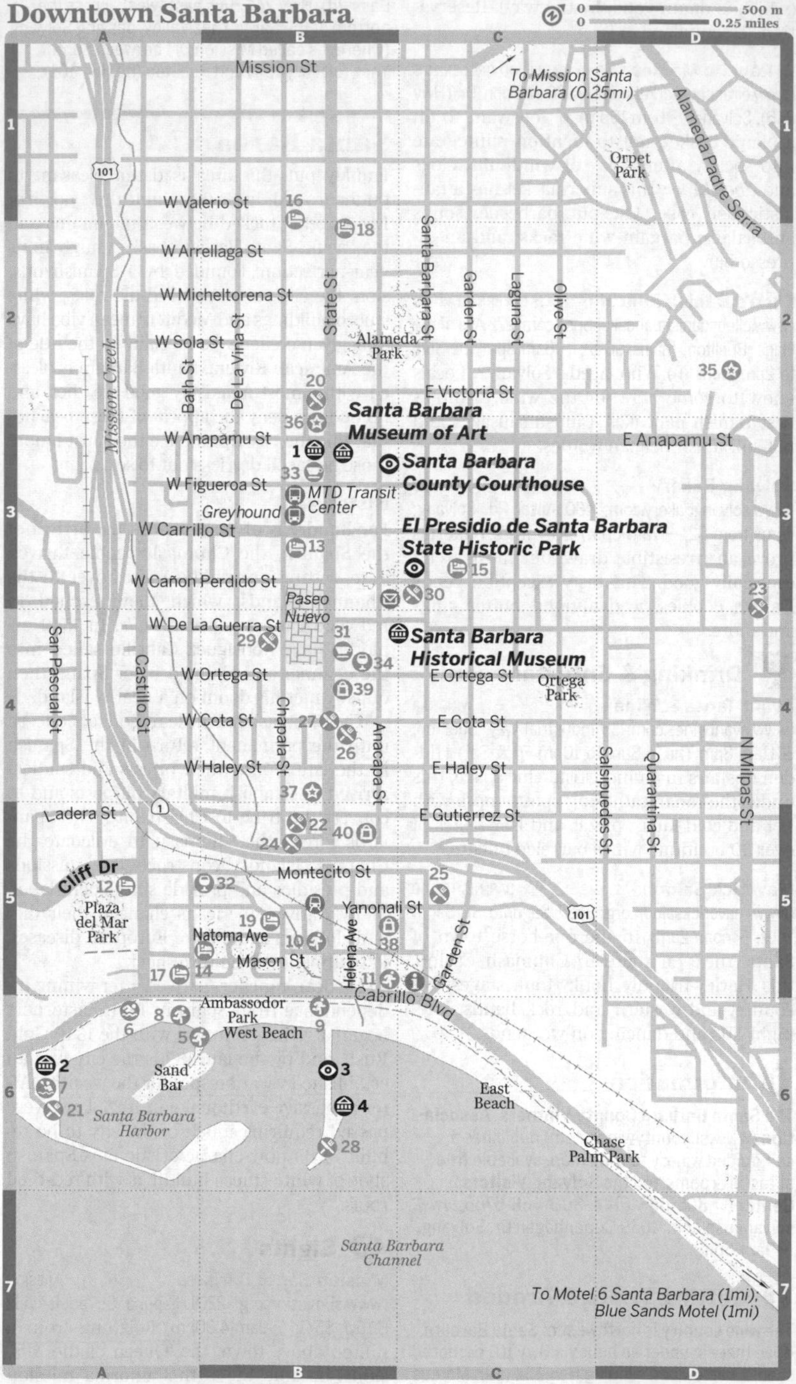

Downtown Santa Barbara

Top Sights

El Presidio de Santa Barbara State Historic Park ... C3
Santa Barbara County Courthouse ... B3
Santa Barbara Historical Museum ... B4
Santa Barbara Museum of Art ... B3

Sights

1 Karpeles Manuscript Library ... B3
2 Santa Barbara Maritime Museum ... A6
3 Stearns Wharf ... B6
4 Ty Warner Sea Center ... B6

Activities, Courses & Tours

5 Condor Express ... A6
6 Los Baños del Mar ... A6
7 Paddle Sports ... A6
8 Santa Barbara Sailing Center ... A6
9 Santa Barbara Trolley (Main Stop) ... B6
10 Wheel Fun ... B5
11 Wheel Fun ... B5

Sleeping

12 Brisas del Mar ... A5
13 Canary Hotel ... B3
14 Harbor House Inn ... B5
15 Inn of the Spanish Garden ... C3
16 James House ... D1
17 Marina Beach Motel ... A5
18 Presidio Motel ... B2
19 Santa Barbara Tourist Hostel ... B5

Eating

20 Bouchon ... B2
21 Brophy Bros ... A6
22 D'Angelo Pastry & Bread ... B5
23 El Buen Gusto ... D3
24 Lilly's Taquería ... B5
25 Metropulos ... C5
Olio Pizzeria ... (see 20)
26 Palace Grill ... B4
27 Santa Barbara Farmers Market ... B4
28 Santa Barbara Shellfish Company ... B6
29 Silvergreens ... B4
30 Sojourner ... C3

Drinking

31 Blenders in the Grass ... B4
32 Brewhouse ... B5
33 French Press ... B3
34 Press Room ... B4

Entertainment

35 Santa Barbara Bowl ... D2
36 Soho ... B3
37 Velvet Jones ... B4

Shopping

38 Channel Island Surfboards ... B5
39 CRSVR ... B4
40 REI ... B5

on the feast day of Saint Barbara in 1786. Occupied by Catholic priests ever since, the mission escaped Mexico's policy of forced secularization. Today it functions as a Franciscan friary, parish church and historical museum. The 1820 stone church has Chumash artwork and beautiful cloisters; its imposing Doric facade, an homage to a chapel in ancient Rome, is topped by twin bell towers. Behind the church is an extensive cemetery – look for skull carvings over the door leading outside – with 4000 Chumash graves and the elaborate mausoleums of early settlers.

El Presidio de Santa Barbara State Historic Park HISTORIC SITE
(805-965-0093; www.sbthp.org; 123 E Cañon Perdido St; adult/child under 17yr $5/free; 10:30am-4:30pm) Founded in 1782 to protect missions between San Diego and Monterey, this fort was Spain's last military stronghold in Alta California. But its mission wasn't solely to protect – the presidio also served as a social and political hub, and as a stopping point for traveling Spanish military. Today this small urban park shelters some of the city's oldest structures, which seem to be in constant need of propping up and restoring. Be sure to stop by the chapel, its interior radiant with kaleidoscopic color. Tickets also include admission to **Casa de la Guerra** (15 E De La Guerra St; noon-4pm Sat & Sun), a 19th-century colonial adobe displaying Spanish-American heritage exhibits.

FREE **Santa Barbara County Courthouse** HISTORIC BUILDING
(1100 Anacapa St; 8:30am-4:45pm Mon-Fri, 10am-4:45pm Sat & Sun) Built in Spanish-Moorish Revival style, it's an absurdly beautiful place to be on trial. The magnificent 1929

courthouse features hand-painted ceilings, wrought-iron chandeliers and tiles from Tunisia and Spain. Step inside the hushed 2nd-floor mural room depicting Spanish colonial history, then climb the 85ft clocktower for arch-framed panoramas of the city, ocean and mountains. Docent-led tours are usually offered at 2pm daily and 10:30am on Monday, Tuesday, Wednesday and Friday.

Santa Barbara Historical Museum MUSEUM
(www.santabarbaramuseum.com; 136 E De La Guerra St; admission by donation; ⏲10am-5pm Tue-Sat, noon-5pm Sun) Embracing a romantic cloistered adobe courtyard, this off-the-beaten-path museum has an endlessly fascinating collection of local memorabilia, ranging from simply beautiful, like Chumash woven baskets and colonial-era textiles, to intriguing, such as an intricately carved coffer once belonging to Junípero Serra. Learn about Santa Barbara's involvement in toppling the last Chinese monarchy, among other interesting footnotes in local history.

Santa Barbara Botanic Garden GARDEN
(www.sbbg.org; 1212 Mission Canyon Rd; adult/child 2-12yr/student $8/4/6; ⏲9am-5pm Nov-Feb, to 6pm Mar-Oct; 👪🐾) Take a soul-satisfying jaunt around this 40-acre botanic garden, devoted to California's native flora. Over 5 miles of partly wheelchair-accessible trails meander through cacti, redwoods and wildflowers past the old mission dam, originally built by Chumash tribespeople. Guided tours are available at 2pm daily and 11am on Saturday and Sunday. Ask for a 'Family Discovery Sheet' from the admission kiosk. Leashed dogs are welcome. See the website or call ahead for directions; it's about a 10-minute drive uphill from the mission.

Santa Barbara Museum of Art MUSEUM
(www.sbma.net; 1130 State St; adult/child 6-17yr $9/6; ⏲11am-5pm Tue-Sun; 👪) Culture vultures delight in these downtown galleries, which hold an impressive, well-edited collection of contemporary Californian artists, modern masters like Matisse and Chagall, 20th-century photography and Asian art, with provocative special exhibits, an interactive children's gallery and a cafe. Sundays are pay-what-you-wish admission.

Santa Barbara Maritime Museum MUSEUM
(www.sbmm.org; 113 Harbor Way; adult/child 1-5yr/youth 6-17yr $7/2/4, all free 3rd Thu of the month; ⏲10am-5pm Thu-Tue Sep-May, to 6pm Jun-Aug; 👪) Even li'l cap'ns will get a kick out of this museum by the yacht harbor. A two-level exhibition hall celebrates Santa Barbara's briny history with historical artifacts and memorabilia, hands-on and virtual-reality exhibits, and a small theater for documentary videos.

FREE **Karpeles Manuscript Library** MUSEUM
(www.rain.org/~karpeles; 21 W Anapamu St; ⏲10am-4pm) Stuffed with historical written artifacts, this museum is an embarrassment of riches for history nerds, science geeks and literary and music lovers. Rotating exhibits often spotlight literary masterworks, from Shakespeare to Sherlock Holmes.

Stearns Wharf LANDMARK
(www.stearnswharf.org) At its southern end, State St runs into Stearns Wharf, once co-owned by tough-guy actor Jimmy Cagney. Built in 1872, it's the West Coast's oldest continuously operating wooden pier. There's 90 minutes of free parking with validation from any shop or restaurant, but it's more fun to walk atop the very bumpy wooden slats.

Beaches

The long, sandy stretch between Stearns Wharf and Montecito is **East Beach**, Santa Barbara's largest and most crowded. At its far end, near the Biltmore hotel, Armani swimsuits and Gucci sunglasses abound at chic, but narrow **Butterfly Beach**.

Between Stearns Wharf and the harbor, **West Beach** is popular with tourists. There **Los Baños del Mar** (☎805-966-6110; 401 Shoreline Dr; admission $6; 👪), a municipal heated outdoor pool complex, is good for recreational and lap swimming, plus a kids' wading pool. Call for opening hours. West of the harbor, **Leadbetter Beach** is the spot for beginning surfers and windsurfers. Climbing the stairs on the west end takes you to **Shoreline Park**, with picnic tables and awesome kite-flying conditions.

Further west, near the junction of Cliff Dr and Las Positas Rd, family-friendly **Arroyo Burro (Hendry's) Beach** has free parking and a restaurant and bar. Above the beach is the **Douglas Family Preserve**, offering cliffside romps for dogs.

Outside town off Hwy 101 you'll find even more spacious, family-friendly **state beaches** (☎805-958-1033; www.parks.ca.gov; per car $10; ⏲sunrise-sunset; 👪), including **Carpinteria State Beach**, about 12 miles southeast of

TOP 5 SANTA BARBARA SPOTS FOR CHILDREN

Museum of Natural History (www.sbnature.org; 2559 Puesta del Sol; adult/child 3-12yr/youth 13-17yr $11/7/8; ⏲10am-5pm; 👪) Stuffed wildlife mounts, glittering gems and a pitch-dark planetarium captivate kids' imaginations. It's about a 10-minute drive uphill from the mission.

Arroyo Burro (Hendry's) Beach (p330) Wide sandy beach, away from the tourist crowds, popular with local families.

Ty Warner Sea Center (www.sbnature.org/seacenter; 211 Stearns Wharf; adult/child 2-12yr/youth 13-17yr $8/5/7; ⏲10am-5pm; 👪) Gawk at a gray whale skeleton, touch tide-pool critters and crawl through a 1500-gallon surge tank.

Santa Barbara Sailing Center (below) Short, one-hour harbor sails let young 'uns see sea lions up close.

Santa Barbara Maritime Museum (p330) Peer through a periscope, reel in a virtual fish or check out the gorgeous model ships.

Santa Barbara, and **Refugio & El Capitán State Beaches**, over 20 miles west in Goleta.

Activities

Surfing, Kayaking, Sailing & Whale-Watching

Santa Barbara's proximity to the wind-breaking Channel Islands makes it a good spot to learn how to ride the waves. Unless you're a novice, conditions are too mellow in summer; swells kick back up in winter. Pro-level **Rincon Point** in Carpinteria has long, glassy, point-break waves, while **Leadbetter Point** is best for beginners. From spring through fall, kayakers can paddle the calm waters of the harbor or the coves of the Gaviota coast, or hitch a ride out to the Channel Islands for more solitude and sea caves. Meanwhile, stand-up paddle boarders can get their feet wet in the city's harbor.

Santa Barbara Sailing Center KAYAKING, SAILING
(☎805-962-2826, 800-350-9090; www.sbsail.com; 133 Harbor Way; rental per hr single/double kayak $10/15, kayaking lessons & tours $55-95, catamaran cruises $10-65) Rents kayaks and leads guided paddles, teaches sailing and offers sunset cocktail and wildlife-watching cruises.

Santa Barbara Adventure Co KAYAKING, SURFING
(☎805-884-9283; www.sbadventureco.com; kayaking tours $50-105, surfing & SUP lessons $99-125) Offers traditional board-surfing and SUP lessons, and leads guided coastal kayaking tours – ask about stargazing floats.

Paddle Sports KAYAKING, SURFING
(☎805-899-4925; www.kayaksb.com; 117b Harbor Way; surfboard rentals $10-30, kayak rentals $25-120, SUP rentals $40-65, 1hr SUP lesson $65, 2hr kayak tour $50) Friendly community-based outfitter, conveniently positioned right at the harbor.

Condor Express BOAT TOURS
(☎805-882-0088, 888-779-4253; www.condorcruises.com; 301 W Cabrillo Blvd; adult/child 5-12yr from $48/25) Runs year-round narrated whale-watching tours, including out to the Channel Islands, aboard a smooth-sailing catamaran.

Cycling

A paved recreational path stretches for 3 miles along the waterfront between Leadbetter Beach and Andrée Clark Bird Refuge, passing Stearns Wharf. **Santa Barbara Bicycle Coalition** (www.sbbike.org) offers free cycling tour maps online.

Wheel Fun CYCLING
(www.wheelfunrentals.com; ⏲8am-8pm) Cabrillo (23 E Cabrillo Blvd); State St (22 State St) Rents beach cruisers, hybrid mountain bikes and cheesy pedal-powered surreys with the fringe on top (local kids like to bomb 'em with water balloons!).

Hang-Gliding & Paragliding

For condor's-eye ocean views, **Eagle Paragliding** (☎805-968-0980; www.eagleparagliding.com) and **Fly Above All** (☎805-965-3733; www.flyaboveall.com) offer paragliding lessons (from $200) and tandem flights ($60 to $200). For hang-gliding lessons and tandem flights, contact **Fly Away** (805-403-8487; www.flyawayhanggliding.com).

Tours

Architectural Foundation of Santa Barbara WALKING TOURS
(805-965-6307; www.afsb.org; adult/child under 12yr $10/free) Nonprofit organization offers 90-minute fascinating guided small-group walking tours of downtown's art, history and architecture, usually on Saturday and Sunday mornings.

Santa Barbara Trolley BUS TOURS
(805-965-0353; www.sbtrolley.com; adult/child 3-12yr $19/8; 10am-5:30pm) Biodiesel trolley buses make a narrated 90-minute one-way loop around major tourist attractions, starting at Stearns Wharf (last departure 4pm). Hop-on, hop-off tickets are valid all day and qualify for small discounts at select attractions.

Festivals & Events

First Thursday CULTURE
(www.santabarbaradowntown.com) On the first Thursday evening of every month, downtown art galleries, museums and theaters come alive for a big street party with live entertainment.

Santa Barbara International Film Festival CINEMA
(http://sbiff.org) Film buffs arrive in droves for screenings of independent US and foreign films in late January and early February.

I Madonnari Italian Street Painting Festival CULTURE
(www.imadonnarifestival.com) Chalk drawings adorn Santa Barbara's mission sidewalks over Memorial Day weekend.

Summer Solstice Celebration CULTURE
(www.solsticeparade.com) Wacky, wildly popular – and just plain wild – performance-art parade and outdoor fun in late June.

Old Spanish Days Fiesta CULTURE
(www.oldspanishdays-fiesta.org) The city gets packed in early August for this long-running but slightly overrated heritage festival featuring rodeos, music and dancing.

Avocado Festival FOOD
(www.avofest.com) In small-town Carpinteria, witness the world's largest guacamole vat in early October, with food and arts-and-crafts vendors and live bands.

Sleeping

Prepare for sticker shock: basic motel rooms by the beach command over $200 in summer. Don't show up without reservations, especially on weekends. Cheaper motels and hotels cluster along upper State St and Hwy 101 between Goleta and Carpinteria.

TOP CHOICE **Inn of the Spanish Garden** BOUTIQUE HOTEL $$$
(805-564-4700, 866-564-4700; http://spanishgardeninn.com; 915 Garden St; d incl breakfast $259-519;) At this elegant Spanish Revival-style downtown hotel, two dozen romantic rooms and suites have balconies and patios overlooking a gracious fountain courtyard. Beds have luxurious linens, bathrooms boast deep soaking tubs and concierge service is top-notch.

Four Seasons Resort – The Biltmore RESORT $$$
(805-969-2261, 800-819-5053; www.fourseasons.com/santabarbara; 1260 Channel Dr; d from $595;) Wear white linen and live like Jay Gatsby at the oh-so-cushy 1927 Biltmore, Santa Barbara's iconic Spanish Colonial–style hotel and spa, overlooking Butterfly Beach. Every detail is perfect, from bathrooms with Mediterranean tiles to hideaway garden cottages for honeymooners. Wi-fi in lobby and poolside only. The resort is a 15-minute drive from downtown via Hwy 101 southbound.

El Capitan Canyon CABINS, CAMPGROUND $$
(805-685-3887, 866-352-2729; www.elcapitancanyon.com; 11560 Calle Real, off Hwy 101; safari tents $155, cabins $225-350;) Go 'glamping' in this woodsy car-free zone near El Capitán State Beach, a 20-mile drive west of Santa Barbara via Hwy 101. Enjoy the great outdoors by day, and rustic safari tents or creekside cedar cabins with heavenly mattresses, gas fireplaces and backyard firepits by night.

Canary Hotel HOTEL $$$
(805-884-0300, 877-468-3515; www.canarysantabarbara.com; 31 W Carrillo St; d from $299;) Downtown's sleekest multi-story hotel has a rooftop pool and a sunset-watching perch for cocktails. Posh accommodations have four-poster Spanish-framed beds and all mod cons, but 'suites' are just over-

sized rooms. Ambient street noise may leave you sleepless. Pet fee $35.

James House B&B $$$
(☎805-569-5853; www.jameshousesantabarbara.com; 1632 Chapala St; r incl breakfast $190-240;) For a traditional B&B experience, revel in this stately Queen Anne Victorian run by a charmingly hospitable owner. All of the antique-filled rooms are sheer elegance, with lofty ceilings, some fireplaces and none of that shabby-chic look. Full sit-down breakfast served.

Harbor House Inn MOTEL $$
(☎805-962-9745, 888-474-6789; www.harborhouseinn.com; 104 Bath St; r $129-335;) All of these brightly lit studios inside a converted motel have hardwood floors, small kitchens and a cheery design scheme. Rates include a welcome basket of breakfast goodies, a DVD library and three-speed bikes to borrow. Pet fee $15.

Agave Inn MOTEL $$
(☎805-687-6009; www.agaveinnsb.com; 3222 State St; r $79-209;) While it's still just a motel at heart, this boutique-on-a-budget property's 'Mexican pop meets modern' motif livens things up with a color palette out of a Frieda Kahlo painting. Family-sized rooms come with kitchenettes and pull-out sofabeds. It's a 10-minute drive north of downtown.

Presidio Motel MOTEL $$
(☎805-963-1355; http://thepresidiomotel.com; 1620 State St; r incl breakfast $119-220;) Presidio is to lodging what H&M is to shopping: a cheap, trendy alternative. Just north of downtown, these crisp, modern motel rooms have panache, with dreamy bedding and art-splashed walls. Noise can be an issue, though. Free loaner beach cruisers.

Brisas del Mar HOTEL $$
(☎805-966-2219, 800-468-1988; www.sbhotels.com; 223 Castillo St; r incl breakfast $145-290; @) Big kudos for the freebies (DVDs, wine and cheese, milk and cookies) and the Mediterranean-style front section, although the motel wing is unlovely. Its sister properties away from the beach may be lower-priced.

State Park Campgrounds CAMPGROUND $
(☎reservations 800-444-7275; www.reserveamerica.com; tent & RV sites $35-50, hike-and-bike sites $10) Under a 30-minute drive from Santa Barbara, Carpinteria, Refugio and El Capitán State Beaches each offer a jam-packed, popular campground with flush toilets, hot showers, BBQ grills and picnic tables. Reserve ahead.

> **SANTA BARBARA'S URBAN WINE TRAIL**
>
> No wheels to head up to Santa Barbara's wine country? No problem! Walk between almost a dozen wine-tasting rooms (and a killer microbrewery, too) near the beach, southeast of downtown. You can join the burgeoning **Urban Wine Trail** (www.urbanwinetrailsb.com) anywhere along its route. Most wine-tasting rooms are open from 11am to 6pm daily.

Marina Beach Motel MOTEL $$
(☎805-963-9311, 877-627-4621; www.marinabeachmotel.com; 21 Bath St; r $115-289; @) Flower-festooned, one-story motor lodge by the sea, with some kitchenettes; pet fee $10.

Blue Sands Motel MOTEL $$
(☎805-965-1624; www.thebluesands.com; 421 S Milpas St; r $99-259;) Kinda kitschy two-story motel just steps from East Beach, with some kitchens; pet fee $10.

Motel 6 Santa Barbara MOTEL $$
(☎805-564-1392, 800-466-8356; www.motel6.com; 443 Corona del Mar; r $85-185;) The very first Motel 6, remodeled with Ikea-esque design; pet fee $10.

Santa Barbara Tourist Hostel HOSTEL $
(☎805-963-0154; www.sbhostel.com; 134 Chapala St; dm $25-43, r $79-139; check-in 2:30-11:15pm; @) Traveling strangers, trains rumbling by and a rowdy bar just steps from your door – it's either the perfect country-and-western song or this low-slung, tattered hostel.

Eating

TOP CHOICE **Bouchon** FRENCH $$$
(☎805-730-1160; www.bouchonsantabarbara.com; 9 W Victoria St; mains $28-36; 5:30-9pm Sun-Thu, to 10pm Fri & Sat) Flavorful French cooking with a seasonal California influence is on the menu at convivial Bouchon (meaning 'wine cork'). Locally grown farm produce and ranched meats marry beautifully with more than 30 regional wines by the glass. Lovebirds, book a table on the candlelit patio.

TOP CHOICE **Santa Barbara Shellfish Company** SEAFOOD $$
(www.sbfishhouse.com; 230 Stearns Wharf; dishes $5-19; ⏲11am-9pm) 'From sea to skillet to plate' best describes this end-of-the-wharf crab shack that's more of a counter joint. Great lobster bisque, ocean views and the same location for 25 years.

Olio Pizzeria ITALIAN $$
(☎805-899-2699; www.oliopizzeria.com; 11 W Victoria St; dishes $3-24; ⏲11:30am-2pm Mon-Sat, 5-10pm Sun-Thu, to 11pm Fri & Sat) Cozy, high-ceilinged pizzeria and enoteca with a happening wine bar. It proffers a tempting selection of crispy pizzas, imported cheeses and meats, traditional antipasti and *dolci* (desserts).

Palace Grill SOUTHERN $$$
(www.palacegrill.com; 8 E Cota St; lunch mains $8-15, dinner mains $16-30; ⏲11:30am-3pm daily, 5:30-10pm Sun-Thu, to 11pm Fri & Sat; 👪) With all the exuberance of Mardi Gras, this N'awlins grill dishes up delectable biscuits and ginormous (if only so-so) plates of jambalaya, gumbo ya-ya and blackened catfish. Act unsurprised if the staff lead diners in a rousing sing-along.

Silvergreens HEALTHY $$
(www.silvergreens.com; 791 Chapala St; dishes $4-10; ⏲7:30am-10pm Mon-Fri, 11am-10pm Sun; 👪🖉) Who says fast food can't be fresh and tasty? With the tag line 'Eat smart, live well,' this sun-drenched cafe makes nutritionally sound (check the calorie counts on your receipt) salads, soups, sandwiches and breakfast burritos.

Brophy Bros SEAFOOD $$
(www.brophybros.com; 119 Harbor Way; mains $9-20; ⏲11am-10pm Sun-Thu, to 11pm Fri & Sat) A longtime favorite for its fresh-off-the-dock seafood, rowdy atmosphere, salty harborside setting and sunset-view deck. Skip the long lines for a table and start knocking back oyster shooters and Bloody Marys at the bar.

El Buen Gusto MEXICAN $
(836 N Milpas St; dishes $3-8; ⏲8am-9pm) While waiting for authentic south-of-the-border tacos, kick back at plasticky booths with an *agua fresca* or cold Pacifico as Mexican music videos and soccer games blare on TVs. *Menudo* (tripe soup) and *birria* (spicy stew) are weekend specials.

D'Angelo Pastry & Bread CAFE $
(25 W Gutierrez St; dishes $2-8; ⏲7am-2pm) This retrolicious downtown bakery with shiny-silver sidewalk bistro tables is a perfect quick breakfast or brunch spot, whether for a buttery croissant and rich espresso or Iron Chef Cat Cora's favorite 'Eggs Rose.'

Sojourner HEALTH FOOD $$
(www.sojournercafe.com; 134 E Cañon Perdido St; mains $8-15; ⏲11am-11pm Mon-Sat, to 10pm Sun; 🖉) This granola-flavored favorite has been doing its all-natural, mostly meatless magic since 1978. Chili-spiced tempeh tacos and ginger tofu wonton pillows are tasty. Fair-

WORTH A TRIP

OJAI

Hollywood director Frank Capra chose the Ojai Valley to represent mythical Shangri-La in his 1937 movie *Lost Horizon*. Today Ojai (pronounced '*oh*-hi', meaning 'moon' to the Chumash) attracts artists, organic farmers, spiritual seekers and anyone ready to indulge in spa-style pampering. Start by wandering around Arcade Plaza, a maze of Mission Revival–style buildings on Ojai Ave (downtown's main drag), alive with arty boutiques and cafes.

Ojai is famous for the rosy glow that emanates from its mountains at sunset, the so-called 'Pink Moment.' The ideal vantage point for catching it is the peaceful lookout **Meditation Mount** (www.meditationmount.org; 10340 Reeves Rd; admission free). Head east of downtown on Ojai Ave (Hwy 150), then take a left at Boccali's farm-stand pizzeria. For hiking trail maps to hot springs, waterfalls and more mountaintop viewpoints, visit the **Ojai Ranger Station** (☎805-646-4348; www.fs.fed.us/r5/lospadres; 1190 E Ojai Ave; ⏲8am-4:30pm Mon-Fri).

Ojai is about 35 miles east of Santa Barbara via Hwys 101 and 150, or 15 miles inland from Ventura via Hwy 33.

trade coffee, local beers and wines and delish desserts.

Lilly's Taquería MEXICAN $
(www.lillystacos.com; 310 Chapala St; dishes from $2; ⌚11am-9pm Mon & Wed-Thu, to 10pm Fri & Sat, to 9:30pm Sun) Almost always a line out the door for *adobada* (marinated pork) tacos.

Metropulos DELI $
(www.metrofinefoods.com; 216 E Yanonali St; dishes $6-10; ⌚8:30am-5:30pm Mon-Fri, 10am-4pm Sat) Artisan breads, cheeses and cured meats, hand-crafted sandwiches and market-fresh salads.

Santa Barbara Farmers Market MARKET $
(www.sbfarmersmarket.org; cnr Santa Barbara & Cota Sts; ⌚8:30am-1pm Sat) Farmers and food vendors also set up along lower State St on Tuesday afternoons.

Drinking

Santa Barbara's after-dark scene revolves around college-age bars and nightclubs on lower State St. Saturday nights here get rowdy.

Brewhouse BREWPUB
(www.brewhousesb.com; 229 W Montecito St; ⌚11am-11pm Sun-Thu, to midnight Fri & Sat;) This rowdy dive down by the railroad tracks crafts its own unique small-batch beers (Saint Bar's Belgian-style rules!) and has cool art and rockin' live music Wednesday to Saturday nights.

Press Room PUB
(http://pressroomsb.com; 15 E Ortega St) This downtown pub attracts a slew of students and European travelers. There's no better place to watch the footie, stuff quarters in the jukebox and be jovially abused by the British bartender.

French Press COFFEE SHOP
(1101 State St; ⌚6am-7pm Mon-Fri, 7am-7pm Sat, 8am-5pm Sun;) This State St coffee shop shames the chains with beans roasted in Santa Cruz, shiny silver espresso machines from Italy and baristas that know how to pull their shots and mix spicy chais.

Blenders in the Grass JUICE, SMOOTHIES $
(www.drinkblenders.com; 720 State St; drinks $3-6; ⌚7am-9pm Mon-Thu, 7am-10pm Fri, 8am-10pm Sat, 8am-9pm Sun) For a quick, healthy burst of energy, pop by this locally owned juice and smoothie bar for a wheatgrass shot or date milkshake.

Hollister Brewing Co BREWPUB
(www.hollisterbrewco.com; Camino Real Marketplace, 6980 Marketplace Dr, off Hwy 101 exit Glen Annie Rd; ⌚11am-10pm) Beer geeks won't regret making the trip out near the UCSB campus to sample unique brews like White Star XPA or Hip Hopimperial ale. It's about a 20-minute drive from downtown via Hwy 101 northbound.

☆ Entertainment

For a calendar of events and live shows, including in downtown's historic movie palaces and theaters, pick up the free weekly *Santa Barbara Independent* (www.independent.com) or Friday's 'Scene' guide from the *Santa Barbara News-Press* (www.sbnewspress.com).

Santa Barbara Bowl MUSIC, COMEDY
(☎805-962-7411; www.sbbowl.org; 1122 N Milpas St) Built by the 1930s New Deal–era WPA labor, this outdoor stone amphitheater grants ocean views from the highest cheap seats. Kick back in the summer sunshine or under the stars during live rock, jazz and folk concerts and stand-up comedy shows, including big-name acts.

Soho MUSIC
(☎805-962-7776; www.sohosb.com; 1221 State St, 2nd level) An unpretentious brick room hosts live music almost nightly, upstairs inside a downtown office complex. Lineups range from indie rock, jazz, folk, funk and world beats to DJs.

Velvet Jones MUSIC, COMEDY
(☎805-965-8676; www.velvet-jones.com; 423 State St) Long-running downtown punk and indie dive for rock, hip-hop, comedy and 18+ DJ nights for the city's college crowd. Many bands stop here between gigs in LA and San Francisco.

Zodo's Bowling & Beyond BOWLING, BILLIARDS
(☎805-967-0128; www.zodos.com; 5925 Calle Real, off Hwy 101 exit Fairview Rd;) With over 40 beers on tap, pool tables and a video arcade (Skee-Ball!), this bowling alley near UCSB is good ol' family fun. Call for schedules of open-play lanes and 'glow bowling' nights. It's a 15-minute drive from downtown via Hwy 101 northbound.

CAR-FREE SANTA BARBARA

If you use public transportation to get to Santa Barbara, you can get valuable hotel discounts, plus get a nice swag bag of coupons for various activities and attractions, all courtesy of **Santa Barbara Car Free** (www.santabarbaracarfree.org).

Shopping

Downtown's **State St** is packed with shops, from vintage clothing to brand-name boutiques; cheapskates stick to lower State St, while trust-fund babies head uptown. For indie shops, dive into the **Funk Zone**, east of State St, just south of Hwy 101.

Channel Islands Surfboards OUTDOORS
(www.cisurfboards.com; 36 Anacapa St) Dying to take home a handcrafted, authentic SoCal surfboard? Down in the Funk Zone, this contempo surf shack turns out innovative pro-worthy board designs, cool surfer threads and beanie hats.

CRSVR SHOES, CLOTHING
(www.crsvr.com; 632 State St) Check this downtown sneaker boutique run by DJs, not just for rare, limited-edition Nikes and other athletic-shoe brands, but also trendy T-shirts, hats and other men's urban styles.

REI OUTDOORS
(www.rei.com; 321 Anacapa St; 10am-9pm Mon-Fri, 10am-7pm Sat, 11am-6pm Sun) West Coast's biggest independent co-op outdoor retailer is the place to pick up active clothing, shoes, sports gear and topographic recreational maps.

Information

Several downtown coffee shops offer free wi-fi.

FedEx Office (www.fedex.com; 1030 State St; per min 20-30¢; 7am-11pm Mon-Fri, 9am-9pm Sat & Sun; @ wi-fi) Pay-as-you-go internet workstations and free wi-fi.

Post office (www.usps.com; 836 Anacapa St; 9:30am-6pm Mon-Fri, 10am-2pm Sat) Full-service.

Public library (www.sbplibrary.org; 40 E Anapamu St; 10am-8pm Mon-Thu, 10am-5:30pm Fri & Sat, 1-5pm Sun; @ wi-fi) Public internet terminals and free wi-fi.

Santa Barbara Cottage Hospital (805-682-7111; http://cottagehealthsystemc.org; cnr Pueblo & Bath Sts; 24hr) Emergency room.

Visitor center (805-965-3021; www.santabarbaraca.com; 1 Garden St; 9am-5pm Mon-Sat, 10am-5pm Sun) Maps, brochures and tourist information at the waterfront.

Getting There & Away

About 10 miles west of downtown off Hwy 101, small **Santa Barbara Airport** (SBA; www.flysba.com; 500 Fowler Rd) is served by American (LA), Frontier (Denver), Horizon (Seattle), United (Denver, LA and San Francisco) and US Airways (Phoenix).

Santa Barbara Airbus (805-964-7759, 800-423-1618; www.sbairbus.com) shuttles between Los Angeles International Airport (LAX) and Santa Barbara (one way/round trip $48/90, 2½ to three hours, eight daily).

Amtrak (www.amtrak.com; 209 State St) is a stop on the daily Seattle–LA *Coast Starlight*. Regional *Pacific Surfliner* trains head south to LA ($25, three hours, six daily) and San Diego ($35, six hours, four daily), or north to San Luis Obispo ($29, 2¾ hours, twice daily). Connecting Amtrak Thruway buses also head north along Hwy 101 via San Luis Obispo and Paso Robles to the San Francisco Bay Area.

Greyhound (www.greyhound.com; 34 W Carrillo St) has a few daily services along Hwy 101 south to LA ($18, three hours) or north to San Francisco ($53, nine hours) via San Luis Obispo ($26, 2¼ hours).

Getting Around

Equipped with front-loading bicycle racks, local buses operated by **Metropolitan Transit District** (MTD; 805-963-3366; www.sbmtd.gov; 1020 Chapala St) cost $1.75 per ride; ask for a free transfer when boarding.

MTD's electric **Downtown Shuttle** runs along State St to Stearns Wharf every 10 to 15 minutes, while the **Waterfront Shuttle** travels from Stearns Wharf west to the harbor and east to the zoo every 15 to 30 minutes. Both routes operate 10am to 6pm daily (also from 6pm to 10pm on Fridays and Saturdays between late May and early September). The fare is 25¢ (transfers free).

In 10 municipal lots and garages around downtown parking is free for the first 75 minutes; each additional hour costs $1.50.

Channel Islands National Park

Don't let this remote park, part of an island chain lying off the SoCal coast, loiter too long on your bucket list. Imagine hiking, kayaking, scuba diving, camping and whale-watching, all amid a raw, end-of-the-world landscape. Rich in unique species of flora and fauna, tide pools and kelp forests, the islands are home to 145 species found nowhere else in the world, earning them the nickname 'California's Galapagos.'

Sights & Activities

Most tourists arrive during summer, when island conditions are hot, dusty and bone-dry. Better times to visit are during the spring wildflower bloom or in early fall, when the fog clears and kayaking conditions are ideal. Winter can be stormy, but it's also great for wildlife watching, especially whales.

Before you shove off from the mainland, stop by Ventura Harbor's NPS Visitor Center (p338) for educational natural-history exhibits, a short video and ranger-led family activity programs on weekends and holidays.

Anacapa Island — ISLAND

If you're short on time, Anacapa Island, which is actually three separate islets, gives a memorable introduction to the islands' ecology. Boats dock on the East Island and after a short climb you'll find 2 miles of trails offering fantastic views of island flora, a historic lighthouse, and rocky Middle and West Islands. Kayaking, diving, tidepooling and seal-watching are popular activities here. After checking out the small museum at the visitors center, ask about ranger-led programs. In summer, scuba divers with videocameras may broadcast live images to TV monitors you can watch.

Santa Cruz Island — ISLAND

The park's largest island (96 sq mi) boasts two mountain ranges. The western three-quarters of the island is managed by the Nature Conservancy and can only be accessed with a permit (apply online at www.nature.org/cruzpermit). But the remaining eastern quarter, managed by the NPS, packs a wallop – ideal if you want an action-packed day trip or overnight camping trip. You can swim, snorkel, scuba dive and kayak. There are rugged hikes too, which are best not attempted midday – there's little shade. It's a 1-mile climb to captivating, but windy Cavern Point.

Santa Rosa Island — ISLAND

Snowy white-sand beaches and a chance to spot hundreds of bird and plant species are among the highlights of Santa Rosa, where seals and sea lions haul out. Hiking trails through grasslands and canyons and along beaches abound, but high winds typically make swimming, diving and kayaking tough for everyone but experts.

San Miguel Island — ISLAND

The most remote of the park's northern islands offers solitude and a wilderness experience, but it's often shrouded in fog and is very windy. Some sections are off-limits to prevent disruption of the fragile ecosystem, which includes a ghostly caliche forest (made of the hardened calcium-carbonate castings of trees and vegetation) and seasonal colonies of seals and sea lions.

Santa Barbara Island — ISLAND

Only 1 sq mile in size, this isolated island is for nature lovers. Big, blooming coreopsis, cream cups and chicory are just a few of the island's memorable plant species. It's also a thriving playground for seabirds and marine wildlife, including humongous elephant

PARADISE LOST & FOUND

Humans have left a heavy footprint on the Channel Islands, originally inhabited by Chumash and Gabrieleño tribespeople. In the 19th century, ranching livestock overgrazed, causing erosion, while rabbits fed on native plants. The US military even used San Miguel as a mid-20th–century practice bombing range. In 1969, an offshore oil spill engulfed the northern islands in an 800-sq-mi slick, killing off uncountable seabirds and mammals. Meanwhile, deep-sea fishing has caused the destruction of three-quarters of the islands' kelp forests.

Despite past abuses, the islands' future is not bleak. Brown pelicans, once decimated by the effects of DDT and reduced to one chick on Anacapa in 1970, have rebounded, and bald eagles were recently reintroduced. On San Miguel, native vegetation has returned a half century after overgrazing sheep were removed. On Santa Cruz, the National Park Service (NPS) and the Nature Conservancy have implemented ambitious multi-year plans to eliminate invasive plants and feral pigs. Information is available from the NPS (☎805-658-5730; www.nps.gov/chis; 1901 Spinnaker Dr, off Harbor Blvd, Ventura; ⏰8:30am-5pm; 👪) and from **Nature Conservancy** (www.nature.org)..

seals and Xantus' murrelets, a bird that nests in cliff crevices. Ask at the island's visitor center about the best diving, snorkeling and kayaking spots.

Tours

Most trips require a minimum number of participants, and may be canceled due to surf and weather conditions.

Island Packers WHALE-WATCHING
(☎805-642-1393; www.islandpackers.com; 1691 Spinnaker Dr, Ventura Harbor; adult/child 3hr cruise from $33/24, full-day trip from $72/54) Offers whale-watching excursions from late December to early April (gray whales) and in summer (blue and humpback whales).

Paddle Sports of Santa Barbara KAYAKING, HIKING
(☎805-899-4925, 888-254-2094; www.kayaksb.com; 117b Harbor Way, Santa Barbara; day trips from $175) Organizes kayaking and hiking excursions to all five islands.

Santa Barbara Adventure Co KAYAKING
(☎805-899-4925, 888-254-2094; www.kayaksb.com; 720 Bond Ave, Santa Barbara; day trips adult/child from $170/150;) Offers both day and overnight sea-kayaking trips to the islands.

Sleeping

Each island has a primitive year-round **campground** (☎reservations 518-885-3639, 877-444-6777; www.recreation.gov; tent sites $15) with pit toilets and picnic tables. Water is available on Santa Cruz and Santa Rosa islands only. Campers must pack everything in and out, including trash. Due to fire danger, campfires are not allowed (enclosed gas campstoves are OK). Advance camping reservations are required.

Information

NPS Visitor Center (☎805-658-5730; www.nps.gov/chis; 1901 Spinnaker Dr, off Harbor Blvd, Ventura; 8:30am-5pm;) On the mainland, at the far end of Ventura Harbor, it's a one-stop shop for books, maps and trip-planning information.

Getting There & Away

Trips may be canceled anytime due to surf and weather conditions. Reservations are essential for weekends, holidays and summer trips.

AIR **Channel Islands Aviation** (☎805-987-1301; www.flycia.com; day trips adult/child from $160/135, campers from $300) runs half-day beach excursions, surf-fishing trips and camper shuttles to Santa Rosa Island, departing from Camarillo or Santa Barbara.

BOAT **Island Packers** (☎805-642-1393; www.islandpackers.com; 1691 Spinnaker Dr, Ventura Harbor; day trips adult/child from $56/39) provides regularly scheduled boat service to all of the islands; campers pay extra. Some departures from Oxnard.

Ventura

The primary departure point for Channel Islands trips, Ventura may not look at first like the most enchanting coastal city, but it has its seaside charms, especially along the beaches and in the historic downtown corridor along Main St, north of Hwy 101.

CHANNEL ISLANDS NPS CAMPGROUNDS

CAMPGROUND NAME	NO OF SITES	ACCESS FROM BOAT LANDING AREA	DESCRIPTION
Anacapa	7	0.5-mile walk with 154 stairs	High, rocky, sun-exposed & isolated
San Miguel	9	Steep 1-mile walk uphill	Windy, often foggy with volatile weather
Santa Barbara	10	Steep 0.5-mile walk uphill	Large, grassy & surrounded by trails
Santa Cruz (Scorpion Ranch)	40	Flat, 0.5-mile walk	Popular with groups, often crowded & partly shady
Santa Rosa	15	Flat, 1.5-mile walk	Eucalyptus grove in a windy canyon

Sights & Activities

San Buenaventura State Beach BEACH
(805-968-1033; www.parks.ca.gov; per car $10; dawn-dusk;) Off Hwy 101, this long, golden strand is perfect for swimming, surfing or just lazing on the sand. Recreational cycling paths connect to more nearby beaches.

Mission San Buenaventura MISSION
(www.sanbuenaventuramission.org; 211 E Main St; adult/child $2/50¢; 10am-5pm Mon-Fri, 9am-5pm Sat, 10am-4pm Sun) Ventura's Spanish colonial roots are in evidence at the final California mission founded by Junípero Serra in 1782. A stroll around this petite parish church is a tranquil experience, leading through a small museum, past statues of saints, centuries-old religious paintings and unusual wooden bells, and around a garden courtyard.

Limoneira AGROTOURISM
(805-525-5541; www.limoneira.com; 1141 Cummings Rd, Santa Paula; tours $20-40) A 20-minute drive outside town, this working ranch and farm is the place to get up close and smell the citrus that Ventura is famous for: lemons. Drop by the historical ranch store and play bocce ball on outdoor courts, or reserve a guided tour of the ranch, the modern packing house and the sea-view fruit and avocado orchards. Call for opening hours.

California Oil Museum MUSEUM
(805-933-0076; www.oilmuseum.net; 1001 E Main St, off Hwy 126, Santa Paula; adult/child 6-17yr/senior $4/1/3; 10am-4pm Wed-Sun) If you've seen the Oscar-winning movie *There Will Be Blood*, then you already know that SoCal's early oil boom was a bloodthirsty business. Examine SoCal's 'black bonanza' with modest historical exhibits that include an authentic 1890s drilling rig and vintage gas pumps. To reach downtown Santa Paula, drive about 13 miles east of Ventura via Hwy 126.

Sleeping & Eating

Midrange motels and high-rise beachfront hotels cluster off Hwy 101 and by Ventura Harbor. Alternatively, keep driving on Hwy 101 southbound to Camarillo, where cheaper roadside chains abound. Back in downtown Ventura, Main St is chock-a-block with taco shops, healthy SoCal-style cafes and globally flavored kitchens.

Brooks CALIFORNIAN $$$
(805-652-7070; www.restaurantbrooks.com; 545 E Thompson Blvd; mains $17-34; 5-9pm Tue-Thu & Sun, to 10pm Fri & Sat) Just off Hwy 101, this chef-driven restaurant serves such high-flying New American cuisine as cornmeal-fried oysters, jalapeño cheddar grits and Maytag blue cheesecake with seasonal berries.

Anacapa Brew Pub BREWPUB $$
(www.anacapabrewing.com; 472 E Main St; mains $9-20; 11:30am-9pm Sun-Wed, to midnight Thu-Sun) Right downtown, this casual brewpub crafts its own microbrews – props to the Pierpoint IPA – and makes a fine pulled-pork sandwich too.

Mary's Secret Garden VEGETARIAN $
(805-641-3663; 100 S Fir St; mains $5-12; 4-9:30pm Tue-Thu, 11am-9:30pm Fri & Sat;) Two blocks east of California St by a pretty park, this internationally spiced vegan haven mixes up fresh juices, smoothies and out-of-this-world cakes.

Drinking

Wine Rack WINE BAR
(www.weaverwines.com; 14 S California St; 4-9pm Mon & Tue, 2-9pm Wed & Thu, noon-10pm Fri & Sat, 2-8pm Sun) At this upbeat wine shop, novices can sidle up to the unpretentious tasting bar, loiter over a tasty cheese plate and listen to live music.

Zoey's Café CAFE $$
(805-652-1137; www.zoeyscafe.com; 185 E Santa Clara St; mains $9-15; 6-9pm Tue-Sat, later on show nights) Cozy coffeehouse that makes pizzas and paninis, and showcases live acts almost nightly, mostly bluegrass, folk and acoustic singer-songwriters.

Shopping

Downtown on Main St, you'll find a terrific assortment of antiques, vintage, secondhand thrift and indie boutique shops.

Patagonia OUTDOOR EQUIPMENT
(www.patagonia.com; 235 W Santa Clara St; 10am-6pm Mon-Sat & 11am-5pm Sun) Ventura is the birthplace of this pioneering outdoor-gear and clothing outfitter, known for its commitment to sustainable, environmentally progressive practices.

Real Cheap Sports OUTDOOR EQUIPMENT
(www.realcheapsports.com; 36 W Santa Clara St; 10am-6pm Mon-Sat, to 5pm Sun) Shh, don't

tell anyone but you can get that brand-name outdoors stuff for less here, including Patagonia factory seconds.

Camarillo Premium Outlets MALL
(www.premiumoutlets.com; 740 E Ventura Blvd, Camarillo; ⏲10am-9pm Mon-Sat & 10am-8pm Sun) For steeply discounted designer duds, drive about 20 minutes from downtown via Hwy 101 southbound to this mall.

Information

Ventura Visitors & Convention Bureau (☎805-648-2075, 800-483-6214; www.ventura-usa.com; 101 S California St; ⏲8:30am-5pm Mon-Fri, 9am-5pm Sat, 10am-4pm Sun) Free information and maps downtown.

Getting There & Away

Ventura's unstaffed **Amtrak station** (www.amtrak.com; cnr Harbor Blvd & Figueroa St) has five daily trains north to Santa Barbara ($12, 40 minutes) and south to Los Angeles ($20, 2¼ hours). **Vista** (☎800-438-112; www.goventura.org) runs several daily Coastal Express buses between Ventura and Santa Barbara ($3, 35 minutes).

Los Angeles

Includes »

Best Places to Eat

» Bottega Louie (p373)

» Osteria Mozza & Pizzeria Mozza (p373)

» Ivy (p375)

» Bazaar (p375)

» Gjelina (p377)

Best Places to Stay

» Standard Downtown LA (p370)

» Hollywood Roosevelt Hotel (p370)

» Beverly Hills Hotel (p371)

» Casa Del Mar (p372)

» Queen Mary Hotel (p372)

Why Go?

Ah, Los Angeles, land of starstruck dreams and Tinseltown magic. You may think you know what to expect from LA: celebrity worship, plastic surgery junkies, endless traffic, earthquakes, wildfires…And true, your waitress today might be tomorrow's starlet and you may well encounter artificially enhanced blondes and phone-clutching honchos weaving lanes at 80mph, but LA is intensely diverse and brimming with fascinating neighborhoods and characters that have nothing to do with the 'Industry' (entertainment, to the rest of us). Its innovative cooking has pushed the boundaries of American cuisine for generations. Arts and architecture? Frank Lloyd Wright to Frank Gehry. Music? The Doors to Dr Dre and Dudamel.

So do yourself a favor and leave your preconceptions in the suitcase. LA's truths are not doled out on the silver screen or gossip rags; rather, you will discover them in everyday interactions. Chances are, the more you explore, the more you'll enjoy.

When to Go

Los Angeles

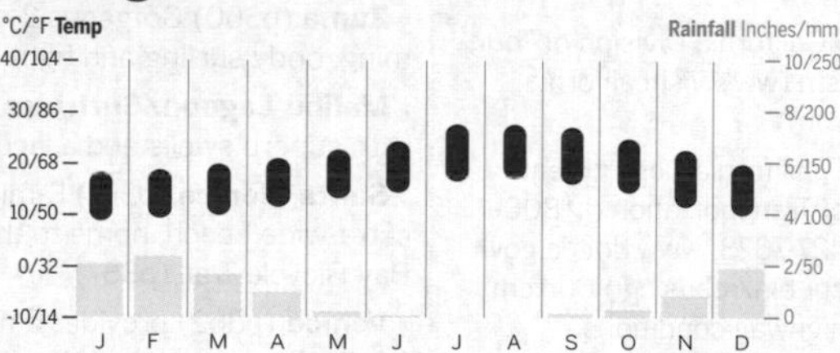

Feb The red carpet is rolled out for the Academy Awards. Prime time for celeb-spotting.

Apr & Sep Most tourists visit when the sun shines the brightest on LA's golden sands.

Oct–Nov & Jan–Mar The region's two distinct wet seasons.

DID YOU KNOW?

At nearly 10 million people, LA is America's largest county in population. It would be the eighth-largest state on its own.

Fast Facts

» **Population of LA** 3.8 million

» **Average temperature low/high in LA** Jan 47/66°F, July 62/82°F

» **LA to Disneyland** 26 miles

» **LA to San Diego** 120 miles

» **LA to Palm Springs** 110 miles

Planning Your Trip

Reserve hotels in prime locations at least three weeks out, especially for summer weekends. Two weeks out, make reservations for popular restaurants. Weekends are toughest, but primo nights for celeb sightings at dining hot spots are actually Tuesday through Thursday.

Resources

» California Division of Tourism (www.visitcalifornia.com)

» California Department of Transportation (☎800-427-7623; www.dot.ca.gov/cgi-bin/roads.cgi) Current highway conditions.

» LA Inc. (http://discoverlosangeles.com) Official tourist bureau website.

» Los Angeles Times (www.latimes.com) The region's newspaper of record.

Actually, Some People do Walk in LA

'No one walks in LA,' the '80s band Missing Persons famously sang. That was then. Fed up with traffic, smog and high gas prices, the region that defined car culture is developing a foot culture. Angelenos are moving into more densely populated neighborhoods and are walking, cycling and taking public transportation.

You may not need a car during your visit if you stay near one of the arty stations on the Metro Red Line, which connects Union Station in Downtown LA to the San Fernando Valley via Koreatown, Hollywood and Universal Studios. Unlimited-ride passes ($5 per day, via stored-value TAP cards) are a downright bargain, and given LA's legendary traffic it's often faster to travel below ground than above. Light-rail lines connect Downtown with Long Beach, Pasadena and East LA. A Culver City line was due to open as we went to press, to be extended to Santa Monica by 2015.

In 2011, the city of Los Angeles authorized construction of an eventual 1,680 miles of bikeways, in addition to those in other cities around the county. Bicycles are permitted on Metro trains and buses are fitted with bike racks.

While eventual plans call for a 'Subway to the Sea' in Santa Monica, for now you'll be busing, biking or – gasp! – driving to Mid-City, Beverly Hills and the beaches.

GRAUMAN'S CHINESE THEATRE

Yes, every other tourist goes there too, but even the most jaded may thrill to matching hand- or footprints with those of the stars, enshrined forever in concrete in front of Grauman's Chinese Theatre in Hollywood (p353).

Top Five LA Beaches

» **El Matador** (off Map p388) Hideaway hemmed by battered rock cliffs and strewn with giant boulders. Wild surf; not suitable for children.

» **Zuma** (p360) Gorgeous 2-mile ribbon of sand for swimming, body surfing and tight bodies.

» **Malibu Lagoon/Surfrider** (p360) Legendary surf beach with superb swells and a lagoon for bird-watching.

» **Santa Monica** (p361) Families escape inland heat on this extra-wide beach, home to the Santa Monica Pier and South Bay Bicycle Trail (p367).

» **Venice** (p362) provides a nonstop parade of friends and freaks. Drum circle in the sand on Sundays.

DON'T MISS

ANGELS FLIGHT

Part novelty act, part commuter train for the lazy, **Angels Flight** (1901; Map p348; www.angelsflight.com; per ride 25¢; ⏲6:45am-10pm) is a funicular billed as the 'shortest railway in the world' (298 feet). The adorable cars chug up and down the steep incline connecting Hill and Olive Sts.

History

Los Angeles' human history began as early as 6000 BC, as home to the Gabrieleño and Chumash tribespeople. Their hunter-gatherer existence ended in the late 18th century with the arrival of Spanish missionaries and pioneers, led by Padre Junípero Serra. Established in 1781, the civilian settlement of El Pueblo de la Reina de Los Angeles (Village of the Queen of the Angels) became a thriving farming community but remained an isolated outpost for decades.

Spain lost its hold on the territory to Mexico in 1821 and, following the Mexican-American War (1846–48), California came under US rule. The city was incorporated on April 4, 1850.

A series of seminal events caused LA's population to swell to two million by 1930: the collapse of the Northern California Gold Rush in the 1850s, the arrival of the railroad in the 1870s, the birth of the citrus industry in the late 1800s, the discovery of oil in 1892, the launch of San Pedro Harbor in 1907, the arrival of the motion picture industry in 1908 and the opening of the LA Aqueduct in 1913. Beginning in WWI, aviation and defense industries helped drive the city's economy through the end of the Cold War. The 10th Summer Olympic Games, held here in 1932, marked LA's coming of age as a world city (10th St was renamed Olympic Blvd in their honor).

After WWII, a deluge of new residents, drawn by reasonably priced housing, seemingly boundless opportunity and reliably fabulous weather, shaped LA into the megalopolis of today. Culturally, LA's freewheeling, free-thinking, free-living lifestyle defined the American consciousness of the 1960s and '70s, a boom culminating in a second Summer Olympics held here in 1984.

LA's growth has not been without its problems, including suburban sprawl and air pollution, though smog levels have fallen annually since records have been kept. Major riots in 1965 and 1992 created distrust between the city's police department and various ethnic groups. Violent crime has since dropped significantly, and in May 2005 Angelenos elected Antonio Villaraigosa, the city's first mayor of Latino descent since 1872.

In the new millennium, traffic, a teetering national economy, struggling public education system and fluctuating real-estate market continue to cloud LA's sunny skies. But all things considered, LA's a survivor.

Sights

Los Angeles may be vast and amorphous, but the areas of visitor interest are fairly well defined. About 12 miles inland, Downtown LA is the region's hub, combining great architecture and culture with global-village pizzazz. Northwest of Downtown, there's sprawling Hollywood and nearby hip 'hoods Los Feliz and Silver Lake. West Hollywood is LA's center of urban chic and the gay and lesbian community, while Long Beach, at six o'clock from Downtown, is a bustling port with big city sophistication. Most TV and movie studios are north of Hollywood in the San Fernando Valley, and to its east Pasadena feels like an all-American small town writ large.

South of Hollywood, Mid-City's main draw is Museum Row, while further west are ritzy Beverly Hills and the Westside communities of Westwood and Brentwood. Santa Monica is the most tourist- and pedestrian-friendly beach town; others include swish-but-low-key Malibu and bohemian Venice.

DOWNTOWN & AROUND

For decades, Downtown was LA's historic core and main business and government district – and empty nights and weekends. No more. Crowds fill Dowtown's performance and entertainment venues, and young professionals and artists have moved by the thousands into new lofts, attracting bars, restaurants and galleries. Don't expect Manhattan just yet, but for adventurous urbanites, now is an exciting time to be Downtown.

Downtown is easily explored on foot or by subway or DASH minibus. Parking is cheapest (about $6 all day) around Little Tokyo and Chinatown.

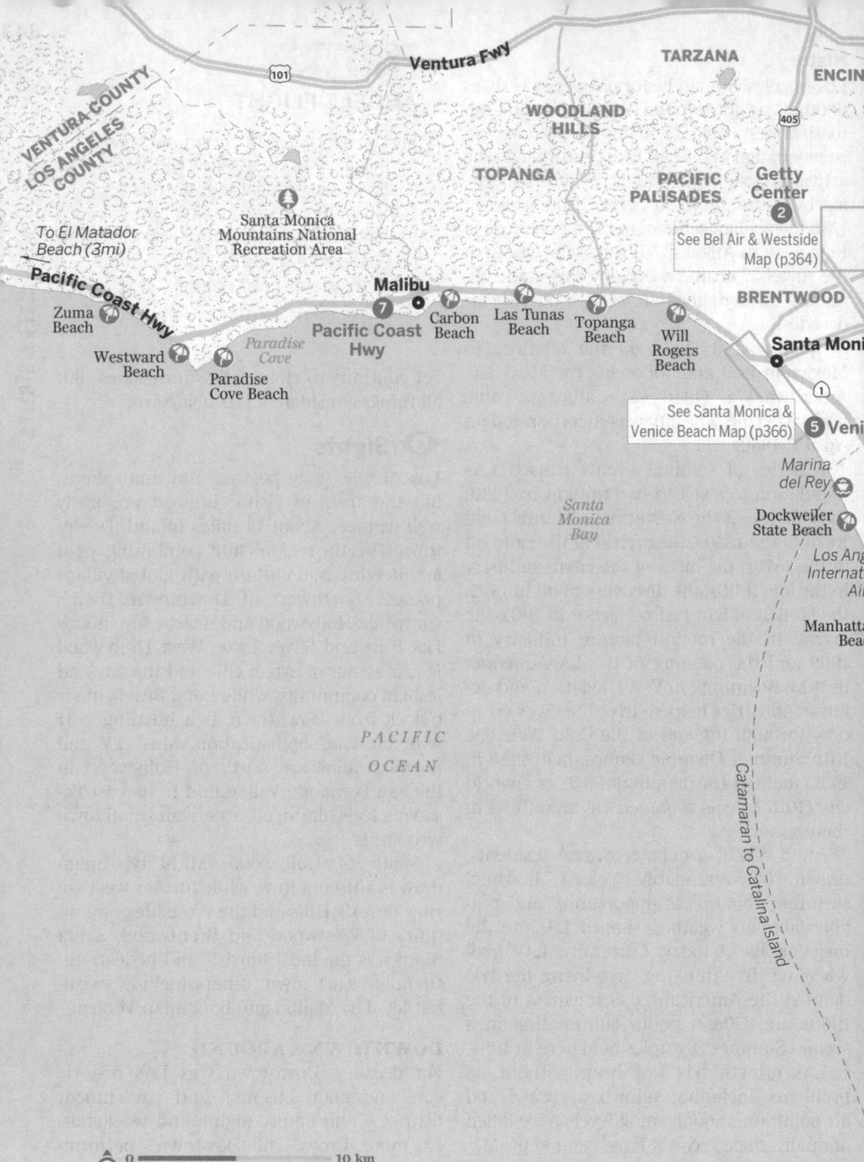

Los Angeles Highlights

1 Go behind the scenes on a **studio tour** (p354)

2 Visit world-famous venues such as the **Walt Disney Concert Hall** (p532), the **Los Angeles County Museum of Art** (p357) and the **Getty Center** (p544)

3 Discover the perfect taco, shrimp dumpling or Korean barbecue at one of thousands of **ethnic restaurants** (p373)

4 Enjoy a picnic and a concert under the stars at the venerable **Hollywood Bowl** (p382)

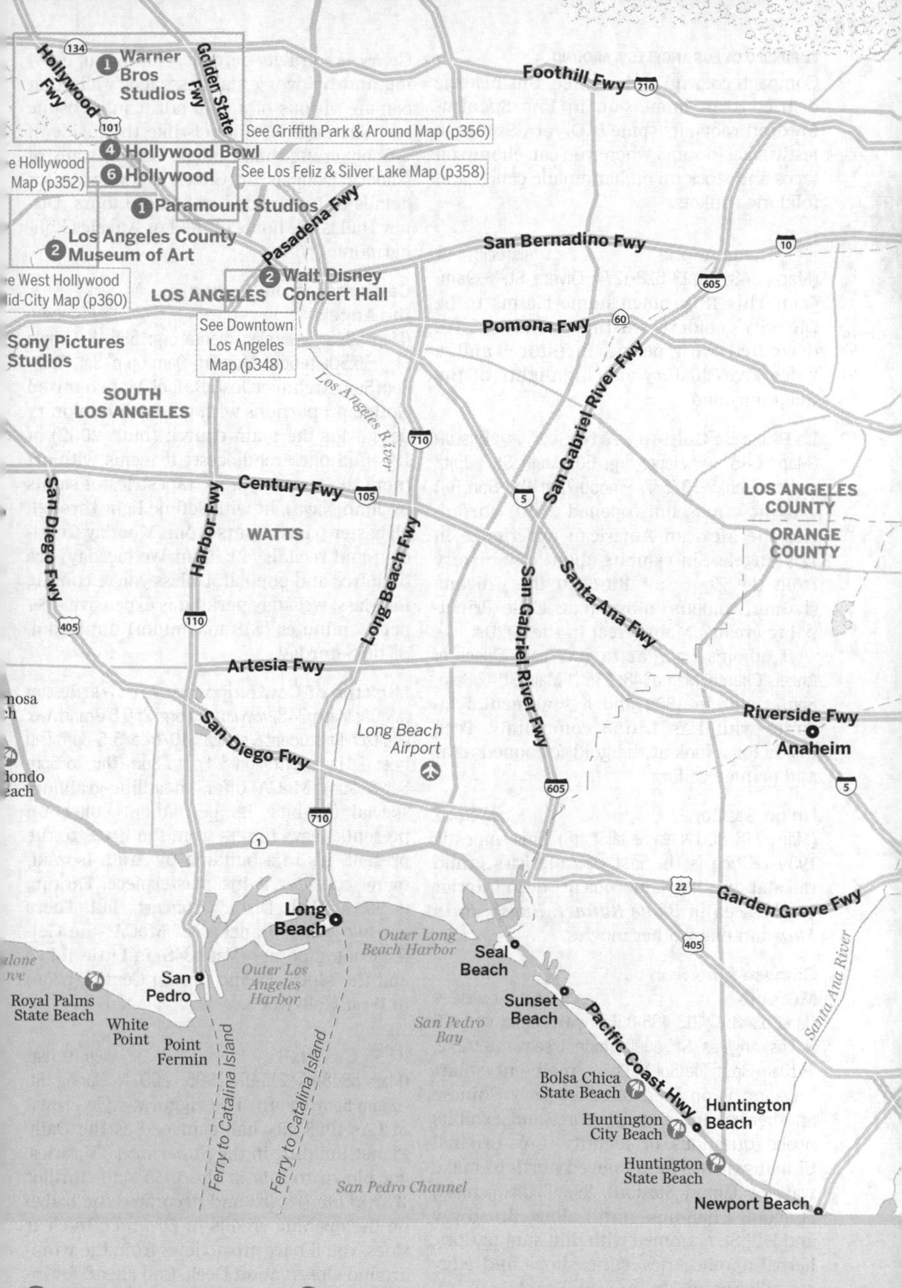

5 Bask with the bronzed, buff, bicyclists, 'bladers and buskers in **Venice** (p362)

6 Mingle with the beau monde in a hip **Hollywood** bar or club (p380)

7 Hot-rod the breathtaking **Pacific Coast Highway** in **Malibu** (p360)

EL PUEBLO DE LOS ANGELES & AROUND

Compact, colorful and car-free, this historic district is an immersion in LA's Spanish-Mexican roots. Its spine is **Olvera Street**, a festive tack-o-rama where you can chomp on tacos and stock up on handmade candy and folkloric trinkets.

FREE Avila Adobe HISTORIC HOME

(Map p348; ☎213-628-1274, Olvera St; ⏰9am-4pm) This 1818 ranch home claims to be the city's oldest existing building. It's decorated with period furniture, and a video gives history and highlights of the neighborhood.

La Plaza de Cultura y Artes CULTURAL MUSEUM

(Map p348; www.lapca.org; 501 Main St; adult/student/senior $9/5/7; ⏰noon-7pm Wed-Sun; P) This new museum (opened 2010) chronicles the Mexican–American experience in Los Angeles, in exhibits about city history from the Zoot Suit Riots to the Chicana (Latina women's) movement. Calle Principal re-creates Main Street in the 1920s.

It adjoins **La Placita** (Our Lady Queen of Angels Church; Map p348; 535 N Main St; ⏰8am-8pm), built in 1822 and a sentimental favorite with LA's Latino community. Peek inside for a look at the gold-festooned altar and painted ceiling.

Union Station LANDMARK

(Map p348; 800 N Alameda St; P) This majestic 1939 edifice is the last of America's grand rail stations; its glamorous art deco interior can be seen in *Blade Runner*, *Bugsy*, *Rain Man* and many other movies.

Chinese American Museum CULTURAL MUSEUM

(Map p348; ☎213-485-8567; www.camla.org; 425 N Los Angeles St; adult/student/senior $3/2/2; ⏰10am-3pm Tue-Sun) This small but smart museum is on the site of an early Chinese apothecary and general store, and exhibits probe questions of identity. LA's original Chinatown was here (moved north to make way for Union Station). 'New' **Chinatown** is about a half-mile north along Broadway and Hill St, crammed with dim sum parlors, herbal apothecaries, curio shops and edgy art galleries on **Chung King Road**.

FREE Walt Disney Concert Hall CONCERT HALL, ARCHITECTURE

(Map p348; www.laphil.com; 111 S Grand Ave) This gleaming concert venue, designed by Frank Gehry, is a gravity-defying sculpture of curving and billowing stainless-steel walls that conjure visions of a ship adrift in a cosmic sea. The auditorium feels like the inside of a finely crafted instrument clad in walls of smooth Douglas fir. Check the website for details of free guided and audio tours. Disney Hall is the home of the Los Angeles Philharmonic (p382).

Cathedral of Our Lady of the Angels CHURCH

(Map p348; www.olacathedral.org; 555 W Temple St; ⏰6:30am-6pm Mon-Fri, 9am-6pm Sat, 7am-6pm Sun) Architect José Rafael Moneo mixed Gothic proportions with bold contemporary design for the main church (built 2002) of LA's Catholic archdiocese. It teems with art (note the contemporary tapestries of saints by John Nava), lit with serene light through alabaster panes. Tours (1pm, Monday to Friday) and recitals (12:45pm Wednesday) are both free and popular. Unless you're coming for Mass, weekday parking is expensive – $4 per 15 minutes ($18 maximum) until 4pm, $5 on Saturday.

Museum of Contemporary Art ART MUSEUM

(MoCA; Map p348; www.moca.org; 250 S Grand Ave; adult/child/student & senior $10/free/5, 5-8pm Thu free; ⏰11am-5pm Mon & Fri, to 8pm Thu, to 6pm Sat & Sun) MoCA offers headline-grabbing special exhibits; its permanent collection presents heavy hitters from the 1940s to the present. It's in a building by Arata Isozaki; many consider it his masterpiece. Parking is $9, at Walt Disney Concert Hall. There are two other branches of MoCA: the Geffen Contemporary (Map p348) in Little Tokyo and the MoCA Pacific Design Center (p355) in West Hollywood.

FREE City Hall ARCHITECTURE

(Map p348; ☎213-978-1995; 200 N Spring St; ⏰8am-5pm Mon-Fri) The ziggurat-style crown of LA's 1928 city hall cameoed as the Daily Planet Building in the *Superman* TV series, got blown to bits in the 1953 sci-fi thriller *War of the Worlds* and decorated the badge on the opening credits of *Dragnet*. In clear skies, you'll have great views from the wraparound Observation Deck. Call ahead for information on guided tours.

FREE Wells Fargo History Museum MUSEUM

(Map p348; www.wellsfargohistory.com; 333 S Grand Ave; ⏰9am-5pm Mon-Fri) Continuing

10 DOWNTOWN LA GLAMOUR BUILDINGS

In addition to Walt Disney Concert Hall and the Cathedral of Our Lady of the Angels, architecture buffs shouldn't leave Downtown without checking out some of the following gems.

» **Richard J Riordan Central Library** (1922; 630 W 5th St) Bertram Goodhue, inspired by the discovery of King Tut's tomb the same year, incorporated numerous Egyptian motifs. The Tom Bradley Wing is an eight-story glass atrium added in 1993 and named for a former mayor.

» **US Bank Tower** (1989; 633 W 5th St) The tallest building west of Chicago has 73 floors and juts 1017 feet up. Designed by Henry Cobb, an architect from the New York firm of IM Pei, the tower was attacked by an alien spaceship in the 1996 movie *Independence Day.*

» **Caltrans Building** (2004; 100 S Main St) Headquarters of District 7 of the California Department of Transportation. Santa Monica-based architect Thom Mayne won the 2005 Pritzker Prize, the Oscar of architecture, for this futuristic design. Neon stripes on the facade recall head- and tail-lights whizzing along a freeway, and the windows open or close depending on the outside temperature and angle of the sun.

» **One Bunker Hill** (1931; 601 W 5th St) The reliefs above the entrance to this 12-story art deco moderne office tower recall the building's former occupant, the Southern California Edison company, depicting energy, light and power. In the 40ft-high lobby are 17 types of marble, gold-leaf ceilings and a mural by Hugo Ballin, a set designer for Cecil B DeMille.

» **Millenium Biltmore Hotel** (1923; 515 S Olive St) Overlooking Pershing Square, this is one of LA's grandest hotels. Designed by the team that also created New York's Waldorf Astoria, it has hosted presidents, political conventions and eight Academy Awards ceremonies. It boasts carved and gilded ceilings, marble floors, grand staircases and styles from Renaissance to Baroque to Neoclassical.

» **Oviatt Building** (1928; 617 S Olive St) This art deco gem was conceived by the mildly eccentric James Oviatt, owner of a men's clothing store here (now Cicada restaurant). Oviatt fell in love with art deco on a visit to Paris and had carpets, draperies and fixtures shipped from France, including the purportedly largest shipment of etched decorative glass by René Lalique ever to cross the Atlantic.

» **Fine Arts Building** (1927; 811 W 7th St) This 12-story Walker & Eisen structure is a visual feast inside and out. The facade is awash in floral and animal ornamentation, and sculptures peer down from arcaded upstairs windows. The cathedral-like lobby is especially striking. Built in Spanish Renaissance style, it has a galleried mezzanine from which large sculptures representing the arts gaze down.

» **High School for the Visual and Performing Arts** (2008; aka High School No. 9; cnr N Grand Ave & W Cesar Chavez Blvd) The metal cladding on the exterior – by Austrian architecture firm Coop Himmelb(l)au – echoes the Walt Disney Concert Hall a few blocks away, as if to inspire the students. Look for a spiral ramp protruding skyward from the roof.

» **Historic Movie Theaters** Until eclipsed by Hollywood in the mid-1920s, Broadway was LA's entertainment hub, with a dozen-plus movie palaces in a riot of styles – beaux arts to East Indian to Spanish Gothic – on the National Register of Historic Places. Standouts include the 1931 **Los Angeles Theater** (Map p348; 615 S Broadway), where Charlie Chaplin's *City Lights* premiered, and the 1926 **Orpheum Theater** (Map p348; 842 S Broadway), which more recently has hosted *American Idol* auditions. See them on one of the excellent tours offered by the Los Angeles Conservancy (p369), or through its Last Remaining Seats film series of Hollywood classics on their big screens.

Downtown Los Angeles

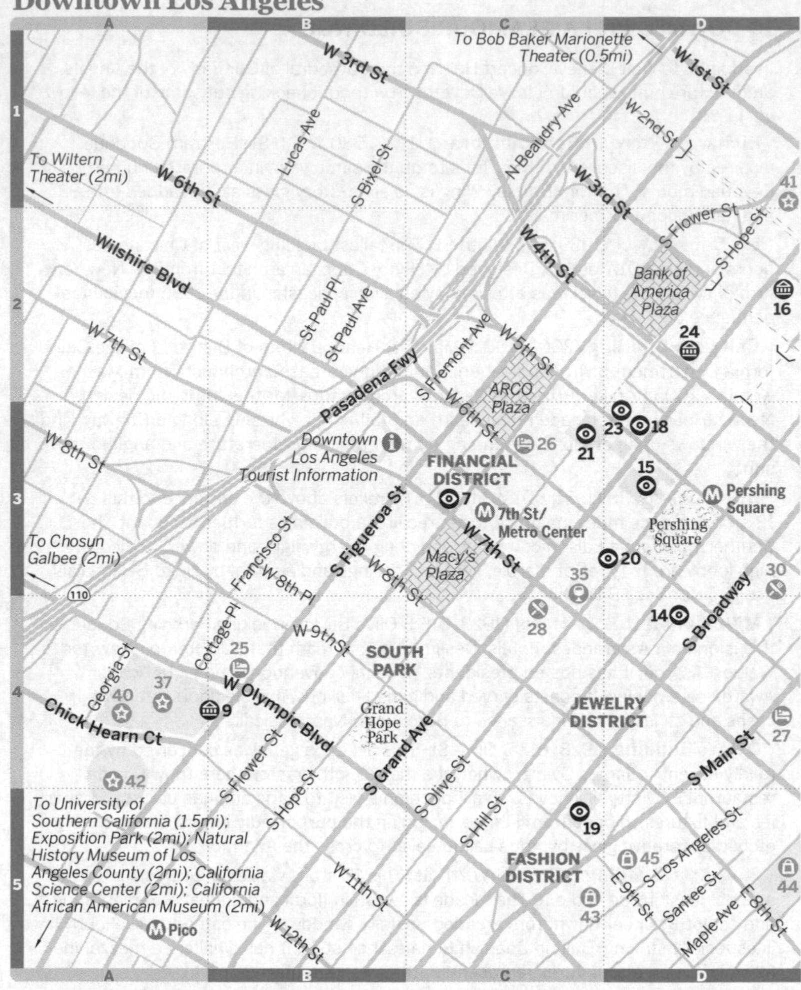

south along Grand Ave is this small but intriguing museum, which relives the Gold Rush era with an original Concord stagecoach, a 100oz gold nugget and a 19th-century bank office.

Dodger Stadium BASEBALL STADIUM

(Map p348; losangeles.dodgers.mlb.com; 1000 Elysian Park Ave; tour adult/child 4-14yr/senior $15/10/10; ⏲tours 10am & 11:30am except during day games) Just north of Chinatown sits this beloved, 56,000-seat baseball park, home of the Los Angeles Dodgers (see p383). Tours (up to 90 minutes) visit the press box, dugout, field, Dugout Club and training center.

LITTLE TOKYO

Little Tokyo is a contemporary but attractive mix of Buddhist temples and Japanese shops and eateries, as you'd expect. There's also an increasingly lively **Arts District** drawing a young, adventurous crowd who live and work in makeshift studios in abandoned warehouses and support a growing number of restaurants nightspots. Stop into the **Little Tokyo Koban** (Map p348; ☎213-

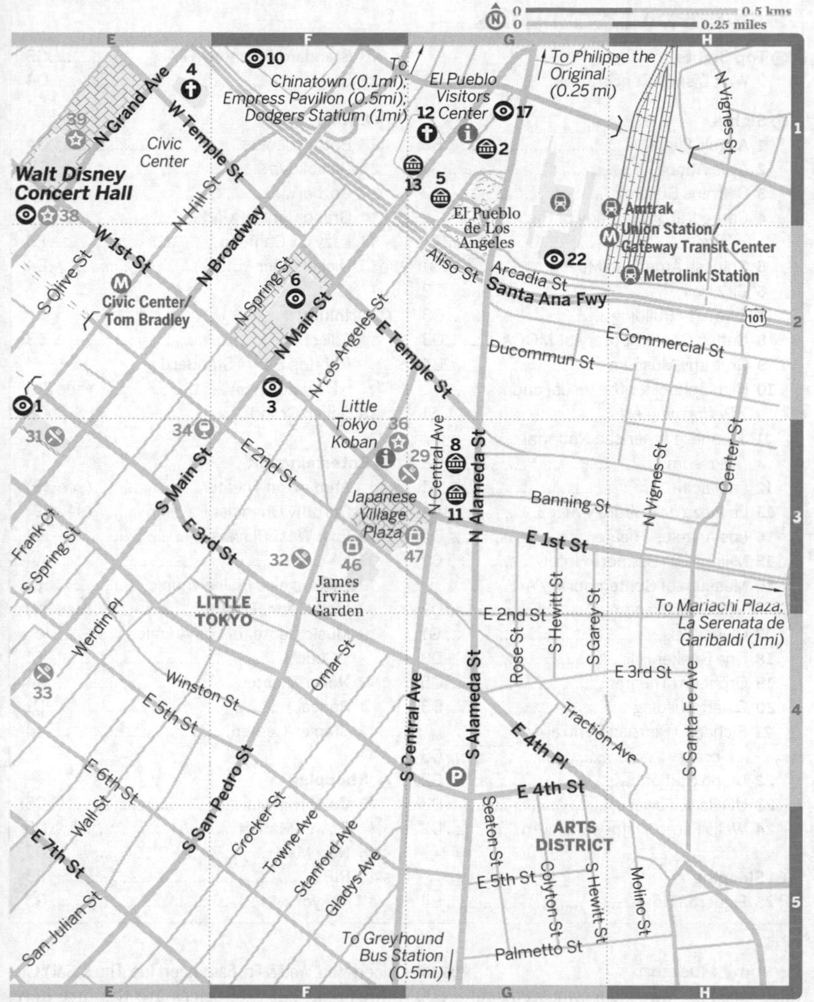

613-1911; 307 E 1st St; ⏲10am-6pm Mon-Sat) visitors center for maps and information.

Japanese American National Museum MUSEUM

(Map p348; www.janm.org; 369 E 1st St; adult/seniors & students $9/5; ⏲11am-5pm Tue, Wed & Fri-Sun, to 8pm Thu) Brims with objects of work and worship, photographs, art and even a uniform worn by *Star Trek* actor (and Japanese-American) George Takei. Special focus is given to the painful chapter of the WWII internment camps.

SOUTH PARK

The southwestern corner of Downtown, South Park isn't a park but an emerging neighborhood, including Staples Center arena (p383), LA's Convention Center and LA Live, which includes a dozen restaurants, live-music venues, a 54-story hotel tower and the 7100-seat Nokia Theatre, home to the MTV Music Awards and *American Idol* finals. This is also where you'll find the Fashion District (see p385).

Parking is in private lots ($8 to $20). South Park is near the Metro Blue Line light-rail.

Downtown Los Angeles

Grammy Museum MUSEUM
(Map p348; www.grammymuseum.org; 800 W Olympic Blvd; adult/child/senior & student $12.95/10.95/11.95; 11:30am-7:30pm Mon-Fri, 10am-7:30pm Sat & Sun) The highlight of LA Live. Music lovers will get lost in interactive exhibits, which define, differentiate and link musical genres, while live footage strobes from all corners. You can glimpse GnR's bass drum, Lester Young's tenor, Yo Yo Ma's cello and Michael's glove. Interactive sound chambers allow you and your friends to try your hand at mixing and remixing, singing and rapping.

Downtown LA Flower Market MARKET
(Map p348; www.laflowerdistrict.com; Wall St btwn 7th & 8th Sts; admission Mon-Fri $2, Sat $1; 8am-noon Mon, Wed & Fri, 6am-noon Tue, Thu & Sat) Cut flowers at cut-rate prices are the lure here, where a few dollars gets you armloads of Hawaiian ginger or sweet roses, a potted plant or elegant orchid. The market is busiest in the wee hours when florists stock up. Bring cash.

EXPOSITION PARK

A couple miles south of Downtown, family-friendly Exposition Park (off Map p348) started as an agricultural fairground in 1872 and now contains three fine museums, a lovely **Rose Garden** (admission free; 9am-sunset mid-Mar–Dec) and the 1923 **Los Angeles Memorial Coliseum**, best known as venue for the 1932 and 1984 Summer Olympic Games. The **University of Southern California**

(USC; www.usc.edu) is just north of the museums. Famous alumni include George Lucas, John Wayne and Neil Armstrong.

DASH minibus 'F' (p388) and the Metro Expo light rail line serve South Park from Downtown. Parking lots start at around $6.

Natural History Museum of Los Angeles County SCIENCE MUSEUM
(off Map p348; www.nhm.org; 900 Exposition Blvd; adult/child/senior & student $12/5/8; ⏲9:30am-5pm; 👪) Take a spin around the world and back in time at this popular museum, inside a baronial building corner (it stood in for Columbia University in the first *Spider-Man* movie). The **Dino Hall** was due to reopen as we went to press. Other crowd-pleasers include stuffed African elephants and the giant megamouth, one of the world's rarest sharks. Historical exhibits include prized Navajo textiles, baskets and jewelry in the **Hall of Native American Cultures**. The **Gem & Mineral Hall**, meanwhile, is a glittering spectacle with a walk-through gem tunnel and more gold than any other such collection in the US. Kids love the hands-on **Discovery Center** and the **Insect Zoo** with its tarantulas, hissing cockroaches and other creepy-crawlies.

FREE **California Science Center** SCIENCE MUSEUM
(off Map p348; www.californiasciencecenter.org; 700 State Dr; ⏲10am-5pm; 👪) At this un-stuffy museum, experience a simulated earthquake, watch baby chicks hatch in an incubator, play virtual reality games, push buttons, switch lights and pull knobs. As we went to press, the museum was preparing to become the permanent home of the **Space Shuttle Endeavour**. Other flying machines include the 1902 *Wright Glider* and the Soviet-made *Sputnik*, the first human-made object to orbit the earth in 1957.

Of the three main exhibition areas, **World of Life** focuses mostly on the human body. You can 'hop on' a red blood cell for a computer fly-through of the circulatory system, ask Gertie how long your colon really is and meet Tess, a giant techno-doll billed as '50 feet of brains, beauty and biology.' The Science Center's **IMAX theater** (☎213-744-7400; adult/child/senior & student $8.25/5/6; 👪) caps off an action-filled day.

Avoid weekday mornings during the school year, when the center typically crawls with school kids.

California African American Museum CULTURAL MUSEUM
(off map p348; www.caamuseum.org; 600 State Dr; admission free; ⏲10am-5pm Tue-Sat, 11am-5pm Sun) This acclaimed museum documents African and African American art and history, especially in California and other western states, further illuminated by an active lecture and performance schedule.

SOUTH LOS ANGELES

The area south of Exposition Park was long known as South Central, a name that quietly went away after the 1992 riots had their epicenter here. Gangs, drugs, poverty, crime and drive-by shootings are just a few of the negative images – not entirely undeserved – associated with this district. This is too bad because South Central (named for Central Ave, which runs through it) was once the proud and prosperous heart of LA's African American community. The upscale shops and restaurants of **Leimert** (luh-*murt*) **Park Village** reflect this heritage, particularly around the intersection of Degnan and 43rd Sts.

Watts Towers MONUMENT
(www.wattstowers.org; 1727 E 107th St; tours adult/child/senior & teen $7/free/3; ⏲tours every 30 mins 11am-3pm Thu & Fri, 10:30am-3pm Sat, 12:30-3pm Sun Oct-Jun, 10:30am-3pm Thu-Sat & 12:30-3pm Sun Jul Sep; Ⓟ) South LA's beacon of pride, the towers rank among the world's greatest monuments of folk art. Italian immigrant Simon Rodia spent 33 years (from 1921 to 1954) cobbling together this whimsical free-form sculpture from a motley assortment of found objects – from green 7-Up bottles to sea shells, rocks to pottery.

HOLLYWOOD, LOS FELIZ & SILVER LAKE

Aging movie stars know that a facelift can quickly pump up a drooping career, and the same has been done with the legendary **Hollywood Blvd** (Map p352), preened and spruced up in recent years. Though it still hasn't recaptured its Golden Age (1920s–1940s) glamour, much of its late-20th-century seediness is gone.

Historic movie palaces bask in restored glory, Metro Rail's Red Line makes access easy, some of LA's hottest bars and nightclubs have sprung up here, and even 'Oscar' has found a permanent home in the Kodak Theatre, part of the vast shopping and entertainment complex called Hollywood & Highland.

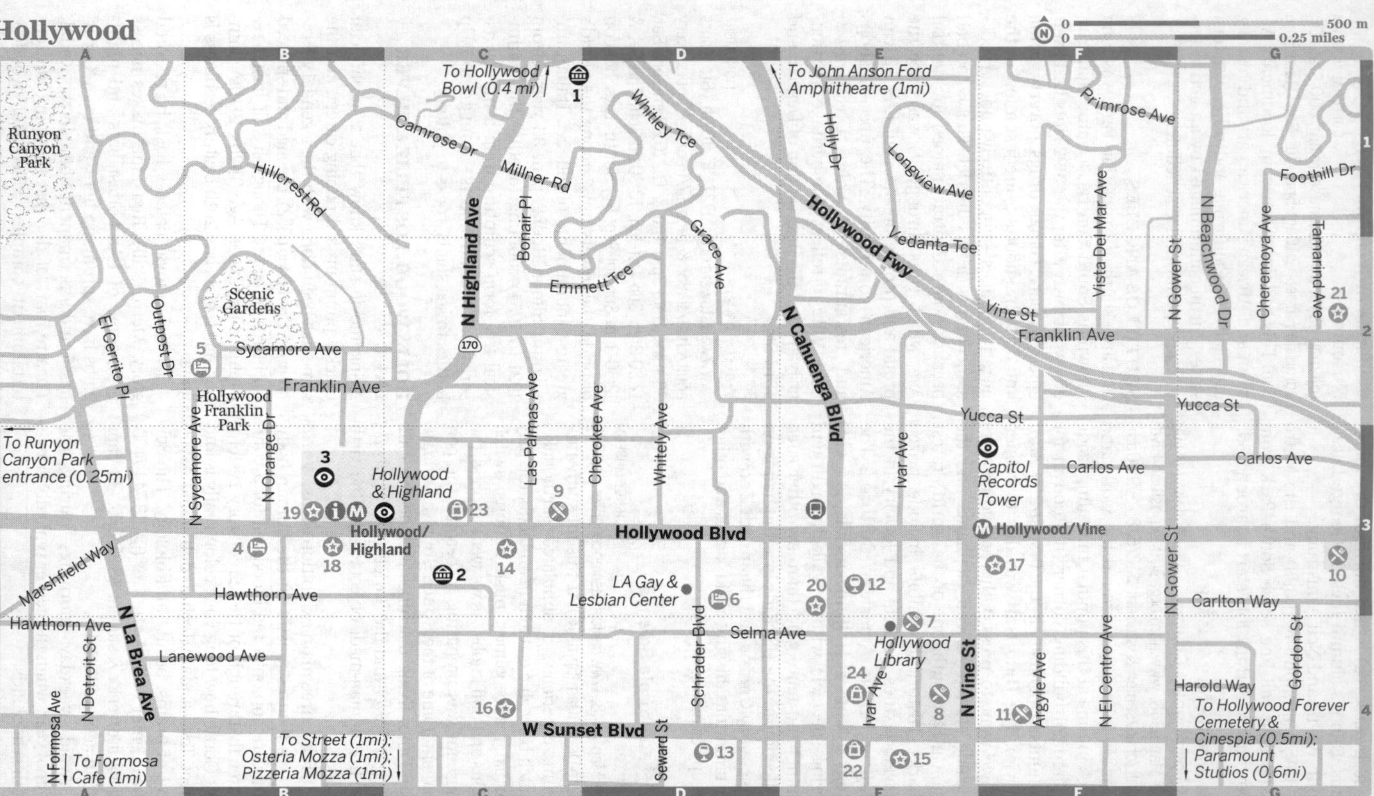
Hollywood
500 m
0.25 miles
To Hollywood Bowl (0.4 mi)
To John Anson Ford Amphitheatre (1mi)
Runyon Canyon Park
To Runyon Canyon Park entrance (0.25mi)
Scenic Gardens
Hollywood Franklin Park
Hollywood & Highland
Capitol Records Tower
Hollywood/Vine
Hollywood/Highland
LA Gay & Lesbian Center
Hollywood Library
To Street (1mi); Osteria Mozza (1mi); Pizzeria Mozza (1mi)
To Formosa Cafe (1mi)
To Hollywood Forever Cemetery & Cinespia (0.5mi); Paramount Studios (0.6mi)
Hollywood Fwy
N Cahuenga Blvd
Hollywood Blvd
W Sunset Blvd
N Highland Ave
N La Brea Ave
N Vine St
Franklin Ave
Yucca St
Tamarind Ave
Foothill Dr
Cheremoya Ave
N Beachwood Dr
Carlos Ave
N Gower St
Carlton Way
Gordon St
Harold Way
Primrose Ave
Vista Del Mar Ave
N El Centro Ave
Argyle Ave
Vine St
Longview Ave
Vedanta Tce
Ivar Ave
Holly Dr
Selma Ave
Grace Ave
Schrader Blvd
Whitley Tce
Whitely Ave
Seward St
Emmett Tce
Cherokee Ave
Millner Rd
Bonair Pl
Las Palmas Ave
Camrose Dr
Hillcrest Rd
Sycamore Ave
N Orange Dr
Hawthorn Ave
Lanewood Ave
N Sycamore Ave
Outpost Dr
El Cerrito Pl
Marshfield Way
N Detroit St
N Formosa Ave

Hollywood

Sights

	Egyptian Theatre	(see 14)
	El Capitan Theatre	(see 18)
	Grauman's Chinese Theatre	(see 19)
1	Hollywood Heritage Museum	C1
2	Hollywood Museum	C3
3	Kodak Theatre	B3

Sleeping

4	Hollywood Roosevelt Hotel	B3
5	Magic Castle Hotel	B2
6	USA Hostels Hollywood	D3

Eating

7	Hollywood Farmers Market	E4
8	Hungry Cat	E4
9	Musso & Frank Grill	C3
10	Palms Thai	G3
11	Waffle	F4

Drinking

12	Beauty Bar	E3
13	Cat & Fiddle	D4

Entertainment

14	American Cinematheque	C3
15	ArcLight & Cinerama Dome	E4
16	Catalina Bar & Grill	C4
17	Drai's	F3
18	El Capitan Theatre	B3
19	Grauman's Chinese Theatre	B3
20	Hotel Café	E3
21	Upright Citizens Brigade	G2

Shopping

22	Amoeba Music	E4
23	Frederick's of Hollywood	C3
24	Space 1520	E4

The most interesting mile runs between La Brea Ave and Vine St, along the **Hollywood Walk of Fame**, which honors more than 2000 celebrities with brass stars embedded in the sidewalk. For interesting historical tidbits about local landmarks, keep an eye out for the sign markers along here, or join a guided walking tour operated by Red Line Tours.

Following Hollywood Blvd east beyond Hwy 101 (Hollywood Fwy) takes you to the neighborhoods of **Los Feliz** (los *fee*-liss) and **Silver Lake**, both boho-chic enclaves with offbeat shopping, funky bars and a hopping cuisine scene.

The Metro Red Line serves central Hollywood (Hollywood/Highland and Hollywood/Vine stations) and Los Feliz (Vermont/Sunset station) from Downtown LA and the San Fernando Valley. Pay-parking lots abound in the side streets. The Hollywood & Highland parking garage charges $2 for four hours with validation (no purchase necessary) from any merchant within the mall or the Hollywood Visitors Center (Map p352).

HOLLYWOOD BOULEVARD

Grauman's Chinese Theatre CINEMA

(Map p352; 6925 Hollywood Blvd) Even the most jaded visitor may thrill in the Chinese Theater's famous forecourt at the heart of the Hollywood Walk of Fame, where generations of screen legends have left their imprints in cement: feet, hands, dreadlocks (Whoopi Goldberg), and even magic wands (the young *Harry Potter* stars). Actors dressed as Superman, Marilyn Monroe and the like pose for photos (for tips), and you may be offered free tickets to TV shows.

El Capitan Theatre CINEMA

(Map p352; ☎323-467-7674; 6838 Hollywood Blvd) Flamboyant theatre hosts Disney Studios first-runs.

Egyptian Theatre CINEMA

(Map p352; ☎323-466-3456; www.egyptiantheatre.com; 6712 Hollywood Blvd) Home of the nonprofit American Cinematheque (p381).

Kodak Theatre THEATER

(Map p352; www.kodaktheatre.com; adult/child & senior $15/10; ⏲10:30am-4pm; closed irregularly) Real-life celebs sashay along the Kodak's red carpet for the Academy Awards – columns with names of Oscar-winning films line the entryway. Pricey 30-minute tours take you inside the auditorium, VIP room and past an actual Oscar statuette. Cirque du Soleil presents **Iris** (www.cirquedusoleil.com; tickets $43-253) here, a new film-themed performance. FYI, the first Academy Awards ceremony was held diagonally across the street in the 1927 Hollywood Roosevelt Hotel.

Hollywood Sign LANDMARK

(Map p356) LA's most recognizable landmark first appeared atop its hillside perch in 1923 as an advertising gimmick for a real-estate development called Hollywood Land. Each letter is 50 feet tall and made of sheet metal. It's illegal to hike up to the sign, but there are many places where you can catch good views, including the Hollywood & Highland shopping and entertainment complex, Griffith Park and the top of Beachwood Dr.

WORTH A TRIP

BEHIND THE CURTAIN

Did you know it takes a week to shoot a half-hour sitcom? Or that you rarely see ceilings on TV because the space is filled with lights and lamps? You'll learn these and other fascinating nuggets about the world of film and TV production while touring a working studio. Action is slowest (and star-sighting potential lowest) during 'hiatus' (May to August). Reservations recommended; bring photo ID.

Paramount Studios (off Map p352; ☎323-956-1777; www.paramountstudios.com/special-events/tours.html; 5555 Melrose Ave, Hollywood; tours $45; ⊙Mon-Fri by reservation) The only studio in Hollywood proper runs two-hour tram tours of its historic lot. Group size is limited to eight per tram, leaving ample opportunity to pepper your guide with questions. No two tours are alike, and access to stages varies daily, but they might include the sets of *Dr Phil* or *Nip/Tuck*. Minimum age 12.

Sony Pictures Studios (☎323-520-8687; www.sonypicturesstudiostours.com; 10202 W Washington Blvd, Culver City; tour $33; ⊙tours 9:30am, 10:30am, 1:30pm & 2:30pm Mon-Fri; P) Two-hour walking tours include possible visits to sound stages where *Men in Black*, *Spider-Man*, *Charlie's Angels* and other blockbusters were filmed. Munchkins hopped along the Yellow Brick Road in the *Wizard of Oz*, filmed when this was the venerable MGM studio. You might even pop in on the set of *Jeopardy!* Minimum age 12.

Warner Bros Studios (Map p356; ☎818-972-8687; www.wbstudiotour.com; 3400 Riverside Dr, Burbank; tours $45; ⊙8:30am-4pm Mon-Fri, extended hr Mar-Sep) This 2¼-hour, fun-yet-authentic look behind the scenes kicks off with a video of WB's greatest hits (*Rebel Without a Cause*, *Harry Potter*, etc) before you travel by mini-tram to sound stages, backlot sets and technical departments, including costumes and set building. The studio museum is a treasure trove of props and memorabilia, including Hogwarts' Sorting Hat. Tours leave roughly every half-hour. Minimum age eight. Parking $7.

Hollywood Museum MUSEUM
(Map p352; www.thehollywoodmuseum.com; 1660 N Highland Ave; adult/student/senior/child $15/12/12/5; ⊙10am-5pm Wed-Sun) The slightly musty museum is a 35,000-sq-ft shrine to the stars, crammed with kitsch, costumes, knickknacks and props from Charlie Chaplin to *Glee*.

Hollywood Bowl & Around AMPHITHEATER
(off Map p352; ☎323-850-2000; www.hollywoodbowl.com; 2301 N Highland Ave; ⊙concerts late Jun-Sep) Summer concerts at the Hollywood Bowl have been a great LA tradition since 1922. This 18,000-seat hillside amphitheater is the summer home of the LA Philharmonic, and is also host to big-name rock, jazz and blues acts. Many concertgoers come early to enjoy a pre-show picnic on the parklike grounds or in their seats (alcohol is allowed). For insight into the Bowl's storied history, visit the **Hollywood Bowl Museum** (off Map p352; www.hollywoodbowl.com/visit/museum.cfm; 2301 N Highland Ave; admission free; ⊙10am-8pm Tue-Sat, 4-7pm Sun mid-Jun–mid-Sep, 10am-5pm Tue-Fri mid-Sep–mid-Jun). The Bowl grounds are open to the public daytimes.

Hollywood Heritage Museum MUSEUM
(Map p352; www.hollywoodheritage.org; 2100 N Highland Ave; adult/child $7/free; ⊙noon-4pm Wed-Sun; P) Across from the Bowl, this museum is inside the horse barn used by the movie pioneer Cecil B DeMille in 1913 and 1914 to shoot *The Squaw Man*, Hollywood's first feature-length film. Inside are exhibits on early filmmaking, including costumes, projectors and cameras, as well as a replica of DeMille's office.

Griffith Park PARK
(Map p356; www.laparks.org/dos/parks/griffithpk; admission free; ⊙6am-10pm, trails close at dusk; P) America's largest urban park is five times the size of New York's Central Park. It embraces an outdoor theater, zoo, observatory, museum, antique trains, golf, tennis, playgrounds, bridle paths, 53 miles of hiking trails, Batman's caves and the Hollywood Sign. The **Ranger Station** (Map p356; 4730 Crystal Springs Dr) has maps.

Kids particularly love the 1926 **Griffith Park Merry-Go-Round** (Map p356; rides $1; ⏲11am-5pm daily May-Sep, 11am-5pm Sat & Sun Oct-Apr; 🚸), with beautifully carved and painted horses sporting real horse-hair tails and vintage railcars and steam locomotives of the **Travel Town Museum** (Map p356; 5200 W Zoo Dr; admission free; ⏲10am-5pm Mon-Fri, to 6pm Sat & Sun; 🚸). **Griffith Park & Southern Railroad** (Map p356; 4400 Crystal Springs Dr; tickets $2.50; ⏲10am-4:30pm Mon-Fri, to 5pm Sat & Sun; 🚸) is a miniature train chugging through a re-created old Western town and a Native American village.

Griffith Observatory OBSERVATORY
(Map p356; www.griffithobservatory.org; 2800 Observatory Rd; admission free, planetarium shows adult/child/senior $7/3/5; ⏲noon-10pm Tue-Fri, 10am-10pm Sat & Sun, closed occasional Tue; P🚸) Above Los Feliz loom the iconic triple domes of this 1935 observatory, which boasts a super-techie planetarium and films in the Leonard Nimoy Event Horizon Theater. During clear night-time skies, you can often peer through the telescopes at heavenly bodies.

Los Angeles Zoo & Botanical Gardens ZOO
(Map p356; www.lazoo.org; 5333 Zoo Dr; adult/child/senior $14/9/11; ⏲10am-5pm; P🚸) Make friends with 1100 finned, feathered and furry creatures, including in the Campo Gorilla Reserve and the Sea Cliffs, which replicate the California coast complete with harbor seals.

Museum of the American West MUSEUM
(Map p356; www.autrynationalcenter.org; 4700 Western Heritage Way; adult/child/students & seniors $10/4/6, free 2nd Tue each month; ⏲10am-4pm Tue-Fri, to 5pm Sat & Sun; P🚸) Exhibits on the good, the bad and the ugly of America's westward expansion rope in even the most reluctant of cowpokes. Star exhibits include an original stagecoach, a Colt firearms collection and a nymph-festooned saloon. Its affiliated **Southwest Museum of the American Indian** (234 Museum Dr) is scheduled to reopen in 2013.

Hollyhock House ARCHITECTURE
(1919; Map p358; www.hollyhockhouse.net; Barnsdall Art Park; adult/student/child $7/3/free; ⏲tours hourly 12:30-3:30pm Wed-Sun; P) An early masterpiece by Frank Lloyd Wright, this house marks the famous architect's first attempt at creating an indoor-outdoor living space in harmony with LA's sunny climate, a style he later referred to as California Romanza. Admission is by tour only.

Hollywood Forever Cemetery CEMETERY
(off Map p352; www.hollywoodforever.com; 6000 Santa Monica Blvd; ⏲8am-5pm; P) Next to Paramount Studios, this cemetery is crowded with famous 'immortals,' including Rudolph Valentino, Tyrone Power, Jayne Mansfield and Cecil B DeMille. Pick up a map ($5) at the flower shop near the entrance. See p381 for details of **film screenings** here. No, really.

FREE **826 LA Time Travel Mart** GALLERY
(off map p358; www.826la.org; 1714 W Sunset Blvd; noon-8pm Mon-Fri, to 6pm Sat & Sun) At first glance, this is a convenience store stocked with products from the past and the future: whale oil (not really) and spice rubs (really), suction-cup clocks and the correct answer in a can ('That looks great on you!'). In reality, proceeds fund a center in the back room specializing in homework help and writing workshops, brainchild of author, screenwriter and McSweeney's founder, Dave Eggers.

WEST HOLLYWOOD

Rainbow flags fly proudly over Santa Monica Blvd. Celebs keep gossip rags happy by misbehaving at clubs on the fabled Sunset Strip. Welcome to the city of West Hollywood (WeHo), 1.9 sq miles of pure personality.

Boutiques on Robertson Blvd and Melrose Ave purvey the sassy and chic for Hollywood royalty, Santa Monica Blvd is gay central, WeHo's eastern precincts are filled with Russian speaking émigrés, and Sunset Blvd bursts with clubs, chichi hotels and views across LA. WeHo's also a hotbed of cutting-edge interior design, particularly along the **Avenues of Art and Design** around Beverly Blvd and Melrose Ave.

Pacific Design Center DESIGN CENTER
(Map p360; www.pacificdesigncenter.com; 8687 Melrose Ave; ⏲9am-5pm Mon-Fri) Some 130 galleries fill the monolithic blue and green 'whales' of the Cesar Pelli–designed Pacific Design Center (a red whale should open by 2012). Visitors are welcome to window-shop, though most sales are to the trade. There's a small offshoot of the **Museum of Contemporary Art** (Map p360, admission free). Parking is $6 per hour.

Griffith Park & Around

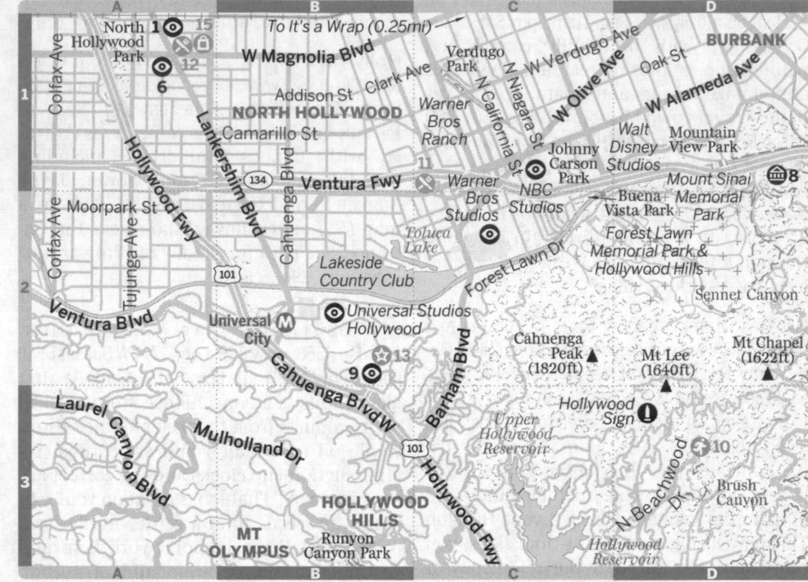

Schindler House ARCHITECTURE
(Map p360; www.makcenter.org; 835 N Kings Rd; adult/senior & student $7/6, 4-6pm Fri free; ⏲11am-6pm Wed-Sun) A point of pilgrimage, which pioneering modernist architect Rudolph Schindler (1887–1953) made his home. It houses changing exhibits and lectures.

Parking lot rates vary widely. Use caution when parking on the street as parking is quite restricted and fervently enforced. WeHo is also served by the DASH bus.

Sunset Strip NEIGHBORHOOD
The famed Sunset Strip – Sunset Blvd between Laurel Canyon Blvd and Doheny Dr – has been a favorite nighttime playground since the 1920s. The **Chateau Marmont** and clubs such as Ciro's (now the **Comedy Store**; p383), Mocambo and the Trocadero (both now defunct) were favorite hangouts for Hollywood high society, from Bogart to Bacall, Monroe to Sinatra. The 1960s saw the opening of **Whisky-a-Go-Go** (☎310-652-4202; 8901 W Sunset Blvd), America's first discotheque, the birthplace of go-go dancing and a launch pad for The Doors, who were the club's house band in 1966. Nearby is the **ANdAZ** (Map p360; ☎323-656-1234; 8401 W Sunset Blvd), which, in its previous incarnation as the Hyatt Hotel, earned the moniker 'Riot House' during the 1970s, when it was the hotel of choice for raucous rock royalty such as Led Zeppelin. At one time, the band rented six floors and raced motorcycles in the hallways.

Today the strip is still nightlife central, although it's lost much of its cutting edge. It's a visual cacophony dominated by billboards and giant advertising banners draped across building facades. More recent places include the **House of Blues** (Map p371); the jet-set **Mondrian hotel** (Map p371), home of the **Sky Bar** (p380); and the **Viper Room** (Map p371), until recently owned by Johnny Depp, where Tommy Lee attacked a paparazzo and, in 1993, actor River Phoenix overdosed.

MID-CITY

Mid-City encompasses an amorphous area east of West Hollywood, south of Hollywood, west of Koreatown and north of I-10 (Santa Monica Fwy). A historic farmers market and a row of top-notch museums are its main attractions. There's plenty of street parking and validated parking at the farmers market and the adjacent Grove shopping mall. The main sights are served by DASH buses on the Fairfax route.

Los Angeles County Museum of Art ART MUSEUM
(Map p360; www.lacma.org; 5905 Wilshire Blvd; adult/child under 17yr/student & senior $15/

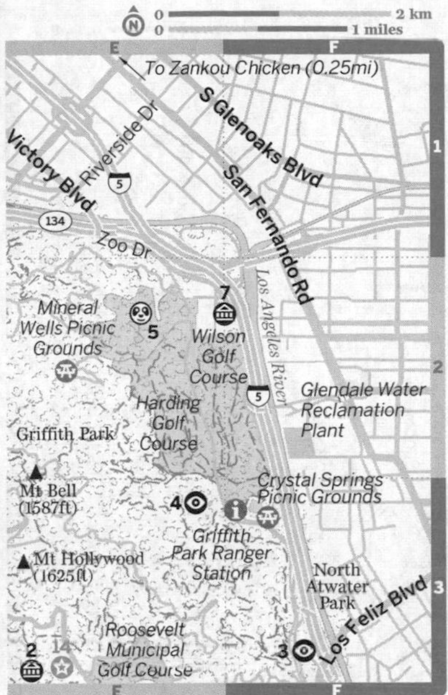

Griffith Park & Around

Sights

1 Academy of Television Arts & Sciences A1
2 Griffith Observatory E3
3 Griffith Park & Southern Railroad F3
4 Griffith Park Merry-Go-Round E3
5 Los Angeles Zoo & Botanical Gardens E2
6 Millennium Dance Complex A1
7 Museum of the American West F2
8 Travel Town Museum D1
9 Universal City Walk B2

Activities, Courses & Tours

10 Sunset Ranch Hollywood D3

Eating

11 Bob's Big Boy C1
12 Eclectic A1

Entertainment

13 Gibson Amphitheatre B2
14 Greek Theatre E3

Shopping

15 Vintage Clothing Store District A1

free/10; ⌚noon-8pm Mon, Tue & Thu, noon-9pm Fri, 11am-8pm Sat & Sun) One of the country's top art museums and the largest in the western USA. The collection in the new Renzo Piano–designed **Broad Contemporary Art Museum** (B-CAM) includes seminal pieces by Jeff Koons, Roy Lichtenstein and Andy Warhol, and two gigantic works in rusted steel by Richard Serra.

Other LACMA pavilions brim with paintings, sculpture and decorative arts: Rembrandt, Cézanne and Magritte; ancient pottery from China, Turkey and Iran; photographs by Ansel Adams and Henri Cartier-Bresson; and a jewel box of a Japanese pavilion. There are often headline-grabbing touring exhibits. Parking is $10.

La Brea Tar Pits HISTORIC SITE

Between 10,000 and 40,000 years ago, tarlike bubbling crude oil trapped saber-toothed cats, mammoths and other now-extinct Ice Age critters, which are still being excavated at La Brea Tar Pits. Check out their fossilized remains at the **Page Museum** (Map p360; www.tarpits.org; 5801 Wilshire Blvd; adult/child/senior & student $11/5/8, free first Tue each month; ⌚9:30am-5pm; 👪). New fossils are being discovered all the time, and an active staff of archaeologists works behind glass. Parking is $7.

Petersen Automotive Museum MUSEUM

(Map p360; www.petersen.org; 6060 Wilshire Blvd; adult/child/student/senior $10/3/5/8; ⌚10am-6pm Tue-Sun; 👪) A four-story ode to the auto, the museum exhibits shiny vintage cars galore, plus a fun LA streetscape showing how the city's growth has been shaped by the automobile. Parking is $8.

BEVERLY HILLS & WESTSIDE

The mere mention of Beverly Hills conjures up images of fame and wealth, reinforced by film and TV. Opulent mansions flank manicured grounds on palm-lined avenues, especially north of **Sunset Blvd**, while legendary **Rodeo Drive** is three solid blocks of style for the Prada and Gucci brigade.

These days much of Beverly Hills' wealth is new money, brought here by Iranian émigrés who've been settling here since the fall of the Shah in the late 1970s. About 25% of the 35,000 residents are of Iranian descent, spawning the nickname 'Tehrangeles.'

Several city-owned parking lots and garages offer up to two hours free parking.

West of Beverly Hills to the Santa Monica city line, the well-to-do LA neighborhoods of

Los Feliz & Silver Lake

Los Feliz & Silver Lake

Sights

1 Hollyhock House A2

Eating

2 El Conquistador C3
3 Umami Burger A2
4 Yuca's B1

Drinking

5 Akbar B3
6 Dresden A1
7 Good Luck Bar B2
8 MJ's D1

Entertainment

9 Little Temple B3
10 Spaceland D3

Shopping

11 Bar Keeper B3
12 Wacko/Soap Plant A2

Brentwood, Bel Air, Westwood and the separate city Culver City are collectively referred to as the Westside.

Getty Center ART MUSEUM
(off Map p364; www.getty.edu; 1200 Getty Center Dr; admission free; ⌚10am-5:30pm Sun & Tue-Thu, to 9pm Fri & Sat) Triple delights: stellar art collection (Renaissance to David Hockney), Richard Meier's soaring architecture and Robert Irwin's ever-evolving gardens. On clear days, add breathtaking views of the city and ocean to the list. Visit in the late afternoon after the crowds have thinned. See also Getty Villa (p361). Parking is $15, or Metro bus 761 stops here.

Paley Center for Media MUSEUM
(www.paleycenter.org; 465 N Beverly Dr; suggested donation adult/child/senior/student $10/5/8/8; ⌚noon-5pm Wed-Sun) TV and radio addicts can indulge their passion at this mind-boggling archive of TV and radio broadcasts

from 1918 through the internet age. Pick your faves, grab a seat at a private console and enjoy. There's an active program of lectures and screenings. It's just south of Little Santa Monica Blvd.

Museum of Tolerance MUSEUM
(www.museumoftolerance.com; 9786 W Pico Blvd; adult/child/student & senior $15/12/11; ⏲10am-5pm Mon-Thu, to 3:30pm Fri, 11am-5pm Sun; P ♿) This museum uses interactive technology to make visitors confront racism and bigotry. There's a particular focus on the Holocaust, including Nazi-era artifacts and letters by Anne Frank. A history wall celebrates diversity, exposes intolerance and champions rights in America. Reservations recommended.

FREE **Annenberg Space for Photography** MUSEUM
(www.annenbergspaceforphotography.org; 2000 Ave of the Stars, No 10; admission free; ⏲11am-6pm Wed-Sun) This fine museum shows special exhibits in a camera-shaped building just west of Beverly Hills, in the skyscraper village known as Century City. Parking is $3.50 from Wednesday to Friday, or $1 on Saturday and Sunday or after 4:30pm daily.

Museum of Jurassic Technology MUSEUM
(www.mjt.org; 9341 Venice Blvd, Culver City; suggested donation adult/student & senior/under 12yr $5/3/free; ⏲2-8pm Thu, noon-6pm Fri-Sun) It has nothing to do with dinosaurs and even less with technology. Instead, madness nibbles at your synapses as you try to read meaning into displays about Cameroonian stink ants, a tribute to trailer parks or a sculpture of the Pope squished into the eye of a needle. It may all be a mind-bending spoof. Or not.

University of California, Los Angeles UNIVERSITY
(Map p364; ☎campus tour reservations 310-825-8764; www.ucla.edu; 405 Hilgard Ave) Westwood is practically synonymous with UCLA, alma mater of Francis Ford Coppola, James Dean, Jim Morrison and multiple Nobel Prize laureates. Campus parking: $11 per day.

Excellent, university-run museums include the **Hammer Museum** (Map p364; www.hammer.ucla.edu; 10899 Wilshire Blvd; adult/child/senior $10/free/5, free Thu; ⏲11am-7pm Tue, Wed, Fri & Sat, to 9pm Thu, to 5pm Sun) with cutting-edge contemporary art exhibits and a courtyard cafe (Hammer parking is $3), and the **Fowler Museum of Cultural History** (Map p364; www.fowler.ucla.edu; admission free; ⏲noon-5pm Wed & Fri-Sun, to 8pm Thu) presenting a rich variety of arts, crafts and artifacts from non-Western cultures.

Gardens include the sprawling **Franklin D Murphy Sculpture Garden** (Map p364), with dozens of works by Rodin, Moore, Calder and other American and European artists, and tranquil **Mildred E Mathias Botanical Garden** (Map p364). The secluded **UCLA Hannah Carter Japanese Garden** (Map p364; www.japanesegarden.ucla.edu; 10619 Bellagio Rd) was closed for renovation as of this writing. Check for reopening.

Westwood Village Memorial Park CEMETERY
(Map p364; 1218 Glendon Ave, Westwood; admission free; ⏲8am-5pm) Tucked among Westwood's high-rises, this postage-stamp-sized park is packed with such famous 6-feet-under residents as Marilyn Monroe, Burt Lancaster and Rodney Dangerfield.

Sawtelle Blvd NEIGHBOURHOOD
Can't make it all the way to Little Tokyo? The smaller Japanese neighborhood around Sawtelle Blvd, between Olympic and Santa Monica Blvds and just west of I-405, is sometimes called **Little Osaka**, after Japan's second city. It's easy to spend an hour or two browsing shops selling *manga,* Japanese trinkets and housewares, going 'hmm?' in the groceries and, of course, enjoying the restaurants. The largest concentration is within a few blocks north of Olympic Blvd.

Skirball Cultural Center MUSEUM
(☎tickets 877-722-4849; www.skirball.org; 2701 N Sepulveda Blvd; adult/child 2-12yr/student/senior $10/5/7/7, Thu free; ⏲noon-5pm Tue, Wed & Fri, to 9pm Thu, 10am-5pm Sat & Sun, closed major Jewish holidays; P ♿) This museum in the Sepulveda Pass beyond the Getty Center has two main attractions. The preschool set can climb the gigantic wooden **Noah's Ark** by noted architect Moshe Safdie, an indoor playground of imaginative creatures made from car mats, couch springs, metal strainers and other recycled items. Entry to Noah's Ark is by timed tickets, which also cover museum admission; advance reservations are recommended. For grown-ups, the permanent exhibit is an engaging view of 4000 years of history, traditions, trials and triumphs of the Jewish people, including replicas of a mosaic floor from an ancient Galilee synagogue and Hitler's racist rant *Mein Kampf.*

West Hollywood & Mid-City

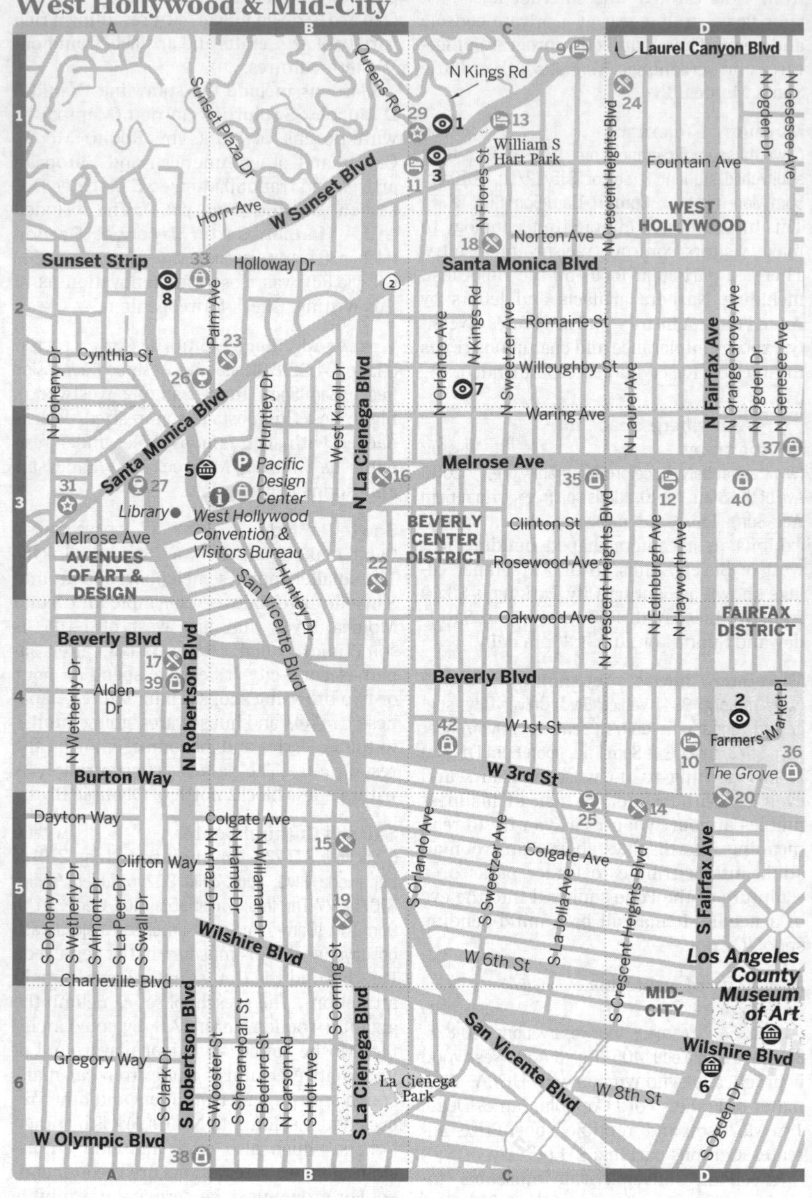

MALIBU

Malibu has been synonymous with celebrities since the early 1930s. Clara Bow and Barbara Stanwyck were the first to stake out their turf in what became known as the **Malibu Colony** and the earliest Hollywood elite to Barbra and Leo have lived here ever since.

Along Malibu's spectacular 27-mile stretch of the Pacific Coast Hwy, where the Santa Monica Mountains plunge into the ocean, are some fine beaches, including **Las**

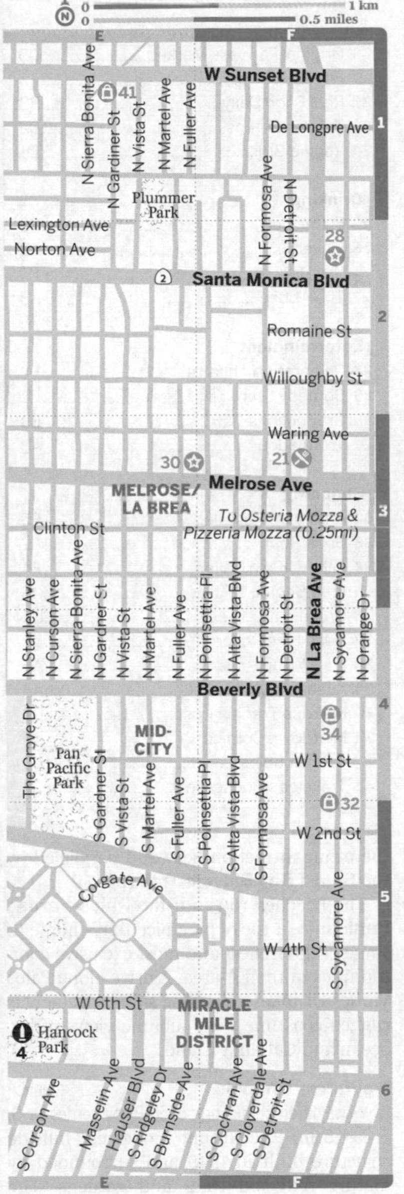

Tunas, **Point Dume**, **Zuma** and the world-famous surfing spot **Surfrider**. Rising behind Malibu is **Malibu Creek State Park**, part of the Santa Monica Mountains National Recreation Area and laced with hiking trails (see p367). Malibu has no real center, but you'll find the greatest concentration of restaurants and shops near the century-old **Malibu Pier**. The most likely star-spotting venue is the **Malibu Country Mart shopping center** (3835 Cross Creek Rd).

Getty Villa ART MUSEUM

(www.getty.edu; 17985 Pacific Coast Hwy; admission free; ⏲10am-5pm Wed-Mon; 🅿) Malibu's cultural star – a replica Roman villa that's a fantastic showcase of Greek, Roman and Etruscan antiquities. Admission is by timed ticket (no walk-ins). See also the Getty Center. Parking is $15.

SANTA MONICA

Santa Monica is the belle by the beach, mixing urban cool with a laid-back vibe.

Tourists, teens and street performers make car-free, chain-store-lined **Third Street Promenade** (Map p366) the most action-packed zone. For more local flavor, shop celeb-favored **Montana Avenue** or down-home **Main Street** (Map p366), backbone of the neighborhood once nicknamed 'Dogtown' as birthplace of skateboard culture. Rent bikes or in-line skates from many outlets along the beach.

There's free two-hour parking in public garages on 2nd and 4th Sts ($3 flat rate after 6pm), and most lines of Santa Monica's Big Blue Bus converge around the Promenade.

Santa Monica Pier AMUSEMENT PARK

(Map p366; www.santamonicapier.org; admission free, unlimited rides under/over age 7 $16/22; ⏲24hr; 👪) Kids love the venerable 1908 pier, where attractions include a quaint 1922 carousel, a tiny aquarium with touch tanks and the **Pacific Park** (www.pacpark.com) amusement park crowned by a solar-powered Ferris wheel.

Bergamot Station Arts Center ART GALLERIES & MUSEUM

(2525 Michigan Ave; ⏲10am-6pm Tue-Sat; 🅿) Art fans gravitate inland toward this avant-garde center, a former trolley stop that now houses 35 galleries and the progressive **Santa Monica Museum of Art** (www.smmoa.org; 2525 Michigan Ave; suggested donation $5; ⏲11am-6pm Tue-Sat).

VENICE

Venice was created in 1905 by eccentric tobacco heir Abbot Kinney as an amusement park, called 'Venice of America,' complete with Italian *gondolieri* who poled visitors around canals. Most of the waterways have

West Hollywood & Mid-City

Top Sights

Los Angeles County Museum of Art ... D6

Sights

1 ANdAZ ... C1
2 CBS Television City ... D4
3 House of Blues ... C1
4 La Brea Tar Pits ... E6
5 MOCA Pacific Design Center ... A3
Page Museum ... (see 4)
6 Petersen Automotive Museum ... D6
7 Schindler House ... C2
8 Viper Room ... A2

Sleeping

9 Chateau Marmont ... C1
10 Farmer's Daughter Hotel ... D4
11 Mondrian Hotel ... C1
12 Orbit Hotel & Hostel ... D3
13 Standard Hollywood ... C1

Eating

¡Loteria! Grill ... (see 20)
14 AOC ... D5
15 Bazaar ... B5
16 Comme Ça ... B3
Gumbo Pot ... (see 20)
17 Ivy ... A4
18 Marix Tex Mex ... C2
19 Matsuhisa ... B5
20 Original Farmers Market ... D5
21 Pink's Hot Dogs ... F3
22 Real Food Daily ... B3
23 Tender Greens ... B2
24 Veggie Grill ... D1

Drinking

25 El Carmen ... C5
26 Eleven ... A2
Sky Bar ... (see 11)
27 The Abbey ... A3

Entertainment

28 Celebration Theatre ... F2
29 Comedy Store ... C1
30 Groundlings ... E3
31 Troubadour ... A3

Shopping

32 American Rag Cie ... F5
33 Book Soup ... A2
34 Fahey/Klein Gallery ... F4
35 Fred Segal ... C3
36 Grove ... D4
37 Head Line Records ... D3
38 It's a Wrap ... A6
39 Kitson ... A4
40 Melrose Trading Post ... D3
41 Meltdown Comics & Collectibles ... E1
42 Traveler's Bookcase ... C4

since been paved over, but those that remain are flanked by flower-festooned villas, easily accessed from either Venice or Washington Blvds.

The hippest Westside strip is funky, sophisticated **Abbot Kinney Boulevard** (Map p366), a palm-lined mile of restaurants, yoga studios, art galleries and eclectic shops selling mid-century furniture and handmade fashions.

There's street parking around Abbot Kinney Blvd, and parking lots ($6 to $15) on the beach.

SOUTH BAY & PALOS VERDES

South of LAX, Santa Monica Bay is lined by a trio of all-American beach towns – **Manhattan Beach, Hermosa Beach** and **Redondo Beach** – with a distinctive laid-back vibe. Pricey, if not lavish, homes come all the way down to the gorgeous white beach, which is the prime attraction here and paralleled by the **South Bay Bicycle Trail** (p367).

The beaches run into the **Palos Verdes Peninsula**, a rocky precipice that's home to some of the richest and most exclusive communities in the LA area. A drive along Palos Verdes Dr takes you along some spectacular rugged coastline with sublime views of the ocean and Catalina Island.

Wayfarers Chapel CHURCH
(www.wayfarerschapel.org; 5755 Palos Verdes Dr S; 8am-5pm) Enchanting modernist hillside structure built in 1949 and surrounded by mature redwood trees and gardens. The work of Lloyd Wright (Frank's son), it is almost entirely made of glass and is one of LA's most popular spots for weddings.

SAN PEDRO

While other LA beachside communities primp, tempt and put on airs, San Pedro (*pee*-droh) feels like what it is: a working port, albeit in the shadow of ritzy Palos Verdes. It began as a lumber port and grew on an influx of Croatian, Italian, Greek, Japanese and Scandinavian fishers. Today their descendants populate this 90,000-strong enclave, part of the largest container port in North America (nearby Long Beach is the second largest).

San Pedro's symbol is the 1874 **Point Fermin Lighthouse** (www.pointferminlighthouse.org; 807 W Paseo del Mar; admission free, donations welcome; ⏲tours 1pm, 2pm, 3pm Tue-Sun), unusually built of wood, like a Victorian home. The impressive WWII-era **Fort MacArthur**(www.ftmac.org; 3601 S Gaffey St; suggested donation adult/child $3/1; ⏲noon-5pm Tue, Thu, Sat & Sun) displays military history through artifacts and weaponry inside a maze-like battery built into the cliffs.

If you enjoy clambering around old ships, head a mile north to the **SS Lane Victory** (www.lanevictory.org; Berth 94; adult/child $3/1; ⏲9am-3pm), a museum vessel that sailed the seven seas from 1945 to 1971. Self-guided tours take in the engine room and the cargo holds. See the website for directions.

Further south, you'll be besieged by shrieking gulls and excited children at **Ports O'Call Village** (Berth 77; admission free; ⏲11am-10pm). Skip the trinket stores and fill up on fresh fish and shrimp at the raucous **San Pedro Fish Market & Restaurant**. Afterwards, hop on a port cruise or join a whale-watching trip (January to March).

Pedro's surfer-sophisticate **Arts District** (6th St, btwn Pacific Ave & Palos Verdes St) perks with coffee shops, art galleries, army-surplus stores and restaurants, many in art deco buildings, including the fabulous 1931 **Warner Grand Theatre** (www.warnergrand.org; 478 W 6th St).

San Pedro is most easily reached by car. Take the 110 Fwy from either Downtown LA or the 405 Fwy.

LONG BEACH

While San Pedro still retains some of its port city edge, Long Beach's has worn smooth in its humming downtown and restyled waterfront. Pine Ave is chockablock with restaurants and clubs popular with everyone from coiffed conventioneers to the testosterone-fuelled frat pack.

The Metro Blue Line (55 minutes) connects Long Beach with Downtown LA, and Passport minibuses (www.lbtransit.org) shuttle you around the major sights for free ($1.25 elsewhere in town).

Queen Mary OCEAN LINER

(www.queenmary.com; 1126 Queens Hwy; adult/child/senior from $25/13/22; ⏲10am-6pm) Long Beach's 'flagship' is this grand (and supposedly haunted!) British ocean liner, permanently moored here. Larger and fancier than the *Titanic,* it transported royals, dignitaries, immigrants and troops during its 1001 Atlantic crossings between 1936 and 1964. Parking is $12.

Aquarium of the Pacific AQUARIUM

(www.aquariumofpacific.org; 100 Aquarium Way; adult/child/senior $25/13/22; ⏲9am-6pm; 👪) Kids will probably have a better time here – a high-tech romp through an underwater world in which sharks dart, jellyfish dance and sea lions frolic. Imagine the thrill of petting a shark! Parking is $8 to $15. *Queen Mary* and aquarium combination tickets cost $36/20 for adult/child three to 11 years.

Museum of Latin American Art ART MUSEUM

(www.molaa.org; 628 Alamitos Ave; adult/child/student & senior $9/free/6, Sun free; ⏲11am-5pm Wed-Sun; P) The only museum in the western USA specializing in contemporary art from south of the border. The permanent collection highlights spirituality and landscapes, and special exhibits are first-rate.

Gondola Getaway BOAT RIDES

(www.gondo.net; 5437 E Ocean Blvd; per couple $85; ⏲11am-11pm) About three miles east of

YOUR 15 MINUTES OF FAME

Come on, haven't you always dreamed of seeing your silly mug on TV? Well, LA has a way of making dreams come true, but you have to do your homework before coming to town. Here are some leads to get you started.

Sitcoms and game shows usually tape between August and March before live audiences. To nab free tickets, check with **Audiences Unlimited** (☎818-260-0041; www.tvtickets.com). For tickets to the *Tonight Show* at **NBC Studios** (Map p356; 3000 W Alameda Ave, Burbank), check www.nbc.com/nbc/footer/Tickets.shtml.

Although many game shows tape in LA, the chances of becoming a contestant are greatest on *The Price is Right*, at **CBS Television City** (Map p360; www.cbs.com/daytime/price; 7800 Beverly Blvd, Mid-City).

Bel Air & Westside

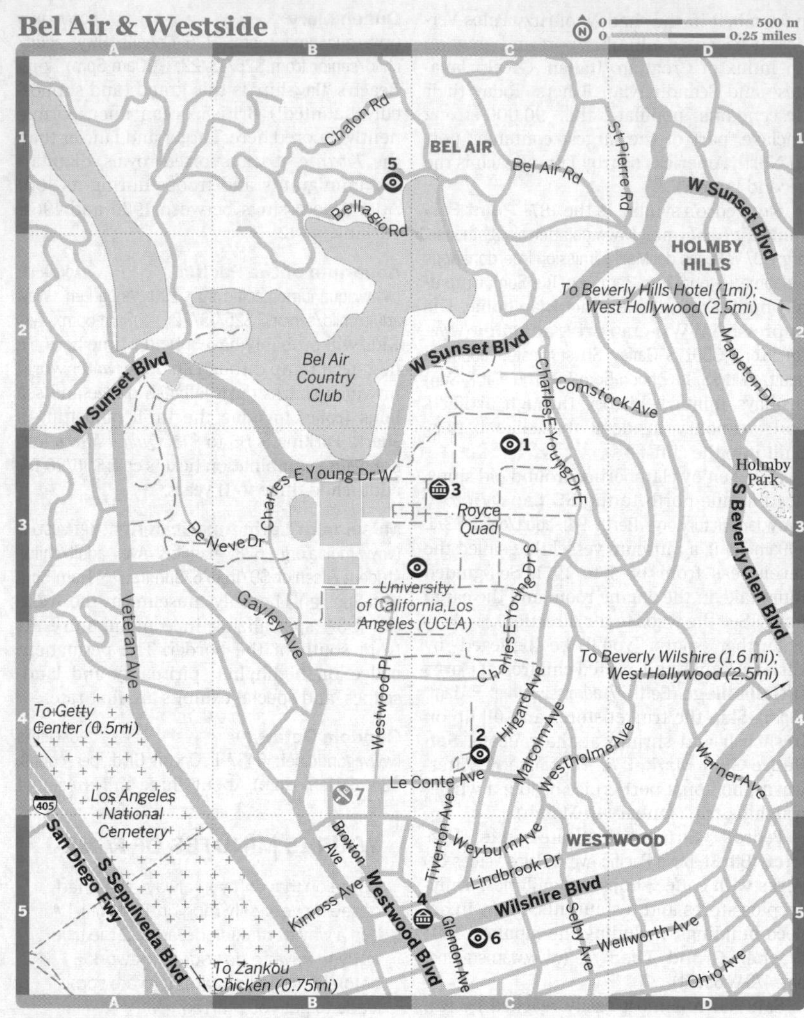

Downtown Long Beach, the upscale neighborhood of canal-laced Naples can be explored via hour-long cruises aboard authentic gondolas.

SAN FERNANDO VALLEY

The sprawling grid of suburbia known simply as 'the Valley' is home to most of the major movie studios, which makes it prime hunting grounds for 'Industry' fans. It's also the world capital of the porn movie industry. An arts district in North Hollywood (NoHo) has given the Valley a hip, artsy side.

Universal Studios Hollywood THEME PARK
(Map p356; www.universalstudioshollywood.com; 100 Universal City Plaza; admission over/under 48in \$77/69; open daily, hours vary;) One of the world's oldest and largest continuously operating movie studios, Universal first opened to the public in 1915, when studio head Carl Laemmle invited visitors at a quaint 25¢ each (including a boxed lunch) to watch silent films being made.

Your chances of seeing an actual movie shoot are approximately nil at Universal's current theme park incarnation, yet generations of visitors have had a ball here. Start

Bel Air & Westside

Sights

1 Franklin D Murphy Sculpture Garden....C3
2 Mildred E Mathias Botanical Garden....C4
3 UCLA Fowler Museum of Cultural History....C3
4 UCLA Hammer Museum....C5
5 UCLA Hannah Carter Japanese Garden....B1
6 Westwood Village Memorial Park....C5

Eating

7 Diddy Riese Cookies....B4

with the 45-minute narrated **Studio Tour** aboard a giant, multicar tram that takes you past working soundstages and outdoor sets such as *Desperate Housewives*. Also prepare to survive a shark attack à la *Jaws* and an 8.3-magnitude earthquake. It's hokey but fun.

Among the dozens of other attractions, **King Kong in 3-D** scares the living daylights, the **Simpsons Ride** is a motion-simulated romp 'designed' by Krusty the Klown, and you can splash down among the dinos of **Jurassic Park**, while **Special Effects Stages** illuminate the craft of movie-making. **Water World** may have bombed as a movie, but the live action show based on it is a runaway hit, with stunts including giant fireballs and a crash-landing seaplane. Note: the single-digit set may be too short or too easily spooked for many attractions.

Allow a full day, especially in summer, as lines can easily take 45 minutes for top attractions. To beat the crowds, invest in the Front of Line Pass ($149).

The adjacent **Universal City Walk** is an unabashedly commercial (yet also entertaining) fantasy promenade of restaurants, shops, bars and entertainment venues. Get your hand stamped if you'd like to return to the park.

Parking is $12, or arrive via Metro Red Line.

NoHo Arts District NEIGHBORHOOD

(www.nohoartsdistrict.com) At the end of the Metro Red Line, **North Hollywood** (NoHo) was a down-on-its-heels neighborhood of artists, but thanks to a redevelopment effort it now boasts some 20 stage theaters in 1 square mile and a burgeoning community of art galleries, restaurants, gyms and vintage clothing stores around them. Most of the theaters are 'Equity waiver houses' – 99 seats or fewer – where members of the Actors' Equity union (some quite famous) can perform at below regular wages, for example to showcase work or talent before heading to larger venues.

The Hall of Fame Plaza at the **Academy of Television Arts & Sciences** (Map p356; ☎818-754-2000; www.emmys.tv; 5200 Lankershim Blvd, North Hollywood; admission free) bursts with busts and life-size bronzes of TV legends (Johnny Carson, Bill Cosby, Lucille Ball et al) and a giant, gleaming Emmy award. **Millennium Dance Complex** (Map p356; www.millenniumdancecomplex.com; 5113 Lankershim Blvd, North Hollywood; classes from $15) trains many of the world's top hip-hop dancers and is open to the public. Vintage clothing stores (many with celebrity clients) line Magnolia Blvd east of Lankershim Blvd.

NoHo is best visited late afternoon through early evening, Thursday through Sunday, when the streets are buzzing with activity around the theaters.

PASADENA

Resting below the lofty San Gabriel Mountains, Pasadena is a genteel city with old-time mansions, superb Arts and Crafts architecture and fine-art museums. Every New Year's Day, it is thrust into the national spotlight during the **Rose Parade**.

The main fun zone is **Old Town Pasadena**, a bustling 20-block shopping and entertainment district in handsomely restored historic Spanish colonial buildings along Colorado Blvd, west of Arroyo Pkwy. Pick up information at the **Pasadena Convention & Visitors Bureau** (☎626-795-9311, 800-307-7977; www.pasadenacal.com; 171 S Los Robles Ave; ⌚8am-5pm Mon-Fri, 10am-4pm Sat). Outside the town center is the **California Institute of Technology** (Caltech; www.caltech.edu; 551 S Hill Ave), one of the world's leading scientific universities and operator of the **Jet Propulsion Laboratory** (JPL; www.jpl.nasa.gov), NASA's main center for robotic exploration of the solar system.

Pasadena is served by the Metro Gold Line from Downtown LA. Pasadena ARTS buses (fare 50¢) plough around the city on seven different routes.

TOP CHOICE **Huntington Library** MUSEUM, GARDENS

(www.huntington.org; 1151 Oxford Rd; adult/child $15/6 Tue-Fri, $20/6 Sat & Sun; ⏲10:30am-4:30pm Tue-Sun Jun-Aug, noon-4:30pm Tue-Fri, plus 10:30am-4:30pm Sat & Sun, Sep-May; P) LA's biggest understatement does have a library of rare books, including a Gutenberg Bible, but it's the collection of great British and French art (most famously Thomas Gainsborough's *Blue Boy*) and exquisite gardens that make it special. The Rose Garden boasts more than 1200 varieties (and a lovely high tea; reserve ahead, adult/child $28/15), the Desert Garden has a Seussian quality, and the Chinese garden has a small lake crossed by a stone bridge.

Norton Simon Museum ART MUSEUM

(www.nortonsimon.org; 411 W Colorado Blvd; adult/child & student/senior $10/free/5; ⏲noon-6pm Wed-Thu & Sat-Mon, to 9pm Fri; P) Stroll west and you'll see Rodin's *The Thinker,* a mere overture to the full symphony of European art at this museum. Don't skip the basement, with fabulous Indian and Southeast Asian sculpture.

Gamble House ARCHITECTURE

(www.gamblehouse.org; 4 Westmoreland Pl; adult/child/student & senior $10/free/7; ⏲admission by tour only noon-3pm Thu-Sun; P) A masterpiece of California craftsman architecture, this 1908 house by Charles and Henry Greene was Doc Brown's home in the movie *Back to the Future*. Admission is by one-hour guided tour.

Pacific Asia Museum ART MUSEUM

(www.pacificasiamuseum.org; 46 N Los Robles Ave; adult/student & senior $9/7; ⏲10am-6pm Wed-Sun; P) This re-created Chinese palace houses nine galleries, which rotate a stellar collection of ancient and contemporary art and artifacts from Asia and the Pacific Islands: Himalayan Buddhas to Chinese porcelain and Japanese costumes.

Pasadena Museum of California Art ART MUSEUM

(www.pmcaonline.org; 490 E Union St; adult/student & senior/child $7/5/free, 1st Fri of month free; ⏲noon-5pm Wed-Sun; P) A progressive gallery dedicated to art, architecture and design created by California artists since 1850. Shows change every few months. Also swing by the **Kosmic Kavern**, a former garage done over by spray-mural pop artist Kenny Scharf.

Santa Monica & Venice Beach

Sights
1 Carousel ... A3
2 Pacific Park Amusement Park ... A3
3 Santa Monica Pier Aquarium ... A3
Third Street Promenade ... (see 16)

Activities, Courses & Tours
4 Perry's Café & Rentals ... A4
5 Perry's Café & Rentals ... A2

Sleeping
6 Casa Del Mar ... A3
7 Embassy Hotel Apartments ... B1
8 HI-Los Angeles/Santa Monica ... B2
9 Hotel Erwin ... A6
10 Viceroy ... B3

Eating
11 3 Square Café & Bakery ... B6
12 Gjelina ... B6
13 Joe's ... B6
14 Library Alehouse ... B5
15 Real Food Daily ... B2
16 Santa Monica Farmers Market ... B2
17 Santa Monica Place ... B2
Umami Burger ... (see 25)

Drinking
18 Chez Jay ... B3
19 Copa d'Oro ... B2
20 Galley ... B4
21 Otherroom ... B6
22 Roosterfish ... B6
23 Ye Old King's Head ... B2

Entertainment
24 Zanzibar ... B2

Shopping
25 Fred Segal ... B2
26 Puzzle Zoo ... B2
Ten Women ... (see 11)

Rose Bowl & Brookside Park STADIUM
(www.rosebowlstadium.com; 1001 Rose Bowl Dr) One of LA's most venerable landmarks, the 1922 Rose Bowl Stadium can seat up to 93,000 spectators, and every New Year's hosts the famed Rose Bowl Game between two top-ranked college football teams. At other times, concerts, special events and the huge monthly **Rose Bowl Flea Market** (p384) bring in the crowds.

The Rose Bowl is surrounded by **Brookside Park**, a broadening of the Arroyo Seco, a now-dry riverbed that runs from the San Gabriel Mountains to Downtown LA. It's a nice spot for hiking, cycling and picnicking. South of the stadium is the **Kidspace Children's Museum** (p368).

Activities

Cycling & In-line Skating

Anyone who's ever watched tourism footage of LA (or the opening of *Three's Company*) knows about skating or riding on the **South Bay Bicycle Trail**. This paved path parallels the beach for 22 miles, from just north of Santa Monica to the South Bay, with a detour around the yacht harbor at Marina del Rey. Mountain-bikers will find the **Santa Monica Mountains** (Map p388) a suitably challenging playground. You'll find lots of good information at www.labikepaths.com.

There are numerous bike-rental shops, especially along the beaches. Prices range from about $6 to $10 per hour and $10 to $30 per day (more for high-tech mountain bikes).

Perry's Cafe & Rentals BICYCLE RENTALS
(Map p366; ☎310-939-0000; www.perryscafe.com; Ocean Front Walk; bikes per hr/day $10/25; ⊙9:30am-5:30pm) Several locations on the bike path. They also rent body boards ($8/17 per hour/day). Cash only.

Hiking

Trails surprisingly close to the city provide instant getaways from the nation's second-largest metropolis.

For a quick ramble, head to **Griffith Park** (Map p356) or **Runyon Canyon** (Map p356; www.runyon-canyon.com), both just a hop, skip and jump from frenzied Hollywood Blvd. The latter is a favorite playground of hip and fitness-obsessed locals and their dogs, which roam mostly off-leash. You'll have fine views of the Hollywood Sign, the city and, on clear days, all the way to the beach. Runyon's southern trailhead is at the end of Fuller St, off Franklin Ave.

Runyon Canyon is on the eastern edge of the 150,000-acre **Santa Monica Mountains National Recreation Area** (Map p388; ☎805-370-2301; www.nps.gov/samo). This hilly, tree- and chaparral-covered park follows the outline of Santa Monica Bay from just north of Santa Monica all the way north across the Ventura County line

DON'T MISS

VENICE BOARDWALK

Freak show, human zoo and wacky carnival, the **Venice Boardwalk** (Ocean Front Walk; Map p366) is an essential LA experience. This cauldron of counterculture is the place to get your hair braided or a *qi gong* back massage, or pick up cheap sunglasses or a woven bracelet. Encounters with bodybuilders, hoop dreamers, a Speedo-clad snake charmer or an in-line-skating Sikh minstrel are pretty much guaranteed, especially on hot summer afternoons. Alas, the vibe gets a bit creepy after dark.

to Point Mugu. **Will Rogers State Historic Park**, **Topanga State Park** and **Malibu Creek State Park** are popular hikes here. The latter has a great trail leading to the set of the hit TV series *M*A*S*H,* where an old Jeep and other leftover relics rust serenely in the sunshine. The trailhead is in the park's main parking lot on Malibu Canyon Rd, which is called Las Virgenes Rd if coming from Hwy 101 (Hollywood Fwy). Parking is $8. For more ideas, consult the Santa Monica Mountains Conservancy (http://smmc.ca.gov).

Horseback Riding

Leave the urban sprawl behind on the forested bridle trails of Griffith Park or Topanga Canyon. All rides are accompanied by an experienced equestrian wrangler. Rates vary, and a 20% tip is customary.

Los Angeles Horseback Riding HORSEBACK RIDING
(☎818-591-2032; www.losangeleshorsebackriding.com; 2661 Old Topanga Canyon Rd, Topanga Canyon) Sunset, day and full-moon rides in the Santa Monica Mountains with fabulous views all around. Reservations required.

Sunset Ranch Hollywood HORSEBACK RIDING
(Map p356; ☎323-469-5450; www.sunsetranchhollywood.com; 3400 Beachwood Dr, Hollywood) Guided tours, including popular Friday-night dinner rides.

Swimming & Surfing

LA pretty much defines beach culture, yet be prepared: the Pacific is generally pretty chilly; in colder months you'll definitely want a wet suit. Water temperatures peak at about 70°F in August and September. Water quality varies; for updated conditions check the 'Beach Report Card' at www.healthebay.org.

For a list of LA's top beaches, see p342.

Surfing novices can expect to pay up to $120 for an up to two-hour private lesson or $65 to $75 for a group lesson, including board and wet suit. Contact the following surfing schools for details:

Learn to Surf LA SURF SCHOOL
(www.learntosurfla.com)

Malibu Long Boards SURF SCHOOL
(www.malibulongboards.com)

Surf Academy SURF SCHOOL
(www.surfacademy.org)

Los Angeles for Children

Keeping the rug rats happy is child's play in LA.

The sprawling Los Angeles Zoo (p355) in family-friendly Griffith Park is a sure bet. Dino fans dig the Page Museum at the La Brea Tar Pits (p357) and Natural History Museum (p351), while budding scientists love the California Science Center (p351) next door. For live sea creatures, head to the Aquarium of the Pacific (p363); teens might get a kick out of the ghost tours of the *Queen Mary* (p363). Special mention goes to Noah's Ark at the Skirball Cultural Center (p359).

Among LA's amusement parks, Santa Monica Pier (p361) is meant for kids of all ages. Activities for younger children are more limited at Universal Studios Hollywood (p364). See the Orange County chapter for Disneyland and Knott's Berry Farm (p407).

Kidspace MUSEUM
(www.kidspacemuseum.org; 480 N Arroyo Blvd, Pasadena; admission $8, ⏲9:30am-5pm Mon-Fri, 10am-5pm Sat & Sun; 🅿👪) Hands-on exhibits, outdoor learning areas and gardens lure the single-digit set. It's best after 1pm, when the field-trip crowd has left.

Bob Baker Marionette Theater PUPPET THEATER
(off Map p348; www.bobbakermarionettes.com; 1345 W 1st St, near Downtown; admission $15, reservations required; ⏲10:30am Tue-Fri, 2:30pm Sat & Sun; 🅿👪) Adorable singing and dancing marionettes have enthralled generations of wee Angelenos.

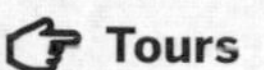

Tours

Esotouric HISTORY, LITERATURE
(☎323-223-2767; www.esotouric.com; bus tours $58) Hip, offbeat, insightful and entertaining walking and bus tours themed around literary lions (Chandler to Bukowski), famous crime sites (Black Dahlia) and historic neighborhoods.

Los Angeles Conservancy ARCHITECTURE, WALKING
(☎213-623-2489; www.laconservancy.org; tours $10) Architectural walking tours, mostly of Downtown LA. Check the website for self-guided tours.

Melting Pot Tours CULINARY, WALKING
(☎800-979-3370; www.meltingpottours.com; tours from $58; ⌚Wed-Sun) Snack your way through the Original Farmers Market and the aromatic alleyways of Old Town Pasadena.

Six Taste CULINARY, WALKING
(☎888-313-0936; www.sixtaste.com; tours $55-65) Walking tours of restaurants in LA neighborhoods, including Downtown, Little Tokyo, Chinatown, Thai Town and Santa Monica.

Out & About GAY, LESBIAN
(www.outandabout-tours.com; tours $60; ⌚Sat & Sun) Enthusiastic guides show landmarks of LA's gay and lesbian history – there's a lot more than you think!

Red Line Tours WALKING, BUS
(☎323-402-1074; www.redlinetours.com; tours from $25) 'Edutaining' walking tours of Hollywood and Downtown using headsets that cut out traffic noise.

Starline Tours BUS
(☎323-463-333, 800-959-3131; www.starlinetours.com; tours from $39) Narrated bus tours of the city, stars' homes and theme parks.

Bikes & Hikes LA CYCLING
(☎323-796-8555; www.bikesandhikesla.com; cycling tours from $44-158) Tours of Hollywood, celebrity homes and the signature, six-hour 'LA in One Day' tour ($158) from WeHo to the beaches.

Festivals & Events

In addition to the following annual events, monthly street fairs include the gallery and shop open houses and food truck meetups of **Downtown LA Art Walk** (www.downtownartwalk.com; ⌚2nd Thu each month) and **First Fridays** (⌚1st Fri each month) on Abbot Kinney Blvd in Venice.

Tournament of Roses PARADE
(☎626-449-4100; www.tournamentofroses.com) New Year's Day cavalcade of flower-festooned floats along Pasadena's Colorado Blvd, followed by the Rose Bowl football game.

Toyota Grand Prix of Long Beach AUTO RACE
(☎888-827-7333; www.longbeachgp.com) Week-long auto-racing spectacle in mid-April drawing world-class drivers.

Fiesta Broadway STREET FAIR
(☎310-914-0015; www.fiestabroadway.la) Mexican-themed fair along historic Broadway in Downtown, with performances by Latino stars. Last Sunday in April.

West Hollywood Halloween Carnival STREET FAIR
(☎323-848-6400; www.visitwesthollywood.com) Eccentric, and often NC-17-rated, costumes fill Santa Monica Blvd, on October 31.

Sleeping

For seaside life, base yourself in Santa Monica, Venice or Long Beach; Long Beach is also convenient to Disneyland and Orange

WORTH A TRIP

RONALD REAGAN LIBRARY & MUSEUM

No matter how you feel about Ronald Reagan (1911–2004), his **presidential library** (www.reaganlibrary.com; 40 Presidential Dr; adult/teen/senior $12/6/9; ⌚10am-5pm; P) is quite fascinating. Galleries cover the arc of the man's life from his childhood in Dixon, Illinois, through his early days in radio and acting to his years as governor of California, although the focus is obviously on his stint as president (1980–88) in the waning years of the Cold War. The museum features re-creations of the Oval Office and the Cabinet Room, Reagan family memorabilia, gifts from heads of state, a nuclear cruise missile and even a graffiti-covered chunk of the Berlin Wall. His grave is on the grounds as well. Get there via the I-405 (San Diego Fwy) north to the 118 (Ronald Reagan Fwy) west; exit at Madera Rd South, turn right on Madera and continue straight for 3 miles to Presidential Dr.

SCENIC DRIVE: MULHOLLAND DRIVE

What to See

The legendary road winds and dips for 24 miles through the Santa Monica Mountains, skirting the mansions of the rich and famous (Jack Nicholson's is at No 12850, Warren Beatty's at No 13671) and delivering iconic views of Downtown, Hollywood and the San Fernando Valley at each bend. Named for its creator, California aqueduct engineer William Mulholland, it's especially pretty just before sunset (go west to east, though, to avoid driving into the setting sun) and on clear winter days when the panorama opens up from the snowcapped San Gabriel Mountains (Map p388) to the shimmering Pacific Ocean.

At the very least, drive up to the Hollywood Bowl Overlook (off Map p352) for classic views of the Hollywood Sign (Map p356) and the beehive-shaped bowl below. Other pullouts offer hiking-trail access, for instance to Runyon Canyon (p367). Note that pulling over after sunset is verboten.

Time & Route

Driving the entire route takes about an hour, but even a shorter spin is worth it. Mulholland Dr runs from the US-101 Fwy (Hollywood Fwy; take the Cahuenga exit, then follow signs) to about 2 miles west of the I-405 (San Diego Fwy). About 8 miles of dirt road, closed to vehicles but not to hikers and cyclists, links it with Mulholland Hwy, which continues a serpentine route through the mountains for another 23 miles as far as Leo Carrillo State Beach.

County. Cool-hunters and party people will be happiest in Hollywood or WeHo; culture-vultures, in Downtown. Expect a lodging tax of 12% to 14%; always inquire about discounts. Rates quoted here are for high season.

DOWNTOWN

TOP CHOICE Standard Downtown LA HOTEL $$
(Map p348; ☎213-892-8080; www.standardhotel.com; 550 S Flower St; r from $165; ❄@🛜🏊) This 207-room design-savvy hotel in a former office building goes for a young, hip and shag-happy crowd – the rooftop bar fairly pulses – so don't come here with kids or to get a solid night's sleep. Mod, minimalist rooms have platform beds and peek-through showers. Parking is $33.

Figueroa Hotel HISTORIC HOTEL $$
(Map p348; ☎213-627-8971, 800-421-9092; www.figueroahotel.com; 939 S Figueroa St; r $148-184, ste $225-265; ❄@🛜🏊) A rambling 1920s oasis across from LA Live, the Fig welcomes guests with a richly tiled Spanish-style lobby that segues to a sparkling pool and buzzy outdoor bar. Rooms, furnished in a world-beat mash-up of styles (Morocco, Mexico, Zen...), are comfy but varying in size and configuration. Parking is $12.

Stay HOSTEL $
(Map p348; ☎213-213-7829; www.stayhotels.com; 636 S Main St; dm $35, r with/without bath $80/60; P@🛜🏊👪) Occupying the first three floors of Hotel Cecil, Stay has groove factor, with marble floors, baby-blue walls and a frosted-glass, faux-flower wall in the wired lobby. Rooms have retro furnishings and bedspreads, iPod docks and safety-orange accent walls. Most accommodations have shared baths with marble showers.

HOLLYWOOD

Hollywood Roosevelt Hotel HOTEL $$$
(Map p352; ☎323-466-7000, 800-950-7667; www.hollywoodroosevelt.com; 7000 Hollywood Blvd; r from $269; ❄@🛜🏊) This venerable hotel has hosted elite players since the first Academy Awards were held here in 1929. It pairs a palatial Spanish lobby with sleek Asian contemporary rooms, a busy pool scene and rockin' restos: Public and 25 Degrees burger bar. Parking is $33.

Magic Castle Hotel HOTEL $$
(Map p352; ☎323-851-0800, 800-741-4915; www.magiccastlehotel.com; 7025 Franklin Ave; r $154-304; ❄🛜🏊👪) Walls are thin, but this renovated former apartment building around a courtyard boasts contemporary furniture, attractive art, comfy bathrobes and fancy bath amenities. Most rooms have a separate

living room. For breakfast: freshly baked goods and gourmet coffee on your balcony or poolside. Ask about access to the namesake private club for magicians. Parking is $10.

USA Hostels Hollywood HOSTEL $
(Map p352; ☎323-462-3777, 800-524-6783; www.usahostels.com; 1624 Schrader Blvd; incl breakfast & tax dm from $30-40, r from $70-85; ❄@📶) Not for introverts, this energetic hostel puts you within steps of Hollywood's party circuit. Make new friends during staff-organized barbecues, comedy nights and tours, or during free pancake breakfast in the guest kitchen.

WEST HOLLYWOOD & MID-CITY

Mondrian HOTEL $$$
(Map p360; ☎323-650-8999; www.mondrianhotel.com; 8440 W Sunset Blvd; r $295-375, ste $405-495; ❄@📶🏊) This Ian Schrager hotel has been the place to be since the attached Sky Bar's '90s heyday, with sleek wood floors and billowy white linens, dangling chandeliers, tinted orange and pink glass accents, rain showers and down duvets. And let's not forget the model-licious staff. Parking is $32.

Standard Hollywood HOTEL $$
(Map p360; ☎323-650-9090; www.standardhotel.com; 8300 W Sunset Blvd; r $165-250, ste from $350; ❄@📶🏊) This white-on-white property on the Sunset Strip is a scene with Astroturf-fringed pool offering a view across LA and sizable shagadelic rooms with silver beanbag chairs, orange-tiled bathrooms and Warhol poppy-print curtains. Parking is $29.

Farmer's Daughter Hotel MOTEL $$
(Map p360; ☎323-937-3930; www.farmersdaughterhotel.com; 115 S Fairfax Ave; r $219-269; ❄@📶🏊👪) Opposite the Original Farmers Market, Grove and CBS Studios, this perennial pleaser gets high marks for its sleek 'urban cowboy' look. Adventurous lovebirds should ask about the No Tell Room… Parking is $18.

Chateau Marmont HISTORIC HOTEL $$$
(Map p360; ☎323-656-1010; www.chateaumarmont.com; 8221 W Sunset Blvd; r $415, ste $500-875; ❄📶🏊) Its French-flavored indulgence may look dated, but this faux-chateau has long attracted A-listers – from Greta Garbo to Bono – with its legendary discretion. The garden cottages are the most romantic. Parking is $28.

Orbit Hotel & Hostel HOSTEL $
(Map p360; ☎323-655-1510; www.orbithotel.com; 7950 Melrose Ave; dm $35, r$75-85; P❄@📶) Fun-seekers should thrive at this retro-styled hostel within staggering distance of hip shopping, boozing and dancing. Meet up with fellow travelers over movie nights, Sunday barbecues and clubbing (shuttle available). Dorms sleep six in full-size beds, while private rooms have a TV and bathroom.

BEVERLY HILLS & WESTSIDE

TOP CHOICE **Beverly Hills Hotel** HOTEL $$$
(Map p364; ☎310-276-2251, 800-283-8885; www.beverlyhillshotel.com; 9641 Sunset Blvd; r from $530; ❄@📶🏊) The legendary Pink Palace from 1912 oozes opulence. The pool deck is classic, the grounds are lush, and the Polo Lounge remains a clubby lunch spot for the well heeled and well dressed. Rooms are comparably old-world, with gold accents and marble tiles. Parking is $33.

Avalon Hotel HOTEL $$
(Map p364; ☎310-277-5221; www.avalonbeverlyhills.com; 9400 W Olympic Blvd; r $228-370; ❄@📶🏊) Mid-Century Modern gets a 21st-century spin at this fashion-crowd fave – Marilyn Monroe's old pad in its days as an apartment building. The beautiful, moneyed and metrosexual now vamp it up in the chic restaurant-bar overlooking a sexy hourglass-shaped pool. Rooms facing the other direction are quieter. Parking is $30. It's near the corner of Olympic Blvd and Beverly Dr.

Beverly Wilshire HOTEL $$$
(off Map p364; ☎310-275-5200; www.fourseasons.com/beverlywilshire; 9500 Wilshire Blvd; r $495-545, ste $695-1795; ❄@📶🏊👪) It has anchored the corner of Wilshire Blvd and Rodeo Dr since 1928, yet amenities are very much up-to-the-minute, both in the original Italian Renaissance wing and in the newer addition. And yes, this is the very hotel from which Julia Roberts first stumbled then strutted in *Pretty Woman*. Parking costs $33.

MALIBU

Malibu Beach Inn INN $$$
(☎310-456-6444; www.malibubeachinn.com; 22878 Pacific Coast Hwy; r from $325; 📶) If you want to live like a billionaire, stay with one. Hollywood mogul David Geffen has plunked megabucks into this intimate hacienda near his home on Carbon Beach. Its 47 super-deluxe ocean-facing rooms are sheathed in

soothing browns and outfitted with fireplaces, a handpicked wine selection and Dean & Deluca gourmet goodies. Parking is $23. It's just west of Sweetwater Canyon Dr.

Leo Carrillo State Beach Campground CAMPING $

(800-444-7275; www.reserveamerica.com; 35000 W Pacific Coast Hwy; campsite $35;) This shady, kid-friendly site gets busy in summer, so book early, especially on weekends. It has 140 sites, flush toilets and coin-operated hot showers. A long sandy beach, offshore kelp beds and tide pools are all great for exploring. Enter about 0.3 of a mile west of Malibu Pier.

SANTA MONICA & VENICE

Casa Del Mar HOTEL $$$

(Map p366; 310-581-5533; www.hotecasadelmar.com; 1910 Ocean Way, Santa Monica; r $425-1275;) A historic brick hotel built beachside in 1926. Powder-blue rooms have wood-floor entryways, four-poster beds and marble bathrooms with soaker tubs. The lobby bar gets a good crowd in both summer and winter when the fireplace roars. Parking is $34.

Viceroy HOTEL $$$

(Map p366; 310-260-7500, 800-622-8711; www.viceroysantamonica.com; 1819 Ocean Ave, Santa Monica; r from $370;) Ignore the high-rise eyesore exterior and plunge headlong into *Top Design*'s Kelly Wearstler's campy 'Hollywood Regency' decor and color palette from dolphin gray to mamba green. Look for poolside cabanas, Italian designer linens, and a chic bar and restaurant. Parking is $33.

Hotel Erwin HOTEL $$

(Map p366; 310-452-1111; www.jdvhotels.com; 1679 Pacific Ave, Venice; r from $169;) A worthy emblem of Venice. Rooms aren't the biggest and in most there's a low traffic hum, but you're steps from the beach and your room features graffiti- or anime-inspired art and honor bar containing sunglasses and '70s-era soft drinks. The rooftop bar offers spellbinding coastal vistas. Parking is $28.

Embassy Hotel Apartments BOUTIQUE HOTEL $$

(Map p366; 310-394-1279; www.embassyhotelapts.com; 1001 3rd St, Santa Monica; r $169-390;) This hushed 1927 Spanish-colonial hideaway delivers charm by the bucket. A rickety elevator takes you to units oozing old-world flair and equipped with internet. Kitchens make many rooms well suited to do-it-yourselfers. No air-con.

HI Los Angeles-Santa Monica HOSTEL $

(Map p366; 310-393-9913; www.lahostels.org; 1436 2nd St, Santa Monica; r $26-30;) Near the beach and Promenade, the location is the envy of much fancier places. Its 200 beds in single-sex dorms and bed-in-a-box doubles with shared bathrooms are clean and safe; party people are better off in Hollywood.

LONG BEACH

Queen Mary Hotel CRUISE SHIP $$

(562-435-3511; www.queenmary.com; 1126 Queens Hwy, Long Beach; r $110-395;) Take a trip without leaving the dock aboard this grand ocean liner (p363). Staterooms brim with original art deco details – avoid the cheapest ones that are on the inside. Rates include admission to guided tours. Parking is $12 to $15.

Hotel Varden BOUTIQUE HOTEL $$

(562-432-8950, 877-382-7336; www.thevardenhotel.com; 335 Pacific Ave; r from $109;) The designers clearly had a field day with their modernist renovation of the 35 diminutive rooms in this 1929 hotel: tiny desks, tiny sinks, lots of right angles, cushy beds, white, white and more white. Rates include a simple continental breakfast and wine hour. It's a block from Pine Avenue's restaurants and night spots. Parking is $10.

PASADENA

Bissell House B&B B&B $$

(626-441-3535; www.bissellhouse.com; 201 S Orange Grove Blvd; r $155-255;) Sumptuous antiques, sparkling hardwood floors and a crackling fireplace make this romantic, six-room 1887 Victorian B&B on 'Millionaire's Row' a bastion of warmth and hospitality. If you don't like flowery decor, book the Prince Albert room. The Garden Room comes with a Jacuzzi for two.

Saga Motor Hotel HISTORIC MOTEL $$

(626-795-0431; www.thesagamotorhotel.com; 1633 E Colorado Blvd; r $79-135 incl breakfast;) One of the best bets on Pasadena's 'motel row' on historic Route 66, this well-kept vintage inn (built in 1957) has comfortable, spotless rooms. The nicest are near the good-sized pool orbited by plenty of chaises and chairs for soaking up the SoCal sunshine. Extra-large units available for families.

Eating

LA's culinary scene is one of the world's most vibrant and eclectic. You'll have no trouble finding high-profile restaurants helmed by celebrity chefs, whipping up farmers-market-fresh California fare, and ethnic neighborhoods covering huge swaths also mean authentic international cooking.

Reservations are recommended for dinner, especially at top-end places.

DOWNTOWN

Downtown's restaurant scene has exploded in the past few years. Great neighborhoods for browsing include 7th St east of Grand Ave, Little Tokyo (not just for Japanese cuisine anymore), **LA Live** (Map p348), and the food stalls of the **Grand Central Market** (Map p348; 317 S Broadway; ⏲9am-6pm).

Bottega Louie ITALIAN **$$**
(Map p348; ☎213-802-1470; www.bottegalouie.com; 700 S Grand Ave; mains $11-18; ⏲breakfast, lunch & dinner) The wide marble bar has become a magnet for the artsy loft set and office workers alike. The open-kitchen crew, in chef's whites, grills house-made sausage and wood-fires thin-crust pizzas in the white-on-white, big-as-a-gym dining room. Always busy, always buzzy.

Lazy Ox Canteen GASTROPUB **$$**
(Map p348; ☎213-626-5299; www.lazyoxcanteen.com; 241 S San Pedro St; appetizers $4-16, mains $21-21; ⏲lunch & dinner) Where Little Tokyo is headed, culinarily: contemporary tapas in post-industrial digs. Think grilled squid with garbanzo beans, brick-roast mussels and fantastic burgers and vegetarian dishes. Pair them with something from the creative beer and wine list.

Gorbals NEW AMERICAN **$$**
(Map p348; ☎213-488-3408; www.thegorbalsla.com; 501 S Spring St; small plates $8-17; ⏲6pm-midnight Mon-Wed, 6pm-2am Thu-Sat) *Top Chef* winner Ilan Hall tweaks traditional Jewish comfort food: bacon-wrapped matzoh balls, potato latkes with smoked applesauce, *gribenes* (fried chicken fat) served BLT style. It's hidden in the back of the Alexandria Hotel lobby.

Nickel Diner DINER **$**
(Map p348; www.5cdiner.com; 524 S Main St; mains $8-14; ⏲8am-3:30pm Tue-Sun, 6pm-11pm Tue-Sat) In Downtown's boho historic district, this red-vinyl joint feels like a throwback to the 1920s. Ingredients are 21st century, though: artichokes stuffed with quinoa salad, burgers piled with poblano chiles. Must-try dessert: maple-glazed bacon donut.

> **LA'S MOVEABLE FEASTS**
>
> In 2009, Korean-born, LA-raised chef Roy Choi began roving the streets of LA in a food truck, selling Korean grilled beef inside Mexican tacos and tweeting the locations, and a trend was born. His Kogi truck spawned some of LA's most creative mobile kitchens – Brazilian to Singaporean, southern BBQ, Vietnamese *banh mi* sandwiches and grilled cheese sandwiches topped with short ribs and mac and cheese. Now hundreds of gourmet food trucks plough the city streets (standouts include Kogi, the Grilled Cheese Truck and the Dim Sum Truck), and no street fair, lunch break or pub crawl is complete without them. Check out www.trucktweets.com for each day's locations.

Philippe the Original DINER **$**
(off Map p348; www.philippes.com; 1001 N Alameda St; sandwiches $6-7.50; ⏲6am-10pm; Ⓟ) LAPD hunks, stressed-out attorneys and Midwestern vacationers all flock to this legendary 'home of the French dip sandwich,' dating back to 1908 at the edge of Chinatown. Order your choice of meat on a crusty roll dipped in *au jus*, and hunker down at the tables on the sawdust-covered floor. Coffee is just 10¢ (no misprint). Cash only.

HOLLYWOOD, LOS FELIZ & SILVER LAKE

Osteria Mozza & Pizzeria Mozza ITALIAN **$$$**
(off Map p360; ☎323-297-0100; www.mozza-la.com; 6602 Melrose Ave, Mid-City; mains Osteria $17-29, Pizzeria $10-18; ⏲lunch & dinner) Reserve weeks ahead at LA's hottest Italian eatery, run by celebrity chefs Mario Batali and Nancy Silverton. Two restaurants share the same building: a wide-ranging menu at the Osteria, and precision-made pizzas baked before your eyes at the Pizzeria (☎323-297-0101, 641 N Highland Ave).

Musso & Frank Grill BAR, GRILL **$$**
(Map p352; ☎323-467-7788; 6667 Hollywood Blvd; mains $12-35; ⏲11am-11pm Tue-Sat) Hollywood history hangs thickly in the air at the boulevard's oldest eatery. Waiters balance platters of steaks, chops, grilled liver and other

EATING LA: ESSENTIAL ETHNIC NEIGHBORHOODS

Taking nothing away from LA's top-end eateries, some of the city's greatest food treasures are its ethnic restaurants. With some 140 nationalities in the county, we can just scratch the surface, but here are some of the most prominent neighborhoods for authentic cuisine and fun things to do nearby.

» **Little Tokyo** Downtown LA; Essential dish: steaming bowl of ramen at **Daikokuya** (Map p348; www.daikoku-ten.com; 327 E 1st St; ⏲11am-2.30pm & 5pm-midnight Mon-Sat). While there: shop for J-pop culture at Tokyo (114 Japanese Village Plaza).

» **Chinatown** Downtown LA; Essential dish: dim sum at **Empress Pavilion** (off Map p348; www.empresspavilion.com; 2nd fl, 988 N Hill St; dim sum per plate $2-6, most mains $10-25; ⏲10am-2:30pm & 5:30-9pm, to 10pm Sat & Sun). While there: view contemporary art in galleries along Chung King Rd.

» **Boyle Heights (Mexican)** East LA; Essential dish: gourmet tortilla soup at **La Serenata de Garibaldi** (off Map p348; www.laserenataonline.com; 1842 E 1st St; mains $10-25; ⏲11:30am-10:30pm Mon-Fri, 9am-10:30pm Sat & Sun). While there: listen to mariachis at Mariachi Plaza.

» **Koreatown** West of Downtown LA; Essential dish: barbecue cooked at your table with lots of *banchan* (side dishes) at **Chosun Galbee** (www.chosungalbee.com; 3300 Olympic Blvd; mains $12-24; ⏲11am-11pm). While there: browse the giant Koreatown Galleria mall (Olympic Blvd and Western Ave) for housewares and more food.

» **Thai Town** East Hollywood; Essential dish: curries with accompaniment by an Elvis impersonator at **Palms Thai** (Map p352; www.palmsthai.com; 5900 Hollywood Blvd; mains $6-19; ⏲11am-midnight Sun-Thu, to 2am Fri & Sat). While there: pick up a flower garland at Thailand Plaza shopping center (5321 Hollywood Blvd).

dishes harking back to the days when cholesterol wasn't part of our vocabulary. Service is smooth, so are the martinis.

Street FUSION **$$**
(off Map p352; ☎323-203-0500; www.eatatstreet.com; 742 N Highland Ave; dishes $7-17; ⏲lunch & dinner) From Singapore's *kaya* toast (with coconut jam and a soft fried egg) to Ukrainian spinach dumplings and Syrian lamb kafta meatballs, celeb chef Susan Feniger's hot spot offers small plates of global street food in upmarket environs.

Hungry Cat SEAFOOD **$$**
(Map p352; ☎323-462-2155; www.thehungrycat.com; 1535 Vine St, Hollywood; mains $10-27; ⏲lunch & dinner; P) This kitty is small and sleek and hides out in the heart of Hollywood. It fancies fresh seafood and will have you salivating for hunky lobster roll, portly crab cakes and savory fish-*du-jour* specials. The Pug Burger – slathered with avocado, bacon and blue cheese – is a worthy meaty alternative. There's a second location by the beach in Santa Monica (☎310-459-3337, 100 W Channel Rd, Santa Monica; ⏲dinner nightly, brunch Sat & Sun).

Waffle NEW AMERICAN **$**
(Map p352; ☎323-465-6901; www.thewaffle.us; 6255 W Sunset Blvd; most mains $9-12; ⏲6:30am-2:30am Sun-Thu, to 4:30am Fri & Sat) After a night out clubbing, do you really feel like filling yourself with garbage? Us, too. But the Waffle's 21st-century diner food – cornmeal-jalapeño waffles with grilled chicken, carrot cake waffles, mac and cheese, samiches, heaping salads – is organic and locally sourced, so it's (almost) good for you.

Umami Burger BURGERS **$$**
(Map p358; www.umamiburger.com; 4655 Hollywood Blvd; burgers $9-17; ⏲lunch & dinner; P) With a spacious brick interior framed by rusted iron, this is by far the grooviest Umami in the fledgling empire. It does the staples everyone loves (the Umami, the SoCal and the Truffle), as well as a *carnitas* (Mexican braised pork) and a Jurky (jerk turkey) burger. The wine bar offers $4 artisan drafts or glasses of wine, and $5 'smash burgers' at happy hour (3pm to 7pm). Other locations include the Space 1520 shopping mall and the Fred Segal fashion boutique in Santa Monica.

Yuca's TAQUERIA $
(Map p358; www.yucasla.com; 2056 Hillhurst Ave, Los Feliz; tacos $1.75-2, burritos $2.50-4, tortas $3.50; ⏲lunch & dinner Mon-Sat; P) Location, location, location…is definitely not what lures people to this parking-lot snack shack. But the tacos, *tortas,* burritos and other Mexi faves have earned the Herrera family the coveted James Beard Award.

El Conquistador MEXICAN $$
(Map p358; ☎323-666-5136; www.elconquistador restaurant.com; 3701 W Sunset Blvd, Silver Lake; mains $9-16.50; ⏲lunch Tue-Sun, dinner daily) Wonderfully campy Mexican cantina that's perfect for launching yourself into a night on the razzle. The margaritas are potent, so be sure to fill your belly with tasty nachos, *chiles rellenos* (stuffed peppers, usually with cheese, but anything goes) and quesadillas to sustain your stamina.

WEST HOLLYWOOD & MID-CITY

Ivy AMERICAN $$$
(Map p360; ☎310-274-8303; www.theivyla.com; 113 N Robertson Blvd; mains $20-38; ⏲11:30am-11pm Mon-Fri, 11am-11pm Sat, 10am-11pm Sun) In the heart of Robertson's fashion frenzy, the Ivy's picket-fenced porch and rustic cottage are *the* power lunch spot. Chances of catching B-lister (possibly A-lister) babes nibbling on a carrot stick or studio execs discussing sequels over the lobster omelet are excellent.

Original Farmers Market MARKET $
(Map p360; cnr 3rd St & S Fairfax Ave; 👪) The market hosts a dozen worthy, budget-priced eateries, most *alfresco.* Try the classic diner Du-par's, Cajun-style cooking at the Gumbo Pot, ¡Loteria! Mexican grill or Singapore's Banana Leaf.

Comme Ça FRENCH $$
(Map p360; ☎323-782-1178; www.commecares taurant.com; 8479 Melrose Ave, West Hollywood; mains breakfast $8-14, lunch $12-25, dinner $19-28; ⏲8am-midnight) 'Bistro cooking' way understates the case at this vibrant, all-day Francophile eatery. Look for *croque madame, moules frites,* a cheese bar and a raw bar, all from Michelin-starred chef David Myers. Plus there's old-world bartending; the penicillin cocktail will cure what ails you with scotch, ginger, lemon and honey.

AOC WINE BAR $$$
(Map p360; ☎323-653-6359; www.aocwinebar.com; 8022 W 3rd St, Mid-City; mains $4-14; ⏲dinner) The small-plate menu at this stomping ground of the rich, lithe and silicone-enhanced will have you noshing happily on sweaty cheeses, homemade charcuterie and such richly nuanced morsels as braised pork cheeks. Huge list of wines by the glass.

Marix Tex Mex MEXICAN $
(Map p360; www.marixtexmex.com; 1108 N Flores St; mains $9-19; ⏲11:30am-11pm) Many an evening in Boystown has begun with flirting on Marix's patios over kick-ass margaritas, followed by fish tacos, fajitas, chipotle chicken sandwiches, and all-you-can-eat on Taco Tuesdays.

Veggie Grill VEGETARIAN $
(Map p360; www.veggiegrill.com; 8000 W Sunset Blvd; mains $7-9.50; ⏲11am-11pm; ✍) If Santa Fe crispy chickin' or a carne asada sandwich don't sound vegetarian, know that this cheery local chain uses seasoned vegetable proteins (mostly tempeh). Try sides of 'sweetheart' sweet potato fries or steamin' kale with miso dressing.

Pink's HOT DOGS $
(Map p360; www.pinkshollywood.com; 709 N La Brea Ave, Mid-City; dishes $3.45-6.20; ⏲9:30am-2am Sun-Thu, to 3am Fri & Sat) Folks have been queuing at this corner hot-dog stand since 1939, the specialty is gut-busting chili dogs ($3.45); lines are long all day, especially after nights on the prowl.

BEVERLY HILLS & WESTSIDE

TOP CHOICE **Bazaar** SPANISH $$$
(Map p360; ☎310-246-5555; 465 S La Cienega Blvd; dishes $8-18; ⏲brunch 11am-3pm Sat & Sun, 6pm-11pm daily) In the SLS Hotel, the Bazaar dazzles with over-the-top design by Philippe Starck and 'molecular gastronomic' tapas by José Andrés. Caprese salad pairs cherry tomatoes with mozzarella balls that explode in your mouth, or try cotton-candy foie gras or a Philly cheesesteak on 'air bread.' Caution: those small plates add up.

Spago CALIFORNIAN, FUSION $$$
(☎310-385-0880; www.wolfgangpuck.com; 176 N Cañon Dr, Beverly Hills; mains $43-150; ⏲lunch Mon-Sat, dinner daily) Wolfgang Puck practically defined California cuisine for SoCal, and his flagship emporium has long been tops for A-list celebrity-spotting and fancy eating. Try to score a table on the lovely patio and prepare your taste buds to do cartwheels over fusion pork chops, porcini, pasta and pizzas. Reservations essential. It's north of Wilshire Blvd.

Matsuhisa JAPANESE $$$
(Map p360; ☎323-659-9639; www.nobumatsuhisa.com; 129 S La Cienega Blvd; dishes $5-36; ⏰lunch Mon-Fri, dinner Mon-Sun) Chef Nobu Matsuhisa has gone on to conquer the world with Nobu restaurants in major food capitals. The legend began here on La Cienega's Restaurant Row. There's always something fresh and innovative alongside old standbys such as lobster ceviche and sushi adorned with cilantro and jalapeño.

Yakitoriya JAPANESE $$
(☎310-479-5400; 11301 W Olympic Blvd, West LA; dishes $2.50-27; ⏰dinner; 👪) Simple and real, this chef-owned and family-operated *yakitori* (Japanese grilled chicken) joint crafts tender and savory grilled-chicken skewers. It's one of several tasty Japanese spots north of Olympic Blvd on Sawtelle Blvd.

Nate 'n Al's DELI $$
(www.natenal.com; 414 N Beverly Dr, Beverly Hills; dishes $6.50-13; ⏰breakfast, lunch & dinner) Dapper seniors, chatty girlfriends, financial planners and even Larry King have kept this New York–style deli busy since 1945. The huge menu boasts what may quite possibly be the best pastrami on rye, lox and bagels and chicken soup this side of Manhattan.

Tender Greens ORGANIC $
(www.tendergreensfood.com; 9523 Culver Blvd, Culver City; dishes $10.50; ⏰lunch & dinner; 🖉) Herbivore or meathead, your tastebuds will be doing somersaults when treated to the carefully composed salads, tossed as you move down the line. The ahi tuna niçoise and grilled flatiron steak are fabulous, and the chicken soup is soul-restoring. Ingredients are sourced from local providers. See website for other locations in Hollywood, WeHo (Map p360) and Pasadena.

Shamshiri PERSIAN $$
(www.shamshiri.com; 1712 Westwood Blvd, Westwood; appetizers $4.-16, mains $13-24; ⏰lunch & dinner; Ⓟ) One of a string of Persian kitchens in Westwood, these guys bake their own flatbread for wrapping chicken, beef and lamb shwarma, kebabs and falafel. They also do salad and vegan stews. Great-value lunch specials.

Versailles CUBAN $
(www.versaillescuban.com; 10319 Venice Blvd, Culver City; mains $11-15; ⏰lunch & dinner; Ⓟ) There's nothing fancy about this country-style Cuban eatery, but that barely matters when the garlic sauce (served with everything from roast chicken to fish) is so celestial. Many dishes come with rice, beans and fried plantains. Also at 1415 S La Cienega Blvd in West LA (☎310-289-0392).

Diddy Riese Cookies DESSERT $
(Map p364; ☎310-208-0448; www.diddyriese.com; 926 Broxton Ave, Westwood; cookies 35¢; ⏰10am-midnight Mon-Thu, to 1am Fri, noon-1am Sat, to midnight Sun) No night out in Westwood is complete without Diddy's bargain-priced ice-cream sandwiches ($1.50). Choose from over a dozen ice-cream flavors between 10 fresh-baked cookie options.

MALIBU

Reel Inn SEAFOOD $$
(www.reelinnmalibu.com; 18661 Pacific Coast Hwy; fresh grilled fish $12-25; ⏰lunch & dinner; Ⓟ) Across PCH from the ocean, this shambling shack with counter service and picnic tables serves up fish and seafood for any budget and many styles, including grilled, fried or Cajun. The coleslaw, potatoes and Cajun rice (included in most meals) have fans from Harley riders to beach bums and families. It's an easy detour from Topanga State Park or the Getty Villa (p361).

Inn of the Seventh Ray ORGANIC $$$
(☎310-455-1311; www.innoftheseventhray.com; 128 Old Topanga Canyon Rd; mains $24-55; ⏰lunch & dinner; Ⓟ🖉) If you've lived through the '60s, you might experience flashbacks at this New Agey hideaway in an impossibly idyllic setting in Topanga Canyon. All of the food is organic, much of it raw, most of it meat-free and some rather esoteric. Crispy vegan duck anyone?

SANTA MONICA & VENICE

Santa Monica's Third Street Promenade and Main St, as well as Abbot Kinney Blvd in Venice, are all happy hunting grounds for browsing.

TOP CHOICE **Gjelina** CALIFORNIAN $$
(Map p366; ☎310-450-1429; www.gjelina.com; 1429 Abbot Kinney Blvd, Venice; dishes $8-25; ⏰lunch & dinner) Whether you carve out a slip on the communal table between the hipsters and yuppies or get your own slab of wood on the rustic stone terrace, you will dine on delicious and imaginative small plates (think chanterelles and gravy on toast or raw yellowtail spiced with chili and mint,

LA'S FABULOUS FARMERS MARKETS

In a city as big as LA, it's easy to forget that California is America's most productive agricultural state. Nearby farmers, top-name chefs and locavore home-cooks come together at dozens of certified farmers markets. Here are just some standouts.

Santa Monica (Map p366; www01.smgov.net/farmers_market; 8:30am-1pm Wed & Sat cnr 3rd St Promenade & Arizona Ave, 9:30am-1pm Sun cnr Main St & Ocean Park Blvd) Cream of the crop. Serious gourmets and high profile chefs gather over everyday produce and exotica from Asian vegetables to heirloom tomatoes, herbs and lotions and potions made from them, raw cheeses and organically raised meat.

Hollywood (Map p352; www.farmernet.com; cnr Ivar & Selma Aves; 8am-1pm Sun) Some 90 farmers set up stalls alongside vendors of prepared foods, including Mexican, Caribbean and espresso. Artisans and street musicians round out the experience.

and drenched in olive oil and blood orange), and sensational thin-crust, wood-fired pizza.

3 Square Café & Bakery CALIFORNIAN $
(Map p366; 310-399-6504; 1121 Abbot Kinney Blvd, Venice; mains $8-20; cafe 8am-10pm Mon-Thu, to 11pm Fri, 9am-11pm Sat, to 10pm Sun, bakery 7am-7pm) Tiny, modernist cafe at which you can devour Hans Röckenwagner's German-inspired pretzel burgers, gourmet sandwiches and apple pancakes. Bakery shelves are piled high with rustic breads and fluffy croissants.

Library Alehouse PUB $$
(Map p366; www.libraryalehouse.com; 2911 Main St, Santa Monica; mains $12-20; 11:30am-midnight) Locals gather as much for the food as the 29 beers on tap, in the wood-paneled dining room or cozy back patio. Angus burgers, fish tacos and hearty salads sate the 30-something regulars.

Real Food Daily VEGETARIAN $
(www.realfood.com; Map p366; 514 Santa Monica Blvd, Santa Monica; mains $10-14; lunch & dinner;) Are you tempted by tempeh? Salivating for seitan? Vegan cooking queen Ann Gentry sure knows how to give these meat substitutes the gourmet treatment. Start things off with lentil-walnut pâté, move on to the vegan club sandwich with Caesar salad, then finish up with a rich tofu cheesecake. Also in West Hollywood (Map p360; 414 N La Cienega Blvd).

Father's Office PUB $$
(off 1018 Montana Ave; dishes $6-16; 5pm-1am Mon-Thu, 4pm-2am Fri, noon-2am Sat, to midnight Sun) This elbow-to-elbow pub packs 'em in for LA's chic-est burger: a dry-aged beef number dressed in smoky bacon, sweet caramelized onion and an ingenious combo of Gruyère and blue cheese. Pair it with fries served in a mini-shopping cart and a mug of handcrafted brew chosen from three dozen on tap. Downside: service can be snooty. Also in Culver City (310-736-2224; 3229 Helms Ave).

Joe's CALIFORNIAN $$$
(Map p366; www.joesrestaurant.com; 1023 Abbot Kinney Blvd, Venice; mains lunch $13-18, dinner $26-30; lunch Tue-Sun, dinner daily) Like a good wine, this charmingly unpretentious restaurant only seems to get better with age, and has a new Michelin star to prove it. Owner-chef Joe Miller consistently serves great and gimmick-free seasonal Cal-French food. Choicest tables are out on the patio with the waterfall fountain. Three-course lunch menus are a steal at $18.

Santa Monica Place SHOPPING CENTER $$
(Map p366; www.santamonicaplace.com; 3rd fl, Cnr Third St & Broadway, Santa Monica;) We wouldn't normally eat at a mall, but the indoor-outdoor dining deck sets standards: Latin-Asian fusion at Zengo (think Peking duck tacos), sushi at Ozumo, wood-oven-baked pizzas at Antica. Most restaurants have seating with views across adjacent rooftops – some to the ocean. Stalls in the market do *salumi* to soufflés.

LONG BEACH & SAN PEDRO

San Pedro Fish Market & Restaurant SEAFOOD $$
(www.sanpedrofishmarket.com; 1190 Nagoya Way, San Pedro; meals $13.50; breakfast, lunch & dinner; P) Seafood feasts don't get any more rootsy and decadent than at this family-run, harbor-view institution. Pick from the day's catch, have it spiced and cooked to order with potatoes, tomatoes and peppers,

lug your tray to a picnic table, fold up your sleeves and devour meaty crabs, plump shrimp, slimy oysters, melty yellowtail and tender halibut. Don't forget to ask for buttery garlic bread and a pile of extra napkins.

Number Nine VIETNAMESE $
(www.numberninenoodles.com; 2118 E 4th St, Long Beach; mains $7-9; noon-midnight) Maximalist portions of Vietnamese noodles and five-spice chicken with egg roll, in minimalist surrounds on Retro Row. Meats and poultry are sustainably raised.

George's Greek Café GREEK $$
(www.georgesgreekcafe.com; 135 Pine Ave, Long Beach; mains $8-19; 11am-10pm Sun-Thu, to 11pm Fri & Sat) George himself may greet you at the entrance on the generous patio, heart of the Pine Ave restaurant row, both geographically and spiritually. Locals cry *'Opa!'* for the *saganaki* (flaming cheese) and lamb chops.

Alegria SPANISH $$
(www.alegriacocinalatina.com; 115 Pine Ave, Long Beach; tapas $5-11, mains $7-20;) Long Beach's busy Pine Ave nightlife district, trippy, technicolor mosaic floor, trompe l'oeil murals and an eccentric art nouveau bar form an appropriately spirited backdrop to Alegria's vivid Latino cuisine. The tapas menu is great for grazers and the paella a feast for both eyes and stomach. There's even live flamenco some nights.

SAN FERNANDO VALLEY

Asanebo SUSHI $$$
(818-760-3348; 11941 Ventura Blvd, Studio City; dishes $3-21; lunch Tue-Fri, dinner Tue-Sun) Ventura Blvd in Studio City is Sushi Row, which locals will tell you has the highest concentration of sushi restaurants in America. Asanebo stands out and has a Michelin star to prove it; think halibut sashimi with fresh truffle or kanpachi with miso and Serrano chilies.

Zankou Chicken ARMENIAN $
(off Map p356; www.zankouchicken.com; 1001 N San Fernando Rd, Burbank; mains $8-11; 10am-10pm) Lip-smacking Armenian-style rotisserie chicken, best paired with vampire-repellent garlic sauce. Also in Westwood (off Map p364; 310-444-0550; 1716 Sepulveda Blvd).

Eclectic CALIFORNIA-ITALIAN $$
(Map p356; www.eclecticwinebarandgrille.com; 5156 Lankershim Blvd, North Hollywood; mains $8-32; lunch & dinner) An anchor of NoHo's Arts District (p365), this loft-style space is as diverse as its name suggests (though trends Italian) with pasta and pizza to BLTs and rack of lamb. It's best, though, for people-watching after a show, when the casts come in and hold court.

Bob's Big Boy DINER $
(Map p356; www.bigboy.com; 4211 Riverside Dr, Burbank; mains $6-9; 24hr; P) This landmark 1950s coffee shop has been doing comfort food (patty melts, half-pound burgers, mac and cheese, great fries and shakes) since way before it became retro-fashionable.

PASADENA & SAN GABRIEL VALLEY

Saladang Song THAI $$
(www.saladangsong.com; 383 S Fair Oaks Ave; dishes $10-18; breakfast, lunch & dinner; P) Soaring concrete walls with artsy, cut-out steel insets hem in the outdoor dining room of this modern Thai temple. Even simple curries become extraordinary at Saladang Song, and look for unusual breakfast soups.

Burger Continental MIDDLE EASTERN $
(626-792-6634; www.burgercontinental.com; 535 S Lake Ave, Pasadena; mains $9-14; breakfast, lunch & dinner; P) What sounds like a patty-and-bun joint is in reality Pasadena's most beloved Middle Eastern nosh spot. Nibble on classic hummus, dig into sizzling kebab dinners or go adventurous with the Moon of Tunis platter (chicken, gyros and shrimp in filo). Live bands and belly dancers provide candy for ears and eyes. Great patio.

Drinking

Hollywood has been legendary sipping territory since before the Rat Pack days. Nowadays bartenders are as creative as they were back then, even if your taste is Budweiser. Hollywood Blvd and the Sunset Strip are classic bar-hopping grounds, but there's plenty of good drinking going on in the beach cities and Downtown as well.

DOWNTOWN

Edison BAR
(Map p348; www.edisondowntown.com; 108 W 2nd St, enter off Harlem Alley; 5pm-2am Wed-Fri, 6pm-2am Sat) *Metropolis* meets *Blade Runner* at this industrial-chic basement boîte, where you'll sip mojitos surrounded by turbines from Edison's days as a boiler room. It's all tarted up nicely with cocoa leather couches and three cavernous bars. No athletic wear, flip-flops or baggy jeans.

OUT & ABOUT IN LA

The rainbow flag flies especially proudly in 'Boystown,' along Santa Monica Blvd in West Hollywood, which is lined with dozens of high-energy bars, cafes, restaurants, gyms and clubs, and is especially busy Thursday through Sunday. Most places cater to gay men. Beauty reigns supreme here and the intimidation factor can be high unless you're buff, bronzed and styled…or a 'fag hag.'

Elsewhere, the gay scenes are considerably more laid-back. Silver Lake, LA's original gay enclave, has evolved from largely leather and Levi's to encompass both cute hipsters of all ethnicities and an older contingent. Long Beach also has a significant gay neighborhood.

If nightlife isn't your scene, the gay community has plenty of ways to meet, greet and engage. **Will Rogers Beach** ('Ginger Rogers' to her friends) in Santa Monica is LA's unofficial gay beach. Run with **Frontrunners** (www.lafrontrunners.com), take a tour of gay history (p369), hike with **Great Outdoors** (www.greatoutdoorsla.org), catch a show at the **Celebration Theatre** or a concert by the amazing **Gay Men's Chorus of Los Angeles** (www.gmcla.org).

Long Beach Pride Celebration (www.longbeachpride.com; ⏲late May), is a warm-up for **LA Pride** (www.lapride.org; ⏲mid-Jun), a weekend of nonstop partying and a parade down Santa Monica Blvd, attended by hundreds of thousands.

Following are some nightlife classics to get you started. For more, consult free listings mags or www.losangeles.gaycities.com.

LA's essential gay bar and restaurant is **The Abbey** (Map p360; www.abbeyfoodandbar.com; 692 N Robertson Blvd; mains $9-24; ⏲9am-2am). Take your pick of preening and partying spaces spanning from a leafy patio to a slick lounge, and enjoy flavored martinis, mojitos and upscale pub grub.

Eleven (Map p360; www.eleven.la; 8811 Santa Monica Blvd; mains $13-29; ⏲6-10pm Tue-Sun, 11am-3pm Sat & Sun) This glam spot occupies a historic building, serves New American cuisine and offers different theme nights, from Musical Mondays to high-energy dance parties; check the website for club nights.

Akbar (Map p358; www.akbarsilverlake.com; 4356 W Sunset Blvd) Best jukebox in town, a casbah atmosphere, and a crowd that's been known to change from hour to hour – gay, straight or just hip, but not too-hip-for-you. Some nights, the back room's a dance floor; other nights, you'll find comedy, craft-making or 'Bears in Space'.

MJ's (Map p358; www.mjsbar.com; 2810 Hyperion Ave) Popular contempo hangout for dance nights, 'porn star of the week' and cruising. Young but diverse crowd.

Oil Can Harry's (www.oilcanharrysla.com; 11502 Ventura Blvd, Studio City) If you've never been country-and-western dancing, you'll be surprised at just how sexy it can be, and Oil Can's is the place to do it, three nights a week, with lessons for the uninitiated. Saturday night: retro disco.

Roosterfish (Map p366; www.roosterfishbar.com; 1302 Abbot Kinney Blvd, Venice) The Westside's last remaining gay bar, the 'Fish has been serving the men of Venice for over three decades, but still feels current and chilled, with a pool table and back patio. Friday nights are busiest.

Silver Fox (www.silverfoxlongbeach.com; 411 Redondo Ave, Long Beach) Despite its name, all ages frequent this mainstay of gay Long Beach, especially on karaoke nights. It is a short drive from shopping on Retro Row.

Seven Grand BAR
(Map p348; www.sevengrand.la; 515 W 7th St) It's as if hipsters invaded mummy and daddy's hunt club, amid the tartan-patterned carpeting and deer heads on the walls. Whiskey is the drink of choice: choose from over 100 from Scotland, Ireland and even Japan.

Rooftop Bar@Standard Downtown LA BAR
(Map p348; 550 S Flower St; ⏲noon-1:30am) The scene at this outdoor lounge, swimming in a sea of skyscrapers, is libidinous, intense and more than a bit surreal. There are vibrating waterbed pods for lounging, hot-bod servers and a pool for cooling off if it all gets too steamy. Velvet rope on weekends.

HOLLYWOOD, LOS FELIZ & SILVER LAKE

Formosa Cafe BAR
(off Map p352; ☎323-850-9050; 7156 Santa Monica Blvd, Hollywood) Bogie and Bacall used to knock 'em back at this watering hole, and today you can use all that nostalgia to soak up mai tais and martinis.

Dresden PIANO BAR
(Map p358; www.thedresden.com; 1760 N Vermont Ave, Los Feliz; 4pm-2am Mon-Sat, to midnight Sun) If Formosa had Bogie and Bacall, Dresden has the songster duo Marty & Elayne, who've been there for almost as long. They're an institution (watch them perform 'Muskrat love') – you saw them singing 'Stayin' alive' in *Swingers*.

Good Luck Bar BAR
(Map p358; ☎323-666-3524; 1514 Hillhurst Ave, Los Feliz; 7pm-2am Mon-Fri, 8pm-2am Sat & Sun) The clientele is cool, the jukebox loud and the drinks seductively strong at this cult-ish watering hole decked out in Chinese opium-den carmine red. The baby-blue Yee Mee Loo and Chinese herb-based whiskey are popular choices.

Cat & Fiddle PUB
(Map p352; www.thecatandfiddle.com; 6530 Sunset Blvd; ⏲11:30am-2am; P) From Morrissey to Frodo, you never know who might be popping by for Boddingtons or Sunday-night jazz. Still, this Brit pub with leafy beer garden is more about friends and conversation than faux-hawks and deal-making.

Beauty Bar BAR, NAIL SALON
(Map p352; www.beautybar.com; 1638 N Cahuenga Blvd; ⏲9pm-2am Sun-Wed, 6pm-2am Thu-Sat) Still beautilicious after all these years, this pint-sized, retro cocktail bar is the place for having your nails painted in lurid pink while catching up on gossip and getting liquefied on martinis ($10, 7pm to 11pm Thursday to Saturday).

WEST HOLLYWOOD

WeHo is the epicenter of LA's gay scene (see the boxed text, p379), but there's a cluster of other venues frequented by hipsters of all sorts.

Sky Bar BAR
(Map p360; ☎323-848-6025; 8440 W Sunset Blvd, West Hollywood) The poolside bar at the Mondrian hotel has made a virtue out of snobbery. Unless you're exceptionally pretty, rich or are staying at the hotel, chances are relatively slim that you'll be imbibing expensive drinks (from plastic cups no less, because of the pool) with the ultimate in-crowd.

El Carmen TEQUILA BAR
(Map p360; ☎323-852-1552; 8138 W 3rd St, Mid-City; ⏲5pm-2am Mon-Fri, 7pm-2am Sat & Sun) Beneath mounted bull heads and *lucha libre* (Mexican wrestling) masks, this tequila temple dispenses cocktails based on over 100 tequilas. Industry-heavy crowd.

SANTA MONICA & VENICE

Copa d'Oro LOUNGE
(Map p366; www.copadoro.com; 217 Broadway; ⏲6pm-2am Mon-Fri, 8pm-2am Sat & Sun) Old-school, handcrafted cocktails from a well of top-end liquors and a produce bin of fresh herbs, fruits, juices and a few veggies too. The rock tunes and the smooth, dark ambience don't hurt.

Ye Olde King's Head PUB
(Map p366; ☎310-451-1402; www.yeoldekingshead.com; 116 Santa Monica Blvd, Santa Monica; ⏲8am-2am) Unofficial headquarters of Santa Monica's big British expat community, complete with darts, soccer (er, football) on the TV (er, telly), traditional English breakfast and the best fish and chips in town.

Otherroom BAR
(Map p366; ☎310-396-6230; 1201 Abbot Kinney Blvd, Venice; ⏲5pm-2am) Dark, loud and industrial, this loftlike lounge screams 'Soho transplant' but is actually a laid-back lair for local lovelies, artists and professionals. Only beer and wine are served, but the selection is tops and handpicked; sometimes the crowd is too.

For bars that ooze history, pop into **Chez Jay** (Map p366; ☎310-395-1741; 1657 Ocean Ave, Santa Monica) or the **Galley** (Map p366; ☎310-452-1934; 2442 Main St, Santa Monica), both classic watering holes with campy nautical themes.

★ Entertainment

LA's nightlife is lively, progressive and multifaceted. You can hobnob with hipsters at a trendy dance club, groove to experimental sounds in an underground bar, skate along the cutting edge at a multimedia event in an abandoned warehouse or treat your ears to a concert by the LA Philharmonic. Mainstream and fringe theater, performance art and comedy clubs all thrive. Even seeing a movie can be a deluxe event.

The freebie *LA Weekly* and the *Los Angeles Times* Calendar section are your best sources for plugging into the local scene. Buy tickets at box offices or through **Ticketmaster** (☎213-480-3232; www.ticketmaster.com). Half-price tickets to many shows are sold online by **LAStageTIX** (www.theatrela.org).

Cinemas

Moviegoing is serious business in LA; it's not uncommon for viewers to sit through the end credits, out of respect for friends and neighbors. In addition to the classic Hollywood theaters like Grauman's Chinese and El Capitan, venues listed here are noteworthy for their upscale atmosphere. Movie ticket prices run between $12 and $15, a little less before 6pm. Tickets for most theaters can be booked online or through **Moviefone** (☎from any LA area code 777-3456).

ArcLight CINEMA

(Map p358; ☎323-464-4226; www.arclightcinemas.com; 6360 W Sunset Blvd, Hollywood) This cineastes' favorite multiplex offers plush seating and no commercials before films (only trailers). Look for the landmark geodesic Cinerama Dome.

American Cinematheque CLASSIC CINEMA

(☎323-466-3456; www.americancinematheque.com) Hollywood (Map p352; Egyptian Theatre, 6712 Hollywood Blvd); Santa Monica (off Map p366; Aero Theatre, 1328 Montana Ave) Eclectic film fare from around the world for serious cinephiles, often followed by chats with the actors or director.

Cinespia OUTDOOR SCREENINGS

(off Map p352; www.cemeteryscreenings.com; 6000 Santa Monica Blvd, Hollywood; ⏲Sat & Sun May-Oct) Screenings 'to die for,' projected on the wall of the mausoleum at Hollywood Forever Cemetery (p355). Bring a picnic and cocktails (yes, alcohol is allowed!) to watch classics with a hipster crowd. A DJ spins until showtime.

Live Music

Following are some of our favorite live-music clubs. Cover charges vary widely. Unless noted, venues are open nightly and only open to those 21 or older.

Troubadour LIVE MUSIC

(Map p360; www.troubadour.com; 9081 Santa Monica Blvd, West Hollywood; ⏲Mon-Sat) The Troub did its part in catapulting the Eagles and Tom Waits to stardom, and it's still a great place to catch tomorrow's headliners. The all-ages policy ensures a mixed crowd that's refreshingly low on attitude. Mondays are free.

Spaceland LIVE MUSIC

(Map p358; www.clubspaceland.com; 1717 Silver Lake Blvd, Silver Lake) Mostly local alt-rock, indie, skate-punk and electrotrash bands take the stage here in the hopes of making it big. Beck and the Eels played some of their early gigs here.

Catalina Bar & Grill JAZZ

(Map p358; www.catalinajazzclub.com; 6725 W Sunset Blvd, Hollywood; cover $12-35, plus dinner or 2 drinks; ⏲Tue-Sun) LA's premier jazz club has a ho-hum location but top-notch acts, including Ann Hampton Calloway and Karen Akers.

McCabe's Guitar Shop ACOUSTIC

(off Map p366; www.mccabes.com; 3101 Pico Blvd; tickets $8-22; ⏲8pm Fri & Sat, 11am & 7pm Sun) This mecca of musicianship sells guitars and other instruments, and in the postage-stamp-sized back room the likes of Jackson Browne and Liz Phair have performed live and unplugged. It hosts a popular Matinee Kids' Show Sundays at 11am.

Hotel Cafe LIVE MUSIC

(Map p352; www.hotelcafe.com; 1623-1/2 N Cahuenga Blvd; tickets $10-15) The 'it' place for handmade music sometimes features big-timers such as Suzanne Vega, but it's

BIG-NAME ACTS

» **Staples Center** (Map p348; www.staplescenter.com; 1111 S Figueroa St, Downtown)

» **Nokia Theatre** (Map p348; www.nokiatheatrelive.com; 1111 S Figueroa St, Downtown)

» **Gibson Amphitheatre** (Map p356; ☎818-622-4440; www.hob.com; 100 Universal City Plaza, Universal City)

» **Wiltern Theater** (off Map p348; www.livenation.com; 3790 Wilshire Blvd)

» **Greek Theatre** (Map p356; www.greektheatrela.com; 2700 N Vermont Ave, Griffith Park)

» **John Anson Ford Amphitheatre** (off Map p352; www.fordtheatres.org; 2580 E Cahuenga Blvd, Hollywood; ⏲May-Oct)

really more of a stepping stone for message-minded newbie balladeers. Get there early and enter from the alley.

Babe & Ricky's BLUES
(www.bluesbar.com; 4339 Leimert Blvd, Leimert Park) Mama Laura has presided over LA's oldest blues club for nearly four decades. The Monday-night jam session, with free food, often brings the house down.

Nightclubs

To confirm all your clichés about Los Angeles, look no further than a nightclub in Hollywood or West Hollywood. Come armed with a hot bod, a healthy attitude or a fat wallet in order to impress the armoire-sized goons presiding over the velvet rope. Clubs in other neighborhoods are considerably more laid-back, but most require you to be at least 21 (bring picture ID). Cover ranges from $5 to $20. Doors are usually open from 9pm to 2am.

Drai's CLUB
(Map p352; www.draishollywood.com; 6250 Hollywood Blvd; ⌚10pm-3am Tue-Sat) The W Hotel rooftop is the domain of this classic Vegas after-hours club. If you dig bling and surgical enhancements, hip-hop and the sweaty pulse of a packed dance floor, you will be in Shangri La. Wednesday and Friday are the big nights.

Little Temple CLUB
(Map p358; www.littletemple.com; 4519 Santa Monica Blvd; ⌚9pm-2am Wed-Sun) This Buddha-themed lounge still brings global grooves to the people via live acts and local DJs. Fans of good reggae, funk and Latin rhythms shake their collective ass here. Admission prices vary.

Zanzibar WORLD MUSIC
(Map p366; www.zanzibarlive.com; 1301 5th St, Santa Monica; cover $7-10; ⌚Tue-Sun) Beat freaks will be in heaven at this groovetastic den dressed in a sensuous Indian-African vibe with a shape-shifting global DJ lineup that goes from Arabic to Latin to African depending on the night. The crowd is just as multiculti.

Performance Arts

Hollywood Bowl AMPHITHEATER
(off Map p352; ☎323-850-2000; www.hollywoodbowl.com; 2301 N Highland Ave, Hollywood; tickets $1-105; ⌚late Jun-Sep) One of those quintessential LA summer experiences, the Bowl is the LA Phil's summer home and also a stellar place to catch big-name rock, jazz, blues and pop acts. Come early for a preshow picnic (alcohol is allowed).

Los Angeles Philharmonic ORCHESTRA
(Map p348; www.laphil.org; 111 S Grand Ave, Downtown) The world-class LA Phil performs classics and cutting-edge works at the Walt Disney Concert Hall, under the baton of Venezuelan phenom Gustavo Dudamel.

Redcat THEATER
(Map p348; ☎213-237-2800; www.redcat.org; 631 W 2nd St, Downtown) Part of the Walt Disney Concert Hall complex, this venue presents a global feast of avant-garde and experimental theater, performance art, dance, readings, film and video.

Theater

Believe it or not, there are more live theaters in LA than in New York. Venues range from a 1000-plus seats down to 99-seat-or-less 'Equity waiver' houses, so named because actors can showcase themselves or new works free of the rules of the Actors' Equity union. Following are some of the leaders:

Music Center of Los Angeles County THEATER
(Map p348; ☎213-628-2772; www.musiccenter.org; 135 N Grand Ave) This blocks-long triple-threat comprises the **Dorothy Chandler Pavilion**, home of the LA Opera led by Placido Domingo, the multiple Tony and Pulitzer award winning horseshoe-shaped **Mark Taper Forum** and the **Ahmanson Theatre** known for big Broadway road shows. Phone for $20 'Hot Tix.' Parking is $9.

Actors' Gang THEATER
(www.theactorsgang.com; 9070 Venice Blvd, Culver City) Cofounded by Tim Robbins, this socially mindful troupe has won many awards for its bold and offbeat interpretations of classics and new works pulled from ensemble workshops.

East West Players THEATER
(Map p348; www.eastwestplayers.org; 120 N Judge John Aiso St, Little Tokyo; tickets $23-38) Founded in 1965, this pioneering Asian American ensemble presents modern classics as well as premieres by local playwrights. Alumni have gone on to win Tony, Emmy and Academy awards.

Will Geer Theatricum Botanicum AMPHITHEATER
(www.theatricum.com; 1419 N Topanga Canyon Blvd, Malibu) Enchanting summer repertory in the woods. It's up Topanga Canyon Blvd, about 6.3 miles from Pacific Coast Highway.

Celebration Theatre GAY, LESBIAN
(Map p360; www.celebrationtheatre.com; 7051 Santa Monica Blvd, West Hollywood) One of the nation's leading producers of gay and lesbian plays, winning dozens of awards.

Comedy

Little surprise that LA is one of the world's comedy capitals. If the club serves dinner and you're not eating, many clubs require a two-drink minimum order on top of the cover charge (usually $5 to $20). Except where noted, you must be 21 or older to get in.

Upright Citizens Brigade COMEDY
(Map p352; www.ucbtheatre.com; 5919 Franklin Ave; admission up to $10) Founded in New York by *SNL* alums including Amy Poehler, this sketch-comedy group cloned itself in Hollywood in 2005 and is arguably the best improv theater in town.

Groundlings COMEDY
(Map p360; www.groundlings.com; 7307 Melrose Ave, Mid-City) This improv school and company launched the careers of Lisa Kudrow, Jon Lovitz, Will Ferrell and other top talent. Improv night on Thursday brings together the main company, alumni and surprise guests. All ages.

Comedy Store COMEDY
(Map p360; www.thecomedystore.com; 8433 W Sunset Blvd, West Hollywood) From Chris Tucker to Whoopi Goldberg, there's hardly a famous comic alive that has not at some point performed at this classic, which was a gangster hangout in an earlier life.

Comedy & Magic Club COMEDY
(www.comedyandmagicclub.com; 1018 Hermosa Ave, Hermosa Beach) Best known as the place where Jay Leno tests out his *Tonight Show* shtick most Sunday nights. Reservations required; 18 and over.

Sports

Dodger Stadium BASEBALL
(off Map p348; www.dodgers.com; 1000 Elysian Park Dr, Downtown) LA's Major League Baseball team plays from April to October in this legendary stadium.

Staples Center BASKETBALL, ICE HOCKEY
(Map p348; www.staplescenter.com; 1111 S Figueroa St, Downtown) All the high-tech trappings fill this flying-saucer-shaped home to the Lakers, Clippers and Sparks basketball teams, and the Kings ice hockey team. Headliners – Britney Spears to Katy Perry – also perform here.

Shopping

Fashion-forward fashionistas (and paparazzi) flock to Robertson Blvd (between Beverly Blvd and W 3rd St) or Melrose Ave (between San Vicente and La Brea) in West Hollywood, while bargain hunters haunt Downtown's Fashion District (see the boxed text, p385). If money is no object, Beverly Hills beckons with international couture, jewelry and antiques, especially along Rodeo Dr, which is ground central for groovy tunes. East of here Silver Lake has cool kitsch and collectibles, especially around Sunset Junction (Hollywood and Sunset Blvds). Santa Monica has good boutique shopping on high toned Montana Ave and eclectic Main St, while the chain store brigade (H&M to Banana Republic) has taken over Third Street Promenade. In nearby Venice, you'll find cheap and crazy knickknacks along the Venice Boardwalk, although locals prefer Abbot Kinney Blvd with its fun mix of art, fashion and new-age emporiums.

Fahey/Klein Gallery GALLERY
(Map p360; www.faheykleingallery.com; 148 S La Brea Ave; ⏲10am-6pm Tue-Sat) Vintage and contemporary fine-art photography by icons such as Annie Leibovitz, Bruce Weber and the late, great rock and roll shutterbug, Jim Marshall.

Ten Women GALLERY
(Map p366; www.tenwomengallery.com; 1237 Abbot Kinney Blvd) This bright, whimsical gallery is a collective of two dozen female artists and craftswomen who paint, weave wire, blow glass and create beautiful material magic. They also take turns behind the counter.

Fred Segal CLOTHING
West Hollywood (Map p360; ☎323-651-4129; 8100 Melrose Ave; P); Santa Monica (Map p366; ☎310-458-9940; 500 Broadway; P) Cameron and

> **IT'S A WRAP**
>
> Dress like a movie star – in their actual clothes! Packed-to-the-rafters **It's a Wrap** Mid-City (Map p360; www.itsawrap.com; 1164 S Robertson Blvd) and Burbank (Map p356; 3315 W Magnolia Blvd) sells wardrobe castoffs – tank tops to tuxedos – worn by actors and extras working on TV or movie shoots. Tags are coded, so you'll know whose clothing you can brag about wearing.

Gwyneth are among the stars kitted out at this kingpin of LA fashion boutiques, where you can also stock up on beauty products, sunglasses, gifts and other essentials.

Kitson CLOTHING

(Map p360; ☎310-859-2652; 115 S Robertson Blvd, West Hollywood) If you like to stay ahead of the fashion curve, pop into this hip haven chock-full of tomorrow's outfits and accessories, many of them by local labels. It's a major stop for celebs on a shopping prowl.

American Rag Cie VINTAGE

(Map p360; www.amrag.com; 150 S La Brea; ⏰10am-9pm Mon-Sat, noon-7pm Sun; P) This industrial-flavored warehouse-sized space has kept trend-hungry stylistas looking fabulous since 1985. Join the vintage vultures in their hunt for second-hand leather, denim, T-shirts and shoes. It also has some new gear. It's not cheap, but it is one hell of a browse. We particularly enjoyed the period homewares in the Maison Midi wing.

RIF SHOES

(Map p348; www.rif.la; 334 E 2nd St; ⏰noon-7pm) A hip-hop spiced consignment shoe store and your one-stop shop for new and used limited edition, imported and old-school sneaks.

Jewelry District JEWELRY

(Map p348; www.lajd.net; Hill St, Downtown) For bargain bling head to this bustling downtown district, between 6th & 8th Sts, where you can snap up watches, gold, silver and gemstones at up to 70% off retail, even if they're unlikely to be seen on the red carpet.

Rose Bowl Flea Market FLEA MARKET

(www.rgcshows.com; 1001 Rose Bowl Dr, Pasadena; admission $8-20; ⏰5am-4:30pm 2nd Sun of the month) The 'mother' of all flea markets with more than 2500 vendors; held monthly.

Melrose Trading Post FLEA MARKET

(Map p360; www.melrosetradingpost.com; Fairfax High School, 7850 Melrose Ave, West Hollywood; admission $2; ⏰9am-5pm Sun) Good weekly flea market that brings out hipsters in search of retro treasure.

Amoeba Music MUSIC

(Map p352; www.amoeba.com; 6400 W Sunset Blvd, Hollywood; ⏰10:30am-11pm Mon-Sat, 11am-9pm Sun; P) Our friends call it 'Hot-moeba' for good reason: all-star staff and listening stations help you sort through over half a million new and used CDs, DVDs, videos and vinyl, and there are free in-store live shows.

Head Line Records MUSIC

(Map p360; www.headlinerecords.com; 7706 Melrose Ave, Mid-City; ⏰noon-8pm) The ultimate source for punk and hardcore.

Bar Keeper MIXOLOGY

(Map p358; www.barkeepersilverlake.com; 3910 W Sunset Blvd; ⏰noon-6pm Mon-Thu, 11am-7pm Fri & Sat, to 6pm Sun) Eastside mixologists now have their dream habitat. Here are all manner of stemware, absinthe fountains, shakers, mixers and vessels needed to pour fine cocktails.

Puzzle Zoo TOYS

(Map p366; www.puzzlezoo.com; 1413 Third St Promenade, Santa Monica; ⏰10am-9pm Sun-Thu, to 11pm Fri & Sat) Encyclopedic selection of puzzles, board games and toys, including every imaginable *Star Wars* figurine this side of Endor.

Wacko/Soap Plant POP CULTURE

(Map p358; www.soapplant.com; 4633 Hollywood Blvd, Los Feliz; ⏰11am-7pm Mon-Wed, to 9pm Thu-Sat, noon-6pm Sun) Billy Shire's emporium of camp and kitsch has been a fun browse since 1976. Pick up hula-girl swizzle sticks, a Frida Kahlo mesh bag, an inflatable globe or other, well, wacky stuff.

Meltdown Comics & Collectibles COMICS

(Map p360; ☎323-851-7283; www.meltcomics.com; 7522 W Sunset Blvd, West Hollywood; ⏰11am-9pm, 10am-10pm Wed) LA's coolest comics store beckons with indie and mainstream books, from Japanese manga to graphic novels by Daniel Clowes of *Ghost World* fame. The Baby Melt department stocks rad stuff for kids.

Frederick's of Hollywood LINGERIE

(Map p352; www.fredericks.com; 6751 Hollywood Blvd; ⏰10am-9pm Mon-Sat, 11am-7pm Sun) This legendary inventor of the cleavage-enhancing push-up bra and the G-string also sells everything from chemises to crotchless panties, all tastefully displayed with no need to blush.

Space 1520 MALL

(Map p352; www.space1520.com; 1520 N Cahuenga Blvd; ⏰11am-9pm Mon-Fri, 10am-10pm Sat, to 9pm Sun; P) The hippest mini-mall in Hollywood, this designer construct of brick, wood, concrete and glass is home to classic and trend-setting mini-chains such as Umami Burger and the Hennesy & Ingalls art and design bookstore.

LA'S FASHION DISTRICT DEMYSTIFIED

Nordstrom's semiannual sale? Barney's warehouse blowout? Mere child's play to serious bargain shoppers, who save their best game for Downtown LA's **Fashion District** (Map p348; ☎213-488-1153; www.fashiondistrict.org), a frantic, 90-block trove of stores, stalls and showrooms where discount shopping is an Olympian sport. Basically, the district is subdivided into specialty areas:

Designer knockoffs (Santee & New Alleys) Enter on 11th St between Maple Ave and Santee St.

Children (Wall St) Between 12th St and Pico Blvd.

Jewelry and accessories (Santee St) Between Olympic Blvd and 11th St.

Men and bridal (Los Angeles St) Between 7th and 9th Sts.

Textiles (8th St) Between Santee and Wall Sts.

Women (Los Angeles St) Between Olympic and Pico Blvds; also at 11th St between Los Angeles and San Julian Sts.

Shops with signs reading 'Wholesale Only' or *'Mayoreo'* are off-limits to the public. Haggling is OK, but don't expect more than 10% or 20% off, and most vendors accept only cash. Refunds or exchanges are rare, so choose carefully; many items are 'seconds,' meaning they're slightly flawed. Most stores don't have dressing rooms. Hours are generally 9am to 5pm Monday to Saturday; many stores are closed on Sunday except on Santee Alley.

On the last Friday most months (except during trade shows or around holidays; call to confirm), snap up amazing deals when dozens of designer showrooms open to the public for 'sample sales,' 9am to 3pm in and around the **New Mart** (Map p348; ☎213-627-0671; 127 E 9th St, Downtown), which specializes in contemporary and young designers, and the **California Mart** (Map p348; ☎213-630-3600; 110 E 9th St, Downtown), one of the largest apparel marts in the country, with 1500 showrooms.

Information

Dangers & Annoyances

Despite what you see in the movies, walking around LA is generally safe. Crime rates are lowest in Westside communities such as Westwood through Beverly Hills, as well as in the beach towns (except parts of Venice) and Pasadena.

Downtown's Skid Row, an area roughly bounded by 3rd, Alameda, 7th and Main Sts, has plenty of homeless folks, as does Santa Monica, though they usually avoid you if you avoid them.

Bookstores

$1 Bookstore (www.odbstore.com; 248 Pine Ave, Long Beach; ⏰10am-9pm Sun-Thu, 9am-10pm Fri, 10am-10pm Sat) Groovy warehouse of fiction and non, comics, textbooks and magazines. And, yes, everything is $1.

Book Soup (Map p360; www.booksoup.com; 8818 W Sunset Blvd, West Hollywood) Frequent celeb sightings.

Distant Lands (www.distantlands.com; 56 S Raymond Ave, Pasadena) Treasure chest of travel books, guides and gadgets.

Traveler's Bookcase (Map p360; www.travelersbookcase.com; 8375 W 3rd St, Mid-City) Just what it says.

Vroman's (www.vromansbookstore.com; 695 E Colorado Blvd, Pasadena) SoCal's oldest bookstore (since 1894) and a favorite with local literati.

Emergency

Emergency number (☎911) For police, fire or ambulance service.

Rape & Battering Hotline (☎800-656-4673)

Internet Access

Coffee shops, including the local chain **Coffee Bean & Tea Leaf** (www.cbtl.com), offer wi-fi with a purchase. Libraries offer free access. Below are some main branches; phone or surf for branch locations.

Los Angeles Public Library (☎213-228-7000; www.lapl.org; 630 W 5th St, Downtown; wi-fi)

Santa Monica Public Library (☎310-458-8600; www.smpl.org; 601 Santa Monica Blvd; wi-fi)

Internet Resources

Daily Candy LA (www.dailycandy.com) Little bites of LA style.

Discover Los Angeles (http://discoverlosangeles.com) Official tourist office site.

Gridskipper LA (www.gridskipper.com/travel/los-angeles) Urban travel guide to the offbeat.

LA Observed (www.laobserved.com) News blog that rounds up – and often scoops – other media.

LA.com (www.la.com) Clued-in guide to shopping, dining, nightlife and events.

Thrillist (www.thrillist.com) A *DailyCandy* for guys.

Media

For entertainment listings magazines, see p381.

KCRW 89.9 fm (www.kcrw.org) Santa Monica–based National Public Radio (NPR) station with cutting-edge music and well-chosen public affairs programming.

KPCC 89.3 fm (www.kpcc.org) Pasadena-based NPR station with intelligent local talk shows.

LA Weekly (www.laweekly.com) Free alternative news and listings magazine.

Los Angeles Magazine (www.losangelesmagazine.com) Glossy lifestyle monthly with useful restaurant guide.

Los Angeles Times (www.latimes.com) The west's leading daily and winner of dozens of Pulitzer Prizes. Embattled but still useful.

Medical Services

Cedars-Sinai Medical Center (☎310-423-3277; 8700 Beverly Blvd, West Hollywood; ⊙24hr emergency)

Rite-Aid pharmacies (☎800-748-3243; ⊙some 24hr) Call for the nearest branch.

Money

Travelex (☎310-659-6093; US Bank, 8901 Santa Monica Blvd, West Hollywood; ⊙9am-5pm Mon-Thu, to 6pm Fri, to 1pm Sat)

Post

Call ☎800-275-8777 or visit www.usps.com for the nearest branch.

Telephone

LA County is covered by 10 area codes (some shared with neighboring counties). Dial 1 plus the area code before the final seven digits, even when calling within the same area code.

Tourist Information

Beverly Hills (☎310-248-1015, 800-345-2210; www.lovebeverlyhills.org; 239 S Beverly Dr, Beverly Hills; ⊙8:30am-5pm Mon-Fri)

Downtown LA (☎213-689-8822; http://discoverlosangeles.com; 685 S Figueroa St; ⊙8:30am-5pm Mon-Fri)

Hollywood (☎323-467-6412; http://discoverlosangeles.com; Hollywood & Highland complex, 6801 Hollywood Blvd; ⊙10am-10pm Mon-Sat, to 7pm Sun)

Long Beach (☎562-628-8850; www.visitlongbeach.com; 3rd fl, One World Trade Center; ⊙11am-7pm Sun-Thu, 11:30am-7:30pm Fri & Sat Jun-Sep, 10am-4pm Fri-Sun Oct-May)

Santa Monica (☎310-393-7593, 800-544-5319; www.santamonica.com) Visitor center (1920 Main St; ⊙9am-6pm); Information kiosk (☎1400 Ocean Ave; ⊙9am-5pm Jun-Aug, 10am-4pm Sep-May)

Getting There & Away

Air

Los Angeles International Airport (LAX; www.lawa.org; 1 World Way, Los Angeles) is one of the world's busiest, located on the coast between Venice and the South Bay city of Manhattan Beach. Of its eight terminals, most international airlines operate out of Tom Bradley International Terminal. Free shuttles to other terminals and hotels stop outside each terminal on the lower level. A free minibus for the mobility-impaired can be ordered by calling ☎310-646-6402.

Locals love **Bob Hope Airport** (BUR; www.bobhopeairport.com; 2627 N Hollywood Way, Burbank), commonly called Burbank Airport, in the San Fernando Valley. It has delightful art deco style, easy-to-use terminals and proximity to Hollywood, Downtown and Pasadena.

To the south, on the border with Orange County, **Long Beach Airport** (LGB; www.longbeach.gov/airport; 4100 Donald Douglas Dr, Long Beach) is convenient for Disneyland. **Ontario International Airport** (ONT; www.lawa.org/ont; 2900 E Airport Dr, Ontario), is approximately 35 miles east of Downtown LA.

Bus

LA's hub for **Greyhound** (☎213-629-8401, 800-231-2222; www.greyhound.com; 1716 E 7th St) is in an unsavory part of Downtown, so avoid arriving after dark. Bus 18 makes the 10-minute trip to the 7th St metro station with onward service across town, including Metro Rail's Red Line to Hollywood; bus 620 Rapid takes you across town to Santa Monica via Wilshire Blvd.

Greyhound buses serve San Diego approximately hourly ($19, 2¼ to 3¾ hours). They also have about four daily buses to/from Santa Barbara ($18, 2¼ to 2¾ hours), about a dozen to/from San Francisco ($56.50, 7¼ to 12¼ hours), and about a half-dozen to Anaheim ($11, one hour). Some northbound buses stop at the terminal in **Hollywood** (☎323-466-6381; 1715 N Cahuenga Blvd), and a few southbound buses also pass through **Long Beach** (☎562-218-3011; 1498 Long Beach Blvd).

For more information, see p514 and p516.

Car & Motorcycle

All the major international car-rental agencies have branches at airports and throughout Los

Angeles (see p516 for central reservation numbers). If you haven't booked, use the courtesy phones in airport arrival areas at LAX. Offices and lots are outside the airport, reached by free shuttles.

Eagle Rider (☎888-600-6020; www.eaglerider.com; 11860 S La Cienega Blvd, Hawthorne; ⏲9am-5pm), just south of LAX, and **Route 66** (☎310-578-0112, 888-434-4473; www.route66riders.com; 4161 Lincoln Blvd, Marina del Rey; ⏲9am-6pm Tue-Sat, 10am-5pm Sun & Mon) rent Harleys. Rates start from $140 per day, with discounts for longer rentals.

Train

Amtrak trains roll into Downtown's historic **Union Station** (☎800-872-7245; www.amtrak.com; 800 N Alameda St) from across California and the country. The *Pacific Surfliner* travels daily to San Diego ($36, 2¾ hours), Santa Barbara ($29, 2¾ to 3¼ hours) and San Luis Obispo ($40, 5½ hours). See p519 for full details.

Getting Around

To/From Airports

LOS ANGELES INTERNATIONAL AIRPORT

At LAX, door-to-door shared-ride vans operated by **Prime Time** (☎800-473-3743; www.primetimeshuttle.com) and **Super Shuttle** (☎310-782-6600; www.supershuttle.com) leave from the lower level of all terminals. Typical fares to Santa Monica, Hollywood or Downtown are $20, $25 and $16, respectively. **Disneyland Express** (☎714-978-8855; www.grayline.com) travels at least hourly between LAX and Disneyland-area hotels for one way/round trip $22/$32.

Curbside dispatchers will summon a taxi for you. There's a flat fare of $46.50 to Downtown LA. Otherwise, metered fares ($2.85 at flag fall plus $2.70 per mile) average $30 to Santa Monica, $42 to Hollywood and up to $90 to Disneyland. There is a $4 surcharge for taxis departing LAX.

LAX Flyaway Buses (☎866-435-9529; www.lawa.org/flyaway) depart LAX terminals every 30 minutes, from about 5am to midnight, nonstop to both Westwood ($5, 30 min) and Union Station ($7, 45 min) in Downtown LA.

Other **public transportation** is slower and less convenient but cheaper. From the lower level outside any terminal, catch a free shuttle bus to parking lot C, next to the LAX Transit Center, hub for buses serving all of LA. You can also take shuttle bus G to Aviation Station and the Metro Green Line light rail, from where you can connect to the Metro Blue Line and Downtown LA or Long Beach (40 minutes).

Popular routes (trip times given are approximate and depend on traffic):

DOWNTOWN Metro Buses 42a or 439 West ($1.50, 1½ hours)

HOLLYWOOD Metro bus 42a West to Overhill/La Brea, transfer to Metro bus 212 North ($3, 1½ hours)

VENICE & SANTA MONICA Big Blue Bus 3 or Rapid 3 ($1, 30 to 50 minutes)

BOB HOPE AIRPORT

Typical shuttle fares are Hollywood $23, Downtown $24 and Pasadena $23. Cabs charge about $20, $30 and $40, respectively. Metro Bus 222 goes to Hollywood (30 minutes), while Downtown is served by Metro Bus 94 South (one hour).

LONG BEACH AIRPORT

Shuttle services cost $35 to the Disneyland area, $40 to Downtown LA and $29 to Manhattan Beach. Cabs cost $45, $65 and $40, respectively. Long Beach Transit Bus 111 makes the trip to the Transit Mall in downtown Long Beach in about 45 minutes. From here you can catch the Metro Blue Line to Downtown LA and points beyond.

Bicycle

Most buses have bike racks and bikes ride for free, although you must securely load and unload it yourself. Bikes are also allowed on Metro Rail trains except during rush hour (6:30am to 8:30am and 4:30pm to 6:30pm, weekdays). For rental places, see p367.

Car & Motorcycle

Unless time is no factor or money is extremely tight, you'll probably find yourself behind the wheel. Driving in LA doesn't need to be a hassle (a GPS device helps), but be prepared for some of the worst traffic in the country during rush hour (roughly 7:30am to 9am and 4pm to 6:30pm).

Parking at motels and cheaper hotels is usually free, while fancier ones charge from $8 to $36. Valet parking at nicer restaurants, hotels and nightspots is commonplace, with rates ranging from $2.50 to $10.

For local parking recommendations, see each of the neighborhoods in the Sights section.

Public Transportation

Trip-planning help is available via LA's **Metro** (☎800-266-6883; www.metro.net), which operates about 200 bus lines and six subway and light-rail lines:

BLUE LINE Downtown (7th St/Metro Center) to Long Beach.

EXPO LINE Downtown (7th St/Metro Center) to Culver City, via Exposition Park (scheduled opening: winter 2011–12).

GOLD LINE Union Station to Pasadena and East LA.

GREEN LINE Norwalk to Redondo Beach, with shuttle to LAX.

PURPLE LINE Downtown to Koreatown.

RED LINE Union Station to North Hollywood, via Downtown, Hollywood and Universal Studios.

Tickets cost $1.50 per boarding (get a transfer when boarding if needed). There are no free transfers between trains and buses, but 'TAP card' unlimited ride passes cost $5/20/75 (plus $1 for the reusable card) per day/week/month. Purchase train tickets and TAP cards at vending machines in stations, or visit www.metro.net for other vendors.

Local **DASH minibuses** (☎your area code + 808-2273; www.ladottransit.com; 50¢) serve Downtown and Hollywood. Santa Monica-based **Big Blue Bus** (☎310-451-5444; www.bigbluebus.com, $1) serves much of the Westside and LAX. Its Line 10 Freeway Express connects Santa Monica with Downtown LA ($2; one hour).

Taxi

Except for taxis lined up outside airports, train stations, bus stations and major hotels, it's best to phone for a cab. Fares are metered: $2.85 at flag fall plus $2.70 per mile. Taxis serving the airport accept credit cards, though sometimes grudgingly. Some recommended companies:

Checker (☎800-300-5007)

Independent (☎800-521-8294)

Yellow Cab (☎800-200-1085)

AROUND LOS ANGELES

Six Flags Magic Mountain & Hurricane Harbor

Velocity rules at **Six Flags Magic Mountain** (Map p388; www.sixflags.com/parks/magicmountain; 26101 Magic Mountain Parkway, Valencia; adult/child under 4ft $62/37; ⊙check website;) about 30 miles north of LA off I-5 (Golden State Fwy), an amusement park with dozens of baffling ways to go up, down and inside out, fast to faster.

Teens and college kids get their jollies on the 16 bone-chilling roller coasters, including the aptly named **Scream**, which goes through seven loops, including a zero-gravity roll and a dive loop, with you sitting in a floorless chair. If you've got a stomach of steel, don't miss **X2**, where cars spin 360 degrees while hurtling forward and plummeting all at once. Many rides have height restrictions ranging from 36in to 58in, but there are tamer rides for the elementary-school set, plus shows, parades and concerts for all ages.

On hot summer days, little ones might be more in their element next door at **Six Flags Hurricane Harbor** (www.sixflags.com/parks/hurricaneharborla; 26101 Magic Mountain Parkway;

Around Los Angeles

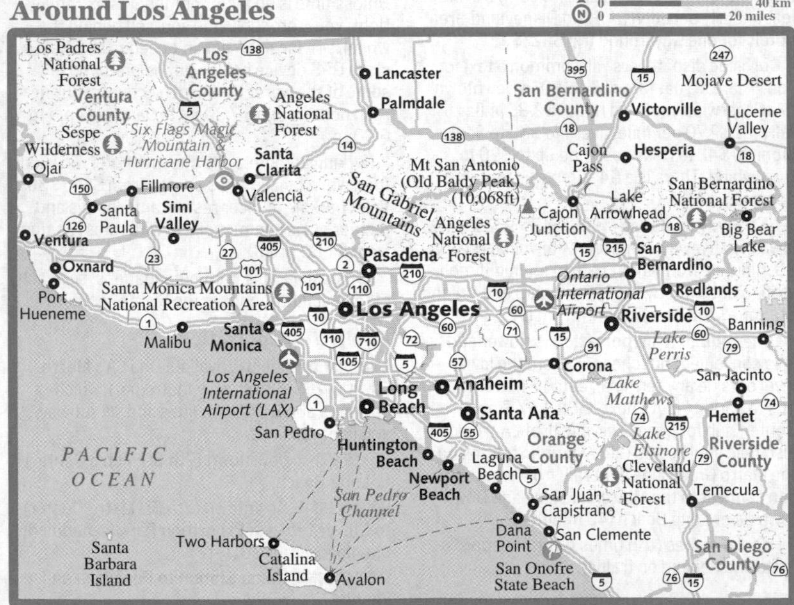

adult/child under 4ft $35/25;), a jungle-themed 22-acre water park with a tropical lagoon, churning wave pools and wicked high-speed slides.

Check the website for discounts. If you don't have your own transport, look for organized tour flyers in hotels. Parking is $15.

Catalina Island

Mediterranean-flavored Catalina is just '26 miles across the sea,' as the old song by The Four Preps goes, but it feels an ocean away from LA. Even if it sinks under the weight of day-trippers in summer, stay overnight and you'll feel the ambience go from frantic to romantic.

Part of the Channel Islands, Catalina has a unique ecosystem and history. Until the late 19th century, it was alternately a hangout for sea-otter poachers, smugglers and Union soldiers. Chewing-gum magnate William Wrigley Jr purchased it in 1919 and brought his Chicago Cubs baseball team here for spring training. In 1924, bison were imported for the shooting of a western (*The Vanishing American*); today their descendants form a managed herd of about 250. Of the island's sun-baked hillsides, valleys and canyons, 88% is owned by the Santa Catalina Island Conservancy, ensuring that most of it remains free of development, though open for visitors.

For more information, see the **Catalina Visitors Bureau** (310-510-1520; www.catalina.com; Green Pier, Avalon).

Sights & Activities

Most tourist activity concentrates in the pint-sized port town of Avalon, where a yacht-studded harbor hems in a tiny downtown with shops, hotels and restaurants. The only other settlement is remote Two Harbors in the backcountry, which has a general store, dive and kayak center, snack bar and lodge.

Avalon's most recognizable landmark is the 1929 art deco hall **Casino** (310-510-0179; 1 Casino Way), not a gambling casino but a cinema and ballroom still in use. Fabulous murals, a twinkling domed ceiling and history can be seen via an amusing one-hour tour (adult/child two to 12 $17.50/14.25). Tour tickets also include admission to the **Catalina Island Museum** (www.catalinamuseum.org; 1 Casino Way; adult/child/senior $5/2/4; 10am-5pm) downstairs, which has modest exhibits about island history.

Catalina's protected, hilly interior, filled with flora, fauna and memorable vistas of the rugged coast, sandy coves and LA coastline, may only be explored on foot, mountain bike or organized tour. Pick up maps and compulsory permits at the **Catalina Island Conservancy** (310-510-2595; www.catalinaconservancy.org; 125 Claressa Ave; biking permit adult/student $35/25, hiking permit free; 8:30am-4:30pm, closed for lunch). Hikers might hop on the **Airport Shuttle** (310-510-0143; adult/child round-trip $25/20, reservations required; from 5 times daily) to the hilltop airport, a popular starting point as you're hiking downhill virtually the whole 10 miles back to Avalon. There's very little shade so bring a hat, sunscreen and plenty of water.

Avalon's sliver of a beach along Crescent Ave gets packed, and it's not much better at palm-tree-lined **Descanso Beach** (admission $2), a beach club with a bar and restaurant that's a short walk north of the Casino. Nearby, though, is some of SoCal's finest kayaking.

There's good **snorkeling** at Lovers' Cove and at Casino Point Marine Park, a marine reserve that's also the best shore dive. Rent gear at any of these locations or on Green Pier.

Tours

Discovery Tours (310-510-2500; www.visitcatalinaisland.com) and **Catalina Adventure Tours** (310-510-2888; www.catalinaadventuretours.com) both offer scenic tours ($16 to $79) of Avalon, the coastline, the interior countryside and the fish-rich underwater gardens from a glass-bottom boat. A two-hour **zip-line tour** ($113) takes you on five separate lines, up to 600 feet above ground and as fast as 55mph. This popular attraction can book out a month or more in advance, so make reservations as soon as you have your travel dates set.

Sleeping & Eating

Rates soar on weekends and between May and September, but at other times they're about 30% to 60% lower than what's listed here.

Hotel Metropole BOUTIQUE HOTEL **$$$**
(800-300-8528; www.hotel-metropole.com; 205 Crescent Ave; r from $249) The newest and grooviest spot in Avalon. Oceanfront rooms are huge, with wood floors, fireplaces,

soaker tubs and sea views. Its M restaurant does creative fusion such as duck breast and oyster mushrooms coated in blood orange molasses.

Hermosa Hotel & Cottages COTTAGES $
(☎310-510-1010, 877-453-1313; www.hermosahotel.com; 131 Metropole St; r without bath $45-75, cottage with bath $65-170) Tidy, central, home-style and diver-friendly collection of compact wooden rooms and cottages (some dating back to 1896). Some rooms have kitchenettes and air-con.

Campgrounds CAMPING $
(☎310-510-8368; www.visitcatalinaisland.com/camping; tent sites per adult/child $14/7) The best way to get up close and personal with the island's natural beauty and possibly bison. There are several campgrounds, including one about 1.5 miles from central Avalon (Hermit Gulch); Little Harbor is especially scenic. Reservations required.

Ristorante Villa Portofino ITALIAN $$
(☎310-510-2009; 101 Crescent Ave; mains $15-35; ⏰dinner) The restaurant at the Villa Portofino hotel serves Italian specialties that would be at home at top LA restaurants, such as *mezzaluna di pollo* (chicken-filled pasta) and *vitello al marsala* (veal in mushroom and marsala wine sauce). All served with a view of the harbor.

Cottage DINER $
(www.menu4u.com/thecottage; 603 Crescent Ave; sandwiches & burgers $8-11; ⏰breakfast, lunch & dinner) Huge breakfasts, sandwiches and American, Italian and Mexican favorites are served here.

Casino Dock Cafe CAFE $
(www.casinodockcafe.com; 1 Casino Way; appetizers $6-12, sandwiches, burgers & hot dogs $4-10; ⏰breakfast & lunch) Casual waterfront hangout, good for a beer and a simple meal.

Getting There & Around

It takes about 1½ hours to get to Catalina from any of several coastal ports.

Catalina Express (☎800-481-3470; www.catalinaexpress.com; adult/child round-trip $69.50/54) Ferries to Avalon from San Pedro, Long Beach and Dana Point in Orange County and to Two Harbors from San Pedro. Up to 30 services daily.

Catalina Marina del Rey Flyer (☎310-305-7250; adult/child round-trip $54/42) Catamaran to Avalon and Two Harbors from Marina del Rey in LA. Schedules vary seasonally.

Catalina Passenger Service (☎800-830-7744; www.catalinainfo.com; adult/child round-trip $68/51) Catamaran to Avalon from Newport Beach in Orange County.

Most places in Avalon are within a 10-minute walk. The Avalon Trolley (single ride/day pass $2/6) operates along two routes, passing all major sights and landmarks.

Big Bear Lake

Big Bear Lake and the towns in its surrounding valley (total population 21,000) are family-friendly and versatile holiday destinations, drawing ski bums and boarders in winter, and hikers, mountain-bikers and water-sports enthusiasts the rest of the year. About 99 miles northeast of LA, it's a popular getaway.

Big Bear is approached by **Rim of the World Drive** (Hwy 18), which climbs, curves and meanders through 37 miles of the **San Bernardino National Forest** to the town of San Bernardino. Views are spectacular on clear days. The forest is hugely popular with weekend warriors, but from Monday to Thursday you'll often have trails and facilities to yourself, and can also benefit from lower accommodation prices.

Activities

Most of Big Bear is sandwiched between the lake's south shore and the mountains. The main thoroughfare, Big Bear Blvd (Hwy 18), is lined with motels, cabins and businesses. It skirts the pedestrian-friendly 'Village,' which has cutesy shops, restaurants and the Big Bear Lake Resort Association. The ski resorts are east of the Village. North Shore Blvd (Hwy 38) is quieter and provides access to campgrounds.

Hiking

In summer, people trade their ski boots for hiking boots and hit the forest trails. If you only have time for one short hike, make it the **Castle Rock Trail**, which is a 2.4-mile round-trip offering superb views. The first half-mile is pretty steep but the trail flattens out somewhat after that. The trailhead is off Hwy 18 on the western end of the lake. Also popular is the moderate **Cougar Crest Trail** (5 miles round trip), starting near the Discovery Center, which links up with the **Pacific Crest Trail** (PCT) after about 2 miles and offers views of the lake and Holcomb

Valley. Most people continue eastward for another half-mile to the top of **Bertha Peak** (8502ft) for a 360-degree view of Bear Valley, Holcomb Valley and the Mojave Desert.

Mountain-Biking

Big Bear is a mountain-biking mecca, with over 100 miles of trails and fire roads. It hosts several pro and amateur races each year. A good place to get your feet in gear is along the aptly named 9-mile **Grandview Loop**, which starts at the top of Snow Summit, easily reached via the **Scenic Sky Chair** (one way/round trip without bike $8/12, with bike one way/day pass $12/25). One of the best single-track rides is the intermediate 13-mile **Grout Bay Trail**, which starts on the north shore.

Bear Valley Bikes (909-866-8000; 40298 Big Bear Blvd; half-/full day from $30/40), near the Alpine Slide amusement park, is a good rental place.

Skiing

With an 8000ft ridge rising above the lake's southern side, Big Bear usually gets snow between mid-December and March or April, and has two ski mountains with the same parent: **Bear Mountain** (909-585-2519; www.bearmountain.com) and **Snow Summit** (909-866-5766; www.snowsummit.com), both off Hwy 18. Bear Mountain, the higher of the two, has a vertical drop of 1665 feet (1200 feet at Snow Summit), and is an all-mountain freestyle park, while Snow Summit focuses on traditional downhill skiing. Altogether the mountains are laced by over 60 runs and served by 26 lifts, including four high-speed quads. An adult lift ticket costs half-/full day $46/56 Monday to Friday, $59/69 on Saturday and Sunday. One ticket buys access to both resorts, which are linked by a free shuttle. Ski and boot rentals cost around $25.

Water Sports

Swim Beach, near the Village, has lifeguards and is popular with families. For a bit more privacy, rent a boat, kayak or waverunner and get out on the water. A pretty destination is **Boulder Bay** near the lake's western end. Rent boats at **Holloway's** (909-866-5706; www.bigbearboating.com; 398 Edgemoor Rd).

Cantrell Guide Service FISHING
(909-585-4017) Cantrell guarantees a catch – or your money back. You'll need a fishing license, available at sporting stores around town, and there's a three-hour minimum for boat hire (per hour $75).

Alpine Slide AMUSEMENT PARK
(www.alpineslidebigbear.com; 800 Wild Rose Ln; prices vary; vary) Great for families, this small fun park has a water slide (day pass $12), a wheeled downhill bobsled ride, a go-cart track and a miniature golf course.

 Tours

Take a 20-mile self-guided tour through the Holcomb Valley, the site of Southern California's biggest Gold Rush in the early 1860s on the Gold Fever Trail. The dirt road is negotiable by mountain bikes and practically all vehicles. Budget two to four hours, stops included. The Big Bear Discovery Center has a free pamphlet describing 12 sites of interest along this route.

Guided tours are offered by **Off-Road Adventures** (909-585-1036; www.offroadadventure.com) to a variety of landscapes including Butler Peak, a mountaintop crowned by a historic fire lookout tower for panoramic views.

Sleeping

Rates are highest in the winter peak and lowest in summer. Big Bear Lake Resort Association books accommodations for $20 per reservation.

Big Bear has five **US Forest Service campgrounds** (800-444-6777; www.recreation.gov), open spring to fall (dates vary), most on the North Shore, with potable water and flush toilets.

Knickerbocker Mansion B&B $$
(909-878-9190, 800-388-4179; www.knickerbockermansion.com; 869 Knickerbocker Rd; r $125-280; P @) Secluded from the tourist fray of the Village, innkeepers Thomas and Stanley have poured their hearts into this ornate B&B with nine rooms and two suites inside a hand-built 1920s log home and a converted carriage house. Breakfasts are to die for, and fine dinners are served on Fridays and Saturdays (make reservations).

Grey Squirrel Resort CABINS $$
(909-866-4335, 800-381-5569; www.greysquirrel.com; 39372 Big Bear Blvd; r $94-218; P @) On the main road into town, amid pines, this delightful throwback, built in 1927, has an assortment of classic mountain cabins named for woodland creatures and sleeping

two to 14. All have kitchen and the nicest come with fireplace, sundeck and Jacuzzi.

Northwoods Resort HOTEL $$
(909-866-3121, 800-866-3121; www.northwoodsresort.com; 40650 Village Dr; r $139-169;) 'Resort' may be a bit overblown, but this 148-room inn is your best bet in town for mod-cons. Mineshaft-style timber beamed hallways lead to motel-style rooms (warning: thin walls). The large pool is heated year-round. The restaurant (mains lunch $10 to $15, dinner $10 to $32) has sandwiches, steaks, pizzas and tables on the pond-adjacent patio.

Castlewood Theme Cottages COTTAGES $$
(909-866-2720; www.castlewoodcottages.com; 547 Main St; r $49-319;) Bored with bland motel rooms? Your fantasies can go wild in these well-crafted, clean and amazingly detailed cabins, complete with Jacuzzi tubs and costumes. Let your inner Tarzan roar, fancy yourselves Robin and Marian or Antony and Cleopatra, or cavort among woodland fairy-folk or an indoor waterfall. It's cheesy, wacky and, oddly, fun. Kids are not allowed.

Big Bear Hostel HOSTEL $
(909-866-8900; www.bigbearhostel.com; 541 Knickerbocker Rd; dm $25-30, r per person from $35;) Grayson, a mountain-biker and snowboarder enthusiast, and a fount of local info, oversees this 49-bed inn. Furnishings and bedding are standard-issue – but hey, man, it's a hostel – and there's a deck for lounging with views of the lake. Linens are provided, though BYOT (towel).

Eating & Drinking

Grizzly Manor Cafe DINER $
(909-866-6226; 41268 Big Bear Blvd; mains $3-9; breakfast & lunch;) You'll feel like you've stepped into a backwoods sitcom at this buzzy locals' hangout, about a quarter mile east of the Village. Breakfasts are bear-sized (look for pancakes bigger than the plate), staff irreverent, walls covered with whacky stickers and prices small.

Himalayan SOUTH ASIAN $
(www.himalayanbigbear.com; 672 Pine Knot Ave; mains $8-16; lunch & dinner;) Homey spot for authentic dishes from Nepal and India. Momo (Tibetan-style dumplings) are a refreshing start, while chicken soup is thick with garlic, onion and tomato. Tandoori chicken and chicken *saag* (with pureed spinach) are also popular.

Peppercorn Grille ITALIAN-AMERICAN $$
(www.peppercorngrille.com; 553 Pine Knot Ave; mains $12-34; lunch & dinner) Locals and visitors alike swear by the Italian-inspired American fare for a fancy meal at this cute cottage in the Village: brick-oven baked pizzas, pastas, chicken breast stuffed with artichoke and spinach, steak, lobster and homemade desserts such as tiramisu.

Information

Drivers need to obtain a National Forest Adventure Pass if parking on forest land. Passes are available at the Big Bear Discovery Center.

Tourist Information

Big Bear Discovery Center (909-382-2790; www.bigbeardiscoverycenter.com; 40971 North Shore Dr (Hwy 38), Fawnskin; 8:30am-4:30pm Thu-Mon) Operated in cooperation with the US Forest Service, the center offers outdoor information, exhibits & guided tours.

Big Bear Lake Resort Association (909-866-7000, 800-424-4232; www.bigbear.com; 630 Bartlett Rd; 8am-5pm Mon-Fri, 9am-5pm Sat & Sun) Maps, information and room reservations.

Getting There & Away

From I-10 take I-210 and CA-330 (in Highland) to CA-18 (in Running Springs). To avoid serpentine mountain roads, CA-38 near Redlands is longer but relatively easy on the queasy.

Mountain Area Regional Transit Authority (MARTA; www.marta.cc) buses connect Big Bear with the Greyhound bus station in San Bernardino ($10; three times Monday to Friday, once Saturday), with connections to LA ($13, 1¼ hours).

Disneyland & Orange County

Includes »

Best Places to Eat

- Bluewater Grill (p414)
- French 75 Bistro & Champagne Bar (p418)
- Sabatino's Sausage Company (p414)
- Napa Rose (p404)
- Nick's Deli (p409)

Best Places to Stay

- Shorebreak Hotel (p410)
- Disney's Grand Californian Hotel & Spa (p402)
- Newport Channel Inn (p414)
- Casa Laguna Inn (p417)
- Montage (p417)

Why Go?

Once upon a time, long before the Real Housewives threw lavish pool parties and the rich teens of MTV's *Laguna Beach* screamed at each other on our TV screens, Orange County's public image was defined by an innocent animated mouse. Even in his wildest imagination, Walt Disney couldn't have known that Mickey would one day share the spotlight with Botoxed socialites and rich kids driving Porsches along the sunny Pacific Coast Hwy. But Walt might have imagined the bigger picture – those same catfighting teens are now adults and will be bringing their little ones to Disneyland soon.

These seemingly conflicting cultures, plus a growing population of Vietnamese and Latino immigrants seeking the American dream, form the county's diverse population of more than three million. And while there's truth to the televised stereotypes, look closer – there are also deep pockets of individuality and open-mindedness keeping the OC real.

When to Go

Anaheim

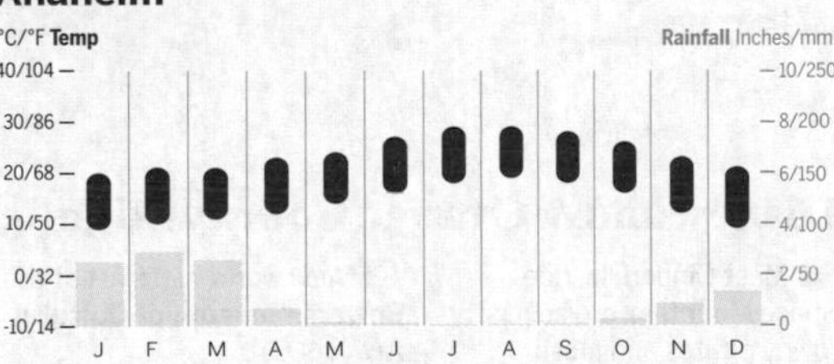

May Spring break draws crowds, then numbers drop until Memorial Day. Sunny and balmy days.

Jul & Aug Summer vacation and beach season peak. Surfing and art festivals by the coast.

Sep Blue skies, cooler temperatures inland, fewer crowds at the theme parks.

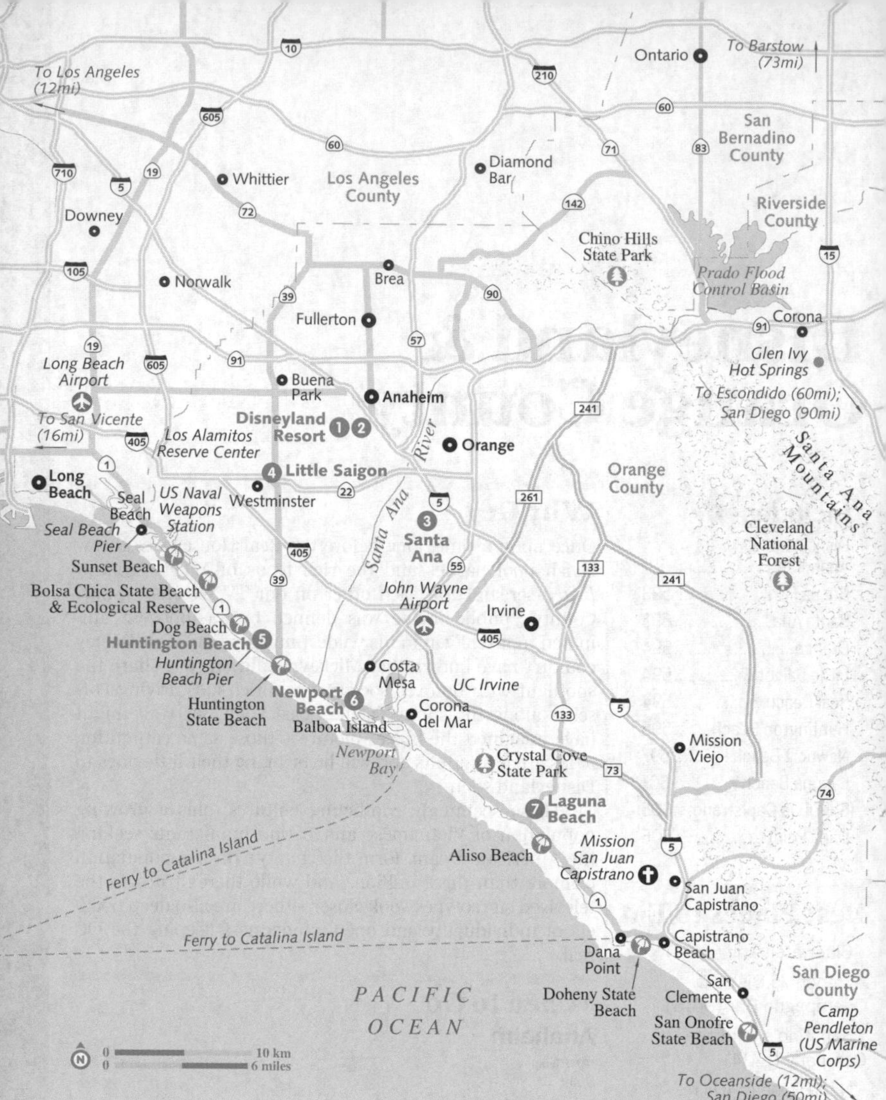

Disneyland & Orange County Highlights

1. Meet Cinderella, ride Space Mountain, cruise past rowdy pirates and finish the day with fireworks at **Disneyland park** (p397)
2. Join an eager crowd of Pixar enthusiasts and visit **Cars Land** (p402), a brand-new section of Disney California Adventure park
3. View world-class art at the **Bowers Museum of Cultural Art** (p407)
4. Go for pho in the Vietnamese enclave of **Little Saigon** (p408)
5. Watch the pros hit the waves in Surf City, USA, also known as **Huntington Beach** (p409)
6. Shop the boutiques, ride a bicycle along beach paths and watch beautiful people in **Newport Beach** (p411)
7. Check out the bohemian-chic art scene of Laguna Beach with the **First Thursdays Art Walk** (p417) or, in summer, at the **Festival of the Arts** (p418)

Getting There & Around

Air

If you're heading to Disneyland or the Orange County beaches, avoid always-busy Los Angeles International Airport (LAX) by flying in to the easy-to-navigate **John Wayne Airport** (SNA; ☎949-252-5200; 18601 Airport Way; www.ocair.com) in Santa Ana. The airport is 8 miles inland from Newport Beach, via Hwy 55, near the junction of I-405 (San Diego Fwy). Airlines serving Orange County include Alaska, American, Continental, Delta, Frontier, Northwest, Southwest, United and US Airways.

Long Beach Airport (LGB; ☎562-570-2600; www.longbeach.gov/airport; 4100 Donald Douglas Dr), to the north just across the county line, is a handy alternative.

From John Wayne Airport, Orange County bus 76 runs west to South Coast Plaza and Huntington Beach, and southeast to Fashion Island in Newport Beach. To get to Orange County from Long Beach Airport, take Long Beach bus 111 to the Long Beach Transit Center. Catch Orange County bus 60 to 7th and Channel and transfer to Orange County bus 1, which travels along the Orange County coast.

For information on shuttle services, see p406.

Bus

The **Orange County Transportation Authority** (OCTA; ☎714-636-7433; www.octa.net; ⊙info line 7am-8pm Mon-Fri, to 7pm Sat & Sun) runs county-wide bus service. Buses generally run from about 5am to 10pm weekdays, with shorter hours on weekends. The fare is $1.50 per ride or $4 for a day pass. You can buy both types of tickets onboard, and you'll need exact change. Look for OCTA bus system maps and schedules at train stations and online. To get schedule information by phone, call during the hours noted above; there is no after-hours automated phone service.

Although it would not be time efficient to explore all of Orange County by bus, hopping on OCTA bus 1 – which runs along the coast between Long Beach and San Clemente – is a cheap and easy way to visit the county's oceanfront communities. Bus 1 runs roughly every half-hour on weekdays (4:30am to 10pm) and every hour on weekends (5:30am to 7:20pm).

Car

The easiest way to get around is by car, but avoid driving on the freeways during the morning and afternoon rush hours (7am to 10am and 3pm to 7pm).

Train

Fullerton, Anaheim, Orange, Santa Ana, Irvine, Laguna Niguel, San Juan Capistrano and San Clemente are all served by Amtrak's Pacific Surfliner (p519).

A one-way trip from LA to Anaheim ($14) takes about 40 minutes, and the trip to San Juan Capistrano from LA ($20) is one hour and 20 minutes. From San Diego, it takes one hour and 20 minutes to get to San Juan Capistrano ($21), and two hours to get to Anaheim ($27). The Pacific Surfliner runs about every hour between 6am and 5pm weekdays and between 7am and 5pm on weekends.

DISNEYLAND & ANAHEIM

Mickey is one lucky mouse. Created by animator Walt Disney in 1928, he caught a ride on a multimedia juggernaut (film, TV, publishing, music, merchandising and theme parks) that's made him an international superstar. Plus, he lives in the Happiest Place on Earth, a slice of 'imagineered' hyperreality where the streets are always clean, the employees – called cast members – are always upbeat and there's a parade every day of the year. It would be easy to hate the guy but since opening the doors to his Disneyland home in 1955, he's been a thoughtful host to millions of guests.

But there are grounds for discontent. Every ride seems to end in a gift store, prices are high and there are grumblings that management could do more to ensure affordable local housing for employees as well as cover health insurance for more workers at its hotels. (With 20,000 workers on payroll, Disneyland Resort is the largest private employer in Orange County.) But the parade marches on and for the millions of kids and

> DON'T MISS
>
> **IS IT A SMALL WORLD AFTER ALL?**
>
> Pay attention to the cool optical illusion along Main Street, USA. As you look from the entrance up the street toward Sleeping Beauty Castle, everything seems far away and larger-than-life. When you're at the castle looking back, everything seems closer and smaller. This technique is known as forced perspective, a trick used on Hollywood sets where buildings are constructed at a decreasing scale to create an illusion of height or depth. Welcome to Disneyland.

FASTPASS: THE INS AND OUTS

Even if you don't have a smartphone app (p406) to update you with current wait times at the theme parks' rides and attractions, you can still significantly cut your time in line with FASTPASS.

Walk up to a FASTPASS ticket machine – located near the entrance to select theme park rides – and insert your park entrance ticket or annual passport. You'll receive a slip of paper showing the 'return time' for boarding (always at least 40 minutes later). Then show up within the window of time printed on the ticket and join the ride's FASTPASS line, where a cast member will check your FASTPASS ticket. There'll still be a wait, but it's shorter (typically 15 minutes or less). Hang on to your FASTPASS ticket until you board the ride, just in case another cast member asks to see it.

Even if you're running late and miss the time window printed on your FASTPASS ticket, you can still try joining the FASTPASS line. Cast members are rarely strict about enforcing the end of the time window, but showing up before your FASTPASS time window is a no-no.

You're thinking, 'what's the catch,' right? When you get a FASTPASS, you will have to wait at least two hours before getting another one (check the 'next available' time printed at the bottom of your ticket). So make it count. Before getting a FASTPASS, check the display above the machine, which will tell you what the 'return time' for boarding is. If it's much later in the day, or doesn't fit your schedule, a FASTPASS may not be worth it. Ditto if the ride's current wait time is just 15 to 30 minutes.

Some Disneyland fans have developed strategies for taking advantage of the FASTPASS system. For example, for now there's nothing to prevent you from simultaneously getting FASTPASSes at both Disneyland Park and Disney's California Adventure. As long as you have a Park Hopper ticket and don't mind doing a *lot* of walking between the two parks, you can bounce back and forth between a dozen or so of the most popular rides and attractions all day long.

families who visit every year, Disneyland remains a magical experience.

History

Having celebrated its 55th anniversary, Disneyland still aims to be the 'Happiest Place on Earth,' an expression coined by Walt Disney himself when the 'theme park' (another Disney-ism) first opened on July 17, 1955. Carved out of Anaheim's orange and walnut groves, the park's construction took just one year. But Disneyland's opening day was a disaster. Temperatures over 100°F (about 40°C) melted asphalt underfoot, leaving women's high heels stuck in the tar. There were plumbing problems, which made all of the drinking fountains quit working. Hollywood stars didn't show up on time, and more than twice the number of expected guests – some 28,000 by the day's end – crowded through the gates, some holding counterfeit tickets. But none of this kept eager Disney fans away for long; more than 50 million tourists visited in its first decade alone.

During the 1990s, Anaheim, the city surrounding Disneyland, undertook a staggering $4.2 billion revamp and expansion, cleaning up run-down stretches and establishing the first US police force specifically for guarding tourists. (They call it 'tourist-oriented policing.') The cornerstone of the five-year effort was the addition of a second theme park in 2001, Disney California Adventure (DCA). Adjacent to the original Disneyland Park, DCA was designed to pay tribute to the state's most famous natural landmarks and cultural history. More recently Downtown Disney, an outdoor pedestrian mall, was added and at the time of writing, major construction was underway at DCA. This ever-expanding ensemble is called the Disneyland Resort.

Nearby roads have been widened, landscaped and given the lofty name 'the Anaheim Resort.' In 2008, Anaheim GardenWalk opened on Katella Ave within walking distance of the park. This outdoor mall, though lacking personality, brings a welcome array of sit-down restaurants to the Disney-adjacent neighborhood.

Sights & Activities

You can see either Disneyland park or DCA in a day, but going on all the rides requires at least two days (three if visiting both parks), as waits for top attractions can be an hour or more. To minimize wait times, especially in summer, arrive midweek before the gates open and use the Fastpass system (p396), which assigns boarding times for selected attractions. A variety of multiday passes are available. Check the website for discounts and seasonal park hours. Parking is $15.

DISNEYLAND PARK

As you push through the turnstiles (note the giant floral Mickey) at the entrance of **Disneyland park** (714-781-4565/4400; www.disneyland.com; 1313 Harbor Blvd, Anaheim; 1-day pass Disneyland Park or DCA adult/child 3-9yr $80/74, both parks $105/99;), look for the sign above the nearby archway leading to Main Street, USA. It reads, 'Here you leave today and enter the world of yesterday, tomorrow and fantasy,' an apt but slightly skewed greeting that's indicative of the upbeat, slightly skewed 'reality' of the park itself. But it's a reality embraced by the millions of children who visit every year.

Spotless, wholesome Disneyland is still laid out according to Walt's original plans: **Main Street, USA**, a pretty thoroughfare lined with old-fashioned ice-cream parlors and shops, is the gateway into the park.

Main Street, USA

Fashioned after Walt's hometown of Marceline, MO, bustling Main Street, USA resembles a classic turn-of-the-20th-century all-American town. It's an idyllic, relentlessly cheerful representation complete with a barbershop quartet, penny arcades, ice-cream shops and a steam train.

If you're visiting on a special occasion, stop by City Hall to pick up oversized buttons celebrating birthdays, anniversaries and those 'Just Married.' There's also an Information Center here. Nearby there's a station for the **Disneyland Railroad**, a steam train that loops the park and stops at four different locations.

There's plenty of shopping along Main Street, but you can save that for the evening as the stores remain open after the park's attractions close. The same goes for the antique photos and history exhibit at **Disneyland Story: Presenting Great Moments with Mr. Lincoln**, on your right as you enter the park – younger children won't be interested, but adults will enjoy learning more about Walt's ambitions, plans and personal history.

Main Street ends in the **Central Plaza**, the hub of the park from which the eight different lands (such as Frontierland and Tomorrowland) can be reached. **Sleeping Beauty Castle** lords over the plaza, its towers and turrets fashioned after Neuschwanstein, a Bavarian castle owned by Mad King Ludwig. One difference? The roof here was placed on backward.

Tomorrowland

What did the future look like to Disney's 1950s imagineers? Visiting Tomorrowland suggests a space-age community where monorails and rockets are the primary forms of transportation. In 1998 this 'land' was revamped to honor three timeless futurists – Jules Vern, HG Wells, and Leonardo da Vinci – while major corporations like Microsoft and HP sponsor futuristic robot shows and interactive exhibits in the **Innoventions** pavilion.

The retro high-tech **monorail** glides to a stop in Tomorrowland, its rubber tires traveling a 13-minute, 2.5-mile round-trip route to Downtown Disney. Right away, kiddies will want to shoot laser beams on **Buzz Lightyear's Astro Blaster** adventure. Then jump aboard the **Finding Nemo Submarine Voyage** to search for Nemo from within a refurbished submarine and rumble through an underwater volcanic eruption.

The recently reimagineered **Star Tours** clamps you into a Starspeeder shuttle for a wild and bumpy 3D ride through the desert canyons of Tatooine on a space mission with several alternate storylines, so you can ride it again and again. **Space Mountain**, Tomorrowland's signature attraction and one of the USA's best roller coasters, hurtles you into complete darkness at frightening speed.

Another classic is **Captain EO**, a short 3D sci-fi film starring a young Michael Jackson. The film was shown at Disneyland in the late '80s and into the '90s; after the superstar's death, Disney started rescreening the film as a tribute. Catch this one if you can; adults in particular will get a kick out of

TOP FIVE THEME-PARK AREAS FOR YOUNG KIDS

- Fantasyland (p399)
- Mickey's Toontown (p399)
- Paradise Pier (p402)
- Critter Country (p400)
- Cars Land (p402)

Disneyland Resort

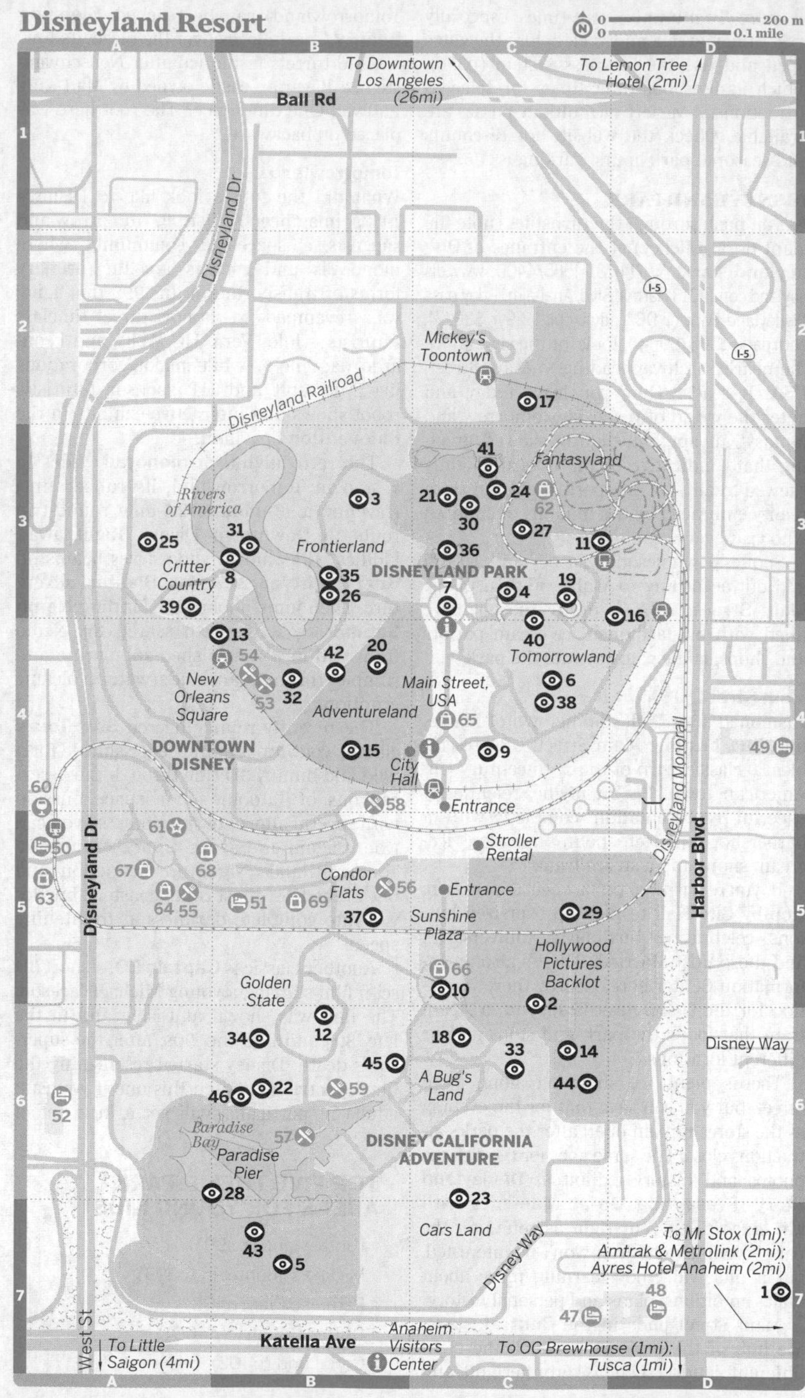

0 200 m
0 0.1 mile
To Downtown Los Angeles (26mi)
To Lemon Tree Hotel (2mi)
Ball Rd
Disneyland Dr
Mickey's Toontown
Disneyland Railroad
Fantasyland
Rivers of America
Frontierland
Critter Country
DISNEYLAND PARK
Tomorrowland
New Orleans Square
Adventureland
Main Street, USA
DOWNTOWN DISNEY
City Hall
Entrance
Stroller Rental
Disneyland Monorail
Harbor Blvd
Condor Flats
Entrance
Sunshine Plaza
Hollywood Pictures Backlot
Golden State
A Bug's Land
Disney Way
Paradise Bay
Paradise Pier
DISNEY CALIFORNIA ADVENTURE
Cars Land
Disney Way
To Mr Stox (1mi); Amtrak & Metrolink (2mi); Ayres Hotel Anaheim (2mi)
West St
To Little Saigon (4mi)
Katella Ave
Anaheim Visitors Center
To OC Brewhouse (1mi); Tusca (1mi)

Disneyland Resort

Sights

1 Anaheim GardenWalk D7
2 Animation Building C5
3 Big Thunder Mountain Railroad B3
4 Buzz Lightyear's Astro Blaster C3
5 California Screamin' B7
6 Captain EO C4
7 Central Plaza C3
8 Davy Crockett's Explorer Canoes B3
9 Disneyland Story: Presenting Great Moments with Mr Lincoln C4
10 ElecTRONica C5
11 Finding Nemo Submarine Voyage C3
12 Grizzly River Run B6
13 Haunted Mansion B4
14 Hyperion Theater C6
15 Indiana Jones Adventure B4
16 Innoventions D3
17 It's a Small World C2
18 It's Tough to Be a Bug C6
19 Jedi Training Academy C3
20 Jungle Cruise B4
21 King Arthur Carousel C3
22 Little Mermaid Ariel's - Undersea Adventure B6
23 Luigi's Roamin' Tires C6
24 Mad Tea Party C3
25 Many Adventures of Winnie the Pooh A3
26 Mark Twain Riverboat B3
Mater's Junkyard Jamboree ..... (see 23)
27 Matterhorn Bobsleds C3
28 Mickey's Fun Wheel B6
29 Monsters, Inc: Mike & Sulley to the Rescue! C5
30 Mr. Toad's Wild Ride C3
31 Pirate's Lair on Tom Sawyer Island B3
32 Pirates of the Caribbean B4
33 Princess Dot Puddle Park C6
Radiator Springs Racers ..... (see 23)
34 Redwood Creek Challenge Trail B6
35 Sailing Ship Columbia B3
36 Sleeping Beauty Castle C3
37 Soarin' over California B5
38 Space Mountain C4
39 Splash Mountain A3
40 Star Tours C4
41 Storybook Land Canal Boats C3
42 Tarzan's Treehouse B4
43 Toy Story Mania B7
44 Twilight Zone Tower of Terror C6
45 Walt Disney Imagineering Blue Sky Cellar B6
46 World of Color B6

Sleeping

47 Alpine Inn C7
48 Candy Cane Inn D7
49 Carousel Inn & Suites D4
50 Disneyland Hotel A5
51 Disney's Grand Californian Hotel & Spa B5
52 Disney's Paradise Pier Hotel A6

Eating

53 Blue Bayou B4
54 Café Orleans B4
55 Catal Restaurant A5
56 La Brea Bakery B5
Napa Rose ..... (see 51)
57 Pacific Wharf Food Court B6
58 Picnic Area B4
59 Wine Country Trattoria B6

Drinking

60 ESPN Zone A4
Golden Vine Winery ..... (see 59)
Nava Rose Lounge ..... (see 51)
Uva Bar ..... (see 55)

Entertainment

61 House of Blues A5

Shopping

62 Bibbidi Bobbidi Boutique C3
63 Compass Books A5
64 Disney Vault 28 ..... A5
65 Emporium C4
66 Greetings from California C5
67 Lego Imagination Center A5
68 LittleMissMatched A5
69 World of Disney B5

watching a still-innocent Michael – kids will like his adorable animated pals – under the direction of Francis Ford Coppola. Look for Anjelica Huston in a delightful cameo.

Fantasyland

Behind Sleeping Beauty Castle, Fantasyland is filled with the characters of classic children's stories – it's also your best bet for meeting princesses and other characters in costume. If you only see one attraction in Fantasyland, visit **"it's a small world"**, a boat ride past hundreds of creepy Audio-Animatronics children from different cultures, now joined by Disney characters, all singing the annoying theme song in an astounding variety of languages. Another classic, the **Matterhorn Bobsleds** is a steel-frame roller coaster that mimics a bobsled ride down a mountain. The **Storybook Land Canal Boats** is a narrated boat cruise past hand-crafted miniatures of famous Disney stories, including straw and brick houses from *Three Little Pigs,* the Alpine village from *Pinocchio* and the royal city of Agrabah from *Aladdin.*

Fans of old-school attractions will also get a kick out of the *Wind in the Willows*–inspired **Mr. Toad's Wild Ride**, a loopy jaunt in an open-air jalopy through London. Younger kids love whirling around the **Mad Tea Party** teacup ride and the **King Arthur Carrousel**, then cavorting with characters in nearby **Mickey's Toontown**, a topsy-turvy minimetropolis where kiddos can traipse through Mickey's and Minnie's houses.

Frontierland

In the wake of the successful *Pirates of the Caribbean* movies, Tom Sawyer Island – the only attraction in the park personally designed by Uncle Walt – was re-imagined as **Pirate's Lair on Tom Sawyer Island** and now honors Tom in name only. After a raft ride to the island, wander among roving pirates, cannibal cages, ghostly apparitions and buried treasure. Or just cruise around the island on the 18th-century replica **Sailing Ship Columbia** or the **Mark Twain Riverboat**, a Mississippi-style paddle wheeler. The rest of Frontierland gives a nod to the rip-roarin' Old West with a shooting gallery and the **Big Thunder Mountain Railroad**, a mining-themed roller coaster.

Adventureland

Adventureland loosely derives its style from Southeast Asia and Africa. The hands-down highlight is the jungle-themed **Indiana Jones Adventure**. Enormous Humvee-type vehicles lurch and jerk their way through the wild for spine-tingling encounters with creepy crawlies and scary skulls in re-creations of stunts from the famous film trilogy. (Look closely at Indy during the ride: is he real or Audio-Animatronics?) If you can, get a seat in the front of the car.

Nearby, little ones love climbing the stairways of **Tarzan's Treehouse**. Cool down with a **Jungle Cruise** where exotic Audio-Animatronics animals from the Amazon, Ganges, Nile and Irrawaddy Rivers jump out and challenge your boat's skipper. The cruise narration's somewhat forced humor can be grating, but kids don't mind.

New Orleans Square

Chicory coffee, jazz bands, wrought-iron balconies, mint juleps and beignets – must be New Orleans. (It's Walt Disney's version, of course, so the drinks are alcohol-free and the beignets are shaped like Mickey Mouse.) New Orleans was Walt and his wife Lilian's favorite city, and he paid tribute to it by building this charming square. **Pirates of the Caribbean**, the longest ride in Disneyland (17 minutes) and the inspiration for the movies, opened in 1967 and was the first addition to the original park. Today, you'll float through the subterranean haunts of tawdry pirates where artificial skeletons perch atop mounds of booty, cannons shoot across the water, wenches are up for auction and the mechanical Jack Sparrow character is creepily lifelike. At the **Haunted Mansion**, '999 happy haunts' – spirits and goblins, shades and ghosts – evanesce while you ride the Doom Buggy through web-covered graveyards of dancing skeletons. The Disneyland Railroad stops at New Orleans Square.

Critter Country

Tucked behind the Haunted Mansion, Critter Country's main attraction is **Splash Mountain**, a flume ride that transports you through the story of Brer Rabbit and Brer Bear, based on the controversial 1946 film *Song of the South.* Right at the big descent, a camera snaps your picture. Some visitors lift their shirts, earning the ride the nickname 'Flash Mountain,' though R-rated pics are destroyed. Just past Splash Mountain, hop in a mobile beehive on the **Many Adventures of Winnie the Pooh**. Nearby on the Rivers of America, you can paddle **Davy Crockett's Explorer Canoes** on summer weekends.

DISNEY CALIFORNIA ADVENTURE

'The other park,' Disney California Adventure (DCA; ☎714-781-4565/4400; www.disneyland.com; 1313 Harbor Blvd, Anaheim; 1-day pass Disneyland Park or DCA adult/child 3-9yr $80/74, both parks $105/99; 👪), which opened in 2001, is located just across the plaza from Disneyland's mon-

DON'T MISS

DISNEYLAND FIREWORKS, PARADES & SHOWS

Magical, the fireworks spectacular above Sleeping Beauty Castle, happens nightly around 9:30pm in summer; for the rest of the year, check the online schedule to find out when and where evening fireworks are happening. In winter, artificial snow falls on Main Street, USA after the fireworks. However, the extremely short **Celebrate! A Street Party** parade down Main Street, USA is forgettable – there's no need to plan around it.

At the **Princess Fantasy Faire** in Fantasyland, your little princesses and knights can join the Royal Court and meet some Disney princesses. Storytelling and coronation ceremonies happen throughout the day in summer. Younglings can learn to harness 'The Force' at Tomorrowland's **Jedi Training Academy**, which accepts Padawans several times daily in peak season.

Fantasmic!, an outdoor extravaganza on Disneyland's Rivers of America, may be the best show of all, with its full-size ships, lasers and pyrotechnics. Arrive early to snag the best seats, which are down front by the water, or splurge and reserve **balcony seating** (☎714-781-4400; adult/child $59/49) upstairs in New Orleans Square, which includes premium show seating, coffee and desserts . Book up to 30 days in advance.

Verify all show times once you arrive in the park; also see p403 for events at Disney's California Adventure.

ument to fantasy and make-believe. An ode to Californian geography, history and culture – or at least a sanitized G-rated version of it – DCA covers more acres than Disneyland and feels less crowded, even on summer weekend afternoons. If the original theme park leaves you feeling claustrophobic and jostled – or, gasp!, bored – you'll like this park better, with its more modern rides and attractions. DCA's critics, on the other hand, say that the newer park feels a lot less magical than Disneyland park.

Even though the park is only a decade old, the Disney honchos are pushing to expand and improve it. At the moment, DCA is undergoing a $1.1 billion building spree that's set to finish in 2012. The park remains open during construction. Some of the brand-new attractions have already rolled out, like the epic **World of Color** water show and the **Little Mermaid – Ariel's Undersea Adventure** ride, while others, like **Cars Land** (based on the Disney/Pixar classic), are hotly anticipated.

SUNSHINE PLAZA

The entrance to DCA was designed to look like an old-fashioned painted-collage postcard. As you pass through the turnstiles, note the gorgeous mosaics on either side of the entrance. One represents Northern California, the other Southern California. After passing under the Golden Gate Bridge, you'll arrive at Sunshine Plaza, where a 50ft-tall sun made of gold titanium 'shines' all the time (heliostats direct the rays of the real sun onto the Disney sun). According to the plans, Sunshine Plaza will soon be replaced by an homage to a 1920s Los Angeles streetscape, complete with a red trolley running down the street into what will be renamed 'Hollywoodland.'

Hollywood Pictures Backlot

With its soundstages, movable props and studio store, Hollywood Pictures Backlot is designed to look like the backlot of a Tinseltown studio. If you're early you'll have an unobstructed view of the forced-perspective **mural** at the end of the street, a sky-and-land backdrop that looks, at least in photographs, like the street keeps going.

The big attraction, however, is **The Twilight Zone Tower of Terror**, a 13-story drop down an elevator chute situated in a haunted hotel – which eerily resembles the historic Hollywood Roosevelt Hotel in Los Angeles. From the upper floors of the tower, you'll have views of the Santa Ana Mountains, if only for a few heart-pounding seconds. Less brave children can navigate a taxicab through 'Monstropolis' on the **Monsters, Inc: Mike & Sulley to the Rescue!** ride heading back toward the street's beginning.

In the air-conditioned **Animation Building** you can have a live conversation with Crush, the animated sea turtle from Finding Nemo. In addition, aspiring artists can learn how to draw like Disney in the Animation Academy, discover how cartoon artwork becomes 3D at the Character Close-Up or simply be amazed by the interactive Sorcerer's Workshop.

Changes are ahead, but not all have been announced to the public; this theme-park area will soon be reimagineered as 'Hollywoodland'.

A Bug's Land

Giant clover, rideable insects and oversized pieces of fake litter give kids a view of the world from a bug's perspective. Attractions here, which were designed in conjunction with Pixar Studios' film *A Bug's Life* in mind, include the 3D **It's Tough to Be a Bug!** – kids will love putting on a pair of 'bug eyes.' **Princess Dot Puddle Park**, where guests can splash around and enjoy the spray of sprinklers and drenching fountains, is a relief on a sweltering summer's day.

Golden State

On first impression, the concept behind this part of the park – celebrating California's cultural and scientific achievements – doesn't sound too thrilling. But Golden State is home to one of DCA's coolest attractions, **Soarin' over California**, a virtual hang-gliding ride, which uses Omnimax technology that lets you float over landmarks such as the Golden Gate Bridge, Yosemite Falls, Lake Tahoe and Malibu. (It's part of **Condor Flats**, a nod to the state's aerospace industry.) Enjoy the winds on your face as you soar and keep your nostrils open for smells of the sea, orange groves and pine forests. **Grizzly River Run** takes you 'rafting' down a faux Sierra Nevada river; you *will* get wet so try it on a warm day.

Nearby, kids can tackle the **Redwood Creek Challenge Trail**, with its 'Big Sir' redwoods, wooden towers and lookouts, and rock slide and climbing traverses. You can also get a behind-the-scenes look at what's in the works next for Disneyland's theme parks inside the **Walt Disney Imagineering Blue Sky Cellar**.

Paradise Pier

The brand-new attraction here is the **Little Mermaid – Ariel's Undersea Adventure** ride, in which guests board giant clam shells and descend below the waves (so to speak, with the help of elaborate special effects) into a colorful underwater world. The wicked Ursula, more than 7ft tall and 12ft wide, is a force to be reckoned with.

This section of the park was designed to look like a combination of all the beachside amusement piers in California. The state-of-the-art **California Screamin'** roller coaster resembles an old wooden coaster, but it's got a smooth-as-silk steel track: it feels like you're being shot out of a cannon. Awesome. Just as popular is **Toy Story Mania!**, a 4D ride with lots of old-fashioned arcade games. Want a bird's-eye view of the park? Head to **Mickey's Fun Wheel**, a 15-story Ferris wheel where gondolas pitch and yaw (unless you've requested one of the stationary ones).

Cars Land

Look for this brand-new area of DCA, designed around the popular Disney/Pixar movie *Cars* and expected to open sometime in 2012. Take a tractor ride through **Mater's Junkyard Jamboree**, steer your bumper car through **Luigi's Flying Tires** or ride along with the wacky **Radiator Springs Racers**. Route 66–themed gift shops and diners will take on that special glow of nostalgia underneath neon lights in the evening.

DOWNTOWN DISNEY

This quarter-mile-long pedestrian mall feels longer than it is, mostly because it's packed with stores, restaurants, entertainment venues and, in summer, hordes of people. The shops and restaurants are mostly chains and there are very few stores with individual character. On summer evenings, musicians perform outside.

Sleeping

Anaheim gets most of its hotel business from Disneyland tourism, but the city is also a year-round convention destination. Room rates spike accordingly, so the following rates fluctuate. Most properties offer packages combining lodging with tickets to Disneyland or other local attractions, and some run shuttles to the park. Prices listed are for standard double rooms during high season. Many hotels have family rooms that sleep up to six people.

For the full Disney experience, splurge and stay right at the **resort** (☎reservations 714-956-6425; www.disneyland.com). Be aware that the three Disney hotels charge an additional resort fee of $14 per day, which covers parking, internet access and other amenities. The Disneyland Hotel is nothing special but is currently under renovation (stay tuned).

TOP CHOICE **Disney's Grand Californian Hotel & Spa** LUXURY HOTEL **$$$**
(☎714-635-2300; http://disneyland.disney.go.com/grand-californian-hotel; 1600 S Disneyland Dr; d $384-445;) Along the prom-

DON'T MISS

DCA SHOWS & PARADES

Disney California Adventure (DCA) has one major advantage over the original Disneyland park – the live entertainment here is more varied and often more impressive. The premier show is **World of Color**, a dazzling nighttime display of lasers, lights and animation projected over Paradise Bay. It's so popular, you'll need a FASTPASS ticket (see p396). Otherwise, **reserved seating** (☎714-781-4400; per person $15) includes a picnic meal; make reservations up to 30 days in advance. Tip: if you're here in summer and have a Park Hopper ticket, see World of Color first, then head over to Disneyland Park for the fireworks and to catch the later show of Fantasmic!

During the day, don't miss the **Pixar Play Parade**, led by race car Lightning McQueen from *Cars* and featuring energetic, even acrobatic appearances by characters from other popular animated movies like *Monsters, Inc, The Incredibles, Ratatouille, Finding Nemo* and *Toy Story*. Be prepared to get squirted by aliens wielding water hoses.

Also popular is **Disney's Aladdin – A Musical Spectacular**, a 40-minute one-act extravaganza based on the movie of the same name. It's in the Hyperion Theater on the Hollywood Studios Backlot. Sit in the mezzanine for the best view of the Magic Carpet. Teens will prefer the nearby **ElecTRONica**, a street party–style show with live DJs, lasers, martial artists and dancing. Check the online calendar for dates and times.

enade of Downtown Disney, you'll see the entrance to this splurgeworthy craftsman-style hotel offering family-friendly scavenger hunts, swimming pools bordered by private cabanas and its own entrance to DCA. Non-guests can soak up some of the hotel's glamour by stopping for lunch or a glass of wine at **Napa Rose**, the onsite wine bar and eatery – **Disney Dining** (☎714-781-3463) handles reservations.

Disney's Paradise Pier Hotel HOTEL **$$**
(☎714-999-0990; www.disneyland.com; 1717 S Disneyland Dr; r $290-370; @☎≋🚸) From some rooms at Paradise Pier, you can see fireworks and DCA's fabulous World of Color show – a major perk for those traveling with small children with early bedtimes. Sunbursts, surfboards and a giant superslide are all on deck at the Paradise Pier Hotel, the cheapest, but maybe the most fun, of the Disney hotel trio. Kids will love the beachy decor, not to mention the rooftop pool and the tiny-tot video room filled with mini Adirondack chairs. Rooms are just as spotlessly kept as at the other hotels and are decorated with colorful fabrics and custom furniture. The hotel connects directly to DCA.

Candy Cane Inn MOTEL **$$**
(☎714-774-5284; www.candycaneinn.net; 1747 S Harbor Blvd; r $123-144; ❄☎≋🚸) Bright bursts of flowers, tidy grounds and a cobblestone drive welcome guests to this cute motel, which is also adjacent to the main gate at Disneyland. Rooms have all the mod cons, plus down comforters and plantation shutters. It's a top choice and booking well ahead of time is strongly advised.

Carousel Inn & Suites HOTEL **$$**
(☎714-758-0444; www.carouselinnandsuites.com; 1530 S Harbor Blvd; r $139-239; ❄☎≋🚸) Recently remodeled, this four-story hotel makes an effort to look stylish, with upgraded furniture and pots of flowers hanging from the wrought-iron railings of its exterior corridors. The rooftop pool has great views of Disneyland parks' fireworks.

Alpine Inn MOTEL **$$**
(☎714-535-2186; www.alpineinnanaheim.com; 715 W Katella Ave; r $86-189; ❄≋) Connoisseurs of kitsch will love this snow-covered motel with its A-frame exterior and glistening 'icicles' – framed by palm trees of course. On the border of DCA, the inn has views of the Ferris wheel and is close to a shuttle stop. Rooms are on the older side but clean, and there are five family-friendly suites.

Lemon Tree Hotel HOTEL **$$**
(☎866-311-5595; http://lemon-tree-hotel.com; 1600 E Lincoln Ave; r $89-119, ste $159; ❄☎≋) Disneygoers and road-trippers appreciate the great value and communal BBQ facilities at this Aussie owned inn. The simple but appealing accommodations include studios with kitchenettes and a two-room, three-bed suite with a kitchen that's ideal for families.

Ayres Hotel Anaheim HOTEL $$
(☎714-634-2106; www.ayreshotels.com/anaheim; 2550 E Katella Ave; r $129-149;) For something a bit more upscale but still affordable, try this French country-style hotel where amenities include complimentary evening receptions, large flat-screen TVs and pillow top beds.

Eating

For both parks, call **Disney Dining** (☎714-781-3463; ⏲7am-9pm) if you need to make dining reservations, have dietary restrictions or want to inquire about character dining (Disney characters work the dining room and greet the kids). For a birthday, call to ask about decorate-your-own-cake parties and birthday meals (you'll need to order 48 hours ahead).

There are dozens of dining options inside the theme parks; it's part of the fun to hit the walk-up food stands for treats like huge dill pickles, turkey legs and sugar-dusted churros. Park maps use the red apple icon to indicate restaurants where you can find healthy foods and vegetarian options.

DISNEYLAND PARK

Blue Bayou CAJUN $$$
(☎714-781-3463; New Orleans Sq; lunch $22-40; ⏲11:30am-park closure) Surrounded by the 'bayou' inside Pirates of the Caribbean, this place is famous for its Monte Cristo sandwiches at lunch and Creole and Cajun specialties at dinner. Make reservations. Whatever the time of day, you'll feel like you're dining outside under the stars, while the ride's boats floating peacefully by.

Café Orleans SOUTHERN $
(New Orleans Sq; mains $11-20; ⏲11am-park closure) Jambalaya and virgin mint juleps served cafeteria-style. Have lunch under the pavilion while listening to live music.

DISNEY CALIFORNIA ADVENTURE

In addition to the following option, there is a good food court at Pacific Wharf.

Wine Country Trattoria ITALIAN $$
(Golden Vine Winery, Golden State; mains $12-25; ⏲11am-6pm) DCA's best place for a relaxing sit-down lunch serves wonderfully appetizing Italian pasta, salads, gourmet sandwiches and wines by the glass.

DOWNTOWN DISNEY

La Brea Bakery BAKERY, CAFE $
(1556 Disneyland Dr; breakfast $5-20; ⏲8am-11pm) This branch of one of LA's top bakeries serves up great sandwiches and salads. Express items under $10.

Napa Rose CALIFORNIAN $$$
(☎714-781-3463; Disney's Grand Californian Hotel & Spa, 1600 S Disneyland Dr; mains $32-45; ⏲5:30-10pm) Disney's – and one of the OC's – finest restaurants occupies a soaring Arts and Crafts–style dining room overlooking DCA's Grizzly Peak. There's a special emphasis on pairing native ingredients with native wines. Enter from Downtown Disney or through DCA. Reservations strongly recommended.

Catal Restaurant CALIFORNIAN, ITALIAN $$$
(☎714-774-4442; www.patinagroup.com/catal; 1580 S Disneyland Dr; breakfast $9-14, dinner $23-38; ⏲8am-10pm;) The chef cooks up a fusion of Californian and Mediterranean cuisines (squid-ink pasta with lobster, grilled ahi with curry sauce) at this airy two-story restaurant decorated in a sunny Mediterranean-Provençal style with exposed beams and lemon-colored walls. Reserve ahead for balcony seating.

ANAHEIM

The 2008 opening of **Anaheim GardenWalk** (☎714-635-7400; www.anaheimgardenwalk.com; 321 W Katella Ave), an outdoor mall on Katella Ave one block east of Harbor Blvd, brought a welcome influx of sit-down eateries within walking distance of the park. Yes, it's heavy on chain restaurants and it's a long walk away, but dining options beyond Downtown Disney are so scarce we won't complain. Other nearby options are listed here.

Tusca CALIFORNIAN, ITALIAN $$
(www.tusca.com; Hyatt Regency Orange County, 11999 Harbor Blvd, Garden Grove; mains $11-24; ⏲6:30am-2pm & 5-10pm) You know Anaheim's dining scene isn't too exciting when we recommend dining inside a chain hotel. But Tusca's crispy handmade pizzas and seasonally inspired pastas prepared by a northern Italian chef – with herbs and veggies grown on the hotel's rooftop – justify the detour. Meanwhile, lobby-level **OC Brewhouse** pours California microbrews.

Mr Stox CALIFORNIAN $$
(☎714-634-2994; www.mrstox.com; 1105 E Katella Ave; mains lunch $12-20, dinner $20-42; ⏲11:30am-2:30pm Mon-Fri, 5:30pm-10pm Mon-Sat, to 9pm Sun) For country club ambience, settle into one of the oval booths and savor some of Anaheim's best California Cuisine. Mains include prime rib, duck and rack of

lamb, plus a fair number of seafood and vegetarian options. Wear nice shoes and make reservations.

Drinking & Entertainment

DISNEYLAND RESORT

After a long day of waiting in lines and snapping pictures with princesses, harried parents might be wondering where they can get a drink in this town. You can't buy any alcohol in Disneyland Park, but you can at DCA, Downtown Disney and Disney's trio of resort hotels.

Uva Bar WINE BAR
(www.patinagroup.com/catal; 1580 S Disneyland Dr; ⌚11am-10pm;) Named after the Italian word for grape, this bar resembling a Paris metro station is Downtown Disney's best outdoor spot to tipple wine, nibble Cal-Mediterranean tapas and people-watch. There are 40 wines available by the glass.

Golden Vine Winery WINE BAR
(Golden State; ⌚11am-park closure) This centrally located terrace is a great place for relaxing and regrouping in DCA. Nearby at Pacific Wharf, walk-up window **Rita's Baja Blenders** whips up frozen cocktails.

Napa Rose Lounge WINE BAR
(Disney's Grand Californian Hotel & Spa, 1600 S Disneyland Dr; ⌚5:30-10pm) Raise a glass to Napa as you nosh on pizzettas, artisan cheese plates and Scharffen Berger chocolate truffle cake.

ESPN Zone SPORTS BAR
(www.espnzone.com; 1545 Disneyland Dr; ⌚11am–11pm Sun-Thu, to 12am Fri-Sat) Show up early and score a personal leather recliner at this sports and drinking emporium with 175 TVs. Ball-park food and couch-potato classics make up an all-American menu.

House of Blues LIVE MUSIC
(☎714-778-2583; www.houseofblues.com; 1530 S Disneyland Dr; ⌚11am – 1:30am) House of Blues occasionally gets some heavy-hitting rock, pop, jazz and blues concerts. Call or check online for showtimes and tickets.

Shopping

DISNEYLAND PARK & DISNEY CALIFORNIA ADVENTURE

Every section of the Disney parks has its own shopping options tailored to its own particular themes – Davy Crockett, New Orleans, the Old West, Route 66 or a seaside amusement park. The biggest theme park stores – Disneyland Park's **Emporium** (Main Street, USA) and DCA's **Greetings from California** – have a mind-boggling variety of souvenirs, clothing and Disneyana, from T-shirts to mouse ears. Girls go wild at the **Bibbidi Bobbidi Boutique** (☎reservations 714-781-7895; Fantasyland; ⌚open by reservation only), where princess makeovers – including hairstyle, makeup and gown – don't come cheap.

Don't bother carrying your purchases around all day; store them at the Newsstand (Main Street, USA), Star Trader (Tomorrowland), Pioneer Mercantile (Frontierland) or Engine Ear Toys (DCA). If you're staying at Disneyland, have packages sent directly to your hotel – you can even pay for your purchases with your keycard.

DOWNTOWN DISNEY

Most shops in Downtown Disney open and close with the parks.

Disney Vault 28 CLOTHING, GIFTS
Hipster gear from distressed T-shirts with edgy Cinderella prints to black tank tops patterned with white skulls. Features Disney boutique lines like Kingdom Couture and Disney Vintage.

LittleMissMatched CLOTHING, GIFTS
Quirky-cool apparel for girls; the specialty is colorful mismatched socks sold in packs of three, so it'll never matter if you lose one.

Lego Imagination Center CLOTHING, GIFTS
Just what it says. Featuring hands-on exhibits and all the latest Lego building sets.

World of Disney SOUVENIRS
Pirates and princesses are hot at this minimetropolis of merchandising. Don't miss the special room dedicated to Disney's villains.

Compass Books BOOKS
Decorated in the style of an old-school NYC Explorers' Club, this shop stocks best sellers, manga paperbacks and travel tomes from an independent local bookseller.

Information

FASTPASS & Single Riders

With a bit of preplanning, you can significantly cut your wait time for popular attractions. One option is using the FASTPASS system (p396). If you're traveling solo, ask the greeter at the entrance to the ride if there's a single-rider line;

you can often head to the front of the queue. Availability may depend on the crowd size.

Internet Resources

Mouse Wait (www.mousewait.com) This free iPhone app offers up-to-the-minute updates on ride wait times and what's happening in the parks.

Touring Plans (www.touringplans.com) The 'unofficial guide to Disneyland' since 1985, this online resource offers no-nonsense advice, a crowd calendar and a 'lines app' for most mobile devices.

Medical Services

Western Medical Center Anaheim (☎714-533-6220; www.westernmedanaheim.com; 1025 S Anaheim Blvd; ⏰24hr) Emergency room available 24/7.

Stroller Rental

Rent a stroller for $15 per day ($25 for two strollers) outside the main entrance of Disneyland park. Rental strollers may be taken into both theme parks.

Tickets & Opening Hours

Both parks are open 365 days a year, but park hours depend on the marketing department's projected attendance numbers. You can access the **current calendar** (☎recorded info 714-781-4565, live assistance 714-781-7290; www.disneyland.com) by phone or online. During peak season (mid-June to early September) Disneyland Park's hours are usually 8am to midnight. The rest of the year it's open from 10am to between 8pm and 11pm. DCA closes at 9pm in summer, earlier in the low season.

One-day admission to either Disneyland or DCA costs $80 for adults and $74 for children aged three to nine. To visit both parks in one day costs $105/99 per adult/child. Multiday Park Hopper Tickets cost $173/161 for two days, $214/198 for three days, $234/216 for four days and $246/226 for five days. Ticket prices increase annually, so check the website for the latest information. You may also be able to buy discounted tickets online.

For parking, see p406.

Tourist Information

Anaheim Visitors Center (☎714-765-8888; www.anaheimoc.org; 800 W Katella Ave; ⏰8am-5pm Mon-Fri) Just south of DCA at the Anaheim Convention Center. Offers information on county-wide lodging, dining and transportation. No public internet access. Best to walk here to avoid a parking fee of $10 per day.

Central Plaza Information Board (☎714-781-4565; Main Street, USA, Disneyland park) One of several information centers in the theme parks.

Getting There & Away

Air

See p395 for information on air connections.

Southern California Gray Line/Coach America (☎714-978-8855; www.graylineanaheim.com) runs the Disneyland Resort Express between LAX and Disneyland-area hotels at least hourly (one way/round-trip to LAX $20/30). It also serves John Wayne Airport (SNA) in Santa Ana ($15/25).

Bus

Frequent departures are available with **Greyhound** (☎714-999-1256; 100 W Winston Rd) to and from downtown LA ($8 to $15, about one hour) and to San Diego ($14 to $27, 2½ hours).

Car

Disneyland Resort is just off I-5 on Harbor Blvd, about 30 miles south of downtown LA. The park is roughly bordered by Ball Rd, Disneyland Dr, Harbor Blvd and Katella Ave. Giant, easy-to-read overhead signs indicate which ramps you need to take for the theme parks, hotels or Anaheim's streets.

All-day parking costs $15. Enter the 'Mickey & Friends' parking structure from southbound Disneyland Dr at Ball Rd. (It's the largest parking structure in the world, with a capacity of 10,300 vehicles.) Take the tram to reach the parks; follow the signs. The lots stay open one hour after the parks close.

The parking lots for Downtown Disney are reserved for shoppers and have a different rate structure: the first three hours are free, with an additional two more free hours if you have a validation from a table-service restaurant or the movie theater. After that it's $6 per hour, up to $30 a day. Downtown Disney also has valet parking for an additional $6, plus tip.

Train

If you're arriving by train, you'll stop at the **depot** (2150 E Katella Ave) next to Angel Stadium, a quick shuttle or taxi ride east of Disneyland. **Amtrak** (☎714-385-1448; www.amtrak.com) and **Metrolink** (☎800-371-5465; www.metrolinktrains.com) commuter trains connect Anaheim to LA's Union Station ($14, 50 minutes) and San Diego ($27, two hours).

Getting Around

Bus

The bus company **Anaheim Resort Transit** (ART; ☎714-563-5287, 888-364-2787; www.rideart.org) provides frequent service between Disneyland and hotels in the immediate area, saving headaches parking and walking. An all-day pass costs $4 per adult and $1 per child aged three to nine. You must buy the pass before boarding; pick one up at one of a dozen kiosks (exact cash or credit card) or online. If you hop on without a pass, you can pay $3 onboard for a one-way trip. Service starts one hour before Disneyland opens and ends half an hour after it closes.

Many hotels and motels have free shuttles to Disneyland and other area attractions; ask before booking.

Monorail

Take the monorail from Tomorrowland to the Disneyland Hotel, across from Downtown Disney, and save about 20 minutes of walking time. It's free if you've bought a park admission ticket.

AROUND DISNEYLAND

If the relentless cheeriness of Disneyland starts to grate on your nerves, there are several entertaining – even kitschy – alternatives within 5 miles of the parks. Anaheim's streets are laid out in an easy-to-navigate grid, with most neighborhoods flowing seamlessly from one to another.

Buena Park

Knott's Berry Farm AMUSEMENT PARK
(☎714-220-5200; www.knotts.com; 8039 Beach Blvd; adult/child 3-11yr & senior $57/25; ⏱from 10am, closing hours vary; 👪) They drop off kids by the busload at this Old West–themed park. Just 4 miles northwest of Anaheim off the I-5, Knott's is smaller and less frenetic than the Disneyland parks, but it can be fun, especially for roller coaster fanatics, young teens and kids who love the *Peanuts* gang. Opening hours vary seasonally so call ahead or check online. Also check the website for the latest discounts; some can be substantial. Parking costs $14.

The park opened in 1940 when Mr Knott's boysenberries (a blackberry-raspberry hybrid) and Mrs Knott's fried-chicken dinners attracted crowds of local farmhands. Mr Knott built an imitation ghost town to keep them entertained. Eventually they hired local carnival rides and charged admission. Mrs Knott kept frying chicken but the rides and Old West buildings became the main attraction.

Today the park keeps the Old West theme alive with shows and demonstrations at Ghost Town, but it's the thrill rides that draw the crowds. Nearby, the suspended, inverted **Silver Bullet** screams through a corkscrew, a double spiral and an outside loop. From the ground, look up to see the dirty socks and bare feet of suspended riders who've removed their shoes. The **Xcelerator** is a '50s-themed roller coaster that blasts you from 0mph to 82mph in only 2.3 seconds. There's a hair-raising twist at the top. One of the tallest wooden roller coasters in the world – and the largest attraction in the park's history – is the 118ft-tall **GhostRider**, in which riders climb into 'mining cars' for a thrilling journey. **Camp Snoopy** is a kiddie wonderland populated by the Peanuts characters and family-friendly rides.

In October Knott's hosts what is regarded as SoCal's best and scariest Halloween party. On select dates from late September to Halloween, the park closes at 5:30pm and reopens at 7pm as Knott's Scary Farm. Terrifying mazes and creepy shows – not to mention 1000 roaming monsters – keep things scary.

Next to Knott's is the affiliated water park **Knott's Soak City USA** (☎714-220-5200; www.knotts.com; adult/child 3-11yr & senior $27/22; ⏱mid-May–Sep; 👪).

Medieval Times Dinner & Tournament SPECTATOR SPORT
(☎714-521-4740; www.medievaltimes.com; 7662 Beach Blvd; adult/child $58/36; ⏱daily, show times vary; 👪) Hear ye, hear ye! Gather ye clans and proceed forthwith to Medieval Times for an evening of feasting and performance in 12th-century style. Guests root for various knights as they joust, fence and show off their horsemanship (on real live Andalusian horses). Dinner is OK; the show's the thing.

Santa Ana

Discovery Science Center MUSEUM
(☎714-542-2823; www.discoverycube.org; 2500 N Main St; adult/child & senior $18/13; ⏱10am-5pm; 👪) This fantastic science center has more than 100 interactive displays in exhibit areas that include Dynamic Earth, The Body and Dino Quest. Step into the eye of a hurricane – you hair will get mussed – or grab a seat in the Shake Shack for a 6.9 quake. Heading south on the I-5 from Disneyland (about 5 miles), look for the 10-story cube seemingly balanced on one of its points. Parking costs $4.

Bowers Museum of Cultural Art MUSEUM
(☎714-567-3600; www.bowers.org; 2002 N Main St; permanent collection adult/child $12/9; ⏱10am-4pm Tue-Sun) The Bowers may be small, but the place draws major crowds with its tantalizing, high-quality special exhibits; at the time of writing, offerings included 'The Art and Craft of the American Whaler' and a

collection of Chinese objects borrowed from the Shanghai Museum. This Mission-style museum also has a rich permanent collection of pre-Columbian, African, Oceanic and Native American art. Special exhibits may require separate tickets, which have cost as much as $27 per adult; the museum is free on the first Sunday of each month.

Orange

For a pleasant dose of small-town life complete with a wide selection of mom-and-pop restaurants and shops, drive 1.5 miles south from Disneyland on S Harbor Blvd then turn left on Chapman Ave, following it east about 3.5 miles to Old Towne Orange in the City of Orange. Old Towne was originally laid out by Alfred Chapman and Andrew Glassell who, in 1869, received the 1-sq-mile piece of real estate in lieu of legal fees. Built around a pretty plaza at the intersection of Chapman Ave and Glassell St, it's got the most concentrated collection of antiques shops in Orange County.

You can enjoy breakfast inside a former gas station at the **Filling Station** (www.fillingstationcafe.com; 201 N Glassell St; mains $4-12; ⏲9am-5pm), now serving gourmet scrambles and pancake sandwiches instead of unleaded. For lunch or dinner, nab a patio table at **Felix Continental Cafe** (www.felixcontinentalcafe.com; 36 Plaza Sq; mains lunch $5-12, dinner $7-14; ⏲11am-10pm Mon-Fri, from 8am Sat & Sun). This longtime favorite serves spiced-just-right Caribbean, Cuban and Spanish dishes, most accompanied by a hefty serving of black beans or rice. Disneyland's imagineered Main Street, USA will lose a little luster after you slurp a chocolate malt at the counter inside **Watson Drug & Soda Fountain** (www.watsonsdrugs.com; 116 E Chapman Ave; ⏲6:30am-9pm Mon-Sat, 8am-8pm Sun), a 100-year-old diner and soda shop.

Little Saigon

If you head a few miles southwest of Disneyland, you'll drive into the city of Westminster near the junction of I-405 and Hwy 22. Home to a large Vietnamese population, the community has carved out its own vibrant commercial district around the intersection of Bolsa and Brookhurst Aves. At its heart is the **Asian Garden Mall** (www.asiangardenmall.com; 9200 Bolsa Ave), a behemoth of a structure packed with 400 ethnic boutiques, including herbalists and jade jewelers. On weekend evenings in summer, there's a night market from 7pm to midnight with vendors, food and live entertainment.

If you're here at lunchtime, browse the photo menus at the casual eateries on the lower level toward the mall's north entrance. The mini food court offers a variety of noodle and vegetable dishes and the *pho ga* (chicken noodle soup) is superb.

Another popular restaurant is **Brodard** (www.brodard.net; 9892 Westminster Ave, Garden Grove; mains under $13; ⏲8am-9pm, closed Tue), where half the fun is finding the place. The restaurant is known for its *nem nuong cuon,* rice paper wrapped tightly around a Spam-like pork paste and served with a light special sauce. It's oddly addictive. From Disneyland, follow Harbor Blvd south for 3.5 miles. Turn right at W 17th St, which becomes Westminister Ave, and cross Brookhurst Ave. At the mall on your left, drive behind the 99 cent store and continue to the restaurant's red awning.

ORANGE COUNTY BEACHES

An inviting string of beaches and coastal communities lines Orange County's 42-mile coast, each of them boasting a distinctly different set of charms. The six major towns, starting with Seal Beach in the north, are linked by the **Pacific Coast Hwy** (PCH; Hwy 1) and grow increasingly scenic – and some may say ritzy – as you continue south.

From Seal Beach, PCH passes scruffy Sunset Beach, surfing-crazed Huntington Beach, ritzy Newport Beach and Corona del Mar before rolling into the cliff-and-cove-dotted artists' enclave of Laguna Beach. Just south, Dana Point draws the yacht crowd, while end-of-the-county San Clemente returns to the small-town vibe – and one awesome, border-hugging surf spot.

In summer, accommodations book up far in advance, prices rise and some properties impose minimum two- or three-night stays.

Seal Beach

In the pageant for charming small towns, Seal Beach enjoys an unfair advantage over the competition: 1.5 miles of pristine beach glittering like an already won crown. And that's without mentioning its three-block Main St – a lineup of locally owned restaurants, mom-and-pop stores and indie coffeehouses that are refreshingly low on attitude and high on welcoming charm.

Main St spills into **Seal Beach Pier**, which extends 1885ft out over the ocean. The beach faces south here and, except for the offshore oil rigs (which locals seem to easily tune out), it's very pleasant. The mild waves make it a great place to learn how to surf before heading to more challenging waves further south. Good thermal winds make the coast here a prime spot for kite-surfing. For surfing lessons, look for the marked van owned by **M&M Surfing School** (☎714-846-7873; www.mmsurfingschool.com; 3hr group lesson $65) usually parked in the lot north of the pier.

The one hotel that's within walking distance of the beach is **Pacific Inn** (☎562-493-7501, 866-466-0300; www.pacificinn-sb.com; 600 Marina Dr; r from $159;). The recently renovated rooms have down comforters and complimentary wi-fi; there's also a sunny central pool.

As for food, most of the restaurants on Main St are worthy of recommendation. In the morning, we suggest **Nick's Deli** (223 Main St; mains $5-8; 7am-7pm Mon-Fri, to 4pm Sat & Sun) for the county's best breakfast burritos (they sell about one per minute). Everybody's favorite for fresh fish is **Walt's Wharf** (www.waltswharf.com; 201 Main St; mains lunch $8-15, dinner $13-27; 11am-3:30pm & 4-9pm); some people even drive here from LA. Walt's gets packed on weekends and you can't make reservations for dinner, but it's worth the long wait for the oak-fire-grilled seafood and steaks, served with delicious sauces.

Huntington Beach

In June 2011, the mayor of Huntington Beach (HB) presented the 'key to the city' to surfing legend Kelly Slater – an event that tells you everything you need to know about this beach community. HB has been a surf mecca for nearly a century, starting in 1914 when Hawaiian-Irish surfing star George Freeth (brought to California by pioneer developer Henry Huntington) gave demonstrations of the exotic sport off the coast. In recent years, HB's surfing image has been heavily marketed, with city fathers even getting a bit aggro (surfer slang for 'territorial') in their efforts to ensure exclusive rights to the now-trademarked nickname 'Surf City, USA.' The moniker originally came from Jan and Dean's 1963 pop hit by the same name. But the sport is big business, with buyers for major retailers coming here to see what surfers are wearing and then marketing the look.

Commercial development along Main St has left downtown with a vaguely prefab feel, but the bland facades are frequently enlivened by sidewalk-surfing skateboarders and inebriated barflies whooping it up from the street's numerous bars. Just look around at the beautiful blonde people playing volleyball on the sand or skating along the beach paths – HB is still the quintessential place to celebrate the coastal SoCal lifestyle.

In late July, the city hosts the **US Open of Surfing** (www.usopenofsurfing.com), a six-star competition drawing more than 600 surfers, 400,000 spectators and a minivillage of concerts, motocross demos and skater jams.

Sights & Activities

Surfing in Huntington Beach is competitive; control your longboard or draw the ire of territorial locals. Surf north of the pier and consider **M&M Surfing School** (☎714-846-7873; www.mmsurfingschool.com; 3hr group lesson $65) for lessons (and a bodyguard). For kitesurfing instruction, try **Kitesurfari** (☎714-964-5483; www.kitesurfari.com; 18822 Beach Blvd; 3hr lesson from $180). If you just want to watch surfers in action, walk down to **Huntington City Beach** at the foot of the pier. Just south is **Huntington State Beach**, the place to build a beach bonfire. Buy wood at nearby concessionaires then stake out a concrete fire ring. Romp with your dog in the surf at **Dog Beach**, northwest of Goldenwest St. Huntington Beach prides itself on being a dog-friendly community: the visitors center has full listings of the city's dog parks and cafes and shops that cater to canines.

International Surfing Museum MUSEUM
(☎714-960-3483; www.surfingmuseum.org; 411 Olive Ave; suggested donation $2; noon-5pm Mon & Wed-Fri, to 9pm Tue, 11am-6pm Sat & Sun) A small but interesting collection of surf-related memorabilia can be found at this museum just off Main St. Exhibits chronicle the sport's history with photos, surfboards and surf music. The museum also hosts film screenings and special events; check the website for details.

Bolsa Chica State Ecological Reserve NATURE RESERVE
(☎714-846-1114; sunrise-sunset) Just north of HB, PCH looks out onto Bolsa Chica State Ecological Reserve. At first glance it may

look rather desolate (especially with the few small oil wells scattered about), but this restored salt marsh is an environmental success story teeming with bird life – according to reports, 321 of Orange County's 420 bird species have been spotted here in the past decade. These 1700 acres have been saved from numerous development projects over the years by a band of determined locals. A 1.5-mile loop trail starts from the parking lot on PCH. There's a small **interpretative center** (3842 Warner Ave; 9am-4pm Tue-Fri, 10am-3pm Sat & Sun) near the intersection of PCH and Warner.

Sleeping

There aren't many budget option in HB, especially in summer when nothing-special motels hike their prices to ridiculous levels. If you want budget accommodation, head inland toward I-405.

TOP CHOICE Shorebreak Hotel LUXURY HOTEL $$$
(714-861-4470; www.shorebreakhotel.com; 500 Pacific Coast Hwy; r from $224;) Stunning and sleek, the brand-new Shorebreak – the latest from Joie de Vivre, the popular California boutique hotel chain – is the hands-down winner for the coolest place to stay near the water. There's an airy patio with several fire pits, a state-of-the-art fitness center, an evening wine reception for guests, and 157 rooms with flat-screen TVs and decks or balconies (some of which face the sea). There's even a 'Beach Butler' to book your surfing lessons for you.

Hotel Huntington Beach HOTEL $
(714-891-0123, 877-891-0123; www.hotelhb.com; 7667 Center Ave; r from $85;) This eight-story hotel, which looks like an office building, is decidedly sans personality and a bit worn, but the rooms are clean and perfect for get-up-and-go travelers (the hotel's adjacent to I-405).

Comfort Suites HOTEL $$
(714-841-1812; www.comfortsuiteshuntington beach.com; 16301 Beach Blvd (Hwy 39); r $100-120;) Hot breakfast items such as scrambled eggs and bacon, plus free parking and complimentary wi-fi, make this chain worth a mention. The rates are pretty reasonable for comfortable, if not particularly distinctive, rooms. Closer to I-405 than the beach: you'll have to drive away from the water for about 10 minutes to reach the hotel.

Sun 'n Sands MOTEL $$
(714-536-2543, www.sunnsands.com; 1102 Pacific Coast Hwy; r $149-189, mini-ste $229-269;) This mom-and-pop motel would cost well under $100 a night anywhere east of town, but its location across from the beach lets it get away with absurdly high rates. The place offers views of the Huntington Beach Pier, but it probably goes without saying that it can get pretty loud here at night.

Eating & Drinking

It's easy to find a bar in HB. (Walk up Main Street in the early evening and it might seem like there's nothing *but* bars in this town.)

Sugar Shack BREAKFAST $
(www.hbsugarshack.com; 2131/2 Main St; mains $5-10; 6am-4pm Mon, Tue & Thu, to 8pm Wed, to 5pm Fri-Sun) The sidewalk patio is the place to sit at this Main St stalwart for some of HB's best people-watching. And if you're here really early, you might catch surfer dudes donning their wetsuits. The $5.55 breakfast special comes with two pancakes, an egg and bacon or a sausage. Sign up for a table at the clipboard on the outside wall.

Chronic Tacos MEXICAN $
(www.eatchronictacos.com; 328 11th St; mains under $8; 8am-9pm) For surfer haute cuisine, mosey into this sticker-covered shack and request a made-to-order Fatty Taco, then settle in for one of the best Mexican meals around. With the Dead playing on the stereo, a couple of surf bums shooting pool and chatty, laid-back staff, you might just never leave. You'll see other locations scattered across SoCal.

Park Bench Cafe BREAKFAST, CAFE $
(www.parkbenchcafe.com; 17732 Goldenwest St; mains breakfast $6-10, lunch $9-11; 7:30am-2pm Tue-Fri, to 3pm Sat & Sun;) A short drive east on Goldenwest St from PCH lands you at this shady outdoor cafe in Huntington Central Park. If you're traveling with Fido, he can order the Hound Dog Heaven patty off the dog menu.

RA Sushi SUSHI $$
(www.rasushi.com; 155 5th St; mains $10-18; 11am-11pm Tue-Fri) The sushi is so-so at this stylish clublike eatery across the street from the beach; the real draw is the budget-friendly happy hour (3pm to 7pm Monday through Saturday) with a long menu of discounted appetizers and Asian-style tapas from pork gyoza and crunchy calamari rolls

(each $5) to hot sake ($2) and vodka martinis ($5).

Deville PUB, BURGERS $
(424 Olive Ave; mains $4-9; ⌚11am-11pm Mon-Fri, from 10am Sat & Sun) This dark, down-to-earth pub – across the street from the International Surfing Museum – is a local favorite, thanks to delicious $5 burgers and $1 beers. It's on the small side, so it stays a little quieter than some of the loud bars on Main St.

Duke's AMERICAN $$
(www.dukeshuntington.com; 317 Pacific Coast Hwy; lunch $9-15, dinner $20-30; ⌚noon-10pm Tue-Sat, 5-10pm Mon; 👪) It's definitely touristy, but this Hawaiian-themed restaurant – named after surfing legend Duke Kahanamoku – is also fun and offers up some of the best views around. Start things off with the poke-roll appetizer then pick your fish and seasoning from a long list of choices. If you're just in the mood for drinks, try the Barefoot Bar downstairs.

Beachfront 301 AMERICAN $$
(www.beachfront301.com; 301 Main St; mains $8-18; ⌚10am-late; 👪) This laid-back corner bar and grill is renowned for its lively happy hour (all day Monday and 3pm to 9pm Tuesday through Friday) with bargain food and drink specials. Offerings include $3 Baja-style chicken tacos and onion rings; $5 will buy you a veggie pizza, Santa Fe chicken wrap or double cheeseburger.

Information

Huntington Beach Convention and Visitors Bureau (☎714-969-3492; www.surfcityusa.com; Suite 208, 301 Main St; ⌚9am-5pm Mon-Fri) provides tourist maps and other information.

Newport Beach & Around

Pop culture representations of Newport Beach – rich kids driving sports cars on *The OC*, an earnest George Michael Bluth working at the frozen banana stand on *Arrested Development* – are surprisingly realistic. Indeed, Orange County's ritziest beach community is filled with beautiful, moneyed people. The locals, almost uniformly fresh-faced and sun-kissed, are the last word in resort wear – you'll be hard-pressed to find even one brooding, pimply-faced smoker in a too-large sweater. And yes, there are frozen bananas (though Newport's classic summertime treat is actually the Balboa Bar, a square of vanilla ice cream dipped into chocolate and served on a stick).

So why visit Newport? Because the local environment is particularly lovely. The city surrounds a pretty natural harbor that's one of the largest for pleasure craft in the US. Balboa Peninsula, which faces the harbor on one side and the open ocean on the other, offers fantastically wide beaches. At almost any hour of the day, you'll see a steady stream of cyclists, joggers and skaters on paved beach paths that extend as far as the eye can see. Just southeast of Newport is the chichi beach community of Corona del Mar and the historic Crystal Cove State Park.

For a more down-to-earth vibe, follow Hwy 55 south onto Balboa Peninsula. Six miles long and a quarter-mile wide, the peninsula is home to white-sand beaches, a number of hotels, seafood restaurants and stylish homes – and lots of surfers catching oceanside waves.

Hotels, restaurants and bars cluster around the peninsula's two piers: **Newport Pier**, near its western end, and **Balboa Pier**, at the eastern end. The oceanfront strip teems with beachgoers and the people-ogling is great.

Sights & Activities

Lovell House HISTORIC BUILDING
(1242 W Ocean Front) One of Newport Beach's most architecturally significant homes, this 1926 house sits beside the beach bike path. Designed by seminal modernist architect Rudolph Schindler, it was built using site-cast concrete frames and wood.

Balboa Fun Zone AMUSEMENT PARK
(www.thebalboafunzone.com; 603 E Bay Ave; ⌚11am-9pm Sun-Thu, to 10pm Fri & Sat) Opposite the Balboa Pier on the harbor side of the peninsula, visitors can hop aboard the iconic Ferris wheel (you'll catch great views of the sea from the top) or take a spin on the carousel, which has been around since 1936.

Newport Harbor Nautical Museum MUSEUM
(☎949-675-8915; www.nhnm.org; Balboa Fun Zone, 600 E Bay Ave; adult/child $4/2; ⌚11am-6pm Sun-Thu, to 7pm Sat) This lively nautical museum features model ships, maritime memorabilia and a kid-friendly wing with a 'Touch Tank' where visitors can interact with sea creatures (sea stars, bat stars, sea urchins) found in the region's tidepools. The nearby **Balboa Pavilion**, a landmark dating from 1905, is beautifully illuminated at night.

Newport Beach

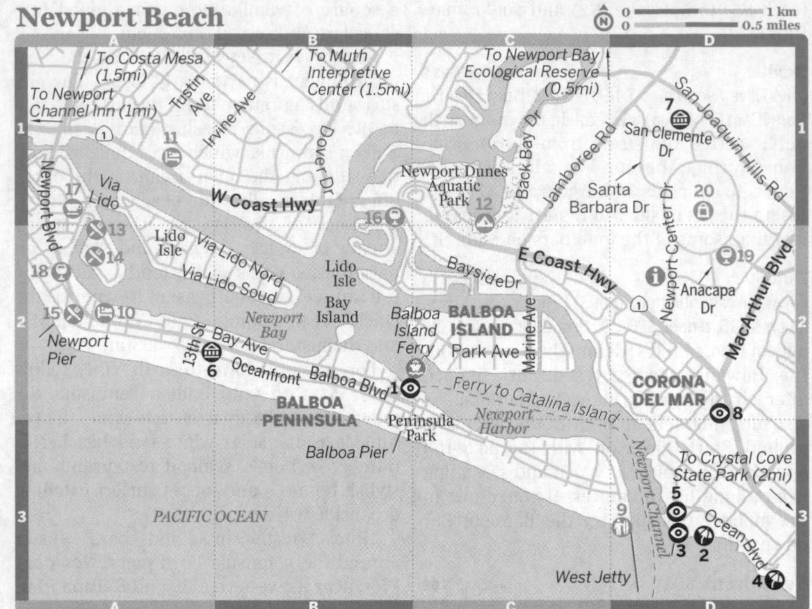

Wedge SURFING

At the very tip of the peninsula, by the West Jetty, the Wedge is a bodysurfing and knee-boarding spot famous for its perfectly hollow waves that can get up to 30ft high. Look for the small crowd watching the high-octane action from the shore. But beware venturing in yourself – the waves are shore-breakers and regularly smash bodysurfers against the sand like rag dolls.

Balboa Island ISLAND

In the middle of the harbor sits the island that time forgot. Its streets are still largely lined with tightly clustered cottages built in the 1920s and '30s when this was a summer getaway from LA. The 1.5-mile promenade that circles the island makes a terrific car-free stroll or jog. Near the Ferris wheel on the harbor side, the **Balboa Island Ferry** (www.balboaislandferry.com; 410 S Bayfront; adult/child/car & driver $1/0.50/2; ⌚6:30am-midnight) shuttles passengers across the bay. The ferry lands at Agate Ave, about 11 blocks west of Marine Ave, which is lined with swimwear boutiques, Italian trattorias and cocktail bars.

Orange County Museum of Art MUSEUM

(☎949-759-1122; www.ocma.net; 850 San Clemente Dr; adult/child under 12yr $12/free; ⌚11am-5pm Wed & Fri-Sun, to 8pm Thu) Less than a mile from Fashion Island, this engaging museum highlights California art and cutting-edge contemporary artists with exhibits rotating through its two large gallery areas every four to six months. There's also a sculpture garden, an eclectic gift shop and a theater screening classic, foreign and art-related films.

Corona del Mar NEIGHBORHOOD

This ritzy bedroom community, perched on the privileged eastern bluffs of the Newport Channel, has some of the best coastal views in SoCal. It also includes a high-end stretch of PCH, with trendy shops and restaurants, as well as **Corona del Mar State Beach** (☎949-644-3151; www.parks.ca.gov; ⌚5am-10pm), which lies at the foot of rocky cliffs. Parking costs $15, even more on peak summer holidays. If you're early (or lucky), try to nab a free parking spot above the beach on Ocean Blvd.

Lookout Point sits above the beach along Ocean Blvd near Heliotrope Ave. Locals throw sunset cocktail parties here, but be discreet with your chardonnay: technically, open containers are illegal. Stairs lead to **Pirate's Cove**, which has a great, waveless beach and is ideal for families. Scenes from *Gilligan's Island* were shot here. A bit further east on Ocean Blvd is **Inspiration Point**, another nice spot to enjoy the view.

Newport Beach

Sights

1 Balboa Fun Zone....B2
Balboa Pavilion....(see 1)
2 Corona del Mar State Beach....D3
3 Inspiration Point....D3
4 Little Corona del Mar Beach....D3
5 Lookout Point....D3
6 Lovell House....A2
Newport Harbor Nautical Museum....(see 1)
7 Orange County Museum of Art....D1
Pirate's Cove....(see 5)
8 Sherman Library & Gardens....D2

Activities, Courses & Tours

9 Wedge....D3

Sleeping

10 Bay Shores Peninsula Hotel....A2
11 Holiday Inn Express....A1
12 Newport Dunes Waterfront Resort & Marina....C1

Eating

13 Bluewater Grill....A2
14 Sabatino's Sausage Company....A2
15 Sol Grill....A2

Drinking

16 3-Thirty-3 Waterfront....B1
17 Alta Coffee Warehouse....A1
18 Cassidy's Bar & Grill....A2
19 Muldoon's....D2

Shopping

20 Fashion Island....D1

Children love the tide pool just east at **Little Corona del Mar Beach**.

Corona del Mar's prize attraction is the compact **Sherman Library & Gardens** (949-673-2261; www.slgardens.org; 2647 E Coast Hwy; adult/child $3/1, Mon admission free; gardens 10:30am-4pm daily, library 9am-4:30pm Tue-Thu). The gardens are manicured, lush and bursting with color. The small, noncirculating research library holds a wealth of California historical documents, as well as paintings by early California landscape artists. If you're here around lunchtime, dine in full view of the gardens at the French-inspired **Café Jardin** (949-673-0033; 11:30am-2pm Mon-Fri; set menu $20-25).

Crystal Cove State Park PARK
(949-494-3539; www.crystalcovestatepark.com; Pacific Coast Hwy; 6am-sunset) Once you get past the parking lots ($15), it's easy to forget you're in a crowded metropolitan area at this state park, where visitors are treated to 2000 acres of undeveloped woodlands and 3.5 miles of coastline. Everyone thought the hilltops were part of the state park too, until the Irvine Company, the actual landowner, bulldozed them to make room for McMansions that are the dream of many OC residents. For a more discreet, short-term stay, reserve one of the park's inland campsites (it's a 3-mile hike each way) with **Reserve America** (800-444-7275; www.reserveamerica.com; tent sites $20).

Newport Bay Ecological Reserve NATURE RESERVE
Inland from the harbor, where runoff from the San Bernardino Mountains meets the sea, the brackish water of the Newport Bay Ecological Reserve supports more than 200 species of birds. This is one of the few estuaries in Southern California that has been preserved, and it's an important stopover on the Pacific Flyway. The **Muth Interpretive Center** (949-923-2290; www.ocparks.com/unbic; 2301 University Dr; 10am-4pm Tue-Sun;), near Irvine Ave and just out of view of the parking lot, is made from sustainable materials. Inside, you'll find displays and information about the 752-acre reserve, as well as a kid-friendly activity room with a number of small, snake-and-spider-filled terraria. For guided tours with naturalists and weekend kayak tours of the Back Bay (from $20 per person) contact the **Newport Bay Naturalists & Friends** (949-640-6746; www.newportbay.org).

Sleeping

Rates drop by as much as 40% (or more) in winter. Those listed here are for high season.

Newport Dunes Waterfront Resort & Marina CAMPGROUND $
(949-729-3863; www.newportdunes.com; 1131 Back Bay Dr; tent & RV sites with hookups from $64, cottages from $146; @) Welcome to RV heaven. Besides hookups, Newport Dunes has a pool, a spa, game rooms and a small beach on one of Newport's brackish lagoons. For those without a Winnebago, the tiny cottages are a good deal, especially in the low season. There are a few campsites. In

the lobby, look for the concrete handprints of several cast members from the now-canceled show *The OC;* the memorial was booted from its former spot of glory at the visitors bureau.

Newport Channel Inn MOTEL $$
(800-255-8614; www.newportchannelinn.com; 6030 W Coast Hwy; r $109-200;) Cyclists love this two-story motel's proximity to the beach bike path, which is just across the street. Other perks include large rooms, a big common sundeck and genuinely friendly owners. The large A-framed room 219 sleeps up to seven. Top budget choice that works well for traveling groups.

Bay Shores Peninsula Hotel HOTEL $$
(949-675-3463, 800-222-6675; www.thebestinn.com; 1800 W Balboa Blvd; d $179-300;) *Endless Summer* surf murals. Freshly baked cookies. Shelves of free movies. This three-story hotel has a fun, beach-minded hospitality that makes the surfing lifestyle seem accessible – even if you're a middle-aged landlubber who's never touched a board in your life.

Holiday Inn Express MOTEL $$
(800-308-5401; www.hienewportbeach.com; 2300 W Coast Hwy; r $190-219;) There's not much in the way of local charm, but this Holiday Inn branch is good value. Rooms have up-to-date furnishings and extras such as microwaves and refrigerators. Centrally located on PCH between major attractions.

Eating

TOP CHOICE **Bluewater Grill** SEAFOOD $$
(www.bluewatergrill.com; 630 Lido Park Dr; mains $8-30; 11am-10pm Mon-Thu, to 11pm Fri & Sat, 10am-10pm Sun) This casual yet elegant New England–style seafood eatery, occupying a quiet spot on the edge of the bay, is a hit with locals thanks to the spacious patio seating, raw oyster bar, fresh grilled swordfish and the famous house clam chowder. Try the ceviche lettuce wraps at lunchtime or come for happy hour (3:30pm to 6:30pm Monday through Friday) at the nautical-themed bar.

Sabatino's Sausage Company ITALIAN $$
(www.sabatinoschicagosausage.com; 251 Shipyard Way; mains $10-27; 11am-10pm Mon-Fri, from 8:30am Sat & Sun) Around the corner from Bluewater Grill is this pleasantly rustic Italian restaurant with checkered tablecloths and free-flowing red wine. Famous for Sicilian-style sausage – you'll see a stream of locals coming in to buy it at the central deli counter – Sabatino's also turns out savory seafood stews and pasta tossed with fresh clams and mussels. If you're with a few people, be sure to order the sizzling sausage platter (grilled with sauteed peppers and onions) to start. Note that Sabatino's is tucked away on the bayside; though it's not far from the beach, it's also not on the way anywhere.

Sol Grill SEAFOOD, AMERICAN $
(www.solgrill.com; 110 McFadden Pl; mains $5-25; 5-10pm Tue-Sun;) This down-to-earth bar and eatery, specializing in ahi chowder, lobster ravioli and fruity sangria, has brightly painted walls and an unpretentious atmosphere. There's live music and candlelight in the evenings. The place feels refreshingly bohemian – especially considering the location just across the street from the Newport Pier – and the prices are more than fair.

Drinking

Ruby's Crystal Cove Shake Shack CAFE, JUICE BAR
(949-464-0100; 7703 E Coast Hwy; shakes under $5; 10am-sunset) This been-here-forever wooden milkshake stand is now owned by the Ruby's Diner chain, but the shakes and the ocean view are just as good as ever. It's located just east of the Crystal Cove/Los Trancos entrance to the state park.

Alta Coffee Warehouse COFFEE SHOP
(www.altacoffeeshop.com; 506 31st St; 7am-11pm Sun-Thu, to midnight Fri & Sat) Regulars hang their mug on the wall at this cozy coffee shop housed in an inviting bungalow. Try the iced toffee coffee or come for a lunchtime salad on the patio.

Muldoon's PUB
(www.muldoonspub.com; 202 Newport Center Dr; 11:30am-late Tue-Sat, 10:30am-3pm Sun) The SoCal Irish tradition continues at lively Muldoon's, which anchors a small strip mall across the street from Fashion Island.

Cassidy's Bar & Grill BAR
(2603 Newport Blvd; 11am-late) This centrally located dive bar does cheap, strong drinks, addictive cheeseburgers (add its signature hot pepper sauce for a kick) and specials like juicy ribs or chicken. By noon – even on a weekday – most of the barstools are already taken. Located at the intersection of Balboa and Newport Blvds.

WORTH A TRIP

COSTA MESA

It takes a lot to drag Newport Beach locals away from their beloved sand and sea. But if there's one thing they love even more than sailing, biking and stand-up paddleboarding, it's looking fabulous – so they all make frequent pilgrimmages to the land-locked suburb of Costa Mesa to do some serious credit card damage at **South Coast Plaza** (☎800-782-8888; www.southcoastplaza.com; 3333 Bristol St). This sprawling shopping complex is home to 300 luxury stores – it attracts 25 million visitors a year and reports annual sales approaching $1.5 billion. Boutiques such as Chanel and Rolex do their part to keep the numbers high.

If you're not ready to drop a thousand dollars on a bikini and sandals, consider a visit to the **Lab** (☎714-966-6660; www.thelab.com; 2930 Bristol St; ⏲10:30am-9pm Mon-Sat, 11am-6pm Sun), an ivy-covered, outdoor 'anti-mall' where indie shoppers can sift through vintage clothing, trendy styles and eclectic tennis shoes. Pop into the Lab's sultry Cuban-inspired eatery **Habana** for mojitos, or head next door to the '60s-style bar and Southern-inspired small plates at **Memphis Cafe** (www.memphiscafe.com). You'd be hard-pressed to find a place this moody and stylish anywhere in sunny Newport.

3-Thirty-3 Waterfront BAR, LOUNGE
(www.3thirty3nb.com; 333 Bayside Dr; ⏲11:30am-2am Mon-Fri, from 9am Sat & Sun) Perfect for a low-key happy hour with friends (try the gourmet sliders and fries), this stylish harborside lounge morphs into the stereotypical Newport 'scene' as the night rolls on – think Botoxed former beauties and overtanned yachtsmen, all on a midnight prowl. On weekend mornings, there's a happening brunch with a mix-your-own Bloody Mary bar and gigantic breakfast burritos.

Shopping

A string of tiny boutiques lines PCH in Corona del Mar. On Balboa Island, Marine Ave is lined with unassuming (but not cheap) shops in a village-like atmosphere.

Fashion Island MALL
(www.shopfashionisland.com; 401 Newport Center Dr; ⏲10am-9pm Mon-Fri, to 7pm Sat, 11am-6pm Sun) Sometimes referred to as Fascist Island, this chic mall has nearly 200 stores and is the draw here for serious shopping. Its breezy, Mediterranean-style walkways are lined with specialty stores, national chains, upscale kiosks, restaurants and the occasional koi pond and fountain. Anchor stores include Bloomingdales, Macy's and Neiman Marcus. There's a small indoor section, Atrium Court, with a Barnes & Noble.

Information

Your best bet for information? Order the visitors guide from the website before arrival from the **Newport Beach Conference and Visitors' Center** (☎949-719-6100; www.newportbeach-cvb.com; Suite 120, 1200 Newport Center Dr; ⏲9am-5pm).

Getting Around

OCTA (☎714-560-6282; www.octa.net) bus 71 stops at the corner of PCH and Hwy 55, and goes south to Palm St beside the Balboa Pier. It departs about every 45 minutes and the trip between Newport Pier and Balboa Pier is about eight minutes. Bus 57 goes north to South Coast Plaza in Costa Mesa. It runs roughly every 30 minutes daily from the Newport Transportation Center on San Nicolas Dr (near Fashion Island) to South Coast Plaza. The trip takes about 25 minutes.Check current schedules online.

The local fare is $1.50 per trip, cash only. It can be purchased from OCTA fareboxes or the bus driver – you'll need exact change. A one-day pass, available from the driver, costs $4.

Laguna Beach

If you've ever wanted to step into a painting, a sunset stroll through Laguna Beach might be the next best thing. But hidden coves, romantic cliffs, azure waves and waterfront parks aren't the only aesthetic draw. Public sculptures, arts festivals and gallery nights imbue the city with an artistic sensibility you won't find elsewhere in SoCal. Most locals here, though wealthy, are also live-and-let-live, and there's a palpable artistic *joie de vivre* in the air that increases the sense of fun (the kids of MTV's *Laguna Beach* being the one troubling exception).

Laguna Beach

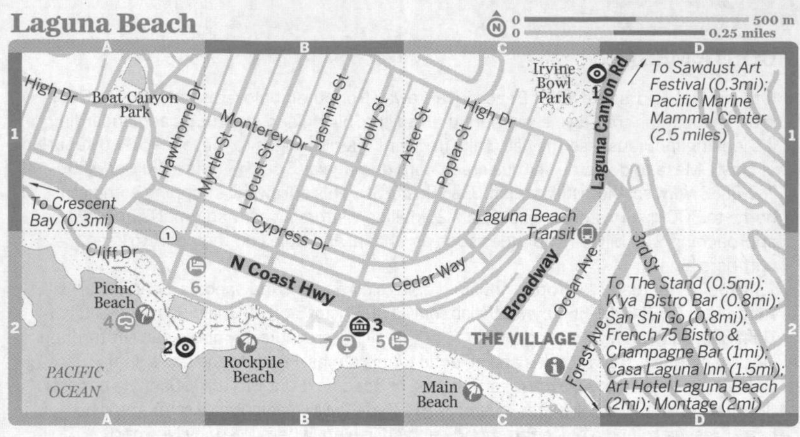

Laguna Beach

Sights
1 Festival of the Arts C1
2 Heisler Park A2
3 Laguna Art Museum B2

Activities, Courses & Tours
4 Diver's Cove A2

Sleeping
5 Inn at Laguna Beach B2
6 Laguna Cliffs Inn A2

Drinking
7 Las Brisas B2

The city's natural beauty was a siren's call for San Francisco artist Norman St Clair, who discovered Laguna around 1910 and stayed on to paint its surf, cliffs and hills. His enthusiasm attracted other artists who, influenced by French impressionism, came to be known as the 'plein air' (open air) school.

Partly tucked into canyons and partly arrayed on oceanfront bluffs, Laguna is also a refreshing change from the OC's beige-box architecture, with a combination of classic Arts and Crafts cabins and bold (if at times garish) modern homes. There's even a distinct downtown, known as the Village, with shops, art galleries and restaurants.

While Laguna swells with tourists on summer weekends, there are plenty of uncrowded beaches once you move away from downtown and the adjacent Main Beach.

Sights & Activities

Laguna stretches for about 7 miles along Pacific Coast Hwy. Shops, restaurants and bars are concentrated along a quarter-mile stretch in the Village, along three parallel streets: Broadway, Ocean Ave and Forest Ave.

Laguna Art Museum MUSEUM
(949-494-8971; www.lagunaartmuseum.org; 307 Cliff Dr; adult/child under 12yr/student $12/free/10; 11am-5pm, later in summer) This breezy museum has changing exhibits, usually featuring one or two California artists, plus a permanent collection heavy on California landscapes, vintage photographs and works by early Laguna artists. The museum also makes an effort to support new artists and runs an excellent foreign film series.

The museum is a centrally located stop on the **First Thursdays Art Walk** (949-683-6871; www.firstthursdaysartwalk.com; museum admission free; 5-9pm). During this convivial monthly event, numerous galleries open their doors for an evening of art, music and special exhibits.

Pacific Marine Mammal Center NATURE CENTER
(www.pacificmmc.org; 20612 Laguna Canyon Rd; 10am-4pm;) A nonprofit organization dedicated to rescuing and rehabilitating injured or ill marine mammals, this center northeast of town has a small staff and many volunteers who help nurse rescued pinnipeds – mostly sea lions and seals – before releasing them back into the wild. There are several outside pools and holding

pens – but remember, this is a rescue center, not SeaWorld. Still, it's educational and heart-warming. Admission is by donation and anything you buy in the gift shop (say, a stuffed animal) helps.

Beaches

With 30 public beaches and coves, Laguna is perfect for do-it-yourself exploring. Although many beaches are hidden from view by multimillion-dollar homes, a sharp eye will reveal one of the numerous stairways leading to the sand. Traveling south from the Village on PCH, pick an oceanside cross street and see what you can find.

Located at the western end of Broadway, **Main Beach** has benches, tables, restrooms and volleyball and basketball courts. It's also the best beach for swimming. Northwest of Main Beach, it's too rocky to surf; tidepooling is best. (Tidepool etiquette: tread carefully and don't pick up any living thing that you find in the rocks.)

Just northwest of Main Beach, follow the path to the grassy, bluff-top **Heisler Park** for sweeping views of the craggy coves and deep blue sea. Bring your camera. Drop down below the park to **Diver's Cove**, a deep, protected inlet popular with snorkelers and, of course, divers. Northwest of town, **Crescent Bay** has big hollow waves good for bodysurfing, but parking is difficult here; try the bluffs atop the beach.

Tours

The visitors center has brochures detailing self-guided tours. *The Heritage Walking Companion* is a tour of the city's architecture with an emphasis on bungalows and cottages. The self-guided *Tour Laguna by Bus* gives a more general overview.

First Thursdays Art Walk WALKING
(949-683-6871; www.firstthursdaysartwalk.com; admission free) On the first Thursday of the month, downtown gets festive during these walks, which includes 40 local galleries and the Laguna Art Museum from 6pm to 9pm. Shuttles run from the museum to various clusters of galleries.

Sleeping

Most hotels in Laguna are on PCH, and traffic can be loud. If you're sensitive ask for a room away from the street or use earplugs. There are no budget lodgings in summer, but it's the best place in the OC for charming, noncorporate digs. Summer rates are listed. Come fall, they drop significantly.

Casa Laguna Inn B&B **$$$**
(800-233-0449; www.casalaguna.com; 2510 S Coast Hwy; r from $300) Laguna's B&B gem is built around a historic 1920s Mission-revival house surrounded by lush, manicured, mature plantings. Rooms are inside former artists' bungalows built in the 1930s and '40s; all have delicious beds, some have Jacuzzi tubs. There's a full breakfast, and evening wine and cheese.

Laguna Cliffs Inn INN **$$$**
(949-497-6645; www.lagunacliffsinn.com; 475 N Coast Hwy; r $209-379) Be it good feng shui, friendly staff, comfy beds or proximity to the ocean, something just feels right at this 36-room inn. From the big green pillows on the bed and the flat-screen TVs to the hardwood floors, the decor is a nice mix of new, comfy and clean. For a relaxing close to the day, settle in to the outdoor Jacuzzi with your honey as the sun drops over the ocean. Formerly known as By the Sea Inn.

Montage RESORT **$$$**
(949-715-6000, 866-271-6953; www.montagelagunabeach.com; 30801 S Coast Hwy; d from $580) Widely regarded as the most luxurious and fashionable resort in the area, Montage is an indulgent place to hide away with your lover in a secluded bungalow. Even if you're not staying, come for a spa treatment or a cocktail and check out the lobby art and the spectacular sunburst-inlaid swimming pool. At the resort's southern end, there's underground public parking and a public walkway that loops around the grounds atop the bluffs overlooking the sea, and grants access to the sandy shore.

Art Hotel Laguna Beach HOTEL **$$**
(877-363-7229; www.arthotellagunabeach.com; 1404 N Coast Hwy; r from $154) One mile north of downtown near Crystal Cove State Park, this simply furnished 28-room hotel boasts appealing extras like free wi-fi, free parking, a handful of oceanview rooms and a deck with a brand-new Jacuzzi.

Inn at Laguna Beach HOTEL **$$$**
(949-497-9722; www.innatlagunabeach.com; 211 N Coast Hwy; r $199-599) This three-story white concrete hotel at the north end of Main Beach walks the fine line between hip and homey, with personable finesse. All

DON'T MISS

LAGUNA ART FESTIVALS

With a 6-acre canyon as its backdrop, Laguna's landmark event is the **Festival of Arts** (949-494-1145; www.foapom.com; 650 Laguna Canyon Rd; adult/student & senior $7/4; from 10am Jul & Aug), a two-month celebration of original artwork in almost all its forms. The 140 exhibiting artists – all approved pursuant to a juried selection process – display art ranging from paintings to handcrafted furniture to scrimshaw. Started in the 1930s by local artists who needed to drum up buyers, the festival now attracts patrons and tourists from around the world. In addition to the art, there are free daily artists workshops, docent tours and live entertainment. For a slightly more indie-minded art show, look for the **Sawdust Art Festival** (949-494-3030; www.sawdustartfestival.org; 935 Laguna Canyon Rd; adult/child/senior $7.75/3.25/6.25; 10am-10pm Jul & Aug) across the street.

The most thrilling part of the main festival is the **Pageant of the Masters** (949-497-6582; www.pageanttickets.com; admission $15-100; 8:30-11:30pm nightly Jul & Aug), where human models blend seamlessly into re-creations of famous paintings. It began in 1933 as a sideshow to the main festival. Tickets generally go on sale around the beginning of December the previous year and sell out before the year ends. You may be able to snag last-minute cancellations at the gate.

rooms have a fresh, clean look enhanced by French blinds and thick featherbeds. Some have balconies overlooking the water. Watch the extra charges – parking costs $20 per day, the resort fee is another $25.

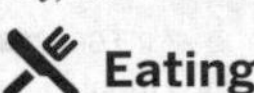

Eating

French 75 Bistro & Champagne Bar FRENCH $$
(949-494-8444; www.french75.net; 1464 S Coast Hwy; mains $19-35; 4:30-11pm) Fantastic coq au vin, chocolate souffle, and icy champagne cocktails (half-price at the bar everyday from 4:30pm to 6:30pm) are the main draws at this refined but friendly bistro. It's a choice spot for a romantic evening out; reservations recommended.

San Shi Go SUSHI $$
(1100 S Coast Hwy; mains $10-25; 11:30am-2pm Tue-Fri, 5-10pm Mon-Thu, 5-11pm Fri & Sat) This slightly hidden sushi spot has ocean views from some of the tables; more importantly, the rainbow roll and lemon salmon roll practically melt in your mouth. For a more authentic experience, sit at the sushi bar and ask the chef to make you something special (ie a roll that's not on the menu).

The Stand VEGAN $
(238 Thalia St; mains $6-12; 7am-7pm;) This tiny tribute to vegan cuisine reflects what's best about Laguna living – it's friendly, unassuming and filled with indie spirit. The long menu includes hummus-and-guac sandwiches, sunflower-sprout salads and bean-and-rice burritos. For a snack, try a smoothie or the corn tortilla chips and salsa. Grab a spot on the wooden patio.

Drinking & Entertainment

K'ya Bistro Bar COCKTAIL BAR
(www.kyabistro.com; 1287 S Coast Hwy) This chic rooftop bar does killer cocktails (strawberry balsamic martini, anyone?) and tasty small plates. Perched atop the La Casa del Camino Hotel, the bar is noteworthy for its beautiful coastal views and friendly vibe. Follow the crowds through the hotel lobby and take the elevator to the top. As for mojitos, there are five on the cocktail menu, including mango and wild berry.

Las Brisas COCKTAIL BAR
(949-497-5434; www.lasbrisaslagunabeach.com; 361 Cliff Dr) Locals roll their eyes at the mere mention of this tourist-heavy spot, but out-of-towners flock here for a good reason: the blufftop view of the beach. Sip margaritas while you stare at the crashing waves from the glassed-in patio; the image of the coast will leave an indelible impression. Cocktail hour gets packed; make reservations.

Information

Laguna Beach Library (949-497-1733; www.ocpl.org; 363 Glenneyre St; 10am-8pm Mon-Wed, to 6pm Thu, 10am-5pm Fri & Sat;) Free wi-fi and walk-in computer and internet access.

Laguna Beach Visitors Center (949-497-9229; www.lagunabeachinfo.org; 381 Forest Ave; 10am-4pm Mon-Fri) The staff at this visitors center is very helpful, and one wall here is filled with maps, brochures, bus schedules and coupons.

 Getting There & Around

To reach Laguna Beach from the I-405, take Hwy 133 (Laguna Canyon Rd) southwest. Laguna is served by **OCTA** (☎714-560-6282; www.octa.net) bus 1, which runs along the coast from Long Beach to San Clemente.

Number one piece of advice? Bring lots of quarters to feed the meters. Laguna is hemmed in by steep canyons, and parking is a perpetual problem. In and around the Village you'll find a few outdoor change machines (there's one on Cliff Dr by Heisler Park). If you're spending the night, leave your car at the hotel and ride the local bus. Parking lots in the Village charge $10 to $20 or more per entry and fill up early during summer.

Laguna Beach Transit (www.lagunabeachcity.net; 375 Broadway) has its central bus depot on Broadway, just north of the visitors center in the heart of the Village. It operates three routes at hourly intervals (approximately 7am to 6pm Monday through Friday, 9am to 6pm Saturday). Routes are color-coded and easy to follow but subject to change. For tourists, the most important route is the one that runs along PCH. Pick up a brochure and schedule at your hotel or the visitors center. Rides cost 75¢ (exact change). All routes are free during July and August. No Sunday service.

San Juan Capistrano

Famous for the swallows that annually return here from their winter migration on March 19 (though sometimes they arrive a bit early), San Juan Capistrano is also home to the 'jewel of the California missions.'

Sights & Activities

Mission San Juan Capistrano HISTORIC SITE
(☎949-234-1300; www.missionsjc.com; 31882 Camino Capistrano, cnr Ortega Hwy; adult/child/senior $9/5/8; ⏲8:30am-5pm) Located about 10 miles southeast and inland of Laguna Beach, this beautiful mission was built around a series of 18th-century arcades, all of which enclose photogenic fountains and lush gardens. The charming Serra Chapel – whitewashed outside and decorated with vivid frescoes inside – is considered the oldest building in California. It's the only chapel still standing in which Padre Junípero Serra gave Mass. He founded the mission on November 1, 1776 and tended it personally for many years. Particularly moving are the remains of the Great Stone Church, almost completely destroyed by an earthquake in 1812 that killed 42 Native Americans worshipping inside. Plan to spend at least an hour looking around. Admission includes a worthwhile free audio tour with interesting stories narrated by locals.

To celebrate the swallows' return from their South American sojourn, the city puts on the **Festival of the Swallows** every year. The birds nest in the walls of the mission until around October 23. They're best observed at feeding time, usually early in the morning and late afternoon to early evening.

Los Rios Historic District DISTRICT
One block west, next to the Capistrano train depot, is this picturesque assemblage of cottages and adobes housing cafes and gift shops.

 Eating

Ramos House Cafe CAFE $$
(www.ramoshouse.com; 31752 Los Rios St; mains $13-17, weekend brunch $35; ⏲8:30am-3pm Tue-Sun; 🍷) Famous for earthy comfort food flavored with herbs from the nearby garden, Ramos House is the best spot for breakfast or lunch near the Mission. To find it, walk across the railroad tracks at the end of Verdugo St and turn right. Promptly reward yourself with cinnamon-apple beignets, basil-cured salmon or pulled-pork sandwiches with sweet-potato fries.

Tea House on Los Rios CAFE $$
(www.theteahouseonlosrios.com; 31731 Los Rios St; mains $13-27; ⏲11am-5pm Wed-Fri, 10am-5pm Sat & Sun) Made for ladies who lunch – or sip tea – and their significant others. Think flower-covered trellis, a table-dotted porch and dainty settings, but the menu isn't all cucumber sandwiches. There's also prime rib, shepherd's pie and beer on offer.

 Entertainment

Coach House LIVE MUSIC
(☎949-496-8930; www.thecoachhouse.com; 33157 Camino Capistrano) Long-running live-music venue which features a roster of local and national rock, indie, alternative and retro bands; expect a cover charge of $15 to $40 depending on who's playing. Recent performers include Robben Ford, Aimee Mann and the Gin Blossoms.

SCENIC DRIVE: CRYSTAL COVE TO DOHENY STATE BEACH

This quiet stretch of the Pacific Coast Highway (PCH) offers gorgeous ocean views, a classic roadside milkshake stand, dramatic cliffs, Orange County's (the OC) prettiest beach town, and options to get out of the car and hit the hiking trails.

What to See

Start at the forested coastal paradise of Crystal Cove State Park (p413) and head south on the PCH, stopping for a chocolate milkshake at Ruby's Crystal Cove Shake Shack (p414). The stand, though now owned by a chain, is an old-fashioned OC classic. Enjoy sea views as you continue south towards Laguna Beach. Stop for mango ceviche or chips and salsa with stunning views at Las Brisas (p418), then continue driving through the Village. Continue along the PCH towards Dana Point and the family-friendly Ocean Institute (p420) before ending up at Doheny State Beach (p420) to splash around the tidepools, set up an afternoon picnic or ride bikes along the beach paths.

The Route

The Pacific Coast Highway (Hwy 1) from Crystal Cove State Park south to Doheny State Beach.

Time & Mileage

Fifteen miles, 35 minutes without stops and one to two hours or more if you pull over frequently.

Worthy Detours

Hike the trails high above the ocean in Crystal Cove State Park or head inland from Laguna Beach to tour the beautiful Mission San Juan Capistrano (p419).

Getting There & Away

From Laguna Beach, ride **OCTA** (☎714-560-6282; www.octa.net) bus 1 south to Dana Point. At the intersection of PCH and Del Obispo St, catch bus 91 northbound toward Mission Viejo. Buses run every 30 to 60 minutes and the trips takes about an hour. You'll have to pay the one-way fare ($1.50, exact change) twice.

The Amtrak depot is one block south and west of the mission; you could arrive by train from LA or San Diego in time for lunch, visit the mission and be back in the city for dinner.

Drivers should exit I-5 at Ortega Hwy and head west for about a quarter of a mile.

Dana Point & Around

Nineteenth-century adventurer Richard Dana called Dana Point 'the only romantic spot on the coast.' Nowadays its yacht-filled marinas don't inspire immediate thoughts of romance, but it is a pleasant place to wander if you enjoy maritime history and family-oriented attractions. Most of the action occurs around the man-made harbor on Dana Point Harbor Dr, just off PCH.

The kid-friendly **Ocean Institute** (☎949-496-2274; www.ocean-institute.org; 24200 Dana Pt Harbor Dr; adult/child $6.50/4.50, extra for cruises; ⏲10am-3pm Sat & Sun; 👪) includes replicas of historic tall ships, maritime-related exhibits and a floating research lab. Specific trips include a marine-wildlife cruise aboard the RV *Sea Explorer* (adult/child $35/22) and a Pyrate Adventure Sail – with a cast of pirates – on the 118ft *Spirit of Dana Point* tall ship.

Just as fun may be nearby **Doheny State Beach** (☎949-496-6172; www.parks.ca.gov, www.dohenystatebeach.org; ⏲6am-8pm Nov-Feb, to 10pm Mar-Oct; 📶👪), where you'll find picnic tables, grills, volleyball courts, a bike path and surf that's good for swimming, surfing and diving. They also allow **beach camping** (☎800-444-7275, international callers 916-638-5883; www.reserveamerica.com; tent & RV sites $25-45). Day-use parking is $15.

Dedicated surfers won't mind the 1-mile hike to world-renowned **Trestles**, just south of the town of **San Clemente** and north of San Onofre State Beach, bordering the San Diego County line. It's a natural surfbreak that consistently churns out perfect waves. Check out www.surfrider.org for more information on the potential extension of a nearby toll road that could affect the waves. Exit off I-5 at Los Christianos Rd.

San Diego

Includes »

Best Places to Eat

» Prado (p449)
» Puerto La Boca (p448)
» George's at the Cove (p451)
» Bread & Cie (p449)

Best Places to Stay

» Hotel del Coronado (p446)
» Hotel Indigo (p446)
» La Pensione Hotel (p446)
» Inn at Sunset Cliffs (p447)
» Crystal Pier Hotel (p447)

Why Go?

There's a certain arrogance that comes with living on the SoCal coast, a breezy confidence that springs from the assumption that your life is just, well, *better* than everyone else's. No offense – it just is. But as far as coastal snobs go, San Diegans are the ones we like the most. Whether it's a battle-tested docent sharing stories on the USS *Midway* or a no-worries surf diva helping you catch a wave, folks here are pretty willing to share the good life.

The only problem is that with 70 miles of coastline and a near-perfect climate, it's tough to decide where to start. Exploring maritime history, biking the beach paths, microbrewery hopping, ball games, horse races, Japanese gardens? Killer whales? When in doubt, do as the locals do and just take it easy – grab a fish taco and a surfboard and head for the beach.

When to Go

San Diego

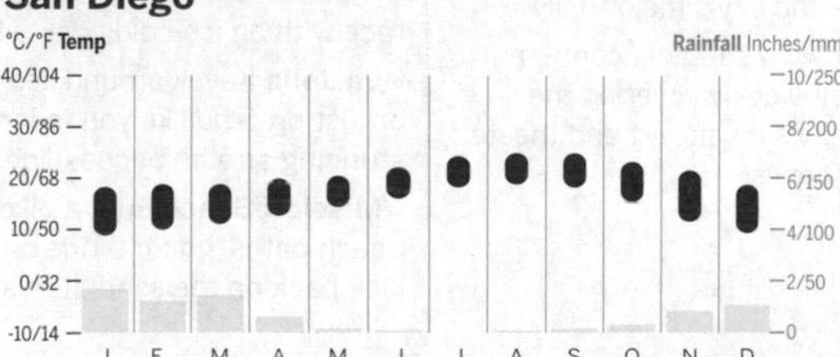

Jun–Aug High season. Temperatures and hotel rates are highest. Beware of cloudy weather.

Sep–Oct & Mar–May Shoulder seasons; moderate hotel rates. Chilly evenings and sunny days.

Nov–Feb Low season. But it's still sunnier in San Diego than almost anywhere else in the USA.

DON'T MISS...

The chance to glimpse rhinos, giraffes, and ostriches in their (almost) natural habitat at the San Diego Zoo Safari Park.

Fast Facts

» **Population** 1.3 million

» **Average high temperature in San Diego** Jan 65°F, Jul 76°F

» **San Diego to Tijuana** 18 miles

Planning Your Trip

As your San Diego visit approaches, look online for coupons and special promotions for SeaWorld and the Zoo. If you'd rather skip the stress of southern California traffic, book a hotel room downtown – you can take the trolleys to get around instead.

Resources

» www.sandiego.org – the official San Diego resource for travelers

» www.signonsandiego.com – the city's major daily

» www.sdreader.com – an alt-weekly covering the city's music, art and theater scenes

Green San Diego: the 'finest city on earth?'

San Diegans hold their fair city in high esteem. And by the looks of it, they're devoted to protecting their beautiful beaches and clear, sunny skies: sustainable building and ecofriendly businesses are on the rise, and the laid-back metropolis recently became the home of North America's first all-electric car-sharing program.

GOURMET SAN DIEGO

Though wine connoisseurs and foodies often head elsewhere in California to taste, swirl and sip, San Diego is a gourmet destination in its own right. Local chefs, farmers and brewmasters have slowly but steadily added flavor to a culinary scene that, thanks to the city's location near the border, has long been associated with one-dimensional Mexican food.

On almost any day of the week, you'll find organic farmers selling their plump avocados, strawberries and basil at **farmers markets** scattered throughout San Diego's neighborhoods. While you pick out your peaches and parsley, you'll likely bump shoulders with the kitchen staff from stylish but down-to-earth eateries like **JRDN** (p451) of Pacific Beach or **whisknladle** (p451) of La Jolla. Meanwhile, at **microbreweries** around the city, brewmasters are turning out award-winning India Pale Ales and barley wine. Taste their concoctions at any bar downtown, or drive out to the microbreweries' onsite **tasting rooms**; we recommend **AleSmith** or **The Lost Abbey** (p452). Go ahead, raise your glass to the city's underrated food and drink scene – the secret's not out yet.

San Diego's Best Beach Moments

» **Coronado** Walk barefoot in the soft white sand in front of the glamorous old Hotel del Coronado, then sit on the terrace with an ice-cold cocktail and stare out at the ocean.

» **La Jolla** Kayak around sea caves, snorkel near the shore or just pretend like you're in the Mediterranean along this stunning stretch of coastline.

» **Mission Beach** Rent a bike and ride along the endless beach paths, go for a ride on a vintage roller coaster or just kick back on the sand at this lively, family-friendly beach.

History

Evidence of human habitation in the region dates back to 18,000 BC. By the time the Spanish explorer Juan Rodriguez Cabrillo sailed into San Diego Bay in 1542 – the first European to do so – the region was divided peaceably between the Kumeyaay and Luisenõ/Juanenõ peoples. Their way of life continued undisturbed until Junípero Serra and Gaspar de Portolá arrived in 1769. They founded a mission and a military fort on the hill now known as the Presidio, making it the first permanent European settlement in California.

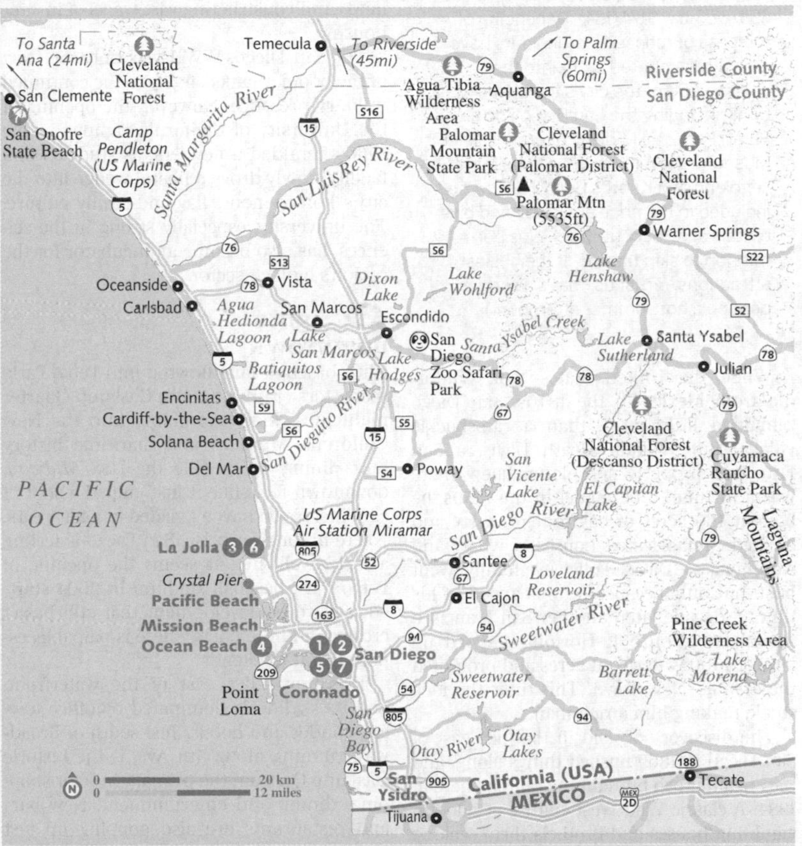

San Diego Highlights

1. Explore the nation's largest urban cultural park, **Balboa Park** (p426), then go for margaritas on the lively Spanish-style patio of the **Prado** (p449)

2. Wander the 4-acre flight deck and get lost in the snaking corridors of the **USS Midway** (p426), an impressive aircraft carrier parked along the Embarcadero

3. Kayak through the eerily beautiful sea caves along the coast of **La Jolla Cove** (p444)

4. Eat your way through **Ocean Beach** (p450), feasting on fish tacos, juicy burgers and other classic SoCal street foods

5. Come face-to-face with the King of the Jungle at the **San Diego Zoo Safari Park** (p428)

6. Learn to hang ten off **La Jolla Shores** (p443).

7. Bar-hop through the happening nightlife scene of the **Gaslamp** (p451), stopping for a drink at rooftop lounges and down-to-earth dive bars

GO SAN DIEGO CARD

If you're planning on doing significant sightseeing in San Diego, it's wise to pick up the **Go San Diego Card** (☎866-628-9032; www.smartdestinations.com; adult/child 1-day $69/58, 2-day $99/87, 3-day $174/134). Depending on the pass purchased, cardholders have steeply discounted entry into their choice of 50 of the city's top attractions, including the San Diego Zoo and Safari Park, the Midway Aircraft Carrier Museum, the Air and Space Museum, Legoland and Knott's Berry Farm. Also included in the price are kayak and bike rentals at select outfitters, plus permission to skip the line at the busiest attractions. (Trust us, that's a serious perk on a hot summer afternoon.)

When the United States took California from Mexico in the 1840s, San Diego remained little more than a ramshackle village. But William Heath Davis, a San Francisco property speculator, knew there was a fortune to be made. In the 1850s, he bought 160 acres of bayfront property and erected prefabricated houses, a wharf and warehouses. 'Davis' Folly' eventually went bust, but only because he was ahead of his time. A decade later, another San Francisco speculator, Alonzo E Horton, snapped up almost 1000 waterfront acres and promoted the area as 'New Town.' This time, the idea stuck, making him a rich man.

The discovery of gold in the hills east of San Diego in 1869 pushed things along, and the ensuing rush brought the railroad here in 1884. A classic Wild West culture of saloons, gambling houses and brothels thrived along 5th St in the Gaslamp Quarter. When gold played out, the economy took a nosedive, and the city's population plummeted yet again.

When San Francisco hosted the successful Panama-Pacific International Exposition (1914), San Diego responded with its own Panama-California Exposition (1915–16), hoping to attract investment to a city with a deepwater port, a railroad hub and a perfect climate – but virtually no industry. To give San Diego a unique image, boosters built exhibition halls in the romantic, Spanish colonial style that still defines much of the city today.

However, it was the bombing of Pearl Harbor in 1941 that made San Diego. The US Pacific Fleet needed a mainland home for its headquarters. The top brass quickly settled on San Diego, whose excellent deep-water port affords protection in almost all weather. The military literally reshaped the city, dredging the harbor, building landfill islands and constructing vast tracts of instant housing.

For San Diego, WWII was only the start of the boom, thanks largely to the continued military presence. However, the opening of the University of California campus in the 1960s heralded a new era, as students and faculty slowly drove a liberal wedge into the city's homogenous, flag-and-family culture. The university, especially strong in the sciences, has also become an incubator for the region's biotech sector.

Sights

DOWNTOWN

With baseball fans flowing into Petco Park, scenesters cramming into Gaslamp Quarter nightclubs, kids scrambling into the New Children's Museum and maritime history buffs lining up outside the USS *Midway*, downtown feels like it just gulped a shot of caffeine. If you haven't visited in a few years, you're in for a surprise. San Diego is feeling a little, well, hip. It seems the opening of Petco Park baseball stadium in 2004 started a wave of development that still hasn't crested, and the energy here is palpable, especially on weekends.

Downtown lies east of the waterfront, and its skyline is dominated by office towers, condos and hotels. Just south of Broadway, running along 5th Ave, is the historic Gaslamp Quarter, the primary hub for shopping, dining and entertainment. New bars and restaurants are also popping up just north of Petco Park in edgy East Village. To the west lies the Embarcadero district, a nice spot for a bayfront jog or a stroll through historic sea-faring vessels. A short walk north lands you in Little Italy, where mom-and-pop eateries alternate with high-end design stores.

Soon after his arrival in San Diego in 1867, San Francisco speculator Alonzo Horton purchased 960 acres of land stretching south from Broadway to the waterfront and east to 15th St – for a grand total of $265. While respectable businesses went up along Broadway, the 5th Ave area became known as The Stingaree, a notorious red-light district filled with saloons, bordellos, gambling halls and opium dens.

By the 1960s it had declined to a skid row of flophouses and bars, but the neighborhood's very seediness made it so unattractive to developers that many of the older buildings survived when others around town were being razed. When developers turned their eyes toward the area in the early 1980s, preservationists organized to save the old brick and stone facades from the wrecking ball. The city stepped up, contributing trees, benches, wide brick sidewalks and replica 19th-century gas lamps. Restored buildings (built between the 1870s and the 1920s) became home to restaurants, bars, galleries, shops and theaters. The 16-acre area south of Broadway between 4th Ave and 6th Ave is designated a National Historic District and development is strictly controlled.

These days, the Gaslamp Quarter is enjoying a second, post-Petco wave of revitalization and growth, one characterized by a youthful, stylish energy. Upscale hotels and sleek restaurants are making ever-more-frequent debuts, while new rooftop bars and velvet-rope clubs are fending off (or creating) long lines of martini-craving scenesters. The neighborhood isn't a total hipster haven – yet – and a smattering of dive bars are working hard to keep things real.

The commercial focal point of downtown is **Westfield Horton Plaza** (Map p430; Broadway & 4th Sbr; P), a five-story mall designed by Los Angeles architect Jon Jerde, who also designed Universal City Walk. Inside, toy-town arches, post-modern balconies and an asymmetrical floor plan – all surrounding an open-air atrium – are reminiscent of an MC Escher drawing.

William Heath Davis House HISTORIC BUILDING
(Map p430; ☎619-233-4692; www.gaslampquarter.org; 410 Island Ave; adult/senior $5/4; ⏲10am-6pm Tue-Sat, 9am-3pm Sun) For a taste of local history, peruse the exhibits inside this museum; the saltbox house was the onetime home of William Heath Davis, the man credited with starting the development of modern San Diego. Upstairs, look for the hidden prohibition-era still. Self-guided tours are available and the foundation also offers **guided walking tours** (adult/student & senior $10/8; ⏲11am Sat) of the quarter.

San Diego Chinese Historical Museum MUSEUM
(Map p430; ☎619-338-9888; www.sdchm.org; 404 3rd Ave; admission $2; ⏲10:30am-4pm Tue-Sat, from noon Sun) This was the heart of San Diego's former Chinatown. The museum occupies the attractive Chinese Mission Building, built in the 1920s, as well as a contemporary annex completed in 2004. Exhibits include a former warlord's 40-piece wood-carved bed – assembled without nails – as well as the ornate, ultratiny slippers worn by women with bound feet.

Museum of Contemporary Art MUSEUM
(Map p430; ☎858-454-3541; www.mcasd.org; 1001 & 1100 Kettner Blvd; adult/student/senior $10/free/5; ⏲11am-5pm Thu-Tue, to 7pm third Thu each month, with free admission 5-7pm) This modern art museum emphasizes minimalist and pop art, conceptual works and cross-border art. The original branch, open since the 1960s, is in La Jolla (p441). Tickets are valid for seven days in all locations.

New Children's Museum MUSEUM
(Map p430; ☎619-233-8792; www.thinkplaycreate.org; 200 W Island Ave; adult & child/senior/child under 1yr $10/5/free; ⏲10am-4pm Mon, Tue, Fri & Sat, to 6pm Thu, noon-4pm Sun) With concrete

HAUNTED SAN DIEGO

Don't let the sunshine and happy people fool you: San Diego has an unnerving number of haunted homes and hotels. (Do the ghosts know something we don't about this shiny coastal city?) Take the **Horton Grand Hotel** (p446), built on the site of the 19th-century Seven Buckets of Blood Saloon. According to hotel lore, a local troublemaker was shot in a room above the saloon, and his ghost now haunts the hotel's Room 309, playing tricks on maids and causing some guests to check out at 2am. A jilted woman allegedly walks the halls at the **Hotel del Coronado** (p436) and appears on the TV screen in the room where her heart was broken. Then there's the **Whaley House** (p433), certified haunted by the US Department of Commerce, where staff and guests claim to have seen apparitions, even in the daytime.

floors, soaring walls, and mod furnishings and decor, this revamped interactive museum is engaging for kids and adults; it earns kudos for its environmentally sustainable features. Part art studio, part children's museum, and part modern art gallery, the museum displays artist-created exhibits that encourage kids of all ages to think about art, react to it, and create it.

LITTLE ITALY

Like any 'Little Italy' worth its salt, San Diego's version offers friendly pizzerias with red and white checkered tablecloths, unpretentious espresso bars, mom-and-pop delis, and family-friendly businesses. It's a place where San Diegans come to while away a sunny afternoon. The pedestrian-friendly neighborhood is perched on a small rise of land east of the Embarcadero, north of Ash St.

The neighborhood's always been community minded, beginning in the mid-19th century, when Italian immigrants, mostly fishermen and their families, first started settling here. The tight-knit neighborhood had its heyday in the 1920s, when Prohibition opened up new business opportunities (read 'bootlegging').

The construction of I-5 in 1962 – right beside Little Italy – disrupted the community. The hardiest of the old family businesses survived, mingling easily beside the chichi restaurants and specialty shops. You'll find the busiest patio tables on the eastern side of **India Street** (Map p430), a prime spot for a glass of Chianti.

EMBARCADERO

Heading west from downtown, cross the tram tracks to enter a 500yd-wide stretch of landfill that culminates with the Embarcadero. This wide pedestrian strip hugs the bay, offering breezy views of the water and an impressive line-up of ships and vessels, not to mention a few overpriced restaurants. It's also the launch point for the ferry to Coronado, the site of a public fishing pier, and the home of the San Diego Convention Center. Designed by Canadian avant-garde architect Arthur Erickson, the building – which some say was inspired by an ocean liner – stretches for a half-mile.

Maritime Museum MUSEUM

(Map p430; ☎619-234-9153; www.sdmaritime.com; 1492 N Harbor Dr; adult/child/senior $14/8/11; ⏲9am-8pm, to 9pm late May-early Sep; 👪) The 100ft masts of the square-rigger tall ship *Star of India* – one of seven vessels open to the public here – make this museum easy to find. Built on the Isle of Man and launched in 1863, the restored ship plied the England-India trade route, carried immigrants to New Zealand, became a trading ship based in Hawaii and, finally, worked the Alaskan salmon fisheries. Nowadays she's taken out once a year for a sail, making her the oldest active ship in the world.

Kids can learn the Pirate's Code at the small but engaging pirate's exhibit below deck on the HMS *Surprise*. For the highest wow-per-square-foot factor, squeeze into the museum's B-39 Soviet attack submarine. (Take note: the sub is a claustrophobe's nightmare.) If you do venture in, check out the torpedo tubes. In a last-ditch attempt to escape a crippled sub, sailors would blast from these tubes as human torpedoes. Metered parking and $10 day lots are nearby.

USS Midway Museum MUSEUM

(Map p430; ☎619-544-9600; www.midway.org; Navy Pier; adult/child/senior & student $18/10/15; ⏲10am-5pm; 👪) A short walk south is the Embarcadero's heavyweight attraction, the USS *Midway*, clocking in with a total weight of 69,000 tons. Commissioned in 1945, the ship is the Navy's longest-serving aircraft carrier, seeing action in Vietnam and the first Gulf War. It opened as a museum in 2004. An engaging self-guided audio tour – filled with first person accounts from former crewmen – takes visitors on a maze-like climb through the engine room, the brig, the galley and the 4-acre flight deck, where an impressive lineup of fighter jets – including an F-14 Tomcat – await up-close inspection. For an eagle-eye view of the flight deck and San Diego Bay, take the docent-led tour of the Island Superstructure, which includes stops in the bridge and flight control. Parking costs $5 to $7.

Seaport Village PLAZA

(Map p430; ☎619-235-4014; www.seaportvillage.com; ⏲10am-10pm summer) Continue south to this open-air tourist promenade which is technically neither a Seaport nor a Village. Filled with outdoor restaurants and knick-knack shops (if you need a coffee mug or T-shirt, come here), it's a pretty place to relax, listen to live music or look at the water.

BALBOA PARK

The rumors are true: Balboa Park is, in fact, the largest urban cultural park in the US. While we're spouting statistics, it's also the

Metropolitan San Diego

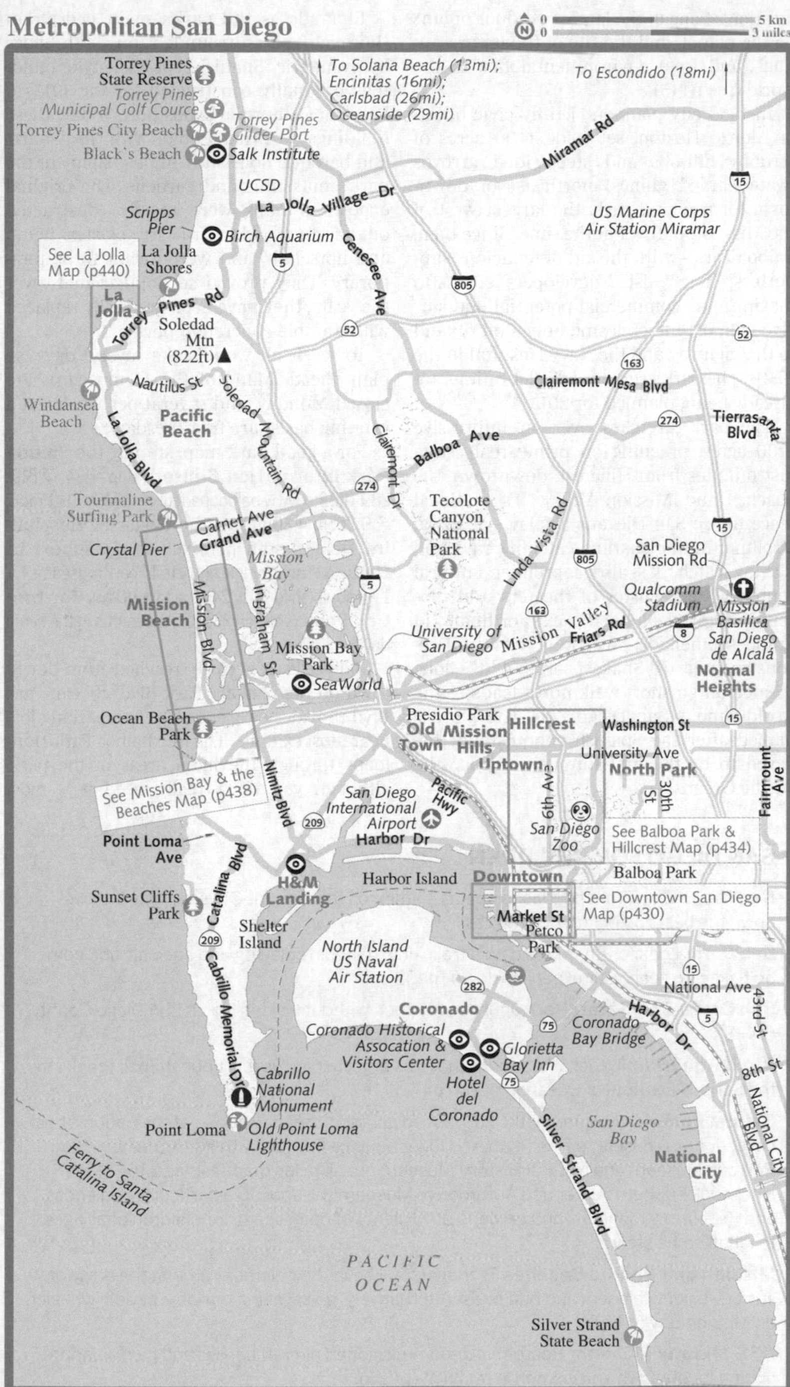

0 5 km
0 3 miles
Torrey Pines State Reserve
Torrey Pines Municipal Golf Cource
Torrey Pines City Beach
Torrey Pines Gilder Port
Black's Beach
Salk Institute
UCSD
To Solana Beach (13mi); Encinitas (16mi); Carlsbad (26mi); Oceanside (29mi)
To Escondido (18mi)
Miramar Rd
La Jolla Village Dr
US Marine Corps Air Station Miramar
Scripps Pier
Birch Aquarium
See La Jolla Map (p440)
La Jolla Shores
Genesee Ave
La Jolla
Torrey Pines Rd
Soledad Mtn (822ft)
Nautilus St
Soledad Mountain Rd
Windansea Beach
Pacific Beach
La Jolla Blvd
Clairemont Mesa Blvd
Tierrasanta Blvd
Clairemont Dr
Balboa Ave
Tourmaline Surfing Park
Garnet Ave
Grand Ave
Crystal Pier
Mission Bay
Tecolote Canyon National Park
Linda Vista Rd
San Diego Mission Rd
Qualcomm Stadium
Mission Basilica San Diego de Alcalá
Mission Beach
Mission Blvd
Ingraham St
Mission Bay Park
University of San Diego
Mission Valley
Friars Rd
SeaWorld
Normal Heights
Ocean Beach Park
Presidio Park
Old Town
Mission Hills
Hillcrest
Washington St
Uptown
University Ave
North Park
30th St
Fairmount Ave
See Mission Bay & the Beaches Map (p438)
Nimitz Blvd
San Diego International Airport
Pacific Hwy
6th Ave
San Diego Zoo
See Balboa Park & Hillcrest Map (p434)
Harbor Dr
Point Loma Ave
Catalina Blvd
H&M Landing
Harbor Island
Downtown
Balboa Park
Sunset Cliffs Park
See Downtown San Diego Map (p430)
Market St
Petco Park
Shelter Island
North Island US Naval Air Station
Cabrillo Memorial Dr
National Ave
43rd St
Coronado
Harbor Dr
Coronado Historical Assocation & Visitors Center
Glorietta Bay Inn
Coronado Bay Bridge
Hotel del Coronado
Cabrillo National Monument
8th St
Point Loma
Old Point Loma Lighthouse
San Diego Bay
National City Blvd
National City
Silver Strand Blvd
Ferry to Santa Catalina Island
PACIFIC OCEAN
Silver Strand State Beach

location of one of the largest outdoor organs on the planet, and the site of the largest annual (and free) environmental fair in the world (see p445).

In 1868 city planners, led by civic booster Alonzo Horton, set aside 1400 acres of scrubby hilltops and steep-sided arroyos (water-carved gullies) northeast of downtown for use as a park, the largest west of the Mississippi River at the time. Since then, Balboa Park – with the aid of tenacious supporters – has resisted developers' efforts to maximize its commercial potential and survived almost intact, losing only a bit of land to the highway and the Navy Hospital in the 1950s. The park's centennial celebrations are already being planned for 2015.

The park stretches over an impressive 1200 acres, preening on prime real estate just minutes from Hillcrest, downtown, the beaches and Mission Valley. It's an ideal place to see San Diegans at play – jogging, strolling, in-line skating, catching rays and playing catch. It's also a premier cultural center, with a cluster of theaters and museums arrayed along the extraordinary El Prado promenade. Nearby is a faithful reconstruction of Shakespeare's Old Globe theater, and a short walk north leads to the world-famous San Diego Zoo. The park is named after the Spanish conquistador believed to be the first European to see the Pacific Ocean.

El Prado is the park's main pedestrian thoroughfare, surrounded on both sides by romantic Spanish colonial-style buildings originally constructed for the 1915–16 Panama-California Exposition. Today, these buildings – ornamented with beaux-arts and baroque flourishes – house many of the park's museums and gardens. The original exposition halls were mostly constructed out of stucco, chicken wire, plaster, hemp and horsehair, and were meant to be temporary. They proved so popular that, over the years, they have been gradually replaced with durable concrete replicas.

To see it all would take several days, so plan ahead. Many of the 15 museums are closed Monday, and several per week (on a rotating basis) are free Tuesday.

For a good park map, stop by the **Balboa Park Information Center** (Map p434; ☎619-239-0512; www.balboapark.org; 1549 El Prado; ⌚9:30am-4:30pm) in the House of Hospitality. Helpful staff here sell the **Passport to Balboa Park** (single entry to 14 park museums for 1 wk adult/child $45/24) and the **Stay-for-the-Day Pass** (your choice of 5 museums in the same day for $35).

Balboa Park is easily reached from downtown on bus 7 along Park Blvd. By car, Park Blvd provides easy access to free parking lots near most exhibits. The free Balboa Park Tram loops through the main areas of the park, although you don't really need it – most

SAN DIEGO FOR CHILDREN

San Diego Zoo From pandas to koalas, flamingos to Elephant Odyssey, this is paws-down the best zoo in America (p429).

SeaWorld Look for Shamu and pals frolicking, penguins playing and specials and combo tickets to keep your expenses down (p438).

San Diego Zoo Safari Park Journey to Africa without leaving North San Diego County (p428).

Birch Aquarium La Jolla Aquarium that's as entertaining as it is educational, thanks to the Scripps Institute of Oceanography (p441).

Balboa Park After exploring the zoo, spend an additional day at one of the nation's best collections of museums. The Reuben H Fleet Science Center (with IMAX theater), Model Railroad Museum and Natural History Museum are all tailor-made for kids, the Marie Hitchcock Puppet Theater and Automotive Museum will appeal to particular audiences, and the plazas, fountains and gardens offer plenty of open space for children of all ages to let off some steam.

Mission and Pacific Beaches Teenagers will be in their element among the array of surfers, bikers, 'bladers and buff bods. Alternatively, go kayaking or ride a paddle wheeler on Mission Bay (p439).

USS Midway Museum Board this decommissioned aircraft carrier and gain an appreciation for our men and women in uniform (p426).

WORTH A TRIP

SAN DIEGO ZOO SAFARI PARK

How close can you get to the animals at this 1800-acre **open-range zoo** (☎760-747-8702; www.sandiegozoo.org; 15500 San Pasqual Valley Rd, Escondido; general admission incl tram adult/child $40/30; ⊙opens 9am, closing times vary; 👪) just 30 miles northeast of downtown? Consider this sign near the Lowlands Gorilla Habitat: 'In gorilla society prolonged eye contact is not only impolite, but it's considered a threat. Please respect the social signals of our gorillas and do not stare at them directly.' Seems we're so close we need to be reminded of our manners. But the sign is indicative of the experience here, where protecting and preserving wild animals and their habitats – while educating guests in a soft-handed manner – is the primary goal.

For a minisafari, hop aboard The Journey into Africa biodiesel tram for a drive through the world's second-largest continent. Sit on the left-hand side for slightly better views of the rhinos, giraffes, ostriches and other herbivores (by law, predators can't share space with prey). To enjoy close-up views of big cats, follow signs to the 33,000 sq ft Lion Camp and the Safari Walk Backcountry – and pray there's not a park-disrupting earthquake. Combination tickets with the San Diego Zoo are $76/56.

And for the wildlife lover who has everything? Book the **Roar & Snore** (☎619-718-3000; tickets adult/child $180/150; ⊙seasonal) camping experience on a hilltop where families sleep in canvas tents overlooking the East African–style plains and their wild inhabitants.

To get to the park take the freeway to the Via Rancho Parkway exit, turn right and continue to San Pasqual Rd. Turn right and follow signs to the park. Parking costs $10. For bus information contact **North San Diego County Transit District** (☎619-233-3004, from northern San Diego 800-266-6883; www.gonctd.com).

attractions are within an easy stroll of each other.

California Building & Museum of Man — MUSEUM

From the west, El Prado passes under an archway and into an area called the California Quadrangle, with the **Museum of Man** (Map p434; ☎619-239-2001; www.museumofman.org; Plaza de California; adult/child 3-12yr/youth 13-17yr/senior $12.50/5/8/10; ⊙10am-4:30pm) on its northern side. This was the main entrance for the 1915 exposition, and the building was said to be inspired by the churrigueresque church of Tepotzotlán near Mexico City. California Building's single tower, sometimes called the **Tower of California**, is richly decorated with blue and yellow tiles, and has become a symbol of San Diego itself. Inside, the museum specializes in anthropology, with a focus on Native American cultures, particularly those in the American Southwest.

San Diego Zoo — ZOO

(Map p434; ☎619-231-1515; www.sandiegozoo.org; 2920 Zoo Dr; adult/child with guided bus tour & aerial tram ride $40/30; ⊙opens 9am, closing times vary; 👪) If it slithers, crawls, stomps, swims, leaps or flies, chances are you'll find it in this world-famous zoo in northern Balboa Park. Since its opening in 1916, the zoo has also pioneered ways to house and display animals that mimic their natural habitat, leading to a revolution in zoo design and, so the argument goes, to happier animals. In its efforts to re-create those habitats, the zoo has also become one of the country's great botanical gardens. Experts trick San Diego's near-desert climate to yield everything from bamboo to eucalyptus to Hawaiian koa. The plants don't just provide pleasant cover for cages and fences; many are grown specifically to feed the zoo's more finicky eaters.

Today, the zoo is home to thousands of animals representing 800-plus species in a beautifully landscaped setting. Perennial favorite **Polar Bear Plunge** (just remodeled) wows crowds with up-close, underwater views of the bears through thick glass walls. Other hotspots are **Elephant Odyssey** and **Panda Canyon**, where a live narrator shares facts about pandas at the outdoor viewing area here and, more importantly, keeps the line moving.

Arboreal orangutans and siamangs peacefully coexist in the **Lost Forest.** Don't miss the vast **Scripps Aviary** and **Owens Rain Forest Aviary**, where carefully placed feeders (and remarkably fearless birds) allow for close-up viewing. To note: if you didn't like Hitchcock's *The Birds*, the aviaries might be

Downtown San Diego

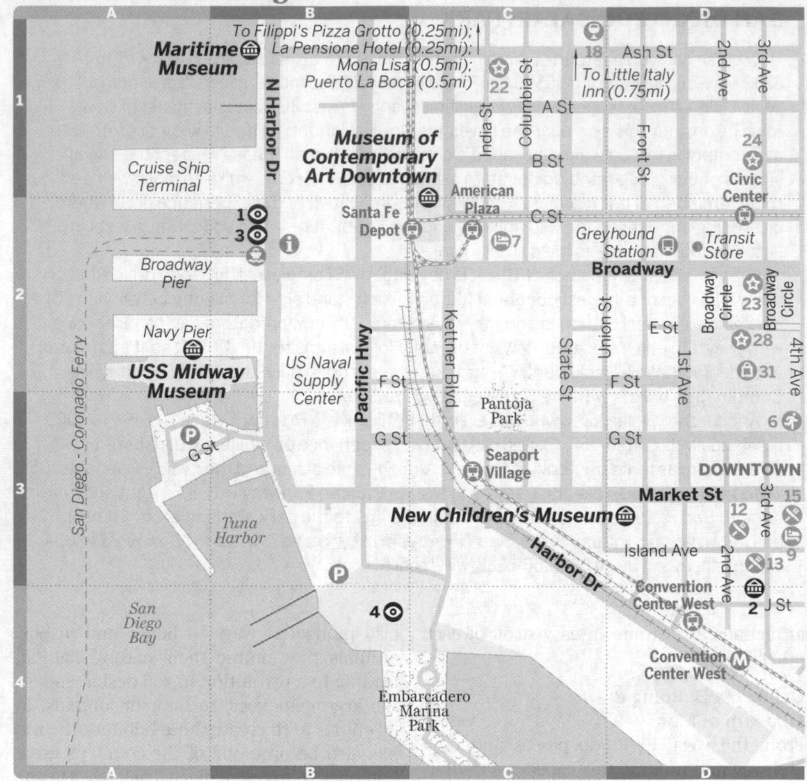

a less than enjoyable experience. The koalas in the **Outback** have proved so popular that Australians may be surprised to find them an unofficial symbol of San Diego. Less cuddly is the Komodo dragon in the reptile house, an Indonesian lizard that grows up to 10ft long.

At **Discovery Outpost**, youngsters can pet small critters and watch animal shows. Visitors of all ages will enjoy viewing 'zoo babies,' the park's newest arrivals.

Arrive early, when the animals are most active. There's a large, free parking lot off Park Blvd that starts filling fast right at opening time. Write down where you parked, as it can be confusing at the end of the day. Bus 7 will get you there from downtown. If you would like to leave the zoo and return, staff will stamp your hand. If you're not in a hurry, take the 35-minute double-decker bus tour first thing in the morning to get oriented. You'll also pick up intriguing facts about the animals – grizzlies can run the length of a football field in six seconds!

San Diego Natural History Museum MUSEUM

(Map p434; ☎619-232-3821; www.sdnhm.org; 1788 El Prado; adult/child/senior $17/11/15; ⏲10am-5pm; 👪) Seventy-five million years of SoCal fossils are the subject of one of the museum's newer permanent exhibits, Fossil Mysteries, which opened at the museum in 2006. Ongoing and upcoming exhibits cover climate change in polar regions and the ancient bond between horses and humans. At the time of writing, the museum had just received a $7 million state grant to build a permanent exhibit about the natural habitats of southern California.

San Diego Air & Space Museum MUSEUM

(Map p434; ☎619-234-8291; www.sandiegoairandspace.org; 2001 Pan American Plaza; adult/child/student & senior $16.50/6/13.50; ⏲10am-5:30pm

Jun-Aug, to 4:30pm Sep-May) One look at the banged-up silver pod inside the rotunda of this museum, at the end of Pan American Plaza, and you'll be glad you chose not to become an astronaut. The pod, known as Gumdrop, is the Apollo 9 command module used in a 1969 mission to test the lunar module before the first moon landing. Exhibits here trace the history of aviation, providing plenty of close-up views of planes with dangerous names – Flying Tiger, Cobra and Skyhawk – plus a few reproductions. Moon rocks and a space suit are also cool.

San Diego Museum of Art MUSEUM
(Map p434; ☎619-232-7931; www.sdmart.org; 1450 El Prado, Plaza de Panama; adult/child/senior $12/4.50/9; ⏲10am-5pm Tue-Sat, noon-5pm Sun, to 9pm Thu Jun-Sep) The building's architect, San Diegan William Templeton Johnson, chose the 16th-century Spanish plateresque style, which gets its name from heavy ornamentation that resembles decorated silverwork. The permanent collection holds a number of paintings by European masters (a few of the Spanish old masters are represented by sculptures on the building's facade), as well as noteworthy American landscape paintings and a fine collection of Asian art. The **Sculpture Garden** has pieces by Alexander Calder and Henry Moore. Check the website to see if a 'Cocktail & Culture' night is coming up – the evening event ($15) features cocktails, DJs, and a pre-tour of upcoming exhibits.

FREE **Timken Museum of Art** MUSEUM
(Map p434; ☎619-239-5548; www.timkenmuseum.org; 1500 El Prado; ⏲10am-4:30pm Tue-Sat, from 1:30pm Sun) It's not just the impressive collection of European old masters that makes the Timken stand out from its Balboa Park peers. The Timken is special because its simple exterior stands in bold contrast to the park's ubiquitous Spanish colonial style. It's also free. Paintings are from the Putnam Foundation collection and include works by Europeans Rembrandt, Rubens, El Greco, Cézanne and Pissarro, and Americans John Singleton Copley and Eastman Johnson.

Balboa Park Gardens GARDENS
(Map p434) Balboa Park is home to nine gardens, most clustered just south of El Prado. The **Alcazar Garden**, a formal Spanish-style garden, is tucked in a courtyard across from the Old Globe, south of El Prado, while the **Palm Canyon**, which has more than 50 species of palms, is a short stroll south. For a tranquil stroll or a bit of meditation, the **Japanese Friendship Garden** (☎619-232-2721; www.niwa.org; adult/student & senior $4/3; ⏲10am-4pm Tue-Sun, to 5pm in summer), just north of Spreckels Organ Pavilion, is a convenient retreat. A short path winds past a koi pond, rippling water and the Exhibit House with a glass-walled meditation room overlooking the Zen Garden.

Spreckels Organ Pavilion LANDMARK
(Map p434) South of Plaza de Panama, an extravagantly curved colonnade provides shelter for one of the world's largest outdoor organs. Donated by the Spreckels family of sugar fortune and fame, the pipe organ – which has more than 4500 pipes – came with the stipulation that San Diego must always have an official organist. Free concerts are held at 2pm every Sunday.

Downtown San Diego

Top Sights
- Maritime Museum ... B1
- Museum of Contemporary Art Downtown ... C1
- New Children's Museum ... D3
- USS Midway Museum ... A2

Sights
1. Hornblower Cruises ... B2
2. San Diego Chinese Historical Museum ... D4
3. San Diego Harbor Excursion ... B2
4. Seaport Village ... B4
5. William Heath Davis House ... E3

Activities, Courses & Tours
6. Another Side of San Diego ... D3

Sleeping
7. 500 West Hotel ... C2
8. HI San Diego Downtown Hostel ... E3
9. Horton Grand Hotel ... D3
10. Hotel Indigo ... F3
11. USA Hostels San Diego ... E3

Eating
12. Café 222 ... D3
13. Candelas ... D3
14. Hodad's ... F2
15. La Puerta ... D3
16. Oceanaire Seafood Room ... E4

Drinking
17. Altitude Sky Lounge ... E4
18. Extraordinary Desserts ... C1
19. Star Bar ... E2
20. Tipsy Crow ... E2
21. Wine Steals East Village ... E4

Entertainment
22. Anthology ... C1
23. Arts Tix ... D2
24. Civic Theatre ... D1
25. Croce's Restaurant & Jazz Bar ... E2
26. Gaslamp 15 ... E3
27. Petco Park ... F4
- San Diego Opera ... (see 24)
28. San Diego Repertory Theatre ... D2
29. San Diego Symphony ... E1

Shopping
30. Le Travel Store ... E3
31. Westfield Horton Plaza ... D2

Reuben H Fleet Science Center MUSEUM
(Map p434; ☎619-238-1233; www.rhfleet.org; 1875 El Prado; adult/child & senior $10/8.75; ⏰10am-varies; 👪) Family-oriented hands-on museum and **Imax theater** (incl Science Center adult/child $14:50/11.75). The exhibits at this hands-on science center include the energy-focused So Watt! and the galaxy-minded Origins in Space, where colorful Hubble images of colliding galaxies are particularly mesmerizing.

Mingei International Museum MUSEUM
(Map p434; ☎619-239-0003; www.mingei.org; 1439 El Prado; adult/child/senior $7/4/5; ⏰10am-4pm Tue-Sun) Exhibits folk art from around the globe; don't miss the lovely museum store here.

Museum of Photographic Arts MUSEUM
(Map p434; ☎619-238-7559; www.mopa.org; 1649 El Prado; adult/child/senior $8/free/6; ⏰10am-5pm Tue-Sun) Exhibits fine-art photography and hosts an ongoing film series.

San Diego Model Railroad Museum MUSEUM
(Map p434; ☎619-696-0199; www.sdmrm.org; 1649 El Prado; adult/senior/student $7/6/3; ⏰11am-4pm Tue-Fri, 11am-5pm Sat & Sun; 👪) One of the largest of its kind with brilliantly 'landscaped' train sets.

San Diego Automotive Museum MUSEUM
(Map p434; ☎619-231-2886; www.sdautomuseum.org; 2080 Pan-American Plaza; adult/child/senior $8/4/6; ⏰10am-5pm) It's all about polished chrome and cool tailfins at this museum.

OLD TOWN

In 1769 Padre Junípero Serra and Gaspar de Portola established the first Spanish settlement in California on Presidio Hill, overlooking the valley of the San Diego River. Spanish soldiers built adobe homes and started families at the southwestern base of the hill, and in 1821 the community, with 600 citizens, became the first official civilian Spanish settlement – called a pueblo – in California. It remained the city center until a devastating fire in 1872, after which the city's main body moved to the downtown.

Today, this area below Presidio Hill is called Old Town, and it presents life as it was between 1821 and 1872. Although it is neither very old (most of the buildings are reconstructions), nor exactly a town (more like a leafy suburb), it's a more-or-less faithful copy of San Diego's original nucleus, offering a pedestrian plaza surrounded by historic buildings, shops, a number of restaurants and cafes, and a good opportunity to explore San Diego's early days.

The Old Town Transit Center, on the trolley line off Taylor St just east of Congress St at the western edge of Old Town, is a stop for the *Coaster* commuter train, the San Diego Trolley (blue and green lines) and buses. Old Town Trolley tours stop southeast of the plaza on Twiggs St.

Old Town State Historic Park visitor center MUSEUM

(☎619-220-5422; www.parks.ca.gov; Robinson-Rose House, 4002 Wallace St; ⏰10am-5pm; P) At the western end of the Plaza de las Armas close to the entrance of the Old Town State Historic Park. It houses memorabilia and books about the era as well as a diorama depicting the pueblo in 1872. If you're really interested in the historical background, take a guided tour, which leaves from the visitors center at 11am and 2pm. A row of small, historical-looking buildings (only one is authentically old) line the southern border of the plaza and some house souvenir and gift shops. There's plenty of free parking next to the Old Town Transit Center, about a block away.

Whaley House HISTORICAL BUILDING

(☎619-297-7511; www.whaleyhouse.org; 2476 San Diego Ave; adult/child/senior $6/4/5; ⏰10am-9:30pm Jun-Aug, 10am-5pm Mon & Tue, 10am-9:30pm Thu-Sat Sep-May) We can't guarantee what you'll see at this lovely Victorian home (and the city's oldest brick building), two blocks northeast of the Old Town perimeter. It's served as a courthouse, theater and private residence, but that's not the cool part. What's intriguing is that the house was *officially* certified as haunted by the US Department of Commerce. Guides here claim ghostly encounters occur even during the day, from observing figures with no faces to hearing talking behind them (when no one's there) to learning that a visitor's camera batteries have drained while in the house. Ask the informative guides to share their stories.

Presidio Hill PARK

(Map p427) The walk from Old Town east along Mason St to the top of Presidio Hill rewards you with excellent views of San Diego Bay and Mission Valley – just don't depend on the most horribly marked trail in all of California to get you there! At the end of Mason St, if you obey the arrow pointing left, you'll follow a series of historic trail markers that *supposedly* end up at the Serra Museum. If you follow the arrow pointing up Presidio Hill, turn left at the dirt trail at the top and you might stumble upon the **Fort Stockton Memorial**. American forces occupied the hill in 1846, during the Mexican-American War, and named it for American commander Robert Stockton. A flagpole, cannon, some plaques and earthen walls form the memorial. If you turn right at the top of the hill, the path leads to Presidio Dr. Follow it to the **El Charro Statue**, a bicentennial gift to the city from Mexico depicting a Mexican cowboy on horseback. Nothing remains of the original Presidio structures.

Junípero Serra Museum MUSEUM

(☎619-232-6203; www.sandiegohistory.org; 2727 Presidio Dr; adult/child/student & senior $6/2/4; ⏰10am-5pm Sat & Sun, varying hours Mon-Fri; P) A Spanish colonial–style structure designed by William Templeton Johnson in 1929. The museum has a small but interesting collection of artifacts and pictures from the mission and rancho periods.

Mission Basilica San Diego de Alcalá MISSION

(Map p427; ☎619-281-8449; www.missionsandiego.com; 10818 San Diego Mission Rd; adult/child/student & senior $3/1/2; ⏰9am-4:45pm) Though the first California mission was established on Presidio Hill near Old Town, Padre Junípero Serra decided in 1773 to move upriver several miles, closer to a better water supply and more arable land. In 1784 the missionaries built a solid adobe and timber church, but it was destroyed by an earthquake in 1803. The church was promptly rebuilt, and at least some of it still stands on a slope overlooking Mission Valley. With the end of the mission system in the 1830s, the buildings were turned over to the Mexican government. The buildings were later used as US army barracks before falling into disrepair. Some accounts say that they were reduced to a facade and a few crumbling walls by the 1920s. Extensive reconstruction began in 1931, and the pretty white church

Balboa Park & Hillcrest

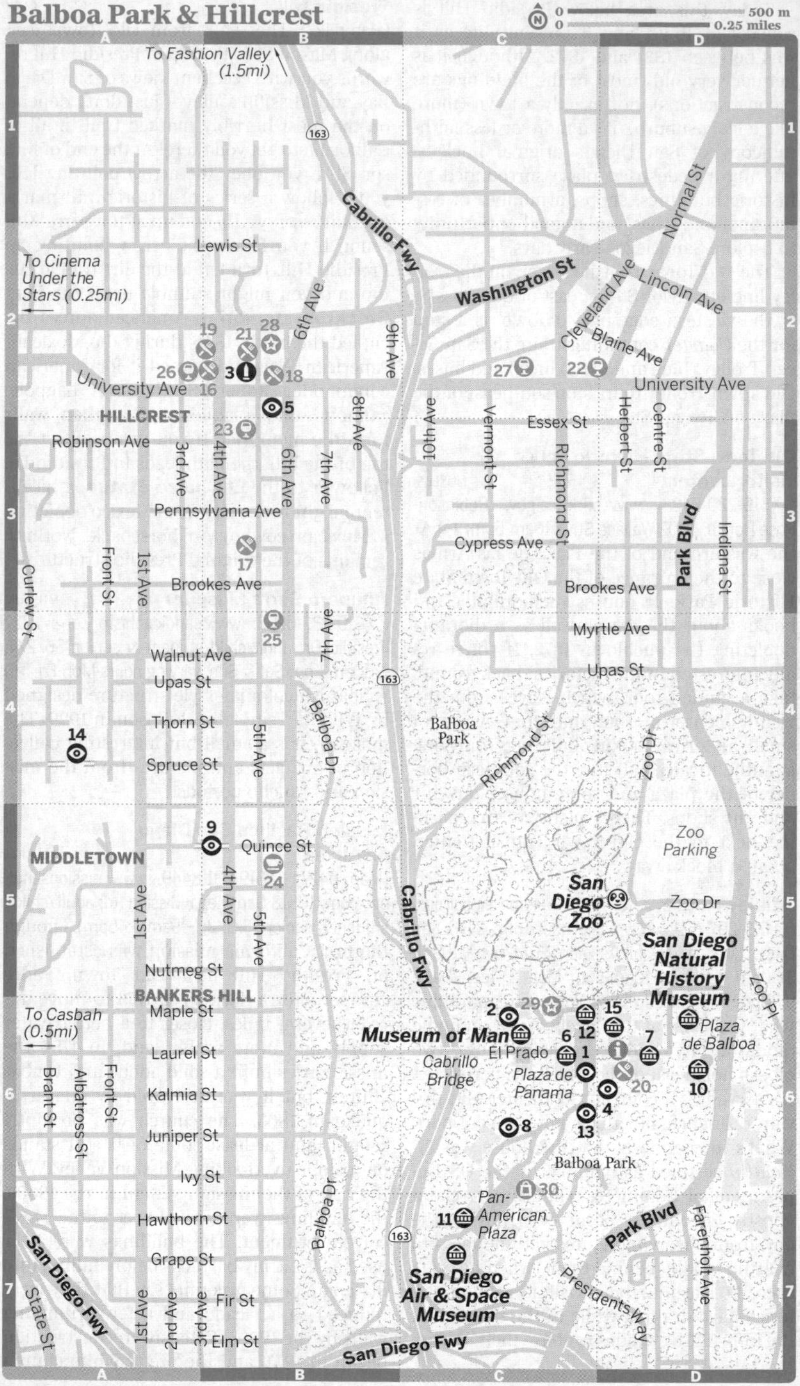

Balboa Park & Hillcrest

Top Sights
- Museum of Man C6
- San Diego Air & Space Museum C7
- San Diego Natural History Museum D6
- San Diego Zoo D5

Sights
1. Alcazar Garden C6
2. California Building C6
3. Hillcrest Gateway B2
4. Japanese Friendship Garden D6
5. Kahn Building B2
6. Mingei International Museum C6
7. Museum of Photographic Arts D6
8. Palm Canyon C6
9. Quince St Bridge B5
10. Reuben H Fleet Science Center D6
11. San Diego Automotive Museum C7
- San Diego Model Railroad Museum .... (see 7)
12. San Diego Museum of Art C6
13. Spreckels Organ Pavilion C6
14. Spruce St Footbridge A4
15. Timken Museum of Art D6

Eating
16. Bread & Cie B2
17. Hash House a Go Go B3
18. Khyber Pass B2
19. Kous Kous B2
20. Prado D6
21. Saigon on Fifth B2
- Tea Pavilion .... (see 4)

Drinking
22. Baja Betty's C2
23. Brass Rail B3
24. Extraordinary Desserts B5
25. Nunu's Cocktail Lounge B4
26. Urban Mo's A2
27. Wine Steals C2

Entertainment
28. Landmark Hillcrest Cinemas B2
29. Old Globe Theater C6

Shopping
30. United Nations International Gift Shop C6

and the buildings you see now are the result of the thorough restoration.

Inside, a bougainvillea-filled garden offers a tranquil spot for meditation, and nearby tile panels that depict the crucifixion are moving in their simplicity. In the museum, a glass case holds items unearthed at the site, ranging from old spectacles to buttons to medicine bottles. In fact, don't be surprised if you see an archaeologist sifting through the dirt just outside. Look for old photographs and artifacts set up beside their dig site – currently across from the visitors center – when they're working. Come at sunset for glowing views over the valley and the ocean beyond.

The mission is two blocks north of I-8 via the Mission Gorge Rd exit just east of I-15. After exiting, take a left just past Roberto's at San Diego Mission Rd (on the right it's called Twain Ave) and follow it to the mission. You can take the trolley to the Mission stop, walk two blocks north and turn right onto San Diego Mission Rd.

UPTOWN

Just east of Old Town, between Mission Valley to the north and downtown to the south, is Uptown. As you head north from downtown along the west side of Balboa Park, you arrive at a series of bluffs that, in the late 19th century, became San Diego's most fashionable neighborhood – only those who owned a horse-drawn carriage could afford to live here. Known as Bankers Hill after some of the wealthy residents, these upscale heights had unobstructed views of the bay and Point Loma before I-5 went up.

Spruce Street Footbridge & Quince Street Bridge BRIDGE

(Map p434) As you head northward toward Hillcrest consider a detour across the 375ft **Spruce Street Footbridge**. Note that the 1912 suspension bridge, built over a deep canyon between Front St and Brant St, wriggles beneath your feet. But don't worry; it was designed that way. The nearby **Quince Street Bridge**, between 4th Ave and 3rd Ave, is a wood-trestle structure built in 1905 and refurbished in 1988 after community activists vigorously protested its slated demolition.

HILLCREST

Just up from the northwestern corner of Balboa Park, you hit **Hillcrest** (Map p434), the heart of Uptown. The neighborhood began its life in the early 20th century as a

WORTH A TRIP

NORTH PARK

The hip-right-now neighborhood of North Park, a gentrifying, Bohemian-light enclave just east of Hillcrest, is getting press for its eco-friendly dining and drinking scene. The big North Park sign at 30th and University Aves marks the center of the action. Carnivores with a conscience flock to **The Linkery** (www.thelinkery.com; 3794 30th St; mains $10-25; ⌚5-11pm Mon-Thu, noon-midnight Fri, 11am-midnight Sat, 11am-10pm Sun) for a vast selection of local microbrews and a daily changing menu of housemade sausages and hand-cured meats from sustainably raised animals. Nearby, **Alchemy** (www.alchemysandiego.com; 1503 30th St; mains $13-25; ⌚4pm-midnight Sun-Thu, 4pm-1am Fri & Sat, 10am-2pm Sat & Sun) features a spin-the-globe menu of local ingredients from small plates – try the Parmesan frites with garlic aioli – in an art-filled blondwood room.

For something sweeter, there's **Heaven Sent Desserts** (www.heavensentdesserts.com; 3001 University Ave; ⌚11am-11pm Tue-Thu, to midnight Fri & Sat, to 10pm Sun) for tarts, tiramisu and chunky chocolate chip cookies. For a great indie coffeehouse, walk a block west to high-ceilinged **Caffé Calabria** (www.caffecalabria.com; 3933 30th St; ⌚6am-3pm Mon & Tue, to 11pm Wed-Fri, 7am-11pm Sat & Sun), which has freshly roasted coffee and wood fire-baked Neapolitan pizzas. You'll see North Park's energy and diversity if you spend an hour or two sitting at one of the cafe's sunny patio tables.

modest middle-class suburb. Today, it's San Diego's most bohemian district, with a decidedly urban feel, despite the suburban visuals. It's also the headquarters of the city's gay and lesbian community. University Ave and 5th Ave are lined with coffeehouses, fashion-forward thrift shops and excellent restaurants in all price ranges.

For a tour, begin at the **Hillcrest Gateway** (Map p434), which arches over University Ave at 5th Ave. On 5th Ave between University Ave and Washington St is the multiplex **Landmark Hillcrest Cinemas** (Map p434) and lots of restaurants and shops. Go east on University Ave to see the 1919 **Kahn Building** (Map p434) at No 535; it is an original Hillcrest commercial building with a kitschy facade. Then head south on 5th Ave to find a variety of cafes, friendly gay bars, vintage clothing shops and independent bookstores, many with a good selection of nonmainstream publications.

CORONADO

In 1885 Coronado Island wasn't much more than a scrappy patch of land sitting off the coast of what's now downtown San Diego. Home to jackrabbits and the occasional tycoon that rowed over to shoot them, Coronado was not a postcard-worthy destination. But what a difference three years makes. In February 1888, the Hotel del Coronado – at the time the largest hotel west of the Mississippi – welcomed its very first guests. Today, the hotel and its stunning surroundings are the primary reasons to visit this well-manicured community.

The city of **Coronado** (Map p427) is now connected to the mainland by the graceful 2.12-mile Coronado Bay Bridge (opened in 1969), as well as by a narrow spit of sand known as the Silver Strand, which runs south to Imperial Beach and connects Coronado to the mainland. The large North Island US Naval Air Station occupies a northern tip of the island.

The **Coronado Visitors Center** (Map p427; ☎619-437-8788; www.coronadovisitorcenter.com; 1100 Orange Ave; ⌚9am-5pm Mon-Fri, 10am-5pm Sat & Sun) conducts a walking tour ($12), starting from the **Glorietta Bay Inn** (Map p427; 1630 Glorietta Blvd), near Silver Strand Blvd, at 11am Tuesday, Thursday and Saturday. The visitors center also has information on special-interest tours (Coronado Tree Tour, Coronado by gondola, etc). We recommend picking up the pamphlet for a self-guided tour of Coronado's public artworks.

The **Coronado Historical Assocation**, housed in the same space as the visitors center, runs 90-minute **tours** (☎619-437-8788; $15; ⌚10:30am Tue & Fri, 2pm Sat & Sun) of the historic Hotel del Coronado. Reserve ahead.

Hotel del Coronado HISTORIC BUILDING

(1500 Orange Ave) This iconic hotel, familiar today with its whitewashed exterior, red conical towers, cupolas and balconies, sprang from the vision of two of the aforementioned jackrabbit hunters, Elisha Babcock and HL Story, who bought the island for $110,000. They cooked up the idea of building a grand hotel as a gimmick to entice people to buy parcels of land on the island. Coronado land sales were a booming success and construction began on the hotel in 1887. Craftsmanship and innovation were strong points – the Del was the first hotel to have electric lights – as was sheer determination to finish it. The hotel had its grand opening, with 399 completed rooms, in February 1888 (although work on the property continued for two more years). Though the hotel was a success, Babcock and Story couldn't keep up with the bills and by 1900 millionaire John D Spreckels bankrolled the island into one of the most fashionable getaways on the west coast.

Guests have included 11 US presidents and world royalty – pictures are displayed in the history gallery downstairs from the lobby. The hotel, affectionately known as The Del, achieved its widest exposure in the 1959 movie *Some Like It Hot,* which earned its lasting association with Marilyn Monroe. Today, the hotel still exudes a snappy, look-at-me exuberance that makes guests and day-trippers alike feel as though they've been invited to the jazziest party in town.

Coronado Ferry FERRY
(Map p427; ☎619-234-4111; www.sdhe.com; each way $4.25; ⏰9am-10pm) Hourly ferry shuttles between the Broadway Pier on the Embarcadero to the Coronado Ferry Landing at the foot of First Street, where **Bikes & Beyond** (☎619-435-7180; rental per 1 2 hrs $25; ⏰9am-8pm, call for seasonal hours) rents bicycles.

POINT LOMA

Cabrillo National Monument MONUMENT
(Map p427; ☎619-557-5450; www.nps.gov/cabr; per car $5, per person $3; ⏰9am-5pm; P) For spectacular views of downtown San Diego, Coronado and San Diego Bay, take a half-day to visit on the southern tip of Point Loma, the handily placed peninsula that provides shelter to the bay. This hilltop monument is also the best place in San Diego to see the gray whale migration (January to March) from land. Historically, this is the spot where Portuguese conquistador Juan Rodriguez Cabrillo landed in 1542 – making him the first European to step on the United States' western shores. A small museum highlights his travels. The 1854 **Old Point Loma Lighthouse**, atop the point, is furnished with typical lighthouse furniture from the 1880s. Displays reveal the lonely, hard life (endless maintenance, sleepless nights) of the lighthouse keeper. Gearheads will want to check out the massive 5ft 2in 3rd Order Fresnel lens weighing 1985lb. On the ocean side of the point, drive or walk down to the **tide pools** to look for anemones and starfish.

OCEAN BEACH

In Ocean Beach, the beach bums and the restaurants are a little scruffier than those in coastal communities to the north. And the pier? It just doesn't seem to care that it's not all that photogenic. But therein lies the charm of this Bohemian neighborhood just south of I-8 and Mission Beach. You can get tattooed, shop for antiques, and walk into a restaurant shirtless and barefoot and nobody cares. You can also enjoy the best cheap eats in town and maybe grab a nice sunset or a little surfing. All with a minimum of surf-god pretension.

Newport Ave, which runs perpendicular from the beach, is the main drag, passing surf shops, bars, music stores, java joints, and used-clothing and secondhand furniture stores. The street ends a block from the half-mile-long **Ocean Beach Pier** (Map p438), an excellent spot for fishing or a breath of fresh air.

Just north of the pier, near the end of Newport Ave, is the central beach scene, with volleyball courts and sunset barbecues. A bit further north is **Dog Beach** (Map p438), where Fido can run unleashed around the marshy area where the San Diego River meets the sea. A few blocks south of the pier is **Sunset Cliffs Park**, a great spot to watch the sun dipping below the horizon.

There are good surf breaks at the cliffs and, to the south, off Point Loma. Under the pier, the brave slalom the pilings. If you're new to the area, beware of the rips and currents, which can be deadly.

MISSION BAY

While San Diego is famous generally as a watersports mecca, the actual heart of the sailing, windsurfing and kayaking scene is Mission Bay, shimmering in sun-dappled glory at the end of the San Diego River just west of the I-5.

In the 18th century, the mouth of the river formed a shallow bay when the river flowed, and a marshy swamp when it didn't; the Spanish called it False Bay. After WWII, a combination of civic vision and coastal engineering turned the swamp into a 7 sq mile playground, with 27 miles of shoreline and 90 acres of public parks. With financing from public bonds and expertise from the Army Corps of Engineers, the river was channeled to the sea, the bay was dredged, and millions of tons of sludge were used to build islands, coves and peninsulas. A quarter of the land created has been leased to hotels, boatyards and other businesses, providing ongoing city revenue. Today, Mission Bay Park, at 4235 acres, is the largest man-made aquatic park in the US.

SeaWorld AQUARIUM, AMUSEMENT PARK

(Map p427; ☎800-257-4268, 619-226-3901; www.seaworld.com/seaworld/ca; 500 SeaWorld Dr; adult/child 3-9yr $70/62; ⏲9am-10pm Jul–mid-Aug, to 11pm Fri-Sun, shorter hours rest of year; 👪) Along with the zoo, SeaWorld is one of San Diego's most popular attractions, and Shamu has become an unofficial mascot for the city itself (not to be a spoilsport, but for the record, several killer whales here perform under the name Shamu). SeaWorld has a shamelessly commercial feel, but it's undoubtedly entertaining and even educational. Its popularity means you should plan on long waits for rides, shows and exhibits during peak seasons.

SeaWorld's claim to fame is its live shows, which feature trained dolphins, seals, sea lions and killer whales. Current hits are **Blue Horizons**, a bird and dolphin extravaganza, and **One Ocean**, featuring Shamu and his killer whale amigos leaping, diving and gliding. At the time of writing, the aquatic (and acrobatic) show **Cirque de la Mer** was scoring rave reviews. There are also zoolike animal exhibits and a few amusement-park-style rides.

In **Penguin Encounter**, you'll smell the 250 tuxedoed show-offs before you see them. Here, penguins share a habitat that faithfully simulates Antarctic living conditions. Nearby, dozens of sharks glide overhead as you walk through a 57ft acrylic tube at **Shark Encounter**. Species include reef sharks and sand tiger sharks, some impressively large. Word of warning: the shark habitat gets very crowded.

Amusement-park-style rides – there aren't too many – include **Wild Arctic**, a simulated helicopter flight, and **Journey to Atlantis**, a combination flume ride and roller coaster that ends with a 60ft plunge – you'll get wet if you sit in the front seat.

Discount coupons are available, and you can find deals by buying tickets online, but

Mission Bay & the Beaches

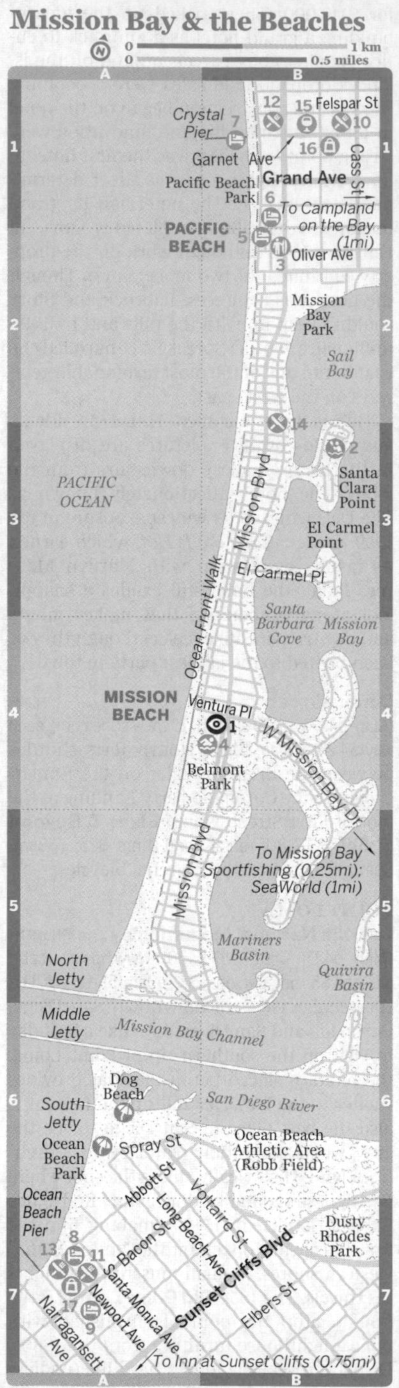

Mission Bay & the Beaches

the extras add up – parking costs $14 and food is expensive ($2.79 for a regular soda). Ways to get the best value: a re-entry stamp (you can go out for a break and return later – good during late-opening hours in summer) or buy a combination ticket. Check the SeaWorld website for promotions.

The park is easy to find by car – take Sea World Dr off I-5 less than a mile north of where it intersects with I-8. Take bus 9 from downtown. Tickets sales end 90 minutes before closing time.

MISSION BEACH & PACIFIC BEACH

If you want to enjoy a quintessential California beach day, the 3 mile-long swath of sand between the South Mission Jetty and Pacific Beach Point is the best place. The wide beach fills fast on summer weekends with determined sun-worshippers, families and surfers.

Planning-wise, be prepared for 'June Gloom' cloud cover early in the summer, when a stubborn marine layer typically hides the sun and makes June the least sunny month here.

Up in Pacific Beach (or PB) the activity spreads further inland, especially along **Garnet Ave** (Map p438), where hordes of 20-somethings toss back brews and gobble cheap tacos. It gets hoppin' on Taco Tuesdays. At the ocean end of Garnet Ave, **Crystal Pier** (Map p438) is worth a look. Built in the 1920s, it's home to San Diego's quirkiest hotel (p447), which consists of a cluster of Cape Cod–style cottages built out over the waves. Surfing is more demanding around Crystal Pier, where the waves are steep and fast.

Ocean Front Walk BOARDWALK

(Map p438) The beachfront boardwalk teems year-round with joggers, in-line skaters, cyclists and a few brave dog-walkers. It's a primo spot for people-watching. One block off the beach, Mission Blvd, which runs up and down the coast, consists of block after block of surf shops, burger joints, beach bars and '60s-style motels. The surf is a beach break, good for beginners, bodyboarders and bodysurfers.

Belmont Park AMUSEMENT PARK

(Map p438; ☎858-488-1549; www.belmontpark.com; admission free, rides $2-6, unlimited rides adult/child $27/16; ⊙from 11am; P 👪) The family-style amusement park in the heart of Mission Beach has been here since 1925. When the park was threatened with demolition in the mid-1990s, concerted community action saved the large indoor pool known as the **Plunge** (Map p438) and the classic wooden **Giant Dipper roller coaster** (Map p438; per person $6; ⊙from 11am), which might just shake the teeth right out of your mouth. Other rides include bumper cars, a tilt-a-whirl, a carousel and the popular FlowRider, a wave machine for simulated surfing.

Cheap Rentals BICYCLE RENTAL, WATER SPORTS

(☎858-488-9070; www.cheap-rentals.com; 3689 Mission Blvd) To get around, consider renting a bike or in-line skates. This place, at the corner of Santa Clara Pl, rents everything from bicycles, skates and baby joggers (all per hour/day $5/12) to surfboards ($15 per day) and kayaks ($40 per day); it also accepts advance reservations, crucial in summer for late sleepers.

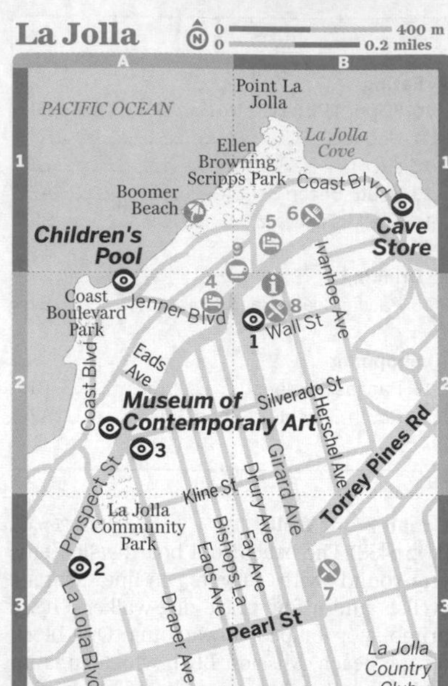

La Jolla

Top Sights

- Cave Store ... B1
- Children's Pool ... A2
- Museum of Contemporary Art ... A2

Sights

1 Athenaeum Music & Arts Library ... B2
2 Bishop's School ... A3
3 La Jolla Woman's Club ... A2

Sleeping

4 Grande Colonial Hotel ... A2
5 La Valencia ... B1

Eating

6 George's at the Cove ... B1
7 Harry's Coffee Shop ... B3
8 Whisknladle ... B2

Drinking

La Sala ... (see 5)
9 Living Room Coffeehouse ... B1

LA JOLLA

Locals like to say that the name La Jolla (la hoya) is derived from the Spanish for 'the jewel.' One look at the tidy parks, upscale boutiques and glitzy restaurants clustered downtown and the appropriateness of this explanation is immediately apparent. Some challenge this claim, however, saying that the indigenous people who lived in the area until the mid-19th century called it 'Mut la Hoya, la Hoya' – the place of many caves. It's this second explanation that's more intriguing to outdoor enthusiasts and fun-loving families because the sea caves, sandy coves and marine life here make it a fantastic place to kayak, dive, snorkel and tide-pool.

Technically part of San Diego, La Jolla feels like a world apart, both because of its radical affluence as well as its privileged location above San Diego's most photogenic stretch of coast. The community – generally stretching from Pacific Beach north past Torrey Pines to Del Mar – first became fashionable when Ellen Browning Scripps moved here in 1897. The newspaper heiress acquired much of the land along Prospect St, which she then donated to various community uses, including **Bishop's School** (Map p440; cnr Prospect St & La Jolla Blvd) and the **La Jolla Woman's Club** (Map p440; 715 Silverado St). She also hired Irving Gill to set the architectural tone – an elegant if unadorned Mediterranean style noted by its arches, colonnades, palm trees, red-tile roofs and pale stucco.

Bus 30 connects La Jolla to downtown via the Old Town Transit Center.

LA JOLLA VILLAGE & THE COAST

La Jolla Village, known locally as 'the Village,' sits atop a bluff lapped by the Pacific on three sides. There's little interaction between the compact downtown and the sea, although you can catch lovely glimpses of Pacific blue from a few of the fancy rooftop restaurants. The main thoroughfares, Prospect St and Girard Ave, are lined with boutiques, galleries and jewelry stores.

For a camera-worthy stroll, take the half-mile bluff-top path that winds above the shoreline a few blocks west of the Village. Near the path's western end is the **Children's Pool** (see boxed text, p443), off Coast Dr near Jenner Blvd. Here, a jetty funded by Ellen Browning Scripps protects the beach from big waves.

Continuing northeast, you'll reach Point La Jolla, at the path's eastern end, and **Ellen Browning Scripps Park** (Map p440), a tidy expanse of green lawns and palm trees. It's a great place to read, relax with your kids or watch the sunset. A short walk north leads to picnic tables and grills plus views of **La Jolla Cove** just below the path. This gem of a beach provides access to some of the best snorkeling around; it's also popular with rough-water swimmers.

Athenaeum Music & Arts Library LIBRARY
(Map p440; ☎858-454-5872; www.ljathenaeum.org; 1008 Wall St; ⏲10am-5:30pm Tue-Sat, to 8:30pm Wed; Ⓟ) Housed in a small but graceful Spanish renaissance structure near the intersection of Prospect St and Girard Ave, the library hosts small art exhibits and concerts. There's also a good selection of art and music books in the library plus a few used books (including current fiction) for sale.

Museum of Contemporary Art MUSEUM
(MCASD; Map p440; ☎858-454-3541; www.mcasd.org; 700 Prospect St; adult/student/senior $10/free/5; ⏲11am-5pm Thu-Tue, to 7pm third Thu each month, with free admission 5-7pm) The La Jolla branch of the small but excellent museum shows world-class exhibitions that rotate every six months. Originally designed by Irving Gill in 1916 as the home of Ellen Browning Scripps, the building was renovated by Philadelphia's postmodern architect Robert Venturi. Overall, MCASD holds more than 4000 works of art created after 1950 in its collection. Inside, the Krichman Family Gallery offers a superb view of the ocean below. Outside, Nancy Rubin's *Pleasure Point* sculpture bursts with boats – from kayaks to canoes to paddleboards. Tickets are good for one week at all museum locations.

San Diego-La Jolla Underwater Park Ecological Reserve DIVING, SNORKELING
Look for the white buoys offshore from Point La Jolla north to Scripps Pier that mark this protected zone with a variety of marine life, kelp forests, reefs and canyons (see p443). Waves have carved caves into the sandstone cliffs east of the cove.

Cave Store CAVE
(Map p440; ☎858-459-0746; www.cavestore.com; 1325 Coast Blvd; adult/child $4/3; ⏲10am-5pm) For a spooky mini-adventure, continue walking north on Coast Blvd. Here, 145 wooden steps descend a dank, man-made tunnel (completed in 1905) to the largest of the caves, Sunny Jim Cave. From its marine-ripe interior, you can watch kayakers paddling off-shore.

Windansea Beach BEACH
(Map p427) A popular, not-for-beginners surf spot, 2 miles south of downtown (take La Jolla Blvd south and turn west on Nautilus St). Locals here can be aggressive toward outsiders. If you brave their ire, you'll find that the surf's consistent peak – a powerful reef break – works best at medium to low tide. Immediately south at **Big Rock**, at the foot of Palomar Ave, is California's version of Hawaii's Pipeline, which has steep, hollow tubes. The name comes from the large chunk of reef protruding just offshore – a great spot for tide pooling at low tide.

LA JOLLA SHORES

Called 'the Shores,' this area northeast of La Jolla Cove is where La Jolla's cliffs meet the wide, sandy beaches that stretch north to Del Mar. To reach the **beach** (Map p427), take La Jolla Shores Dr north from Torrey Pines Rd and turn west onto Ave de la Playa. The waves here are gentle enough for beginner surfers, and kayakers can launch from the shore without much problem.

Some of the best beaches in the county are north of the Shores at **Torrey Pines City Beach** (Map p427). At extreme low tides (about twice a year), you can walk from the Shores north to Del Mar along the beach. The **Torrey Pines Glider Port** (Map p427) at the end of Torrey Pines Scenic Dr is the place for hang gliders and paragliders to launch themselves into the sea breezes that rise over the high cliffs. It's a beautiful sight – tandem flights are available if you can't resist trying it (p445). Below, **Black's Beach** (Map p427), is a storied clothing-optional venue – though bathing suits are technically required, most folks don't seem to know that; there's a gay section at the far (north) end.

Birch Aquarium AQUARIUM
(Map p427; ☎858-534-3474; http://aquarium.ucsd.edu; 2300 Exhibition Way; adult/child/student & senior $12/8.50/9; ⏲9am-5pm; Ⓟ👪) Off N Torrey Pines Rd, this aquarium has brilliant displays about the marine sciences and marine life. The **Hall of Fishes** has more than 60 fish tanks simulating marine environments from the Pacific Northwest to the tropics of Mexico and the Caribbean. Divers feed leopard sharks, garibaldi, sea bass and eels in the 70,000-gallon kelp tank during half-hour shows; check the website for times. The 13,000-gallon shark tank holds white-tip and black-tip reef sharks and others

native to tropical reef habitats. There's a small touch-tank tide pool in back.

From downtown San Diego and La Jolla, take bus 30.

FREE Salk Institute ARCHITECTURE

(Map p427; ☎858-453-4100 ext 1287; www.salk.edu; 10010 N Torrey Pines Rd; ⊙architectural tours noon-Mon-Fri, reservations required) Jonas Salk, the pioneer of polio prevention, founded the Salk Institute in 1960 for biological and biomedical research. San Diego County donated 27 acres of land, the March of Dimes provided financial support and Louis Kahn designed the building. Completed in 1965, it is a masterpiece of modern architecture, with its classically proportioned travertine marble plaza and cubist, mirror-glass laboratory blocks framing a perfect view of the Pacific. The Salk Institute attracts the best scientists to work in a research-only environment. The facilities have been expanded, with new laboratories designed by Jack McAllister, a follower of Kahn's work. Bus 101 follows N Torrey Pines Rd from the University Town Center (UTC) transit center.

Torrey Pines State Natural Reserve WILDLIFE RESERVE

(Map p427; ☎858-755-2063; www.torreypine.org; 12600 N Torrey Pines Rd; car $10; ⊙8am-dusk) Birders, whale-watchers, hikers and those seeking great coastal views will want to amble through this tree-studded reserve that preserves the last mainland stands of the Torrey pine *(Pinus torreyana),* a species adapted to sparse rainfall and sandy, stony soils that's only found here and on Santa Rosa Island in Channel Islands National Park. Steep sandstone gullies are eroded into wonderfully textured surfaces, and the views over the ocean and north to Oceanside are superb, especially at sunset. The reserve is on the Pacific Flyway, making it a popular pit stop for migrating birds.

The main access road, Torrey Pines Park Rd, off N Torrey Pines Rd (bus 101) at the reserve's northern end, winds its way up to a simple adobe – built as a lodge in 1922 by (drum roll) Ellen Browning Scripps – which is now a **visitors center** (⊙9am-6pm mid-March–Oct, to 4pm Nov–mid-Mar) – with displays on the local flora and fauna. Rangers lead nature walks from here at 10am and 2pm on weekends.

Admission is free if you enter on foot. Several walking trails wind through the reserve and down to the beach. For a good sampling of reserve highlights, plus good whale-watching spots, staff recommend the ⅔-mile Guy Fleming loop trail.

Torrey Pines Municipal Golf Course GOLF

(Map p427) Crowds swarmed the area for the historic, Tiger Woods–winning US Open golf tournament in June 2008. Located just north of the glider port, Torrey Pines is only the second public course to ever host the event.

University of California, San Diego UNIVERSITY

(UCSD; Map p427) The 1200-acre campus of the University of California San Diego was established in 1960 and now enrolls more than 22,000 undergraduates. Known for its math and science programs, the respected university lies on rolling coastal hills in a park-like setting, with many tall and fragrant eucalyptus trees shading the campus. Its most distinctive structure is the space-agey **Geisel Library**, a visually stunning upside-down pyramid of glass and concrete whose namesake, Theodor Geisel, is better known as Dr Seuss, creator of the *Cat in the Hat*. He and his wife, longtime residents of La Jolla, contributed substantially to the library. A collection of his drawings and books are displayed on the ground level in March.

For an engaging fusion of art and exercise, stroll the **Stuart Collection** of outdoor sculptures dotting the campus. Pick up the Stuart Collection brochure and map from the library's helpful information desk. From the eastern side of the library's 2nd level, an allegorical snake created by artist Alexis Smith winds around a native California plant garden, past an enormous marble copy of John Milton's *Paradise Lost*. Other works include Niki de Saint Phalle's *Sun God,* Bruce Nauman's *Vices & Virtues* (which spells out seven of each in huge neon letters), and a forest containing poem-reciting and music-singing trees. Most installations are near the Geisel Library.

The **UCSD bookstore**, located at the Price Center, has helpful staff and excellent stock that includes travel, religion, arts, sci-fi and California history. Inside the Mandell Weiss Center for the Performing Arts, the **La Jolla Playhouse** (☎858-550-1010; www.lajollaplayhouse.org) is known for high-quality productions.

The best access to campus is off La Jolla Village Dr or N Torrey Pines Rd (bus 30 from downtown). Pick up a campus map at Gil-

SEALS VS SWIMMERS

The **Children's Pool** (Map p440) was created in the early 1930s when the state deeded the area to the city with the proviso that it be used as a public park and children's pool. As part of the arrangement, Ellen Browning Scripps paid for a protective 300ft seawall. Then came the seals, drawing tourists but gradually nudging out swimmers. Animal rights groups want to protect the cove as a rookery while some swimmers and divers want the seals – whose presence raises bacteria levels in the water to unsafe levels – removed. In 2005 the California Superior Court ruled that the seals had to go. The US Appeals Court refused to hear an appeal by animal activists in 2008, and the California Supreme Court has done the same. In the last few years, it's been a constant battle between animal activists, City Council and the State Court – the State Court ordered the seals to be removed in 2009, then City Council called for the seals' habitat to be roped off, a temporary solution that was ended due to an insufficient budget. Activists keep up the fight, manning an information table near the pool's entrance. Visit www.savesandiegoseals.com to learn more.

man Dr Visitor Center. Parking is free on weekends. During the week, look for a metered spot just north of the library.

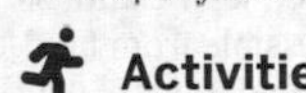

Activities

Surfing

San Diego has great surf spots for all skill levels, but the water can get crowded. Several spots, particularly Sunset Cliffs and Windansea, get especially territorial and you could get taunted unless you're an awesome surfer.

Fall brings the strong swells and offshore Santa Ana winds. In summer, swells come from the south and southwest, and in winter from the west and northwest. Spring brings more frequent onshore winds, but the surfing can still be good.

Beginners looking for classes and board rentals should try Mission or Pacific Beaches, where the waves are gentle. North of the Crystal Pier, Tourmaline Surfing Park (Map p427) is an especially good place to take your first strokes.

The best surf breaks, from south to north, are at Imperial Beach (south of Coronado, especially in winter); Point Loma (reef breaks, which are less accessible but less crowded; best in winter); Sunset Cliffs in Ocean Beach (a bit territorial); Pacific Beach; Big Rock (California's Pipeline); Windansea (hot reef break, best at medium to low tide; locals can be territorial); La Jolla Shores (beach break, best in winter); and Black's Beach (a fast, powerful wave). In North County (Map p458), there are breaks at Cardiff State Beach, San Elijo State Beach, Swami's, Carlsbad State Beach and Oceanside.

Bodysurfing is good at Coronado, Mission Beach, Pacific Beach and La Jolla Shores.

Pacific Beach Surf School SURFING
(Map p438; 858-373-1138; www.pacificbeachsurfschool.com; 4150 Mission Blvd, Suite 161; private/semi-private lessons per person $80/65) Learn to hang 10 at surf school or just rent a board and wetsuit (half-day $25) at San Diego's oldest surf shop.

Surf Diva SURFING
(858-454-8273; www.surfdiva.com; 2160 Avenida de la Playa) In La Jolla, the wonderful women here offer two-day weekend workshops for gals of all ages ($165 per person) and private classes for gals and guys ($60 per 90 minutes per person, price decreases with added students). They take newbies into the easygoing waves at nearby La Jolla Shores.

Diving & Snorkeling

Divers will find kelp beds, shipwrecks (including the *Yukon,* a WWII destroyer) and deep canyons just off the coast of San Diego County.

A number of commercial outfits teach scuba courses, sell or rent equipment, fill tanks and run boat trips to nearby wrecks and islands.

San Diego-La Jolla Underwater Park Ecological Reserve SNORKELING, DIVING
For some of the state's best and most accessible (no boat needed) diving and snorkeling, just a few kicks from La Jolla Cove. With an average depth of 20ft, the 6000 acres of look-but-don't-touch underwater real estate are home to the bright orange garibaldi,

HIKE TO CITYWIDE VIEWS

A popular trail leads to the top of 1592ft **Cowles Mountain** (www.mtrp.org) near San Diego State University. On this two-hour summit bagger (3 miles round trip), you'll pass joggers, dog-walkers and moms with toddlers, all hoping to catch sweeping views that can stretch from La Jolla south to Coronado on a clear day. From I-8, take the College Ave north exit, following College Ave to Navajo Rd. Take a right onto Navajo Rd and drive almost 2 miles, turning left onto Goldcrest Dr then enter the parking lot.

California's protected state fish (there's a fine for poaching one). Further out, you'll see forests of giant California kelp (which can increase its length by up to 2ft per day) and the 100ft-deep La Jolla Canyon.

OEX Dive & Kayak WATER SPORTS
(☎858-454-6195; www.oexcalifornia.com; 2243/2132 Avenida de la Playa, La Jolla) For gear or instruction, including spear seminars and stand-up paddleboard lessons, head to this one-stop resource.

Fishing

If you're over 16 years of age, you'll need a state fishing license, except when fishing from an ocean pier (one/two/10 days $14/22/43). Call a recorded service on ☎619-465-3474 for fishing information. An ocean enhancement stamp ($5) is currently required for 10-day trips but not one- or two-day trips.

The most popular public fishing piers are Imperial Beach Municipal Pier, Embarcadero Fishing Pier at the Marina Park, Shelter Island Fishing Pier, Ocean Beach Pier and Crystal Pier at Pacific Beach. The best time of year for pier fishing is from about April to October. Offshore catches can include barracuda, bass and yellowtail. In summer albacore is a special attraction.

For guided fishing try the following outfitters. Prices do not include license and tackle (about $10 to $15).

H&M Landing FISHING
(Map p427; ☎619-222-1144; www.hmlanding.com; 2803 Emerson St, Shelter Island) Half-day trips just off the coast cost $46 per person. See the website for full day-trip and multiday trip options.

Mission Bay Sportfishing FISHING
(off Map p438; ☎619-222-1164; 1551 West Mission Bay Dr) This friendly outfitter offers half-day trips from around $40 per adult (less for children). See website for overnight tuna fishing trips and boat rental information.

Boating

Rent power and sailboats, sailboards, kayaks and Waverunners on Mission Bay. Experienced sailors can charter yachts and sailboats for trips on San Diego Bay and out into the Pacific. You'll find the following charter companies on Harbor Islands (on the west side of San Diego Bay near the airport).

Family Kayak KAYAKING
(☎619-282-3520; www.familykayak.com) Ocean kayaking is a good way to see sealife and explore cliffs and caves inaccessible from land. This company offers a guided tour of San Diego Bay (per adult/child $42/17).

Mission Bay Sportcenter KAYAKING, BOATING
(Map p438; ☎858-488-1004; www.missionbaysportcenter.com; 1010 Santa Clara Pl). A sailboat costs $24/72/96 per hour/four hours/full day and a single kayak is $13/39/44.

Whale-Watching

From mid-December to late February, gray whales pass San Diego on their way south to Baja California and again in mid-March on their way back to Alaskan waters. Their 12,000-mile round-trip journey is the longest migration of any mammal on earth.

There's a bluff-top viewing area at Cabrillo National Monument (Map p427), the best place to observe the whales from land. You'll also find whale-related film and exhibits year-round and, seasonally, whale-centric ranger programs. Southwest of the Old Point Loma Lighthouse is a small glass-walled shelter, where you can watch the whales breach (bring binoculars). Further north, Torrey Pines State Reserve (p442) and La Jolla Cove (p440) are also good whale-watching spots.

H&M Landing CRUISE
(p444) Three-hour whale-watching boat trips (adult/child $25/17.50) and six-hour blue whale–watching cruises (adult/child $80/55) are offered seasonally.

Hornblower Cruises CRUISE
(Map p430; ☎888-467-6256; www.hornblower.com; tour per adult/child/senior $40/20/33) Offers a seasonal 3½-hour tour.

Hang Gliding

Torrey Pines Glider Port ADVENTURE SPORTS
(Map p427; ☎858-452-9858; www.flytorrey.com; 2800 Torrey Pines Scenic Dr; tandem paraglider flights/hang glider flights per person $150/200) Don't let age keep you from a tandem paraglide with an instructor. Instructors have lifted off with three-years-olds and 99-year-olds at this world-renowned gliding center by the sea, where most rides last between 20 and 25 minutes. The difference between paragliding and hang gliding? With paragliding, the instructor and passenger remain in a seated position under a soft 'wing,' while hang gliders fly in a prone position under a triangular wing.

Experienced pilots can fly here if they are USHGA members and/or have on them a temporary 30-day USGHA membership card.

Tours

Look for brochures with discounts or check online for deals.

Another Side of San Diego WALKING, BOAT
(Map p430; ☎619-239-2111; www.anothersideofsandiegotours.com; 300 G St) This highly rated tour company does Segway tours of Balboa park, horseback riding on the beach and Gaslamp food tours.

Hike, Bike, Kayak San Diego CYCLING
(☎858-551-9510, 866-425-2925; www.hikebikekayak.com; 2246 Avenida de la Playa, La Jolla) Just what it says.

Old Town Trolley Tours TROLLEY
(☎619-298-8687; www.trolleytours.com; adult/child $34/17) Not to be confused with the Metropolitan Transit System's rail trolleys, these open-air, hop-on-hop-off buses loop to the main attractions in and around downtown and in Coronado. Tickets for the orange-and-green trolleys are good for unlimited all-day travel. Board in Old Town. Tours run every 30 minutes.

San Diego Harbor Excursion BOAT
(Map p430; ☎619-234-4111; www.sdhe.com; 1050 N Harbor Dr; adult/child from $22/11) A variety of bay and harbor cruises.

Festivals & Events

For the most current list, contact the San Diego Convention & Visitors Bureau.

Kiwanis Ocean Beach Kite Festival KITES
(www.oceanbeachkiwanis.org) Kite-making, decorating, flying and competitions at Ocean Beach on the first Saturday in March.

EarthFair FAIR
(www.earthdayweb.org/EarthFair.html) The world's largest annual – and free – environmental fair draws upwards of 60,000 visitors each year on April's Earth Day. Don't miss the fantastic Food Pavilion.

San Diego County Fair FAIR
(www.sdfair.com) Over 1.4 million attended this huge county fair in 2011, held from mid-June to July 4; features headline acts and hundreds of carnival rides and shows at the Del Mar Fairgrounds in Del Mar.

US Open Sandcastle Competition QUIRKY
(www.usopensandcastle.com) You won't believe what can be made out of sand at the amazing sandcastle-building competition held mid-July in Imperial Beach, south of Coronado.

San Diego Gay Pride GAY, LESBIAN
(www.sdpride.org) The city's gay community celebrates in Hillcrest and Balboa Park at the end of July.

Comic-Con International COMICS
(www.comic-con.org) America's largest event for collectors of comic, pop culture and movie memorabilia at the San Diego Convention Center. Late July.

December Nights CAROLS
(www.balboapark.org) Festival in Balboa Park includes crafts, carols and a candlelight parade in the park.

Harbor Parade of Lights CULTURAL
(www.sdparadeoflights.org) More than 100 decorated, illuminated vessels float in procession on the harbor on two Sunday evenings in December.

Sleeping

High-season summer rates for double-occupancy rooms are listed in this section. The prices drop significantly between September and June, often by 40% or more. Budget travelers should consider cheaper lodgings in neighboring Mission Valley.

DOWNTOWN

Despite its recent popularity, downtown still has some great, quirky budget options. It's also where you'll find several independently run midrange lodgings, from boutique hotels to B&Bs, and the bulk of the city's high-end palaces.

USA Hostels San Diego HOSTEL **$**
(Map p430; 619-232-3100, 800-438-8622; www.usahostels.com; 726 5th Ave; dm/d incl breakfast from $28/72;) In a former Victorian-era hotel, this convivial Gaslamp hostel has cheerful rooms, a full kitchen and an inviting movie room. Rates include a pancake breakfast and laundry facilities; the nightly family-style dinner costs $5.

HI San Diego Downtown Hostel HOSTEL **$**
(Map p430; 619-525-1531; www.sandiegohostels.org/downtown; 521 Market St; incl breakfast dm $29-32, d with/without bath $93/77;) Friendly, helpful staff coordinate lots of activities and tours at this bustling, mazelike hostel. Located in the heart of the Gaslamp Quarter, this former Victorian-era hotel is close to public transportation and nightlife. Rates include a pancake breakfast, 24-hour access (including kitchen facilities), a laundry room and lockers (bring your own lock).

La Pensione Hotel BOUTIQUE HOTEL **$**
(off Map p430; 800-232-4683; www.lapensionehotel.com; 606 W Date St; r $100; P) At this four-story Little Italy hotel, rooms are built around a frescoed courtyard – a pleasant place to sip coffee from the adjacent cafe. Thanks to extensive renovations in 2010, the hotel looks fresh and stylish, even if rooms are on the small side. The location can hardly be beat, but if you have a car, there's complimentary parking under the building.

Little Italy Inn B&B **$$**
(off Map p430; 619-230-1600; www.littleitalyhotel.com; 505 W Grape St; incl breakfast r with shared/private bath $89/109, 2-room apt from $149;) If you can't get enough of Little Italy's charm, this pretty B&B is an ideal place to hang your hat. The 23-room Victorian-style inn boasts comfortable beds, cozy bathrobes in each room, a casual European-style breakfast and wine socials on weekend evenings.

Hotel Indigo BOUTIQUE HOTEL **$$**
(Map p430; 619-727-4000; www.hotelsandiegodowntown.com; 509 9th Ave; r from $146; P@) The first LEED-certified hotel in San Diego, Hotel Indigo is smartly designed and ecofriendly. The design is contemporary but colorful; guest rooms feature huge floor-to-ceiling windows, spa-style baths and large flat-screen TVs. Parking is $35.

500 West Hotel HOSTEL, GUESTHOUSE **$**
(Map p430; 619-231-4092; www.500westhotelsd.com; 500 W Broadway; s/d with shared bath from $50/62; @) Budget-minded hipsters go for the tiny rooms, bright decor and communal kitchen inside this 1920s beaux arts YMCA building.

Horton Grand Hotel HISTORIC HOTEL **$$**
(Map p430; 619-544-1886, 800-542-1886; www.hortongrand.com; 311 Island Ave; r $149-269; @) This Gaslamp classic, dating from 1886 and once the home of Wyatt Earp, has Victorian-era furnishings and marble fireplaces.

CORONADO

Hotel del Coronado LUXURY, HISTORIC HOTEL **$$$**
(Map p427; 619-435-6611, 800-468-3533; www.hoteldel.com; 1500 Orange Ave; r from $325; P@) You probably don't *need* to take the antique elevator – complete with uniformed operator – to your 2nd-floor room but 'the Del' is so darn charming you won't want to miss a bit of its history. The 120-year old hotel combines tradition (p436), luxury and access to the city's most stunning beach. Amenities include two pools, a full-service spa, fitness center, shops, restaurants and manicured grounds. Note that half the accommodations are not in the main Victorian-era hotel, but in an adjacent seven-story building constructed in the 1970s. For a sense of place, book a room in the original hotel. Watch the fees, though. There's a $25 daily resort fee that includes use of the broadband in your room, local phone calls and access to the fitness center. Parking is another $25.

Coronado Inn MOTEL **$$**
(619-435-4121, 800-598-6624; www.coronadoinn.com; 266 Orange Ave; r $119-159, ste with kitchen $179-199; P@) It feels like home – in a good way – at this tidy, motel-style property wrapped around a small parking lot on Orange Ave near the ferry. Relax under the palm trees by the pool or grill your own fish on the communal barbecue.

OCEAN BEACH & POINT LOMA

Inn at Sunset Cliffs HOTEL $$
(Map p438; ☎619-222-7901, 866-786-2543; www.innatsunsetcliffs.com; 1370 Sunset Cliffs Blvd, Point Loma; r from $175; P ❄ @ ☎ ≋) Hear the surf crashing onto the rocky shore at this breezy charmer wrapped around a flower-bedecked courtyard. Newly renovated rooms are light-filled but on the small side; recent efforts to decrease the hotel's water and plastic consumption have made the place greener.

Ocean Beach Hotel HOTEL $$
(Map p438; ☎619-223-7191; www.obhotel.com; 5080 Newport Ave, Ocean Beach; d from $129; ❄ @ ☎) This recently remodeled hotel is just across the street from the beach. Spotless guest rooms are on the smaller side; the French provincial look is a bit dated but all feature refrigerators and complimentary wi-fi.

Ocean Beach International Hostel HOSTEL $
(Map p438; ☎800-339-7263; www.californiahostels.com; 4961 Newport Ave; dm incl breakfast $35; @ ☎) A large peace sign signals the cheapest sleeping option in the neighborhood, only a couple of blocks from the ocean. It's a fun, slightly rundown place reserved for international travelers and students, with bonfires, barbecues, free linens, and surfboard rentals. They'll arrange free transportation from the airport, train station or bus terminal.

MISSION BAY & PACIFIC BEACH

Crystal Pier Hotel QUIRKY, HISTORIC HOTEL $$$
(Map p438; ☎800-748-5894; www.crystalpier.com; 4500 Ocean Blvd; d cottage from $300, 3-night minimum; P ☎) White clapboard cottages with flower boxes and blue shutters are the draw at this popular hotel, and not just because they're picturesque. The cottages – dating from 1936 – are special because they sit atop the pier itself, offering one-of-a-kind views of coast and sea. Newer, larger cottages sleep more people, but the older units are the best. Book well in advance for summer reservations.

Banana Bungalow HOSTEL $
(Map p438; ☎858-273-3060; www.bananabungalow.com; 707 Reed Ave; dm/r $35/150; @ ☎) The Bungalow has a top beachfront location that's just a few blocks from the Garnet Ave bar scene. It's reasonably clean, though pretty basic, and it gets rowdy. A communal, made-for-keggers patio overlooks the boardwalk and Mission Beach. It's more of a party scene than other city hostels.

Campland on the Bay CAMPGROUND $
(Map p438; ☎800-422-9386; www.campland.com; 2211 Pacific Beach Dr; tent & RV sites $52-142; P ☎ ≋ 👪) This kid-friendly campground, with more than 40 acres fronting Mission Bay, also has a restaurant, two pools, a small grocery, a marina, boating rentals and full RV hook-ups. The location is great, but the tent area can be pretty sorry – try to avoid the shadeless, dusty sites.

Beach Cottages HOTEL, BUNGALOWS $$$
(Map p438; ☎858-483-7440; www.beachcottages.com; 4255 Ocean Blvd; r from $285, cottages from $300; P @ ☎ ≋ 👪) This picturesque family-owned complex comprises 17 cozy, 1940s-era beachfront cottages, plus motel-style rooms in the main building.

OLD TOWN

Old Town Inn HOTEL $$
(☎800-643-3025; www.oldtown-inn; 4444 Pacific Hwy; incl breakfast r $90-135, with kitchen $145-155; P ❄ @ ☎ ≋) Rooms look a bit dark when compared to those in the shiny hipster hotels downtown, but otherwise this simple, mission-style motel has a lot to recommend it. Centrally located off the I-5, on the opposite side of the interstate from the Old Town Transit Center, it's an easy walk to Old Town. Sturdy mattresses, an on-site laundry, and complimentary wi-fi, parking and continental breakfast round out the appeal.

LA JOLLA

It's hard to find a cheap room here, even on weekdays off-season. Less expensive options, including a handful of midrange chains and the occasional family-run motel, can be found south of town along La Jolla Blvd. Longer stays yield lower rates.

La Valencia HISTORIC HOTEL $$$
(Map p440; ☎858-454-0771, 800-451-0772; www.lavalencia.com; 1132 Prospect St, La Jolla; r $285-515, ste $695; P ❄ @ ☎ ≋) For Old Hollywood style, book a room at this pink 1926 Mediterranean-style palace. The 116 rooms are compact – befitting the era – but the hotel wins for Old Hollywood romance; recent ecofriendly efforts add to the charm. Even if you can't afford to sleep with the ghosts of Depression-era Hollywood, have a drink in **La Sala**, the elegant Spanish revival lounge. Parking is $32.

DON'T MISS

FISH TACOS

The ingredients of this SoCal staple are always the same: a soft tortilla topped with fish, salsa, cabbage and special sauce. It's the preparation that makes San Diego's addition to the culinary lexicon – the fish taco – so interesting. Ralph Rubio, who founded his namesake fish-centric fast-food chain **Rubio's Fresh Mexican Grill** (www.rubios.com) in 1983, is credited with popularizing the dish. Who serves the city's best version? Perennial frontrunners include the piled-high bad boys at **South Beach Bar & Grille** (p450) in Ocean Beach, where the lightly fried mahi mahi is the fish of choice. Then there are the uber-fresh grilled fish tacos at **Blue Water Seafood Market & Grill** (www.bluewater.sandiegan.com; 3667 India St). The deep-fried fish taco at longtime chain **Roberto's** (www.robertos.us) is a corndog-sized piece of fried fish that is sure to ruin any diet. Minichain **Brigantine** (www.brigantine.com; 1333 Orange Ave) also has a devoted following.

Grande Colonial Hotel LUXURY HOTEL **$$$**
(Map p440; ☎888-828-5498; www.thegrandecolonial.com; 910 Prospect St; r $255-500, ste from $325;) Warm colors, simple prints and classic furnishings set a conservative but sophisticated mood at the popular Grande Colonial, demure step-sister to the pink palace just down the road. There's been a hotel on the site for almost a century, and its central location makes it a perfect home base for exploring. Accommodating staff add to the ambience. Parking is $22 a day.

Eating

San Diego's not a foodie capital like some California cities, though the dining scene is becoming increasingly dynamic. As a rule of thumb, you'll find haute cuisine and fine steakhouses in the Gaslamp, casual seafood along the beaches, ethnic food in and around Hillcrest, and tacos and margaritas, well, everywhere. For full listings of sustainable San Diego eating options, look for a free copy of the seasonal magazine *Edible San Diego.*

DOWNTOWN & EMBARCADERO

It seems new restaurants are opening weekly in the Gaslamp Quarter, particularly in and around the trendy hotels surrounding nearby Petco Park – reservations are recommended. If you're in the mood for Italian, just take a stroll along Little Italy's India Street and choose the most inviting sidewalk table.

Café 222 BREAKFAST **$**
(Map p430; ☎619-236-9902; www.cafe222.com; 222 Island Ave; mains $7-11; ⏲7am-1:45pm;) This small, airy breakfast spot is renowned for pumpkin waffles, orange pecan pancakes and farm-fresh egg scramblers. The French toast stuffed with peanut butter and bananas was featured on the Food Network.

TOP CHOICE **Puerto La Boca** ARGENTINE **$$**
(off Map p430; ☎619-234-4900; www.puertolaboca.com; 2060 India St; mains lunch $8-12; dinner $15-45; ⏲11am-10pm Mon-Thu, to 11pm Fri, noon-11pm Sat, 1-8:30pm Sun;) This classy, new-on-the-scene Argentine eatery in Little Italy is surprisingly authentic: come for grilled chorizo and steak, fried empanadas, garlicky mussels, and a glass of Malbec or Torrontés. Happy hour food and wine specials (4:30 to 7:30pm Monday to Saturday and all day Sunday) are a bargain.

C Level SEAFOOD **$$**
(☎619-298-6802; www.islandprime.com; 880 Harbor Island Dr; mains $14-30; ⏲from 11am-late) The food is as aesthetically pleasing as the view from this Harbor Island patio lounge with sweeping vistas of the bay and downtown. Here, carefully crafted salads, sandwiches and light seafood fare are winning rave reviews. The uber-rich lobster and fontina BLT – dunked in lobster bisque – is a top choice. The Social Hour (3:30 to 5:30pm Monday to Friday) offers $5 'bites and libations.' C Level is located on the tip of Harbor Island, which juts into the bay near the airport; to get here, take N Harbor Dr north from the Gaslamp Quarter and Embarcadero.

Filippi's Pizza Grotto PIZZERIA **$$**
(Map p430; www.realcheesepizza.com; 1747 India St; mains $11-20; ⏲11am-10pm Sun-Thu, to 11:30pm Fri & Sat) Regularly lauded by locals for its pizza, this old-school Italian joint – think red-and-white checked tablecloths, tiny booths, small deli up front – often has a line out the door. Look for a **second location** (Map p438; 962 Garnet Ave) in Pacific Beach.

Candelas MEXICAN $$$

(Map p430; ☎619-702-4455; www.candelas-sd.com; 416 3rd Ave; mains $18-53; ⊙5-11pm) Upscale 'rustic' decor, flattering lighting, attentive waiters and savory Mexican specialties – from beef tenderloin au gratin (with blue cheese) to jumbo prawns flamed with tequila – make Candelas one of downtown's most romantic dining experiences. Don't be surprised if someone pops the question at the adjacent table. Now there's a **second location** (1201 1st St) in Coronado.

The Oceanaire Seafood Room SEAFOOD $$$

(Map p430; ☎619-858-2277; www.theoceanaire.com; 400 J St; mains $24-40; ⊙5-10pm Sun-Thu, to 11pm Fri & Sat) The look is art-deco ocean liner and the service is just as refined, with an oyster bar (get them for a buck during happy hour, 5 to 6pm Monday to Friday) and inventive creations, including Maryland blue crab cakes and horseradish-crusted Alaskan halibut.

La Puerta MEXICAN $

(Map p430; www.taco619.com; 560 4th Ave; mains $7-10; ⊙11:30am-2am Mon-Sat, from 10am Sun) Toss back Coronas, enchiladas and fresh guacamole at this shadowy Mexican bar that looks like the inside of a vampire's lair.

Mona Lisa DELI, ITALIAN $

(Map p430; www.monalisalittleitaly.com; 2061 India St; mains lunch $6-9, dinner $12-18; ⊙11am-10pm Mon-Sat, from 3pm Sun) This traditional Italian eatery and deli is the place to dig into veal piccata or pick up picnic fixings.

BALBOA PARK

TOP CHOICE **Prado** MEDITERRANEAN, AMERICAN $$

(Map p434; ☎619-557-9441; www.pradobalboa.com; 1549 El Prado; mains lunch $10-15, dinner $21-34; ⊙11:30am-3pm Mon-Fri & from 5pm Tue-Sun, 11am-3pm Sat & Sun; 👪) This classic lunch spot in the museum district of Balboa Park serves up fresh Mediterranean cuisine like steamed mussels, shrimp paella and grilled portobello sandwiches. Breezy outdoor seating and the Mexican-tiled interior are equally inviting; happy hour food and drink specials (4 to 6pm Tuesday to Friday) are a steal.

Tea Pavilion ASIAN $

(Map p434; 2215 Pan American Way; mains $5-10; ⊙10am-5pm, later in summer) Enjoy a quick and spicy noodle bowl – or a simple cup of tea – under an umbrella at this low-key eatery next to the Japanese Garden.

OLD TOWN

Old Town overflows with lively Mexican restaurants, but only a few are reasonably authentic. Still, the pretty outdoor seating and ice-cold margaritas can make for a fun lunch or evening out.

Old Town Mexican Café MEXICAN $

(☎619-297-4330; www.oldtownmexcafe.com; 2489 San Diego Ave; mains $4-15; ⊙7am-2am; 👪) Watch the staff turn out fresh tortillas in the window while waiting for a table. Besides breakfast (great *chilaquiles* – soft tortilla chips covered with mole), there's *pozole* (spicy pork stew), avocado tacos and margaritas at the festive central bar.

HILLCREST & MISSION HILLS

You'll find lots of ethnic dining options in and around Hillcrest: wander around University Ave and 5th Ave for an overview. Restaurants here tend to be more casual than downtown – and better value.

Bread & Cie BAKERY $

(Map p434; www.breadandciecatering.com; 350 University Ave; mains $6-10; ⊙7am-7pm Mon-Fri, to 6pm Sat, 9am-6pm Sun; 👪) A delightful sensory overload of aromatic fresh bread, chattering locals and pastry-filled trays awaits inside this bustling Hillcrest crossroads. Daily breads include black olive and walnut raisin. Try the almond croissant or the ridiculously rich and oversized *pain au chocolat*.

Kous Kous MOROCCAN $$

(Map p434; www.kouskousrestaurant.com; 3940 4th Ave; mains $14-20; ⊙5pm-late; 🖉) Entering this otherworldly Moroccan eatery is like stepping onto another continent: the dining room is seductively illuminated by glowing lanterns, dinner guests sit on jewel-toned cushions drinking exotic cocktails, the aroma of ginger, nutmeg and foreign spices hangs in the air. Don't miss the lamb sausage or the B'stila roll (saffron chicken baked with honey, cinnamon and almonds in phyllo dough).

Khyber Pass MIDDLE EASTERN $$

(Map p434; www.khyberpassandiego.com; 523 University Ave; mains $14-30; ⊙11:30am-10pm; 🖉) Afghan tapestries and moody photos set the tone in this tall-ceilinged space, with adventuresome Afghan cooking. Never had it? Think Indian meets Middle Eastern, with yogurt curries, kababs and stews.

TO MARKET, TO MARKET

Swinging by the local farmers market to pick up your eggs and basil is *so Californian*. So it's no surprise that San Diego has a street market (or two or three) for almost every day of the week. For full listings of where the hipsters are eating tamales and foodies shop for avocados and ginger root, visit the San Diego Farm Bureau website at www.sdfarmbureau.org.

» Tuesday – **Coronado Farmers Market** (1st St & B Ave, Ferry Landing; ⌚2:30-6pm) and **UCSD La Jolla Farmers Market** (Town Square; ⌚10am-2pm)

» Wednesday – **Ocean Beach Farmers Market** (4900 Newport Ave, ⌚4-8pm) and **Carlsbad Farmers Market** (Roosevelt St & Carlsbad Village Dr, ⌚1-5pm)

» Thursday – **North Park Farmers Market** (3151 University & 32nd St, ⌚3-7pm) and **SDSU Farmers Market** (Campanile Walkway near Love Library, ⌚10am-3pm)

» Friday – **Imperial Beach Farmers Market** (Seacoast Dr, Pier Plaza; ⌚2-7:30pm) and **Mission Hills Farmers Market** (Falcon St & W Washington; ⌚3-7pm)

» Saturday – **Little Italy Mercato** (Date St & Kettner; ⌚9am-1:30pm) and **Del Mar Farmers Market** (1050 Camino del Mar; ⌚1-4pm)

» Sunday – **Gaslamp Farmers Market** (400 block of 3rd Ave, ⌚9am-1pm), **Hillcrest Farmers Market** (3960 Normal & Lincoln Sts; ⌚9am-2pm), **Point Loma Farmers Market** (Cañon & Rosecrans; ⌚9:30am-2:30pm) and **Solana Beach Farmers Market** (410 S Cedros Ave; ⌚1-5pm)

Saigon on Fifth VIETNAMESE **$$**
(Map p434; 3900 5th Ave; mains $11-16; ⌚11am-midnight; P) For good Vietnamese, try this elegant but not overbearing place.

Hash House a Go Go BREAKFAST **$$**
(Map p434; www.hashhouseagogo.com; 3628 5th Ave; mains breakfast & lunch $8-17, dinner $15-39; ⌚7:30am-2pm daily, 5:30-9pm Tue-Sun) Does this fantastically popular breakfast joint merit the hype (and long lines)? One way to find out – the portions are massive, so consider sharing your flapjacks.

CORONADO

Coronado Brewing Company PUB **$$**
(www.coronadobrewingcompany.com; 170 Orange Ave; mains $10-22; ⌚10:30am-late) The delicious house brew (the Pilsner-style Coronado Golden) goes well with the pizzas, pastas, sandwiches and fries at this good-for-your-soul, bad-for-your-diet bar and grill near the ferry. Try the $9 beer tasting.

1500 Ocean SEAFOOD **$$$**
(Map p427; ☎619-522-8490; www.dine1500ocean.com; Hotel del Coronado; 1500 Orange Ave; mains $18-45; ⌚5:30-9pm Tue-Thu, to 10pm Fri-Sun) Bright marigolds border the veranda at the Del's most romantic restaurant, adding a cheerful splash of color to palm-framed views of the sea. Come here to impress someone, celebrate or simply revel in your good fortune over duck confit or seared scallops.

OCEAN BEACH

OB is the place to go for the city's best cheap eats. Most places are on Newport Ave.

Hodad's BURGERS **$**
(Map p438; www.hodadies.com; 5010 Newport Ave, Ocean Beach; burgers $4-9; ⌚5am-10pm) If there was a glossy magazine called *Beach Bum Living*, then legendary Hodad's, with its surfboards- and-license-plates decor, communal wooden tables and baskets of burgers and fries, would score the very first cover. Many say the succulent burgers are the best in town. Add an order of onion rings and you'll go home happy. A **second location** (Map p430; 945 Broadway Ave) recently opened downtown.

South Beach Bar & Grille MEXICAN, CALIFORNIAN **$**
(Map p438; www. southbeachob.com; 5059 Newport Ave; mains $8-10; ⌚11am-1am Sun-Thu, to 2am Fri & Sat) Maybe it's the lightly fried mahi mahi. Or the kickin' white sauce. Or the layer of cabbage and salsa. Whatever the secret, the fish tacos at this beachside bar and grill stand out in a city of awesome fish tacos. On Fridays, follow the noise to this festive watering hole in a nondescript building at the end of Newport Ave.

MISSION BAY & PACIFIC BEACH

You can eat well on a tight budget in these two coastal communities. Both have a young, mostly local scene; PB has the bulk of the restaurants, especially along Garnet Ave.

The Mission BREAKFAST, LATIN AMERICAN $

(Map p438; 3795 Mission Blvd; dishes $7-11; ⏲7am-3pm; 🌱👪) Savor the famously delicious coffee or homemade cinnamon bread for breakfast – or kick back with Chino-Latino lunch specialties that include ginger sesame wraps and rosemary potatoes with salsa and eggs. Other locations have popped up around town: **The Mission SoMa** (1250 J St) and **The Mission North Park** (2801 University Ave).

JRDN SEAFOOD, CALIFORNIAN $$$

(Map p438; www.jrdn.com; Tower 23, 723 Felspar St; mains breakfast $10-18, lunch $9-18, dinner $23-46; ⏲7am-11am Mon-Fri, 9am-4pm Sat & Sun, 5-10pm daily) Sustainably farmed meats and seafood join local veggies for a plate-topping farmers market at chic, vowel-disdaining JRDN, where you can choose futuristic decor indoors or ocean views outdoors. Try dry scallops with crabmeat risotto, miso halibut and green-onion creamers (aka mashed potatoes).

LA JOLLA

La Jolla is a major haute-cuisine outpost, but there are some good budget and mid-range options, too.

Harry's Coffee Shop DINER $

(Map p440; www.harryscoffeeshop.com; 7545 Girard Ave; dishes $5-12; ⏲6am-3pm; 👪) Classic coffee shop serving all-American fare with vinyl booths and a posse of regulars, from blue-haired socialites to sports celebs.

whisknladle MODERN AMERICAN $$

(Map p440; ☎858-551-7575; www.whisknladle.com; 1044 Wall St; mains brunch & lunch $12-19, dinner $15-30; ⏲11:30am-9:30pm Mon-Fri, from 10am Sat & Sun) whisknladle serves up carefully selected and seasoned 'slow food' – fresh fare simply prepared. The breezy covered patio is the main dining area, and there's only a small bar – and artsy wall of empty wine bottles – inside. Dinner menu favorites include chorizo date fritters and charred bone marrow (tastes far better than it sounds). For lunch, try the locally harvested mussels with fries.

George's at the Cove MODERN AMERICAN $$

(Map p440; ☎858-454-4244; www.georgesatthecove.com; 1250 Prospect St; mains $11-48; ⏲11am-11pm) Chef Trey Foshee's Euro-Cal cuisine is as dramatic as this eatery's oceanfront location. George's has graced just about every list of top restaurants in California. Three venues allow you to enjoy it at different price points: **George's Bar** (lunch mains $9-16), **Ocean Terrace** (lunch mains $11-18) and **George's California Modern** (dinner mains $28-48). Walk-ins welcome at the bar, but reservations are recommended for the latter two.

Drinking

If you want to explore the city's alive-and-kicking bar scene, head to the Gaslamp for rooftop bars atop fashionable hotels, Hillcrest for bohemian and gay-friendly watering holes, and the beaches for casual bars where surfers and college kids down cheap beers and tacos.

TOP CHOICE **Wine Steals** WINE BAR

(Map p434; ☎619-295-1188; www.winestealssd.com; 1243 University Ave, Hillcrest) Laid-back wine tastings (go for a flight or choose a bottle off the rack in the back), live music, gourmet pizzas and cheese platters bring in a nightly crowd to this low-lit wine bar. Look for two newer branches in San Diego, **Wine Steals East Village** (Map p430; 793/5 J Street, Downtown) and **Lounge-Point Loma** (2970 Truxtun Rd, Point Loma).

TOP CHOICE **Cafe 1134** CAFE $

(1134 Orange Ave, Coronado; mains $8-10; ⏲9am-7pm) This cool coffeeshop on Coronado's main drag offers more than your morning fix: think delicious Greek-style egg scramblers, grilled panini, spinach salads, high-end teas and a wine and beer list. Prices are slashed as part of the 'Money Wise Menu' on Sunday, Monday and Tuesday evenings.

Starlite COCKTAIL BAR

(www.starlitesandiego.com; 3175 India St, Mission Hills) Slightly out of the way – don't worry, the drive is worthwhile – is this hipster cocktail haven with top-notch house creations and a lively central bar. The list changes frequently: just try anything made with ginger beer. From the Gaslamp/downtown, take I-5 N to exit 17B, then follow India St for 0.5 miles. Starlite will be on your right.

SAN DIEGO MICROBREWERIES

San Diegans take their craft beers seriously – even at a dive bar, you might overhear local guys talking about hops and cask conditioning. Various microbreweries on the city outskirts specialize in India Pale Ale (IPA) and Belgian-style brews; the following venues are beer-enthusiast favorites.

Stone Brewing Company (760-471-4999; www.stonebrew.com; 1999 Citracado Pkwy, Escondido; 11am-9pm). Take a free tour before a guided tasting of Oaked Arrogant Bastard Ale and Stone Barley Wine.

Lost Abbey (800-918-6816; www.lostabbey.com; 155 Mata Way 104, San Marcos; 1-6pm Wed-Thu, 3-9pm Fri, noon-6pm Sat & Sun). More than 20 brews ($1 per taste) are on tap in the tasting room – try Lost and Found Abbey Ale.

AleSmith (858-549-9888; www.alesmith.com; 9368 Cabot Dr; 2-7pm Thu-Fri, noon-6pm Sat, to 4pm Sun). Wee Heavy and the potent Old Numbskull ($1 per taste) are the standout brews.

Living Room Coffeehouse COFFEE SHOP
(Map p440; www.livingroomcafe.com; 1010 Prospect St, La Jolla; 6am-midnight) This popular cafe serves spinach salads, quiche lorraine, and apricot strudel and has a great central position in the heart of the Village. There's a **second location** (2541 San Diego Ave) in Old Town and several others around town.

Extraordinary Desserts CAFE
(Map p434; 619-294-2132; www.extraordinarydesserts.com; 2929 5th Ave, Hillcrest; 8:30am-11pm Mon-Thu, to midnight Fri, 10am-midnight Sat, 10am-11pm Sun;) For those with a sweet tooth, Karen Krasne's treasure trove of stylishly decadent pastries – fruit-topped tarts, chunky cookies, creamy chocolate cheesecake and unforgettable bread pudding, to name a few – is heaven. There's organic coffee and wine, too, and cozy couches where you can share your treats with friends. There's a **second location** (1430 Union St) with a full bar in Little Italy.

Altitude Sky Lounge COCKTAIL BAR
(Map p430; www.altitudeskylounge.com; 660 K St) The Marriott's rooftop bar is our favorite. It may have the *de rigueur* firepits and sleek decor, but unlike other open-air lounges, the vibe is friendly, not hipper-than-thou. Sightlines to Petco Park are superb.

Tipsy Crow BAR, LOUNGE
(Map p430; www.thetipsycrow.com; 770 5th Ave, Downtown) There are three distinct levels at this historic Gaslamp building that's been turned into an atmospheric watering hole: the main floor with its long mahogany bar, the lounge-like 'Nest' (thought to be the site of a former brothel), and the brick-walled 'Underground' with a dance floor and live music acts.

Nunu's Cocktail Lounge COCKTAIL BAR
(Map p434; www.nunuscocktails.com; 3537 5th Ave, Hillcrest) Dark and divey, this hipster haven started pouring when JFK was president and still looks the part with its curvy booths, big bar and lovably kitsch decor.

Cosmopolitan Restaurant & Hotel BAR
(www.oldtowncosmo.com; 2660 Calhoun St, Old Town) The service is spotty, but the historic Old Town atmosphere (the house dates from the 1820s) makes the 3pm to 6pm happy hour appealing.

Pacific Beach Bar & Grill BAR
(Map p438; 858-272-4745; 860 Garnet Ave, Pacific Beach) This classic attracts a young, party-hearty crowd to its long wooden tables, patios and big central bar.

Star Bar BAR
(Map p430; 619-234-5575; 423 E St) Down-and-divey Star Bar: the place where dreams come to die.

☆ Entertainment

The Thursday editions of the free weekly *San Diego Reader* and the Night & Day section of the San Diego *Union Tribune* list the latest movies, theater shows, gallery exhibits and music gigs in the area. From a kiosk outside Horton Plaza, **Arts Tix** (Map p430; 858-381-5595; www.sdartstix.com; 3rd Ave & Broadway, Downtown; 9:30am-5pm Tue-Thu, 9:30am-6pm Fri & Sat), sells half-price tickets for same-day evening performances as well as discounts tickets to other events.

There's a thriving theater culture in San Diego. Book tickets at the box office or with Arts Tix.

TOP CHOICE **Cinema Under the Stars** CINEMA
(off Map p434; ☎619-295-4221; www.topspresents.com; 4040 Goldfinch St, Mission Hills; 👪) Catch classic films, both new and old – from *An Affair to Remember* to the latest Harry Potter installment – at this family-friendly outdoor theater. Heatlamps, reclining chairs and fleece blankets are provided.

San Diego Opera OPERA
(Map p430; ☎619-533-7000; www.sdopera.com; Civic Theatre, cnr 3rd Ave & B St) This fine company presents high quality, eclectic programming under the direction of maestro Karen Keltner.

Anthology LIVE MUSIC
(Map p430; ☎619-595-0300; www.anthologysd.com; 1337 India St; cover free-$60) Near Little Italy, Anthology presents live jazz, blues and Indie music in a swank supper-club setting, from both up-and-comers and big-name performers.

San Diego Symphony CLASSICAL MUSIC
(Map p430; ☎619-235-0804; www.sandiegosymphony.com; 750 B St) Nearly a century old, this accomplished symphony presents classical and family concerts at the Copley Symphony Hall. Starting in June, performances move to the Embarcadero Marina Park South for the lively outdoor Summer Pops season.

Casbah LIVE MUSIC
(Map p434; ☎619-232-4355; www.casbahmusic.com; 2501 Kettner Blvd; cover free-$20) Liz Phair, Alanis Morissette and the Smashing Pumpkins all rocked this funky Casbah on their way up the charts; catch local acts and headliners like Bon Iver.

La Jolla Playhouse THEATER
(☎619-550-1010; www.lajollaplayhouse.com; UCSD, 2910 La Jolla Village Dr) Classic and contemporary plays.

Landmark Hillcrest Cinemas CINEMA
(Map p434; ☎619-819-0236; www.landmarktheatres.com; 3965 5th Ave, Hillcrest) Regularly shows new arthouse, foreign films and classics in the boxy, postmodern Village Hillcrest Center.

Croce's Restaurant & Jazz Bar JAZZ, LIVE MUSIC
(Map p430; www.croces.com; cnr 5th Ave & F St) Ingrid Croce's tribute to her late husband Jim, this busy restaurant and club hosts great nightly jazz, blues and R&B performers.

Gaslamp Stadium 15 CINEMA
(Map p430; ☎619-232-0400; www.readingcinemasus.com; 701 5th Ave) A downtown cinema showing current-release movies.

Old Globe Theatre THEATER
(Map p434; ☎619-234-5623; www.theoldglobe.org; Balboa Park) Three venues stage Shakespeare, classics and contemporary plays.

San Diego Repertory Theatre THEATER
(Map p430; ☎619-544-1000; www.sdrep.org; Lyceum Theatre, 79 Horton Plaza) Avant-garde, multicultural and a musical or two.

Petco Park STADIUM
(Map p430; ☎619-795-5011, tickets 877-374-2784; www.padres.com; 100 Park Blvd) Home of the San Diego Padres Major League Baseball team. The season lasts from April to early October. Behind-the-scenes stadium **tours** (⏲10:30am, 12:30pm & 2:30pm Tue-Sun May-Aug, 10:30am & 12:30pm Apr & Sep, subject to game schedule) are possible year-round.

Qualcomm Stadium STADIUM
(Map p427; ☎619-280-2121; www.chargers.com; 9449 Friars Rd, Mission Valley) The San Diego Chargers National Football League team plays here: the season runs August through January.

Shopping

Though San Diego isn't known for shopping, you'll find plenty to purchase in this town if you're so inclined. Local fashionistas head to the upscale boutiques of La Jolla, shoppers in search of colorful housewares like the museum stores at Balboa Park and the Mexican artisan stands of Old Town, hipsters hit the secondhand clothing racks in Hillcrest and Ocean Beach, and kids find stuffed Shamus at SeaWorld. Surf shops and bikini boutiques dot the coastal communities.

The San Diego Trolley green line (or your car) takes you to each of three large malls in Mission Valley, visible just north of I-8 and bordering Hotel Circle.

GAY & LESBIAN NIGHTLIFE

Interestingly, many historians trace the roots of San Diego's thriving gay community to the city's strong military presence. During WWII, amid the enforced intimacy of military life, gay men from around the country were suddenly able to create strong (if clandestine) social networks. After the war, many stayed.

In the late 1960s, a newly politicized gay community began to make the Hillcrest neighborhood its unofficial headquarters. Here you'll find the highest concentration of bars catering to lesbians and gays. The scene is generally more casual and friendly than in San Francisco and LA.

Baja Betty's (Map p434; www.bajabettyssd.com; 1421 University Ave) Gay owned and straight friendly, this restaurant-bar is always a party with a just-back-from Margarita-ville vibe (and dozens of tequilas to take you back there) alongside dishes like Mexi-queen queso dip & You Go Grill swordfish tacos.

Brass Rail (Map p434; www.thebrassrailsd.com; 3796 5th Ave) The city's oldest gay bar has a different music style nightly, from Latin to African to Top 40.

Urban Mo's (Map p434; www.urbanmos.com; 308 University Ave) Equal parts bar and restaurant, Mo's isn't particularly known for great food, service or prices, but it's popular nonetheless for its thumping club beats, casual vibe, dance floor and happy hours.

TOP CHOICE Bazaar del Mundo Shops HOMEWARES, HANDICRAFTS
(www.bazaardelmundo.com; 4133 Taylor St, Old Town) Housed in a romantic hacienda-style building in Old Town, these lively shops specialize in high-quality Latin American artisan wares, folk art, Mexican jewelry and home accessories.

United Nations International Gift Shop HOMEWARES, HANDICRAFTS
(p434; United Nations Bldg, 2171 Pan American Plaza, Balboa Park) Fair-trade gifts and housewares from Africa and Latin America.

Pangaea Outpost MARKET
(Map p438; www.pangaeaoutpost.com; 909 Garnet Ave, Pacific Beach) This funky indoor marketplace features 70 funky miniboutiques and craft stores – think surf-baby tanks, hand-painted wine glasses and bright Oaxacan figurines.

Westfield Horton Plaza Center MALL
(Map p430; Broadway & 4th St, Downtown; P) For general shopping downtown, Horton Plaza has the highest concentration of shops and a variety of casual eateries.

Fashion Valley MALL
(off Map p434; www.simon.com; 7007 Friars Rd) Furthest west, home to Tiffany & Co, Burberry, Louis Vuitton, Kiehl's, Restoration Hardware, and department stores Neiman Marcus, Saks Fifth Avenue, Macy's and Nordstrom.

South Coast Surf Shop CLOTHING, OUTDOOR EQUIPMENT
(Map p438; www.southcoast.com; 5023 Newport Ave) Surf dudes staff the counter at this beach apparel and surf-gear shop in Ocean Beach that carries a good selection of Quiksilver, Hurley, Billabong and O'Neill for men and women.

Le Travel Store BOOKS
(Map p430; 745 4th Ave) Excellent selection of maps, travel guides and accessories.

Information

Dangers & Annoyances

San Diego is fairly safe, though you should be cautious venturing east of 6th Ave in downtown – especially after dark. Hostile panhandling is the most common problem.

Emergency & Medical Services

Scripps Mercy Hospital (619-294-8111; www.scripps.org; 4077 5th Ave, Hillcrest; 24hr) Has a 24-hour emergency room.

Internet Access

All city-operated libraries provide free internet and wireless access; no library card is required. Check www.sandiego.gov/public-library to see various use policies.

Media

KPBS 89.5FM (www.kpbs.org) Public radio, high-quality news and information.

San Diego Reader (www.sdreader.com) On Thursdays, look for this alt-weekly with the latest on the active music, art and theater scenes.

San Diego Union-Tribune (www.signonsandiego.com) The city's major daily.

Money

You'll find ATMs throughout San Diego.

Travelex (619-235-0901; 177 Horton Plaza, Downtown; 10am-7pm Mon-Fri, to 6pm Sat, 11am-4pm Sun) For foreign-currency exchange.

Post

For local post office locations, call 800-275-8777 or log on to www.usps.com.

Downtown post office (Map p430; 619-232-8612; 815 E St; 8:30am-5pm Mon-Fri)

Tourist Information

Balboa Park Visitors Center (Map p434; 619-239-0512; www.balboapark.org; 1549 El Prado; 9:30am-4:30pm) In the House of Hospitality. Sells park maps and the Passport to Balboa Park (adult/child $45/24, with zoo admission $77/42), which allows one-time entry to 14 of the park's museums within seven days.

San Diego Visitor Information Centers (619-236-1212, 800-350-6205; www.sandiego.org) Downtown (Map p430; cnr W Broadway & Harbor Dr; 9am-5pm Jun-Sep, 9am-4pm Oct-May); La Jolla (7966 Herschel Ave; 11am-5pm, possible longer hr Jun-Sep & Sat & Sun) The downtown location is designed for international visitors.

Old Town State Historic Park Visitor Center (619-220-5422; www.parks.ca.gov; Robinson-Rose House, Old Town 10am-5pm; P) For information about state parks in San Diego County, head to the Robinson-Rose House at the western end of the plaza.

Getting There & Away

Air

San Diego International Airport-Lindbergh Field (SAN; Map p427; 619-231-2100; www.san.org; 3225 N Harbor Dr) Because of the limited length of runways, most flights into this airport are domestic. It sits just 3 miles from downtown and plane-spotters will be thrilled watching planes come in over Balboa Park for landing. Coming from overseas, you'll likely change flights – and clear US Customs – at one of the major US gateway airports, such as LA, Chicago or Miami.

Bus

Greyhound (Map p430; 619-515-1100; www.greyhound.com; 120 W Broadway, Downtown) Serves San Diego from cities all over North America. There are hourly direct buses to Los Angeles (one way/round-trip $19/31, two to three hours). Service between San Diego and San Francisco (one way $72 to $90, 11 to 13 hours, six to eight daily) requires a transfer in LA.

Car & Motorcycle

The region's main north-south highway is I-5, which parallels the coast from the Camp Pendleton Marine Corps Base in the north to the Mexican border at San Ysidro in the south. The I-8 runs east from Ocean Beach, through Mission Valley, past suburbs including El Cajon, and on to the Imperial Valley and, eventually, Arizona.

Train

Amtrak (800-872-7245; www.amtrak.com) Runs the *Pacific Surfliner* several times daily to Los Angeles ($36, three hours) and Santa Barbara ($41, 5½ hours) from the **Santa Fe Depot** (Map p430; 1055 Kettner Blvd, Downtown). Amtrak and **Metrolink** (800-371-5465; www.metrolinktrains.com) commuter trains connect Anaheim to San Diego ($27, two hours).

Getting Around

While many people get around by car (and the city's fairly easy to navigate), it's possible to enjoy an entire vacation here using buses, trolleys and trains operated by the **Metropolitan Transit System** (MTS; 619-233-3004; www.sdmts.com).

To/From the Airport

Bus 992 ('the Flyer,' $2.25) operates at 10- to 15-minute intervals between the airport and Downtown, with stops along Broadway. Airport shuttles such as **Super Shuttle** (800-974-8885; www.supershuttle.com) charge about $8 to $10 to Downtown. A taxi fare to Downtown from the airport is $10 to $15.

Bicycle

Some areas around San Diego are great for biking, particularly Pacific Beach, Mission Beach, Mission Bay and Coronado.

All public buses are equipped with bike racks and will transport two-wheelers free. Inform the driver before boarding, then stow your bike on the rack on the tail end of the bus. For more information telephone 619-685-4900.

For rentals try Cheap Rentals (p439).

Boat

San Diego Harbor Excursion operates a **water taxi** (619-235-8294; www.sdhe.com; per person one way $7; 9am-9pm Sun-Thu, to 11pm Fri & Sat) serving Harbor Island, Shelter Island, Downtown and Coronado. It also runs the hourly **Coronado Ferry** (619-234-4111; www.sdhe.com; per person one way $4.25; 9am-10pm) shuttling between Broadway Pier on the Embar-

TIJUANA, MEXICO

Times are tough in Tijuana. For years 'TJ' has been a cheap, convivial destination just south of the border, popular with hard-partying San Diegans, Angelenos and sailors. Drug-related violence and too-frequent fatal shoot-outs, however, have turned once-bustling tourist areas into near ghost towns.

The government has taken steps to turn things around, but efforts haven't met with much success. Indeed, the heavy presence of armed soldiers clad in bulletproof vests tends to inspire fear, not confidence, in foreign guests. On the other hand, intrepid tourists who stay low-key (avoid flashy jewelry and stay aware of your surroundings) will find authentic dining experiences, great cultural attractions and an otherwise welcoming populace.

After descending from the pedestrian bridge at the border, stop by the San Ysidro Border crossing **visitor center** (www.tijuanaonline.org; ⌚9am-6pm) for a map. Pass through the turnstile and follow the street toward the **Tijuana Arch**. After a 10-minute walk, you'll arrive at the blocks-long Av Revolution (La Revo). La Revo's once-raucous streets are decidedly light on revelers, although you'll still find plenty of souvenir shops, low-priced pharmacies and liquor stores. There's no need to change your money, as nearly all businesses accept US dollars.

A short drive away is **Centro Cultural Tijuana** (CECUT; ☎01-664-687-9600; www.cecut.gob.mx; cnr Paseo de los Heroes & Av Independencia), a modern cultural center showcasing highbrow concerts, theater, readings, conferences and dance recitals. Inside the Centro Cultural the **Museo de las Californias** provides an excellent history of Baja California from prehistoric times to the present, including the earliest Spanish expeditions, the mission period, the Treaty of Guadalupe Hidalgo, irrigation of the Colorado River and the advent of the railroad. Signage is in English.

Travelers really interested in Tijuana can book a down-to-earth day tour through **Turista Libre** (www.turistalibre.com), an offbeat travel agency whose slogan is 'No narco warfare. No strolls down hooker row. No donkey shows. No gringo stereotypes. Lo mejor del alternaturismo.'

An easy way to get to Tijuana is via the San Diego Trolley on the blue line, which runs from Old Town to downtown to San Ysidro ($2.50, about 30 minutes). From the San Ysidro stop, follow the pedestrian bridge mentioned above. You can also drive to the border, but it's better to leave your car on the US side. Traffic in Tijuana is frenetic, parking is competitive, and there will likely be a long wait to cross back into the States. If you do drive, buy daily Mexican car insurance at a US office on Via San Ysidro and Camino de la Plaza.

US citizens not planning to go past the border zone (ie beyond Ensenada, or 20km to 30km/12.4 miles to 18.6 miles from the border, depending on location), or planning to stay in the border zone more than 72 hours, don't need a visa. All visitors, however, must bring their passport and US visa (if needed) for re-entry to the US.

cadero to the ferry landing at the northern end of First St. Headed to a Padres game? Park at the Coronado ferry landing and take SDHE's **PETCO Shuttle** (one way $4.25, game days) across the water to the stadium.

Public Transportation

BUS

The MTS covers most of the metropolitan area, North County, La Jolla and the beaches. It's most convenient if you're staying downtown and not partying until the wee hours. Get a free *Regional Transit Map* from the Transit Store.

For route and fare information, call **MTS** (☎619-233-3004, 24hr recorded info 619-685-4900, in San Diego 511). For online route planning, visit www.sdmts.com. Fares are $2.25 for most trips; express routes cost $2.50. Exact fare is required on all buses; drivers cannot make change. The **Transit Store** (Map p430; ☎619-234-1060; Broadway & 1st Ave; ⌚9am-5pm Mon-Fri) has route maps, tickets and Day Tripper passes for $5/9/12/15 for one/two/three/four days. Single-day passes are available for purchase on board buses.

Useful routes to/from downtown and Old Town:

ROUTE 3 Hillcrest, UCSD Medical Center, Balboa Park

ROUTE 7 Balboa Park, Zoo

ROUTE 30 Old Town, Pacific Beach, La Jolla

ROUTE 35 Old Town, Ocean Beach

ROUTE 901 Coronado, PETCO Park

Car

All the big-name rental companies have desks at the airport, but lesser-known ones may be cheaper. Shop around – prices vary widely. Check the company's policy before taking the car into Mexico.

For contact information for the big-name rental companies, see p516. Smaller, independent companies in Little Italy like **West Coast Rent A Car** (☎619-544-0606; www.westcoastrentacar.net; 834 W Grape St) offer cheaper rates for older rental cars; a one-day rental goes for about $35.

Taxi

Taxi fares start at $2.20 for the first one-tenth mile and $2.30 for each additional mile. Some established companies:

Orange Cab (☎619-291-3333; www.orangecabsandiego.com)

Yellow Cab (☎619-234-6161; www.driveu.com)

Train

Coaster commuter trains ($4.50 to $5.50) run from downtown's **Santa Fe train depot** (Map p430) up the coast to North County, stopping in Solana Beach, Encinitas, Carlsbad and Oceanside. Before entering North County, it stops at the Old Town Transit Center and Sorrento Valley, where there are Coaster Connections throughout Torrey Pines. Buy self-validating tickets from Coaster stations. Machines accept cash and credit cards.

There are 11 daily trains in each direction Monday to Friday; the first trains leave Oceanside at 5:15am and the Santa Fe depot at 6:31am; the last ones depart at 5:35pm and 7:03pm, respectively. Six trains run on Saturdays, four on Sundays and holidays.

For information, contact **North San Diego County Transit District** (☎619-233-3004, from North County 800-266-6883; www.gonctd.com).

Trolley

San Diego's trolleys are an efficient, convenient and typically safe way to travel. They're also fun, especially for kids. There are three lines – blue, orange and green. Blue Line trolleys head south to San Ysidro (last stop, just before Tijuana, Mexico) and north to Old Town Transit Center. The Green Line runs east through Mission Valley, past Fashion Valley to Qualcomm Stadium and Mission San Diego de Alcala. The Orange Line connects the Convention Center and Seaport Village with downtown.

Trolleys run between about 4:15am and midnight at roughly 15-minute intervals during the day and half-hour intervals in the evening. A one-way trolley route costs $2.50; buy tickets at vending machines on station platforms.

NORTH COUNTY COAST

The North County Coast feels like summer camp: loads of outdoor activities, gorgeous natural surroundings and a laid-back approach to daily life. If there's a real emergency, the big city is less than an hour away.

'North County,' as locals call it, begins at pretty Del Mar, just north of La Jolla and Torrey Pines, and continues up the coast through Solana Beach, Encinitas and Carlsbad (home of Legoland) before hitting Oceanside, largely a bedroom community for Camp Pendleton Marine Base. The communities hug the shore and overlook fantastic beaches (with lots of good surf spots). They also offer a variety of unique attractions, including the Del Mar Racetrack, the Chopra Center and Legoland.

As you drive north on Hwy 101, coastal cliffs and coves gradually give way to wide sandy shores. A constant companion is the railroad tracks, and though the trains can be distracting, they do make it easy to glide up here for a day trip. By car via I-5 in nonrush-hour traffic, Del Mar is only 20 to 30 minutes from San Diego, Oceanside 45 to 60 minutes.

ℹ Getting There & Around

For the most scenic approach, take N Torrey Pines Rd to Del Mar. Driving north along the coast, S21 changes its name from Camino del Mar to Coast Hwy 101 to Old Hwy 101 to Carlsbad Blvd. If you're in a hurry or headed to Los Angeles, the parallel I-5 is quicker. Traffic can snarl everywhere during rush hour, however, as well as during race or fair season when heading toward the Del Mar Racetrack.

Bus 101 departs from University Towne Centre near La Jolla and follows the coastal road to Oceanside; for information call the **North County Transit District** (NCTD; ☎760-966-6500; www.gonctd.com).

The NCTD also operates the *Coaster* commuter train, which originates at the Santa Fe Depot in downtown San Diego and travels north, stopping in Old Town, Solana Beach, Encinitas, Carlsbad and Oceanside. Train travel is an easy and convenient way to visit the north coast communities because most stations are right in town and close to the beach. See p457.

North County Coast

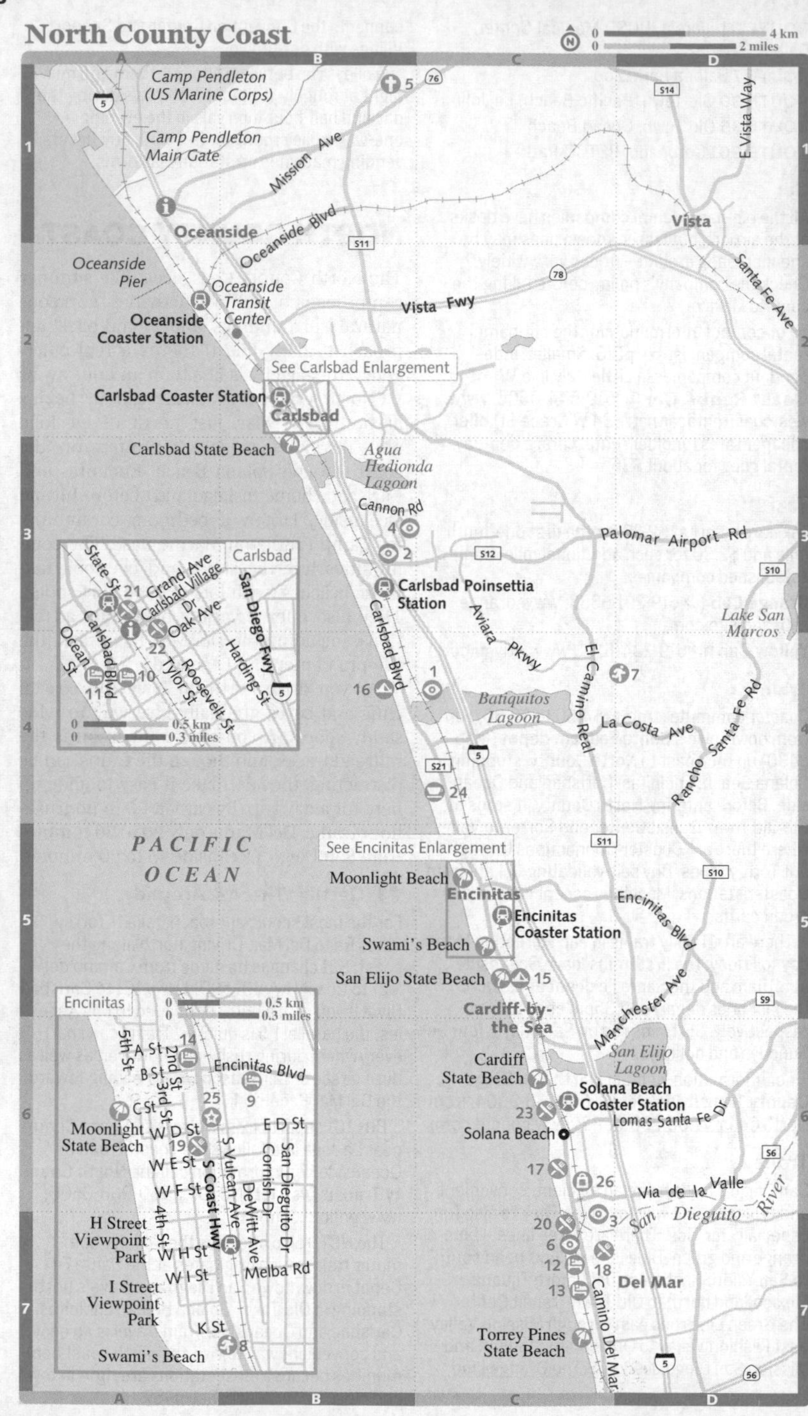

Camp Pendleton
(US Marine Corps)
Camp Pendleton
Main Gate
Mission Ave
Oceanside
Oceanside Blvd
Oceanside
Pier
Oceanside
Transit
Center
Oceanside
Coaster Station
Vista
Vista Fwy
Santa Fe Ave
E Vista Way
See Carlsbad Enlargement
Carlsbad Coaster Station
Carlsbad
Carlsbad State Beach
Agua
Hedionda
Lagoon
Cannon Rd
Palomar Airport Rd
Carlsbad Poinsettia
Station
Carlsbad Blvd
Aviara
Pkwy
El Camino Real
Lake San
Marcos
Batiquitos
Lagoon
La Costa Ave
Rancho Santa Fe Rd
Carlsbad
State St
Grand Ave
Carlsbad Village
Dr
Oak Ave
San Diego Fwy
Carlsbad Blvd
Ocean
St
Tylor St
Roosevelt St
Harding St
PACIFIC
OCEAN
See Encinitas Enlargement
Moonlight Beach
Encinitas
Encinitas
Coaster Station
Swami's Beach
San Elijo State Beach
Encinitas Blvd
Cardiff-by-
the Sea
Manchester Ave
San Elijo
Lagoon
Cardiff
State Beach
Solana Beach
Coaster Station
Lomas Santa Fe Dr
Solana Beach
Via de la Valle
San Dieguito River
Del Mar
Camino Del Mar
Torrey Pines
State Beach
Encinitas
5th St
A St
2nd St
B St
3rd St
Encinitas Blvd
C St
Moonlight
State Beach
W D St
E D St
W E St
S Coast Hwy
S Vulcan Ave
Cornish Dr
San Dieguito Dr
DeWitt Ave
W F St
H Street
Viewpoint
Park
4th St
W H St
W I St
Melba Rd
I Street
Viewpoint
Park
K St
Swami's Beach

North County Coast

Sights
1 Batiquitos Lagoon Nature Center C4
2 Carlsbad Ranch B3
3 Del Mar Racetrack & Fairgrounds C6
4 Legoland California B3
5 Mission San Luis Rey de Francia B1
6 Seagrove Park C7

Activities, Courses & Tours
7 Chopra Center for Wellbeing D4
8 Self-Realization Fellowship Retreat & Hermitage B7

Sleeping
9 Best Western Encinitas Inn & Suites B6
10 Best Western Plus Beach View Lodge A4
11 Carlsbad Inn Beach Resort A4
12 L'Auberge del Mar C7
13 Les Artistes Inn C7
14 Moonlight Beach Motel A6
15 San Elijo State Beach Campground C5
16 South Carlsbad State Park Campground B4

Eating
17 Beach Grass Café C6
18 Del Mar Plaza C7
19 El Q'ero A6
Harvest Ranch Market .... (see 18)
20 Jake's del Mar C7
21 Le Passage A3
22 Pizza Port Carlsbad A3
23 Pizza Port Solana Beach C6

Drinking
Carruth Cellars .... (see 26)
24 Pannikin Coffee & Tea C4

Entertainment
25 La Paloma Theatre A6

Shopping
26 Cedros Design District C6

Del Mar

North County's ritziest seaside suburb, Del Mar has good, if pricey, restaurants, high-end boutiques and a fabled horse-racing track that's also the site of the annual county fair in June. Downtown Del Mar (sometimes called 'the Village') extends for about a mile along Camino del Mar. Fifteenth St crosses Camino del Mar at the tasteful **Del Mar Plaza**, the city's unofficial hub, where you'll find restaurants, shops and upper-level terraces that look out to sea.

Sights & Activities

Seagrove Park PARK

At the beach end of 15th St, this park overlooks the ocean. Despite the occasional whooshing train on the adjacent train tracks, this little stretch of tidy beachfront lawn is a favorite gathering place for locals and a good spot for a picnic.

Del Mar Racetrack & Fairgrounds HORSE RACING

(☎858-755-1141; www.dmtc.com; 2260 Jimmy Durante Blvd; admission $5-20) Founded in 1937 by a number of Hollywood luminaries, including Bing Crosby and Jimmy Durante. The lush gardens and pink, Mediterranean-style architecture are a visual delight. Get gussied up for the horse races, which run from mid-July to early September.

California Dreamin' BALLOONING

(☎800-373-3359; www.californiadreamin.com; per person from $178) Brightly colored hot-air balloons are a trademark of the Del Mar's northern skies. Come here for a sunset flight.

Sleeping

L'Auberge del Mar LUXURY HOTEL $$$

(☎800-245-9757; www. laubergedelmar.com; 1540 Camino Del Mar; r from $450; P) This ecofriendly beachfront resort offers chic but simple guest rooms in shades of sand, sea and sky. The sunset view from the terrace and swimming pool – where an outdoor cocktail bar opens to the public – is probably the finest in Del Mar.

Les Artistes Inn QUIRKY, INN $$

(☎858-755-4646; www.lesartistesinn.com; 944 Camino del Mar; r from $105; P) One of the less expensive options (comparatively speaking) in Del Mar is this bohemian inn with Southwestern-style adobe architecture, Buddha statues in the courtyard, and a rustic central fireplace. Each of the 12 rooms is inspired by, and named for, a different famous artist.

SCENIC DRIVE: CARLSBAD TO DEL MAR

This pretty coastal drive takes you through the quaint towns of San Diego's North County, past a few notable geographic landmarks, past a design-minded shopping district, and ends up on a terrace with (you guessed it) a stunning ocean view.

What to See

Start in the village of Carlsbad (p461). Drive south along Carlsbad Blvd towards the Batiquitos Lagoon (p462), one of California's last remaining tidal wetlands. Continue south to Encinitas and stop for your caffeine fix at Pannikin Coffee and Tea (p461) along the PCH. Follow Hwy 101 past the San Elijo Lagoon and onto Solana Beach and the colorful Cedros Design District (p460) where you can pull over and browse the design books and home decor. While you're there, pick up a bottle of locally produced wine at Carruth Cellars (p460). Finish heading south on the dramatic downhill slope into Del Mar, stopping for sunset cocktails on the terrace at ecofriendly L'Auberge del Mar (p459)

The Route

Carlsbad Blvd south to Vulcan Ave, continuing south to North Coast Hwy 101 to Camino del Mar in Del Mar – the trick is to stay on the coastal road and never exit onto the freeway.

Time & Mileage

17 miles, 22 minutes without stops and one to two hours or more if you pull over frequently.

Eating

Jake's del Mar SEAFOOD **$$**
(☎858-755-2002; www.jakesdelmar.com; 1660 Coast Blvd; mains lunch $10-18, dinner $10-37; ⊙11:30am-9pm, from 4pm Mon) Just north of Seagrove Park is ever-popular Jake's, exuding a clubby feel with its wood-planked ceiling, historic photos, and rich old guys enjoying seafood chowder, crusted sea bass, filets and lobster tail. Great views of kids and volleyball players on the beach.

Harvest Ranch Market MARKET **$**
(www.harvestranchmarkets.com; 1555 Camino Del Mar; ⊙8am-9pm) To craft your own meal, try this place in the Del Mar Plaza for high-quality groceries and sandwiches for the beach. Check the sign outside for upcoming **wine tastings** ($10-20 per person; ⊙usually 4-6pm Thu & Fri, from 3pm Sat).

Solana Beach

Solana Beach may not be as posh as its southern neighbor, but it has lovely beaches as well as the **Cedros Design District** (Cedros Ave), a blocks-long avenue filled with home-furnishing stores, art and architecture studios, antiques shops and handcrafted-clothing boutiques.

Beach Grass Cafe (www.beachgrasscafe.com; 159 S Hwy 101; mains $6-15; ⊙7am-3pm daily, 5-9pm Sun-Thu; ✎) A local favorite for breakfast, Beach Grass Cafe's bestsellers include pineapple pancakes and macacha taco omelets.

Pizza Port (www.pizzaport.com; 135 N Hwy 101; mains $8-15) This branch of the popular local pizza and microbrew chain is across the street from the train station.

Carruth Cellars (☎858-847-9463; www.carruthcellars.com; 320 S Cedros Ave; ⊙noon-9pm Mon-Sat, to 6pm Sun) Taste Sonoma syrah and locally produced cheeses at this friendly urban winery.

Cardiff-by-the-Sea

The stretch of restaurants, surf shops and new age–style businesses just south of Encinitas (and technically part of that city) on the Pacific Coast Hwy – called 'Cardiff' by locals – is known for its surfing and laid-back crowds.

Cardiff is also home to **San Elijo Lagoon** (☎760-436-3944; www.sanelijo.org), an ecological preserve (almost 1000 acres) popular with bird-watchers for herons, coots, terns, ducks, egrets and about 250 more species. Nearly 7 miles of trails lead through the area. The nature center is at 2710 Manchester Ave.

At **Cardiff State Beach** (☎760-753-5091; www.parks.ca.gov; ⊙7am-sunset), just south of

Cardiff-by-the-Sea, the surf break on the reef is mostly popular with longboarders. A little further north, **San Elijo State Beach** has good winter waves.

San Elijo State Beach Campground (☎760-753-5091, reservations 800-444-7275; www.parks.ca.gov,reserveamerica.com; tent/RV sites $26/39;) Overlooks the surf at the end of Birmingham Dr.

Encinitas

Golden lotus domes mark the southern border of Encinitas on South Coast Hwy 101, setting an offbeat tone that permeates this funky little beach town. Since Paramahansa Yoganada founded his **Self-Realization Fellowship Retreat & Hermitage** here in 1937, the town has been a magnet for healers, seekers and hardcore surfers. The gold lotus domes of the hermitage also border the turnout for **Swami's**, a powerful reef break favored by territorial locals. If you practice yoga, meditation or just want a nice place to stretch your legs, stroll the hermitage's **Meditation Garden** (215 K St; www.yogananda-srf.org; 9am-5pm Tue-Sat, 11am-5pm Sun), which has wonderful ocean vistas.

The heart of Encinitas lies north of the hermitage between E and D Sts. Apart from the outdoor cafes, bars, restaurants and surf shops, the town's main attraction is **La Paloma Theatre** (☎760-436-7469; www.lapalomatheatre.com; 471 S Coast Hwy 101), built in 1928. La Paloma shows current movies nightly and *The Rocky Horror Picture Show* every Friday at midnight.

Sleeping

Moonlight Beach Motel MOTEL **$$**
(☎760-753-0623; www.moonlightbeachmotel.com; 233 2nd St; r $135-170;) Upstairs rooms have private decks and partial ocean views at this mom-and-pop motel, 1½ blocks from the sea and the kiddie-minded park at Moonlight Beach. Some furnishings could use upgrading, but rooms are clean, quiet and have furnished kitchens.

Best Western Encinitas Inn & Suites HOTEL **$$**
(☎760-942-7455; www.bwencinitas.com; 85 Encinitas Blvd; r $160-210;) With an exterior caught somewhere between treehouse-modern and adobe-mission, it's a nice surprise to find well-appointed, spacious rooms boasting all modern conveniences and up-to-date furnishings.

Eating & Drinking

El Q'ero PERUVIAN **$$$**
(☎760-753-9050; www.qerorestaurant.com; 564 S Coast Hwy; mains lunch $10-18, dinner $32-48; 11:30am-3pm & from 5pm Tue-Sun) Inside this tiny Peruvian charmer, red-tile floors, bright print tablecloths and boldly colored paintings set a convivial mood, but ah, it's the food that makes us happiest. Perfectly seasoned dishes like papa *lomo saltado* (flatiron steak with garlic, cracked pepper and sautéed onions) and *aji gallina* (tender chicken in toasted walnut and chili sauce) bring out the best flavors of Peru. And yes, 'slow food' aptly describes the cooking process, but it's well worth the wait. Make reservations for dinner.

Pannikin Coffee & Tea CAFE **$**
(www.pannikincoffeeandtea.com; 510 N Coast Hwy; 6am-6pm) As far as indie coffee shops go, this yellow former train station is a prime example of what works. Large patio dotted with Adirondack chairs? Check. Chalkboard list of coffee and teas? Check. Lots of muffins and desserts on display? Check. Quirky decor plus a well-planted inspirational quote or two? Check.

Carlsbad

While Carlsbad may be known for Legoland, a theme park built on our love for joinable

WHAT THE ...?

Discretion may be the better part of small talk when it comes to the much-maligned 'Magic Carpet Ride' statue erected on the west side of Hwy 101 at Chesterfield Dr in 2007. The intent was to commission a statue celebrating the surfing lifestyle – presumably something cool. The $120,000 result? A gangly young man with his arms awkwardly outstretched, trying to maintain his balance on the board. An object of derision and pranksters ever since, he's been draped in a Mexican wrestling mask and a bikini top. Judge for yourself: he's holding tight beside San Elijo State Beach.

plastic blocks, it's the natural attractions here that may be the most stunning, from long, sandy beaches to a 50-acre flower field to a flora-and-fauna filled lagoon.

The community got its start when train service arrived in the 1880s, building up a solid four square block downtown rather than stretching along the highway like most North County towns. Early homesteader John Frazier, a former ship's captain, sank a well and found water with a high mineral content, supposedly identical to that of spa water in Karlsbad, Bohemia (now the Czech Republic). He built a grand spa hotel that prospered until the 1930s.

Carlsbad is bordered by I-5 and Carlsbad Blvd, which run north-south. You'll find many of the community's hotels and restaurants clustered on or near Carlsbad Village Dr, the east-west road connecting I-5 and Carlsbad Blvd.

Sights & Activities

Legoland California AMUSEMENT PARK
(760-918-5346; www.california.legoland.com; 1 Legoland Dr; adult/child $69/59; opens 10am, closing hours vary;). Modeled loosely after the original in Denmark, Legoland California is a fantasy environment built on the backs of an army of joinable plastic building blocks. Geared toward younger kids, expect to spend most of the day here.

In the **Land of Adventure** area of the park, a 16ft Pharaoh made from 300,000-plus Legos guards the new Lost Kingdom Adventure. Inside, families can laser-blast targets from a moving car. A longtime highlight includes **Miniland**, where the skylines of major metropolitan cities have been spectacularly re-created entirely of Legos. Elsewhere, many activities are geared specifically to kids, such as face painting, boat rides and scaled-down roller coasters. Combination passes are available to the adjacent water park and aquarium.

From I-5, take the Legoland/Cannon Rd and follow the signs. From downtown Carlsbad or downtown San Diego, take the *Coaster* to the Carlsbad Village Station and hop on bus 344 straight to the park. Parking costs $12.

Carlsbad Ranch GARDENS
(760-431-0352; www.theflowerfields.com; 5704 Paseo del Norte; adult/senior/child $10/9/5; 9am-6pm) From early March to early May, nearly 50 acres of flower fields of Carlsbad Ranch come ablaze in a vibrant sea of carmine, saffron and snow-white ranunculus blossoms. The fields are two blocks east of I-5; take the Palomar Airport Rd exit, go east, then left on Paseo del Norte Rd.

Batiquitos Lagoon NATURE RESERVE
(760-931-0800; www.batiquitosfoundation.org; 7380 Gabbiano Ln; 9am-12:30pm Mon-Fri, to 3pm Sat & Sun) One of the last remaining tidal wetlands in California, Batiquitos Lagoon separates Carlsbad from Encinitas. A self-guided tour lets you explore area plants, including the prickly pear cactus, coastal sage scrub and eucalyptus trees, as well as lagoon birds, such as the great blue heron and the snowy egret. To get to the Nature Center follow Poinsettia Lane east past the I-5 turn and go right onto Batiquitos Dr, then turn right onto Gabbiano Lane, taking it to the end.

Chopra Center for Wellbeing SPIRITUAL
(760-494-1600; www.chopra.com; 2013 Costa del Mar; 7am-8pm Mon-Fri, to 6pm Sat & Sun) This den of tranquility and personal empowerment offers free tea to those browsing several shelves of books by alternative-health guru Deepak Chopra and acolyte David Simon. The welcoming (but no-pressure) center, located on the lush grounds of La Costa Resort & Spa, offers Ayurveda-based programs and workshops as well as yoga classes and personal consultations.

Sleeping & Eating

South Carlsbad State Park Campground CAMPGROUND $
(760-438-3143, reservations 800-444-7275; www.parks.ca.gov; 7201 Carlsbad Blvd; tent & RV sites $35-50;) Three miles south of downtown, this campground has 222 tent and RV sites and a bluff-top perch above the beach. Spots go fast; start calling months before your desired date.

Best Western Plus Beach View Lodge HOTEL $$
(760-729-1151; www.beachviewlodge.com; 3180 Carlsbad Blvd; d $152-215;) An Arts and Crafts–style lobby with great ocean views welcomes guests to this small, friendly Best Western that's just across Hwy 101 (called Carlsbad Blvd here) from the beach. Three floors wrap around a small courtyard and pool. (The 'Plus' means the place is nicer than your average Best Western.)

Carlsbad Inn Beach Resort LUXURY HOTEL $$$
(760-434-7020, 800-235-3939; www.carlsbadinn.com; 3075 Carlsbad Blvd; d from $240;) This upscale Tudor-style hotel and time-share

property sits just across from the beach. Guests have access to an elaborate calendar of events and activities from stand-up paddle-boarding ($15 per person) to yoga ($5), wine tasting ($5) and sailing ($45 per person).

Pizza Port PIZZERIA, PUB **$**
(www.pizzaport.com; 571 Carlsbad Village Dr; mains $8-20; ⏲11am-10pm Sun-Thu, to midnight Fri & Sat;) Pizza Port is like the general store of yore, an easygoing hub where everybody seems to swing by at some point. The main draw inside this surfboard-adorned mini-warehouse are the homebrewed beers and thick, buttery, almost fluffy slices, ranging from standard pepperoni to 'anti-wimpy' gourmet pies (margherita, garlic veggie).

Le Passage FRENCH **$$**
(www.lepassagefrenchbistro.net; 2961 State St; mains lunch $10-16, dinner $16-32; ⏲11:30am-3pm & 5pm-late Tue-Fri, noon-3pm & 5pm-late Sat) This welcoming country French bistro is a retreat from the ocean fray and a nice place to bump it up a notch (just a bit) from T-shirts and flip-flops. There's a rustic exposed-brick interior and cozy back patio where guests can enjoy baked brie and lavender roasted chicken.

Oceanside

Just outside the giant Camp Pendleton Marine Base, Oceanside lacks the charm of Encinitas and Carlsbad, but the wide beaches and fine surf continue unabated. Amtrak,

WORTH A TRIP

TEMECULA

According to the menu at the Swing Inn Cafe, 'Temecula' was a Native American word meaning 'The Valley of Joy.' That label certainly holds true today, with tourists flocking here for weekends filled with wine tasting, gambling and a bit of Old West style shopping.

Located in Riverside County, about one hour north from downtown San Diego, the area was a ranching outpost for Mission San Luis Rey in the 1820s, later becoming a stop along the Butterfield stagecoach line. But perhaps most interesting is the region's recent history. Marketing itself as a stylish wine country community, the town successfully lured newcomers with its small-town charms.

Tourists come to wander five-block Front St, the heart of Old Town Temecula, where faux Old West facades front a line-up of restaurants, antique dealers and wine shops. This is motorcycle country, so don't be surprised to hear Harleys rumbling up behind you. For cheap diner-style eats check out the aforementioned **Swing Inn Cafe** (www.swinginncafe; 28676 Old Town Front St; ⏲5am-9pm), where two eggs, two hotcakes and two strips of bacon will set you back six bucks. The hickory-smoked pork at nearby **Sweet Lumpy's BBQ** (www.sweetlumpys.com; 41915 3rd St; mains $7-20; ⏲11am-8pm Tue-Fri, from 8am Sat & Sun) was voted best barbecue in the Inland Empire. As for Old Town shopping, you'll find flavored olive oils and free samples at **Temecula Olive Oil Company** (www.temeculaoliveoil.com; 28653 Old Town Front St). Next door at **Temecula House of Jerky** (www.getmyjerky.com; 28655 Old Town Front St) look for ostrich, buffalo and venison jerky in addition to the usual teeth-pulling suspects. **Country Porch** (28693 Old Town Front St) is an atmospheric antiques market where you can shop for vintage sunglasses or cowboy boots.

Wine tasting is popular in the rolling hills about 10 minutes east of Old Town. **Wilson Creek** (☎951-699-9463; www.wilsoncreekwinery.com; 35960 Rancho California Rd; tastings $12-15; ⏲10am-5pm) makes almond champagne (infused with almond oil in the fermentation process) and a chocolate-infused port. Further afield, **Leonesse Cellars** (☎951-302-7601; www.leonessecellars.com; 38311 De Portola Rd; tastings $14; ⏲11am-5pm) offers award-winning viognier and Melange des Reves, plus sweeping views from its Tudor-esque tower. For a tour, try **Grapeline Temecula** (☎888-894-6379; www.gogrape.com; tasting-inclusive tour $98 per person). Visit www.temeculawines.org for links to the wineries' websites – many offer two-for-one tasting coupons.

To see Temecula by air, contact **California Dreamin'** (☎800-373-3359; www.californiadreamin.com) for an air balloon ride (from $178 per person). Of course, you could just blow off the wine, jerky and balloons and head straight to California's largest casino, **Pechanga Resort & Casino** (☎877-711-2946; www.pechanga.com; 45000 Pechanga Pkwy) where your perception of the Valley of Joy may depend on the spin of the wheel.

Greyhound, the *Coaster* and MTS buses stop at the **Oceanside Transit Center** (235 S Tremont St). Another crowd-getter is the **California Welcome Center** (☎760-721-1101, 800-350-7873; www.oceansidechamber.org, www.californiawelcomecenter.org; 928 N Coast Hwy; 9am-5pm), which has loads of brochures and coupons for local attractions, as well as maps and information about the San Diego area and the entire state.

Nearby, stretch your legs on the wooden **Oceanside Pier**, which extends 1942ft out to sea. **Mission San Luis Rey de Francia** (☎760-757-3651; www.sanluisrey.org; 4050 Mission Ave; adult/child/senior $5/3/4; 9am-5pm Mon-Fri, from 10am Sat & Sun), lies 4 miles inland. Founded in 1798, it was the 18th of the 21 California missions and, as the largest California mission, was dubbed 'King of the Missions.' It was also the most successful in recruiting Native American converts. After the Mexican government secularized the missions, San Luis fell into ruin; only the adobe walls of the 1811 church are original. Inside, exhibits highlight work and life in the mission, with some original religious art and artifacts. Ruins of the *lavanderia* (the Luiseno Indian laundry) and mission soldiers' barracks are visible in front. From I-5, follow Hwy 76 about 4 miles east. The mission is on the left at the Rancho del Oro exit.

Understand Coastal California

population per sq mile

California | Los Angeles | San Francisco

≈ 240 people

Coastal California Today

Californians by the Numbers

» Population 37.3 million

» Foreign-born residents 27%

» Residents who don't speak English at home 40%+

People & Politics

Even if you've seen it in the movies, coastal California may still be a shock. Venice Beach skateboarders, Humboldt hippies, Marin County wild-mushroom hunters, 'Bezerkely' professors and Silicon Valley millionaires aren't on different channels. They all live here, where tolerance for other's beliefs, be they conservative, liberal or wacky, is the social glue.

Today, the most divisive political hot potato may be same-sex marriage, and the proposed voter-approved constitutional amendment to ban it, which remains tied up in legal battles. Medical marijuana is old news for Californians, who approved a state proposition allowing its use back in 1996 – although the proliferation of raids on MMJ dispensaries and rumors of Mexican cartel intervention have raised eyebrows.

Environmental Roots

There's no denying that California's culture of conspicuous consumption is exported via Hollywood flicks and reality TV (hello, *Real Housewives of Orange County*!). But since the 1960s, Californians have trailblazed another, 'greener' way by choosing more sustainable foods and low-impact lifestyles, preserving old-growth forests with tree-sitting activism, declaring urban nuclear-free zones, pushing for environmentally progressive legislation and establishing the biggest US market for hybrid vehicles.

That shouldn't really come as a surprise. It was Californians who originally helped kick-start the world's conservation movement in the midst of the 19th-century industrial revolution, with laws curbing industrial dumping, swaths of prime real estate set aside as urban green space, and pristine wilderness protected by national and state parks. Today, even conservative California politicians prioritize environmental issues on their agendas – at least as much as the state's current economic woes allow.

Top Films

» *Maltese Falcon* (1941)

» *Sunset Boulevard* (1950)

» *The Graduate* (1967)

» *Chinatown* (1974)

» *Boyz n the Hood* (1991)

» *LA Confidential* (1997)

» *Sideways* (2004)

Top Downloads

» 'California Dreaming' – Mamas and the Papas

» 'Surfer Girl' – Beach Boys

» '(Sittin' on) The Dock of the Bay' – Otis Redding

» 'California Soul' – Fifth Dimension

» 'Los Angeles' – X

» 'Straight Outta Compton' – NWA

» 'California Gurls' – Katy Perry

» 'Californication' – Red Hot Chili Peppers

» 'California Love' – 2Pac

belief systems
(% of population)

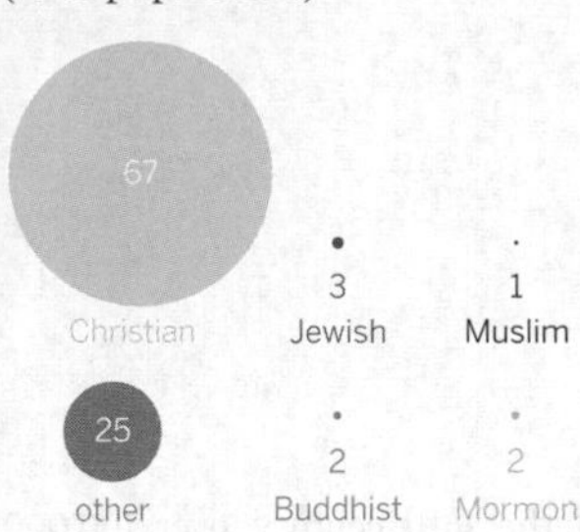

if California were 100 people

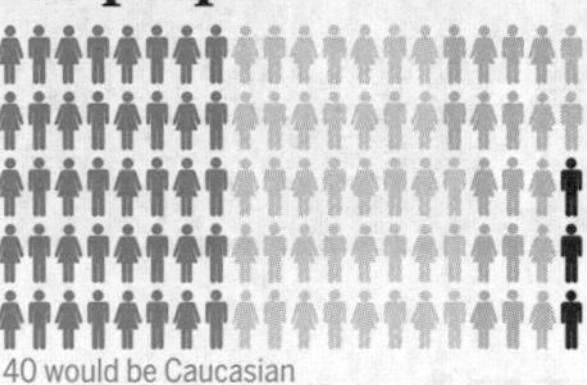

40 would be Caucasian
38 would be Latino
13 would be Asian American
6 would be African American
3 would be other

Fast Companies, Slow Economy

You might not get a word in edgewise when it comes to discussing the environment with a local, but California's technological innovations need no introduction by anyone. Perhaps you've heard of PCs, iPods, Google and the internet? The home of Silicon Valley and a burgeoning biotech industry, Northern California is giving Southern California's gargantuan entertainment industry a serious run for its money.

But even these industries haven't been enough to salvage the state's ravaged economy, which has spiraled out of control with the national subprime mortgage-lending crisis and lingering US recession. California's ongoing budget crisis has resulted in deep cuts in environmental protections, education, social services and other public programs, including state parks. While Governor Jerry Brown (Democrat) and state legislators argue about austerity measures, Californians are trying to live with the nation's highest employment rate and gas prices.

Growing Pains

The biggest problem California faces is growth itself. Because of the Golden State's adaptability and charms, the human wave of domestic migration and international immigration continues to crest. Many Americans and immigrants who heed the mid-19th-century advice to 'Go West, young man!' today find themselves winding up on California's shores.

With this burgeoning humanity come the skyrocketing costs of living and real estate. Public transportation is often inadequate, so everyone hits the tortured freeways. Sheer human impaction is a palpable force and begs the question that Rodney King asked in 1992: 'People, I just want to say, you know, can we all get along?' Like California's economic future, the answer to that famous question remains unknown.

California's Money Matters

» GDP $1.9 trillion (13% of USA)

» Annual medical-marijuana taxes $105 million

» Average per-capita income $29,020

» Median single-family home price $479,200

» Unemployment 12.1%

Dos and Don'ts

» Do expect distracted, enraged and unpredictable California freeway drivers to cut you off.

» Do slather on sunblock.

» Do tip when appropriate.

» Don't smoke indoors.

» Don't get tanked while wine tasting.

Go Outside

» If you want to do like locals do, get back to nature. More than 60% of Californians say they've hugged a tree, nearly 25% have tried surfing and at least one out of every five skinny dips on occasion.

Tribal Casinos

» Though Native Californian tribal reservations account for less than 1% of the total land in the state, voter-approved 1998 state Proposition 5, allowing gambling on reservations, generates almost $7 billion annually.

History

When European explorers arrived in the 16th century, over 100,000 Native Americans called this land home, speaking over 100 diverse languages and living in small villages along the coast, at seasonal mountain camps or nomadically in the desert.

Spanish conquistadors combed through what they called 'Alta California' (Upper California, as opposed to Baja, or Lower California) in search of a fabled 'city of gold' but left the territory alone after failing to find it. Not until the Mission Period (1769–1810) did Spain make a serious attempt to settle the land, establishing 21 Catholic missions for conversion purposes, and presidios (military forts) to keep out other would-be foreign colonizers.

After winning independence from Spain in 1821, Mexico briefly ruled California until it was trounced by the fledgling United States in the 1846–48 Mexican-American War. The discovery of gold soon sent the territory's population soaring from 14,000 to 92,000 by 1850, when California became the 31st US state.

Thousands of imported Chinese laborers helped complete the transcontinental railroad in 1869, which opened up markets on both coasts and further spurred migration to the Golden State. Mexican immigrants arrived during the 1910–21 Mexican Revolution and again during WWII to fill labor shortages.

During WWII, military-driven industries developed, while anti-Asian sentiments led to the internment of many Japanese Americans, especially those living in San Francisco and Los Angeles. Reacting against the banal complacency of post-WWII suburbia, 1950s beatniks and 1960s hippies flocked to California spreading poetry and free love, and in the '70s, Gay Pride activists kept the social revolution going.

The internet revolution, spurred by Silicon Valley near San Francisco, rewired the economy and led to a 1990s boom in overspeculated stocks. When the bubble burst in 2000, it plunged the state's economy into cha-

Top History Books

» *California: A History* (Kevin Starr)

» *A World Transformed: Firsthand Accounts of California Before the Gold Rush* (Joshua Paddison)

» *Cadillac Desert: The American West and Its Disappearing Water* (Marc Reisner)

TIMELINE

Around 15,000 BC

First people start crossing from Asia into North America via the Bering Strait land bridge. The bones of a human found on California's Santa Rosa Island date back 11,000 years.

AD 1542

Portuguese navigator Juan Rodríguez Cabrillo and his Spanish crew become the first Europeans to sight the mainland of New Spain's west coast, anchoring in today's San Diego Bay.

1769

Spain attempts to colonize California when Padre Junípero Serra and Captain Gaspar de Portolá lead an expedition to establish the first Catholic missions in Alta California, starting in San Diego.

os, especially when deregulation of the electricity market led to rolling blackouts and sky-high power bills.

In the new millennium, meltdowns on Wall Street and the lingering US recession have caused a staggering financial crisis that California has yet to bounce back from. Ballistic population growth, pollution and traffic are other vexing issues. Meanwhile, the need for public education and prison reform builds, and the conundrum of illegal immigration from Mexico, which fills a critical labor shortage, remains unsolved.

California's First Peoples

Immigration is hardly a new phenomenon here: human beings have been migrating to California for millennia. Many archaeological sites have yielded evidence, from large middens of seashells along the beaches to campfire sites on the Channel Islands, that a diversity of indigenous tribes have been living along this coast for up to 12,000 years.

Northern coastal tribes such as the Tolowa, Ohlone, Yurok and Pomo used redwood trees to build dugout canoes and fished for salmon. Chumash villages dotted the southern coast, from where tribespeople voyaged out to the Channel Islands. Furthest south, the nomadic Kumeyaay tribe hunted, foraged and fished along the coast near present-day San Diego.

Traditionally, most Native Californian tribes made and used earthenware pots, fishing nets, bows with arrows and spears with chipped-stone points, while crafting animal skins and plant fibers into clothing. The most developed craft was weaving baskets, often with intricate geometric designs; some baskets were so tightly woven they could even hold water.

Despite pockets of armed resistance and violent revolts, indigenous tribes were made to construct the Spanish missions and presidios in the late 18th and early 19th centuries. Native Californians were further dispossessed of tribal lands during the Mexican colonial and early American periods. Not until the 20th century when the US federal government began to recognize tribes as sovereign nations did indigenous populations once driven almost to the point of disappearing begin to rebound.

Political activism, including the 'Red Power' protests of the American Indian Movement (AIM) starting in the late 1960s, led to a cultural renaissance and secured some of California's tribes economic assistance from state and federal agencies. Deprived of their traditional land base and means of livelihood long ago, many modern tribes have turned to casino gaming to alleviate unemployment and poverty.

ETYMOLOGY

The precise etymology of 'California' has never been convincingly established, though many think it derives from a 16th-century Spanish romance novel about a legendary island, fabulously rich in gold and inhabited only by black women warriors ruled by Queen Califia.

A New World for Europeans

Following the conquest of Mexico in the early 16th century, the Spanish turned their attention toward exploring the edges of their new empire. In 1542 the Spanish crown engaged Juan Rodríguez Cabrillo, a Portuguese

1781

Mexican governor of California, Felipe de Neve, and a tiny band of settlers set out from Mission San Gabriel and trek just 9 miles away to found Los Angeles.

1821

Mexican independence ends Spanish colonial dreams. Mexico inherits 21 Catholic missions in various states of disrepair, but quickly reorganizes Alta California into ranchos (land grants).

1826–32

Teenage Kit Carson helps blaze the Santa Fe Trail, which eventually leads to Los Angeles through 900 miles of rattlesnake-filled high desert and plains guarded by Native American tribes.

1848

After winning the Mexican-American War and signing the Treaty of Guadalupe Hidalgo, the US takes control of Alta California, luckily just as gold is discovered in the Sierra Nevada foothills.

explorer and retired conquistador, to lead an expedition up the West Coast to find the fabled golden land beyond Mexico's west coast.

When Cabrillo sailed into San Diego Bay in 1542, he and his crew became the first Europeans to see mainland California. Staring back at them from shore were the Kumeyaay. Cabrillo's ships sat out a storm in the harbor, then sailed northward. They made a stop at the Channel Islands where Cabrillo fell ill, died and was buried. The expedition continued as far as Oregon, but returned with no evidence of a city of gold. Unimpressed Spanish colonial authorities ignored California for the next 50 years.

The English privateer Sir Francis Drake later sailed up the California coast in 1579. He missed the entrance to San Francisco Bay, but pulled in near what is today called Point Reyes to repair his ship, which was practically bursting with the weight of plundered Spanish silver. The coastal Miwok believed the English mariners to be the spirits of dead relatives returned from the afterworld. Drake quickly claimed their land for Queen Elizabeth, named it Nova Albion (New England) and sailed on to other adventures, journeying north up the Pacific coast to Alaska.

Top Spots for Native American History

- Patrick's Point State Park, North Coast
- Chumash Painted Cave State Historic Park, Santa Barbara
- Museum of the American West, Los Angeles
- Museum of Man, San Diego

The Mission Impossible

In the late 18th century, as Russian ships came to California's coast in search of sea-otter pelts, and British trappers and explorers spread throughout the West, Spain grew worried that these other newcomers might pose a threat to their colonial claims. Conveniently, the Catholic Church was anxious to start missionary work among California's indigenous peoples, so church and state combined forces to found a chain of Spanish missions and presidios near the coast.

A sorry lot of about 100 missionaries and soldiers, met by military commander Gaspar de Portolá and Franciscan priest Junípero Serra, limped ashore at San Diego Bay in 1769. The men had just spent several weeks at sea sailing from Baja California; about half had died en route and many of the survivors were sick or near death. It was an inauspicious beginning for Mission San Diego de Alcalá, the first of the chain of 21 California missions.

If you're wondering about the traditions and lifestyles of California's Native American tribes, find answers in the readable natural history guide *California Indians and Their Environment*, by Kent Lightfoot and Otis Parrish.

Ostensibly, the presidios' purpose was to protect the missions and deter foreign intruders. The idea was to have Native American converts live inside the missions, learn trade and agricultural skills, and ultimately establish pueblos (small towns). But these garrisons created more threats than they deterred, as the soldiers aroused local hostility by raiding and looting tribal camps and kidnapping and raping indigenous women. Not only were the presidios militarily weak, but their weaknesses were well known to Russia and Britain, and they didn't strengthen Spain's claims to California.

1850

After debate about whether it would be a slaveholding or free state (Congress chooses the latter), California enters the Union. Its first constitution is written in both Spanish and English.

1869

A golden spike is nailed in Utah, completing the first transcontinental railroad linking California with the East Coast. Gold is uncovered outside San Diego, unleashing a 30-year mining frenzy.

» Chinatown, San Francisco

1882

The US Chinese Exclusion Act suspends new immigration from China, denies citizenship to those already in the country and sanctions racially targeted laws that stay on the books until 1943.

Ultimately, the mission period was a failure. The Spanish population remained small; the missions achieved little more than mere survival; foreign intruders were not deterred much; and more Native Americans died from European diseases, culture shock and conscript labor than were converted. Several of California's original Spanish missions still stand today, though a few are in ruins – some toppled by earthquakes, others broken by forced secularization under Mexican rule.

From Mexico to Manifest Destiny

When Mexico gained independence from Spain in 1821, many of that new nation's people looked to California to satisfy their thirst for private land. By the mid-1830s all but one Spanish mission had been secularized so that Mexican governors could dole out hundreds of free land grants, or ranchos, that were largely given over to livestock to supply the profitable trade in hide and tallow. The new landowners, called rancheros or Californios, prospered and became the social, cultural and political elite.

Meanwhile, American explorers, trappers, traders, whalers, settlers and other pioneering opportunists showed increasing interest in California, seizing on economic prospects that the rancheros largely ignored. Some US citizens who started businesses in the Mexican territory of Alta California even converted to Catholicism, married locals and successfully assimilated into local ranchero society.

Impressed by California's potential wealth and hoping to fulfill the promise of Manifest Destiny (the USA's imperialist doctrine to extend its borders from coast to coast), President Andrew Jackson sent an emissary to offer the financially strapped Mexican government $500,000 for California in 1835. Though American settlers were by then showing up by the hundreds, Jackson's emissary was tersely rejected.

By 1836 Texas had seceded from Mexico and declared itself an independent republic. Ten years later, the US declared war on Mexico following disputes over the US annexation of Texas. By July, US naval units occupied every port on the California coast, including Monterey, the capital of Alta California. When US troops captured Mexico City in September 1847, ending the war, the Mexican government had little choice but to cede much of its northern territory. The Treaty of Guadalupe Hidalgo, signed on February 2, 1848, turned over what is now California to the USA.

Don't-Miss Missions

- San Juan Capistrano (best exemplary architecture)
- Santa Barbara (never secularized)
- San Diego (oldest)
- La Purísima (most complete restoration)
- San Carlos Borroméo de Carmelo (Padre Serra's tomb)

Eureka! The Gold Rush Is On

By remarkable coincidence, gold was discovered at Sutter's Creek, in California's Sierra Nevada foothills, little more than a week before the signing of the Treaty of Guadalupe Hidalgo ended the Mexican-American War. By 1849 surging rivers of wagon trains were creaking into California filled with miners, pioneers, savvy entrepreneurs, outlaws and

1892

Oil is discovered by Edward Doheny in downtown LA, near where Dodger Stadium stands today, sparking a major oil boom. Within a decade, LA's population doubles to over 100,000 people.

April 18, 1906

A massive earthquake levels entire blocks of San Francisco in less than a minute, setting off fires that rage for three days. Survivors start rebuilding immediately.

1913

The Los Angeles Aqueduct, built under the direction of city engineer William Mulholland, starts supplying a thirsty metropolis with water controversially taken from the eastern Sierra Nevada.

June 29, 1925

At 6.44am, a 6.3-magnitude earthquake levels most of downtown Santa Barbara, killing 13 people. The city purposefully rebuilds in Spanish colonial style, with its now signature red-tile roofs.

prostitutes, all seeking their fortunes. In 1850, less than two years after being ceded by Mexico, California became the USA's 31st state.

Overnight wealth and a flood of new immigrants from around the world stimulated every aspect of California life, from banking and construction to journalism and agriculture. But mining also damaged the land: hills were stripped bare, erosion wiped out vegetation, streams silted up and mercury washed down rivers all the way into San Francisco Bay. Meanwhile, San Francisco became a hotbed of gambling, prostitution, drink and chicanery, giving rise to its moniker 'the Barbary Coast,' an allusion to Africa's north coast where pirates preyed upon Mediterranean ships.

In 1860, California vicariously experienced a second boom after the discovery of the Comstock silver lode, discovered east of the Sierra Nevada in present-day Nevada. Exploiting this mother lode required deep-mining techniques, which in turn necessitated California's big-shouldered industrial companies, stocks, trading and speculation. In fact, San Francisco made more money speculating on silver than Nevada did mining it: huge mansions sprouted on the city's Nob Hill, and California's new business tycoons became renowned for their unscrupulous audacity.

BLUE JEANS

In 1873, German immigrant and San Francisco store owner Levi Strauss received a patent for his hard-wearing, riveted denim pants, originally designed for California's gold prospectors – and, voilà! – American blue jeans were born.

Riches from Railroads & Real Estate

Opening the floodgates to massive migration into the West in 1869, the transcontinental railroad shortened the trip from New York to San Francisco from two months to less than four days, elevating the latter to California's metropolitan center. Meanwhile, Southern California's parched climate, its distance from water resources, and relatively small population made it less attractive to profit-minded railroad moguls, though wheeling and dealing finally resulted in a spur line to LA in 1876.

By this time, rampant speculation had raised land prices in California to levels no farmer or immigrant could afford. The railroad brought in products that undersold goods made in California, while some 15,000 Chinese laborers – no longer needed for railroad construction work or mining – flooded the labor market, especially in San Francisco. A period of anti-foreign discrimination and unrest ensued, which culminated in federal legislation banning Chinese immigration outright in 1882.

Much of the land granted to railroads was flipped and sold in big lots to speculators who also acquired, with the help of corrupt politicians and bureaucrats, much of the farmland intended for new settlers. A major share of California's agricultural land was consolidated in the hands of a few city-based landlords, establishing the still-existing pattern of industrial 'agribusiness' rather than small family farms, and solidifying an ongoing need for large-scale irrigation projects and cheap migrant farm labor.

1927

The Jazz Singer premieres in Los Angeles as the world's first feature-length 'talkie' movie, signaling the decline of the silent-film era. Worldwide movie demand kicks off Hollywood's Golden Age.

WITOLD SKRYPCZAK/LONELY PLANET IMAGES ©

» Hollywood Walk of Fame

1934

A longshoremen's strike in San Francisco ends with dozens of labor activists shot or beaten by police. After mass funeral processions and a citywide strike, shipping magnates meet union demands.

1941

Following Japan's attack on Pearl Harbor on December 7, the US enters WWII. In February 1942, US Executive Order 9066 banishes 120,000 Japanese Americans to internment camps, including in California.

Labor & Military Might

The Great Depression saw another wave of immigrants, this time of American farm families from drought-struck Great Plains states who were fleeing the Dust Bowl. In the promised land of California, they often found social discrimination against 'Okies' and only scant pay and deplorable working conditions at agribusinesses. Outbreaks of social and labor protest led to the rapid growth of the Democratic Party in California, as well as growing trade unions for blue-collar workers.

Many of California's Depression-era public works projects that were sponsored by the federal government have had lasting benefits, including construction of the ambitious San Francisco–Oakland Bay Bridge, the restoration of historic Spanish missions and improvements to highways and parklands. But it was really California's cutting-edge aviation industry – pumped up by billions of dollars from US military contracts – that really helped boost the state out of the Great Depression.

California's workforce permanently changed in WWII, when women and African Americans were recruited for wartime industries and Mexican workers were brought in to fill agricultural labor shortages. San Diego became the headquarters of the entire US Pacific Fleet, while Southern California aircraft manufacturing plants turned out planes by the thousands. Military contracts attracted an international elite of engineers, who would later launch California's high-tech industry.

After WWII, many service people settled on the West Coast. Within a decade after the war, California's population had grown by 40%, almost reaching 13 million. The state's military-industrial complex continued to prosper during the Cold War, providing jobs in everything from avionics and missile manufacturing to nuclear submarine maintenance. Military spending peaked in the 1980s under ex-California governor and then US president Ronald Reagan, lasting until the end of the Cold War.

The Academy Award-winning 2007 film *There Will Be Blood* is adapted from Upton Sinclair's book *Oil!*, about fictional California oil magnate Daniel Plainview, whose story is based on real-life SoCal tycoon Edward Doheny.

Social Movers & Shakers

Unconstrained by the burden of traditions and promoted by film and TV, California has been a leader in new attitudes and social movements. During the affluent 1950s, the Beat movement in San Francisco's North Beach railed against the banality and conformity of suburban life, instead choosing bohemian coffeehouses for jazz, poetry and pot.

When the postwar baby boomers came of age, many hippies took up where the Beat generation left off, heeding 1960s countercultural icon Timothy Leary's counsel to 'turn on, tune in, and drop out.' Sex, drugs and rock and roll ruled the day. With the foundations for social revolution already laid, protestors marched against the Vietnam War and for civil rights in the late 1960s, then again for gay liberation in the '70s.

A noir film masterpiece, *Chinatown* (1974) is the fictionalized yet surprisingly realistic account of the brutal early-20th-century water wars that were waged to build Los Angeles and San Francisco.

July 17, 1955

In Anaheim, Disneyland opens to guests and bad press, as crowds swarm the theme park, plumbing breaks, temperatures soar over 100°F (38°C) and ladies' high-heeled shoes sink into the still-soft asphalt.

1969

UCLA professor Len Kleinrock sends data from a computer in Los Angeles to another at Stanford University, typing just two characters before the system crashes. The internet is born.

1977

San Francisco Supervisor Harvey Milk becomes the first openly gay man elected to US public office. Milk sponsors a gay-rights bill before his 1978 murder by political opponent Dan White.

October 17, 1989

The 6.9-magnitude Loma Prieta Earthquake hits near Santa Cruz, destroying a two-level section of the Interstate 880, collapsing a section of San Francisco's Bay Bridge and resulting in 63 deaths.

Since the 1980s, California has become synonymous with a healthy lifestyle obsession, with more aerobics classes and self-actualization workshops than you could shake a shaman's stick at. Inline skating, snowboarding and mountain biking rose to fame here first. Be careful what you laugh at, though: from pet rocks to soy burgers, California's flavor of the month is often next year's global trend.

Nobel Prize-winning novelist John Steinbeck's *The Grapes of Wrath* narrates the epic journey of the Joad family as they struggle to escape the Dust Bowl and reach California by motoring along Route 66.

High-Tech Booms & Busts

In the 1950s, Stanford University in Palo Alto needed to raise money to finance postwar growth, so it built an industrial park and leased space to high-tech companies like Hewlett-Packard, which formed the nucleus of Silicon Valley. In 1971 Intel invented the microchip, and in 1976 Apple invented the first personal computer, paving the way for the global internet revolution of the 1990s.

By the late 1990s, an entire dot-com industry had boomed in Silicon Valley, and companies nationwide jumped on the dot-com bandwagon following the exponential growth of the web. Many reaped huge overnight profits from start-ups, fueled by misplaced optimism, only to crash with equal velocity at the turn of the millennium.

No place in America was more affected by the demise of the dot-coms in 2000 than California. That same year also brought widespread power shortages and rolling blackouts to California, which were caused by Enron's illegal manipulation of markets. But before the truth came out, Republican malcontents fingered then-Governor Gray Davis and called for a special recall election that ousted him.

To read more about the garage-workshop culture of Silicon Valley go to www.folklore.org, which covers the crashes and personality clashes that made geek history.

Enter Arnold Schwarzenegger – Californians will always forgive a movie star more easily than a politician. Although a Republican, Schwarzenegger's actions pointed out that he intended to govern from California's political center, notably when it came to environmental issues. He fought to pass legislation that helped California lead the nation in cutting greenhouse emissions, even as US President and fellow Republican George W Bush rejected the Kyoto Protocol.

Then came the unraveling of the US subprime mortgage-lending crisis, which triggered the stock-market crash of 2008 and mired the entire nation in a recession. Massive unemployment devastated California, once the world's sixth-largest economy. By 2010 the state was so broke that it had issued IOU slips to creditors and newly elected Governor Jerry Brown, a liberal Democrat, was forced to make massive cuts to social services, education and state parks funding.

1992

Three of four white police officers charged with beating African American Rodney King are acquitted by a predominantly white jury. Following the trial, Los Angeles endures six days of riots.

2003

Body builder and movie actor Arnold Schwarzenegger announces his Republican candidacy for governor on *The Tonight Show with Jay Leno*. In October's recall election, he wins with 4.2 million votes.

2008

Four years after San Francisco Mayor Gavin Newsom officiated same-sex marriage, California voters narrowly pass Proposition 8, a constitutional ban on same-sex marriages.

2012

Due to California's fiscal crisis, statewide budget cuts slash many social services, as well as public education; overcrowded prisons release some nonviolent female prisoners;.

California Flavor

As you graze the Golden State, eating everything from surfer-worthy fish tacos to foraged-ingredient urban tasting menus, you'll often have cause to compliment the chef – but they're quick to turn around and share the praise with local farmers, ranchers, fishers and artisan food producers. Almost anything can and does grow in California's fertile valleys; rain-soaked coastal pastures provide grazing territory for livestock; sun-drenched vineyards overflow with prized grapes; and with more than 1000 miles of coastline, seafood just doesn't get much fresher than this.

California Cuisine: Then & Now

To really strike up a conversation with a Californian, skip asking about the weather (or worse, the economy) and instead start right in on the food. Say, 'So where's a good place for a taco around here?' and everyone within earshot will have an opinion. Californians proselytize about their food and idolize homegrown chefs like rock stars. And after a few bites you may begin to understand why.

'Let the ingredients speak for themselves!' is the rallying cry of California cuisine. Heavy French sauces and fussy molecular-gastronomy foams need not apply, as dishes are prepared with a light touch. Mulling over menus often means taking a political stand on issues close to many Californians' hearts: organic and non-GMO crops, veganism, grass-fed versus grain-fed meat, biodynamic vineyards and fair-trade coffee. It's no accident that the term 'locavore' – meaning people who buy and eat food grown locally – was invented here.

Some Pacific species have been overfished to near-extinction, disrupting local aquaculture. For good choices and also items to avoid on local seafood and sushi-bar menus, check the Monterey Bay Aquarium's Seafood Watch List (www.montereybayaquarium.org/cr/seafoodwatch.aspx), now available as a free mobile app.

What's with All that Fusion?

Beyond exceptionally rich dirt, California has another culinary advantage: an experimental attitude toward food that dates from its Wild West days. Most '49ers (mid-19th-century gold miners) were men not accustomed to cooking for themselves, as seems obvious from such early mining-camp culinary experiments as jelly omelets and chop suey, an American Chinese noodle dish with a name derived from the Cantonese expression 'odds and ends.' But the Gold Rush era also introduced Californians to Cantonese-style dim sum and the first US Italian restaurant, opened in San Francisco in 1886.

Some 150 years later, fusion is not a fad but second nature in California, where chefs can hardly resist adding local twists to international flavors, with creative infusions from new immigrant communities. Remember that California once belonged to Mexico, and Californian takes on Mexican classics remain go-to comfort foods for many people. Californian cross-pollination has also yielded wilder fusion experiments: just witness the Korean taco, with marinated beef, picked vegetables and rice wrapped up in a Mexican corn tortilla.

Alice Waters' California Food Revolution

Local, seasonal eating is hitting the US mainstream, but in California it started 40 years ago. As the turbulent 1960s wound down, many disillusioned idealists concluded that the revolution was not about to be delivered on a platter – but California's pioneering organic farmers weren't about to give up the idea. In 1971, Alice Waters opened Chez Panisse in a converted house in Berkeley, with the then-radical notion of making the most of California's seasonal, all-natural, sustainably produced bounty – and diners quickly tasted the difference.

What are your best bets on local menus? Given coastal California's varied regional cuisine, that depends on where you are, and the time of year. For what's ripe and in season right now, check www.cuesa.org/page/seasonal-foods.

Today, Waters' credo of organic, seasonal, locally grown cuisine has inspired countless other kitchens to follow suit. Eating 'green' like a slow-food loving 'locavore' isn't a tall order in coastal California, where weekly certified farmers markets, natural-foods grocery stores and organic farm co-ops abound. Many top chefs make a point of using organic, seasonal produce whenever possible and only order fish, meat or poultry from local, sustainable sources. Bottled water shipped over from Fiji or France? No, thank you; filtered tap water will be just fine.

Vegetarians, Vegans & an Omnivore's Feast

To all you beleaguered vegetarians: relax, you are not an afterthought in California cuisine, which revolves around seasonal produce instead of the usual American meat and potatoes. Long before actress Alicia Silverstone (of *Clueless* fame) championed a vegan diet in her cookbook *The Kind Diet* and website (www.thekindlife.com), California restaurants were catering to vegans. Bakeries, bistros, cafes, coffee shops and even mom-and-pop counter joints are usually prepared for meat-free, dairy-free, gluten-free and/or eggless requests and menu substitutions.

To find vegetarian and vegan restaurants and health-food stores throughout coastal California, consult the free online directory at Happy Cow (www.happycow.net).

Although California may have more vegetarians and vegans per capita than any other US state, many locals ardently love meat. Trendsetting restaurants' menus proudly herald the names of local farms that supply grass-fed, free-range and hormone-free beef, pork, lamb, chicken, duck and even American heritage-breed turkeys. Not only does being grass-fed improve the meat's texture and flavor, but it's more ecofriendly, since livestock aren't forced to consume a crop that requires vast amounts of water, fuel and electricity to grow and process into feed.

Food Fight! West Coast vs East Coast

It's true, California's food fixations are easily exaggerated, but not every Californian demands grass-fed burgers with heirloom tomato ketchup. When New York chefs David Chang and Anthony Bourdain mocked California cuisine as merely putting an organic fig on a plate, Californian chefs turned the tables, saying that New York needs to get out more often and actually try some Mission figs – one of hundreds of heirloom varietals cultivated by Californians since the 18th century.

UC Berkeley professor Michael Pollan's groundbreaking book *The Omnivore's Dilemma: A Natural History of Four Meals* (2007) traces exactly where the food a contemporary Bay Area family eats comes from, all the way down the food chain from McDonald's fast food to a DIY foraged, hunted and farmed feast.

East–West Coast foodie rivalries are rowdy, with culinary pundits tracking James Beard Awards (the culinary Oscars) like sportscasters ranking pro teams. California chefs are breaking boundaries, expanding beyond historic Cal-Mex and Cal-Italian fusion to more newly-minted hyphenated cuisines: Cal-Vietnamese, Cal-Moroccan, even Cal-Ecuadorian. Meanwhile, New York menus have been looking suspiciously Californian, citing local farms and introducing specialty organics from (where else?) California.

California Cooking Courses

Take California's signature dishes home, with leading California chefs sharing their culinary secrets in workshops and classes at the following places:

Culinary Institute of America at Greystone (p175) Weekend baking and cooking classes, chef demonstrations and wine-tasting seminars in Napa Valley.
Le Cordon Bleu (www.chefs.edu) 'Master Chef' classes land you in culinary boot camp, or just dabble in holiday baking or Mediterranean, Asian and Latin American cuisine.
New School of Cooking (www.newschoolofcooking.com) Learn ethnic cooking from the pros in LA, anything from traditional Cuban flavors to Italian pasta-making to Thai street food.
Cheese School of San Francisco (www.cheeseschoolsf.com) This North Beach kitchen lets you experiment with making homemade mozzarella and perfectly pairing artisan cheeses with wine, beer and even whiskey.
Ramekins Sonoma Valley Culinary School (p187) In downtown Sonoma, stuff your own sausage, dip into Mexican cooking or join a winemaker or brewmaster for dinner.
Cavallo Point Cooking School (www.cavallopoint.com) Seasonal, sustainably themed cooking classes showcase local chefs and organic, fresh farmers-market fare.
Laguna Culinary Arts (www.lagunaculinaryarts.com) Home-chef classes for all skill levels, plus wine and cheese tastings and date-night DIY dinners for couples.
Relish Culinary Adventures (p208) Cooking demos and hands-on baking, cheese-making and dinner-party workshops in the Russian River Valley's wine country.
Sushi Academy (www.sushi-academy.com) Apprentice in the art of finessing raw fish and Japanese sake tasting in LA.
Montecito Country Kitchen (www.mckcuisine.com) Near Santa Barbara, this chefs gourmet-food shop puts on seasonal, farm-to-table cooking classes and farmers-market demonstrations.

Some high-end cookware shops such as **Williams-Sonoma** (www.williams-sonoma.com) and **Sur la Table** (www.surlatable.com) also offer casual introductory cooking classes.

Edible Regional Specialties

San Francisco Bay Area

Today, San Francisco's adventurous eaters support the most award-winning chefs and restaurants per capita of any US city – five times more restaurants than New York, if anyone's keeping score – and 25 farmers markets in San Francisco alone, more than any other US city. Some San Francisco food novelties have had extraordinary staying power, including ever-popular *cioppino* (seafood stew), chocolate bars invented by the Ghirardelli family, and sourdough bread, with original Gold Rush–era mother dough still yielding local loaves with that distinctive tang. Beyond the obvious Pacific Rim influences, from Chinese dim sum to Japanese *izakaya* (gastropubs), no SF chef's tasting menu is complete without some foraged ingredients – such as wild chanterelle mushrooms found beneath Bay Area oak trees – and plates of artisan cheeses such as Point Reyes blue and fresh oysters from Marin County over the Golden Gate Bridge.

FOOD & WINE FESTIVALS

February

San Francisco Chronicle Wine Competition (www.winejudging.com) The world's stiffest competition of American wines, with tastings and gourmet food vendors.

May

Castroville Artichoke Festival (www.artichoke-festival.org) 3D 'agro-art' sculptures, chef demos and a food-and-wine expo near Monterey.

May

Cooking for Solutions (www.montereybayaquarium.org) Celebrity chefs showcase sustainably farmed and fished ingredients to benefit the Monterey Aquarium.

July

LA Street Food Fest (http://lastreetfoodfest.com) Let the food trucks come find you for a change (finally!) in Pasadena.

September

San Diego Festival of Beer (http://sdbeerfest.org) One of the coast's biggest gatherings of microbrewers.

September/ October

Sonoma County Harvest Fair (www.harvestfair.org) Wine competition and tastings, artisan food marketplace, cooking demos and championship grape-stomping in Santa Rosa.

November

San Diego Bay Wine & Food Festival (www.worldofwineevents.com) Winemaker dinners and tasting seminars, cooking classes with celebrity chefs and a bottle auction.

FINDING FOOD TRUCKS & POP-UP EATERIES

Sure, there have always been taco trucks in California. But recently, a gourmet street-food revolution has taken over, especially in LA and San Francisco. Whatever you're craving, from Korean BBQ to Indian *dosa*, haute grilled cheese to good ol' fried chicken, there's probably a restaurant-on-four-wheels serving it. To find trucks coming soon to a curb near you, search for 'food truck' and your location on Twitter. Come prepared with cash and sunblock: most trucks are cash-only, and lines for popular trucks can take 15 to 20 minutes.

More maverick urban kitchens have been popping up in more unexpected places such as art galleries, warehouses and storefronts. Chefs at these 'pop-ups' prepare wildly creative meals around a theme, for example, Asian street food or winemakers' dinners. Adventurous eaters seek out overnight taste sensations on Twitter, www.eater.com and www.chowhound.com. But be prepared for some downsides: pop-ups often charge restaurant prices, but without advance menus, quality control, health-inspected facilities or professional service. Bring cash and arrive early: most pop-ups don't accept credit cards, and popular dishes run out fast.

Napa & Sonoma Wine Country

With a world-beating reputation for local wines established in the 1970s, today NorCal's wine country has top-flight restaurateurs and artisan cheesemakers and olive-oil producers to sustain woozy visitors in desperate need of sustenance after a day of tippling. In 1994, Chef Thomas Keller transformed a historic Yountville saloon into the French Laundry, now an international gastronomic landmark, showcasing garden-grown organic produce and casual elegance in multicourse feasts. Other chefs eager to make their names and fortunes among free-spending wine-country visitors have since flocked to the Napa and Sonoma Valleys, where farm-to-table cuisine is the byword in rustic-chic kitchens. Sonoma hasn't forgotten its origins as a Mexican *pueblo* (town) either: you can still spot taco trucks rolling by vineyards.

Cook your own fabulous meals by shopping from the produce stalls and artisan food stands at farmers markets across the state. To find a certified California-grown farmers market near you, search www.cafarmersmarkets.com.

North Coast

In the 1970s, San Francisco hippies headed back to the land along the North Coast, seeking a more self-sufficient lifestyle, reviving traditions of making breads and cheeses from scratch and growing their own everything. Early adopters of pesticide-free farming, NorCal's hippie homesteaders innovated hearty, organic cuisine with a health-minded, global-fusion twist. Today, in pro-medical marijuana Mendocino and Humboldt Counties, farms are *very* serious about 'No Trespassing' signs – beware!

You can still taste the influence of traditional Native Californian cuisine on the North Coast. In addition to fishing, hunting game and making bread from acorn flour, Northern California tribes also carefully cultivated crops and gathered bonanzas of berries and wildflower honey. Today, fearless foragers have identified hundreds of edible plants, though spots for wild mushrooms remain closely guarded local secrets.

Central Coast

Most of California's produce is grown in the hot, irrigated Central Valley south of the Bay Area, but road-tripping epicureans tend to mistakenly bolt through this sunny stretch to reach LA in time for dinner – if only to make it past the stinky cattle feedlots strung out along Hwy 101 without losing their appetites.

But those urban snobs are missing out on some of California's freshest seafood around Monterey, Morro and San Luis Bays off Hwy 1, excellent wine tasting from the Santa Cruz Mountains down to Paso Robles and

Santa Barbara, and worthy farmstand produce pit stops, like for Watsonville strawberries, Cayucos oranges, Carpinteria avocados and Ventura lemons, as well as more rare local seafood delicacies such as farm-raised red abalone and oysters.

Much of the inland Central Valley remains dedicated to large-scale agribusiness, but industrial and family-owned farms that have converted to organic production have helped make California the top US producer of organics. Meanwhile, a cornucopia of weekly farmers markets and exuberant food festivals year-round prove that farm-to-table cooking is not just a fad here.

For coupons and deals on coastal California restaurants, check Open Table (www.opentable.com), Blackboard Eats (http://blackboardeats.com), Restaurants.com (www.restaurants.com), Living Social (www.livingsocial.com), Groupon (www.groupon.com) and Yelp (www.yelp.com).

Los Angeles & Southern California

There's no telling which came first in LA: the chefs or the stars. Perhaps no one has done as much to popularize California's fusion-style cuisine nationwide as peripatetic Austrian-born chef Wolfgang Puck, who began his career as a celebrity restaurateur upon launching Beverly Hill's Spago in 1982. Reservations at private chefs tables are now as sought-after as entry into velvet-roped nightclub VIP areas.

As with certain Hollywood blockbusters, trendy LA restaurants don't always live up to the hype – for LA's most brutally honest opinions, check www.laweekly.com and www.eater.com. Then follow in-the-know locals to Koreatown for flavor-bursting *kalbi* (marinated barbecued beef short ribs), East LA for tacos *al pastor* (marinated, fried pork) and Little Tokyo for ramen noodles made fresh daily, to name just a few worthy global bites.

California produces nearly all the nation's grapes and almonds, 75% of its strawberries and half its tomatoes. But dairy products are the real cash cow, bringing in $6 billion annually.

When it comes to fresh seafood, Angelenos were enthusiastically picking up sushi and sashimi with their chopsticks when most of America dismissed raw fish as foreign food not to be trusted. Wanna know the quickest way to start a fight in LA today? Ask Angelenos who they think the city's best sushi chef is. Farther south, San Diego may not have an official food, but the entire city obsesses about where to get the best fish tacos. All along the SoCal coast from Malibu to La Jolla, surf-and-sun lovers cruise Hwy 1 in search of the ultimate wave – and the perfect seafood shack.

Made in California: Wine & Beer

Powerful drink explains a lot about California. Mission vineyards planted in the 18th century gave California a taste for wine, which led settlers to declare an independent 'Bear Flag Republic' in the Mexican settlement of Sonoma one drunken night in 1846. The Gold Rush era soon brought a rush on the bar: by 1850, San Francisco had one woman per 100 men, but 500 saloons shilling hooch.

Where ripe avocados, fresh fruits and crunchy nuts grow in SoCal, there's always something unusual thrown into the salad bowl. Contemporary classics invented here include the Cobb salad (invented in Hollywood), the Caesar salad (invented in Tijuana, Mexico) and the Chinese chicken salad (popularized in LA during the health-conscious 1970s).

Today, California's traditions of wine, beer and cocktails are converging in saloon revivals, wine-bar trends and microbrewery booms. North America's only indigenous beer-brewing style originated right here, and grapes thrive from the Napa and Sonoma Valleys north to Mendocino and south along the coast to Santa Barbara and beyond.

Growing Up on the Grapevine

Mission-grown communion wine was fine for Sundays, but when imported French wine was slow to arrive during California's Gold Rush era, two Czech brothers named Korbel started making their own bubbly in 1882. Drinkers began switching their loyalty to wines made from locally grown grapes and, by the end of the century, California vintages were winning medals at Paris expositions. Some of California's heritage vinestock survived federal scrutiny during Prohibition, on the specious grounds that grapes were needed for Christian sacramental wines back east – a bootlegging bonanza that kept speakeasies well supplied.

CHRIS BURROUGHS: TASTING-ROOM MANAGER

The long-time tasting-room manager at Santa Barbara's Alma Rosa Winery is already familiar to moviegoers for his appearance in the 2004 indie hit *Sideways* as – what else? – a cowboy-hat-wearing tasting-room manager. He shared a few smart wine-tasting tips with us.

» Novices, never fear. Don't let a lack of wine savvy keep you away. Winemakers enjoy sharing their passion and knowledge, and beginners are often their favorite guests.

» Travel light. Most tasting rooms aren't equipped for large crowds. Traveling in small groups of less than six people means you'll have more time to chat with the staff.

» Less is more. Don't keep a scorecard on the number of wineries visited. Spend time at only a handful of tasting rooms on any given day. Wine drinking is a social vehicle (not a mobile party crawl).

» Stay open-minded. At most tasting rooms you'll sample six wines: three whites and three reds. Don't tell the staff you never drink chardonnay – who knows, the wine you try that day may change your mind.

» Don't be a jerk. Be friendly. Smoking and heavy perfume? Not so considerate of others – and smoking dulls your wine-tasting senses, besides.

Jonathan Gold, restaurant critic for the *LA Weekly*, won the Pulitzer Prize for criticism in 2007, the first time a restaurant critic won this award. To find out where Gold is eating these days, pick up the free alternative weekly tabloid newspaper anywhere around town, or visit www.laweekly.com.

California had a lamentable international reputation for mass-market plonk and bottled wine spritzers by 1976, when upstart wineries in Napa Valley and the Santa Cruz Mountains suddenly gained international status. Stag's Leap Wine Cellars cabernet sauvignon, Chateau Montelena chardonnay and Ridge Monte Bello cabernet sauvignon beat venerable French wines to take top honors at a landmark blind tasting by international critics now known as the Judgment of Paris. Today, the Napa and Sonoma Valleys north of San Francisco Bay continue to produce some of California's most prestigious wines, thanks to cool coastal fog, sunny valleys, rocky hillsides and volcanic soils that mimic wine-growing regions across France and Italy.

Sustainable Vines & Wines

During California's dot-com boom of the late 1990s, owning a vineyard became the ultimate Silicon Valley status symbol. Believing the dread phylloxera blight had been conquered with the development of resistant California rootstock AxR1, it seemed like a solid investment – until phylloxera made a catastrophic comeback, and infected vines across the state had to be dug out from the roots. But disaster brought breakthroughs: winemakers rethought their approach from the ground up, replanting organically and trialing biodynamic methods to keep the soil healthy and pests at bay.

Today such sustainable winemaking processes have become widespread across California, establishing regional rules for 'green' winemaking and pursuing international Demeter certification for biodynamic wines. Renegade winemakers are experimenting with natural-process winemaking methods such as wild-yeast fermentation, bringing the thrill of the unexpected to their tasting rooms. Owls for pest management, sheep for weed control and solar panels atop LEED-certified buildings are all increasingly common features of California's eco-savvy wineries.

California's Other Wine Countries

There is no time like the present to wine taste across California, with a broad variety of heirloom, imported and experimental varietals that are true expressions of this vibrant, varied landscape. Every year California sells more than 563 million gallons of wine – enough to fill more than 850 Olympic-sized swimming pools – and California wines now account for more than 60% of all the wine consumed in the USA. Surprisingly, most grapes are not grown and most wines are not made in the famous Napa and Sonoma Valleys.

California has 112 distinct AVAs, or American Viticulture Areas, which are known for different varietals and have developed distinct winemaking styles. Some standout wine regions of Northern California are just a grape's throw (okay, about an hour's drive) from movie-star Napa and Sonoma. In northern Sonoma County, Healdsburg is the gateway to the Alexander Valley, known for its cellar-worthy cabernet sauvignon and chardonnay, and the Dry Creek Valley, which favors zinfandel and sauvignon blanc. West of Hwy 101 nearer the coast, the Russian River Valley is famed for its fruit-forward pinot noir, accounting for almost 20% of that varietal statewide. Farther north in rural Mendocino County, you can follow back roads through the Anderson Valley to taste more delicate, soft-spoken pinot noir, riesling and gewürztraminer.

On the Central Coast, the Santa Cruz Mountains produce complex cabernet sauvignon and pinot noir, with some of the oldest wineries in all of California. Around Santa Barbara, pinot noirs, chardonnays and Rhône varietals from the Santa Maria and Santa Ynez Valleys are also blessed with sun, cooling ocean breezes and morning mists. In Paso Robles, one of California's fastest-growing wine regions, growers are making the most of their vineyards' sunny dispositions with bold syrah, zinfandel and renegade red blends. Nearby, in San Luis Obispo, the Edna Valley's family-owned wineries craft crisp chardonnay and delicate pinot noir.

California's southernmost wine region is in Temecula, where some vineyards were originally planted by Spanish missionaries in the early 19th century. There, at the edge of the desert outside San Diego, less than 100 miles from the Mexico border, Rhône and Spanish varietals thrive in the heat.

The movie *Bottle Shock* (2008) takes liberties with the true story of the Judgment of Paris, but it captures the rule-breaking flavor of the early days of winemaking in Sonoma and Napa in the 1970s.

The outlandish film *Sideways* (2004) captures the folly and passion of California's wine-snob scene. It was a critical hit, but California winemakers have a love/hate relationship with it for praising pinot noir at merlot's expense.

Building Better Brews

Blowing off some steam after work took on new meaning during California's Gold Rush era, when entrepreneurs trying to keep up with the demand for drink started brewing ales at steamy higher temperatures, because they lacked ice refrigeration. The result was an amber color, rich, malted flavor and such powerful effervescence that when a keg was tapped, steam sometimes escaped. San Francisco's Anchor Brewing Company has made its Anchor Steam amber ale this way since 1896.

Fast forward to the 21st century: California today boasts over 200 craft brewers, with one in every nine US microbreweries established here, especially along the North Coast (see p229). Snobbery is not just reserved for California's foodies and wine lovers: many beer drinkers fuss just as much over their monk-brewed triple Belgians and the relative merits of 'hoppiness.' You won't get attitude for ordering beer with a fancy meal – many California sommeliers are happy to suggest beer pairings, and some restaurants offer special tasting menus to accompany signature local beers, especially on the North Coast.

For quality small-batch brews you won't find elsewhere, any self-respecting California city has at least one craft brewery or brewpub of note, while specialty beer bars proudly offer dozens of California and West Coast microbrews on tap. These days, California's craft breweries are increasingly canning instead of bottling to make their beer cheaper, greener and more widely distributed at supermarkets and liquor stores statewide.

California's latest and greatest wines and winemaking trends are covered by *Wine Enthusiast*'s West Coast editor, Steve Heimoff, on his own blog: http://stevehei moff.com.

The People & Way of Life

In the dream-world California, you wake up, have your shot of wheatgrass, and roll down to the beach while the surf's up. Lifeguards wave to you as they go jogging by in their bikinis. You skateboard down the boardwalk to your yoga class, where everyone admires your downward dog. A taco truck pulls up with your favorite: low-carb sustainable line-caught tilapia fish tacos with organic mango chipotle salsa.

Napping on the beach afterward, you awake to find a casting agent hovering over you, blocking your sunlight, imploring you to star in a movie based on a best-selling comic book. You say you'll have your lawyer look over the papers, and by your lawyer you mean your roommate who plays one on TV. The conversation is cut short when you get a text to meet up with some friends at a bar.

If you happen to overhear some California slang you're, like, totally confused by, consult the awesome Urban Dictionary (www.urbandictionary.com) for all the uncensored, street-worthy definitions. Word out.

That casting agent was a stress case – she wanted an answer in, like, a month – so you swing by your medical marijuana dispensary and a tattoo parlor to get 'Peace' inscribed on your bicep as a reminder to yourself to stay chill. At the bar, you're called onstage to play a set with the band, and afterward you complain to the drummer about how the casting agent harshed your mellow. She recommends a wine-country getaway, but you're already doing that Big Sur primal-scream chakra-cleansing retreat this weekend.

You head back to your beach house to update your status on your Facebook profile, simultaneously alerting your 10,000 Twitter followers to the major events of the day: 'Killer taco, solid downward dog, peace tattoo, movie offer.' Then you repeat your nightly self-affirmations: 'I am a child of the universe…I am blessed, or at least not a New Yorker…tomorrow will bring sunshine and possibility…om.'

Regional Identity

Now for the reality check: any Northern Californian hearing your California fantasy is bound to get huffy. What, political protests and open-source software inventions don't factor in your dreams? Huh, typical SoCal slacker. But Southern Californians will roll their eyes at the silicone-and-spray-tan stereotypes: they didn't create NASA's Jet Propulsion Lab and almost half the world's movies by slacking off. For newcomers, it helps to think of California as two states: SoCal and NorCal. Where you choose to live here makes a statement about who you are.

Feel free to believe everything you've ever heard about Californians, so long as you realize the stereotypes are always exaggerated. Sure, tweens snap chewing gum in the shopping malls of the San Fernando Valley north of LA, blond surfers shout 'Dude!' across San Diego beaches, hippies and Rastafarians gather for drum circles in San Francisco's Golden Gate Park, and tree huggers toke on joints in the North Coast woods but, all in all, it's hard to peg the population. (Although there's truth in at least one more stereotype: over 60% of Californians admit to having hugged a tree.)

Four out of every five Californians live near the coast rather than inland, even though not every beach is sunny or even swimmable. The odds of that increase the further south you go, thus SoCal's inescapable associations with surf, sun and prime-time TV soaps like *Baywatch* and *The OC*. Although nobody can agree on exactly where to draw the line between SoCal and NorCal, the invisible cultural border falls somewhere along the Central Coast between San Francisco and LA.

According to a 2008 Cambridge University study, creativity, imagination, intellectualism and mellowness are all defining personality characteristics of Californians compared with inhabitants of other states. (New Yorkers were found to be notably 'neurotic' and 'unfriendly.')

San Francisco & North Coast

In the San Francisco Bay Area, the politics are liberal and the people open-minded, with a strong live-and-let-live ethic and passionate devotion to the outdoors. In overwhelmingly wealthy and white Marin County, there's a tremendous sense of civic pride that sometimes borders on narcissism. San Francisco is more of a melting pot, but there aren't a lot of lower-income citizens since rents are so high. The East Bay, especially Oakland and Berkeley, and San Jose to the south are more ethnically diverse.

Woodsy types live further up along the North Coast. Think buffalo-plaid flannel. There aren't a lot of people way up there – and there's not a lot of money floating around either. Conservative radio stations shout on several strong frequencies. At the other end of the political spectrum, you'll also find some of the state's most progressive liberals and borderline eco-fanatics way up north. If you spot a beat-up old Volvo chugging along the highway, chances are it's running on biodiesel, possibly recycled French-fry grease from fast-food restaurants. There's lots of DIY ingenuity around here.

Central Coast

The hard-to-classify Central Coast, with its smaller pockets of population, starts near wacky, left-of-center Santa Cruz and stretches all the way south to surreally beautiful, posh Santa Barbara. Along the way, Hwy 1 winds past working-class Monterey, made famous in John Steinbeck's novels; the bohemian Big Sur coast, where beatnik artists, hippies and back-to-landers stake their homestead claims; the conservative upper-crust villages of Carmel-by-the-Sea and Cambria, where the 'newly wed and nearly dead' have built multimillion-dollar homes; and the laid-back, liberal college town of San Luis Obispo, halfway between San Francisco and LA via Hwy 101.

Los Angeles & Southern California

LA has a reputation for racial tension, possibly because it's so much more diverse than other coastal cities. Yet the unease also likely reflects the disparity between haves and have-nots, for example, between Beverly Hills mansions and the ghettoes of South Central. Composed of dozens of independent cities, LA is impossible to generalize about, but one thing is for sure: almost everybody drives. In terms of social status, you're nothing – and sometimes literally nowhere – without a car.

Can San Diego's outwardly carefree appearance belie a seamy noir underbelly? Get the dirt in *Under the Perfect Sun: The San Diego Tourists Never See* (2003), by Mike Davis, Kelly Mayhew and Jim Miller.

Between LA and San Diego lies Orange County, where beautifully bronzed, buff bodies soak up rays on the sands. But make no mistake about it: it's no beach bums' paradise here. Until recent waves of immigration tipped the scales toward liberal voters, the politics 'behind the Orange Curtain' were overwhelmingly conservative. Republicans were welcomed with open arms at $2000-a-plate fundraising dinners, and many people still live in gated communities that have limited tolerance for outsiders. This conservative political trend extends south to San Diego, which also has a sizable US military population.

Lifestyle

Self-help, fitness and body modification are major industries throughout SoCal and NorCal, successfully marketed since the 1970s as 'lite' versions of religious experience – all the agony and ecstasy of the major religious brands, without all those heavy commandments. Exercise and good food help keep Californians among the fittest in the nation. Yet almost 250,000 Californians are apparently ill enough to merit prescriptions for medical marijuana. MMJ dispensaries have proliferated up and down the coast, and they now outnumber Starbucks coffee shops in some places.

But few coastal Californians can afford to spend their entire day tanning, sipping lattes, doing yoga and getting high, what with UVB rays, the rent and gas prices to consider. Most Californians live in their car, not their house. The average Californian commutes almost 30 minutes each way to work, and spends at least $1 out of every $5 earned on car-related expenses. But California has zoomed ahead of the national energy-use curve with smog-checked cars and by buying more hybrid and fuel-efficient cars than any other state. Despite a bad rap for smoggy skies, two of the 25 US cities with the cleanest air are actually in California (kudos, San Luis Obispo and Salinas!).

SoCal Inventions

- Space Shuttle
- Mickey Mouse
- Whitening toothpaste
- Hula hoop (or at least its trademark)
- Barbie
- Skateboard and surfboard technology
- Cobb salad

Housing & Homelessness

Few Californians can afford a coastal dream home by the beach, as most rent rather than own on a median household income of $56,134 per year. Eight of the 10 most expensive US housing markets are in California, and in the number-one most expensive area, La Jolla in San Diego County, the average house price is $1.875 million.

Yet Californian cities – especially San Francisco and San Diego – consistently top national quality-of-life indexes. Almost half of all Californians live in cities, while most of the rest live in suburbs, where the cost of living is just as high, if not higher: Marin County, just north of San Francisco, is the country's most costly place to live.

Homelessness is not part of the California dream, but it's a reality for at least 160,000 Californians. Some are teens who have run away or been kicked out by their families, but the largest contingent of homeless Californians are US military veterans – almost 30,000 in all. What's more, in the 1970s mental-health programs were cut, and state-funded drug-treatment programs were dropped in the 1980s, leaving many Californians with mental illnesses and substance-abuse problems with no place to go.

Also standing in line at homeless shelters are the working poor, unable to cover medical care and high rent on minimum-wage salaries.

THE WAY CALIFORNIANS TALK: IT'S COMPLICATED

Political correctness thrives along the coast. In fact, most people are so determined to get along that it can be hard to find out what somebody really thinks. This increases the further south you go, reaching its Zen-like zenith of 'niceness' in San Diego.

Self-help jargon has thoroughly infiltrated the daily language of coastal Californians. For example, the word 'issue' is constantly bandied about. Generally this is a way to refer to someone else's problems without implying that the person has...well, problems.

The mantra 'Can't we all just get along, man?' flies out the window on busy freeways. Take a deep breath before putting the key in the ignition. Expect to encounter unpredictable drivers with road rage who won't hesitate to cut you off, then flip you the 'bird.'

If someone you just met says 'Let's get together sometime,' in most parts of the world that means, 'Call me.' Not in California. It may be just a nicety. Often the other person never calls and, if you do, you may never hear back. Don't take it *too* personally.

MARRIAGE EQUALITY

Forty thousand Californians were already registered as domestic partners when, in 2004, San Francisco Mayor Gavin Newsom started issuing marriage licenses to same-sex couples in defiance of a California same-sex marriage ban. Four thousand same-sex couples promptly got hitched by the Bay. The state ban was nixed by California courts in June 2008, but a few months later, California voters narrowly passed Proposition 8, which amended the state's constitution to explicitly prohibit same-sex marriage.

Following the election, protests against Proposition 8 were staged statewide, including in San Francisco and LA. Civil-rights activists immediately filed suit to challenge the constitutionality of the proposition in court. In August 2010, more controversy erupted when US District Court Judge Vaughn Walker, himself gay (a legally irrelevant issue, but politically persuasive to some in the court of public opinion), overturned Proposition 8. The judge stayed his ruling pending further appeals and a California Supreme Court hearing in late 2011.

Meanwhile California's reputation as a haven of LGBT (lesbian/gay/bisexual/transgender) tolerance is lagging behind other states that have already legalized same-sex marriage, including Massachusetts, New Hampshire, Vermont, Connecticut, Iowa and New York, as well as the District of Columbia and two Native American tribes in Oregon and Washington states. Whatever the final outcome of the legal battle over Prop 8, California can still claim a decades-long history of being in the vanguard of the GLBT civil-rights movement. Find out more at San Francisco's GLBT History Museum (p64).

Rather than addressing the underlying causes of homelessness, some California cities have criminalized loitering, panhandling, even sitting on sidewalks. However, local charities continue to provide essential backup for the homeless.

Population: Who Lives Here?

Immigration

With 37 million residents, California is the most populous US state: one in every nine Americans lives here. It's also one of the fastest-growing states, with three of America's 10 biggest cities (Los Angeles, San Diego and San Jose) and over 350,000 new arrivals very year. If you were the average Californian, statistically speaking, you'd be a Latina woman, aged about 34, living in densely populated LA, Orange or San Diego Counties, and speaking more than one language. There's a one in four chance you were born in another country, and even if you were born in the US, the odds are 50/50 you moved here from another state.

One of every four immigrants to the USA lands in California, with the largest segment coming from Mexico. Most legal immigrants to California are sponsored by family members who already live here. In addition, an estimated two million undocumented immigrants currently live in California. But this is not a radical new development: before California became a US state in 1850, it was a territory of Mexico and Spain, and historically most of the state's growth has come from immigration, legal or otherwise.

Since 1988, California's prison population has increased by more than 200%, mostly for drug-related crimes. More than four out of every 1000 Californians are currently in jails, many of which are now so dangerously overcrowded that federal courts have mandated the release of some prisoners.

Multiculturalism

Many coastal Californians idealize their state as an easygoing multicultural society that gives everyone a chance to live the American dream. No one should be expected to give up their cultural or personal identity just to become Californian. The Chicano Movement, Gay Pride and black power all built political bases here during the social and civil-rights activism heyday of the 1960s and '70s.

While equal opportunity may be a shared goal, in practice it's very much a work in progress. Historically, California's Chinatowns, Japantowns and other immigrant enclaves were often created by segregationist sentiment, not by choice. Even racially integrated metropolitan areas of coastal California can be quite segregated in terms of income, language, education and perhaps most ironically (given the state's position as a high-tech industry leader in Silicon Valley), internet access.

As of the 2010 census, California's Latino and Asian populations were steadily increasing. More than 30% of the country's Asian American population currently lives in California, and Latino residents are expected to become California's majority ethnic group by 2020. But California's pop culture already reflects the composite identity of the state more clearly than any number-crunching census taker.

California Babylon: A Guide to Sites of Scandal, Mayhem and Celluloid in the Golden State (2000) by Kristan Lawson and Anneli Rufus is a guilty-pleasure guide to infamous and bizarre locations throughout the state.

Latino identity is deeply enmeshed in everyday life, from Tejano tunes and taco trucks to the ex-Governator's catchphrase in *Terminator II: Judgement Day:* 'Hasta la vista, baby.' Despite being just 6.6% of the population and relatively late arrivals with the WWII shipping boom, African Americans have also defined California's pop culture, from jazz and hip-hop to fashion, sports and beyond.

New & Old Religions

Maybe the bond holding this state of confusion together isn't a shared ethnic background or common language: it's choosing to be Californian. Along with that comes the freedom to choose your religion, if any. Although Californians are less churchgoing than the American mainstream, and one in five Californians professes no religion at all, it remains one of the most religiously diverse states. About a third of Californians are Catholic, due partly to a large Latino population, while another third are Protestant. But there are also more than 500,000 Muslims in Southern California alone; LA has the second-largest Jewish community in North America; and the state claims the most Buddhists living anywhere outside Asia.

In his column 'iAsk a Mexican!,' *OC Weekly* columnist Gustavo Arellano tackles such questions as why Mexicans swim with their clothes on, alongside weighty social issues involving immigrants' rights. Read it at www.ocweekly.com.

Despite their proportionately small numbers, California's alternative religions and utopian communities dominate the popular imagination, from modern-day pagans to new-age healers. California made national headlines in the 1960s with gurus from India, in the 1970s with Jim Jones' People's Temple and Erhard Seminars Training (EST) and in the 1990s with Heaven's Gate doomsday UFO cult in San Diego. Around since 1954, the controversial Church of Scientology is still seeking acceptance with celebrity proponents from movie-star Tom Cruise to musician Beck.

California is also a stronghold of fundamentalist and evangelical Christian churches, which have proliferated for the last century. In 1924 the world's first broadcast preacher, Aimee Semple McPherson, opened her own radio station to spread the word from LA's Angelus Temple, home of the Foursquare Church, a Pentecostal Christian sect. She pioneered the way for other 20th-century radio and televangelists like the Schullers of Orange County's Crystal Cathedral and Harold Camping, the Oakland radio minister and numerologist who predicted that the Rapture would happen in 1994, then in 1998 and again – twice! – in 2011.

Sports

California has more professional sports teams than any other state. For proof that locals do get excited about sports, go ahead and just try to find tickets before they sell out for a San Diego Chargers football, San Francisco Giants baseball or Los Angeles Lakers basketball game. You can score less-expensive tickets more easily for pro women's (WNBA) basketball in Los Angeles, pro hockey in Anaheim and San Jose, and pro soccer in LA and San Jose. Minor-league baseball teams also play up and down the coast; look out for the winning San Jose Giants.

According to a recent study, Californians are less likely to be couch potatoes than other Americans, but when one Californian team plays another, the streets are deserted and all eyes glued to the tube. The biggest grudge matches are between football's San Francisco '49ers and Oakland Raiders, basketball's LA Lakers and LA Clippers, and baseball's San Francisco Giants and LA Dodgers. College-sports rivalries, such as UC Berkeley's Cal Bears versus the Stanford Cardinals, or the USC Trojans against the UCLA Bruins, are just as insanely passionate.

Even if you're not a sports buff, you may find something that catches your eye in California.

Surfing is the coast's coolest spectator sport, with waves sometimes reaching 100ft at the annual Mavericks competition near Half Moon Bay, south of San Francisco.

Now an Olympic sport, professional beach volleyball started at LA's Santa Monica Beach in the 1920s, and tournaments are still held every summer in SoCal.

Horse racing is a tradition at Del Mar Racetrack on San Diego's North County Coast and Santa Anita Racetrack near LA.

Over 200 different languages are spoken in California, with Spanish, Chinese, Tagalog, Persian and German in the top 10. Almost 40% of state residents speak a language other than English at home.

Music & the Arts

California supports thriving music and arts scenes that aren't afraid to be completely independent, even outlandish at times. Even Californians acknowledge that their music is eclectic, ranging from pitch-perfect opera to off-key punk. Meanwhile, critics have tried and failed to find any consistency in the styles and schools of art and architecture that have flourished here – but in the context of California, the most racially and ethnically diverse US state, that variety makes perfect sense. Life in California has always been about telling stories, too, whether on the written or digital-inked page or on the magical screens of movies and TV.

Music

A walk down a city street here can sound like the world's most eclectic iPod set to shuffle. Much of the recording industry is based in Los Angeles, but today's troubled pop princesses and airbrushed boy bands are only here thanks to all the tuneful revolutions that preceded them.

Swing, Jazz, Blues & Soul

Swing swept over California in the 1930s and '40s, as big bands sparked a lindy-hopping craze in LA and sailors on shore leave hit San Francisco's underground, integrated jazz clubs. As California's African American community grew with the 'Great Migration' and during the WWII shipping and manufacturing boom, the West Coast blues sound emerged, especially in San Francisco and Oakland. Down south, Texas-born bluesman T-Bone Walker worked in LA's Central Ave clubs before making hit records of his electric guitar stylings for Capitol Records.

Waiting for the Sun: Strange Days, Weird Scenes and the Sound of Los Angeles, by British rock historian Barney Hoskyns, follows the twists and turns of the SoCal music scene from Nat King Cole to NWA.

With Beat poets riffing over improvised bass-lines and audiences finger-snapping their approval, the cool, 1950s West Coast jazz of Chet Baker and Dave Brubeck emerged from San Francisco's North Beach neighborhood. In the African American cultural hub of LA's Central Avenue, the hard bop of Charlie Parker and Charles Mingus kept the SoCal scene alive and swinging. In the 1950s and '60s California, doo-wop, rhythm and blues, and soul music were all in steady rotation at nightclubs in South Central LA, the 'Harlem of the West.' Soulful singer Sam Cooke started his own hit-making record label, attracting major soul and gospel talent to LA.

First Rockers, Folkies & Funk Masters

California's first homegrown rock and roll talent to make it big in the 1950s was Richie Valens, whose 'La Bamba' was a rockified version of a Mexican folk song. Dick Dale (aka 'The King of the Surf Guitar') started experimenting with reverb effects in Orange County in the 1950s, then topped the charts with his band the Del-Tones in the early '60s, influencing everyone from the Beach Boys to Jimi Hendrix.

When Joan Baez and Bob Dylan had their Northern California fling in the early 1960s, Dylan plugged in his guitar and played folk rock.

Janis Joplin and Big Brother & the Holding Company developed their shambling musical stylings in San Francisco, splintering folk rock into psychedelia. Emerging from that same San Francisco mélange, Jefferson Airplane remade Lewis Carroll's children's classic *Alice's Adventures in Wonderland* into the psychedelic hit 'White Rabbit.'

Meanwhile, Jim Morrison and the Doors and the Byrds blew minds on LA's famous Sunset Strip. The epicenter of LA's psychedelic rock scene was the Laurel Canyon neighborhood, just uphill from the Sunset Strip and the legendary Whisky A-Go-Go nightclub. Sooner or later, many of these 1960s rock and roll headliners wound up overdosing on drugs. The original jam band the Grateful Dead stayed together until guitarist Jerry Garcia's passing in a Marin County rehab clinic in 1995.

In the early 1970s, the Mexican-fusion sounds of Santana emerged from San Francisco and funk bands War from Long Beach and Sly & the Family Stone, which got their groove on in the Bay area before moving to LA, bounced up the charts.

Punk, Post-Punk & Pop

From the late 1970s to the mid-1980s, LA band X bridged punk and new wave, while local punk radio station KROQ rebelled against the tyranny of pop playlists. LA crossover bands such as Bad Religion and Suicidal Tendencies rocked the '80s, as did all-female bands the Bangles and the Go-Gos, new wavers Oingo Boingo and alt-rockers Jane's Addiction. On avant-garde Frank Zappa's 1982 single *Valley Girl,* his 14-year-old daughter Moon Unit taught the rest of America to say 'Omig*o*-o-od!' like an LA teen.

By the 1990s alternative rock acts such as Beck and Weezer had gained national traction. Berkeley revived punk in the '90s, including with Grammy Award–winning Green Day. Down south, a key '90s band was the ska-punk-alt-rock No Doubt, of Orange County (which later launched the solo career of lead singer Gwen Stefani). SoCal rock stars of the new millennium include San Diego–based pop-punksters Blink 182 and punk-funk sensation Red Hot Chili Peppers, rockin' LA since the '80s.

Wanna hear the next breakout indie band before they make it big? Tune into the 'Morning Becomes Eclectic' show on Southern California's KCRW radio station for live in-studio performances and musician interviews. Listen anywhere online (www.kcrw.com), download KCRW's free podcasts or buy the mobile app.

Rap & Hip-Hop Rhythms

Since the 1980s, LA has been a hotbed for West Coast rap and hip-hop. Eazy E, Ice Cube and Dr Dre released the seminal NWA (Niggaz with Attitude) album, *Straight Outta Compton,* in 1989. Death Row Records, cofounded by Dr Dre, has launched megawatt rap talents including Long Beach bad boy Snoop Dog and the late Tupac Shakur, who began his rap career in Marin County and was fatally shot in 1996 in Las Vegas, in a suspected East Coast/West Coast rap feud.

Throughout the 1980s and '90s, California maintained a grassroots hip-hop scene closer to the streets in LA and in Oakland. In the late 1990s, the Bay Area birthed the 'hyphy movement,' a reaction against the increasing commercialization of hip-hop, and underground artists like E-40. Also hailing from Oakland, Michael Franti & Spearhead blend hip-hop with funk, reggae, folk, jazz and rock stylings into messages for social justice and peace. In LA, no hip-hop band has risen farther up the *Billboard* pop charts than the Black Eyed Peas, anchored by Fergie and will.i.am.

On Location: Film & TV

Try to imagine living in a world without Orson Welles whispering 'Rosebud,' Judy Garland clicking her heels three times, John Travolta dancing in his white suit or the Terminator telling us that 'I'll be back.' Shakespeare claimed that 'all the world's a stage,' but in California, it's actually more of a film or TV set. Every palm-lined boulevard or beach in SoCal seems to come with its own IMDB.com filming resume. And no wonder: in any given year some 40 TV shows and scores of movies use Californian locations, not including all of those shot on LA studio backlots.

It's a myth that most movie production ever took place in Hollywood, the Industry's social hub. Of the major motion-picture studios, only Paramount Pictures stood in Hollywood proper, albeit surrounded by block after block of production-related businesses such as lighting and post-production. The high cost of filming has sent location scouts beyond LA's San Fernando Valley (where most movie and TV studios are found) and north of the border to Canada. A few production companies are based in San Francisco, including Francis Ford Coppola's American Zoetrope.

With increasing regularity, Hollywood films feature California as both a setting and a topic and, in some cases, almost as a character. LA especially loves to turn the camera on itself, often with a film-noir angle. SoCal is also a versatile backdrop for edgy cable TV dramas such as HBO's *Entourage*, an exposé of A-list Hollywood life, and reality TV shows such as MTV's *The Hills,* about rich, gorgeous 20-somethings in LA.

Film Festivals

» AFI Fest (www.afi.com/afifest/), Los Angeles

» LA Film Fest (www.lafilmfest.com)

» Outfest (www.outfest.org), Los Angeles

» San Francisco International Film Festival (www.sffs.org)

» Sonoma International Film Festival (www.sonomafilmfest.org)

Animated Magic

A young cartoonist named Walt Disney arrived in LA in 1923, and five years later his first breakout hit, *Steamboat Willie,* starred a mouse named Mickey. That film spawned the Disney empire, and dozens of other animation studios have followed suit with films, TV shows and special effects. Among the most-loved are Warner Bros (Bugs Bunny and the *Looney Tunes* gang), Hanna-Barbera (*The Flintstones, The Jetsons, Scooby-Doo*) and DreamWorks (*Shrek, Madagascar, Kung-Fu Panda).*

In San Francisco, George Lucas' Industrial Light & Magic hires high-tech wizards to produce computer-generated special effects for block-busters such as the *Star Wars,* Indiana Jones, *Terminator* and Harry Potter series. Pixar Animation Studios, located just across the Bay in Emeryville, has produced a string of animated box-office hits including *Toy Story, Finding Nemo, Cars* and *Ratatouille.*

Literature

Californians read more than movie scripts: they make up the largest market for books in the US, and read much more than the national average. You've probably already read books by Californians without knowing it, for example, Ray Bradbury's 1950s dystopian classic *Fahrenheit 451;* Alice Walker's Pulitzer Prize–winning *The Color Purple*; Ken Kesey's quintessential '60s novel *One Flew Over the Cuckoo's Nest*; UC Berkeley professor Maxine Hong Kingston's *The Woman Warrior*; Michael Chabon's Pulitzer Prize-winning *The Amazing Adventures of Kavalier*

HOLLYWOOD GOLDEN YEARS

The Industry, as it's called, grew out of the humble orchards of Hollywoodland, a residential neighborhood of Los Angeles, where entrepreneurial moviemakers (including many European immigrants) established studios. In 1913, the first full-length Hollywood feature, a silent Western drama called *The Squaw Man,* was shot by director Cecil B de Mille. The silent-movie era gave way to 'talkies' when 1927's *The Jazz Singer* premiered in downtown LA, ushering in Hollywood's glamorous Golden Age.

During the 1930s and '40s, American literary lions such as F Scott Fitzgerald, Dorothy Parker, Truman Capote, William Faulkner and Tennessee Williams did stints as Hollywood screenwriters. In the 1950s, during the anticommunist 'Red Scare' of the Cold War era, the federal government's House Un-American Activities Committee investigated and subsequently blacklisted many Hollywood actors, directors and screenwriters, some of whom left for self-imposed exile in Europe, never to return.

and Clay; or Dave Eggers, the Bay area hipster behind *McSweeney's* quarterly literary journal.

Few writers nail California culture as well as Joan Didion. She's best known for her collection of essays, *Slouching Towards Bethlehem,* which takes a caustic look at 1960s flower power and Haight-Ashbury. Tom Wolfe also put '60s San Francisco in perspective with *The Electric Kool-Aid Acid Test,* which follows Ken Kesey's band of Merry Pranksters, who began their acid-laced 'magic bus' journey near Santa Cruz. By that time, the Beat generation of writers had already fired up San Francisco's North Beach literary scene beginning in the 1950s, including with Allen Ginsberg's epic poem *Howl* and Jack Kerouac's iconic novel *On the Road*. In the early 1970s, Charles Bukowski's semiautobiographical novel *Post Office* captured down-and-out downtown LA, while Richard Vasquez's *Chicano* took a look at the Latino barrio. Up north, the serial-style *Tales of the City,* by Armistead Maupin, was a frothy taste of 1970s San Francisco, following the lives of colorful characters, gay and straight.

Arguably the most influential author to ever emerge from California was social realist John Steinbeck. Published in the 1930s, his first California novel, *Tortilla Flat,* takes place in Monterey's Mexican American community, while his masterpiece, *The Grapes of Wrath,* tells of the struggles of migrant farm workers. Closer to the coast, San Francisco and LA became capitals of pulp detective novels, which were often turned into classic Hollywood noir films. Dashiell Hammett (*The Maltese Falcon*) made San Francisco's fog a sinister character. The king of hard-boiled crime writers was Raymond Chandler (*The Big Sleep*), who thinly disguised Santa Monica as shadowy Bay City. A contemporary renaissance of noir crime fiction has been masterminded by James Ellroy (*LA Confidential*) and Walter Mosley (*Devil in a Blue Dress*), whose Easy Rawlins detective novels are set in LA's South Central 'hood.

Director Alfred Hitchcock set some of his best thrillers in coastal California, including *Vertigo* (1958), with unforgettable shots of San Francisco's Golden Gate Bridge and Muir Woods, and *The Birds* (1963), mostly filmed in Bodega Bay.

Acclaimed writers from John Muir to Gary Snyder have written about California's awe-inspiring scenery. Look for their work in two outstanding anthologies, *Natural State: A Literary Anthology of California Nature Writing* and *Unfolding Beauty: Celebrating California's Landscapes*.

Architecture

California has long adapted imported international styles to fit the local climate and available materials. Today, unexpected elements are almost everywhere you look: tiled Mayan art deco facades in LA, chinoiserie streetlamps in San Francisco, English country cottages in Carmel-by-the-Sea or Japanese hipped roofs on SoCal suburban bungalows. California's architecture was postmodern before the word existed.

Spanish Missions & Victorian Queens

In the late 18th century, the first Spanish missions were built around courtyards, using materials that Native Californians and colonists found on hand: adobe, limestone and grass. Many missions crumbled into disrepair under Mexican rule in the early 19th century, but the style remained practical for the climate and many Californian settlers later adapted it into the rancho adobe style.

During the mid-19th-century gold rush, California's nouveau riche imported materials to construct grand mansions matching European fashions, and raised the stakes with ornamental excess. Many millionaires favored the gilded Queen Anne style. Outrageous examples of Victorian architecture, including 'painted ladies' and 'gingerbread' houses, can be found in San Francisco, Ferndale and Eureka.

Peaking between 1890 and 1915, Spanish colonial and Mission revival styles rejected frilly Victorianism in favor of simple, classical lines that harkened back to California's past, with arched doors and windows, long covered porches, fountains, courtyards, adobe walls and red-tiled roofs. Several SoCal train depots showcase this style, as do buildings in downtown Santa Barbara and San Diego's Balboa Park.

For a memorable ramble through California in the company of contemporary literati from Pico Iyer to Michael Chabon, read *My California: Journeys by Great Writers,* edited by Donna Wares. Proceeds from online purchases (www.angelcitypress.com/myca.html) support the California Arts Council.

Arts & Crafts to Art Deco

Simplicity was also the hallmark of California's early-20th-century Arts and Crafts style. Influenced by Japanese design principles and England's Arts and Crafts movement, its woodwork and handmade touches marked a deliberate departure from the Industrial Revolution. Pasadena architects Charles and Henry Greene and the Bay Area's Bernard Maybeck and Julia Morgan popularized the versatile one-story bungalow, with overhanging eaves, outdoor terraces and sleeping porches.

Cosmopolitan California couldn't be limited to any one set of international influences. In the 1920s, the international art deco style took elements from the ancient world – Mayan glyphs, Egyptian pillars, Babylonian ziggurats – and flattened them into modern motifs to cap stark facades and outline skyscrapers, especially in downtown Oakland and LA. In the '30s, streamline moderne kept decoration to a minimum and mimicked the aerodynamic look of ocean liners and airplanes.

Jim Heimann's *California Crazy & Beyond: Roadside Vernacular Architecture* is a romp through the zany, whimsical building-blocks world of California, where lemonade stands look like giant lemons and motels are shaped like tepees.

Naked Modernism

Clothing-optional California has never been shy about showcasing its assets. Starting in the 1960s, California embraced the stripped-down, glass-wall aesthetics of the International Style championed by Bauhaus architects Walter Gropius and Ludwig Mies van der Rohe and Le Corbusier. After moving to LA, Austrian-born Richard Schindler and Richard Neutra adapted this minimalist modern style to residential houses with open floorplans and floor-to-ceiling windows perfectly suited to SoCal's see-and-be-seen culture. Neutra and Schindler were influenced by the earlier work of Frank Lloyd Wright, who designed LA's Hollyhock House in a style he dubbed 'California Romanza.' Together with Charles and Ray Eames, Neutra also contributed to the experimental Case Study Houses, several of which still jut out of the LA landscape and are often used as filming locations, as seen in *LA Confidential*.

Postmodern Evolutions

True to its independent-minded nature, California veered away from strict high modernism to add unlikely postmodern shapes to the local landscape. Richard Meier made his mark on West LA with the Getty Center, a cresting white wave of a building atop a sunburned hilltop. Canadian-born Frank Gehry relocated to Santa Monica, and his billowing, sculptural style for LA's Walt Disney Concert Hall winks cheekily at shipshape Californian streamline moderne.

San Francisco has lately championed a brand of postmodernism by Pritzker Prize–winning architects that magnifies and mimics California's great outdoors, especially in Golden Gate Park. Swiss architects Herzog & de Meuron clad the MH de Young Memorial Museum in copper, which

LATINO MURALS: TAKING IT TO THE STREETS

Beginning in the 1930s, when the federal Works Progress Administration sponsored schemes to uplift and beautify cities across the country, murals came to define Californian cityscapes. Mexican muralists Diego Rivera, David Alfaro Siqueiros and José Clemente Orozco sparked an outpouring of murals across LA that today number in the thousands. Rivera was also brought to San Francisco for murals at the San Francisco Art Institute, and his influence is reflected in the interior of San Francisco's Coit Tower and scores of murals lining the Mission District, now being expanded by Precita Eyes (www.precitaeyes.org). Murals gave voice to Chicano pride and protests over US Central American policies in the 1970s, notably in San Diego's Chicano Park and East LA murals by collectives such as the East Los Streetscapers.

will slowly oxidize green to match its park setting. Nearby, Renzo Piano literally raised the roof on sustainable design at the LEED platinum-certified California Academy of Sciences, capped by a living garden.

Visual Arts

The earliest European artists were trained cartographers accompanying Western explorers, although their images of California as an island show more imagination than scientific rigor. This mythologizing tendency continued throughout California's mid-19th-century Gold Rush era, as Western artists alternated between caricatures of Wild West debauchery and manifest-destiny propaganda urging pioneers to settle the golden West. The completion of the Transcontinental Railroad in 1869 brought an influx of romantic painters, who painted epic California wilderness landscapes. In the early 1900s, homegrown colonies of California Impressionist plein-air painters emerged, most famously at Laguna Beach and Carmel-by-the-Sea.

With the invention of photography, the improbable truth of California's landscape and its inhabitants was revealed. Pirkle Jones saw expressive potential in California landscape photography after WWII, while San Francisco native Ansel Adams' sublime photographs had already started doing justice to Yosemite. Adams founded Group f/64 with Edward Weston from Carmel and Imogen Cunningham in San Francisco. Berkeley-based Dorothea Lange turned her unflinching lens on the plight of Californian migrant workers in the Great Depression and Japanese Americans forced to enter internment camps in WWII, producing poignant documentary photos.

As the postwar American West became crisscrossed with freeways and divided into planned communities, Californian painters captured the abstract forms of manufactured landscapes on canvas. In San Francisco Richard Diebenkorn and David Park became leading proponents of Bay Area Figurative Art, while San Francisco–born sculptor Richard Serra captured urban aesthetics in massive, rusting monoliths resembling ship prows and industrial Stonehenges. Pop artists captured SoCal's ethos of conspicuous consumerism through Wayne Thiebaud's still-life gumball machines, British émigré David Hockney's acrylic paintings of LA pools and Ed Ruscha's canvas and film studies.

To see contemporary California art at its most experimental, browse the gallery scenes in downtown LA and Culver City or San Francisco's SoMa neighborhood.

Oddball Architecture

- Hearst Castle, San Simeon
- Tor House, Carmel-by-the-Sea
- Theme Building, LAX Airport
- Binoculars Building, Venice Beach
- Solvang, Santa Barbara Wine Country
- Winchester Mystery House, San Jose

Redwoods & Wild Things

From misty redwood forests and rocky headlands to sunny beaches and arid canyons, coastal California is home to a bewildering variety of ecosystems. In fact, 30% of all plant and reptile species and almost half of all of bird and mammal species that inhabit the entire country are found in California, which boasts the highest biodiversity in North America. This is also a land of record-breaking superlatives, starting with Earth's tallest trees, coast redwoods.

Although the staggering numbers of land and sea animals, boundless virgin forests and wildflower fields that greeted California's early settlers are now mostly a thing of the past, it's still possible to see wildlife thriving along the coast in the right places and at the right times of year, from emerald hillsides blanketed by golden poppies to migratory gray whales and monarch butterflies. Some of coastal California's endemic species of flora and fauna are but shadow populations today, hovering at the edge of survival, pushed up against the state's ever-burgeoning human population.

Marine Superstars

Peak mating season for northern elephants seals along the Pacific coast just happens to coincide with Valentine's Day (February 14).

Spend even one day along California's coast and you may spot pods of bottle-nosed dolphins and porpoises swimming and doing acrobatics in the ocean. Playful sea otters and harbor seals typically stick closer to shore, especially around public piers and protected bays. Since the 1989 earthquake, loudly barking sea lions have been piling up on San Francisco's Pier 39, much to the delight of ogling tourists. Other excellent places to see wild pinnipeds include Point Lobos State Natural Reserve just south of Monterey, Point Reyes National Seashore in Marin County and the Channel Islands National Park, offshore from Southern California.

Once threatened by extinction, gray whales now migrate in growing numbers along California's coast. Adult whales live up to 50 years, are longer than a city bus and can weigh up to 40 tons, making quite a splash when they dive below or leap out of the water. In summer, the whales feed in Arctic waters between Alaska and Siberia. During autumn, they move south down the West Coast of Canada and the US to sheltered lagoons in the Gulf of California in Mexico. During their biannual 6000-mile migration, these whales are spotted off California's coast between December and April. For whale-watching tips and boat tours, see p35.

Also hunted almost to extinction by the late 19th century for their oil-rich blubber, northern elephant seals have made a remarkable comeback along California's coast. Observe elephant seals from a safe distance and do not approach or otherwise harass these unpredictable wild animals, who surprisingly move faster on the sand than you can. In winter, the behemoth bulls engage in mock – and sometimes real – combat, all the while making odd guttural grunts, while their harems of females and young pups look on. Año Nuevo State Reserve, north of Santa Cruz, is a protected breeding ground, and there's a smaller rookery at Point Reyes, north of San Francisco, but California's biggest colony of northern elephant seals hauls out by Point Piedras Blancas near Hearst Castle, south of Big Sur.

Mighty Mammals on Land

California's most symbolic animal – it graces the state flag – is the grizzly bear. Grizzlies once roamed California's beaches and grasslands in large numbers, eating everything from whale carcasses to acorns, but were extirpated in the early 1900s after relentless persecution. All that remains now are the grizzlies' smaller cousins, black bears. These burly omnivores, which feed on berries, nuts, roots, grasses, insects, eggs, small mammals and fish, are rarely seen outside forests in the mountains farther inland.

As European settlers moved into California in the 1800s, many other large mammals fared almost as poorly as grizzlies. Immense herds of tule elk were particularly hard hit, having been hunted to near-extinction by the 1860s. A small remnant herd of tule elk was moved to Point Reyes National Seashore in 1973, where the population has since rebounded.

Mountain lions hunt throughout California, especially in woodsy areas teeming with deer. Solitary lions, which can grow 8ft in length and weigh 175lb, are formidable predators. A few attacks on humans have occurred, usually where human encroachment pushes hungry lions to their limits – for example, at the boundaries between wilderness and rapidly developing suburbs.

If you can't tell your white-tailed kite from your double-crested cormorant, or a tufted sea lion from a whiskered harbor seal, pick up one of the excellent California Natural History Guides published by the University of California Press (www.californianaturalhistory.com), which are compact enough to carry in a daypack.

Feathered Friends & Butterflies

California lies on major migratory routes for over 350 species of birds, which either pass through the state or linger during winter. It's an essential stop on the migratory Pacific Flyway between Alaska and Mexico, and almost half of North America's bird species use coastal and inland refuges for rest and refueling. You can spot a huge variety of birds year-round at California's beaches, estuaries, wetlands and bays (see p38).

Year-round avian residents along California's coast include gulls, grebes, terns, cormorants, sandpipers and little sanderlings that chase receding waves along the shore, looking for critters in the freshly turned sand. A few of California's beaches are closed between March and September to protect endangered western snowy plovers, who lay their eggs

EYEING E-SEALS

Northern elephant seals follow a precise calendar. In November and December, adult male 'bull seals' return to their favorite California beaches and start the ritual struggles to assert superiority; only the largest, strongest and most aggressive 'alpha' males gather a harem. In January and February, adult females, already pregnant from last year's beach antics, arrive and give birth to their pups, then mate with dominant males, who promptly depart on their next feeding migration. Talk about 'love 'em and leave 'em'!

At birth an elephant seal pup already weighs about 75lb, and while being fed by its mother it puts on a whopping 10lb a day. Female seals leave the beach in March, abandoning their offspring. For one or two months the young seals, now known as 'weaners,' lounge around in groups, gradually teaching themselves to swim, first in tidal pools, then in the sea. The 'weaners' depart by May, having lost 20% to 30% of their weight. Between June and October, elephant seals of all ages and both sexes return in smaller numbers to their colony's preferred beaches to molt.

in exposed ground scrapes in the sand. Snowy plovers are easily frightened by humans, dogs and noisy off-highway vehicles (OHV), which can cause them to run off and abandon their eggs to burn in the sun.

As you drive along the Big Sur coast, look skyward to spot the largest flying bird in North America, the endangered California condor (see p296), which also soars over Pinnacles National Monument inland. Also keep an eye out for regal bald eagles, which have regained a foothold on the Channel Islands, and sometimes spend their winters at Big Bear Lake outside LA. The northern spotted owl, today a threatened species due to destructive logging practices, is protected inside the North Coast's Headwaters Forest Reserve.

The Audubon Society's California chapter website (http://ca.audubon.org) has helpful birding checklists, a newsy blog, and descriptions of key species and important birding areas statewide.

Another iconic species that takes flight in coastal California, monarch butterflies are gorgeous orange creatures that follow amazing long-distance migration patterns in search of milkweed, their only source of food. Tens of thousands of monarchs hibernate here in winter, notably along the Central Coast at Santa Cruz, Pacific Grove and Pismo Beach.

Going Native: Trees & Flowers

Imagine almost all of California's coast from the Oregon border south to Santa Cruz covered with stands of coast redwoods. Today less than 5% of these old-growth forests remain, yet scientists have recently found that their complexity matches that of tropical rain forests. Officially the world's tallest trees, coast redwoods are towering giants with spongy red bark, flat needles and olive-sized cones that rely on fog as their primary water source. On the damp forest floor beneath them, look for sword ferns, redwood sorrel and velvety green mosses.

In 2006 the world's tallest tree was discovered in Redwood National Park (its location is being kept secret). It's named Hyperion and stands a whopping 379ft tall.

More rare native plant species in coastal California include Monterey and Torrey pines, gnarled trees that have adapted to harsh coastal conditions such as high winds, sparse rainfall and sandy, stony soils. They too derive much of their water from the billowing coastal fog. Today, Torrey pines grow only at Torrey Pines State Reserve near San Diego and in Channel Islands National Park, home to dozens more endemic plant species. Catalina Island is also a hot spot for biodiversity: there you'll find Catalina ironwood and mahogany trees and the Catalina live-forever (a succulent).

California's myriad flowering plants are both flamboyant and subtle. Many species are so obscure or similar-looking that only a botanist could tell them apart. But add them all together in the spring and you end up with riotous carpets of wildflowers. Those famous 'golden hills' of California are actually the result of many plants drying up in preparation for the long, dry summer. Here plants have adapted to long periods of almost no rain by growing prolifically during California's mild wet winters, springing to life with the first rains in fall and blooming as early as February, peaking between March and May.

Earthquakes & the Land

The third-largest US state after Alaska and Texas, California covers over 155,000 sq miles, making it larger than 85 of the world's smallest nations. It's bordered to the north by woodsy Oregon, to the east by desert-dry Nevada and Arizona, to the south by subtropical Baja California, Mexico, and by 840 miles of Pacific shoreline to the west.

Shake, Rattle 'n' Roll

California is a complex geological landscape formed from fragments of rock and earth crust scraped together as the North American continent drifted westward over hundreds of millions of years. The crumpled Coast Ranges, the depressed Central Valley and the still-rising Sierra Nevada mountains all provide evidence of gigantic geological forces exerted as the continental and ocean plates crushed together.

Everything changed about 25 million years ago, when the ocean plates stopped colliding and instead started sliding against each other. Today California sits on one of the world's major earthquake fault zones, on the dramatic edge of two moving plates: the Pacific Plate, consisting of the Pacific Ocean floor and much of California's coastline, and the continental North American Plate.

The primary boundary between these two plates is the massive San Andreas Fault, which runs for over 650 miles and has spawned numerous smaller faults that extend their treacherous fingers toward California's shoreline. Because this contact zone doesn't slide smoothly, but catches and slips irregularly, it rattles California with an ongoing succession of tremors and earthquakes. Walk the Earthquake Trail at Point Reyes National Seashore for an up-close look at plate tectonics – notice how a fence jumped 16ft during just one earthquake!

Curious about all the rumbling along the San Andreas Fault? Check out *A Land in Motion* by Michael Collier for a photographic overview of the subject, or get the bejeezus scared out of you by Marc Reisner's part journalistic, part imaginative book, *A Dangerous Place: California's Unsettling Fate*.

California's Monster Quakes

California's most famous earthquake, in 1906, measured 7.9 on the Richter scale and demolished San Francisco, leaving more than 3000 people dead. The San Francisco Bay Area made headlines again in 1989 when the Loma Prieta earthquake (magnitude 6.9), which lasted just 15 seconds, caused a section of the Bay Bridge and I-880 in Oakland to collapse. Today, you can walk right up to the epicenter of the Loma Prieta quake in Forest of Nisene Marks State Park, south of Santa Cruz.

Los Angeles' last 'big one' was in 1994, when the Northridge quake (magnitude 6.7) caused parts of the freeways and the scoreboard at Anaheim Stadium to fall down. With its epicenter in the San Fernando Valley, the Northridge quake's seismic waves were felt as far away as Las Vegas, Nevada. Dozens of deaths, thousands of injuries and estimated damages of $25 billion make it the most costly quake in California history.

According to the US Geological Survey, the odds of a magnitude 6.7 or greater earthquake hitting California within the next 30 years is 99.7%.

Lay of the Land

California's northern boundary lies at the same Mediterranean latitude as Rome, Italy, while its southern edge lies at the same desert latitude as Tel Aviv, Israel. Much of the state remains a biological island cut off from the rest of North America by the Sierra Nevada range. As on other 'islands' in the world, evolution here has created unique plants and animals under these biologically isolated conditions. As a result, California ranks first in the nation for its number of endemic plants, amphibians, reptiles, freshwater fish and mammals. For more about coastal California's wildlife, see p494.

Curious to know more about the geological forces that have shaped California? Throw copies of *Roadside Geology of Northern and Central California*, by David Alt, and *Geology Underfoot in Southern California*, by Robert Sharp, on to the back seat of your car.

Ranging Along the Coast

Much of California's coast is fronted by rugged coastal mountains that capture life-giving moisture from summertime fog and winter's water-laden storms. Called the Coast Ranges, these mountain chains run north and south along most of the shoreline, plunging west into the wild Pacific Ocean and rolling east toward the sea-level Central Valley.

Over 120in of rain a year fall in the northernmost reaches of the Coast Ranges and, in some places, persistent summer fog contributes another 12in of precipitation. Nutrient-rich soils and abundant moisture foster forests of towering trees (where they haven't been logged, that is), including stands of towering coast redwoods growing as far south as Big Sur and all the way north into Oregon.

San Francisco divides the Coast Ranges roughly in half, with the foggy North Coast remaining sparsely populated. The Central and Southern California coasts have a balmier climate and, as a result, many, many more people, especially in urban areas from LA to San Diego. South of Santa Barbara, the Coast Ranges are linked to the mightier Sierra Nevada by the Transverse Ranges, one of the USA's only east–west mountains ranges.

Southern California

Southern California is a hodgepodge of smaller mountain ranges and desert basins. The desert-like Los Angeles Basin fronts the ocean and is partly surrounded by mountains. San Diego, on the edge of another

EARTHQUAKE SAFETY TIPS

Earthquakes happen all the time in California, but most are so tiny they are detectable only by sensitive seismological instruments. In the unlikely event that you're caught in a serious shaker:

» If indoors, get under a desk or table or stand in a doorway.

» Protect your head and stay clear of windows, mirrors or anything that might fall.

» Don't head for elevators or go running into the street.

» If you're in a shopping mall or large public building, expect the alarm and/or sprinkler systems to come on.

» If outdoors, get away from buildings, trees and power lines.

» If you're driving, pull over to the side of the road away from bridges, overpasses and power lines. Stay inside the car until the shaking stops.

» If you're on a sidewalk near buildings, duck into a doorway to protect yourself from falling bricks, glass and debris.

» Prepare for aftershocks.

» Turn on the radio and listen for bulletins.

» Use the telephone only if absolutely necessary. Keep cell (mobile) phone networks free for emergency services personnel.

COASTAL CALIFORNIA'S TOP 10 NATIONAL & STATE PARKS

PARK	FEATURES	ACTIVITIES	BEST TIME
Big Sur's State Parks (p293)	vertical sea cliffs, pocket beaches, redwood forests, waterfalls, California condors, migrating whales	hiking, horseback riding, beachcombing, bird-watching, swimming	May-Oct
Channel Islands National Park (p336)	rocky islands with steep cliffs, elephant seals, sea lions, otters, foxes, wildflowers	snorkeling, diving, kayaking, hiking, bird-watching	Apr-Oct
Crystal Cove State Park (p413)	sandy beaches, tide pools, woodlands, mule deer, bobcats, great horned lizards, hermit crabs, hummingbirds	swimming, surfing, snorkeling, diving, hiking, mountain-biking	Jun-Sep
Golden Gate National Recreation Area (p104)	beaches, tide pools, forests, grassy headlands, sand dunes, wetlands, harbor seals, sea lions, migratory whales, brown pelicans, peregrine falcons, mission blue butterflies	hiking, cycling, mountain-biking, bird-watching, swimming, surfing, kayaking, self-guided historical site tours	May-Sep
Mendocino Headlands State Park (p225)	coastal bluffs, rugged beaches, wildflowers, migrating whales	nature walks, beachcombing, hiking, kayaking, fishing	May-Sep
Muir Woods National Monument (p115)	towering stands of old-growth redwood trees, black-tailed deer, banana slugs, northern spotted owls	nature walks, hiking	Apr-Oct
Point Lobos State Natural Reserve (p290)	rocky headlands, beaches, coves, grassy meadows, woodlands, seals, sea lions, sea otters, migratory whales	hiking, bird-watching, snorkeling, scuba diving, kayaking	May-Oct
Point Reyes National Seashore (p119)	windswept beaches, lagoons, grassy headlands, tule elk, northern elephant seals, migrating whales	hiking, bird-watching, kayaking, mountain-biking	May-Oct
Redwood National & State Parks (p260)	virgin redwood groves, fern forests, pristine beaches, Roosevelt elk, bald eagles, northern spotted owls, Steller's sea lions	hiking, backpacking, kayaking, cycling, scenic drives	May-Sep
Torrey Pines State Natural Reserve (p442)	rugged ocean bluffs, saltwater marsh and lagoon, rare Torrey pine forest, great blue herons, migrating whales	hiking, bird-watching, swimming, surfing, fishing	Apr-Oct

plateau about 120 miles south of LA, borders Tijuana, Mexico. Mountains just east of San Diego continue south down the spine of northern Baja California in Mexico. Unlike LA and San Francisco, San Diego gets the majority of its water supply not from the Sierra Nevada Mountains but from the Colorado River, which partly defines the state border between California and Arizona.

National & State Parks

Browse through over 66,000 aerial photos covering almost every mile of California's wildly rugged and developed coastline, from the Oregon to the Mexican border, at www.californiacoastline.org.

The majority of Californians rank outdoor recreation as vital to their quality of life, and the amount of preserved lands has steadily grown due to important pieces of legislation passed since the 1960s, including the landmark 1976 California Coastal Act, which saved the coastline from further development, and the controversial 1994 California Desert Protection Act, which angered many ranchers, miners and off-roaders. Today, **California State Parks** (www.parks.ca.gov) protects nearly a third of the state's coastline, along with redwood forests, lakes, desert canyons, waterfalls, wildlife preserves and historical sites.

In recent years, federal and state budget shortfalls and chronic underfunding have been partly responsible for widespread park closures, limiting visitor services and steadily increasing park-entry and outdoor recreation fees. Even so, it's still in California's economic best interests to protect wilderness, as recreational tourism consistently outpaces competing 'natural resource extraction' industries such as mining. As this book went to press, 70 state parks were slated to shut their gates in 2012.

Some of California's parks are also being loved to death. Overcrowding severely affects the parks' natural environments and makes it increasingly difficult to balance public access with conservation. At popular SoCal beach parks during summer, it's almost impossible to find a parking space, let alone space on the sand. To avoid the biggest crowds and reduce your impact on parks, try to visit during the shoulder seasons (ie spring and fall) and take public transportation or cycle there.

Take a virtual field trip all around the Golden State courtesy of the myriad links put together by the California Geological Survey at www.conservation.ca.gov/cgs/geotour.

Alternatively, other natural areas of coastal California, including those managed by the **National Park Service** (www.nps.gov/state/CA), may go relatively untouched most of the year, which means you won't have to reserve permits, campsites or accommodations months in advance. Just inland from the coast, several national forests in California, run by the **US Forest Service** (USFS; www.fs.fed.us/r5/), are less-trammeled areas worth exploring. National wildlife refuges (NWR), favored by bird-watchers, are managed by the **US Fish & Wildlife Service** (USFWS; www.fws.gov/refuges). More remote wilderness tracts are overseen by the **Bureau of Land Management** (BLM; www.blm.gov/ca/st/en.html).

Sustainable California

Although California is in many ways a historical success story, development and growth have often come at great environmental cost. Starting in 1849, Gold Rush miners tore apart the land in their frenzied quest for the 'big strike,' ultimately sending more than 1.5 billion tons of debris, and uncalculated amounts of poisonous mercury, downstream into the Central Valley, where rivers and streams became clogged and polluted.

Today, tons of particulate matter spew into the air from automobile and diesel emissions, reducing air quality and hiding the sun in urban areas, especially in LA. The ocean is overfished, open-space land is disappearing beneath asphalt and landfills, and tankers occasionally leak oil into the sea. California is now the most-populous US state – with over 70% of residents living in coastal counties – which puts a tremendous strain on its finite natural resources.

So, is this paradise found actually lost? Not yet. California's conservationists and environmental activists, biodynamic farmers and vineyard owners, high-tech innovators in the renewable energy and alternative fuel industries, and progressive-minded legislators, civic leaders and voters are all taking steps together to 'green' the future.

Founded in 1892 with naturalist John Muir serving as its first president, the Sierra Club (www.sierraclub.org/ca) was the USA's first conservation group and it remains the nation's most active, offering educational programs, genial group hikes, outdoor-activity trips and volunteer vacations.

Water, Water, Where?

Water, or the lack thereof, has long been at the heart of California's epic environmental struggles and catastrophes. Despite campaigning by the state's greatest environmental champion, John Muir, the Tuolumne River was dammed in 1923, flooding the Hetch Hetchy Valley inside Yosemite National Park, so that the burgeoning population of San Francisco could have drinking water. Likewise, the diversion of water to Los Angeles from the Eastern Sierra via aqueducts starting in 1913 has contributed to the destruction of Owens Lake and its fertile wetlands, and the degradation of Mono Lake.

Statewide the damming of rivers and capture of water for houses and farms has destroyed countless salmon runs and drained marshlands. The Central Valley, for example, today resembles a dust bowl, and its underground aquifer is in poor shape. Dams along the Colorado River send millions of acre-feet of water per year to San Diego and much of the rest of Southern California via hundreds of miles of aqueducts, as they wreak havoc on the ecosystem and decimate local fish populations.

Regardless of where the water comes from, there never seems to be enough to satisfy demand by thirsty Californians. Both global warming and persistent droughts critically affect the state's winter snowpack. If it doesn't snow heavily enough in the Sierra Nevada during winter, there won't be enough snow left in spring to melt and fill the reservoirs that supply coastal cities and inland farms. Homeowners are slowly learning to conserve water; for example, with outdoor xeriscaping and dry gardens that don't require irrigation. And you will too: look for low-flow showerheads and low-flush toilets in hotel rooms.

Fighting for Clean Air, Land & Energy

Although air quality in California has improved markedly in past decades, it still ranks among the worst in the USA. Along much of the coast, air pollution is alleviated by the prevailing westerly winds that blow clean air in off the Pacific. But travel inland, especially across the LA Basin, and the air often takes on a thick haze, obscuring vistas and creating health hazards.

At the same time, California leads the nation in automobile emissions control and ownership of hybrid and alternative-fuel vehicles, from Priuses and plug-ins to biodiesel cars that chug along on recycled fast-food cooking oil. Toxic clean-up and reclamation of abandoned industrial areas and military sites has also created urban 'green spaces' that help Californians breathe more easily.

Southern California would not exist as it does today without water. Marc Reisner's must-read *Cadillac Desert: the American West and its Disappearing Water* examines the contentious, sometimes violent, water wars that gave rise to modern California.

Recently, voters have funded construction of solar-power plants, which already produce 500 megawatts of electricity statewide, and there's even talk of harnessing the tremendous tidal flows of the Pacific to generate more 'clean' energy. By law, California must get 33% of its energy from renewable resources by 2020, the most ambitious target of any US state so far.

Coastal California cities are also leading the way when it comes to the mantra 'reduce, reuse, recycle.' Take San Francisco, for example, which plans to recycle *all* of its trash by the year 2020 and has already instituted citywide composting of perishable organic matter under its zero-waste 'landfill avoidance' policy.

Native Wildlife vs Alien Invaders

Once a biodiverse 'island' protected by the Pacific Ocean and the Sierra Nevada Mountains, California has been overrun by alien species introduced by foreigners ever since Spanish colonists arrived in the late 18th century, right up through the Gold Rush era and post-WWII boom. Significantly altered and compromised habitats, both on land and water, make easy targets for invasive plants and animals, including highly aggressive species that damage California's ecosystems and economy.

In San Francisco Bay alone, one of the most important estuaries in the world, there are now over 230 alien species choking the aquatic ecosystem and in some areas they already comprise as much as 95% of the total biomass. Pushing out native flora all along the coast, ice plant – that ropy green groundcover with purple-and-white flowers that creep over beach dunes and take over headlands – originally came from South Africa. Volunteers all along the coast are kept busy pulling out invasive alien plants.

During construction of California's 19th-century railways, fast-growing eucalyptus trees were imported from Australia to make railroad ties, but the wood proved poor and split when driven through with a stake. The trees now grow like weeds, fueling summertime wildfires with their flammable, explosive seed capsules. Even California's snails come from far away, brought here in the 1850s from France to produce *escargot*. Now they're everywhere, along with Atlantic crabs, which destroy native oyster beds.

Out of necessity but also by choice, California has become a leader in wildlife and ecosystem conservation. The Monterey Bay National Marine Sanctuary harbors North America's deepest underwater canyon and alone protects more than 340 species of fish and 30 species of marine mammals, including migratory whales. All along the coast, protecting and restoring native habitats, tagging and monitoring endangered wildlife and innovating captive-breeding-and-release programs are all showing hopeful results.

Survival Guide

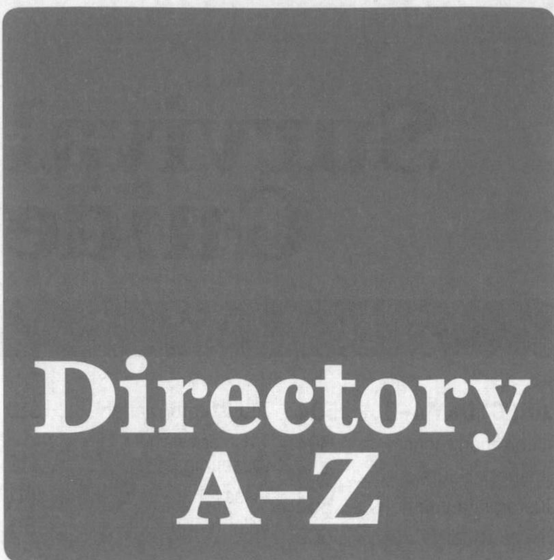

Accommodations

Amenities

» In many coastal areas, budget and midrange accommodations may only offer fans in guest rooms. Where air-conditioning is available, the ❄ icon appears with our reviews.

» Accommodations offering online computer terminals for guests are designated with the internet icon (@). When wireless internet access is offered, the wi-fi icon (wi-fi) appears. There may be a fee for either service. Look for free wi-fi hotspots in public areas (eg lobby).

» Many lodgings are now exclusively nonsmoking. Where they still exist, smoking rooms are often unrenovated and in undesirable locations. Expect a hefty 'cleaning fee' ($100 or more) if you light up in designated nonsmoking rooms.

» For environmentally friendly lodgings, look for the sustainable icon (leaf). Also browse properties denoted by two palm trees in the online directory of the **California Green Lodging Program** (www.dgs.ca.gov/travel/Programs/GreenLodgingDirectory.aspx).

Rates & Discounts

» Budget-conscious accommodations include campgrounds, hostels and motels. Because midrange properties generally offer better value for money, most of our recommendations fall into this category.

» This guide lists accommodations in order of author recommendation. Rates are categorized as $ (under $100), $$ ($100 to $200) or $$$ (over $200). Unless noted, rates do not include lodging taxes, averaging more than 10%.

» Rates quoted in this book are for summer high season, from June to August. Demand and prices spike even higher around major holidays and festivals, when some properties may also impose multiday minimum stays.

» Generally, midweek rates are lower except in hotels geared toward weekday business travelers, which lure leisure travelers with weekend deals.

» Discount cards (p506) and auto-club membership (p516) may entitle you to 10% off standard rates at participating hotels and motels.

» Look for freebie ad magazines packed with hotel and motel discount coupons at gas stations, highway rest areas, tourist offices and online at **Roomsaver.com** (www.roomsaver.com).

» Bargaining may be possible for walk-in guests without reservations, especially during off-peak times.

Reservations

» Reservations are recommended for weekend and holiday travel year-round, and every day during summer high season.

» If you book a reservation by phone, always get a confirmation number and ask about the cancellation policy before you give out your credit-card information.

» If you plan to arrive late in the evening, call ahead on the day of your stay to let them know. Hotels overbook, but if you've guaranteed the reservation with your credit card, they should try to accommodate you somewhere else.

B&Bs

If you want an atmospheric alternative to impersonal motels and hotels, bed-and-breakfast inns typically inhabit fine old Victorian houses or other heritage buildings, bedecked with floral wallpaper and antique furnishings. People who like privacy may find B&Bs too intimate.

Rates may include a cooked breakfast, but occasionally breakfast is *not* provided (never mind what the name 'B&B' suggests). Amenities vary widely, but rooms with TV and telephone are the exception; the cheapest units share bathrooms. Standards are high at places certified by the **California Association of Bed & Breakfast Inns** (www.cabbi.com).

Most B&Bs require advance reservations and don't

accept drop-in guests; always call ahead. Smoking is generally prohibited and children are usually not welcome. Expect minimum-stay requirements, especially on weekends and in peak season.

Camping

In coastal California, camping is much more than just a cheap way to spend the night; the best campsites let you wake up on the beach or under a canopy of redwood trees. Most public and private campgrounds are open year-round, including these types:

Primitive campgrounds Usually campsites have fire pits, picnic tables and access to drinking water and vault toilets; most common in national forests (USFS) and on Bureau of Land Management (BLM) land.

Developed campgrounds Typically found in state and national parks, these offer more amenities, including flush toilets and occasionally hot showers.

Private campgrounds Catering mainly to RVers with hot showers, swimming pools, wi-fi and family camping cabins; tent sites may be sparse and uninviting.

Walk-in (environmental) sites Providing more peace and privacy, a few public-lands campgrounds reserve these sites for long-distance hikers and cyclists.

Many campgrounds accept reservations for all or some of their sites, while a few are strictly first-come, first-served. Overnight fees range from $10 or less for the most primitive and remote campsites to $65 or more for developed oceanfront sites with RV pull-throughs and full hookups.

To search for campground locations and amenities, check current availability and make reservations, try these sites:

Recreation.gov (☎518-885-3639, 877-444-6777; www.recreation.gov) Camping and cabin reservations for national parks, national forests, BLM land etc.

ReserveAmerica (☎916-638-5883, 800-444-7275; www.reserveamerica.com) Reservations for California state parks, East Bay and Orange County regional parks and some private campgrounds.

Kampgrounds of America (KOA; http://koa.com) National chain of reliable but pricey campgrounds offering full facilities, including for RVs.

Hostels

Coastal California has 16 hostels affiliated with **Hostelling International USA** (HI-USA; ☎301-495-1240; www.hiusa.org). Dorms in HI hostels are typically gender-segregated and alcohol and smoking are prohibited. HI-USA membership cards (adult/senior $28/18 per year, free for under-18s) entitle you to $3 off per night.

California also has dozens of independent hostels, particularly in coastal cities. They generally have more relaxed rules and often no curfew. Some hostels include a light breakfast in their rates, arrange local tours or offer pick-ups at transportation hubs. Facilities typically include mixed dorms, semi-private rooms with shared bathrooms, communal kitchens, lockers, internet access and coin-op laundry.

Dorm-bed rates average $25 to $40 per night, including taxes. Reservations are always a good idea, especially in high season. Most hostels take reservations online or by phone. Some hostels say they accept only international travelers, basically to keep out homeless locals, but US travelers who look like they'll fit in with other guests may be admitted, especially during slower times. A passport, HI-USA card or international plane ticket should help establish your credentials.

Hotels & Motels

» At midrange motels and hotels, expect clean, comfortable rooms with a private bathroom and such standard amenities as a cable TV, telephone, coffeemaker and perhaps a microwave and mini fridge.

» Top-end hotels and resorts offer more amenities and perhaps a scenic oceanfront location or historical ambience. Pools, fitness rooms, business centers and full-service restaurants and bars are all standard.

» Rooms are often priced by the size and number of beds. A room with a king-sized bed or two double or queen-sized beds usually costs more.

» There is often a small surcharge for the third and fourth adult, but children

PRACTICALITIES

» **Electricity** 110/120V AC, 50/60Hz

» **Newspapers** *Los Angeles Times* (www.latimes.com), *San Francisco Chronicle* (www.sfgate.com), *San Jose Mercury News* (www.mercurynews.com)

» **Radio** National Public Radio (NPR), lower end of FM dial

» **TV** PBS (public broadcasting); cable: CNN (news), ESPN (sports), HBO (movies), Weather Channel

» **Video** NTSC standard (incompatible with PAL or SECAM); DVDs coded region 1 (USA & Canada only)

» **Weights & Measures** Imperial

under a certain age (this varies) may stay free. Cribs or rollaway cots may cost extra.

» Beware that suites or 'junior suites' may simply be oversized rooms; ask about the layout when booking.

» Recently renovated or larger rooms, or those with a view, are likely to cost more. Descriptors like 'oceanfront' and 'oceanview' are liberally used, and you may need a periscope to spot the surf.

» Rates may include breakfast, which could be just a stale donut and wimpy coffee, an all-you-can-eat hot and cold buffet, or anything in between.

» Some motels and hotels are entirely smokefree, meaning you're not allowed to smoke anywhere on the property, not even outside (within a certain distance).

Business Hours

Unless otherwise noted with reviews, standard opening hours for listings in this guide are as follows:

Banks 8:30am-4:30pm Mon-Thu, to 5:30pm Fri, sometimes 9am-12:30pm Sat

Bars 5pm-midnight, sometimes to 2am Fri & Sat

Businesses 9am-5pm Mon-Fri, some post offices 9am-noon Sat

Nightclubs 10pm-2am Thu-Sat

Restaurants 7am-10:30am, 11:30am-2:30pm & 5-9:30pm daily, some later Fri & Sat

Shops 10am-6pm Mon-Sat, noon-5pm Sun; shopping malls keep extended hours

BOOK YOUR STAY ONLINE

For more accommodations reviews by Lonely Planet authors, check out hotels.lonelyplanet.com. You'll find independent reviews, as well as recommendations on the best places to stay. Best of all, you can book online.

Customs Regulations

Currently, non-US citizens and permanent residents may import the following:

» 1L of alcohol (if you're over 21 years old)

» 200 cigarettes (one carton) or 50 (non-Cuban) cigars (if you're over 18)

» $100 worth of gifts

Amounts higher than $10,000 cash, traveler's checks, money orders and other cash equivalents must be declared. Don't even think about bringing illegal drugs.

For more complete, up-to-date information, check with **US Customs and Border Protection** (www.cbp.gov).

Discount Cards

For discounts for children and families, see p40.

American Association of Retired Persons (AARP; ☎888-687-2277; www.aarp.org; annual membership $16), Advocacy group for Americans 50 years and older offers member discounts (usually 10%) on hotels, car rentals and more.

American Automobile Association (AAA; ☎877-428-2277; www.aaa.com; annual membership from $48) Members of AAA and its foreign affiliates (eg CAA, AA) qualify for small discounts (usually 10%) on Amtrak trains, car rentals, motels and hotels, chain restaurants, shopping, tours and theme parks.

Southern California CityPass (www.citypass.com; adult/child 3-9yr from $276/229) If you're visiting theme parks, this discount card covers three-day admission to Disneyland and Disney's California Adventure and one-day admission each to Universal Studios and SeaWorld, with another day at either the San Diego Zoo or Safari Park. Passes are valid for 14 consecutive days after first use; purchase online in advance for the lowest prices.

Go Los Angeles Card (one-day pass adult/child 3-12yr $60/50) and **Go San Diego Card** ($70/59) both include admission to major SoCal theme parks (but not Disney), while the **Go San Francisco Card** ($55/40) covers museums, bicycle rental and a Bay cruise. You have to do *a lot* of sightseeing over multiple days to make these passes even come close to paying off. To grab the best deals, purchase online at www.smartdestinations.com before your trip.

International Student Identity Card (ISIC; www.isic.org; $22) Offers savings on airline fares, travel insurance and local attractions for full-time students. For nonstudents under 26 years of age, an **International Youth Travel Card** (IYTC; $22) grants similar benefits. Both cards are issued by student unions, hostelling organizations and budget travel agencies.

Student Advantage Card (☎877-256-4672; www.studentadvantage.com; $23) This is for international and US students and it offers 15% savings on Amtrak and 20% with Greyhound, plus discounts of 10% to 20% on selected airlines and at some chain shops, hotels and motels.

Seniors People over the age of 65 (sometimes 55, 60 or 62) often qualify for the same discounts as students; any ID showing your birth ate should suffice as proof of age.

Electricity

Food

In this book, restaurant prices usually refer to an average main course at dinner:

Budget ($) Dinner mains under $10.

Midrange ($$) Most dinner mains $10 to $20.

Top End ($$$) Dinner mains over $20.

These prices don't include drinks, appetizers, desserts, taxes or tip. Note the same dishes at lunch will usually be cheaper, maybe even half-price.

Lunch is generally served between 11:30am and 2:30pm, and dinner between 5pm and 9:30pm daily, though some restaurants close later, especially on Friday and Saturday nights. If breakfast is served, it's usually between 7am and 10:30am; some diners and coffee shops keep serving breakfast into the afternoon, or all day. Weekend brunch is a laidback affair, usually available from 10am until 3pm on Saturdays and Sundays. Full opening hours are given with all restaurant reviews in this book.

Here are some more things to keep in mind:

» Only a handful of top-end restaurants require more than a dressy shirt, slacks and a decent pair of shoes; most budget and midrange places are California-casual.

» Tipping 15% to 20% is expected anywhere you receive table service.

» Smoking is illegal indoors; some restaurants have patios or sidewalk tables where lighting up is tolerated, though don't expect your neighbors to be happy about secondhand smoke.

» You can bring your own wine to most restaurants, but expect to pay a 'corkage' fee of $15 to $30. Lunches rarely include booze, though a glass of wine or beer, while uncommon, is usually acceptable.

» If you ask the kitchen to divide a plate between two (or more) people, there may be a small split-plate surcharge.

» Vegetarians and travelers with food allergies or medical issues are in luck – most restaurants are used to catering to specific dietary needs.

» If you're dining out with kids, see p40.

For more information on California cuisine, see p475.

Gay & Lesbian Travelers

California is a magnet for LGBTQ (lesbian/gay/bisexual/transgender/queer) travelers. The hot spots are San Francisco's Castro neighborhood (p90); West Hollywood (WeHo), Silver Lake and Long Beach in LA (p379); the Hillcrest area of San Diego (p454); and Guerneville (p201) and Calistoga (p177) in Napa and Sonoma wine country.

California offers gays and lesbians extensive domestic rights but currently stops short of the legalization of same-sex marriage. Although homophobic bigotry exists, widespread tolerance is the norm up and down the California coast, except for some small towns, where 'don't ask, don't tell' is still the unspoken social policy.

Helpful Resources

Advocate (www.advocate.com/travel) Online news and gay travel features.

Damron (www.damron.com) Advertiser-driven gay travel guides, with digital editions and a 'Gay Scout' mobile app.

Gay.com Daily Travel (www.gay.net/travel) City guides, travel news and special events coverage.

Gay & Lesbian Yellow Pages (www.glyp.com) Ads for local restaurants, bars and clubs plus a free 'Gay Yellow Pages' mobile app.

Gay & Lesbian National Hotline (☎888-843-4564; www.glnh.org; ⏲1-9pm Mon-Fri, 9am-2pm Sat) For counseling and referrals of any kind.

Gay Travelocity (www.travelocity.com/gaytravel) LGBT travel articles and hotel, guided tour and activity bookings.

Out Traveler (www.outtraveler.com) Free online magazine for travel news, destination guides and upcoming events.

Purple Roofs (www.purpleroofs.com) Online directory of LGBT accommodations.

Health

See also Safe Travel (p509) and Travel Insurance (p508).

Healthcare & Insurance

» Medical treatment in the USA is of the highest caliber, but the expense could kill you. Many health-care professionals demand payment at the time of service, especially from out-of-towners or international visitors.

» Except for medical emergencies (in which case call ☎911 or go to the nearest 24-hour hospital emergency room, or ER), phone around to find a doctor or an urgent-care center that will accept your insurance.

» Some health-insurance policies require you to get pre-authorization over the phone for medical treatment before seeking help. Keep all medical receipts and documentation for billing and insurance claims and reimbursement later.

» Carry any medications you may need in their original containers, clearly labeled. Bring a signed, dated letter from your doctor describing all medical conditions and medications (including generic names).

Insurance

For automobile insurance, see p516.

Travel Insurance

Getting travel insurance to cover theft, loss and medical problems is highly recommended. Some policies do not cover 'risky' activities such as scuba diving, motorcycling and skiing so read the fine print. Make sure the policy at least covers hospital stays and an emergency flight home.

Paying for your airline ticket or rental car with a credit card may provide limited travel accident insurance. If you already have private health insurance or a homeowners or renters policy, find out what those policies cover and only get supplemental insurance. If you have prepaid a large portion of your vacation, trip cancellation insurance may be a worthwhile expense.

Worldwide travel insurance is available at www.lonelyplanet.com/travel_services. You can buy, extend and claim online anytime – even if you're already on the road.

Internet Access

» Internet cafes listed throughout this guide typically charge $6 to $12 per hour for online access.

» With branches in coastal cities and most towns, **FedEx Office** (☎800-463-3339; www.fedex.com) offers internet access at self-service computer workstations (20¢ to 30¢ per minute) and sometimes free wi-fi, plus pay-as-you-go digital-photo printing and CD-burning stations.

» Accommodations, cafes, restaurants, bars etc that provide guest computer terminals are identified in this book by the internet icon @; the wi-fi icon (wi-fi) indicates that wireless access is available. There may be a fee for either service.

» Wi-fi hot spots (free or fee-based) can be found at major airports; many hotels and motels and a few campgrounds; and some tourist information centers, coffee shops, bars, restaurants and shopping malls.

» Public libraries have internet terminals, but online time may be limited, advance sign-up required and a nominal fee charged for out-of-network visitors. Increasingly libraries now offer free wi-fi.

Legal Matters

Drugs & Alcohol

» Possession of under 1oz of marijuana is a misdemeanor in California. Possession of any other drug or more than an ounce of weed is a felony punishable by lengthy jail time. For foreigners, conviction of any drug offense is grounds for deportation.

» Police can give roadside sobriety checks to assess if you've been drinking or using drugs. If you fail, they'll require you to take a breath, urine or blood test to determine if your blood alcohol is over the legal limit (0.08%). Refusing to be tested is treated the same as if you had taken and failed the test.

» Penalties for driving under the influence (DUI) of drugs or alcohol range from license suspension and fines to jail.

» It's illegal to carry open containers of alcohol inside a vehicle, even if they're empty. Unless they're full and still sealed, store them in the trunk.

» Consuming alcohol anywhere other than at a private residence or licensed premises is a no-no, which puts most parks and beaches off-limits (although many campgrounds do allow it).

» Bars, clubs and liquor stores often ask for photo ID to prove you are of legal drinking age. Being 'carded' is standard practice; don't take it personally.

Police & Security

» If you are stopped by the police, be courteous. Don't get out of the car unless asked. Keep your hands where the officer can see them (eg on the steering wheel).

» There is no system of paying fines on the spot. Attempting to pay the fine to the officer may lead to a charge of attempted bribery.

» For traffic violations the ticketing officer will explain the options to you. There is usually a 30-day period to pay a fine; most matters can be handled by mail.

» If you are arrested, you have the right to remain silent and are presumed innocent until proven guilty. Everyone has the right to make one phone call. Foreign travelers who don't have a lawyer, friends or family to help should call their embassy or consulate; the police can provide the number upon request.

» For police, fire and ambulance emergencies, dial ☎911. For nonemergency police assistance, call directory assistance (☎411) for the number of the nearest local police station.

» Due to security concerns about terrorism, never leave your bags unattended, especially not at airports, bus and train stations or on public transportation.

» Carrying mace or cayenne-pepper spray is legal in California, as long as the spray bottle contains no more than 2.5oz of active product. Federal law prohibits it from being carried on planes.

Smoking

» Smoking is generally prohibited inside all public buildings, including airports, shopping malls and train and bus stations.

» There is no smoking allowed inside restaurants, although it may be tolerated at outdoor patio or sidewalk tables (if you don't see an ashtray, ask first).

» At hotels, you must specifically request a smoking room, but note some properties are entirely nonsmoking by law.

» In some cities and towns, smoking outdoors within a certain distance of any public business is now forbidden.

Money

» For US dollar exchange rates and setting your trip budget, see p18. For tipping, see p510.

» Most people do not carry large amounts of cash for everyday use, relying instead on credit and debit cards. Some businesses refuse to accept bills over $20.

» Most ATMs are connected to international networks and offer decent foreign-exchange rates. Expect a minimum surcharge of $2.50 per transaction, plus any fees charged by your home bank.

» Exchange money and traveler's checks (the latter have fallen out of use) at major airports, big-city banks and currency-exchange offices such as **American Express** (www.americanexpress.com).

» Outside major coastal cities, exchanging money may be a problem, so make sure you have a credit card and sufficient cash.

» It's almost impossible to rent a car, book a room or buy tickets over the phone without a credit card. Visa, MasterCard and American Express are widely accepted.

Post

The **US Postal Service** (USPS; ☎800-275-8777; www.usps.com) is inexpensive and reliable.

For sending important letters or packages overseas, there's **Federal Express** (FedEx; ☎800-463-3339; www.fedex.com) or **UPS** (☎800-782-7892; www.ups.com).

Public Holidays

On the following national holidays, banks, schools and government offices (including post offices) are closed, and transportation, museums and other services operate on a Sunday schedule. Holidays falling on a weekend are usually observed the following Monday.

New Year's Day January 1

Martin Luther King Jr Day Third Monday in January

Presidents' Day Third Monday in February

Easter Sunday March/April

Memorial Day Last Monday in May

Independence Day July 4 (aka Fourth of July)

Labor Day First Monday in September

Columbus Day Second Monday in October

Veterans' Day November 11

Thanksgiving Day Fourth Thursday in November

Christmas Day December 25

School Holidays

Colleges take a one- or two-week 'spring break' around Easter, sometime in March or April. Some hotels and resorts, especially at beaches and near SoCal's theme parks, raise their rates during this time. School summer vacations run from early June to late August, making July and August the busiest travel months in coastal California.

Safe Travel

Despite its seemingly apocalyptic list of dangers – guns, violent crime, riots – coastal California is a reasonably safe place to visit. The greatest danger is posed by car accidents (buckle up – it's the law). There's also the dramatic, albeit unlikely, possibility of a natural disaster such as a tsunami or a large-magnitude earthquake (for the latter, see p497).

Wildlife

» Never feed or approach wild animals. Disturbing or harassing protected species (eg many marine mammals) is a crime, subject to enormous fines.

» Mountain lion (see p495) attacks on humans are rare. If you encounter one, stay calm, pick up small children, face the animal and retreat slowly. Try to appear larger by raising your arms or grabbing a stick. If the lion behaves menacingly, shout or throw rocks at it. If attacked, fight back aggressively.

» Snakes and spiders are common, and not just in wilderness areas. Always look inside your shoes before putting them back on outdoors, especially when camping. Snake bites are rare, but usually occur when a snake is stepped on or provoked (eg picked up or poked with a stick). Antivenom is available at most hospitals.

Telephone

Cell (Mobile) Phones

You'll need a multiband GSM phone in order to make calls in the USA. Popping in a prepaid rechargeable SIM card is usually cheaper than using your own network. SIM cards are sold at telecommunications and electronics stores, which also sell inexpensive prepaid phones, including some airtime. You can rent a cell phone in San Francisco or LA from **TripTel** (☎877-874-7835; www.triptel.com); pricing plans vary, but are typically expensive.

Dialing Codes

» US phone numbers consist of a three-digit area code followed by a seven-digit local number.

» When dialing a number within the same area code, only use the seven-digit number.

» Long-distance or toll-free calls must be preceded by dialing ☎1.

» For direct international calls, dial ☎011 plus the country code plus the area code (usually without the initial '0') plus the local phone number.

» If you're calling from abroad, the country code for the US is ☎1 (the same as Canada, but international rates apply between the two countries).

Payphones & Phonecards

Where payphones still exist, they're usually coin-operated, although some may only accept credit cards (eg in state or national parks). Local calls cost 50¢ minimum. For long-distance and international calls, prepaid phonecards are sold at convenience stores, supermarkets, newsstands and electronics stores.

Time

California is on **Pacific Standard Time** (GMT minus eight hours). When it's noon in LA, it's 3pm in New York, 8pm in London and 5am (the next day) in Sydney.

Daylight Saving Time (DST) starts on the second Sunday in March, when clocks are set one hour ahead, and ends on the first Sunday in November.

Tipping

Tipping is *not* optional. Only withhold tips in cases of outrageously bad service.

Airport skycaps & hotel bellhops $2 per bag, minimum per cart $5

Bartenders 10% to 15% per round, minimum $1 per drink

Concierges Nothing for providing simple information, but up to $20 for securing last-minute restaurant reservations, sold-out show tickets etc

Housekeeping staff $2 to $4 daily, left under the card provided; more if you're messy

Parking valets At least $2 when handed back your car keys

Restaurant servers & room service 15% to 20%, unless a gratuity is already charged

Taxi drivers 10% to 15% of metered fare, rounded up to the next dollar

Tourist Information

For pretrip planning, peruse the info-packed website of the **California Travel and Tourism Commission** (www.visitcalifornia.com).

This state-run agency also runs several **California Welcome Centers** (www.visitcwc.com), where staff dispense maps and brochures and can help find accommodations.

Almost every coastal city and town has a local visitors center or a chamber of commerce where you can pick up maps, brochures and information.

For helpful tourist information websites, see p19.

Travelers with Disabilities

More populated areas of coastal California are reasonably well-equipped for travelers with disabilities, but facilities in smaller towns and rural areas may be quite limited.

Communications & Accessibility

» Telephone companies provide relay operators (dial ☎711) for the hearing impaired.

» Many banks provide ATM instructions in Braille.

» Most intersections have dropped curbs and sometimes audible crossing signals.

» The Americans with Disabilities Act (ADA) requires public buildings built after 1993 to be wheelchair-accessible, including restrooms.

» Motels and hotels built after 1993 must have at least one ADA-compliant accessible room; state your specific needs when making reservations.

» For nonpublic buildings built prior to 1993, including hotels, restaurants, museums and theaters, there are no accessibility guarantees; call ahead to find out what to expect.

» Most national and many state parks and some other outdoor recreation areas offer paved or boardwalk nature trails that are wheelchair-accessible.

Transportation

» All major airlines, Greyhound buses and Amtrak trains can accommodate travelers with disabilities, usually requiring 48 hours advance notice.

» Major car-rental agencies offer hand-controlled vehicles and vans with wheelchair lifts at no extra charge, but you must reserve these well in advance.

» For wheelchair-accessible van rentals, try **Wheelchair Getaways** (☎800-638-1912; www.wheelchairgetaways.com) in LA, San Diego and San Francisco or **Mobility Works** (☎877-275-4915; www.mobilityworks.com) in LA, Pasadena and San Jose.

» Local buses, trains and subway lines usually have wheelchair lifts.

» Seeing-eye dogs can accompany passengers on public transportation.

» Taxi companies have at least one wheelchair-accessible van, but you'll usually need to call the dispatcher for one and then wait, sometimes quite a while.

Helpful Resources

Access Northern California (www.accessnca.com) Extensive links to accessible-travel resources, publications, tours and transportation, including outdoor recreation opportunities and car and van rentals, plus a searchable lodgings database and an events calendar.

Access San Francisco (www.onlyinsanfrancisco.com/plan_your_trip/access_guide.asp) Free downloadable accessible travel guide (somewhat dated, but still useful).

Access Santa Cruz County (www.sharedadventures.com/access_guide.htm) Slightly outdated, but still handy bilingual (English/Spanish) accessible travel guide (US shipping $3).

Accessible San Diego (http://asd.travel) Downloadable city guide booklet ($3, print version $5) that's updated annually.

California Coastal Conservancy (www.wheelingcalscoast.org) Free accessibility information covering beaches, parks and trails along the entire coast, plus downloadable wheelchair riders' guides to the San Francisco, Los Angeles and Orange County coasts.

California State Parks (http://access.parks.ca.gov) Online searchable map and database for finding accessible features at parks statewide.

Flying Wheels Travel (☎877-451-5006; www.flyingwheelstravel.com) Full-service travel agency.

Los Angeles for Disabled Visitors (discoverlosangeles.com/guides/la-living/) Tips for accessible sightseeing, entertainment, museums, theme parks and transportation.

Theme-Park Access Guide (www.mouseplanet.com/tag) An insider's view of Disneyland and other Southern California theme parks 'on wheels.'

Visas

All of the following information is highly subject to change. Depending on your country of origin, the rules for entering the USA keep changing. Double-check current visa requirements *before* coming to the USA.

Currently, under the US Visa Waiver Program (VWP), visas are not required for citizens of 35 countries for stays up to 90 days (no extensions) as long as your passport meets current US standards (see p513).

Citizens of VWP countries must also register with the Electronic System for Travel Authorization (ESTA; $14) online (https://esta.cbp.dhs.gov/esta) at least 72 hours before travel. Once approved, the registration is valid for up to two years or until your passport expires, whichever comes first.

Citizens from all other countries or whose passports don't meet US standards will need to apply for a visa in their home country. The process costs a nonrefundable $140, involves a personal interview and can take several weeks, so apply as early as possible.

For more information, check with the **US Department of State** (http://travel.state.gov/visa).

Volunteering

Volunteering might just provide some of your most memorable experiences – you'll get to interact with locals and the land and sea in ways you never would just passing through coastal California. Casual, drop-in volunteer opportunities are most common in cities. You can register online with a number of organizations:

HandsOn Bay Area (www.hoba.org)

LA Works (www.laworks.com)

One Brick (www.onebrick.org)

OneOC (www.oneoc.org) Orange County

Santa Cruz Volunteer Center (www.scvolunteercenter.org)

Volunteer San Diego (www.volunteersandiego.org)

For more opportunities, browse local alternative weekly newspapers and **Craigslist** (www.craiglist.org).

Helpful Resources

California Volunteers (www.californiavolunteers.org) State volunteer directory and matching service, with links to national service days and long-term AmeriCorps programs.

Habitat for Humanity (www.habitat.org) Nonprofit organization helps build homes for impoverished families, including weekend and week-long projects.

Idealist.org (www.idealist.org) Free searchable database with short- and long-term volunteer work.

Sierra Club (www.sierraclub.org) Day or weekend projects and longer volunteer vacations (including for families) focusing on conservation; annual membership $25.

TreePeople (www.treepeople.org) Organizes group tree-planting, invasive weed-pulling and eco-restoration projects around LA, from urban parks to wildfire-damaged forests.

Volunteer Match (www.volunteermatch.org) Free searchable listings of short- and long-term local volunteering opportunities.

Worldwide Opportunities on Organic Farms (www.wwoofusa.org) Long-term volunteering opportunities on organic farms in California; online membership fee $30.

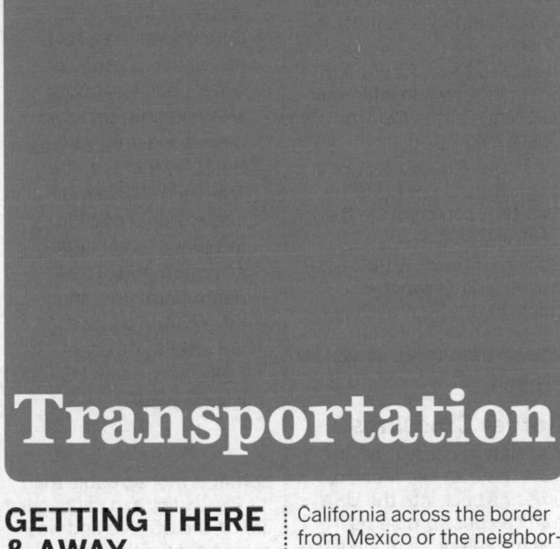

Transportation

GETTING THERE & AWAY

Getting to coastal California by air or overland by car, bus or train is easy, although it's not always cheap. Flights and tours can be booked online at www.lonelyplanet.com/bookings.

Entering the Region

California is an important agricultural state. To prevent the spread of pests and diseases, certain food items (including meats, fresh fruit and vegetables) may not be brought into the state. Bakery items, chocolates and hard-cured cheeses are admissible. If you drive into California across the border from Mexico or the neighboring states of Oregon, Nevada or Arizona, you may have to stop for a quick inspection and questioning by California Department of Food and Agriculture agents.

Under the US Department of Homeland Security (DHS) registration program, **US-VISIT** (www.dhs.gov/us-visit), almost all visitors (excluding, for now, many Canadian, some Mexican citizens and also children under age 14) will be digitally photographed and have their electronic (inkless) fingerprints scanned upon arrival; the process typically takes just a minute. For Mexico land-border crossings, turn to p514. For US customs for all international arrivals, see p506. For visa requirements, see p511.

Passport

» Under the Western Hemisphere Travel Initiative (WHTI), all travelers must have a valid machine-readable (MRP) passport when entering the USA by air, land or sea.

» The only exceptions are for most US citizens and some Canadian and Mexican citizens traveling *by land* who can present other WHTI-compliant documents (eg pre-approved 'trusted traveler' cards). For details, check www.getyouhome.gov.

» All foreign passports must meet current US standards and be valid for at least six months longer than your intended stay.

» MRP passports issued or renewed after October 26, 2006 must be e-passports (ie have a digital photo and integrated chip with biometric data). For more information, consult www.cbp.gov/travel.

Air

» To get through airport security checkpoints (30-minute wait times are standard), you'll need a boarding pass and photo ID.

» Some travelers may be required to undergo a secondary screening, involving hand pat-downs and carry-on-bag searches.

» Airport security measures restrict many common items

CLIMATE CHANGE & TRAVEL

Every form of transport that relies on carbon-based fuel generates CO_2, the main cause of human-induced climate change. Modern travel is dependent on aeroplanes, which might use less fuel per kilometer per person than most cars but travel much greater distances. The altitude at which aircraft emit gases (including CO_2) and particles also contributes to their climate change impact. Many websites offer 'carbon calculators' that allow people to estimate the carbon emissions generated by their journey and, for those who wish to do so, to offset the impact of the greenhouse gases emitted with contributions to portfolios of climate-friendly initiatives throughout the world. Lonely Planet offsets the carbon footprint of all staff and author travel.

(eg pocketknives) from being carried on planes. Check current restrictions with the **Transportation Security Administration** (TSA; ☎866-289-9673; www.tsa.gov).

» Currently, TSA requires that all carry-on liquids and gels be stored in 3oz or smaller bottles placed inside a quart-sized clear plastic zip-top bag. Exceptions, which must be declared to checkpoint security officers, include medications.

» All checked luggage is screened for explosives. TSA may open your suitcase for visual confirmation, breaking the lock if necessary. Leave your bags unlocked or use a TSA-approved lock like **Travel Sentry** (www.travelsentry.org).

Airports

Coastal California's primary international airports:

Los Angeles International Airport (LAX; www.lawa.org/lax) Southern California's largest and busiest airport, 20 miles southwest of downtown LA, near the coast.

San Francisco International Airport (SFO; www.flysfo.com) Northern California's major hub, 15 miles south of downtown, on San Francisco Bay.

Regional airports serving domestic flights, with limited international services:

Mineta San José International Airport (SJC; www.flysanjose.com) In San Francisco's South Bay.

Oakland International Airport (OAK; www.flyoakland.com) In San Francisco's East Bay.

San Diego International Airport (SAN; www.san.org) Four miles northwest of downtown San Diego.

Domestic flights also arrive at regional airports:

Bob Hope Airport (BUR; www.bobhopeairport.com) In Burbank, Los Angeles County.

John Wayne Airport (SNA; www.ocair.com) In Santa Ana, Orange County.

Long Beach Airport (LGB; www.lgb.org) In Los Angeles County.

Monterey Peninsula Airport (MRY; www.montereyairport.com) On the Central Coast.

San Luis Obispo County Regional Airport (SBP; www.sloairport.com) On the Central Coast.

Santa Barbara Municipal Airport (SBA; www.flysba.com) On the Central Coast.

Land

Border Crossings

It's relatively easy crossing from the USA into Mexico; it's crossing back into the USA that can pose problems if you haven't brought all of the required documents. Check the ever-changing passport (p513) and visa (p511) requirements *before* traveling.

On the US–Mexico border between San Diego and Tijuana, San Ysidro is the world's busiest border crossing. US citizens and residents do not require a visa for stays of 72 hours or less within the border zone (ie as far south as Ensenada). For more details about traveling to Tijuana, see p456.

> **WARNING!**
>
> As of April 2011, the **US State Department** (http://travel.state.gov) has issued a issued a travel warning about Mexican drug-cartel violence and crime along the US–Mexico border. Travelers should exercise extreme caution in Tijuana, avoid large-scale gatherings and demonstrations, and refrain from venturing out after dark, especially in cars with US license plates.

BUS

» US-based **Greyhound** (☎800-231-2222; www.greyhound.com) and **Greyhound México** (☎800-010-0600; www.greyhound.com.mx) have cooperative service, with direct buses between Mexico and California.

» Northbound buses from Mexico can take some time to cross the US border, since US immigration may insist on checking every person on board.

CAR & MOTORCYCLE

» Unless you're planning an extended stay in Tijuana, driving across the Mexico border is more trouble than it's worth. Instead park your car on the US side and walk across or take the trolley from San Diego (see p456).

» If you do decide to drive across, you must purchase Mexican car insurance either beforehand or at the border crossing. Bring your vehicle's registration papers, US liability insurance and driver's license.

» If you're renting a car or a motorcycle in the USA, ask if the agency allows its vehicles to be taken across the Mexican border; chances are it doesn't.

» Expect long waits at the border, especially on weekends and holidays and during summer. **US Customs & Border Protection** (http://apps.cbp.gov/bwt/) tracks current wait times at every Mexico border crossing.

» Occasionally the authorities of either country decide to search a car *thoroughly*. Remain calm and be polite.

Bus

Greyhound (☎800-231-2222; www.greyhound.com) is the major long-distance bus company, with routes throughout the USA, including to/from California. It has recently stopped service to many small towns; routes trace major highways and stop at larger population centers.

For more details about Greyhound, including on-board amenities, fares and reservations, see p516.

Train

Amtrak (☎800-872-7245; www.amtrak.com) operates a fairly extensive rail system throughout the USA. Fares vary according to the type of train and seating (eg reserved or unreserved coach seats, business class, sleeping compartments).

Trains are comfortable, if slow and occasionally delayed, and are equipped with dining and lounge cars on long-distance routes.

Amtrak routes to/from California:

California Zephyr Daily service between Chicago and Emeryville (from $149, 52 hours), near San Francisco, via Denver, Salt Lake City, Reno and Sacramento.

Coast Starlight Travels the West Coast daily from Seattle to LA (from $104, 35 hours) via Portland, Sacramento and Oakland; wi-fi may be available on board.

Southwest Chief Daily departures between Chicago and LA (from $149, 44 hours) via Kansas City, Albuquerque and Flagstaff.

Sunset Limited Thrice-weekly service between New Orleans and LA (from $138, 47 hours) via Houston, San Antonio, El Paso and Tucson.

For more details about Amtrak, including fares, reservations and intra-California routes and rail passes, see p519.

GETTING AROUND

Most people drive around California, although you can also fly (if time is limited) or save money by taking buses or trains, the latter often following scenic routes.

Air

Several major US carriers fly within California, although the expense involved only makes it worthwhile if you have to travel long distances in a hurry. Intra-California flights are often operated by regional subsidiaries, such as American Eagle, Delta Connection and United Express. Alaska Airlines and partner Horizon Air serve many regional California airports, as do popular low-cost airlines Southwest and JetBlue. Virgin America currently flies out of San Francisco, Los Angeles and San Diego.

For airports, see p514.

Bicycle

Although it's a nonpolluting 'green' way to travel, cycling coastal California's roads demands a high level of fitness and the long distances involved make it difficult to cover much ground very fast. Come prepared for weather extremes, from chilly coastal fog and rainstorms to intense heat in summer, which is peak season for bicycle touring.

Helpful Resources

Adventure Cycling Association (www.adventurecycling.org) Excellent online resource for purchasing bicycle-friendly maps, long-distance route guides and gadgets.

Better World Club (☎866-238-1137; www.betterworldclub.com) Annual membership ($40, plus $12 enrollment fee) entitles you to two 24-hour emergency roadside pickups with transportation to the nearest bike repair shop within a 30-mile radius.

California Department of Transportation (www.dot.ca.gov/hq/tpp/offices/bike) Road rules, safety tips and links to statewide bicycle advocacy groups.

Road Rules

» Cycling is allowed on all roads and highways – even along freeways if there's no suitable alternative (eg frontage roads); all mandatory exits are marked.

» Some cities have designated bicycle lanes, but make sure you have your wits about you when venturing out into heavy traffic.

» Cyclists must follow the same rules of the road as vehicles. Don't expect drivers to always respect your right of way, however.

» Wearing a helmet is mandatory for bicycle riders under 18 years old.

» Ensure you have proper lights and reflective gear, especially at night and in fog.

Transporting Bicycles

» Greyhound transports bicycles as luggage (surcharge $30 to $40), provided the bicycle is disassembled and placed in a box ($10, available at some terminals).

» Most of Amtrak's *Pacific Surfliner* trains feature on-board racks where you can secure your bike unboxed. Reserve a spot for your bicycles when buying tickets (surcharge $5 to $10).

» On Amtrak trains without racks, bikes must be put in a box ($15) and checked as luggage (fee $5). Not all stations or trains offer checked-baggage service, though.

» Before flying, you'll need to disassemble your bike and box it as checked baggage; contact airlines directly for details, including surcharges (typically $50 to $100 or more).

Boat

Boats won't get you around coastal California, although there are a few offshore routes, notably to Catalina Island from LA and Orange County and to Channel Islands National Park from

Ventura or Oxnard, north of LA. On San Francisco Bay, regular ferry routes operate between San Francisco and Sausalito, Larkspur, Tiburon, Angel Island, Oakland, Alameda and Vallejo.

Bus

Greyhound (☎800-231-2222; www.greyhound.com) buses are an economical way to travel between major cities and to points along the coast, but won't get you off the beaten path or to state or national parks. Frequency of service varies from 'rarely' to 'constantly,' but the main routes have service several times daily.

On Greyhound buses, the best seats are typically near the front away from the bathroom. Limited amenities include freezing air-con (bring a sweater) and slightly reclining seats; select buses have electrical outlets and wi-fi. Smoking on board is prohibited. Long-distance buses stop for meal breaks and driver changes.

Bus stations are typically dreary places, often in dodgy areas; if you arrive at night, take a taxi into town. In small towns where there is no bus station, know exactly where and when the bus arrives, be obvious as you flag it down and pay the driver with exact change.

Costs

For lower fares, purchase tickets seven to 14 days in advance. Round trips and Monday through Thursday bus travel may be cheaper.

Discounts on unrestricted full fares are available for seniors over 62 (5% off), students (20%) with a Student Advantage Card (p506) and children aged two to 11 (25%).

Special promotional discounts, such as 50% off companion fares, are often available on the Greyhound website; restrictions (eg blackout periods) may apply.

Reservations

It's easy to buy tickets online with a credit card, then pick them up (bring photo ID) at the terminal. You can also buy tickets over the phone or in person. Greyhound terminal ticket windows accept credit and debit cards, traveler's checks and cash.

General boarding is first-come, first-served. Buying tickets in advance doesn't guarantee a seat on any particular bus unless you also purchase priority boarding (fee $5, available at some terminals). Otherwise, arrive at least one hour prior to the scheduled departure to get a seat; allow extra time on weekends and holidays.

Car, Motorcycle & RV

California's love affair with cars runs deep, and it's here to stay: the state is so big, public transportation can't cover it. For flexibility and convenience, you'll want a car, although rental rates and fuel prices can eat up a good chunk of your trip budget.

Automobile Associations

For 24-hour emergency roadside assistance, free maps and discounts on lodging, attractions, entertainment, car rentals and more:

American Automobile Association (AAA; ☎877-428-2277; www.aaa.com) Walk-in offices throughout California, add-on coverage for RVs and motorcycles, and reciprocal agreements with international affiliates (eg CAA) – bring your membership card from home.

Better World Club (☎866-238-1137; www.betterworldclub.com) Supports environmental causes and offers add-on emergency roadside assistance for cyclists.

Driver's License

» Visitors may legally drive a car in California for up to 12 months with their home driver's license.

» If you're from overseas, an International Driving Permit (IDP) will have more credibility with traffic police and simplify the car-rental process, especially if your license doesn't have a photo or isn't written in English.

» To drive a motorcycle, you'll need a valid US state motorcycle license or a specially endorsed IDP.

» International automobile associations can issue IDPs, valid for one year, for a fee. Always carry your home license together with the IDP.

Fuel

» Gas stations in California, nearly all of which are self-service, are ubiquitous, except in national parks and some sparsely populated coastal areas.

» Gas is sold in gallons (one US gallon equals 3.78L). At press time, the cost for mid-grade fuel ranged from $3.75 to $4.25.

Insurance

California law requires liability insurance for all vehicles. When renting a car, check your home auto-insurance policy or your international travel-insurance policy (p508) to see if you're already covered. If not, expect to pay around $20 per day.

Insurance against damage to the car itself, called Collision Damage Waiver (CDW) or Loss Damage Waiver (LDW), costs another $20 per day; the deductible may require you to pay the first $100 to $500 for any repairs. Some credit cards cover this, provided you charge the entire cost of the car rental to the card; check with your credit-card issuer first to determine the extent of coverage and policy exclusions.

Rental

CARS

To rent your own wheels, you'll typically need to be at least 25 years old, hold a valid driver's license and have a major credit card, *not* a check or debit card. A few companies may rent to drivers under 25 but over 21 for a surcharge (around $25 per day). If you don't have a credit card, large cash deposits are occasionally accepted.

With advance reservations, you can often get an economy-size vehicle with unlimited mileage from around $30 per day, plus insurance, taxes and fees. Weekend and weekly rates are usually more economical. Airport locations may have cheaper rates but higher add-on fees; if you get a fly-drive package, local taxes may be extra when you pick up the car.

Rates generally include unlimited mileage, but expect surcharges for additional drivers and one-way rentals. Child or infant safety seats are compulsory (reserve them when booking), costing about $10 per day (or $50 per rental).

Major international car-rental companies include:

Alamo (☎877-222-9075; www.alamo.com)

Avis (☎800-331-1212; www.avis.com)

Budget (☎800-527-0700; www.budget.com)

Dollar (☎800-800-3665; www.dollar.com)

Enterprise (☎800-261-7331; www.enterprise.com)

Fox (☎800-225-4369; www.foxrentacar.com)

Hertz (☎800-654-3131; www.hertz.com)

National (☎877-222-9058; www.nationalcar.com)

Thrifty (☎800-847-4389; www.thrifty.com)

If you'd like to minimize your carbon footprint, a few major car-rental companies (eg Avis, Budget, Enterprise, Fox, Hertz and Thrifty) offer 'green' fleets of hybrid or biofueled rental cars, but these fuel-efficient models are in short supply. Reserve well in advance and expect to pay significantly higher rates. Also consider the following:

Simply Hybrid (☎323-653-0011, 888-359-0055; www.simplyhybrid.com) In Los Angeles. Free delivery and pick-up from some locations with three-day minimum rental.

Zipcar (☎866-494-7227; www.zipcar.com) Currently available in 21 California locations, this car-sharing club charges usage fees (per hour or daily), including free gas, insurance (damage fee of up to $500 may apply) and limited mileage. Apply online (foreign drivers OK); annual membership $50, application fee $25.

To find and compare independent car-rental companies, try **Car Rental Express** (www.carrentalexpress.com). Independent agencies that may rent to drivers under 25 include:

Rent-a-Wreck (☎877-877-0700; www.rentawreck.com) Minimum rental age and surcharges vary by location.

ROAD DISTANCES (miles)

	Anaheim	Arcata	Bakersfield	Death Valley	Las Vegas	Los Angeles	Monterey	Napa	Palm Springs	Redding	Sacramento	San Diego	San Francisco	San Luis Obispo	Santa Barbara	Sth Lake Tahoe
Arcata	680															
Bakersfield	135	555														
Death Valley	285	705	235													
Las Vegas	265	840	285	140												
Los Angeles	25	650	110	290	270											
Monterey	370	395	250	495	535	345										
Napa	425	265	300	545	590	400	150									
Palm Springs	95	760	220	300	280	110	450	505								
Redding	570	140	440	565	725	545	315	190	650							
Sacramento	410	300	280	435	565	385	185	60	490	160						
San Diego	95	770	230	350	330	120	465	520	140	665	505					
San Francisco	405	280	285	530	570	380	120	50	490	215	85	500				
San Luis Obispo	225	505	120	365	405	200	145	265	310	430	290	320	230			
Santa Barbara	120	610	145	350	360	95	250	370	205	535	395	215	335	105		
Sth Lake Tahoe	505	400	375	345	460	480	285	160	485	260	100	600	185	390	495	
Yosemite	335	465	200	300	415	310	200	190	415	325	160	430	190	230	345	190

Ten branches, mostly in the LA and San Francisco Bay areas.

Super Cheap Cars (www.supercheapcar.com) No surcharge for drivers ages 21 to 24; daily fee applies for under-21s. Three locations in the San Francisco Bay Area and Los Angeles and Orange Counties.

For wheelchair-accessible van rentals, see p510.

MOTORCYCLES

Depending on the model, renting a motorcycle costs $100 to $200 per day plus taxes and fees, including helmets, unlimited miles and liability insurance; one-way rentals and collision insurance (CDW) cost extra. Discounts may be available for three-day and weekly rentals. Required credit-card security deposits start over $1000.

Motorcycle rental agencies include:

Dubbelju (☎415-495-2774, 866-495-2774; www.dubbelju.com; 689-A Bryant St, San Francisco) Harley-Davidson, BMW, Japanese-import and electric motorcycles for rent.

Eagle Rider (☎888-900-9901; www.eaglerider.com) Nationwide company with eight locations in coastal California; one-way rental surcharge $250.

Route 66 (☎310-578-0112, 888-434-4473; www.route66riders.com; 4161 Lincoln Blvd, Marina del Rey) Harley-Davidson rentals in LA's South Bay.

RECREATIONAL VEHICLES

Gas-guzzling RVs remain popular despite high fuel prices and being cumbersome to drive. It's easy to find RV campgrounds with electricity and water hookups, but in cities, RVs are a nuisance, because there are few places to park or plug them in. That said, they do solve transportation, accommodation and cooking needs in one fell swoop.

Book RVs as far in advance as possible. Rental costs vary by size and model, but you can expect to pay over $100 per day. Rates often don't include mileage (from 35¢ per mile), bedding or kitchen kits (rental fee $50 to $100), vehicle prep ($100 surcharge) or taxes.

RV rental agencies include:

Cruise America (☎480-464-7300, 800-671-8042; www.cruiseamerica.com) A dozen pick-up locations all along the coast.

El Monte (☎562-483-4956, 888-337-2214; www.elmonterv.com) Mostly in the LA and San Francisco Bay areas; ask about AAA discounts.

Happy Travel Campers (☎310-928-3980, 800-370-1262; www.camperusa.com) In LA and San Francisco.

Moturis (☎877-297-3687; www.moturis.com) In San Francisco, LA and San Diego.

Road Bear (☎818-865-2925, 866-491-9853; www.roadbearrv.com) In LA and San Francisco.

Road Conditions & Hazards

For up-to-date highway conditions in California, including road closures and construction updates, contact **Caltrans** (☎800-427-7623; www.dot.ca.gov).

In rural areas, livestock sometimes graze next to unfenced roads. These areas are typically signed as 'Open Range.' Where wild animals frequently appear roadside, you'll see signs with the silhouette of a leaping deer. Take these signs seriously, particularly at night.

In coastal areas thick fog may impede driving – slow down and if it's too soupy, get off the road. Along ocean cliffs and on curvy mountain roads, watch out for falling rocks, mudslides and avalanches that could damage or disable your car.

Coastal highways with precarious cliffsides may wash out in winter, sometimes for months at a time. If you see signs that read, 'Expect long delays 40 miles ahead,' or 'Hwy 1 closed north of Hearst Castle,' heed their warnings but don't panic. If you have lodging reservations, call ahead and ask if any local detours are available.

Road Rules

» Drive on the right-hand side of the road.

» Talking on a cell (mobile) phone while driving is illegal.

» The use of seat belts is required for drivers, front-seat passengers and children under age 16.

» Infant and child safety seats are required for children under six years old or weighing less than 60lbs.

» All motorcyclists must wear a helmet. Scooters are not allowed on freeways.

» High-occupancy (HOV) lanes marked with a diamond symbol are reserved for cars with multiple occupants, sometimes only during morning and afternoon rush hours.

» Unless otherwise posted, the speed limit is 65mph on freeways, 55mph on two-lane undivided highways, 35mph on major city streets and 25mph in business and residential districts and near schools.

» Except where indicated, turning right at red lights after coming to a full stop is permitted, although intersecting traffic still has the right of way.

» At four-way stop signs, cars proceed in the order in which they arrived; if two cars arrive simultaneously, the one on the right has the right of way. When in doubt, politely wave the other driver ahead.

» When emergency vehicles (eg ambulances, fire trucks) approach from either direction, carefully pull over to the side of the road.

» California has strict anti-littering laws; throwing

trash from a vehicle merits a $1000 fine.

» Driving under the influence of alcohol or drugs is illegal (see p508).

» It's illegal to carry open containers of alcohol inside a vehicle, even empty ones. Unless containers are full and still sealed, store them in the trunk.

Local Transportation

California's biggest coastal cities have local bus, cable-car, trolley, train, light-rail and/or subway systems. Larger coastal towns and counties operate commuter-bus systems, usually with limited evening and weekend services. Elsewhere, public transportation to rural towns and to state and national parks can be sparse.

Bicycle

» San Francisco, Santa Barbara, San Luis Obispo and Santa Cruz are among California's most bike-friendly communities, as rated by the **League of American Bicyclists** (www.bikeleague.org).

» Bicycles may be transported on many local buses and trains, sometimes during noncommute hours only.

» You can rent bikes by the hour, the day or the week in coastal cities and many towns. Rentals start around $10 per day for beach cruisers up to $45 or more for mountain bikes (credit-card security deposit of $200 or more required).

Taxi

» Taxis are metered, with flag-fall fees of $2.50 to $3.50 to start, plus $2 to $3 per mile. Credit cards may be accepted.

» Taxis may charge extra for baggage and/or airport pick-ups.

» Drivers expect a 10% to 15% tip, rounded up to the next dollar.

» Taxis cruise busy urban areas, but elsewhere you may need to call for one.

Train

Amtrak (☎800-872-7245; www.amtrak.com) runs comfortable, if occasionally tardy, trains to major California cities and some SoCal coastal towns. Amtrak's Thruway buses provide onward connections from many train stations. Smoking is prohibited on board trains and buses.

Amtrak routes within California:

Coast Starlight Chugs north–south almost the entire length of the state; wi-fi may be available. Daily stops include LA, Santa Barbara, San Luis Obispo, Paso Robles, Salinas, San Jose and Oakland.

Pacific Surfliner Over a dozen daily trains ply the San Diego–LA route (via Anaheim, home of Disneyland). Six trains continue north to Santa Barbara, with three going all the way to San Luis Obispo. The trip itself, which hugs the coastline for much of the route, is a visual treat. Bicycle and surfboard racks may be available on board.

Costs

Purchase tickets at train stations, by phone or online. Fares depend on the day of travel, the route, the type of seating, etc. Fares may be slightly higher during peak travel periods, eg, during summer and around holidays. Round-trip tickets cost the same as two one-way tickets.

Usually seniors over 62 and students with an ISIC or Student Advantage Card (p506) receive a 15% discount, while up to two children aged two to 15 who are accompanied by an adult get 50% off. AAA members save 10%. Special promotions can become available anytime, so check the website or ask.

Reservations

Reservations can be made any time from 11 months in advance to the day of departure. In summer and around holidays, trains sell out quickly, so book tickets as early as possible. The cheapest coach fares are usually for unreserved seats; business-class fares typically come with reserved seats.

Train Passes

» Amtrak's California Rail Pass costs $159 ($80 for children aged two to 15).

» The pass is valid on all trains (except certain long-distance routes) and most connecting Thruway buses for seven days of travel within a 21-day period.

» Passholders must make advance reservations for each leg of travel and obtain hard-copy tickets prior to boarding.

behind the scenes

SEND US YOUR FEEDBACK

We love to hear from travelers – your comments keep us on our toes and help make our books better. Our well-traveled team reads every word on what you loved or loathed about this book. Although we cannot reply individually to postal submissions, we always guarantee that your feedback goes straight to the appropriate authors, in time for the next edition. Each person who sends us information is thanked in the next edition – and the most useful submissions are rewarded with a free book.

Visit **lonelyplanet.com/contact** to submit your updates and suggestions or to ask for help. Our award-winning website also features inspirational travel stories, news and discussions.

Note: We may edit, reproduce and incorporate your comments in Lonely Planet products such as guidebooks, websites and digital products, so let us know if you don't want your comments reproduced or your name acknowledged. For a copy of our privacy policy visit lonelyplanet.com/privacy.

OUR READERS

Many thanks to the travelers who used the last edition and wrote to us with helpful hints, useful advice and interesting anecdotes:

Björn Ahrens, Diana Frattali-Moreno, Michael Kelly Jr, Pauline Ondei, Cynthia C Rignanese and Mark & Courtney Tate.

AUTHOR THANKS

Sara Benson

Without everyone at Lonely Planet and all of my co-authors, this book would never have seen such smooth sailing. I'm grateful to everyone I met on the road who shared their local expertise and tips. Big thanks to all of my coastal friends and family in the Golden State. PS to MSC Jr: Are you ready for more midnight drives and moonlight hikes along the Big Sur coast?

Andrew Bender

Suki Gear, Alison Lyall and Sam Benson for the opportunity and their good cheer and advice. Thanks also to Adrienne Costanzo, Karen Grant, Corey Hutchison and Bella Li for their assistance on this book.

Alison Bing

Suki Gear and Sam Benson, whose guidance, insight and support make any tricky mental backbend possible. Shameless California bear hugs to John Vlahides and Robert Landon for setting giddily high writing standards, to fearless leaders Brice Gosnell and Heather Dickson at Lonely Planet, to the Sanchez Writers' Grotto, and above all to Marco Flavio Marinucci, whose kindness and bracing espresso make everything possible.

Nate Cavalieri

Thanks to my partner Florence Chien for joining my research travels through Northern California and giving a careful read to this text. Thanks to Ben Calhoun and Catrin Einhorn for sheltering me while this text was completed. Thanks also to the lovely people at Lonely Planet and particularly for the enthusiasm of commissioning editor and mentor Suki Gear.

Bridget Gleeson

Thank you to my lovely sister Molly, my brother-in-law Germán, and my dear friend Starla Silver for their hospitality when I'm passing through California – and to all their friends for their endless dining and drinking suggestions. Thanks, as well, to my mother Margaret, who always serves as my faithful travel companion.

Beth Kohn

All the usual suspects get thanks again, especially the fabulous multitasking Suki Gear and the dynamo known as Sam Benson. California cohorts and experts this time around included Agent 'Pedal-to-the-metal' Moller, Felix 'Hella Loves Oakland' Thomson, Jenny 'Stink' G, Dillon 'The Scientist' Dutton and Julia 'Wawona' Brashares, plus all the helpful and patient park rangers.

John A Vlahides

I owe heartfelt thanks to my commissioning editor, Suki Gear, and co-authors, Sam Benson and Alison Bing, for their wonderful help and always-sunny dispositions. Kate Brady, Steven Kahn, Karl Soehnlein, Kevin Clarke, Jim Aloise and Adam Young – you kept me upbeat and laughing when things seemed impossible. And to you, the readers: thank you for letting me be your guide to the Wine Country. Have fun. I know you will.

ACKNOWLEDGMENTS

Climate map data adapted from Peel MC, Finlayson BL & McMahon TA (2007) 'Updated World Map of the Köppen-Geiger Climate Classification', *Hydrology and Earth System Sciences*, 11, 163344.

Cover photograph: Wildflowers bloom along the California coastline, Kodiak Greenwood/ Getty Images. Many of the images in this guide are available for licensing from Lonely Planet Images: www.lonelyplanetimages.com.

This Book

This 4th edition of *Coastal California* was coordinated by Sara Benson. This guidebook was also researched and written by Andrew Bender, Alison Bing, Nate Cavalieri, Bridget Gleeson, Beth Kohn and John A Vlahides.

This guidebook was commissioned in Lonely Planet's Oakland office, and produced by the following:

Commissioning Editor Suki Gear

Coordinating Editors Susie Ashworth, Justin Flynn

Coordinating Cartographer Valentina Kremenchutskaya

Coordinating Layout Designer Carlos Solarte

Managing Editors Annelies Mertens, Anna Metcalfe

Senior Editor Angela Tinson

Managing Cartographers Shahara Ahmed, Alison Lyall

Managing Layout Designer Chris Girdler

Assisting Editors Holly Alexander, Jackey Coyle, Elizabeth Anglin, Bella Li

Assisting Layout Designers Virginia Moreno, Wibowo Rusli

Cover Research Naomi Parker

Internal Image Research Sabrina Dalbesio

Thanks to Sasha Baskett, Jessica Boland, Brigitte Ellemor, Ryan Evans, Yvonne Kirk, Trent Paton, Kirsten Rawlings, Diana Von Holdt, Gerard Walker

000 Map pages
000 Photo pages

000 Map pages
000 Photo pages

N

O

T

U

V

W

Y

Z

how to use this book

These symbols will help you find the listings you want:

- Sights
- Beaches
- Activities
- Courses
- Tours
- Festivals & Events
- Sleeping
- Eating
- Drinking
- Entertainment
- Shopping
- Information/ Transport

These symbols give you the vital information for each listing:

- Telephone Numbers
- Opening Hours
- Parking
- Nonsmoking
- Air-Conditioning
- Internet Access
- Wi-Fi Access
- Swimming Pool
- Vegetarian Selection
- English-Language Menu
- Family-Friendly
- Pet-Friendly
- Bus
- Ferry
- Metro
- Subway
- London Tube
- Tram
- Train

Reviews are organised by author preference.

Look out for these icons:

TOP CHOICE Our author's recommendation

FREE No payment required

A green or sustainable option

Our authors have nominated these places as demonstrating a strong commitment to sustainability – for example by supporting local communities and producers, operating in an environmentally friendly way, or supporting conservation projects.

Map Legend

Sights
- Beach
- Buddhist
- Castle
- Christian
- Hindu
- Islamic
- Jewish
- Monument
- Museum/Gallery
- Ruin
- Winery/Vineyard
- Zoo
- Other Sight

Activities, Courses & Tours
- Diving/Snorkelling
- Canoeing/Kayaking
- Skiing
- Surfing
- Swimming/Pool
- Walking
- Windsurfing
- Other Activity/ Course/Tour

Sleeping
- Sleeping
- Camping

Eating
- Eating

Drinking
- Drinking
- Cafe

Entertainment
- Entertainment

Shopping
- Shopping

Information
- Post Office
- Tourist Information

Transport
- Airport
- Border Crossing
- Bus
- Cable Car/ Funicular
- Cycling
- Ferry
- Metro
- Monorail
- Parking
- S-Bahn
- Taxi
- Train/Railway
- Tram
- Tube Station
- U-Bahn
- Other Transport

Routes
- Tollway
- Freeway
- Primary
- Secondary
- Tertiary
- Lane
- Unsealed Road
- Plaza/Mall
- Steps
- Tunnel
- Pedestrian Overpass
- Walking Tour
- Walking Tour Detour
- Path

Boundaries
- International
- State/Province
- Disputed
- Regional/Suburb
- Marine Park
- Cliff
- Wall

Population
- Capital (National)
- Capital (State/Province)
- City/Large Town
- Town/Village

Geographic
- Hut/Shelter
- Lighthouse
- Lookout
- Mountain/Volcano
- Oasis
- Park
- Pass
- Picnic Area
- Waterfall

Hydrography
- River/Creek
- Intermittent River
- Swamp/Mangrove
- Reef
- Canal
- Water
- Dry/Salt/ Intermittent Lake
- Glacier

Areas
- Beach/Desert
- Cemetery (Christian)
- Cemetery (Other)
- Park/Forest
- Sportsground
- Sight (Building)
- Top Sight (Building)

Bridget Gleeson

Disneyland & Orange County, San Diego Though she travels all over Latin America to write about glaciers, penguins and giant turtles, the sunshine and sailboats of southern California always draw Bridget back to the USA. She covers food, wine, hotels and adventure travel for *Afar*, *Budget Travel*, *Jetsetter*, Mr & Mrs Smith and *Delta Sky*.

Read more about Bridget at:
lonelyplanet.com/members/bridgetgleeson

Beth Kohn

Marin County & the Bay Area A lucky long-time resident of San Francisco, Beth lives to be playing outside or splashing in big puddles of water. For this guide, she hiked and biked Bay Area byways, lugged a bear canister along the John Muir Trail and selflessly soaked in hot springs – for research purposes, of course. An author of Lonely Planet's *Yosemite, Sequoia & Kings Canyon National Parks* and *Mexico* guides, you can see more of her work at www.bethkohn.com.

John A Vlahides

Napa & Sonoma Wine Country John A Vlahides co-hosts the TV series *Lonely Planet: Roads Less Travelled*, screening on National Geographic Channels International. John studied cooking in Paris, with the same chefs who trained Julia Child, and is a former luxury-hotel concierge and member of *Les Clefs d'Or*, the international union of the world's elite concierges. He lives in San Francisco, where he sings tenor with the San Francisco Symphony, and spends free time skiing the Sierra Nevada. For more, see johnvlahides.com and twitter.com/johnvlahides.

Read more about John at:
lonelyplanet.com/members/johnvlahides

OUR STORY

A beat-up old car, a few dollars in the pocket and a sense of adventure. In 1972 that's all Tony and Maureen Wheeler needed for the trip of a lifetime – across Europe and Asia overland to Australia. It took several months, and at the end – broke but inspired – they sat at their kitchen table writing and stapling together their first travel guide, *Across Asia on the Cheap*. Within a week they'd sold 1500 copies. Lonely Planet was born.

Today, Lonely Planet has offices in Melbourne, London and Oakland, with more than 600 staff and writers. We share Tony's belief that 'a great guidebook should do three things: inform, educate and amuse'.

OUR WRITERS

Sara Benson

Coordinating Author, Central Coast After graduating from college in Chicago, Sara jumped on a plane to California with just one suitcase and $100 in her pocket. She has bounced around the Golden State ever since, including just about everywhere between San Francisco and LA. She paddled, hiked, cycled and drove all along the Central Coast while researching this guide. The author of 50 travel and nonfiction books, Sara has contributed to Lonely Planet's *USA*, *California* and *Hawaii* guides. Follow more of her adventures online at www.indietraveler.blogspot.com and www.indietraveler.net, and follow her on Twitter (@indie_traveler).

Read more about Sara at:
lonelyplanet.com/members/sara_benson

Andrew Bender

Los Angeles Andy is a true Angeleno, not because he was born in Los Angeles but because he's made it his own. Two decades ago, this native New Englander packed up the car and drove cross-country to work in film production, and eventually realized the joy was in the journey (and writing about it). His work has since appeared in the *Los Angeles Times*, *Forbes*, more than two dozen LP titles and on his blog, www.wheres-andy-now.com. Current obsessions: discovering LA's next great ethnic enclave, and winter sunsets over the bike path in Santa Monica.

Alison Bing

San Francisco Author, arts commentator and adventurous eater Alison was adopted by California 16 years ago. By now she has done everything you're supposed to do here and a few things you're definitely not, including talking up LA bands in San Francisco bars and falling in love on the 7 Haight bus. Alison holds a graduate degree in international diplomacy, which she regularly undermines with opinionated commentary in magazines, newspapers, on public radio and in more than 20 books.

Nate Cavalieri

North Coast & Redwoods A native of central Michigan, Nate lives in Northern California and has crisscrossed the region's back roads by bicycle, bus and rental car on a quest for the biggest trees, the best camping and the hoppiest pints of beer. In addition to authoring guides on California and Latin America for Lonely Planet, he writes about music and professional cycling. He's the Jazz Editor at Rhapsody Music Service. Photos from his travels in Northern California and other writing can be found at www.natecavalieri.com.

Read more about Nate at:
lonelyplanet.com/members/natecavalieri

OVER PAGE MORE WRITERS

Published by Lonely Planet Publications Pty Ltd
ABN 36 005 607 983
4th edition – April 2012
ISBN 978 1 74179 981 1

10 9 8 7 6 5 4 3 2 1
Printed in China